S0-AUX-268

Contents

1 Introduction and hints 9

Introduction, 9
Where to go, 11
Transport and travelling, 11
Timetabling a visit, 12
Highlights, 13
How to go, 16
Best time to visit, 16
Health, 16
What to take, 16
Money, 17
Getting there, 18
Safety, 18
Women travelling alone, 19
Travelling with children, 19
Where to stay, 19
Food and drink, 20
Getting around, 20
Language, 21
Tourism: counting the costs, 22

2 Malaysia 29

Horizons 31
The land, 35
Geography, 35
Climate, 36
Flora and fauna, 38
Diving, 46
Peninsular Malaysia's west coast, 46
Peninsular Malaysia's east coast, 47
East Malaysia, 48
History, 48
Pre-colonial Malaya, 48
The colonials arrive, 50
British Malaya emerges, 50
The Japanese occupation, 55
The British return, 56
The rise of Communism, 57
The road to Merdeka, 58
Racial politics in the 1960s, 59
Art and architecture, 61
Culture, 63
People, 63
Religion, 72
Language and literature, 76
Dance, drama and music, 78
Crafts, 81
Modern Malaysia, 84
Politics, 84
Economy, 92

Kuala Lumpur 99
History, 99
The colonial core and the national mosque, 106
Chinatown, 109
Lake Gardens area, 110
Jalan Ampang, 111
Around the city area, 113
Excursions, 114
Tours, 120
Local information, 120

Northern Peninsular Malaysia 142
Horizons, 142
Barisan Titiwangsa and the hill stations, 142
Genting Highlands, 142
Fraser's Hill, 145
Cameron Highlands, 147
Tanah Rata, 153
Brinchang, 156
Ipoh, 158
Lumut, 165
Pulau Pangkor, 166
Kuala Kangsar, 170
Taiping, 171
Bukit Larut (Maxwell Hill), 174
Penang (Pulau Pinang), 175
Georgetown, 179
Batu Ferringhi and Teluk Bahang, Penang, 194
Alor Star, 199
Kangar, 204
Pulau Langkawi, 205

Southern Peninsular Malaysia 214
Horizons, 214
Seremban, 216
Port Dickson, 218
Melaka, 220
Johor Bahru (JB), 241

The Peninsular's East Coast 252
Horizons, 252
Mersing, 255
Pulau Tioman, 258
Pulau Rawa, 268
Other islands, 268

Endau Rompin National Park, 270
Pekan, 272
Kuantan, 273
Taman Negara, 281
Kuala Lipis and the Kenong Rimba National Park, 286
Kampung Cerating, 287
Kemasik, 291
Kuala Abang, 291
Rantau Abang, 292
Marang, 295
Kuala Terengganu, 297
Kota Bharu, 306
Coast to coast, 316

Borneo Horizons 319
The Land, 319
Geography, 319
Climate, 320
Flora and fauna, 321
History, 328
Culture, 329
People, 329
Religion, 330
Books on Borneo, 331

Sarawak 333
Horizons, 335
Kuching, 354
Dami Peninsula, 374
Bako National Park, 376
Bandar Sri Aman, 380
Sibu and the Rejang River, 383
Kapit, 386
Belaga, 392
Bintulu and Niah Caves, 396
Similajau National Park, 399
Niah National Park, 400
Miri and the Baram River, 404
Marudi, 409
Gunung Mulu National Park, 410
Bario and the Kelabit Highlands, 419
Limbang and Lawas, 420

Sabah 422
Horizons, 422
Kota Kinabalu, 434
Tunku Abdul Rahman Park, 447
South of Kota Kinabalu, 448
Tambunan, 448
Keningau, 451
Tenom, 452
Beaufort, 455
Pulau Labuan, 456
Papar 462
The North and Gunung Kinabalu Park, 463
Kota Belud, 463
Kudat, 464
Gunung Kinabalu Park, 467
Ranau and Kundasang, 473
Poring Hot Springs, 474
The East Coast, 475
Sandakan, 475
Turtle Islands National Park, 483
Sepilok Orang-utan Sanctuary and Rehabilitation Centre, 486
Kinabatangan River, 487
Lahad Datu, 489
Danum Valley Conservation Area, 491
Semporna, 492
Sipadan Island Marine Reserve, 494

Information for travellers 422
Air travel, 510
Before travelling, 499
Best time to visit, 500
Bus, 516
Car and motorbike hire, 518
Cash, 501
Clothing, 504
Communications, 520
Conduct, 504
Cookery courses, 510
Cost of living, 501
Credit cards, 501
Currency regulations, 503
Customs, 503
Duty free allowance, 503
Entertainment, 522
Food and drink, 508
Further reading, 526
Getting around, 510
Getting there, 502
Health, 501
Holidays and festivals, 522
Hours of business, 505
Language, 520
Malaria, 501
Media, 522
Money, 501
Official time, 506
On arrival, 504
Postal services, 520
Prohibited items, 503
Safety, 506
Shopping, 506
Telephone services, 512
Trains, 512
Travellers cheques, 502
Vaccinations, 501
Visas, 499
When to go, 500
Where to stay, 507

3 Brunei 529

Horizons 530
The land, 530
History, 533
Culture, 542
Modern Brunei, 543

Bandar Seri Begawan 549
Omar Ali Saifuddien Mosque, 550
Kampon Ayer, 550
Royal Regalia building, 552
Brunei History Centre, 553
Excursions, 554
Istana Nurul Iman, 554
Damuan Park, 554
Brunei Museum, 554
Muzium Teknologia Melayu, 555

Tours, 555
Local information, 555

Around Brunei 559
Temburong District, 559
Muara, 560
Tutong, 561
Seria, 561
Kuala Belait, 562

Parks and walks 562

Information for travellers 564
Airport tax, 566
Before travelling, 564
Best time to visit, 564
Boat, 568
Bus, 567
Car hire, 568
Clothing, 566
Communications, 568
Conduct, 566
Credit cards, 565
Currency, 565
Customs, 566
Duty free allowance, 566
Entertainment, 568
Food and drink, 567
Further reading, 569
Getting around, 567
Getting there, 565
Health, 564
Holidays and festivals, 569
Hours of business, 565
Language, 568
Money, 565
Official time, 566
On arrival, 566
Postal services, 568
Prohibited items, 566
Safety, 566
Shopping, 566
Telephone services, 568
Vaccinations, 564
Visas, 564
When to go, 564
Where to stay, 567

4 Singapore 571

Horizons 574
The land, 575
Geography, 575
Climate, 576
Flora and fauna, 576
History, 577
Early records, 577
Raffles steps ashore, 579
From fishing village to international port, 582
The Japanese occupation, 584
After the war, 586
Art and architecture, 588
Culture, 595
People, 595
Religion, 600
Language, 602
Dance, drama and music, 603
Modern Singapore, 603
Politics, 603
Economy, 613

Places of interest 627
The Colonial Core and the Singapore River, 631
The port, 641
Orchard Road, 643
Chinatown, 646
Little India, 654
Arab Street, 657
Around Singapore Island, 659

Singapore's islands 670
Sentosa, 670
St John's and Kusu Island, 674
Other islands to the South, 675
Islands to the Northeast, 675

Tour and tour operators 676

Local information 678
Accommodation, 678
Places to eat, 686
Airline offices, 695
Banks & money changers, 695
Churches, 696
Embassies & consulates, 696
Entertainment, 696
Hospitals & medical services, 698
Post & telecommunications, 698
Shopping, 698
Sports, 704
Tour companies & travel agents, 706

Information for travellers 707
Airport information, 711
Airport tax, 712
ATMs, 708
Before travelling, 707
Best time to visit, 707
Bus, 718
Car hire, 719
Clothing, 712
Communications, 719
Conduct, 712
Credit cards, 708
Currency, 708
Customs, 710
Duty free allowance, 710
Entertainment, 721
Food and drink, 713
Further reading, 724
Getting around, 717
Getting there, 708
Goods and services tax refunds, 708
Health, 707
Holidays and festivals, 721
Hours of business, 712
Language, 719
Malaria, 707
Mass Rapid Transit, 717
Media, 721
Medical facilities, 707
Money, 708

Official time, 712
On arrival, 711
Postal services, 720
Prohibited in
Singapore, 712
Safety, 713
Telephone services, 720
Vaccinations, 707
Visas, 707
When to go, 707
Where to stay, 713

5 Rounding up 727

Acknowledgements, 727
Reading and listening, 727
The Internet, 729
Short wave radio, 731
Useful addresses, 732
Malaysian words and
phrases, 737
Food glossary, 740
Distinctive fruits, 740
Health, 742
Travelling with children, 749
Weights and measures, 752
Glossary, 753
Tinted boxes, 761
Illustrations, 768
Index, 769
Maps, 782

We try as hard as we can to make each Footprint Handbook as up-to-date and accurate as possible but, of course, things always change. Many people write to us with new information, amendments or simply comments. Please do get in touch. In return we will send you details of our special guidebook offer.

See page 767 for more information.

Malaysia, Singapore & Brunei

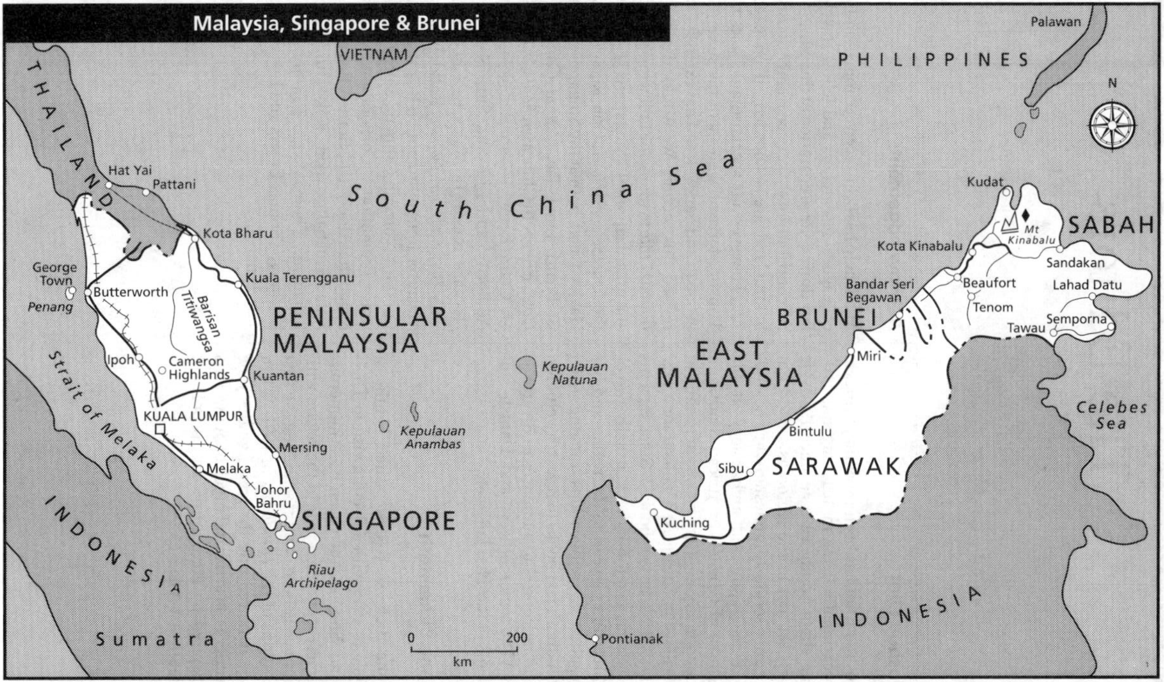

The Editors

Joshua Eliot

Joshua Eliot has been travelling through, occasionally living in, teaching and writing about Southeast Asia since 1980. He first set foot in the region as a child but became seriously interested when he studied geography and archaeology at the School of Oriental & African Studies in London. By the time he was deposited in a village in Northeast Thailand for a year in 1981-82, he was hooked. Since then his work has taken him back, usually two or three times a year, to the region and has resulted in publications ranging from children's text books to research volumes, and in lectures to audiences as diverse as NATO senior officers and Danish students of the Thai language.

Jane Bickersteth

Jane Bickersteth first visited Southeast Asia in 1979 with a fleeting visit to Thailand. She has since been back numerous times, spending a year in the region with her newly born child researching the first editions of the *Handbooks* in 1991. When she is not editing the travel guides Jane works as an artist and much of her work is inspired by the cultures and peoples of Southeast Asia.

Acknowledgements

Much help has been received from friends, colleagues, researchers and fellow travellers during the preparation of this edition. All contributions have been tremendously helpful and are acknowledged on page 727. However our special thanks goes to Tamsin Morrison who spent the summer in Sabah and Sarawak and has extensively revised this section. We would also particularly like to thank the following people and organizations. In Singapore: Jo Tan at the *Four Seasons Hotel*; Goh Kersing and Hayley Wood, both at the Singapore Tourist Board; Janet Tao, *Conrad Centennial Hotel*; Elizabeth Chin, *Merchant Court Hotel*; Colin Leuw, Urban Redevelopment Authority; and Lim Sun Sun, National Heritage Board. In Malaysia: Chow Kai Wah, *Berjaya Resort Tioman*; Rafidi Ismail, Malaysia Tourist Promotion Board, Kuala Lumpur; Noredah Othman, Sabah Tourism Promotion Corporation, Kota Kinabalu; Albert Teo, Borneo Eco Tours, Kota Kinabalu; Voon Kok Hui, Kota Kinabalu; Thomas and Kimmy Nalo, Kuching; Thomas Enters and Lay Cheng Tan, Penang.

Introduction and hints

THE 'MALAY ARCHIPELAGO' is a term intimately associated with the mystery of the East. It conjures up images of sultans, head-hunters and pirates; munificent jungles brimming with exotic life; clippers cutting through the warm waters of the South China Sea; and of explorers discovering new tribes while planters sit on verandahs taking tiffin and, perhaps later, a pink gin or two. The Europeans most closely associated with the Malay Archipelago are sepia tinted: Alfred Russel Wallace, the great Victorian naturalist; Joseph Conrad, the novelist, who spent the years 1883-1888 sailing these waters; and Thomas Stamford Raffles who founded Singapore – and lost his wife.

Today's Malay Archipelago is somewhere very different. Singapore's go-downs have been replaced by towering glass and steel office blocks. The rickshaw pullers, who rarely lived long enough to see middle age, have become English-speaking workers with incomes among the highest in the world and a health system that sustains them well into old age. Malaysia, thrusting and self-confident, is following where Singapore has been, with a mission to transform itself into a developed country by 2020. And then there is Brunei, where the so-styled 'richest man in the world' bestows on his fortunate population a welfare state without parallel. The people of today's Malay Archipelago stand out clearly, their images stark and bright, and their characters pragmatic: Lee Kuan Yew, the architect of modern Singapore and a man with a fiercesome intellect; and Dr Mahathir Mohamad,

Prime Minister of Malaysia, possessed with a desire to sweep away the past and build a new 21st-century Malaysia.

Both these worlds, in a sense, wait for the visitor. The world of Wallace, Conrad and Raffles is still there to be found up-river in the forests of Sabah and Sarawak, in the kampongs of the east coast of the Peninsula, and in the side streets of Melaka. Similarly, the world inhabited by Lee and Mahathir is here, showcased in the slick bars, hotels and restaurants of Singapore and Kuala Lumpur, in the efficient transportation systems, and the flickering computer screens.

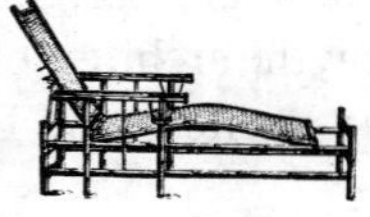

Where to go

THE THREE countries covered in this book are split into two land areas, divided by some 600 km of the South China Sea. Half of Malaysia occupies the Malay Peninsula, with Singapore at its southern extremity, while the other half, consisting of the East Malaysian states of Sabah and Sarawak, takes up the western portion of the island of Borneo, with the Sultanate of Brunei Darussalam neatly sandwiched between the two East Malaysian states.

The Peninsula and Borneo offer wildly different visions of environment, life and livelihood in the region. Even to begin to grasp this diversity it is necessary to visit both areas and combine a visit to the Peninsula (West Malaysia) and Singapore with a trip to the East Malaysian states of Sabah or Sarawak. Of course many people decide to concentrate their attentions on the jungles and upriver tribal groups of Borneo, or on the historic cities of the Peninsula, for instance, and there are good reasons to be selective in this manner. But for those intent on combining the two 'faces' of the region in one visit, timetabling requires a little more thought.

TRANSPORT AND TRAVELLING

Singapore and the Peninsula

The transport infrastructures in Singapore and on the Malay Peninsula are well developed and because the Peninsula is less than 1,000 km from north to south, and considerably less from east to west, travelling even from one extremity to the other by road (or rail) can be achieved comparatively painlessly in less than a day. Although West Malaysia and Singapore may account for the great bulk – around 80% – of the population of the three countries covered here, in terms of land area East Malaysia and Brunei are considerably bigger.

The main transport glitch to bear in mind, and it is only a minor one, is the barrier presented by the Barisan Titiwangsa, a range of mountains that runs down the centre of the Peninsula. As a result, north-south communication is easier than east-west. This is particularly true in the northern half of the Peninsula where the Barisan Titiwangsa is at its most imposing.

Because population centres, including the capital Kuala Lumpur, and industrial activity are concentrated on the western side of the Peninsula, the roads here are generally faster – although the traffic is much heavier too. The east coast's roads are fine and have been greatly improved over recent years.

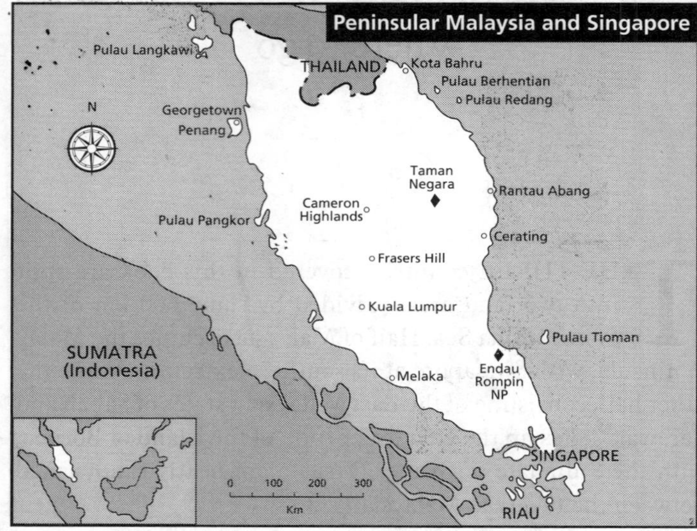

Given the concentration of people and economic activity on the Peninsula, public transport is generally good, frequent and cheap. Singapore has a superb public transportation system, and because the government restricts private car ownership the roads are wonderfully clear of traffic jams. Kuala Lumpur is another story; congestion is terrible and catching a taxi at peak periods can be enormously frustrating (businesspeople with a meeting to make, take note!). Phase I of the Light Rail Transit System (or LRT) began operating in 1996 and the first section of Phase II is due to open in time for the Commonwealth Games (which KL is hosting) in 1998. So far the LRT appears to have had only a marginal impact on congestion, although the Phase II extension may improve the situation.

East Malaysia (Sarawak and Sabah) and Brunei

Travelling around East Malaysia and Brunei by road is more difficult than on the Peninsula. Roads are few, their condition is often poor, and public transport is less well developed. To get to some towns, taking a plane is occasionally the only sensible option. The population of the area have traditionally used rivers as arteries of communication and they still provide the main links between many regional centres. But river transport can be slow (although there are terrifyingly fast speedboats) and it is also affected by the seasons. In the dry season, when water levels are low, some services stop entirely.

Because many people visit East Malaysia to travel upriver and stay in tribal longhouses and explore the magnificent national parks, providing ample time to return to base is essential. Brunei, although its coastal roads are good, has a poor public transportation system and the bus service is sporadic and limited. The reason? Most Bruneians own their own cars so there is little local demand for public transport.

TIMETABLING A VISIT

As the above has hinted, getting around Peninsular Malaysia and Singapore is not difficult and even making the trip from Kota Bharu at the northern extremity of the east coast, down to Melaka, towards the southern end of the west coast, need only take a day's travelling by road. Air links between the major towns are clearly faster still. However, many visitors with only a fortnight, say, in the area wonder whether it is possible to combine a trip to Peninsular Malaysia and Singapore with a visit to East Malaysia and Brunei. This requires a little more thought. There are regular domestic air connections between the Peninsula and the major cities of East Malaysia and Brunei, and from there with smaller towns in the Bornean interior. For those intending, for example, to fly to Kota Kinabalu, stay a few days at Tanjung Aru Beach, and then return, taking in East and West Malaysia should pose no difficulties. However, if intending to do more than this, such as climbing Mount Kinabalu, travelling upriver on the Baram, Rejang or Skrang rivers, or hiking through one of the national parks, then a little more leeway in terms of time is required. A minimum period to just begin to scratch the surface would be 1 week, preferably 10 days to 2 weeks. Of course some people spend weeks and weeks in just one area and still profess to have seen only a fraction of what is on offer.

HIGHLIGHTS

Hill Stations

The Peninsula and Singapore: Fraser's Hill and the Cameron Highlands offer a taste of colonial Malaya, and there are good walks around the Cameron Highlands. The Genting Highlands is more ersatz and kitsch, a favourite haunt of KL's nouveau riche. Maxwell Hill is the quietest of the hill stations.

Wildlife and Jungle

The Peninsula and Singapore: the national parks of the peninsula do not compare with those of East Malaysia. Nonetheless, Taman Negara and the Endau Rompin National Park are both well worth visiting. Rantau Abang on the east coast is a stretch of shoreline where turtles come to lay their eggs.

East Malaysia and Brunei: Sarawak, Sabah and Brunei offer a wealth of parks and conservation areas. Some, like the Semonggoh Orang Utan Sanctuary and the Bako National Park outside Kuching, and the Sepilok Orang Utan Rehabilitation Centre and the Turtle Islands National Park outside Sandakan are accessible as day trips. Other parks, like the Niah and Gunung Mulu national parks for example, require several days to explore properly.

Trekking

The Peninsula and Singapore: there are good jungle treks in Taman Negara and in the Endau Rompin National Park, and hiking in the Cameron Highlands.

East Malaysia and Brunei: most of East Malaysia's parks offer hiking trails, but the best are in the Niah, Gunung Mulu and Gunung Kinabalu national parks. Climbing Mount Kinabalu, to be at the summit for sunrise, is one of the most popular hikes.

Natural features

East Malaysia and Brunei: the caves at the Niah and Gunung Mulu national parks, and Gunung Kinabalu (Malaysia's highest mountain) are stupendous natural features worth visiting for themselves.

Beaches

The Peninsula and Singapore: Penang has a wide selection of hotels and facilities, and some may view it as over-developed. Langkawi, though more recently 'discovered', has also developed rapidly in recent years. Also off the west coast is Pulau Pangkor. Tioman, off the Peninsula's east coast, is less developed than Langkawi and Penang and there are also numerous other islands which are less touched by the hands of humans still. On the Peninsula itself, Kampung Cerating is the best known beach resort, which still

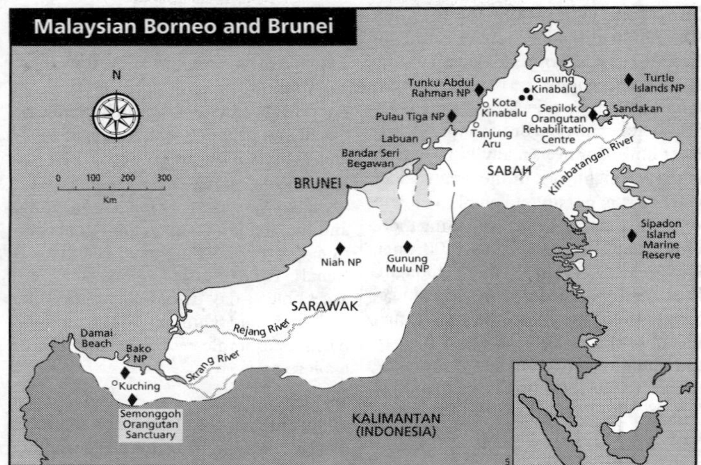

has a backpacker-feel to it, although it is hardly off the beaten track. There are also other groups of hotels and chalets dotted up and down the east coast.

East Malaysia and Brunei: East Malaysia and Brunei do not have beach 'resorts' to compare with those – at least in scale – of the Peninsula. However, there are some fine beaches and excellent snorkelling and diving, especially in the Tunku Abdul Rahman National Park and at Sipadan Island Marine Reserve. Small resorts include those at Damai, north of Kuching; Tanjung Aru, outside Kota Kinabalu; and Labuan.

Diving

For more details see page 46.

The Peninsula and Singapore: dive sites off the Peninsula are not world class although there are some very good places to learn to scuba dive including Pulau Paya, Pulau Pangkor, Tioman, the Pulau Sibu archipelago, Pulau Redang and Pulau Perhentian.

East Malaysia and Brunei: there are some world class dive sites in East Malaysia including Pulau Sipadan, Pulau Layang-Layang, the Tunku Abdul Rahman and Turtle Islands national parks, Pulau Tiga and Labuan.

Historical sites

The Peninsula and Singapore: Melaka is one of Malaysia's two historic gems. There are buildings dating from the Portuguese and Dutch periods, as well as some fine Chinese shophouses. Georgetown, the capital of Penang, is Malaysia's second city of architectural and historical note with probably the finest assembly of Sino-colonial architecture in the region.

Culture

The Peninsula and Singapore: traditional Malay culture is best preserved on the east coast, and especially in the Malay heartland of Kelantan (Kota Bharu) with its rural kampongs and thriving craft industry.

East Malaysia and Brunei: the Sarawak Cultural Village near Kuching offers an anaesthetized vision of tribal life and culture; the upriver 'tribes' and longhouses give a taste of the real thing. The Rajang, Skrang, and Kinabatanagan rivers, dotted with towns and small tribal settlements, are all worth exploring by boat.

Shopping

The Peninsula and Singapore: Singapore is renowned as a shopping Mecca. In terms of picking up a bargain this is today largely undeserved, although the range of goods is vast. KL is the best place to buy the full range of handicrafts from batik to blowpipes, although prices are higher than at their source. The east coast is the centre of the Peninsula's Malay handicraft industry, particularly Kelantan (Kota Bharu).

East Malaysia and Brunei: Sabah and Sarawak are the places to find tribal handicrafts. Many are on sale in the main towns, although smaller communities potentially offer the best buys.

Cuisine and nightlife

The Peninsula and Singapore: Singapore's restaurants, bars and nightlife are varied and abundant. Though Kuala Lumpur is not on the same level of sophistication as Singapore, it also has a very good range of restaurants.

Museums

The Peninsula and Singapore: Singapore has a fine collection of museums and art galleries, most of them meticulously managed. Kuala Lumpur's museums are less impressive but worth visiting. Sentosa in Singapore, an entertainment complex rather than a museum, is also noteworthy.

East Malaysia and Brunei: surprisingly, perhaps the best museum in the region is the Sarawak Museum in Kuching with its superb ethnographic collection.

NB The above is only a selection of places of interest and is not exhaustive. It is designed to assist in planning a trip to the region. Any 'highlight' list is inevitably subjective.

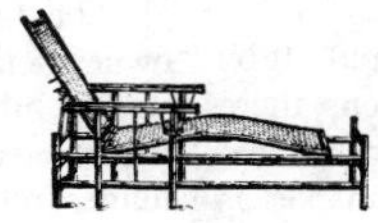

How to go

BEST TIME TO VISIT

The Malaysian government announced that it no longer has an 'off season' for tourism. This attempt to even-out arrivals has not, however, changed the pattern of the seasons. Temperatures at sea level uniformly range between 25° and 30°. Rainfall shows more variability although the seasons are not nearly as marked as they are further north, in Thailand, and south, in Indonesia.

On the west coast of the Peninsula, the pattern of rainfall through the year is least varied as it is protected from the north-east monsoon by the shadowing effect of the Barisan Titiwangsa. See the climate graphs on pages 99 (Kuala Lumpur), 147 (Cameron Highlands), 175 (Penang), 221 (Melaka), and 243 (Johor Bahru). The east coast of the Peninsula, however, bears the full brunt of the north-east monsoon and rainfall is concentrated in the months of November, December, January and February. See the climate graphs on pages 255 (Mersing), 273 (Kuantan), 297 (Kuala Terengganu), and 306 (Kota Bharu).

East Malaysia and Brunei have a similar pattern of rainfall, with December, January and February being the wettest months, although this becomes less marked travelling north-east into Sabah. See the climate graphs on pages 46 (Kuching) and 18 (Kota Kinabalu).

Although many people are put off by the prospect of tropical monsoons, there are advantages of travelling in the wet season, especially now that transport is not so influenced by the state of the weather. Generally during the low season visitors can take advantage of discounted hotel prices and in East Malaysia and Brunei river transport is cheapest and fastest when the river's are high. Some river services do not run during low water at the end of the dry season.

HEALTH

In Singapore, medical care is first class but expensive. Health care in Malaysia and Brunei is also of a high standard. Most doctors speak English even in smaller towns, and the general run of ailments can be adequately treated.

For a comprehensive roundup of health related issues see page 742.

WHAT TO TAKE

Travellers usually take too much. Almost everything is available in the main towns and cities – and often at a lower price than in the West. Remoter areas, are inevitably, less well supplied.

Suitcases are not appropriate if you are intending to travel overland by bus. A backpack, or even better a travelpack (where the straps can be zipped out of sight), is recommended. Travelpacks have the advantage of being hybrid backpacks-suitcases; they can be carried on the back for easy porterage, but they can also be taken into hotels without the owner being labelled a 'hippy'. **NB** For serious hikers, a backpack with an internal frame is still by far the best option for longer treks.

In terms of clothing, dress in Southeast Asia is relatively casual – even at formal functions. Suits are not necessary except in a few of the most expensive restaurants. However, although formal attire may be the exception, dressing tidily is the norm. Women particularly should note that in many areas of Malaysia and Brunei, they should avoid offending Muslim sensibilities and dress 'demurely' (ie keep shoulders covered and wear below-knee skirts or trousers). This is particularly true on the east coast of the Peninsula, especially in Kelantan, but does not generally apply in most beach resorts. It is usually warm (except in highland areas), so only one thin sweater or sweatshirt is necessary. Cotton clothes are most appropriate: they are light, dry quickly, and are cool. A sarong is useful when bathing in public or lounging in the evening – but it is best to buy one after arrival.

There is a tendency, rather than to take inappropriate articles of clothing, to take too many of the same article. Laundry services are cheap, and the turn-around rapid. It is also worth remembering that clothes are cheap should something fall apart or get lost.

Checklist

Bumbag
Earplugs
First aid kit
Insect repellent and/or electric mosquito mats, coils
International driving licence
Passports (valid for at least 6 months)
Photocopies of essential documents
Short wave radio
Spare passport photographs
Sun protection
Sunglasses
Swiss Army knife
Torch
Umbrella
Wet wipes
Zip-lock bags

Those intending to stay in budget accommodation might also include:
Cotton sheet sleeping bag
Money belt
Padlock (for hotel room and pack)
Sarong (or buy on arrival)
Soap
Student card
Toilet paper
Towel
Travel wash

For women travellers
A supply of tampons (although these are available in most towns)
A wedding ring for single female travellers who might want to help ward off the attentions of amorous admirers.

MONEY

Travellers cheques denominated in most major currencies can be easily exchanged in Malaysia, Singapore and Brunei. A small amount of cash (in US$) can also be useful in an emergency. Keep it separate from your TCs. Most credit cards are accepted in Malaysia, and money can also be drawn from ATMs (Automatic Teller Machines) with a 'PIN' number.

NB The Malaysian currency, the ringgit, weakened considerably during 1997. This is likely to result in higher prices (in ringgit terms) for many goods and services.

ISIC

Anyone in full-time education is entitled to an International Student Identity Card (ISIC). These are issued by student travel offices and travel agencies across the world and offer special rates on all forms of

Exchange rates (December 1997)

	US$	£	DM
Brunei (dollar)	1.63	2.70	0.92
Indonesia (rupiah)	4,580	7,575	2,583
Malaysia (ringgit)	3.74	6.19	2.11
Singapore (dollar)	1.63	2.70	0.92

transport and other concessions and services. The ISIC head office is: ISIC Association, Box 9048, 1000 Copenhagen, Denmark, T (45) 33 93 93 03.

WORKING ABROAD

It is sometimes possible to arrange work in the region. Contact Jobs Abroad in the UK for further information. They will also arrange work permits, visas etc.

GETTING THERE

AIR

Many airlines offer non-stop flights from European cities. The scheduled flying time from London to Singapore is 13 hours on direct flights, but may be up to 20 hours on flights with more than one stop. Many of the world's top airlines fly the Southeast Asian routes and standards are therefore high. From North America's west coast there are direct flights from Los Angeles and Vancouver.

Discounts

It is possible to obtain significant discounts, especially outside European holiday times, most notably in London. Shop around and book early. It is also possible to get discounts from Australasia, South Asia and Japan. Note that 'peak season' varies from airline to airline – many using 8-10 bands. This means one airline's high season may not be another's.

Air passes

Discover Malaysia Air Pass This is a US$199, 21-day pass for up to five sectors on any internal flight, including Sabah and Sarawak. (Or US$99 for just Peninsula Malaysia.) The pass must be used in conjunction with at least one international sector on Malaysia Airlines and purchased prior to departure outside Malaysia. As the terms change frequently, check with a good travel agent before booking flights – the above was valid to 31 December 1997. Be particularly careful to check any restrictions on either international or internal flights.

SEA

Few people arrive in island Southeast Asia by sea, despite the fact every country is a maritime nation. There are few regular oceanic passenger ships to Malaysia, Brunei or Singapore. However, there are daily international ferry links between Singapore and Batam Island, Sumatra, Indonesia; and between Peninsular Malaysia and various ports on the Sumatran 'mainland'. Boats also run between Singapore and Peninsular Malaysia, although most people take the causeway; and between Brunei and East Malaysia. Finally, there are regular connections between Langkawi and the Thai port of Satun.

For those interested in booking a passage on a cargo ship travelling to the region, contact the Strand Cruise Centre, Charing Cross Shopping Concourse, The Strand, London WC2N 4HZ, T 0171-836-6363, F 0171-497-0078. Another company booking berths on freighters is Wagner Frachtschiffreissen, Stadlerstrasse 48, CH-8404 Winterthur, Switzerland, T (052) 242-1442, F (052) 242 1487.

OVERLAND

There are road links between Thailand and Peninsular Malaysia, and Peninsular Malaysia and Singapore (the latter via a 1.2 km causeway). There are also overland links between the Borneo states of East Malaysia (Sabah and Sarawak) and Brunei and Kalimantan (Indonesia). The most commonly used border crossings are those separating Malaysia from Thailand to the north, and Singapore to the south. Regular buses and trains ply these routes.

SAFETY

Confidence tricksters

Most common of all are confidence tricksters: people selling fake gems and antiques, informal currency exchange services offering surprisingly good rates, and card sharps. Confidence tricksters are, by definition, extremely convincing and persuasive. Time, as they say, is cheaper in Southeast Asia than it is in the West, and people are willing to invest long hours lulling tourists into a false sense of security. Be suspicious of any offer than seems too good to be true. That is probably what it is.

Theft

Thieves favour public transport; confidence tricksters frequent popular tourist destinations. Personal valuables – money, TCs, passports, jewellery – should be kept safe. Do not leave valuables in hotel rooms; place them in a safe deposit box if possible, or keep them with you.

Drugs

Penalties are harsh; in Malaysia and Singapore the death penalty applies for trafficking in even modest quantities.

Police

Report any incident that involves you or your possessions. In general, police will act promptly and properly.

Prisoners Abroad

Prisoners Abroad is a charity dedicated to supporting UK nationals in prison abroad. As the charity writes: "Arrest, trial and imprisonment are devastating in a familiar environment, supported by family and friends. Abroad it is much worse." Young men and women caught with drugs may find themselves facing sentences of 10 years or more, often in appalling conditions. Volunteers can help Prisoners Abroad, and similar organizations, by becoming a pen pal, donating a magazine subscription, or sending books, for example. If you or a friend find yourself in the unfortunate position of being in jail, or facing a jail term, then contact the charity at: Prisoners Abroad, Freepost 82, Roseberry Avenue, London EC1B 1XB, UK, T (+44) (0)171 833-3467, F (+44) (0)171 833-3460. Further information on the charity and its work can also be obtained from the above address.

WOMEN TRAVELLING ALONE

Women travelling alone face greater difficulties than men or couples. The general advice given above should be observed even more carefully. Young Southeast Asian women rarely travel without a partner, so it is believed to be strange for a western woman to do so. Western women are often believed to be of easy virtue – a view perpetuated by Hollywood and in local films, for example. To minimize the pestering that will occur, dress modestly – particularly in staunchly Muslim areas such as the east coast of Peninsular Malaysia. Comments, sometimes derogatory, will be made however carefully you dress and act; simply ignore them. Toiletries such as tampons are widely available in the main towns and cities of the region.

TRAVELLING WITH CHILDREN

Many people are reluctant to visit Southeast Asia with young children, but for Malaysia, Singapore and Brunei it need not be regarded as 'out of the question'. See page 749 for more advice and background.

WHERE TO STAY

The main towns and tourist destinations in Malaysia and Singapore offer a wide range of accommodation. Some of the finest hotels in the world are to be found in these countries and are moderately priced by western standards. Mid-range and budget accommodation are also generally of a relatively good standard – and in many towns it is also possible to get a dorm bed for just a few ringgit. However, outside the main towns and tourist areas, accommodation can be surprisingly limited – restricted to one or two 'Chinese' hotels with neither budget places for backpackers, nor more expensive establishments. In Brunei, budget accommodation is not available, and hotel rates are high.

Camping

Camping is becoming increasingly popular in Malaysia and Singapore. Most national parks offer camping facilities and they are generally good. Outside national parks however, there are very few dedicated camping grounds. Southeast Asians find it strange that anyone should want to camp out when it is possible to stay in a hotel.

FOOD AND DRINK

Food

Food in Malaysia and Singapore is generally good, and excellent value for money. Levels of hygiene are reasonable – particularly in Singapore. All towns have local restaurants and stalls serving cheap, tasty and nourishing dishes.

In tourist areas and more expensive hotels, western food is also widely available. In areas popular with backpackers, so-called travellers' food is also available: dishes such as chocolate fudge cake, pancakes, fruit shakes (or 'smoothies'), and garlic toast. Across the region, fruit can be a life-saver. It is varied, cheap, exotic, safe to eat (if peeled oneself) and delicious.

Water

Bottled water is also easily obtainable in these countries. It is only advisable to drink water straight from the tap in Singapore.

GETTING AROUND

AIR

Services are efficient and safe, although considerably more expensive than the overland alternatives. See page 18 for details on the Discover Malaysia Air Pass.

TRAIN

Travelling third class is often the cheapest way to get from A to B, while first class (air-conditioned) is more comfortable (and safer) than travelling by bus (although usually slower). **NB** Theft can be a problem on long-distance train journeys.

ROAD

Road is the main mode of transport in most areas, with the exception of some parts of East Malaysia. **Buses** link nearly all towns, however small. In much of Malaysia (except the Borneo states of Sabah and Sarawak), Brunei and Singapore roads are good, and air-conditioned 'VIP' buses are available on the more popular routes. These are considerably cheaper than travelling by air. Non air-conditioned buses and other vicarious forms of transport are cheaper still, but usually slower and more uncomfortable. **NB** Security can be a problem on long-distance bus journeys.

CAR HIRE

Cars for self-drive hire are available from reputable firms. Motorists drive on the left, and standards of driving are reasonably high (compared with neighbouring Indonesia and Thailand). While it is usual in Indonesia and Thailand for foreign visitors to hire a driver as well as a car, in Malaysia it is much more common for visitors to drive themselves.

DRIVE AROUND MALAYSIA WITH ...

FOR RESERVATIONS:
Tel: (603) 230 7788
Fax: (603) 232 0077

RENTAL LOCATIONS:
- *Kuala Lumpur, Shangri-La Hotel*
- *Kuala Lumpur Airport*
- *Penang Airport*

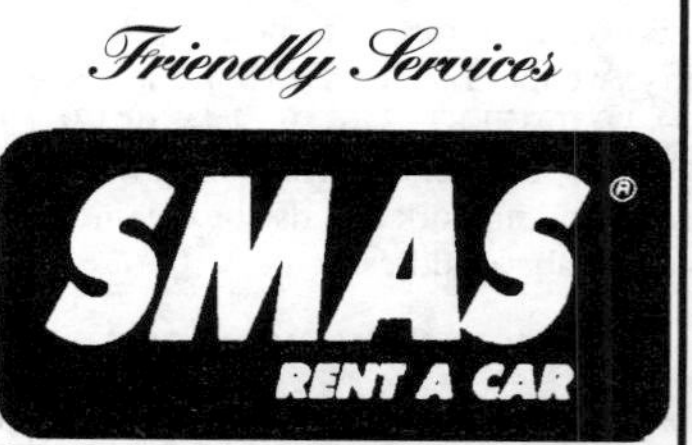

HITCHHIKING AND CYCLING

Hitchhiking is not common in Southeast Asia, although it is easy in Malaysia and Brunei. However there are small but increasing numbers of visitors who tour Indonesia and Malaysia by **bicycle**. It is strongly recommended that bicyclists arrange their route on minor roads; drivers use the hard shoulder. See pages 518 for further information on bicycling in Malaysia.

BOAT

There are regular ferries to off-shore islands and Malaysian passenger ferries link the main port towns of the Peninsula with Singapore, Sabah and Sarawak. In East Malaysia, river-craft are sometimes a more usual mode of transport than road.

LANGUAGE

English is widely spoken in Singapore and Malaysia. Off the tourist track in Malaysia, it is useful to be able to speak a few words of Malay.

Tourism: counting the costs

"Tourism is like fire. It can either cook your food or burn your house down". This sums up the ambivalent attitude that many people have regarding the effects of tourism. It is the largest foreign exchange earner in countries like Thailand, and the world's largest single industry; yet many people in receiving countries would rather tourists go home. Tourism is seen to be the cause of polluted beaches, rising prices, loose morals, consumerism, and much else besides.

The word 'tourist' is derived from 'travail', meaning work or torment. Travail, in turn, has its roots in the Latin word *tripalium*, which was a three-pronged instrument of torture. For many people struggling through interior Borneo this etymology should strike a chord. And yet, as *The Economist* pointed out in a survey of the industry in 1991:

> "The curse of the tourist industry is that it peddles dreams: dreams of holidays where the sun always shines, the children are always occupied, and where every evening ends in the best sex you have ever had. For most of its modern life, this has been matched by a concomitant dreaminess on the part of its customers. When asked, most tourists tell whopping lies about what they want on holiday..." (Economist, 1991).

Most international tourists come from a handful of wealthy countries. Half from just five countries (the USA, Germany, the UK, Japan and France) and 80% from 20 countries. This is why many see tourism as the new 'imperialism', imposing alien cultures and ideals on sensitive and unmodernized peoples. The problem, however, is that discussions of the effects of tourism tend to degenerate into simplifications – culminating in the drawing up of a checklist of 'positive' and 'negative' effects, much like the one on page 26. Although such tables may be useful in highlighting problem areas, they also do a disservice by reducing a complex issue to a simple set of rather one dimensional 'costs' and 'benefits'. Different destinations will be affected in different ways; these effects are likely to vary over time; and different groups living in a particular destination will feel the effects of tourism in different ways and to varying degrees. At no time or place can tourism (or any other influence) be categorized as uniformly 'good' or 'bad'. Tourism can take an Australian backpacker on US$5 a day to a village on the east coast of Peninsular Malaysia, an American tourist to luxury hotels in the city state of Singapore where a room can cost over US$200 a night, and a Malaysian Muslim to the southern Thai cities of Hat Yai and Songkhla on a long weekend.

SEARCHING FOR CULTURE

Southeast Asia is one of the richest cultural areas in the world, and many tourists are attracted to the region because of its exotic peoples. These include the Dayaks of Borneo. When cultural erosion is identified, the tendency is to blame this on tourists and tourism. Turner and Ash have written that tourists are the "suntanned destroyers of culture", while Bugnicourt argues that tourism:

"...encourages the imitation of foreigners and the downgrading of local inhabitants in relation to foreign tourists; it incites the pillage of art work and other historical artefacts; it leads to the degeneration of classical and popular dancing, the profanation and vulgarization of places of worship, and the perversion of religious ceremonies; it creates a sense of inferiority and a cultural demoralization which 'fans the flames of anti-development' through the acquisition of undesirable cultural traits" (1977).

The problem with views like this is that they assume that change is bad, and that indigenous cultures are unchanging. It makes local peoples victims of change, rather than masters of their own destinies. It also assumes that tourism is an external influence, when in fact it quickly becomes part of the local landscape. Cultural change is inevitable and on-going, and 'new' and 'traditional' are only judgements, not absolutes. Thus new cultural forms can quickly become key markers of tradition. Tourists searching for an 'authentic' experience are assuming that tradition is tangible, easily identifiable and unchanging. It is none of these.

'Tribal' people wearing American baseball caps are assumed to have succumbed to western culture. But such changes really say next to nothing about an individual's strength of identity. There are also problems with identifying cultural erosion, let alone linking it specifically with tourism, rather than with the wider processes of 'modernisation'. This is exemplified in the case of Bali where tourism is paraded by some as the saviour of Balinese culture, and by others as its destroyer. Michel Picard in his paper "'Cultural tourism' in Bali" (1992) writes:

"No sooner had culture become the emblematic image of Bali [in the 1920s] than foreign visitors and residents started fearing for its oncoming disappearance. ...the mere evocation of Bali suggested the imminent and dramatic fall from the 'Garden of Eden': sooner of later, the 'Last Paradise' was doomed to become a 'Paradise Lost'" (Picard, 1992:77).

Yet the authorities on Bali are clearly at a loss as to how to balance their conflicting views:

"...the view of tourism held by the Balinese authorities is blatantly ambivalent, the driving force of a modernisation process which they welcome as ardently as they fear. Tourism in their eyes appears at once the most promising source of economic development and as the most subversive agent for the spread of foreign cultural influences in Bali" (Picard,1992:85).

TOURIST ART: FINE ART, DEGRADED ART

Tourist art, both material (for instance, sculpture) and non-material (like dances) is another issue where views sharply diverge. The mass of inferior 'airport' art on sale to tourists demonstrates, to some, the corrosive effects of tourism. It leads craftsmen and women to mass-produce second rate pieces for a market that appreciates neither their cultural or symbolic worth, nor their aesthetic value. Yet tourism can also give value to craft industries that would otherwise be undermined by cheap industrial goods. The geographer Michael Parnwell has argued with respect to the poor Northeast of Thailand, the craft tradition should be allied with tourism to create vibrant rural industries. The corrosive effects of tourism on arts and crafts also assumes that artists and craftsmen are unable to distinguish between fine pieces and pot-boilers. Many produce inferior pieces for the tourist market while continuing to produce for local demand, the former effectively subsidising the latter.

Some researchers have also shown how there is a tendency for culture to be 'invented' for tourists, and for this to then become part of 'tradition'. Michel Picard has shown in the case of Bali how dances developed for tourists are now paraded as paragons of national cultural heritage. The same is true of art, where the anthropologist Lewis Hill of the Centre for

South-East Asian Studies at the University of Hull has demonstrated how objects made for the tourist market in one period are later enthusiastically embraced by the host community.

ENVIRONMENT AND TOURISM

The environmental deterioration that is linked to tourism is due to a destination area exceeding its 'carrying capacity' as a result of overcrowding. But carrying capacity, though an attractive concept, is notoriously difficult to pin down in any exact manner. A second dilemma facing those trying to encourage greater environmental consciousness is the so-called 'tragedy of the commons', better described in terms of Chinese restaurants. When a group of people go to a Chinese restaurant with the intention of sharing the bill, each customer will tend to order a more expensive dish than he or she would normally do – on the logic that everyone will be doing the same, and the bill will be split. In tourism terms, it means that hotel owners will always build those few more bungalows or that extra wing, to maximize their profits, reassured in the knowledge that the environmental costs will be shared among all hotel owners. So, despite most operators appreciating that over-development may 'kill the goose that lays the golden eggs', they do so anyway. Penang, off Peninsular Malaysia's west coast, is a classic example. By the late 1980s, the sea near the main stretch of hotels was too polluted to swim safely. In short, tourism contains the seeds of its own destruction.

But many developing countries have few other development opportunities. Those in Southeast Asia are blessed with beautiful landscapes and exotic cultures, and tourism is a cheap development option. Other possibilities cost more to develop and take longer to take-off. It is also true that 'development', however it is achieved, has cultural and environmental implications. For many, tourism is the

Tourism development guidelines

- Tourism should capitalize on local features (cultural and natural) so as to promote the use of local resources.
- Attention should be given to the type of tourist attracted. A mix of mass and individual will lead to greater local participation and better balance.
- Tourist development should be integrated with other sectors. Co-ordination between agencies is crucial.
- Facilities created should be made available to locals, at subsidised rates if necessary.
- Resources such as beaches and parks must remain in the public domain.
- Different tourists and tourist markets should be exploited so as to minimize seasonal variations in arrivals and employment.
- A tourist threshold should be identified and adhered to.
- Environmental impact assessments and other surveys must be carried out.
- Provision of services to tourists must be allied with improvements in facilities for locals.
- Development should be focused in areas where land use conflicts will be kept to a minimum.
- Supplies, where possible, should be sourced locally.
- Assistance and support should be given to small-scale, local entrepreneurs.

least environmentally corrosive of the various options open to poor countries struggling to achieve rapid economic growth.

THE 'POST-TOURIST' AND THE TRAVELLER

In the last few years a new tourist has appeared; or at least a new type of tourist has been identified – the 'post-tourist'. The post-tourist is part of the post-modern world. He or she is aware that nothing is authentic; that every tourist experience is new and different; that tourism begins at home, in front of the television. The whole globe is a stage on and in which the post-tourist can revel; the crass and crude is just as interesting and delightful as the traditional and authentic to the post-tourist. He – or she – is abundantly aware that he is a tourist, not a brave and inquisitive searcher for culture and truth; just another sunburnt, probably over-weight, almost certainly ignorant foreigner spending money to have a holiday (not a travel 'experience') in a foreign country. Paradoxically this lack of apparent discernment is what is seen to identify the post-tourist as truly discerning. Feifer, in 1985, stated that the post-tourist is well aware he is "not a time-traveller when he goes somewhere historic; not an instant noble savage when he stays on a tropical beach; not an invisible observer when he visits a native compound. Resolutely 'realistic', he cannot evade his condition of outsider". Of course, all this could be discounted as the meaningless meanderings of a group of academics with little better to do than play with words and ideas. But, there is something akin to the post-tourist of the academic world beginning to inhabit the real world of tourism. These people might have once been described as just cynics, marvelling in the shear ironies of life. They are tourists for whom tourism is a game to be taken lightly; people who recognize that they are just another 'guest', another consumer of the tourist experience. No-one, and nothing, special.

The 'traveller' in contrast to the post-tourist finds it hard even to think of him or herself as a tourist at all. This, of course, is hubris built upon the notion that the traveller is an 'independent' explorer somehow beyond the bounds of the industry. Anna Borzello in an article entitled 'The myth of the traveller' in the journal *Tourism in Focus* (no. 19, 1994) writes that "Independent travellers cannot acknowledge – without shattering their self-image – that to many local people they are simply a good source of income. ...[not] inheritors of Livingstone, [but] bearers of urgently needed money". Although she does, in writing this, grossly underestimate the ability of travellers to see beyond their thongs and friendship bracelets, she does have a more pertinent point when she argues that it is important for travellers realistically to appraise their role as tourists, because: "Not only are independent travellers often frustrated by the gap between the way they see themselves and the way they are treated, but unless they acknowledge that they are part of the tourist industry they will not take responsibility for the damaging effects of their tourism."

GUIDE BOOKS AND TOURISM

Guide books themselves have been identified by some analysts as being part of the problem. They are selective in two senses. First, they tend to selectively pick destination areas, towns and regions. This is understandable: one book cannot cover all the possibilities in a country. Then, and second, they selectively pick sights, hotels and restaurants within those places. Given that many travellers use guide books to map out their journey, this creates a situation where books determine the spatial pattern of tourist flows. As John McCarthy writes in *Are sweet dreams made of this? Tourism in Bali and Eastern Indonesia* (1994, IRIP: Victoria, Australia):

> "Such is the power of guide books that, unless they are carefully written, one writer's point of view can determine the

commercial success or failure of a hotel or restaurant for years after. Even when the enterprise changes, the loathing or love of a travel writer who passed through a village 3 years ago remains too potent a testimony" (page 93).

There are no easy answers to this. If guide books were more diverse; if travellers really were more independent; and if guide books were not so opinionated and subjective, then this would all help in spreading the tourism phenomenon. But

A tourism checklist

Costs	Benefits
Vulnerable to external developments – eg oil price rises, 1991 Gulf War.	Diversifies an economy and is usually immune to protectionism. Requires few technical and human resources and is a 'cheap' development option. Requires little infrastructure.
Erodes culture by debasing it; strong cultures overwhelm sensitive ones (often tribal).	Gives value to cultures and helps in their preservation.
Leads to moral pollution with rising crime and prostitution.	Changing social norms are not due solely, or even mostly to tourism.
Often concentrated in culturally and environmentally sensitive areas, so effects are accentuated.	Helps to develop marginal areas that would otherwise 'miss out' on development.
Lack of planning and management causes environmental problems.	Poor planning and management is not peculiar to tourism and can be rectified.
Foreigners tend to dominate; costs of involvement are high so local people fail to become involved and benefit.	Costs of involvement can be very low; tourism is not so scale-dependent as other industries.
Tourism increases local inequalities. Jobs are usually seasonal and low-skilled. Economic leakages mean revenue generated tends to accrue to foreign multi-nationals.	Leakage is less than with many other industries; local involvement generally greater and value added is significant.
Tourism is not sustainable; tourism ultimately destroys tourism because it destroys those attributes that attracted tourists in the first place.	Tourism is not monolithic; destination areas evolve and do not have to suffer decay.

none of these is likely: guide books exist to 'guide'; humans are by nature subjective; and the notion of the free spirit 'traveller' has always, in the most part, been a mirage brought on by a romantic collective sense of what tourism *should* be. One answer is for books to become more specialist, and certainly one identifiable trend is towards guide books covering sub-national regions – East Malaysia, Singapore, and Kuala Lumpur, for example. It seems that people are now more willing to spend an extended period of time exploring one area, rather than notching up a large number of 'must do's'. Although even such specialist books also tend to suffer from the dangers of selectivity noted above, those people who do spend a longer period of time in an area are in a position to be more selective themselves, and to rely more on their own experiences rather than those of a guide book writer who may have visited a town in a bad mood 3 years previously.

In the opening page to his *Illustrated guide to the Federated Malay States*, Cuthbert Woodville Harrison wrote:

> "It has become nowadays so easy and so common a venture to cross the world that the simple circum-navigation of the globe 'merely for wantonness' is very rapidly ceasing to be in fashion. But as the rough places of the earth become smooth to the travellers, and they no longer fear 'that the gulfs will wash us down', there is growing amongst them a disposition to dwell awhile in those lands whose climate and inhabitants most differ from ours. The more completely such places are strange to us the more do they attract us, and the more isolated they have lived hitherto, the more do we feel called upon to visit them now."

Cuthbert Woodville Harrison's book was published in 1923.

SUGGESTED READING AND TOURISM PRESSURE GROUPS

In the UK, **Tourism Concern** aims to "promote greater understanding of the impacts of tourism on host communities and environments", "to raise awareness of the forms of tourism that respect the rights and interests of [local] people", and to "work for change in current tourism practice". Annual membership is £15.00 which includes subscription to their magazine *In Focus*. Tourism Concern, Froebel College, Roehampton Lane, London SW15 5PU, T (0181) 878-9053.

The most up-to-date book examining tourism in Southeast Asia is: Hitchcock, Mike *et al.* (edits) (1993) *Tourism in South-East Asia*, Routledge: London.

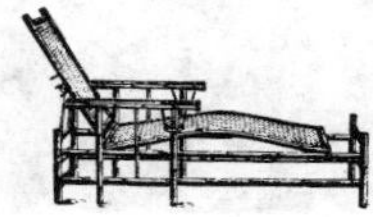

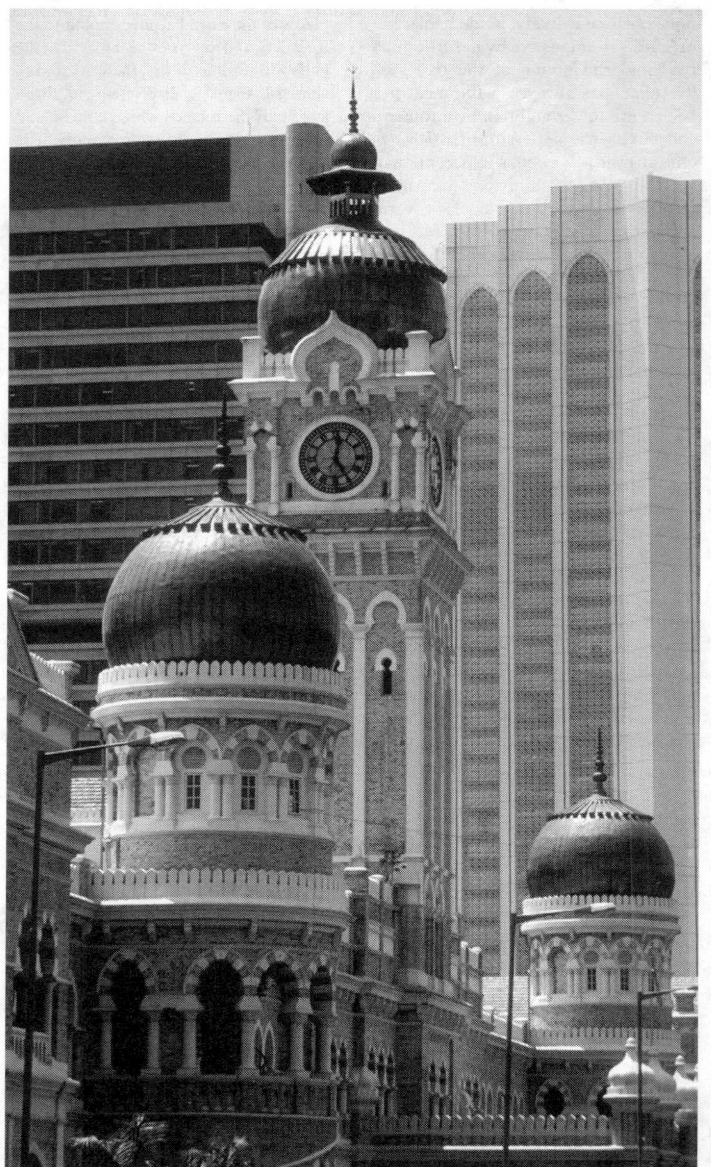

Malaysia

Horizons	31	Borneo Horizons	318
Kuala Lumpur	99	Sarawak	333
Northern Peninsular Malaysia	142	Sabah	422
Southern Peninsular Malaysia	214	Information for travellers	499
The Peninsular's East Coast	252		

THE POPULAR image of Malaysia – or more likely 'Malaya' – is one of tropical rainforests, honourable and proud Malays, intrepid rubber planters and industrious Chinese working in a country of monstrous butterflies and stifling tropical heat. The reality is that Malaysia has undergone fundamental social and economic change since the British left the land of Joseph Conrad's Captain William Lingard and Alfred Russel Wallace's orang utan. People are more likely to make semi-conductors than tap rubber trees, and just as likely to live in modern condominiums than in atap-roofed houses in a Malay *kampong*. Malaysia can no longer be classed as a 'developing' country – it is a self-confident nation whose time has come. A country that has been more than ready to confront the perceived self-serving hypocrisy of the West and to present itself as speaking for the interests of the collective 'Third World'. It may still, in the phrase of the Malaysian Tourist Promotion Board, be 'Fascinating Malaysia', but expect to be Fascinated Unexpectedly.

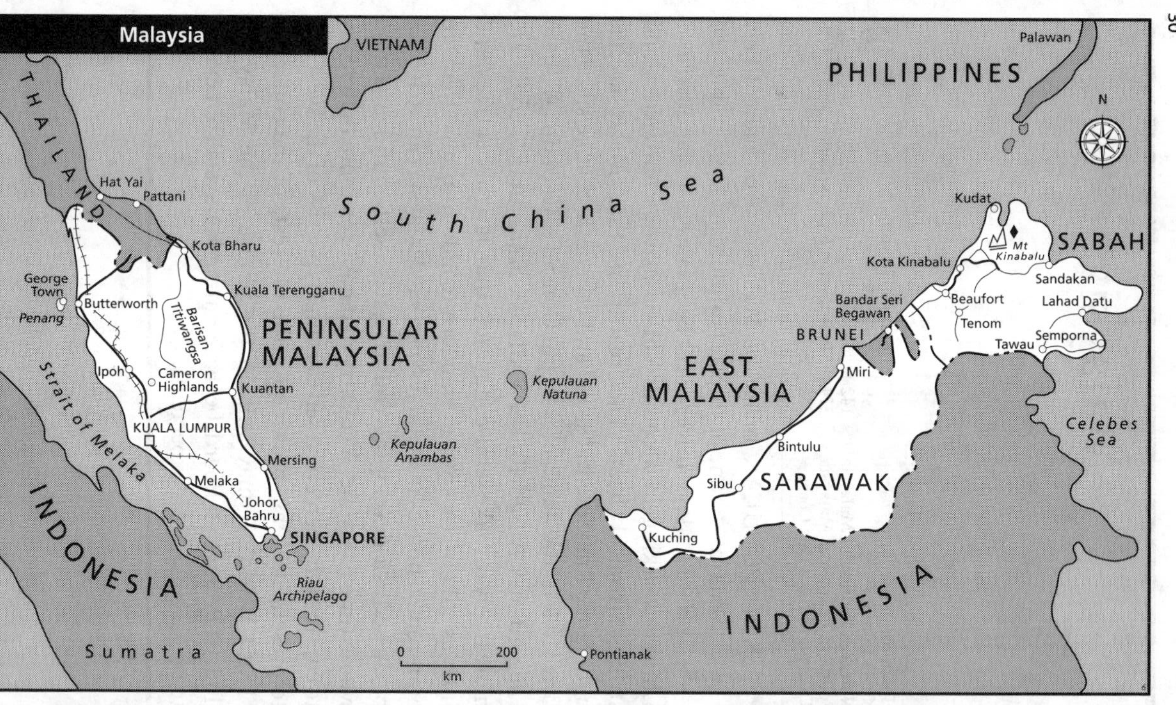
Malaysia
VIETNAM
PHILIPPINES
Palawan
N
THAILAND
Hat Yai
Pattani
South China Sea
Kota Bharu
Kuala Terengganu
George Town
Penang
Butterworth
Barisan Titiwangsa
PENINSULAR MALAYSIA
Ipoh
Cameron Highlands
Kuantan
Strait of Melaka
KUALA LUMPUR
Mersing
Melaka
Johor Bahru
SINGAPORE
INDONESIA
Riau Archipelago
Sumatra
Kepulauan Natuna
Kepulauan Anambas
0 200
km
Kudat
Mt Kinabalu
SABAH
Kota Kinabalu
Sandakan
Bandar Seri Begawan
Beaufort
Lahad Datu
Tenom
BRUNEI
Semporna
Tawau
EAST MALAYSIA
Miri
Celebes Sea
Bintulu
Sibu
SARAWAK
Kuching
INDONESIA
Pontianak

Horizons

The land	35	Art & architecture	61
Diving in Malaysia	46	Culture	63
History	48	Modern Malaysia	84

ON 31 AUGUST 1997 Malaysia turned 40. Over the four decades since independence the country has been transformed from a poor, undeveloped British colony reliant on the export of primary products like rubber and tin to a self-confident industrializing nation with a burgeoning middle class and an increasingly sophisticated economy. The figures, as they say, speak for themselves: between 1970 and 1995 per capita income rose ten-fold to RM10,000, the number of children dying before the age of one was cut from 40/1,000 live births to 10 and, most striking of all, the number of people living in poverty in Peninsular Malaysia was reduced from one in two to less than one in ten. Malaysia has become a country where people – and especially the prime minister, Mahathir Mohamad – think big. He has set out a vision which will bring Malaysia developed country status by 2020, and he is forever cajoling his people to join him in the effort.

Malaysia's economy – and, by implication, its Prime Minister – came in for a mauling during 1997 as Thailand's economic crisis rebounded on other economies in the Asian region (see page 96 for more details). The ringgit weakened, projected economic growth rates were cut, and some prestigious projects were delayed or shelved. The whiff of schadenfreude was thick in the air as Western journalists wrote of 'The end of the miracle', 'Asian tigers burning, burning not so bright', and 'Falling dragons'.

Malaysia is sometimes called 'the lucky country of Asia' because it is so richly endowed with natural resources. It has the world's largest tin deposits, extensive oil and gas reserves and is cloaked in rainforest containing valuable tropical hardwoods. Until very recently, the economy

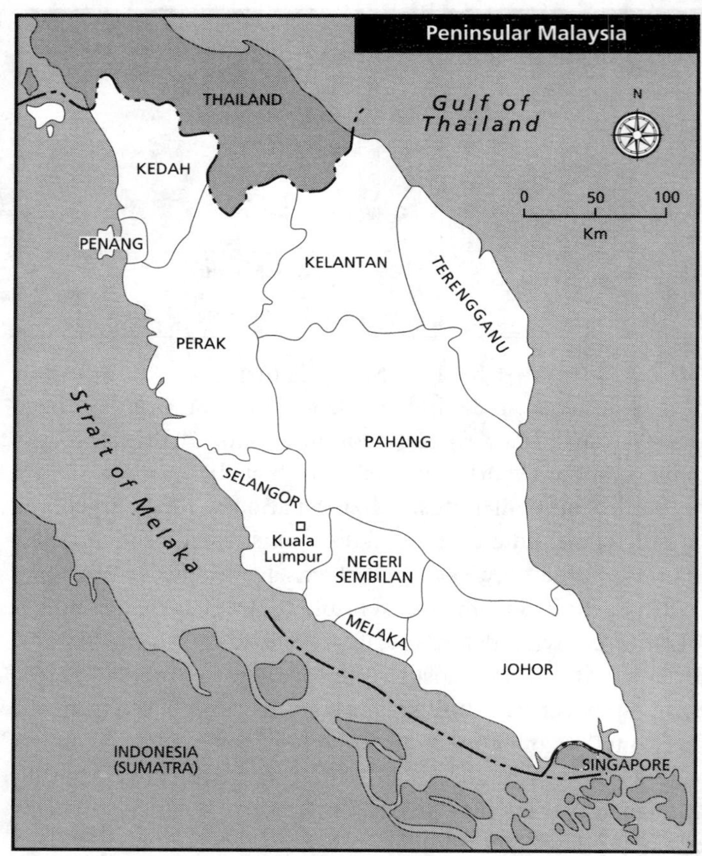

was heavily dependent on these resources and plantation crops such as palm oil, natural rubber, pepper and cocoa. But in the late 1980s and early 1990s, a sudden explosion of industrial growth, spearheaded by a surge in manufacturing, changed the complexion of Malaysia's economy beyond recognition. In 1992, Michael Vatikiotis, Kuala Lumpur correspondent for *The Far Eastern Economic Review*, wrote: "Malaysia in many ways forms the leading edge of social change in Southeast Asia. ... Prime Minister Dr Mahathir Mohamad has captivated his people with a vision of a developed Malaysia by 2020. Deploying this distant vision of the future has allowed Malaysians to think of themselves as becoming a nation of airline pilots and nuclear physicists by 2020."

Malaysia is a young country – until the end of the last century there was just a collection of divided coastal sultanates around the peninsula and three colonial trading settlements. The British grouped the different states into a federation, but

Biggest = best: Malaysia's race for the skies

Malaysia, one of the world's fastest growing and most self-confident nations, seems intent on dominating the *Guinness Book of Records*. The country now boasts:

- The world's tallest flagpole at 100m in Merdeka Square, Kuala Lumpur
- The Petronas Twin Towers in Kuala Lumpur, rising through 88 storeys to 450m. On their completion in 1996 the towers claimed the title of the tallest building(s) in the world. The Petronas Twin Towers are part of the Kuala Lumpur City Centre project which, when completed, will have no fewer than 22 office blocks.
- Asia's tallest tower, the KL Tower, at 421m which opened on 1 October 1996.
- The Bakun Hydroelectric Dam in the East Malaysian state of Sarawak. Preparatory work began in 1995 and when it is completed (there is still a chance it won't be) it will be the highest HEP dam in the world and the largest such project in Southeast Asia, generating 2,400 megawatts. The cost? A paltry US$6bn and 10,000 people uprooted.
- In 1995 Prime Minister Mahathir lay the foundation stone for Putrajaya, Malaysia's new capital city 35 km south of Kuala Lumpur. It is due for completion in 2005, will support a population of 250,000, and has a price tag of a cool US$8bn. Along with the new international airport and Cyberjaya, both under construction near Putrajaya, the total cost is projected at US$20bn.

Standard Chartered Securities in Kuala Lumpur drew up a list of the 31 largest projects Malaysia had embarked upon or had announced it was undertaking. Totting up the cost, the bill came to M$163bn or US$65bn. **NB** With the weakening of the Malaysian economy during 1997 some of these projects have been delayed or shelved.

Malaysia did not emerge in its present form until 1965, 8 years after independence from the British. Today the Federation of Malaysia includes the 11 peninsular states together with Sabah and Sarawak on the island of Borneo (East Malaysia). Singapore left the federation in 1965 after an unsuccessful 2-years experiment. The politically dominant Malays of the peninsula had felt uncomfortable with the destabilizing effect of Singapore's mainly Chinese population on the country's racial equation and the uncomfortable marriage of convenience came to an end.

A favourite Malaysian dish is *rojak* – a tossed salad with many different ingredients. It is not uncommon to hear the rojak analogy applied to Malaysia's exotic ethnic mix of Malays, Chinese, Indians and indigenous tribes. The country's cultural blend makes Malaysia interesting, but it is also a potentially volatile mixture. Yet only once since independence in 1957 has the communal melting pot boiled over. Today, most Malaysians are too young to remember the 1969 race riots, although they have lived with their consequences ever since. The government's affirmative action policies have attempted to lessen the economic disparities between the races (see page 90) and have given the Malays – the economic underdogs – a helping hand. Over the years, non-Malays have complained bitterly about discrimination against them by the Malay-led government, but somehow, tensions have been kept below boiling point. Today, there is much more inter-mixing between Malaysians from all ethnic backgrounds; many of them are more interested in cashing in on the economic boom than worrying about race. When Malaysia celebrated 35 years of nationhood in August 1992, Dr Mahathir said that on independence, many had predicted that its multiracial,

Putting Malaya on the map

The names of most of Malaysia's states are older than the name Malaya – until the 1870s the scattered coastal sultanates were independent of each other. Many of the Malay areas were colonized by Sumatrans long ago and it is possible that the word 'Melayu' – or 'Malay' – derives from the Sungai Melayu (Melayu River) in Sumatra. The name in turn is derived from the Dravidian (Tamil) word *malai*, or 'hill'. As the Malays are coastal people, the paradox is explained by their pre-Islamic religion, which is thought to have been based on a cult in which a sacred mountain took pride of place.

The Graeco-Roman geographer Ptolemy called the Malay peninsula *Aurea Chersonesus* – 'The Golden Chersonese': it was the fabled land of gold. By the early 1500s, European maps were already marking Melaka and Pulau Tioman, which were well known to Chinese mariners. During the Portuguese and Dutch colonial periods, the whole peninsula was simply labelled 'Malacca', and the town was the only significant European outpost until the British took possession of Penang in 1786. There was very little mapping of the peninsula until the early 19th century, and the names of states only gradually appeared on maps over the course of the 17th and 18th centuries.

According to cartographic historian RT Fell, the first maps of the interior of the peninsula, beyond the bounds of the British Straits Settlements, did not appear until the late 19th century. In 1885 the Survey Department was founded and charged with mapping the interior – one of the tasks William Cameron was undertaking when he stumbled across the highland plateau named after him that same year. But right into the 20th century, large tracts of mountainous jungle were still unexplored.

multicultural and multireligious society would collapse. "Malaysia has proven to the world", he said, "that its multiracial nature has not prevented it from achieving progress and success. We must continue to cooperate and be united."

The government of Dr Mahathir has ushered in an era of undreamt of economic growth. He has capitalized on the boom his policies helped create by promoting his coalition government as the one and only hope for a stable and prosperous Malaysia. He is widely regarded as the architect of Malaysia's success. In the most recent general election in April 1995, the Front won an unprecedented 64% of the vote – translating into 161 of 192 parliamentary seats. The foreign investors on whom the Malaysian economy increasingly relies continue to vote with their feet. Today Malaysians are bristling with self-confidence in their new-found prosperity, which is a key ingredient of the social glue that binds the country's plural society.

Malaysia may soon be a 'Newly Industrialized Economy' (NIE) – the level of development which bridges the grey area between the Third World and the industrialized countries. Many nations would give anything to be dubbed an NIE – it signifies the fact they they have 'made it'. But the Malaysian government is in no rush to acquire the label, suspecting that NIE status would be used as a pretext for western trading partners to withdraw special trade privileges.

The tourism industry plays a crucial role in Malaysia's economy. The country is endowed with good beaches, coral reefs, ancient jungle, mountains and hill resorts, islands and, these days, hundreds of golf courses. It also has a handful of urban attractions: notably Penang's beautifully preserved Chinatown and Melaka's architectural heritage. As the world's largest exporter of sawn timber Malaysia's logging industry has earned the country notoriety among environmentalists. The industry is riddled with corruption and the Malaysian government admits to problems enforcing its surprisingly stringent forestry policies. But a substantial part of Malaysia's land area is forested (especially in the states of East Malaysia) and the government has been enthusiastically promoting eco-tourism; there are several magnificent national parks, both on the peninsula and in the East Malaysian states of Sarawak and Sabah. In Sarawak there are also many jungle tribes, whose culture has remained remarkably intact.

For an historical introduction to Sarawak see page 335, and for Sabah see page 423.

THE LAND

GEOGRAPHY

Malaysia covers a total land area of 329,054 sq km and includes Peninsular Malaysia (131,587 sq km) and the Borneo states of Sarawak (124,967 sq km) and Sabah (72,500 sq km). Geologically, both the peninsula and Borneo are part of the Sunda shelf, although the mountains of the peninsula were formed longer ago than those in Borneo. This 'shelf', which during the Pleistocene ice age was exposed forming a land bridge between the two havles of the country, was inundated as the glaciers of the north retreated and sea levels rose.

The Malay peninsula is about 800 km north-south, has a long narrow neck, a tapered tail and a bulging, mountainous, middle. The neck is called the **Kra Isthmus**, which links the peninsula to the Southeast Asian mainland. The isthmus itself is in southern Thailand – Peninsular Malaysia comprises only the lower portion of the peninsula and covers an area larger than England and a little smaller than Florida. Nestled into the southernmost end of the peninsula is the island of Singapore, separated from the peninsula by the narrow Strait of Johor. The thin western coastal plain drains into the Strait of Melaka, which separates the peninsula from Sumatra (Indonesia) and is one of the oldest shipping lanes in the world. The eastern coastal lowlands drain into the South China Sea.

The **Barisan Titiwangsa** (Main Range) comprises the curved jungle-clad spine of Peninsular Malaysia. It is the most prominent of several, roughly parallel ranges running down the peninsula. These subsidiary ranges include the Kedah-Singgora Range in the north-west; the Bintang Range (stretching north-east from Taiping), the Tahan Range (which includes the peninsula's highest mountain, Gunung Tahan, 2,187m). In the northern half of the peninsula, the mountainous belt is very wide, leaving only a narrow coastal strip on either side.

The Main Range – or Barisan Titiwangsa – runs south from the Thai border for nearly 500 km, gradually receding as it approaches the coastal plain, near Melaka. The average elevation is about 1,000m and there are several peaks of more than 2,000m. The southern end of the range is much narrower and the mountains, lower; the most prominent southern 'outlier' is Gunung Ledang (Mount Ophir) in Johor. Until just over a century ago, when William Cameron first ventured into the mountains of the Main Range, this was uncharted territory – British colonial Malaya was, in fact, little more than the west coastal strip. Not only was the west coast adjacent to the important trade routes (and therefore had most of the big towns), its alluvial deposits were also rich in tin. Because roads and railways were built along this western side of the peninsula during the colonial period, it also became the heart of the plantation economy.

In addition to the mountain ranges, the Malay peninsula also has many spectacular limestone outcrops. These distinctive outcrops are mainly in the Kuala

Climatic variations: yes, we have no monsoons

One of the problems frustrating Peninsular Malaysia's east coast states in their efforts to promote tourism is the weather. Although coconut palms sway gently over sun-splashed sandy beaches most of the year round, the northeast monsoon starts to blow just as the northern hemisphere's Christmas holidays get underway and antipodeans start thinking about their summer getaways. State authorities contend that the November to March monsoon is blown out of all proportion in the minds of western tourists (and most Malaysians for that matter).

Tourism Malaysia says too much is made of the word 'monsoon' and points the finger at Club Med – which owns an idyllic private beach at Cerating in Pahang – for reinforcing the problem by shutting down during the northeast monsoon season. The tourism committee in Northeast Terengganu state has gone as far as to ban the use of the word altogether because they believe it has created a stigma among tourists and investors. They say 'rainy weather' is a perfectly adequate description. Others might consider this an understatement: more than 600 mm of rain has fallen on parts of the E coast within a single day. It also ignores the fact that there are also dry monsoons.

On the other side of the peninsula, however, states occasionally suffer from too little rain. In 1991, for example, there was a water-crisis in Melaka – the worst for 30 years – and on behalf of the state government, the Chief Minister contracted an American company, TJC-Atmos Engineers, to help resolve the problem. The company was promised more than M$3mn if it created enough rain to fill the local reservoir. But after claiming to have produced rain on 30 separate occasions over a 2-month period, Kuala Lumpur's Meteorological Services Department (MSD) dismissed the company's techniques as 'unscientific' and said any rain was a natural consequence of the SW monsoon.

The director of TJC-Atmos claimed to use 'etheric engineering techniques' to attract clouds, by "manipulating the *qi* [or subtle life-force] in the atmosphere". He had developed the techniques while investigating Unidentified Flying Objects in the 1950s and described himself as 'a hi-tech *bomoh*' (Malay witch doctor). The director of the MSD took a dim view of his 'metaphysical' techniques however and TJC-Atmos Engineering left Malaysia empty-handed.

Lumpur area (such as Batu Caves and those in and around Templer Park) and in the Kampar Valley near Ipoh, to the north. The erosion of the limestone has produced intricate solution-cave systems, some with dramatic formations. The vegetation on these hills is completely different to the surrounding lowland rainforest.

Malaysia's year-round rainfall has resulted in a dense network of rivers. The peninsula's longest river is the Sungai Pahang, which runs for just over 400 km. Most rivers flood regularly – particularly during the northeast monsoon season – and during the heavy rain the volume of water can more than double in the space of a few hours. It is thought that the flooding of Malaysian rivers has become more pronounced due to logging and mining. Waterfalls are very common features in Peninsular Malaysia; these occur where rivers, with their headwaters in the hills, encounter resistant (usually igneous) rocks as they cut their valleys.

CLIMATE

The Malay peninsula has an equatorial monsoon climate (for more details on the climatic features of Sabah and Sarawak, see page 320). Temperatures are uniformly high throughout the year – as is humidity – and rainfall is abundant and well distributed, although it peaks during the northeast monsoon period from November to February.

Mean annual temperature on the coastal lowlands is around 26°C. The mean daily minima in the lowlands is between 21.7°C and 24.4°C; the mean daily maxima is between 29.4°C and 32.8°C. The maxima are higher and the minima, lower, towards the interior. In the Cameron Highlands, the mean annual temperature is 18°C. Temperatures dip slightly during the north-east monsoon period. The highest recorded temperature, 39.4°C, was taken on Pulau Langkawi in March 1931. The lowest absolute minimum temperature ever recorded on the peninsula was in the Cameron Highlands in January 1937 when the temperature fell to 2.2°C. The Cameron Highlands also claims the most extreme range in temperature – the absolute maximum recorded there is 26.7°C.

The developed west coast of the peninsula is sheltered from the northeast monsoon which strikes the east coast with full force between November and February. The east coast's climatic vagaries have reinforced its remoteness: it is particularly wet and the area north of Kuantan receives between 3,300 mm and 4,300 mm a year. About half of this falls in the northeast monsoon period. The northwest coast of the peninsula is also wet and parts receive more than 3,000 mm of rain a year. Bukit Larut (Maxwell Hill), next to Taiping has an annual rainfall of more than 5,000 mm. The west coast receives its heaviest rainfall in March and April. October and April are the transitional months between the southwest and northeast monsoons.

Thunderstorms provide most of Malaysia's rainfall. In the most torrential downpour ever recorded in Kuala Lumpur 51 mm of rain fell in 15 minutes. Heavy rain like this causes serious soil erosion in areas which have been cleared of vegetation.

In the more heavily populated coastal districts of the peninsula, the temperature is ameliorated by sea breezes which set in about 1000 and gather force until early afternoon. In the evenings, a land breeze picks up. These winds are only felt for distances up to 15 km inland. Another typical weather feature on the Malay peninsula is the squall – a sudden, violent

The universal stimulant – the betel nut

Throughout the countryside in Southeast Asia, and in more remote towns, it is common to meet men and women whose teeth are stained black, and gums red, by continuous chewing of the 'betel nut'. This, though, is a misnomer. The betel 'nut' is not chewed at all: the three crucial ingredients that make up a betel 'wad' are the nut of the areca palm (*Areca catechu*), the leaf or catkin of the betel vine (*Piper betel*), and lime. When these three ingredients are combined with saliva they act as a mild stimulant. Other ingredients (people have their own recipes) are tobacco, gambier, various spices and the gum of *Acacia catechu*. The habit, though also common in South Asia and parts of China, seems to have evolved in Southeast Asia and it is mentioned in the very earliest chronicles. The lacquer betel boxes of Burma and Thailand, and the brass and silver ones of Indonesia and Malaysia, illustrate the importance of chewing betel in social intercourse. Galvao in his journal of 1544 noted: "They use it so continuously that they never take it from their mouths; therefore these people can be said to go around always ruminating". Among westernized Southeast Asians the habit is frowned upon: the disfigurement and ageing that it causes, and the stained walls and floors that result from the constant spitting, are regarded as distasteful products of an earlier age. But beyond the elite it is still widely practised.

storm characterized by sharp gusts of wind. These can be very localized in their effect, very unpredictable and, from time to time, very hazardous to light fishing vessels. Squalls are caused by cool air (either from sea breezes in the late morning or land breezes in the evening) undercutting warmer air; squall lines are marked by stacks of cumulo-nimbus clouds. Most squalls occur between May and August; the ones that develop along the west coast between Port Klang and Singapore during this period are called 'Sumatras' and produce particularly violent cloudbursts. Most Sumatras occur at night or in the early morning, while squalls between November and February usually occur in the afternoon.

Climate charts: graphs of rainfall and temperature are provided on the following pages: **Peninsular Malaysia**: Kuala Lumpur page 99; Cameron Highlands page 147; Penang page 175; Melaka page 221; Johor Bahru page 243; Mersing page 255; Kuantan page 273; Kuala Terengganu page 297; Kota Bharu page 306: **East Malaysia**: Kuching page 354; Kota Kinabalu page 434.

FLORA AND FAUNA

Originally 97% of Malaysia's land area was covered in closed-canopy forest. According to the government, about 56% of Malaysia is still forested – although it is difficult to ascertain exactly how much of this is primary rainforest. Only 5% of the remaining jungle is under conservation restrictions. The Malaysian jungle, which, at about 130 million years old, is believed to be among the oldest forest in the world, supports more than 145,000 species of flowering plant (well over 1,000 of which are already known to have pharmaceutical value), 200 mammal species, 600 bird species and countless thousands of insect species. The rainforest is modified by underlying rock-type (impervious rocks and soils result in swamp forest) and by altitude (lowland rainforest gives way to thinner montane forest on higher slopes). All the main forest types are represented on the peninsula; these include mangrove swamp forest, peat swamp forest, heath forest, lowland and hill mixed *Dipterocarp* forest and montane forest. Where primary forest has been logged, burned or cleared by shifting cultivators or miners, secondary forest grows up quickly. The fields

Nepenthes – the jungle's poisoned chalice

There are about 30 species of insectivorous pitcher plants in Malaysia; they come in all shapes and sizes – some are bulbous and squat, some are small and elegant, others are huge and fat. All are killers, and are among the handful of insect-eating plants in the world. Pitcher plants grow on poor soils, either in the mountains or in heath (*kerangas*) forest. The Malay name for the *Nepenthes* family is *periuk kera* – or 'monkey cups'. The Chinese call them after the tall wicker baskets used to take pigs to market – *shu long cao*. The plants remain sealed until they have begun to secrete the fluids which help them supplement their meagre diet. One of these liquids is sweet and sticky and attracts insects; the other, which builds up at the bottom, digests each victim which ventures in. The 'lid' opens invitingly when the plant is ready for business and it is virtually impossible for insects to escape – the pitcher plant's waxed interior offers little traction for the uphill climb and the upper lips, past the overhanging ridge, are serated and very slippery. This plant amazed the first Europeans to visit the Malay archipelago. George Rumphius, the German naturalist, thought it one of nature's freaks when he travelled through the region at the end of the 17th century. Two centuries later, the British naturalist, Frederick Burbridge, wrote that seeing the plants "was a sensation I shall never forget – one of those which we experience but rarely in a whole lifetime".

Durian: king of fruits

In Southeast Asia, the durian is widely regarded as the most delicious of fruits – to the horror of many foreign visitors). In his book *The Malay Archipelago* (1869), Alfred Russel Wallace describes it in almost orgiastic terms:

"The consistence and flavour are indescribable. A rich butter-like custard highly flavoured with almonds gives the best general idea of it, but intermingled with it come wafts of flavour that call to mind cream-cheese, onion sauce, brown sherry and other incongruities. Then there is a rich glutinous smoothness in the pulp which nothing else possesses, but which adds to its delicacy. It is neither acid, or sweet, nor juicy, yet one feels the want of none of these qualities, for it is perfect as it is. It produces no nausea or other bad effect, and the more you eat of it the less you feel inclined to stop. In fact to eat Durian is a new sensation, worth a voyage to the East to experience."

cultivated by shifting cultivators are known as swiddens – a word which is derived from an old English term meaning 'burnt field'. In Malaysia, the secondary regrowth is known as *belukar*. It can take up to 250 years before climax rainforest is re-established. The pioneer plant species colonizing abandoned *ladang* (sites cleared by shifting cultivators) is called *lalang* (elephant grass).

Mammals

The continual development of forested areas has destroyed many habitats in recent years. Malaysia's, and Asia's, biggest mammal is the Asiatic elephant. Adult elephants weigh up to 3-4 tonnes; they are rarely seen, although the carnage caused by a passing herd can sometimes be seen in Taman Negara (the National Park). For more detail on elephants, see page 326. One of the strangest Malayan mammals is the tapir, with its curled snout – or trunk – and white bottom. The starkly contrasting black and white is good camouflage in the jungle, where it is effectively concealed by light and shade. Young tapirs are dark brown with light brown spots, simulating the effect of sun-dappled leaf-litter.

Other large mammals include the common wild pig and the bearded pig, and the *seladang* (or gaur) wild cattle; the latter live in herds in deep jungle. There are two species of deer on the Malay peninsula: the *sambar* (or *rusa*) and the *kijang* (barking deer); the latter gets its English name from its dog-like call. The mouse deer (*kanchil* and *napoh*) are not really deer; they are hoofed animals, standing just 20 cm high. The mouse deer has legendary status in Malay lore – for example, the Malay Annals tell of Prince Parameswara's decision to found Melaka on the spot where he saw a mouse deer beat off one of his hunting dogs (see page 221). Despite their reputation for cunning, they are also a favoured source of protein.

Malaysia's most famous carnivore is the tiger – *harimau* in Malay. Tigers still roam the jungle in the centre of the peninsula, and on several occasions have made appearances in the Cameron Highlands, particularly during the dry season, when they move into the mountains to find food. Other members of the cat family are the clouded leopard and four species of wild cat: the leopard cat, the golden cat, the flat-headed cat and the marbled cat. Other jungle animals include the Malayan sun bear (which have a penchant for honey), the *serigala* (wild dog), civet cats (of which there are many different varieties), mongooses, weasels and otters.

The ape family includes the white-handed gibbon (known locally as *wak-wak*), the dark-handed gibbon (which is rarer) and *siamang*, which are found in more mountainous areas. The five species of monkeys are the long-tailed macaque, pig-tailed macaque, and three species of leaf monkey (langur) – the banded, dusky and silvered varieties. Malaysia's cutest animal is the little slow loris, with its huge sad eyes and lethargic manner; among the most exotic is the flying lemur, whose legs and tail are joined together by a skin membrane. It parachutes and glides from tree to tree, climbing each one to find a new launch-pad.

Malaysia has several species of fruit bats and insect-eating bats, but the best-known insect-eater is the pangolin (scaly anteater), the animal world's answer to the armoured car. Its scales are formed of matted hair (like rhinoceros horn) and it has a long thin tongue which it flicks into termite nests. More common jungle mammals include rodents, among which are five varieties of giant flying squirrels. Like the flying lemur, these glide spectacularly from tree to tree and can cover up to about 500m in one 'flight'.

Birds

In ornithological circles, Malaysia is famed for its varied bird-life. The country is visited by many migratory water birds, and there are several wetland areas where the Malayan Nature Society has set up bird-watching hides; the most accessible to Kuala Lumpur is the Kuala Selangor Nature Park (see page 118). Migratory birds winter on Selangor's mangrove-fringed mudflats from September to May. There are also spectacular birds of prey, the most common of which are the hawk eagles and brahminy kites. Among the most fascinating and beautiful jungle species are the crested firebacks, a kind of pheasant; the kingfisher family, with their brilliantly coloured plumage; the hornbills (see page 327); greater racquet-tailed drongos – dark blue with long, sweeping tails; and black-naped orioles, saffron-coloured lowland residents. There are also wagtails, mynas, sunbirds, humming birds (flower-peckers), bulbuls, barbets, woodpeckers and weaver-birds. The latter makes incredible, finely woven, hanging tubular nests from strips of grass.

Reptiles

The kings of Malaysia's reptile population are the giant leatherback turtles (see page 293), hawksbill and green turtles (see page 484); there are several other species of turtle and three species of land tortoise. The most notorious reptile is the estuarine crocodile (*Crocodilus porosus*) – which can grow up to 8m long. The Malayan gharial (*Tomistoma schlegeli*) is a fish-eating, freshwater crocodile which grows to just under 3m. Lizards include common house geckos (*Hemidactylus frenatus* – or *cikcak* in Malay), green crested lizards (*Calotes cristatellus*), which change colour like chameleons, and flying lizards (*Draco*), which have an extendable undercarriage allowing the lizard to glide from tree to tree. Monitors are the largest of Malaysian lizards, the most widespread of which is the common water monitor (*Varanus salvator*), which can grow to about 2.5m.

The Malaysian jungles also have 140 species of frogs and toads, which are more often heard than seen. Some are dramatically coloured, such as the appropriately named green-backed frog (*Rana erythraea*) and others have particular skills, such as Wallace's flying frog (*Rana migropalmatus*) which parachutes around on its webbed feet.

Of Malaysia's 100-odd land snakes, only 16 are poisonous; all 20 species of sea snake are poisonous. There are two species of python, the reticulated python (*Python reticulatus*) – which can grow to nearly 10m in length and has iridescent black and yellow scales – and the short python (*Python curtus*), which rarely grows more than 2.5m and has a very thick, rusty-brown body. Most feared are the venomous snakes, but the constrictors can also pose a threat to humans. On Wednesday 6 September 1995 a rubber tapper was found in the process of being swallowed by a 7m python near the town of Semagat, about 150 km southeast of Kuala Lumpur. The unfortunate victim's brother found the snake at its repast and called the police who shot the creature.

It was, though, too late. The snake – which weighed 140 kg – had crushed Ee Heng Chuan who had suffered multiple fractures. Fang marks on Heng Chuan's legs led the authorities to suspect that the rubber tapper had been caught while he was resting, possibly asleep. Trapped within the snake's powerful coils – its body measured 30 cm in diameter – Heng Chuan would have found it impossible to escape. This episode, it should be added, was exceptional and led to the python (not just this one, the species in general) receiving a good deal of largely unjustified bad press. As Kiew Bong Heang, Associate Professor of Zoology at the Universiti Malaya remarked, the python is "a nice creature if it's not eating you".

Among the most common non-poisonous snakes is the dark brown house snake (*Lycodon aulicus*) which likes to eat geckos and the common Malayan racer (*Elaphe flavolineata*), which grows to about 2m and is black with a pale underbelly. The most beautiful non-poisonous snakes are the paradise tree snake (*Chrysopelea paradisi*), which is black with an iridescent green spot on every scale and the mangrove snake (*Boiga dendrophilia*) which grows to about 2m long and is black with yellow stripes. The former is famed for its gliding skills: it can leap from tree-to-tree in a controlled glide by hollowing its underbelly, trapping a cushion of air below it. In the jungle it is quite common to see the dull brown river snake which goes by the unfortunate name of the dog-faced water snake (*Cerberus rhynchops*); it has a healthy appetite for fish and frogs.

The most feared venomous snake is the king cobra (*Naja hannah*) which grows to well over 4m long and is olive-green with an orange throat-patch. They are often confused with non-poisonous rat snakes and racers. The king cobra eats snakes and lizards – including monitor lizards. Its reputation as an aggressive snake is unfounded but its venom is deadly. Both the king cobra and the common cobra (*Naja naja*) are hooded; the hood is formed by loose skin around the neck and is pushed outwards on elongated ribs when the snake rears to its strike posture.

Other poisonous snakes are: the banded krait (*Bungarus fasciatus*) with its distinctive black and yellow stripes and the Malayan krait (*Bungarus candidus*) with black and white stripes. Kraits are not fast movers and are said to bite only under extreme provocation. Coral snakes (of the genus *Maticora*) have extremely poisonous venom, but because the snake virtually has to chew its victim before the venom can enter the bite (its poison glands are located at the very back of its mouth), there have been no recorded fatalities. Pit vipers have a thermo-sensitive groove between the eye and the nostril which can detect warm-blooded prey even in complete darkness. The bite of the common, bright green Wagler's pit viper (*Trimeresurus wagleri*) is said to be extremely painful, but is never fatal. They have broad, flattened heads; adults have yellow bars and a bright red tip to the tail.

Insects

Malaysia has a literally countless population of insect species; new ones are constantly being discovered and named. There are 120 species of butterfly in Malaysia. The king of them is the male Rajah Brooke's birdwing (*Troides brookiana*) – the national butterfly – with its iridescent, emerald zig-zag markings on jet-black velvety wings. It was named by Victorian naturalist Alfred Russel Wallace after his friend James Brooke, the first White Rajah of Sarawak (see page 338). The males can be found along rivers while the much rarer females (which are less-spectacularly coloured), remain out of sight among the treetops.

There are more than 100 other magnificently coloured butterflies, including the black and yellow common birdwing, the swallowtails and swordtails, the leaf butterflies (which are camouflaged as leaves when their wings are folded) such as the blue and brown saturn and the rust, white and brown tawny rajah. Among the most beautiful of all is the delicately patterned Malayan lacewing (*Cethosia hypsea*) with its jagged markings of red, orange, brown and white. There are several butterfly farms around the country, including in Kuala Lumpur (see page 119), Penang (see page 195) and the butterfly capital of Malaysia, the Cameron Highlands (see page 158).

The most spectacular moths are the huge atlas moth (*Attacus atlas*) and the swallow-tailed moth (*Nyctalemon patroclus*); these can often be found on exterior walls illuminated by strip-lights late at night, particularly in remoter parts of the country.

The Malaysian beetle population is among the most varied in the world. The best known is the rhinoceros beetle (*Oryctes rhinoceros*), which can grow to nearly 6 cm in length and is characterized by its dramatic horns. The empress cicada (*Pomponia imperatoria*) is the biggest species in Malaysia and can have a wingspan of more than 20 cm. The male cicada is the noisiest jungle resident. The incredible droning and whining noises are created by the vibration of membranes in the body, the sound of which is amplified in the body cavity.

One of the most famous insects is the praying mantis. In *Malayan animal life*, MWF Tweedie writes: "They owe their name to the deceptively devotional appearance of their characteristic pose, with the fore legs held up as if in prayer. In reality the mantis is, of course, waiting for some unwary insect to stray within reach; if it does, the deadly spined fore limbs will strike and grasp and the mantis will eat its victim alive, daintily, as a lady eats a sandwich." There are several other species of mantis, and the most intriguing is the flower mantis (*Hymenopus coronatus*) which is bright pink and can twist and extend itself to resemble a 4-petalled flower, a camouflage which protects it from predators, while attracting meals such as bees.

Of the less attractive insect life, it is advisable to be wary of certain species of wasps and hornets. The most dangerous is the slender banded hornet (*Polistes sagittarius*) which is big (3 cm long) and has a black and orange striped abdomen. Its nests are paper-like, and hang from trees and the eaves of houses by a short stalk. They are extremely aggressive and do not need to be provoked before they attack.

Fireflies – flashers in the forest

There are plenty of fireflies (*Lampyridae*) in Malaysia. But the ones which sit in the trees along the Selangor River, to the west of Kuala Lumpur, are special. They flash in synch – thousands of them go on and off like Christmas-tree lights. Although there are a few reported instances of this happening elsewhere in Southeast Asia, Kampong Kuantan, near Kuala Selangor (see page 118), is the best place to witness the phenomenon, which many visitors suspect is a clever electric hoax. The Lampyrid beetle which exhibits the synchrony is the *Pteroptyx malaccae*, which grows to about 9 mm in length and emits flashes at the rate of just over one per second. In the days before batteries, villagers used to put the fireflies in bottles to serve as torches. Because they stick to the same trees – which are chosen because they are always free of *keringga* weaving ants (see below) – local fishermen are said to use them as navigational beacons. Only the males are synchronous flashers, and scientists have yet to come up with an explanation for their behaviour. The females, which are the first to settle in the trees, shortly after sunset, emit dimmer light, and the males, which fly around the water level as it gets dark, join the females which respond to their flashes. The light is produced by cells on the firefly's lower abdomen.

Environment – mud-slinging in the greenhouse

Malaysia is spending US$10mn a year on a slick public relations counter offensive to the anti-tropical timber lobby in the West. That's a lot of money – until compared with the US$4.5bn it earns every year from its trees. For the past decade, Malaysia has been the world's biggest exporter of tropical timber.

But the bald figures disguise the fact that the export of raw logs has been reduced by about half in recent years, in line with Malaysia's policy of sustainable forestry management. In 1991 a government minister defended Malaysia's logging policy by saying that "it's not our responsibility to supply the West with oxygen." But things have changed since then – the government has gone green. While continuing to expose western hypocrisy in environmental matters, Malaysia has done much to clean up its own back yard. Most importantly, it has undertaken to reduce log production to sustainable levels, following apocalyptic warnings of what might happen if it didn't.

Malaysia now claims to be practising selective logging techniques (see page 412), felling a maximum of 7-12 trees per hectare. Critics have long alleged, however, that Malaysia's forestry laws are being flouted by illegal loggers and corrupt timber concessionaires. The government's answer to these allegations was the introduction in 1993 of tough new laws involving heavy fines and lengthy custodial sentences for poachers and illegal loggers. Concessionaires – who's ranks include sultans and senior politicians – are now liable for the same fines and sentences. Forest rangers will be empowered to arrest and will have the back-up of the police and the army.

The government insists that its stricter policies were not motivated by pressure from the West. It simply says that it would not be so stupid or greedy as to kill the goose that lays the golden egg and it maintains that sustained-yield harvesting means its forests will be there in perpetuity.

The government has long railed against western nations for their double standards over the environment. Its line is that because industrialized countries have already cleared their forests in the name of development, why shouldn't Malaysia be free to do the same? At the Earth Summit in Rio de Janeiro in June 1992, the Prime Minister, Dr Mahathir Mohamad, noted that poor countries have been told to preserve their forests and other genetic resources for research purposes. He said: "This is the same as telling these countries that they must continue to be poor because their forests and other resources are more precious than the people themselves". In the wake of Rio, hopes that a new global environment fund would help cover the costs of enforcing environmental protection, have been dashed. Dr Mahathir says western countries have reneged on their undertaking.

There are still holes in Malaysia's forestry policies; adequately policing large tracts of forest against illegal loggers is impossible. Local environmental groups continue to call for greater accountability and a crackdown on corruption. A small elite of extremely wealthy, corrupt and powerful men still control much the timber trade. But even the government's critics concede that great strides have been made in environmental protection. Until the rest of the world recognizes this, the government has sworn to keep making its point: that the people who created the greenhouse effect should not be throwing stones.

The golden wasp (*Vespa auraria*) is found in montane jungle – notably the Cameron Highlands, and, like the hornet above, will attack anything coming near its nest. The wasp is a honey-gold colour, it nests in trees and shrubs and its sting is vicious. There are several other wasp species which attack ferociously, and stings can be extremely painful. One of the worst is the night wasp (*Provespa anomala*), which is an orangy-brick colour and commonly flies into houses at night, attracted by lights. Bee stings can also be very serious, and none more so than that of the giant honey bee, which builds pendulous combs on overhanging eaves and trees. It is black with a yellow mark at the front end of the abdomen; multiple stings can be fatal.

Another insect species to be particularly wary of is the fire ant (*Tetraponera rufonigra*). It has a red body and a big black head; it will enthusiastically sting anything it comes into contact with, and the pain is acute. Weaver ants (*Oecophylla smaragdina*) are common but do not sting. Instead, their powerful jaws can be used as jungle sutures to stitch up open wounds. The bites alone are very painful, and the ant (which is also known as the *kerengga*) adds insult to injury by spitting an acidic fluid on the bite. It is difficult to extract the pincers from the skin, and once attached, the ant will not let go. The biggest of all ants, the giant ant (*Camponotus gigas*), can be nearly 3 cm in length; (it is also variously known as the elephant ant and the 'big-bum ant'). They are largely nocturnal, however, so tend to cause less trouble in the jungle.

Other jungle residents worth avoiding are the huge, black and hairy *Mygalomorph* spiders, whose bodies alone can be about 5 cm long. Their painful bites cause localized swelling. Scorpions are dangerous but not fatal. The biggest scorpion, the wood scorpion (*Hormurus australasiae*) can grow to about 16 cm long; it is black, lives under old logs and is mainly nocturnal. In rural areas, the particularly paranoid might shake their shoes for the spotted house-scorpion (*Isometrus maculatus*), which is quite common. Centipedes (*Chilopoda*) have a poisonous bite and can grow up to about 25 cm in length. The Malaysian peninsula is malaria-free, although the *Aedes*, tiger mosquito, with its black and white striped body and legs, is a daytime mosquito that carries dengue fever (see page 748).

The environmental costs of growth

As Malaysia has become more wealthy, and the middle class has burgeoned, so environmental concerns have gained greater prominence. In 1993 the Department of the Environment released figures revealing that of Peninsular Malaysia's 116 major rivers, 85 were either 'biologically dead' or 'dying'. Air quality is also a source of concern, especially in the Klang Valley, an agglomeration of industrial activity around Kuala Lumpur. Environmental Impact Assessments (EIAs) are now, in theory, compulsory for every development project, but most companies undertake to do them only grudgingly – if at all – and then place them on a shelf to gather dust. The claim that, as a developing country, Malaysia can ill-afford the 'luxury' of such things is wearing very thin as wealth spreads with each year of 8% growth. The government recognizes that the environment is fast becoming a political issue, and like any good political party which thinks it has identified a bandwagon with a fair number of votes attached, is trying to climb aboard.

Most accounts of Malaysia's environmental problems – some would characterize it as a 'crisis' – concentrate on the East Malaysian states of Sarawak and Sabah. In a sense the peninsular is a lost cause: deforestation has been so extensive that the only large areas remaining are already gazetted as national parks. In East Malaysia, though, there is a sense that if only logging could be better controlled then the natural wealth of Malaysian Borneo could be preserved. The background to this issue and the flora and fauna of Borneo are discussed in detail in the introductions to Borneo and the states of Sabah and Sarawak.

Scorched earth, bitter winds – the great fires of 1997

The stupendous fires that blazed across the Indonesian island of Sumatra and Indonesian Borneo brought hazardous conditions to Malaysia. In Sarawak the government considered evacuating the entire population of over 2 million people – but wondered where to put them. The airport in Kuching was closed and residents rushed to stockpile water and basic necessities. Schools, factories and government offices stayed shut as the smog became a threat to health. Fishermen did not venture out on the seas. Visibility became so bad that people stopped using their vehicles – even in the middle of the day. The state government of Sarawak declared a state of emergency and advised people to stay indoors. But even in their own homes people could not escape the acrid smoke and hospitals filled with people suffering from aggravated respiratory and heart compaints. The Air Pollution Index reached 851 at 1300 on the 24th September. A figure of 300 is considered 'hazardous' and it was estimated that even a figure of 200-300 is equivalent to smoking 20 cigarettes a day. In Kuala Lumpur the Air Pollution Index broke through the 300 mark and some foreign embassies and companies began evacuating their staff. Satellite images showed that by late September the smog stretched over 3,000 km from east to west, affecting six countries and afflicting perhaps 70 million people.

Though the fires are concentrated in Indonesia, the Malaysian government has not escaped criticism. The failure of the government to introduce a coherent zoning policy or to control car emissions has been attacked. And there seems little doubt that pollution from cars and industry has combined with the smoke from the fires to produce a particularly

unpleasant concoction leading to eye irritation, asthma attacks, headaches and breathing difficulties. In 1994 the Malaysian cabinet was presented with a Clean Air Action Plan but it was rejected as potentially undermining the country's industrialization efforts. At the beginning of November the Malaysian government even went so far as to muzzle academics, ordering them not to talk to the press about the ill effects of the smog. This followed one (inaccurate) report that breathing the haze was like smoking 40 cigarettes a day (up from 20 a few weeks earlier!).

Although Singapore was less effected by the fires in Indonesia, even there the air became unpleasant to breath. Rosemary Richter reporting from the Republic wrote of the experience of breathing the polluted air as 'unbelievably unpleasant' adding that it was like 'inhaling hot cotton wool fibres' and 'living inside a wet blanket redolent of a refuse tip'. Other correspondents reported on the bitter smell, oppressive darkness, watering eyes, the layer of soot that covered everything, the choking sensation, and the itching skin. One Indonesian minister estimated that 20 million Indonesians were suffering from aggravated respiratory problems because of the smog and some environmentalists were even predicting an increase in cancer in two or three decades time because of the carcinogens that are present in the smoke. To put it bluntly: while a few people will die as a direct result of the smog, many more will die prematurely.

What may be remarkable to many Westerners was the time it took before the politics of blame took hold. President Suharto apologized to his fellow Asean nations at an environment conference in September 1997, but criticism from Malaysia and Singapore, the two countries most affected after Indonesia, was astonishingly muted. It was the media in the two countries, chiivied on by an irate public making their feelings known through newspaper letter columns and radio talk shows, that encouraged the governments of Malaysia and Singapore to take a more forthright stance. Warren Fernandez in Singapore's *Straits Times* wrote at the peak of the crisis that it was time to put aside Asean's usual chumminess: "This will entail their being able to set aside traditional inhibitions – diplomatic niceties, worries about national sensitivities, the so-called 'Asean-way' of not interfering in each other's affairs – to take steps to deal with a common problem that transcends national borders. At the beginning of October, President Suharto issued a second apology to his neighbours but once again the problem was described as 'natural' and 'environmental'. The president was not willing to take responsibility for a disaster which most academics and commentators believe has been hugely aggravated by human actions – or inaction. He also seemed to take some action, revoking the licences of 29 timber and plantation companies. But the impression remained among the public in the region that the Indonesian government was driven by more powerful interests than public opinion and, more to the point, was powerless to put out the fires in any case. It is probably appropriate to leave the last words to the Imam of the Central Mosque in the city of Pontianak in Kalimantan, for he probably best articulated what many people in the region felt: 'Allah is giving us a warning'.

DIVING IN MALAYSIA

PENINSULAR MALAYSIA'S WEST COAST

Generally, the diving off the west coast of Peninsular Malaysia is the least spectacular in the country. However, as the bulk of Malaysia's population live near here, it is the most accessible from Kuala Lumpur and other important centres. The islands of the Paya archipelago offer the best diving opportunities.

Diving seasons in Malaysia

West coast, Peninsular Malaysia	November-May
East coast, Peninsular Malaysia	March-October
East Malaysia (Sabah & Sarawak)	March-September*

*__NB__ Diving conditions at Pulau Sipadan are generally good year-round.

Pulau Paya

This is an archipelago of islands to the north of Penang and south of Langkawi (see page 209). It is now protected as an underwater reserve, having being gazetted in 1985. The principal islands are Paya, Kacha, Lembu and Segantan and they support a marine flora and fauna that includes 36 genera of hard corals, 92 other marine invertebrates and 45 genera of fish. On **Pulau Paya** itself, the waters off the rocky southwest tip offer the best diving; the corals here are particularly good (with semi-precious black coral in deeper waters). Barracuda, grouper, jack and garfish are regularly seen in deeper waters. Facilities include an information centre and bathroom facilities. Camping is allowed (if the authorities are informed beforehand – see the Paya entry in the Langkawi section for further information), but there is no accommodation available; the nearest hotels are on Langkawi to the north, or Penang to the south. Further expansion is planned however.

Other west coast dive sites

Less well-known and developed dive sites off the west coast of the Peninsula include **Pulau Sembilan**, **Pulau Pangkor** and **Pulau Pangkor Laut**, situated not far from the town of Lumut (see page 166).

PENINSULAR MALAYSIA'S EAST COAST (FROM SOUTH TO NORTH)

Pulau Tioman

The waters around Tioman itself have been devastated in recent years through over-fishing and the uncontrolled activities of tourists. However, it is a convenient base to visit islands in the area including **Pulau Tulai**, **Labas**, **Chebeh** and **Sepoi** (see page 258).

Pulau Sibu Archipelago

This is a group of islands off Mersing in Johore province and includes **Pulau Rawa** (see page 268), **Babi Hujung**, **Babi Tengah**, **Babi Besar**, **Tinggi**, **Mentinggi** and **Sibu** (see page 268). They are all included within a single marine park and with the exception of Babi Hujung and Mentinggi, offer basic accommodation.

Pulau Tenggol

This is the largest of a small group of islands, still relatively undeveloped and unspoilt. The range and number of fish here is impressive. Particularly noteworthy are the spectacular sunken cliffs. There is no accommodation available (see page 303).

Pulau Kapas

Like Pulau Perhentian this is an area suited to snorkelling and shallow dives (3-10m). The beaches are good and there is accommodation available (see page 295).

Pulau Redang

The dive sites around the protected Pulau Redang island group (consisting of 9 islands), 45 km off the Terengganu coast, are numerous and varied and are considered some of the best in Malaysia. There are an estimated 500 species of coral, 1,000 species of bivalves and some 3,000 species of fish, and the star of the show is a resident whale shark. There are also large schools of red snapper and other fish. The beaches of the islands that constitute the Pulau Redang Marine Park are nesting sites for the hawksbill and rarer green turtles. A fishing village on stilts occupies one end of the island, but there is no dedicated tourist accommodation (see page 303 and box on page 295).

Pulau Perhentian

Shallow water snorkelling is excellent here, and in July and August dolphins and pilot whales migrate through the waters fringing the island. Accommodation in 'A' frame huts available (see page 304).

Distant islands

Pulau Aur and **Pulau Pemanggil** are situated 15 km apart about 65 km off the east coast of the Peninsula to the south of Tioman. Their remoteness has meant that they are the least disturbed diving locations in the area (see page 268).

EAST MALAYSIA

Pulau Layang-Layang

The most memorable feature here is a 2,000m sea wall; the oceanic position means that sharks and pelagic fish are common (see page 445).

Tunku Abdul Rahman Park

This park includes five pristine islands – **Gaya**, **Sapi**, **Manukan**, **Mamutik** and **Sulug**. The beaches are excellent and the coral and marine life good. They are also the most easily accessible dive spots of quality from Kota Kinabalu, lying about 20 minutes by boat from the state capital. Accommodation is available on two of the islands, Mamutik and Manukan (see page 447).

Pulau Mantanani

A group of islands off Sabah's west coast of which Pulau Mantanani is the largest. Sharks and large pelagic fishes abound and the area is also a renowned fishing location.

Pulau Mengalum

This island is 70 km west of Kota Kinabalu and fish include marlin and sail fish along with the more usual grouper, wrasse and snapper.

Pulau Tiga

This dive spot comprises three islands that lie within the boundaries of a 15,864 hectare park gazetted in 1978, 50 km southwest of Kota Kinabalu. Marine life includes turtles, tuna, dolphin and sting-rays. The islands themselves support populations of monkeys and monitor lizards, as well as a mud volcano (see page 462). The park is primarily a research area for naturalists and so tourist facilities are intentionally kept to a minimum. Camping is allowed, but visitors need to bring their own food.

Turtle Islands National Park

This national park was created in 1977 and encompasses three islands – **Pulau Selingaan**, **Gulisan** and **Bakkungan Kecil**. As the popular name of the park suggests, it was gazetted to protect the rare green and hawksbill turtles. The peak period for egg laying is August to October for the green turtle and February to April for the hawksbill. Pulau Selingaan is the only island with accommodation (see page 483).

Labuan

The duty free island of Labuan is a good base for visiting surrounding islands and dive spots. Because Labuan was a focus of military activity during World War Two, there are a number of wrecks here including Japanese and US warships (the latter probably the USS Salute) (see page 456).

Pulau Sipadan

Sipadan is probably the best-known dive site in east Malaysia because of its stunning 700m sea wall. Because Sipadan is an oceanic island, fish such as manta rays and large schools of barracuda are commonly seen here while they are rare elsewhere (see page 494).

HISTORY

PRE-COLONIAL MALAYA

With the arrival of successive waves of Malay immigrants about 5 millennia ago, the earliest settlers – the *Orang Asli* aboriginals (see page 71) – moved into the interior. The Malays established agricultural settlements on the coastal lowlands and in riverine areas and from very early

The kris: martial and mystic masterpiece of the Malay world

The kris occupies an important place in Malay warfare, art and philosophy. It is a short sword – the Malay word *keris* means dagger – and the blade may be either straight or sinuous (there are over 100 blade shapes), sharpened on both edges. Such was the high reputation of these weapons that they were exported as far afield as India. Krisses are often attributed with peculiar powers – one was reputed to have rattled violently before a family feud. Another, kept at the museum in Taiping, has a particularly bloodthirsty reputation. It would sneak away after dark, kill someone, and then wipe itself clean before miraculously returning to its display cabinet. Because each kris has a power and spirit of its own, they must be compatible with their owners. Nor should they be purchased – a kris should be given or inherited.

The fact that so few kris blades have been unearthed has led some people to assume that the various Malay kingdoms were peaceful and adverse to war. The more likely explanation is that pre-Muslim Malays attributed such magical power to sword blades that they were only very rarely buried. The art historian Jan Fontein writes that "the process of forging the sword from clumps of iron ore and meteorite into a sharp blade of patterned steel is often seen as a parallel to the process of purification to which the soul is subjected after death by the gods".

The earliest confirmed date for a kris is the 14th century – they are depicted in the reliefs of Candi Panataran and possibly also at Candi Sukuh, both on Java. However, in all likelihood they were introduced considerably earlier – possibly during the 10th century.

Krisses are forged by beating nickel or nickeliferous meteoritic material into iron in a complex series of laminations (iron from meteors is particularly prized because of its celestial origin). After forging, ceremonies are performed and offerings made before the blade is tempered. The *empu*, or swordsmith, was a respected member of society, who was felt to be imbued with mystical powers. After forging the blade, it is then patinated using a mixture of lime juice and arsenicum. Each part of the sword, even each curve of the blade, has a name and the best krisses are elaborately decorated. Inlaid with gold, the cross-pieces carved into floral patterns and animal motifs, grips made of ivory and studded with jewels, they are works of art.

But they were also tools of combat. In the Malay world, a central element of any battle was the amok. Taken from the Malay verb *mengamok*, the amok was a furious charge by men armed with krisses, designed to spread confusion within the enemy ranks. Amok warriors would be committed to dying in the charge and often dressed in white to indicate self-sacrifice. They were often drugged with opium or cannabis. It was also a honourable way for a man to commit suicide. Alfred Russel Wallace in *The Malay Archipelago* (1869) writes: "He grasps his kris-handle, and the next moment draws out the weapon and stabs a man to the heart. He runs on, with the bloody kris in his hand, stabbing at everyone he meets. 'Amok! Amok!' then resounds through the streets. Spears, krisses, knives and guns are brought out against him. He rushes madly forward, kills all he can – men, women and children – and dies overwhelmed by numbers...". The English expression 'to run amok' is taken from this Malay word.

Recommended reading: Frey, Edward (1986) *The Kris: mystic weapon of the Malay world*, OUP: Singapore.

on, were in contact with foreign traders, thanks to the peninsula's strategic location on the sea route between India and China. Although the original tribal inhabitants of Malaya were displaced inland, they were not entirely isolated from the coastal peoples. Trade relations in which 'up-river' tribal groups exchanged forest products for commodities like salt and metal implements with 'downstream' Malays, were widespread (see box on page 320). Malay culture on the peninsula reflected these contacts, embracing Indian cultural traditions, Hinduism among them. In the late 14th century, the centre of power shifted from Sumatra's Srivijayan Empire across the Strait to Melaka (see page 220). In 1430, the third ruler of Melaka embraced Islam, and became the first sultan; the city quickly grew into a flourishing trading port. By the early 1500s, it was the most important entrepôt in the region and its fame brought it to the attention of the Portuguese, who, in 1511, ushered in the colonial epoch. They sacked the town and sent the sultan fleeing to Johor, where a new sultanate was established (see page 242). But because of internal rivalries and continued conflict with the Acehnese and the Portuguese, Johor never gained the prominence of Melaka, and was forced to alternate its capital between Johor and the Riau archipelago (see page 243).

THE COLONIALS ARRIVE

The Portuguese were the first of three European colonial powers to arrive on the Malay peninsula. They were followed by the Dutch, who took Melaka in 1641 (see page 220 for a history of Melaka). When Holland was occupied by Napoleon's troops at the end of the 18th century, Britain filled the vacuum, and the British colonial era began. Historian John M Gullick writes: "The main effects of European control were, firstly, to break the sequence of indigenous kingdoms and to disrupt the trade system upon which they had been based; secondly to delimit colonial spheres of influence and thereby to fix the subsequent boundaries of the national states which are heirs to colonial rule; and lastly to promote economic development and establish the infrastructure of government and other services which that development required; mass immigration from India and China was an incidental consequence of economic development."

During the 17th century, the Dutch came into frequent conflict with the Bugis – the fiercesome master-seafarers who the Dutch had displaced from their original homeland in South Sulawesi. In 1784, in league with the Minangkabau of West Sumatra, the Bugis nearly succeeded in storming Melaka and were only stymied by the arrival of Dutch warships. The Bugis eventually established the Sultanate of Selangor on the west coast of the peninsula and, in the south, exerted increasing influence on the Johor-Riau sultans, until they had reduced them to puppet-rulers. By then however, offshoots of the Johor royal family had established the sultanates of Pahang and Perak. The Minangkabau-dominated states between Melaka and Selangor formed a confederacy of nine states – or Negeri Sembilan (see page 216). To the northeast, the states of Kelantan and Terengganu came under the Siamese sphere of influence.

BRITISH MALAYA EMERGES

The British occupied Dutch colonies during the Napoleonic Wars, following France's invasion of the Netherlands in 1794. Dutch King William of Orange, who fled to London, instructed Dutch governors overseas to end their rivalry with the British and to permit the entry of British troops to their colonies in a bid to keep the French out. Historian William R Roff writes: "From being an Indian power interested primarily ... in the free passage of trade through the Malacca Straits and beyond to China, the East India Company suddenly found itself possessor not merely of a proposed naval station on

A woodcut depicting Admiral Cornelis Matelieff's 1606 siege of Melaka

Penang island but of numerous other territorial dominions and responsibilities. Nor were some of the company's servants at all reluctant to assume these responsibilities and, indeed to extend them."

The British had their own colonial designs, having already established a foothold on Penang where Captain Francis Light had set up a trading post in 1786 (see page 175). The Anglo-Dutch Treaty of London, which was signed in 1824, effectively divided maritime Southeast Asia into British and Dutch spheres of influence. Britain retained Penang, Melaka (which it swapped for the Sumatran port of Bengkulu) and Singapore – which had been founded by Stamford Raffles in 1819 (see page 580) – and these formed the Straits Settlements. The Dutch regained control of their colonial territories in the Indonesian archipelago. Britain promised to stay out of Sumatra and the Dutch promised not to meddle in the affairs of the peninsula, thus separating two parts of the Malay world whose histories had been intertwined for centuries.

The British did very little to interfere with the Malay sultanates and chiefdoms on the peninsula, but the Straits Settlements grew in importance – particularly Singapore, which soon superceded Penang, which in turn, had eclipsed Melaka. Chinese immigrants arrived in all three ports and from there expanded into tin mining which rapidly emerged as the main source of wealth on the peninsula. The extent of the tin-rush in the mid-19th century is exemplified in the town of Larut in north-western Perak. Around 25,000 Chinese speculators arrived in Larut between 1848 and 1872. The Chinese fought over the rights to mine the most lucrative deposits and organized into secret societies and *kongsis*,

Malaysia's monarchs – the public swings against the sultans

Malaysia's nine hereditary rulers, who take it in turn to be king, represent the greatest concentration of monarchs in the world. In 1993 they were at the forefront of the most heated political controversy that Malaysia has seen in years. The battle royal ended in mid-March 1993 with the opposition Democratic Action Party voting with the government to remove the sultans' personal immunity from prosecution. For Prime Minister Dr Mahathir Mohamad, the 1993 Constitutional Amendment Bill was a personal victory. He had long made it known that he regarded the country's nine traditional rulers as a residual anachronism in modern Malaysia. A further constitutional amendment in May 1994 drove that victory home. It makes clear that from now on, the king can only act on the advice of the government. And even if the king does not approve of legislation passed by the government, it becomes law anyway after 30 days.

Malaysia's sultans emerged in the 14th and 15th centuries as the rulers of the small rivermouth states – or *negeri* – that grew up around the peninsula's coasts. The word 'sultan' is a Turkish term for the Malay *Yang di-Pertuan* – literally, 'He who is made Lord'. Sultans wielded more than temporal authority (*kuasa*); they were vested with an aura of sanctity and magical authority, or *dualat*. Malaya's sultans came through the British colonial period and the Japanese interregnum with their status and powers surprisingly intact. The post-war British government was forced by Malay lobbyists to adhere to the principle set by colonial administrator Sir Hugh Clifford in 1927: "The States were, when the British government was invited by their rulers and chiefs to set their troubled houses in order, Muhammadan monarchies: such they are today, and such they must continue to be".

On independence in 1957, Malaysia became a constitutional monarchy, with the king elected for a 5-year term from among the ranks of the sultans. In 1969, following race riots, the government amended the Sedition Act to make it an offence to question the position or prerogatives of traditional rulers. But in 1983, Prime Minister Mahathir provoked a constitutional crisis when he curtailed the power of the king by removing the monarch's right to veto legislation.

Most of Malaysia's rulers have expensive tastes and some live jet-setting playboy lifestyles. Many have used their position to amass prodigious wealth. Several sultans and their wayward offspring fitted snugly into the polo-set and the golfing and yachting elites, frequenting glitzy nightclubs, attended by retinues of security men. Traditional Malays considered such behaviour unacceptable in light of the sultans' traditional position as the upholders of Islamic values. One or two sultans added to their unsavoury reputation by committing acts of violence, safe in the knowledge that they would not be prosecuted. Resentment over such acts could never be articulated without falling foul of the Sedition Act. The activities of some contemporary rulers are not without precedent. In the 17th century, Sultan Mahmud of Johor was notorious for his cruelty, which included shooting men at random to test a new gun. On one occasion he ordered a pregnant woman to be ripped apart because she had eaten a jackfruit from his garden. In the end the woman's husband ran the sultan through with a *kris* with the full support of palace officials.

Until very recently it has not been possible to print the alleged crimes of Sultan *Mahmud*'s modern successors in the house of Johor. But in early 1993 a government MP referred in parliament to 23 incidents since 1972 involving today's Sultan

Mahmud of Johor and his son, the Rajah Muda Abdul Majid Idris. The most notorious of these concerned the death of a caddie on the Cameron Highlands golf course. Sultan Mahmood allegedly killed him by smashing his head with a club after the caddie sniggered at a duffed shot. On another occasion a man was shot and killed after an argument with the prince in a Johor Bahru nightclub. Abdul Majid was convicted for this but was pardoned by his father.

Other sultans' disregard for various facets of the law of the land was highlighted by His Royal Highness Tuanku Ismail Petra Ibni Al-Marhum Sultan Tahya Petra of Kelantan. He managed to import 30 luxury cars duty-free. In March 1992, he eluded customs officials by claiming he was taking his new Lamborghini Diablo for a test-drive. Following that incident, the government took full advantage of its ownership of most national newspapers by devoting pages and pages to exposés of the sultans' flamboyant lifestyles. The M$200mn it cost Malaysian tax-payers each year to maintain them was broken down in detail. It emerged that entire hospital wards were reserved for their exclusive use. More than M$9mn was spent on new cutlery and bedsheets for the King – a sum which the *New Straits Times* said would have built two new hospitals or 46 rural clinics or 46 primary schools.

Malaysia's defence minister, Najib Razak, added to the stable of royal anecdotes in 1993 when he revealed that a certain unnamed sultan had ordered a Royal Malaysian Navy Commander to jump ship and swim to shore in front of his assembled crew. His sin? To disturb the sultan's windsurfing by churning up too much wake. Coincidentally, the Sultan of Johor is an avid windsurfer.

Dr Mahathir gambled that the unveiling of such royal scams would swing public opinion in favour of constitutional amendments. The Prime Minister had long lost patience with the sultans over their interference in politics and business. He was particularly angered by the Sultan of Kelantan who backed the state's Islamic opposition's campaign against his government in the 1990 general election. In July 1992 his government agreed a 'code of conduct' with the sultans, but they refused to accept constitutional amendments undermining their powers. Mahathir responded by withdrawing royal privileges such as their generous financial stipends. In Jan 1993, parliament passed amendments removing their legal immunity. Deadlock ensued as Malaysian law said the sultans had to approve legislation affecting their position. Finally, after a tense stand-off, the government and the sultans agreed to a compromise. The sultans secured an undertaking that no ruler would be taken to court without the Attorney General's approval.

Mahathir emerged from the fray with his executive powers strengthened and his no-nonsense reputation enhanced. The sultans' reputation, by contrast, has been severely dented. As one commentator noted, "the palace doors have been thrown open", adding that public prying into royal affairs is unlikely to cease.

In April 1994 Sultan Ja'afar ibni Abdul Rahman of Negri Sembilan, took over from the Sultan of Perak as the next king. Tunka Ja'afar is Malaysia's 10th king; he is an Oxford-educated former diplomat. The new king has an air of authority and respectability. His first statement was that of a responsible environmentalist, urging Malaysian factories to clean up industrial waste.

which by the 1860s, were engaged in open warfare. At the same time, the Malay rulers in the states on the peninsula were busily taxing the tin traders while in the Straits Settlements, British investors in the mining industry put increasing pressure on the Colonial Office to intervene in order to stabilize the situation. In late-1873 Britain decided it could not rule the increasingly lawless and anarchic states by remote control any longer and the western-central states were declared a British protectorate. In his account of British intervention, William R Roff quotes a Malay proverb: 'Once the needle is in, the thread is sure to follow'.

In 1874, the Treaty of Pangkor established the Residential system whereby British officers were posted to key districts; it became their job to determine all administrative and policy matters other than those governing Islam and Malay custom. This immediately provoked resentment and sparked uprisings in Perak, Selangor and Negeri Sembilan, as well as a Malay revolt in 1875. The revolts were put down and the system was institutionalized; in 1876 these three states plus Pahang became the Federated Malay States. By 1909 the north states of Kedah, Perlis, Kelantan and Terengganu – which previously came under Siamese suzerainty – finally agreed to accept British advisers and became known as the Unfederated Malay States. Johor remained independent until 1914 (see page 243). The British system of government relied on the political power of the sultans and the Malay aristocracy: residents conferred with the rulers of each state and employed the aristocrats as civil servants. Local headmen (known as *penghulu*) were used as administrators in rural areas.

Meanwhile, the British continued to encourage the immigration of Chinese, who formed a majority of the population in Perak and Selangor by the early 1920s. Apart from the wealthy traders based in the Straits Settlements, the Chinese immigrants were organized (and exploited) by their secret societies, which provided welfare services, organized work gangs and ran local government. In 1889 the societies were officially banned, and while this broke their hold on political power, they simply re-emerged as a criminal underworld. In the Federated Malay States, there was an eight-fold population increase to 1.7 million between 1891 and 1931. Even by 1891 the proportion of Malays had declined to a fraction over a third of the population, with the Chinese making up 41.5% and Indians – imported as indentured labourers by the British (see page 68) – comprising 22%. To the south, Johor, which in the late 1800s was not even a member of the federation, had a similar ethnic balance.

For the most part, the Malay population remained in the countryside and were only gradually drawn into the modern economy. But by the 1920s Malay nationalism was on the rise, partly prompted by the Islamic reform movement and partly by intellectuals in secular circles who looked to the creation of a Greater Malaysia (or Greater Indonesia), under the influence of left-wing Indonesian nationalists. These Malay nationalists were as critical of the Malay elite as they were of the British colonialists. The elite itself was becoming increasingly outspoken for different reasons – it felt threatened by the growing demands of Straits-born Chinese and second-generation Indians for equal rights.

The first semi-political nationalist movement was the *Kesatuan Melayu Singapura* (Singapore Malay Union), formed in 1926 (see page 598). The Union found early support in the Straits Settlements where Malays were outnumbered and there was no sultan. They gradually spread across the peninsula and held a pan-Malayan conference in 1939. These associations were the forerunners of the post-war Malay nationalist movement. In the run-up to World War Two the left-wing split off to form the *Kesatuan Melayu Muda* – the Union of Young Malays, which was strongly anti-British and whose leaders were arrested by the colonial authorities in 1940. The Chinese were more interested in business than politics and any political interests were focused on China. The middle class supported the Chinese nationalist Kuomintang (KMT), although it was eventually banned by the British, as it was becoming an obvious focus of anti-colonial sentiment. The KMT allowed Communists to join the movement until 1927, but in 1930 they split off to form the Malayan Communist Party (MCP) which drew its support from the working class.

THE JAPANESE OCCUPATION

Under cover of darkness on the night of 8 December 1941, the Japanese army invaded Malaya, landing in South Thailand and pushing into Kedah, and at Kota Bharu in Kelantan (see page 311). The invasion – which took place an hour before the attack on Pearl Harbour – took the Allies in Malaya and 'Fortress' Singapore completely by surprise. The Japanese forces had air, land and sea superiority and quickly overwhelmed the Commonwealth troops on the peninsula. Militarily, it was a brilliant campaign, made speedier by the fact that the Japanese troops stole bicycles in every town they took, thus making it possible for them to outpace all Allied estimates of their likely rate of advance.

By 28 December they had taken Ipoh and all of northern Malaya. Kuantan fell on the 31st, the Japanese having sunk the British warships *Prince of Wales* and *Repulse* (see page 274) and Kuala Lumpur on 11 January 1942. They advanced down the east coast, centre and west coast simultaneously and by the end of the month had taken Johor Bahru and were massed across the strait from Singapore. By 15 February they had forced the capitulation of the Allies in Singapore (see page 584). This was a crushing blow, and, according to Malaysian historian Zainal Abidin bin Abudul Wahid, "the speed with which the Japanese managed to achieve victory, however temporary that might have been, shattered the image of the British, and generally the 'whiteman', as a superior people". Right up until the beginning of World War Two, the British had managed to placate the aristocratic leaders of the Malay community and the wealthy Chinese merchants and there was little real threat to the status quo. The Japanese defeat of the British changed all that by altering the balance between conservatism and change. Because Britain had failed so miserably to defend Malaya, its credentials as a protector were irrevocably tarnished.

For administrative purposes, the Japanese linked the peninsula with Sumatra as part of the Greater East Asia Co-prosperity Sphere. All British officials were interned and the legislative and municipal councils swept aside. But because the Japanese had lost their command of the seas by the end of 1942, nothing could be imported and there was a shortage of food supplies. The 'banana' currency introduced by the Japanese became worthless as inflation soared. Japan merely regarded Malaya as a source of raw materials, yet the rubber and tin industries stagnated and nothing was done to develop the economy.

After initially severing sultans' pensions and reducing their powers, the Japanese realized that their cooperation was necessary if the Malay bureaucracy was to be put to work for the occupation government (see page 52). The Indians were treated well – they were seen as a key to fighting the British colonial regime in India. But Malaya's Chinese – while they were not rounded up and executed as they were in Singapore (see page 586) – were not trusted. The Japanese, however, came to recognize the importance of the Chinese community in oiling the wheels of the economy. The Chinese Dalforce militia (set up by the Allies as the Japanese advanced southwards) joined the Communists and other minor underground dissident groups in forming the Malayan People's Anti-Japanese Army. British army officers and arms were parachuted into the jungle to support the guerrillas. It was during this period that the Malayan Communist Party (MCP) broadened its membership and appeal, under the guise of a nationwide anti-Japanese alliance.

The brutality of the Japanese regime eased with time; as the war began to go against them, they increasingly courted the different communities, giving them more say in the run of things in an effort to undermine any return to colonial rule. But the Japanese's favourable treatment of Malays and their general mistrust of the Chinese did not foster good race relations between the two. A Malay paramilitary police force was put to work to root out Chinese who were anti-Japanese, which exacerbated inter-communal hostility. The Japanese never offered Malaya independence but allowed Malay nationalist sentiments to develop in an effort to deflect attention from the fact they had ceded the North Malay states of Kedah, Perlis, Kelantan and Terengganu to Thailand.

THE BRITISH RETURN

During the war, the British drew up secret plans for a revised administrative structure in Malaya. The plan was to create a Malayan Union by combining the federated and unfederated states as well as Melaka and Penang, leaving Singapore as a crown colony. Plans were also drawn up to buy North Borneo from the Chartered Company (see page 425) and to replace the anachronous White Rajahs of Sarawak (see page 338) with a view to eventually grouping all the territories together as a federation. As soon as the Japanese surrendered in September 1945, the plan was put into action. Historian Mary Turnbull notes that "Malaya was unique [among western colonies] because the returning British were initially welcomed with enthusiasm and were themselves unwilling to put the clock back. But they were soon overwhelmed by the reaction against their schemes for streamlining the administration and assimilating the different immigrant communities."

A unitary state was formed on the peninsula and everyone, regardless of race or origin, who called Malaya 'home', was accorded equal status. But the resentment caused by British high-handedness was the catalyst which triggered the foundation of the United Malays National Organization (UMNO) which provided a focus for opposition to the colonial regime and, following independence, formed the ruling party. Opposition to UMNO – led by the Malay ruling class – forced the British to withdraw the Union proposal – the sultans refused to attend the installation of the governor and the Malays boycotted advisory councils. Mary Turnbull notes that the Malayan Union scheme was "conceived as a civil servant's dream but was born to be a politician's nightmare". Vehement Malay opposition prompted negotiations with Malay leaders which hammered out the basis of a Federation of Malaya which was established in February 1948. It was essentially the same as the Union in structure, except that it recognized the sovereignty of the sultans in the 11 states and the so-called 'special position' of the Malays as the indigenous people of Malaya. The federation had a strong central government (headed by a High Commissioner) and a federal executive council.

In this federal system, introduced in 1948, non-Malays could only become Malaysian citizens if they had been resident in Malaya for a minimum of 15 out of the previous 25 years, were prepared to sign a declaration of permanent settlement and were able to speak either Malay or English. This meant only 3 million of Malaya's 5 million population qualified as citizens, of whom 78% were Malay, 12% Chinese and 7% Indian. Historian Mary Turnbull says that while the British believed they had achieved their objective of common citizenship (even on more restricted terms), they had, in reality "accepted UMNO's concept of a Malay nation into which immigrant groups would have to be integrated, and many difficulties were to develop from this premise".

THE RISE OF COMMUNISM

The Chinese and Indian communities were not consulted in these Anglo-Malay negotiations and ethnic and religious tensions between the three main communities were running high, unleashing the forces of racialism which had been lying dormant for years. Because their part in the political process had been ignored, many more Chinese began to identify with the Malaysian Communist Party (MCP) which was still legal. It was not until the Communist victory in China in 1949 that the Chinese began to think of Malaya as home. During the war the MCP had gained legitimacy and prestige as a patriotic resistance movement. The MCP's *de facto* military wing, the MPAJA, had left arms dumps in the jungle, but the Communist leadership was split as to whether negotiation or confrontation was the way forward. Then in 1947 the MCP suffered what many considered to be a disastrous blow: its Vietnamese-born secretary-general, Lai Teck, absconded with all the party's funds having worked as a double agent for both the Japanese and the British. He was suspected of having betrayed the entire MCP central committee to the Japanese in 1942. The new 26-years-old MCP leader, former schoolmaster Chin Peng, immediately abandoned Lai's soft approach.

In June 1948 he opted for armed rebellion, and the Malayan Communist Emergency commenced with the murder of three European planters. According to John Gullick, the historian and former member of the Malayan civil service, it was called an 'Emergency' because the Malayan economy was covered by the London insurance market for everything other than war. Premiums covered loss of stock, property and equipment through riot and civil commotion, but not through civil war, so the misnomer continued throughout the 12-years insurrection. Others say it got its name from the Emergency Regulations that were passed in June 1948 which were designed to deny food supplies and weapons to the Communists.

The Emergency was characterized by indiscriminate armed Communist raids on economic targets – often rubber estates and tin mines – and violent ambushes which were aimed at loosening and undermining central government control. Chinese 'squatters' in areas fringing the jungle (many of whom had fled from the cities during the Japanese occupation) provided an information and supply network for the Communists. In 1950 the British administration moved these people into 500 'New Villages', where they could be controlled and protected. This policy – known as 'The Briggs Plan' after the Director of Operations, Lt-Gen. Sir Harold Briggs – was later adopted (rather less successfully) by the Americans in South Vietnam.

In much the same way as they had been caught unprepared by the Japanese invasion in 1941, the British were taken by surprise and in the first few years the MCP (whose guerrillas were labelled 'CTs' – or Communist Terrorists) gained the upper hand. In 1951 British morale all but crumbled when the High Commissioner, Sir Henry Gurney, was ambushed and assassinated on the road to Fraser's Hill (see page 145). His successor General Sir Gerald Templer took the initiative, however, with his campaign to 'win the hearts and minds of the people'. Templer's biographer, John Cloake, gave him Japanese General Tomoyuki Yamashita's old sobriquet 'Tiger of Malaya' (see page 585), and there is little doubt that his tough policies won the war. In his book *Emergency Years*, former mine-manager Leonard Rayner says the chain-smoking Templer "exuded nervous energy like an overcharged human battery". Within 2 years the Communists were on the retreat. They had also begun to lose popular support due to the climate of fear they introduced – although the Emergency did not officially end until 1960.

Historians believe the Communist rebellion failed because it was too slow to take advantage of the economic hardships in the immediate aftermath of World War Two and because it was almost exclusively Chinese. It also only really appealed to the Chinese working class and alienated and shunned the Chinese merchant community and Straits-born Chinese.

THE ROAD TO MERDEKA

The British had countered the MCP's claim to be a multi-racial nationalist movement by accelerating moves towards Malayan independence – which Britain promised, once the Emergency was over. The only nationalist party with any political credibility was UMNO. Its founder, Dato' Onn bin Jaafar wanted to allow non-Malays to become members, and when his proposal was rejected, he resigned to form the Independence of Malaya Party. The brother of the Sultan of Kedah, Tunku Abdul Rahman, took over as head of UMNO and to counter Onn's new party, he made an electoral pact with the Malayan Chinese Association (MCA) and the Malayan Indian Congress (MIC). With the MCP out of the picture, the Chinese community had hesitantly grouped itself around the MCA. The Alliance (which trounced Onn's party in the election) is still in place today, in the form of the ruling *Barisan Nasional* (National Front). After sweeping the polls in 1955, the Alliance called immediately for *merdeka* – independence – which the British guaranteed within 2 years.

With independence promised by nonviolent means, Tunku Abdul Rahman offered an amnesty to the Communists. Together with Singapore's Chief Minister, David Marshall (see page 587) and Straits-Chinese leader Tan Cheng Lock (see page 231), he met Chin Peng in 1956. But they failed to reach agreement and the MCP fled through the jungle into the mountains in southern Thailand around Betong. While the Emergency was declared 'over' in 1960, the MCP only finally agreed to lay down its arms in 1989, in a peace agreement brokered by Thailand. The party had been riven by factionalism and its membership had dwindled to under 1,000. In 1991, the legendary Chin Peng struck a deal with the Malaysian government allowing the former guerrillas to return home.

Historian Mary Turnbull writes: "When Malaya attained independence in 1957 it was a prosperous country with stable political institutions, a sound administrative system and a good infrastructure of education and communications – a country with excellent resources and a thriving economy based on export agriculture and mining". Under the new constitution, a king was to be chosen from one of the nine sultans, and the monarchy was to be rotated every 5 years. A 2-tier parliament was set up, with a *Dewan Rakyat* (People's House) of elected representatives and a *Dewan Negara* (Senate) to represent the state assemblies. Each of the 11 states had its own elected government and a sultan or governor.

Politicians in Singapore made it clear that they also wanted to be part of an independent Malaya, but in Kuala Lumpur, UMNO leaders were opposed to a merger because the island had a Chinese majority. (A straight merger would have resulted in a small Chinese majority in Malaya.) Increasing nationalist militancy in Singapore was of particular concern to UMNO and the radical wing of the People's Action Party, which was swept to power with Lee Kuan Yew at its head in 1959 (see page 587), was dominated by Communists. Fearing the emergence of 'a second Cuba' on Malaysia's doorstep, Tunku Abdul Rahman proposed that Singapore join a greater

Malaysian Federation, in which a racial balance would be maintained by the inclusion of Sarawak, Brunei and British North Borneo (Sabah). Britain supported the move, as did all the states involved. Kuala Lumpur was particularly keen on Brunei joining the Federation on two scores: it had Malays and it had oil. But at the eleventh hour, Brunei's Sultan Omar backed out, mistrustful of Kuala Lumpur's obvious designs on his sultanate's oil revenues and unhappy at the prospect of becoming just another sultan in Malaya's collection of nine monarchs (see page 52).

Prime Minister Tunku Abdul Rahman was disheartened, but the Malaysia Agreement was signed in July 1963 with Singapore, Sarawak and Sabah. Without Brunei, there was a small Chinese majority in the new Malaysia. The Tunku did not have time to dwell on racial arithmetic, however, because almost immediately the new federation was plunged into an undeclared war with Indonesia – which became known as *Konfrontasi*, or Confrontation (see page 341) – due to President Sukarno's objection to the participation of Sabah and Sarawak. Indonesian saboteurs were landed on the peninsula and in Singapore and there were Indonesian military incursions along the borders of Sabah and Sarawak with Kalimantan. Konfrontasi was finally ended in 1966 after Sukarno fell from power. But relations with Singapore – which had been granted a greater measure of autonomy than other states – were far from smooth. Communal riots in Singapore in 1964 and Lee Kuan Yew's efforts to forge a nation-wide opposition alliance which called for 'a democratic Malaysian Malaysia' further opened the rift with Kuala Lumpur. Feeling unnerved by calls for racial equality while the Malays did not form a majority of the population, Tunku Abdul Rahman expelled Singapore from the federation in August 1965 against Lee Kuan Yew's wishes (see page 588).

RACIAL POLITICS IN THE 1960s

The expulsion of Singapore did not solve the racial problem on the peninsula, however. Because the Malay and Chinese communities felt threatened by each other – one wielded political power, the other economic power – racial tensions built up. Resentment focused on the enforcement of Malay as the medium of instruction in all schools and as the national language and on the privileged educational and employment opportunities afforded to Malays. The tensions finally exploded on 13 May 1969, in the wake of the general election.

The UMNO-led Alliance faced opposition from the Democratic Action Party (DAP) which was built from the ashes of Lee Kuan Yew's People's Action Party. The DAP was a radical Chinese-dominated party and called for racial equality. Also in opposition was *Gerakan* (the People's Movement), supported by Chinese and Indians, and the Pan-Malayan Islamic Party, which was exclusively Malay and very conservative. In the election, the opposition parties – which were not in alliance – deprived the Alliance of its two-thirds majority in parliament; it required this margin to amend the constitution unimpeded. Gerakan and DAP celebrations provoked counter-demonstrations from Malays and in the ensuing mayhem hundreds were killed in Kuala Lumpur.

The government suspended the constitution for over a year and declared a **State of Emergency**. A new national ideology was drawn up – the controversial New Economic Policy (see page 90) – which was an ambitious experiment in social and economic engineering aimed at ironing out discrepancies between ethnic communities. The *Rukunegara*, a written national ideology aimed at fostering nation-building, was introduced in August 1970. It demanded loyalty to the king and the constitution, respect for Islam and observance of the law and morally acceptable behaviour. All discussion

Pityamit one: from guerrilla camp to holiday camp

The Malayan Emergency was one of the few insurgencies which the Communists lost. But their shelling, ambushes, bombings and assassinations cost the lives of more than 10,000 soldiers and civilians over 40 years. The Emergency started just after the Second World War. At its peak, tens of thousands of Commonwealth troops were pitted against an estimated 3,500 Communists – most of whom were Chinese – in the Malayan jungle. Newly independent Malaysia pronounced the Emergency officially over in 1960. They had the Communists on the run. The guerrillas fled across Malaysia's jungled frontier into South Thailand – but once ensconsed there, they held out for another 30 years against both the Malaysian and Thai armies.

Most of their secret camps were never found. The Communists had laced the border itself with booby trap devices and regularly launched attacks and ambushes across the border. The people on the frontline of the war were the residents of the Malaysian border town of Pengkalan Hulu (formerly Keroh), which means 'forward base'. Many attrocities were committed in and around the town, which was still under curfew until well into the 1980s. The Communists also made themselves unpopular in Thailand, where they demanded protection money from local businesses around Betong. They never surrendered, but finally, in 1989, they reached what was known as "an honourable settlement" with the Malaysian and Thai governments, bringing to an end one of the world's longest-running insurgencies. Realizing that most of the former guerrillas would be unwilling to return to their homeland, King Bhumipol of Thailand offered them land around their former camps and built them houses. One of those camps, Pityamit I, has now opened to the public for the first time. Like others in the vicinity, nobody knew it was there until recently.

Having laid down their Kalashnikovs, former revolutionaries now take tourists round their old jungle stronghold. Some sell herbal medicine and soft drinks to the tourists; others have become vegetable farmers at the Highland Friendship Cooperative (the camp's new name). The trees which once afforded them thick cover from helicopter gunships have been chopped down and the steep hillsides have been planted out. About 1,200 former fighters have now settled into their new lives but few have any regrets about their old ones as members of the Communist Party of Malaya's pro-Moscow splinter group. "Money is important", one of them told a visiting journalist. "Without it you can't do anything." They are happy to regail tourists with tales of the jungle. Some have been living in it since 1948. Although they admit that Communism world-wide appears to have failed, they urge those who are prepared to listen not to jump to hasty conclusions. "The final decisions should be up to our sons and grandsons."

of the Malays' 'special position' was banned as was discussion about the national language and the sovereignty of the sultans. In the words of historian John Gullick, "Tunku Abdul Rahman, whose anguish at the disaster had impeded his ability to deal with it effectively," resigned the following month and handed over to Tun Abdul Razak. Tun Razak was an able administrator, but lacked the dynamism of his predecessor. He did, however, unify UMNO and patched up the old Alliance, breathing new life into the coalition by incorporating every political party except the DAP and one or two other small parties into the newly named *Barisan Nasional* (BN), or National Front. In 1974 the Barisan won a landslide majority.

Tun Razak shifted Malaysia's foreign policy from a pro-western stance to non-alignment and established diplomatic relations with both Moscow and Beijing. But within Malaysia, Communist paranoia was rife: as Indochina fell to Communists in the mid-1970s, many Malaysians became increasingly convinced that Malaysia was just another 'domino' waiting to topple. There were even several arrests of prominent Malays (including two newspaper editors and five top UMNO politicians). But when Chin Peng's revolutionaries joined forces with secessionist Muslims in South Thailand, the Thai and Malaysian governments launched a joint clean-out operation in the jungle along the frontier. By the late 1970s the North Kalimantan Communist Party had also been beaten into virtual submission too (see page 342). In 1976 Tun Razak died and was succeeded by his brother-in-law, Dato' Hussein Onn (the son of Umno's founding father). He inherited an economy which was in good shape, thanks to strong commodity prices, and in the general election of 1978, the BN won another comfortable parliamentary majority. 3 years later he handed over to Dr Mahathir Mohamad (see profile, page 88) who in April 1995 secured yet another term in office having won a massive majority in Parliament (see Modern Malaysia page 89).

ART AND ARCHITECTURE

Unlike the countries of mainland Southeast Asia and its neighbour, Indonesia, Malaysia is not known for its art and architecture. Arriving at Kuala Lumpur's Sabang International Airport and driving into town, there is apparently scarcely anything worth an aesthetic second glance. Many of Malaysia's artistic treasures have either been torn down to make way for modern buildings with scarcely a concrete ounce of artistic merit, or have simply rotted away through sheer neglect. However, the country is far from being the artistic desert that a cursory glance might suppose. The sadness, though, is that much of what is deemed to be 'worth seeing' (ie a 'sight') is not Malaysian *per se*, but colonial. The most attractive towns – notably Georgetown (Penang) and Melaka – are notable mainly for their Chinese shophouses, and Dutch, Portuguese and English colonial buildings. Vernacular Malay houses must be sought out more carefully; few are preserved, and most are being demolished to make way for structures perceived to be more fitting of a thrusting young country on the verge of developed nation status.

In his book *The Malay House*, architect Lim Jee Yuan writes that traditional houses, which are built without architects, "reflect good housing solutions, as manifested by the display of a good fit to the culture, lifestyle and socio-economic needs of the users; the honest and efficient use of materials; and appropriate climatic design". Classic Malay houses are built of timber and raised on stilts with wooden or bamboo walls and an *atap* roof – made from the leaves of the nipah palm. It should have plenty of windows and good ventilation – the interior is usually airy and bright. It is also built on a prefabricated system and can be expanded to fit the needs of a growing family. Malay houses are usually simple, functional and unostentatious, and even those embellished by woodcarvings blend into their environment. Lim Jee Yuan says "the Malay house cannot be fully appreciated without its setting – the house compound and the kampung". Kampung folk, he says, prefer "community intimacy over personal privacy" which means villages are closely knit communities.

Most Malays on the peninsula traditionally lived in pile-houses built on stilts along the rivers. The basic design is called the bumbung panjangi ('long roof'), although there are many variations and hybrids; these are influenced both by the Minangkabau house-forms (of West Sumatra) and by Thai-Khmer designs. The differences in house-styles between regions is mainly in the shape of the roof. The bumbung panjang is the oldest, commonest, simplest and most graceful, with a long gable roof, thatched with atap. There are ventilation grills at either end, allowing a throughflow of air. From the high apex, the eaves slope down steeply, then, towards the bottom, the angle lessens, extending out over the walls. Bumbung panjang are most commonly found in Melaka, but the design is used widely throughout the peninsula.

These days it is more usual to find the atap replaced with corrugated zinc roofs which require less maintenance and are a measure of status in the community. But zinc turns houses into ovens during the day, makes them cold at night and makes a deafening noise in rainstorms. On the east coast of the peninsula, the use of tiled roofs is more common. Towards the north, Thai and Khmer influences are more pronounced in roof style. As in Thai houses, walls are panelled; there are also fewer windows and elaborate carving is more common. Because Islam proscribes the use of the human figure in art, ornamental woodcarvings depict floral and geometric designs as well as Koranic calligraphy. Most are relief-carvings on wood panels or grilles. In Melaka, colourful ceramic tiles are also commonly used as exterior decoration.

The oldest surviving Malay houses date from only the 19th century. The traditional design is the rumah berpanggung, which is built high off the ground on stilts with an A-shaped roof. The basic features include:

- *Anjung*: covered porch at the top of entranceway stairs where formal visitors are entertained.
- *Serambi gantung*: verandah, where most guests are entertained.
- *Rumah ibu* ('the domain of the mother of the house'): private central core of the house, with raised floor level, where the family talks, sleeps, prays, studies and eats (particularly during festivals).
- *Dapur*: kitchen, always at the back, and below the level of the rest of the house; most meals are taken here. The dapur is connected to the rumah ibu by the *selang*, a closed walkway. Near the dapur, there is usually a *pelantar*, with a washing area for clothes, a mandi and a toilet.

The best places to see traditional Malay houses are Melaka and Negeri Sembilan, on the west coast, and Terengganu and Kelantan states to the northeast. Minangkabau influence is most pronounced in Negeri Sembilan state, between Kuala Lumpur and Melaka. There, houses have a distinctive, elegant, curved roofline, where the gable sweeps up into 'wings' at each end – the so-called Minangkabau 'buffalo horns'.

Today the traditional Malay house has lost its status in the kampung – now everyone wants to build in concrete and brick. Many planned modern kampungs have been built throughout Malaysia, with little regard for traditional building materials or for the traditional houseforms. Lim Jee Yuan writes that: "Unless there are positive steps taken to uplift the status of the traditional Malay house ... it is bound for extinction in the near future despite its superior design principles and suitability to our environmental, economic and socio-cultural needs". Many like-minded architects despair of the 'vulgarization' of the Malay houseform, which has been used as an inspiration for many modern buildings (notably in Kuala Lumpur, see page 101). The curved Minangabau roof, for example, which has been borrowed for everything from modern bank buildings to tollbooths, has merely become a cultural symbol, and has been deprived of its deeper significance.

Peranakan

The Straits Chinese (Peranakan) communities of Melaka, Penang and Singapore developed their own architectural style to match their unique cultural traditions (see page 230). The finest Peranakan houses can be seen along Jalan Tun Tan

The Malay istana – royals on the riverside

The Malay word *istana* derives from the Sanskrit for 'sleeping place' – but the Malay sultans adopted it as the term for their royal palaces. Because Malay sultanates were usually focused on the mouths of rivers, the istanas were normally sited on a prominent point on the riverbank, along which the sultan's powerbase extended. This meant they were prone to flooding, however, and over the centuries, a number slipped into the river – notably in Perak. The 16th century *Sejarah Melayu* (Malay Annals) provide a description of Sultan Mansur Shah's palace in Melaka (see page 229). The building has been reconstructed from notes and historical data and now serves as Melaka's *Muzium Budaya* (Cultural Museum). The original palace was said to have had a 7-tiered roof and 12 halls; it was razed to the ground by the invading Portuguese in 1511.

Traditionally, istanas included everything from the sultan's private quarters (at the rear) to the state administrative and cultural centre. They also doubled as forts in time of war. The sultan's concubines lived in outhouses, dotted around the compound, which also included the mosque and the *rumah wakaf* – the lodging house for commoners (such as the Istana Jahar in Kota Bharu, which is now the Kelantan State Museum). There are several other istanas in Kelantan and Terengganu states, all dating from the 19th century. The most impressive of the surviving istanas are the Istana Lama Sri Menanti and the Istana Ampang Tinggi in Negri Sembilan (see page 216), the Istana Balai Besar in Kedah – one of the grandest and best-preserved on the peninsula, and now the state museum – and the Istana Kenangan at Kuala Kangsar in Perak, which is now the Royal Museum (see page 170). There are only 11 wooden palaces remaining in Malaysia, and none of them houses a royal family any longer.

Cheng Lock in Melaka (see page 232), notably the Baba-Nyonya Heritage Museum. Typical Peranakan houses were long and narrow, and built around a central courtyard. Their interiors are characterized by dark, heavy wood and marble-topped furniture, often highly decorated, and made by Chinese craftsmen who were brought over from China.

Immigrant Chinese

For background on Chinese temple architecture and the basic principles of geomancy (*feng shui*), see page 595.

CULTURE

PEOPLE

Visitors sometimes get confused over the different races that make up Malaysia's population. All citizens of Malaysia are 'Malaysians'; they are comprised of Malays, Chinese and Indians as well as other 'tribal' groups, most of whom live in the East Malaysian states of Sabah and Sarawak (see page 329).

Malaysia has a total population approaching 20 million, of who 83% lives on the peninsula, 8% in Sabah and 9% in Sarawak. Statistics on the ethnic breakdown of Malaysia's multi-racial population tend to differ and because politics is divided along racial lines, they are sensitive figures. For Malaysia as a whole, Malays make up roughly 52% of the population, Chinese 29%, Indians 8% and indigenous tribes 11%. The Malays and indigenous groups are usually lumped together under the umbrella term ***bumiputra*** – or 'sons of the soil'. So in the country as a whole, 'bumis' – as they are popularly known – account for 63% of the population. On the peninsula the figure is slightly less, with bumis comprising 58% of the inhabitants there, while the Chinese make up 31% and Indians 9%.

In theory being a *bumi* bestows certain advantages. The New Economic Policy or NEP (see page 90), introduced after the race riots in 1969, discriminates in favour of the indigenous population – mostly the Malays, but also the non-Malay tribal peoples of East Malaysia and the Orang Asli of the peninsula. They receive preferential treatment when it comes to university places, bumi entrepreneurs have an inside track securing government contracts, and they also benefit from discounts on houses. However there have been stories of non-Malay bumiputras not being accorded the affirmative action rights of Malay bumis. In 1997, for example, it was revealed that an Iban ('tribal' Dayak from East Malaysia) man was refused the 5-7% discount which bumis are entitled to when he tried to buy a house in Melaka. The federal government was appalled but many commentators were not altogether surprised. What it means to qualify as a bumi has never been adequately defined. It appears that for some people being a bumi not only means being indigenous, it also means being Muslim, and many of the non-Malay bumis are Christian.

Malaysia's population is growing by about 2.5% per annum. Since 1970, the bumiputra population has grown fastest, and, on the peninsula, their proportion of the total population has increased from 53%. In the same period, the proportion of the Chinese population has declined from 36% while the proportion of Indians has remained roughly the same. Mahathir announced at the beginning of the 1990s that for Malaysia to become an industrialized country, it would need a strong domestic market, so he encouraged Malaysians to procreate – his once suggested target was a population of 70 million by 2010, up from 17 million in 1990. The target date has subsequently been revised to 2095. The higher average fertility rate of the Malay compared with the Chinese population means that the delicate racial balance that was such a potential source of instability at independence is becoming less of a worry. It has been estimated that by 2020 the bumiputra population will comprise 70% of the total population of the country. The fear that the Chinese might represent a political threat to Malay domination is receding as each year passes.

Malays

The Malay people probably first migrated to the peninsula from Sumatra. Anthropologists speculate that the race originally evolved from the blending of a Mongoloid people from Central Asia with an island race living between the Indian and Pacific oceans. They are lowland people and originally settled around the coasts. These 'Coastal Malays' are also known as 'Deutero-Malays'. They are ethnically similar to the Malays of Indonesia and are the result of intermarriage with many other racial groups, including Indians, Chinese, Arabs and Thais. They are a very relaxed, warm-hearted people who had the good fortune to settle in a land where growing food was easy. For centuries they have been renowned for their hospitality and generosity as well as their well-honed sense of humour. When Malays converted to Islam in the early 15th century, the language was written in Sanskrit script which evolved into the Arabic-looking *Jawi*.

Because Malays were traditionally farmers and were tied to rural kampungs, they remained insulated from the expansion of colonial Malaya's export economy. Few of them worked as wage labourers and only the aristocracy, which had been educated in English, were intimately involved in the British system of government, as administrators. "... In return for the right to develop a modern extractive economy within the *negeri* [states] by means of alien immigrant labor," writes historian William R Roff, "the British undertook to maintain intact the position and prestige of the ruling class and to refrain from catapulting the Malay people into the modern world". Rural Malays only began to enter the cash economy when they started to take up rubber cultivation on their smallholdings – but this was not until after 1910. In 1921, less than 5% of Malays lived in towns.

On attaining independence in 1957, the new constitution allowed Malays to be given special rights for 10 years. The idea was that this would allow the Malay community to become as prosperous as the Chinese 'immigrants'. To this end, they were afforded extra help in education and in securing jobs. The first economic development plan focused on the rural economy, with the aim of improving the lot of the rural Malays. It was the Malay community's sense of its own

Running amok

The word *amok* is one of the few Malay words to have been embraced by the English language, most obviously used in the expression 'to run amuck'. Amok refers to aberrant behaviour which, at least until the early 20th century, was prevalent among the Malay peoples. There are two forms of amok – martial amok, where it is used as an honourable tactic of warfare (martial amok was also common in India), and solitary amok. It is the latter which has attracted the most attention, as it appears to occur suddenly, without warning, and with little apparent reason. The earliest reference to solitary amok occurs in the work of Nicolo Conti dating from the early 15th century. All references agree that it is a frenzied, murderous and usually unselective attack on all and everyone that an amok-runner or *pengamok* might meet, and that it almost always ended in the death of the attacker, such is the madness of the violence. Some authorities have attributed amok to social alienation (amok-runners are usually new arrivals in an area); others to the disgrace of penury that might force a person into slavery; some to the effects of drugs (this was the usual colonial explanation, as the cause is clear and easily understood); others to some deep-seated grief (for example following the death of a man's wife or child); while still others have maintained that it is religiously motivated. Within the Malay social context, the amok-runner was viewed as a person with a certain honour: the act itself, although it might well lead to the death of innocent bystanders, was seen as an honourable escape from some dire situation.

The British in Malaya tended to view *pengamok* in western terms, and to moralize about their crimes. On 8 July 1846, Sunan, a respectable Malay housebuilder ran amok in Penang. According to the judicial disposition at his trial:

> "... before he [Sunan] was arrested [he] killed an old Hindu woman, a Kling, a Chinese boy, and a Kling girl about 3 years old in the arms of its father, and wounded two Hindus, three Klings, and two Chinese, of whom only two survived."

He had, apparently, been devastated by the death of his wife and only child. Nonetheless, the magistrate sentenced the man with the words:

> "The sentence of the Court therefore is, that you, Sunan, be remanded to the place from whence you came, and that on the morning of Wednesday next you be drawn from thence on a hurdle to the place of execution, and there hanged by the neck until you are dead. Your body will then be handed over to the surgeons for dissection, and your mangled limbs, instead of being restored to your friends for decent interment, will be cast into the sea, thrown into a ditch, or scattered on the earth at the discretion of the Shreriff. And may God Almighty have mercy on your miserable soul!"

Source of quote: Spores, John C (1988) *Running amok: an historical inquiry*, Ohio University Center for International Studies: Athens, Ohio.

weakness in comparison with the commercial might of the Chinese that led to ethnic tensions erupting onto the streets in May 1969. Following the race riots, the Malays were extended special privileges in an effort to increase their participation in the modern economy (see page 90). Along with indigenous groups, they were classed as bumiputras, usually shortened to 'bumis' – a label many were able to use as a passport to a better life.

Chinese

The Chinese community accounts for about a third of Malaysia's population. In 1794, just 8 years after he had founded Georgetown in Penang, Sir Francis Light wrote: "The Chinese constitute the most valuable part of our inhabitants: ... they possess the different trades of carpenters, masons, smiths, traders, shopkeepers and planters; they employ small vessels. They are the only people from whom a revenue may be raised without expense and extraordinary effort by the government. They are a valuable acquisition ..." Chinese immigrants went on to become invaluable members of the British Straits Settlements – from the early 1820s they began to flood into Singapore from China's southern provinces (see page 584). At the same time they arrived in droves on the Malay peninsula, most of them working as tin prospectors, shopkeepers and small traders.

Although the great bulk of Chinese in Malaysia arrived during the massive immigration between the late 19th and early 20th centuries, there has been a settled community of Chinese in Melaka since the 15th century. Many arrived as members of the retinue of the Chinese princess Li Poh who married Melaka's Sultan Mansur Shah in 1460 (see page 233). Over the centuries their descendants evolved into a wealthy and influential community with its own unique, sophisticated culture (see page 230). These **Straits Chinese** became known as ***Peranakans*** (which means 'born here'); men were called **Babas** and women, **Nyonyas**. When Peranakans began to be known as such is not known. Baba came into common useage during the 19th century and it is thought that Peranakan was already a well-established label at that time. 'Baba' does not seem to be of Chinese origin but is probably derived from Arabic, or perhaps Turkish, roots. To begin with Baba was used to refer to all local-born foreigners in Malaya, whether they were ethnic Chinese, Indians or Europeans. However, before long it became solely associated with the Straits Chinese.

The centres of Peranakan Chinese culture were the Straits Settlements of Melaka, Penang and Singapore. There were, however, significant differences between the communities in the three settlements. For example, Nyonya food in Penang shows culinary influences from Thailand, while food in Melaka and Singapore does not.

The Peranakans of Malaysia and Singapore saw their futures being intimately associated with the British. They learnt the English language, established close links with the colonial administration system and colonial businesses, and even their newspapers were written in English rather than Chinese. With the massive infusion of new Chinese blood from the mainland beginning at the end of the 19th century there emerged a 2-tier Chinese community. The Peranakans were concentrated in the commercial and professional sectors, and the 'pure' Chinese in the manual sectors. But as the 20th century progressed so the influence of the Peranakans declined. Competition from non-Baba Chinese became stronger as their businesses expanded and as sheer weight of numbers began to tell. The Straits Chinese British Association (SCBA) was eclipsed by the Malaysian Chinese Association (MCA) as a political force and the Peranakans found themselves marginalized. As this occurred, so the Babas found themselves the object, increasingly, of derision by non-Baba Chinese. They were regarded as having

The new breed: farewell to the old Malaise

In recent years, the easy-going Malay *kampong* world of old wooden houses, water buffalo and coconut curries has clashed head-on with modern Malaysia and its hi-tech office towers, 6-lane highways and polypropelene refineries.

For the past 30 years, the government has done just about everything in its power to coax Malays out of the villages and into the cities in an effort to catapault them into the modern economy. The New Economic Policy formalized this attempt to increase the Malays' stake of national wealth. But because life was made easy for them, many massaged the system to their advantage, and arrived on top of the heap having expended comparatively little effort. This engendered much resentment.

The racial quotas introduced by the NEP still have not been met — even with all the scholarships and free directorships, Malays do not comprise a third of the corporate workforce. But today, in Kuala Lumpur's penthouse boardrooms and behind the terminals in dealing rooms, a new breed of Malay professional has begun to appear. At last, they are there not because they are Malay but because they are good.

There is a Malay phase associated with this phenomenon: *kurang ajar*. It is coarse language – if you accuse someone of being *kurang ajar*, it means they are extremely rude, ignorant and ill-bred. Not long ago, the phrase was actually banned in the Malaysian parliament after one opposition MP used it to describe a member of the government. But with a little good-humoured antiseptic, the quality of *kurang ajar* has come to represent the new assertiveness of the 1990s Malay. A Malay who is more critical, more analytical, more willing to stand up for his – or her – rights and a Malay who is more able. Enter bumiputras with attitude: the New Malay. Anwar Ibrahim, the relatively youthful, confident, clean-cut, urbane deputy Prime Minister, has emerged as a role model for the aspiring New Malay.

Although immersed in the wheeling and dealing of modern progressive Malaysia, the boomtown bumiputra has not entirely forsaken his kampong roots. Lat, Malaysia's favourite cartoonist, has a series of books on the theme of the rural Malay struggling to keep pace with the times. His opinion is that every mobile-phone-wielding, Rayban-clad, BMW-driving KL yuppy is really a kampong kid at heart. And to be sure, every weekend and public holiday, the highways and airports become clogged as the new city species – *balek kampung* – head back to their villages.

'sold out' their Chinese roots and become ridiculous in the process. Today the Straits Chinese, in terms of political and economic power, have become – to a large extent – an irrelevance.

Today Peranakan culture is disappearing. Few Baba Chinese identify themselves as Baba; they have become Chinese Malaysians. Only in Melaka (and to some extent in Singapore) does the Baba cultural tradition remain strong. In Penang the numbers of people who see their Baba roots as anything but historical are dwindling. But although Peranakan culture is gradually disappearing, it has left an imprint on mainstream Malaysian culture. For example the custom among Peranakan women of wearing the *sarong* and *kebaya* has become subsumed within Malay tradition and has, in the process, become inter-ethnic. Baba cuisine has also been incorporated within Malay/Chinese cuisine.

The Peranakans may be the most colourful piece in Malaysia's Chinese mosaic, but the vast majority of modern

Malaysia's prosperous Chinese population arrived from China rather later, as penniless immigrants. They left China because of poverty, over-population and religious persecution – and were attracted by the lure of gold. In the mid-19th century, these newly arrived immigrants came under the jurisdiction of secret societies and *kongsis* – or clan associations. Some of the most striking examples of the latter are in Penang (see, for example the Khoo Kongsi, page 183). The secret societies sometimes engaged in open warfare with each other as rival groups fought over rights to tin mining areas.

The overseas Chinese have been described as possessing these common traits: the ability to smell profits and make quick business decisions; a penchant for good food (they prefer to sit at round tables to facilitate quicker exchange of information); and a general avoidance of politics in favour of money-making pursuits. Like most stereotypes, these characteristics break down when put to the detailed test but at a certain level of generalization, hold true. It is also true to say – broadly speaking – that the Chinese population felt little loyalty to their host society. At least, that is, until the 1949 Communist take-over in China, which effectively barred their return. Despite the community's political and economic gripes and traumas in the intervening years (see page 90), Chinese culture has survived intact and the community enjoys religious freedom; Chinese cuisine is enthusiastically devoured by all races and the mahjong tiles are still clacking in upstairs rooms. Today about 80% of Chinese schoolchildren attend private Chinese primary schools – although all secondary and tertiary education is in Malay.

Indians

Indian traders first arrived on the shores of the Malay peninsula more than 2,000 years ago in search of Suvarnadvipa, the fabled Land of Gold. There was a well established community of Indian traders in Melaka when the first sultanate grew up in the 1400s – there was even Tamil blood in the royal lineage. But most of the 1.5 million Indians in modern Malaysia – who make up nearly 9% of the population – are descendants of indentured Tamil labourers shipped to Malaya from South India by the British in the 19th century. They were nicknamed 'Klings' – a name which today has a deeply derogatory connotation. Most were put to work as coolies on the roads and railways or as rubber tappers.

A 100 years on, four out of five Indians are still manual labourers on plantations or in the cities. This has long been explained as a colonial legacy, but as modern Malaysia has grown more prosperous, the Tamils have remained at the bottom of the heap. Other Indian groups – the Keralans (Malayalis), Gujeratis, Bengalis, Sikhs and other North Indians, who came to colonial Malaya under their own volition, are now well represented in the professional classes. The South Indian Chettiar money-lending caste, which was once far more numerous than it is today, left the country in droves in the 1930s. Their confidence in British colonial rule was shaken by events in Burma, where anti-Indian riots prompted tens of thousands of Chettiars to return to India. While most of Malaysia's Indian community are Hindus, there are also Indian Muslims, Christians and Sikhs. In Melaka there is a small group of Indians with Portuguese names – known as Chitties.

Today the chanted names of the Hindu pantheon echo around the cool interior of the Sri Mariamman Temple in the heart of Kuala Lumpur as they have since its construction in 1873. But large numbers of Tamils still live in the countryside, where they still make up more than half the plantation workforce. Because the estates are on private land, they fall outside the ambit of national development policies and Malaysia's economic boom has passed them by. The controversial

New Economic Policy (see page 90) gave Malays a helping hand, and although it was aimed at eradicating poverty generally, it did not help Indians much – who often, and justifiably, feel that they are the group who have missed out most. They lack the economic clout of the Chinese, and the political might of the Malays, and can, it seems, conveniently be forgotten.

The new policy document which replaced the NEP in 1991 officially recognizes that Indians have lagged behind in the development stakes. Education is seen as the key to broadening the entrepreneurial horizons of Tamils, getting them off the plantations, out of the urban squatter settlements and into decent jobs. But in the privately-run Tamil shanty schools on the estates,

Malay magic and the spirits behind the prophet

Despite the fact that all Malays are Muslims, some traditional, pre-Islamic beliefs are still practiced by Malays – particularly in the northeast of the peninsula, the conservative Islamic heartland. The *bomoh* – witch doctor and magic-man – is alive and well in modern Malaysia. The use of *ilmu* (the malay name for magic), which is akin to voodoo, is still widely practiced and bomohs are highly respected and important members of kampong communities. Consulting bomohs is a commonplace event; they are often called in to perform their ancient rituals – sometimes they are contracted to bring rain or to determine the site of a new house; on other occasions to make fields (or married couples) fertile or to heal sickness. The healing ceremony is called the *main puteri*: there are certain illnesses which are believed to be caused by spirits – or *hantu* – who have been offended and must be placated.

The bomoh's job is to get the protective, friendly spirits on his side, in the belief that they can influence the evil ones. He knows many different spirits by name; some are the spirits of nature, others are spirits of ancestors. Many bomohs are specialists in particular fields. Some, known as *pewangs*, traditionally concentrated on performing spells to ensure fruitful harvests or safe fishing expeditions. Bomohs are still consulted and contracted to formulate herbal remedies, charms, love potions and perform traditional massage (*urut*). The *belian* – or shaman – specializes in more extreme forms of magic conducting exorcisms and spirit-raising seances, or *berhantu*. In Kelantan, a bomoh who acts as a spirit medium is known as a *Tok Peteri* and once a spirit has entered him, during a seance, his assistant, called the *Tok Mindok*, is required to question the spirit, present offerings and address the spirit in a secret language of magic formulae. Seances are always held in public – in front of the whole village – and are held after evening prayers.

Manipulation of the weather is one area where the magic is still widely used. The government has been known to employ a *pewang* to perform rituals designed to keep rain from falling during large public events. In 1991 actors from Kuala Lumpur's Instant Café Theatre Company called on a bomoh to ensure their open-air production of *A Midsummer Night's Dream* was not washed out. The only occasion on which rain interupted the play was during an extra performance, not covered in the bomoh's contract.

All natural and inanimate objects are also capable of having spirits and Malays often refer to them using the respectful title *Datuk*. Other spirits, like the *pontianak* (the vampire ghost of a woman who dies in childbirth) are greatly feared. Any suspicion of the presence of a pontianak calls for the immediate intervention of a belian, who is believed to inherit his powers from a *hantu raya* – great spirit – which attaches itself to a bloodline and is subsequently passed from generation to generation.

The practice of Islam: living by the Prophet

Islam is an Arabic word meaning 'submission to God'. As Muslims often point out, it is not just a religion but a total way of life. The main Islamic scripture is the Koran or Quran, the name being taken from the Arabic *al-qur'an* or 'the recitation'. The Koran is divided into 114 *sura*, or 'units'. Most scholars are agreed that the Koran was partially written by the Prophet Mohammad. In addition to the Koran there are the hadiths, from the Arabic word *hadith* meaning 'story', which tell of the Prophet's life and works. These represent the second most important body of scriptures.

The practice of Islam is based upon five central tenets, known as the Pillars of Islam: Shahada (profession of faith), Salat (worship), Zakat (charity), *saum* (fasting) and Haj (pilgrimage). The mosque is the centre of religious activity. The two most important mosque officials are the *imam* – or leader – and the *khatib* or preacher – who delivers the Friday sermon.

The **Shahada** is the confession, and lies at the core of any Muslim's faith. It involves reciting, sincerely, two statements: 'There is no god, but God', and 'Mohammad is the Messenger [Prophet] of God'. A Muslim will do this at every **Salat**. This is the daily prayer ritual which is performed five times a day, at sunrise, midday, mid-afternoon, sunset and at night. There is also the important Friday noon worship. The Salat is performed by a Muslim bowing and then prostrating himself in the direction of Mecca (in Malaysian *kiblat*, in Arabic *qibla*). In hotel rooms throughout there is nearly always a little arrow, painted on the ceiling – or sometimes inside a wardrobe – indicating the direction of Mecca and labelled kiblat. The faithful are called to worship by a mosque official. Beforehand, a worshipper must wash to ensure ritual purity. The Friday midday service is performed in the mosque and includes a sermon given by the *khatib*.

the drop-out rate is double the national average. Critics accuse the Malaysian Indian Congress (MIC), which is part of the ruling coalition, of perpetating this system in an effort to garner support. Because Indians are spread throughout the country and do not form the majority in any constituency, the plantations have been the MIC's traditional support base. It is not in the MIC's interests to see them move off the estates.

But things are beginning to change on the plantations – an unprecedented national strike in 1990 guaranteed plantation workers a minimum wage for the first time. Workers are becoming more assertive and aware of their individual and political rights. A new party, the Indian Progressive Front, has drawn its support from working class Indians. It seems that these stirrings of new assertiveness represent rising aspirations on the estates – which will have to continue to rise if the Tamils are ever going to escape from their plantation poverty trap, which one prominent Indian leader refers to as 'the green ghetto'. In 1970 ethnic Indians controlled about 1.1% of the country's wealth. By 1992, at the end of the 20-year NEP, this figure had declined to 1%. It has been estimated that two-thirds of Indians still live in poverty and for the Indians the NEP has been largely irrelevant. While Malays have enjoyed cumulative gains from the NEP and the Chinese have seen their slice of the cake grow in size if not in proportion, the Indian community have been left trailing and marginalized – a classic 'excluded' community. As government minister Datuk Ling Liong Sik remarked in an inteview in late 1995, "They're in the position of the Malays in the 1950s" suggesting that "the time may come for an NEP for Indians".

A third essential element of Islam is **Zakat** – charity or alms-giving. A Muslim is supposed to give up his 'surplus' (according to the Koran); through time this took on the form of a tax levied according to the wealth of the family. In Malaysia there is no official Zakat as there is in Saudi Arabia, but good Muslims are expected to contribute a tithe to the Muslim community.

The fourth pillar of Islam is **saum** or fasting. The daytime month-long fast of Ramadan is a time of contemplation, worship and piety – the Islamic equivalent of lent. Muslims are expected to read one-thirtieth of the Koran each night. Muslims who are ill or on a journey have dispensation from fasting, but otherwise they are only permitted to eat during the night until "so much of the dawn appears that a white thread can be distinguished from a black one".

The **Haj** or Pilgrimmage to the holy city of Mecca in Saudi Arabia is required of all Muslims once in their lifetime if they can afford to make the journey and are physically able to. It is restricted to a certain time of the year, beginning on the 8th day of the Muslim month of Dhu-l-Hijja. Men who have been on the Haj are given the title *Haji*, and women *hajjah*.

The Koran also advises on a number of other practices and customs, in particular the prohibitions on usury, the eating of pork, the taking of alcohol, and gambling. There is quite a powerful Islamic revival in Malaysia and Brunei. The use of the veil is becoming *de rigeur* in Brunei and increasingly in Malaysia. The Koran says nothing about the need for women to veil, although it does stress the necessity of women dressing modestly. In Indonesia, the practices and customs are not strictly interpreted.

Orang Asli (Aboriginals)

While the Malay population originally settled on the coasts of the peninsula, the mountainous, jungled interior was the domain of the oldest indigenous groups – the aboriginals. They are a sinewy, dark-skinned race, characterized by their curly hair and are probably of Melanesian origin – possibly related to Australian aborigines. During the Pleistocene ice age, when a land-bridge linked the Philippines to Borneo and mainland Southeast Asia, these people spread throughout the continent. Today they are confined to the mountains of the Malay peninsula, North-east India, North Sumatra, the Andaman Islands and the Philippines. The Negrito aboriginals – who in Malay are known as *Orang Asli*, or 'Indigenous People' – were mainly hunter-gatherers. As the Malays spread inland, the Orang Asli were pushed further and further into the mountainous interior. Traditionally, the Negritos did not build permanent houses – preferring makeshift shelters – and depend on the jungle and the rivers for their food.

A second group of Orang Asli, the *Senoi* – who are also known as the *Sakai* – arrived later than the Negritos. They practised shifting cultivation to supplement their hunting and gathering and built sturdier houses. The third aboriginal group to come to the peninsula were the Jakuns – or proto-Malays – who were mainly of Mongoloid stock. They were comprised of several subgroups, the main ones being the Mantera and Biduanda of Negeri Sembilan and Melaka and the Orang Ulu, Orang Kanak and Orang Laut ('Sea People') of Johor. Their culture and language became closely linked to that of the coastal Malays and over the centuries, many of them assimilated into Malay society. Most practised shifting cultivation; the Orang Laut were fishermen.

In Siddhartha's footsteps: a short history of Buddhism

Buddhism was founded by Siddhartha Gautama, a prince of the Sakya tribe of Nepal, who probably lived between 563 and 483BC. He achieved enlightenment and the word *buddha* means 'fully enlightened one', or 'one who has woken up'. Siddhartha Gautama is known by a number of titles. In the West, he is usually referred to as *The Buddha*, ie the historic Buddha (but not just Buddha); more common in Southeast Asia is the title *Sakyamuni*, or Sage of the Sakyas (referring to his tribal origins).

Over the centuries, the life of the Buddha has become part legend, and the Jataka tales which recount his various lives are colourful and convoluted. But, central to any Buddhist's belief is that he was born under a *sal* tree (*Shorea robusta*), that he achieved enlightenment under a bodhi tree (*Ficus religiosa*) in the Bodh Gaya Gardens, that he preached the First Sermon at Sarnath, and that he died at Kusinagara (all in India or Nepal).

The Budda was born at Lumbini (in present-day Nepal), as Queen Maya was on her way to her parents' home. She had had a very auspicious dream before the child's birth of being impregnated by an elephant, whereupon a sage prophesied that Siddhartha would become either a great king or a great spiritual leader. His father, being keen that the first option of the prophesy be fulfilled, brought him up in all the princely skills (at which Siddhartha excelled) and ensured that he only saw beautiful things, not the harsher elements of life.

Despite his father's efforts Siddhartha saw four things while travelling between palaces – a helpless old man, a very sick man, a corpse being carried by lamenting relatives, and an ascetic, calm and serene as he begged for food. These episodes made an enormous impact on the young prince, and he renounced his princely origins and left home to study under a series of spiritual teachers. He finally discovered the path to enlightenment at the Bodh Gaya Gardens in India. He then proclaimed his thoughts to a small group of disciples at Sarnath, near Benares, and continued to preach and attract followers until he died at the age of 81 at Kusinagara.

Malaysia's aborigines have increasingly been drawn into the modern economy. Along with the Malays, they are classified as *bumiputras* and as such, became eligible, as with other tribal groups in East Malaysia, for the privileges extended to all bumiputras following the introduction of the New Economic Policy (NEP) in 1970 (see page 90). In reality, however, the NEP offered few tangible benefits to the Orang Asli, and while the government has sought to integrate them – there is a Department of Aboriginal Affairs in Kuala Lumpur – there is no separate mechanism to encourage entrepreneurism among the group.

RELIGION

Islam

Malays are invariably Muslims and there is also a small population of Indian Muslims in Malaysia. (For more background on Islam, see page 70). The earliest recorded evidence of Islam on the Malay peninsula is an inscription in Terengganu dating from 1303, which prescribed penalties for those who did not observe the moral codes of the faith. Islam did not really gain a foothold on the peninsula, however, until Sri Maharaja of Melaka – the third ruler – converted in 1430 and changed his name to Mohamed Shah (see page 221). He retained many of the ingrained Hindu traditions of the royal court and did not attempt to enforce Islam

In the First Sermon at the deer park in Sarnath, the Buddha preached the Four Truths, which are still considered the root of Buddhist belief and practical experience. These are the 'Noble Truth' that suffering exists, the 'Noble Truth' that there is a cause of suffering, the 'Noble Truth' that suffering can be ended, and the 'Noble Truth' that to end suffering it is necessary to follow the 'Noble Eightfold Path' – namely, right speech, livelihood, action, effort, mindfulness, concentration, opinion and intention.

Soon after the Buddha began preaching, a monastic order – the *Sangha* – was established. As the monkhood evolved in India, it also began to fragment as different sects developed different interpretations of the life of the Buddha. An important change was the belief that the Buddha was transcendent: he had never been born, nor had he died; he had always existed and his life on earth had been mere illusion. The emergence of these new concepts helped to turn what up until then was an ethical code of conduct, into a religion. It eventually led to the appearance of a new Buddhist movement, Mahayana Buddhism which split from the more traditional Theravada 'sect'.

Despite the division of Buddhism into two sects, the central tenets of the religion are common to both. Specifically, the principles pertaining to the Four Noble Truths, the Noble Eightfold Path, the Dependent Origination, the Law of Karma and nirvana. In addition, the principles of non-violence and tolerance are also embraced by both sects. In essence, the differences between the two are of emphasis and interpretation. Theravada Buddhism is strictly based on the original Pali Canon, while the Mahayana tradition stems from later Sanskrit texts. Mahayana Buddhism also allows a broader and more varied interpretation of the doctrine. Other important differences are that while the Thervada tradition is more 'intellectual' and self-obsessed, with an emphasis upon the attaining of wisdom and insight for oneself, Mahayana Buddhism stresses devotion and compassion towards others.

as the state religion. The Arab merchant ships which made regular calls at Melaka probably brought Muslim missionaries to the city. Many of them were Sufis – belonging to a mystical order of Islam which was tolerant of local customs and readily synthesized with existing animist and Hindu beliefs. The adoption of this form of Islam is one reason why animism and the Muslim faith still go hand in hand in Malaysia (see below). Mohamad Shah's son, Rajah Kasim was the first ruler to adopt the title 'Sultan', and he became Sultan Muzaffar; all subsequent rulers have continued to preserve and uphold the Islamic faith. The Portuguese and Dutch colonialists, while making a few local converts to Christianity, were more interested in trade than proselytizing.

The British colonial system of government was more 'progressive' than most colonial regimes in that it barred the British Residents from interfering in 'Malay religion and custom'. So-called Councils of Muslim Religion and Malay Custom were set up in each state answerable to the sultans. These emerged as bastions of Malay conservatism and served to make Islam the rallying point of nascent nationalism. The Islamic reform movement was imported from the Middle East at the turn of the 19th century and Malays determined that the unity afforded by Islam transcended any colonial authority and the economic dominance of immigrant groups. The ideas spread as increasing numbers of Malays made the Haj to Mecca, made possible by the advent of regular steamer services. But gradually the sultans and the Malay aristocracy – who had done well out of British rule – began to see the Islamic renaissance as a threat.

On Fridays, the Muslim day of prayer, Malaysian Muslims congregate at mosques in their 'Friday best'. The 'lunch hour' starts at 1130 and runs through to about 1430 to allow Muslims to attend the mosque; in big towns and cities, Friday lunchtimes are marked by traffic jams. In the fervently Islamic east coast states, Friday is the start of the weekend. Men traditionally wear *songkoks* – black velvet hats – to the mosque and often wear their best sarung (sometimes *songket*) over their trousers. Those who have performed the Haj pilgrimage to Mecca wear a white skullcap. However, at least until recently (see below), Malaysia's Islam has been moderate by Middle Eastern standards. Traditionally, for example, women were not required to wear the head scarf or *tudung*.

But Malaysia has emerged as an outspoken defender of Muslims and Islamic values around the world. While hosting a banquet in honour of the visiting former British Prime Minister, John Major, in late 1993, the Malaysian premier, Dr Mahathir Mohamad, shocked his audience with a blunt full-frontal attack on western intransigence over the plight of Bosnian Muslims. He urged him to "reconsider Britain's position before the situation in Bosnia-Herzegovina is forever cemented in history as the blackest catastrophe of the modern world". Malaysia has put its money where its mouth is in welcoming Bosnian Muslim refugees and staging conferences on the Bosnian situation. On other occasions, Dr Mahathir has made outspoken attacks on western attitudes towards Islam, in which, he says, Muslims are cast as pariahs and bogeymen.

Although not disingenuous, all this was viewed by observers as part of the Prime Minister's efforts to polish his own Islamic credentials. At home, Dr Mahathir's government feels threatened by the rise of fundamentalist sentiments – particularly in the north-eastern state of Kelantan, where the Islamic government has approved a bill calling for the introduction of a strict Islamic penal code (see page 306). Hard-line Islam is perceived as a threat to secular society in Malaysia. The deputy Prime Minister, Anwar Ibrahim – once a young Islamic firebrand himself – has become an

The Ramayana and Mahabharata

Across much of Southeast Asia, the Indian epics of the Ramayana and Mahabharata have been translated and adapted for local consumption. The stories of the **Mahabharata** are the more popular. These centre on a long-standing feud between two family clans: the Pandawas and the Korawas. The feud culminates in an epic battle during which the five Pandawa brothers come face to face with their 100 first cousins from the Korawa clan. After 18 days of fighting, the Pandawas emerge victorious and the eldest brother becomes king. The plays usually focus on one or other of the five Pandawa brothers, each of whom is a hero.

The **Ramayana** was written by the poet Valmiki about 2,000 years ago. The 48,000 line story tells of the abduction of the beautiful Sita by the evil king, Ravana. Sita's husband Rama, King of Ayodhia, sets out on an odyssey to retrieve his wife from Ravana's clutches, finally succeeding with the help of Hanuman the monkey god and his army of monkeys. Today it is rare to see the Ramayana performed; the orchestra needs to be large (and is therefore expensive), and in the case of *wayang* few puppet masters have a sufficiently large collection of puppets to cover all the characters.

eloquent proponent of Islamic moderation. He has appealed in articles submitted to international newspapers for less rhetoric in the name of political expediency from Muslim leaders around the world and for greater understanding of Islam in the West.

In 1994, Dr Mahathir was forced to clamp down on a fundamentalist Islamic sect known as **Al Arqam** with 10,000 followers, an estimated 200,000 sympathizers, and assets of RM15mn in businesses ranging from property firms to textile factories. Ashaari Muhammed, the leader of the sect, was arrested after being deported from Thailand and then held in detention under the Internal Security Act. Unlikely liberals leapt to defend Mr Ashaari who taught that women should be kept in their place, and operated his sect almost like a secret society. Why the Prime Minister should have issued an order for Mr Ashaari's arrest was a point of dispute. The Prime Minister's office maintained that the sect's teachings were 'deviationist' – as also argued by the National Fatwah Council – and that he threatened state security. To begin with the government even suggested that the sect had a 313-man 'death squad'. Opponents maintained that his arrest was more to do with domestic politics: Al Arqam was attracting middle class Malays, just the sort of people who are the bedrock of UMNO's support. The arrest was not, in their view, anything to do with religion, but a great deal to do with politics. Nonetheless, the government is very firm over the acceptable limits of Islam. People voicing support for the sect or wearing their garb can be arrested, and their publications are banned. Later the government backtracked on the 'death squad' allegations, but nonetheless were able to get Ashaari Muhammed to renounce his teachings on television, thereby preventing him becoming a martyr.

It seems that Mahathir is concerned that radical Islam might destabilize Malaysia's delicate racial and religious cocktail. Sects like Al Arqam, and the spread of Shia theology, are closely watched by a government that wishes to maintain its secular credentials and to control what has been termed 'creeping Islamization'. In mid-1997, Mahathir showed his displeasure at the enforcement of a *fatwa* in the state of Selangor banning all beauty contests. In June, three Malay contestants were arrested and handcuffed on stage after they had competed in the Miss Malaysia Petite contest. The prime minister rebuked the religious officials who had exceeded their 'little powers'. Earlier he had set in motion a wide-ranging review of Islamic jurisprudence or *fiqh*. In confronting the clerics and their supporters Mahathir has taken on a powerful conservative group which is closely allied with the opposition PAS. But if there is anyone in Malaysia with the accumulated prestige to challenge the *ulamas* (Muslim theologians) openly, it is Mahathir.

Buddhism

While Buddhism is the formal religion of most of Malaysia's Chinese population, many are Taoists, who follow the teachings of the three sages – Confucius, Mencius and Lao Tse. Taoism is characterized by ancestor worship and a plethora of deities. As with Islam, this has been mixed with animist beliefs and spirit worship forms a central part of the faith. For more background on Buddhism see the box on page 72.

Hinduism

Hindu (and Buddhist) religions were established on the Malay peninsula long before Islam arrived. Remains of ancient Hindu-Buddhist temples dating from the kingdom of Langkasuka in the early years of the first millennium have been found in the Bujang Valley, at the foot of Gunung Jerai (Kedah Peak) in Kedah (see page 200). The majority of Malaysia's Indian population is Hindu, although there are also many Indian Muslims.

LANGUAGE AND LITERATURE

Bahasa Melayu (literally, 'Malay Language') – or to give the language its official title, *Bahasa Kebangsaan* ('National Language') – is an Austronesian language which has been the language of trade and commerce throughout the archipelago for centuries. It is the parent language of – and is closely related to – modern Indonesian. In 1972, Indonesia and Malaysia came to an agreement to standardize spelling – although many differences still remain.

Modern Malay has been affected by a succession of external influences – Sanskrit from the 7th century, Arabic from the 14th and English from the 19th century. These influences are reflected in a number of words, most of them of a religious or technical nature. All scientific terminology is directly borrowed from the English or Latin. However, there are many common everyday words borrowed from Arabic or English: *pasar*, for example, comes from the Arabic *bazaar* (market) and there are countless examples of English words used in Malay – particularly when it comes to modern modes of transport – *teksi*, *bas* and *tren*. Where a Malay term has been devised for a 20th century phenomenon, it is usually a fairly straightforward description. An alternative word for train, for example is *keretapi* (literally 'fire car') and the word for aeroplane is *kapalterbang* (flying ship).

From the 7th century, the Indian Pallava script was in restricted use, although few examples survive. The *Jawi* script, adapted from Arabic, was adopted in the 14th century, with the arrival of Muslim traders and Sufi missionaries in Melaka. To account for sounds in the Malay language which have no equivalent in Arabic, five additional letters had to be invented, giving 33 letters in all. Jawi script was used for almost all Malay writings until the 19th century, and romanized script only began to supplant Jawi after World War Two. Many older Malays still read and write the script and it is not uncommon to see it along the streets. Some Chinese-owned banks, for example, have transliterated their names into Jawi script so as to make Malays feel a little more at home in them.

Tikus Rahmat: Malaysian racial relations in rat form

Tikus Rahmat or *Blessed Rat* written by Hassan Ibrahim and first published in 1963 is the only Malay novel in satire form and it is modelled closely on George Orwell's *Animal Farm*. The novel is based on relations between various groups of rats in Tikusia Raya (Ratland), each of which is symbolic of the different races in Malaysia. The similarities between the inhabitants of Tikusia Raya and the stereotypical view of the races of Malaysia are clear. The farm rats or *tikus ladang* symbolize the Chinese: they are the newcomers; they play the role of the middleman; and they are hard-working and diligent. The novelist also writes that they are: "... capable in the art of cheating as it is their way of life, taught by their parents since birth."

The valley rats or *tikus lembah* are the Malays. They are the poorest rats, whose interests are continually sacrificed in the interests of the rest of the population. But they are also very religious and humble. Needless to say, the other rats view them as lazy good-for-nothings.

The farm rats insist that their own language – cok cak – be used as the *lingua franca* of Tikusia Raya and in an election the farm rats win a majority. The valley rats rebel against the results of the election and attack and kill the rich white rats (symbolizing white people) and farm rats. The few that survive this epic rat battle agree to settle their differences and follow the Prophet Solomon (Muhammad). Although the novel was written before the 1969 race riots, parts of the story coincidentally mirror the tragic events of that year.

Making a wayang kulit puppet

Wayang kulit puppets are made of buffalo hide, preferably taken from a female animal of about 4 years of age. The skin is dried and scraped, and then left to mature for as long as 10 years to achieve the stiffness required for carving. After carving, the puppet is painted in traditional pigments. In carving the puppet, the artist is constrained by convention. The excellence of the puppet is judged according to the fineness of chisel-work and the subtlety of painting. If the puppet is well made it may have *guna* – a magical quality which is supposed to make the audience suspend its disbelief during the performance. Puppets accumulate *guna* with age; this is why old puppets are preferred to new ones.

Each major character has a particular iconography, and even the angle of the head and the slant of the eyes and mouth are important in determining the character. Some puppets may be called on to perform a number of minor parts, but in the main a knowledgeable wayang-goer will be able to recognise each character immediately.

The *cempurit* or rods used to manipulate the puppet are made of buffalo horn while the studs used to attach the limbs are made of metal, bone or bamboo. Court puppets might even be made of gold, studded with precious stones.

Malay literature is thought to date from the 14th century – although surviving manuscripts written in Jawi only date from the beginning of the 15th century. The first printed books in Malay were produced by European missionaries in the 17th century. The best known of Malay literary works are the 16th century *Sejara Melayu* or Malay Annals; others include the romantic *Hikayat Hang Tuah* and the 19th century *Tuhfat al-Nafis*.

The first of Malaysia's 'modern' authors was the 19th century writer Munshi Abdullah – who has lent his name to a few streets around the country. Although he kept to many of the classical strictures, Abdullah articulated a personal view and challenged many of the traditional assumptions underlying Malay society. His best known work was his autobiography, *Hikayat Abdullah*. However, it was not until the 1920s that Malayan authors began to write modern novels and short stories. Among the best known writers are Ahmad bin Mohd. Rashid Talu, Ishak Hj. Muhammad and Harun Aminurrashid. Their work laid the foundations for a expansion of Malaysian literature from the 1950s and today there is a prodigious Malay-language publishing industry.

Since independence, the government has promoted Bahasa Melayu at the expense of Chinese dialects and English. However in 1994 Prime Minister Mahathir signalled a switch in strategy when he declared that university courses in the sciences and technology would be taught in English rather than Bahasa. The emphasis on Bahasa is regarded to some extent as yesterday's battle – the battle to build a national, Malaysian identity. Today's battle is to produce an educated workforce conversant and at home in the world of international business – in other words, people who can use English. When comparisons are made between Malaysian and other overseas students, Malaysian students come out poorly. This is one reason why so many wealthy Malays and Chinese send their children to private English language schools – including ministers who in public used to defend the use of Bahasa Melayu in state schools. Now the government appears to have realized the necessity for state schools and universities to reintroduce English. The announcement that a London University campus in Kuala Lumpur would be built is perhaps indicative of this liberalization in education policies.

(Not that the process is necessarily one-way: in mid-1997 the government ruled that Islamic civlization would become a mandatory course for all university students – they would need to take and pass it in order to graduate. Needless to say, non-Muslim Malaysians, and some Muslim Malaysians, thought this a step backwards and going against the trend towards a modern, outward-looking, and inclusive Malaysia. Later it was announced that the course would also include study of other Asian civilizations.)

DANCE, DRAMA AND MUSIC

Wayang Kulit *Wayang* means 'shadow', and the art form is best translated as 'shadow theatre' or 'shadow play'. Shadow plays were the traditional form of entertainment in Malay kampungs. Although film and television have replaced the *wayang* in many people's lives – especially the young – they are still performed in some rural parts of the peninsula's east coast and are regular fixtures at cultural events. Some people believe that the wayang is Indian in origin, pointing to the fact that most of the characters are from Indian epic tales such as the Ramayana and Mahabharata (see page 74).

By the 11th century *wayang* was well-established in Java. A court poet of the Javanese King Airlangga (1020-1049), referred to wayang in *The meditation of King Ardjuna*:

"There are people who weep, are sad and aroused watching the puppets, though they know they are merely carved pieces of leather manipulated and made to speak. These people are like men, thirsting for sensual pleasures, who live in a world of illusion; they do not realize the magic hallucinations they see are not real".

It seems that by the 14th century the art form had made the crossing from the Javanese Majapahit Empire to the courts of the Malay Peninsula and from there spread to kampungs across the country.

There are many forms of wayang – and not all of them are, strictly-speaking, shadow plays – but the commonest and oldest form is the wayang kulit. Kulits are finely carved and painted leather, 2-dimensional puppets, jointed at the elbows and shoulders and manipulated using horn rods. In order to enact the entire repertoire of 179 plays, 200 puppets are needed. A single performance can last as long as 9 hours. The plays have various origins. Some are animistic, others are adapted from the epic poems. The latter are known as 'trunk' tales or *pondok* and include the Ramayana. Others have been developed over the years by influential puppet masters. They feature heroic deeds, romantic encounters, court intrigues, bloody battles, and mystical observations, and are known as *carangan* or 'branch' tales.

The gunungan or Tree of Life, is an important element of wayang theatre. It represents all aspects of life, and is always the same in design: shaped like a stupa, the tree has painted red flames on one side and a complex design on the other (this is the side which faces the audience). At the base of the tree are a pair of closed doors, flanked by two fierce demons or *yaksas*. Above the demons are two garudas and within the branches of the tree there are monkeys, snakes and two animals – usually an ox and a tiger. The gunungan is placed in the middle of the screen at the beginning and end of the performance – and sometimes between major scene changes. During the performance it stands at one side, and flutters across the screen to indicate minor scene changes.

Traditionally, performances were requested by individuals to celebrate particular occasions – for example the seventh month of pregnancy (*tingkep*) – or to accompany village festivities. Admission was free, as the individual commissioning the performance would meet the costs. Of course, this has changed now and tourists invariably have to pay an entrance charge.

In the past, the shadows of the puppets were reflected onto a white cotton cloth stretched across a wooden frame using the light from a bronze coconut oil lamp. Today, electric light is more common – a change which, in many people's minds, has meant the unfortunate substitution of the flickering, mysterious shadows of the oil lamp, with the constant harsh light of the electric bulb. There are both day and night wayang performances. The latter, for obvious reasons, are the most dramatic, although the former are regarded as artistically superior.

The audience sits on both sides of the screen. Those sitting with the puppet master see a puppet play; those on the far side, out of view of the puppet master and the accompanying gamelan orchestra, see a shadow play. It is possible that in the past, the audience was segregated according to sex: men on the to' dalang's side of the screen, women on the shadow side.

The puppet-master is known as the *to' dalang*; he narrates each story in lyrical classical Malay – with a great sense of melodrama – and is accompanied by a traditional gamelan orchestra of gongs, drums, *rebab* (violins) and woodwind instruments. He slips in and out of different characters, using many different voices throughout the performances, which lasts as long as 3-4 hours. The words *to' dalang* are said to be derived from *galang*, meaning bright or clear, the implication being that the to' dalang makes the sacred texts understandable. He sits on a plinth, an arm's length away from the cloth screen. From this position he manipulates the puppets, while also narrating the story. Although any male can become a to' dalang, it is usual for sons to follow their fathers into the profession. The to' dalang is the key to a successful performance: he must be multi-skilled, have strength and stamina, be able to manipulate numerous puppets simultaneously, narrate the story, and give the lead to the accompanying gamelan orchestra. No wonder that an adept to' dalang is a man with considerable status.

Chinese classical street operas (wayang) date back to the 7th century. They are performed in Malaysia by troupes of roving actors during Chinese festivals, particularly during the seventh lunar month, following the Festival of the Hungry Ghosts. For more details on the wayang, see page 603.

Dance

Silat (or, more properly, *bersilat*) is a traditional Malay martial art, but is so highly stylized that it has become a dance form and is often demonstrated with the backing of a percussion orchestra. *Pencak silat* is the more formal martial art of self-defence; *seni silat* is the graceful aesthetic equivalent. A variety of the latter is commonly performed at ceremonial occasions – such as Malay weddings – it is called *silat pulut*. Silat comprises a fluid combination of movements and is designed to be as much a comprehensive and disciplined form of physical exercise as it is a martial art. It promotes good blood circulation and deep-breathing, which are considered essential for strength and stamina. The fluidity of the body movements require great suppleness, flexibility and poise. Malaysia's best known silat gurus live along the east coast.

The ***Mak Yong*** was traditionally a Kelantanese court dance-drama, performed only in the presence of the sultan and territorial chiefs. The dance is performed mainly by women (the mak yong being the 'queen' and lead dancer), and is accompanied by an orchestra of gongs, drums and the *rebab* (violin). There are only ever two or three male dancers who provide the comic interludes. The dance is traditionally performed during the Sultan of Kelantan's birthday celebrations. Unlike the wayang kulit shadow puppet theatre (above), the stories are not connected to the Hindu epics; they are thought to be of Malay origin. Other Kelantanese court dances include: the *garong*, a lively up-tempo dance by five pairs of men and women, in a round (a *garong* is a bamboo cow bell). The *payang*, a folk dance, is named after the distinctive east coast fishing boats; traditionally it was danced on the beach while waiting for the kampung fishing fleet to return.

The ***joget*** dance is another Malay art form which is the result of foreign cultural influence – in this case, Portuguese. It has gone by a variety of other names, notably the *ronggeng* and the *branyo*. It is traditionally accompanied by the gamelan orchestra. In 1878, Frank Swettenham (the first British Resident at Kuala Lumpur, but then, a young colonial officer) witnessed a performance of the joget, which he described in his book *Malay Sketches*. "Gradually raising themselves from a sitting to a kneeling posture, acting in perfect accord in every motion, then rising to their feet, they began a series of figures hardly to be exceeded in grace and difficulty, considering that the movements are essentially slow, the arms, hands and body being the performers, whilst the feet are scarcely noticed and half the time not visible. ..."

Arab traders were responsible for importing the ***zapin*** dance and Indonesians introduced the ***inang***. Immigrants from Banjarmasin (South Kalimantan), who arrived in Johor in the early 1900s, brought with them the so-called Hobbyhorse Dance – the ***Kuda Kepang*** – which is performed at weddings and on ceremonial occasions in Johor. The hobbyhorses are made of goat or buffalo skin, stretched over a rotan frame. There are countless other local folk dances around Malaysia, usually associated with festivals – such as the ***wau bulan*** kite dance in Kelantan.

The **Lion Dance** is performed in Chinese communities, particularly around Chinese New Year, and the dances are accompanied by loud drums and cymbals, so are hard to miss. The lion dance actually originated in India, where tame lions were led around public fairs and festivals to provide entertainment along with jugglers. But because lions were in short supply, dancers with lion masks took their place. The dance was introduced to China during the Tang Dynasty. The lion changed its image from that of a clown to a symbol of the Buddha and is now regarded as 'the protector of Buddhism'. The lion dance developed into a ceremony in which demons and evil spirits are expelled (hence the deafening cymbals and drums).

Bharata Natyam (Indian classical dance) is performed by Malaysia's Indian community and is accompanied by Indian instruments such as the *tambura* (which has four strings), the *talam* (cymbals), *mridanga* (double-headed drum), *vina* (single stringed instrument) and flute. In Malaysia, the Temple of Fine Arts in Kuala Lumpur is an Indian cultural organization which promotes Indian dance forms. The Temple organizes an annual Festival of Arts (see page 133).

Music and musical instruments

Traditional Malay music, which accompanies the various traditional dances, offers a taste of all the peninsula's different cultural influences. The most prominent of these were Indian, Arab, Portuguese, Chinese, Siamese and Javanese – and finally, western musical influence which gave birth to the all-pervasive genre 'Pop Melayu' – typically melancholic heavy rock. Traditional musical instruments reflect similar cultural influences, notably the *gambus* or lute (which has Middle Eastern origins and is used to accompany the *zapin* dance), the Indian harmonium, the Chinese *serunai* (clarinet) and gongs, the *rebana* drums, also of Middle Eastern origin, and the Javanese *gamelan* orchestra. Because Malays have traditionally been so willing to absorb new cultural elements, some of their traditional art forms have been in danger of extinction. Most traditional Malay instruments are percussion instruments; there are very few stringed or wind instruments. There are six main Malay drums, the most common of which is the cylindrical, double-headed *gendang*, which is used to accompany wayang kulit performances and silat. Other drums include the *geduk* and the *gedombak*; all three of these are played in orchestras.

Rebana, another traditional Malay drum, is used on ceremonial occasions as well as being a musical instrument. Traditionally, drumming competitions would be held following the rice-harvesting season (in May) and judges award points for timing, tone and rhythm. The best place to see the rebana in action is during Kelantan's giant drum festivals at the end of June. The drums are made from metre-long hollowed-out logs and are brightly painted. In competitions, drummers from different kampungs compete against each other in teams of up to 12 men. Traditionally the rebana was used as a means of communication between villages, and different rhythms were devised as a sort of morse code to invite distant kampungs to weddings or as warnings of war. *Kertok* are drums made from coconuts whose tops are sliced off and replaced with a block of *nibong* wood (from the sago palm) as a sounding board; these are then struck with padded drumsticks.

There are three main gongs; the biggest and most common, the *tawak* or *tetawak* is used to accompany wayang kulit shadow puppet theatre and Mak Yong dance dramas. The other smaller gongs are called *canang* and also accompany wayang kulit performances. The only Malay stringed instrument is the *rebab*, a violin-type instrument found throughout the region. The main wind instrument is the *serunai*, or oboe, which is of Persian origin and traditionally accompanies wayang kulit and dance performances. Its reed is cut from a palm leaf.

The ***Nobat*** is the ancient royal orchestra which traditionally plays at the installation of sultans in Kedah, Perak, Selangor, Terangganu and Brunei. It is thought to have been introduced at the royal court of Melaka in the 15th century. The instruments include two types of drums (*negara* and *gendang*), a trumpet (*nafiri*), a flute (*serunai*) and a gong. The Nobat also plays at the coronation of each new king, every 5 years.

CRAFTS

The Malay heartland, on the east coast of Peninsular Malaysia, is the centre of the handicraft industry – particularly Kelantan. An extensive variety of traditional handicrafts, as well as batiks, are widely available in this area, although they are also sold throughout the country, notably in Kuala Lumpur and other main towns (see individual town entries). In East Malaysia, Sarawak has an especially active handicraft industry (see page 351).

Kites Kite-making and kite-flying (or *main wau*) are traditional pursuits in the northern Malaysian states of Perlis, Kedah, Kelantan and Terengganu. Malaysia's most famous kite is the crescent-shaped Kelantanese *wau bulan* (moon kite) which has a wingspan of up to 3m and a length of more than 3m; they can reach altitudes of nearly 500m. Bow-shaped pieces of bamboo are often secured underneath, which make a melodious humming noise (*dengung*) in the wind. Wau come in all shapes and sizes however, and scaled-down versions of wau bulan and other kites can be bought. It is even possible to find batik-covered *wau cantik* or *wau sobek*, which are popular wall-hangings but make for awkward hand-luggage. There are often kite-flying competitions on the east coast, where competitors gain points for height and manoeuvering skills. Kites are also judged for their physical attributes, their ability to stay in the air and their sound. Most kite-flying competitions take place after the rice harvest in May, when kampungs compete against each other. On the east coast, all kites are known as *wau*, a word which, it is said, is derived from the arabic letter of the same sound, which is shaped like a kite. Perhaps the most recognizable one is Terengganu's *wau kucing* (cat kite), which Malaysia Airlines adopted as its logo. There are also *wau daun* (leaf kites) and *wau jala budi* (which literally means 'the net of good deeds kite'). Elsewhere in Malaysia, kites are known as *layang-layang* (literally, 'floating objects').

Tops Top spinning (*main gasing*) is another traditional form of entertainment, still popular in rural Malay kampungs – particularly on the east coast of the peninsula. There are two basic forms of tops. The heart-shaped *gasing jantung* and the flattened top, *gasing uri*. The biggest tops have diameters as big as frisbees and can weigh more than 5 kg; the skill required in launching a top is considerable. To launch the larger tops requires wrapping them in a tightly coiled 4m long rope which is smeared with resin. Once spinning, the top is scooped up on a wooden batton and left to spin on top of a small wooden post – sometimes for as long as 2 hours. Some tops have added metal or lead, and these are used in top-fighting events. Top-making is a precision-craft, and each one can take up to 3 days to make; they are carved from the upper roots and stem-bases of merbau and afzelia trees.

Woodcarving Originally craftsmen were commissioned by sultans and the Malay nobility to decorate the interiors, railings, doorways, shutters and stilts of palaces and public buildings. In Malay woodcarving, only floral and animal motifs are used as Islam prohibits depiction of the human form. But most widely acclaimed are the carved statues of malevolent spirits of the Mah Meris, an Orang Asli tribe.

Batik (*Batek*) The word *batik* may be derived from the Malay word *tik*, meaning 'to drip'. It is believed that batik replaced tatooing as a mark of status in the Malay archipelago. (In eastern Indonesia the common word for batik and tattoo are the same.)

Although batik-technology was actually imported from Indonesia several centuries ago, this coloured and patterned cloth is now a mainstay of Malaysian cultural identity. Malaysian batik are very different from their Indonesian counterparts, which are, on the whole, much darker; the best Malaysian batiks come from the east coast states, particularly Kelantan.

Traditionally, the wax was painted onto the woven cloth using a *canting* (pronounced 'janting'), a small copper cup with a spout, mounted on a bamboo handle. The cup is filled with melted wax, which flows from the spout like ink from a fountain pen – although the canting never touches the surface of the cloth. Batik artists have a number of canting with various widths of spout, some even with several spouts, to give varied thicknesses of line and differences of effect.

The canting was probably invented in Java in the 12th century, whereupon it replaced the crude painting stick, enabling far more complex designs to be produced. Inscriptions from this period refer to *tulis warna*, literally 'drawing in colour', which was probably some sort of resist dyeing technique similar, but ancestral, to batik. Cloth produced using a canting should be labelled *tulis* (literally, to write) and one sarong length can take from 1 to 6 months to complete. Reflecting the skill and artistry required to produce such batik, waxers used to be called *lukis* or painters. Drawing the design with a canting is a laborious process and has largely been replaced by stamping.

In the mid-19th century the 'modern' batik industry was born with the invention (in Java, but quickly adopted in Malaysia) of the *cap* (pronounced 'jap'). This is a copper, sometimes a wooden stamp which looks something like a domestic iron, except that it has an artistically patterned bottom, usually made from twisted copper and strips of soldered tin. Dripping with molten wax, the jap stamps the same pattern across the length and breadth of the cloth, which is then put into a vat of dye. The waxed areas resist the dye and after drying, the process is repeated several times for the different colours. The cracking effect is produced by crumpling the waxed material, which allows the dye to penetrate the cracks. The cloth is traditionally printed in 12m lengths.

The cap revolutionized batik production. As Wanda Warming and Michael Gaworski say in their book *The world of Indonesian textiles* "... it took a small cottage industry, a fine art, an expression of Javanese sensibilities, and a hobby for aristocratic women, and turned it into a real commercial enterprise". With the invention of the cap, so there evolved a parallel cap-making industry. Old copper stamps have become collectors' pieces. Not only did the cap speed-up production, it also took the artistry out of waxing: waxers merely stamp the design onto the cloth.

Recent years have seen a revival of hand-painted batiks (*batik tulis*), particularly on silk. Price depends on the type of material, design, number of colours used and method employed: factory-printed materials are cheaper than those made by hand. Batik is sold by the *sarung*-length or made up into shirts – and other items of clothing.

Distinguishing hand-drawn from stamped batik It can be hard differentiating drawn (*tulis*) and stamped (*cap*) batik, particularly in the case of the repetitious geometric designs of Central Java. Look for irregular lines and examine repetitive motifs like flowers carefully – stamped batik will show no variation. On poorly-executed stamped cloth, there may be a line at the point where two stamps have been imperfectly aligned. **NB** There is also machine printed cloth with traditional batik designs: this can be identified by the clear design and colour on one side only; batik, whether drawn or printed, will have the design clearly revealed on both sides of the fabric.

Kain songket is Malaysia's 'cloth of gold', although it is also woven in other parts of the region, particularly coastal southern Sumatra. Originally cloth made from a mix of cotton and silk was inter-woven with supplementary gold or silver thread. Today imitation thread is generally used although the metallic thread from old pieces is also removed to provide yarn for new lengths. Some more enterprising weavers have also reportedly used plaited copper wire or yarns thinly coated in metal to achieve the desired effect.

The songket evolved when the Malay sultanates first began trading with China (where the silk came from) and India (where the gold and silver thread derived). Designs are reproduced from Islamic motifs and Arabic calligraphy. It was once exclusive to royalty, but is used today during formal occasions and ceremonies (such as weddings). In Kelantan, Terengganu and Pahang the cloth can be purchased directly from workshops. Prices increase with the intricacy of the design and the number of threads used. Each piece is woven by hand and different weavers specialize in particular patterns – one length of cloth may be the work of several weavers.

Pewterware Pewter-making was introduced from China in the mid-19th century; it was the perfect alloy for Malaysia, which until recently, was the world's largest tin-producer: pewter is 95% tin. Straits tin is alloyed with antimony and copper. The high proportion of tin lends to the fineness of the surface. Malaysia's best pewter is made by Selangor Pewter, which has factories in KL and Singapore. It is made mainly into vases, tankards, water jugs, trays and dressing table ornaments. The Selangor Pewter factory on the outskirts of KL (see page 119) employs about 400 craftsmen and has a good showroom. Selangor pewter was started in 1885 by Yong Koon, a Chinese immigrant from Swatow province who came to Malaya by junk. Using the ample supply of tin, he started making items for ancestral worship, such as incense burners and joss-stick holders. The third generation of the Yong family now runs the operation. The dimpling effect is made by tapping the surface with a small hammer. Selangor Pewter is the world's biggest pewter manufacturer.

Wayang kulit (shadow puppets – see above) are crafted from buffalo-hide and represent figures from the Indian epic tales. They are popular handicrafts as they are light and portable. See page 77 for a description of making a puppet.

Silverware Silverwork is a traditional craft and is now a thriving cottage industry in Kelantan. It is crafted into brooches, pendants, belts, bowls and rings. Design patterns incorporate traditional motifs such as *wayang kulit* (see above) and hibiscus flowers (the national flower). The Iban of Sarawak also use silver for ceremonial headdresses and girdles, and some Iban silvercraft can be found for sale on the peninsula.

MODERN MALAYSIA

POLITICS

Prime Minister Mahathir and UMNO

Malaysia's economy has boomed in recent years and with the creation of a *nouveau riche* middle class, there have been hopes that a more open political system might evolve. But the government does not readily tolerate dissent and during the premiership of Dr Mahathir Mohamad power has, in fact, become increasingly concentrated in the hands of the government. Dr Mahathir is aware that his political dominance hinges largely on economic success, and as Malaysia's 'economic miracle' is unlikely to crumble in the immediate future, so it is equally unlikely that Dr Mahathir and the United Malays National Organization (UMNO) will lose their grip on power. This was forcibly illustrated in the general election of April 1995 when the National Front (a coalition of parties of which UMNO is the leading member) won an unprecedented 64% of the vote, winning a landslide of 161 seats in the 192-seat parliament. As Jomo KS, an economist at the University of Malaya and one of Malaysia's leading political and economic commentators, was quoted as saying: "Make no mistake, this can only be interpreted as a thundering endorsement of Mahathir and no one else. He's got the mandate to lead the country into the 21st century."

Dr Mahathir, as leader of the United Malays National Organization (UMNO), heads the *Barisan Nasional* (BN), or National Front coalition, has won every election since coming to power in 1981. At present the BN is a coalition of 14 parties, but there is no question who leads and dominates the coalition: UMNO. It is notable that Mahathir's hold on power is only really challenged from within UMNO; the other members of the BN would not risk speaking out against the premier and it sometimes seems as though they are only along for the ride.

The most serious challenge to Mahathir's leadership came in 1987 when he narrowly retained his premiership following a contest with the then trade and industry minister Tunku Razaleigh Hamzah. The same year, Mahathir became embroiled in an education controversy after non-Chinese administrators were appointed to Chinese schools. In an atmosphere of rising political tension, the government used the draconian Internal Security Act (a legislative hangover from the British administration which allows for unlimited detention without trial), to arrest more than 100 opponents. The clampdown was known as Operation Lalang. The Prime Minister dealt with his opponents within UMNO by excluding them when he formed a new party – UMNO Baru (or New UMNO) – which is still just known as UMNO. Since then, Mahathir has consolidated his position and the strength of the economy has enabled him to promote himself as the architect of Malaysia's new-found prosperity.

In 1990, for the first time in the 33 years since Malaysian independence, the BN coalition faced a credible multi-racial opposition. The opposition alliance was led by Tunku Razaleigh Hamzah, the former UMNO cabinet minister (and member of the Kelantan royal family) who had challenged Mahathir for the UMNO leadership in 1987, and lost. His faction broke away from UMNO and called itself Semangat '46 – or 'Spirit of '46', the year in which UMNO had been founded. In the run-up to the election, Semangat struck electoral pacts with the predominantly Chinese Democratic Action Party (DAP) and, separately, the conservative Parti Islam, whose powerbase was in the Northeast Malay heartland of Terengganu and Kelantan states. Despite much speculation that the opposition would unseat the ruling BN coalition – or at least, deprive it of its crucial two-thirds majority in parliament – Dr Mahathir won a landslide victory, securing 127 seats in the 180-seat parliament. A two-thirds majority allows the government to amend the constitution and has been Mahathir's measuring stick for electoral success.

The 1995 general election

The 1995 general election results illustrate that Mahathir's grip on power is probably even tighter than it was in 1990. It was quite simply the Front's greatest victory since independence in 1957. The opposition DAP saw its seats in parliament decline from 20 to 9, Semangat '46 from 8 to 6, Sabah's PBS from 13 to 8, while the Parti Islam or PAS managed to maintain its presence at 7. The only blots on Mahathir's – and the Front's – copybook was their inability to dislodge the PAS in their east coast stronghold of Kelantan, and to make more substantial inroads into the PBS vote in the East Malaysian state of Sabah. In Kelantan, the PAS still controls the state government having won 35 of the 43 seats (see page 306). Sabah is a different story. After suffering the defection of the Christian dominated ruling party in the State, Dr Mahathir swore vengeance. In March 1994 he finally got it, dislodging the State's besieged Chief Minister despite his having won a state election 3 weeks previously (see page 432).

1995 Election results

	Parliamentary seats Election results	
	1990	**1995**
National Front (BN)	127	161
Democratic Action Party (DAP)	20	9
Semangat '46	8	6
Parti Islam (PAS)	7	7
Parti Bersatu Sabah (PBS)	3	8
Others	4	0

NB A two-thirds majority allows the government to amend the constitution.

Mahathir achieved this following the defection of several PBS members of the state assembly to the National Front. The April 1995 election, however, showed that the defection of individual politicians to the Front does not necessarily translate into a similar shift in votes. The PBS won eight seats, in the process defeating some of those who had defected to the Front the previous year. The Front may have won 12 of the 20 parliamentary seats, but in three the PBS ran them very close. Despite the close call in Sabah however, the 1995 elections leave Kelantan as the lone state in opposition hands.

In the Western media there was some discussion as to whether the elections were 'fair'. They were fair in the sense that the electorate was freely allowed to vote, without intimidation, and the votes themselves were tallied fairly. However, the fact that television is state-controlled, the press is cowed because papers must apply annually for a permit to publish (most, in any case, are controlled by UMNO interests), and public rallies are banned, made it extremely difficult for the opposition to get its message across. Lim Kit Siang, leader of the opposition DAP said before the poll that it was the most 'unfair and unclean' election in Malaysian history. Christopher Thomas in the London *Times* went so far as to write that "The massive victory leaves Malaysian democracy discredited in western eyes because of the heavy-handed tactics

Drugs trafficking – stiff punishment

Malaysia is well known around the world for its stringent laws against drugs. As they fill in their immigration forms, visitors cannot fail to notice the bold block capitals reading: "BE FOREWARNED – DEATH FOR DRUG TRAFFICKERS UNDER MALAYSIAN LAW". At entry points to Malaysia there are prominent posters repeating this warning, the words emblazoned over an ominous picture of a noose. World attention focuses on Malaysia whenever westerners go to the gallows, but they represent a tiny fraction of those hanged for drug trafficking offences. Since 1983 about 150 prisoners have been hanged and about 4,000 arrested under Section 39(B) of the Dangerous Drugs Act; about a quarter of those face execution within the next few years. Malaysia's biggest-ever mass-hanging of traffickers took place at Taiping jail in May 1990 when eight Hong Kong people were executed.

The Dadah Act – *dadah* is the Malay word for drugs – stipulates a mandatory death sentence upon conviction for anyone in possession of 15 or more grams of heroin or morphine, 200g of cannabis or hashish or 40g of cocaine. Those caught with more than 10g of heroin or 100g of cannibis are deemed to be traffickers and face lengthy jail sentences and flogging with a rotan cane. Following the execution of two Australians in 1986, the then Australian Prime Minister, Bob Hawke, branded the Malaysian government 'barbaric'. A similar outcry resulted from the hanging of a Briton in 1987 – the British opposition even called for a trade embargo of Malaysia. But Malaysian Prime Minister Dr Mahathir Mohamad – who is a medical doctor and as such has taken the Hypocratic Oath – has consistently refused to bow to international pleas for clemency. In a British television documentary in 1991, *The Prime Minister, the junkie and the boys on death row*, he said: "We have to carry out this death penalty because it would not be fair to those who had already been hanged and their families."

employed to achieve it, and confirms a tendency to authoritarianism in what is traditionally a feudal society." In writing this, Thomas, reporting for a western audience, was failing to understand Malaysian politics in Asian terms, and also failing to sufficiently acknowledge that despite the authoritarian attitude of the government it still has a massive popular mandate to govern. It is not by accident that perhaps the most widely admired recent British politician in Malaysia is Margaret Thatcher.

The succession: life after Mahathir

Before the election in 1995, there was talk that **Anwar Ibrahim**, the youthful Finance Minister who was elected as deputy Prime Minister in November 1993, and in the process became the designated successor to Dr Mahathir, was anxious to take over the leadership. Since his election to the post of Finance Minister, Anwar had succeeded in a number of high-profile tasks – including engineering the BN take over in Sabah and the management of the Anglo-Malaysian trade dispute (see box page 88). These successes helped to bolster his position in the party and create a platform for an assault on the leadership.

Although the scale of Mahathir's 1995 election victory – for it was his personal victory just as much as it was a victory for the party – quietened talk of resignation and succession for a while it was not long before mutterings of dissent surfaced once more within the ranks of UMNO – and Anwar Ibrahim's was the name on many people's lips. Mahathir's peace moves towards his former bitter rival Tunku Razaleigh Hamzah (see above), the president of opposition party Semangat '46, were probably motivated by a desire to thwart Anwar just as much as a wish to reunite the mainstream Malay cause. In October 1996 Razaleigh returned to the UMNO fold, bringing with him almost 200,000 supporters. It was widely assumed that in the elections to UMNO's Supreme Council a month later Mahathir would reward Razaleigh with a seat on the council. He was disappointed.

Recent political machinations, labyrinthine though they may be, seem to have emphasized one thing: that Anwar seems Mahathir's likely successor (although two other contenders are the Minister for Education and the Minster of Defence). In May 1997 Mahathir took a 2-month break from prime ministerial duties and, significantly, Anwar took over as Acting Prime Minister during his absence. His performance was generally given high marks, strengthening his position as leader-in-waiting. Mahathir was 71 in 1997, has been at the top for 16 years now, has had one heart by-pass operation, and people – without being too ghoulish – are beginning to count the years. The most widely backed date for his resignation is 1999.

This took on a new urgency in 1997 with the slide in Malaysia's economy – and the slide in Mahathir's reputation. The skilled manner in which Anwar soothed foreign investors fears and appeared, in the process, to contradict the prime minister was taken by some as a further boost to his reputation – and his leadership credentials. But it also led Anwar's enemies to act. In September a series of anonymous 'poison pen' letters circulated among UMNO officials accusing Anwar of infidelity and homosexuality. Almost no one put any store by the letters, but the fact that they were written is significant. It is unlikely that Mahathir will step down. The most widely backed date for Mahathir's resignation is 1999 when UMNO must hold its own party elections.

The political opposition

With the Front in control, talk turned to **the role of the opposition** – indeed, the continued relevance of an opposition. The leader of the DAP, Lim Kit Siang said that "he accepted the people's verdict". Semangat '46, according to one leading political commentator, had been "basically wiped out". Dr Mahathir himself was quoted as saying that the opposition does still have a role to play but "not the politics of destruction nor that of playing to the gallery. ... We want constructive criticism and engagement, not shouting your head off." With this, Dr Mahathir was saying much the same as the leader of Singapore's People's Action Party. In 1995, Prime Minister Goh of Singapore said that he welcomed "well-meaning people who put forth their views in a very well-meaning way", but anything presumed to be snide or mocking would be dealt a "very, very hard blow from the government in return".

The difficulty for the Chinese population – or at least this is how some **Chinese Malaysians** see the issue – is how to make a difference. Should they vote for one of the Chinese political parties – Gerakan and the Malaysian Chinese Association (MCA) – that are members of the ruling coalition and hope to change things from the 'inside'? Or should they vote for one of the Chinese opposition parties and challenge from 'outside'? Their critics maintain that Gerakan and the MCA are too meek and not sufficiently assertive in representing the interests of the Chinese within the BN. Some would go even further and say they have sold out to the UMNO money-go-round. On the other hand, the opposition parties, with the exception of the PAS (which, in any case, is non-Chinese), are so ineffectual that they are not in a position to make a difference. The hope held by some is that racial politics may whither as Malaysia develops and affluence spreads. Vision 2020, Mahathir's long-term development plan (see below), envisages that by that date there will be a united Malaysian 'race' with a "sense of common and shared destiny". The persistence of ethnic divisions in other, already affluent countries might lead one to doubt this admirable objective.

Mahathir Mohamad – recalcitrance rules OK

He's blunt; he's abrasive and he's headstrong. His detractors regularly acuse him of autocratic tendencies. His supporters talk of a man of conviction. Over the past decade, Prime Minister Dr Mahathir Mohamad has curtailed the power of the judiciary, clamped down on the press, jailed his critics and removed the privileges enjoyed by Malaysia's nine hereditary monarchs. In the international arena, Mahathir has emerged as the self-appointed champion and spokesman for the developing world. He made a name for himself in 1992 by vociferously defending Malaysia's environmental record at the Earth Summit in Rio de Janeiro (see page 43). And Dr M has a virulent dislike of the western media.

The Malaysian Prime Minister dominated news headlines in Britain in early 1994 when he ordered the cancellation of British contracts in Malaysia worth US$6bn. He had taken offence at London newspaper allegations that senior Malaysian politicians were corrupt. (Ironically, after claiming an apology from the British press, Mahathir himself in 1996 was decrying the corruption in Malaysia's body politic while senior members of his party, UMNO, were resigning for assorted nefarious activities.) The papers may have dubbed him "the Prickliest Premier in the East", but Mahathir has put Malaysia firmly on the world map. "If you can't be famous," he said "then at least be notorious!"

For all the notoriety born of his possibly Machiavellian manoeuvering, the Malaysian premier is also sensitive to criticism. He is a home-grown, made-in-Malaysia product and is quick to seize on any opportunity to lash out at what he sees as the condescending, neo-colonialist attitudes of the West. Today, a slight against him appears to be perceived as a national slur. For Mahathir has become the CEO for Malaysia Inc. He has continued to win elections because with him has come the political stability and prosperity which has kept most Malaysians happy. He's also imbued them with a new self-confidence – particularly the Malays. Britain got its first taste of Mahathir's wrath a decade ago after the British government raised fees for foreign students. His no-nonsense response was to instruct Malaysians to "Buy British Last". In November 1993, the Australian Prime Minister, Paul Keating, tangled with him. He branded Mahathir "recalcitrant" for his refusal to attend a regional summit. That remark nearly provoked a trade war. In the end, Keating was forced to apologize – too much was at stake.

Politics is a game which Mahathir is good at and one in which he has always proved controversial. During Malaysia's race riots of May 1969, he gained notoriety as a rabble-rouser and outspoken critic of Tunku Abdul Rahman, Malaysia's first Prime Minister. He outlined his extreme pro-Malay views in a book, *The Malay Dilemma*, which was promptly banned. Ironically, Mahathir himself is not fully Malay: his father was an Indian Muslim. But his pro-Malay views struck a chord and through

Money politics and corruption

The entrenched position of UMNO and the BN has, in the eyes of the government's critics, allowed **money politics** and political patronage to flourish. It is argued that the use of political power to dispense favours and make money has become endemic, so much so that it is accepted as just another part of the political landscape. In 1995 Datuk Rafidah Aziz, the highly respected minister of International Trade and Industry, revealed in court that her son-in-law, a son of Prime Minister Mahathir, and a brother of Deputy Prime Minister Anwar Ibrahim had all benefited from share allocations which fell under her largesse. Such allocations are permitted – indeed encouraged – as the early 1970s, he fought his way into the upper echelons of the political hierarchy. Mahathir entered the cabinet as education minister and by 1976 had become deputy prime minister. Over the next 5 years, he gained a reputation as a dynamic Malay leader with a sense of purpose. In 1981 Mahathir was elected President of the politically dominant United Malays National Organisation (UMNO); the President automatically becomes Prime Minister.

Unlike his predecessors, Mahathir climbed the political ladder without the help of aristocratic connections. He was the first Malaysian leader not to have been educated in the West – he trained as a medical doctor at the University of Singapore. And he had humble origins; he was born in a small Malay kampung house, next door to an ice factory, on the outskirts of Alor Star in Kedah. In his school days, during the Japanese occupation, the young Mahathir worked as a stallholder at the local market, where he sold ginger drinks and bananas. His first stall was torn down by Japanese soldiers. He revealed all this in 1991, while attempting to convince stallholders in the same market of the wisdom of turning it into a modern shopping complex.

From his first day in office, Mahathir gained respect for his determination to root out corruption, although the rise of money-politics – a consequence of his policy to promote Malay businesses – undermined this. One of his first actions was to loosen Malaysia's ties with the Commonwealth – particularly with Britain, through the 'Buy British Last' campaign, in which he instructed Malaysians to 'Look East' instead to the booming economies of Japan, S Korea and Taiwan. He stressed the importance of self-reliance and one of Mahathir's enduring legacies will be the Proton Saga, the national car (see page 116). It has become the ultimate symbol of the new high-tech 'Made-in-Malaysia' image the Prime Minister has been so keen to promote.

Mahathir has won a string of impressive election victories – most recently in 1995 – and has weathered both economic recession and criticism of his sometimes abrasive and often autocratic style. His health is the one wild card: he suffered a big heart attack in 1989 and in 1997 celebrated his 71st birthday. But so far at least, whenever there have been the merest glimpse of a threat Mahathir has out manoeuvred his opponent with consommate skill and not a little ruthlessness.

More than anything, Mahathir has changed the way Malaysian's, and especially Malays, think about themselves. When he came to power, Malays were all to ready to put themselves down, to admit defeat to the more assiduous Chinese. Now Malaysians are self-confident and willing not just to compete with the Chinese on a level playing field but to take their new-found confidence into the international arena and to play – and win.

part of the effort to increase bumiputra representation in the economy. But the scale to which relatives and political supporters benefit is questioned. Mahathir announced a new code of conduct for senior officials and politicians in early 1995 in an attempt to foster greater probity.

Nonetheless, the years since have seen a gradual drip, drip of scandal which has threatened to take the shine off Malaysia's glossy image. This so incensed Prime Minister Mahathir that in an UMNO address in October 1996 he wept as he warned party members that money politics and corruption 'would destroy the country'. Critics have suggested that UMNO's unquestioned political supremacy has created the conditions

The new economic policy – Malaysia's recipe for racial harmony

Just over 2 decades ago Malaysia's Malay-led government woke up to the fact that Malays and indigenous groups – collectively called *bumiputras*, or 'sons of the soil' – made up more than half the country's population but owned just 2% of corporate equity. Their average income was also less than half that of non-Malays. The Malay elite worked in the civil service, but most Malays were poor farmers. Economic power was concentrated in the hands of foreigners and urban Chinese while rural Malays lived on, or under, the breadline. The Chinese virtually ran the economy – they were the bankers, brokers and businessmen. In 1970, in the wake of the bloody race riots in which hundreds died (see page 59), the controversial New Economic Policy, or NEP, was introduced. The NEP aimed to wipe out poverty irrespective of race and completely restructure society by putting the Malay, Chinese and Indian communities on an equal footing. The idea was to abolish racial stereotyping, making it more difficult to associate a person's job with the colour of his or her skin.

The NEP was designed to prevent a recurrence of the bloodletting by keeping multiracial Malaysia intact. It offered Malays, the economic underdogs, a chance to catch up and encouraged them to move to the cities. Racial quotas were introduced to raise their stake in the economy to at least 30%. They were granted scholarships and directorships, they were pushed into managerial jobs, subsidized, goaded and given a ticket to get rich quick – which many did. But because the NEP favoured the Malays, it antagonized almost everyone else. For 20 years, the NEP was denounced as racist by its critics and flagrantly abused by many of those it tried to help. The policy was an invitation to bribery and corruption and the hijacking and exploitation of the NEP by wealthy bumiputras alienated non-Malays and fanned resentment.

But the NEP's targets were not met. Although poverty has been markedly reduced since 1970, the bumiputras' stake in the economy was a fraction over 20% in 1995 instead of the targeted 30%. While the jump from 2% to 20% is enormous, only 7% of that is in the hands of individuals – most is owned by big bumiputra investment companies, institutions and government trust agencies. A sizeable chunk of the remainder is concentrated in the hands of a stratum of bumiputra fat

where corruption and money politics can flourish. In 1996 it was alleged that people in positions of power had managed to manipulate the legal system. The United Nations Centre for Human Rights released a press statement saying: "Complaints are rife that certain highly placed personalities in Malaysia ... are manipulating the Malaysian system of justice and thereby undermining the due administration of independent and impartial justice by courts." The statement referred to a series of allegations that litigants had managed to select judges of their own choice. In an address to the UMNO Supreme Council in May 1997 shortly after two senior UMNO leaders had been sacked in connection with missing funds, Mahathir pointedly said "We will not defend anyone who's corrupt". A few months earlier on 22 December 1996, to the intense embarrassment of the Prime Minister, Muhammad Muhammad Taib, Chief Minister of Selangor, was detained trying to leave Brisbane, Australia with close to US$1 million in cash stashed into a suitcase – an offence under Australian law. Muhammad rather feebly explained to a packed and incredulous press conference that the money had been entrusted to him by his brothers to buy property on Australia's Gold Coast.

cats who act as 'sleeping partners' in big firms. Today, the government admits that the biggest income disparities in Malaysia are within the bumiputra community itself. There are still relatively few high-calibre Malays with relevant management qualifications and experience to fill the posts available.

In the months before the NEP expired in 1990, many Malays were arguing for the continuation of the policy; they must still be given special treatment, they said, to enable them to catch up. However much the Chinese have been disadvantaged by the policy, their robust business acumen has meant that they are far from being a downtrodden minority. Even the NEP's most outspoken critics accept the need to rectify Malaysia's socio-economic imbalances, but they say the solution does not lie in a programme discriminating along racial lines.

The spectre of a repeat of the 1969 race riots has been constantly raised by the government in an effort to promote racial harmony – but today Malaysians look to the Los Angeles riots of 1992 as an example of unwanted mayhem, rather than 1969. There is little doubt that despite the abuses of political patronage, the bumiputras are now in a better position to compete. A fairly large number of bumiputras have become leading lights in Kuala Lumpur's business and financial community. As a group, Malays are more self-confident and more competitive than they were in 1970; they are also less prone to cast themselves as a disenfranchised majority.

In 1991, the old policy was replaced with the New Development Policy (NDP), which formalized a more liberal strategy. The NDP sets no deadline for the achievement of the 30% bumiputra ownership target – although it is still there. The new policy uses incentives instead of quotas – in the words of one commentator, it uses 'more carrot and less stick'. The emphasis now is on ensuring that bumiputras retain and build on the wealth they have accumulated. The government now wants to wean Malays off government hand-outs and patronage but it appears to believe that until the dependency syndrome has completely disappeared, bumiputras should be protected. Most Malaysians have welcomed the change in emphasis, but critics still maintain the NDP is just old wine in a new bottle.

He continued: "I do not feel any sense of wrong-doing in this matter and if it is an offence, it is a technical one ...".

The anti-corruption drive continued through the year and by the middle of 1997 a chief minister (the above Muhammad Muhammad Taib), a deputy minister and a host of government officials and UMNO party stalwarts had been sacked or had resigned. Anwar Ibrahim, the Prime Minister's number two, responded to Mahathir's fears by heading an anti-corruption drive to root out the guilty and announced that the powers of the Anti-Corruption Agency would be strengthened. By all accounts there are more than a few unusually wealthy politicians pacing the deep shag pile of their luxury apartments considering their futures. Although no one considers Mahathir himself to be among the guilty, there are those who suggest that the Prime Minister's style and his emphasis on wealth creation has helped to promote corruption. Chandra Muzaffar, a political scientist at the Science University of Malaysia in Penang, for example, argues that "He's created a culture that places undue emphasis on wealth accumulation for its own sake. The new heroes are all corporate barons."

Social ills

Another challenge for the government is how to curb the growth of what Prime Minister Mahathir has termed 'social ills'. For a country which has argued that 'Asian values' have permitted it to modernize without the social and moral degradation evident in the West, this is a sensitive subject. Research has revealed a surge in drug taking (particularly recreational drugs like Ecstasy), illegitimate pregnancies, wife abuse, gangsterism and incest. Moreover, this research seems to show that the problem is predominantly concentrated among Malays. Never one to shy away from a problem, however embarrassing, Mahathir has bluntly pointed out: "In terms of population breakdown, the Malays form 55% while the Chinese make up about 25% and Indians, 10%. But when comparing social problems, the Malays account for 67%, while Chinese involvement is only 16%." State and national government have rushed to introduce legislation to control this rash of ills. For example, smoking by anyone under 18 may soon be prohibited and nightclubs in many states have to shut early.

Racial relations in the New Malaysia

Since the race riots of 1969 relations between Malaysia's Malay and Chinese populations have dominated political affairs. Now that Malaysia is fast attaining economic maturity a debate is beginning to emerge about whether it is time to consign racial politics, and racial quotas, to the dust heap. Prime Minister Mahathir's Vision 2020 (see page 96), which sets out a path to developed country status by 2020, significantly talks of a 'Malaysian race working in full and equal partnership'. There is no mention here of 'bumiputras' and 'Chinese Malaysians', but of a single Malaysian identity which transcends race.

Not everyone agrees with this vision. There are those who note that the communal peace which has descended on the nation since 1969 has been based on a fast-growing economy in which everyone has gained even while the portions of the cake alloted to each group have changed. But what if the economy slows? – as it may do given the country's current economic problems. Then, these critics argue, the old racial animosities and conflicts will quickly re-emerge. Others, like Sarawak's state minister for tourism James Masing, would like to see a plural society where difference is respected and accepted. "To say I'm Iban", Masing explains, "doesn't mean I'm any less Malaysian."

Foreign relations

In **foreign affairs** Malaysia follows a non-aligned stance and is fiercely anti-Communist. This, however, has not stopped its enthusiastic investment in Indochina and Myanmar (Burma). Malaysia is a leading light in the Association of Southeast Asian Nations (ASEAN), and Mahathir has made his mark as an outspoken champion of the developing world. As such, he has frequently clashed with the West. Malaysia needs continued foreign investment from industrialized countries, but Dr Mahathir remains deeply suspicious of western motives and intentions.

Malaysia's most delicate relations are with neighbouring Singapore, a country with which it is connected by history and also by water pipelines and a causeway. For a few years Singapore was part of the Malaysian Federation – until it was ejected in 1965 – and Singapore's status as a largely Chinese city state makes for an uneasy relationship with Malay-dominated Malaysia. In 1997 mutual sensitivities were made all too clear in a spat which threatened to escalate into a major diplomatic conflict. The cause? A dispute over whether Johor Bahru was a safe place or not (see page 625).

ECONOMY

Malaysia has an abundance of natural resources. Today, though, tin-mining, rubber and palm oil are declining in importance, and while the country's oil, gas and timber wealth are valuable sources of revenue, the manufacturing sector has become the powerhouse of the economy. At the same time, the services sector is booming, and tourism is now the third largest foreign exchange earner. Malaysia has one of the fastest-growing economies in the world. The World Bank defines Malaysia as an upper-middle-income country. In 1995 GNP per capita was US$3,890, placing Malaysia in the ranks of the World Bank's Upper Middle Income grouping of countries. In terms of purchasing power parity, this translates into a per capita income of PPP$9,020. To put this into perspective, Portugal in 1995 had a PPP income of under $12,670.

There is a Malay saying which goes: *ada gula, ada semut* ('where there's sugar, there's ants') – and from the late 1980s foreign investors swarmed to Malaysia, thanks to its sugar-coated investment incentives as well as its cheap land and labour, its good infrastructure and political stability.

The evolution of the Malaysian economy

In the late 1800s, as the British colonial government developed the infrastructure of the Federated Malay States, they built a network of roads, railways, telephones and telegraphs which served as the backbone of the export economy. In the 50 years following 1880, export earnings rose 30-fold. Most of the tin mines and plantations were in the hands of British-owned companies and remained foreign-owned until the Malaysian government restructured foreign equity holdings in the 1970s.

On independence in 1957, resource-rich Malaysia's future looked bright and foreign investment was encouraged, the capitalist system maintained and there was no threat to nationalize industry. The first national development plan aimed to expand the agricultural sector and begin to reduce dependence on rubber, which, even then, was beginning to encounter competition from synthetic alternatives. But rubber and tin remained the main economic props. In 1963, when the Federation of Malaysia was formed, only 6% of the workforce was employed in industry and 80% of exports were contributed by tin, rubber, oil palm, timber, and oil and gas.

The structure of Malaysia's economy has been radically altered since independence, and particularly, since the 1980s. Commodity exports such as rubber and palm oil, which were the mainstay of the post-colonial economy, having declined in significance and, within 30 years, this sector is unlikely to contribute more than 6% of Malaysia's export earnings. A turning point was 1987, when agriculture was overtaken by the manufacturing sector in terms of contribution to Gross Domestic Product. Manufacturing output has almost tripled in 25 years – thanks mainly to the fact that Malaysia has been the darling of foreign investors. The value of manufactured exports is growing even faster; today they are approaching three-quarters of Malaysia's export earnings. The country that used to be the world's biggest producer of rubber and tin is now the world's leading producer of semi-conductors and a/c units. In May 1993, another landmark was created in Malaysia's economic history: the Malaysia Mining Corporation, one of the country's biggest remaining tin producers, pulled out of tin mining. Tin production costs have increased while the price of tin has slumped. In 1990 there were still 141 tin mines in Malaysia; by 1993 there were only 50.

But the type of products Malaysia manufactures is also undergoing rapid change. One of the main reasons for this is Malaysia's labour squeeze. The main industrial boom zones (the Klang Valley around Kuala Lumpur, Johor and Penang) are already suffering shortages, and while infrastructural developments have just about kept pace with the flood of foreign manufacturing investment, the labour pool is drying up. Unemployment in 1996 was only 2.7% – in practical terms zero – and the government has been forced to recruit blue-collar migrant labourers from Thailand, Bangladesh, Myanmar (Burma) and Indonesia. Most of these immigrant workers are still employed in the plantation sector, but increasingly they are being brought in to man the production lines. In 1993 factories faced a labour shortage of 22,000 workers, and it was estimated in 1995 that the electronics sector alone will require 320,000 new workers before the end of the decade. To some extent this yawning gap is being met by hundreds of thousands of illegal immigrants; in July 1992 the government forced illegals to register or face deportation, realizing it could no longer turn a blind eye to the labour-smuggling racket. But the general failure of this policy is reflected in the figures for 1996: an estimated 1.75 million migrant workers – in a country with a workforce of 8 million – of whom just 750,000 are in the country and working legally. Nor is it just a case of a shortage of blue-collar workers: demand for skilled white-collar staff means that poaching and job-hopping are becoming endemic.

The flood of foreign workers easing Malaysia's labour squeeze is, in the process, creating some quite severe inter-ethnic squabbles. Bangladeshis, for example, are popularly credited with bringing diseases to Malaysia while being in the country for the added purpose of snaring a Malay wife thereby becoming Malaysian via the back door. Fights often break out between migrant workers and Malay youths. The fact that Bosnian Muslims have been made welcome in Malaysia while Bangladeshi Muslims are cold-shouldered has led commentators to accuse some Malays of thinly disguised racism.

The rate at which wages have risen in recent years has also meant that more labour-intensive industries now find it considerably cheaper to locate in neighbouring Thailand or Indonesia. To prevent this drain of investment, the government is trying to do two things. First, to encourage companies to invest in more 'backward' states in the Federation – including Sabah and Sarawak in East Malaysia – where labour is cheaper. And second, to encourage firms to 'upgrade' into more skill- and capital-intensive activities. This is the trick that Singapore tried in the late 1970s with its so-called Second Industrial Revolution – and which led, in part, to the recession of 1985 (see page 620). To achieve this second aim, the government has become increasingly selective with the sorts of industries it allows to locate in the country.

The **New Development Policy (NDP)**, unveiled in 1991 (see box) promotes hi-tech industries, higher value-added production, skills development and increased productivity and is the basis of the government's economic development strategy. It is a much more economically and socially liberal document than its predecessor, the New Economic Policy. Through it, the government tacitly concedes that without continued inflows of foreign capital, Malaysia's ambitious targets will not be realized. The NDP envisages a fourfold increase in the value of private-sector investment by 2000 and the private sector – both local and foreign – has been charged with spearheading economic growth and enhancing the country's industrial profile. The Ministry of International Trade and Industry has energetically promoted the concept of 'Malaysia Incorporated' in its effort to foster consultation and dialogue with the private sector and the all-important foreign investors. This has helped cut the red tape. Since Mahathir adopted his 'Look East' policy in the 1980s (instead of relying solely on trade links with the West), most of Malaysia's foreign investment has come from the East. In 1994 approved foreign investment in manufacturing alone amounted to RM11.2bn. The largest investor was Taiwan (RM2.9bn), followed by Japan (RM1.8bn) and the US (RM1.3bn). Most of this investment was concentrated in three sectors and in three areas of the country: electronics, chemicals and textiles, and Selangor (around the capital Kuala Lumpur), Penang and Johor.

Evidence of the growing maturity of the Malaysian economy can be seen in the degree to which the country – Malaysia Inc. – is pursuing its industrial ambitions in the global arena. Between 1991 and mid-1996 US$7.1 billion was invested in enterprises off-shore. This ranged from the acquisition of Lotus sports cars in Britain, to timber operations in New Zealand, Guyana and Canada, and construction in Albania and Uruguay.

Transforming the economy

A key element in Malaysia's development strategy is how to manage the transition from a production centre where comparative advantage is based on labour cost to an economy where high levels of education and skills provide the industrial impetus. Malaysia invariably looks across to Singapore as both a role model in this regard and as a competitor.

One of Prime Minister Mahathir's favourite programmes is the so-called MSC or 'Multimedia Super Corridor' – an attempt to build an Oriental Silicon Valley on a 15 km-by-50 km stretch of land south of KL. Like most of Malaysia's plans, the MSC will not come cheap. It will cost US$800 million just to provide the optical communications infrastructure. When you add in the new administrative capital of Putrajaya and associated international airport, both currently under construction, along with a technological centre predictably called Cyberjaya, the bill comes to US$20 billion. As Daniel Ng of Sun Microsystems was quoted as saying: "It's as if someone said, 'What would be the perfect Silicon Valley?' and then built it."

There are critics and sceptics aplenty. There are those who say Malaysia lacks the human resources to justify such grandiose plans. There are only 0.02 computers per capita (Singapore has nearly ten times more) and out of 49 countries listed in the 1996 *Global Competitiveness Report*, Malaysia ranks only 28th in terms of computer literacy. Part of the problem is perceived to be the culture of education in the country. Gary Silverman in the *Far Eastern Economic Review* (1996) writes of a professor of history at the University of Malaya:

> "Khoo Kay Kim has a rare complaint: he gets too much respect. Every day at work, Khoo is surrounded by people who hang on his every word, agree with what he says and repeat his statements virtually verbatim months later. It's making him nervous ... he's haunted by the silence in his classroom."

Malaysian students are not expected to challenge or contradict their teachers, but to conform. This is perceived to be unhealthy if Malaysia is to become a thinking economy where people are creative and innovative. More practically, Malaysian graduates are often not sufficiently fluent in English to take full advantage of the IT revolution. This dates back to the 1970s when the government switched from English to Bahasa Malaysia as the medium of instruction in secondary schools. Further, the tertiary level enrollment rate in Malaysia is low: just 7.2% of the relevant age group are in higher education.

Tourism

Tourism has grown to assume a critical role in Malaysia's economy in the past few years. In 1990, Malaysia launched itself into big league tourism with a bang, joining the swelling ranks of Southeast Asian countries to host 'tourism years'. Visit Malaysia Year (VMY) was a big success: 7.4 million tourists arrived – half as many again as in 1989 and receipts rose 61% to US$1.5bn. This made tourism Malaysia's third biggest earner after manufacturing and oil – up from sixth position the previous year. Now Prime Minister Dr Mahathir Mohamad calls tourism "Malaysia's goldmine"; he says there should be "no saturation point" and wants a 3-fold increase in tourist arrivals by the end of the 1990s.

While the vast majority of tourists still come from neighbouring Singapore and Thailand, the government is targeting the big spenders – the 'high-yield markets' like the Japanese, who spend 70% more than the average tourist. Smart new hotel and resort complexes are springing up around the country and scores of golf courses are being carved out of the jungle. Until fairly recently, the government paid scant regard to the lower-middle end of the tourism market, favouring sparkling new 5-star complexes instead. The government thought VMY 1990 such a success that it decided to do it all over again in 1994. Malaysia was once again aggressively promoted abroad, this time under the slogan 'Visit Malaysia Naturally', with an eye on the eco-market. More colourful extravaganzas filled the calendar as locals shrugged off a feeling of déjá vu. Although VMY 1994 was not quite the success of VMY 1990, 7.2 million visitors arrived in the country during the year, spending RM9 billion.

Mapping out the future: Vision 2020

The NDP, unveiled in 1991, is a 10-year policy which forms part of Mahathir's longer term economic blueprint appropriately labelled 'Wawasan 2020' or 'Vision 2020'. This aims to quadruple per-capita income, double the size of the economy and make Malaysia a fully developed industrialized country by the end of the second decade of the next century. Vision 2020 is full of lofty ambitions, grand goals and fuzzy rhetoric. But although it might read more like a corporate mission statement than a well-defined policy, given Malaysia's successes over the last quarter century it would be a brave person who rejected it as unachieveable. To meet the targets, the economy must average 7% growth a year: the average rate of growth of the economy since 1970 has been almost 7.5% per year. The fear over the last few years has not been that growth will be too slow to meet Vision 2020's ambitious target, but rather that it has been too rapid.

Since the late 1980s, the economy has grown so fast that it has been in danger of overheating – inflation has been rising steadily and the trade balance is deep in the red. In the 3 years between 1993 and 1995 the economy grew by an average of 9.1%. The rate of GDP growth in 1996 was 8.2% and the forecast for 1997 was of a similar pace of growth. Many analysts have been privately hoping for a slowdown, to enable the government to catch up and the spending public to cool out. The current account deficit in 1995 was US$7 bn, or nearly 9% of GNP, and the overall balance of payments deficit stood at nearly US$2bn. Because foreign investment and government borrowing were not sufficient to finance this deficit, the central bank had to dip into its foreign exchange reserves – something that bankers and investment analysts regarded with some alarm. One foreign bank described the government's economic management as 'Noddynomics' – a characterization which, needless to say, left ministers a trifle peeved. But the Central Bank, Bank Negara Malaysia, has kept a tight grip on money and in 1996 the current account deficit improved to 5.5% of GNP. Indeed, the alarmist perspective of many reports in 1995 was replaced by a tone of optimism about Malaysia's immediate economic prospects during 1996 and into 1997.

Falling tigers

This optimism was rudely shaken by the collapse of the Thai economy in July 1997, leading to the devaluation of the baht and the acceptance of a US$15 billion IMF rescue package. Though Thailand's problems were uniquely serious there were enough commonalities to cause concern in KL's financial district: a high current account deficit; a currency linked to the US$; a booming property sector; and a lack of transparency in some aspects of financial management.

It was these similarities with Thailand – and perhaps also a sense that the economies of Asean, having boomed together would also fall together – which led currency speculators to attack the ringgit. Initially Bank Negara, the central bank, frantically bought ringgit. Then the authorities seemed to decide to let the market take its course and allowed the currency to trade within a wider band.

Prime Minister Mahathir, predictably, blamed perfidious currency speculators and in particular George Soros, the Hungarian-born billionaire who was instrumental in forcing Sterling (£) out of the ERM and thereby gained the epithet 'the man who broke the Bank of England'. Mahathir has allegedly compared speculators to drug dealers, labelling them anarchists, saboteurs and rogues (*The Economist*, 2 August 1997). It is perhaps also significant that Soros funds a foundation which campaigns against the SLORC in Myanmar (Burma) while Mahathir was one of the key supporters of Burma's entry into the Asean fold. In July at their annual meeting, the nine Asean foreign ministers released a joint communiqué stating that the currency crisis was due to the "well co-ordinated efforts [by speculators] to destabilize ASEAN currencies for self-serving purposes". *The Economist* opined that blaming Soros for Thailand's plight was "rather like condemning an undertaker for burying a suicide".

Mahathir imposed various currency and trading controls to try and beat the speculators but, if anything, this seemed to make matters worse, causing foreign investors to loose confidence and the KL stock market to slump alarmingly. By November the KL stock market had lost 50% of its capitalization in 8 months. Each time Mahathir came out fighting the ringgit would take another battering and Malaysia's bankers would turn their faces to the sky in despair. One Asian diplomat was quoted as saying: "You'd think he know when to step back". With

Malaysia: fact file

Geographic

Land area	330,000 sq km
Arable land as % of total	15%
Average annual rate of deforestation	2.5%
Highest mountain, Gunung Kinabalu	4,101m
Kuala Lumpur	
Average rainfall	2,250 mm
Average temperature	26°C

Economic

GNP/person (1995)	US$3,890
GDP/person (1995, PPP*)	US$9,020
GNP growth (/capita, 1985-1995)	5.7%
GDP growth 1996	8.2%
GDP growth 1997	8% (est)
% labour force in agriculture	27%
Total debt (% GNP)	43%
Debt service ratio (% exports)	8%
Military expenditure (% GNP)	4.8%

Social

Population (mid-1995)	20.1 million
Population growth rate (1990-95)	2.4%
Adult literacy rate	83%
Mean years of schooling	5.6 years
Secondary School enrolment as % of age group (male/female)	61%/56%
Population living on $1/day (1981-1995)	5.6%
Rural population as % of total	46%
Growth of urban population (1980-95)	4.3%/year

Health

Life expectancy at birth	71 years
Population with access to clean water	90%
Population with access to sanitation	94%
Infant mortality (/1,000 live births)	12
Total fertility rate (1995)	3.4

* PPP = Purchasing Power Parity (based on what it costs to buy a similar basket of goods and services in different countries).

Sources: UNDP (1995) *Human Development Report 1995*, OUP: New York; World Bank (1997) *World Development Report 1997* , OUP: New York; and other sources.

Calling names

Soros on Mahathir

- Mahathir is 'a menace to his own country' and a 'loose cannon'
- Mahathir was using Soros 'as a scapegoat to cover up his own failure'

Mahathir on Soros and currency speculators

- Currency trading is 'unnecessary, unproductive and immoral'
- Foreign investors are 'ferocious beasts'
- Soros is 'a moron'

all the uncertainty surrounding Malaysia's economic fortunes in the wake of the Thai financial debacle, so greater pessimism has crept into commentators' predictions about the future.

Although it was the prime minister's battle with Soros et al. which gained the column inches, Malaysia's financial difficulties are likely to have some far more important implications. To begin with, there was talk in late 1997 of ending the close links that have evolved between business and government where contracts are agreed according to 'negotiated' rather than 'competitive' tender. It also seems that some of the more grandiose projects that have Mahathir's support – like the Bakun Dam and Putrajaya, Malaysia's new administrative capital – may be delayed. In mid-October 1997 Anwar Ibrahim released the 1998 budget: he forecast 7% GDP growth in 1998, significantly higher than most independent analysts who projected 5%-6%. The fear is that the implications of Malaysia's tussle with economic forces and foreign speculators has not quite sunk in.

What may be surprising is that many Malaysians – as well as Thais and Indonesians – agree with their prime minister. The currency attacks, the austerity measures forced on Thailand and Indonesia by the IMF, are seen as a Western imperialist plot: a way of pushing Asia back in its place.

Kuala Lumpur

JUST over a century ago, Kuala Lumpur was nothing more than a collection of atap-roofed huts in a jungle clearing. Its history therefore starts in the British colonial period: the city's most imposing Moorish-style buildings date from the turn of the century.

HISTORY

Kuala Lumpur means 'muddy confluence' in Malay – as apt a description today as it was in the pioneer days of the 1870s. This romantic name refers to the Klang and Gombak rivers that converge in the middle of the city – there is also some evidence that the *kopi-susu*-coloured Gombak was once known as the *Sungai Lumpur*. Kuala Lumpur, which nearly everyone knows as KL, has grown up around the Y-shaped junction of these rivers in the area called *Ulu Klang* – the upper reaches of the Klang River.

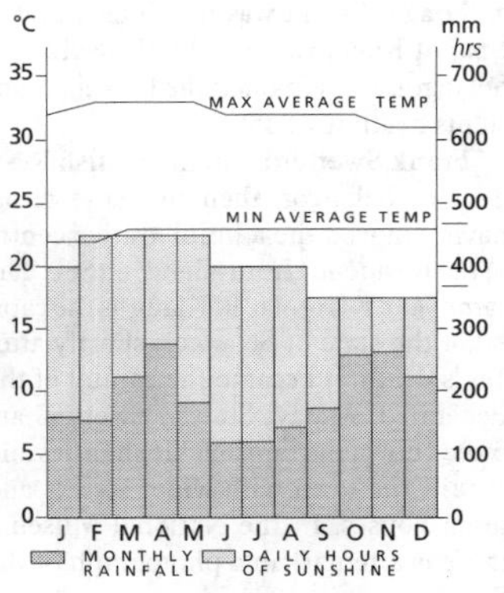

Climate: Kuala Lumpur

In the space of a century, KL grew from a trading post and tin mining shanty into a colonial capital. Today, it is a modern, cosmopolitan business hub and the centre of government. But it may not entirely have outgrown its pioneering tin-town mentality: rumour has it that the speculators were still looking for tin when the subterranean carpark was built beneath the Padang at Merdeka Square in the mid-1980s.

In 1857, members of the Selangor Royal family – including Rajah Abdullah, the Bugis chief of the old state capital of Klang – mounted an expedition to speculate for tin along the upper reaches of the Klang River. Backed by money from Melakan businessmen, 87 Chinese prospectors travelled up the river by raft to the confluence of the Klang and the Gombak. After trekking through dense jungle they stumbled across rich tin deposits near what is now Ampang. 69 miners on this first expedition died of malaria within a month.

This did not stop Rajah Abdullah from organizing a second expeditionary

Kuala Lumpur highlights

Museums and historical sights The centre of colonial Kuala Lumpur includes several **Moorish-style buildings** (page 108); **National Art Gallery** (page 108); **Muzium Negara** (the National Museum) (page 110).

Mosques and temples **Masjid Jame**, the old Moghul-style mosque (page 106); the modern **Masjid Negara** (the National Mosque) (page 108); **Sri Mahamariamman Hindu Temple** (page 110); **Chan See Shu Yuen Temple** (page 110); **Sze Ya Temple** (page 110).

Other sights **Chinatown**, which retains much of its original turn-of-the-century architecture and comes alive each night with its *pasar malam* (night market) (page 109); **Batu Caves**, high on the cliff-face of a limestone massif, and focus of Hindu pilgrimage (page 114); **Templer Park**, a 1,200-hectare tract of jungle (page 114).

Shopping Kuala Lumpur's Art Deco-style **central market** has been converted into a lively focus for the local artistic community and contains shops and stalls selling art and handicrafts (page 108); the **Chinatown street market** (*pasar malam*) sells everything from ten-cent trinkets and cheap T-shirts to inexpensive leather goods and copy watches (page 109).

Sport **Royal Selangor Club** for golf (page 137); a water theme park at **Sunway Lagoon and adventure park** at **The Mines** (page 137).

Nightlife Kuala Lumpur is very lively after dark, with scores of excellent bars, nightclubs and discos (page 133).

labour force, which succeeded in mining commercial quantities of tin, taking it downriver to Klang. Until then Malaya's tin-mining industry had been concentrated in the Kinta Valley near Ipoh, to the north. At about this time, the invention of canning as a means of preserving food led to strong world demand for tin. Spotting a good business opportunity, two Chinese merchants opened a small trading-post at the confluence in 1859. One of them, Hiu Siew, was later appointed *Kapitan Cina* – the first headman of the new settlement. But secret society rivalry between the Hai San (which controlled KL) and the Ghee Hin (which controlled a nearby settlement) retarded the township's early development. Malaria also remained a big problem and fires regularly engulfed and destroyed parts of the town.

By the mid-1860s, KL, which was still predominantly Chinese, began to prosper under the guiding hand of its sheriff, **Yap Ah Loy**. He was a Hakka gang leader from China, who arrived in Melaka in 1854, fought in Negri Sembilan's riots at Sungai Ujong (see page 217), then went to KL in 1862 where he became a tin magnate – or *towkay* – and ran gambling dens and brothels. But he emerged as a respected community leader and in 1868, at the age of 31, he was appointed *Kapitan Cina* of Kuala Lumpur by the Sultan of Selangor. He remained the headman until his death in 1885.

Frank Swettenham, the British Resident of Selangor, then took the reins, having moved the administrative centre of the Residency from Klang in 1880. The same year, KL replaced Klang as the capital of the state of Selangor; shortly after Yap's death, it became the capital of the Federated Malay States. Swettenham pulled down the ramshackle shanties and rebuilt the town with wider streets and brick houses. In the National Museum there is a remarkable photograph of the Padang area in 1884, showing a shabby line of atap huts where the Sultan Abdul

Samad Building is today. By 1887 the new national capital had 518 brick houses and a population of 4,050. By 1910, when the magnificent Moorish-style railway station was completed, the city's population had risen more than 10-fold; nearly four-fifths of the population was Chinese. The town continued to grow in the following decades, becoming increasingly multiracial in character, as the British educated the Malay nobility, then employed them as administrators. The Indian population also grew rapidly; many were brought from South India to work on the roads and railways and the plantations in the Klang Valley.

In World War Two, the city was bombed by the Allies, but little real damage was incurred. The Japanese surrendered in KL on 13 September 1945. 3 years later, there was a massive influx of squatters into the city, with the start of the Communist Emergency. The city area quickly became overcrowded, so in 1952 Petaling Jaya, KL's satellite town was founded to relieve the pressure. It subsequently went on to attract many of Malaysia's early manufacturing industries. Following the end of the Emergency, Malaya became the Federation of Malaysia on 31 August 1957. Independence was declared by the late Prime Minister Tunku Abdul Rahman ('Papa Malaysia') in the brand new Merdeka Stadium.

Modern Kuala Lumpur

In 1974, the 243 sq km area immediately surrounding the city was formerly declared the Federal Territory of Kuala Lumpur, with a separate administration from its mother-state of Selangor. Today, KL's population is approaching 1.5 million, and although one of the smallest capitals in Southeast Asia, it is a rapidly growing business centre, its industrial satellites gaining the lion's share of the country's manufacturing investment. The economic boom that started in the late 1980s has caused a building boom that rivals Singapore's. In downtown KL, old and new are juxtaposed – and the digger and pile driver seem to be nowhere far from eye sight or ear shot. The jungled backdrop of the copper-topped clock tower of the Supreme Court of a century ago has been replaced by scores of stylish high-rise office blocks, dominated by the soaring, angular-roofed Maybank headquarters. The Victorian Moorish and Moghul-style buildings, the Art Deco central market and cinemas and the Chinese shophouses stand in marked contrast to these impressive new skyscrapers. The most recent addition to the modern skyline is the Petronas Twin Tower, also known as KLCC (Kuala Lumpur City Centre), which when it was completed in 1996 was the tallest building in the world at 88 storeys and 421m. The bridge connecting the two towers claims the title of the highest bridge in the world. When it was under construction in 1995 and 1996 the contractors were completing a floor every 4 days – and were being paid RM2.2 million a day. The structure was designed by American architect Cesar Pelli and the surrounding park by the Brazilian landscape artist Roberto Marx.

There have been efforts to create a 'new Malaysian architecture', to lend the city a more integrated look and a national identity. Such buildings include the modern-Islamic National Mosque, the National Museum and the Putra World Trade Centre (the latter two have *Minangkabau*-style roofs) and the 34-storey Dayabumi complex, by the river, with its modern Islamic latticed arches. At the same time, KL has also been trying to cultivate a 'garden city' image like neighbouring Singapore; from the top of its sky-scrapers, KL looks green and spacious, although green areas are fast being taken over by building developments.

For years, KL enjoyed a reputation as the least-congested capital in Southeast Asia. But this has changed of late. As if to finally cement this transition from provincial outpost to thrusting capital, in September

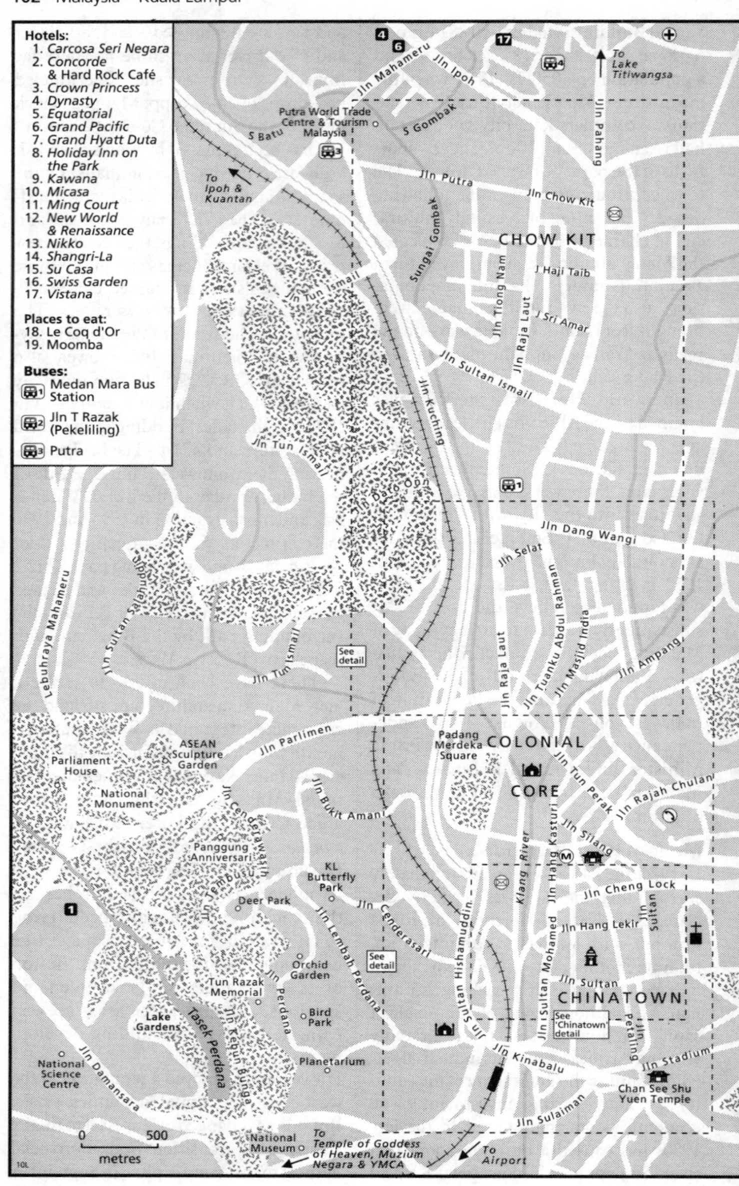
Hotels:
1. Carcosa Seri Negara
2. Concorde & Hard Rock Café
3. Crown Princess
4. Dynasty
5. Equatorial
6. Grand Pacific
7. Grand Hyatt Duta
8. Holiday Inn on the Park
9. Kawana
10. Micasa
11. Ming Court
12. New World & Renaissance
13. Nikko
14. Shangri-La
15. Su Casa
16. Swiss Garden
17. Vistana
Places to eat:
18. Le Coq d'Or
19. Moomba
Buses:
1 Medan Mara Bus Station
2 Jln T Razak (Pekeliling)
3 Putra
Jln Mahameru
Jln Ipoh
To Lake Titiwangsa
Putra World Trade Centre & Tourism Malaysia
S Batu
S Gombak
Jln Pahang
To Ipoh & Kuantan
Jln Putra
Jln Chow Kit
Sungai Gombak
CHOW KIT
J Haji Taib
Jln Tiong Nam
Jln Raja Laut
J Sri Amar
Jln Tun Ismail
Jln Sultan Ismail
Jln Kuching
Jln Dato Onn
Jln Dang Wangi
Jln Selat
Jln Tuanku Abdul Rahman
Jln Masjid India
Jln Sultan Salahuddin
Lebuhraya Mahameru
See detail
Jln Ampang
Jln Parlimen
Padang Merdeka Square
COLONIAL CORE
ASEAN Sculpture Garden
Parliament House
National Monument
Jln Cenderawasih
Jln Bukit Aman
Jln Tun Perak
Jln Rajah Chulan
Jln Silang
Panggung Anniversari
Jln Tembusu
KL Butterfly Park
Deer Park
Jln Cenderasari
Klang River
Jln Hang Kasturi
Jln Cheng Lock
Jln Hang Lekir
Jln Sultan
Jln Lembah Perdana
Orchid Garden
Tun Razak Memorial
Jln Perdana
Bird Park
Jln Sultan Hishamuddin
Jln Sultan Mohamed
CHINATOWN
See 'Chinatown' detail
Jln Petaling
Lake Gardens
Tasek Perdana
Jln Kebun Bunga
Jln Kinabalu
Jln Stadium
National Science Centre
Jln Damansara
Planetarium
Chan See Shu Yuen Temple
Jln Sulaiman
0 500 metres
National Museum
To Temple of Goddess of Heaven, Muzium Negara & YMCA
To Airport

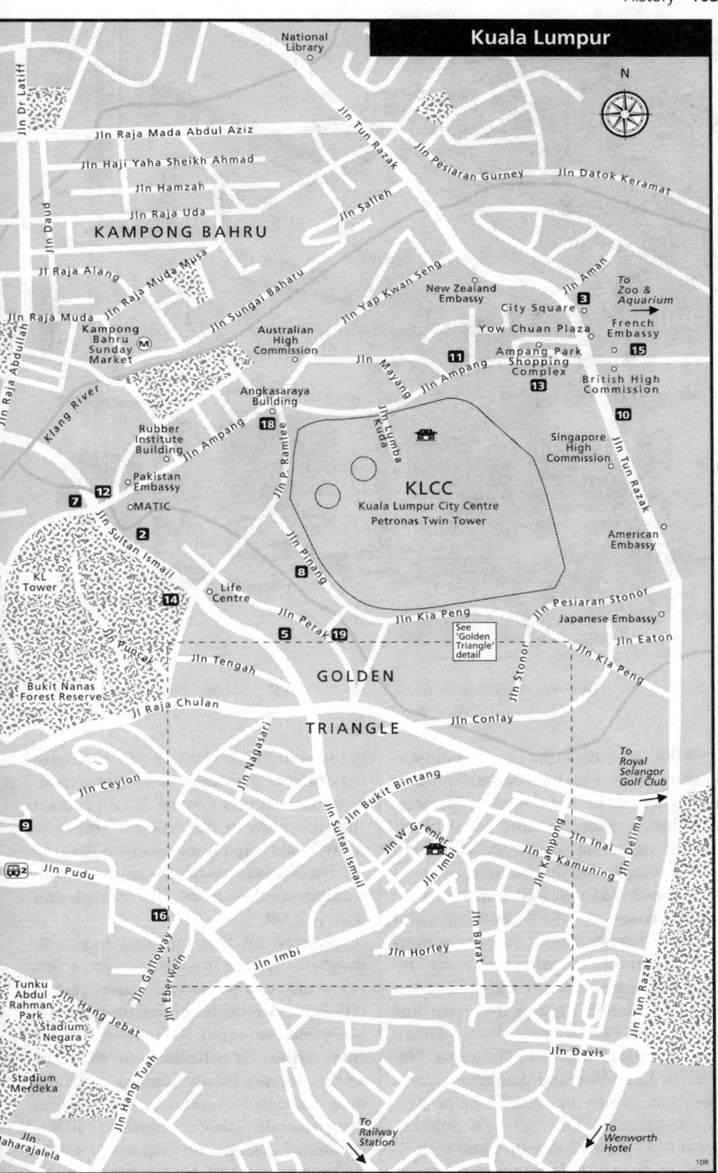
Kuala Lumpur
N
National Library
Jln Dr Latiff
Jln Raja Mada Abdul Aziz
Jln Haji Yaha Sheikh Ahmad
Jln Hamzah
Jln Raja Uda
Jln Daud
KAMPONG BAHRU
Jl Raja Alang
Jln Raja Muda Musa
Jln Raja Muda
Jln Raja Abdullah
Kampong Bahru Sunday Market
Jln Sungai Baharu
Jln Tun Razak
Jln Pesiaran Gurney
Jln Datok Keramat
Jln Salleh
Jln Yap Kwan Seng
New Zealand Embassy
Jln Aman
To Zoo & Aquarium
City Square
Yow Chuan Plaza
French Embassy
Australian High Commission
Jln Mayang
Jln Ampang
Ampang Park Shopping Complex
British High Commission
Klang River
Angkasaraya Building
Rubber Institute Building
Jln Ampang
Jln P. Ramlee
Jln Lumba Kuda
Singapore High Commission
Jln Tun Razak
Pakistan Embassy
MATIC
KLCC
Kuala Lumpur City Centre
Petronas Twin Tower
Jln Sultan Ismail
American Embassy
Jln Pinang
KL Tower
Life Centre
Jln Pesiaran Stonor
Jln Perak
Jln Kia Peng
Japanese Embassy
See 'Golden Triangle' detail
Jln Eaton
Jln Puncak
Jln Tengah
Jln Kia Peng
GOLDEN
Jln Stonor
Bukit Nanas Forest Reserve
Jl Raja Chulan
TRIANGLE
Jln Conlay
Jln Nagasari
To Royal Selangor Golf Club
Jln Ceylon
Jln Bukit Bintang
Jln Sultan Ismail
Jln W Grenier
Jln Inai
Jln Imbi
Jln Kampong
Jln Kamuning
Jln Delima
Jln Pudu
Jln Barat
Jln Horley
Jln Imbi
Jln Galloway
Jln Eberwein
Tunku Abdul Rahman Park
Jln Hang Jebat
Stadium Negara
Jln Tun Razak
Jln Davis
Stadium Merdeka
Jln Hang Tuah
To Railway Station
To Wenworth Hotel
Jln Maharajalela
3
11
15
13
10
18
12
7
2
8
14
5
19
9
16

The town residence (in Jalan Pudu) of the last Captain China, drawing by RD Jackson, c1910

1998 KL will host the XVI Commonwealth Games. This has provoked numerous large scale development projects including a dozen or more 5-star hotels (KL is expecting an influx of around 60,000 tourists for the Games), the construction of the Light Rail Transit or LRT which connects the Commonwealth Games village to the city, and a new international airport 45 km south of the city (due for completion in 1998). Phase I of the LRT system linking the main bus terminals of Putra Centre (Sultan Ismail Station) and Puduraya (Puduraya Station) to Loke Yew and Ampang is complete but is only marginally helping to ease congestion. The 'network' only extends to a single 12 km-long line with 13 stops, so most of KL's commuters are not yet served. Phase II which will run south may help to provide a more comprehensive mass transit system. It is a project that has been in the pipeline since the early 1980s when it was decided that the KL basin was geologically unsuited to an underground railway. Its completion date is 1999.

Frankly, all this building has done much to detract from what, just a few years ago, was a relatively quiet capital city. But as well as becoming increasingly noisy and congested, KL is also suffering from serious air pollution – or 'the haze' as it is known locally. The cause of the haze is widely thought to be the fires that burn uncontrollably in Sumatra (and Kalimantan) during the Summer months (between July and September). At the

The only legal Hash in Malaysia

Around the turn of the century, the annual dare in colonial KL involved swimming from the Royal Selangor Club terrace to the State Secretariat and back when the Klang River flooded the Padang. But the *Spotted Dog*, as the club was affectionately known, was also home to another eccentric sporting event which caught on around the world. The **Hash**, a cross-country chase – which is invariably followed by a drinking bout – was started in 1938, when the Selangor Club was the preferred watering hole for colonial bachelors. A Mr GS Gisbert, having drunk too much at the Long Bar, went for a jog around the Padang to sober up. In no time, Mr Gilbert's Hash had a band of disciples who took to the new sport with varying degrees of seriousness.

The run, named after the Club's dining room, the Hash House, ventured into the countryside surrounding KL where 'hounds' chased 'hares' – along a paper trail. The KL hash, known as the 'mother hash' to **Hash House Harriers** around the world (there are now 300 clubs in more than 60 countries) normally involves runs of 3-8 km, which are usually fairly jovial affairs. Most big Malaysian towns have a Hash and there are several branches in KL – men-only, women-only and mixed. Although popular among expatriates, many locals participate these days and visitors are welcome. (For details, contact Kuala Lumpur Hash House Harriers, PO Box 10182, KL; T 2484846.)

end of 1994, pollution levels at Shah Alam, a suburb of KL, reached '500'. '300' is deemed hazardous by the authorities. Visibility was down to 400m, making landings at KL's airport difficult. But though the root cause of the haze may be fires in Indonesia, it is when this smoke mixes with car fumes and other emission that it becomes downright dangerous. Locals also note the convenience of being able to blame fires in another country for pollution problems at home: it means the authorities don't have to do anything about it. Whenever environmentalists have suggested ways to reduce pollution in the capital they have got nowhere. Instead, while KL hospitals fill up with children suffering from bronchial problems, the health ministry feebly recommends that Malaysians wear surgical masks and give up exercising outside. "But", as S Jayasankaran wrote in 1997, "the ministry can't advise them to stop breathing."

Orientation

The streets to the north of the Padang – the cricket pitch in front of the old Selangor Club, next to the new Merdeka Square – are central shopping streets with modern department stores and smaller shops.

The colonial core is around the Padang and down Jalan Raja and Jalan Tun Perak. East of the Padang, straight over the bridge on Lebuh Pasar Besar is the main commercial area, occupied by banks and finance companies. To the southeast of Merdeka Square is KL's vibrant Chinatown.

To find a distinctively Malay area, it is necessary to venture further out, along Jalan Raja Muda Musa to Kampung Baru, to the northeast.

To the south of Kampung Baru, on the opposite side of the Klang River, is Jalan Ampang, once KL's 'millionaires' row' – where tin towkays and sultans first built their homes. The road is now mainly occupied by embassies and high commissions. To the southeast of Jalan Ampang is KL's so-called Golden Triangle, to which the modern central business district has migrated. In recent years the city's residential districts have been expanding out towards the jungled hills surrounding the KL basin, at the far end of Ampang, past the zoo to the north, and to Bangsar, to the southwest. KL has become a city of condominiums, which have sprung up everywhere from the centre of town to these outlying suburbs. Greater Kuala Lumpur sprawls out into the Klang Valley, once plantation country and now home to the industrial satellites of Petaling Jaya and Shah Alam.

The most recent – and grandiose – development is Putrajaya, Malaysia's new administrative capital, which is being hacked out of plantations 35 km south of KL. When it is completed in 2005, Putrajaya's projected population will be 250,000, although its first bureaucrats are due to be relocated from congested KL as soon as 1998. The city will cost a cool US$8bn. Other developments in this area to the south of KL include the new international airport which will open in 1998 (45 km from KL) and the Cyberjaya, the heart of Malaysia's much vaunted Multimedia Super Corridor.

PLACES OF INTEREST

KL's sights are spread thinly over a wide area which makes life difficult for the visitor. Any distance on foot is a bit of trial, with uneven and hazardous – sometimes non-existent – pavements. (Like other Southeast Asian cities, with the notable exception of Singapore, the internal combustion engine rules and little consideration seems to be given to the lowly pedestrian, either by drivers or planners.) The bus system is not easily deciphered and congested streets means that jumping in a taxi can make for a tedious wait in a traffic jam. Taxis are probably your best option however – try and insist drivers use their meters, although do not be surprised if they simply refuse point blank.

THE COLONIAL CORE AND THE NATIONAL MOSQUE

At the muddy confluence of the Klang and Gombak rivers where KL's founders stepped ashore, stands the Masjid Jamek, formerly the National Mosque (main entrance on Jalan Tun Perak). Built in 1909, English architect, A B Hubbock's design was based on that of a Moghul mosque in North India. The mosque has a walled courtyard – or *sahn* – and a 3-domed prayer hall. It is striking with its striped white and salmon-coloured brickwork and domed minarets, cupolas and arches. Surrounded by coconut palms, the mosque is an oasis of peace in the middle of modern KL, as is testified by the number of Malays who sleep through the heat of the lunchtime rush-hour on the prayer hall's cool marbled floors. Open 0900-1100, 1400-1600 daily.

Behind the mosque, from the corner of Jalan Tuanku Abdul Rahman and Jalan Raja Laut, are the colonial-built public buildings, distinguished by their grand, Moorish architecture. All were the creation of A C Norman, a colleague of Hubbock's, and were built between 1894 and 1897. The photogenic former State Secretariat, now called the **Sultan Abdul Samad – or SAS – Building**, with its distinctive clock tower and bulbous copper domes, houses the Supreme Court. To the south of here is another Moorish building awaiting renovation, to become a **Textile Museum**, T 2917136 for information.

Sultan Abdul Samad Building faces onto the **Padang** on the opposite side of the road, next to **Merdeka Square**. The old Selangor Club cricket pitch is the venue for Independence Day celebrations. The centrepiece of Merdeka Square is the tallest flagpole in the world (100m high) and the huge Malaysian flag that flies from the top can be seen across half the city, particularly at night when it is floodlit. The Padang was trimmed to make way for the square, which is also the venue for impromptu rock concerts and is a popular meeting place. A shopping complex has been built underneath the square.

The very British mock-Tudor **Royal Selangor Club** fronts the Padang and was the centre of colonial society after its construction in 1890. Much of the building was damaged by a fire in the late 1960s and the north wing was built in 1970. The

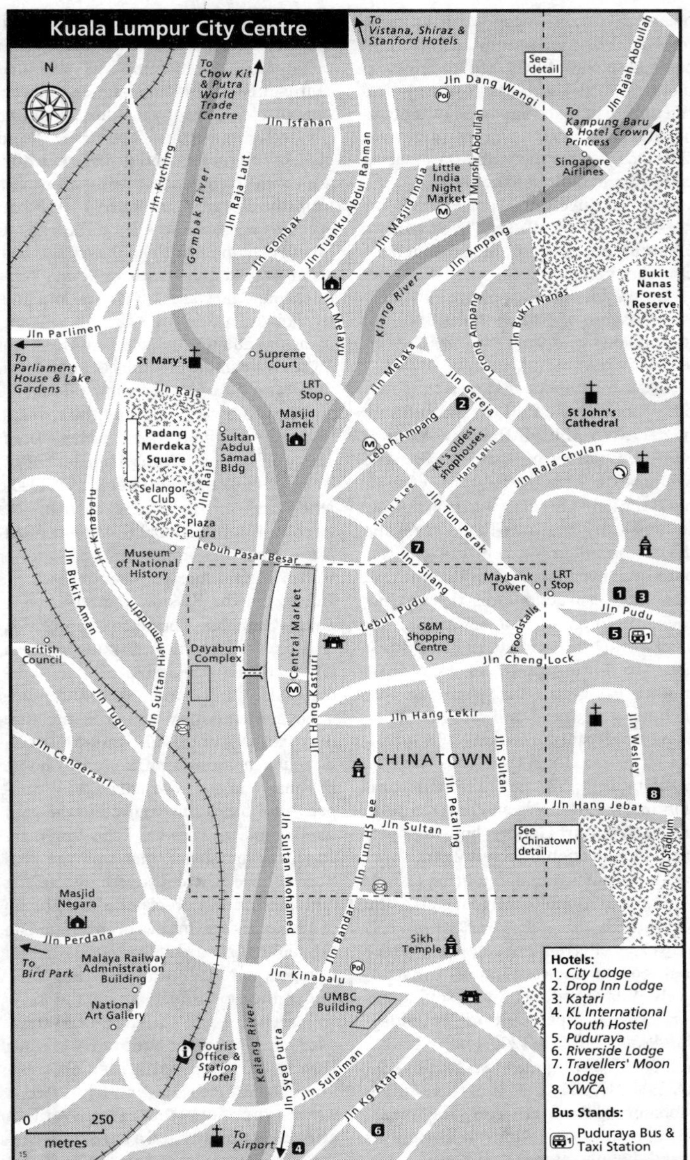
Kuala Lumpur City Centre
N
To Vistana, Shiraz & Stanford Hotels
To Chow Kit & Putra World Trade Centre
See detail
Jln Dang Wangi
Jln Rajah Abdullah
Jln Isfahan
To Kampung Baru & Hotel Crown Princess
Singapore Airlines
Jln Kuching
Gombak River
Jln Raja Laut
Jln Tuanku Abdul Rahman
Little India Night Market
Jl Munshi Abdullah
Jln Masjid India
Jln Gombak
Jln Ampang
Bukit Nanas Forest Reserve
Jln Bukit Nanas
Lorong Ampang
Klang River
Jln Melayu
Jln Parlimen
To Parliament House & Lake Gardens
St Mary's
Supreme Court
LRT Stop
Jln Melaka
Jln Gereja
St John's Cathedral
Jln Raja
Padang Merdeka Square
Sultan Abdul Samad Bldg
Masjid Jamek
Leboh Ampang
KL's oldest shophouses
Hang Lekiu
Jln Raja Chulan
Selangor Club
Jln Raja
Plaza Putra
Tun H S Lee
Jln Tun Perak
Jln Kinabalu
Museum of National History
Lebuh Pasar Besar
Jln Silang
Maybank Tower
LRT Stop
Jln Bukit Aman
Jln Sultan Hishamuddin
Central Market
Lebuh Pudu
Foodstalls
Jln Pudu
S&M Shopping Centre
British Council
Dayabumi Complex
Jln Cheng Lock
Jln Hang Kasturi
Jln Tugu
Jln Hang Lekir
Jln Wesley
Jln Cendersari
CHINATOWN
Jln Sultan
Jln Petaling
Jln Hang Jebat
Jln Sultan Mohamed
Jln Tun HS Lee
Jln Sultan
See 'Chinatown' detail
Jln Stadium
Masjid Negara
Jln Perdana
Jln Bandar
Sikh Temple
To Bird Park
Malaya Railway Administration Building
Jln Kinabalu
UMBC Building
National Art Gallery
Tourist Office & Station Hotel
Kelang River
Jln Syed Putra
Jln Sulaiman
Jln Kg Atap
0 250 metres
To Airport
Hotels:
1. City Lodge
2. Drop Inn Lodge
3. Katari
4. KL International Youth Hostel
5. Puduraya
6. Riverside Lodge
7. Travellers' Moon Lodge
8. YWCA
Bus Stands:
1 Puduraya Bus & Taxi Station

Selangor Club is still a gathering place for KL's VIPs. It has one of the finest colonial saloons, filled with trophies and pictures of cricket teams. Non-members can only visit if accompanied by a member and the famous Long Bar (known as 'The Dog') – which contains a fascinating collection of old photographs of KL – is still an exclusively male preserve. On the north side of the Padang is **St Mary's Church**, one of the oldest Anglican churches built in 1894.

On the south side of Merdeka Square is a **Museum of National History**, limited displays, open 0900-1800, daily, T 2944590.

In 1910 Hubbock designed the fairy-tale Moorish-style **Railway Station** and, in 1917, the **Malaya Railway Administration Building**, opposite. Beneath the Islamic exterior of the former, the building is similar to the glass and iron railway stations constructed in England during the Victorian era – except this one was built by convict labour. It is said that the station's construction was delayed because the original roof design did not meet British railway specifications – it had to be able to support 1m of snow. The interior has been refurbished and now includes restaurants and souvenir stalls.

Also opposite the station on Jalan Sultan Hishamuddin is the former *Majestic Hotel*, built in 1932. Saved from demolition in 1983, it has been converted into the **National Art Gallery**, housing a permanent collection of about 2,000 works by Malaysian artists and touring exhibitions. For a chronological tour start at the top of the building and work down. It is a diverse collection but refreshing to see that most of the work retains a distinctively Malay spirit, some of it exciting and very original. Open 1000-1800 Monday-Sunday. Closed 1200-1500 Friday. T 2300157. *Getting there*: Sri Jaya bus 30, 47, 238, 247, 251, 252, 337 (from Sultan Mohammad Bus Station) or Mini Bus 22, 33, 35, 38 (from Bangkok Bank Bus Stand, Lebuh Pasar).

To the north of the railway station and the art gallery is **Masjid Negara** (National Mosque), the modern spiritual centre of KL's Malay population and the symbol of Islam for the whole country. Abstract, geometric shapes have been used in the roofing and grillwork, while the Grand Hall is decorated with verses from the Koran. Completed in 1965, it occupies a 5-hectare site at the end of Jalan Hishamuddin. The prayer hall has a star-shaped dome with 18 points, representing Malaysia's 13 states and the five pillars of Islam. The 48 smaller domes emulate the great mosque in Mecca. The single minaret is 73m tall and the grand hall can accommodate 8,000 people. An annex contains the mausoleum of Tun Abdul Razak, independent Malaysia's second Prime Minister. Open 0900-1800 Saturday-Thursday, 1445-1800 Friday. Muslims can visit the mosque from 0630-2200. Women must use a separate entrance.

North of the mosque, back towards the Padang, is the 35-storey, marble **Dayabumi Complex**. Located on Jalan Raya, it is one of KL's most striking modern landmarks. It was designed by local architect Datuk Nik Mohamed, and introduces contemporary Islamic achitecture to the skyscraper era. The government office-cum-shopping centre used to house Petronas, the secretive national oil company, which has since moved to the even more grandiose Petronas Twin Tower. Try getting permission to stand on the 30th floor helipad where a superb, but fading (and increasingly obsolete) pictorial map of all the city's sights has been painted on the rooftop. Next door to the Dayabumi Complex is the General Post Office.

On the opposite bank to the Dayabumi complex, is the **Central Market**, a former wet market built in 1928 in Art Deco-style, tempered with 'local Baroque' trimmings. In the early 1980s it was revamped to become a focus for KL's artistic community and a handicraft centre – KL's version of London's Covent

Garden or San Francisco's Fisherman's Wharf. It is a warren of boutiques, handicraft and souvenir stalls – some with their wares laid out on the wet market's original marble slabs – and is now a bit of a tourist trap, although it is definitely worth visiting for a one-stop buying spree. On the second level of the market are several restaurants and a small hawker centre.

CHINATOWN

(See map, page 121.) Southeast of the Central Market, lies Chinatown, roughly bounded by Jalan Bandar, Jalan Petaling and Jalan Sultan. It was the core of Yap Ah Loy's KL (see page 100) and is a mixture of crumbling shophouses, market stalls, coffee shops and restaurants. This quarter wakes up during late afternoon (after about 1630) and evening, when its streets become the centre of frenetic trading and haggling. Jalan Petaling (and parts of Jalan Sultan) are transformed into an open air night market (*pasar malam*) and food stalls selling Chinese, Indian and Malay delicacies, fruit stalls, copy watch stalls, music cassettes, leather bag stalls and all manner of impromptu boutiques line the streets. Jalan Hang Lekir, which straddles the gap between Jalan Sultan and Jalan Petaling, is full of popular Chinese restaurants and coffee shops. Off the north side of Jalan Hang Lekir, there is a lively covered fruit and vegetable market in two intersecting arcades.

South of Jalan Hang Lekir, tucked away on Jalan Tun H S Lee (Jalan Bandar)

Petaling Street on a quiet day; the processional route of Chinese feast days, drawing by RD Jackson, C1910

is the extravagantly decorated **Sri Mahamariamman Temple**, incorporating gold, precious stones and Spanish and Italian tiles. It was founded in 1873 by Tamils who had come to Malaya as contract labourers to work in the rubber plantations or on the roads and railways. Its construction was funded by the wealthy Chettiar money-lending caste, and it was rebuilt on its present site in 1985. It has a silver chariot dedicated to Lord Murugan (Subramaniam), which is taken in procession to the Batu Caves (see page 114) during the Thaipusam festival, when Hindu devotees converge on the temple. The best time to visit is on Friday lunchtimes, from 1230, when Muslims head off to the mosques. Large numbers flock to the temple to participate in the ritual; this is usually preceded by about half an hour's chanting, accompanied by music. In testament to Malaysia's sometimes muddled ethnic and religious mix, it is not uncommon to find Chinese devotees joining in the ceremony.

There are two prominent Chinese temples in the Chinatown area. The elaborate **Chan See Shu Yuen Temple**, at the southernmost end of Jalan Petaling was built in 1906 and has a typical open courtyard and symmetrical pavilions. Paintings, woodcarvings and ceramic sculptures decorate the façade. It serves both as a place of worship and as a community centre. The older **Sze Ya Temple**, close to the central market on Lebuh Pudu, off Jalan Cheng Lock, was built in the 1880s on land donated by Yap Ah Loy. He also funded the temple's construction and a photograph of him sits on one of the altars. Ancestor worship is more usually confined to the numerous ornate clan houses (*kongsis*); a typical one is the **Chan Kongsi** on Jalan Maharajalela, near the Chan See Shu Yuen Temple.

South of Chinatown, off Jalan Stadium is the 50,000-capacity **Merdeka Stadium**, the site of Malaysia's declaration of independence on 31 August 1957 (*merdeka* means 'freedom' in Malay). National and international sports events are held at the stadium (the famous Mohammad Ali vs. Joe Bugner fight was staged here in 1975) as well as the annual international Koran reading competition, held during Ramadan.

LAKE GARDENS AREA

Overlooking Jalan Damansara, near the south tip of the Lake Gardens, is the **Muzium Negara** (National Museum), with its traditional *Minangkabau*-style roof, and two large murals of Italian glass mosaic either side of the main entrance. They depict the main historical episodes and cultural activities of Malaysia. The museum's displays of photographs, models, artefacts and dioramas (with English-language texts) are excellent introductions to Malaysia's history, geography, natural history and culture. A Straits Chinese house from Melaka has been reconstructed in one gallery and the possessions and collections of various sultans are on show in another. The *Kris* exhibit is worth seeing and the fauna section is good. Over the next few years there is talk that the present museum building will become the Museum of Culture and a Museum of Natural Science may open near Titiwangsa Lake Gardens, on the city's north outskirts. Admission RM1. Open 0900-1800 Monday-Sunday. Closed 1200-1430 Friday. T 2826255.

Close to the museum is the south entrance to the man-made **Lake Gardens** (Taman Tasek Perdana), a 91.6-hecatare park, a joggers' paradise and popular city escape. Pedal boats can be hired on the main lake (Tasek Perdana) at the weekend. The Gardens also hold a Hibiscus Garden (Taman Bunga Raya) with over 500 species, an Orchid Garden (Taman Bunga Orkid) which has over 800 species and is transformed into an orchid market at weekends, children's playgrounds, picnic areas, restaurants and cafés, and a small deer park. At the north end of the Lake Gardens is the **National Monument**. Located at the far side of Jalan

Parlimen, it provides a good view of Parliament House. The memorial, over 15m tall, with its dramatically-posed sculpted figures, is dedicated to the heroes of Malaya's 12-years Communist Emergency (see page 57). The state of emergency was lifted in 1960, but members of the banned Communist Party managed to put a bomb under the memorial in 1975. Below the monument is a sculpture garden with exhibits from all over ASEAN – the Association of South East Asian Nations.

The showpiece of the Lake Gardens is the **Taman Burung** or **Bird Park**. Opened in 1991 in an effort to out-do neighbouring Singapore's famous Jurong Bird Park, this aviary is twice the size of Jurong, and encloses over 2,000 birds of 200 species, from ducks to hornbills. Spread out over 8 acres of naturally landscaped gardens, most of the birds are free and very accustomed to being around people. The hornbill area is particularly exciting. It houses seven varieties of hornbill, most of which are local. A further 10 acres is under development and will eventually provide spacious enclosures for birds currently in cages. Reference centre, refreshment kiosk and binoculars for hire. Admission RM5, child RM2. Open 0800-1800 Monday-Sunday.

The Kuala Lumpur Butterfly Park, is a 5 minute drive from the main entrance of the Lake Gardens, coming in from Jalan Parlimen. It is a miniature jungle which is home to almost 8,000 butterflies, from 150 species. There are also small mammals, amphibians and reptiles, and rare tropical insects in the park. There is an insect museum and souvenir shop on the site. Admission adult RM5, child RM2. RM1 admission to film. Open 0900-1700 Monday-Friday and 0900-1800 Saturday and Sunday.

On the southeast edge of the park is **Tun Razak Memorial**, the former residence of Malaysia's revered second prime minister, the late Tun Abdul Razak, whose great, great, great, great, great grandfather, Sultan Abdullah of Kedah, ceded Penang to the British (see page 177). In recognition of his services – he is popularly known as the father of Malaysia's development – his old home has been turned into a memorial with the aim of preserving his documents, speeches, books and awards, including his collection of walking sticks and pipes. T 2912111. Open 0900-1800 Tuesday-Sunday. Closed 1200-1500 Friday. At the southern end of the Lake Gardens is the **National Planetarium**. The planetarium has a theatre with a 20m diameter dome screen where the Space Science Show and Sky movies are projected. Other facilities include an exhibition hall, an observatory, a viewing gallery. Admission, Space Science Show adult RM3, child RM2, Sky movie adult RM6, child RM4, exhibition RM1. Open 1000-1700 Tuesday-Friday, 1000-1900 Saturday, Sunday, closed 1200-1430 Friday. First space show 1100. T 2735484.

The modern 18-storey **Parliament House** and its Toblerone-shaped House of Representatives is on the west fringe of the gardens. When parliament is in session, visitors may observe parliamentary proceedings (permission must be formally obtained beforehand), and must be smartly dressed. In years gone by, many of the administrative arms of government were housed in the State Secretariat (now renamed the Sultan Abdul Samad Building) on the Padang. Most of the main government ministries are now situated in scruffy 1960s suburban office blocks off Jalan Duta, to the west.

Getting to Lake Gardens: Buses 244 and 250 from Sultan Mohammed Bus Station and minibus 18, 21, 46, 48 from Jalan Tun Perak. Taxis away from the park can be difficult to obtain – it may be worth chartering one to wait for you or booking one in advance.

JALAN AMPANG

Jalan Ampang became the home of KL's early tin millionaires and an important leafy adjunct to the colonial capital. The styles of its stately mansions ranged from Art Deco and mock-Palladian to Islamic. Today many of these buildings have become embassies and consulates. One of the lovelier **Art Deco-style buildings** now houses the **Rubber Research Institute**. Another of Jalan Ampang's fine old buildings is the old **Coq D'Or restaurant**, formerly the residence of a Chinese tin mogul, and still a great place for dinner and 'stengahs' on the terrace (*setengah* is Malay for 'half', and became the colonial term for shots of whisky and water). Further into town, another renovated house is now the **Malaysian Tourist Information Centre (MATIC)**, T 2643929. It was the headquarters of the Japanese Imperial Army during World War Two, but was originally built in 1935 by Eu Tong Seng, a wealthy Chinese rubber planter and tin mogul. Matic is a one-stop visitors centre, as well as having a tourist information counter, it has money changing facilities, an express bus ticketing counter, reservations for package holidays, a souvenir shop, Malay restaurant, cultural shows every Tuesday, Thursday and Sunday at 1530, and audio visual shows. The intersection of Jalan Ampang and the old circular road, Jalan Tun Razak, has become a booming shopping area in the shape of Ampang Park and City Square shopping centres.

The old Selangor Turf Club racecourse, which lies to the south-east of this intersection, is the focus of extraordinary redevelopment in the guise of the **KLCC** or **Kuala Lumpur City Centre** project –

Kuala Lumpur's golden triangle

High-rise development came late to KL but has rapidly gained a foothold; the city's offices, hotels and new shopping complexes are mostly concentrated in the 'Golden Triangle', on the east side of the city, near the former race course which is now being developed as the KLCC (Kuala Lumpur City Centre). When completed it will be one of the largest real estate developments in the world. Covering a 40-ha site, the first phase of the KLCC project is already well underway, although it will be another 10-15 years before the scheme is finally completed. The first phase includes the construction of the Petronas Twin Towers, 88-storeys high and 450m tall, which on completion made it the tallest building in the world. The pair of gleaming pinnacles are joined at the 41st and 42nd floor by the Skybridge which is a remarkable 170m above street level. It is almost 60m long, weighs 750 tonnes and is supported by a 2-hinge arch. The towers will provide 427,500 square metres of office space, an art gallery, an 850-seat concert hall, and a Petroleum Discovery Centre. The Ampang Tower, a mere 50-storey office block, is part of phase one, as is a crescent-shaped retail and entertainment centre on the junction of Jalan Ampang and Jalan P Ramlee, the 20-storey Esso Tower, a 20-hectare park with a children's playground and the *Mandarin Oriental Hotel* which will be a 5-star establishment with over 600 rooms. Jalan Bukit Bintang and Jalan Sultan Ismail was where the first modern hotels and shopping complexes went up – the *Regent*, the *Hilton*, the *Equatorial*, *Holiday Inn*, *Shangri-La* and *Concorde*. More recently the area around Jalan Ampang and Jalan Tun Razak has been transformed into a commercial centre; several towers have sprung up in the area in recent years, including the MBf building and the extraordinary hour-glass-shaped Pilgrims' Building, which coordinates the annual Haj and looks after the pilgrims' funds. There are several further developments planned for the Golden Triangle before the Commonwealth Games, including a new *Sheraton* and *Hyatt* both 5-star tower block hotels. One of the newest shopping plazas in the Golden Triangle is *Star Hill Plaza* on Jalan Bukit Bintang, next to the new 5-star *Marriott Hotel*.

a 'city within a city', set on a 40 hectare site. High-rise development came comparatively late to KL, but now that it has arrived the city's developers and planners seem intent on making up for lost time. Many of the most grandiose projects are concentrated in the KLCC area and none is more grandiose than the **Petronas Twin Towers**. This pair of 88 storey, 421m-high towers was designed by Cesar Pelli using Islamic-inspired geometric motifs. On its completion in 1996 the towers became the tallest building(s) in the world. The gleaming pinnacles are joined at the 41st and 42nd storeys by a Skybridge which itself is a remarkable 170m above street level. The bridge is almost 60m long, weighs 750 tonnes and is supported by a two hinge arch. Gazing up at the Skybridge, it is hard not to wonder – and hope – that the engineers got their maths right and the contractors stuck to their brief. In March 1997 'Spiderman', a Frenchman whose life work seems to be to scale tall buildings the world over, was arrested whilst ascending Tower 1 of the Petronas Twin Towers. Using no safety gear, he had reached the 60th floor before the police were able to apprehend him. (In November 1996 he was arrested in Hong Kong after scaling the tallest building there.) The towers provide 427,500 sq metres of office space, an art gallery, an 860-seat concert hall, and a Petroleum Discovery Centre. Other buildings that constitute Phase I of the KLCC development include: the **Ampang Tower** (a miserly 50-storeys tall); **Suria KLCC**, a crescent-shaped retail and entertainment centre with six levels of shopping, restaurants and a 13 screen cineplex; the 30-storey Esso Tower; a 20 hectare park with a children's playground, jogging track and bird sanctuary; and the 600 plus room *Mandarin Hotel*.

Near the intersection of Jalan Ampang and Jalan Sultan Ismail atop Bukit Nanas stands the **KL Tower**, or **Menara KL**. This 421m-high telecommunications tower is the tallest such tower in Asia and the third tallest in the world – and, characteristically, the brain-child of PM Dr Mahathir Mohammed. A trip up to the observation deck should head most peoples' list of 'things to do', as the view from the top is astonishing, giving the visitor an idea of the sheer scale of development taking place in the city – in particular in the KL City Centre area. Admission RM8, RM4 for children, T 2085421. Open 1000-2130, Monday-Sunday. At ground level, there are several shops and fast food restaurants and a mini amphitheatre. Above the viewing platform is the *Seri Angkasa* revolving restaurant. Excellent Malay cuisine and one revolution every 60 minutes so diners get to see the whole city between hors d'oeuvre and ice cream – should they remember to raise their heads from the trough. T 2085055 for reservation. *Getting there*: no public transport – take a taxi or walk from one of the surrounding roads.

AROUND THE CITY AREA

The US$150mn **Putra World Trade Centre** (Kompleks Seni Budaya, Jalan Conlay), to the north of the city centre on Jalan Tun Ismail, took nearly 15 years to materialize, but when it opened in 1985, Malaysia proudly announced that it was finally on the international convention and trade fair circuit. The luxurious complex of buildings includes the *Pan-Pacific Hotel*, a sleek 41-storey office block and an exhibition centre, adorned with a traditional *Minangkabau* roof. The headquarters of Prime Minister Dr Mahathir Mohamad's ruling United Malays National Organization (UMNO) occupies the top floors and there is a tourist information centre on the second floor.

The **Karyaneka Handicraft Centre** (Kompleks Seni Budaya) is on Jalan Conlay to the east of the city centre (see Around the Golden Triangle map). A small museum illustrates batik, weaving and pottery processes. Craft demonstrations from 1000-1800. There is a selection of crafts for sale from each of the 13 states of Malaysia – popular tour group spot. Open 0900-1800 Monday-Sunday. *Getting there*: minibus or intrakota no.40 from Jalan Tuanku Abdul Rahman.

East of the Karyaneka Handicraft Centre, on Jalan Bukit Bintang, is the **Jade Museum**. This small museum houses a private collection of 80 jade artefacts from China. Replicas and jade souvenirs are for sale. Or, so it seems: in 1997 a case of tourists being sold fake rubies was under investigation by the police and it is likely that the authorities will take action against the museum. Admission RM10. Open 1000-1900 Monday-Sunday. *Getting there*: Sri Jaya bus 18 from Klang Bus Station.

Thean Hou Temple or the **Temple of the Goddess of Heaven** is situated at Jalan Klang Lama (off Jalan Tun Sambathan, to the southwest of the city). Perched on a hill, it has a panoramic view over KL. A contemporary Buddhist pagoda and Buddha images are enshrined in the octagonal hall. It stands between a sacred Bodhi tree and a Buddhist shrine, built by Sinhalese Buddhists in 1894. *Getting there*: minibus 27 from Kelang bus terminal to Jalan Syed Putra.

EXCURSIONS

North

Batu Caves are a system of caverns set high in a massive limestone outcrop 13 km north of KL – they were 'discovered' by American naturalist William Hornaby in the 1880s. In 1891 Hindu priests set up a shrine in the main cave dedicated to Lord Subramaniam and it has now become the biggest Indian pilgrimage centre in Malaysia during the annual Thaipusam festival (see page 522) when over 800,000 Hindus congregate here.

The main cave is reached by a steep flight of 272 steps. Coloured lights provide illumination for the fantasy features and formations of the karst limestone cavern. There are a number of other less spectacular caves in the outcrop, including the Museum Cave (at ground level) displaying elaborate sculptures of Hindu mythology (RM1). During World War Two, the Japanese Imperial Army used some of the caves as factories for the manufacture of ammunition and as arms dumps; the concrete foundations for the machinery can be seen at the foot of the cliffs. *Getting there*: Intrakota or minibus 11 from Central Market. The caves are a short walk off the main road.

Templer Park is about 10 km further on up the main road from the turn-off to the Batu Caves. Covering 500 hectares, it serves as Kuala Lumpur's nearest jungle playground, apart from the tiny Bukit Nanas Forest Reserve in the middle of the city. It opened as a park in 1954 and is named after the last British High Commissioner of Malaya, Sir Gerald Templer, 'the Tiger of Malaya', who oversaw the tactical defeat of the Communist insurgents during the Emergency (see page 57). The park is dominated by several impressive 350m-high limestone hills and outcrops, the biggest being **Bukit Takun** and **Bukit Anak Takun** (similar to the Batu Caves outcrop).

There are extensive networks of underground passages and cave systems within the hills, thought to have formed 400 million years ago. Unfortunately a huge new floodlit golf course has impinged on the north boundaries of the park making access to some of these massifs more difficult – and another 180 hectares golf resort is being developed. The park has a wide variety of jungle flora and fauna. Templer Park is a popular venue for boy scout and youth camps and tends to attract swarms of day-trippers at weekends – although most of them do not venture much beyond the car park and picnic area. Nearby are the **Kanching Falls** (sometimes incorrectly referred to as Templer Park Falls) – a drop of 300m in several stages and a good place for swimming. *Getting there*: buses Len Omnibus 66, 78, 83 or 81 from Pudu Raya bus terminal (RM1.20).

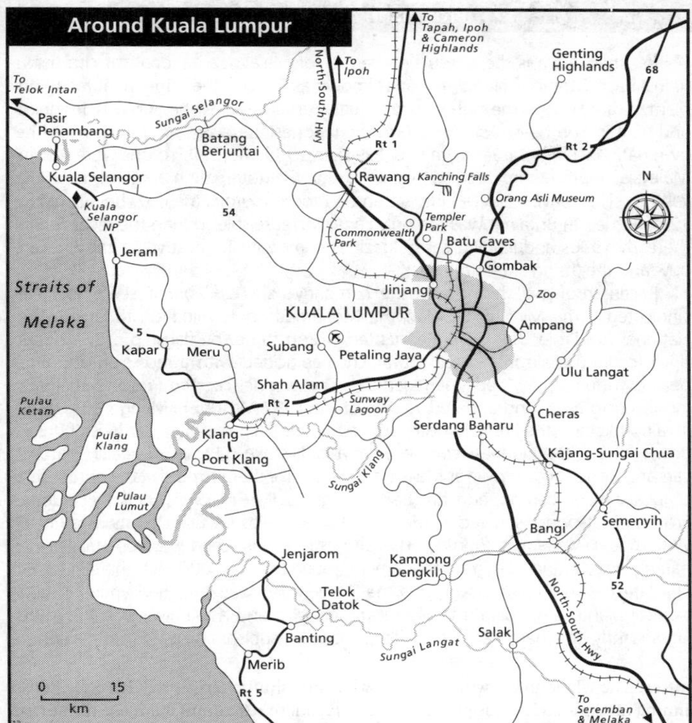

Taman Tasek Titiwangsa 10 minutes north of KL is a man-made lake with facilities for boating, horse riding, tennis, badminton, model car racetrack and a seafood restaurant.

The **Orang Asli Museum** is 25 km north of KL on the old Gombak Road. It preserves the traditions of Malaysia's indigenous Orang Asli aboriginals – there are about 60,000 living on the peninsula. Displays give the background on the 18 different tribes and their geographical dispersal. There are also models of Orang Asli village houses and a souvenir shop attached to the museum selling Orang Asli crafts. T 6892122. Open 0900-1700 Saturday-Thursday. Closed Friday. Admission free. *Getting there*: City Liner bus 174 from Lebuh Ampang terminus (RM1.50). It is possible to do a **jungle canopy walk** at the Forestry Research Institute of Malaysia (FRIM) at Kepong, some 30 minutes north of KL, on the Jabayan Perhutanan. However, it is important to book with the FRIM (T 6357315), as it can be closed. Speak with Ms Terry Ong.

West and Southwest

Petaling Jaya, 15 km southwest of KL, is a thriving industrial satellite and middle-class dormitory town for the capital and is known as PJ. It was initially built to provide low-cost housing for squatter resettlement but is now a city in its own right, with shopping and administration

Proton: driving the flag

Shah Alam is the production centre for Malaysia's national car company, Perusahaan Otomobil Nasional, better known as Proton. The huge manufacturing plant, located just off the highway from Kuala Lumpur, makes the only cars designed and built in Southeast Asia (although the Indonesian government announced its own national car programme in mid-1996). In 1995 140,500 Protons were sold in Malaysia, representing around two-thirds of the total car market of 225,000 vehicles. They have made an impact abroad too – Protons are now being sold in 12 countries. In Britain it was the only car to increase sales during the recession in the early 1990s and leading car magazines named it 'the best value car you can buy' and the 'rising star in the East'.

Recent profits at home and the company's success abroad seem to have vindicated Prime Minister Dr Mahathir Mohamad's determination to launch the National Car Project in 1984. He wanted Proton to be the flagship of Malaysia's drive for industrialization but his brainchild coincided with a recession and was nearly written-off by inept management. The original car, the Proton Saga, is a locally-customized and updated version of the 1982 Mitsubishi Mirage. "They say it's a boring car," the Prime Minister admitted. "On the other hand, it doesn't break down either." The Japanese company has a 17% stake in Proton. In reality Proton's cars are not as home-grown as Malaysians would like them to be, but the proportion of locally made components has been rising rapidly – in 1993, 65% by value of Proton's parts were sourced in Malaysia. In 1993, Proton unveiled its racey new Wira model – meaning 'warrior'. The car has been launched in Europe under the name 'Persona' and Proton's management hoped to sell 20,000 units there in 1996. The latest model to be unveiled is the Tiara which was launched amidst 7,000 tropical plants, a simulated tropical thunderstorm and a rainbow in April 1996. Significantly, the Tiara has been built without Mitsubishi's help – Proton went to

centres. The whole town, with its streets running in semi-circles, was planned on a drawing board, but despite its unimaginative street names (or rather, numbers), is not as sterile as it might sound. In recent years it has become quite lively, with its own nightlife scene and several gourmet restaurants, many of which cater for PJ's expatriate and wealthy Malaysian population. Mainly frequented by businessmen, as the airport is close by. **Accommodation A+** *Allson Sunway Lagoon Resort*, Jalan Lagun Timur, Bandar Sunway, Petaling Jaya, T 7358886, F 7365688, brand new dazzling resort, the world's largest surf 'n wave pool, health and spa club, 3 tennis courts, squash, 170m man-made beach, annexed to Sunway Capitol Shopping Centre – one of the largest in Malaysia, and located near Sunway Lagoon water theme park, kiddy camp, shuttle service to KL, coffee house, Japanese restaurant, Chinese restaurant, American/Italian restaurant, poolside bar, recommended. **A+** *Hyatt Regency Saujana Hotel & Country Club*, 2 km Subang International Airport Highway, Petaling Jaya, T 7461234, F 7462789, 5 minutes from the airport and 2 minutes from the golf course (it has two 18-hole championship courses), low-rise hotel set in landscaped gardens, it is a particularly convenient stop-over for early-morning flights, provides shuttle service to and from airport. **A+** *Pan Pacific Glenmarie Resort*, Jalan Sultan, T 7039090, F 7032728, new resort hotel with 300 rooms set in 450 acres, 10 minutes drive from Subang Airport, all sports facilities include 2 golf courses, Olympic-sized swimming pool, squash and tennis courts. **A+** *Petaling Jaya Hilton*, 2 Jalan Barat,

Citroën for the basic design and technology. It seems that Mahathir and Malaysian executives at Proton have been disappointed at the level and rate of technology transfer from Mitsubishi and so have begun to look elsewhere for help.

In common with Malaysia's bumiputra Malay majority, the car enjoys certain privileges and advantages in the marketplace that other makes do not. It is exempt from the hefty duty other car assemblers pay on imported kits. The government has also set a compulsory profit margin on all car sales, which means no price wars and, for Proton, no competition. This level of protection should end soon as Malaysia's membership of the World Trade Organization (WTO) obliges the government to cut import duties. With other cars competing with Proton on something close to a level playing field, Proton's outdated technology and sometimes poor build quality may make Malaysia's roads a little more varied in terms of the cars they carry.

In December 1991 Dr Mahathir unveiled his wish to make an even cheaper 660cc Made-in-Malaysia saloon in conjunction with the Daihatsu Company of Japan. Production of the car, which is based on the Daihatsu *Mira*, and named the *Kancil* (Mouse Deer) began in September 1994. The Prime Minister did not ask Mitsubishi to help build the car but created a new firm – Perusahaan Otomobil Kedva or Perodva, literally the Second Vehicle Enterprise, in alliance with Daihatsu. In February 1995 Mahathir signed a deal with Japan's Kawasaki Heavy Industries to make 90cc motorbikes. And then, in October 1996, Proton bought the British sports car maker Lotus. In buying this world famous marque for just US$80 million, Proton and Malaysia Inc have gained access to a wealth of engineering and design expertise. Significantly, Proton are building a training centre near Lotus in Norfolk, England, so that its engineers and designers can learn from Lotus' years of experience. Presumably this will lead, in a few years, to a Lotus-derived Proton sports car.

T 7559122, F 7553909, a/c, restaurant, pool. **A** *Holiday Villa*, 9 Jalan SS 12/1, Subang Jaya, T 7338788, F 7337449, a/c, restaurant, pool. **A** *Merlin Subang*, Jalan 5512/1, Subang Jaya, T 7335211, F 7331299, a/c, restaurant, pool. **A** *Subang Airport Hotel*, Kompleks Airtel Fima, T 7462122, F 7461097, a/c, restaurant, pool. **B** *Shah's Village Motel*, 3 & 5 Lorong Sultan, T 7569702, F 7557715, a/c, restaurant. *Grand City* is a good Indian restaurant near the University Hospital. *Getting there*: buses to most parts of Petaling Jaya can be boarded at Bangkok Bank stop and Kelang bus terminal (RM0.60).

Shah Alam, the new state capital of Selangor, is situated between KL and Port Klang. It has the reputation as Malaysia's best planned city and is an ultra-modern showpiece town. The skyline is dominated by the State Mosque, Masjid Sultan Salahuddin Abdul Aziz Shah which has a huge blue aluminium dome, said to be the largest in the world. Completed in 1988, it is reputed to be the largest mosque in Southeast Asia and can accommodate up to 16,000. There is an interesting museum here. **Accommodation A** *Holiday Inn*, Plaza Perangsang, Persiaran Perbandaran, T 5503696, F 5503913, a/c, restaurant, rooftop pool, ugly highrise, but only 15 minutes drive from Subang Airport. *Getting there*: from Kelang bus station (1 hour) or by taxi (RM20).

Klang, 30 km southwest of KL, is a royal town with a magnificent mosque and attractive royal palace, the **Istana Alam Shah** set in well cared for grounds. No public admittance, but the palace can be seen from the road, Klang had been the capital of Selangor for centuries before the tin mining town of Kuala Lumpur assumed the mantle in 1880. Klang was the name for the whole state of Selangor at the time when it was one of the *Negri Sembilan* – the nine states of the Malay Federation. The town is also known as Kelang; it is thought to derive from an old Sumatran word for tin. Today **Port Klang** (which used to be known as Port Swettenham, after former British Resident Frank Swettenham) is KL's seaport and is a busy container terminal. Klang is also an important service centre for nearby rubber and palm oil plantations, which in the early decades of the 20th century, spread the length of the Klang Valley to KL.

The **Gedung Rajah Abdullah** warehouse, built in 1857, is one of the oldest buildings in the town. (Rajah Abdullah was the Bugis Chief who first dispatched the expedition to the upper reaches of the Klang River, which resulted in the founding of KL.) In 1991 it was turned from an historical museum into Malaysia's first tin-mining museum. Open 0900-1600 Monday-Sunday. Closed 1200-1445 Friday. There is also a **fort** in Klang, built by Rajah Mahdi (a rival of Raja Abdullah), which guarded the entrance to the Klang valley from its strategic position overlooking the river.

The town is well known for its seafood; most of the restaurants are close to the bus terminal. Ferries leave from Klang for offshore islands such as Pulau Ketam (see below), Pulau Morib (golf course, see page 137) and Pulau Angsa. *Getting there*: buses 51, 58, 225 (Kelang Bus Co) from Kelang bus terminal (RM1.70) or by train, 1½ hours.

Pulau Ketam (Crab Island), off Port Klang is like a downmarket Venice, Malaysian-style, with the whole village on stilts over the fetid water. Good spot for seafood. *Getting there*: bus to Port Klang (RM2), ferry from Port Klang 1 hour (RM4), T 3314713.

Kuala Selangor is on the banks of the Sungai Selangor, about 60 km north of Klang on the coast road. In the last century, it was a focal point of the Sultanate of Selangor. The Dutch built two fortresses there in 1784 which they used to blockade the river, Sungai Selangor, in retaliation for Sultan Ibrahim of Selangor's attacks on Melaka. Nearly a century later, in 1871, British gunboats bombarded the forts – then occupied by Malays – for several hours, marking the first British intervention in the Selangor Civil War, over the possession of the tin-rich Klang Valley. The two fortresses are on the hills overlooking the Sungai Selangor estuary. The larger of the two, **Fort Altingberg**, on Bukit Melawati, serves as a royal mausoleum and museum. Open daylight hours Monday-Sunday.

The fort overlooks the **Kuala Selangor Nature Park**, 250 hectares of coastal mangrove swamp and wetland. It has several observation hides and more than 156 bird species – including bee eaters, kingfishers and sea eagles – have been recorded. There are also leaf monkeys. It is one of the best places to see Malaysia's famous synchronized fireflies – the only fireflies in Southeast Asia which manage to co-ordinate their flashing (see page 42). The fireflies are best observed on a moonless night, from about 1 hour after sunset. The actual riverside site is about 8 km from Kuala Selangor, near a village called Kampung Kuantan. A boat trip can be taken from Kampung Kuantan (RM2 each, 4 per boat), T 8892403/8892294. **Accommodation** The Society runs chalets in the Park (which is a short walk from the last bus stop). 'A'-frames RM15 (accommodates 2); chalets RM25-30 (accommodates 4). These must be booked in advance (see below) – a few days in advance for weekend visitors. There are also two small bus station hotels (**D-E**), rooms with bathrooms. *Getting there*: regular direct buses from KL's Puduraya bus terminal (Platform 24) to Kuala Selangor (RM3.50). Taxis can be chartered from there to Kampung Kuantan (wait and return RM25-30; whole car). The *Malayan Nature Society*, which operates the Nature Park will also arrange private transport to Kampung Kuantan and back for about the same price. This must be pre-arranged by booking with their KL Office (T 8892294 before 1700; T 8892403 after 1700).

South

Mines Wonderland is adjacent to the site of the new Sepang International Airport in Sungai Besi about 20 minutes south of KL. This adventure playground has been constructed on a 60 hectare plot which used to be the largest tin-mining lake in the world. Attractions include a Snow House, where you can see sculptures carved out of ice by artists from China. Alternatively, take a ride on a water taxi or see the Musical Fountain or any of the other sound and light attractions. Admission: RM25 adults, RM15 children. Open: 1600-2300 Monday-Sunday. Batu 10 1/2, Jalan Sungai Besi, T 9425010. The whole 'Mines Resort City' consists of a sizeable conference centre set within a a 5-star hotel, a 'Beach Resort' (no beach here), a shopping mall, a business park, an international standard gold course, and a new residential development. *Getting there*: mini bus 65 from Kota Raya or Toong Foong Bus 110, or a taxi via the KL-Seremban Expressway. There are also all-in tours which service the major hotels with a special coach. T 2488820 for more information. **Accommodation L-A+** *Palace of the Golden Horses*, Jalan Kuda Emas, The Mines Resort City, T 9436633, F 9436622, e-mail: mtaylor@mol.net.my, set on the old tin-mining lake, a 400 plus room hotel, with luxury fittings, range of cuisine, state-of-the-art conference centre, exquisite spa, fitness centre, free-form lagoon pool, children's camp. The closest 5-star hotel to the new airport. **A+** *Mines Beach Resort and Spa*, Jalan Dulang, The Mines Resort City, T 9436688, F 9435555, e-mail: MBR@signature.com.my. Furnished to a high standard, the resort has even managed to achieve a sandy beach. Low rise hotel in well landscaped gardens, a pleasant alternative to the bustle of KL. **A** *Mint*, 8th Rm, KL-Seremban Highway, T 943 8888, F 943 8889, new ugly block of over 400 rooms, sizeable pool, health centre, business centre, convenient for Mines Exhibition Centre and Wonderland, and for the new airport.

East

Malaysian Armed Forces Museum, on Jalan Gurney, exhibits pictures, paintings, weapons – including those captured from the so-called Communists Terrorists (CTs) during the emergency. Open 1000-1800 Monday-Thursday and Saturday. *Getting there*: minibus 19 (RM0.60).

Royal Selangor Complex on Jalan Pahang, in Setapak Jaya, to the north of the city, is the biggest pewter factory in the world, employing over 500 craftsmen. Royal Selangor was founded in 1885, using Straits tin (over 95%) which is alloyed with antimony and copper. Visitors can watch demonstrations of hand-casting and pewter working. Visitors can also see jewellery making and the handpainting of bonded porcelain. One of the most photographed sights at the complex is the massive pewter tankard outside the building. It is in the Guinness Book of Records as the largest in the world. As well as the Setapak Jaya Complex, there are showrooms throughout the city (see page 135). Open 0900-1600 Monday-Sunday. *Getting there*: Len Seng Bus from Lebuh Ampang Bus Station 12 or 10 (RM0.70).

National Zoo & Aquarium is 13 km from the centre of KL, down Jalan Ampang to Ulu Klang. The zoo encompasses a forest and a lake and houses 1,000 different species of Malaysian flora and fauna in addition to collections from elsewhere in the world. It also has an aquarium with over 80 species of marine life. Admission adult RM4, child RM1. Open 0900-1700 Monday-Sunday. *Getting there*: Len Seng bus 170, Len Chee 177, Sri Jaya 255 from Jalan Ampang or minibus 17 from Chowkit (RM0.50).

TOURS

Many companies offer city tours, usually of around 3 hours, which include visits to Chinatown, Muzium Negara (the National Museum), the Railway Station, Thean Hou Temple, Masjid Negara (the National Mosque), the Padang area and Masjid Jame – most of which cost in the region of RM25. City night tours take in Chinatown, the Sri Mahmariamman Temple and a cultural show (RM55). Other tours on offer visit sights close to the city such as Batu Caves, a batik factory and the Selangor Pewter Complex (RM25) as well as day trips to Melaka, Port Dickson, Fraser's Hill, Genting Highlands and Pulau Ketam (RM40-80). Most of these tour companies offer tours to destinations around the peninsula. *Helicopter tours* of the city are now run by *Mofaz Air* from Bukit Lanjan, Taman Tun Dr Ismail on weekdays and from Taman Tasik Titiwangsa on Sun. Trips last 15 minutes and cost RM100 per person, with a maximum of 4-6 people per helicopter. Another air tour company are *Asia Tenggara Aviation Services*, T 6264613, offering tours 7 days/week 0800-1830 – note that aerial photography is not allowed.

For a jungle tour with a difference there is *UBAT* (*Utan Bara Adventure Team*), Unit 286-03-08, The Heritage, Jalan Pahang, T 4225124, F 4226125. The people who run this outfit are ex-security personnel and the names of their tours speak for themselves: 'Cross country jungle survival course' (4-7 days, US$180-350 per person), 'Jungle wilderness medicine camp' (5 days, US$250), 'Mountain trekking' (5 days, US$200), '35 km Taman Negara Jungle Trail' (US$200), 'Expeditions into the jungle to locate downed US and Japanese aircraft', etc.

LOCAL INFORMATION

● Accommodation

Room rates in KL's top hotels escalated as the economy boomed in the early 1990s. With the forthcoming Commonwealth Games imminent (1998), many new hotels have been, or are being, constructed. It has been estimated that the number of beds in 3, 4 and 5-star hotels will more than double between 1997 and 2000-2002. This will mean a glut of rooms, falling occupancy rates, and therefore falling room rates: a fall of 5-20% has been forecast. Of course it may not come to that, but the likelihood is a drop, or at least a stagnation, in room rates.

> **Prices: L** over RM500; **A+** RM260-500; **A** RM130-260; **B** RM65-130; **C** RM40-65; **D** RM20-40; **E** RM10-20; **F** Below RM10

By international standards KL's hotels are excellent value for money, but because of the city's growing traffic problems, the location of a hotel has become an increasingly important consideration. Most top hotels are between Jalan Sultan Ismail and Jalan P Ramlee, in KL's so-called 'Golden Triangle'. South of Jalan Raja Chulan, in the Bukit Bintang area, there is another concentration of big hotels. **Corporate discounts** of 10-15% are usually on offer; even if you are just on holiday, you are likely to qualify for the reduced rates by simply giving your company's name. This however may be outweighed by the 'plus plus' that is quoted on top of rates by most hotels ('plus plus' is 10% service charge and 5% government tax).

NB Some top hotels drastically reduce their room rates during the weekends. If you are staying in the larger, a/c hotels and are a non-smoker, it is possible to request a room on a non-smoking floor. Rooms with a/c generally have non-opening windows, making it difficult to freshen the air. Many of the cheaper hotels are around Jalan Tunku Abdul Rahman, Jalan Masjid India and Jalan Raja Laut, all of which are within easy walking distance of the colonial core of KL, lieing north-east of the Padang. There are also cheap hotels in the Chinatown area.

City centre: most of these hotels are in and around Chinatown, a bustling area where KL's colonial roots have not been entirely olditerated. Fairly central for sight-seeing but relatively distant from the CBD. **A+** ***Holiday Inn City Centre***, Jln Raja Laut, T 2939233, F 2939634, a/c, Szechuan restaurant, coffee house, pool, squash, health club, gymnasuim, big enough hotel, but inside everything is rather bijou – the lobby is squashed, the swimming pool tiny and the fitness and business centres on the miniature side. **A** ***Heritage***, Banguanan Stesen Keretapi, Jln Sultan Hishamuddin, T 2735588, F 2732842 part of the magnificent Moorish-style railway station. It has recently been redeveloped and has managed to retain some of its colonial splendour, but disappointingly the

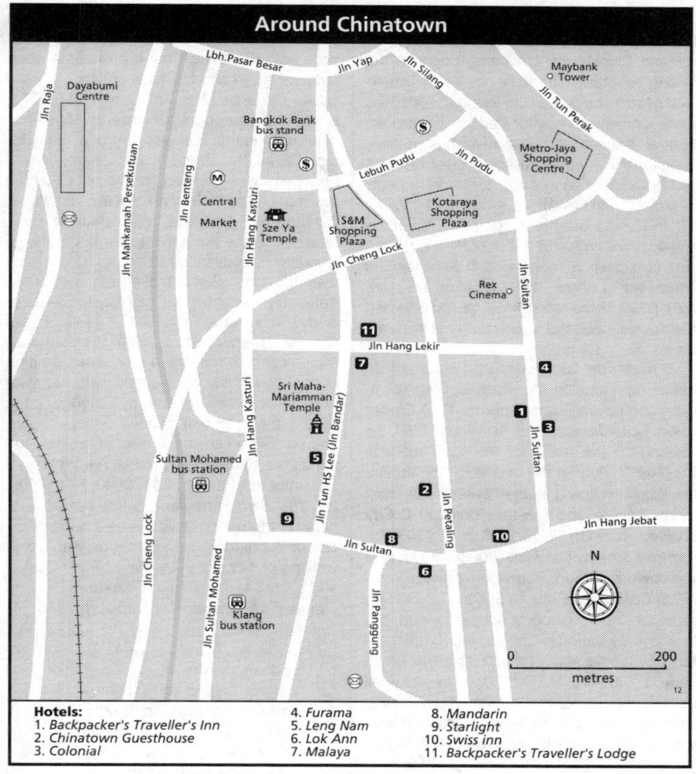

standard rooms have been furnished in a contemporary style. **A** *Malaya*, Jln Hang Lekir, T 2327722, F 2300980, a/c, restaurant, 1970s hotel with central location in Chinatown, pretty characterless. **A** *Mandarin*, 2-8 Jln Sultan, T 2303000, F 2304363, a/c, restaurant, in Chinatown, used by businessmen, not as plush as its name suggests (it is not a part of the Mandarin group), but is clean, with an interesting location and is reasonable value for money. **A** *Swiss Inn*, 62 Jln Sultan, T 2323333, F 2016699, a/c, café, smart hotel, well run, 30s Malaya-style furnishings, in good position in the heart of Chinatown. **A-B** *Katari*, 38 Jln Pudu, T 2017777, F 2017911, a/c, restaurant, small hotel opposite Puduraya bus terminal, small, clean rooms, with showers only, price including American breakfast, reductions available, friendly staff, safe place to leave luggage.

B *Furama*, Komplek Selangor, Jln Sultan, T 2301777, F 2302110, a/c, restaurant, health centre, another uninspired hotel with the benefit of a central location in the heart of Chinatown, reasonable rates, geared, as name suggests, mainly to Japanese visitors. **B** *Lok Ann*, 118A Jln Petaling, T 2389544, a/c, clean, large rooms, centrally located in Chinatown. **B** *Madura Inn*, 285-7 Jln Tuanku Adbul Rahman, T 2948589, F 2948385, a/c, good value, rooms are large with good bathrooms, TV and mini-bar, curry house next door. **B** *Puduraya*, 4th Flr, Puduraya Bus Station, Jln Pudu, T 2321000, F 2305567, a/c, restaurant, breakfast included, clean, but nothing to recommend it other than its convenience for early morning departures and late night arrivals.

C-D *Starlight*, 90-92 Jln Hang Kasturi, T 2389811, a/c, well situated for Central Market and Chinatown, but being opposite the Kelang Bus Station, it can be noisy. **C-D** ***Travellers' Moon Lodge***, 36c Jln Silang, T 2306601, some a/c, conveniently located for Chinatown, Central Market and Puduraya bus station, popular with budget travellers, breakfast and bed bugs included in price, some dorm beds, dirty place with tiny cubicle rooms. **C-D** *YWCA*, 12 Jln Hang Jebat (to the east of Chinatown and south of Jln Pudu), T 2383225, a/c, restaurant, also caters for couples. **C-D** *Backpackers Travellers' Lodge*, 158 Jln Tun HS Lee, T 2010889, some rooms have a/c and attached bathrooms, clean and a good choice in this area, dorms (**F**).

D *Riverside Lodge*, 80A Jln Rotan, of Jln Kampung Attap, to the south of Chinatown, clean and sizeable rooms, dorms (**F**). **D** *Chinatown Guesthouse*, 2nd Flr, Wisma BWT, Jln Petaling (in the centre of the *pasar malam*), T 2320417, right in the middle of Chinatown, travel bulletin board, budget guesthouse, most rooms are quiet and have fans, dorm (**E**). **D** *City Lodge*, 1st to 4th Flr, 16 Jln Pudu, T 2305275, some a/c, small windowless rooms, some rooms with own bathroom, rather run-down, dorms (**E**). **D** *Colonial*, 39-45 Jln Sultan, T 2380336, some a/c, noisy, as rooms are partitioned, but in a central location in Chinatown, complimentary Chinese tea at any time. **D** *Kawana*, 68 Jln Pudu, T 2386714, F 2302120, some a/c, small barrack-like rooms, but very clean, communal toilets and showers, run by camp Indian fellow, some dorm beds (**E**). **D** *Leng Nam*, 165-167 Jln Tun HS Lee, T 2301489, small hotel, fan only, communal showers. **D** *Drop Inn Lodge*, 1-3 Jln Tun HS Lee, T 2386314, some a/c, 13 rooms, basic and quite dirty – no windows in a/c rooms – but with the advantage of being very central. **D-F** *Backpackers' Travellers' Inn*, 2nd Flr, 60 Jln Sultan (opposite *Furama Hotel*), T 2382473, some a/c, centrally and conveniently located in Chinatown next to excellent stalls/restaurants, popular and professionally run by Stevie, rooms are small but generally clean, ranging from non-a/c dorm rooms to a/c rooms with attached showers, good facilities for the traveller including left luggage, washing and cooking facilities, recommended. **E** *The Travellers Station*, right next to railway station, T 2735588, ext 3070, e-mail: station1@tm.net.my, one of the few backpackers places left, basic but friendly, some dorm rooms, but showers available.

Chow Kit area: a good choice for businessmen using the Putra World Trade Centre. The next door Mall Shopping Centre provides a good range of shops and fast food outlets.

A+ *Dynasty*, 218 Jln Ipoh, T 4437777, F 4436688, a/c, pool, Chinese or Mediterranean restaurants, business centre, a short distance from the World Trade Centre, all the luxury you would expect for the price – and a rooftop heli-pad. **A+** *Pan Pacific*, Jln Putra, T 4425555, F 4417236, a/c, restaurant, pool, attached to the Putra World Trade Centre, so favoured by convention delegates, good views over the city, excellent dim sum restaurant, irritatingly uncentral for sightseers. **A+** *Legend*, 100 Jln Putra, T 4429888, F 4430700, a/c, Chinese, Japanese and health food restaurants, pool, health centre, like a monstrous creation out of Lego, this hotel is legendary in size, with 600 rooms and apartments, and a lobby on the 9th Flr, the hotel was opened by Joan Collins and pursues a film-star image, all facilities and reductions sometimes available. **A+** *Vistana*, 9 Jln Lumut, off Jln Ipoh, T 4428000, F 4411400, a/c, *Thai Barn Restaurant*, coffee house, business centre, pool, classic business hotel of excellent standard but unpretentious, within easy walking distance of Putra World Trade Centre, and a RM2 taxi ride from Chinatown, recommended. **A** *Grand Centrepoint*, 316 Jln Tuanku Abdul Rahman, T 2933988, F 2943688, a/c, Island Bar, café, 100-room hotel, very clean, stylish primary colour decor, good for business people on a tight(ish) budget. **A** *Grand Continental*, Jln Belia/Jln Raja Laut, T 2939333, F 2939732, a/c, restaurant, pool, not really in the big league, except so far as it has 328 unremarkable rooms, impersonal atmosphere, but reasonable facilities, similar, but much larger, to nearby *Plaza Hotel*. **A** *Grand Pacific*, Jln Ipoh/Jln Sultan Ismail, T 4422177, F 4426078, a/c, restaurant, not very grand, but delightful views of the highway (drivers have good views into hotel bedrooms), an old hotel, rather the worse for wear, on the edge of the city centre, with none of the facilities which one might expect from newer hotels – a plus point are the competitive room rates. **A** *Plaza*, Jln Raja Laut, T 2982255, F 2920959, a/c, restaurant, 160-room hotel offering competitive rates, price includes buffet breakfast and use of sauna. **A** *Stanford*, 449 Jln Tuanku Abdul Rahman, T 2919833, F 2936482, a/c, coffee house, business centre, on a lively thoroughfare with plenty of shops and stalls, small but comfortable rooms, discounts available in low season, recommended.

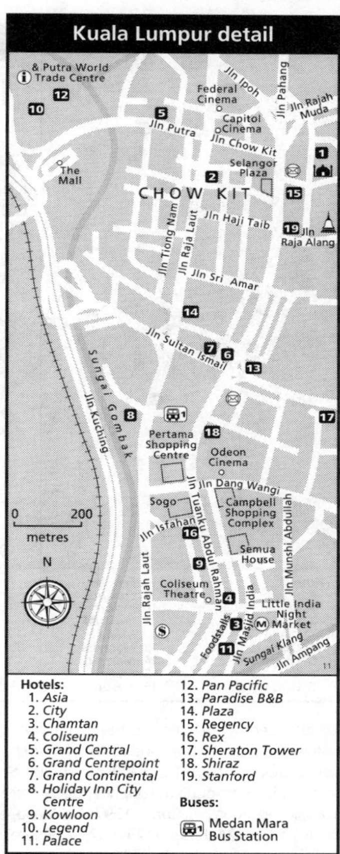

B *Asia*, 69 Jln Haji Hussein, T 2926077, F 2927734, a/c, restaurant, established joint means it remains popular, karaoke bar, good value for money. **B** *City*, 366 Jln Raja Laut, T 4414466, F 4415379, a/c, restaurant, 101 rooms, refurbished in 1993, does not look much from the exterior, but rooms are clean with good hot water showers, professional management, competitively priced – most guests are Malaysians, recommended. **B** *Grand Central*, 63 Jln Putra/Jln Raja Laut, T 4413011, F 4424758, a/c, clean but drab middle-market hotel with 138 rooms and little to recommend it bar reasonable room rates.

C *Sentosa*, 316 Jln Raja Laut, T 2925644, a/c, simple, Chinese-run, value for money. **C-D** *Paradise Bed and Breakfast*, 319 Jln Tuanku Abdul Rahman, T 2922872, F 2924532, some a/c, restaurant, shared bathrooms, well run bed and breakfast, on good city bus routes, price including breakfast, travel agency in hotel can arrange discounts for alternative hotels in KL if this one isn't suitable, recommended by travellers.

Golden Triangle: a big shopping and business area, dominated by new high-rise hotels, shopping malls and office blocks. **L** *Shangri-La*, 11 Jln Sultan Ismail, T 2322388, F 2301514, a/c, Chinese, Japanese and French restaurants, small, rather old-fashioned pool, health club, sauna, jacuzzi, tennis, with its grand marble lobby and 720 rooms, the *Shang* has remained KL's ritziest hotel despite the arrival of swish upstart competition; constantly hosting political leaders and assorted royalty for dinner, big bright rooms, good bar (styled after English pubs), but its best feature is its ground floor *Gourmet Corner* deli, which stocks a great variety of European food, recommended. **L-A+** *Hilton*, Jln Sultan Ismail, T 2482322, F 2442157, a/c, restaurant, pool, all facilities but not quite as good as others in this league, when returning to the hotel by taxi, specify '*KL Hilton*', otherwise you are liable to end up in the *PJ Hilton* (in Petaling Jaya), recommended. **L-A+** *Istana*, 73 Jln Raja Chulan, T 2419988, F 2440111 a/c, Chinese, Japanese and Italian restaurants, pool, this striking, almost grotesquely extravagant hotel in the heart of KL's business district, all facilities. **A+** *Equatorial*, Jln Sultan Ismail (opposite MAS building), T 2617777, F 2619020, a/c, restaurant (excellent Cantonese), pool, one of KL's earlier international hotels, the *Equatorial* has had several revamps over the years, its 1960s-style coffee shop has metamorphosed into one the best hotel coffee shops in town, open 24 hours (see below), with an international news agency in the basement, the hotel is the favoured repose of visiting journalists. Choose a room at the back to reduce disturbance by traffic noise, two no smoking floors. **A+** *Federal*, 35 Jln Bukit Bintang, T 2489166, F 2482877, a/c, Indian restaurant, revolving restaurant, ice-cream bar, cafés, bowling, shopping arcade, business centre, pool, when it first opened in the early 1960s, it was the pride of KL: its *Mandarin Palace* restaurant was rated as the most elegant restaurant in the Far East, it is still good, but does not compare with the world-class glitz that KL

has attracted of late, and it is having difficulty matching up to the newer hotels. **A+** ***Marriott***, 183 Jln Bukit Bintang, T 2459000, F 2453000, next to KL's most opulent shopping plaza *Star Hill*, still under construction in 1997. **A+** ***Melia***, 16 Jln Imbi, T 2428333, F 2426623, Chinese and Spanish restaurants, 300 plus rooms, pool, health centre, not quite up to the standard of many of the other big hotels which charge around the same prices but nonetheless a very reasonable place to stay. **A+** ***Park Royal***, Jln Sultan Ismail, T 2425588, F 2414281, a/c, restaurant, pool, formerly called *The Regent*, the hotel underwent major cosmetic surgery in 1989, allowing it to charge more for its good range of facilities, although it often offers promotions with rates in **A** category. **A+** ***Regent***, 160 Jln Bukit Bintang, T 2418000, F 2421441, a/c, Western, Cantonese and Japanese restaurants, beautiful pool, gym with Roman baths, children's pool, a/c squash courts, health club, business centre (open until midnight), the ultimate hotel in KL – it won the 'Best Hotel in Malaysia' award the year it opened in 1990, all suites have butler service and the rooms and bathrooms are lavishly appointed, the enormous lobby is designed around a pool of cascading water, recommended. **A+** ***Swiss Garden***, 117 Jln Pudu, T 2413333, F 2415555, a/c, Chinese restaurant, tiny pool, fitness centre with limited equipment, business centre, Blue Chip Lounge – a classy bar with live band and a computer terminal linked to the KL Stock Exchange, popular for their cocktail of the month, grand addition to first class hotels in KL, with 310 rooms and 15 storeys, but disappointing facilities. **A+** ***New World***, 128 Jln Ampang, T 2636888, F 2631888. 520 rooms in this new horror. Good sized rooms and nice bathrooms but all a bit ostentatious. Shares its spectacular pool with the *Renaissance Hotel* next door. **A+** ***Renaissance***, corner of Jln Ismail and Jln Ampang, T 2622233, F 2631122. 400 rooms in this new hotel, with over-the-top lobby of massive black marble pillars. Furnishings in rooms are verging on the pretentious, but the bathrooms are nice, lovely pool makes up for all of this and there are two tennis courts. The ballroom seats 1400. **A** ***Agora***, 106-110 Jln Bukit Bintang, T 2428133, F 2427815, a/c, restaurant, small 50-room hotel, located on busy intersection in shopping area of Golden Triangle, rooms on the front tend to be noisy, interesting design incorporating Greek columns and elegant furnishings. **A** ***Cardogan***, 64 Jln Bukit Bintang, T 2444856, F 2444865, a/c, coffee house, health centre, business centre, dark wood interior. 61 rather bare rooms and small shower rooms attached. Price includes tax and breakfast. **A** ***Concorde***, 2 Jln Sultan Ismail, T 2442200, F 2441628, a/c, restaurant, decent sized lengths pool, gym, it is the old *Merlin* (the first big modern hotel in KL) masquerading behind a face-lift and rather sterile interior decor, 4 good restaurants and a coffee shop and the *Hard Rock Café* attached to it. **A** ***Fortuna***, 87 Jln Berangan, T 2419111, F 2418237, a/c, coffee house with live band, health centre, just off Bukit Bintang, behind *McDonalds*, good value for money, recommended. **A** ***Holiday Inn on the Park***, Jln Pinang, T 2481066, F 2481930, a/c, restaurant, large pool and garden area, located across the road from a string of lively bars, *'Satay station'* restaurant is a train carriage in the forecourt. The 'Park' to which its title refers, is now a building site. **A** ***Bintang Warisan***, 68 Jln Bukit Bintang, T 2488111, F 2482333, a/c, coffee house, nice little hotel, limited number of standard price double bedrooms. Good clean but quite basic small rooms.

B ***Emerald***, 166 Jln Pudu, T 2429233, F 2445774, a/c, noisy location, on edge of Golden Triangle, reasonably maintained, considering this Chinese hotel is nearly 20 years old, strong Asian feel, attached bathrooms with hot water. **B** ***Imperial***, 76-80 Jln Changkat Bukit Bintang (Jln Hicks), T 2481422, F 2429048, a/c, restaurant, well priced Chinese hotel in an otherwise pricey part of town, well located for shopping centres but at this price don't expect a gem. **B** ***Park Royal***, 80 Jln Bukit Bintang, T 2427288, a/c, reasonable value for this more expensive area of town, popular restaurant. **B** ***Sungei Wang***, 74-76 Jln Bukit Bintang, T 2485255, F 2424576, a/c, Thai restaurant, a small and very average hotel, but well-run, friendly and good value for money – discounts available. **B** ***The Lodge***, Jln Sultan Ismail, T 2420122, F 2416819, a/c, restaurant, small pool, small hotel on busy junction, surrounded by tower blocks, large rooms with 50s fittings – rather unusual for KL. **B** ***The Malaysia***, 67-69 Jln Bukit Bintang, T 2428033, F 2428579, a/c, restaurant, a rather jaded hotel amidst all the glitz, faded wallpaper, limited facilities, but a lot cheaper than many. Unsuccessful attempt at international style.

C ***Tai Ichi***, 78 Jln Bukit Bintang, T 2427533, F 2310162. Another little hotel in this strip. Nothing in particular to recommend it.

Jalan Ampang: a relatively new commercial district, it runs along the northern edge of the new KLCC (see box, page 112) making it a good position for anyone doing business here. See map, page 103. **L-A+** ***Crown Princess***, City Square Centre, Jln Tun Razak, T 2625522, F 2624492, a/c, pool on 10th Flr, 10th Flr restaurant good for 'High Tea' buffet, *Taj* Indian restaurant on 11th Flr, lobby lounge with baby grand piano, cafés, Vietnamese restaurant on 11th Flr, Szechuanese restaurant, business centre, adjacent shopping centre with 168 shops, opulent decor, over 500 spacious rooms with panoramic views, recommended. **L-A+** ***Mi-Casa Hotel Apartments***, 368b Jln Tun Razak (near junction with Jln Ampang), T 2618833, F 2611186, a/c, restaurant, pool, shopping arcade, hair salon, dentist and doctor, children's pool, jacuzzi, tennis, squash, gym, sauna, children's playhouse, business centre, first rate, especially for longer stays, KL's only apartment hotel with suites which include fully equipped kitchen with utensils and sitting room, Italian restaurant, Tapas Bar, recommended. **A+** ***De Palma***, Ampang Point, T 4707070, full facilities including fully equipped gym and spa, coffee house serves local and western food, has sister hotels in Shah Alam and Sepang. **A+** ***Radisson Plaza***, 138 Jln Ampang, T 4668866, F 4669966, another new addition and no details yet. **A** ***Ming Court***, Jln Ampang, T 2618888, F 2623428, a/c, restaurant, good pool, room rate includes a good buffet breakfast, spacious rooms, some with a view of the Petronas Twin Towers. **A+** ***Nikko***, 165 Jln Ampang, T 2611111, F 2611122, a/c, pool, Japanese and Chinese restaurants, near city square and Ampang Shopping centres. **A+** ***Su Casa***, 222 Jln Ampang, T 4513833, F 4521031, a/c, restaurant, pool, business centre, store, serviced apartment suites with fully equipped kitchens for business people intending a slightly longer stay than is usual, weekly and monthly rates are negotiable, prices are slightly cheaper here than at the sister hotel *MiCasa*.

Little India (see map, page 123): **B** ***Chamtan***, 62 Jln Masjid India, T 2930144, F 2932422, a/c, restaurant, clean and reasonable value, a well run establishment and a good location, recommended. **B** ***Kowloon***, 142-146 Jln Tuanku Abdul Rahman, T 2934246, F 2926548, a/c, coffee house, health centre, clean, value for money, rooms facing the main street are noisy, recommended. **B** ***Palace***, 46-1 Jln Masjid India, T 2986122, F 2937528, a/c, café, deli corner, shopping arcade, good lively location, but very average hotel.

D ***Coliseum***, 100 Jln Tuanku Abdul Rahman, T 2926270, some a/c, restaurant, rather run-down colonial hotel, if arriving outside hours, knock on one of the side doors, large, simply furnished rooms and a famous bar and restaurant (see below) and friendly staff, but no attached bathrooms and incredibly noisy a/c. **D** ***Tivoli***, 134 Jln Tuanku Abdul Rahman, T 2924108, fan only, restaurant, not as good as the *Rex* or the *Coliseum* on the same stretch of road.

Others: **L** ***Carcosa Seri Negara*** (see map, page 102), Taman Tasek Perdana, T 2821888, F 2827888, a/c, restaurant, pool, former residence of the British High Commissioner and built in 1896, it is now a luxury hotel, where Queen Elizabeth II stayed when she visited Malaysia during the Commonwealth Conference in 1989 and where other important dignitaries, presidents and prime ministers are pampered on state visits, situated in a relatively secluded wooded hillside and overlooking the Lake Gardens there are just 13 suites served by over 100 staff, recommended. **L** ***Pan Pacific KL International Airport Hotel***, T 3394688, F 3395787, a 450-room hotel opening as this book went to press, right next to the new airport at Sepang, so convenient for stop-overs, should provide all the luxury you could demand, with pool, fitness centre, tennis court, spa, business centre, several restaurants. **L** ***Pan Pacific Glenmarie Resort***, T 7031000, F 7041000 for more details, a new golf resort in the suburbs of KL, due to open as this book went to press, close to the airport and half an hour from the city centre, it will boast two 18 hole golf courses, a pool and spa, business centre and guests will be able to use the Clubhouse, providing an Olympic size pool, tennis and squash courts, fitness centre etc. Just under 300 rooms in this low rise resort, choice of dining and a quieter atmosphere away from the city centre.

A ***Concorde Inn***, Sepang, within the new airport site, T 8431118, F 8432118, a/c, TV, pool, tennis court, food court, restaurants, health and fitness centre, over 400 rooms, presently under construction. **A** ***Wenworth***, Jln Yew, T 9833888, F 9828088, a/c, Chinese restaurant, café, roof pool, health spa, simple but comfortable rooms, good location for North-South highway – approaching KL from the south, it is one of the first hotels in the city, the surrounding Pudu area is fast being developed with old shophouses giving way to tower blocks and two new shopping centres (Phoenix Plaza and the Leisure Mall), in the pipeline, breakfast is included in room tariff and there is a monthly food promotion, not surprisingly this hotel won the 1994/95 Malaysian Tourism Award for its excellence in services for its price category, a RM4 taxi ride will get you to the City Centre and Golden Triangle, recommended.

B ***Matri Inn***, 235 Jln Tun Sambanthan, near KL-Klang Highway, 50470 Brickfields, T 2731097, F 2731569, a/c, café, run by an Indian family, good Indian food. **B** ***YMCA***, 95 Jln Padang Belia/Jln Kandang Kerbau, T 2741439, F 2740559, good facilities – sports facilities, language courses, shop – neutralized by inconvenient location in Brickfields district on the southwest outskirts, off Jln Tun Sambathan, it is, however, within sniffing distance of Raju's tandoori ovens (see *Sri Vani's Corner*, Places to eat), dormitory for men only (**D**) also private rooms. *Getting there*: minibus 12.

C ***Kuala Lumpur International Youth Hostel***, 21 Jln Kampung Attap, a/c, on the south-eastern edge of KL, near the railway station and tucked in behind some big bank buildings, good hawker stalls nearby to serve office staff but reports are that the rooms are dirty and noisy – a last resort.

Homes away from home: run by the *Asian Overland Service*, the Homes Away from Home programme gives visitors first-hand experience of Malaysian life by staying in fishing kampungs, rubber plantations, tin mines or pensioners' homes, RM45/day including pick-up service, accommodation and 2 meals. Contact ***Asian Overland Services***, 33M Jln Dewan Sultan Sulaiman Satu, T 2925622, F 2925209; ***Village Home Stay***, 178 Jln Tuanku Abdul Rahman, T 2920319.

● Places to eat

Many of KL's big hotels in the Jln Sultan Ismail/Bukit Bintang areas serve excellent value buffet lunches and offer a selection of local and international dishes. One of the best ways to sample various cuisines is to graze among the foodstalls.

Prices: ♦♦♦♦ over RM40; ♦♦♦ RM13-40; ♦♦ RM5-13; ♦ under RM5

Malay: ♦♦♦***Nelayan Floating Restaurant***, Titiwangsa Lake Gardens, good but expensive. ♦♦♦***Seri Melayu***, 1 Jln Conlay, T 2451833, open 1100-1500, 1900-2300 (reservations recommended for groups of four or more – it seats 500), the best Malay restaurant in town in traditional Minangkabau-style building, the brain-child of Malaysian PM Datuk Seri Dr Mahatir Mohamad, beautifully designed interior in style of Negeri Sembilan palace, don't be put off by cultural shows or big groups – the food's still worth it, very popular with locals too, individual dishes expensive, buffet at RM35 (or RM70 for dinner) best bet (more than 50 dishes) with promotions featuring cuisine from different states each month, those arriving in shorts will be given a sarong to wear, recommended. ♦♦♦***Seri Angkasa***, at the top of the KL Tower (see map, page 103), T 2085055, a sister hotel to *Seri Melayu*. The tower revolves, achieving a full rotation in 60 minutes. Good food, booking advisable for the evenings. There is also a good value buffet lunch available. ♦♦♦***Spices***, *Concorde Hotel*, 2 Jln Sultan Ismail, T 2442200, open 1130-1500, 1830-2300, closed Sun, unlike its name, the food is not overly spicy, eclectic Asian cuisine as well as traditional Malay, 4-piece band background music, a/c indoors or poolside outdoors, *se-tengah* – stiff whisky drink popular in colonial times – features on their varied drinks list. ♦♦***Jamal Bersaudara***, Jln Raja Abdullah, Kampung Baru. ♦♦***Rasa Utara***, Bukit Bintang Plaza, Jln Bukit Bintang. ♦♦***Wan Kembang*** (Cik Siti), 24 Jln 14/22, Petaling Jaya (in front of the mosque), specializing in Kelantanese food. ♦***Satay Anika***, Ground Floor, Bukit Bintang Plaza, Jln Bukit Bintang, fast food satay, recommended. ♦***Sate Ria***, 9 Jln Tuanku Abdul Rahman, fast food. ♦***Malay 'buffet'***, Jln Gereja, opposite Jln Tun HS Lee. Very good value little restaurant.

Chinese: ♦♦♦♦***Dynasty Garden Chinese Restaurant***, Lot M72-75, Mezzanine Flr, Plaza Yow Chuan, Jln Tun Razak. ♦♦♦♦***The Museum***, *The Legend Hotel*, The Mall, Putra Place, T 4429888, open 1200-1500, 1830-2230, aims to look like a museum, with Chinese antiques and columns everywhere, although many display cabinets still to be filled, Teochew and Cantonese cuisine, adventurous food promotions, winner of Malaysian Tourism and Promotion best Chinese award. ♦♦♦♦***Golden Phoenix***, *Hotel Equatorial*, Jln Sultan Ismail, T 2617777, open 1200-1430, gourmet Chinese establishment, mock Chinese courtyard setting. ♦♦♦♦***Lai Ching Yuen***, *The Regent Hotel*, Jln Bukit Bintang, T 2418000, set in mock Chinese pavilion, holder of four Malaysian Tourism Gold Awards for consistently fine cuisine, popular with Chinese gourmets, luxury table settings, revolving solid granite table centres. ♦♦♦♦***Shang Palace***, *Shangri-La Hotel*, Jln Sultan Ismail, T 2322388, open 1200-1430, 1900-2300, dim sum lunch of over 40 varieties costs around RM50, check food promotions for evening meals.

♦♦♦***Ampang Yong Tau Foo***, 53 Jln SS2/30, Petaling Jaya, T 7753686, *yong tau foo* (stuffed beancurd dishes) in a coffee shop, recommended, closed Mon. ♦♦♦***The Blossom***, *Swiss Garden Hotel*, 117 Jln Pudu, T 2413333, open 1130-1430, 1830-2230, 40 varieties of dim sum, tiger prawns a house speciality, good selection of pork dishes, abalone and birds' nests only for those on hefty expense accounts. ♦♦♦***Cha Yuan Teahouse***, 5B Jln SS2/67, Petaling Jaya, traditional Chinese teahouse offers light meals and tea prepared by tea-master Paul Lim, recommended. ♦♦♦***Hai Tien Lo***, *Pan Pacific Hotel*, Jln Putra, T 4425555, open 1200-1500, 1900-2300, excellent dim sum, steamed fish with suet, recommended. ♦♦♦***Marco Polo***, Wisma Lim Foo Yong, 86 Jln Raja Chulan, T 2412233, open 1200-1500, 1900-2300, extensive menu, barbecue roast suckling pig recommended, 70s style decor, very busy lunchtimes. ♦♦♦***Oriental Bowl***, 587 Leboh Pudu, T 2025577, a/c restaurant above Chinese spice shop, convenient location for Central Market, rather formal atmosphere. ♦♦♦***Overseas***, G2, Central Market, Jln Hang Kasturi, T 2746407, Cantonese restaurant, very popular with locals. Good range of dishes (*dim sum* particularly recommended, 0800-1500), excellent barbecue and roast meats as well as vegetarian dishes in generous portions and pleasant location, recommended. ♦♦♦***Tsui Yuen***, 5th Flr, *Hilton Hotel*, Jln Sultan Ismail, T 2482322, open 1200-1430, 1900-2230, main attraction is the lunchtime *dim sum*, weekend 'all you can eat' promotions also worth checking and good value set meals.

♦♦***Balakon***, half way to Kajang, near Sungai Besi (take Seremban highway, exit to left at Taman Sri Petaling – before toll gates, right at T-junction, over railway line and past Shell and Esso stations, turn left towards Sungai Besi tin mine, then branch right to Balakong, the restaurant is signposted), it is little more than a tin shed (with a fruit stall outside) but is famed among KL's epicurians for its deep-fried paper-wrapped chicken, wild boar curry and vinegar pork shank, recommended. ♦♦***Cameleon Vegetarian Restaurant***, 1 Jln Thamboosamy (off Jln Putra, near The Mall and *Pan Pacific*), Thai and Chinese, good *kway teow*, but vegetarians with carnivorous instincts rate the soyabean roast duck and various other ersatz meat and fish dishes whose presentation (and sometimes taste) is convincing. ♦♦***Esquire Kitchen***, Level 1, Sungai Wang Plaza, Jln Sultan Ismail, T 2485006, dumplings and pork dishes good value, Shanghai dishes popular. ♦♦***Hokkaido***, 68 Jln Lumut, off Jln Ipoh, T 4411316, open 1800-0200, located at north end of town, opposite *Vistana Hotel*, good genuine fare, not fancy, tables outside, pleasant retreat from shopping plazas and hotel complexes, recommended. ♦♦***Sin Kiew Yee***, Jln Hang Lekir (Jln Cecil, between Jln Petaling and Jln Sultan, Chinatown), mouthwatering dishes, good value for money, tables on pavement, recommended. ♦♦***Westlake***, Jln Sultan, highly rated for its Hokkien *mee* and *mee hun*, mixed with raw egg. ♦♦***Yook Woo Hin***, 100 Jln Petaling, cheap dim sum in the middle of Chinatown – until 1400.

♦***Nam Heong***, 54 Jln Sultan, Hainanese chicken rice. ♦***Seng Nam***, Lebuh Pasar Besar, Hainanese. The steamboats in the restaurant area of Chinatown are worth sampling at one of out-door tables.

Nyonya: ♦♦♦♦***Baluchi's***, 3 Jln SS21/60, Petaling Jaya, T 7190879 (advisable to take taxi; ask for Damansara Utama Shophouse Complex), North Indian cuisine, modest decor but excellent food; chicken tikka, tandoori chicken, prawn *masala* and *palak paneer* particularly recommended; freshly baked naan, recommended.

♦♦♦***Bangles***, 60A Jln Tuanku Abdul Rahman, T 2986770, reckoned to be among the best North Indian tandoori restaurants in KL, often necessary to book in the evenings, recommended. ♦♦♦***Bon Ton***, 7 Jln Kia Peng, T 2413611, open 1200-1500, 1900-2400, good Eastern Nyonya set menu, some western dishes such as chicken pie, set in a '30s colonial bungalow, just south of KLCC, recommended. ♦♦♦***Dondang Sayang***, 12 Lower Ground Floor, The Weld, Jln Raja Chulan, T 2613831; also branch at 28 Jln Telawi Lima, Bangsar Baru, T 2549388, popular and reasonably priced restaurant with big Nyonya menu. ♦♦♦***Kapitan's Club***, 35 Jln Ampang, T 2010242, open 1100-1500, 1800-2230, spacious restaurant decorated with straits woodwork, staff in traditional outfits, 'top hats', the house speciality is a tasty pastry and egg dish, Kapitan chicken is popular, Malay dishes also available.

♦♦***Sri Penang***, Lower Ground Floor, Menara Aik Hua, Changkat Raja Chulan (Jln Hicks), variety of Nyonya and North Malaysian dishes.

Indian and Pakistani: ♦♦♦♦***The Taj***, *The Crown Princess Hotel*, 11th Flr, City Square Centre, Jln Tun Razak, T 2625522, open 1200-1500, 1900-2300, closed Sat lunch, stylish Anglo-Raj decor, live Indian muzak, open view kitchen, winner of '93 Tourism Malaysia Gold Award for Best Indian Restaurant, New Delhi chefs create first rate Indian cuisine, vegetable samosas and tandooris – meat and veg – are excellent, recommended. ♦♦♦***Bombay Palace***, 388 Jln Tun Razak, next to US Embassy, T 2454241, open 1200-1500, 1830-2300, good quality North Indian food in tasteful surroundings with staff in traditional Indian uniform, menu including vegetarian section. ♦♦♦-♦♦***Restoranua Jime***, next door to *Paradise B+B*, Jln Tunku Abdul Rahman, specializing in Moghul food and tandooris, recommended.

♦♦***Annalakshmi***, 46 Lorong Maarof, Bangsar Baru, T 2823799, excellent Indian vegetarian restaurants run by the Temple of Fine Arts, dedicated to the preservation of Indian cultural heritage in Malaysia, the buffet is particularly recommended. ♦♦***Kampung Pandan***, 1st Flr, Central Market, specialist in fish-head curry. ♦♦***Sri Vani's Corner*** (*Raju's*), Jln Tun Sambathan 4 (next to *YMCA* tennis courts), overgrown hawker stall rated among its dedicated clientele as the best place for tandooris and oven-baked naan in KL, recommended. ♦♦***Valentine Roti***, 6 Jln Semark (close to the National Library), this place was fortunate enough to be reviewed in the *Far Eastern Economic Review* and was billed as the best Roti restaurant in town, Ilango Arokias-amy's rotis are a treat, light and flaky, and as he says "I think God wanted me to do this".

♦***Alhmdoolilla***, 12 Jln Dang Wangi, rated for its rotis. ♦***Lay Sin Coffee Shop***, 248 Jln Tun Sambathan, banana leaf.

Japanese: ♦♦♦♦***Keyaki***, *Pan Pacific Hotel*, Jln Putra, T 4425555, open 1200-1500, 1900-2300, good set meals, excellent sashimi and sushi made with fish flown from Japan twice weekly, highly rated, but extremely expensive. ♦♦♦♦***Nadaman***, *Shangri-La Hotel*, 11 Jln Sultan Ismail, T 2322388, *Shang* quality and *Shang* prices.

♦♦♦***Chikuyo-Tei***, Plaza See Hoy Chuan, Jln Raja Chulan, T 2300729, open 1200-1500, 1830-2230, housed in a basement, good value set meals, quality teppanyak, seafood and steak. ♦♦♦***Munakata***, 2nd Flr, Menara Promet,

Jln Sultan Ismail, T 2417441. ♦♦♦*Tykoh Inagiku*, Ground Floor, Kompleks Antarabangsa, Jln Sultan Ismail (between *Equatorial* and *Hilton hotels*), T 2482133.

♦♦*Sushi King*, Lower Ground Flr, The Mall, Jln Putra, T 4428205 and 63 Jln Sultan Ismail, T 2417312, spotlessly clean sushi bar, prices from 50c to RM3/sushi. ♦♦*Teppanyaki*, 2nd Flr, Sungai Wang Plaza, Jln Bukit Bintang and Lot 10, Jln Sultan Ismail, basement, excellent Japanese fast food, set meal for RM10.

Korean: ♦♦♦*Koryo-Won*, Kompleks Antarabangsa, Jln Sultan Ismail, T 2427655 (between *Hilton* and *Equatorial* hotels), excellent barbecues – particularly when washed down with Jung Jong rice wine, recommended. ♦♦♦*Korean Restaurant*, 24 Jln Medan Imbi, T 2446163, open 1100-1500, 1800-2300, small restaurant off Jln Imbi, lashings of garlic, friendly staff.

Thai: ♦♦♦*Barn Thai*, 370B Jln Tun Razak (opposite *MiCasa Hotel*), T 2446699, open 1200-1430, 1900-0300, very tastefully decorated Thai style 'Jazzaurant' with excellent live music, extensive Thai menu, hot and sour seabass and mango salad are specialities, recommended, also a more subdued but equally tasteful outlet in the *Vistana Hotel*, 9 Jln Lumut, off Jln Ipoh, T 4428000. ♦♦♦*Sawasdee Thai Restaurant*, *Holiday Inn on the Park*, Jln Pinang, T 2481066. ♦♦*Cili Padi Thai Restaurant*, 2nd Flr, The Mall, Jln Putra, T 4429543, soups and seafood are excellent, recommended speciality: King Solomon's Treasure (chicken wrapped in pandan leaves), closes 2200 sharp, recommended. ♦♦*Restoran Miyako*, Level 5, Kota Raya Complex, Jln Cheng Lock, T 2022822, excellent Thai food – some of the best outside Thailand, recommended. *Johnny's Thai Steamboat*, basement of Bukit Bintang Plaza.

Vietnamese: ♦♦♦♦*Mekong*, 11th Flr, *Crown Princess Hotel*, City Square Centre, Jln Tun Razak, T 2625522, well-appointed, serving authentic Indo-Chinese cuisine with specialities from Vietnam and Thailand. ♦♦♦*Restoran Sri Saigon*, 53 Jln 552/30, Petaling Jaya, T 7753681, genuine Vietnamese dishes. ♦♦♦*Vietnam House*, 6th Flr Sogo Pernas, T 2941726, open 1200-2100, genuine Vietnamese chef and many ingredients flown from Vietnam, spring rolls and chicken with lemon grass are recommended.

International: ♦♦♦♦*Carcosa Seri Negara*, Persiaran Mahameru, Taman Tasek Perdana (Lake Gardens), T 2306766 (reservations), built in 1896 to house the British Administrator for the Federated Malay States, Carcosa offers English-style high tea in a sumptuous, colonial setting, expensive and Italian lunches and dinners are also served in the Mahsuri dining hall on fine china plates with solid silver cutlery, Continental and Malay cuisine, high tea (recommended) RM25 (1530-1800, Mon-Sun). ♦♦♦♦*Ciao*, 428 Jln Tun Razak, T 9854827, open 1200-1430, 1900-2230, closed Mon, authentic tasty Italian food served in a beautifully renovated bungalow, recommended. ♦♦♦♦*Flamenco*, 1 Jln U-Thant, T 4517507, open 1100-2400, excellent South Mediterranean food, good paella, daily specialities. ♦♦♦♦*Jake's*, 21 Jln Setiapuspa, Medan Damansara, off Jln Damansara, towards PJ, T 2545677, open 1200-1500, 1830-2300, Jake's steaks are highly rated in KL, served by cowboys and cowgirls, recommended. ♦♦♦♦*Lafitte*, *Shangri-La Hotel*, 11 Jln Sultan Ismail, T 2322388, open 1200-1500, 1900-2300, best French restaurant in Malaysia, but very expensive, recommended. ♦♦♦♦*Melaka Grill*, *Hilton Hotel*, Jln Sultan Ismail, T 2482322, open 1200-1500, 1900-2300, closed Sat and Sun lunch, well-established, popular business lunch venue, good quality international cuisine. ♦♦♦♦*Pour Toi*, 36 Jln Walter Grenier, T 2455836, a new Golden Triangle restaurant, French cuisine, fun decor, well-balanced menu, RM15 corkage if you bring your own wine. ♦♦♦♦*Sakura Café & Cuisine*, 165-169 Jln Imbi, excellent variety of Malay, Chinese and Indian dishes including fish-head curry, located in an area with many other good cheap restaurants, recommended.

♦♦♦*TGI Friday's*, Life Centre, Jln Sultan Ismail, T 2637762, open 1130-2400, cocktails and American food, good value for money, though lacks atmosphere perhaps because they've been here for 30 years. ♦♦♦*Coliseum Café*, 100 Jln Tuanku Abdul Rahman (Batu Rd), next door to the old Coliseum Theatre, long-famed for its sizzling lamb and beef steaks, Hainanese (Chinese) food and Western-style (mild) curries, all served by frantic waiters in buttoned-up white suits, during the communist Emergency, planters were said to come here for gin and curry, handing their guns in to be kept behind the bar, it is easy to believe it, recommended. ♦♦♦*D'Ribeye*, Ground Floor, Central Market, Jln Hang Kasturi, good atmosphere, good steak and offering good value, full of businessmen at lunchtime. ♦♦♦*Hard Rock Café*, Ground Floor, *Wisma Concorde Hotel*, T 2444062, open 1130-0200, 2 Jln Sultan Ismail, one of the best places for top-quality American burgers, steaks and salads, good value, recommended. ♦♦♦***Le Coq D'Or***, 121 Jln Ampang, T 2429732, European/Malay, former residence of a rich mining towkay with a porticoed veranda and Italian marble, western, Chinese and Malay cooking, great atmosphere of crumbling grandeur, best known for its steaks and mixed grills, recommended (♦♦♦), Sam's Curry Lunch (Indian buffet, Sun 1230-1400), excellent à la carte selection of Malaysian dishes, include *nasi lemak* and *rendang*, open 24 hours, recommended. ♦♦♦***L'Escargot***, Lot 253, The Mall, 2nd Flr, 100 Jln Putra, T 4431988, open 1200-2200, good set menu, and authentic French atmosphere. ♦♦♦***Marble Arch***, *Hotel Grand Continental*, Jln Raja Laut, T 2939333, open 1100-1500, 1800-2300, good buffet lunches (RM25) and set meals during food promotions when chefs are on hand from the country being promoted. ♦♦♦***The Jump***, Ground Flr, Wisma Inai 241, Jln Tun Razak, T 2450046, open 1100-2230, American fare prepared by US chef, good value, popular with foreigners, good cocktail band and live music venue. ♦♦♦***The Ship***, 40 Jln Sultan Ismail, very dark interior, extensive menu of steaks, chicken, salads – the stone grills are particularly popular. Open from lunch until 0230. ♦♦♦***Uno's***, corner of Jln Kia Peng, reasonable Italian pasta restaurant downstairs with disco/bar above which is the unchallenged nocturnal playground of KL's rich and famous. ♦♦♦-♦♦***Moomba***, Ground floor, UOA Centre, 19 Jln Pinang, T 2628226. Australian bar and restaurant, selection of sandwiches, ribs, pasta, pies. Trendy businessman's lunch spot, but good value. ♦♦♦-♦♦***Roadhouse Grill***, 42 Jln Sultan Ismail. Cheap and cheerful American fare. Open 1130-2400.

♦♦***Riverbank***, Ground floor, Central Market. 'Hearty American Fare' – which just about says it all – burgers, sandwiches etc. ♦♦***Caleos***, 1 Jln Pinang, pastas and pizzas, Napoli-style seafood, upstairs bar and karaoke lounge. ♦♦***Equatorial Coffee Shop***, Basement, *Equatorial Hotel*, Jln Sultan Ismail, recommended Malay curry buffets 1230-1400, Mon-Sat. ♦♦***Federal Hotel Revolving Restaurant***, Jln Bukit Bintang, was once one of KL's tallest buildings, now rather dwarfed but still a good spot for icecream sundaes with a view. ♦♦***Lodge Coffee Shop***, Jln Sultan Ismail, good value for money – particularly local dishes: *nasi goreng*, curries and buffets, recommended. ♦♦-♦***Lakshmi Villas***, Leboh Ampang, excellent vegetarian food, try the *dosai masala* – pancakes stuffed with vegetables and accompanied by a lentil sauce.

Seafood: ♦♦♦***Bangsar Seafood Village***, Jln Telawi Empat, Bangsar Baru, T 254555, open 1200-1430, 1800-2300, large restaurant complex with reasonably priced seafood, fresh from tanks that line the inside of the restaurant, specialities include crab in butter sauce and Thai-style tiger prawns (and a good satay stall). ♦♦♦***Eden Village***, 260 Jln Raja Chulan, wide-ranging menu, but probably best known for seafood, resembles a glitzy Minangkabau palace with garden behind, cultural Malay, Chinese and Indian dances every night, less touristy outlet in PJ 25-31 Jln 5322/23, Damansara Jaya, T 7193184. ♦♦♦***Hai Peng Seafood Restaurant***, Taman Evergreen, Batu Empat, Jln Klang Lama (Old Klang Rd), the smallest and least assuming restaurant in a row of Chinese shophouses (red neon sign), but one of the very best seafood restaurants in Malaysia, where the Chinese community's seafood connoisseurs come to eat (the other seafood restaurants in the cluster include *Chian Kee*, *Pacific Sea Foods* and *Yee Kee* – most of which are good, but not as good as *Hai Peng*), its specialities include butter crab (in clove and coconut), belacan crab, sweet and sour chilli crab and bamboo clams, the *siu yit kum* (small gold-leaf tea) is a delicious, fragrant Chinese tea, which is perfect with seafood, open until 0100, recommended. ♦♦♦***Studio 123***, 159 Jln Ampang, easily missed – it's opposite the *Ming Court Hotel*, unassuming place with friendly staff and excellent, good value food, recommended.

♦♦***MASs***, 228 Jln Dua A, Subang, Selangor, T 7461200, well out of town, past Subang airport's Terminal 2, and strung out along the road running beside Runway One are about 10 seafood restaurants, they all do a brisk turnover, and there is not much between them; they all serve seafood and each has its own speciality, *MASs* is the one with the front end of an MAS jumbo jet on the roof, recommended. ♦♦***New Ocean***, 29B Medan Imbi (off Jln Imbi and Jln Hoo Teik Ee), good seafood restaurant just round the corner from the Sungai Wang and Lot 10 shopping complexes. ♦♦***Unicorn***, 1st Flr, Annex Block, Lot 10 Shopping Centre, Jln Sultan Ismail, T 2441695, open 1100-1500, 1800-0400, big, smart Chinese seafood restaurant in the Lot 10 complex, just by the footbridge to Sungai Wang, good stop for shoppers. **NB** For additional seafood entries, see also Port Klang and Pulau Ketam (see page 118).

Teahouses: Traditional Chinese teahouse opposite *Sungai Wang Hotel* on Jln Bukit Bintang.

Foodstalls: ***Ampang Park Shopping Complex***, (along Jln Tun Razak), popular, but small centre, with good variety of stalls; ***Brickfields*** (Jln Tun Sambathan), string of small outdoor restaurants; ***Central Market*** (Top Floor), Jln Hang Kasturi, excellent, but small centre with good *nasi campur* (lunchtimes); ***Jalan Raja Alang*** and ***Jalan Raja Bot*** stalls, off Jln Tuanku Abdul Rahman (Chow Kit area), mostly Malay stalls; stalls set up along ***Jalan Haji Hussein*** when the market closes at 1800 and stays open until 0200; ***Lorong Raja Muda Food Centre***, off Jln Raja Muda, on the edge of Kampung Baru, mainly Malay food; ***Medan Hang Tuah***, The Mall (Top Floor), Jln Putra (opposite the *Pan Pacific Hotel*); ***Munshi Abdullah Food Complex***, off Lorong Tuanku Abdul Rahman (near *Coliseum*), good satay; ***Puduraya Bus Station***, Jln Pudu, good variety of stalls, open at all hours; *Lot 10 Shopping Complex*, Jln Sultan Ismail, excellent choice of food here, if you can tolerate the high volume music; ***Sunday Market***, Kampung Baru (main market actually takes place on Sat night), many Malay hawker stalls, Jln Masjid India.

● Bars

There is no shortage of good watering holes in KL; many have live Filipino and local cover bands, and others have discotheques attached. An increasing number of bars are now being taken over by karaoke.

Barn Thai, 370B Jln Tun Razak, T 2446699, self-styled 'Jazzaurant', Bangkok-type wooden bar with panelled interior and tasteful Thai decor, some of KL's best live acts with excellent jazz, drinks are expensive, also serves good Thai food, recommended; ***Betelnut***, Jln Pinang, T 2416455, Thur ladies night, located in the ruins of a former colonial bungalow in a strip of bars and clubs which are not as good, disco in main house, but relaxed outdoor bar, recommended; ***Bull's Head***, Ground Flr, Central Market, Jln Hang Kasturi, T 2746428, large bar with the darkened atmosphere of a London pub inside and with tables on the terrace outside, convenient for shopping in Central Market; ***Bier Keller***, German pub and restaurant, Ground Flr, Menara Haw Par (next to *Shangri-La Hotel*), Jln Sultan Ismail, T 2013313, authentic German draft beer served in stylish glasses, wide range of Shnapps, salty German food, recommended; ***Cathy's Place***, Wisma Stephen, Jln Sultan Ismail, T 2481794, cheap beer and a regular expat crowd; ***Centrepoint***, Jln Setiapuspa, Medan Damansara, off Jln Damansara, lively bar with live music every night; ***Coliseum***, 100 Jln Tuanku Abdul Rahman, the bar, which has a number of long-term residents who never seem to move, is the haunt of Malaysia's star cartoonist, Lat (his Coliseum sizzling steak cartoon hangs on the wall along with his carricatures of regulars), the so-called *Planters' Bar* used to be the gathering point for colonial rubber planters and tin miners then became the hangout of war correspondents during the Malayan Emergency, the bar is frequented by everyone from diplomats and businessmen to backpackers, it is a pleasant old-time bar which opens for business before lunch and shuts at 2200 sharp, recommended; ***English Pub***, *Shangri-La Hotel*, not as naff as it sounds, and popular with visiting business people, happy hour 1730-1930, live band 2030-2230, full size pool table.

Hard Rock Café, Basement and Ground Floor Wisma Concorde, 2 Jln Sultan Ismail, T 2444152, the *Hard Rock*, with its Harley Davidson chopper posing on the rooftop, opened in 1991 and quickly became one of the most popular and lively bars in town, good atmosphere and small disco floor, recommended; ***London Pub***, Lorong Hampshire, off Jln Ampang (behind *Ming Court Hotel*), continuing KL's obsession with recreating English pubs, this one, part-owned by a London Cockney is not a mock-Tudor half-timbered mess, it has a good atmosphere and a regular darts competition; ***Ronnie Q's Pub***, 32 Jln Telawi Dua, Bangsar Baru, popular with expats and locals, great sporting moments with international cricket and rugby videos; ***Shark Club***, 23 Jln Sultan Ismail, T 2417878, trendy bar and café open 24 hours daily, live band in basement after 2030 Mon-Sat, American and Mexican food, giant screen for latest sports events, darts, and boasts the longest bar in KL; ***Solutions***, City Square Centre, Jln Tun Razak, T 2621689, happy hours 1600-2200, popular after-work spot; ***Tapas Bar***, *MiCasa Hotel*, 368b Jln Tun Razak (near junction with Jln Ampang), serves what are arguably the best margaritas in KL, recommended; ***Titiwangsa Bar***, *Carcosa Seri Negara Hotel*, Taman Tasek Perdana; ***Traffic Lights***, 42 Jln Sultan Ismail (near Bukit Bintang junction), music (sometimes live) and attached grill.

● Airline offices

Aeroflot, Ground Floor, Wisma Tong Ah, 1 Jln Perak, T 2613231; **Air India**, Bangunan Ankasa Raya, 123 Jln Ampang, T 2420166; **Air Lanka**, UG4 Bangunan Perangasang Segemai, Jln Kampung Attap, T 2740211; **Alitalia**, Plaza See Hoy Chan, Jln Raja Chulan, T 2380366; **America West Airlines**, UBN Tower, 10 Jln P Ramlee, T 2387057; **American Airlines**, Bangunan

Angkasa Raya, 123 Jln Ampang, T 2480644; **Bangladesh Biman**, Subang International Airport, T 7461118; **British Airways**, Mezz Flr, See Hoy Chan Plaza, Jln Raja Chulan, T 2426177; **Cathay Pacific**, UBN Tower, 10 Jln P Ramlee, T 2383377; **China Airlines**, Level 3, Bangunan Amoda, 22 Jln Imbi, T 2427344; **Czechoslavak Airlines**, 12th Flr, Plaza Atrium, 10 Lorong P Ramlee, T 2380176; **Delta Airlines**, UBN Tower, Jln P Ramlee, T 2324700; **Garuda**, Suite 3.01, Level 3, Menara Lion, Jln Ampang, T 2622811, opposite Ampang Park Shopping Mall; **Japan Airlines**, 1st Flr, Pernas International, Lot 1157, Jln Sultan Ismail, T 2611728; **KLM**, Shop 7, Ground Floor, President House, Jln Sultan Ismail, T 2427011; **Korean Air**, 17th Flr, MUI Plaza, Jln P Ramlee, T 7465700; **Lufthansa**, 3rd Flr, Pernas International Bldg, Jln Sultan Ismail, T 2614646/2614666; **MAS**, UMBC Bldg, Jln Sulaiman, T 2610555; MAS Bldg, 33rd Flr, Jln Sultan Ismail, T 7463000; Dayabumi Complex, T 2748734, The Mall, World Trade Centre, Level 3 T 4426759; **Northwest Airlines**, UBN Tower, Jln P Ramlee, T 2433542; **Pelangi Airways**, 18th floor, Technology Resources Tower, 161B Jln Ampang, T 2624446, F 2624515; **Philippine Airlines**, 104-107 Wisma Stephens, Jln Raja Chulan, T 2429040; **PIA**, Ground Floor, Angkasa Raya Bldg, 123 Jln Ampang, T 2425444; **Qantas**, UBN Tower, 10 Jln P Ramlee, T 2389133; **Royal Brunei**, 1st Flr, Wisma Merlin, Jln Sultan Ismail, T 2307166; **Royal Jordanian**, 8th Flr, Mui Plaza, Jln P Ramlee, T 2487500; **Sabena**, 1st Flr, Wisma Stephens, Jln Raja Chulan, T 2425820; **Saudi**, c/o *Safuan Travel & Tours*, 7 Jln Raja Abdullah, T 2984566; **Scandinavian Airlines**, Bangunan Angkasa Raya, 123 Jln Ampang, T 2426044; **Singapore Airlines**, Wisma SIA, 2 Jln Sang Wangi, T 2923122; **Thai International**, Kuwasa Bldg, 5 Jln Raja Laut, T 2937100; **Turkish Airlines**, *Hotel Equatorial*, 20 Jln Sultan Ismail, T 2614055; **United Airlines**, Bangunan MAS, Jln Sultan Ismail, T 2611433; **UTA French Airlines**, Plaza See Hoy Chan, Jln Raja Chulan, T 2324179; **Virgin Atlantic**, 77 Jln Bukit Bintang (2nd Flr), T 2430322/3.

● Banks & money changers

There are money changers in all the big shopping centres and along the main shopping streets. Most branches of the leading Malaysian and foreign banks have foreign exchange desks, although some (eg Bank Bumiputra) impose limits on charge card cash advances. The following addresses are for bank headquarters: **Bank Bumiputra**, Menara Bumiputra, Jln Melaka, T 2988011; **Bank of America**, 1st Flr, Wisma Stephens, Jln Raja Chulan, T 2021133; **Chase Manhattan**, 1st Flr, Bangunan Pernas International, Jln Sultan Ismail; **Hongkong & Shanghai Banking Corporation**, 2 Leboh Ampang (off Jln Gereja), T 2300744; **Maybank**, 100 Jln Tun Perak, T 2308833; **Public Bank**, Bangunan Public Bank, 6 Jln Sultan Sulaiman (off Jln Syed Putra), T 2741788; **Standard Chartered Bank**, 2 Jln Ampang, T 2326555; **United Malayan Banking Corporation**, Bangunan UMBC, Jln Sultan Sulaiman (off Jln Syed Putra), T 2309866.

● Churches

Times of English-language Sun services: *Baptist Church*, 70 Cangkat Bukit Bintang, 0830, 0945; *St Andrews International Church*, 31 Jln Raja Chulan, 0900, 1100; *St John's Cathedral (Roman Catholic)*, 5 Jln Bukit Nanas, 0800, 1030, 1800; *St Mary's (Anglican) Church*, Jln Raja, 0700, 0800, 0930 (family Eucharist), 1800; *Wesley Methodist Church*, 2 Jln Wesley, 0815, 1030, 1800.

● Embassies & consulates

Australia: 6 Jln Yap Kwan Sweng, T 2423122; **Austria**: 7th Flr, MUI Plaza, Jln P Ramlee, T 2484277; **Belgium**: 4th Flr, Wisma DNP, 12 Lorong Yap Kwan Seng, T 2485733; **Brunei Darussalam**: 8th Flr, Wisma Sin Heap Lee (next to the *Crown Princess Hotel*), Jln Tun Razak, T 2612800; **Canada**: 7th Flr, Plaza MBS, 172 Jln Ampang, T 2612000; **China**: 229 Jln Ampang, T 2428495; **Czechoslovakia**: 32 Jln Mesra (off Jln Damai), T 2427185; **Denmark**: 22nd Flr, Bangunan Angkasa Raya, 123 Jln Ampang, T 2022101; **Finland**: 15th Flr, MBF Plaza, Jln Ampang, T 2611088; **France**: 196 Jln Ampang, T 2484318; **Germany**: 3 Jln U Thant, T 2429666; **India**: 2 Jln Taman Duta, off Jln Duta, visas take 3-4 days; **Indonesia**: 233 Jln Tun Razak, T 9842011; **Italy**: 99 Jln U Thant, T 4565122; **Japan**: 11 Persiaran Stonor, off Jln Tun Razak, T 2427044; **Laos**: 108 Jln Damai, off Jln Ampang, T 2483895; **Myanmar (Burma)**: 5 Jln Taman U Thant Satu, T 2423863; **Netherlands**: 4 Jln Mesra (off Jln Damai), T 2485151; **New Zealand**: 193 Jln Tun Razak, T 2382533; **Norway**: 11th Flr, Bangunan Angkasa Raya, Jln Ampang, T 2420144; **Pakistan**: Jln Ampang, in front of Tourist Centre; **Papua New Guinea High Commission**: 1 Lorong Ru Kedua (off Jln Ampang), T 2455145; **Philippines**: 1 Chnagkat Kia Peng, T 2484233; **Poland**: 495, 4½ mile, Jln Ampang, T 4576733; **Romania**: 114 Jln Damai,

T 2423172; **Singapore**: 209 Jln Tun Razak, T 2616277; **Spain**: 200 Jln Ampang, T 2484868; **Sweden**: 6th Flr, Angkasa Raya Bldg, 123 Jln Ampang, T 2485433; **Switzerland**: 16 Persiaran Madge, T 2480622; **Thailand**: 206 Jln Ampang, T 2488333; **Turkey**: Bangunan Citi 1, Jln Perumahan Gurney, T 2986455; **UK**: 185 Jln Ampang, T 2482122; **USA**: 376 Jln Tun Razak, T 2489011; **USSR**: 263 Jln Ampang, T 4560009; **Vietnam**: Vietnam House, 4 Persiaran Stonor, T 2484036.

● Entertainment

Art galleries: KL is gradually becoming a centre for local and some international artists, but the art market is not exactly flourishing, and much of the art work around is mediocre. Some of the main galleries include: ***Anak Alam Art Gallery***, 905 Pesiaran Tun Ismail off Jln Parliamen; ***AP Art Gallery***, Ground Floor, Central Market, off Jln Hang Kasturi; ***Artfolio Gallery***, 1st Flr City Square, Jln Tun Razak, T 2623339; ***Art House***, 2nd Flr, Wisma Stephens, Jln Raja Chulan, T 2482283; ***Balai Seni***, Menara Maybank, Jln Tun Perak, T 2321416; ***Fine Arts Gallery***, Yow Chuan Plaza, Jln Tun Razak; ***Galericitra***, 1st Flr, Shopping Arcade, *Shangri-La Hotel*, Jln Sultan Ismail; ***National Art Gallery***, Jln Sultan Hishamuddin, T 2300157; ***Rupa Gallery***, Lot 158 Menara Dayabumi, Jln Sultan Hishamuddin.

Contemporary Malaysian art can be seen at ***Art Salon***, 4 Jln Telawi Dua, Bangsar Baru, open Tues-Sun, T 2822601 for information on the latest show.

Cinemas: open daily from 1100. The first showing is usually a 1300 matinee with the last show at 2115 (midnight show Sat). For What's On, the *Sun* paper publishes details. Tickets range from RM2-4. *Cineplex*, small cinema complexes are increasingly popular and many are incorporated into the burgeoning shopping plaza, tickets cost RM8-10. Screenings listed in *The New Straits Times*, and the *Star*. Main cinemas: ***Capitol***, Jln Raja Laut, T 4429051; ***Cathay***, Jln Bukit Bintang, T 2429942; ***Cathay Cineplex***, The Mall, T 4426122; ***Coliseum***, Jln Tuanku Abdul Rahman, T 2925995; ***Federal***, Jln Raja Laut, T 4425014; ***Odeon***, Jln Tuanku Abdul Rahman, T 2920084; ***Odeon Cineplex***, Central Square, T 2308548; ***President***, Sungai Wang Plaza, Jln Sultan Ismail, T 2480084; ***Rex***, Jln Sultan, T 2383021.

Cultural shows: ***Eden Village***, 260 Jln Raja Chulan, Malay, Indian and Chinese dancing every night; ***Malaysian Tourist Information Complex*** (Matic), 109 Jln Ampang, T 2434929, shows on Tues, Thurs and Sun at 1530; ***Seri Melayu Restaurant***, 1 Jln Conlay, traditional Malay folk dances and singing in KL's best Malay epicurean experience, (see page 127) traditional music starts at 2000, dancing at 2045, ends 2130; ***Temple of Fine Arts***, 116 Jln Berhala, Brickfields, T 2743709, this organization, set up in Malaysia to preserve and promote Indian culture, stages cultural shows every month with dinner, music and dancing, the *Temple* organizes an annual Festival of Arts (call for details), which involves a week-long stage production featuring traditional and modern Indian dance (free – "... the Temple believes art has no price"), it also runs classes in classical and folk dancing and teaches traditional musical instruments.

Language courses: available at many places (see Yellow Pages), but not cheap. *Time Spoken Language Centre*, 226-227 2nd Flr, Campbell Complex, T 2921595, recommended but not especially based on 'travelling bahasa', flexible schedules.

Nightclubs and discos: since the mid-1980s, with the rise of the local yuppy, KL has shaken off its early-to-bed image and now has a slightly more lively club scene. Several old colonial buildings have been converted into night spots. The *Metro* section in *The Star* is devoted to what's on where. Most nightclubs and discos in KL used to be open until 0300 during the week and until 0400 on Fri nights and weekends. But at the beginning of 1997 the government, worried at the proliferation of so-called 'social ills', introduced new regulations stipulating that nightspots must close by 0100. This has been a bit of a dampener on what was in danger of becoming a really zany club scene. In the past few years, Jln Pinang, once a backstreet of crumbling bungalows, has emerged as a late-night strip of bars. There are also hundreds of karaoke lounges around KL. Bangsar Baru to the west of the city centre, not far from the University of Malaya, is probably the hippest area of town with around 20 bars and nightclubs. It is frequented mostly by Malaysians. ***Baze 2***, Yow Chuan Plaza, Jln Tun Razak, popular for its R&B, acid jazz, and dance mixes, happy hour 2100-2300, Wed ladies night, RM30 cover charge; ***Boom Boom Room***, 11 Lorong Ampang, off Jln Gereja, usually heaving by the weekend, disco plays up-to-the-minute tracks, busy upstairs bar with live show, dance and dirty jokes, RM15-20 cover, recommended; ***Betelnut***, Jln Pinang, very popular bar/disco complex, behind the disco clubhouse is a spacious outdoor bar area, *Betelnut* is the best in a strip of bars just down from the *Holiday Inn on the Park*, Thur ladies night, recommended; ***Cee Jay's***, Ground Floor, Menara SMI, 6 Lorong P Ramlee (behind *Shangri-La Hotel*), *Cee Jay's* has a good bar and a restaurant, sports bar with screens, pool, darts, but is best known for its live music, with classy local acts playing covers; ***Club Oz***, lower lobby, *Shangri-La Hotel*, Jln Sultan Ismail, professional DJs, predominantly Chinese control, not cheap – cover RM15-30; ***Club Syabas***, 1 Lorong Sultan, Petaling Jaya, the club's renowned *DV8* disco is very popular with KL ravers, as is the karaoke, recommended, cover charge RM12-15; ***Faces***, 103 Jln Ampang, also in an old colonial house, cover RM16; ***Deluxe Nite Club***, Rooftop, Ampang Park Shopping Centre, Jln Ampang, huge hostess bar ("every inch of the way we will make you feel like a Emperor"), Chinese bands (imported from Hong Kong and Taiwan) perform every night; ***Legends***, 1 Jln Kia Peng, particularly popular with local KL crowd and again, in an old converted bungalow; ***The Jump***, Ground Flr, Wisma Inai 241, Jln Tun Razak, one of the latest additions to the club scene, performance bartendering, live bands, jazz nights, popular Wed ladies night, RM20 cover; ***Modesto's***, 1d Lorong Perak, off Jln P Ramlee, trendy night spot, small dance floor, ladies night Wed, pizzas and Italian food; ***Tin Mine***, Basement, *KL Hilton*, Jln Sultan Ismail, one of the few old nightclubs still going strong, small dance floor and backgammon for the less energetic, has a reputation as a hostess hangout, recommended, cover charge RM26++.

Theatre: ***Actor's Studio Theatre***, Plaza Putra, underneath Merdeka Square.

● Hospitals & medical services

Hospitals: *Assunta Hospital*, Petaling Jaya, T 7923433; *City Medical Centre*, 415-427 Jln Pudu, T 2211255; *Damai Service Hospital*, 115-119 Jln Ipoh, T 4434900; *Pudu Specialist Centre*, Jln Baba, T 2429146; *Tung Shin Hospital*, 102 Jln Pudu, T 2321655. All have casualty wards open 24 hours.

● Libraries

National Library, Jln Tun Razak, T 2923144; ***British Council Library***, Jln Bukit Aman, T 2987555; ***Lincoln Resource Centre***, 376 Jln Tun Razak, T 2420291.

● Post & telecommunications

Area code: 03.

General Post Office: Dayabumi Complex, Jln Sultan Hishamuddin (Poste Restante).

Overseas telephone service: *Kedai Telekom* at the airport; *Kaunter Telegraf STM*, Wisma Jothi, Jln Gereja; Ground Floor, *Syarikat Telekom Malaysia*, Bukit Mahkamah.

Assisted International Calls: T 108; **Directory Enquiries**: T 103; **Telegram Service**: T 104; **Fire**: T 994; **Immigration**: Jln Pantai Bharu, T 7578155; **KL Tourist Police**: T 2496593; **Police/ambulance**: T 999; **Telegram Services**: T 104; **Trunk Calls Assistance**: T 101; **Weather Report**: T 1052.

● Shopping

As recently as the early 1980s Malaysians and KL's expatriates used to go on shopping expeditions to neighbouring Singapore – KL just was not up to it. These days however, the city has more or less everything, with new shopping complexes springing up every year. They are not concentrated in any particular area – and ordinary shopping streets and markets are also dotted all around the city.

Antiques: ***Oriental Spirit***, northern end, 1st Flr, Central Market, T 3272160. A stunning emporium of mostly mainland Southeast Asian treasures. Quite pricey but the interior is an Aladdin's Cave of goodies and is well worth a look for the imaginative way in which it's been laid out, recommended; Bangsar Town Centre is also renowned for its antiques;

Artefacts: for a general range of Southeast Asian artefacts, the best areas are Jln Ulu Klang, Jln Pudu and Bangsar Town Centre. ***Tibetan Treasures***, 16 Changkat Bukit Bintang, for antique Tibetan furniture and paintings.

Batik: ***Aran Novabatika Malaysia***, 174 Ground Floor, Ampang Park Shopping Centre, Jln Ampang; ***Batik Bintang***, Lobby Arcade, *Federal Hotel*, Jln Bukit Bintang; ***Batik Corner***, Lot L1.13, The Weld Shopping Centre, 76 Jln Raja Chulan, excellent selection of sarong lengths and ready-mades in batiks from all over Malaysia and Indonesia; ***Batik Malaysia***, 114 Jln Bukit Bintang, Mun Loong, 113 Jln Tunku Abdul Rahman; ***Batik Permai***, Lobby Arcade, *Hilton Hotel*, Jln Sultan Ismail; ***Central Market***, Jln Hang Kasturi, hand-painted silk batik scarves downstairs, many shops sell batik in sarong lengths; ***Evolution***, G24, Citypoint, Dayabumi Complex, Jln Sultan Hishamuddin, T 2913711 fashionable range of readymades and other batik gift ideas by designer Peter Hoe; ***Faruzzi Weld Shopping Centre***, Jln Raja Chulan (also at 42B Jln Nirwana, just off Jln Tun Ismail) exclusive and original batiks, recommended; ***Globe Silk Store***, 185 Jln Tuanku Abdul Rahman; ***Heritage***, 38 1st Flr, has a big selection of very original Kelantanese batiks (RM15-90/m), most ordinary batiks cost about RM7/m; ***Khalid Batik***, 48, Ground Floor, Ampang Park Shopping Centre, Jln Ampang; there are several shops on Jln Masjid India; there are two batik factories which welcome visitors – the East Coast Batiks Factory, No 1, 8½ mile, T 6891948 and No 15, Jln Cahaya 15, Taman Cahaya, Ampang, T 9840205.

Books: *Berita Book Centre* and ***MPH Bookstores***, Bukit Bintang Plaza, 1st Flr and Gd Flr respectively, Jln Bukit Bintang; ***Bookazine***, Damansara Heights 8 Jln Batai; ***Kinokuniya***, Isetan Dept Store, 2nd Flr, 50 Jln Sultan Ismail: ***Minerva Book Store***, 114 Jln Tunku Abdul Rahman; ***Popular Book Co***, Jln Petaling, Jln Hang Lekir, Sungai Way Plaza; ***Times Books***, Yow Chuan Plaza, 6-7 Jln Tun Razak and Weld Shopping Complex, good selection of English language books; *Second-hand bookshop* on 1st Flr of Central Market.

Cameras: **Sungai Wang Plaza**, Jln Sultan Ismail, Golden Triangle.

Carpets and rugs: **KL Plaza**, Jln Bukit Bintang, Golden Triangle; **Ampang Park Shopping Complex**, Jln Ampang; **City Square**, Jln Tun Razak, northeast of Golden Triangle.

Clothing: for **designer clothing** and accessories: **Starhill Shopping Centre**, Jln Bukit Bintang, Golden Triangle; Lot 10 on the corner of Jln Sultan Ismail and Jln Bukit Bintang, Golden Triangle. ***Sogo***, Jln Tuanku Abdul Rahman. For **custom-made clothing**: **Sungai Wang Shopping Plaza**, Jln Sultan Ismail, Golden Triangle. For **discount branded fashions**: **Sungai Wang Plaza**, Jln Sultan Ismail; the **Weld Shopping Centre**, Jln Raja Chulan, near the KL Tower; **City Square**, Jln Tun Razak, northeast of Golden Triangle.

Computers: **Imbi Plaza**, Jln Imbi, Golden Triangle.

Electrical items: **Sungai Wang Plaza**, Jln Sultan Ismail.

Fabrics: Jln Tuanku Abdul Rahman; ***Lot 10***, Jln Bukit Bintang; ***Semua House***, Lorong Tuanku Abdul Rahman (at northern end of Jln Masjid India); Ampang Shopping Complex, Jln Ampang.

Furniture: ***Oriental Style***, southern end of Central Market, 1st Flr and at 64 Jln Hang Kasturi, reproduction Asian furniture. Pricey. ***Oriental Spirit***, northern end of Central Market, 1st Flr, antique furniture. Expensive but beautiful objects. **Rattan furniture** available from Bangsar Town Centre, Ampang Point and Wisma Stephens.

Gems (Gold, pearls and precious gems): Petaling St; Lot 10, Jln Bukit Bintang; City Square, Jln Tun Razak; ***Semua House***, Lorong Tuanku Abdul Rahman (at northern end of Jln Masjid India).

Gems (semi-precious gems, jade and porcelain): **KL Plaza**, Jln Bukit Bintang; **Ampang Shopping Complex**, Jln Ampang; **Petaling Street**; **Lot 10**, Jln Bukit Bintang.

Handicrafts: much of the handicrafts are imported from Indonesia. ***Aked Ibu Kota***, Jln Tuanku Abdul Rahman, shopping centre with wide variety of goods including local handicrafts; ***Amazing Grace***, G-3P Yow Chuan Plaza, Jln Tun Razak; ***Andida Handicraft Centre***, 10 Jln Melayu; ***Central Market***, Jln Hang Kasturi, the old wet market is now full of handicrafts stalls, not always the cheapest but big selection; ***Eastern Dreams***, 101A Jln Ampang; *Oriental Style*, Central Market, 1st Flr, selection of upmarket baskets, pots, brassware. Quite pricey but worth a look; ***Golden Triangle***, Central Market, 1st Flr, Cornucopia of wooden figures; ***Borneo Crafts***, Central Market, 1st Flr, mostly wooden pieces, good selection of puppets and boxes; ***Karyaneka Handicraft Village***, Kompleks Seni Budaya, Jln Conlay, government-run, exhibiting and selling Malaysian handicrafts; ***Lavanya Arts***, 116A Jln Berhala Brickfields, run by the Temple of Fine Arts of *Annalakshmi* vegetarian restaurant fame, which aims to preserve Malaysia's Indian heritage, the shop sells Indian crafts: jewellery, bronzes, wood carvings, furniture, paintings and textiles; ***Lum Trading***, 123 Jln SS2/24 SEA Park, Petaling Jaya, baskets and bambooware, 64 Jln Tun Perak; ***Malaysian Arts***, 23 Jln Bukit Bintang; ***South China Seas***, Level 4 Metro Jaya, Jln Bukit Bintang; for **Chinese arts and handicrafts** the areas to look are along Jln Tuanku Abdul Rahman and Bangsar Town Centre.

Indian knick-knacks: incense, Indian silks, saris, jasmine, jewellery all available along Jln Melayu. Nepalese trinkets from Petaling St.

Mosquito nets: 3rd Flr, Supermarket in the UDA Ocean Building. Camping stall in Central Market.

Optical Goods: *Sungei Wang Plaza*, Jln Sultan Ismail; ***Lot 10***, Jln Bukit Bintang; ***KL Plaza***, Jln Bukit Bintang.

Pewter: *Dai-Ichi Arts and Crafts*, 122 Mezanine Flr, *Parkroyal Hotel*, Jln Sultan Ismail/Jln Imbi; ***KL Arts & Crafts***, 18 Ground Floor, Central Market, Jln Hang Kasturi; ***Royal Selangor Pewter Showrooms***, 231 Jln Tuanku Abdul Rahman, T 2986244.

Shoes: custom made shoes available from Jln Tuanku Abdul Rahman.

Watches: Lot 10, Jln Bukit Bintang; Sungai Wang Plaza, Jln Sultan Ismail; KL Plaza, Jln Bukit Bintang. Jln Petaling is the best place for the 'genuine copy' watch.

Markets and shopping streets: ***Central Market***, next to Jln Hang Kasturi is a purpose built area with 2 floors of boutiques and stalls selling just about every conceivable craft. For example, pewter, jewellery, jade, wood, ceramics. Stalls of note include one which sells all kinds of moulds and cutters for baking, a wonderful spice stall, another one for nuts and a third for dried fruits. One shop called *Collectibles* sells old watches, brass pieces, bird cages – worth a look. See sections on antiques and furniture for details on other shops. ***Chow Kit*** (Jln Haji Hussein), just off Jln Tuanku Abdul Rahman, is a cheap place to buy almost anything – it doubles as a red light district, although this area is rapidly being developed and its image 'cleaned-up', the extensive wet market on Jln Haji Hussein is scheduled to be re-located to make way for building. ***Jalan Melayu*** is another interesting area for browsing – Indian shops filled with silk saris, brass pots and Malay shops specializing in Islamic paraphernalia such as *songkok* (velvet Malay hats) and prayer rugs as well as herbal medicines and oils. ***Jalan Tuanku Abdul Rahman*** (Batu Rd) was KL's best shopping street for decades and is transformed into a pedestrian mall and night market every Sat after 1730, KL's original department store, *Globe Silk Store*, is on Jln Tuanku Abdul Rahman. ***Kampung Baru Sunday Market (Pasar Minggu)***, off Jln Raja Muda Musa (a large Malay enclave at the north end of KL) is an open air market which comes alive on Sat nights, Malays know it as the Sun market as their Sun starts at dusk on Sat – so don't go on the wrong night), a variety of stalls selling batik sarongs, bamboo birdcages and traditional handicrafts compete with dozens of food stalls, the Pasar Minggu has largely been superceded by Central Market as a place to buy handicrafts however. ***Leboh Ampang***, off Jln Gereja was the first area to be settled by Indian immigrants and today remains KL's 'Little India', selling everything from samosas to silk saris. ***Pasar Malam***, Jln Petaling, Chinatown is a night market full of copy watches, pirate cassettes and cheap clothes. ***Pudu Market***, bordered by Jln Yew, Jln Pasar and Jln Pudu, is a traditional wet market selling food and produce – mainly patronized by Chinese.

Shopping complexes Jalan Sultan Ismail/Bukit Bintang: the majority of KL's shopping complexes are to be found in this area, they include – east to west: ***Star Hill Plaza***, Jln Bukit Bintang, prestigious marble clad shopping centre houses *Tang's Department Store* (of Singapore fame) and many designer boutiques. ***Lot 10***, Jln Sultan Ismail, distinctive emerald green façade, Isetan Department Store, British India, Moschino, Knickerbox, other mid-range boutiques plus an excellent food court. ***Bukit Bintang Plaza***, corner of Jln Bukit Bintang and Jln Sultan Ismail, houses the popular department store – Metrojaya, a Marks & Spencers and a labyrinth of other shops, which lead into Sungai Wang. ***Sungai Wang Plaza***, Jln Sultan Ismail, one of largest complexes in KL, houses over 500 shops and Parkson Grand Department Store, food court in basement. ***Imbi Plaza***, corner of Jln Sultan Ismail and Jln Imbi, good for computers. **Ampang**: centre of complexes on east edge of city – ***Yow Chuan Plaza***, JLn Tun Razak, antiques, curios, souvenirs and designer goods, linked to *City Square* next door which has a Metrojaya department store and Toys 'R' Us. ***Ampang Park***, Jln Tun Razak, opposite City Square, noted for its jewellery boutiques. **Jalan Tuanku Abdul Raaman**: ***Sogo Pernas Department Store***, largest department store in Southeast Asia on 10 floors. ***Pertama Shopping Complex***, wide range of shops from souvenirs to fashion and a basement bazaar. **Jalan Putra**: ***The Mall***, right across from Putra World Trade Centre, quite trendy, large shopping mall, good for fashion, Yaohan Department Store, Starlight Express indoor theme park,lots of fast food outlets, *Delifrance*, *Pizza Hut* etc. **Others**: ***The Weld***, corner of Jln Raja Chulan and Jln P Ramlee, quite a few food outlets here, large *Times Bookstore*, *Reject Shop*, *Art Gallery* and selection of fashion/leather shops etc. ***Subang Parade***, Subang Jaya, houses Parkson Grand Department Store and Toys 'R' Us, amusement park and fast food outlets. ***Kota Raya Shopping Complex***, Jln Cheng Lock, cut-price goods.

● Sports

Badminton: ***Bangsar Sports Complex***, Jln Terasek Tiga, Bangsar Baru, T 2546065; ***YMCA***, 95 Jln Padang Belia, off Jln Tun Sambathan, Brickfields, T 2741349, Jln Tun Razak Multipurpose Hall, T 4231158.

Bowling: ***Federal Bowl***, *Federal Hotel*, Jln Bukit Bintang, T 2489166. ***Leisure Mall Bowling***, Cheras Leisure Mall, Jln Manis, 6 Taman Segar, T 9323866. ***Miramar Bowling Centre***,

Wisma Miramar, Jln Wisma Putra, T 2421863. ***Pekeliling Bowl***, Yow Chuan Plaza, Jln Tun Razak, T 2430953.

Golf: *Plaza Putra Indoor Golf Centre*, underground complex in Dataran Merdeka, golfers can select from 7 prestigious international courses from a computerized menu, T 4432541. ***Kelab Golf Negara***, Subang (near Subang International Airport), two 18-hole courses, green fees RM200, T 7760388. ***Royal Selangor Golf Club***, Jln Kelab Golf, off Jln Tun Razak, exclusive championship course (including two 18-hole courses and one 9-hole), one of the oldest in the country, non-members can only play on weekdays, green fees RM210 (without membership introduction), T 9848433. ***Saujana Golf & Country Resort***, Subang (near Subang International Airport), two 18-hole championship courses, green fees RM170 weekdays, RM290 weekends, T 7461466. ***Sentul Golf Club***, 84 Jln Strachan, Sentul, built in 1928, recently refurbished and a swimming pool added, green fees RM30 weekdays, RM50 weekends, T 4435571. ***Templer Park Country Club***, 21 km north of KL, fully floodlit course for 24-hours golf, frequented by Japanese golf package tourists, developed and part-owned by Japanese company, the more environmentally-minded have complained that the course has ruined the north end of Templer Park, jungled limestone outcrops now divide the fairways, green fees, RM150 weekdays, RM200 weekends, T 6919617.

Health centres: *Fitness International*, *Parkroyal Hotel*, Jln Sultan Ismail. ***Good Friend Health Centre***, 33 Jln Tun Sambathan 5. ***Recreation Health Centre***, 4th Flr, *Furama Hotel*, Komleks Selangor, Jln Sultan Ismail.

Roller skating: *Fun World Roller Disco*, 1st Flr Asiajaya Shopping Complex, Petaling Jaya.

Snooker: *Jade Snooker Centre*, GBC Plaza, Jln Ampang, T 4570345. ***Snooker Paradise***, Kompleks Kotaraya.

Spectator sports: Cricket, rugby and hockey are played on the Padang, in the centre of KL, most weekends. Football and badminton are Malaysia's most popular sports. Inter-state Malaysia Cup football matches are played at the ***Merdeka Stadium*** and the Stadium on Jln Stadium, off Jln Maharajalela. The (rather more successful) Selangor team play at the new Shah Alam Stadium – Sat and Tues 2030 kick-off. RM10 entrance fee. A colourful (and safe) experience. One-way taxi RM15-20, need to ask taxi driver to wait for you as it is difficult getting back into town.

Squash: *Bangsar Sports Complex*, Jln Terasek Tiga, Bangsar Baru, T 2546065.

Swimming: all international-class hotels in KL have their own pools for guests. Public pools charge a nominal fee. ***Bangsar Sports Complex***, Jln Terasek Tiga, Bangsar Baru, T 2546065, open Mon-Sat 0800-1300, closed Sun; ***Weld Swimming Pool***, Jln Raja Chulan. ***Public pool***, next to Chinwoo Stadium, off Jln Hang Jebat.

Tennis: *Kelana Jaya Sports Complex*, Lot 1772, Taman Tasek Subang, Kelana Jaya; ***YMCA***, 95 Jln Padan Belia, Brickfields.

Watersports: *Sunway Lagoon and Adventure Park*, T 7356000, a new 'theme park', with plenty of entertainment both in and out of the water, admission RM15 (RM10 for children), open 1200-2030 Mon, Wed, Thur, 1200-2200 Fri, 1000-2000 Sat, Sun and public holidays. *Getting there*: from Klang bus station, Sri Jaya Bus 252B USJ or Klang Bus 51. ***The Mines***, Sungai Besi Tin Mine (T 9487402, admission: weekdays adult RM8, child RM4, weekends adult RM12, child RM6), 20 minutes drive from KL, before the toll booths on highway to Seremban, exit on left (at Taman Sri Petaling), turn right at T-junction, over the railway line and past Shell and Esso stations towards Serdang and Kajang, signposted to the left, located in what was the biggest tin mine in the world, in clean, turquoise water and beneath dramatic rocky cliffs. Recently developed as a 200 acre recreational park which boasts a snow house where the temperature is regulated to create all year round snow. Other amusements include a roller coaster, water screen, laser show and a musical fountain.

● Tour companies & travel agents

Most of the big hotels have their own in-house travel agents and ticketing agencies. For domestic flights it can be cheaper to buy tickets through ticketing agencies rather than going to MAS headquarters on Jln Sultan Ismail. If you are staying in a hotel, many ticketing agencies will deliver the tickets to your room. There are plenty of travel agents in the Angkasaraya Building on the corner of Jln Ampang and Jln Ramlee. For slightly different mid-range tours, try *Dee Travel*, Central Market, T 2019699. For student/cheap outbound tickets, *MSL* is recommended near the *Grand Central Hotel*, T 4424722 or *STA*, 5th Flr, Magnum Plaza, Jln Pudu, T 2489800; *Ecstasy Travel*, 754 Jln Sentul, T 4425688, organizes country and city tours for about RM25 for a 3-hour trip; *Thomas Cook*,

Level 18, Menara Lion, Jln Ampang (near *Nikko Hotel*), T 2649252. MATIC (see below in tourist offices section) provide a telephone booking service for Taman Negara Resort, on T 2643929, ext 113

● Tourist offices

Tourism Malaysia, Information Centre, Level 2, Putra World Trade Centre, 45 Jln Tun Ismail, T 4411295, T 2935188, F 2935884, and **Tourist Information Desks**, Terminals 1 & 2, Subang International Airport, T 7465707, as well as the **Information Counter** at the Railway Station, T 2746063; **KL Visitors Centre**, 3 Jln Sultan Hishamuddin, T 2301369 (next to the National Art Gallery), a non-governmental tourist association, not particularly conveniently located and their most useful publication is an A3 map of the city – which is available from the Tourism Malaysia offices in any case; **Malaysian Tourist Information Centre (MATIC)**, 109 Jln Ampang, T 2643929, F 2621149, located in an opulent mansion formerly belonging to a Malaysian planter and tin miner, information on all 13 states, cultural performances and demonstrations of traditional handicrafts, it also provides money-changing facilities.

● Useful information

Wildlife and National Parks Department, Km 10, Jln Cheras, T 9052872, F 9052873.
American Express, 18th Flr, **The Weld** (near KL Tower), Jln Raja Chulan, T 2130000.

● Transport

Butterworth 383 km, Cameron Highlands 219 km, Ipoh 217 km, Melaka 148 km, Johor Bahru 365 km, Singapore 393 km, Kuantan 274 km, Kuala Terengganu 491 km, Kota Bharu 657 km. KL is not an easy place to get around; walking is hazardous, the bus system is labyrinthine and if you manage to find a taxi with an amenable driver, you'll probably get stuck in a queue. The only solution in some cases is the new LRT (Light Rail Transit), but it's still in its early stages and its single line has only a limited number of stops.

Local Walking: the pedestrian, evidently, is not very high on the list of priorities for the Malaysian urban planner. Many roads, especially outside the central city are built without pavements – making walking both hazardous and difficult. In addition, with the exception of the area around Central Market, Chinatown and Dayabumi, distances between places are too great to cover comfortably on foot – because of lack of pavements, heavy pollution and the humid hot climate. **Bus**: an **Intrakota** bus map should be available gratis from City Hall, but when we visited KL they were reprinting and the tourist board didn't know the new bus system. Intrakota has taken over most routes now but it's not a particularly easy system to grasp. For enquiries, T 7172727. Prices are RM0.60-0.90. **LRT (Light Rail Transit)**: the overhead railway is taking a while to establish itself as a viable form of public transport, as stops are still limited. It currently runs over 12 km and 13 stations, but extensions to the system are due for completion in 1998 and 1999. The trains operate between 0600 and 2400 with a frequency of a train every 3-5 minutes during peak hours and every 8-15 minutes during off-peak hours. Fares range from RM0.75 (one-two stops) to RM2.95; stored value tickets to the value of RM20 or RM50 are also available saving hassle for those using the system regularly. To travel from Ampang to Sultan Ismail takes around 20 minutes; from Ampang to Miharja, 12 minutes. Phase 2 of the LRT will comprise a line from Chan Sow Lin south to Komanwel (the Commonwealth Games Village) adding 7 new stations. This is due for completion before the Commonwealth Games in 1998. A second part of Phase 2 will

DRIVE FROM GATEWAY CITY TO SEE

FOR RESERVATIONS:
Tel: (603) 230 7788
Fax: (603) 232 0077

RENTAL LOCATION:
• *1st Floor, Shangri-La Hotel, Kuala Lumpur*

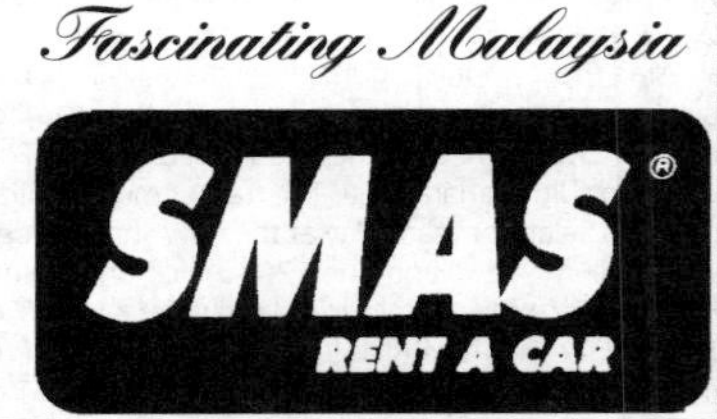

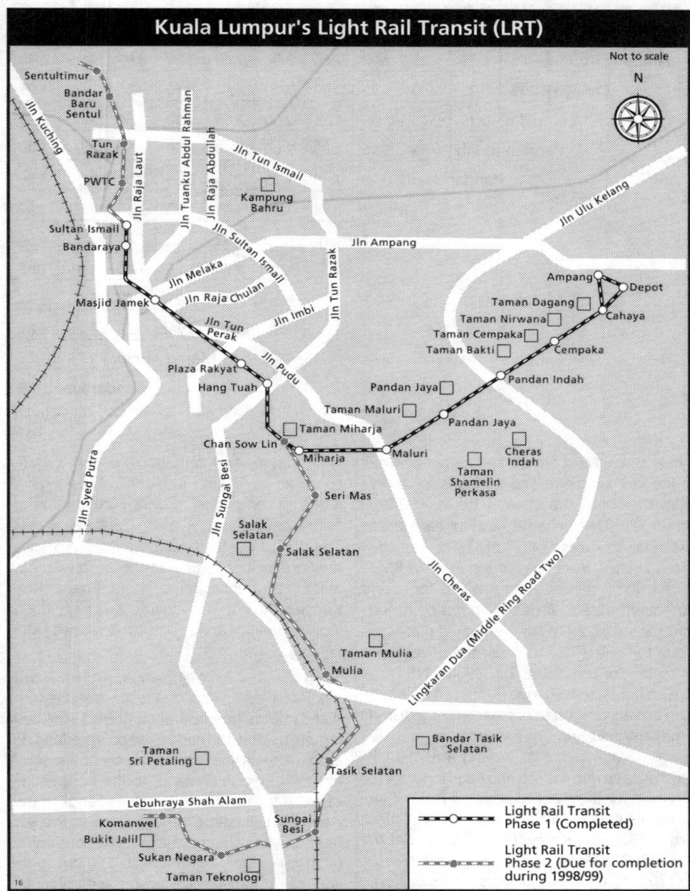

continue north from Sultan Ismail to Sentul Timor, adding four stops, and is due for completion in 1999. **Commuter trains**: the alternative to the LRT for north-south travel in the city is to hop on a commuter train. The three city stops are Putra, near the World Trade Centre, Bang Negara, and the Railway Station. Trains leave every 15-30 minutes (RM1); **Car hire**: **Apex, Budget, Hertz, Mayflower, National, SMAS, Thrifty, Tomo Express, Toyota** and **U-Drive** all have desks at Subang Airport. **Avis**, T 2417144, F 2429650; **Economy Car Rental (ECR)**, T2925427, F 2927888; **Hakikat**, T 2448404; **Hawk**, T 2646455, F 2646466; **Hertz**, T 2486433, F 2428481; **Mayflower**, T 6221888, F 6279282; **National**, T 2480522, F 2482823; **Orix**, T 2423009, F 2423609; **Sintat**, T 2457988, F 2456057; **SMAS**, T 2307788, F 2320077; **Thrifty**, T 2488877, T 7469778 (Airport), F 2424907. For breakdown problems the **Automobile Association of Malaysia (AAM)** is on T 2625777 or T 2625358. **Taxi**: KL is one of the cheaper cities in Southeast Asia for taxis; there are taxi stands

Light Rail Transit (LRT) fares (1997)

Ampang	0.75	0.75	1.35	1.35	2.00	2.00	2.00	2.00	2.50	2.95	2.95	2.95
Cahaya		0.75	0.75	1.35	1.35	2.00	2.00	2.00	2.50	2.50	2.95	2.95
Cempaka			0.75	0.75	1.35	1.35	2.00	2.00	2.50	2.50	2.50	2.95
Pandan Indah				0.75	1.35	1.35	2.00	2.00	2.50	2.50	2.50	2.50
Pandan Jaya					0.75	1.35	1.35	2.00	2.50	2.50	2.50	2.50
Maluri						0.75	1.35	1.35	1.85	2.50	2.50	2.50
Miharja							0.75	1.35	1.85	1.85	2.50	2.50
Pudu								0.75	1.25	1.85	1.85	1.85
Hang Tuah									1.25	1.25	1.85	1.85
Plaza Rakyat										1.25	1.25	1.85
Masjid Jamek											1.25	1.25
Bandaraya												1.25
Sultan Ismail												

all over town. Most are a/c and metered: RM2 for the first kilometre and 10 cents for every 200m thereon. Extra charges between 2400 and 0600 (50% surcharge), and for each extra passenger in excess of 2, RM1 for luggage placed in boot. Waiting charges are now RM2 for the first 2 minutes and RM0.10 for every subsequent 45secs. Taxis should not be hailed from the street; there are designated places to queue for one. (Try and) insist the driver uses the meter. For complaints T 2539044. **NB** During rush hours, shift change (3-ish) or its raining, it can be very difficult to persuade taxis to travel to the centre of town. The answer is to negotiate a price (locals claim that waving a RM10 bill helps) or jump into the cab and feign ingorance; it is illegal for them not to accept a fare within the city limits. For 24-hours taxi service: ***Comfort***, T 7330507; ***Koteksi***, T 7815352; ***Sakti***, T 4420848; ***Selangor***, T 2936211; ***Telecab***, T 2110211; ***KL Taxi Drivers' Association***, T 2215252; ***Mesra***, T 4421019. A RM1 surcharge is made for a phone booking. If you are desperate for a taxi go to the nearest hotel and rent a limousine. The cost varies from RM35 to RM60.

Air Subang International Airport is 24 km from KL. Buses 47 and 343 connect the airport with central KL. Taxis to town cost about RM30; coupons available from the 'limousine' counter outside the arrivals hall. Connections to most other capitals in Southeast Asia (see Transport to and from Malaysia, page 502 for more information on the airport, transport and facilities). Note that a new international airport is under construction 45 km south of KL at Sepang and is due for completion in 1998. Further information available on T (03) 2538588, F (03) 2535671. MAS flights to other Malaysian destinations include regular connections with Alor Star, Ipoh, Johor Bahru, Kota Bharu, Kota Kinabalu, Kuala Terengganu, Kuantan, Kuching, Labuan, Lahad Datu, Langkawi, Miri, Penang, Tawau.

Train Central Railway Station, Jln Hishamuddin, T 2747435. Left luggage office on Platform 4 and information desk at Platform 1. The desk is quite helpful and can advise on schedules. KL is on the main line from Singapore to the south and Butterworth (Penang) to the north; some of these trains go on through to Bangkok (see page 502). To get on the east coast line you have to go to Gemas, the junction south of KL or to Kuala Lipis or Mentakab 150 km to the west of KL. Regular connections with Alor Star, Butterworth, Taiping, Ipoh, Tapah Rd (for Cameron Highlands), Tampin, Gemas, Johor Bahru and Singapore. Tourists on production of their passport, can buy a KTM rail pass which offers unlimited rail travel, although it is not valid on the Thai system. For more information T 2757267, or refer to the timetables and fare charts on pages 513-516.

Road Bus: KL's main bus terminal is **Puduraya** on Jln Pudu. Buses leave here for destinations across the Peninsula as well as to Singapore and Thailand. Most large bus companies have their offices inside the terminal, above the departure

Selected Ekspres National bus fares from KL

From Kuala Lumpur	(M$)
Alor Setar	21.20
Butterworth	17.10
Batu Pahat	10.90
Ipoh	9.40
Johor Bahru	16.50
Kangar	23.40
Kemaman	13.50
Kota Bahru	25.00
Kuantan	12.10
K Terengganu	21.60
Kuala Perlis	23.40
Muar	8.50
Penang	18.50
Singapore	17.80
Taiping/KK	13.20

NB 1997 fares quoted

hall, including the biggest, *Ekspres Nasional*. *Ekspres Nasional* also have a ticket counter at the Malaysia Tourist Infomation Centre on Jln Ampang and many hotels and guesthouses will arrange tickets too – which saves on a journey to Puduraya. There are also quite a number of bus offices opposite the terminal along Jln Pudu and, due to overcrowding within, quite a few buses drop off and pick up along that strip of road. It is best to book tickets the day before leaving (although same day departure is usually possible) and during peak holiday periods several days in advance. **NB** Avoid buying tickets from touts; only go to the counters. There is an information desk at the terminal, along with a Post Office, tourist police booth, left luggage office (open 0800-2200 Mon-Sun, RM1.50/ item/day) and foodstalls. Though most travellers find that Puduraya serves their travelling needs – the key exception being those wishing to visit Taman Negara National Park – KL has a number of other bus terminals. The **Pekeliling Station**, T 4421256 is in the north of the city, off Jln Tun Razak. Buses to Pahang State leave from here including Jerantut (for Taman Negara) and Kuala Lipis which do not depart from Puduraya. Other destinations include Kuantan and the Genting Highlands. The **Putra Station**, T 4429530, facing the Putra World Trade Centre, serves the East Coast and there are connections with destinations in Kelantan, Terengganu and Pahang including Kuantan, Kuala Terengganu and Kota Bharu. Buses to Penang, Ipoh and Johor Bahru leave from **Medan Mara**. Regular connections with Singapore, Johor Bahru, Melaka, Butterworth (and Penang, 5 hours), Ipoh, Kuantan, Kota Bharu. Finally the small **Klang Station** in Chinatown, on Jln Hang Kasturi, serves Port Klang and the suburb of Shah Alam.

Outstation taxis: leave from Jln Pudu, outside the Puduraya bus station. Share taxis run to most large towns on the Peninsula and fares are about double those of equivalent bus journeys. As there are no scheduled departures it is a case of turning up and seeing which taxis have space and where they are going.

Northern Peninsular Malaysia

Horizons	142	Penang (Pulau Pinang)	175
Barisan Titiwangsa and the hill stations	142	Alor Star	199
Ipoh to Butterworth	158	Kangar	204
Taiping	171	Pulau Langkawi	205

THE MAIN ROAD north from Kuala Lumpur is a straightforward journey up the Peninsula's heavily populated west coast. The north-south Highway – Malaysia's equivalent of the autobahn – cuts inland, avoiding the coast which is skirted by mangrove swamps and mudflats. Rubber and oil palm plantations line the route and open-cast tin mines and dredges are a common sight, particularly in the Kinta Valley, south of Ipoh. From Butterworth, the road leaves the plantations behind and enters the ricebowl states of Kedah and Perlis. The latter produces over half Malaysia's rice output, with the help of the Muda irrigation scheme.

BARISAN TITIWANGSA AND THE HILL STATIONS

Brisan Titiwangsa and the Hill Stations On the road north, Peninsular Malaysia's mountainous jungled backbone lies to the east. It is called the Barisan Titiwangsa – or Main Range. It is largely unsettled – apart from the old British hill stations (Fraser's Hill, Cameron Highlands and Maxwell Hill) and scattered Orang Asli aboriginal villages. During the Malayan Emergency in the late 1940s and early 1950s, the Communist guerrillas operated from jungle camps in the mountains and later used the network of aboriginal trails to infiltrate the peninsula from their bases in southern Thailand.

GENTING HIGHLANDS

The Genting Highlands, just 51 km north-east of KL, is the city's closest hill resort and a popular source of entertainment, Las Vegas-cum-Disneyland style. Genting Highlands was first developed as a resort in the 1960s by a prominent Malaysian businessman, Tan Sri Lim Goh Tong. At the time, investing in construction at an altitude of 2,000m above sea level was considered a hair-brain idea. Building the tortuous and impossibly steep road

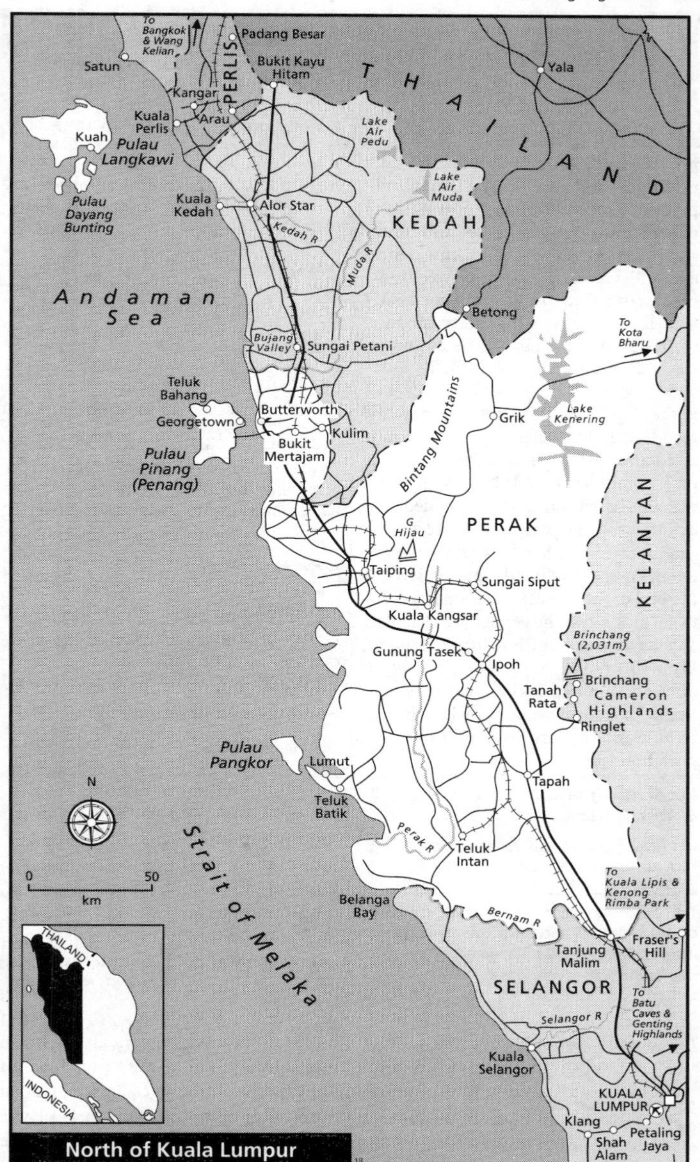

North of Kuala Lumpur

through the dense, jungle-covered hills, took 7 years alone. However, the idea took off, and the government conceded to allow Malaysia's only casino to operate here.

The resort's main attraction is the Casino de Genting which is one of the largest in the world, with endless rows of slot machines, games tables and even a computerized race track where it is possible to bet on Royal Ascot. The decor is glitzy – red plush and glittering chandeliers abound. Occasional grand sweeps are made: last year an Indonesian put a RM4 keno token into a machine and came away with 1.5 million ringgit. The casino attracts an estimated 30,000 clients a day and provides the main source of revenue in the Highlands. Other attractions in the resort include a theme park, which is rated amongst the best in Malaysia. The park comprises an outdoor theme park which is being constantly expanded, and an indoor theme park and leisure zone to cater for wet-weather days, which are frequent in the Highlands, particularly at the end of the year. It takes at least a day to get around all the venues – and at least as long to work out how to get around. With this bonanza of entertainment on offer, not surprisingly, weekends and public holidays are very busy; Chinese New Year and Hari Raya are two of the peak holidays.

Local information

● Accommodation

Prices: L over RM500; **A+** RM260-500; **A** RM130-260; **B** RM65-130; **C** RM40-65; **D** RM20-40; **E** RM10-20; **F** Below RM10

The accommodation at Genting Highlands comes under the umbrella of the *Genting Highlands Resorts*. Weekends and holidays have the disadvantage of having to queue at check in and out times, it is best to visit on a weekday if possible.

A-B *Awana Golf & Country Resort*, T 2113015, F 2113555, 10 km below the main resort peak, the 30-storey octagonal tower dominates the resort, overlooking an 18-hole golf course, all rooms have fans (a/c not needed at this altitude), bath, TV and balconies offering panoramic views, facilities including a heated pool, tennis, gymnasium, sauna, children's library, coffee house, restaurant, cocktail lounge and golf (see Sport), recommended. **A** *Genting Hotel*, T 2111118, F 2111888, located in the heart of the action, deluxe Genting Club rooms, a heated pool and jacuzzi, restaurant, coffee house and easy access to all the resort facilities. **A** *Highlands Hotel*, T 2112812, F 2113535, massive (900 rooms), new and very smart, it calls its decor London-style. **A-B** *Kayangan Apartments*, units designed to accommodate extensive families, the smallest unit has 3 rooms and sleeps 6, the 4-room unit sleeps 8 – splitting the costs between a group, rates/head are in the **B-C** category. **A-B** *Resort Hotel*, T 2111118, F 2113535, mainly caters for tour groups and is rated as a 3-star outlet. **A-B** *Ria Apartments*, a 2-room unit sleeps 4 and in low season is priced at the lower end of the **A** range, a 3-room unit is even more economical and sleeps 6, either unit can take an additional 2 extra beds at a charge of RM20 each. **B** *Theme Park Hotel*, T 2111118, F 2113535, the first hotel to be built at the resort, but recently refurbished, and as its name suggests, the rooms overlook the outdoor theme park.

● Places to eat

Prices: ♦♦♦♦ over RM40; ♦♦♦ RM13-40; ♦♦ RM5-13; ♦ under RM5

Eating places are all within the resort which caters for most tastes and budgets.

Awana Golf & Country Resort: ♦♦♦♦*Japanese Restaurant*, recommended for sushi. ♦♦♦♦*Sails Grill*, 2nd flr, successfully achieves the romantic, candle-lit look combined with dark wood and ethnic masks, excellent quality, international cuisine, 5-star service, recommended. ♦♦♦*Genting Theatre Restaurant*, 2nd flr, tables arranged around the stage, eat while watching a show. ♦♦♦*Korean Restaurant*. ♦♦♦-♦♦*Rajawali Coffee House*. ♦♦*Restaurant Kampung*, lobby floor, traditional Malay fare, good value buffet and set lunch. ♦♦*Sidewalk Café*, lobby floor, a 24-hour coffee shop.

Highlands Hotel: ♦♦♦*The Bistro*, continental food, pizza. ♦♦♦-♦♦*Good Friends Restaurant*, Chinese food.

Indoor Theme Park: over 20 fast food outlets, including ♦♦*KFC*, ♦♦*McDonalds* and ♦♦*Theme Park Noodle House*.

Resort Hotel: ♦♦*Resort Café*, all-day á la carte and buffet breakfast, lunch and dinner.

Theme Park Hotel: ♦♦*Happy Valley Restaurant*, large and very popular Chinese restaurant.

● Banks & money changers
Maybank, *Genting Hotel*.

● Entertainment
Casino de Genting, *Genting Hotel*: formal dress, tie for men or hire a batik shirt at the door, blackjack, baccarat, roulette, Tai-Sai amongst the table games, slot machines, computerized racing, the International Room, for card-holders only, caters for more serious players. ***Indoor Theme Park***, the usual video games as well as a Virtual Reality Dungeon, 3-D Experience and Space Odyssey 2020 – their most recent simulator addition, a World Train Ride for the less techno-minded, and plenty of rides for tots. ***Leisure Zone***, 32-lane computerized bowling alley – the second largest in Malaysia, table tennis, snooker. ***Outdoor Theme Park***, the most recent additions are the Corkscrew Roller Coaster and the Rolling Thunder Mine Train, a monorail makes a circuit of the park and offers good views on a clear day, a cable car runs across the park – also good for views. ***Big Rock Disco Café***, the main disco at the resort.

● Post & telecommunications
Area code: 03.

General Post Office: *Genting Hotel*.

● Sports
Golf: *Awana Golf & Country Resort*, Km 13, T 2113015, F 2113535, 18-hole, international class course featuring bunkers, ponds and streams, putting green, 3-tiered driving range, open daily 0730-1730, green fees RM100 weekdays, not open to public at weekends, driving range.

Horse riding: *Awana Horse Ranch*, T 2112026, open daily 0800-1800, pony rides for children, jumps, horse trekking.

● Transport
51 km from KL, 131 km from Kuantan.

Bus: the resort operates an a/c express bus service between the KL Puduraya bus station and Genting Highlands. The service runs every 30 minutes at peak times and hourly at other times from 0800 to 1800 with an extended service on Sun and public holidays to 1900. The journey takes 1 hour and costs RM5, inclusive of the cable car which runs from near the *Awana Hotel* to the resort at the peak. The ticketing office at Puduraya is at counter 43, and buses leave from platform 13. For advance reservations T (03) 2326863. A free shuttle service operates every 2 hours between the *Awana* and the *Resort Hotel*. An hourly, 24-hour, free shuttle service connects the *Resort Hotel*, *Genting Hotel* and *Ria Apartments*. **Cable car**: the 'flying carpet cable car' operates between the resort at the peak and a station near *Awana*. It runs every 20 minutes between 1200 and 2030 on Mon, 0830 and 2030 Tues to Fri, and 0830 to 2130 weekends and public holidays. Travelling time is 12 minutes and the one way fare is RM3. For enquiries T (03) 2111118, ext 7751. There are plans to build a cable car from Batu caves, just outside KL, to the cable car station at the *Highlands Hotel*, which will cut travelling time considerably.

FRASER'S HILL (BUKIT FRASER)

Fraser's Hill is named after Englishman Louis James Fraser, who ran a gambling den, traded in tin and opium and operated a mule train in these hills at the end of the 19th century. He went on to manage a transport service between Kuala Kubu and Raub. Before Mr Fraser lent his name to it, the seven hills were known as Ulu Tras. The development of the hill station began in the early 1920s.

It was along the road from Kuala Bubu Bharu that Sir Henry Gurney, the British High Commissioner, was ambushed and killed by Communist insurgents during the Malayan Emergency in 1951 (see page 57). A few years earlier British soldiers were involved in the massacre of suspected Communist sympathizers near Kuala Kubu. They shot dead a number of rubber tappers from a local village. There are a number of Orang Asli villages along rivers and tracks leading from the twisting road up the hill.

Fraser's Hill, 1,524m above sea-level, is close enough to KL to be a favoured weekend resort. And because it was easily accessible by train from Kuala Kubu Road, it was a popular weekend retreat long before the Cameron Highlands. Most of colonial Malaya's big companies – such as Sime Darby, Guthries' and Harrisons & Crosfield – built holiday bungalows among the hills. More and more luxury bungalows are now being built here to cater for wealthy Malaysians, but it is still more tranquil and attractive than Genting. Although it is not as varied as the Cameron Highlands by way of attractions, there is one trail (a 3-hour walk) which starts just to the south of the tennis courts and ends at the *Corona Nursery Youth Hostel*, good opportunities for bird watchers and wild flower enthusiasts, a golf course, tennis courts and gardens. Swimming at Jeriau waterfalls is limited as the concrete pool has all but silted up so that the water is only knee deep, but standing under the powerful waterfall is very refreshing.

Local information

● Accommodation

Prices: L over RM500; **A+** RM260-500; **A** RM130-260; **B** RM65-130; **C** RM40-65; **D** RM20-40; **E** RM10-20; **F** Below RM10

Many of the hotels have recreation facilities such as tennis, squash, riding, snooker.

A ***Fraser's Pine Resort***, Fraser's Condominium, Jln Kuari Bukit, T 3622122, F 3622288, reservations T 7832577, F 7836108, price includes tax and breakfast, 1,2 and 3 bed apartments, the latter split between 3 couples brings rates down to **B** category, bit of an eyesore, and rather damp rooms, as the block has been built into the hillside. **A** ***Merlin Inn Resort***, Jln Lady Guilemard, T 3622300, F 3622284, a/c, TV, minibar, bath, in-house movie, tea and coffee-making facilities, restaurant, pool. **A** ***Silverpark Holiday Resort***, Jln Lady Maxwell, T 3622888, F 3622185, reservations T 2916633, apartments only, no cooking facilities, associated with De Club golf course, pool, restaurant, children's playground. **A** ***Ye Olde Smokehouse Hotel***, T 3622226, F 3622035, small 13-room hotel in the Olde English style of the *Smokehouse*, Cameron Highlands.

B ***Fraser's Hill Development Corporation***, T 3622311, F 3622273, the organization manages the ***Puncak Inn***, next to the bus stop, an unspecial 27-room hotel, and a series of 3 to 4-bedroom bungalows, including the ***Temerloh***,unusual circular but rather tatty chalets divided into 2 large rooms. ***Raub***; ***Pekan***. ***Jelai*** and ***Rompin***, rates are charged/room and an additional fixed rate is available for 3 daily meals, hiking and bird-watching tours are arranged.

C ***Gap Resthouse***, 8 km before Fraser's Hill, restaurant (good Chinese food, poor western and Malay-Indian food), recently renovated but still excellent value and a very characterful place to stay, recommended. **C** ***Seri Berkat Rest House***, T 03-8041026 (book through district office), another colonial building with high ceilings and big rooms.

E ***Corona Nursery Youth Hostel***, T 3622225.

● Places to eat

Prices: ♦♦♦♦ over RM40; ♦♦♦ RM13-40; ♦♦ RM5-13; ♦ under RM5

Chinese: ♦♦♦***Kheng Yuen Lee Eating Shop***, sports club.

International: ♦♦♦***Old Smokehouse***, similar to Cameron Highlands establishment, serving English style dishes such as Beef Wellington and Devonshire cream teas, recommended. ♦♦♦***Restoran Puncak***, below *Puncak Inn*. ♦♦♦***Temerloh Steak House***, Temerloh Bungalow.

● Bars

Ye Olde Tavern, above the *Puncak Inn*, Fraser's answer to an English inn, with log fire.

● Banks & money changers

It is possible to change money at **Maybank**, *Merlin Hotel*, also **Malaysia Bank**, along from *Merlin Hotel* entrance in the same complex of shops.

● Sports

Golf: ***De Club at Fraser's***, 18-hole course for members, 9-hole course for public, green fees RM40 weekdays, RM50 weekends, T 382777.

Horse riding, paddle boats: for hire on Allan's Water.

● **Post & telecommunications**
Area code: 09.

● **Tourist offices**
Fraser's Hill Development Corporation Office between golf club and the *Merlin Hotel*, maps and general information available.

● **Transport**
104 km from KL.

Local Bicycles: for hire from Fraser's Hill Development Corporation Office, RM4/hour. **Road Bus**: bus station at Kuala Bubu Bharu. Regular connections with KL, change here to Fraser's Hill. Bus only runs at 0800 and 1200 from Kuala Bubu Bharu to Fraser's Hill and returns at 1000 and 1400. **Car**: one way traffic system operates 8 km from Fraser's Hill: uphill traffic gets right-of-way on the odd hours, downhill traffic on the even hours. **Taxi**: shared taxis go direct to Fraser's Hill. KL (RM15).

CAMERON HIGHLANDS

The Cameron Highlands is the biggest and best known of Malaysia's hill stations. It lies on the northwest corner of Pahang, bounded by Perak, to the west, and Kelantan to the north. On the jungly 1,500m plateau the weather is reassuringly British – unpredictable, often wet and decidedly cool – but when the sun blazes out of an azure-blue sky, the Camerons are hard to beat. Daytime temperatures average around 23°C, and in the evening, when it drops to 10°C and the hills are enveloped in swirling cloud – 'the white witch' – pine log fires are lit in the hilltop holiday bungalows.

In the colonial era the mountain resort was a haven for home-sick, over-heated planters and administrators. Its temperate climate induced an eccentric collection of them to settle and retire in their Surrey-style mansions where they could prune their roses, tend their strawberries, sip G & Ts on the lawn, stroll down to the golf course or nip over to Mr Foster's mock-Tudor Smokehouse for a Devonshire cream tea. The British Army also had a large presence in Tanah Rata until 1971 – their imposing former military hospital (now reverted to being a Roman Catholic convent) still stands on the hill overlooking the main street. To the left of the road leading into Tanah Rata from Ringlet are a few remaining Nissen huts from the original British army camp.

While most of the old timers – the likes of Stanley Foster, Captain Bloxham (who nursed racehorses at his bougainvillaea-fringed 'spelling station' at Ringlet) and Miss Gwenny Griffith-Jones (founder of Singapore's Tanglin School) – have now gone to rest, they bequeathed an ambience which the Camerons has yet to shake off. Miss 'Griff' had been one of the original pioneers, trudging up through the jungle from Tapah on an oxcart, when they first cut the hair-pinned road in the 1930s.

Half a century elapsed between the discovery of the highland plateau and the arrival of the first settlers. William Cameron, a government surveyor, first claimed to have stumbled across "a fine plateau ... shut in by lofty mountains" while on a mapping expedition in 1885. In a letter in which he gave an account of this trip, he wrote: "[I saw] a sort of vortex in the mountains, while for a wide area we have gentle slopes and plateau land". The irony was that Cameron's name was bestowed on a place he never set eyes on. He probably came across the smaller plateau area farthest from Tanah Rata, known as Blue Valley. The highland plateau itself was discovered years later by a

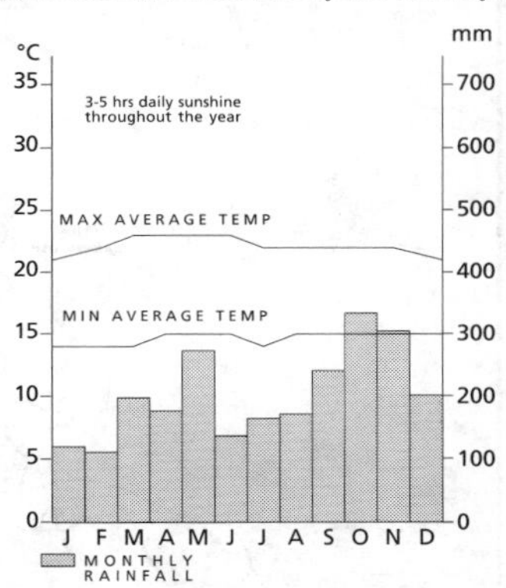

Climate: Cameron Highlands

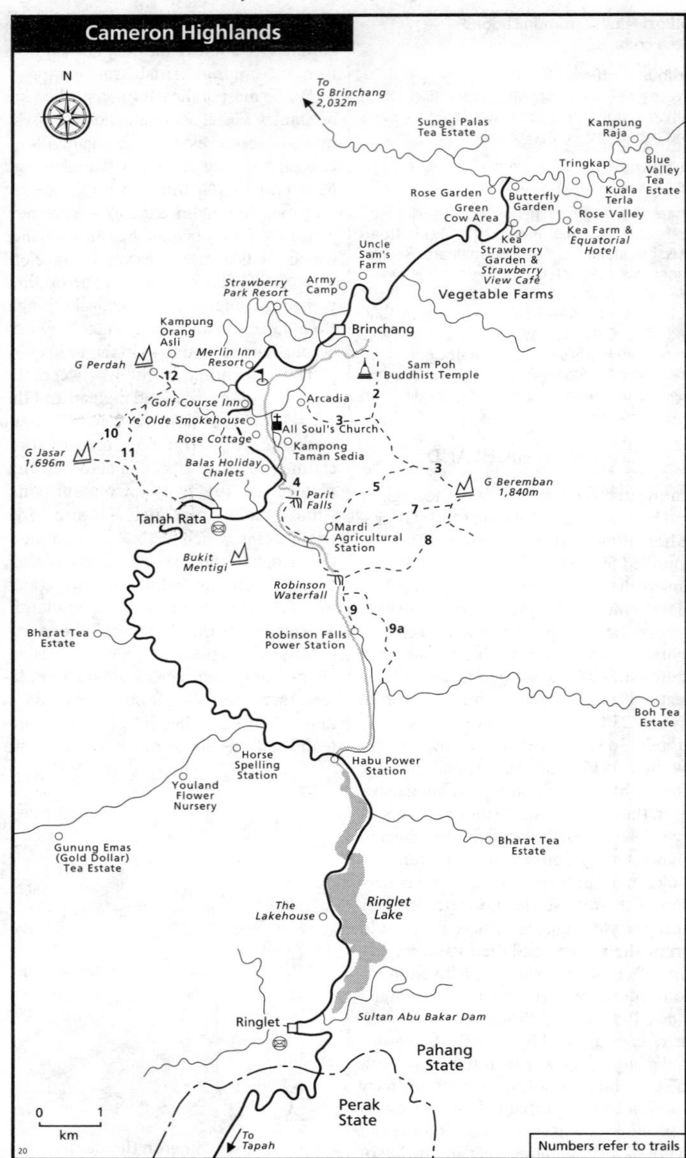
Cameron Highlands
N
To
G Brinchang
2,032m
Sungei Palas
Tea Estate
Kampung
Raja
Blue
Valley
Tea
Estate
Tringkap
Kuala
Terla
Rose Garden
Butterfly
Garden
Green
Cow Area
Rose Valley
Kea Farm &
Equatorial
Hotel
Kea
Strawberry
Garden &
Strawberry
View Café
Uncle
Sam's
Farm
Army
Camp
Strawberry
Park Resort
Vegetable Farms
Brinchang
Kampung
Orang
Asli
Merlin Inn
Resort
G Perdah
Sam Poh
Buddhist Temple
Golf Course Inn
Arcadia
Ye Olde Smokehouse
All Soul's Church
Rose Cottage
Kampong
Taman Sedia
G Jasar
1,696m
Balas Holiday
Chalets
G Beremban
1,840m
Parit
Falls
Tanah Rata
Mardi
Agricultural
Station
Bukit
Mentigi
Robinson
Waterfall
Robinson Falls
Power Station
Bharat Tea
Estate
Boh Tea
Estate
Horse
Spelling
Station
Habu Power
Station
Youland
Flower
Nursery
Gunung Emas
(Gold Dollar)
Tea Estate
Bharat Tea
Estate
The
Lakehouse
Ringlet
Lake
Sultan Abu Bakar Dam
Ringlet
Pahang
State
Perak
State
0 1
km
To
Tapah
Numbers refer to trails
1
2
3
3
4
5
7
8
9
9a
10
11
12
20

Cameron Highlands tea plantations

The Cameron Highlands provide an ideal climate for tea-growing. There are several large and well-established tea estates, including the **Bharat** and **Gold Dollar** tea estates, located in the lower Highlands between Ringlet and Tanah Rata, and the **Blue Valley** tea estate in the upper Highlands. The largest and best known estate in the Highlands is the **Boh Plantation** (Boh tea is the standard household brand in most Malaysian homes) which has 1,200 hectares of mature tea plantations. Both the **Fairlie** (lower Highlands) and the **Sungei Palas** (upper Highlands) operate free guided tours of their factories, every hour or so, daily except Monday (the factories have no tea to process on a Monday, as no tea gets plucked on a Sunday). The Sungei Palas is probably the more attractive of the two, perched high on the steep, green hills above Brinchang, and is less inundated with visitors (see page 158 to get there).

Like all Cameronian tea estates, Boh Plantations (lower Highland) employ a hard-core of tea pluckers whose forebears originally came from South India. Many of the workers are third or fourth generation having been brought here in the late 1920s to start the first plantations. The workers live in self-contained quarters on the estates, most of which have their own shops and school. The original tea plants also came from India, mainly Darjeeling stocks, many of which are still productive. Now bonsai specimens, they can be recognized by their thick trunks and dark green leaves. Bushes planted from the 1960s onwards are mainly cloned varieties and have much lighter coloured leaves.

During the 1920s, the Cameron Highlands were under the control of a British Governor. The founder of the Boh Plantations, John Archibald Russell (known to his friends as Archie), was the son of a British government official. In conjunction with Mr AB Milne, an old tea planter from Ceylon, in 1927, JA Russell applied for and was granted a concession of land in the Cameron Highlands. This became the Boh Estate, which was carved out of virgin jungle, an extraordinary feat considering that the work was carried out without machinery and only with the assistance of mules.

In the 1920s, tea plucking and processing was also an all-manual process. Nowadays, machinery is used, although it is still manually intensive, with an average of 6 to 10 people required to look after each acre of plantation. Part of the reason for the intensity of manual labour is that the tea bushes are grown on slopes that in places are so precipitous that machinery is almost impossible to use: 45 degree slopes are commonplace. However, on the whole, the workers use a plucking machine, a hefty gadget requiring two men to hold it, while double blades slice off the top-most shoots which are blown into a bag, otherwise hand shears are used. Plucking takes place year round every 15-25 days, depending on growth which tends to be slower during the rainy season. Maintenance is a year round task too. The bushes need to be regularly fertilized and weeded, while pruning takes place every 3 years.

The green tea leaf is weighed (the pluckers are paid per kg) before being taken to the factory to be processed where every 5 kg of green leaf produces around 1 kg of tea. The first process in the factory is to whither the leaves under artificial blowers, for 12-16 hrs, depending on the moisture content. The leaves are then rolled, or broken up using a rotary blade, and graded before being put into trays for fermentation. Finally the tea is fired in an oven, the timing of which is critical, before being graded for a second time. The tea is mostly packaged in KL, from where it is distributed, mainly to local destinations as the quantity is limited.

Jungle walks: Cameron Highlands

The Cameron Highlands is great walking country – although many of the longer trails were closed in the 1970s when the army found secret food dumps for the Communist Party of Malaya, which used the Main Range as its insurgency route from its bases near Betong in South Thailand. Despite the CPM calling a halt to hostilities in 1990, the trails have not reopened. There are however a handful of not-so-strenuous mountains to climb and a number of jungle walks. Cameronian trails are a great place for people unfamiliar with jungle walks. They are also very beautiful.

Basic sketch maps of trails, with numbered routes, are available at the Tourist Information kiosk in Tanah Rata and from most hotels. Walkers are advised to take plenty of water with them as well as a whistle, a lighter and something warm. It is very easy to lose your way in jungle – and the district officer has had to call out Orang Asli trackers on many occasions over the years to hunt down disoriented hikers. Always make sure someone knows roughly where you are going and approximately what time you are expecting to get back.

There is a centuries-old Orang Asli trail leading from Tanjung Rambutan, near Ipoh, up the Kinta River into the Main Range. One branch of this trail goes north to the summit of Gunung Korbu (2,183m), 16 km away. When William Cameron and his warrior companion Kulop Riau left on their elephant-back expedition into the mountains, they followed the Kinta River to its source, and from the summit of nearby Gunung Calli, saw Blue Valley 'plateau'. Cameron's view of the plateau that would later bear his name was obscured by two big mountains, Irau (the roller-coaster-shaped one) and Brinchang.

At 2,032m, **Gunung Brinchang** is the Highlands' highest peak and the highest point in Malaysia accessible by road. The area around the communications centre on the summit affords a great panorama of the plateau, although it spends most of its life shrouded in cloud. The road up the mountain veers left in the middle of Boh's Sungei Palas tea estate past Km 73. From the top of Brinchang it is possible to see straight down into the Kinta valley, on the other side. Ipoh is only 15 km away, as the hornbill flies. There is an old and rarely used trail up Gunung Brinchang from the back of the old airstrip (behind the army flats) at the top end of Brinchang town.

Malay warrior named Kulop Riau who accompanied Cameron on his mapping expeditions. Cameron's report engendered much excitement. Sir Hugh Low, who 34 years earlier had made the first attempt at Sabah's Gunung Kinabalu, was by then the Resident of Perak. He wanted to develop the newly reported highland area as "a sanitorium, health resort and open farmland". Two decades elapsed before the first pioneers made their way up to the so-called 'Cameron's Land'.

Hot on the heels of the elderly gin and Jaguar settlers (most of them insisted on solid British cars for the mountain roads) came the tea planters and vegetable farmers. The cool mountain climate was perfect for both. The forested hillsides were shaved to make way for more tea bushes and cabbages and the deforestation appears to have affected the climate. The local meteorological station reports that the average temperature has risen 2° in the past 50 years. The weather has also become more unpredictable – torrential downpours and landslides are no longer confined to the monsoon months of November and December. But the mountain air is still bracing enough to entice thousands of holiday makers to the Camerons

Gunung Beremban (1,840m) makes a pleasant hike, although its trails are well worn. It can be reached from Tanah Rata (trail No 7 goes up through the experimental tea in the MARDI station past the padang off Jalan Persiaran Dayang Endah), Brinchang (trail No 2 leads up from behind the Sam Poh Buddhist temple – a more arduous route), or the golf course (follow trail No 3 past the Arcadia bungalow where the road stops) – this is the easiest. Allow about 4 hours to get up and down. There is a good view down Tanah Rata's main street from the top. It is also possible to climb Gunung Beremban from Robinson Falls (trail No 8 leads off trail No 9). The trail heading for the latter is from the very bottom of the road leading past MARDI from Tanah Rata.

Gunung Jasar (1,696m), between the golf course and Tanah Rata, is a pleasant – but gentler – walk of about 3 hours (trail No 10). The trail goes from half way along the old back road to Tanah Rata near the meteorological station (the road – Jalan Titiwangsa – leaves Tanah Rata from behind a hotel (south of town) and emerges at the golf course, on the corner next to the Golf Course Hotel). The Jasar trail also forks off to **Bukit Perdah** (trail No 12, which branches off the Jasar trail) 2-3 hours to the top and back. The path down from the summit comes out on a road leading back into the top end of Tanah Rata.

The trails to **Robinson Falls** (trail No 9, 1 hour walk) and **Parit Falls** (trail No 4, 30 minutes walk) are more frequently trampled. The trail branches off to No 9a which leads down to the Boh tea estate road near Ringlet Lake. The walk to the Boh tea estate is a long one, but it is possible to hitch along the road or catch a bus (great views when you get there). Tours every hour. The estate is closed on Monday, and closed at 1700 on other days, the last bus leaves the factory at 1730. The short trail to Parit Falls starts behind the *Garden Hotel* and mosque on the far side of Tanah Rata's padang and ends up below the Slim army camp. Parit Falls is a small waterfall in between the two, with what was once a beautiful jungle pool before it became cluttered with day-trippers and their rubbish.

There are hundreds of other trails through the Camerons, traversing ridges and leading up almost every hill and mountain. Most are *Orang Asli* paths, some date from the Japanese occupation in World War Two (these are marked by barbed wire) and some aren't really trails at all – beware.

from the steamy plains. Today coach-loads of Singaporeans wind their way up the mountain roads and, together with well-heeled KL businessfolk, fork out extortionate sums for weekends in timeshare apartments and endless rounds of golf.

The Camerons' most talked-about visitor arrived in March 1967 for a quiet sojourn in Moonlight bungalow, perched on a hilltop above the golf course. The disappearance of the US-born Thai silk emperor, art collector and military intelligence agent Jim Thompson from a lonely Cameronian backroad, propelled the hill resort into the headlines. Teams of Orang Asli trackers combed the jungle in vain while detectives, journalists and film-makers toyed with credible explanations: he had been given a new identity by the CIA; he had been kidnapped and smuggled from the highlands in the boot of a Thai taxi; he had been eaten by a tiger. The fate of Thompson, the Lord Lucan of Southeast Asia, is still a mystery.

Places of interest

Most of the tourist attractions in the Cameron Highlands are on and around the plateau but there are a handful of sights on the road from Tapah. These are listed in order from the bottom of the mountain up. There are three main townships in the Highlands: Ringlet, Tanah Rata – literally 'flat land' – and Brinchang (in order as you go up). The latter two are in the plateau area, either side of the golf course. Unfortunately, the Cameron Highlands is no longer a peaceful bolthole in the sky. Frenetic development is turning the area, in critics' eyes, into a building site where forest is fast making way for golf courses and luxury tourist developments. When Prime Minister Dr Mahathir's plan for a new road from Ipoh to the Cameron Highlands is put underway, further expansion can be expected. At present the road from Tapah is the only way up and down; this road runs through Perak until it reaches Ringlet, and the Perak state authorities are unlikely to spend much money upgrading it as Pahang state accrues all the financial returns of Cameron Highlands' tourism.

Tapah is a centre for making the large bamboo baskets that are used to collect the tea. The town itself is very small, a single street of dilapidated shophouses with a couple of basic hotels including the **E** *Bunga Raya* (T 05-4011436) and **E** *Hotel Utara* (T 05-4012299), and a few eating places, including *KFC*. *Getting there*: the bus station in Tapah is on Jalan Raja, just off the main road. There are hourly connections with Tanah Rata as well as occasional departures for KL and Penang. Most long distance bus departures from Tapah (including KL, Melaka, Penang, Kuantan, and Lumut as well as connections with Hat Yai in southern Thailand) are from the *Caspian Restaurant* on the main highway. The Tapah Road Railway Station is about 10 km from town.

Kuala Woh, a jungle park with a swimming pool, fishing and natural hot pools, is only 13 km from Tapah, on the road to the Camerons and has a basic camping area.

Lata Iskandar Waterfall (22½ km from Tapah) is a beautiful jungle waterfall, right by the roadside, which has been ruined by commercial ventures capitalizing on the picnic spot, although it is a good place to pick up the local terracotta pottery, crafted Kampung Kerayung. The **19th Mile**, further up the hill, is a more pleasant spot for a stop-off. To the right of the little shop, a path leads along the side of the river, up into the jungle, past Orang Asli villages, waterfalls and jungle pools. Good for birdwatching and butterflies.

The first township on the road to the Cameron Highlands is **Ringlet**, just inside Pahang state. It was relocated to its present site in the 1960s when the original village was flooded to make way for the Sultan Abu Bakar hydro-electric scheme. *Ringlet* is the Semai aboriginal word for a jungle tree. The town itself is basically unattractive, the apartment blocks erected here in the 60s now looking very shabby. The *Lakehouse Hotel* is located here (see accommodation), and there are a couple of basic hotels – the *Hotel Cathay* and the *Hotel da Restoran Sha* – which have rooms in the **D** category. There is also a cluster of hawker stalls in the town centre and a well-used temple.

After Ringlet, the road follows a wide river to a large murky brown lake, connected to a hydro-electric dam. The lake is overlooked by the famous *Lakehouse*, a tudor-style country house, formerly the home of Colonel Stanley Foster and now a cosy 18-room hotel. The lake is also overlooked by a row of food and souvenir stalls. At the Habu power station, a road leads right to two of the tea growing estates of the Boh Plantations. The original Boh Estate is 6 km from the junction and the Fairlie Estate is 12 km. The latter offers free guided tours of the factory (almost every hour, Tuesday-Sunday).

Youland Nursery is on the road to Gold Dollar tea estate, left off the main road to Tanah Rata from Ringlet (milestone 32). At the same turn-off there is a racehorse spelling station, formerly owned by Cameronian pioneer Captain Bloxham. Before reaching Tanah Rata, on the right is a waterfall and picnic spot, on the left is the *Cameron Bharat* tea shop which has a fine view over the Bharat tea estate.

TANAH RATA

Tanah Rata, a further 5 km up the mountain, at 1,440m, is the biggest of the three Cameronian towns. Having said this, it is still not very large, comprising a row of shophouses straddled along the main road where there are two or three restaurants, imitating British cafés with fish and chips on most menus. It is a friendly little town, with a resort atmosphere rather like an English seaside town. There are also several souvenir shops, including the *Yung Seng Souvenir Shop* which is more up-market than the others and has an interesting selection of well-priced asli crafts, ranging from blow-pipes to wood-carvings. It is also worth looking in local shops for teas from surrounding estates.

Tours

Well-priced half day tours of the area are organized by *Bala's Holiday Chalets* (see Accommodation) which saves on trying to negotiate the highlands by public transport.

Local information

● Accommodation

Prices: L over RM500; **A+** RM260-500; **A** RM130-260; **B** RM65-130; **C** RM40-65; **D** RM20-40; **E** RM10-20; **F** Below RM10

NB It should be noted that during public holidays, accommodation gets fully booked and prices rise by 30-50%. It is also busy at peak school holiday periods – Apr, Aug and Dec. The most economic form of accommodation is to share a bungalow between a group of people. Most bungalows have gardens, logfires and are away from the towns.

A+-A *The Lakehouse*, T 4956152, F 4956213, Tudor-style country house, final brain child of Colonel Stanley Foster, 18 rooms with antique furnishings, four poster beds and en suite bathrooms, overlooking lake, restaurant serving English food, Cameron Bar and Highlander Lounge both have English country pub atmosphere, a great place to stay and reasonable value considering. **A+-A** ***Merlin Inn Resort***, T 4911211/4911205, F 4911178, excellent position overlooking the golf course, north of Tanah Rata, 100 rooms extension completed in early 1997, there are other more atmospheric places to stay at this price. **A+-A** *The Smokehouse Hotel*, T 4911215, F 4911214, recently completely refurbished, preserving its home counties ethos and 'ye olde English' style of old time resident Colonel Stanley Foster, it is modelled on its namesake, the Smokehouse in Mildenhall (UK), rooms are first class, there is an original red British telephone box in the garden, restaurant serves expensive English food. **A** ***Heritage***, T 4913888, F 4915666, located just south of Tanah Rata next to the Convent School, the newest quality hotel in the Cameron Highlands, with a rather bland international look, out of keeping with its surroundings, 170 spacious rooms, bath, TV, in-house video, mini-bar, tea and coffee-making facilities, Chinese restaurant, coffee house, sauna, health centre, squash, tennis. **A** ***Strawberry Park Resort***, T 4911166, F 4911949, magnificent setting above Tanah Rata, dominating a hilltop with its 8 blocks of walk-up rooms and apartments, built in Tudor/Swiss-chalet style, interior is starting to look dated, rooms are designed to hold maximum capacity, even the smallest studio rooms and 1-room apartments can sleep 4 people, all rooms with bath (inadequate water heaters), TV, in-house video, fridge, tea and coffee-making facilities, resort facilities include indoor pool (the only one in the Cameron Highlands), tennis, squash, sauna, indoor games rooms, mini-putting green, children's play area, 7 km jogging track, *Monroe's Pub* (with the only disco in the Cameron Highlands and karaoke rooms), Coffee House, *Tudor Grill* steakhouse, Chinese restaurant, recommended. **A-B** ***New Garden Inn***, Jln Masjid, T 4915170, F 4915169, 47 rooms in 3 separate buildings, of which the Old Scottish House is the only one with any character, generally outdated decor, facilities include a cinema in the former Dalat School – used by children of US forces in Vietnam, restaurant, games room.

B ***Cool Point***, Jln Dayang Indah, T 4914914, F 4914070, a tacky interpretation of the Tudor style and rather dated decor, but comfortable, TV, tea and coffee-making facilities, restaurant. **B** ***Golf Course Inn***, T 4911411, by the golf course, 30-room concrete building, rooms with TV, fridge, bath, bar, games room, children's playground, restaurant. **B-C** ***Orient***, 38 Jln Besar, T 4911633, located above *The Orient* Chinese restaurant, recommended. **B-C** ***Roselane***, 44 Jln Besar, T 4912377, above the *Roselane* coffee shop, large comfortable rooms. **B-D** ***Bala's***

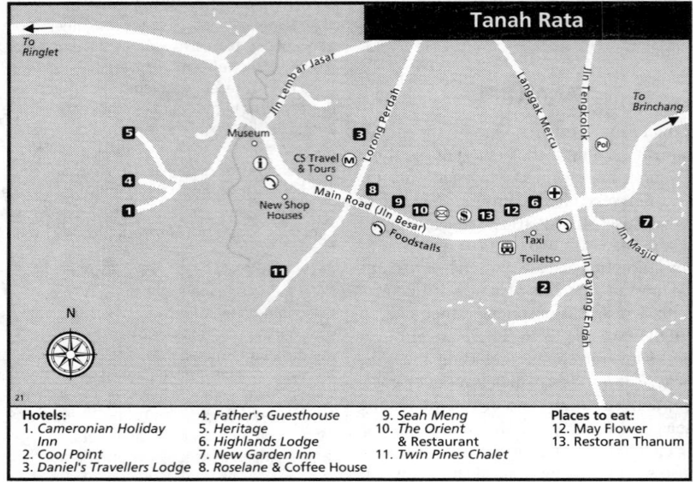

Holiday Chalets, T 4911660, 1 km outside Tanah Rata on road to Brinchang (RM3 taxi ride), not chalets at all, but a rambling colonial house (formerly a British school) with character and a pleasant garden, rooms a little dank and run down, private bathrooms with hot water (sporadically available), great view, Bala knows the Camerons well, there is a pinboard with information on jungle walks and the latest gen from travellers, common sitting-rooms, log fires, good atmosphere but relying on reputation, reasonably-priced restaurant.

C ***Cameron***, 29 Jln Besar, T 4911160, uninspiring. **C** ***Rumah Rehat***, Jln Dayang Endah, T 4911254, exceptionally nice little resthouse, tends to get overbooked by government employees so it pays to book in advance, tennis court, recommended. **C-D** ***Seah Meng***, 39 Jln Besar, T 4911618, fairly typical Chinese hotel with little atmosphere but the rooms are kept spotless. **C-D** ***Cameron Highlands Resthouse***, T 4911066, restaurant, must book first, well run. **C-D** ***Cameronian Holiday Inn***, 16 Jln Mentigi, T 4911327, restaurant, garden, TV, games, sitting area, hot showers in more expensive rooms, this is one of the better mid-budget places in town with a large lawn and a suitably relaxing atmosphere, dorm bed also available (**F**). **C-E** ***Twin Pines Chalet***, 2 Jln Mentigi, T 4912169, popular guesthouse at top end of town, hot showers, clean and friendly, rooms and dorm, bus tickets and tours bookable here, good source of information although its once peaceful outlook has been marred by a shopping centre development.

D ***Father's Guesthouse***, Jln Gereja, T 4912484, near the convent, up a long flight of steps, very basic and rather run-down although some of the rooms seem to have received a facelift in the last few months, dorm beds available, good communal sitting area. **D-E** ***Daniel's Travellers Lodge***, 9 Lorong Perdah, T 4915823, F 4915828, new, clean and friendly place to stay, lots of useful information available and a good place to eat, dorm beds (**F**). **D-E** ***Papillon Guesthouse***, Jln Mentigi, T 4914069, newish place close to the *Twin Pines Chalet*, good-sized rooms and dorm beds available, friendly and enthusiastic management.

E-F ***Highlands Lodge***, T 4911922, near the hospital, noisy, rooms and dorm.

Bungalows: rates are for whole bungalow, per night unless stated; most prices include resident cook. Rates may vary according to season – discounts on request. Most of the bungalows are dotted around the town, in the countryside, with their own gardens. There are a great many to choose from, the following gives an idea of the type of range available: **A+** ***Fair Haven***; **A+** ***Golf View Villa***; **A** ***Highlands Villa***; **B** ***Gunder Singh***; **B** ***Lutheran Bungalow***; **D** ***Rumah Tetamu Sri Pahang***.

Places to eat

Prices: ◆◆◆◆ over RM40; ◆◆◆ RM13-40; ◆◆ RM5-13; ◆ under RM5

Chinese: ◆◆◆-◆◆*Mayflower*, 22 Jln Besar, specialize in Highland steamboat, seafood, popular with locals. ◆◆*The Orient*, 38 Jln Besar, steamboat and soups are popular, good value set lunch. ◆◆*The Oriental Melody*, 44 Jln Besar, popular.

Indian: ◆◆-◆*Thanum*, 25 Jln Besar, claypot and Hainam chicken rice recommended, excellent breakfast rotis and murtabak, chairs and tables outside. ◆*Kumar*, good value banana leaf, popular breakfast spot. ◆*Restoran No 14*, on the main road, very popular place doing good thalis and dosas at good prices.

International: ◆◆◆◆*Lakehouse*, traditional English food, typical Sun lunch fare and cream teas. ◆◆◆◆*Smokehouse*, similar to *Lakehouse*, favourites include: beef Wellington, roast beef, Yorkshire pudding, steak and kidney pie, and Devonshire cream teas. ◆◆◆*Merlin*, international menu, and pleasant atmosphere but not very good value. ◆◆*Bala's*, in Bala's Holiday Chalets (see above), good breakfasts and vegetarian dinners, also a popular stop for cream teas. ◆◆*Roselane Coffee House*, western and local food, set meals are good value.

Foodstalls: ◆◆-◆Next to the bus station, opposite the main row of shops on Jln Besar, serve good selection of Malay, Indian and Chinese food.

Banks & money changers

All the banks are on Jln Besar. They include: **Arab-Malaysian Finance, Hong Kong Shanghai Bank, Maybank, Sampanian National** and **Visa Finance Berhad**. It is also possible to change money at **CS Travel & Tours**, next to *Roselane Hotel* and *Coffee House* on Jln Besar.

Entertainment

The only nightlife as such takes place in the *Strawberry Park Resort* where there is the only disco in town, karaoke, and a bar. The hotel bars at the *Lakehouse* and *Smokehouse* are also popular venues for their country pub atmosphere and air of exclusivity.

Hospitals & medical services

Hospitals: opposite gardens at north end of town, on Jln Besar, T 4911966.

Places of worship

Anglican: *All Souls' Church*, between Kampung Taman Sedia and golf course. Converted army Nissen hut with lych-gate in memory of Miss Griffeths Jones. Services 1030 Sun.

Post & telecommunications

Area code: 05.
General Post Office: next to the *Orient Hotel & Restaurant*, Jln Besar.

Sports

Golf: *Cameron Highlands Golf Club*, T 4911126, located to the north of Tanah Rata, connected by a pleasant footpath from the town, founded in 1885 by the British surveyor William Cameron, the 18-hole golf course is magnificently appointed, occupying pride of place in the centre of the plateau, surrounded by jungled hills, it is a favourite haunt of Malaysian royalty, green fees: RM40 weekdays, RM60 weekends and public holidays, RM18 caddy fee, T 4911126. Note that players are expected to wear appropriate clothing, which rules out singlets and revealing shorts.

Tennis: courts across the road from golf clubhouse, rackets and balls on hire at clubhouse shop.

Tour companies & travel agents

CS Travel & Tours, 47 Jln Besar, T 4911200, F 4912390, local tours, air/train/bus tickets, accommodation reservations.

Tourist offices

Tourist Information Centre, on the right as you come into Tanah Rata, poor source of information. Open: 0800-1615 Mon-Thur, 0800-1215 and 1445-1615 Fri, 0800-1245 Sat. There is a small museum attached to the tourist office. The *Orang Asli* exhibit is worth a browse. Book lending scheme available at office.

Useful addresses

District office: T 4911455, alert this office if someone you know is long-overdue after a jungle walk.
Police: T 4911222, opposite gardens at north end of town.

Transport

214 km from KL, 121 km from Ipoh. **NB** Those who suffer from travel sickness are advised to take some anti-nausea medication before setting out on the mountain road.

Local Bus/taxis: nearly all the buses from Tapah (last bus 1600) go through Ringlet, Tanah Rata and on to Brinchang and it is easy enough to climb aboard one of the buses that do this route through the day. Rex buses go from Tanah Rata to the farthest outpost on the mountain. Taxis are available for local travel – they can be chartered for about RM15 per hour. It is also possible just to take a seat in a taxi, going from Tanah Rata to Brinchang, for example. Taxi and local bus station (T 4911485) on either side of the Shell station in Tanah Rata. To order a taxi: T 4911234/4912355. **Car hire**: because visitors pose a serious insurance problem on the mountain roads, the car rental business is not well developed in the Camerons. The only one available is semi-official: contact Ravi at *Rainbow Garden Centre* (between *The Smokehouse* and Tanah Rata), T 491782. If you are driving, remember to sound your horn at bends and beware the lorries that hurtle along. If you are wondering why there are lorries on the road it is because there is a large replantation project underway as well as construction work.

Train The nearest station to the Camerons is Tapah Rd in Tapah, 67 km from Tanah Rata. Regular connections with Ipoh, KL, Butterworth 5 a day, 6 hours.

Road Bus: a daily bus leaves KL's Puduraya terminal, for the Cameron Highlands, at 0830, 5 hours, but it gets heavily booked. The *Bintang Mas* bus service operate direct a/c buses from KL to Tanah Rata (leaving from Jln Pudu, at the foot of the 'pedestrian bridge' to the Puduraya bus station), departing 0900 and 1530 daily (T 2324285). Most other buses for the Cameron Highlands leave from Tapah, 67 km from Tanah Rata in the Camerons, regular hourly connections with Brinchang and Tanah Rata and with Sungai Palas and Kampung Raja (in the north of the Camerons). Tickets for the return journey can be booked at travel agents or at the bus station in Tanah Rata. There are 2 daily express buses from the Camerons to KL, leaving at 0830 and 1530, and one express bus to Georgetown, Penang, 0930. Regular connections from Tapah with Ipoh, KL, Butterworth, Kuantan, Melaka (5 hours), Singapore. Can reserve tickets at *CS Travel & Tours*, Tanah Rata. **NB** Buses coming down from the Camerons tend to be more expensive.

BRINCHANG

In recent years Brinchang, 7 km beyond Tanah Rata, on the far side of the golf course, has grown fast: since the mid-1980s several new hotels have sprung up, mainly catering for mass-market Malaysian Chinese and Singaporean package tourists. It is not a very beautiful little town, although the central square with craft centre has a certain character.

Places of interest

Sam Poh Buddhist Temple, a popular sight with Chinese visitors who arrive by the coach load, the temple is located just outside Brinchang, along Jalan Pecah Batu, overlooking the golf course. It is backed by the Gunung Beremban hills, and comprises both a temple and monastery which were built here in 1971. Emphasis is on size and grandeur, with a monumental double gates with dragons at either side leading into the complex. The inner chamber with its six red-tiled pillars holds a vast golden effigy of a Buddha.

Local information

● Accommodation

Prices: L over RM500; **A+** RM260-500; **A** RM130-260; **B** RM65-130; **C** RM40-65; **D** RM20-40; **E** RM10-20; **F** Below RM10

NB It should be noted that during public holidays, accommodation gets fully booked and prices rise by 30-50%. It is also busy at peak school holiday periods – Apr, Aug and Dec. The most economic form of accommodation is to share a bungalow between a group of people. Most bungalows have gardens, logfires and are away from the towns. For budget traveller Tanah Rata has a better selection of acommodation.

A *Country Lodge*, T 4913071, F 4911396, located on hillside above Brinchang, typical black and white Tudor-style, decor rather on the severe side, parquet floors and rattan furniture, spacious standard and deluxe rooms as well as suites, restaurant, karaoke lounge. **A** *Rosa Passadena*, T 4912288, F 4912688, large mock-Tudor block, dominates Brinchang town centre, 120 rooms, bath, TV, in-house video, mini-bar, safe, restaurant, karaoke lounge; **A** *Rose Cottage*, T 4911173, bungalow. **A-B** *Jasmine Holiday Apartments*, 40 Jln Besar, T 4912408, overlooking the main square, attractive, furnished flats of varying cost and size with cooking facilities, barbecue and rooftop garden, recommended.

B *Hill Garden Lodge*, 15-16 Jln Besar, T 4912988, F 4912226, bath, TV, clean and comfy, rooms facing street noisy, discounts available in off-peak season. **B** *Parkland Hotel*, T 4911299, F 4911399, modern 30-room hotel at edge of town, bath, TV, café, restaurant, good value for money, recommended. **B-C** *Brinchang Hotel*, 36 Jln Besar, T 4911755, F 4911246, clean and comfortable, hot showers, TV, discounts available. **B-C** *Kowloon Hotel*, 34-35

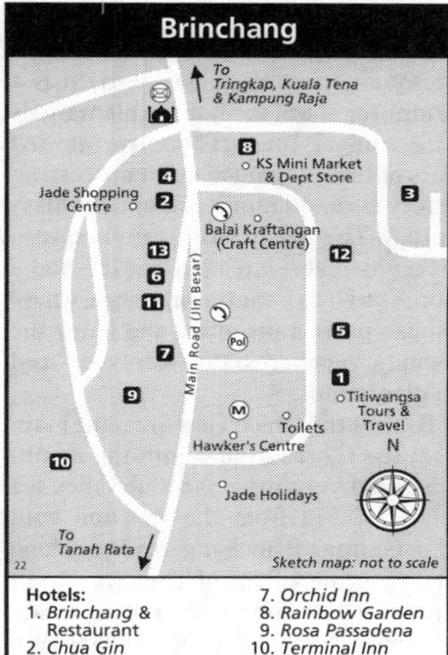

Jln Besar, T 4911366, F 4911803, above popular Chinese restaurant, good value for money, recommended. **B-C** ***Rainbow Garden Hotel***, Lot 25, T 4914628, F 4914668, brand spanking new, 36 good value comfortable rooms.

C ***Hotel Plastro***, 19 Jln Besar, T 4911009, mediocre. **C-D** ***Orchid Inn***, 30 Jln Besar, T 4912102, brand new, very clean and simple but attractive, good central position, good value family rooms, recommended. **C-D** ***Terminal Inn***, T 4912203, one of the newer budget hotels in Brinchang, good value family rooms with TV and water heater, dorm also available, very clean, recommended.

D ***Hotel Chua Gin***, 11 Jln Besar, T 4911801, small and spartan, but clean, good value family rooms.

● Places to eat

Prices: ◆◆◆◆ over RM40; ◆◆◆ RM13-40; ◆◆ RM5-13; ◆ under RM5

Chinese: ◆◆*Brinchang*, below hotel of same name on Jln Besar, popular for its steamboat, good selection of vegetable dishes, recommended. ◆◆*Kowloon*, busy restaurant, red tablecloths and clean tiled floors, menu priced according to size of portion, lemon chicken and steamboat are popular, recommended. ◆◆*Kwan Kee*, next door to *Hotel Lido*, good steamboat. ◆◆*Silverstar*, on the other side of *Hotel Lido*, not special.

Indian: ◆◆*Shal's Curry House*, 25 Jln Besar, upmarket coffee shop serving top quality Indian cuisine, excellent South Indian claypot dishes, sweet and savoury thosai, peanut, honey or banana roti good for breakfast, run by former manager of the *Smokehouse*, attractive presentation on real banana leaf, some tables and chairs outside, overlooking square, recommended.

International: ◆◆◆*Parkland*, Grill restaurant in *Parkland Hotel*, steaks, breakfast menu (◆◆). ◆◆◆*Ferns Restaurant*, *Rosa Passadena Hotel*, western and oriental, good value buffet.

Foodstalls: hawker stalls in the central square, open after 1600, good for satay and roti.

● Banks & money changers

Public Bank, next to *Hill Garden Lodge*.

● Entertainment

Apart from a couple of karaoke bars that have recently sprung up in the town, any nightlife that exists takes place in the *Rosa Passadena Hotel*.

● Hospitals & medical services

See Tanah Rata, page 155.

● Post & telecommunications

Area code: 05.

General Post Office: opposite the Petronas petrol station at the north end of the town.

● Sports

Golf: *Cameron Highlands Golf Club*, see Tanah Rata, page 155.

● Tour companies & travel agents

Jade Holidays, 37a & b Jln Bandar, T 4912318, F 4912071, local tours, air/bus tickets, accommodation bookings, jungle trekking; ***Titiwangsa Tours & Travel***, 36 Jln Besar, T 4912122, F 4911246, similar services to *Jade Holidays*.

● Tourist offices

See Tanah Rata, page 155.

● Useful addresses

Police: in central square, next to children's playground.

● Transport

See Tanah Rata, page 155.

Local: taxis are available for local travel – they can be chartered for about RM15 per hour. For travel between Tanah Rata, Brinchang and Tapah it is easy enough to climb aboard one of the buses that do this route through the day.

Up the hill from Brinchang the Cameron Highlands becomes one big market garden and the terrain becomes increasingly steep and hilly. One of the first market gardens outside Brinchang, just after the army camp on the left, is *Uncle Sam's Farm*. The farm specializes in the cultivation of the Kaffir Lily, as well as strawberries, oranges, apples and a selection of cactii. Beyond Uncle Sam's, 4 km up the road from Brinchang, there is a large market selling local produce to eager customers from the plains below.

The Cameronian climate is particularly suited to the cultivation of vegetables more usually associated with temperate climates. Cabbages, cauliflowers, carrots and tomatoes – as well as fruit such as strawberries and passion fruit – are taken by truck from the Camerons to the supermarkets of Kuala Lumpur and Singapore. **Kea Farm**, with its neatly terraced hillsides, is down the first right turn after the market area. At the Kea turning, on the main road, Kea Farm has a small shop and café and restaurant called the *Strawberry View*. **Accommodation A+** *Equatorial Hill Resort*, T 4961777, F 4961333, a monstrosity of 500 plus rooms, perched on the hillside, very mock Tudor in style, all the facilities of a 4-star hotel – heated pool, tennis, squash, bowling alley, Cineplex, not exactly an intimate little place.

Butterfly garden is past the Kea Farm turning. Admission RM2.50. Open 0800-1700 Monday-Sunday. There is a large shop attached to the garden, where everything from framed dead butterflies to Cameronian souvenirs (beetles embedded in key rings) is on sale. Outside there are fruit and vegetable stalls – all very popular with Chinese visitors.

The **rose garden** is 2 km further up the mountain. To get there, take the first left turn after the butterfly farm, on Jalan Gunung Brinchang, at what is known as the Green Cow area – a village there was burned to the ground by the Communists during the insurgency. A few kilometres beyond the Rose Garden, continue up Jalan Gunung Besar, which is a very picturesque narrow road, on the right is a turning for one of the Boh tea plantations – the Sungai Palas. There are guided tours of the Sungai Palas tea processing factory every 10 minutes from Tuesday-Sunday. The newly built visitors centre has a video about tea cultivation and a shop, as well as a charming terrace where you can order a pot of tea and enjoy the dramatic view across the steeply terraced tea plantations.

Back at the Green Cow area, the main road, the C7, continues into the mountains, finally ending at the Blue Valley Tea Estate, 13 km from the junction with Jalan Gunung Brinchang. Midway along the C7, at the village of Trinkap, a right turn leads to a large rose-growing establishment, Rose Valley, open 0800-1800 daily, adults RM3, children RM1.50. It boasts 450 varieties of rose including the thornless rose, the black rose, and the green rose, said to be the ugliest of the rose family. It also has a cactus plantation where some of the plants are 40 years old and lays claim to having the largest flower vase in Malaysia.

IPOH TO BUTTERWORTH

IPOH

The northern state of Perak is known for its tin ore (mainly in the Kinta Valley) and Ipoh, its capital, is Malaysia's third city with a population of about 500,000. The city is situated in the Kinta Valley, between the Main Range and the Keledang Mountains, to the west. Ipoh is named after the abundance of the huge, elusive ipoh (or upas) trees that once grew there; the Orang Asli tribes procured the poison for their blowpipe darts from its fabled lethal sap. It was known as the deadliest poison in the world. The city also has an abundance of imposing limestone outcrops. These jungle-topped hills, with their precipitous white cliffs, are riddled with passages and caves, many of which have been made into cave temples.

Perak: the silver state that grew rich on tin

Perak is nicknamed the 'Silver State' because *perak* is the Malay for silver. This was, according to one account, a misnomer, as the locals mistook their plentiful tin ore for silver. All the way through the Kinta and Perak river valleys, huge areas of sand lie bleached and desolate, after the tin dredges have passed over them. A more likely derivation of Perak's name is from the word *bharat*, meaning 'west'. In maps prior to 1561 the area is marked as 'Perat' – historians speculate this may be a corruption of Bharat. The state became 'the senior state of the federation' in colonial Malaya – before its governmental role passed to Kuala Lumpur at the end of the 19th century.

Perak's ancient name was Gangga-Negara, a Sanskrit word, meaning 'City on the Ganges'... in this case referring to an ancient kingdom centred on the estuary of the Perak River, where the village of Bruas is today. Gangga-Negara was the capital of this powerful kingkom, referred to by an Arab chronicler as far back as 644AD. It is said that many Buddha statues have been found in the area. Gangga-Negara was the site chosen by the Bendahara rulers of old Melaka who founded the Perak dynasty. The settlement was finally sacked by Rajendra Chola, the son of the first Hindu ruler of Kedah – who also destroyed Temasek, which in later life re-emerged as Singapore.

In its early days, Ipoh's citizens became wealthy on the back of the tin mining industry. In 1884 the Kinta Valley tin rush brought an influx of Chinese immigrants to Ipoh; many made their fortunes and built opulent town houses. Chinese immigrants have bequeathed what is now one of Malaysia's best-preserved Chinatowns (the 'Old Town'). In the 1880s Ipoh vied with Kuala Lumpur to be the capital of the Federated States of Malaya, and long after KL took the title, Ipoh remained the commercial 'hub of Malaya'. The city has long had an active 'flesh trade': there are frequent roundups of Thai and Burmese prostitutes who are smuggled across Malaysia's north border.

Few tourists spend long in Ipoh – most are en route to Penang, KL or Pulau Pangkor. Those who do stay rarely regret it: there are excellent Chinese restaurants (a speciality is the rice noodle dish, *Sar Hor Fun* which literally means 'melts in your mouth'), Buddhist temples and examples of Straits Chinese architecture. It is also a good place to pick up Chinese imported goods, such as baskets and chinaware. The shophouses on and around Jalan Yau Tet Shin make for good browsing. Ipoh also has a handful of very well-established bakers. On Jalan Raja Eleram the two bakeries here have been in the business for well over 50 years. They specialize in French bread, buns and cakes.

Places of interest

The Kinta River, spanned by the Hugh Low Bridge, separates the old and new parts of town. The **Old Town** is centred along the river between Jalan Sultan Idris Shah and Jalan Sultan Iskander Shah and is known for its old Chinese and British colonial architecture particularly on Jalan Sultan Yusuf, Jalan Leech and Jalan Treacher.

Prominent landmarks include the **Birch Memorial**, a clock tower erected in memory of the first British resident of Perak, J W W Birch. His murder, in 1875, was one of colonial Malaya's first anti-British incidents and the three perpetrators, after being hanged, promptly became local heroes – which they remain. The four panels decorating the base of the tower depict the development of civilization; the upper part of the tower holds a bust of JWW Birch who was, local history relates, not well liked in the

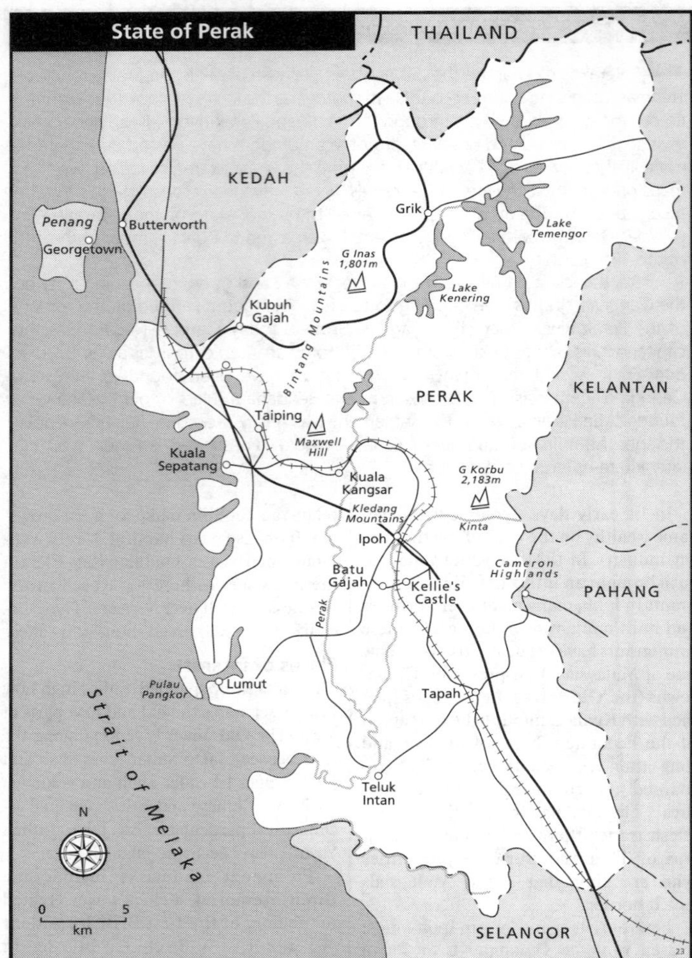

area. The Moorish-style **railway station** (off Jalan Kelab), built in 1917, bears close resemblance to its Kuala Lumpur counterpart, and is known as the 'Taj Mahal' of Ipoh. The *Station Hotel* has recently reopened and is a colonial classic worth noticing. **Ipoh Town Hall**, with its Palladian façade, stands opposite. A solitary ipoh (or *upas*) tree, after which the city is named, stands in the centre of **Taman DR Seenivasagam** (a park north of the centre). The park also contains an artificial lake and a children's playground. There are also **Japanese Gardens**, complete with a typical Japanese carp pond, nearby on Jalan Tambun. Open 1600-2000 Monday-

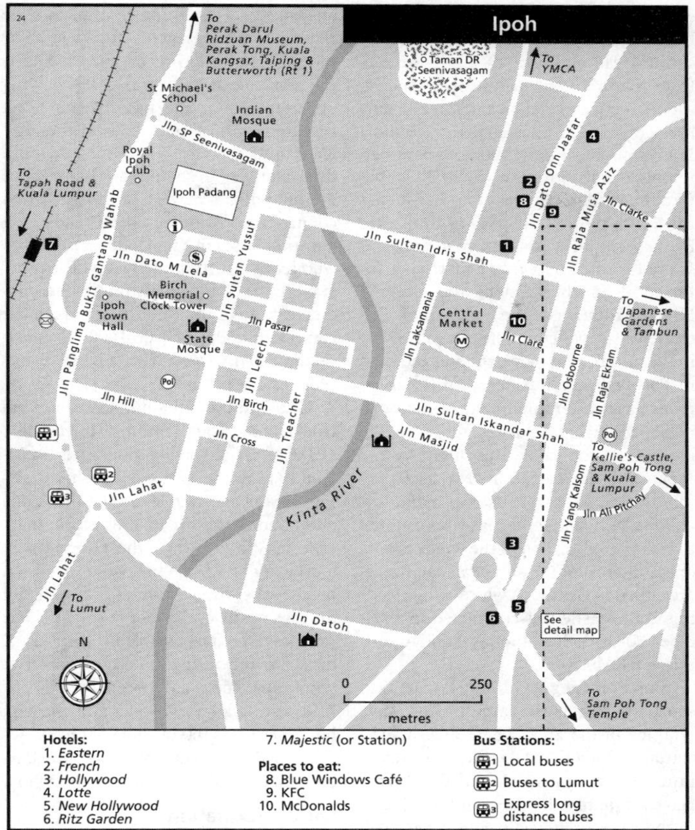

Friday, 0900-2000 Saturday and Sunday. The **Geological Museum**, on Lorong Hariman (out of town centre), was set up in 1957. It is known for its exhibition of tin ore and collection of fossils and precious stones as well as over 600 samples of minerals. Open 0800-1615 Monday-Friday, 0800-1245 Saturday. On Jalan SP Seenivasagam there is an old colonial mission **school** with an impressive white stone façade and an Indian **mosque** next door.

Heading out of town, past St Michael's School, on Jalan Panglima Bukit Gantang Wahab, after about 500m on the right is an elegant, white colonial building which houses the **Perak Darul Ridzuan Museum**. The building which is over 100-years-old, once the home of Malay dignitaries of Kinta, now houses a collection that illustrates the history of Ipoh, and mining and forestry within the state. Open 0900-1600 Saturday-Wednesday, 0900-1200 Thursday.

Excursions

Kellie's Castle, down the road to Batu Gajah, just to the south of Ipoh, is the eccentric edifice of Scotsman William Kellie Smith, a rubber tycoon in the late 19th century. He shipped in Tamil workers from South India to build his fanciful Moorish-style mansion, and after an outbreak of fever, he allowed them to build a Hindu temple – the Sri Maha Mariamman temple – in the grounds, about 500m before the castle. Another story has it that Mr Smith built the temple in 1902 after his prayers for a son and heir were answered – after 6 years of marriage. An image of Smith is among the sculpted Hindu pantheon on the temple roof. The castle was never completed as Smith left in the middle of its construction and died in Portugal on a business trip (local rumour has it, after inhaling the smoke of a poisoned cigar). During the war the grounds of the castle were used by the Japanese as an execution area; locals say that the tall trees were used as makeshift gallows. No wonder the place is presumed to be haunted: although the wine cellar is open, the rest of the subterranean rooms are closed to visitors. A white bridge leading to the castle was completed in 1994. Open: 0830-1930, Monday-Sunday. Admission RM0.50.

Sam Poh Tong at Gunung Rapat, 5 km south of Ipoh, is the largest of the cave temples in the area. There are Buddha statues among the stalactites and stalagmites. The temple was founded 100 years ago by a monk who lived and meditated in the cave for 20 years; and it has been inhabited by monks ever since. The only break was during the Japanese occupation when the cave was turned into a Japanese ammunition and fuel dump. There is a pond at the entrance where locals release turtles to gain merit while young boys sell turtle food to earn money. Open: 0730-1800, Monday-Sunday. *Getting there*: Kampar bus (no 66, RM1).

Perak Tong, 6½ km north of Ipoh on Jalan Kuala Kangsar, is one of the largest Chinese temples in Malaysia. Built in 1926 by a Buddhist priest from China, the temple houses over 40 Buddha statues and mystical traditional Chinese-style murals depicting legends. It is visited by thousands of pilgrims every year and is the most ornately decorated of the many cave temples at the base of the 122m limestone hill. A path beyond the altar leads into the cave's interior and up a brick stairway to an opening 100m above ground with a view of the surrounding countryside. Another climb leads to a painting of Kuan Yin, Goddess of Mercy, who looks out from the face of the limestone cliff. A 15m-high reinforced concrete statue of the Buddha stands in the compound. Open 0900-1600 Monday-Sunday. *Getting there*: Kuala Kangsar bus (90¢) or city bus no 3.

Gua Tambun (Tambun Cave) is 3 km from Ipoh, near Tambun. Traces of a 10,000 years-old civilization were discovered here in the 1930s. The ochre drawings on the cave walls and the limestone cliffs depict the life of prehistoric man, especially interesting is the 'Degong' fish, a drawing of a large fish which feeds on meat, rather like a piranha. Tambun Hot Springs nestle at the foot of the hill. The Japanese were responsible for their initial development during the occupation. Two swimming pools have been built – one filled with luke warm water and one with hot. Open 0900-1600 Monday-Sunday. Admission RM5. Open 1500-2400 Monday-Sunday. *Getting there*: Tambun bus (90¢).

Local information

● Accommodation

Prices: L over RM500; **A+** RM260-500; **A** RM130-260; **B** RM65-130; **C** RM40-65; **D** RM20-40; **E** RM10-20; **F** Below RM10

A *Casuarina*, 18 Jln Gopeng, out of town, T 2505555, F 2508177, over 200 rooms, a/c, restaurant, pool, Ipoh's finest but not central. **A** *Central*, 26 Jln Ali Pitchay, T 255142, a/c, recently upgraded. **A** *Excelsior*, 43 Jln Clarke, T 2536666, F 2536012, a/c, restaurants, new tower block, one of tallest buildings in Ipoh, added in 1994, the hotel now has over 150 rooms. **A** *A-House Ipoh Station Hotel* aka *Majestic Hotel*, Bangunan Stesyen Keretapi, Jln Panglima Bukit Gantang Wahab, T 2555605, F 2553393, a/c, restaurant, pool, 100 rooms,

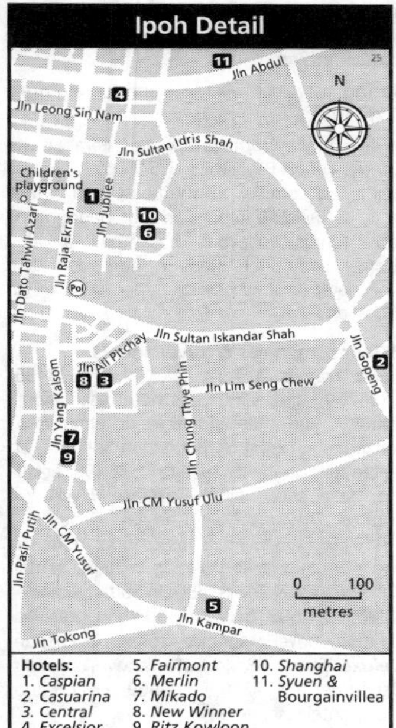

newly-furbished and managed by the Singapore-based A-House group of hotels, old colonial-style decor has been retained, good range of facilities from in-house movies to a health service, well run and priced. **A** *Syuen*, 88 Jln Sultan Abdul Jalil, T 2538889, a/c, 10 food and beverage outlets, central new hotel, 300 rooms, overlooking the bourgainvillea park, a/c, TV, minibar, comfortable and well-furbished rooms, discotheque – the *Car Disco* – one of Malaysia's new night spots, pool, business centre, sauna, tennis, recommended.

B *Eastern*, 118 Jln Sultan Idris Shah, T 2543936, F 2501468, small and rather grim '70s building, a/c, restaurant. **B** *Fairmont*, 10-12 Jln Kampar, T 2559999, a/c, restaurant. **B** *French*, 60-62 Jln Dato Onn Jaafar, T 2533111, another uninspiring small concrete block, a/c, restaurant. **B** *Mikado*, 86-88 Jln Yang Kalsom, T 2555855, a/c, restaurant. **B** *Ritz Garden*, 78 Jln C M Yussuf, T 2547777, a/c, bath, TV, in-house video, mini-bar, coffee house, health centre, sauna, not exactly oozing character but the rooms are well priced. **B** *Tambun Inn*, 91 Jln Tambun, T 577211, 4 km from city centre, most rooms are deluxe double which are priced at upper end of **B** category but offer good value, TV, a/c, in-house video, health centre, karaoke lounge. **B-C** *Ritz Kowloon*, 92-96 Jln Yang Kalsom, T 2547778, a/c, TV, in-house video, safe, tastefully furnished rooms, recommended.

C *Caspian*, 6-10 Jln Jubilee, T 2542324, a/c, hot water, basic furnishings, very clean and functional. **C** *Fair Park*, 85 Jln Kamaruddin Isa, T 2547129, the newest budget hotel in Ipoh, near DBI Sports Centre, recommended. **C** *Lotte*, 97 Jln Dato Onn Jaafar, T 2542215, a/c. **C** *Merlin*, 92-98 Jln Clare, T 2541351, a/c, restaurant. **C-D** *New Hollywood*, 72-76 Jln Yussuf, T 2415404, restaurant, kept clean and the room rates are good but there is little to mark this place out in any way. **C** *Robin*, 106-110 Jln Clare, T 2413755, a/c, recommended. **C** *YMCA*, 211 Jln Raja Musa Aziz, take a small path along the river to get here, T 2540809, tennis courts, dorm (**E**) beds available, this place is good value and the grounds as well as the rooms are spacious, but the location is inconvenient.

D *Cathay*, 90-94 Jln CM Yussuf, south of town, T 2413322, some a/c and private bathrooms, noisy and rather grubby, reasonable value and friendly manager, plenty of furniture, security poor. **D** *Golden Inn*, 17 Jln Che Tak, T 2530866, a/c, efficiently run, recommended. **D** *New Winner*, 32-38 Jln Ali Pitchay, T 2415177, some a/c, good value and very clean. **D** *Shanghai*, 85 Jln Clarke, fan only, restaurant, clean and central, recommended.

E *Ipoh*, 163 Jln Sultan Idris Shah, T 2548663, fan only. **E** *Mei Lai*, 7 Jln Raja Chulan, T 861729, some a/c, inconvenient location, but a good place.

● Places to eat

Prices: ◆◆◆◆ over RM40; ◆◆◆ RM13-40; ◆◆ RM5-13; ◆ under RM5

Ipoh is well known for its Chinese food, especially Ipoh chicken rice and *kway teow* – liquid and fried versions. The pomelo and the seedless guava are both grown in the state of Perak, and the state is also known for its delicious groundnuts.

Malay: ◆◆◆*Perwira*, Medan Gopeng, 3 km south of town centre, before Sam Poh Tong. ◆◆◆*Sabar Menanti*, Jln Raja Musa Aziz. ◆◆◆*Semenanjung*, Jln Sultan Idris Shah.

Chinese: ◆◆◆*Central*, 51-53 Cowan St. ◆◆*Foh San*, Jln Osbourne, dim sum. ◆◆*Kawan*, Jln Sultan Iskandar Shah, also Malay and Indian dishes. ◆◆*Kok Kee*, 272 Jln Sultan Iskandar Shah. ◆◆*Ming Court*, 36 Jln Leong Sin Nam, dim sum. ◆◆*Mung Cheong*, 511 Jln Pasir Putih,

Cantonese. ♦♦*Nam Thim Tong*, Mile 3.5 Gopeng Rd, Chinese, vegetarian, serve ersatz meat dishes made of soya bean. ♦*Chuan Fong*, 175 Jln Sultan Iskandar, speciality: curry laksa. ♦*Foh San*, 2 Osbourne St, popular for Hong Kong dim sum, served 0600-1200. ♦*Woh Heng Coffee Shop*, Osbourne St, good rice and noodles.

Indian: ♦♦♦*Comfy Corner*, 61 Jln Pasar. ♦♦♦*Gopal Corner*, Buntong. ♦♦♦*Guru's Chapati*, *Cheong Seng Restaurant Complex*, Lebuh Raya Ipoh, Punjabi, recommended. ♦♦♦*Krishna Bhawan*, 8 Jln Lahat. ♦♦*Majeedia*, Jln Dendahara/Jln Leong Boon Swee. ♦♦*Shal's Curry House*, 4 Jln Dato Maharaja Lela, a/c, excellent South Indian food and good vegetarian dishes, recommended. ♦*Mohamad Ibrahim*, 786 Jln Yang Kalsom, speciality: *mee rebus*.

International: ♦♦♦♦*Royal Casuarina Coffee House*, and *Il Ritrove*, Italian restaurant specializing in naivelle cuisine, 18 Jln Gopeng. ♦♦♦*Blue Window Café*, 56 Jln Dato Onn Jaafar, western food, aspires to 'romantic' atmosphere. ♦♦♦*Station Hotel Coffee House*, Jln Kelab. ♦♦*Excelsior Hotel Coffee House*, 43 Jln Clarke. ♦♦*Ever Fresh Juice Station*, 21 Jln Mustapha al Bakri, good fresh juice bar.

Foodstalls: Jalan Clarke, Jalan Dewan, Ipoh Garden, Jalan Sultan Idris Shah, mainly Chinese stalls. *Railway Station*, Jln Kelab, recommended. *Wooley Food Centre*, Canning Gardens.

Fastfood: *McDonalds* and *KFC* on Jln Dato Onn Jaafar.

● Airline offices

MAS, Lot 108 Bangunan Seri Kinta, Jln Sultan Idris Shah, T 2414155; **Pelangi Air**, Sultan Azian Shah Airport, T 3124770, F 3132725.

● Banks & money changers

Bank Bumiputra, **Malayan Banking**, **Hock Hua Bank**, and **Maybank** are all on Jalan Sultan Idris Shah; **UMBC**, **Oriental Bank** and **Public Bank**, are on Jln Yang Kalsom; in the new town, along Jln Sultan Yussuf there is a **Southern Bank**, **Hong Kong Bank**, **Standard Chartered**, and **Bank of Commerce**. *K & C Travel* (see below) also have foreign exchange facilities.

● Post & telecommunications

Area code: 05.
General Post Office: next to the railway station on Jln Panglima Bukit Gantang Wahab.

● Sports

Golf: *Royal Perak Golf Club*, Jln Sultan Azlan Shah, 3 km from town centre, 18-hole course laid out on 172 acres, only open to visitors on weekdays, members only at weekends and holidays, green fees RM150, caddy fee RM20, clubhouse facilities include bowling alley, cards and billiards room, bar.

Racing: races held every Sat and Sun at *Perak Turf Club*.

Swimming: *DBI Sports Complex*, Perak Sports Centre, Lebuh Raya Thivy, T 5460651. Largest swimming complex in Southeast Asia. Other facilities include: tennis, indoor badminton, table tennis, volleyball, basketball, a velodrome rugby pitch, stadium. Admission RM1 weekdays, RM2 weekends. Open 0900-2100 Mon-Sun.

● Tour companies & travel agents

Fiyen Travels, 1-3 Jln Che Tak, T 533455, F 506709, sightseeing tours, hotel reservations, domestic and international air ticketing; *Reliance*, Lot 1-12 1st Flr, Bangunan Sri Kinta, Jln Sultan Idris Shah, T 518711, F 538458, ticketing, travel shop, travel insurance; *HWA Yik Tour & Travel*, 23 Jln Che Tak, T 504060, F 530118, tours, hotel reservation, domestic and international air ticketing, mini-bus rental; *K & C Travel & Tours*, 250 Jln Sultan Iskandar, T 506999, F 502154, airline ticketing, hotel reservation, travel insurance, foreign exchange; *Deluxe Tours*, 58 Jln Dato Tahwil Azhar (Jln Osbourne), T 537260, F 508969, air ticketing, tours, hotel reservations.

● Tourist offices

None of Ipoh's three tourist offices offer much in the way of help and assistance, bar a map. **Ipoh City Council Tourist Office**, Jln Abdul Adil, open: 0800-1245 and 1400-1615 Mon-Thur, 0800-1212 and 1400-1615 Fri, 0800-1245 Sat. **Perak Tourist Information Centre**, State Economic Planning Unit, Pejabat Setiausaha Kerajaan, Jln Panglima Bukit Gantang Wahab, open 0800-1245, 1400-1615 Mon-Thur, 0800-1215, 1445-1615 Fri, 0800-1245 Sat, closed Sun, T 2412957, F 2418173; **Tourist Information**, *Casuarina Hotel*, 18 Jln Gopeng, T 2532008.

● Transport

205 km from KL, 161 km from Butterworth.

Local Car hire: **Avis**, Sultan Azian Shah Airport, T 206586; **Hertz**, *Royal Casuarina Hotel*, 18 Jln Gopeng, T 2505533, and Sultan Azlan Shah Airport, T 3127109.

Air Sultan Azlan Shah Airport, T 3122459, approximately 15 km south of town, RM10 taxi ride. Regular connections with Johor Bahru, Kota Bharu, Kota Kinabalu, KL and Kuching on MAS and with Johor Bahru on Pelangi Air.

Train Ipoh is on the main north-south line. Five daily connections with Butterworth and KL, T 2540481. See page 512 for timetable.

Road Bus: Ipoh is on the main north-south road and is well connected. The bus terminal is at the intersection of Jln Kelab, Kidd and Silbin (known as Medan Kidd), a short taxi trip from the town centre. Buses to Taiping, and Kuala Kangsar leave from the local bus terminal. Regular connections with Butterworth (RM7.10), KL (3 hours, RM9.40), Alor Star (RM11.90), Kuantan, Sungai Petani (RM8.80), Johor Bahru (RM25.80), Kangar (RM14.00), Kuala Perlis (RM14.00), Taiping, Lumut and Tapah (90 minutes). There are also services to Kota Bharu (RM17.10) and Grik/Gerik. An express coach company has a booking office at 2 Jln Bendahara, T 535367. They operate a daily service to Singapore, Johor Bahru, KL, Butterworth, Penang, Lumut, Alor Star and Kuala Kangsar. **Taxi**: shared taxis leave from beside the bus station. KL, Butterworth, Taiping, Alor Star, Tapah. If you want to order a taxi try the Nam Taxi Company, 15 Jln Raja Mus Aziz, T 2412189.

International connections Air: MAS provide quite a few international connections from Ipoh. Daily connections on Pelangi Air with Medan, Sumatra, Indonesia. **Road Bus**: connections with Hat Yai in southern Thailand and Singapore.

LUMUT

Lumut is primarily a base for the Royal Malaysian Navy which has a population of around 25,000, compared to the populace of 1,000 in Lumut itself. Lumut is also a transit point for Pulau Pangkor, and in recent years it has also begun tentatively to develop as a holiday destination in its own right. The *Orient Star*, a new international class hotel looms large on the coast where the former government resthouse used to stand, apartment blocks are rearing their ugly heads on Bukit Engku Busu, the hill backing the town, and Lumut has most definitely forsaken its sleepy fishing village identity for a busy seaside town. The town is at its zenith during the *Pesta Laut*, a sea festival, which takes place every August at nearby Teluk Batik.

The naval base houses the **Royal Malaysian Navy Museum**, which really speaks for itself. Open: Monday-Thursday, Saturday-Sunday. **Teluk Batik**, which is 7 km south of Lumut, is a popular beach spot (often used by the naval base), with chalets, food stalls and changing rooms backing the sweeping, sandy bay. There is another good sandy beach at **Teluk Rubiah** which is a further 6 km south. It is near the Teluk Rubia Royal Golf Club (T 2619555) which has a pool and tennis courts in addition to the golf course.

Local information

● Accommodation

Prices: L over RM500; **A+** RM260-500; **A** RM130-260; **B** RM65-130; **C** RM40-65; **D** RM20-40; **E** RM10-20; **F** Below RM10

A+-A *The Orient Star*, Lot 203 and 366, Jln Iskandar Shah, T 6834199, F 6834223, 150 a/c rooms, TV, in-house video, mini fridge, free-form pool with swim-up bar, paddling pool, gymnasium, jet-ski hire, bicycle hire, coffee house, bar, palatial in size and decor, pleasantly furnished rooms with balconies and sea views – but no beach. **A+** *Swiss-Garden Resort*, due to open early in 1997 promises "an idyllic seaside retreat for leisure, golfing, exhilarating watersports, business meetings and conferences".

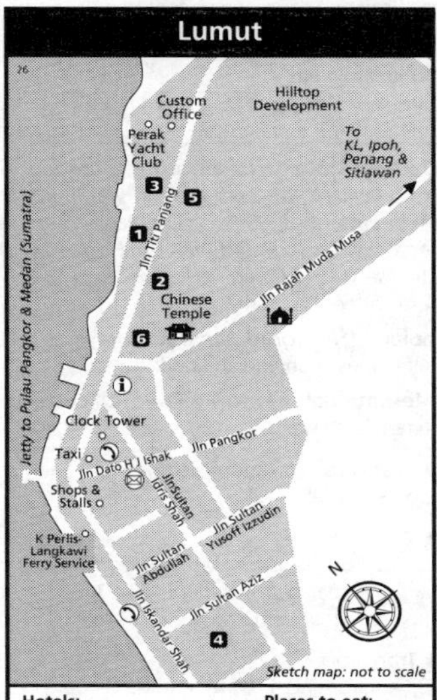

B *Lumut Country Resort*, Jln Titi Panjang, T 6835009, F 6835396, 44 a/c rooms, swimming pool, paddling pool, tennis courts, does not stand up to the *Orient Star* and is soon to be overshadowed by the *Blue Bay Resort* under construction next door, but has some attractive features such as hand-printed batik bed covers and wooden floors, good value. **B** *Hotel Manjun Permai*, Lot 211-213, Jln Iskandar Shah, T 6834934, F 6834937, a/c, comfortable, but decor on the tacky side. **B-C** *Harbour View Hotel*, Lot 13 and 14, Jln Titi Panjang, T 6837888, F 6837088, small hotel on main road along sea front, a/c, TV, mini fridge, tea and coffee-making facilities.

C *Hotel Indah*, 208 Jln Iskandar Shah, T 6835064, F 6834220, one of the newest budget hotels on the main road along the coast, a/c, TV, hot shower, adjoining coffee house, simply furbished and clean with pleasant views over the esplanade. **C-D** *Lumut Villa Inn*, Batu 1, Jln Sitiawan, T 6835982, F 6836563, inconveniently located outside the town if you do not have your own transport, but good value for money, rooms without a/c in **D** category.

D-E *Phin Mum Hooi*, 93 Jln Titi Panjang, T 6835641, the cheapest place around, rooms are clean and the management friendly, not far from the jetty.

● Places to eat

Prices: ♦♦♦♦ over RM40; ♦♦♦ RM13-40; ♦♦ RM5-13; ♦ under RM5

Chinese: ♦♦♦*Ocean Seafood Restaurant*, 115 Jln Tit Panjang, a/c, specializes in seafood. ♦♦♦-♦♦*Sin Pinamhui*, 93-95 Jln Titi Panjang, traditional Chinese food. ♦♦*Phin Lum Hooi*, next to Chinese Temple on Jln Titi Panjang, cheap Chinese coffee shop fare.

Indian: ♦♦*Restoran Samudera Raya*, 39 Jln Sultan Idris Shah, Indian and Malay food.

International: *Kentucky Fried Chicken*, Jln Sultan Abdullah.

● Post & telecommunications

Area code: 05.

● Tourist offices

Lumut Tourist Information Centre, Jln Titi Panjang (near petrol station), T 6834057, not open on a regular basis.

● Transport

183 km from KL, 170 km from Butterworth, 83 km from Ipoh.

Road Bus: the bus station is in the centre of town, a few minutes' walk from the jetty. Regular connections with Ipoh, KL and Butterworth and less regular connections with Melaka and Tapah (for the Cameron Highlands). **Taxi**: services available to Ipoh, KL and Butterworth.

International connections with Singapore: buses also run between Lumut and Singapore.

Sea Ferry: regular crossings, at least every 30 minutes from 0645 to 2000 from Lumut Jetty to Pangkor village on Pangkor Island. Return fare is RM4 for adult and RM2 for child, crossing takes under an hour. Crossings every 2 hours from 0845 to 1830 to Pan Pacific Resort at north end of Pangkor Island. Return fare is RM6 for adult and RM3 for child. For further information contact *Lumut Ferry Station*, T 935541, or *White Yellow Black Ferry*, Kompleks Kraftangan and Pusat Pemandu Pelancong, T 934062.

International connections with Sumatra: Kuala Perlis Langkawi Ferry Service or *KPLFS* (T 6854258) run a service between Lumut and Belawan, Medan's port in Sumatra, Indonesia. The service leaves Lumut at 1000 on Thur and returns from Belawan on Wed at 1100, 3½ hours. *Indomas Express* also operates boats on this route. Fare for both companies is RM90 one way, RM160 return and both include bus connections between Belawan and Medan. In Medan tickets for *Indomas* can also be booked through *Tobali Tour and Travel*, Jln Juanda Baru 52 and for *KPLFS* through *Indoma Citra Agung*, Jln Katamso 33D.

PULAU PANGKOR

Pangkor, just 7 km across the straits from Lumut, is one of the most easily accessible islands in Malaysia. It was on board a British ship anchored off the island that the historic Treaty of Pangkor was signed in 1874, granting the British entry into the Malay states for the first time. Before World War Two the island was used as a leper colony and now has a population of 25,000.

There is old Pangkor with its fishing villages (Pangkor is one of the largest fish suppliers in Peninsular Malaysia) – Sungai Pinang Kecil, Sungai Pinang Besar and Pangkor (main village), and modern Pangkor to the north with a modern luxury resort. To the southwest is the tiny island of Pankgor Laut. The main island is pretty but gets very busy, particularly at weekends and during school holidays, as it is one of the few places on the west coast with good beaches. It is disappointing compared with some of the peninsula's east coast islands however, and could open up even more to tourists if the new airport at Teluk Dalam beach is ever finalized (it was recently closed for safety reasons).

Some of the best beaches and coral can be found on nearby islands – such as **Emerald Bay** on Pangkor Laut, a private island only open to guests of the resort there (see Accommodation). (Emerald Bay is the spot where F Spencer Chapman escaped from Malaya after 3 years fighting the Japanese behind enemy lines – all recounted in his book *The jungle is neutral*.) There are some hidden beaches on the main island: north of **Pasir Bogak**, the most developed beach, turtles lay their eggs right on **Teluk Ketapang** beach (mainly during

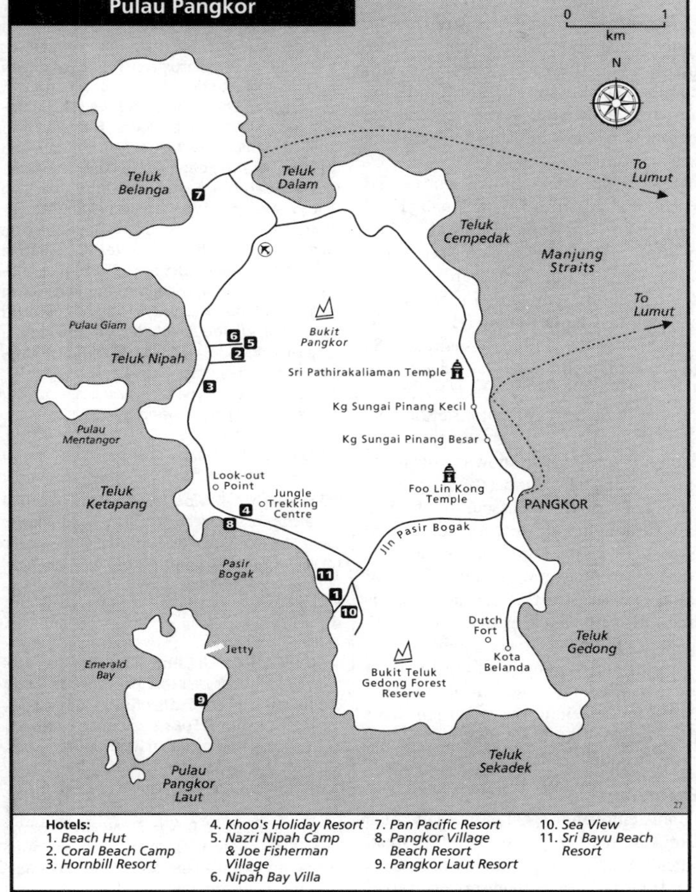

May, June and July); north of this are two of the nicest beaches, (Teluk Nipah) **Coral Bay** and (Teluk Belanga) **Golden Sands**. The most popular beach is at Pasir Bogak. Visitors can also take boats to Pulau Mentangor and Pulau Sembilan.

There are good walks round the island; it takes nearly a day to walk all the way round; by bicycle, half a day, and by motorcycle 2-3 hours. For such a small place, circumnavigating the island is surprisingly entertaining. The west coast is comparatively secluded with stretches of quiet beach and the odd fishing settlement, while the east coast hums with commercial activity – like boat building and fish processing – and because the population is so ethnically diverse, there is a lot of variety.

There is a South Indian temple, **Sri Pathirakaliaman**, at Sungai Pinang Kecil and the **Foo Lin Kong Temple** at the foot of Sungai Pinang Besar, with a miniature Great Wall of China in the garden. To the south at Teluk Gedung there are ruins of a Dutch fort, **Kota Belanda**. It was built by the Dutch East India Company in 1680 to protect Dutch interests, especially the rich tin traders, from attack by Malay pirates. It was heavily fortified and apparently its cannon could protect the whole Strait of Dinding also known as the Manjung Straits. The Dutch were forced to leave the fort after an assault by the Malays although they reoccupied it from 1745-1748. Little more than a shell of the former building now remains. Pangkor village is also attractive. Its main street is lined with stores selling dried fish packaged in pink plastic bags. There are also souvenir shops – mostly selling T-shirts – and a handicraft centre. One or two of the coffee houses along the street still have their original marble topped tables and straits wooden chairs.

Excursions

Pulau Sembilan lies 27 km south of Pulau Pangkor. there are a group of nine small islands and outcrops here, which offer good marine life and diving opportunities.

Local information

● Accommodation

Prices: L over RM500; **A+** RM260-500; **A** RM130-260; **B** RM65-130; **C** RM40-65; **D** RM20-40; **E** RM10-20; **F** Below RM10

Most of the mid and upper range accommodation is at Pasir Bogak and can be reached from Pangkor village by taxi. Many of the budget places are at Teluk Nipah on the west coast which require a rather longer taxi ride in one of the vehicles belonging to Pangkor's taxi mafia. Note that room rates are discounted during the week – especially the more expensive hotels.

Pasir Bogak: **A+** *Sri Bayu Beach Resort*, T 6851929, F 6851050, chalet accommodation only, oriental style decor, a/c, TV, bath, coffee-making facilities, pool, tennis, karaoke, restaurant, children's club, rather over-priced but the best place to stay on Pasir Bogak. **B** *Beach Hut*, T 6851159, a/c, restaurant, watersports, one of the older hotels here and the years are beginning to show, set in a garden close to the beach. **B** *Seaview*, T 6851605, a/c, restaurant, watersports, fishing, boat trips, breakfast included in room rate. **B-C** *Beach Hotel*, T 939159. **B** *Khoo's Holiday Resort*, T 6851164, restaurant, chalets on the hill and rooms in a block, with or without a/c, sea tours arranged. **B-E** *Pangkor Village Beach Resort*, T 6852227, a/c chalet (**B**) inclusive breakfast and dinner, A-frames (**D**), longhouse (**E**) (max 10 people), all inclusive of breakfast, near the main cluster of food stalls in Pasir Bogak, can be noisy and the tents are hot during the day; **E** *Pangkor Anchor*, T 6851363, cheap and rather shabby 'A' frame huts, not far from *Khoo's Holiday Resort*.

Teluk Nipah: **A-B** *Nipah Bay Villa*, T 6852198, a/c, attractive wooden cottages, well equipped, room rate includes all meals, so the deal is pretty good and this place also has a welcoming atmosphere. **A-B** *Hornbill Resort*, T 6852005, F 6852006, all rooms with sea views, a/c, TV, hot shower, seafood restaurant, popular bar with local and imported brews, and recommended at sunset. **B-D** *Coral Beach Camp*, T 6852711, A-frame huts (**D**), with additional cost for bathroom, family rooms split between 5 (**D**), organize watersport, motorbike hire. **B** *Sukasuka Beach Resort*, T 6852494, simple bamboo chalets with attached facilities. **D** *Joe Fisherman Village*, T 6852389, one of the most popular budget places to stay with simple 'A' frame chalets, bicycles for hire, meals available. **D** *Nazri Nipah Camp*, T 6852014, pretty similar to *Joe Fisherman's* and as they are virtually next door it is easy enough to check them both out.

Pangkor Laut: **L-A+** *Pangkor Laut Resort*, Pangkor Laut Island, T 6991100, F 6991200, Malaysia's top resort, officially opened in 1994 by Luciano Pavarotti who is quoted as saying: "I almost cried when I saw how beautiful God had made this paradise." Alan Whicker put the event on film, calling it 'Pavarotti in Paradise', and the Prime Minister of Malaysia chose to spend his birthday here, all this acclaim is no exaggeration, the *Pangkor Laut Resort* is idyllic. Pile chalets, a blend of Malay and Balinese architecture, are magnificently set, either over the sea (linked by wooden walkways) or on the jungled hillside, each is beautifully furbished, with carved wood and rattan work, luxurious bathrooms with recessed tubs and orchids floating on the water's surface for your arrival, a/c, mini-bar (ice buckets regularly delivered), tea/coffee-making facilities, CD player (TV in lounge only), immaculate kimonos, fresh fruit. Other facilities include well-stocked library (books and CDs), 3 swimming pools, squash, watersports, health club, gymnasium, sauna, spa, jacuzzi. A steep hike, or a short shuttle ride, takes you to Emerald Bay, one of the most perfect sandy bays in Malaysia. Eating at the resort is also a delight, top quality seafood at the *Fisherman's Cove*, steamboat at *Uncle Lim's*, or western fare at the *Sumudra* where chimes blow in the breeze. The wildlife on Pangkor Laut is also remarkably abundant and diverse – from hornbills to macaques – and the jungle treks are recommended. If you can afford it, Pangkor Laut is not to be missed, recommended.

Other places: **A+-A** *Pan Pacific Resort*, Teluk Belanga, T 6851091, F 6851852, resv@pprp.po.my, a/c, restaurants, 2 pools, limited golf course, tennis courts, watersports, limited business facilities, excellent location on wide sandy bay, 250 rooms of varying standard and price, to get there take a ferry to the Pan Pacific Jetty from where a hotel minibus takes you the short journey to the resort.

● Places to eat

Prices: ♦♦♦♦ over RM40; ♦♦♦ RM13-40; ♦♦ RM5-13; ♦ under RM5

Most hotels and chalets have their own restaurants and most guests end up eating where they are staying. Seafood is always on the menu.

Chinese: ♦♦*Fook Heng*, Pangkor village, simple coffee shop but excellent quality Chinese food, seafood prices are high. ♦♦*Guan Guan*, Pangkor village, specializes in seafood. ♦♦*Wah Mooi*, Sungai Pinang Kecil, steamed carp recommended by locals.

Seafood: *Ye Lin Seafood Garden*, 200 Jln Pasir Bogak, popular outdoor restaurant, prides itself on its low prices.

Foodstalls: on Pasir Bogak and Teluk Nipah.

● Banks & money changers

Large hotels will change money and there's a **Maybank** in Pangkor village.

● Post & telecommunications

Area code: 05.

● Sports

Golf: *Pan Pacific Resort*, T 6851091, Teluk Belanga, Golden Sands, 9-hole, on the coast, green fees RM50; ***Pangkor Yacht Club***, Teluk Gedong, T 6853478, F 6853480, watersports facilities, including jet skis, sailing and snorkelling, also organize fishing trips and round island tours.

● Transport

90 km southwest of Ipoh.

Local Buses/taxis: there are taxis, most of which are actually minibuses (Kereta Isewa), from Pangkor village to accommodation at Pasir Bogak as well as to Teluk Nipah and the *Pan Pacific Resort*. There is also a local bus service but this is not regular and locals usually take all the seats. For information contact the bus office in Pangkor village: Syarikat Kenderan Sri Pangkor, T 6851178, which is near the jetty. **Motorbikes/bicycles**: it is possible to hire motorbikes from Pangkor village for RM20-30/day. Soon Seng Motor is one of several companies in the village that hire out motorbikes. They are at 12 Main Rd (near jetty), T 6851269, and also have a branch at Standard Camp, Pantai Pasir Bogak, T 6851878. Bicycles are available from many of the chalet operations, RM10/day.

Air In 1991 work started on the construction of a small airport at Kampung Teluk Dalam; direct flights between KL, Penang, Johor Bahru and Singapore were operating in 1993 but the airstrip was subsequently closed for safety reasons. Following the lengthening of the runway, flights by Pelangi Air should have been operating once more – although as of mid-1997 these had yet to materialize.

Sea Boat: ferries leave from Lumut jetty. Connections every 15-30 minutes to Pangkor jetty (RM4 return), also regular connections with *Pan Pacific Resort* jetty close to Golden Sands (RM6 return). The first boat to Pangkor is at 0645 and the last at 1930. From Pangkor, the first boat leaves at 0630 and the last 1410. For further information contact the *Pan Silver Ferry*, 1a Jln Besar, Pangkor, T 6851046, F 6851782. **Ferry**: there are inter-island ferries or it is possible to hire fishing boats from the main villages. Large hotels will organize trips to the islands.

KUALA KANGSAR

Kuala Kangsar, half way between Ipoh and Taiping, is a royal town. It lies on the Kangsar River, a tributary of the Perak River. On the east bank of the Kangsar River lies the home of the Sultan of Perak. To get there, find the main roundabout in the town which has a distinctive clock tower at its centre, and head southeast towards the gates marking the start of the road to the palace estate. The road twists alongside the Perak River where there is also a back walkway for those on foot. The first monument that you come to is the **Ubudiah Mosque**, built on the slopes of Bukit Chandan. Completed in 1917, it is one of the most beautiful mosques in the country with its golden domes and elegant minarets. Next to it are the graves of the Perak royal family. Present members of the Perak royal family are resident in the beautiful **Istana Iskandariah** (and south bank of the Perak), which was built in 1930 sits on the summit of Bukit Chandan, overlooking the Perak River and Ubudiah Mosque. It is a massive marble structure with a series of towers, topped by golden onion domes set among trees and rolling lawns. It is not open to the public, but the former palace, Istana Kenangan (next door to the current Istana), is now the **Museum di Raja** and exhibits royal regalia. It is a fine example of Malay architecture and was built by Sultan Idris of Perak between 1913 and 1917 without recourse to any architectural plans or a single nail. Open 0930-1900 Saturday-Wednesday, 0930-1245 Thursday, closed Friday. In the vicinity of the palaces are several **traditional grand wooden Malay homes**, which used to house court officials. There is also another **former palace** (not open to public), near the Ubudiah Mosque. This grand white building was erected in 1903 for the 28th Sultan of Perak, and is now used as a school. Besides these grand buildings, in the grounds of the district office near the Agricultural Department, is one of the first three rubber trees planted in Malaysia. HN Ridley, also known as 'Crazy Ridley' was responsible for developing Kuala Kangsar as a rubber planting district. He obtained rubber seeds from London's Kew Gardens and brought them, first to Singapore, and then to Kuala Kangsar where the seeds were sown in 1877, when Sir Hugh Low was British President

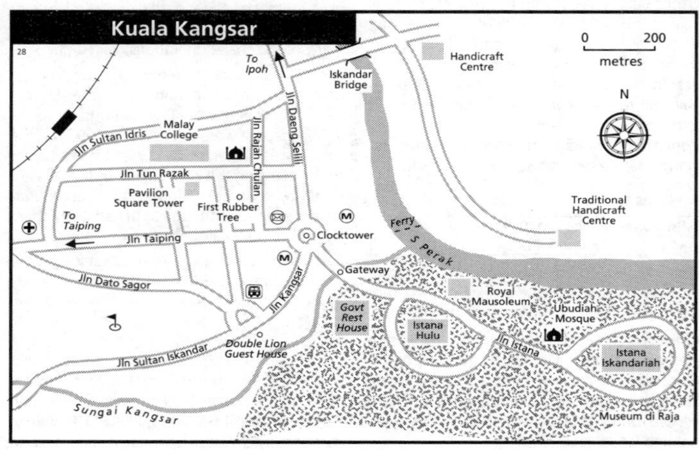

in Perak. The sole tree to remain is now marked with a memorial plaque to Ridley. Across the road from Kuala Kangsar's famed rubber tree is a charming pavilion, built in 1930 as a viewing gallery from which the sultan could watch polo on the padang. The padang is also overlooked by the red roofed building of the Malay college. Considered the Eton of Malaysia, the school was built in 1905 for the children of the Perak royal family. During the Japanese occupation in World War Two, the college was turned into administration offices for the Japanese Imperial Army who interrogated and subsequently beheaded anyone found to be a traitor. A school once again in the 1950s, it attracted a celebrated crowd – Anthony Burgess taught here (see **Further reading** on page 526 for a listing of his novels with a Malaysian theme).

Across the Perak River (20 sen ferry ride) there is a village where **traditional pottery-making** goes on, mostly within the Handicraft Centre there. The pottery is earthenware and fired in padi husk which gives it a rich black colour. The traditional product of the potteries is the labu sayong, a water pitcher, in the shape of a gourd.

Local information

● Accommodation

Prices: L over RM500; **A+** RM260-500; **A** RM130-260; **B** RM65-130; **C** RM40-65; **D** RM20-40; **E** RM10-20; **F** Below RM10

There are very few places to stay in Kuala Kangsar, none is particularly desirable apart from the *Rest House*, and all are small – the largest hotel has 14 rooms. Although Kuala Kangsar is not a popular stopover spot, due to the limited number of rooms, it is best to book in advance.

B *Rest House (Rumah Rehat Kuala Kangsar*, Bukit Candan, T 7763872, pleasant position just inside the gates to the palace road, old colonial mansion, poor value restaurant but excellent views.

D *Mei Lai*, 7f Jln Raja Chulan, T 7761729. **D** *Tin Heong*, 34 Jln Raja Chulan, T 7762066. **D-E** *Double Lion*, 74 Jln Kasa, T 7761010, some a/c, an alternative to the *Rest House* and a pleasant enough place to stay with large rooms, some overlooking the river.

● Post & telecommunications

Area code: 05.

General Post Office: Jln Taiping, near the clock tower.

● Sports

Canoeing: 3-day canoe safaris depart from Kuala Kangsar and follow the Perak for almost its entire length to the Cherendoh dam. For further information contact, No 3 MDKK, Jln Tebing, T 7769717.

● Transport

50 km northwest of Ipoh, 123 km south of Butterworth and 270 km from KL.

Train the station is out of town to the northeast, on Jln Sultan Idris. Trains every 2 hours from Ipoh and trains on the KL-Butterworth route also stop here.

Road Bus: the bus terminal is in the centre of town on Jln Raja Bendahara. Regular connections with Ipoh, Butterworth, KL, Lumut and Taiping. There is also one morning departure a day for Kota Bharu on the east coast. **Taxi**: taxis leave from close to the bus station for destinations including Butterworth, KL, Ipoh and Taiping.

TAIPING

Taiping, with a backdrop of the Bintang Mountains, is the old capital of Perak and one of the oldest towns in Malaysia. Around 1840, Chinese immigrants started mining tin in the area, and the town, as its name suggests, is predominantly Chinese. In the 1860s and 70s the Larut district of Taiping – then known as Kelian Pauh – was the scene of the 'Perak War', caused by bloody feuding between two rival Chinese secret societies – the Hai San and Ghee Hin – over rights to the rich tin deposits. The fighting between these Hakka and Hokkien groups resulted in British armed intervention and when it subsided, the town was renamed *thai-peng* – or 'everlasting peace'. It is the only big Malaysian town with a Chinese name.

In the *Straits Times* in 1933, colonial administrator G L Peet wrote: "What a pleasant town Taiping is! I first saw it some years ago on a rainy, cool evening, when the air was laden with the scent of flowering

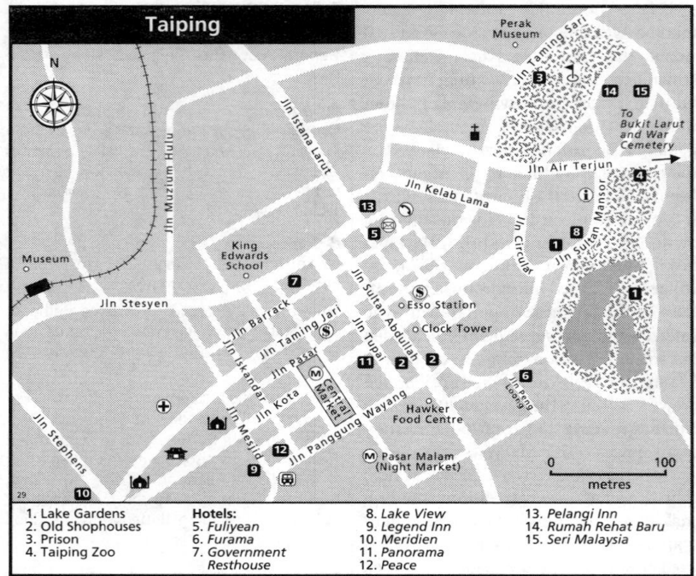

angsana trees and golden light bathed the slopes of the *ijau* [green] range. Taiping ... has the feeling of being lived in for a long time. It was a thriving and well-appointed town when Ipoh was still a Chinese village, when Seremban was in the same state and when Kuala Lumpur was just beginning to take on some semblance of permanence and solidity."

The Japanese built a prison in Taiping during the war (next to the Lake Garden), which was then converted into a rehabilitation centre for captured Communist Terrorists during the Emergency. Some of the executions carried out under Malaysia's draconian drugs legislation now take place in Taiping jail (see page 86).

Today the town has a run-down feel about it and many new buildings have replaced the former shophouses which are laid out on a monotonous grid plan. The streets are wide and the traffic noisy – probably one of the main reasons for coming here is to visit Maxwell Hill (see below). Nonetheless there is more colonial era architecture here than in many of Malaysia's towns. Jalan Iskandar has some fine examples of Chinese shophouse architecture and there are also some attractive colonial-era buildings including the former District Office on Jalan Kota.

Places of interest

As early as 1890 the **Lake Garden** or **Taman Tasik** was set up on the site of an abandoned tin mine. It is very lush due to the high rainfall and is the pride of the town. Covering 66 hectares, the park lies at the foot of Bukit Larut (Maxwell Hill). At one end of the park is **Taiping Zoo**, which is one of the oldest in Malaysia and boasts over 800 animals, including Malaysian elephants, tigers and hornbills. Open 0830-1830 daily. Admission: adult RM2, child RM1. Early morning, some locals use the park for their tai chi exercises. Rowing boats for hire on lake. Built in

1883, the lovely colonial **Perak Museum** (on the Butterworth Road, opposite the prison) is the oldest museum in Malaysia. It contains a collection of ancient weapons, aboriginal implements, stuffed animals and archaeological finds. Open 0900-1700 Saturday-Thursday, 0900-1215, 1445-1700 Friday. Near the museum is **All Saints' Church**. Built of wood in 1889, it is the oldest Anglican church in Malaysia. The graveyard contains graves of early settlers and those who died in the Japanese prisoner-of-war camp nearby. The **Ling Nam Temple** on Station Street is worth a visit for the Chinese antiques inside and is said to be the oldest Chinese temple in Perak state. The **railway station** on Jalan Steysen – now a school – is the oldest in Malaysia and holds a museum.

Excursions

Kuala Sepetang lies 16 km west of Taiping and contains a Mangrove Forest Museum, the first of its kind in Malaysia. The site lies in 40,700 hectares of mangrove swamp – more than half the swamp area in Peninsular Malaysia. The museum aims to highlight foresty operations in Malaysia.

The foot of **Bukit Larut** or **Maxwell Hill** is just 2 km or so east of Lake Gardens and most people climb the hill, whether on foot or by Land Rover, as a day excursion from Taiping (see next entry for details). *Getting there*: a taxi to the Land Rover station at the foot of the hill should cost around RM5.

Local information

● Accommodation

Prices: L over RM500; **A+** RM260-500; **A** RM130-260; **B** RM65-130; **C** RM40-65; **D** RM20-40; **E** RM10-20; **F** Below RM10

A-B *Legend Inn*, 2 Jln Long Jaafar, T 8060000, F 8066666, 8B-room block, bath, TV, video channel, coffee house, plushest place in town with well-equipped rooms.

B *Fuliyean*, 14 Jln Barrack, T 8068648, a/c, TV, bath, quite new and good value, rooms kept very clean. **B** *Meridien*, 2 Jln Simpang, T 8081133, a/c, TV, shower, coffee house, restaurant. **B** *Panorama*, 61-79 Jln Kota, T 834111, a/c, TV, in-house video, bath, mini fridge, coffee-making facilities, joined to a 3-storey supermarket, the *Fajar*, restaurant. **B** *Seri Malaysia*, 4 Jln Sultan Mansor, T 8069502, one of the new chain of budget hotels, located outside the town, near the Lake Gardens, spotlessly clean – to the point of being sterile.

C *Furama*, 30 Jln Peng Loong, T 821077, a/c, restaurant, recommended. **C-D** *New Resthouse (Rumah Rehat Baru)*, 1 Jln Sultan Mansor, Taman Tasek, T 8072044, a/c or fan, restaurant, situated a little out of town and the new block is hardly attractive but the rooms are large, with attached bathrooms, it overlooks the Lake Gardens and is good value, recommended.

D *Ann Chuan*, 25 Jln Kota, T 8075322, a/c or fan, restaurant. **D** *Government Resthouse*, Jln Residensi (opposite King Edwards School), T 822044, restaurant, recommended. **D** *Lake View*, opposite Lake Gardens, 1a Jln Circular, T 8074941, a/c, very noisy karaoke but cheap and clean. **D** *Merlin*, 73 Jln Halaman Pasar, T 8075833, restaurant. **D** *Nanyung*, 129-131 Jln Pasar, T 8074488, a/c or fan. **D** *Peace*, 32 Jln Iskandar, T 8073379, lots of character, basic and noisy, good value. **D** *Town*, 320 Jln Kota, T 8071166, basic.

● Places to eat

Prices: ♦♦♦♦ over RM40; ♦♦♦ RM13-40; ♦♦ RM5-13; ♦ under RM5

Chinese: ♦♦♦*Dragon Phoenix*, Jln Kota. ♦♦♦*Malaysia Restoran*, 36 Jln Eastern. ♦♦*Kum Loong*, 45-47 Jln Kota, good dim-sum 0500-0800. ♦♦*Prima Restaurant*, 21-23 Jln Kota. ♦*Kedai Kopi Sentosa*, Jln Kelab Cina, good Teow Chiew noodles.

Indian: number of places along Jln Pasar and Jln Panggung Wayang selling the usual array of biryani dishes and roti.

International: ♦♦♦*Nagaria Steak House*, 61 Jln Pasar, dark interior, popular for beer-drinking. ♦♦♦*Panorama*, 61-79 Jln Kota, mediocre western food and steak house.

Foodstalls: large night market on Jln Panggung Wayang. *Hawker Centre* in Metro Arcade (Shopping Centre), 54 Medan Simpang (5 km from town centre, on road to Kuala Kangsar). *Malay hawker stalls* on Jln Tupai. Burger, rice and fried chicken stalls near foot of Bukit Larut (Maxwell Hill).

● Banks & money changers

Bank Bumiputra and **UMBC** on Jln Kota; **Standard Chartered** at crossroads of Jln Kota and Jln Sultan Abdullah. *Poly Travels*, 53 Jln

Mesjid and *Fulham Tours*, 25 Jln Kelab Cina, have foreign exchange facilities.

● Post & telecommunications
Area code: 05.
General Post Office: Jln Barrack.

● Sport
Golf: *Bukit Jana Golf & Country Club*, Jln Bukit Jana, T 8837500, green fees RM50 weekdays, RM80 weekends. Clubhouse has pool, paddling pool, tennis, squash, kids' playground, card room, restaurant.

● Tour companies & travel agents
Poly Travels, 53 Jln Mesjid, T 820155, ticketing, currency exchange, hotel reservation, tours; *Trans Asia Pacific*, 112 Jln Barrack, T 828451, ticketing, hotel reservation, car hire, package tours; *Fulham Tours*, 25 Jln Kelab Cina, T 823069, ticketing, hotel reservation, licensed money changers.

● Transport
304 km north of KL, 88 km from Butterworth.

Train Station is on the east side of town. Lying on the north-south railway line, there are regular connections with Ipoh, KL and Butterworth. See page 512 for timetable.

Road Bus: the main long-distance bus station is 7 km out of town and getting there means either catching a town bus or a taxi. Regular connections with Butterworth (RM3.80), Ipoh, Sungai Petani (RM5.50) and KL (RM13.20). There is also a morning bus to Kuantan on the east coast. For other connections, change at Ipoh. Local buses for Ipoh, Grik and Kuala Kangsar leave from the local bus station which is much more conveniently located in the centre of town at the intersection of Jln Mesjid and Jln Iskandar.

BUKIT LARUT (MAXWELL HILL)

Bukit Larut, formerly known as Maxwell Hill, 12 km from Taiping, is Malaysia's oldest hill station. At an elevation of 1,034m it is the wettest place in Malaysia – it receives an average of 5,029 mm of rain a year – and was once a tea plantation. Bukit Larut is a small resort with limited facilities compared to the peninsula's other hill stations. The road up was built by prisoners of war during the Japanese occupation in World War Two. It is in such bad repair that it is virtually inaccessible in anything other than a 4WD vehicle, in any case private transport is not permitted. On the way up you pass a **Commonwealth War Cemetery**. Many of the gravestones here are marked December 1941, which was the date a single company from the Argyle Regiment tried to hold back the Imperial Japanese 42nd Infantry on the road north of Kuala Kangsar. Another stop are the **Tea Gardens** at the Batu 3.5 mark – or what is left of them. The administration office is at the Batu 6 marker and about 1 km on from here is the end of the road – at the *Gunung Hijau Rest House*. From here travel is on foot. On clear days, from the top, it is possible to see for miles along the coast. The walk to the summit takes about 30 minutes. Jungle walks near the top of the hill (but leeches are bad). To walk all the way down takes around 2-3 hours.

Local information

● Accommodation
For bungalows it is essential to book in advance (between 0900-1200), T 8077241 or write to Officer in charge, *Bukit Larut Hill Resort*, Taiping.

B *Cendana*. **B** *Tempinis* all between the sixth and seventh milestones.

D *Beringin*.

E *Bukit Larut*, large bathroom, excellent value. **E** *Gunung Hijau*.

Camping: **F** Campsite.

● Places to eat
Food available at ♦♦♦*Gunung Hijau* or *Bukit Larut* guesthouses. At the bungalows, meals can be arranged with the caretaker.

● Transport
The steep walk from Taiping Lake Gardens takes about 2½-3½ hours. **Road** The road is restricted and private cars are not permitted. A Land Rover service runs from the foot of the hill just above the Lake Garden in Taiping, every hour from 0800-1800 (RM2 one way to the administration office, RM2.50 to the Gunung Hijau Rest Stop), T 8077243.

BUTTERWORTH

An industrial and harbour town and base for the Royal Australian Air Force which is billeted here under the terms of the Five Powers Pact. It is the main port for ferries to Penang Island.

• **Accommodation** Butterworth is not a recommended stopping point – most tourists head straight for Penang. **A-B** *Travel Lodge*, 1 Lorong Bagan Luar, T 3333399, a/c, restaurant. **B** *Berlin*, 4802 Jln Bagan Luar, T 3321701, a/c, restaurant. **B-D** *Ambassador*, 4425 Jln Bagan Luar, T 3327788, a/c, restaurant. **B-C** *Kuala Lumpur*, 4448 Lorong Bagan Luar, T 3326199. **D** *Capital*, 3838 Jln Bagan Luar, T 331882. **D** *City*, 4591 Jln Chain Ferry, T 340705. **D-E** *Federal*, 4293-4294 Kampung Bengali, T 3337805, restaurant.

• **Banks & money changers** Maybank and UMBC on Jln Bagan Luar.

• **Transport** 369 km from KL, 386 km from Kota Bharu. Butterworth is the main transport hub for Penang and buses and trains operate into Thailand and down to KL and Singapore. **Train** The railway station is beside the Penang ferry terminal. Regular connections with Alor Star, Taiping, Ipoh, KL and JB. See page 512 for timetable. **Road Bus**: bus station next to the ferry terminal. Regular connections with KL (RM17.10), Taiping, Kuala Kangsar (RM5.60), Melaka, JB (RM33.50), Kota Bharu (RM16.50), Kuala Terengganu, Kuantan and Ipoh, 2 hours. Buses leave every 30 minutes from Butterworth for Kuala Perlis (Langkawi ferry). There are also buses to Keroh, on the border with Thailand, from where it is possible to get Thai taxis to Betong. **Taxi**: taxis leave from next to the ferry terminal. If you take a taxi across to Penang you must pay the taxi fare plus the toll for the bridge. **Sea Ferry**: ferry (pedestrian and car) to Georgetown and leave every 15-20 minutes. **International connections Train** To Bangkok, Thailand (19 hours) and to Singapore (14 hours). Butterworth is one of the main stopovers on the Eastern and Orient Express, which travels in style from Singapore to Bangkok. Passengers disembark here to make the 3 hour trip by ferry and rickshaw to Georgetown.

PENANG (PULAU PINANG)

Penang – or more properly, Pulau Pinang – is the northern gateway to Malaysia and is the country's oldest British settlement. It has been sold to generations of tourists as 'the Pearl of the Orient' but in shape Penang looks more like a frog than a pearl. Penang state also includes a strip of land on the mainland opposite, Province Wellesley – named after Colonel Arthur Wellesley, later to become the Duke of Wellington, who went on to defeat Napoleon at Waterloo. (The 738 sq km Province Wellesley is also known by its Malay name, Seberang Perai.) Georgetown's founder, Captain Francis Light, originally christened Penang 'Prince of Wales Island'. In Malay, *pinang* is the word for the areca nut palm, an essential ingredient of betel nut (see page 37). The palm was incorporated into the state crest in the days of the Straits Settlements during the 19th century. Today Pulau Pinang is translated as 'betel nut island'. Light called Georgetown after George, the Prince of Wales, who later became King George IV as it was acquired on his birthday; most Malaysians know the town by its nickname: *Tanjung*, as it is situated on a sandy headland called Tanjung Penaga.

Before the arrival of Francis Light, who captained a ship for a British trading company, in 1786, Penang was ruled by the Sultan of Kedah. The sultanate had suffered repeated invasions by the Thais from the north and *Orang Bugis* pirates from the sea. Sultan Muhammad Jawa Mu'Azzam Shah II was also beset by a secession crisis and when this turned into a civil war he requested help from Francis Light, then based at Acheen in Sumatra, whom he met in 1771. Light was in search

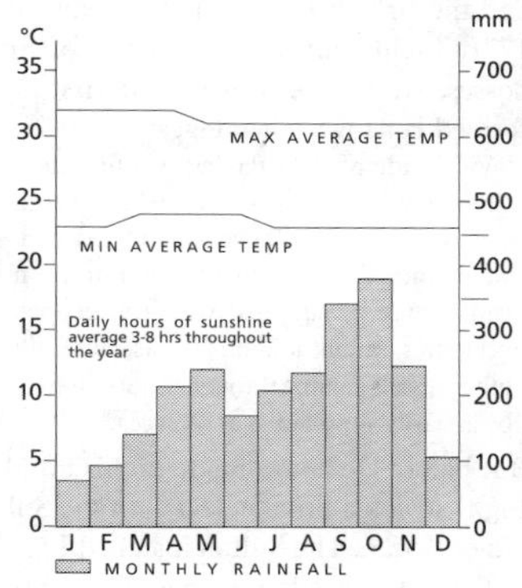

Climate: Penang

Penang highlights

Museums and historical sights **Fort Cornwallis**, on the site of Francis Light's original stockade (page 182); **Penang Museum & Art Gallery**, located in Penang's former English public school, founded in 1816 (page 182); **Khoo Kongsi**, a magnificent and well-preserved Chinese clan association house (page 183).

Temples and mosques **Goddess of Mercy Temple** (Kuan Yin Teng), built by Chinese settlers at the beginning of the 19th century (page 183); **Kek Lok Si** (Monastery of Supreme Bliss) which took 20 years to build and is modelled on a monastery in China (page 186); **Snake Temple** (Temple of the Azure Cloud), built in 1850 and populated by Pit Vipers (page 187); **Sri Mariamann (Hindu) Temple**, built by Georgetown's South Indian community in 1883 (page 183); **Kapitan Kling Mosque**, built in 1800 (page 183); **Wat Chayamangkalaram** (Wat Buppharam) Thai Buddhist temple with Burmese temple opposite (page 184).

Other sights **Chinatown**, one of the liveliest and best-preserved in the region; **Clan Piers**, a Chinese water village, linked to Pengkalan Weld (Weld Quay) by jetties named after different clans (page 183); **Penang Hill**, overlooking Georgetown, with a funicular railway to the top (page 185); **Butterfly Farm**, claiming to be the largest tropical butterfly farm in the world, with more than 120 Malaysian species (page 195).

Beaches **Batu Ferringhi**, the most famous beach in Malaysia, now a hotel strip (page 194); **Muka Head**, on the northwest tip of the island, with a series of secluded coves around a rocky headland (page 195).

Shopping Antiques, basketware, handicrafts and batik (page 198).

Sports Golf, swimming, watersports and sailing – including yacht cruises around the islands of the Langkawi group (page 198).

of a trading base on the north shore of the Strait of Melaka which could be used by his firm, Jordain, Sulivan and De Souza, and the British East India Company. In 1771, Light sent a letter to one of his bosses, De Souza, in which he first described Penang's advantages:

> "Withinside of Pulo Pinang is a fine clear channel of 7 and 14 fathoms which a ship can work anytime. ... There is plenty of wood, water and provisions there, (the European ships) may be supplied with tin, pepper, beetelnut, rattans and birdsnests, and ... all other vessels passing through the Straits may be as easily supplied as at Malacca."

But before De Souza made up his mind, Light struck a private deal with the Sultan of Kedah. The Sultan installed Light in the fort at Kuala Kedah and gave him the title of Deva Rajah, ceding to him control of the Kedah coast as far south as Penang. In turn, Light promised to protect the Sultan from his many enemies.

A frisson between Sultan Muhammad and the East India Company brought developments to a standstill in 1772. Light left Kedah and sailed to Ujung Salang (which English sailors called Junk Ceylon, and is now known as Phuket) where he built up a trading network. 11 years later he finally repaired relations with Kedah and the newly installed Sultan Abdullah agreed to lease Penang to the British – again, in return for military protection. On 11 August 1786, Light formally took possession of Penang. The island was covered in dense jungle and was uninhabited, apart from a handful of Malay fishermen and a few Bugis pirates.

A small township grew up around the camp by the harbour. A wooden stockade

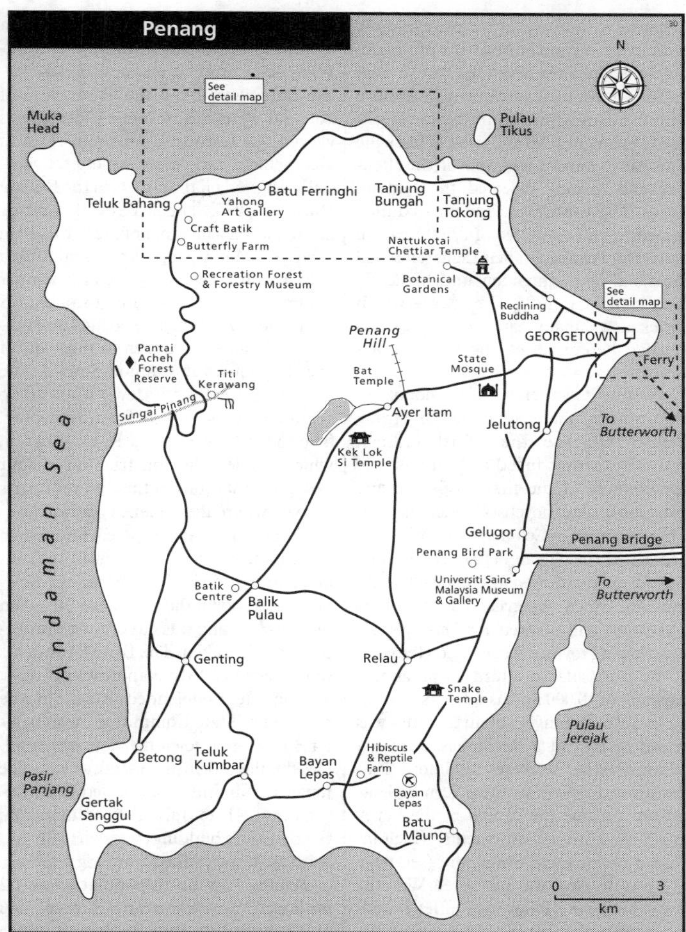

was built to defend the island on the site of the original camp and the cantonment was called Fort Cornwallis, after Marquis Cornwallis, then the Governor-General of India. Light declared Prince of Wales Island a free port to attract trade away from the Dutch, and this helped woo many immigrant traders to Penang. (Penang's status as a free port was only withdrawn in 1969.) Settlers were allowed to claim whatever land they could clear. The island quickly became a cultural melting pot with an eclectic mix of races and religions. By 1789, Georgetown had a population of 5,000 and by the end of the next decade, this had more than doubled.

The Sultan of Kedah was upset that the East India Company had not signed a written contract setting out the terms of Penang's lease. When the Company began to haggle with him over the price and the military protection he had been promised, Sultan Abdullah believed the British were backing out of their agreement. In alliance with the Illanun pirates, the Sultan blockaded Penang in 1790 and tried to force the Company's hand. Light went on the offensive and quickly defeated the Sultan's forces. The vanquished Sultan Abdullah agreed to an annual fee of 6,000 Spanish dollars for Penang. Francis Light remained the island's superintendent until his death, from malaria, in 1794. The disease, which struck down many early settlers, earned Penang the epithet of 'the White Man's Grave'.

Despite Georgetown's cosmopolitan atmosphere, there remained a strong British influence: the British judicial system was introduced in 1801 with the appointment of the first magistrate and judge, an uncle of novelist Charles Dickens. The previous year, Colonel Arthur Wellesley had signed a new Treaty of Peace, Friendship and Alliance with Kedah's new Sultan Diyauddin, which superceded Light's 1791 agreement and allowed for Penang's annexation of Province Wellesley, on the coast of the peninsula, in return for an annual payment of 10,000 Spanish dollars.

In 1805 Penang's colonial status was raised to that of a Residency. A young administrative secretary, Stamford Raffles, arrived to work for the governor. Georgetown became the capital of the newly established Straits Settlements, which included Melaka and Singapore (see page 51). But the glory was shortlived. With the rise of Singapore, following Raffles' founding of the settlement in 1819, Georgetown was quickly eclipsed by the upstart at the southern tip of the peninsula and by the 1830s had been reduced to a colonial backwater. From an architectural perspective, this proved a saving grace: unlike Singapore, Penang retains many of its original colonial buildings and its rich cultural heritage.

In the early 19th century Penang was used as a staging post for the opium trade between India and China. The East India Company auctioned off licences to gambling dens, brothels and opium traders – the latter accounted for about 60% of colonial Penang's revenue. Vice gangs carved out territories for themselves in Georgetown and secret society feuds finally erupted on the streets in the Penang Riots of 1876. The 9 days of fighting started when a member of the White Flag society (a Malay gang) threw a rambutan skin at a Toh-Peh-Kong society member whom he caught peering through his front door. Open warfare ensued and bullet holes can still be seen in the walls of the shophouses in Cannon Square. The riots were finally put down when troop reinforcements arrived from Singapore. The societies were fined RM5,000 each, which funded the construction of four new police stations in the different parts of town where the societies operated.

Colonial Penang prospered, through tin booms and rubber booms, until the outbreak of World War Two. When the Japanese raced down the peninsula on stolen bicycles, Penang was cut off, without being formally taken. The British residents were evacuated to Singapore within days, leaving the undefended island in the hands of a "State Committee", which, after 3 days, put down the riots which followed the British withdrawal. The Japanese administration lasted from December 1941 to July 1945; remarkably, Georgetown's buildings were virtually unscathed, despite Allied bombing attacks.

Penang now has a population of 1.2 million, 53% of whom are Chinese, 35% Malay and 11% Indian. Penang, along with the other two Straits settlements of Melaka and Singapore, was a centre of Peranakan culture. Peranakans, also known as Babas or Straits Chinese, evolved their own unique blend of Malay and Chinese cultures (see page 66). The Babas of Penang, however, have almost disappeared as a distinctive group – although various shops and restaurants play to the Peranakan theme.

Georgetown, the capital of Penang state, is on the northeast point of the island, nearest the mainland; Bayan Lepas Airport is on the southeast tip. The 13 km-long Penang Bridge, linking the island to Butterworth, is half way down the east coast, just south of Georgetown. Batu Ferringhi, now a strip of luxury hotels, is Penang's most famous beach and is on the north coast. In 1970 just 39,454 foreign visitors were recorded as landing on the island. By 1981 this figure had risen to 249,118, and in 1990 – during Visit Malaysia Year – over 630,000 arrived. Nonetheless there are still a handful of small secluded coves with good beaches on the northwest tip of the island. The west of the island is a mixture of jungled hills, rubber plantations and a few fishing kampungs. There are more beaches and fishing villages on the south coast. A short steep mountain range forms a central spine, which includes Penang Hill, overlooking Georgetown, at 850m above sea level.

Although Penang is best known as a beach resort, there is much more here than just sand and (rather dirty) sea. The island is also a cultural and architectural gem with Chinese, Malay and Indian influences. Georgetown has the largest collection of pre-war houses in all Southeast Asia. The Penang Heritage Trust has been established by concerned residents in the face of commercial pressures on Penang's unique heritage. Those interested in Georgetown's architectural heritage should try to get hold of Khoo Su Nin's *Streets of Georgetown, Penang*.

GEORGETOWN

The first four streets of Georgetown – Beach (now known as Lebuh Pantai), Lebuh Light, Jalan Kapitan Kling Mosque (previously Jalan Pitt) and Lebuh Chulia – still form the main thoroughfares of modern Georgetown. Lebuh Chulia was formerly the Cantonese heartland of the Ghee Hin triad, one of the secret societies involved in the 1867 Penang Riots. The older part of town to the west of Weld Quay, in the shadow of Kapitan Kling Mosque, is predominantly Indian.

Georgetown is, however, mainly Chinese; the main Chinatown area is contained by Jalan Kapitan Kling Mosque, Lebuh Chulia, Jalan Penang and Jalan Magazine. The shophouses were built by craftsmen from China: the rituals, burial customs, clan associations, temples and restaurants make up a self-contained Chinese community. Despite the traffic and a skyline pierced by the KOMTAR (Kompleks Tun Abdul Razak) skyscraper, the crowded streets still have plenty of charm. Penang's Chinatown is one of the liveliest in Malaysia; its atmosphere and most of its original architecture remain intact. There are an estimated 12,000 pre-war houses still standing in Georgetown, making the town an architectural gem in Southeast Asian terms.

How Penang has managed to preserve at least some of its heritage while that in other Malaysian towns has been torn down, is linked to a rent control cut – on the statute books for years – which has frozen rents and therefore made redevelopment unprofitable. The houses may be mouldering, but at least they aren't (usually) being demolished. But developers are bringing pressure on the federal government to abolish the Rent Control Act. To alleviate the immediate need for alternative housing and to facilitate adjustments by tenants to payment of rental at market rates, a transitional period has been introduced whereby tenants will have to pay rentals based on a formula provided by the Government. The rates are still lower than the market rates. At the end of the transition period on 31 December 1999, owners are entitled to recover vacant possession of the premises (*The Star*, Section 2. Monday 1 September 1997).

Not all of the island is worthy of 'gem' status however. Pollution and litter have spoiled parts of Penang in recent years. Some beaches are dirty and very few people swim in the sea. The coral which used

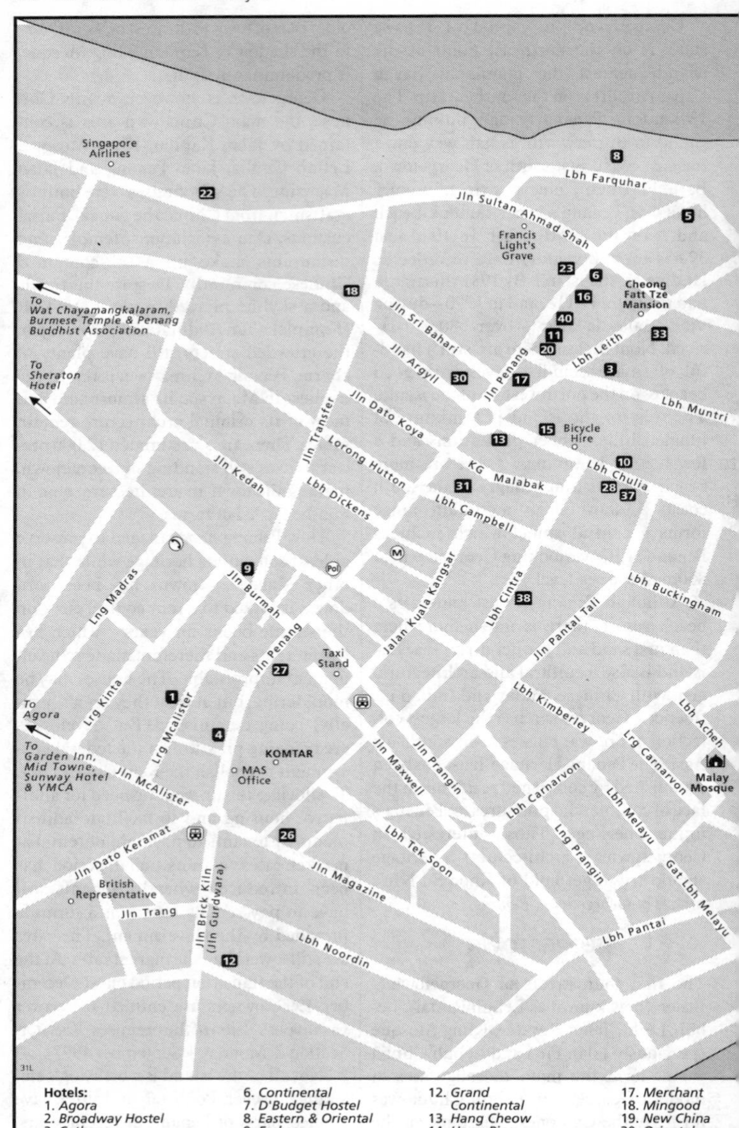

Hotels:
1. *Agora*
2. *Broadway Hostel*
3. *Cathay*
4. *Central*
5. *City Bayview*
6. *Continental*
7. *D'Budget Hostel*
8. *Eastern & Oriental*
9. *Embassy*
10. *Eung Aun*
11. *Federal*
12. *Grand Continental*
13. *Hang Cheow*
14. *Hong Ping*
15. *Lum Thean*
16. *Malaysia*
17. *Merchant*
18. *Mingood*
19. *New China*
20. *Oriental*
21. *Paradise*
22. *Paramount*

Georgetown

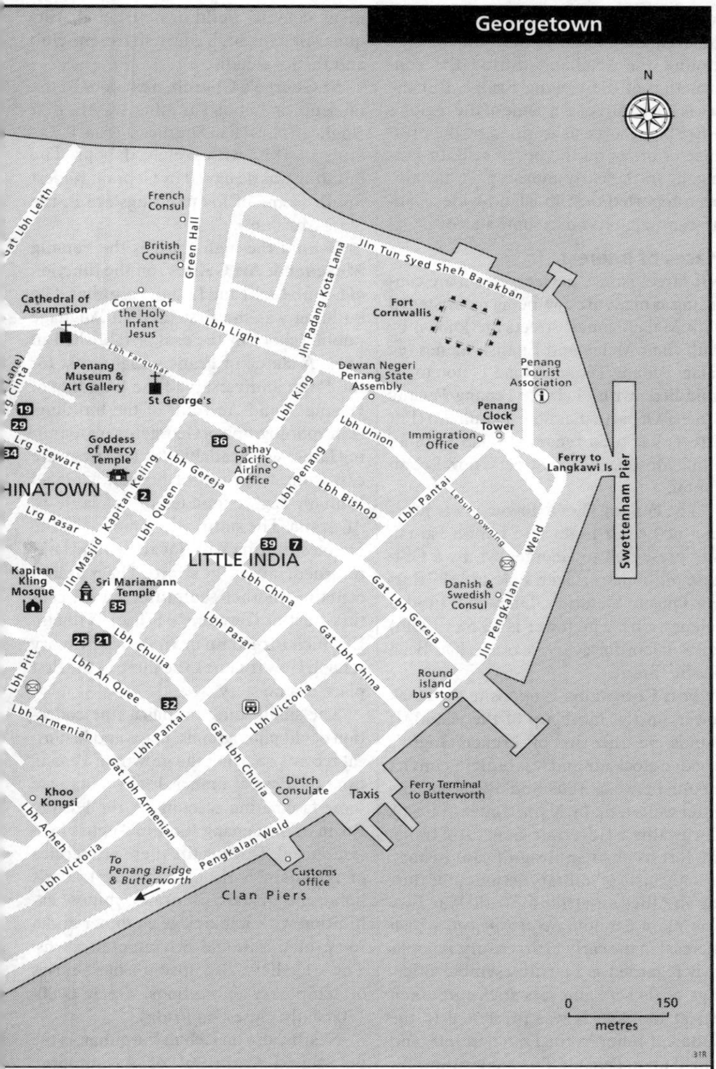

23. *Peking*
24. *Pin Seng*
25. *Plaza Hostel*
26. *Shangri La*
27. *Singapore*
28. *Swiss*
29. *Tiong Wah*
30. *Towne House*
31. *Traverse Inn*
32. *Tye Ann*
33. *Waldorf*
34. *Wan Hai*

Places to eat:

35. Dawood
36. Dragon King
37. English Thai Café
38. Green Planet Café
39. Kaliaman's
40. Maple

to line the shore at Batu Feringghi has all gone, mainly due to the silt washed around the headland during the construction of the Penang Bridge. But the sea is not as dirty as in some of the region's other big resorts, as testified by the presence of otters on the beach at Batu Feringghi in the early morning. It has also been reported that an island-wide clean-up campaign has had some success.

Places of interest

NB Street names in Georgetown are confusing as many are now being rechristened with Malay names; streets are known by both their Malay and English names (eg Jalan Penang/Penang Road – not to be muddled with Lebuh Penang/Penang Street). Of particular note: Lebuh Pitt (Pitt Street) has been renamed Jalan Kapitan Kling Mosque; Beach Street is now Lebuh Pantai.

The **Penang Clock Tower**, at the junction of Lebuh Light and Lebuh Pantai, was presented to Georgetown by a Chinese millionaire, Chen Eok, in 1897 during Queen Victoria's Diamond Jubilee celebrations. The tower is 60 foot (20m) tall – 1 foot for every year she had been on the throne.

Fort Cornwallis is opposite the clock tower, on the north tip of the island. It stands on the site of Francis Light's wooden stockade and was built by convict labour between 1808 and 1810; only its outer walls remain. Named after Marquis Cornwallis, a Governor-General of India, the fort has had an insignificant history. Its only taste of military action came during an Allied air-strike in World War Two. The main cannon, *Serai Rambai*, which was cast in the early 17th century, is popularly regarded as a fertility symbol; offerings of flowers and joss sticks are often left at its base. It was presented to the Sultan of Johor by the Dutch in 1606 and ended up in Penang. The modern amphitheatre hosts concerts and shows. There is an example of a wooden Malay kampung house near the entrance. Open 0830-1800 Monday-Sunday. There are many colonial buildings on Lebuh Farquhar like the high court, mariners' club and the town hall.

St George's Church, next door to the museum on Lebuh Farquhar, was the first Anglican church in Southeast Asia. It was built in 1817 with convict labour. The building was designed by Captain Robert Smith (some of his paintings are in the State Museum).

Behind the high court is the **Penang Museum & Art Gallery**, on the junction of Lebuh Light and Lebuh Farquhar. The building was the first English language public school in the east, established in 1816. A statue of Francis Light, cast for the 150th anniversary of the founding of Penang, stands in front of the building. As no photograph of Georgetown's founding father was available, his features were cast from a portrait of his son, Colonel William Light, founder of Adelaide in Australia. The statue was removed by the Japanese during World War Two and later returned, minus the sword. The museum contains another sculpture: a 19th century bust of Germany's Kaiser Wilhelm II, which turned up in Wellesley primary school. How it came to be there in the first place is a mystery.

The small museum has a fine collection of old photographs, maps and historical records charting the growth of Penang from the days of Francis Light. There are some fascinating accounts in the History Room of the Penang Riots in August 1876 (see above). Downstairs there is a replica of the main hall of a Chinese trader's home and upstairs, a Straits Chinese exhibition with a marriage chamber and a room of traditional ornamental gowns. The art gallery, also upstairs, has a series of temporary exhibitions. Open 0900-1700 daily, closed on Friday.

Nearby, also on **Lebuh Farquhar**, is the twin-spired **Cathedral of Assumption**. This Roman Catholic church houses the only pipe-organ in Penang. The Convent of the Holy Infant Jesus – slightly further east, is the site of Francis Light's original house. Light was Adelaide's architect and planner. His grave can be found on Jalan Sultan Ahmad Shah.

The **Goddess of Mercy Temple** (also known as Kuan Yin Teng) on Jalan Kapitan Kling Mosque/Lorong Steward is a short walk from St George's, in the heart of Georgetown. It was built at the beginning of the 1800s by the island's early Chinese immigrants. Kuan Yin is probably the most-worshipped of all the Chinese deities, and is revered by Buddhists, Taoists and Confucians. The goddess is a Bodhisattva, one who rejected entry into nirvana as long as there was injustice in the world. The goddess is associated with peace, good fortune and fertility – which accounts for her popularity. Kuan Yin is portrayed as a serene goddess with 18 arms – two arms are considered inadequate to rid the world of suffering. The roof-tops are carved to represent waves, on which stand two guardian dragons. Shops in the area sell temple-related goods: lanterns, provisions for the after life (such as paper Mercedes'), joss sticks and figurines.

Although Georgetown is mainly Chinese, it has always had a large population of Indians, living in the city centre. The Hindu **Sri Mariamann Temple**, on Lebuh Queen/Lebuh Chulia, was built in 1883. It is richly decorated and dedicated to the Hindu god Lord Subramaniam. The main statue is strung with gold, silver, diamond and emerald jewellery. It is normally used to lead a chariot procession to the Waterfall Temple during Thaipusam (see page 522). The symbols of the nine planets and the signs of the zodiac are carved into the ceiling. The surrounding area is largely Indian, with money changers and jewellery shops, as well as restaurants and tea-stalls.

There is also a Muslim community in Georgetown and the Indo-Moorish **Kapitan Kling Mosque** (on Jalan Kapitan Kling Mosque) was built by the island's first Indian Muslim settlers around 1800. It was named after the 'kapitan' or headman of the Kling – the South Indian community. As a sight it is rather disappointing.

Straight down Lebuh Chulia is the Chinese water village off Pengkalan Weld. The entrance is through the temple on the quayside. It is known as the **Clan Piers**, as each of the jetties is named after a different Chinese clan. None of the families pays tax as they are not living on land. Rows of junks belonging to the resident traders are moored at the end of the piers.

Armenian Street is worth a wander as this area of the city is being remodelled and conserved because of its historical value; you can see the house of the rich Arab merchant who constructed the mosque opposite the park and a bit further down the road the traditional Chinese house where Dr Sun Yat Sen is said to have planned the Canton uprising.

Khoo Kongsi (on Jalan Acheh, off Lebuh Pitt), is approached through an archway to Cannon Square, and is one of the most interesting sights in Georgetown. A *kongsi* is a Chinese clan house which doubles as a temple and a meeting place. Clan institutions originated in China as associations for people with the same surname. Today they are benevolent organizations which look after the welfare of clan members and safeguard ancestral shrines. Most of the kongsis in Penang were established in the 19th century when clashes between rival clans were commonplace.

The Khoo Kongsi is the most lavishly decorated of the kongsis in Penang, with its ornate Dragon Mountain Hall. It was built in 1898 by the descendents of Hokkien-born Khoo Chian Eng. A fire broke out in it the day it was completed, destroying its roof. It was rebuilt by craftsmen from China and was renovated in the 1950s; the present tiled roof is said to weigh 25 tonnes. The kongsi contains many fine pieces of Chinese art and sculpture, including two huge carved stone guardians which ensure the wealth, longevity and happiness of all who came under the protection of the kongsi. The interior hall houses an image of Tua Sai Yeah, the Khoo clan's patron saint, who was a general during the Ch'in Dynasty in the 2nd century BC. Admission pass from adjoining office. Open 0900-1700 Monday-Friday, 0900-1300 Saturday.

There are other kongsis in Georgetown, although none is as impressive as the Khoo Kongsi. The Chung Keng Kwee Kongsi is on Lebuh Gereja and the Tua Peh Kong Kongsi on Lebuh Armenian. The Khaw Kongsi and the modern Lee Kongsi are both on Jalan Burmah; Yap Kongsi on Lebuh Armenian and the combined kongsi of the Chuah, Sin and Quah clans at the junction of Jalan Burmah and Codrington Avenue. Every kongsi has ancestral tablets as well as a hall of fame to honour its 'sons' or clansmen who have achieved fame in various spheres of life. Today women are honoured in these halls of fame too.

Near the Khoo Kongsi, on Jalan Acheh, is the **Malay Mosque**. Its most noteworthy feature is the Egyptian-style minaret – most in Malaysia are Moorish. In the past it was better known as the meeting place for the notorious White Flag Malays, who sided with the Hokkien Chinese in street battles against the Cantonese (Red Flags) in the Penang Riots of 1867. The hole halfway up the minaret is said to have been made by a cannonball fired from Khoo Kongsi during the clan riots. The mosque is one of the oldest buildings in Georgetown, built in 1808.

Apart from the RM850mn **Penang Bridge** (which, at 13.5 km is the longest bridge in Asia and the third longest in the world) and several new hotels, one of the few visible architectural monuments of the 20th century is **Kompleks Tun Abdul Razak** (**KOMTAR**) on Jalan Penang. This cylindrical skyscraper, which houses the state government offices and a shopping centre, dominates Georgetown. There should be spectacular views of the island and across the straits to the mainland from the 58th floor, but unfortunately the windows are filthy and even if they were clean the smog usually prevents a clear view. There is also a souvenir centre here where the cost of your ticket to ascend the tower (RM5) is offset against any purchase. The viewing gallery encircles the souvenir centre and has coin-operated telescopes. There is also a licensed money changer here.

Outside the town centre on Jalan Burmah is **Wat Chayamangkalaram** (also known as Wat Buppharam), the largest Thai temple in Penang. It houses a 32m-long reclining Buddha, Pra Chaiya Mongkol. There is a 9-storey pagoda behind the temple. The Thais and the Burmese practice Theravada Buddhism as opposed to the Mahayana school of the Chinese. Queen Victoria gave this site to Penang's Thai community in 1845. Opposite Wat Chayamang-kalaram is Penang's only **Burmese temple**. It has ornate carvings and two huge white stone elephants at its gates. The original 1805 pagoda (to the right of the entrance) has been enshrined in a more modern structure. *Getting there*: city bus 2 from Lebuh Victoria terminal.

The **Penang Buddhist Association** is at 182 Jalan Burmah. The Buddha statues are carved from Carrara marble from Italy, the glass chandeliers were made in what was Czechoslovakia and there are paintings depicting the many stages of the Buddha's path to enlightenment. Next door at No 184 is a 1960s Art Deco style building which is a clan hall for the Lee family. Both buildings lie opposite the Chinese recreational club (which is presided over by a statue of Queen Victoria). *Getting there*: city bus 202 from Lebuh Victoria terminal.

Other places of interest in and around Georgetown

Cheong Fatt Tze Mansion, on Lebuh Leith, is now a state monument – albeit in a dilapidated condition. Built by Thio Thiaw Siat, a Kwangtung (Guandong) businessman who imported craftsmen from China, this stately home is one of only three surviving Chinese mansions in this style – the others are in Manila and

Medan. It is privately owned and is not open to the public but still worth marvelling at from the outside.

Jalan Sultan Ahmed Shah (previously Northam Road Mansions) became known as millionaires' row as it was home to many wealthy rubber planters in the wake of the boom of 1911-20. Many of the palatial mansions were built by Straits Chinese in a sort of colonial baroque style, complete with turrets and castellations. Many of them have now gone to seed as they are too expensive to keep up; a few have been lavishly done up by today's generation of rich Chinese businessmen. The largest houses, are the Yeap family mansion, known as the White House, and the Sultan of Kedah's palace.

EXCURSIONS

Around the Island From Georgetown, the round-island trip is a 70 km circuit. It is recommended as a day-trip as there is little or no accommodation available outside Georgetown apart from the north coast beaches.

Batu Ferringhi and **Teluk Bahang** see page 194. The **Butterfly Farm** is close enough to Georgetown to visit in one day using public transport. See page 195.

The **Nattukotai Chettiar Temple**, on Waterfall Road, was built by members of the Indian Chettiar money-lending fraternity, and is the biggest Hindu temple on the island. It is a centre of pilgrimage during the Thaipusam festival (see page 522). *Getting there*: city bus 7 from Lebuh Victoria terminal; get off at the stop before the Botanical Gardens.

The Botanical Gardens, also on Waterfall Road, are situated in a valley surrounded by hills 8 km from Georgetown. The gardens are well landscaped and contain many indigenous and exotic plant species. They were established in 1844. The more interesting plants are kept under lock and key and are open to visitors 0700-1900 Monday-Friday. A path leads from the Gardens' Moon Gate up Penang Hill; the 8 km hike takes about 1½ hours. Open daylight hours Monday-Sunday. *Getting there*: city bus 7 from Lebuh Victoria terminal.

Penang Hill A short distance from Kek Lok Si is the funicular railway, which started operating in 1922. It climbs 850m up Penang Hill; leaves every 30 minutes 0630-2330. (A vintage steam engine is on display at the Penang Museum.) The railway was originally completed in 1899, but on its inauguration by the governor, it didn't work and had to be dismantled. The absence of a paved road up Penang Hill means that its essential qualities of seclusion and peace have been preserved on an island otherwise battered by the forces of commercialism. Penang Hill is about 5°C cooler than Georgetown and was a favoured expatriate refuge before the advent of a/c. Indeed, it was the first colonial hill station developed on Peninsular Malaysia. The ridge on top of Penang Hill is known as Strawberry Hill after Francis Light's strawberry patch. On a clear day it is possible to see the mountains of Langkawi and North Kedah from the top.

Bel Retiro, designed as a get-away for the governor, was the first bungalow to be built on the hill. There is a small hotel, some pleasant gardens, a temple, a mosque and a post office and police station on the top. There are also a few restaurants and a small hawker centre. The hill gets very crowded on weekends and public holidays. A well marked 8 km path leads down to the Moon Gate at the Botanical Gardens (about an hour's walk) from between the post office and the police station – a steep, but delightful, descent, with plenty of places to sit along the way, 1¼ hours' walk. The hill supports the last relic patch of tropical rainforest on Penang and as such is deemed of considerable natural value. The flora and fauna here have been protected since 1960.

In September 1990 a memorandum of understanding was signed between the Penang State Government and Bukit Pinang Leisure Sdn Bhd which proposed to

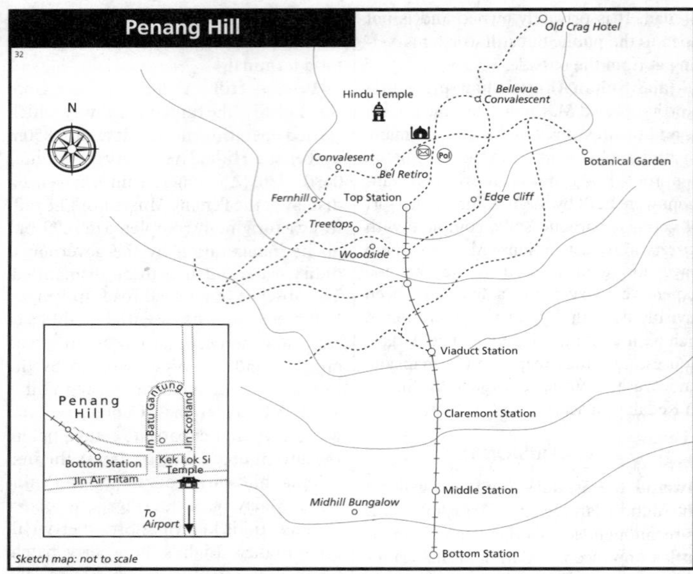

build a waterworld, two large hotels, an adventure park and 'Summit Acropolis'. Although the more extreme elements of the proposal were later dropped following sharp negative public reaction, there remain fears that future development could radically transform Penang Hill. *Getting there*: city bus 1 (from Lebuh Victoria terminal) to Kek Lok Si, then bus 8 to the railway.

State Mosque, Jalan Ayer Itam/Jalan Masjid Negeri, is the largest and newest mosque in Penang and can accommodate 5,000. It was designed by a Filipino architect. Good views from the top of the 57m-high minaret. *Getting there*: city bus 1 from Lebuh Victoria terminal.

Bat Temple at Ayer Itam, is a sanctuary for fruit bats, which hang from the cave roof. The sacred bats are protected by Buddhist monks who guard them zealously. About 60 years ago the wealthy Madam Lim Chooi Yuen, built the bat temple to protect the bats. *Getting there*: city bus 1 from Lebuh Victoria terminal.

Ayer Itam Dam is a pleasant place to relax just above the town. There are several trails around the lake, originally shortcuts to other parts of the island. *Getting there*: city bus 1 (from Lebuh Victoria terminal) then change to 8.

Kek Lok Si Temple (or Monastery of Supreme Bliss), south of Ayer Itam, can be seen from some distance away. It took Burmese, Chinese and Thai artisans, who were shipped in specially, 2 decades to build it. The abbot of the Goddess of Mercy Temple on Lebuh Pitt came from China in 1885 and the landscape around Ayer Itam reminded him of his homeland. He collected money from rich Chinese merchants to fund the construction of the huge temple, modelled on Fok San Monastery in Fuchow, China. On the way up the 'ascending plane' is a turtle pond (turtles are a symbol of eternity).

The temple sprawls across 12 hectares and is divided into three main sections: the Hall of Bodhisattvas, the Hall of Devas and the sacred Hall of the Buddha.

The 7-tier pagoda – or Ban Po, the Pagoda of a Thousand Buddhas – is built in three different styles: the lower follows a Chinese design honouring the Goddess of Mercy, Kuan Yin; the middle is Thai-Buddhist and commemorates to Bee Lay Hood (the Laughing Buddha) and the upper Burmese levels are dedicated to the Gautama or historic Buddha with thousands of gilded statues. The topmost tier contains a relic of the Buddha, a statue of pure gold and other treasures, but it is closed to visitors. All pretty tacky stuff and more than half the complex has been turned into a shopping centre. Admission: voluntary contribution to climb the 30m-high tower. *Getting there*: city bus 1 from Lebuh Victoria terminal.

Penang Bird Park, on Jalan Todak, Seberang Jaya (7 km from the Penang Bridge), includes a huge walk-in aviary (over 200 species of bird). Admission: adult RM4, child RM2. Open 0900-1900 daily. *Getting there*: yellow bus 65 from Pengkalan Weld (Weld Quay).

Universiti Sains Malaysia Museum and Gallery is at Minden (near the Penang Bridge interchange). It has a large ethnographic and performing arts sections with a special exhibition on *wayang kulit* (shadow puppets – see page 78). There is also an art gallery with works by Malaysian artists and visiting temporary exhibitions. Open 0900-1700 Monday-Sunday. *Getting there*: yellow bus 65 from Pengkalan Weld (Weld Quay).

Snake Temple (also known as Temple of the Azure Cloud), was built in 1850 at Bayan Lepas (12 km from Georgetown). Snakes were kept in the temple as they were believed to be the disciples of the deity Chor Soo Kong, to whom the temple is dedicated. The temple was built as the result of a donation from a Scotsman, David Brown, after he was cured by a local priest of an 'incurable disease', using local medicines. Nowadays the reptilian disciples (almost exclusively Wagler's pit vipers) are a bit thin on the ground. The number of snakes in the temple varies from day to day – there are usually more around during festivals. The incense smoke keeps them in a drugged stupor, and most of them have had their fangs extracted. Photographs with (de-fanged) snakes can be posed for in a new annex next door to the temple (RM4). *Getting there*: yellow bus 65 from Pengkalan Weld (Weld Quay).

Batu Maung A Chinese fishing village, near Bayan Lepas, is known for its 'floating' seafood restaurant, built out over the water. *Getting there*: yellow bus 69 (RM0.90). Around the south coast, there are a few beaches and a couple of unremarkable fishing kampungs. The southern beaches are more secluded than the ones along the north coast; the drawbacks are the absence of accommodation and the litter. Veering north towards the centre of the island, however, beyond Barat, is **Balik Pulau**, a good *makan* stop with a number of restaurants and cafés. Around the town, which is known as the "Durian capital" of Penang, there are a number of picturesque Malay kampungs. Further up the west side of the island is the **Pantai Acheh Forest Reserve**, which also has well marked trails into the jungle and to the bays further round, eg Pantai Keracut (1 hour). After the Pantai Acheh junction, and on up a twisting, forested section of road, there is a waterfall with a pleasant pool, suitable for swimming, just off the road (twentieth milestone), called **Titi Kerawang**. *Getting there*: yellow buses 11 or 66 go from Pengkalan Weld (Weld Quay) or Jalan Maxwell in Georgetown to the south of the island. Change at Balik Pulau to bus 76 for Teluk Bahang. From there blue bus 93 to Georgetown. Longer fare stages are RM0.60-RM1.50. As the island buses are infrequent, it is advisable to check departure times at each place to avoid being stranded. It is much easier to explore the kampungs and beaches around the south and west coasts – most of which are off the main road – if you have private transport. Most of them are off the main road

The Bukit Jambul Orchid and Hibiscus Garden is found along Persiaran Bukit Jambul, close to the *Hotel Equatorial* and 5 minutes drive from the airport. As its name suggests, it specializes in orchids and hibiscus. There is also a reptile house here. Admission: RM3 for adults, RM1 for children. Open 1000-1900 Monday-Sunday.

TOURS

The three main tours offered by companies are: the city tour, the Penang Hill and temple tour and the round-the-island tour. All cost RM20-30 and most run every hour.

LOCAL FESTIVALS

May: *Penang Bridge Run* (end of month) open to all visitors.

June: *Penang International Dragon Boat Race*, near Penang Bridge; teams compete from around the region and beyond. *International Beach Volleyball Championship* (end); held on Kital Beach, Batu Ferringhi, next to *Bayview Beach Hotel*.

July: *Penang on Parade*, with three major annual events; details from Tourist Information Centre. *Floral Festival* at KOMTAR. *City parades* by Malays (at Fort Cornwallis), Chinese (at Khoo Kongsi) and Indians (at Market Street).

September: *Penang Lantern Festival* (end), parade with lanterns.

November: *Deepavali Open House*, festivities in Little India.

LOCAL INFORMATION

● Accommodation

Prices: L over RM500; **A+** RM260-500; **A** RM130-260; **B** RM65-130; **C** RM40-65; **D** RM20-40; **E** RM10-20; **F** Below RM10

In Georgetown, most upmarket hotels are concentrated in the Jln Penang area. Most of the cheaper hotels are around Lebuh Chulia and Lebuh Leith.

A+ *Berjaya Georgetown Hotel* T 2277111, F 2267111, one of newest luxury hotels in Georgetown, 330 rooms, part of one-stop Midland Park Complex. All the usual amenities: swimming pool, health centre, several restaurants, business centre. **A+** *Shangri-La*, Jln Magazine, T 2622622, F 2626526, a/c, restaurant, pool, small fitness centre, mostly used by business people rather than tourists, next to KOMTAR. **A+** *Pan Pacific Leader*, new hotel in the 'heart of the financial and business district' which was due to open as this book went to press. 373 rooms and the usual range of amenities including pool and fitness centre. For information T (Singapore) 3394688, F 3395787. **A+-A** *Sheraton*, 3 Jln Larut, T 2267888, F 2266615, 280 rooms, 5-star hotel, special facilities in rooms include direct fax line, electronic safe, iron, newly opened. **A** *Agora*, 202a Lorong Mcalister, T 2266060, F 2267257, formerly *Ming Court*, restaurant, pool. **A** *Eastern & Oriental (E&O)*, 10 Farquhar St, T 2630630, F 2634833, a/c, restaurant, pool, built in 1885 by the Armenian Sarkies brothers, who operated Singapore's *Raffles Hotel* (see page 633) and the *Strand Hotel* in Rangoon (Yangon), Noel Coward and Somerset Maugham figured on former guest lists, closed for renovation expected to reopen in 1998/1999. **A** *Equatorial International*, 1 Jln Bukit Jambal, T 6438111, F 6448998, e-mail: eqp@md.com.my, a/c, restaurant, between the airport and town, on a hill with a view over the Penang Bridge, mostly used by visiting business people as it is conveniently located for Penang's duty-free industrial zone, which lies between it and the airport. A monstrous block of 400 plus rooms with good sports facilities and adjacent 18-hole golf course. **A** *Grand Continental*, 68 Brick Kiln Rd (Jln Gurdwara), T 2636688, F 2630299, a/c, restaurant, pool, health club. **A** *Malaysia*, 7 Jln Penang, T 2633311, F 2631621, a/c, restaurant, dated high-rise hotel, plush decor with coffee house, disco, health centre. **A** *Swiss Inn*, Jln McAlister, not yet opened, international economy class hotel, wide range of business facilities and a roof top pool are planned. **A** *Sunway*, 33 New Lane, T 2299988, F 2292033, pleasant decor, good facilities in rooms, a/c, TV, pulsating shower, in-house video, iron, fridge, complimentary tea/coffee, pool, Jacuzzi, restaurant, tea-house, pub. **A-B** *Garden Inn*, 41 Jln Anson, T 2263655, a/c, restaurant, good hawker centre on the doorstep. **A-B** *Merchant*, 55 Jln Penang, T 2632828, F 2625511, a/c, restaurant, handsomely decorated, smart marble lobby, a/c, TV, in-house video, mini bar, coffee house, trishaws for hire RM15/hour.

B ***Bellevue***, Penang Hill, T 8299600, a/c, restaurant, colonial-style house, cool retreat up on the hill. **B** ***Central***, 404 Jln Penang, T 2266411, F 2271689, a/c, restaurant. **B** ***City Bayview Hotel***, 25a Lebuh Farquhar, T 2633161, F 2634124, a/c, restaurant, pool, revolving restaurant and bar on 14th flr, shabby rooms with uncomfortable beds. **B** ***Continental***, 5 Jln Penang, T 2636388, F 2638718, a/c, restaurant, not great value for money. **B** ***Mid Towne***, 101 Jln Mcalister, T 2269999, F 2295146, new hotel, not very central but good value. **B** ***Mingood***, 164 Argyle Rd, T 2299922, F 2292210, a/c, restaurant, not good value for money. **B** ***Oriental***, 105 Jln Penang, T 2634211/6, a/c, restaurant, dated decor, big rooms and good value, well located with good views from the upper floors, recommended. **B** ***Seri Malaysia***, off Jln Mayang Pasir I, Bandar Bayan Baru, T 6429452, F 6429461, chain budget hotel. **B** ***Towne House***, 70 Jln Penang, T 2638621, chocolate brown and cream block, features an automatic massage chair in lobby, 50 sen, a/c, restaurant.

C ***Cathay***, 15 Lebuh Leith, T 2626271, a/c, large old Chinese house, scrupulously maintained, organizes minibuses to Hat Yai and Phuket (Thailand), coffee shop, recommended. **C** ***Embassy***, 12 Jln Burmah, T 2267515, a/c, restaurant, recommended by travellers. **C** ***Federal***, 39 Jln Penang, T 2634170, good location, near some excellent restaurants, recently revamped, although style is still 1920s. **C** ***Paramount***, 48F Jln Sultan Ahmad Shah, T 2273649, a/c, restaurant, big rooms in run-down colonial house, right on the sea, but not central, recommended. **C** ***Peking***, 50a Jln Penang, T 2636191, once a luxury hotel, now very run-down, a/c, bath, TV. **C** ***Traverse Inn***, 53 Jln Kampung Malabar, T/F 2619858, a/c, new, clean, simple, recommended. **C** ***Waldorf***, 13 Leith St, T 2626140, a/c, bath, dated decor but good value. **C** ***YMCA***, 211 Jln Macalister, T 2288211, a/c, fan only rooms (**D**).

D ***D'Budget Hostel***, 9 Lebuh Gereja, T 2634794, some a/c, roof terrace, laundry, money changer, tea-making, TV, hot water shower, near Medan ferry, clean but sterile, soulless place, quiet, friendly and helpful management, dorm (**E**). **D** ***New China***, 22 Lebuh Leith, T 2631601, large old house set back from the road (overshadowed by *Merchant Hotel*), one of the nicer budget hotels, management helpful for those having trouble procuring Thai visas. **D** ***Paradise***, 99 Lebuh Chulia, T 2628439, F 628441, some a/c, price including breakfast. **D** ***Pin Seng***, 80 Love Lane, T 2619004, original tiled floors and iron beds, fan only, run-down. **D** ***Plaza Hostel***, 32 Lebuh Ah Quee, T 2630570, popular, clean and friendly, lockers, ticketing service (**F** dorm). **D** ***Singapore***, 495h Jln Penang, T 2620323, a/c, basic, next to KOMTAR. **D** ***Tiong Wah***, 23 Love Lane, T 2622057, reasonable value – better than most on Lebuh Chulia in a less frenetic corner of town, shared bathrooms, fan and basin in room, dilapidated. **D-E** ***Eung Aun***, 380 Lebuh Chulia, T 2612333, fan, restaurant, old house set back from the road, basic but popular with clean rooms and friendly service. **D-E** ***Lum Thean***, 422 Lebuh Chulia, T 2614117, restaurant, a/c, Chinese nationalist General Chiang Kai Shek once took refuge here, average Chinese-run hotel. **D-E** ***New Asia***, 110 Jln Pintal Tali, T 2613599, a/c, bar, family run, recommended.

E ***Broadway Hostel***, 35f Lebuh Pitt, T 2628550, clean and basic, some a/c (**D**), dorm (**F**). **E** ***Hang Cheow***, 51 Lebuh Chulia, T 2610810, restaurant, recommended by travellers. **E** ***Hong Ping***, 273B, Lebuh Chulia, above *Coco Island* restaurant, T 2625234, a/c, private bath, TV, bare but quiet rooms. **E** ***Nam Wah***, 381 Lebuh Chulia, T 2610557, old building with character but very basic. **E** ***Swiss***, 431 Lebuh Chulia, T 2620133, a better bet than some of the others in this area, clean and quiet with friendly management, cheap breakfast, next door are motorbikes for hire – (quite cheap at RM15/day), and good selection of books to rent or buy. **E** ***Tye Ann***, 282 Lebuh Chulia, T 2614875, clean but small rooms, hotel staff will help organize Thai visas, now run by 3rd generation of same family, all rooms with fan and basin, dorm (**F**), café. **E** ***Wan Hai***, 35 Love Lane, T 2616853, restaurant, run-of-the-mill budget hotel, motorcycles for hire, visa applications for Thailand and bus tickets to Thailand organized, dorm (**F**), terrace. **E** ***Yeng Keng***, 362 Lebuh Chulia, T 2610610, central but basic, good-sized rooms but hotel is very run down.

● Places to eat

Prices: ◆◆◆◆ over RM40; ◆◆◆ RM13-40; ◆◆ RM5-13; ◆ under RM5

Penang's specialities include *assam laksa* (a hot-and-sour fish soup), *nasi kandar* (a curry), *mee yoke* (prawns in chilli-noodle soup) and *inche kabin* (chicken marinated in spices and then fried).

Malay: best from the stalls. ◆◆◆***Eliza***, 14th Flr, *City Bayview Hotel*, 25a Lorong Farquhar, sumptuous menu eaten in traditional style, seated on pandan mats, good views over the town and coast. ◆◆*Nazir*, 4th level, KOMTAR. ◆◆*Hot Wok*, Desa Tanjung, 125D Jln Tanjung Tokong, Nyonya and local cuisine is a recreated shop-house, recommended. ◆*Spice Café*, 55 Jln Penang (next to *Merchant Hotel*), excellent choice of local food, with Malay, Chinese, Thai and some international.

Chinese: ◆◆◆◆*Shang Palace*, *Shangri La Hotel*, Hong Kong dim sum brunch, Cantonese dishes. ◆◆◆*Dragon King*, 99 Leboh Bishop, comes recommended by travellers. ◆◆◆*Goh Huat Seng*, 59A Lebuh Kimberley, Teochew cuisine, best known for its steamboats. ◆◆◆*Tower Palace*, level 58-60 KOMTAR, good value dim sum. ◆◆*Ang Hoay Loh*, 60 Jln Brick Kiln, Hokkien food: specialities include glass noodles and pork and prawn soups. ◆◆*Lum Fong*, 108 Muntri St, lively coffee shop with an arcaded front, old wooden tables and chairs, good noodles. ◆◆*May Garden*, 70 Penang Rd, good food and very popular. ◆◆*Sin Kheng Hooi Hong*, 350 Lebuh Pantai, Hainanese cuisine, *lor bak* (crispy deep-fried seafood rolls, with sweet-and-sour plum sauce) recommended. ◆◆*Tropics*, *Sunway Hotel*, 33 New Lane, good value steamboat buffet. ◆*Loke Thye Kee*, 2B Jln Burmah, Hainanese cuisine, good place to try *inche kabin* – stewed marinated chicken. ◆*Potbless*, Hutton Lane, *nasi lemale*, banana leaf, steamboat.

Nyonya: Penang and Melaka are the culinary centres of Nyonya cuisine (see page 509). ◆◆*Dragon King*, 99 Lebuh Bishop, family-run business, probably the best Nyonya food in any of the old Straits Settlements, specializes in fish-head curry, good satay, *otak-otak*, curry Kapitan and *kiam chye boey* – a meat casserole, recommended. ◆◆*Nyonya Corner*, 15 Jln Pahang, excellent *otak-otak* (fish marinated in lime and wrapped in banana leaf).

Indian: Penang's 'Little India' is bounded by Lebuh Bishop, Lebuh Pasar and Lebuh King, close to the quay. There is a string of good Indian restaurants along Lebuh Penang, in this area, notably: ***Murugan Vilas***, ***Nava India***, ***Susila*** and ***Veloo Vilas***. They are renowned for their banana-leaf curries. ◆◆◆*Kashmir*, base of *Oriental Hotel*, 105 Jln Penang (**NB** Not Lebuh Penang), North Indian food – usually very busy, recommended. ◆◆◆*Madras New Woodlands Vegetarian Restaurant*, 60 Penang St, North and South Indian food, newly opened and bristling clean. ◆◆*Dawood*, 63 Lebuh Queen (across from Sri Mariamman Temple), Indian Muslim restaurant known for its curries, original 60s decor, Kari Kapitan (chicken curry), and duck are popular, recommended. ◆◆*Kaliaman's*, 43 Lebuh Penang, one of Penang's best Indian restaurants, South Indian food at lunch, Northern Indian food in the evening, not very clean. ◆◆*The Tandoori House*, Lorong Hutton, nicer decor than *Kashmir* (above), evergreen North Indian specialities. ◆*Hameediyah*, 164A Lebuh Campbell, Indian Muslim food, murtabak, rotis, large portions. ◆*Kassim Mustafa*, 12 Lebuh Chulia, basic coffee shop which prides itself in cooking a handful of dishes very well, most trade done between 0500 and 1200, specialities are nasi dalcha (rice cooked with ghee and cinnamon), ayam negro and mutton kurma, recommended. ◆*Kassim Nasi Kandar*, 2-1 Jln Brick Kiln, hot Indian Muslim food, open 24 hours, recommended by locals. ◆*Kedai Kopi Yasmeen*, 177 Jln Penang, simple open-fronted Indian coffee shop, murtabak, roti etc, recommended. ◆*Banana Leaf*, Lebuh Penang, about two blocks south of Lebuh Gereja. Serves excellent southern Indian food notably thali and lassi.

Indonesian: ◆◆*Tambuah Mas*, Level 4 Komtar Tower. ◆*Nasi Padang*, 511 Lebuh Chulia.

Japanese: *The City Bayview* and the *Bellevue* hotels all have Japanese restaurants. The latter serves a good steamboat (last orders 2000). ◆◆◆◆*Kurumaya*, 269 Burma Rd, top quality sushi and sashmi. ◆◆◆*Kong Lung*, 11c Leith St, immaculate traditional decor, teppenyaki and set lunches recommended, recommended. ◆◆◆*Miyabi*, 216 Jln McAlister, well established Japanese restaurant. ◆◆◆*Shin Miyako*, 105 Jln Penang (next to the *Oriental Hotel*), smart-looking restaurant, and reasonably priced for Japanese food.

Thai: ◆◆*Café D'Chiangmai*, 11 Burmah Cross, serves an interesting mixture of Thai and local dishes, renowned for its fish-head curry, popular in the evenings. ◆◆*Thai Food Restaurant*, below *New Pathe Hotel*, Lebuh Light. ◆◆*Yellow Light*, 1C Jln Fettis.

International: ◆◆◆*Beetle Nuts Fun Café*, 9-11 Leith St, in same old block as 20 Leith St, theme is American, tex-mex, trendy. ◆◆*The Brasserie*, *Shangri La Hotel*, Californian cuisine. ◆◆*Café Tower Lounge*, 59th Flr, KOMTAR, buffet lunch, good view over the city and afterwards free entrance to viewing gallery. ◆◆*Coco Island Café*, Lebuh Chulia, good food, popular. ◆◆*Eden Steak House*, Jln Hutton. ◆*Green Planet*, 63 Lebuh Cintra, a backpackers' joint serving classic travellers food. Also provides information, ticketing services, motorbike rental, hot showers, excellent food and helpful owner. ***English Thai Café***, 417b Lebuh Chulia. ***Magnolia Snack***

Bar, Jln Penang. ◆◆***Rainforest Restaurant***, 294a Chulia St, new sister company of *Green Planet*, popular with budget travellers, interesting scrap books of travellers' experiences, wide selection of food – nachos, sandwiches, steak, pizza, apple crumble comes recommended, all home-cooked and no preservatives. ***The Ship Steakhouse***. ***OG Bakery***, Jln Penang. ***Tye Ann Hotel***, Lebuh Chulia, recommended for breakfast.

Seafood: ◆◆◆◆***Eden***, 11B Lorong Hutton, popular chain of restaurants, seafood and grills; ◆◆◆***Grand Garden Seafood***, 164 Jln Penang, seafood market restaurant, outside eating; ◆◆***Lam Kee Seafood***, next to stalls on Esplanade (Padang Kota Lama); ◆◆***Maple***, 106 Jln Penang (near *Oriental Hotel*), same management as *May Garden* and food is in the same league; ◆◆***May Garden***, 70 Penang Rd (next to *Towne House*), reckoned to be among the best seafood restaurants in Georgetown, with an aquarium full of fish and shellfish to choose from, the crab is excellent and *May Garden's* speciality is frogs' legs, fried with chilli and ginger or just crispy, recommended; ◆◆***Ocean-Green***, 48F Jln Sultan Ahmad Shah (in quiet alleyway in front of *Paramount Hotel*), specialities include lobster and crab thermidor, drunken prawns and fresh frogs' legs ('paddy chicken'), lovely location, overlooking fishing boats, recommended. ◆◆***Sea Palace***, 50 Jln Penang (next to *Peking Hotel*), huge menu, popular, a/c, Chinese tableware, good value, recommended.

Coffee shops: most Chinese coffee shops along Jln Burmah and Jln Penang, also some in the financial district along Lebuh Bishop, Lebuh Cina and Lebuh Union. ***Khuan Kew*** and ***Sin Kuan Hwa***, both in Love Lane are particularly popular – the latter is well known for its Hainan chicken rice. The ***Maxim Cakehouse and Bakery*** on Penang Rd is also a popular stop. The oldest in Georgetown is the ***Kek Seng*** (382 Jln Penang), founded in 1906 and still serving *kway teow* soup and colourful *ais-kacangs*.

Foodstalls: Penang's hawker stalls are renowned in Malaysia, and serve some of the best food on the island. (We have received reports though, that many have closed due to a public health drive.) ***Datuk Keramat Hawker Centre*** (also called *Padang Brown*), junction of Anson and Perak roads, this is one of the venues for Georgetown's roving night market – possible to check if it's on by calling tourist information centre (T 2614461), recommended; ***Food Court***, base of KOMTAR; ***Kota Selera Hawker Centre***, next to Fort Cornwallis, off Lebuh Light, recommended; ***Lebuh Keng Kwee***, famed locally for its *cendol* stalls – cocktails of shaved ice, palm sugar and jelly topped with *gula melaka* and coconut milk; ***Lebuh Kimberley*** (called noodle-maker street by the Chinese), good variety of hawker food at night; ***Lorong Selamat Hawker Stalls***, highly recommended by locals; ***Padang Kota Lama/Jalan Tun Syed Sheh Barakbah*** (Esplanade), busy in the evenings, recommended; ***Pesiaran Gurney Seawall*** (Gurney Drive), long row of hawkers opposite the coffee shops, good range of Malay, Chinese and Indian food, very popular in the evenings, recommended. There are also popular stalls along Jln Burmah, Love Lane and at Ayer Itam. Good *roti-canai* opposite *Plaza Hostel*, Lebuh Ah Quee.

● Bars

Anchor bar & poolside bar, *E & O Hotel*, 10 Farquhar St, closed for renovation; ***Carmen's Inn***, 15th Flr, *City Bayview Hotel*, 25a Farquhar St, views over the town and coast, starts turning 1700; ***20 Leith St*** (next to *Waldorf Hotel*), pleasant bar, building is 150-years-old and many original features have been retained, pitchers of Carlsberg, satay and prawn and other light snacks; ***George's***, *Sunway Hotel*, 33 New Lane, quintessentially English, live music.

● Airline offices

Cathay Pacific, AIA Building, Lebuh Farquhar, T 2260411; **MAS**, Kompleks Tun Abdul Razak (KOMTAR), Jln Penang, T 2620011 (the ticket office is on the ground floor, at the southern side of KOMTAR, and can only be entered from outside the complex) or at the airport T 6430811; **Pelangi Airways**, unit 249, 2nd floor, Penang Plaza, 126 Jln Burma, T 2277311, F 2274897; **Singapore Airlines**, Wisma Penang Gardens, 42 Jln Sultan Ahmad Shah, T 2296211; **Thai International**, Wisma Central, 202 Jln Macalister, T 2296250.

● Banks & money changers

Most banks in Georgetown are around the GPO area and Lebuh Pantai. Most money changers are in the banking area and Jln Masjid Kapitan Keling and Lebuh Pantai, close to the Immigration Office. **Bank Bumiputra**, 37 Lebuh Pantai; **Citibank**, 42 Jln Sultan Ahmad Shah; **Hong Kong Bank**, Lebuh Pantai; **Maybank**, 9 Lebuh Union; **Standard Chartered**, 2 Lebuh Pantai. **Hong Kong Bank** issues Thomas Cook TCs and gives cash advances against visa cards.

● Churches

St George's Church, Lebuh Farquhar, services in English 0830 and 1830 every Sun.

● Embassies & consulates

Denmark, Bernam Agencies, Hong Kong Bank Chambers, Lebuh Downing, T 2624886; **France**, 82 Bishop St, Wisma Rajab, T 2629707; **Germany**, Bayan Lepas Free Trade Zone, T 6415707; **Indonesia**, 467 Jln Burmah, T 2274686; **Japan**, 2 Jln Biggs, T 2268222; **Netherlands**, Algemen Bank Nederland, 9 Lebuh Pantai, T 2622144; **Thailand**, 1 Jln Ayer Raja, T 2629484 (visas arranged in 2 days); **UK**, Birch House, 73 Jln Datuk Keramat, T 2625333.

● Entertainment

Discos: most of the big hotels, have in-house nightclubs and discos. Expect to pay cover charges if you are not a guest. ***Celebrity***, 48H Jln Sultan Ahmad Shah; ***Hotlips Disco***, next to *Continental Hotel*; ***Penny Lane***, bottom of *City Bayview Hotel*; ***Xanadu Disco***, next to *Malaysia Hotel*; ***Rockworld***, 1 Drury Lane (off Campbell St), high tech lighting and laser show; ***Street One***, *Shangri La Hotel*, popular with air-hostesses; ***Sol Fun Disco***, 6 Weld Quay, ex-warehouse, techno disco, live band, karaoke, pool, virtual reality games, bar.

Cinemas: *Cathay Cinema* on Jln Penang (between Jln Hutton and Jln Dato Koyah; ***Rex Cinema***, junction of Jln Burmah and Transfer.

● Hospitals & medical services

Hospitals: *General Hospital* (government), Jln Residensi, T 2293333; *Lam Wah Ee Hospital* (private), 141 Jln Batu Lancang, T 6571888.

● Libraries

Penang Public Library, Dewan Sri Pinang, Lebuh Light, T 2622555; ***The British Council***, T 2630330.

● Post & telecommunications

Area code: 04.

General Post Office: Lebuh Pitt, efficient poste restante, also provides a parcel-wrapping service.

Telecoms office (international calls; fax and telex facilities): Jln Burmah.

● Shopping

Shopping in Georgetown requires a lot of wandering around the narrow streets and alleyways off Jln Penang. Main areas are Jln Penang, Jln Burmah and Lebuh Campbell.

Antiques: an Export licence is still required for non-imported goods. Shops on and around Jln Penang with the best ones at the top end opposite *Eastern and Oriental Hotel*, such as the ***Oriental Arts Co***, 3f Penang Rd. Also antique shops along Rope Walk (Jln Pintal Tali). Most stock antiques from Burma, Thailand, Indonesia, Malaysia, Sabah and Sarawak, as well as a few local bargains. ***Eastern Curios***, 35 Lebuh Bishop; ***Kuan Antique***, 7A Aboo Sitee Lane; ***Penang Antique House***, 27 Jln Patani, showcase of Peranakan (Straits Chinese) artefacts – porcelain, rosewood with mother-of-pearl inlay, Chinese embroideries and antique jewellery; ***Saw Joo Aun***, 139 Rope Walk (Jln Pintal Tali), the best in a row of similar shops.

Art Galleries: Georgetown has a College of Art and Music, housed in a grand colonial building on Leith St. Exhibitions are occasionally on view in the College Gallery (7 Leith St, T 2618087). Other galleries in Georgetown including ***The Art Gallery***, 36B Burmah Rd, T 2298219; ***Galerie Mai***, 54 Tung Hing Building, Jln Burmah, T 377504.

Basketry: several shops along Jln Penang, around junction with Jln Burmah.

Batik: *Asia Co*, 314 Jln Penang; ***Maphilindo Baru***, 217 Penang Rd, excellent range of batiks and sarongs (including songket) from Malaysia, Sumatra and Java; ***Sam's Batik House***, 159 Jln Penang; ***Yuyi Batik House***, Level 3, Kompleks Tun Abdul Razak (KOMTAR), Jln Penang. Factory outlet in Teluk Bahang and souvenir shops in Batu Ferringhi.

Books: several bookshops in Lebuh Chulia near *Swiss Hotel* which sell second-hand books. ***Yasin Bookshop***, 417a Lebuh Chulia; ***Parvez Book Store***, 419 Lebuh Chulia (as well as dealing in books they arrange Thai visas and trips, and car/motorbike hire); ***HS Sam Bookstore***, 144 Lebuh Chulia, prides itself on being well-organized and runs a side-line in travel services: Thai visas, bus ticketing, car/bike rental and has a luggage storage; ***MPH Bookstore*** Island Plaza, Jln Tanjong Tokong; ***Times Bookshop***, Penang Plaza, 1st Flr, 126 Burmah Rd; ***Popular Bookshop***, Arked Ria 2, KOMTAR Tower and at Midland Park Complex, Jln Burmah; reasonable selection in Yaohan Department Store in KOMTAR.

Camping gear: *Tye Yee Seng Canvas*, 162 Chulia St, good stock of tents, rucksacks, sleeping bags and beach umbrellas.

Cassettes, electrical and photographic equipment: Jln Campbell, Jln Penang.

CD Roms: fakes available from ***Midland Park Complex***, 6th Flr, Jln Burmah.

Curios and unusual bargains: *Lebuh Chulia*, Bishop and Rope Walk (Jln Pintal Tali). Many of the curios are imported from China and are very well priced. There is a good selection at ***Tan Embroidery Co***, 20 Lebuh Pantai.

Food shops: there are a number of outlets, mostly Chinese-run in Georgetown selling locally produced specialities. Dragon Ball biscuits, pastry balls filled with a mung bean paste are made by ***Wee Ling***, 132 Chulia St; a similar product, including *pong pneah* (pastry filled with molasses or caramel) are made at ***Him Heang***, 162 Jln Burmah; for a selection of unusual pre-packaged products, such as dried mango, jackfruit, nutmeg oil and coconut cookies go to one of the large, a/c outlets of ***Cap Jempol Tropiks***, either at 17 Leith St (next to *Cathay Hotel*), or 50c Penang Rd (next to *Peking Hotel*); Chinese teas and ginseng in a variety of forms are the speciality of ***Eu Yan Sang***, 156 Chulia St, who offer herb-boiling service in a cauldron that bubbles inside the doorway.

Handicrafts: Jln Penang is a good place to start with ***Peking Arts & Crafts*** at 3b, ***Federation Arts & Crafts*** at 3c, and ***China Handicraft Co*** at 3d. ***See Koon Hoe***, 315 Lebuh Chulia sells Chinese opera masks, jade seals and paper umbrellas; ***The Mah Jong Factory*** in Love Lane sells high-quality Mah Jong sets.

Jewellery: Lebuh Campbell and Lebuh Kapitan Klang.

Markets: Penang's night market (1900-2300) changes locations every fortnight. To check venue, call Tourist Information Centre (T 2614461) or refer to the Penang Diary column in the daily newspapers.

Shopping complexes: *Midland Park*, Jln Burmah, opposite Adventist Hospital, amusement arcades, roller skating, bowling alley, several fastfood outlets, hawker food. *Popular Bookshop* and CD Rom shops. ***Island Plaza***, Jln Tanjung Tokong, on road to Batu Ferringhi, upmarket shops – *East India Company, Guess, Fila, Coca Restaurant*, the *Forum*, a Food Court and a new cinema. ***Bukit Jambul Shopping Complex***, close to the airport, good range of shops, food outlets and an ice-rink. ***KOMTAR***, hundreds of boutiques, two department stores, fastfood restaurants, amusement arcade.

Supermarkets: *Gama*, behind the KOMTAR Tower is excellent for stocking up on basics.

Watches: reasonable quality fakes from by the Snake Temple (see page 187).

● Sports

Bowling alley: *Midland Park Complex*, Jln Burmah.

Golf: *Airforce Golf Club*, Butterworth, T 3322632, 9-hole course, green fees weekdays RM20, weekends RM30; ***Bukit Jambul Golf & Country Club***, Jln Bukit Jambul, T 6442255, hilly course, green fees weekdays RM100, weekends RM150; ***Indoor Golf Club***, Level 56, KOMTAR building; ***Penang Turf Club***, Golf Section, Jln Batu Gantong, T 2266701, 18-hole, RM84 weekdays, RM126 weekends; ***Kristal Golf Resort***, Jln Valdor, Seberang Perai Selatan, T 5822280, green fees weekdays RM105, weekends RM150.

Horse racing: *Penang Turf Club*, Jln Batu Gantung, every 2 months.

Ice Rink: *Bukit Jambul Shopping Complex*, close to the airport, RM12 for 2 hours (skate rental extra).

Roller skating: *Midland Park Complex*, Jln Burmah.

Swimming: *Chinese Swimming Club*, between Tanung Bunga and Georgetown (about 8 km from the city). Admission RM2. Open 0900-2045 Mon-Sun. ***Swimwell***, 192 Jln Burmah, T 2291932.

● Tour companies & travel agents

Most of the budget travel agents are along Lebuh Chulia. ***Everrise Tours & Travel***, Lot 323, 2nd Flr, Wisma Central, 202 Jln, T 2264329; ***Georgetown Tourist Service***, 18 Pengkalan Weld, T 2613853, city island tours; ***MSL Travel***, Ming Court Inn Lobby, Jln Macalister, T 2272655 or 340 Lebuh Chulia, T 2616154, student and youth travel bureau; ***North East Travel***, 21 Lebuh Pantai, T 2619563, F 2637149.

● Tourist offices

Penang Tourist Centre, Penang Port Commission Building, Jln Tun Syed Sheikh Barakbah (off Victoria Clocktower roundabout, opposite Fort Cornwallis), T 2616663; **Tourism Malaysia Northern Regional Office**, 10 Jln Tun Syed Sheh Barakbah, round the corner from the Penang Tourist Association (above), T 2620066, T 2619067; **Tourist Information Centre**, 3rd Flr, KOMTAR Tower, Jln Penang, T 2614461, also branch at Batu Ferringhi, outside *Eden Seafood Village* and at Bayan Lepas Airport (T 6430501), the information centre has a list of tour companies in Georgetown.

● Useful addresses

Immigration Office: on the corner of Lebuh Light and Lebuh Pantai, T 2615122.

● Transport

NB Butterworth is the railway stop for Georgetown and Penang; taxis also tend to terminate there, with local taxis making the run across the bridge to the island; long-distance taxis will however cross the bridge for an extra charge.

Local Bicycle hire: rental from the *Eng Ann Hotel* or *Swiss Hotel*, both on Lebuh Chulia, RM20/day. **Bus**: city buses leave from Lebuh Victoria near the Butterworth ferry terminal and serve Georgetown and the surrounding districts. Green, yellow and blue buses leave for various points around the island from Pengkalan Weld (Weld Quay) – next to the ferry terminal or Jln Maxwell. Blue buses go west along the north coast to Tanjung Bungah, Batu Ferringhi and Teluk Bahang. Green buses head towards the centre of the island to Ayer Itam area. Yellow buses go south (including Snake Temple and Bayan Lepas Airport), and then up the west side to Teluk Bahang. Prices from RM0.60 to RM0.90. **Car hire**: **Avis**, Bayan Lepas Airport, T 6439633, *Rasa Sayang Hotel* Lobby, T 8811522; **Budget**, 28 Jln Penang, T 6438891 and Bayan Lepas Airport; **Hertz**, 38 Lebuh Farquhar, T 2635914 and Bayan Lepas Airport; **National Car Rental**, 17 Lebuh Leith, T 2629404; **Orix**, *City Bayview Hotel*, 25A Lebuh Farquhar, T 2618608; **Ruhanmas**, 76 Batu Ferringhi, T 8811023; **SMAS**, Bayan Lepas Airport, T 6452288; **Thrifty** Bayan Lepas Airport, T 6430958; **Tomo**, 386A, 1st Flr Wayton Court, Jln Burmah, T 22665636. **Motorcycle hire**: in Georgetown there are several motorbike rental shops, many of them along Lebuh Chulia. Cost: from about RM20/day depending on size; most are Honda 70s. **Taxi**: taxi stands on Jln Dr Lim Chwee Leong, Pengkalan Weld and Jln Magazine. Fares are not calculated by meter, so agree a price before you set off – short distances within the city cost RM3-6. A trip to the airport costs RM10-12. **Radio taxis**: T 2625721 (at ferry terminal); *CT Radio Taxi Service*, T 2299467/2262441. **Trishaw**: bicycle rickshaws (carry 2 people) are one of the most practical and enjoyable ways to explore Georgetown. Cost RM1/half mile; if taking an hour's trip around town, agree on the route first, bargain and set the price in advance.

Transport to Penang: for details on transport to Penang, see page 198.

BATU FERRINGHI AND TELUK BAHANG, PENANG

The main beach **Batu Ferringhi**, whose hot white sands were once the nirvana of western hippies, has been transformed into an upmarket tropical version of the Costa Brava. There are now at least 10 hotels along the beach strip and graffiti are splashed across the famous Foreigner's Rock. *Ferringhi* – which is related to the Thai word *farang*, or foreigner – actually means 'Portuguese' in Malay. Portuguese Admiral Albuquerque, who captured Melaka in 1511, stopped off at Batu Ferringhi for fresh water on his way down the Straits. And St Francis Xavier is said to have visited Batu Ferringhi in 1545. Towards the end of the 16th century, Captain James Lancaster, who later founded the East India Company in 1600, also came ashore at the beach.

To the majority of today's tourists, Batu Ferringhi *is* Penang. The beach is just over 3 km long but it has been extended to the fishing village of Teluk Bahang at the west end. Most holidaymakers and honeymooners prefer to stick to their hotel swimming pools rather than risk bathing in the sea. Pollution, siltation, and an influx of jellyfish have affected water quality, but of late, the hotels

DRIVE AROUND THE PEARL OF THE ORIENT

FOR RESERVATIONS:
Tel: (603) 230 7788
Fax: (603) 232 0077

RENTAL LOCATIONS:
- Kuala Lumpur, Shangri-La Hotel
- Kuala Lumpur Airport
- Penang Airport

Penang and beyond...

have taken much more care of the beach itself. Despite the explosion of development, Batu Ferringhi still meets most visitors' expectations. With its palms and casuarina trees and its (almost) turquoise water, it retains at least some of its picture-postcard beauty. The hotels offer many different activities: windsurfing, water skiing, diving, sailing and fishing as well as jungle walks and sightseeing tours of the island.

Apart from the string of plush modern hotels, the Batu Ferringhi area also has many excellent restaurants, hawker stalls and handicraft shops. The **Yahong Art Gallery** (58d Batu Ferringhi Road, T 8811251, F 8811093) is on Batu Ferringhi, which displays batik paintings by the Teng (born in China, in 1914) family (the elder Teng is regarded as the father of Malaysian batik painting).

Teluk Bahang is a small fishing kampung at the west end of this north stretch of beach. It is where the Malabar fishermen used to live and has now been dramatically changed by the *Penang Mutiara Beach Resort*. Beyond Teluk Bahang, around **Muka Head**, the coast is broken into a series of small secluded coves separated by rocky headlands; there are several tiny secluded beaches. Some of these are only accessible by boat, which can be hired either from the beach hotels, or from fishermen in Teluk Bahang (much cheaper). Trails also lead over the headland from the fishing kampung. One goes along the coast past the Universiti Malaya Marine Research Station to Mermaid Beach and Muka Head lighthouse (1½ hours); another leads straight over the headland to Pantai Keracut (2 hours). The **Teluk Bahang Recreation Forest** has several well marked trails and a **Forestry Museum**. Open 0900-1300, 1400-1700 Tuesday-Thursday, Saturday and Sunday; 0900-1200, 1445-1700 Friday. **The Butterfly Farm**, a kilometre up the road from the Teluk Bahang junction, claims to be the largest tropical butterfly farm in the world. It has around 4,000 butterflies at any one time, representing over 120 species of Malaysian butterflies. The best time to visit the farm is in the late morning or early afternoon when the butterflies are most active. There is a small but excellent reptile and insect museum next door. The farm is also an important research centre and breeding station. Admission RM5. Open 0900-1700 Monday-Friday, 0900-1800 Saturday and Sunday. There are two **batik factories** along the road near the butterfly farm; visitors welcome. **Craft Bank** is just beyond the Teluk Bahang junction, before the butterfly farm. Batik cloth is sold by the metre in the showroom starting at RM22, while finished garments cost RM45 upwards. Demonstrations of batik block designing, stamp waxing and dyeing.

Local information

● Accommodation

Prices: L over RM500; **A+** RM260-500; **A** RM130-260; **B** RM65-130; **C** RM40-65; **D** RM20-40; **E** RM10-20; **F** Below RM10

The big international hotels all have excellent facilities – including tennis, watersports, sailing and sightseeing tours. They also offer free shuttle services at least once a day to Georgetown. A room glut in the early 1990s – due mainly to the knock-on from recession in the West – has meant several hotels have been offering very competitive deals. With fewer European customers, many turned their attention to the incentive travel business and the Asian market, targeting Singaporeans in particular. Hotels are still going up though. While middle-to-upmarket tourists are spoilt for choice, budget travellers' options on the north coast are rather more limited. Travelling west around the island from Georgetown, the first beach is **Tanjung Bungah**, with only very mediocre swimming. Next is the built-up **Batu Ferringhi**, once a beautiful beach but now, many would argue, over-developed. Continuing west, at the end of the beach strip, is **Teluk Bahang**, a fishing village with a handful of places to stay.

Batu Ferringhi: **A+** *Golden Sands*, T 8811911, F 8811880, a/c, restaurant, pool, popular and central on the beach, arguably the best swimming pool, a *Shangri La* outfit. RM185++ *Parkroyal*, T 8811133, F 8812233, a/c restaurants, attractive pool, large 300-room

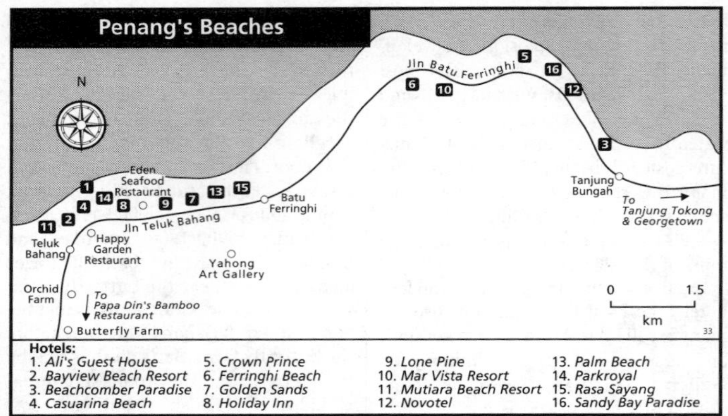

5-star hotel, with excellent facilities especially for families, including children's play area, special children's programmes and baby-sitting. Large airy rooms with sea views. **A+** *Rasa Sayang* T 8811811, F 8811984, a/c, restaurants, pool, one of the *Shangri La* group, winner of Tourism Malaysia 1995 Award for Excellence in Hotel Services, over 500 rooms, probably the most popular along the beach strip, modern interpretation of Minangkabau-style, horseshoe design around central pool and garden area, recommended. **A** *Bayview Beach*, T 8812123, F 8812140, a/c, restaurant, pool, over 400 rooms, pleasant location, away from others on the strip. **A** *Casuarina Beach*, T 8811711, F 8812155, a/c, restaurant, pool, named after the trees which line Batu Ferringhi beach, particularly nice grounds and a good beach. **A** *Ferringhi Beach*, T 8905999, F 8905100, a/c, restaurant, pool, 350 rooms, a/c, minibar, TV, in-house video, overhead bridge to beach, offers golf packages, caters mainly for tour groups. **A** *Holiday Inn Penang*, T 8811601, F 8811389, a/c, restaurant, good pool and beach area. **A** *Mar Vista Resort*, T 8903388, F 8903886, 120 suites all with kitchenette (utensils extra charge), sea views, a/c, TV, dated decor, pool, paddling pool, jacuzzi, Health Club, restaurant. **A** *Palm Beach*, T 8811621, F 8811051, a/c, restaurant, pool. **B** *Lone Pine*, T 8811511, a/c, restaurant, one of the oldest hotels along Batu Ferringhi (opened in 1948), a/c, TV, minibar, pool, reasonably priced, but not up to the standards of its neighbours. **C** *Ah Beng*, 54 C, right on beach, T 8811036, a/c, all rooms have bathrooms, clean. **C** *Ali's*, 53b, T 8811316, alongside *Ah Beng's*, clean and good value. **C** *Baba's*, 52, T 8811686, clean and good value.

Teluk Bahang: **A+** *Penang Mutiara Beach Resort*, Jln Teluk Bahang, T 8852828, F 8852829, a/c, restaurant, pool, over 400 rooms, the last outpost of 5-star luxury along the beach, and a member of the 'Leading Hotels of the World' group, the *Mutiara* (Malay for 'pearl') has landscaped garden, great pool with a bar and every conceivable facility including a children's wonderland, a drink at the *Mutiara* bar costs the same as a huge meal in some nearby restaurants, recommended. **E** *Madame Loh*, near the mosque (left at the roundabout), clean, good atmosphere. **E-F** *Rama's*, 365 Mukim 2, T 811179, homestay-type accommodation, dorm or rooms.

Tanjung Bungah: **A** *Paradise*, T 8908808, F 8908333, another large hotel in the new *Paradise* chain, over 200 rooms, slightly down market to the *Sandy Bay Paradise*, less spacious rooms but lower room rates, a/c, bath, TV, fridge, restaurant – good value buffets. **A** *Crown Prince*, Tanjung Bungah, T 8904111, F 8904777, over 250 rooms, not as good as *Paradise* hotels but sometimes offers good value promotions. **A** *Novotel*, T 8903333, F 8903303, a/c, restaurant, pool, outmoded by the newer *Paradise* hotels. **A** *Sandy Bay Paradise*, 527 Jln Tanjung Bungah, T 8999999, F 8990000, opened in 1995, the *Sandy Bay* is one of Penang's newest 'affordable' luxury hotels, with over 300 rooms, all of which are suites of varying size with kitchenette, balconies, sea views, TV, in-house video, mini-bar, complimentary coffee/tea, a/c and bath, the decor is tasteful and facilities are good, free-form pool, paddling pool, watersports, tennis, squash and gym, 24-hour coffee house and lounge overlooking sea, set around grand open lobby. **B *Motel Sri Pantai***, T 8909728, a/c, restaurant; **E *Loke Thean***, T 8904231.

● Places to eat

Prices: ♦♦♦♦ over RM40; ♦♦♦ RM13-40; ♦♦ RM5-13; ♦ under RM5

Many of the big Batu Ferringhi hotels have excellent restaurants – they have to be good as there is plenty of good quality competition from roadside restaurants. Virtually every cuisine is represented along this stretch.

Malay: ♦♦♦***Shores***, *Paradise Hotel*, Jln Tanjung Bungah, *nasi kandar* and *mee rebus* set lunches. ♦♦***Papa Din's Bamboo***, 124-B Batu Ferringhi (turn left after police station and *Eden Restaurant*, 200m up the kampung road by *Happy Garden Restaurant*), home-cooked Malay fish curries made by loveable bumoh who prides himself on being able to say "thank you" in 30 languages, Papa Din Salat is also a renowned masseur.

Seafood: ♦♦♦***Eden Seafood Village***, 69a Batu Ferringhi, if it swims, *Eden* cooks it – priced according to weight – not cheap, nightly cultural shows, *Eden* has now expanded to include two other big, clean red restaurants, adjacent and opposite the original, the *Ferringhi Village* at 157b and *Penang Village*. ♦♦♦***Pearl Garden***, 78 Batu Ferringhi, affiliated to *Eden*, similar set-up, open courtyard or a/c interior. ♦♦♦***The Catch***, Jln Teluk Bahang, next to *Mutiara Hotel*, Malay, Chinese, Thai and international seafood dishes, huge fish tanks for fresh fish, prawns, crabs, lobster etc, hour-long cultural show daily, pleasant setting, one of the best seafood restaurants on the island, recommended. ♦♦***End of the World***, end of Teluk Bahang beach, huge quantities of fresh seafood, its chilli crabs are superb and its lobster is the best value for money on the island (about RM25 each), pleasant setting on beach, recommended. ♦♦***Happy Garden***, Batu Ferringhi, left after police station and *Eden* restaurant), pretty garden, Chinese and western dishes. ♦♦***Hollywood***, Tanjung Bungah, Batu Ferringhi, great views over the beach, serves *inche kabin* chicken stews and good selection of seafood.

Chinese: ♦♦♦♦***House of Four Seasons***, *Mutiara Beach Resort*, Jln Teluk Bahang, closed Tues, good old-fashioned opulence, black marble, silk and carpets, interesting menu, Cantonese and Szechuan dishes, recommended. ♦♦♦♦***Marco Polo***, *Bayview Beach Resort*, Batu Ferringhi, wide selection of Cantonese dishes, shark's fin is popular, bright lighting and typical Chinese decor with tables set around a courtyard. ♦♦♦***Fok Lok Sow***, *Mar Vista Resort*, Batu Ferringhi, good value buffet (RM22) and 7-course set dinner. ♦♦♦***Shang San***, *Paradise Hotel*, Tanjung Bungah, good value Chinese food, dim sum brunch. ♦♦***Sin Hai Keng***, 551 Tanjung Tokong, overlooks the sea and serves everything from noodles to pork chops, excellent satay.

International: ♦♦♦♦***Feringgi Grill***, *Rasa Sayang Resort*, Batu Ferringhi, popular restaurant, aims to imitate an English club, 3-piece band, specialities include prime US rib of beef served with Yorkshire pudding, expensive but memorable. ♦♦♦♦***La Farfalla***, *Mutiara Beach Resort*, 1 Jln Teluk Bahang, closed Mon, romantic setting overlooking pool, live string band play in background, authentic Italian chef, specialities include beef carpaccio, scallops and lobster. ♦♦♦♦***The Ship***, Batu Ferringhi (next to *Eden*), purpose-built wooden ship with steakhouse inside. ♦♦♦♦***Tiffins***, *Parkroyal Hotel*, Batu Ferringhi, very popular with locals, especially business wishing to impress clients, Nyonya decor, wood carvings and antique furniture, eclectic cooking style, many interesting items, set meal good value (RM37 for 3-course). ♦♦♦***Guan Guan Café***, Batu Ferringhi (opposite Yahong Art Gallery), where backpackers hang out, good value snacks; ♦♦♦***Kokomo***, 1c Jln Sungai Kelian, Tanjung Bungah (opposite *Novotel Hotel*), hip meeting place, light meals and snacks, happy hour 1800-2100. ♦♦♦***Wunderbar***, 37f Jln Cantonment (near Gurney Drive), authentic German restaurant.

Japanese: ♦♦♦♦***Honjin***, *Bayview Beach Resort*, Batu Ferringhi, peaceful Japanese-style setting with a garden at centre of restaurant, good quality food, set meals are best value. ♦♦♦♦***Japanese Restaurant***, *Rasa Sayang Resort*, Batu Ferringhi, typically spartan Japanese decor, two main areas on menu: sushi and sashimi, and teppanyaki.

Thai: ♦♦♦***Dusit Thai***, 92 Batu Ferringhi (next to *Lone Pine Hotel*). ♦♦***Thai Spices***, 62 Cantonement Rd (near Gurney Drive), good value set lunch, good Thai chefs.

● Bars

Beers, *Parkroyal*, Batu Ferringhi, good selection of beers, some draft, low prices, darts and snooker nights; ***Sapphire***, *Ferringhi Beach Hotel*, Batu Ferringhi, 2400-0100, 30% discount on pouring brands and draft beer, Ladies' Night Tues; ***Swing Pub***, *Bayview Beach Resort*, Batu Ferringhi, cross between a pub and a disco.

● Entertainment

Cultural shows: *Eden Seafood Village*, Batu Ferringhi; *Penang Cultural Centre*, near the *Mutiara*, Teluk Bahang, daily Malay Cultural Tour lasting the marathon length of 2½ hours, with Silat demonstraion, handicrafts, traditional game demonstrations, a visit to a Longhouse, the Heritage Gallery and, last but not least, a 45 minute Cultural Show. T 8851175, F 8842449. Theme dinners can be booked at the Istana-Malay Theatre Restaurant, there also facilities for business events. Most of the larger hotels also have cultural shows in evening.

Discos: ***Borsalino***, *Parkroyal*, Batu Ferringhi, 2100-0200; ***Cinta***, *Rasa Sayang Resort*, Batu Ferringhi, 2100-0200; ***Ozone***, *Mar Vista Resort*, Batu Ferringhi, 2100-0200, also karaoke and live band area; ***Shock!***, *Novotel*, Batu Ferringhi, 2100-0200, videotheque, live band, and one of the largest dance floors in Penang.

Traditional massage: ***Papa Din***, 124B Batu Ferringhi (see directions under Malay, Places to eat, above). Health Clubs, such as the ***Do-Club*** in the *Mar Vista Resort*, Batu Ferringhi, in all major hotels offer massage.

● Shopping

Batik: ***Craft Batik***, Mukim 2, Teluk Bahang, batik cloth sold by metre starting at RM22 and as ready-made garments RM45 upwards, demonstrations can be seen to rear of showroom; ***Deepee's Silk Shop***, offering reasonable tailoring service; ***Sim Seng Lee Batik and Handicrafts***, 391 Batu Ferringhi.

● Sports

Sailing: the most popular route is to sail north towards the islands around Langkawi and Turatao. ***Pelangi Cruises***, *Mutiara Beach Resort*, Jln Teluk Bahang, T 8812828/8811305, F 8812829/8811498, 12 yachts, with or without skipper, RM50 pp for 3 hours, RM100 pp for 6 hours, also run overnight cruises, buying fresh fish from fishermen en route. It takes 8-10 hours to Langkawi.

● Transport

Local Boats: boat trips can be arranged through fishermen at Teluk Bahang. Negotiate the price in advance. **Car hire**: **Avis**, *Rasa Sayang Hotel*, Batu Ferringhi; **Hertz**, *Casuarina Beach Hotel*, Batu Ferringhi; **Kasina Baru**, 651 Mukim 2, Teluk Bahang (opposite *Mutiara Beach Resort*), T 8811988; **Mayflower**, *Casuarina Beach Hotel*, Batu Ferringhi; **Ruhanmas**, 157B Batu Ferringhi, T 8811576; **Sintat Rent-a-Car**, *Lone Pine Hotel*, Batu Ferringhi. **Motorbike hire**: quite a few places along Batu Ferringhi all of them clearly signposted on the road.

Road Bus: blue bus 93 goes to Batu Ferringhi/Teluk Bahang from Pengkalan Weld (Weld Quay) or Jln Maxwell in Georgetown. **Taxi**: stands on Batu Ferringhi (eg opposite *Golden Sands Hotel*). The big hotels along the strip are well served by taxis.

● Transport to & from Penang

Air Bayan Lepas Airport is an international airport, 20 km south of Georgetown and 36 km from Batu Ferringhi, T 6434411. **Transport to town**: taxis operate on a coupon system from the airport (30 minutes to Georgetown, RM16) or take yellow bus 83 for either Teluk Bahang (up the west coast) or Georgetown (up the east coast). Regular connections with Johor Bahru, KL, Kota Bharu, Kota Kinabalu, Kuala Terengganu, Kuching, Langkawi and Miri.

Train Station is by the Butterworth ferry terminal, T 2610290/2617125. Advance bookings for onward rail journeys can be made at the station or at the ferry terminal, Pengkalan Weld, Georgetown. From Butterworth: regular connections with Alor Star, Taiping, Ipoh, KL 6 hours, Johor Bahru, see page 512 for timetable.

Road Bus: terminal is beside the ferry terminal at Butterworth. Booking offices along Lebuh Chulia. Some coaches operate from Pengkalan Weld direct to major towns on the peninsula (see Butterworth section). ***Masa Mara Travel*** (54/4 Jln Burmah) is an agent for direct express buses from Penang to Kota Bharu and KL (5 hours, RM18.50). Minibus companies now organize an early morning pick-up from your hotel, to Hat Yai (RM26), from where there are connections north to Thailand. **Car**: the recent completion of the north-south expressway makes the journey from Penang to KL reasonably painless, 4½ hours and a total toll cost of RM25. RM7 toll to drive across the Penang Bridge onto Penang. No payment required for the outward journey. **Taxi**: long-distance taxis to all destinations on peninsula operate from the depot beside the Butterworth ferry on Pengkalan Weld.

Sea Boat: boats from Georgetown for Langkawi Mon-Sun, depart 0800 and return from Langkawi at 1815, 3 hours (RM35 one way, RM60 return). Tickets can be bought from travel agents all over town. Boats leave from Swettenham Pier. Possible to take motor cycle or bicycle (RM10). There is also a weekly overnight service to Langkawi (fortnightly during the monsoon season) from Swettenham Pier. Leaves Georgetown at 2300 and arrives Langkawi at 0700 the next morning. For schedules contact Sanren Delta Marine at *E & O Shopping Complex*, 10 Lebuh Farquhar or Kuala Perlis Ferry Service, PPC Shopping Complex, Pesara King Edward, T 2625630. **Ferry**: passenger and car ferries operate from adjacent terminals, Pengkalan Raja Tun Uda, T 3315780. 24-hours ferry service between Georgetown and Butterworth. Ferries leave every 20 minutes 0600-2400. RM0.40 return. Selasa Express Ferry Company has its office by the Penang Clock Tower, next to the Penang Tourist Office, T 2625630.

● **International connections**

Air Worldwide international connections on MAS, most via Kuala Lumpur.

Train See Butterworth section, see page 175.

Road Bus: express bus agents are along Lebuh Chulia. Regular connections to Bangkok; also connections to Phuket, Hat Yai, Surat Thani. Also some hotels eg *New Asia* and *Cathay* organize minibuses to destinations in Thailand. Bus and ferry to Koh Samui, Krabi and Phuket. **Taxi**: direct taxis from Penang to Thailand: overnight to Hat Yai; Surat Thani for Koh Samui, Krabi (for Phuket).

Sea Boat: there is now a regular ferry service from Georgetown to Langkawi and on to Phuket; check details at Kuala Perlis Ferry service (see below).

To Singapore: **Air** Regular connections with Singapore. **Road Bus**: overnight to Singapore.

To Sumatra, Indonesia: **Air** Regular connections with Medan. **Sea Boat**: A number of companies operate ferries to Belawan (Medan's port) from Swettenham Pier. *Ekspres Bahagia* leave Penang for Medan on Mon and Tues at 0900 and on Wed and Fri at 1000. They depart Medan/Belawan for Penang on Mon and Tues at 1330 and on Thur and Sat and 1000. The fare is RM90/95,000Rp one way, RM160/160,000Rp return, journey time 4½ hours. Note that the Sat departure is often full, so book a ticket beforehand if possible. Their address in Penang is *Ekspres Bahagia*, Ground Floor, Penang Port, Commission Shopping Complex, Jln Pesara King Edward, T 2631943/2635255. Their agent in Medan is *Eka Sukma Wisata Tour and Travel*, Jln Sisingamangaraja 92A. *Perdana Express* is another outfit that runs high speed ferries on the Penang-Medan route. From Penang boats leave on Tues, Thur and Sat at 0900, journey time 4 hours; from Medan they depart on Wed, Fri and Sun at 1000. The fares are the same as *Ekspres Bahagia*. In Penang the *Perdana Express* offices are on the Ground Floor, Penang Port, Commission Shopping Complex, Jln Pesara King Edward; and in Medan, they have their offices at Jln Brig Jend Katamso 35C. *Selasa Express* is yet another company operating ferries between Belawan and Penang. Their office is by the Penang Clock Tower, next to the Penang Tourist Office, T 2625630 and their agent in Medan is *Tobali Tour and Travel*, Jln Juanda Baru 52. All the companies offer free transfer between Belawan and Medan.

ALOR STAR

Alor Star is the capital of Kedah state on the road north to the Thai border. It is the home town of Prime Minister Dr Mahathir Mohamad and is the commercial centre for Northwest Malaysia. Its name, which has been corrupted from Alor Setar, means 'grove of setar trees' (which produce a sour fruit). Kedah is now Malaysia's most important rice-growing state; together with neighbouring Perlis it produces 44% of the country's rice, and is known as *jelapang padi* – 'rice barn country'. Kedah is the site of some of the oldest settlements on the peninsula and the state's royal family can trace its line back several centuries. The ancient Indian names for the state are Kadaram and Kathah, and archaeologists believe the site of the 5th century kingdom of Langkasuka was just to the southeast of Kedah Peak (Gunung Jerai), in the Bujang River valley, half-way between Butterworth and Alor Star (see below).

Places of interest

Alor Star has some interesting buildings, most of which are clustered round the central Padang Besar (Jalan Pekan Melayu/Jalan Raja); apart from them, the town is unremarkable. The most interesting is the state mosque, the Moorish-style **Masjid Zahir**, completed in 1912. Almost directly opposite is the Thai-inspired **Balai Besar**, or audience hall, built in 1898, which is still used by the Sultan of Kedah on ceremonial occasions – it houses the royal

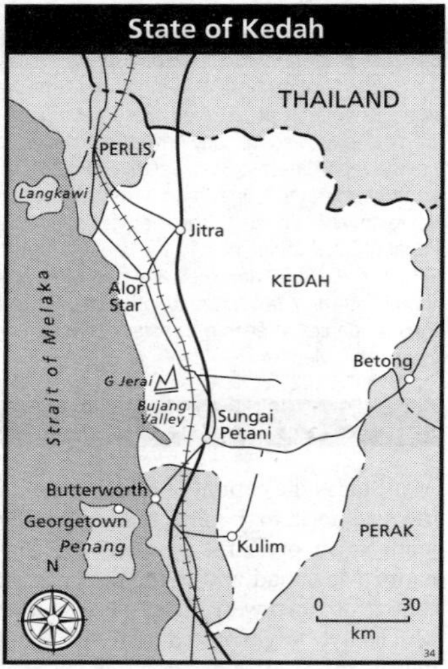

State of Kedah

throne. It is not open to the public. Close to the mosque is the **Balai Seni Negeri**, or State Art Gallery, which contains a collection of historical paintings and antiques. Open 1000-1800, Saturday-Thursday, 1000-1200, 1430-1800 Friday. Further down Jalan Raja is the 400-years-old **Balai Nobat**, an octagonal building topped by an onion dome. This building houses Kedah's royal percussion orchestra or *nobat*; it is said to date back to the 15th century. Again, it is not open to the public.

The **State Museum** (or Muzium Di Raja), styled on the Balai Besar and built in 1936, is on Jalan Bakar Bata. The museum houses exhibits on local farming and fishing practices, a collection of early Sung Dynasty porcelain and some finds from the archaeological excavations in the Bujang Valley (see below). Open 1000-1800 Saturday-Thursday, 0900-1200, 1500-1800 on Friday. The **Pekan Rabu**, or Wednesday market (which is now held all week long) is a good place to buy local handicrafts and try some of the traditional food of Kedah.

Two other places of interest are the **Royal Boat House**, near the Sungai Anak Bukit, west of the clocktower. It houses boats belonging to former rulers of Kedah. For Prime Minister-watchers, the house where Dr Mahathir Mohamad was born has been opened as a museum, giving an insight into his early days. It is to be found at 18 Lorong Kilang Ais, off Jalan Pegawai. Open 0900-1800 Saturday-Thursday, 0900-1200, 1500-1800 Friday.

Excursions

Bujang Valley near the small town of **Sungai Petani**, to the southeast of Kedah Peak (Gunung Jerai), is the site of some of Malaysia's most exciting archaeological discoveries: finds there have prompted the establishment of the Bajung Valley Historical Park (under the management of the National Museum). The name 'Bujang' is derived from a Sanskrit word, *bhujanga* meaning serpent. It is thought to be the site of the capital of the 5th century Hindu kingdom of Langkasuka, the hearthstone of Malay fairytale romance. While the architectural remains are a far cry from those of Cambodia's Angkor Wat, they are of enormous historical significance.

The city is thought to represent one of the very earliest Hindu settlements in Southeast Asia, several centuries before Angkor, and at least 200 years before the founding of the first Hindu city in Java. The capital of Langkasuka is thought to have been abandoned in the 6th century, probably following a pirate raid. There have been some remarkable finds at the site, including brick and marble temple and palace complexes – of both Hindu and Buddhist origin – coins, statues, Sanskrit inscriptions, weapons and jewellery. In 1925 archaeologists stumbled across "a magnificent little granite temple near a beautiful waterfall" on a hillside above the ancient city. One of them, Dr Quarith Wales, the director of the Greater-India Research Committee wrote of the temple: "It had never been robbed, except of images, although the bronze trident of Shiva was found. In each of the stone post-holes were silver caskets containing rubies and sapphires." More than 50 temples have

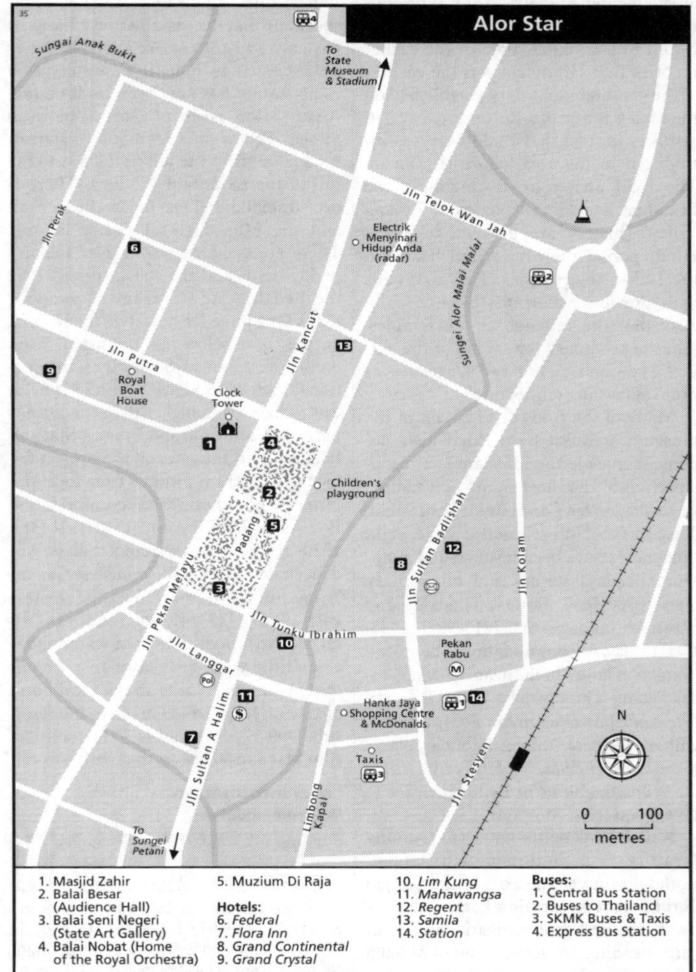

now been unearthed in the Bujang area, most of them buried in soft mud along the river bank.

For several centuries, Indian traders used the city as an entrepôt in their dealings with China. Rather than sail through the pirate-infested Melaka Strait, the traders stopped at the natural harbour at Kuala Merbok and had their goods portered across the isthmus to be collected by ships on the east side. There is speculation that the area of the Sungai Bujang was later used as a major port of the Srivijaya Empire, whose capital was at Palembang, Sumatra. But recent findings by Malaysian archaeologists have begun to contradict some of the earlier theories that Hinduism was the earliest of the great religions to be established on the Malay peninsula. Recently excavated artifacts suggest that Buddhism was introduced to the area before Hinduism. The local archaeologists maintain the Buddhist and Hindu phases of Bujang Valley's history are distinct, with the Hindu period following on much later, in the 10th-14th centuries. This is at odds with previous assertions by archaeologists that the remains of the temples' "laterite sanctuary towers are of the earliest type and ... not yet suggestive of pre-Angkorian architecture".

Many of the finds can be seen in the museum at Bukit Batu Pahat near Bedong; alongside the museum is a reconstruction of the most significant temple unearthed so far, **Candi Bukit Batu Pahat**, Temple of the Hill of Chiselled Stone. Eight sanctuaries have been restored and a museum displays statues and other finds. Open 0900-1600 Monday-Thursday and Saturday-Sunday, 0900-1215 and 1445-1600 Friday. **Accommodation** There are a number of hotels in the nearest town, Sungai Petani. The plushest is the **B** *Sungai Petani Inn*, Jalan Kolam Air, T (04) 4213411, with a/c and pool. Among the budget places is the **D** *Hotel Duta*, 7 Jalan Petri. *Getting there*: change buses at Bedong; easier to take a taxi from Alor Star.

Kedah Peak better known as **Gunung Jerai**) is the highest mountain (1206m) in the northwest and part of the **Sungai Teroi Forest Recreation Park**. The peak has been used as a navigational aid for ships heading down the Strait of Melaka for centuries. It is between the main road and the coast, north of Sungai Petani. In 1884, the remains of a 6th century Hindu shrine were discovered on the summit. It had been hidden under a metre-thick layer of peat, which caught fire, revealing the brick and stone construction, thought to be linked with the kingdom of Langkasuka (above). Archaeologists speculate that the remains may originally have been a series of fire altars. But they are destined to remain a mystery as a radio station has now been built on top. About 3 km north of Gurun, between Sungai Petani and Alor Star, a narrow road goes off to the left and leads to the top of the mountain (11 km). There is even a small hotel just below the summit and the Museum of Forestry on top. There are good views out over Kedah's paddy fields and the coast. In mid-1994 the Kedah State Government scrapped plans for a huge Disney-style theme park on the coast below the mountain. Work on the prestigious US$7bn Jerai International Park was to have begun in June. It was to have been bigger than the Disney parks in California and France. State officials pulled the plug on the project following vociferous protests from local rice farmers and fishermen. **Accommodation** **B** *Gunung Jerai Resort*, T (04) 414311, 1920s resthouse, rooms and chalets, garden, chalets RM99. **B** *Peranginan Gunung Jerai*, Sungai Teroi Forest Recreation Park, T (04) 4223345, a/c, restaurant, attached bathrooms with hot water showers, a little worn but reasonable. *Getting there*: Gunung Jerai is about 4 km north of Garun. Jeeps from Gurun to the resort run 0900-1700. Gurun is 33 km south of Alor Star and 60 km north of Butterworth.

Local information

● Accommodation

Prices: L over RM500; **A+** RM260-500; **A** RM130-260; **B** RM65-130; **C** RM40-65; **D** RM20-40; **E** RM10-20; **F** Below RM10

A *Grand Continental*, Lot 134-141, Jln Sultan Badlishah, T 7335917, F 7335161, a/c, bath, TV, in-house movies, coffee house, business centre, car rental, central location and good discounts from the rack rate usually available.

B *Grand Crystal*, 40 Jln Kampung Perak, T 7313333, F 7316368, a/c, TV, bath, pool, coffee house – like the *Grand Continental*, discounts often on offer. **B** ***Samila***, 27 Jln Kancut, T 7318888, F 7339934, a/c, restaurant, nightclub, a step down from the *Grand Crystal* in terms of price and not as good as the brochure tries to make out, dated. **B** *Seri Malaysia*, Mukim Alor Malai, Daerah Kota Setar, Jln Stadium, T 7308738, F 7307594, 100 rooms, one of the 'amazingly affordable' chain, a/c, TV, shower, tea/coffee-making facility, in-house video, café, clean, functional and good value, located between stadium and public swimming pool at north end of town. **B-C** *Regent*, 1536 Jln Sultan Badlishah, T 7311900, F 7311291, a/c, good value for money, recommended.

C *Mahawangsa*, 449 Jln Raja, T 7321433/7331433, a/c, TV, bath, run-down and not very desirable. **C** *Rumah Rehat* (*Government Resthouse*), 75 Pumpong, T 722422, some a/c, book beforehand as it tends to fill up with government people.

C *Flora Inn*, 8 Kompleks Medan Raja, Jln Pengkalan Kapal, T 7324235, F 73378461, overlooking the Kedah River, a/c, TV, food court, budget rooms (**E**).

D *Federal*, 429 Jln Kancut, T 7330055, a/c, unpleasant. **D** *Station*, 2nd Flr, Jln Stesyen, T 7333855, fan only, laundry, very noisy.

E *Lim Kung*, 36A Jln Langgar, T 722459, fan only, good value.

● Places to eat

Prices: ♦♦♦♦ over RM40; ♦♦♦ RM13-40; ♦♦ RM5-13; ♦ under RM5

Chinese: ♦♦♦*Samila Hotel*, 27 Jln Kancut, recommended. ♦♦*Sri Pumpong*, Jln Pumpong, speciality: barbecued fish.

Indian: ♦♦*Bunga Tanjong*, Jln Seberang, Indian Muslim food, seafood curries.

Thai: ♦♦*Café de Siam*, Jln Kota, lashings of Thai-style seafood. *Kway Teow Jonid*, Jln Stadium (next to the police station), fried *kway teow*, washed down with *teh tarik*.

Foodstalls: *"Garden" Hawker Centre*, Jln Stadium, good range of cuisines, next to stadium, Jln Langgar (in front of cinema); *Old Market* (*Pekan Rabu*), Jln Tunku Ibrahim.

Fast food: *McDonalds*, Jln Langgar; *Kentucky Fried Chicken*, Jln Stadium.

● Airline offices

MAS, 180 Kompleks Alor Star, Lebuhraya Darulaman, T 711106; **Pelangi Airways**, c/o MAS, T 7311106.

● Banks & money changers

Bank Bumiputra, Jln Tunku Ibrahim; **Chartered Bank, Overseas Union Bank** and **UMBC** are all on Jln Raja.

● Post & telecommunications

Area code: 04.

General Post Office: Jln Tunku Ibrahim, near Jln Raja intersection.

● Shopping

Handicrafts: can be found in the Old Market, Pekan Rabu, on Jln Tunku Ibrahim.

● Sport

Golf: *Royal Kedah Club*, Pumpong, green fees RM45 weekdays, RM60 weekends, T 7330467.

● Tourist offices

Kedah State Tourist Office, State Secretariat Building, Jln Sultan Badlisah. Limited selection of brochures.

● Transport

93 km north of Butterworth, 462 km from KL, 409 km from Kota Bharu.

Air The airport is about 10 km north of town. Daily connections on MAS and Pelangi Airways with Kota Bharu and and on MAS with Kuala Lumpur.

Train Station is off Jln Langgar. Regular connections with KL, Butterworth, see page 512 for timetable.

Road Bus: the northern section of the new north-south Highway runs to the Malaysian border crossing at Bukit Kayu Hitam, from where it is easy to cross to Sadao, the nearest Thai town on the other side of the border (see International connections, below). Alor Star has rather a confusion of bus stations. The main bus terminal is about 2 km north of the town centre, off Jln Bakar Bata, and most long distance buses leave from here. Destinations include KL (RM21.20), Melaka, Ipoh (RM11.90), Johor Bahru (RM37.70), Kota Bharu, Kuantan and Kuala Terengganu. Local southbound buses, including buses to Butterworth and Kuala Kedah (for Langkawi), leave from the central bus station in front of the railway station on Jln Stesyen in the centre of town. Local buses also leave from the small station by the taxi stop just off Jln Langgur; long distance connections with Kota Bharu also leave from here. **Taxi**: leave from the stand just south of Jln Langgur, near the centre of town, for Penang, Kuala Kedah (for Langkawi) and Kangar (Perlis).

● International connections

Air connections with Beijing and Guangzhou in China.

Train There is a through-train from Alor Star to Hat Yai in Thailand departing daily at 0619. The international express from Singapore goes through Alor Star but does not stop to pick up passengers. (See Butterworth section for trains to Thailand.)

Road Bus and taxi: most of the buses leave from Penang/Butterworth for Bangkok and other destinations on the Kra Isthmus. There are, though, two direct connections a day between Alor Star and Hat Yai in Thailand following the north-south highway through Changlun to Bukit Kayu Hitam – the easiest way to cross the border. These leave from the small station on Jln Sultan Badlishah, north of the town centre. Alternatively, catch a bus or taxi from Alor Star, following the north-south highway, to Bukit Kayu Hitam, on the border with Thailand. It is then a shortish walk past the paraphenalia of border-dom to the bus and taxi stop where there are connections with the Thai town of Sadao (a few kilometres on) and Hat Yai. A less popular alternative is to travel to Padang Besar (accessible from Kangar in Perlis), where the railway line crosses the border. From here it is an easy walk to the bus or train station for connections to Hat Yai. The other option is to take a taxi from Sungai Petani to Keroh and cross the border into Thailand's red-light outpost at Betong. There are also bus connections with Singapore from the main long distance terminal north of town.

KUALA KEDAH

Historically the town has been an important port for trade with India and there are the ruins of an old fort, built between 1771 and 1780. The fort was built for defence of the state capital from pirate attacks. It fell into the hands of the Siamese army, under the leadership of Raja Ligor in 1821 and was occupied by Siam until 1842, after which it was abandoned. Kuala Kedah is renowned for its seafood stalls. It is also a departure point for Langkawi (see below).

• **Transport** 12 km west of Alor Star. **Road Bus**: buses leave every 30 minutes from Alor Star to Kuala Kedah (RM0.80). **Taxi**: from Alor Star (RM1.50). **Sea Boat**: regular connections with Langkawi. Langkawi ferry leaves 0800, 0930, 1130, 1200, 1330, 1430 and 1600 (RM13).

KANGAR

The state of Perlis, the smallest in Malaysia, is a very picturesque area with limestone outcrops surrounded by paddy. The capital of Perlis is Kangar, a small and unremarkable town with a lively *Pasar Tani*, a Farmers' market every Saturday. There is also a *Pasar Malam*, a night market, which sets up at 1700 every Wednesday. The town is otherwise of little interest, with a few blocks of shabby, modern shophouses and a large concrete shopping centre being developed at its centre. The historical monuments of Perlis, the state mosque and palace,

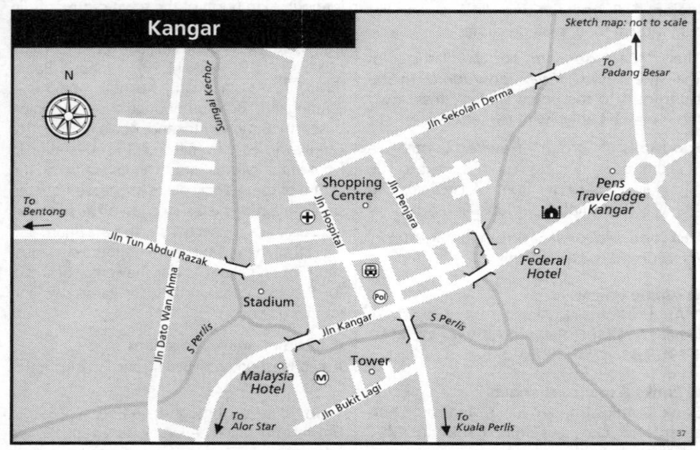

are located 12 km outside the town, in **Arau**, where a Pasar Malam takes place on a Friday.

Local information

● Accommodation

A *Pens Travelodge*, 135 Jln Kangar, T 9767755, F 9761049, 170 rooms, a/c, bath, TV, restaurant, business centre, pool.

C *Federal*, 104b Jln Kangar, T 9766288, F 9766224, 46 rooms, some a/c, shower, TV, restaurant. **C** *Malaysia*, 67 Jln Jubli Perak, T 9761366, a/c, seen better days.

D-E *Ban Cheong*, 79a Jln Besar, T 9761184, cheapest place in town, basic but serviceable.

● Transport

45 km from Alor Star, 138 km from Butterworth.

Road Bus: the bus terminal is on Jln Hospital, near the centre of town. Regular connections with Butterworth, Alor Star, KL (RM23.40), Ipoh (RM14.00), Johor Bahru, Kuantan. Local bus no 56 to Kuala Perlis, no. 59 to Padang Besar. **Taxi**: Alor Star, Kuala Perlis, Butterworth.

KUALA PERLIS

Small fishing port at the delta of the Sungai Perlis. Mainly a jumping-off point for Pulau Langkawi and Phuket (in Thailand). Food stalls by the jetty. It is noted for its local fast food *laksa*. If you miss the boat to Langkawi, the *Soon Hin Hotel* (**E**) is across from the taxi rank or *Pens Hotel* (**B**), Jalan Kuala Perlis, T (04) 9854122. Night Market every Tuesday.

● Transport 14 km from Kangar. **Road Bus and taxi**: both buses and taxis leave from the ferry terminal. Regular connections by bus and taxi with Butterworth, less regular links with Alor Star, KL and Padang Besar (for connections with Thailand, see below) and local buses to Kangar. **High-speed ferry**: departs from Kuala Perlis jetty approximately every hour between 0800 and 1800, the journey takes 45 minutes. *Kuala Perlis Langkawi Ferry Service*, Kuala Perlis, T 9854406.

PADANG BESAR

This is a border town. The railway station platform is very long as half is managed by Thai officials and half by Malaysians. *Pekan Siam*, opposite the railway station, is full of Thai goods and a popular shopping spot for Malaysians.

● Transport 50 km from Kangar. **Road Bus**: the bus station is about 1 km from the border crossing. Regular connections from Kuala Perlis and Kangar. **Taxi**: from Kuala Perlis and Kangar.

PULAU LANGKAWI

The name Langkawi is the last surviving namesake of the ancient kingdom of Langkasuka, known as *negari alang-kah suka* – 'the land of all one's wishes'. The Langkawi group is an archipelago of 99 islands around 30 km off the west coast of Peninsular Malaysia, and Pulau Langkawi itself – by far the largest of the group – is a mountainous, palm-fringed island with scattered fishing kampungs, paddy fields and sandy coves. Some of the islands are nothing more than deserted limestone outcrops rearing out of the turquoise sea, cloaked in jungle, and ringed by coral.

Langkasuka, whose capital is thought to have stood at the base of Kedah Peak, south of Alor Star (see page 202) is mentioned in Chinese accounts as far back as 500 AD. According to a Chinese Liang Dynasty record, the kingdom of 'Langgasu' was founded in the first century and its Hindu king, Bhagadatta, paid tribute to the Chinese Emperor. The names of its kings – known as *daprenta-hyangs* – resurface in Malay legends and fairytales.

In January 1987 the Malaysian government conferred duty-free status on Langkawi to promote tourism on the island. The little airport was upgraded, and the ferry service from Penang was instructed to run regularly. These efforts to turn Langkawi into one of Malaysia's big tourism moneyspinners are bearing fruit as the island is attracting increasing numbers of visitors. The promotion campaign and improved transport links to the mainland means the islands can no longer be touted as 'Malaysia's best kept secret'. New hotels, shopping centres and restaurants have sprouted with typical Southeast Asian speed and, for some former visitors at least, the Langkawi of old is just a memory. But development has been concentrated in a handful of places,

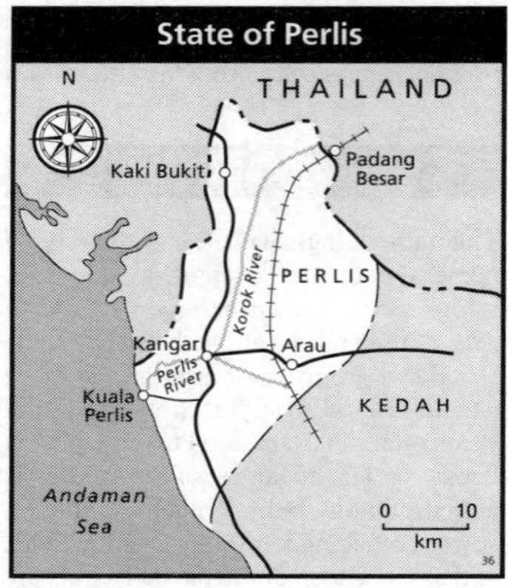

so much of the island remains relatively unspoilt. Budget accommodation is still available and the construction of up-market hotels and resorts means that a broader spectrum of tourists is being attracted. Nearby islands are just starting to develop.

Every so often, Langkawi's beautiful beaches are threatened by oil spills in the nearby Strait of Melaka. Langkawi had a close call in January 1993 when the *Maersk Navigator*, a Danish-owned supertanker carrying 2 million barrels of crude oil to Japan, was in collision with another vessel. One of its tanks was ruptured, the ship burst into flames and oil began gushing into the sea just north of Sumatra. The slick fortunately drifted off into the Indian Ocean where it was broken down with chemical dispersants. But Malaysia's environment minister, Law Hieng Ding predicted that unless there was more rigid policing of the busy waterway, and adequate pollution-prevention measures were enforced, it would only be a matter of time before Malaysia was struck by a pollution disaster.

Kuah, the main town, is strung out along the seafront, and is the landing point for ferries from Satun (Thailand), Kuala Perlis and Kuala Kedah. The town is growing fast and developers have reclaimed land along the shoreline to cope with the expansion. One of the largest developments on the new shores of Kuah is the *Tiara Hotel* with its pink towers and turrets which incorporates a large shopping centre. There is also a new and rather stark park area overlooked by a giant effigy of an eagle on Dataran Lang (Eagle Square), symbol of the island's flight to prosperity. The park area itself, Chogm Park, was built to commemorate the Commonwealth Heads of Government Meeting (CHOGM) in 1989. The old part of Kuah has several restaurants, a few grotty hotels, banks, plenty of coffee shops and a string of duty-free shops, which do a roaring trade in cheap liquor, cigarettes and electronics. There is also an attractive but historically and architecturally unimportant mosque. The town's name 'Gravy' (*Kuah*), is said to derive from a legend about a fight that broke out between two families which fell out over the breaking of a betrothal. Kitchen pots and pans were thrown around and a cooking pot smashed onto *Belanga Pecah* ('broken pot'); its contents splashed all over Kuah. A saucepan of boiling water landed at *Telaga Air Hangat* (the motley hot springs on the north of the island).

It is easy to get round the island at a fairly leisurely pace within a day. The road west to the golf course goes to **Makam Mahsuri**, the tomb of the legendary Princess Mahsuri, in the village of Mawat (12 km from Kuah). The beautiful Mahsuri was condemned to death for alleged adultery in 1355. She protested her innocence and several attempts to execute her failed. According to the legend, the sentence was finally carried out using her own *tombak* (lance) and her severed head bled white blood, thus confirming her innocence. Before Mahsuri died she cursed the island, saying it would remain barren for seven generations. Shortly afterwards, the Thais attacked, killing, plundering, looting and razing all the settlements to the ground. At the time of the Thai attacks, villagers buried their

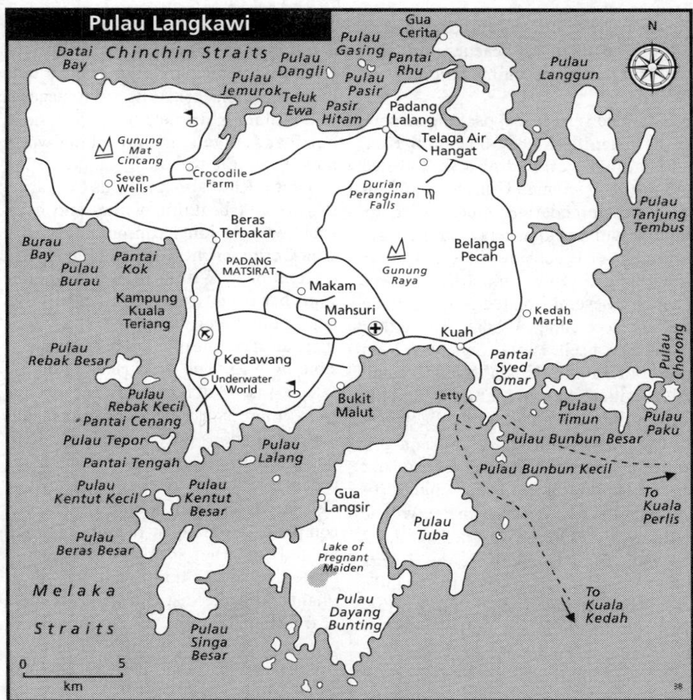

entire rice harvest on Padang Matsirat in Kampung Raja, but the Thais found it and set fire to it too, giving rise to the name Beras Terbakar – the 'field of burnt rice', nearby. The legend is more interesting than the field. The tomb is open 0800-1700, admission RM1.

Southeast of Mahsuri's tomb, past some beautiful paddy fields and coconut groves, are the two main beaches, Pantai Cenang and Pantai Tengah. **Pantai Cenang** is a strip about 2 km long, with budget and mid-range chalet operations, most of which have only a limited length of beachfront, and a few upmarket places. At low tide between November and January a sandbar appears, and it is possible to walk across to the nearby **Pulau Rebak Kecil**. It is also possible to hire boats to the other islands off Pantai Cenang from the beach. Pantai Cenang also has a range of watersport facilities on offer and boasts the *Langkawi Underwater World*, one of the largest aquariums in Asia. It comprises over 100 tanks with over 5,000 types of marine life. The highlight of the aquarium is the 15m long walk-through tunnel tank, open 1000-1930 daily, admission RM10 (RM6 for children), T 9556100. Most of the new beach chalet development is along the 3 km stretch of coast from Pantai Cenang to **Pantai Tengah**, which is at the far southern end, around a small promontory. Pantai Tengah is less developed and quieter than Pantai Cenang. The beaches can get crowded at weekends and during school and public holidays. Pantai Cenang, with the *Pelangi Beach Resort* at the top end, is still one of the nicest beaches on the island and there is accommodation to suit all budgets.

The road west leads, past the airport, to the magnificent bay of **Pantai Kok**, with its dramatic backdrop of the forested and poetically named Gunung Mat Cincang. Accommodation is cheaper here, popular with backpackers, and there are a number of beachside cafés as well as some larger, more up-market resorts. There are several isolated beaches along the bay, accessible by boat from either Pantai Kok itself, Pantai Cenang (12 km away) or Kampung Kuala Teriang, a small fishing village en route. This bay and the surrounding area will sadly be transformed in the next few years, as a golf course is planned and much of the land around Pantai Kok has been bought up – no doubt the backpackers' chalets will be bulldozed too. On the west headland, a 2 km walk from Pantai Kok, the **Telaga Tujuh** waterfalls used to be the island's so-called 'most wonderful natural attraction'. It can no longer claim to be that, as the area has been bought by *Berjaya Leisure Berhad*, 'mother' of *the Berjaya Hotels Group*. A pipeline running next to the pools, and the waterfall, goes all the way to *the Berjaya Beach & Spa Resort* on nearby Burau Bay, so water no longer cascades down a steep hillside, between huge rocks and through a series of seven (*tujuh*) pools (*telaga*); so much for development.

Right on the northwest tip of Langkawi is **Datai Bay**, which has a beautifully landscaped golf course and one of the most sophisticated resorts in Malaysia. Guests also enjoy exclusive access to one of the island's best beaches. It is accessible via a new road, which cuts up through the hills to the coast from the Pantai Kok-Pasir Hitam road. There is a **Crocodile Farm** just beyond the junction, housing more than 1,000 crocodiles. Admission RM6 (RM4 for children), open 0900-1800. There are daily shows at 1115 and 1445, T 9552559. **Pasir Hitam** is at the centre of the north coast, past the Kedah Cement Plant (the island's only industrial monster). As its name suggests, Pasir Hitam is streaked with black sand; but that is about the only thing worth noting about it.

Pantai Rhu (also known as Casuarina Beach) is a beautiful white-sand cove, enclosed by a jungled promontory with **Gua Cerita**, or the 'Cave of Legends', at the end of it. Within the cave, Koranic verse has been written on the walls. Beneath the sheer limestone cliff faces, there are a couple of small beaches accessible by boat. The Thai island Koh Turatao is just 4 km north. Past the *Mutiara Hotel*, there is a collection of foodstalls and small shops next to the beach. It is possible to hire boats and canoes from the beach, which is backed by a small lagoon. **Telaga Air Hangat** is another recently completed tourist attraction, centred around some hot springs. Activities include displays of traditional crafts, elephant and snake 'displays', performances of traditional dance, an 18m long hand-carved river stone mural etc. There is a restaurant and a shop here. Open 1000-1800. Admission RM4, T 9591357. At the ninth milestone, a 3 km-long path branches off to the **Durian Perangin** waterfall, on the slopes of Gunung Raya which rises to 911m.

EXCURSIONS TO NEIGHBOURING ISLANDS

Pulau Dayang Bunting or 'Island of the Pregnant Maiden', is the second largest island in the archipelago, and lies just south of Langkawi. Separated from the sea by only a few metres of limestone, is a freshwater lake renowned for its powers to enhance the fertility of women; unfortunately it is also said to be inhabited by a big white crocodile – although there are no recent reports of white croc attacks and most people swim there unmolested. The myth surrounding this lake involves a beautiful girl named Telani, who became pregnant by the king's son. This indiscretion so angered the god Sang Kelembai that he brought a drought upon the land and turned the new-born baby into a white crocodile. Telani was turned into a rock and the king's son was transformed into an island. To the north of the lake, is the intriguingly named **Gua Langsir** – the 'Cave of the Banshee'. The cave is high on a limestone cliff and is home to a large population of bats. Other nearby islands include **Pulau Bunbun**, **Pulau Beras Besar** and **Pulau Singa Besar** – there is some coral between the last two. Pulau Singa Besar is now a wildlife sanctuary, with about 90 resident bird species, wild boar and a huge population of mouse deer. A network of paths and trails will be built around the island. *Getting there*: boat trips are organized to Pulau Dayang Bunting by many of the larger hotels and travel agents; or boats can be chartered privately from Pantai Cenang. Most trips also include a chance to snorkle off Pantai Singa Besar. Note that visibility is poor between July and September and the sea can be rough.

Pulau Paya, a tiny island (2 km long and 0.25 km wide) about an hour southeast of Langkawi, is part of a marine park (the other islands are **Segantan**, **Kala** and **Lembu**). Just to the south of Payar there is a good coral reef – reckoned to be the best off Malaysia's west coast. A reef platform has been built with an underwater observation chamber and diving facilities (tank and weights RM50, full diving gear RM70, introductory dive RM100), bar and restaurant, souvenir shop. There are basic facilities on the island for day visitors, but those intending to camp on the island require the permission of the Fisheries Management and Protection Office, Wisma Tani, Jalan Mahameru, KL, T 2982011 or Wisma Persekutuan, Jalan Kampung Baru, Alor Star, T 725573. *Getting there*: trips to the islands can be arranged through many of the hotels or tour companies listed below. Several hotels and companies run day-trips to Pulau Payar for RM130-200/head. These islands are also within reach of Kuala Kedah, on the mainland.

Best time to visit The wet season on Langkawi usually spans the months between April to October. Water clarity is poor between July and September – the months of the monsoon – and the sea can be rough.

LOCAL INFORMATION

● Accommodation

Prices: L over RM500; **A+** RM260-500; **A** RM130-260; **B** RM65-130; **C** RM40-65; **D** RM20-40; **E** RM10-20; **F** Below RM10

Langkawi is no longer a haven for backpackers. Even budget accommodation is at the top end of the budget bracket. There are numerous mid- and upper-range places to stay, although people who have sampled accommodation elsewhere in Malaysia claim that prices are high. The island is particularly popular during the months Nov to Feb, and during school holidays. Outside these periods, room rates are often cut.

Kuah: most of the hotels in Kuah itself tend to be rather seedy and poor value for money. Tourists are advised to head straight for the beach resorts. **A+** *City Bayview*, Jln Pandak Mayah, T 9661818, new block dominating Kuah village, 280 rooms with 4-star facilities. **A** *Grand Continental*, Lot 398, Mk Kuah, T 9660333, F 9660288, a/c, TV, in-house movies, tea/coffee-making facilities, restaurant, pool, gymnasium and health club. **A** *Sri Legenda Garden Resort*, Jln Penarak, T 9668919, F 9668980, 250 1 or 2-bedroom suites with kitchenette, dining/living area, balcony, a/c, TV, cassette player, restaurant, pool, children's pool, gym, sauna, tennis, bicycle and car hire, tour arrangements. **A-B** *Hotel Central*, 33 Jln Persiaran Putera, T 9668585, over 100 rooms, a/c, comfortable, discounts sometimes available. **A-B** *Tiara Langkawi*, Pusat Dagangan Kelana Mas, T 9662566, F 9662600, brand new waterfront hotel, 200 well furbished rooms, French-style architecture – reputedly modelled on a castle. **B-C** *Captain Resort*, Lot 82, Jln Penarak, T 9667100, fan, a/c, restaurant, comfortable enough. **B-D** *Malaysia*, 30 Pusat Mas, T 9666298/9668087, a/c, attached bathrooms, basic but good value for money, dorm beds available. **C** *Asia*, 1 Jln Persiaran Putra, T 9666216, a/c, reasonable place with attached bathrooms, 15 minutes walk from

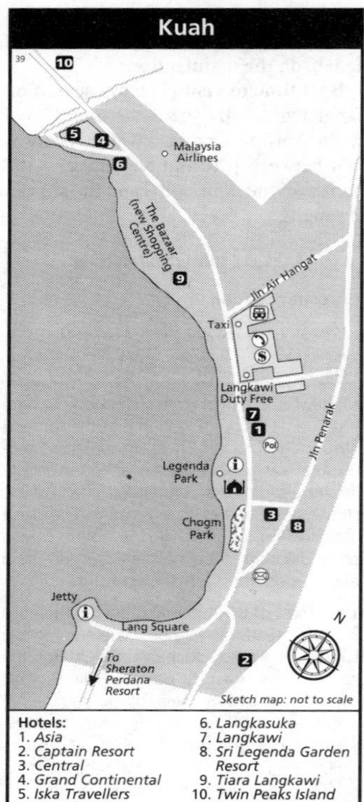

the jetty. **C-D** *Langkawi*, 6-8 Jln Persiaran, T 9666248, some a/c, bathroom outside, basic place, small and airless fan rooms, a/c with attached facilities. **C** *Sri Pulau Motel*, 42c Jln Penarak, T 9667185; **D** *Gaya*, between Kuah and the jetty, T 9667704, fan only, family run, basic but well kept. **D** *Island Motel*, 18 Dundong, T 9667143, a/c and fan, small rooms, bathroom outside (see Tours), hires cars and motorcycles. **D-E** *Iska Travellers Guesthouse*, 47 Taman Sri Pelang, T 9668879, clean and friendly, free transport from ferry, motorbike rental, travel information.

Outside Kuah: **L** *Sheraton Perdana*, Jln Pantai Dato' Syed Omar, T 9666209/9662020, F 9666414, a/c, restaurant, pool, formerly the *Langkawi Island Resort*, has its own private beach with watersports facilities, and all the comforts you would expect of a *Sheraton*. **A+** *Langkasuka Resort*, south of Kuah, T 9556888, F 9555888, a/c, restaurants, attractive pool, over 200 rooms, attractive resort on the beach, watersports. **A** *Beringin Beach Resort*, round the corner from the *Sheraton Perdana*, T 9666966, F 9667770, a/c, restaurant, own private beach, recommended. **A** *Sheraton*, Teluk Nibong, T 9551901, F 9551918, pool overlooking the islands, restaurants, children's centre, health club, watersports activities, rooms arranged in individual Malay-style chalets serviced by resort bus. **A** *Twin Peaks Island Resort*, Jln Kelibang, T 9668255, F 9667458, new wooden chalets surrounding shadeless pool, children's playground, island tours. **B-E** *Langkawi Chalet*, 1 Kampung Penarak, T 9667993.

Pantai Cenang: the most popular of the 3 main beaches, with plenty of hotels and chalets to choose from; some are cramped a little too closely together. Despite the development, it is a picturesque beach. On Pulau Rebak Besar (dubbed Fantasy Island), opposite Pantai Cenang, there is a new resort with 150 chalets, and berthing docks for 200 leisure boats. **A+** *Pelangi Beach Resort*, T 9551001, F 9551122, a/c, restaurant, pool, chalet-styled 5-star resort – guests and their baggage are whisked around in electric cars, holiday camp atmosphere, with daily activities, dirty beach. **A-B** *Semarak Langkawi Beach Resort*, T 9551377, a/c (not always working), good restaurant, simple but attractive rooms and bungalows. **B** *Beach Garden Resort*, T 9551363, F 9551221, a/c, restaurant, pool, apart from the *Pelangi* this is the nicest hotel along this stretch, with thatched roofs, a tiny swimming pool and a wonderful restaurant on the beach, recommended. **B-D** *Sandy Beach*, T 9551308, a/c and fan, restaurant, simple A-frame chalets with more upmarket a/c rooms, good restaurant and friendly staff but now a little run down. **D-E** *Suria Beach Motel*, T 9551776, you get what you pay for.

Pantai Tengah: next beach adjoining Pantai Cenang but not as nice. **A** *Langkawi Holiday Villa*, T 9551701, F 9551504, over 250 rooms, 2 pools, squash, tennis, restaurants and all the amenities you would expect of a first class resort. **B-C** *Sunset Beach Resort*, T 9551751/9552285, a/c, restaurant, some time-share apartments and 24 rooms, good restaurant and bar, recommended. **C-D** *Charlie's*, T 9551200, a/c and fan, restaurant, chalets, at the end of Pantai Tengah, so has a more private stretch of beach, one of the more established places here and often booked up, only 15 rooms, recommended. **C-D** *Delta Motel*,

T 9551891, restaurant, right on the end of the beach, well positioned chalets. **C-D** *Green Hill Beach Motel*, T 9551935, fan, restaurant. **C-D** *Tanjung Mali Beach Resort*, T 9551891, a/c, restaurant, pretty standard but organizes vacuum-packed island tours by what its brochure calls 'hoover craft'.

Pantai Datai: **L** *The Datai*, T 9592500, F 9592600, 2 pools, health club, 40 individual 'villas' each with private sun-bathing terrace, spacious marble bathroom, a/c, bar, minimalist decor offset by Jim Thompson silks from Bangkok, connected by walkways set in 400 ha of primary jungle where hornbills and flying squirrels remain undisturbed, and a further 60 rooms, designed with panache, large rooms with sitting areas and cool wooden floors, own balcony with jungle (and some sea) views, private beach, fine white sand, a wealth of watersports, *Beach Restaurant* serves top quality buffet in the evening, idyllic setting under atap-roofed structure, supported on trunks of original trees that were cleared to make way for resort, *Pavilion Restaurant* on stilts amongst treetops serves Thai food, *Dining Room*, a/c serves Malay and Western food, 18 hole golf course adjacent, attractive, very luxurious resort, recommended.

Pantai Kok: smaller, but more secluded beach and the most popular place for those on a lower budget to stay. **A+** *Berjaya Langkawi Beach Resort*, Burau Bay, T 9591888, F 9591886, Malaysian-style chalets spread over 70 acres of tropical rainforest, some on stilts over water, some on jungled hillside, all serviced by minibuses, each chalet has a/c, TV, CNN, in-house movies, minibar, balcony, massage shower and is very comfortably furbished with oriental carpets and classical furniture, excellent facilities include pool, jacuzzi, Japanese, tennis, watersports, daily organized activities, white sand beach, beach restaurant, Chinese restaurant (a/c) and good value buffet served in Dayang café, inside vast main lobby overlooking sea, surprisingly this 400-room resort manages to feel friendly and not impersonal, moderate value, recommended. **A+-A** *De Lima Resort*, Kuala Muda, T 9551801, F 9551802, restaurants, pool, large hawker centre, shopping mall, 1,200 rooms in chalet-style accommodation. **A** *Burau Bay*, Jln Teluk Burau, T 9591061, F 9551172, a/c, restaurant, at the far end of Pantai Kok, with Gunung Mat Cincang behind it, away from other chalets, twinned with *Pelangi* (but much more attractive), so offers same facilities, excellent value for money, quieter, cleaner beach, recommended. **A** *Mahsuri Beach Resort*, Bukit Tekoh, Jln Pantai Kok, Km 6, T 9552977. **C-D** *Country Beach Motel*, T 9551212, a/c and fan, restaurant, chalets, friendly, boats, bicycles and motorbikes for hire. **C-D** *Dayang Beach Resort*, T 9551058, fan, restaurant. **C-D** *Idaman Bay Resort*, T 9551066/9551212, a/c and fan, restaurant, more upmarket than some of the others along this stretch but set back from the beach with chalets arranged around a pond. **C-D** *Last Resort*, T 9551046, some a/c, good restaurant, name refers to its location rather than its accommodation, the more expensive chalets right on the beach are a good bet, well run by an English-Malay couple, popular, recommended. **C-D** *Mila Beach Motel*, T 9551049, fan, restaurant, 9 nice chalets, manager arranges fishing trips, recommended. **C-D** *Pantai Kok Motel*, T 9551048, some a/c, restaurant, wide range of accommodation at different prices, top end not bad but cheaper rooms are shabby. **D** *Tropica Beach Motel*, T 9551049/9552312, fan, restaurant, on the other side of the road from the beach but the rooms are good value. **C-E** *Memories Chalet*, T 9551118, a/c or fan chalets plus some cheap dormitory accommodation.

Pantai Rhu: the bay has a great view of Thailand's Koh Turatao and other islands. Only 2 hotels and not as popular as the other beaches. **L** *Radisson Tanjung Rhu Resort*, Mukim Air Hangat, T 9591033, F 9591899, exquisitely laid out resort of only 100 rooms with understated decor, beautifully presented, dining on the beach, luxurious facilities, a honeymooners' paradise. **A** *Mutiara Beach Hotel*, T 9556488, a/c, restaurant, pool, smaller of the two hotels here.

● Places to eat

Prices: ♦♦♦♦ over RM40; ♦♦♦ RM13-40; ♦♦ RM5-13; ♦ under RM5

Mee Gulong is Langkawi's speciality: fried noodles cooked with shredded prawns, slices of beef, chicken, carrots, cauliflower are rolled into a pancake, served with a thick potato gravy. Langkawi is also known for its Thai cuisine. Being close to the Thai border, Thai influences even creep into the Malay dishes with the use of hot and spicy ingredients. Thai-styled seafood is also fairly commonplace. Virtually all of the beach hotels have their own restaurants, some of which are excellent; seafood is an obvious choice on Langkawi.

Kuah: there are several Chinese seafood restaurants along the main street in Kuah, all quite good and reasonable value for money. ♦♦*Fortuna*, Dekan Kuah, recommended by locals.

♦♦*Golden Dream Café*, Jln Persiaran Putra (near *Asia Hotel*), good seafood. ♦♦*Orchid*, 3 Dundong Kuah, Chinese. ♦♦*Naga Emas Restaurant*, 31 Pusat Bandar, Jln Pandak Mayah, Thai seafood and steamboat. ♦♦*Noble House*, Lot 23 & 24 Pusat Mas, popular with Thai seafood. ♦♦*Sangkar Ikan*, Jln Pantai Penarak, seafood restaurant and fish farm where you can hire rods (RM4) and catch fish for your own dinner. ♦♦*Sari Seafood*, Kompleks Pasar Lama, built out on stilts over the sea – which is now being reclaimed, vast selection of seafood.

Foodstalls: roadside foodstalls in Kuah, down from *Langkasuka Hotel*, recommended. There is also a collection of stalls behind Langkawi Duty Free.

Pantai Cenang and Pantai Tengah: Of particular note among hotel restaurants are the ♦♦♦♦*Pelangi Beach Resort's* 2 first class international restaurants and the ♦♦♦*Beach Garden Restaurant* next door, which offers a good international selection, beautifully prepared. The latter is right on the beach and is highly recommended. Both are on Pantai Cenang. ♦♦♦*Bon Ton*, a seafront bungalow, near the *Pelangi Beach Resort*, Nyonya and western cuisine, different menus for lunch, afternoon tea and dinner, good homemade cakes and ice cream at tea time, Bali prawns and Nyonya noodles at lunch and Nyonya chicken pie at dinner, good value.

Pantai Datai: ♦♦♦♦*Pavillion*, *The Datai*, Datai Bay, stunning setting on a high terrace in jungle tree tops, top class Thai chefs, papaya salad, excellent seafood. ♦♦♦♦*The Dining Room*, *The Datai*, Datai Bay, quintessentially tasteful in the style of the resort, overlooking turquoise pool and spot lit jungle, French chef combines Malay and western cuisine, interesting menu.

Pantai Kok: ♦♦♦♦*Oriental Pearl*, *Berjaya Langkawi Beach Resort*, Buran Bay, upmarket Chinese restaurant, simple a/c restaurant with ocean views, steamboat recommended.

Elsewhere: ♦♦♦*Barn Thai*, Kampung Belanga Pecah, Mukim Kisap, T 9666699, 9 km from Kuah on road to Padang Lalang, unique restaurant set in Mangrove swamp, reached by 450m wooden walkway, fine wooden building blends with natural surroundings, excellent Thai food, jazz music.

● Airline offices

MAS, Bangunan Tabung Haji, Lot 1598, Mukim Kuah, T 9666622; **Silk Air**, c/o MAS, T 9666622, F9667535.

● Banks & money changers

Maybank and **United Malayan Banking Corporation** are just off the main street in Kuah in the modern shophouse block. Note that banks are open all day Mon-Thur and Sun, but only in the morning on Fri and Sat. Several money changers along the main street, mainly in textile shops. There is also a money changer at Pantai Cenang (across the road from *Sandy Beach* and 100m north), open all day Mon-Thur, Sat and Sun, 1500-2100.

● Entertainment

Nightlife in Langkawi is mainly centred in the larger hotels which offer bars, discos, karaoke and live music. Otherwise there are a few discos including ***Top Ten***, in Kuah, ***Beach Disco***, Kelibang, and ***Dallas***, Jln Penarak, outside Kuah.

● Post & telecommunications

Area code: 04.

General Post Office: at the jetty end of the main street in Kuah.

● Shopping

Duty free shops line the main street in Kuah, alcohol is especially good value. There is a duty free shopping complex at the jetty. The only shop selling alcohol here, ***Sime Duty Free***, is on the 1st flr. Although Langkawi enjoys duty free status there is not much reason to come here for the shopping. At least on a cursory appraisal, the range seems to be limited and the prices hardly bargain basement.

Fishing tackle: shop opposite the *Langasuka Hotel* in Kuah.

Handicrafts: many small shops in Kuah selling textiles. The best-stocked handicraft shop is in front of the *Sari Restaurant* in Kuah, ***Batik Jawa Store***, 58 Pekan Pokok Asam.

● Sports

Golf: ***Langkawi Golf Club***, Jln Bukit Malut. ***Datai Bay Golf Club***, Teluk Datai, T 9592700, F 9592216, green fees RM140, 18-hole course, magnificent fairways, sea-views.

Watersports: the big resorts and hotels all offer watersports facilities. ***Langkawi Marine Sports*** in the centre of Pantai Cenang.

● Tour companies & travel agents

Organized tours around Langkawi and neighbouring islands can be booked through the larger hotels like the *Pelangi Beach Resort* and *Sheraton Perdana*. ***Sala Travel and Tours***, 2 Pokok Asam, Kuah, T 789521 also run tours around the island RM15 (9-12 in minibus) (and to offshore islands). ***Langkawi Coral*** operate a regular Catamaran trip from Kuah (dep 1030) to Pulau Payar (dep 1530). The journey takes 45 minutes and the package costs RM180 adult, RM120 child, T 9667318, F 9667308; ***Indra Travel & Tours***, T 9553791, organize island tours, car/motorbike hire; ***Le Bumbon Island Resort***, T 3332797, organize a variety of tours including island hopping (3 days, 2 nights, RM258, day trip RM35). Many hotels run boat trips and fishing trips round the islands. ***Island Motel***, 18 Dundong, Kuah, T 9667143, arranges snorkelling, fishing and island tours. ***Sheraton Perdana*** runs fishing trips (RM39-180, depending on duration) and diving trips to Pulau Payar (RM220).

● Tourist offices

Langkawi Tourist Information Centre, Jln Pesiaran Putra, Kuah, T 9667789, F 9667889. There is also an information booth at the jetty. Office and booth are open: 0900-1300, 1400-1800, daily.

● Transport

112 km north of Penang, 30 km from Kuala Perlis.

Local Bicycle hire: on the main beaches, RM10-15/day. **Boats**: it is well worth hiring a boat if you can get a large group of people together, otherwise it tends to be expensive – approximately RM150/day. Many of the beach hotels run boat trips to the islands as well as one or two places in Kuah (see Tour companies & travel agents above). Trips to Fantasy Island (opposite Pantai Cenang) leave from the beach next to *Pelangi Resort* (signposted from the road). *Langkawi Marine Sports* in the middle of Pantai Cenang organizes island trips. **Bus**: irregular and undependable and to get to the beaches you often have to walk quite a way from the bus stop, 0700-1815. Kuah to Pantai Cenang every hour 0700-1800, Kuah to Pantai Kok and Burau Bay, every 2 hours from 0800-1630, Kuah to Padang Lalang and Teluk Ewa, every hour, from 0700-1815. **Car hire**: **Mayflower Acme**, *Pelangi Beach Resort*, Pantai Cenang, T 911001; **Tomo Express**, 14 Jln Pandak Maya 4, Pekan Kuah, T 9669252; *Langkawi Island Resort* (see above) and *Island Motel* in Kuah (also see above). Expect to pay about RM80/day. **Motorcycle hire**: motorbikes, usually Honda 70s, are reasonably cheap to hire (RM35/day) and are far-and-away the best way to scoot around the island. Rental shops in Kuah and on all the main beaches. Kuah: *Island Motel*, 18 Dundong, T 9669143. Pantai Cenang: **MBO**, opposite Semarak Langkawi. Pantai Tengah: **ASK**, opposite *Green Hill Beach Motel*. Pantai Kok: *Mila Beach Motel*, T 9551049. *Tropica Beach Motel*, T 9551049. **Taxi**: fares around the island are very reasonable eg jetty-Kuah RM4, Kuah-Pantai Cenang RM12, jetty to Datai Bay RM25-30, the problem is getting hold of one – especially at the jetty.

Air The international airport is the other side of Pantai Cenang, about 30 km from Kuah. *Transport to town*: a taxi to Kuah is RM12 and around RM10 to Pantai Kok. Prices are fixed – coupons on sale in the airport building. Daily connections with Johor Bahru, Kota Kinabalu, KL, Kuching, and Penang on MAS. Silk Air also fly from Singapore. The runway is currently being extended to cater for 747s in the future.

Train (and boat) Take a train to Alor Star (see page 512 for timetable), from there a bus to Kuala Perlis and then the boat to Langkawi.

Road (and boat) It is a 7-8 hour drive or journey from KL to Kuala Perlis; from there catch the boat to Langkawi (see below).

Sea Boat: from Kuah jetty. Timetables subject to seasonal change (fewer boats during the monsoon months, Apr-Sep); ***Lada Ferry Service***, Kuah jetty, T 9667618; ***Kuala Perlis-Langkawi Ferry Service***, Kuah jetty, T 9666950. Regular connections with Kuala Perlis every hour from 0600-1800, 45 minutes. From Kuala Kedah there are boats every 90 minutes or so, 0800-1830, 1 hour. Cheaper for the slow boats. The Kuala Perlis-Langkawi Ferry Service operates daily boats to Penang, leaving at 1800, 2½-3 hours. From Penang, the boat leaves at 0800.

● International connections

Air MAS and Silk Air operate daily connections with Singapore and there are various other irregular international connections. Germany's LTU International Airways now operates a direct, 14-hours, once-a-week (Thur) flight from Munich.

Boat Regular express boat connections with Pak Bara (port 8 km from Satun, Thailand); departures 0830, 1200, 1500 Mon-Sun. Boats leave Satun at 0900, 1300 and 1600. Private yachts also make the journey during the high season; ask at The Last Resort on Pantai Kok for details.

Southern Peninsular Malaysia

Horizons	214	Melaka	220
Seremban	216	Johor Bahru (JB)	241
Port Dickson	218		

THE DRIVE south from Kuala Lumpur through Seremban to Melaka runs on the first-to-be-completed stretch of the much-vaunted north-south Highway and is an easy, pleasant drive through rubber and oil palm plantations, formerly owned by big British companies. Like the route north from KL, the towns are predominantly Chinese, while the rural kampongs are almost exclusively Malay. Negri Sembilan, a confederacy of nine small states united under the British colonial administration as part of the Federated Malay States, is renowned for its Minangkabau-style architecture. This is characterized by buffalo-horn shaped roof peaks, reflecting the influence of the state's first inhabitants who came from Sumatra.

On the coast, southwest of Seremban, off the main highway, is the seaside resort town of **Port Dickson** (PD), which serves as a popular weekend retreat from Kuala Lumpur. The drive southeast from PD to Melaka (Malacca) is much more interesting along the coastal backroads which run through open countryside and Malay kampongs. **Melaka** is one of the Malaysian tourism industry's trump cards, thanks to its Portuguese, Dutch and British colonial history, its rich Peranakan (Straits Chinese) cultural heritage and its picturesque hinterland of rural Malay kampongs. The route south from Melaka

Brand-name Satay from the source

Kajang, about 20 km south of KL on the Seremban road, is named after the palm-leaf canopy of a bullock cart, once ubiquitous and still occasionally seen in Negri Sembilan. At hawker centres all over Malaysia, there are stalls called 'Satay Kajang': the town long ago gained the reputation for the best satay in the country. There are many satay stalls in Kajang today. *Selamat makan!*

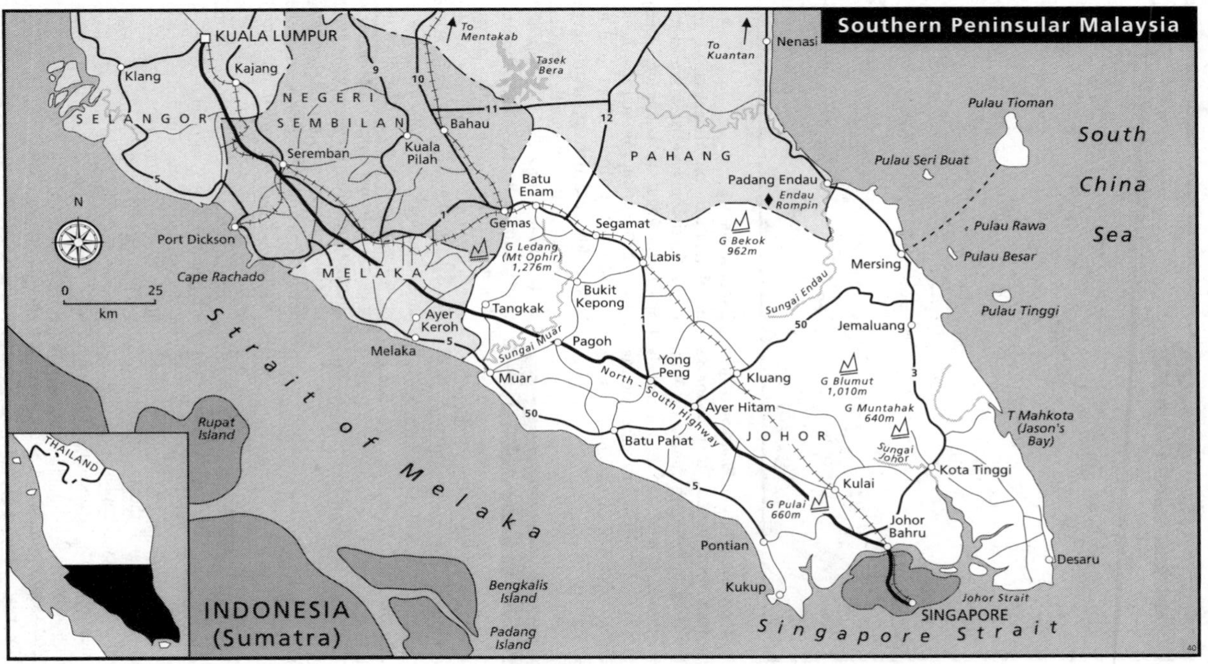
Southern Peninsular Malaysia
South China Sea
Strait of Melaka
Singapore Strait
Johor Strait
SINGAPORE
INDONESIA (Sumatra)
KUALA LUMPUR
Klang
Kajang
Seremban
Port Dickson
Cape Rachado
Kuala Pilah
Bahau
Gemas
Batu Enam
Segamat
Labis
Bukit Kepong
Tangkak
Pagoh
Muar
Sungai Muar
Ayer Keroh
Melaka
Yong Peng
Batu Pahat
Ayer Hitam
Kluang
Pontian
Kukup
Kulai
Johor Bahru
Kota Tinggi
Desaru
Jemaluang
Mersing
Padang Endau
Endau Rompin
Sungai Endau
Nenasi
To Kuantan
To Mentakab
Tasek Bera
SELANGOR
NEGERI SEMBILAN
MELAKA
PAHANG
JOHOR
G Ledang (Mt Ophir) 1,276m
G Bekok 962m
G Blumut 1,010m
G Muntahak 640m
G Pulai 660m
Sungai Johor
North - South Highway
T Mahkota (Jason's Bay)
Pulau Tioman
Pulau Seri Buat
Pulau Rawa
Pulau Besar
Pulau Tinggi
Rupat Island
Bengkalis Island
Padang Island
THAILAND
N
0 25 km

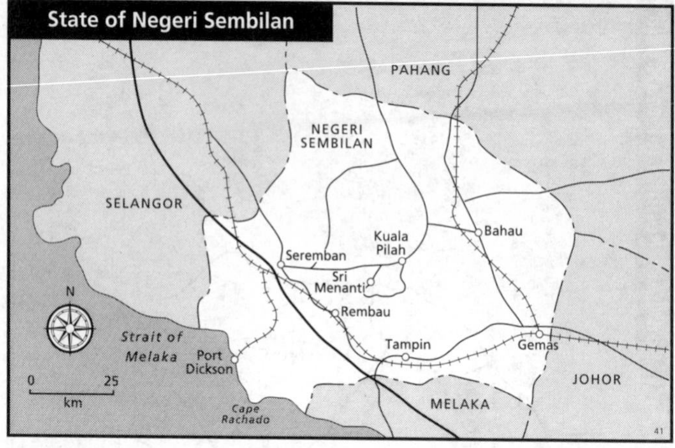

is a pleasant but unremarkable drive through plantation country to **Johor Bahru** (JB), on the southernmost tip of the peninsula. It is a short hop across the causeway from JB to Singapore, and Malaysia's east coast islands and resorts are within easy reach.

SEREMBAN

In 1924 it was shipped to England and exhibited as an example of Malay architecture. On its return it was reassembled near the Lake Gardens in Seremban before being moved to Taman Seni Budaya. The **State Museum** is also part of the complex and is itself a good example of Minangkabau architecture; it is a reconstructed 19th century palace (Istana Ampang Tinggi), a high stilt building with an atap roof. The museum houses a small collection of ceremonial weapons and tableaux depicting a royal wedding and some photographs and other memorabilia from the Emergency. Complex open 1000-1800 Tuesday and Wednesday, 0815-1300 Thursday, 1000-1215, 1445-1800 Friday, 1000-1800 Saturday and Sunday, closed Monday.

Excursions

Sri Menanti, the old Minangkabau capital of Negri Sembilan is 30 km east of Seremban, about 10 km before Kuala Pilah. This area is the Minangkabau heartland. *Sri* is the Minangkabau word for 'ripe paddy', and *Menanti* means 'awaiting' – although it is coloquially translated as 'beautiful resting place'. It was also common for early kings to add the Sanskrit honorific *Sri* to their titles and palaces. The former royal capital is on the upper reaches of Sungai Muar, which meanders through the valley which was known as *Londar Naga* – the tail of the dragon. The **Istana Lama Sri Menanti** is a beautifully carved wooden palace built in Minangkabau style in 1908. It has 99 pillars depicting the 99 warriors of the various *luak-luak* (clans). It was, until 1931, the official residence of the Yang di-Pertuan Besar, the state ruler. On the 4th floor is a display of royal treasures. It is not officially a museum but is open to visitors. Open 1000-1800 Saturday-Wednesday, 0815-1300 Thursday, closed Friday. This royal town also has a large mosque. **Accommodation** Most people come here on a day trip from Seremban, but there is a reasoable resort hotel next to the Istana Lama, the **B** *Sri Menanti*

Minangkabau – the 'buffalo-horn' people from across the water

Negri Sembilan's early inhabitants were immigrants from Minangkabau in Sumatra. They started to settle in the hinterland of Melaka and around Sungai Ujong (modern Seremban) during the 16th and 17th centuries and were skilled irrigated paddy farmers. *Minangkabau* roughly translates as 'buffalo horns' and the traditional houses of rural Negri Sembilan and Melaka have magnificent roofs that sweep up from the centre into two peaks. The Minangkabau architectural style has been the inspiration behind many modern Malaysian buildings, notably the Muzium Negara (National Museum) and the Putra World Trade Centre in Kuala Lumpur.

The Minangkabau introduced Islam, a sophisticated legal system and their matrilineal society to the interior of the Malay peninsula. In 1773 they appealed to the Minangkabau court at Pagar Ruyong in Sumatra to appoint a ruler over them and a Sumatran prince – Raja Melewar – was installed as the first king, or *Yang di-Pertuan Besar* of the confederacy of mini-states, with his capital at Sri Menanti. But Negri Sembilan's four *undang* – territorial chiefs – saw to it that he wielded no real power. In all there were four kings from Sumatra, all of them ineffectual, and the link with Sumatra finally ended in 1824 with the establishment of an indigenous hereditary royal family. The current Sultan of Seremban, educated at Oxford, continues to reside in his palace outside the town.

Resort, T 4976200, with a/c, pool and restaurant and good, well equipped rooms. *Getting there*: United Bus to Kuala Pilah every 15 minutes.

Local information

● Accommodation

Prices: L over RM500; **A+** RM260-500; **A** RM130-260; **B** RM65-130; **C** RM40-65; **D** RM20-40; **E** RM10-20; **F** Below RM10

Seremban has only a handful of hotels, one of which is amongst the best of Malaysia's resort hotels, the ***Allson Klana***. There are 3 mid-range hotels; the rest are basic, Chinese-run establishments which are of an almost uniformly poor quality.

A+ ***Allson Klana Resort***, PT 4388 Jln Penghulu Cantik, Taman Tasik Seremban, T 7629600, F 7639218, once the new KL airport is built at Sepang, the *Allson* will be a good alternative to staying in KL, the airport being only 20 minutes from the new site, set in 18 acres of landscaped gardens the *Allson Klana* is a luxurious and well-established resort hotel, it overlooks one of the largest lagoon shaped pools in Malaysia and has over 200 very comfortable and spacious rooms with a/c, in-house video, shower and bath, mini-bar, other facilities include tennis, health club, sauna, business centre, delicatessen and boutique, outstanding food outlets include *Yuri Japanese Restaurant, Blossom Court Chinese Restaurant* as well as a coffee house.

B ***Tasik***, Jln Tetamu, T 7630994, F 7635355, located next to the Lake Gardens, a/c, TV, shower, restaurant, pool, business centre, seen better days but has a good central position and outlook over the Lake Gardens. **B** ***Carlton Star***, 47 Jln Dato Sheikh Ahmad, T 7625336, F 7620040, good central position, a/c, coffee house, fitness centre, Karaoke lounge, recently refurbished but with a lack of flair and an excess of kitsch. **B** ***Seri Malaysia***, Jln Sungai Ugung, T 7644181, F 7644179, one of the 'ey polivalue for money' chain, good and new but not central.

D ***Happy***, 35 Jln Tunku Hassan, T 7630172, probably the best of the budget places to stay, although that is not saying much, the rooms may be dark but at least they are reasonably clean. **D** ***Golden Hill***, 42 Jln Tuan Sheikh, T 7613760, basic. **D** ***New International***, 126 Jln Tan Sri Manickavasagam, T 7634957, fan only. **D** ***Oriental***, 11 Jln Lemon, T 7630119, restaurant, just about tolerable. **D-E** ***Nam Yong***, 5 Jln Tuanku Munawir, T 7620155, restaurant, grotty hotel, the only plus being the price of the rooms. **D-E** ***Century***, 25-29 Jln Tuanku Munawir, T 7626261.

● Places to eat

Prices: ♦♦♦♦ over RM40; ♦♦♦ RM13-40; ♦♦ RM5-13; ♦ under RM5

Malay: ***Anira***, Kompleks Negeri Sembilan; ***Bilal***, 100 Jln Dato Bandar Tunggal; ***Fatimah***, 419 Jln Tuanku Manawir; ***Flamingo Inn***, 1a Jln Za'aba.

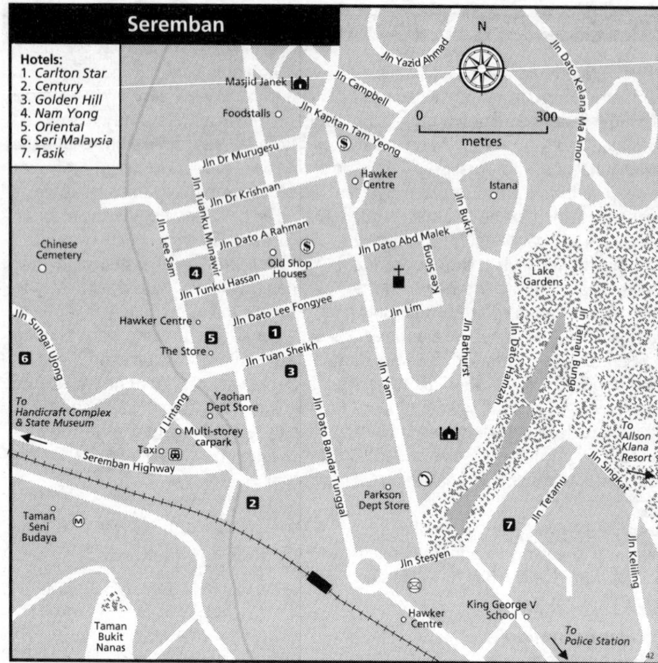

Chinese: ****_**Blossom Court**_, *Allson Klann Resort*, classy Chinese restaurant, expensive-looking decor, popular for extensive range of dimsum, good Peking duck and Cantonese dishes. _**Happy**_, 1 Jln Dato Bandar Tunggal. _**Regent**_, 2391-2 Taman Bukit Labu. _**Seafood**_, 2017-8 Blossom Heights, Jln Tok Ungku; _**Suntori**_, 10-11 Jln Dato Sheikh Ahmad.

Indian: *_**Samy**_, 120 Jln Yam Tuan, banana leaf. _**Anura**_, 97 Jln Tuanku Antah.

Japanese: ****_**Yuri**_, *Allson Klana Resort*, excellent quality, traditional Japanese good, private Tatami rooms, sushi bar, Teppanyaki counter, good value set meals (***).

Foodstalls: _**Jalan Tuanku Antah**_, near the post office; _**Jalan Dr Murugesu**_, opposite Masjid Janek mosque.

● Banks & money changers

Bumiputra, Wisma Dewan Permagaa Melayu; **Maybank**, 10-11 Jln Dato Abdul Rahman; **OCBC**, 63-65 Jln Dato Bandar Tunggal; **Public Bank**, 46 Jln Dato Lee Fong Yee; **Standard & Chartered**, 128 Jln Dato Bandar Tunggal; **UMBC**, 39 Jln Tuanku Munawir.

● Post & telecommunications

Area code: 06.
Post Office: Jln Tuanka Antah.

● Tourist offices

State Economic Planning Unit, 5th Flr Wisma Negeri, T 7622311.

● Transport

62 km south of KL, 83 km north of Melaka.

Train Connections every 2 hours with KL, express service to Singapore, see page 512 for timetable.

Road Bus: new, brightly coloured station on Jln Sungai Ujong. Connections with JB, Melaka, KL, Kota Bharu and Port Dixon. **Taxi**: Port Dickson, KL, Melaka, T 7610764.

PORT DICKSON

Port Dickson – typically shortened to PD – is 32 km from Seremban and is one of the most popular seaside resorts in Malaysia, as testified by all the modern condominium developments. The pace of development

has given the little fishing port a pollution problem in recent years and many people regard the sea as so toxic that it is best not to swim at all. This is a narrow point of the Melaka Strait and large ships use the deep-water channel which cuts close to the Malaysian coast. Rarely a month goes by during which the Malaysian authorities aren't giving chase to tankers which have an increasingly alarming tendency to dump thousands of tonnes of sludge, oil and effluent into the strait. Although for KL's residents it may be a convenient destination for a day trip or weekend, it is, frankly, hard to imagine why those with more time on their hands would wish to come here.

The port town, originally called Tanjung Kamuning, was renamed after Sir Frederick Dickson, British Colonial Secretary and acting Governor in 1890. Port Dickson itself is quiet and undistinguished but to the south is a long sandy beach, stretching 18 km down to the **Cape Rachado** lighthouse, although there are cleaner places to swim in Malaysia. Built by the British on the site of a 16th century Portuguese lighthouse, Cape Rachado has panoramic views along the coast (it is necessary to acquire permission from the Marine Department in Melaka to climb to the top). At **Kota Lukut**, 7 km from Port Dickson, is Raja Jamaat fort, built in 1847 to control the tin trade in the area.

Local information

● Accommodation

Prices: L over RM500; **A+** RM260-500; **A** RM130-260; **B** RM65-130; **C** RM40-65; **D** RM20-40; **E** RM10-20; **F** Below RM10

Because PD is a favourite family getaway for KL's weekenders, beach hotels are often quite full –

and rates are comparatively high. During the week, discounts are sometimes on offer.

A *Bayu Beach Resort*, Batu 4½, Jln Pantai, T 6473703, F 6474362, pool, luxury 300-room beach resort, good watersports facilities, all rooms with a/c, kitchenette, TV, minibar, Chinese restaurant, coffee house, karaoke lounge. **A** *Delta Paradise Lagoon*, 3½ km Jln Pantai, T 6477600, F 6477630, new luxury hotel, the best on the strip, over 200 rooms, all with ocean views, bath, TV, in-house video, mini bar, tea/coffee-making facilities, other amenities include pool, children's playground, tennis, squash, watersports, business centre, coffee house. **A** *Ming Court Beach*, Batu 71/2, Jln Pantai, T 6625244, a/c, restaurant, pool, good range of sports and watersport facilities. **A** *Pantai Dickson Resort*, Batu 12, Jln Pantai, T 405473, a/c, restaurant, pool, beach bungalows. **A** *The Regency*, Batu 5, T 6474090, F 6475016, Minangkabau style architecture, tennis, squash, children's pool, 2 restaurants, business centre. **A** *Tanjung Tuan Beach Resort*, Batu 5, Jln Pantai, T 662013, a/c, restaurant, pool, good sports facilities and weekday discounts. **A-B** *Golden Resort*, Batu 10 Jln Pantai, T 6625176, a/c, restaurant, pool.

B *Seri Malaysia*, Batu 4 Jln Pantai, T 6476070, F 6476028, one of newer additions to this budget chain of hotels, good views across beach and good value, recommended. **B** *Si Rusa Beach Resort*, Batu 7, Jln Pantai, T 6625233, a/c, restaurant, one of the more established places to stay with a good position right on the beach, competition from newer hotels means room rates are competitive. **B** *Travers Pantai Motel*, Batu 9, quiet location facing the sea, charges include breakfast, clean and fairly new.

C *Beach Point Motel*, Batu 9, Jln Pantai, T 6625889, located down a track off main road, a/c, shower, basic but spotlessly clean. **C** *Kong Meng*, Batu 8, Teluk Kemang, T 6625683, restaurant, on the beachfront, reasonable for the price. **C** *Lido*, Batu 8, Jln Pantai, T 662273, restaurant, quiet location, set in large grounds. **C-D** *Merlin*, 218-9 Jln Pantai, T 6623388, restaurant, a/c, shower, run-down. **C-D** *New Hai Tian*, Batu 1, Jln Pantai.

D *Sea View*, Batu 1, Jln Pantai, T 6621811, restaurant.

E *Happy City*, Jln Pasar, T 6623103, a/c or fan, shower, basic. **E-F** *Port Dickson Youth Hostel*, Km 6 Jln Pantai, T 6472188, YHA card holders only (although some non-members seem to land a room), separate dorm for men and women, dining/cooking area, large compound, camping facilities.

● Places to eat

Prices: ♦♦♦♦ over RM40; ♦♦♦ RM13-40; ♦♦ RM5-13; ♦ under RM5

Malay: ♦♦*Santan Berlada*, Batu 1, Jln Pantai.

Chinese: ♦♦*Pantai Ria*, Batu 7½, Jln Pantai, seafood.

Seafood: ♦♦♦*Blue Lagoon*, Cape Rachado (on the way to the lighthouse). ♦♦*Haw Wah Seafood*, Teluk Kamang, simple but clean coffee shop at end of row of modern shophouses on main road, good seafood. ♦♦*Kemang Seafood*, Batu 7, Malay seafood, crab sold by weight (1 kg RM25).

Western: *Kentucky Fried Chicken*, PD centre.

Foodstalls: scattered around town and along Jln Pantai.

● Banks & money changers

Bumiputra, 745 Jln Bharu; **Public**, 866 Jln Pantai; **Standard Chartered**, 61 Jln Bharu.

● Hospitals & medical services

Hospitals: on the waterfront by the bus station, Jln Pantai.

● Post & telecommunications

Area code: 06.

General Post Office: opposite bus station in PD.

● Transport

94 km from KL, 32 km from Seremban, 90 km from Melaka.

Road Bus: station on Jln Pantai, just outside the main centre but buses will normally stop on request anywhere along the beach. Regular connections with KL (RM5) and Melaka. **Taxi**: T 7610764, shared taxis to Melaka, KL and Seremban.

MELAKA (MALACCA)

Thanks to its strategic location on the strait which bears its name, Melaka was a rich, cosmopolitan port city long before it fell victim to successive colonial invasions. Its wealth and influence are now a thing of the past, and the old city's colourful history is itself a major money-spinner for Malaysia's modern tourism industry.

The city was founded by Parameswara, a fugitive prince from Palembang in Sumatra. According to the 16th century *Sejara Melayu* (the Malay Annals), he was a descendent of the royal house of Srivijaya, whose lineage could be traced back to Alexander the Great. Historians, however, suspect that he was really a Javanese refugee who, during the 1390s, invaded and took Temasek (Singapore) before he himself was ousted by the invading Siamese. He fled up the west coast of the peninsula and, with a few followers, settled in a fishing kampung.

The Malay Annals relate how Parameswara was out hunting one day, and while resting in the shade of a tree watched a tiny mouse deer turn and kick one of his hunting dogs and drive it into the sea. He liked its style and named his nearby settlement after the *malaka* tree he was sitting under. Sadly it seems more likely that the name Melaka is derived from the Arabic word *malakat* – or market – and from its earliest days the settlement, with its sheltered harbour, was an entrepôt. Melaka was sheltered from the monsoons by the island of Sumatra, and perfectly located for merchants to take advantage of the trade winds. Because the Strait's deep-water channel lay close to the Malayan coast, Melaka had command over shipping passing through it.

In 1405 a Chinese Muslim Admiral, the eunuch Cheng Ho, arrived in Melaka

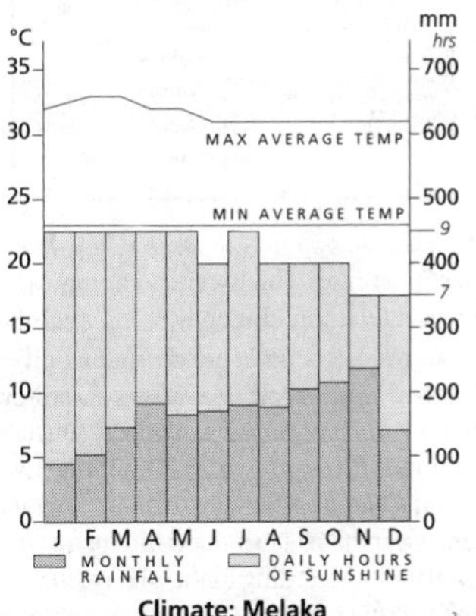

Climate: Melaka

bearing gifts from the Ming Emperor (including a yellow parasol, which has been the emblem of Malay royalty ever since) and the promise of protection from the Siamese. Cheng Ho (Zheng Ho) made seven voyages to the Indian Ocean over the next 3 decades and used Melaka as his supply base. The Chinese gained a vassal state and Melaka gained a sense of security: Parameswara was wary of possible Siamese encroachment. Court rituals, ceremony and etiquette were formalized and an exclusive royal court language evolved. In 1411, 3 years before his death, Parameswara sailed with Cheng Ho to China with a large retinue and was received by the third Ming Emperor, Chu Ti. Melaka's next two rulers continued this tradition, making at least two visits each to China.

But China began to withdraw its patronage in the 1430s, and to make sure Melaka retained at least one powerful friend, the third ruler, Sri Maharaja, married the daughter of the sultan of the flourishing maritime state of Samudra-Pasai in Sumatra. Historian Mary Turnbull says "he embraced Islam and hitched Melaka's fortunes to the rising star of the Muslim trading fraternity". He adopted the name Mohamed Shah, but retained the court's long-standing Hindu rituals and ceremonies. He died without a child from his marriage to the Pasai princess and a succession crisis followed. The rightful royal heir, the

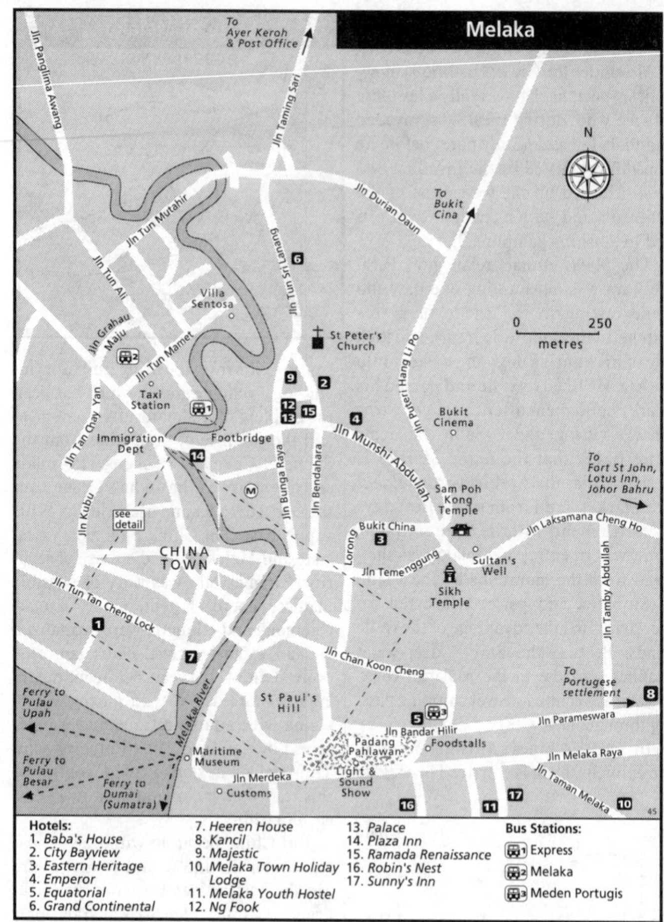

young Rajah Ibrahim was murdered in a palace coup after a year on the throne and Kasim, one of Mohamed's sons by a non-royal marriage declared himself Sultan Muzaffar Shah. Melaka's first proper sultan made Islam the state religion and beat off two Siamese invasions during his reign. Islam was also spreading through the merchant community. In the latter half of the 15th century the faith was taken from Melaka to other states on the peninsula as well as to Brunei and Javanese port cities which were breaking away from the Hindu kingdom of Majapahit.

In the late 15th century, Malay power reached its pinnacle. Muzaffar's successor, Sultan Mansur Shah, extended Melaka's sway over Pahang, Johor and Perak, the Riau archipelago and Sumatra. Contemporary European maps label the entire peninsula 'Malacca'. According to the Malay Annals, the sultan married a Chinese princess in

1460. This marriage and the arrival of the princess and her followers marked the formal beginning of the unique and prosperous Straits Chinese *Peranakan* culture (see page 230).

Another cultural blend that had its roots in medieval Melaka was the Chitty Indian community, the result of Indian merchants inter-marrying with local women, including the Malay nobility. Because foreign traders had to wait several months before the winds changed to allow them to return home, many put down roots and Melaka, 'the city where the winds met', had hundreds of permanent foreign residents. There were no taboos concerning cross-cultural marriage: the polygamous Muslim Sultan Mansur Shah even visited the crumbling Majapahit court in East Java where he cemented relations by his second royal marriage, to the Hindu ruler's daughter.

By the beginning of the 16th century Melaka was the most important port in the region. Foreign merchants traded in Indian and Persian textiles, spices from the Moluccas (Maluku), silk and porcelain from China as well as gold, pepper, camphor, sandalwood and tin. The Malay language became the *lingua franca* throughout the region.

Tales of luxuriance and prosperity attracted the Portuguese. They came in search of trading opportunities and with the aim of breaking the Arab merchants' stranglehold on trade between Europe and Asia. Spices from the Moluccas came through the Strait and whoever controlled the waterway determined the price of cloves in Europe. The Portuguese – known to Melakans as 'the white Bengalis' – combined their quest for riches with a fervent anti-Muslim crusade, spurred by their hatred of their former Moorish overlords on the Iberian peninsula. They arrived in 1509, received a royal welcome and then fled for their lives when Gujerati (Indian) traders turned the Sultan against them. Alfonso d'Albuquerque, the viceroy of Portuguese India, returned 2 years later with 18 ships and 1,400 men. After an initial attempt at reconciliation, he too was beaten off. D'Albuquerque then stormed and conquered the city in July 1511, the year after he seized Goa on India's west coast. The Melakan court fled to Johor where Sultan Ahmad re-established his kingdom.

The Chinese admiral Cheng Ho (Zheng Ho) from an early European print.

The foreign merchants quickly adapted to the new rulers and under the Portuguese the city continued to thrive. Tomé Pires, a Portuguese apothecary who arrived with d'Albuquerque's fleet and stayed 2 years, wrote in his account, *Suma Oriental*: "Whoever is lord of Melaka has his hand on the throat of Venice," adding that "the trade and commerce between different nations for a thousand leagues on every hand must come to Melaka". The port became known as the 'Babylon of the Orient'. Despite the 2-years sojourn of French Jesuit priest St Francis Xavier, Christianity had little impact on the Muslim Malays or the hedonistic merchant community. A large Eurasian population grew up, adding to Melaka's cosmopolitan character; there are still many Pereiras, D'Cruzes, de Silvas, da Costas, Martinezes and Fernandezes in the Melaka phone book.

Back in Lisbon in the early 17th century, the Portuguese monarchy was on the decline, the government in serious debt and successive expeditions failed to acquire anything more than a tenuous hold over the Spice Islands, to the east. The Portuguese never managed to subdue the Sumatran pirates, the real rulers of the Strait of Melaka. As Dutch influence increased in Indonesia, Batavia (Jakarta) developed as the principal port of the region and Melaka declined. The Dutch entered an alliance with the Sultanate of Johor and foreign traders began to move there. This paved the way for a Dutch blockade of Melaka and in 1641, after a 6 months seige of the city, Dutch forces, together with troops from Johor, forced the surrender of the last Portuguese governor.

The Flor de la Mar: sunken treasure beyond measure

From the early years of the first millennium, Chinese junks were plying the *Nanyang* – or the South Seas – and by the 1400s a sophisticated trade network had built up, linking Asia to India, the Middle East and Europe. For three centuries, Melaka was at the fulcrum of the China trade route and even before the Europeans arrived, hundreds of merchants came each year from Arabia, Persia, India, China, Champa, Cambodia, Siam, Java, Sumatra and the eastern Isles. By the early 1500s, more than 100 large ships were anchoring at Melaka every year. It was known as the emporium of the east.

But this trade was not without its casualties and the sunken wrecks littering the coastal waters of the South China Sea and the Strait of Melaka have today given rise to a new, highly profitable industry: treasure hunting. Divers, in league with marine archaeologists and maritime historians, have flocked to the region in recent years. The most publicised find was the 1987 salvage of a cargo of Chinese porcelain from a vessel which sank off the Riau Islands in 1752; the booty was auctioned by Christie's in Amsterdam 2 years later for US$16 million. But treasure hunting carries with it political sensitivities over the ownership of wrecks. Salvage operators have been jailed in Indonesia and salvaged antiquities have been confiscated in Thailand.

But the ultimate sunken treasure trove lies in what remains of the wreck of the *Flor de la Mar*, at the bottom of the Strait of Melaka. The Portuguese vessel, commanded by Admiral Alfonso d'Albuquerque, is thought to be the richest ship ever lost. Having left Lisbon in 1503, Albuquerque plundered his way from Mozambique, the Red Sea and India to the coastal regions of Burma and Thailand. By July 1511, when he anchored off Melaka he had amassed untold riches. After capturing the city, he plundered it.

In his book *The Search for Sunken Treasure*, the treasure hunter Robert F Marx writes: "The spoils the Portuguese took from Malacca stagger the imagination." They included more than 60 tonnes of gold booty in the form of solid gold statues of elephants, tigers, birds and monkeys, all studded with gemstones. There was gilded furniture, gold ingots, gold coins, gold-plated royal litters, chests full of diamonds, rubies and sapphires and several tonnes of Chinese and Arabic coins. And this was just the loot from Sultan Ahmad's palace. Most of it", writes Marx, was loaded onto the *Flor de la Mar* where "it took up so much space that the crew had trouble stowing additional gem-filled chests". In London, Sotheby's auction house tentatively valued the treasure at US$9bn, making it by far the world's richest wreck. Albuquerque stole so much gold that Melaka was left without any coinage. Tin coins were minted instead, for the first time.

Over the next 150 years the Dutch carried out an extensive building programme; some of these still stand in Dutch Square. Melaka was the collecting point for Dutch produce from Sumatra and the Malay peninsula, where the new administration attempted to enforce a monopoly on the tin trade. They built forts on Pulau Pangkor and at Kuala Selangor, north of Klang, to block Acehnese efforts to muscle in on the trade, but the Dutch, like the Portuguese before them, were more interested in trade than territory. Apart from their buildings, the Dutch impact on Melaka was minimal. Their tenure of the town was periodically threatened by the rise of the Bugis, Minangkabaus and Makassarese who migrated to the Malay peninsula having been displaced by the activities of the

Two days after setting off for Portugal, his fleet of four ships ran into a storm at the northeastern tip of Sumatra. Two ships went down, then the *Flor de la Mar* itself hit a reef. Albuquerque survived the shipwreck and managed to salvage a gold sword, a jewel-encrusted crown, a ruby bracelet and a ring which today are on display in a Lisbon museum. The rest was lost in 37m of water. The admiral returned to Portugal on his one remaining ship. With his pilot, who also survived, he drew up a chart indicating where the ship went down – 8 km off Tanjung Jambu Air in Aceh.

It lay there, forgotten, for nearly 500 years. In 1988 an Italian specialist in underwater wrecks and an Australian marine historian claimed to have located the *Flor de la Mar*, hidden under several metres of mud, using satellite imaging. The Indonesian government – in whose territorial waters the wreck lay – then awarded a salvage contract to PT Jayatama Istikacipta, a company linked to the family of President Suharto, which sub-contracted the diving operation to an Australian, arrested in Indonesia the previous year for illegal treasure-hunting. He hired former divers from the British Navy's Special Boat Squadron to join the search. In 1989 they found a couple of wrecked Chinese junks but no *Flor de la Mar* and, in frustration, the operation was called off.

The same year, the Indonesians granted a search permit to a Singapore salvage firm. After a year's fruitless exploration, they hired Robert Marx, who, with the aid of a facsimile of Albuquerque's chart, located the reef which the ship had struck. Numerous artifacts were recovered, but, he writes, "a thorough sonar and magnetometer survey revealed that the main section of the wreck lies in an area the size of five football fields at a depth of 37m under 15m of concrete-like mud."

The discovery sparked a political row. Malaysia and Portugal contested Indonesia's claim to the booty and the matter was passed to the International Court in The Hague for adjudication. Meanwhile, an endless stream of conspiracy stories – none of them confirmed – surrounds the fate of the *Flor de la Mar*. In 1991, it was reported that "powerful interests linked to President Suharto" had harrassed other treasure-hunters researching the location of the wreck and had privately tried to force them to help mount a covert salvage operation. In late-1991, following further reports that Indonesian Navy divers had tried again, Jakarta and Kuala Lumpur reportedly entered a joint-venture agreement. Under it, Malaysia agreed to bear the entire cost of the operation and split the booty 50/50. If any salvage work is currently going on, it is being kept very quiet. There are constant rumours about secret salvage operations circulating among Singapore's commercial diving community, but the matter is so sensitive and the stakes potentially so high that lips are firmly sealed.

Melaka in 1679, from *Borts voyage*.
The buildings are labelled: 1. St Paul's Church; 2. Governor's house; 3. Misericordia bastion; 4. City gates; 5. Middleburgh vantage point; 6. Frederick Hendrick bastion.

Dutch East India Company in Sulawesi and Sumatra. In 1784 Melaka was only saved from a joint Bugis and Minangkabau invasion by the arrival of the Dutch fleet from Europe.

By the late 18th century, the Dutch hold on the China trade route was bothering the English East India Company. In 1795 France conquered the Netherlands and the British made an agreement with the exiled Dutch government allowing them to become the caretaker of Dutch colonies. 4 years later the Dutch East India Company went bankrupt, but just to make sure that they would not be tempted to make a comeback in Melaka, the British started to demolish the fortress in 1807. The timely arrival of Stamford Raffles, the founder of modern Singapore, prevented the destruction from going further, and in 1824, under the Treaty of London, Melaka was surrendered to the British in exchange for the Sumatran port of Bencoolen (Bengkulu).

In 1826 Melaka became a part of the British Straits Settlements, along with Penang and Singapore. But by then, its harbour had silted up and it was a town of little commercial importance. In 1826 it had a population of 31,000 and was the biggest of the settlements; by 1860, although its population had doubled, it was the smallest and least significant of the three. In 1866, a correspondent for the *Illustrated London News* described Melaka (which the British spelled *Malacca*) as "a land where it is 'always afternoon' – hot still, dreamy. Existence stagnates. Trade pursues its operations invisibly ... It has no politics, little crime, rarely gets even two lines in an English newspaper and does nothing towards making contemporary history". In 1867 the Straits Settlements were transferred to direct colonial rule and Melaka faded into obscurity. Strangely, it was the town's infertile agricultural hinterland which helped re-envigorate the local economy at the turn of the century. The first rubber estate in Malaya was started by Melakan planter Tan Chay Yan, who accepted some seedlings from 'Mad' Henry Ridley, director of Singapore's Botanic Gardens (see page 660) and planted out 1,200 hectares in 1896. The idea caught on among other Chinese and European planters and Melaka soon became one of the country's leading rubber producers.

Places of interest

Arriving in Melaka by road, it is not immediately apparent that the city is Malaysia's historical treasure-trove. Jalan Munshi Abdullah, which runs through the middle of the more recent commercial district, is like any Malaysian main street. The taxi station and express bus terminal are away from the central core of old Melaka, and while the old city is quite compact, the town itself is neither as small or medieval-looking as visitors are led to suppose. The historical sights from the Portuguese and Dutch periods are interesting because they are in Malaysia – not because they are stunning architectural wonders. That said, the old red Dutch buildings on the east bank of the river and the magnificent Peranakan architecture and stuccoed shophouses on the west side, lend Melaka an atmosphere unlike any other Malaysian town. It also lays claim to many of the country's oldest Buddhist and Hindu temples, mosques and churches.

Exploring historical Melaka NB It is possible to walk around Melaka's historical sights. There is now an interesting 'trail' – called the **Jerak Warisan Heritage Trail**, which starts at the Tourist Office (details available here); by following this trail the visitor gets to see all the major cultural sights of interest. The route crosses the bridge, to the Baba Nyonya Heritage Museum, takes in all the temples on Jonkers Street and then back across the bridge to Stadthuys, St Paul's Church, St Paul's Hill and the Porta de Santiago Independence Monument. For a 'handout' on the trail, ask at the Tourist Office (see map). A more leisurely way to get around is by trishaw. There are also many places around town which rent bicycles.

The most interesting parts of the old town are close to the waterfront. There are boat tours (see below) down the river through the original port area and past some of the old Dutch houses. On the west bank is **Kampung Morten**, a village of traditional Melakan houses. It was named after a man who built Melaka's wet market and donated the land to the Malays. The main attraction here is Kassim Mahmood's hand-crafted house.

The Dutch colonial architecture in the **town square** is the most striking feature of the riverfront. The buildings are painted a bright terracotta red and are characterized by their massive walls, chunky doors with wrought iron hinges and louvred windows. The most prominent of these is the imposing **Stadthuys**. Completed in 1660, it is said to be the oldest-surviving Dutch building in the East, and served as the official residence of the Dutch governors. The recently renovated building now houses a good **history museum** detailing in maps, prints and photographs the history and development of Malacca/Melaka. Also here are a cultural museum and a literature museum which are of less obvious interest to the average visitor. Admission RM2. Open 0900-1800 Saturday-Thursday 0900-1215, 1445-1800 Friday. Just southwest from Stadthuys, on the river is a half-size replica of the galley that the viceroy of Portuguese India arrived in. The **Tang Beng Swee Clock Tower** looks Dutch but was built by a wealthy Straits Chinese family in 1886. **Christ Church** was built between 1741 and 1753 to replace an earlier Portuguese church, which was by then a ruin (church records date back to 1641). Its red bricks were shipped out from Zeeland in Holland. It is Malaysia's oldest Protestant church and the floor is still studded with Dutch tombstones. The original pews are intact – as are its ceiling beams, each hewn from a single tree trunk more than 15m long. On the altar there is a collection of sacramental silverware bearing the Dutch coat-of-arms. Open Thursday-Tuesday.

On Jalan Kota, which runs in a curve round **St Paul's Hill** from the square, is the **Porta de Santiago**, the remains of the great Portuguese fort **A Famosa**, said to have been built in 4 months flat under Admiral Alfonso d'Albequerque's supervision in 1511. What remains is largely a Dutch reconstruction, the result of repair work carried out following the siege in 1641 – it prominently displays the Dutch East India Company's coat-of-arms. The fort originally sprawled across the whole hill and housed the entire Portuguese administration, including their hospitals and five churches. It was flattened by the British between 1806 and 1808 when they occupied Melaka during the Napoleonic Wars. They wanted to ensure that the fort was not reclaimed by the Dutch. Stamford Raffles arrived for a holiday in Melaka just in time to forestall the destruction of its last remaining edifice.

From behind the gate, a path leads up to the ruins of **St Paul's Church**, built on the site of the last Melakan sultan's istana. The small chapel was originally built by the Portuguese in 1521 and called *Nossa Senhora da Annunciada* – Our Lady of the Anunciation. The body of St Francis Xavier (the 16th century Jesuit missionary who translated the catechism into Malay and visited the church regularly), was temporarily interred in the church vault following his death off the coast of China in 1552. His remains were later sent to Portuguese Goa on the west coast of India. An armless marble statue, erected in 1953, now commemorates Malaysia's best known missionary. The Portuguese added gun turrets and a tower to the church and it became a fortress between 1567 and 1596. During the Dutch seige of Melaka in 1641, it was badly damaged but the invaders repaired it and renamed it St Paul's. It became a Protestant church and remained so until Christ Church was completed in 1753. St Paul's

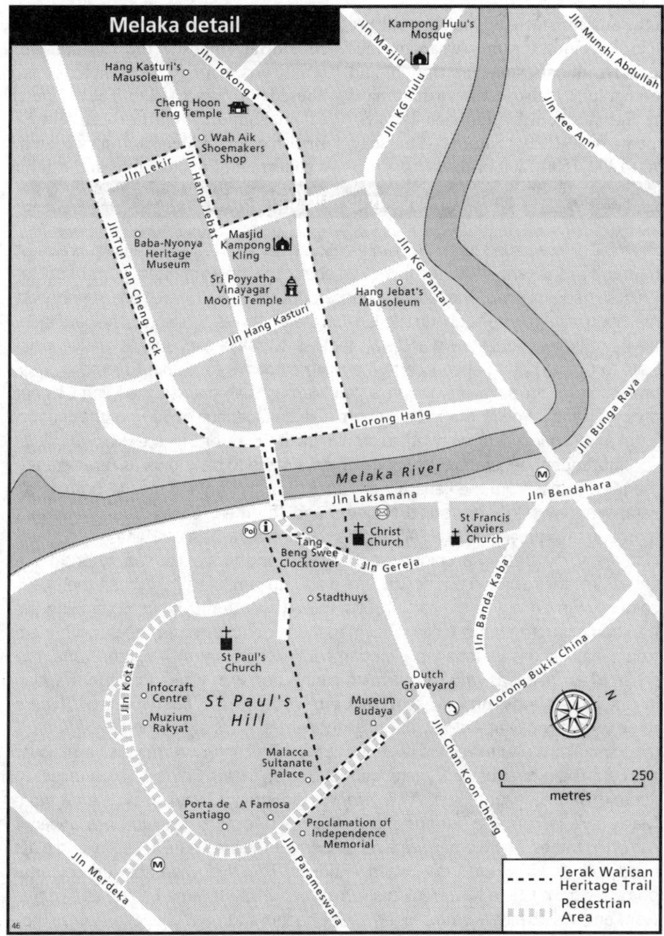

ended its life as a cemetery; it was used as a special burial ground for Dutch nobles, whose tombs line the walls.

A wooden replica of Sultan Mansur Shah's 15th century istana now houses the **Muzium Budaya** (Melaka Cultural Museum) below St Paul's. The palace has been painstakingly reconstructed from a description in the 16th century *Serjarah Melayu* (Malay Annals) and built in 1985 using traditional construction techniques and materials. Mansur – who came to the throne in 1459 – inherited what was reputed to be the finest royal palace in the world, with a roof of copper and zinc in seven tiers, supported by wooden carved pillars. According to the Annals, his magnificent istana was destroyed by fire after being struck by lightning the year after his accession. Exhibits in the museum focus on Melakan culture including clothes, games, weapons, musical instruments, stone inscriptions and photographs. It also features a diorama of the Sultan's court. Admission RM1.50. Open 0900-1800 Saturday-Thursday, 0900-1200, 1500-1800 Friday.

The **Proclamation of Independence Memorial**, opposite the Cultural Museum, was built in 1912 and formerly housed the Malacca Club. The old Dutch colonial building was the social centre of British colonial Melaka. It now contains a collection of photographs and exhibits

The Nyonyas and the Babas

Chinese traders in the *Nanyang*, or South Seas, visited Melaka from its earliest days and by the early 1400s the town was one of the most important ports of call for Chinese trade missions. They arrived between November and March on the northeast monsoon winds and left again in late June on the southwest monsoon. This gave them plenty of time to settle down and start families. Melaka's early sultans made several visits to China, paying obeisance to the Ming emperors to ensure Chinese imperial protection for the sultanate. When Sultan Mansur Shah married the Ming Chinese princess Hang Li Poh in 1460, she brought with her a retinue of 500 'youths of noble birth' and handmaidens who settled around Bukit Cina – or Chinese Hill.

Subsequent generations of Straits Chinese came to be known as *Peranakans* – the term comes from the Bahasa word *anak*, or offspring and means 'born here'. Peranakan women were called Nyonyas and the men, Babas. Sultan Mansur's marriage set a precedent and Peranakans combined the best of Chinese and Malay cultures. They created a unique, sophisticated and influential society and were known for their shrewd business acumen and opulent lifestyles. When the Dutch colonists moved out in the early 1800s, more Chinese moved in, continuing the tradition of intermarriage while clinging to the ancient customs brought with them from China. Jonas Vaughan, a Victorian colonial administrator wrote: "One may see in Malacca Babas who can claim no connection with China for centuries, clad in long jackets, loose drawers, and black skull caps, the very conterparts of Chinese to be seen any day at Amoy, Chusan, or under the walls of Nanking."

Peranakan culture reached its zenith in the 19th century. Although Melaka was the Peranakan hearthstone, there were also large Straits Chinese communities in Penang and Singapore too. The Nyonyas adopted Malay dress – they wore Malay-style jackets and sarongs and were known for their fastidiousness when it came to clothes. The women were renowned for their intricate jewellery and glass beadwork – which are now prized antiques. The Nyonyas imported colourful porcelain from China for ceremonial occasions which became known as Nyonya-ware and was typically emblazoned with phoenix and peony-flower motifs. They also imported craftsmen from China to make their intricate silver jewellery including elaborate belts, hairpins, and pillow end plates.

Peranakan weddings were elaborate affairs; couples were paired off by marriage-brokers, contracted by the groom's parents to consult horoscopes and judge the suitability of the match. If a match proved auspicious, there was a lengthy present-exchanging ritual for the young couple who were not permitted to see each other until they finally got to the nuptial chamber. Wedding rituals often went on for 12 days and ended in a lavish feast before the couple went upstairs and the heavily veiled bride first showed her face to her new husband. As was the custom, he would then say: "Lady, I have perforce to be rude with you", whether he liked what he saw or not, for the marriage had to be consummated immediately.

depicting the run-up to Malaysian independence in 1957. Open 0900-1800 Tuesday-Thursday, Saturday and Sunday, 0900-1200 Friday, closed Monday.

A concrete bridge from the south end of Dutch Square leads to **Chinatown**, the old trading section of Melaka. **Jalan Hang Jebat**, formerly known as **Jonkers Street**, is famous for its antique shops: Nyonya porcelain, Melakan-style 'red and gold' carved furniture, wooden opium beds, Victorian mirrors, antique fans and Peranakan blackwood furniture inlaid with mother-of-pearl. There are

Peranakan architecture is exemplified in the 'Chinese Palladian' townhouses – the best examples of which are in Melaka – with their open courtyards and lavish interiors, dominated by heavy dark furniture, inlaid with marble and mother-of-pearl. Aside from their magnificent homes, one of the Peranakans' most enduring endowments is their cuisine, which is the result of the melding of cultures. The food is spicy but uses lots of coconut milk and is painstakingly prepared – one reason that Nyonya-Baba restaurants are difficult business propositions. Traditionally, would-be brides would have to impress their future mother-in-laws with their kitchen-competence, particularly in their fine-slicing of ingredients. Typical meals, served with rice and *sambal* (crushed chilli fried in oil), include *otak-otak* and *ayam pongteh* and deserts such as iced *chendol*, and *gula melaka* (for details on particular dishes, see page 740).

The cliquey Peranakan upper-class assimilated easily into British colonial society, following the formation of the Straits Settlements in 1826. The billiard-playing, brandy-swilling Babas, in their Mandarin dresses, conical hats, pigtails and thick-soled shoes successfully penetrated the commercial sector and entered public office. Many became professionals: lawyers, doctors and teachers, although they were barred from entering government above the clerical level. "Strange to say," wrote Vaughan, "that although the Babas adhere so loyally to the customs of their progenitors they despise the real Chinamen and are exclusive fellows indeed; [there is] nothing they rejoice in more than being British subjects... They have social clubs of their own to which they will admit no native of China." In Penang they were dubbed 'the Queen's Chinese'. Over the years they evolved their own Malay patois, and, in the 19th century, English was also thrown into their linguistic cocktail. They even devised a secret form of slang by speaking Baba Malay backwards.

Although they chose not to mix with immigrant Chinese, they retained a strong interest in events in China. The Straits Settlements provided a refuge for exiled reformers from the motherland – most notably Dr Sun Yat-sen, who lived in both Singapore and Penang in the early 1900s and became the first president of the Republic of China in 1911.

The Baba community's most famous son was Tan Cheng Lock, who was born into a distinguished Melakan Baba family in 1883. He lent his name to the Peranakans' architectural treasure, Jalan Tun Tan Chen Lock (formerly Heeren Street) in Melaka's Chinatown. Tan served in local government in colonial Melaka from 1912-1935 and vociferously fought British discrimination against the Straits and Malayan Chinese. He charged that the British had done nothing to "foster and strengthen their spirit of patriotism and natural love for the country of their birth and adoption". Tan was the spokesman for Malaya's Chinese community and fought for equality among the races; he founded the Overseas Chinese Association and became a prominent reformist politician in the years leading up to Malaysian independence.

some good examples of Peranakan architecture along the street – notably the renowned Jonkers Melaka Restoran. But none of these Peranakan houses compare with the picturesque **Jalan Tun Tan Cheng Lock**. Named after a leading Melakan Baba, instrumental in pre-independence politics (see box, page 230), it is lined with the Straits Chinese community's ancestral homes and is Melaka's 'Millionaires Row'. Many of the houses have intricately carved doors that were often specially built by immigrant craftsmen from China. Today tour buses exacerbate the local traffic problem which clogs the narrow one-way street, but many of its Peranakan mansions are still lived in by the same families that built them in the 19th century.

One of the most opulent of these houses has been converted into the **Baba-Nyonya Heritage Museum**, 48-50 Jalan Tun Tan Cheng Lock. It is in a well preserved traditional Peranakan town house, built in 1896 by millionaire rubber planter Chan Cheng Siew. Today it is owned by William Chan and his family, who conduct tours of their ancestral home. The interior is that of a typical 19th century residence and all the rooms left as they would have been 100 years ago. The house contains family heirlooms and antiques, including Nyonyaware porcelain and blackwood furniture with marble or mother-of-pearl inlay, and silverware. There is also a collection of traditional wedding costumes, photographs and kitchen utensils. The kitchen sink has the name of William Chan's great grandfather carved on it. The information-packed tours are run regularly throughout the day. Admission RM7. Open 1000-1230, 1400-1630 Saturday-Wednesday, 0900-1200 Thursday.

Wah Aik Shoemaker Shop, 92 Jonkers Street (Jalan Hang Jebat), is Malaysia's most unusual shoe shop. For two generations the Yeo family have been the only cobblers catering for the country's dwindling population of ageing Chinese women with bound feet. The practice, which was considered *de rigeur* for women of noble stock during the Ch'ing Dynasty (1644-1912), was rekindled among the families of nouveau riche Chinese tin towkays during the days of the British Straits Settlements. The process involved binding the feet firmly with bandages before they were fully formed; it was supposed to add to a woman's sensuality, but in reality it just caused a lot of pain. In China, the practice was outlawed in 1912. There are only a handful of women in Malaysia with bound feet, most of them in Melaka and all of them in their 80s or 90s. Mr Yeo Sing Guat makes these *san choon chin lian* (3-inch golden lotus feet) shoes – with brocade on authentic Shanghai Hang Chong silk – for them and as tourist souvenirs; he also makes the Peranakan *kasut manik* 'pearl shoes', sewn with miniature pearl beads.

The **Cheng Hoon Teng Temple**, on Jalan Tokong, was built in 1645 and is the oldest Chinese temple in Malaysia (although there were later additions in 1704 and 1804). The name literally means 'Temple of the Evergreen Clouds' and was founded by Melaka's Kapitan Cina, Lee Wi King from Amoy, a political refugee who fled from China. All the materials used in the original building were imported from China as were the craftsmen who built it in typical South Chinese style. The elaborate tiled roofs are decorated with mythological figures, flowers and birds, and inside there are woodcarvings and lacquer work. The main altar houses an image of Kuan Yin, the Goddess of Mercy (cast in solid bronze and bought from India in the last century), who is associated with peace, good fortune and fertility. On her left sits Ma Cho Po, the guardian of fishermen and on her right, Kuan Ti, the god of war, literature and justice. The halls to the rear of the main temple are dedicated to Confucius and contain ancestral tablets.

Nearby, on Jalan Tukang Emas, is the **Sri Poyyatha Vinayagar Moorthi Temple**, built in 1781 and the oldest Hindu temple in use in Malaysia. It is dedicated to the elephant-headed god Vinayagar (more usually known as Ganesh). Near to this Hindu temple on Jalan Tukang Emas is the **Masjid Kampung Kling**, a mosque built in 1748 in Sumatran style, with a square base surmounted by a 3-tiered roof and pagoda-like minaret. Another 18th century mosque in the same style is the **Masjid Tranquerah**, 2 km out of town on the road to Port Dickson. Next door is an unusual free-standing octagonal minaret with Chinese-style embellishments, in marked contrast to Malaysia's traditional Moorish-style mosques. In the graveyard is the tomb of Sultan Hussein Shah of Johor who, in 1819, signed the cession of Singapore to Stamford Raffles.

St Peter's Church on Jalan Taun Sri Lanang was built in 1710 by descendants of the early Portuguese settlers when the Dutch became more tolerant of different faiths. Iberian design is incorporated in the interior where Corinthian pillars support a curved ceiling above the aisle, similar to churches in Goa and Macau. It is the centre of the Catholic church in Malaysia. Easter candlelit processions to St Peter's seem strangely out of context in Malaysia. Open until 1900 Monday-Sunday.

In 1460 when Sultan Mansur Shah married Li Poh, a Ming princess, she took up residence on Melaka's highest hill, **Bukit Cina**, which became the Chinese quarter. The Malay Annals do not record what became of the Princess's palace but the hill, off Jalan Munshi Abdullah/Jalan Laksamana Cheng Ho, remained in the possession of the Chinese community and because of its good *feng shui* – its harmony with the supernatural forces and the elements – it was made into a graveyard. The cemetery now sprawls across the adjoining hills – Bukit Gedona and Bukit Tempurong – and is the largest traditional Chinese burial ground outside China, containing more than 12,000 graves. Chinese graveyards are often built on hillsides because the hill is said to protect the graves from evil winds; this hill has the added advantage of overlooking water, and the ancestral spirits are said to enjoy the panoramic view over the city and across the Strait of Melaka. Some of the graves date back to the Ming Dynasty but most of these are overgrown or disintegrating.

The hill was ceded in perpetuity to the Chinese by successive colonial governments, but in mid-1991 the city burghers, backed by the Lands and Mining Department, demanded RM10mn in rent arrears, going back 500 years, from the general manager of Cheng Hoon Teng temple, who is responsible for the upkeep of Bukit Cina. Unless the Chinese community paid up in full, the city threatened to repossess the 42 hectares of prime-site real estate it sits on. An impasse ensued which was still unresolved at the time of writing.

At the foot of the hill is an old Chinese temple called **Sam Poh Kong**, built in 1795 and dedicated to the famous Chinese seafarer, Admiral Cheng Ho (see page 221). It was originally built to cater for those whose relatives were buried on Bukit Cina. Next to the temple is the **Sultan's Well** (*Perigi Rajah*), also called the **Hang Li Poh Well**, said to have been sunk in the 15th century. It is believed that drinking from this well ensures a visitor's return to Melaka – but anyone foolhardy to try this today is liable to contract dysentery and instead stay rather longer than they anticipated.

The ruined **Fort St John**, another relic of the Dutch occupation, is to the west of Bukit Cina on Jalan Bendahara (Air Keroh road, off Jalan Munshi Abdullah at *Renaissance Melaka*). Its hilltop location affords some excellent views although its aspect has been spoiled by the water treatment plant and high rise apartment block on either side of it.

The **Portuguese Settlement** (Medan Portugis) at Ujong Pasir, about 3 km from the town centre, is where the descendants of the Portuguese occupiers settled. A

Portuguese community (of sorts) has managed to survive here for nearly 5 centuries; unlike the subsequent Dutch and British colonial regimes, the Portuguese garrison was encouraged to intermarry and generally treat the Malays as social equals. Today these Malaysians of Portuguese descent number around 4,500 (although other estimates are much lower). In the country as a whole, there are thought to be some 20,000. The process of integration was so successful that when the Dutch, after capturing the city in 1641, offered Portuguese settlers a choice between amnesty and deportation to their nearest colony, many chose to stay. In the 1920s, as their distinctive culture was threatened with extinction, the leaders of the community pleaded with the British to allot them a piece of land on which they could settle. A small area of swampland was duly allocated and the neat and well-planned settlement visible today was built, its street named after Portuguese heroes largely unrecognized in Malaysia. The main square, built only in 1985, is a concrete replica of a square in Lisbon – and is visibly ersatz. The descendants of the original settlers still speak a medieval Portuguese dialect called *Cristao* (pronounced 'Cristang'), spoken nowhere else in the world. Today there are just a few tourist-oriented restaurants and shops in the modern Portuguese Square, and cultural shows are staged on Saturday nights (see the Restaurant section below for a listing of recommended places to eat). Other than tourism, the residents of the Portuguese settlement earn their livelihoods by fishing and through a small number of cottage industries including shrimp paste production. The central role that the sea plays in the community's coherence and identity is threatened by a land reclamation project which will cut off its access to the sea. This will destroy the settlement's fishing industry, its fish-based cottage industries and also undermine its attraction to tourists. As Gerard Fernandis remarked in August 1995, "Our history, our culture, songs, dances and food are all linked to the sea", adding that without the sea the "settlement will become an island in a sea of concrete." *Getting there*: bus 17 (RM2). The **Maritime Museum** is housed in a full scale reconstruction of the Portuguese trading vessel Flor de la Mar, on the riverbank, 200m downstream from the River Boat embarkation point. Of all the museums in Melaka, this is one of the better ones – many of the other museums are rather repetitive, but as Melaka's history is the history of sea-trade, this is a more interesting option. It has a collection of models of foreign ships that docked at Melaka during its maritime supremacy from the 14th century to the Portuguese era. The Flor de la Mar itself ended its days on the sea bed just off-shore, laden with treasure that was bound for Portugal (see box on page 224). Admission RM2, open 0900-2100 daily. Open 0900-2100 daily. Entry to the Maritime Museum also gives access to the **Royal Malaysian Navy Museum**, across the road, which displays the salvaged remains of 19th century vessels that have foundered or been sunk in the Melaka Strait as well as more contemporary bits and pieces.

Excursions

Tanjung Kling is about 9 km northwest of Melaka. It is a pleasant drive past beachside kampungs, and Tanjung Kling is a much more relaxing place to stay than in Melaka itself. But because passing tankers have a habit of swilling out their tanks, the sea is muddy and the beach dirty. This does not seem to affect the taste of the seafood and there are several restaurants and hawker stalls along the roadside at **Pantai Kundor**, where there are a number of hotels. Kampung Kling is thought to have got its name from Tamils who originally settled there, having come from Kalingapatam, north of Madras.

• **Accommodation** **L-A+** *Riviera Bay Resort*, 10 km Jalan Tanjung Kling, T 3151111, F 3153333, opened late 1995, classical architecture on a palatial scale, takes the form of a U-shaped building on 14 floors with 450 spacious suites, tastefully decorated in shades of green and all sea-facing, with a/c, TV, in-house movies, tea and coffee-making facilities, mini-bar, other amenities include 3 restaurants under a top Swiss chef, the Bucaneer pub, hair salon, children's playground, watersports, tennis, pool with swim-up bar, paddling pool, recommended. **A** *Mutiara Malacca Beach Resort*, Pantai Kundur, Tanjung Kling, T 3518518, F 3517517, over 218 all-suite units, a/c, TV, mini-bar, kitchenette, spacious but not stylish, 2 restaurants (limited menu), Bubbles Fun Pub, tennis, pool, mountain bikes, watersports, sauna, gymnasium, 20 minutes taxi ride from the centre of Melaka, with views over the Straits and the oil refinery, awful beach and a spartan resort but friendly staff. **A** *Klebang Beach Resort*, 92-1, km 9, Batang Tiga, Tanjung Kling, T 3155888, F 3151713, new, small hotel, clean and comfortable, but unimaginative decor, small free-form pool, paddling pool, children's playground, 2 restaurants. **B** *Shah's Beach Resort*, 9 km, Tanjung Kling, T 3153121, a/c, restaurant, pool, 1950s front with 2 lines of a/c chalets behind, tennis court and pool can be used by non-guests for a fee. **C** *Straits View Lodge*, C-7886, Pantai Kundur, Batu 9, Tanjung Kling, T 514627, F 325788, simple chalets, friendly atmosphere, boat, bike and fishing equipment for hire. **B-C** *Motel Tanjung Kling*, 5855C Pantai Pangkalan Perigi, Tanjung Kling, T 515749, a/c, restaurant. **D** *Westernhay*, Batu 4, Klebang Besar (between Tanjung Kling and Melaka), restaurant, an old colonial-style hotel (formerly a British Army kindergarden) with large, airy rooms and a big garden going down to the beach, recommended. **D-E** *Yashika Traveller Hostel*, Batu 8, Pantai Kundor, restaurant, small but clean rooms, right on the beach. **D-F** *Melaka Beach Bungalow & Youth Hostel*, 739C Spring Gardens, just off the road to Pantai Kundor, T 512935, dormitory and rooms in modern suburbia.

• **Places to eat** ♦*Roti John*, Pantai Kundor, on the seafront, Melaka's Roti John specialist. ♦♦*Yashika Traveller Hostel*, Batu 8, Pantai Kundor, beach restaurant, international. *Getting there*: Patt Hup buses 51, 18, 42 and 47 (buses can be caught from Jalan Tengkera (at the north end of Jalan Tun Tan Cheng Lock, in Melaka); taxi.

Tanjung Bidara is further up the road towards Port Dickson, about 20 km northwest of Melaka. It has a long beach and plenty of hawker stalls; the sea is generally rather dirty.

• **Accommodation A+-B** *Tanjung Bidara Beach Resort*, T 542990, a/c, restaurant, pool, upmarket chalet-style. *Getting there*: Patt Hup buses 51, 18, 42 and 47 (buses can be caught from Jalan Tengkera (at the north end of Jalan Tun Tan Cheng Lock, in Melaka); taxi.

Ayer Keroh, 11 km northeast of Melaka, has a lake, jungle, a golf course and a country club and is just off the highway to KL. It is also the site of **Melaka Zoo** (entrance RM3, RM1 for children), **reptile park** (entrance RM3, children RM1) and **Mini-Malaysia Complex**, where the various states of Malaysia are represented by 13 traditional houses containing works of art and culture (similar to the Karyaneka Handicraft Centre in KL) as well as an Orang Asli village. All the houses look remarkably alike, except the Borneo one. It also stages cultural shows. Overstaffed and badly managed. Mini-ASEAN is next door and is more varied (and included in the ticket price). Admission: RM4, children RM2. All the above sights are open 0900-1800, Monday-Sunday. The Ayer Keroh Golf and Country Club is the longest golf course in Malaysia, with green fees at RM70 for weekdays and RM100 for weekends, T 320822, handicap cards must be produced.

• **Accommodation A-B** *Air Keroh Country Resort*, T 2325211, F 2320422, motel-like atmosphere, a/c, restaurant, pool. **A+-A** *Malacca Village Paradise Resort*, T 2323600, F 2325955, formerly the *Park Plaza*, this is a recent addition to the Paradise chain, popular with Singaporeans at we0ekends, but reduced rates often available during week, over 500 rooms in imposing Malaccan-red buildings, 2 swimming pools, 2 tennis courts, gymnasium, 2 squash courts, recreation centre, health club (good value shiatsu massage), beauty salon, jogging track, children's playground and sand pit, 2 restaurants, all rooms with a/c, bath, mini-bar, tea and coffee-making facilities, TV, in-house video, recommended. **Camping**: only at Ayer Keroh Recreational Forest and at Durian Tunggal Recreational Lake (on the way to Selandar). Admission to Mini Malaysia Complex RM2. Open 0900-1800 Mon-Sun. *Getting there*: bus 19 (known as Townbus 19) every 30 minutes.

Pulau Besar, contrary to its name, is a small, quiet island, about 8 km southeast of Melaka, which is popular at weekends. According to local legend, a princess became pregnant to a Melakan commoner and was banished to the island to die. There is a shrine on the island dedicated to an early Muslim missionary, who is said to have come to Melaka in the 1400s. The island has good beaches (although the sea is not clean and most of the coral is dead) and there are jungle walks. The **Radisson Api Api Marina Village Resort** is still under construction, but the Pandanusa Golf Club, an 18-hole international standard course opened recently with adjoining (**A**) hotel.

• **Accommodation A** *Tapa Nyai Resort*, 37 Jalan Chan Koon Cheng, T 456730, F 236739, located on 22 hectares of the 133-hectare island, a/c, restaurant, RM1.2mn pool complex complete with open-air jacuzzi, deluxe beach resort designed to look like a traditional Melakan village. **D** *Suntan/Sundance Resort*, A frames (with toilet and shower), run by a friendly man who serves great food at good prices. Bookable through an agent near the taxi station. *Getting there*: buses 17 and 25 to Umbai. Boats operate from Umbai Jetty, high speed, a/c catamaran, seats 131. Daily departures from Besar at 1000.

Gunung Ledang (1,276m) – or Mount Ophir – on the east side of the north-south Highway, equidistant from Melaka and Muar and just inside Johor state, is one of the peninsula's best known mountains. It is isolated from the mountains of the Main Range and is sacred to the Orang Asli of Melaka. A Straits Chinese and Malay rumour has it that the mountain is the domain of a beautiful fairy endowed with the local version of the Midas Touch: she has a habit of turning Gunung Ledang's plant-life into gold. The mountain is said to be guarded by a sacred tiger which is possessed by the fairy.

Gunung Ledang is a strenuous climb involving some very steep scrambles, particularly towards the top. In 1884 an expedition reached the summit while trying to demarcate the boundary between Johor and Melaka. Most climbers choose to camp overnight on the summit, although, at a push, it can be done in a day – dawn to dusk. The mountain is surrounded by and covered in virgin jungle, and rises through mossy forest (where there are several varieties of pitcher plant, see page 38) to the rocky summit. Climbers are strongly advised to stick closely to the trails: since 1987, two separate parties of Singaporeans have become lost for several days after straying off the trail. The trail is complex in places and the climb should be carefully planned: would-be climbers are strongly recommended to refer to the detailed trail-guide in John Briggs' *Mountains of Malaysia*, which is available in Singapore and KL bookshops. There are two main trails up the mountain; the best route starts 15 km from Tangkak, just beyond Sagil. Waterfalls (*Air Terjun*) are signposted off the road which leads to Air Penas, an over-popular local picnic spot. The trail begins just beyond the rubber factory. Those attempting the climb without a trail-guide can hire a local guide from Tangkak.

Sadly, the Johor state government has announced plans to build a huge resort on the south slopes to include two 300-room hotels, an 18-hole golf course, 300 holiday chalets and a 'village'. It wants the first phase completed by 1997. *Getting there*: take the Tangkak road from Melaka or the old KL-Johor Bahru trunk road from Segamat. There is a metalled road to the radio station on the lower peak, but this is not open to the public beyond the half-way stage.

Tours

Tickets for the river boat can be purchased from the Tourist Office (45 minutes, RM6) to see the old Dutch trading houses; predictably this area is known as Melaka's 'Little Venice', which does not live up to the description. However, guides are very informative, pointing out settlements and wildlife. Good views of the giant lizards on the banks and plenty of rubbish floating downstream.

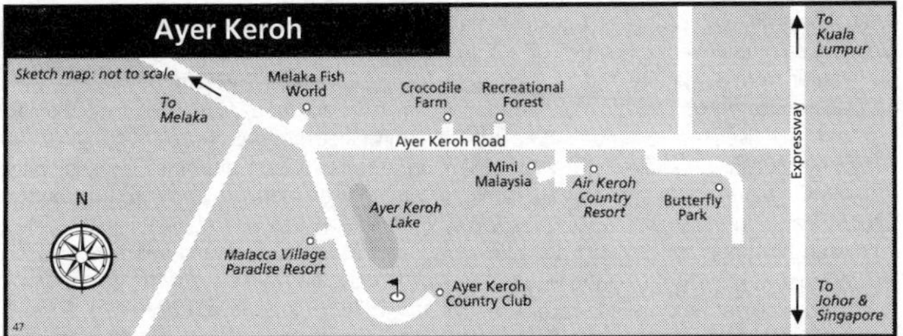

Boat Tours

Boat tours of Melaka's docks, go-downs, wharves and seafront markets run from the quay close to the Tourism Malaysia office. Boats leave when full and usually there is a departure every hour or so between 1000 and 1400 (RM6, RM3 for children).

Local festivals

March/April: *Easter Procession*, (movable) on Good Friday and Easter Sunday, starts from St Peter's Church.

May: *Saint Sohan Singh's Prayer Anniversary* (movable) thousands of Sikhs from all over Malaysia and Singapore congregate at the Melaka Sikh temple, Jalan Temenggong, to join in the memorial prayers.

June: *Pesta San Pedro (Feast of St Peter)* (movable) celebrated at the Portuguese Settlement by fishermen. The brightly decorated fishing boats are blessed and prayers offered for a good season. *Mandi Safar* (movable) bathing festival at Tanjung Kling. *Kite Festival* (movable) on the sea front.

Local information

● Accommodation

Prices: L over RM500; **A+** RM260-500; **A** RM130-260; **B** RM65-130; **C** RM40-65; **D** RM20-40; **E** RM10-20; **F** Below RM10

There's plenty of choice in Melaka but the cheaper hotels tend to be further out of town. There are several nice hotels around Tanjung Kling, like the *Westernhay* (see Excursions, above). There are several good budget hotels at Taman Melaka Raya.

A+ *Equatorial*, Jln Bandar Hilir, T 2828333, F 3089333, monstrous new 500-room block, pools, gym, several restaurants including Chinese, Nyonya and Japanese. Conference facilities. **A+** *Pan Pacific Hotel Malacca*, junction Jln Tun Ali and Jln Hang Tuah, T (Singapore) 3394688, F 3395787 for further information. New hotel which was scheduled to open as this book went to press: 260 rooms, central location, swimming pool and fitness centre, 2 restaurants – the artist's impression does not bode well in terms of architectural merit. **A+** *Ramada Renaissance*, Jln Bendahara, T 2848888, F 2849269, the only 5-star hotel in Melaka, 24-storeys high, it is the tallest building in the town, with 300 rooms all of which are spacious and elegantly appointed with Malaccan wood furniture, a/c, mini-fridge, TV, in-house video and grand views either over the town or to the sea, other amenities include coffee shop, restaurants, fitness centre, pool on the 9th flr, the hotel won the Tourism Malaysia Awards 94/95 for Excellence in Hotel Services First Class Category, recommended. **A+** *Century Mahkota*, Jln Merdeka, T 2812828, F 2812323, on the waterfront next to the Mahkota Parade Shopping and Entertainment Complex, 2 pools, health centre, tennis court, 2 squash courts, mini golf, children's playground, spread out over several towers, the 617 'rooms' are actually suites and apartments, with the usual facilities plus kitchen, good introductory offers may have ceased by the time this book goes to press. **A** *City Bayview*, Jln Bendahara, T 2839888, F 2836699, a/c, restaurant, pool, the rooms visitors are shown are not like the ones they will end up with, the large construction in front of the hotel does not help its image. **A** *Grand Continental*, 20 Jln Tun Sri Lanang, T 2840088, F 2848125, a/c, restaurant, large rooms, good service, buffet for all meals, at a good price, within walking distance of historic part of town, recommended.

B *Emperor*, 123 Jln Munshi Abdullah, T 2840777, F 2838989, a/c, restaurant, pool, good sea view, reasonably clean. **B** *Heeren House*, 1 Jln Tun Tan Cheng Lock, T 2814241, F 2814239, a/c, restaurant, rates include breakfast, 5 a/c nicely furnished rooms in colonial and

Peranakan style, with canopied 4-poster beds (booking recommended) co-owned by a British lecturer from Singapore and his Chinese partner, good afternoon tea, pleasant position in front of the river, recommended. **B** ***Palace***, 201 Jln Munshi Abdullah, T 2825115, F 2848833, a/c, restaurant, rooms are rather lacklustre and on the small size. **B** ***Plaza Inn***, 2 Jln Munshi Abdullah, T 240881, F 249357, a/c, restaurant, high-rise, so good views over town and river, not much else to recommend it though, run down and dirty, poor plumbing and lots of mosquitoes, prices include poor breakfast. **B** ***Straits Meridian***, 1 Jln Malinja, Taman Malinja, towards Ayer Keroh, T 2841166, F 2830030, all suite accommodation. **B-C** ***The Baba House***, 125-127 Jln Tun Tan Cheng Lock, T 2811216, F 2811217, in the centre of Chinatown, a/c, no restaurant, attractive traditional Baba house, rooms quite plain and some overly small but clean, mostly without windows.

C ***Lotus Inn***, 2846 Jln Semabok, T 2837211, F 2837213, a/c, restaurant, east of town. **C** ***Majestic***, 188 Jln Bunga Raya, T 2822367/ 2822455, a/c, restaurant, in a big colonial-style house, with high-ceilinged rooms, plenty of atmosphere and good downtown location, but in a poor state of repair. **C** ***Melaka Sentosa***, 91 Jln Tun Perak, T 2858288, a/c, north of town. **C-D** ***Ng Fook***, 154 Jln Bunga Raya, T 2828055, some a/c, clean but simple rooms.

D ***Chong Hoe***, Jln Tukang Emas, T 2826102, a/c, good location near all the central sights and temples and reasonable value. **D** ***Eastern Heritage***, 8 Jln Bukit Cina, T 233026, great old Chinese building with carved wood and gold inlay, spacious rooms on 2nd Flr, dorm on 3rd Flr, small pool on 1st Flr, batik lessons available, closer to the heart of the city than other low budget places. **D** ***Merryland***, 49 Jln Pasar Baru, T 2820371, a/c. **D** ***New Chin Nam***, 151 Jln Bunga Raya, T 2824962, with a/c but without windows. Rabbit hutches with basin and shower head in room, together with drain (and the smells from all the other rooms and toilets). **D** ***Paradise Hostel***, 4 Jln Tengkerea, T 2830821, a/c, a former hospital, many of the rooms are cubicles with no windows, dormitory, friendly management. **D** ***Pat and Pat's Homestay***, 220 Kampung Bandar Hilar, T 2829153, a genuine homestay, clean and pleasant surroundings (**F** for dorms). **D** ***Trilogy Hostel***, 218a Jln Parameswara Garden, T 2845319, breakfast, TV, laundry, bikes for hire, also has more expensive rooms with bathrooms.

E ***Kancil***, 177 Jln Parameswara (Bandar Hillir), cool and quiet, quiet backyard/garden, bicycles for hire. **E** ***Melaka Town Holiday Lodge***, 148b Taman Melaka Raya, T 2848830, limited breakfast included, hot showers, bikes for hire, laundry service, clean and well looked after, dormitory or rooms, friendly, recommended. **E** ***Melaka Youth Hostel***, 341 Taman Melaka Raya, T 2827915, clean and well run with dorm beds (including an a/c dorm). **E** ***Suan Kee***, 105-107 Jln Bunga Raya, T 223040. **E** ***Sunny's Inn***, 253B Jln Taman Melaka Raya, a couple of single and double rooms and a dorm (**F**), kitchen, bikes for hire, good information, friendly staff, bus tickets, bedbugs prevalent. **E-F** ***Robins Nest***, 205B Jln Taman Melaka Raya, T 2829142, clean and comfortable, helpful proprietor, dorm and rooms.

● Places to eat

Prices: ♦♦♦♦ over RM40; ♦♦♦ RM13-40; ♦♦ RM5-13; ♦ under RM5

Malay: ♦♦***Anda***, 8b Jln Hang Tuah, popular modern coffeeshop, specialities include *ikan bakar* (grilled fish), *sayur masak lemak* (deep-fried marinated prawns) and *rendang*. ♦***Mini***, 35 Jln Merdeka, good for *ikan panggang* (grilled fish with spicy sauce), also *nasi campur*. ♦***Sederhana***, 18A Jln Hang Tuah, near the bus station, good selection of Malay dishes. ♦***Taman***, 10 Jln Merdeka, on the sea front, known for its *ikan assam pedas* – hot (chilli-hot) fish curry.

Chinese: ♦♦♦***Good New World Restoran***, 1319132 Taman Melaka Raya, T 2842528, large and modern, specializes in Cantonese dishes. ♦♦***Dragon Village Restaurant***, 1 Jln Kubu Melaka, T 2815678, in charming old building, popular, although out of the hub of things at the edge of Chinatown. ♦♦***Chop Teo Soon Leng***, 55 Jln Hang Tuah, Teochew cuisine. ♦♦***Keng Dom***, 148 Taman Melaka Raya, T 2826409, renowned for its steamboats. ♦***Bee Bee Hiong***, City Park, Jln Bunga Raya, for fish-ball fans. ♦***Hoe Kee Chicken Rice***, Jln Hang Jebat, Hainanese chicken rice in Chinatown coffee shop, incredibly popular with workers at lunchtime, recommended. ♦***Kim Swee Huat***, 38 Jln Laksamana, big menu with staple western fillers (include travellers' food) as well as local food. ♦***New Oriental Satay and Mee***, 82 Jln Tengkera (road to Tanjung Kling), being a Chinese stall, serves pork satay and other variations such as cuttlefish (*sotong*) satay, also well known for its *yee kiow mee*. ♦***UE Teahouse***, 20 Lorong Bukit Cina, dim sum from early morning until 1200, recommended.

Nyonya: ◆◆◆***Jonkers***, 17 Jln Hang Jebat, old Nyonya house, with restaurant in the old ancestral hall, good atmosphere and excellent food – Nyonya and International, set menu good value at $20 (changes regularly), worth a visit for the house alone but the food is also excellent, recommended. ◆◆◆***Nam Hoe Villa*** (Restoran Peranakan), 317c Klebang Besar (6 km towards Port Dickson), T 3154436, open 1100-1500, 1830-2300, cultural show at 2000 (except Sat), originally the house of a Chinese rubber tycoon, now a restaurant and Peranakan showpiece, all the best known Nyonya dishes are served, buffet. ◆◆◆***Restoran Peranakan Town House***, 107 Jln Tun Tan Cheng Lock, T 245001, same management and concept as *Nam Hoe Villa*. ◆◆◆***Ole Sayang***, 1988199 Taman Melaka Raya, T 2831966, serves all the favourites, including chicken *pongteh* (in sweet and sour spicy sauce), recommended. ◆◆◆***Restoran Manis Sayang***, 617-618 Taman Melaka Raya, T 2813393, traditional Nyonya chicken and fish dishes. ◆◆***Nyonya Makko***, 124 Taman Melaka Raya, T 2840737, located near the bottom of St Paul's Hill, good selection, cheap and friendly, recommended. ◆◆***Heeren House***, 1 Jln Tun Tan Cheng Lock, good value set lunch, cakes, appeals to Western tastes, some Peranakan and Portuguese dishes, a/c, attractive Peranakan furniture.

Indian: ◆◆***Mitchell Raaju Nivaas***, Jln Laksamana, aside from its good curries, this restaurant also offers cooking lessons, RM2, for those who want to make Indian breads and basic curries. ◆◆***Veni***, 34 Jln Temenggong, banana leaf restaurant with good selection of meat curries and vegetarian dishes, roti canai breakfasts. ◆***Banana Leaf***, 42 Jln Munshi Abdullah, South Indian meat curries and vegetarian dishes, biriyani specials on Wed and Sat evenings. ◆***Kerala***, Jln Melaka Raya, good value. ◆***Sri Lakshmi Villas***, intersection of Bendahara and Temenggong, fabulous *dosai masalas* and other good value Indian dishes.

Thai: ◆◆◆***My Place***, 357 Jln Melaka, also some Malay, Chinese and Indian dishes.

Portuguese: most restaurants in the *Medan Portugis* are expensive tourist traps but some of the spicy seafood dishes are worth trying. ◆◆◆***Restaurante d'Nolasco***, 18b Medan Portugis, specializes in Portuguese cuisine. ◆◆◆***Restoran de Lisbon***, Portuguese Square, run by Senhor Alcantra this places comes recommended with its dishes that blend Malaysian and Portuguese cuisines – including devil chicken curry and sea bass roasted in a banana leaf, all washed down with ice cold Portuguese lager or wines, cultural shows Sat evenings. ◆◆◆***San Pedro***, Portuguese Settlement (just off the square), family run and probably the best at the Portuguese settlement, specialities include spicy baked fish, wrapped in banana leaf.

International: ◆◆◆◆***Taming Sari Grill***, *Renaissance Melaka Hotel*, Jln Bendahara, T 2848888, seafood and meat cooked on marble with a little olive oil, served with bread, baked potato and salad. ◆◆***Pandan***, Jln Kota, T 2836858 (behind tourist information office), western and local dishes, claypot noodle a speciality, pleasant location by roadside, friendly staff but over-salted food. Good for juices. ◆◆***Café Sixties***, 12 Jln Melaka Raya 23, Taman Melaka Raya, T 2819507, rock 'n' roll interior, fish 'n' chips, steak, curry and others.

Seafood: *Pengkalan Pernu* (Pernu Jetty), 10 km south on the way to Muar, has several fish restaurants and stalls where you can pick your own fish and have it grilled. North of Melaka, towards Tanjung Kling there are a few Chinese seafood restaurants along the beach. ◆◆◆◆***Bunga Raya Restaurant***, 39-40 Jln Taman, T 2836456, crab, prawn and lobster are house specialities.

Fastfood: *Kentucky Fried Chicken*, Jln Taming Sari and Melaka Plaza, Jln Hang Tuah. *McDonalds*, Soon Seng Plaza, Jln Tun Ali.

Foodstalls: *Satay celup* is a Melakan variation on a Malaysian theme: an assortment of skewered meats, fishballs, quails' eggs, crab, prawns, mussels, mushrooms and yams with traditional peanut sauce. ***Glutton's Corner***, along the old esplanade on Jln Merdeka/Jln Taman: excellent choice of food although the stalls now face a painted wall rather than the sea, thanks to a land reclamation project, ***Prince Satay Celup*** at No 16, recommended; ***Jalan Bendahara***, several noodle stalls and a Mamak man (Indian Muslim) who serves *sup kambing* (mutton soup) and the bits – for marrow suckers (opposite the *Capitol*), Chinese food; ***Jalan Bukit Baru***, just off the main road past the state mosque, mostly Chinese food; ***Jalan Bunga Raya***, stalls (next to Rex Cinema), seafood recommended; ***Jalan Semabok*** (after Bukit Cina on road to JB), Malay-run fish-head curry stall which is a local favourite; ***Klebang Beach***, off Jln Klebang Besar, Tanjung Kling – stalls, with several *ikan panggang* (grilled fish) specialists.

Bakery and softee ice-cream: in basement of *Parkson Grand Department Store & Supermarket*, two more outlets in *Mahkota Parade Shopping Mall*; ***Renaissance Melaka Hotel*** has a good bakery shop in lobby.

● Airline offices

MAS, 1st Flr, Hotel Shopping Arcade, *City Bayview Hotel*, Jln Bendahara, T 2835722. **Pelangi Airways**, Bangunan Terminal, Batu Berendam Airport, T 3174175, F 3173763.

● Banks & money changers

Bumiputra, Jln Kota. **Hong Kong & Shanghai**, Jln Kota. Several banks on Jln Hang Tuah near the bus station and Jln Munshi Abdullah. **Spak Sdn**, 29 Jln Laksamana, T 282674, authorized money changer. **Islah Enterprise**, G 79 Spice Route 27, Mahkota Parade, Jln Merdeka, T 2811488, authorized money changers.

● Entertainment

Cinemas: Jln Bunga Raya for English language films.

Cultural shows: at the Portuguese Settlement every Sat at 2030. Songs and dances including the famous *beranyo*, an excuse for a sing-along and knees-up. ***Nam Hoe Villa*** (Restoran Peranakan), 317c Klebang Besar (6 km towards Port Dickson), T 3154436, 2000 Sun-Fri, ***Taman Mini Malaysia***, Ayer Keroh, 1120 and 1430 Sat, Sun and public hols.

Son et Lumière: ***Melaka Light and Sound Show***, on the Padang, opposite St Paul's Hill, T 011-664166 chronological history of Melaka, an hour long show with a distinctly Malay nationalist perspective, 5 minutes mention of European rule and no mention of the contribution by the Chinese and Indian ethnic communities, not expertly presented. Mon-Sun, 2000 (Malay), 2130 (English) Admission RM5.

● Hospitals & medical services

Hospitals: *Straits Hospital*, 37 Jln Parameswara, T 2835336.

● Post & telecommunications

Area Code: 06.

General Post Office: Melaka's GPO is about 3 km north of the centre of town on Jln Bukit Baru (the continuation of Jln Tun Sri Lanang). Town bus no 19 runs past the GPO. The most convenient **post office** is at JKR430 Jln Laksamana, T 2833840.

● Shopping

Melaka is best known for its antique shops, which mainly sell European and Chinese items.

Antiques: *Jalan Hang Jebat* (formerly Jonker St) is the best place for antiques.

Books: ***Boon Hoong Sports and Bookstore***, 13 Jln Bunga Raya; ***Times Bookshop***, Jaya Jusco Stores, Mukim Bukit Baru. **Book exchange**: Jln Taman Melaka Raya for a good number of English language books.

Clothing: artist Charles Cham sells very original T-shirts from his shop the *Orang Utan House*, 59 Lorong Hang Jebat. His place is hard to miss – a huge orange orang utan is painted on the outside of his shop.

Food: ***Tan Kim Hock Product Centre***, 153 Jln Laksamana Cheng Ho, T 2835322, distinguishable by its colour (pink), this shop is near the *Ramada Renaissance Hotel*, and is a delight for the eye and stomach: cookies and sweets in a great many varieties. Just ask for the 'Dodol Man'; everybody knows who he (Tan Kim Hock) is, a self-made man who became a billionaire with his business. A hotel in town has been named after him.

General: main shopping centres on Jln Hang Tuah and Jln Munshi Abdullah. ***Mahkota Parade Shopping and Entertainment Complex***, including ***Parkson Grand Department Store and Supermarket***, 1 Jln Merdeka, just south of the river mouth, a good choice of shops – the centre won an award for the best shopping centre in the country.

Handicrafts: ***Karyaneka*** (handicraft) centres at ***1 Jalan Laksamana*** and ***Mini Malaysia Complex***, Ayer Keroh. Also ***Crystal D'beaute***, 18 Medan Portugis.

Paintings: ***The Orang Utan House***, 59 Lorong Hang Jebat, paintings by local artist Charles Cham.

Shoes: ***Wah Aik Shoemaker Shop***, 92 Jln Hang Jebat. Shoes are still made here for Chinese grannies with bound feet (see page 232) and tourists.

Woodwork: ***Malacca Woodwork***, 312c Klebang Besar, T 3154468, specialist in authentic reproduction antique furniture including camphor wood chests.

● Sports

Golf: ***Ayer Keroh Golf & Country Club***, 14 km from Melaka, green fees RM70 weekdays; RM100 weekends; ***"A" Famosa Golf Resort***, Jln Kemus, Pulan Sebang, T 560888, located near the Alor Gajah interchange of the north-south expressway, 18-hole course, green fees weekdays RM100, weekends RM150, buggy RM40, caddy RM20.

● Tour companies & travel agents

Annah (Melaka) Tours & Travel, 27 Jln Laksamana, T 2835626; ***AR Tours***, 302a Jln Tun Ali, T 2831977; ***Satik Tour & Travel***, 143 Jln Bendahara, T 2835712.

● **Tourist offices**

Tourism Malaysia, Jln Kota (opposite *Christ Church*), T 2846622, F 2849022. Open 0845-1700 Sat-Thur, 0845-1215 and 1445-1700 Fri. Also tourist information desk at Ayer Keroh, T 3125811.

● **Useful addresses**

Tourist Police: Jln Kota, T 2822222 (close to the Tourism Malaysia office). **Central Police Station**: Jln Kota, T 2825522. **Immigration office**: Bangunan Persekutaan, Jln Hang Tuah, T 2824958/2824955 (for visa extensions).

● **Transport**

149 km from KL, 216 km from Johor Bahru, 90 km from Port Dickson.

Local Bicycle hire: many of the cheaper hotels/hostels rent out bikes, as do one or two shops in town, RM5-8/day. **Buses**: local buses leave from Jln Hang Tuah, right next to the long distance bus station. Less than RM1 round town. There is also an historical shuttle bus which takes tourists through the main historical areas and out to Ayer Keroh. A day pass costs RM5 and this allows three journeys. Hourly departures, 0930-1630. **Car hire**: **Avis**, 124 Jln Bendahara, T 2846710; **Hertz**, *City Bayview Hotel*, Jln Bendahara, T 2828862; **Sintat**, *Renaissance Melaka Hotel*, Jln Bendahara, T 2848888; **Thrifty**, G-5 Pasar Pelancong, Jln Tun Sri Lanang, T 2849471. **Taxi**: all taxis now have meters. There are stands outside major hotels and shopping centres, or T 2823630. Between 0100 and 0600, there is a 50% surcharge. **Trishaws**: mostly for the tourist trade, they congregate at several points in town (there are usually a number near the the tourist information centre on the town square – RM2 for single destination or RM10-15/hour.

Air Airport is at Batu Berendam, 10 km out of town. Town bus no. 65 runs to the airport from the local bus station. Connections on Pelangi Airways with Pekanbaru in Sumatra. **Airport flight information**: T 2822648 (Pelangi T 3851175).

Train Nearest station is at Tampin, 40 km north; Melaka railway enquiry office, T 2823091; Tampin railway station, T 411034. See page 512 for timetable.

Road Bus: long distance buses leave from the terminal on Jln Hang Tuah. Regular connections with KL, Seremban, Port Dickson, Ipoh, Butterworth, Lumut (Pulau Pangkor), Kuantan, Kuala Terengganu, Kota Bharu, Johor Bahru and Singapore. **Taxi**: station opposite the local bus terminal on Jln Gaha Maju, just off Jln Hang Tuah. Vehicles leave for KL, Seremban, Penang, Mersing, Johor Bahru. Passengers for Singapore must change taxis at the long-distance terminal in JB.

● **International connections**

NB It is necessary to secure a visa from the Indonesian Embassy in KL (see page 192) before departing for Sumatra from Melaka.

Air Thrice weekly service on Wed, Fri and Sun by Pelangi Air to Pekanbaru, Sumatra, Indonesia.

Bus Direct bus connections with Singapore, 4 hours.

Sea Ferry: express ferries to Dumai (Sumatra), leave daily from the public jetty on Melaka River, 2 hours, (RM80). Tickets from ***Atlas Travel Service***, Jln Hang Jebat, T 2820777; ***Madai Shipping***, Jln Tun Ali T 2840671; ***Tunar Rapat Utama Express***, 17A Jln Merdeka, T 2832516.

JOHOR BAHRU (JB)

Modern **Johor Bahru** – more commonly called JB – is not a pretty town. It lies on the southernmost tip of the peninsula and is the gateway to Malaysia from Singapore. During the 1980s it became an industrial adjunct to Singapore, attracting land and labour-intensive manufacturing industries (see page 622). Johor's manufacturing boom has brought a measure of prosperity to the state capital and its dingy streets have begun to get a much-needed face-lift. Foreign investors have embarked on property-buying sprees and new hotels, shopping plazas and office complexes have been springing up. The state government's intention is to emulate the development process of neighbouring Singapore.

At weekends JB is jammed with Singaporeans here, it would seem, largely for the sex and/or the shopping – and, perhaps, the chance to escape for a few hours from the stultifying atmosphere of their own clean and green country. During 1997 JB became the subject of a bitter spat between Malaysia and Singapore. In March, Singapore's Senior Minister Lee Kuan Yew suggested that the city was "notorious for shootings, muggings and carjackings". The Malaysian press and some

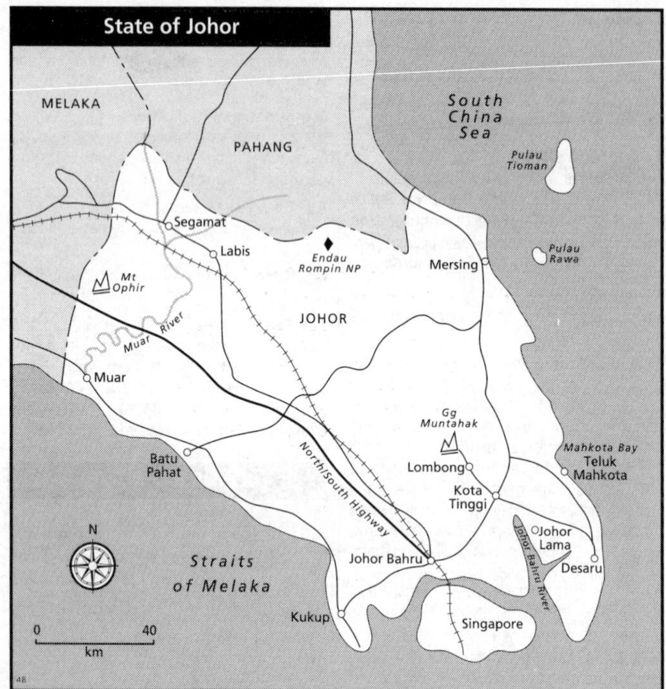

politicians reacted with fury – The Youth head of the ruling United Malays National Party (UMNO) going so far as to accuse Lee of being 'senile and uncouth'. Lee later apologized 'unreservedly'.

The old causeway across the *Selat Tebrau* (Strait of Johor), built in 1924, is still the only land-link to Singapore. It is overburdened with road traffic and also carries the railway and water pipelines: Singapore relies on Johor for most of its water supply. A new bridge is finally being built from Gelang Patah, to the west of JB, to Singapore, which was scheduled for completion in 1995 but is still incomplete. JB is short on tourist attractions but has for many years served as a tacky red-light reprieve for Singaporeans. But Johor's paucity of cultural attractions belies its pivotal role in Malay history.

Following his trouncing by the Portuguese invaders in 1511, Melaka's young Sultan Ahmad fled south with what remained of the royal court, eventually arriving at Bintan in the Riau Archipelago. Ahmad was promptly executed by his father, Mahmud, for gross ineptitude and there then followed 15 years of attrition between the Portuguese and Mahmud, before the Portuguese destroyed his capital at Bintan in 1526. Mahmud died 2 years later and his remaining son became the first Sultan of Perak while his stepson established the Sultanate of Johor near Kota Tinggi, to the east of modern JB.

At the same time, the Sultanate of Aceh, on the north tip of Sumatra, was enjoying a meteoric rise to prominence. Rivalry between Johor and Aceh overshadowed either's hatred of the Portuguese and the Acehnese terrorized Johor for another 60 years, frequently sacking the capital and twice carrying the royal family back to Sumatra as prisoners.

The Johor court was re-established on the Johor River in 1641 and the sultanate grew strong and powerful again as an entrepôt, until the capital was destroyed by the rival Sumatran kingdom of Jambi in 1673. The sultanate moved to Bintan, then back to Kota Tinggi in 1685. But Sultan Mahmud, was a tyrant who frightened off foreign traders; he was also a murderer and sexual pervert and was finally assassinated by his own people, thus ending the centuries-old Melaka Dynasty. Switching its capitals between the Johor River and Riau, the sultanate declined and remained weak throughout the 18th century; the Malay rulers, wracked by in-fighting, were by then firmly under the thumb of the ascendant Buginese and constantly squabbling over trade issues with the Dutch.

In 1818, with the Dutch temporarily absent, due to the Napoleonic Wars, the British resident of Melaka, Colonel William Farquhar, signed a trade pact with the sultan in Riau. Thomas Stamford Raffles was meanwhile looking to set up a British trading post on the south end of the peninsula and after casting around the Riau Archipelago, settled on Singapore. There, in 1819, he signed a deal with Temenggong Abdur Rahman, the sultan's minister on the island, and later with one of two blue-blooded Malays claiming to be Sultan of Johor, allowing the English East India Company to establish a trading post in Singapore.

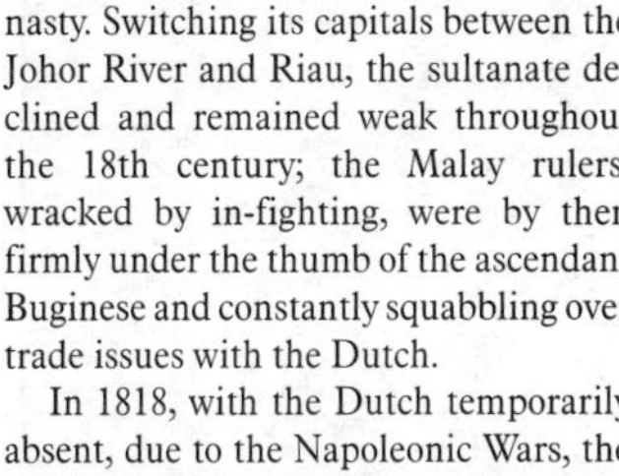

The 1824 Treaty of London, between the British and the Dutch put an end to the Johor-Riau Empire, partitioning it between the two European powers. The Riau side became known as the Sultanate of Lingga, while the Temenggong was left to wield Malay power. Abu Bakar, the grandson of Singapore's Temenggong Abdur Rahman, moved his headquarters to the small settlement of Tanjong Putri in Johor, which he renamed Johor Bahru in 1866. The Anglophile Abu Bakar was known as the Maharajah of Johor until 1877, and in 1885, was recognized as Sultan by Queen Victoria. He developed the state's agricultural economy and, in the early 20th century, Johor attracted many European rubber planters. Sultan Abu Bakar is known as the father of modern Johor, which became the last state to join the colonial Malay Federation, in 1914.

Climate: Johor Bahru

Places of interest

One of the most prominent buildings in JB is the recently renovated **Istana Besar**, the Sultan's former residence on Jalan Tun Dr Ismail (built by Sultan Abu Bakar in 1866). It is now a royal museum – the **Royal Abu Bakar Museum**. Today the Sultan lives in the Istana Bukit Serene, which is on the west outskirts of town (it is not open to the public). The Istana Besar is a slice of Victorian England set in beautiful gardens, overlooking the strait. In the north wing is the throne room and museum containing a superb collection of royal treasures, including hunting trophies, as well as Chinese and Japanese ceramics. It is one of Malaysia's best museums and makes a stay in otherwise unexciting JB worthwhile. Admission US$7,

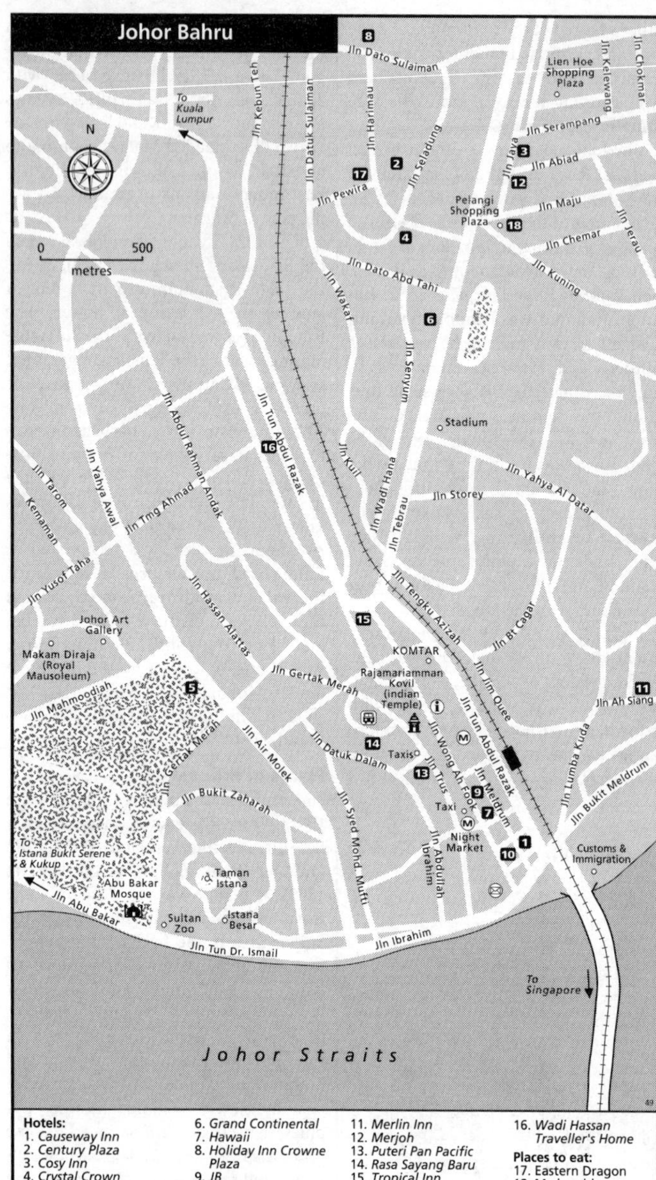

Hotels:
1. *Causeway Inn*
2. *Century Plaza*
3. *Cosy Inn*
4. *Crystal Crown*
5. *Footloose*
6. *Grand Continental*
7. *Hawaii*
8. *Holiday Inn Crowne Plaza*
9. *JB*
10. *Le Tian*
11. *Merlin Inn*
12. *Merjoh*
13. *Puteri Pan Pacific*
14. *Rasa Sayang Baru*
15. *Tropical Inn*
16. *Wadi Hassan Traveller's Home*

Places to eat:
17. Eastern Dragon
18. Mcdonalds

(ringgit equivalent), children under 12 US$3. Open 0900-1800 Monday-Sunday.

Not far away, on Jalan Abu Bakar, is the **Sultan Abu Bakar Mosque**, which faces the Strait of Johor. It was finished in 1900 and clearly reflects the Victorian climate of the period. The mosque can accommodate 2,500 worshippers.

The 32m-high tower of the 1930s **Istana Bukit Serene** on Jalan Skudai – the home of the Sultan of Johore and not open to the public – is only outdone by the 64m tower of the State Secretariat, on Bukit Timbalan, which dominates the town.

Excursions

Kukup, 40 km southwest of Johor on the Straits of Melaka, is a small Chinese fishing kampung renowned throughout the country – and in Singapore – for its seafood (especially prawns and chilli crab). Most of the restaurants, known as *kelong*, are built on stilts over the water. The kampung has become so popular with Singaporeans that coach tours are laid on, and some of the restaurants – notably *Restoran Kukup* – are geared to cater for big groups. Weekend visits are not recommended for this reason. The kampung is also now dominated by a 36-hole golf course, *Kukup Golf Resort*, Pekan Penorok, T 6960952, F 6960961, green fees weekdays RM120, weekends RM165, next to the resort is a new dolphin learning centre where dolphin shows are held. *Getting there*: bus 3 to Pontian Kecil; from there to Kukup by taxi – or take a taxi the whole way (about RM40). A pier has been built at Kukup and direct ferry connections with Tuas in Singapore are likely.

At **Lombong**, below Gunung Muntahak, a series of waterfalls have cut natural swimming pools; the falls are 56 km northeast of JB and 13 km from **Kota Tinggi**, a former royal capital of Johor. Many of the mausoleums of the former sultans of Johor – including that of Mahmud Shah, the last sultan of the Melaka Dynasty – are nearby. The mausoleum of Sultan Mahmud, the feared ruler who was finally assassinated by one of his courtesans (see page 243) is at Kampung Makam (turn right 1 km north of Kota Tinggi, before Desaru sign). The site of the old royal capital of **Johor Lama** ('Old Johor' – as opposed to Johor Bahru, or 'New Johor') is on the east bank of the Johor River, south of Kota Tinggi. Because it was twice burned to the ground, there are no impressive ruins. The site is, however, clearly signposted off the Kota Tinggi-Desaru road (12 km). Just before Telok Sengat, turn right down a laterite track through an oil palm estate. Johor Lama, most of which lies under a rubber tappers' kampung, is 6 km down the track. There is no public transport to the site or to Telok Sengat so it is necessary to charter a taxi. **Accommodation C** *Waterfall Chalet*, Kota Tinggi Waterfall, T 8331146 (must be booked in advance), a/c, reasonably well maintained. **C** *Sri Bayn Resort*, near Telok Sengat (5 km up laterite track through oil palm estate opposite turn-off to Johor Lama), only accessible for those with own transport, possibly the most tranquil and certainly the most remote chalet resort on the peninsula, set on steep hillside overlooking Johor estuary among coconut palms in neat gardens, chalets have balconies and fantastic views, as of mid-1993 the resort had not received official permission to open, check with Tourism Malaysia, T 2223591. In Kota Tinggi there are a number of places to stay including the **D** *Sin May Chun Hotel*, 36 Jalan Tambatan, T 8333573 (spacious, good value rooms) and the **C** *Nasha Hotel*, 40 Jalan Tambatan, T (07) 8338000. **Places to eat** Seafood restaurant and coffee shops in nearby Telok Sengat, recommended. *Getting there*: from JB take bus No 41 to Kota Tinggi (many departures), and from Kota Tinggi bus no. 43 to the waterfall. Or a taxi the whole way.

Desaru holiday resort, set on a 20 km-long beach at Tanjung Penawar, 90 km east of JB, has been aggressively marketed in Singapore – as a result it gets invaded on weekends and public holidays. By the mid-1990 around half a million tourists

Modern Johor: riding on the merlion's tail

Johor is still a predominantly agricultural state, and is Malaysia's leading producer of palm oil, rubber, cocoa and coconuts. But in recent years, Singapore's prosperity has spilled across the 1.2 km causeway linking the island republic with JB. An explosion in foreign manufacturing investment – led by Singapore – has turned Johor into an industrial oasis.

The state planners are as startled as anyone at the suddenness of the transformation: in the past few years Johor has attracted about a quarter of total foreign investment in Malaysia. The industrial estates surrounding JB produce everything from typewriters and televisions to condoms and Kentucky Fried Chickens. Almost everything is immediately exported from JB's Pasir Gudang port. Recently, big Japanese and Taiwanese petrochemicals plants have set up in the state too, one of them near Johor Lama, the site of the old royal capital.

Johor is now the northern point of the so-called 'Growth Triangle' which also incorporates Singapore and parts of Indonesia's Riau Archipelago. The state government, now facing a labour shortage, wants its industries to be increasingly hi-tech, and the Chief Minister has repeatedly stated that he aims to turn his state into a Singapore-clone by the year 2000. Tourism is big in Johor too, mainly because Singaporeans flood across the causeway to get a break from city life. Nearly three-quarters of all tourists visiting Malaysia come from Singapore: each day about 50,000 people cross the causeway to JB.

were visiting the area each year. Although the beach is picturesque, the sea can get very rough, and there is a strong undertow – most holiday-makers stick to their hotel pools. The most popular pursuit here is golf on its beautifully landscaped seaside course. In 1991, in a fit of dollar-driven madness, a consortium of American and Japanese investors proposed transforming Desaru into a resort of obscene proportions at a projected cost of US$1.4bn. Incredibly, they even planned to build a Winter Wonderland with snow and all. Fortunately, it died soon after birth. However, in 1995 a new investor proposed a slightly more modest plan – just US$200mn – to build hotels, more golf courses, a shopping complex et al. So change is in the air.

Accommodation Designed with golf-crazed Singaporeans in mind, although on weekdays, chalet accommodation is reasonable. Budget travellers are better advised to head for Mersing and the off-shore islands. **A+** *Desaru Golf Inn*, T 8221106, F 8221408, a/c, restaurant, pool. **A** *Desaru View*, (PO Box 71, Kota Tinggi), Tanjung Penawar, T 8238221, a/c, restaurant, pool. **A-C** *Desaru Golden Beach Resort*, PO Box 50, Tanjung Penawar, T 8221101, F 8221480, a/c, restaurant, pool, former *Merlin Inn* with standard 4-star facilities, fills up with golfers on weekends, chalets next door are part of same resort (guests can use hotel pool) and are good value during the week. **C** *Tanjung Balau Fishing Village*, T 8221201, F 8221600, dormitory-only accommodation in fishing village just outside Desaru, for those wanting to experience a fisherman's life. *Getting there*: bus 41; regular connections with JB via Kota Tinggi; taxi from JB. Two daily shuttles from most major hotels in Singapore. Regular boats connect Desaru with Changi Point, Singapore to Tanjung Pengileh, where taxis are available to Desaru.

Teluk Mahkota Those taking the road north from Kota Tinggi may be tempted by countless roadside signs to *Jason's Bay Beach Resort* at Teluk Mahkota (25 km off main east coast road from turning 15 km northeast of Kota Tinggi). *Getting there*: bus 300 from Kota Tinggi. Despite its privacy, it is not really worth the bother.

The once-lovely beach is muddy and disappointing; the resort is grimy and rooms smell musty.

Local information

Accommodation

Prices: L over RM500; **A+** RM260-500; **A** RM130-260; **B** RM65-130; **C** RM40-65; **D** RM20-40; **E** RM10-20; **F** Below RM10

JB's top hotels cater for visiting businesspeople and have all the 5-star facilities. Many new hotels were opened in 1996 and in 1997 a *Shangri-La* is due to open. Middle-market and cheaper hotels are as tacky as ever though: the 'hostess girl industry' is big business in JB. Many hotels rent out rooms by the hour. As such facilities are usually prominently advertised, patrons should know what to expect. Though many of these hotels are brothels to locals, for a tourist they are reasonably priced hotels in an otherwise expensive city. Room rates also increase on Fri and weekends. Because most budget travellers don't bother to stop in JB there really isn't much to choose from at the bottom end – except for an array of seedy short-stay hotels.

A+-A ***Holiday Inn Crowne Plaza***, Jln Dato' Sulaiman, Century Garden, T 3323800, F 318884, a/c, restaurant, pool, unhelpfully located on suburban one-way system, frequented by the rich and the royal because of its Szechuan restaurant recently renovated. **A** ***Century Plaza***, Jln Pelanduk, Century Garden, T 3333300, F 3333385, newly-opened, 3-star boutique hotel, 80 comfortable rooms with a/c, TV, in-house video, mini-fridge, tea and coffee-making facilities, soon to be connected by walkway to a health spa. **A** ***Hyatt Regency***, Jln Sungai Chat, T 2221234, over 2 km west of town centre, all the comforts you would expect of the *Hyatt* chain. **A** ***Crystal Crown***, 117 Jln Harimau, Century Garden, T 3334422, F 3343582, a/c, restaurants, TV, tea and coffee-making facilities, minibar, a very recent addition to the town's hotels. **A** ***Grand Continental***, 799 Jln Tebrau, T 3323999, F 3319924, a new addition to the *Grand Continental Chain*, rates include breakfast, rooms with a/c, TV, minibar and tea and coffee-making facilities. **A** ***Merlin Inn***, 10 Jln Bukit Meldrum, T 2237400, a/c, restaurant, comfortable hotel that looks like a truncated Toblerone, with a new wing recently added, good value but cut off from centre of town by railway and flyovers. **A** ***Puteri Pan Pacific***, Jln Trus, T 2233333, F 2236622, e-mail: panpjjb@po.jaring.my, a/c, restaurants, pool, fitness and business centres, good city centre location for those on business, 500 rooms, tennis and squash courts, room rate includes airport transfer, fruit basket and welcome drink. **A** ***Tropical Inn***, 15 Jln Gereja, T 2247888, a/c, restaurant, pool.

B ***Causeway Inn***, 6b Jln Meldrum, T 2248811, a/c, unlike neighbouring premises, this is a clean, quiet, well-run hotel that looks smart and does not overcharge, check the room though because some have no view, recommended. **B** ***Straits View***, 1d Jln Scudai, T 2241400, a/c, restaurant (next door to *Jaws 5*), not much of a Straits View from downstairs rooms but the hotel is clean and the management friendly. **B-C** ***Rasa Sayang Baru***, 10 Jln Dato Dalam, T 2248600, a/c, restaurant, on the outskirts of town, discounts available in off-peak season, recommended.

C ***Cosy Inn*** 38a Jln Jaya, T 331 0891. **C** ***Hawaii***, 23 Jln Meldrum, T 2240633, average Chinese-run hotel – much better value on weekdays when rates are slashed. **C** ***JB Hotel***, 80a Jln Wong Ah Fook, T 2246625/2234788, a/c, clean, reasonably spacious rooms and at this price, good value. **C** ***Hotel Merjoh***, 22 Jln Jaya, T 3334061. **C** ***Le Tian***, 2, A-D Jln Sin Nam, T 2248151 (just off Jln Meldrum), small rooms and chocolate decor doesn't help, but cleaner than most others in the area.

E ***Wadi Hassan Traveller's Home***, 52E Jln Wadi Hassan, restaurant, dorm rooms, family rooms with fan, breakfast included, laundry service, tours organized, good local information, recommended. **E** ***Footloose Homestay***, 4H Jln Ismail, T 2242881, in a quiet area of town outside the city centre, just one private room along with some dorm beds, friendly and well maintained, room rate includes breakfast, this place has come recommended.

Places to eat

Prices: ♦♦♦♦ over RM40; ♦♦♦ RM13-40; ♦♦ RM5-13; ♦ under RM5

JB is best known for its seafood which is considerably cheaper than Singapore, leading scores of Singaporeans to cross the causeway at the weekend to throng the restaurants along the seafront road, Jln Ibrahim, running west from the town centre.

Malay: ♦♦♦***Dapur Rembia***, 1A-2 Jln Mohd Amin (close to *Jaws 5 restaurant*), old bungalow with tables outside. ♦♦***Sedap Corner***, 11 Jln Abdul Samad, Chinese as well as Malay dishes, a good line in fish-head curries. ♦***Wadi Hassan Travellers Home***, good traditional food.

THE BEST SPOT

IN

Tioman

MALAYSIA

The only resort of international standard on one of the most beautiful islands in the region, **Berjaya Tioman Beach Resort**, with its own 18-hole international championship golf course, sprawls over 200 acres. Accommodation comprises 400 rooms and suites in charming Malay chalets equipped with TV, in-house video, CNN, IDD telephone and mini bar.

The resort's 11 food and beverage outlets offer a mouth-watering selection of cuisines from Cantonese fare at Fortune Court to local and Asian delicacies at Sri Nelayan.

State-of-the-art convention facilities cater for groups up to 400 persons while a host of water sports, horseriding, tennis, boat tours and golfing ensure business becomes a pleasure at Berjaya Tioman Beach Resort.

Best Western
Berjaya Tioman Beach Resort
Tioman Island, Malaysia

P.O. Box 4, Mersing, 86807 Johor, Malaysia
Tel: (609) 419 1000 Fax: (609) 419 1718 Toll-free Tel: 800 8836
Toll-free Fax: 800 8826 E-mail: tod@hr.berjaya.com.my

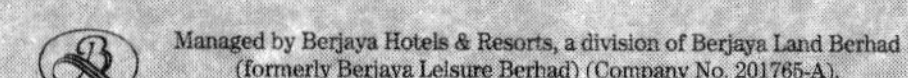

Managed by Berjaya Hotels & Resorts, a division of Berjaya Land Berhad (formerly Berjaya Leisure Berhad) (Company No. 201765-A), a member of the Berjaya Group of Companies

BERJAYA

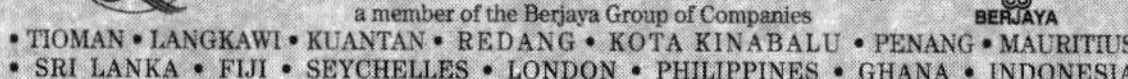

• TIOMAN • LANGKAWI • KUANTAN • REDANG • KOTA KINABALU • PENANG • MAURITIUS • SRI LANKA • FIJI • SEYCHELLES • LONDON • PHILIPPINES • GHANA • INDONESIA

Chinese: ♦♦♦♦***Grand Court Restaurant***, *Hotel Grand Continental*, 3rd flr, T 3345578, good selection including some Cantonese and Nyonya dishes. ♦♦♦***Eastern Dragon Restoran***, 49851 Jln Serigala, Century Garden, T 3319600, very popular. ♦♦♦***Ming Dragon***, G12-14 *Holiday Plaza*, recommended. ♦♦***Teoyuan***, 21 Jln Maju, T331278, a/c, very clean.

Indian: there are some good Indian restaurants in town including the ♦♦***Restoran Nilla*** at 3 Jln Ungku Puan.

Thai: ♦♦♦♦***Manhattan Grill***, Plaza Kotaraya, Jln Trus (opposite Pan Pac), haunt of JB's rich and relatively famous, new grill room with excellent food at half the price of the equivalents across the causeway. ♦♦♦♦***Meisan***, *Holiday Inn JB*, Jln Dato' Sulaiman, Century Garden, superb but expensive spicy Szechuan restaurant. ♦♦♦♦***Selashi***, *Puteri Pan Pacific*, The Kotaraya, top quality Malay cuisine in tastefully decorated, expensive restaurant. ♦♦♦***134 Jalan Serampang***, Taman Pelangi, tables in the garden. ♦♦♦***Jaws 5 Seafood***, 1d Jln Skudai, very popular, next to *Straits View Hotel* and Machinta strip club, the food is very good, but not cheap, specialities include drunken prawns, frogs' legs and chilli crabs, diners may find flashing neons and revolving stage unsettling, recommended. ♦♦♦***Newsroom Café***, Puteri Pan Pacific, The Kotaraya, offering reasonably priced local/continental dishes (enclosed brasserie area called *Editor's Corner*). ♦♦***Medina***, corner of Jln Meldrum and Jln Siew Niam, cheap and delicious murtabak, rotis, fish-head curries etc, open 24 hours.

Foodstalls: ***Tepian Tebrau***, Jln Skudaí (facing the sea beside the *General Hospital*) good for Malay food – satay and grilled fish. There is also good stall food at the long-distance bus terminal and outside the railway station. There is a sprawling outdoor hawker centre right in the centre of town, adjacent to the Plaza Kotaraya on Jln Trus. ***Pantai Lido*** is another well known hawker centre and there is a 'food court' in the *Kompleks Tun Abdul Razak* Jln Wong Ah Fook as well as the *Plaza Kotaraya* on Jln Trus. The night market on Jln Wong Ah Fook is also a great place to sample the full array of stall dishes.

● Airline offices

MAS, 1st Flr Plaza Pelangi, Menara Pelangi, Jln Kuning, Taman Pelangi, T 3341003/3341001 – a little over 2 km from the town centre. **Pelangi Airways**, c/o MAS, Menara Pelangi, Jln Kuning, Taman Pelangi, T 3341001, F 3340043.

● Banks & money changers

Bumiputra, **Hong Kong & Shanghai** and **United Asia** are on Bukit Timbalan. Other big banks are on Jln Wong Ah Fook, several money changers in the big shopping centres and on/around Jln Ibrahim/Jln Meldrum.

● Entertainment

Discos: *Caesar's Palace*, *Holiday Plaza*; ***Millennium***, *Holiday Inn*, Jln Dato Sulaman.

● Hospitals & medical services

Hospitals: *Sultanah Aminah General Hospital*, Jln Skudai.

● Post & telecommunications

Area Code: 07.
Post Office: Jln Tun Dr Ismail.
Telephone office: Jln Trus (opposite the *Puteri Pan Pacific Hotel*).

● Shopping

Books: ***Johore Central Store***, Plaza Kota Raya, Jln Abdullah Ibrahim; ***MPH Bookstore***, Holiday Plaza, Jln Dato Sulaiman; ***Times Bookshop***, Plaza Pelangi, 4th Flr, in Kerry's Department Store, 2 Jln Kuning.

General: large shopping complexes including ***Holiday Plaza***, Jln Datuk Sulaiman; ***Kompleks Tun Abdul Razak*** (KOMTAR), Jln Wong Ah Fook; ***Plaza Pelangi***, Jln Tebrau; ***Sentosa Complex***, Jln Sutera; ***Kotaraya***, off Jln Trus, a pink building situated in the centre of the city, opposite the night market – possibly the best place to shop with a hawker centre upstairs.

Handicrafts: ***Craftown Handicraft Centre***, Jln Skudai; ***Jaro***, Jln Sungai Chat; ***Johorcraft***, Kompleks Kotaraya & Kompleks Tun Abdul Razak, Jln Trus; ***Karyaneka Centre*** at Kompleks Mawar, 562 Jln Sungeai Chat; ***Mawar***, Jln Sultanah Rogayah, Istana Besar. There is also a big new *Johorcraft* complex 1 km before Kota Tinggi on the road from JB selling rather down-market arts and crafts from all over Malaysia. It is aimed at big coach tours from Singapore, has a large restaurant and provides demonstrations of pottery, batik and songkhet production. Open Mon-Sun 0800-1800.

● Sports

Bowling: ***Holiday Bowl***, 2nd Flr Holiday Plaza, Jln Dato Suleiman.

Golf: ***Royal Johor Country Club***, Jln Larkin, T 2233322, green fees RM100 weekdays, RM200 weekends. ***Palm Resort Golf and Country Club***, Jln Persiaran Golf, Off Jln Jumbo (near airport), Senai, T 5996000, F 5996001, course is part of a 5-star resort which includes tennis, squash, bowls, pool, fitness centre, sauna, Japanese baths and luxury hotel and bungalows, green fees weekdays RM135, weekends RM250, caddy fee RM25, buggy RM20.

● Tourist offices

Tourism Malaysia Information Centre, 4th Flr, Tun Abdul Razak Complex, Jln Wong Ah Fook, T 2240288/2223591. Open: 0900-1700 Mon-Sat, 1000-1600 Sun. **Southern Region Tourism Office**, 4th Flr, KOMTAR, T 2223591.

● Useful addresses

Immigration office, 1st Floor, Block B, Wisma Persektuan, Jln Air Molek, T 2244253.

● Transport

134 km from Mersing, 224 km from Melaka.

Local Bus: local buses leave from the main bus terminal on Jln Wong Ah Fook; there is no shortage of local taxis (no meters). **Car hire**: it is much cheaper to hire a car in JB than it is in neighbouring Singapore but check whether the car hire company allows the car to go to Singapore. **Avis**, *Tropical Inn Hotel*, 15 Jln Gereja, T 2244824; **Budget**, Suite 216, 2nd Flr Orchid Plaza, T 2243951; **Calio**, *Tropical Inn*, Jln Gereja, T 2233325; **Halaju Selatan**, 4M-1 Larkin Complex, Jln Larkin; **Hertz**, Room 646, Puteri Pan Pacific Hotel, Jln Salim, T 2237520; **National**, 50-B Ground Floor Bangunan Felda, Jln Sengget, T 2230503 (and at the airport); **Thrifty**, *Holiday Inn*, Jln Dato Sulaiman, T 3332313; **Sintat**, 2nd Flr, Tun Abdul Razak Kompleks (KOMTAR), Jln Wong Ah Fook, T 2227110. **Taxi**: popular and quite cheap.

Air MAS and Pelangi fly into Senai, JB's airport, 20 km north of the city. **Transport to town**: buses every hour (RM1.40), taxis (RM25). For passengers flying MAS to Singapore, there is a shuttle service from the airport to *Novotel Orchid Inn*, Singapore with express immigration clearance. MAS operate an a/c shuttle bus from *Puteri Pan Pacific Hotel* to the airport (RM4). Regular connections on MAS with Ipoh, Kota Kinabalu, Kuala Lumpur, Kuala Terengganu, Kuantan, Kuching, Labuan, Lahad Datu, Miri, Penang and Tawau. Pelangi Airways fly to Ipoh and KL and to destinations in Sumatra (see International connections).

Train The station is on Jln Campbell, near the causeway, off Jln Tun Abdul Razak. Regular connections with KL and all destinations on the west coast, see page 512 for timetable.

Road Bus: the new Larkin bus terminal is inconveniently located 4 km north of the town centre. Regular connections with Melaka, KL (RM16.50), Lumut, Ipoh (RM25.80), Butterworth (RM33.50), Mersing, Kuantan, Kuala Terengganu, Alor Star (RM37.70), Kota Bharu. **Taxi**: the main long-distance taxi station attached to the Larkin bus terminal 4 km north of town. However the old terminal, on Jln Wong Ah Fook, is also still operating and much more convenient. Taxis from here to destinations including KL, Melaka, Mersing and Kuantan.

Sea JB's new ferry terminal to the east of the causeway should now be operating ferry services to Mersing and Tanjung Belungkor.

● International connections

The causeway between JB and Singapore can get jammed, particularly at rush hours although a Special Priority Lane is now open for speedier clearance of tourists. Avoid the causeway at all costs during public holidays.

Air As well as the domestic routes listed above, MAS also operates international connections with Denpasar (Bali), Jakarta, Surabaya, Sandakan and Ujung Pandang, all in Indonesia as well as other worldwide destinations. Pelangi Airways flies daily to Medan and 4 times a week to Padang and Palembang, all in Sumatra, Indonesia.

Train Malaysian and Singapore immigration desks are actually in the Singapore railway station, so for those wanting to avoid delays on the causeway, this is a quick way to get across the border; there are regular commuter trains across to the island, see page 512 for details of timetable.

Road Bus: the Singapore Bus Service between Singapore and JB runs every 10 minutes from 0630 to 2400. The Ban San Terminal (in Singapore) is between Queen St and Rochor Canal Rd. From Singapore, it costs twice as much as from JB, and from JB the Singapore Bus Service takes almost double the time to do the journey. The new JB bus terminal is at Larkin, 4 km north of town towards KL. The 170 Singapore bus and the SBS Johor/Singapore Express only leave from here. To save time at the border, get entry forms for Singapore at the Larkin bus terminal. **Taxi**: Malaysian taxis leave for Singapore from the taxi rank on the first floor of the car park near the KOMTAR building on Jln Wong Ah Fook. They leave when full and go to the JB taxi rank on Rochor Canal Rd in Singapore. Drivers provide immigration forms and take care of formalities making this a painless way of crossing the causeway. Touts also hang around JB's taxi rank offering the trip to Singapore in a private car. They will take you directly to your address in

Singapore, although their geography of the island is not always expert. This is also a fairly cost-effective way to travel and is reliable.

Sea Boat: bumboats leave from various points along Johor's ragged coastline for Singapore; most go to Changi Point (Changi Village), on the northeast of the island where there is an immigration and customs post. The bumboat routes from Tanjung Surat and Tanjung Pengileh to Changi Point make sense for those coming from the east coast, Teluk Makhota (Jason's Bay) or Desaru (taxis to the jetty from Desaru cost RM28). The boats run from 0700-1600 and depart when full (12 passengers). There is now a vehicle ferry from Tanjung Belungkor (JB) to Changi Point 3 times a day, T (65) 3236088. JB's new ferry terminal east of the causeway should now be operating ferry connnections with Changi Point and the World Trade Centre in Singapore, and Batam in Indonesia. The alternatives listed above may be squeezed out as a result.

The Peninsula's East Coast

Horizons	252	Taman Negara	281
Mersing	255	Kampung Cerating	287
Pulau Tioman	258	Kuala Terengganu	297
Endau Rompin National Park	270	Kota Bharu	306
Kuantan	273	Coast to coast	316

IT MIGHT just be on the other side of the peninsula, but Malaysia's east coast could as well be on a different planet than the populous, hectic and industrialized west coast. The coastline of the states of Johor, Pahang, Terengganu and Kelantan is lined with coconut palms, dotted with sleepy fishing kampungs and interspersed with rubber and oil palm plantations, paddy fields, beaches and mangroves. For centuries, the narrow coastal plain between the jungled mountains and the sea, was largely bypassed by trade and commerce and its 60-odd coral-fringed (and largely uninhabited) offshore islands were known only to local fishermen. The east coast is sold by Tourism Malaysia as 'the real Malaysia'.

The mountainous interior effectively cut the east coast off from the west coast, physically, commercially and culturally. The east coast did not have the tin deposits which attracted Chinese speculators and miners to the towns on the other side of the Main Range in the 19th century; and in more recent decades it was left behind as Malaysia joined the development race. The rural parts have been buffered from western influence; traditional kampung lifestyles have been tempered only by the arrival of the electric lightbulb, the outboard motor and the Honda 70. The east coast's fishermen and paddy farmers are Malaysia's most conservative Muslims. In the 1990 general election, the people of Kelantan voted a hard-line Islamic opposition party into power. In the 1995 general election they made the same choice once more. Parti Islam now runs the state government and represents its Kelantan constituencies in federal parliament. The rural Malays of the east coast have not enjoyed much in the way of 'trickledown' from Malaysia's new-found economic

East Coast Malaysia
THAILAND
INDONESIA
N
0
25
km
Tumpat
Pantai Cinta Berahi
Kota Bahru
Pulau Perhentian Kecil
Pulau Perhentian Besar
Sungai Kelantan
Pasir Puteh
Kuala Besut
Pulau Redang
Tanah Merah
Jerteh
Merang
Batu Rakit
Kuala Kerai
G Lawit 1,519m
Kuala Terengganu
Cendering
Lake Kenyir
Marang
KELANTAN
G Chirgoi 863m
TERENGGANU
Rantau Abang
Sungai Dungun
Dungun
Pulau Tenggol
G Perlis 1,279m
G Gagau 1,376m
G Mandi Angin 1,473m
G Tahan 2,187m
Taman Negara National Park
Kerteh
Kuala Tahan
Kemasik
Kemasik Pantai
G Dulang 1,063m
Kemaman
To Kuala Lipis
G Laris 1,073m
Cerating
PAHANG
G Tapis 1,512m
Beserah
Kuantan
South China Sea
Pekan
Mentakab
Temerloh
Sungai Pahang
Lake Chini
Lake Dampar
NEGERI SEMBILAN
Sungai Rompin
Pulau Tioman
Kuala Rompin
Bahau
JOHOR
Endau
To Kuala Lumpur
Endau Rompin National Park
Gemas
Segamat
Sungai Endau
Mersing

Islam on the east coast: fundamental pointers

Because the east coast states are a bastion of Islamic conservatism – which was reinforced by the victory of Parti Islam in Kelantan in the 1995 general election – visitors should be particularly sensitive to the strictures of Islam. Those determined to get an all-over tan should not attempt to acquire it on the east coast's beaches, and women should dress 'respectfully' in public. Many Malay women choose to wear the *tudung* – the veil which signifies adherence to the puritanical lifestyle of the fervently Islamic *dakwah* movement. The east coast stands in contrast to other parts of the peninsula, where this garb is more often a fashion accessory than representative of a lifestyle. In 1988 cultural purists on the east coast began voicing concern about the 'cultural and moral pollution' that tourism brought in its wake. But any resentment that the arrival of western tourists may have sparked seems to have evaporated in the face of the economic opportunities generated.

Malaysia's Islamic powerhouse in Kelantan and Terengganu states poses one possible occupational hazard for tourists – particularly if they travel north-to-south. In these two states, the weekend starts on Thursday lunchtime and everyone drifts back to work on Saturday. By and large, even the Chinese businesses observe the Muslim weekend. This means banks are shut – and those unfortunate to mistime their travels can find themselves arriving in Kuantan just in time for the banks there to close down too. Pahang state observes the Saturday/Sunday weekend. Be warned. In common with other strict Islamic states, there have also been moves in Kelantan to restrict the sale of alcohol, although at present it is still available in Chinese-run shops. Malay-run establishments in Terengganu and Kelantan are barred from serving alcohol. The bars and discos which contribute to a lively nightlife scene on the west coast are conspicuously absent on the east coast. In Kota Bharu even the large hotels do not serve alcohol, and recently there was a petition to form separate queues in supermarkets for men and women. In 1997 the state government in Kelantan went so far as to issue an edict that cinemas keep their lights on when showing films – just in case movie-goers have any amorous intentions. During Ramadan, which is strictly observed, Malay food and beverage outlets remain closed until Muslims break *puasa* (fast) after sundown. Although this means that it is impossible to find a good rendang or satay until the evening, travellers can feast on the amazing variety of colourful *kueh* – or cakes – which are sold at roadside stalls.

prosperity. Although they are *bumiputras* – or 'sons of the soil' (see page 90) – few have reaped the benefits of more than 2 decades of pro-Malay policies.

During World War Two, the Japanese Imperial Army landed at Kota Bharu and sped the length of the peninsula within 6 weeks on stolen bicycles (see page 55). The east coast did not figure prominently during the war, except in the realm of literary fiction, where it starred in Neville Shute's *A Town Like Alice*.

Before and after the war, rubber and oil palm plantations sprang up – particularly in the south state of Johor – which changed the shape of the agricultural economy. But the most dramatic change followed the discovery of large quantities of high-grade crude oil and natural gas off the northeast coast in the 1970s. By the mid-1980s, huge storage depots, gas processing plants and refineries had been built in Terengganu, and the battered old coast road was upgraded to cater for Esso and Petronas tankers. The town of Kerteh, half-way between Kuantan and Kuala Terengganu is a refinery town, built along one of the best beaches on the peninsula. The construction boom and the rig work, helped boost the local economy and provide employment, but the east coast states (bar Johor, which straddles the entire south tip of the peninsula) have singularly failed to attract much industrial investment in the way their west coast neighbours have. Oil money has, however, helped transform the fortunes of Terengganu.

On the whole, the east coast has been less sullied by industrial pollution; the South China Sea is a lot cleaner than the Strait of Melaka. Despite the oil the east coast is still the rural backwater of the peninsula (95% of state revenues from oil go straight into federal coffers in KL). With its jungle, beaches and islands and its strong Malay cultural traditions, it holds many attractions for tourists. The only problem is that during the western world's winter holiday period, the east coast is awash with monsoon flood water, which confines the tourist season to between March and October. Many beach resorts completely close down during these monsoon months as do the offshore islands. The best known tourist attraction on the east coast is the grimy village of Rantau Abang in Terengganu, where leatherback turtles lumber up the beach to lay their eggs between May and October.

Getting to the East Coast

Peninsular Malaysia's east coast can be reached from various points on the west coast. Routes from Butterworth (Penang) and Kuala Kangsar in the north, lead across to Kota Bharu on the northeast coast. The highway from Kuala Lumpur goes to Kuantan (half-way down the east coast) and the railway cuts north from Gemas (south of KL) to Kota Bharu. There are also road routes from KL to the southeast coast. Another common route is to follow the trunk road north from Johor Bahru which hits the east coast at Mersing, the launch-pad for Pulau Tioman and the islands of the Seribuat group.

MERSING

The small fishing port of Mersing is a pleasant but undistinguished little town. Most people are in a hurry to get to the islands and spend as little time as possible in the town, but as fishing boats can only make it out into the sea at high tide, some people will inevitably get stuck here for the night. In the past couple of years a number of good little restaurants have sprung up and Mersing is not an unpleasant place to spend a day or two. The town is evidently prospering, thanks to the through flow of tourists to the islands. A big new plaza opened in 1992 and now accommodates the plethora of tour and ticketing agencies.

The riverside jetty (just out of town to the east) is the jumping-off point for Pulau Tioman, the best known of the east coast's offshore islands. There are, however, 64 islands in total; others that can be reached from Mersing include Pulau Rawa, Pulau Sibu, Pulau Tinggi, Pulau Tengah, Pulau Aur and Pulau Pemanggil (see below).

9 km north of Mersing on the road to Endau, there is a reasonably good beach, **Pantai Air Papan**, signposted off the road. Formerly, the most popular beach was **Sri Pantai**, but it is now stoney and unpleasant.

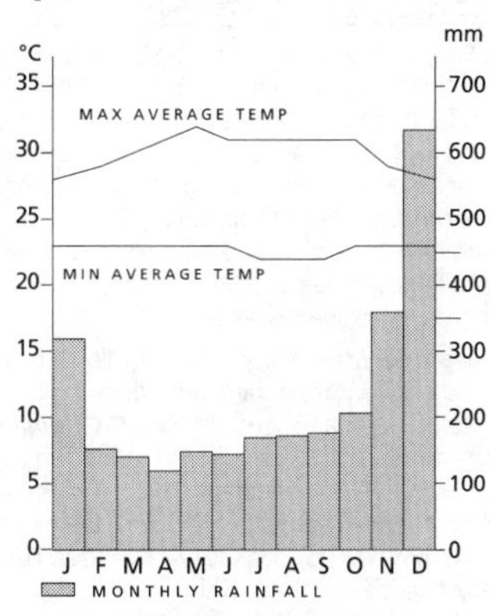

Climate: Mersing

Excursions

Endau Rompin National Park (see page 269).

Air Papan beach, 9 km north of Mersing, passes as the best mainland beach in the area. It is 5 km off the main road north and the beach is about 2 km long, between two headlands. Pantai Air Papan is quite exposed but is backed by lines of casuarina and coconut palms. There is a liberal scattering of rubbish among the trees. There are a number of places at the end of the road offering budget accommodation within the **C-E** range. These include *Teluk Godek Chalet (Lani's Place)*, T 792569 which looks the newest and best; *Mersing Chalet and Restaurant*, T 794194; *Air Papan Chalets*, T 792993. More secluded is *Nusantara Chalet*, 1.5 km north through the kampung which stretches along the beach. There are a few beach-shelters dotted along the beach. *Getting there*: **Bus**: Mersing-Endau bus (No 5) to Simpang Air Papan (turn-off); there is no bus service connecting with the beach, although it is possible to hitchhike. **Taxi**: chartered taxi costs. Arrangements can be made for pick-ups later in the day.

Local information

● Accommodation

Prices: L over RM500; **A+** RM260-500; **A** RM130-260; **B** RM65-130; **C** RM40-65; **D** RM20-40; **E** RM10-20; **F** Below RM10

A *Sutera Emas Villa*, c/o Sutera Emas Tour, No 13 Plaza R & R, Jln Abu Bakar, T 07-7993155, a/c, for those wanting a bit more comfort, this small tour company has 2 fully furnished, self-catering apartments 3 km north of Mersing; **A-B** *Mersing Inn*, 38 Jln Ismail, T 7991919, fairly new, so discounts are available (overpriced at full price), clean and bright, but bathrooms are very small and there's no restaurant.

B *Mersing Merlin Inn*, Batu 1, Jln Endau, T 7991313, a/c, restaurant, pool, decaying concrete block on a hill out of town. **B-C** *Rumah Rehat* (Rest House), 490 Jln Ismail, T 7992102/3, a/c, restaurant, a bit of a walk out of town towards the sea but one of the nicest in Malaysia, overlooking the golf course and the sea, big, clean rooms with views, well-kept garden and airy communal sitting area with balcony, recommended.

C *Country Hotel*, 11 Jln Sulaiman, T 7991799, a/c/fan formerly the *Mandarin Hotel*, very clean and pleasant, but in noisy downtown location near the market and the bus and taxi stands. **C-D** *Embassy*, 2 Jln Ismail, T 7993545/7991301, some a/c, restaurant, very well-kept hotel – scrupulously clean, rooms without TVs considerably cheaper, *Embassy* annexe across the street above *Restoran Keluarga* (basic, cheap rooms), mountain bike hire (RM10/day, RM2/hour) and ticketing, recommended. **C-E** *Kali's Guesthouse*, No 12E Kampung Sri Lalang, T 7993613, fan only, restaurant, arguably the best-kept, friendliest and most relaxed place to stay in Mersing area, rooms range from longhouse dorm to 'A'-frames and bungalows, atap-roofed bar and small Italian restaurant in garden next to beach, managed by Kali (a qualified diving instructor) and two Italians. *Getting there*: Mersing-Endau bus (RM0.40) or taxi RM3, highly recommended. **C-D** *Mersing*, 1 Jln Dato' Mohammed Ali, T 7991004, a/c, restaurant, spartan rooms now a bit tatty, clean enough but *Embassy* a better bet.

D *Golden City*, 23 Jln Abu Bakar, T 7991325, some a/c, near the bus station, clean but a bit run-down. **D** *Wisma Sutera Emas* (*Juni Guesthouse*), c/o Sutera Emas Tour, No 13 Plaza R & R, Jln Abu Bakar, T 7993155, 500m down Kota Tinggi road, guesthouse inside small complex, some a/c, large breakfast included, very friendly owner, recommended. **D-E** *The Cuckoo's Nest*, 9-1 Jln Dato Timor, T 7991060, F 7991060. Price includes breakfast. Recently opened guesthouse jointly owned by a Swiss-Malay couple and an Indian. Dorm beds (**F**), library and snacks available. **D-F** *Farm Guesthouse*, Kampung Tenglu Laut, chalets and dorm in relaxed kampung setting next to muddy beach, all food for extra RM10/day, run by a Malay (Ramli) and his Swiss wife (Marianne). *Getting there*: Mersing-Endau bus (No 5) 7 km north (RM0.45), walk 600m to mosque, turn right for further 300m, taxi RM5.

E *East Coast Hotel*, 43a Jln Abu Bakar, T 7991337, rooms here are reportedly spacious and clean. **E** *Syuan Koong*, 44A Jln Abu Bakar, T 7991135, fan only, some rooms with attached bath, clean and fairly new-looking.

F *Omar Backpackers' Dorm*, Jln Abu Bakar, clean and well looked-after but only 10 beds, excellent information on Sibu and other less visited islands, recommended. **F** *Sheikh Guesthouse*, 1B Jln Abu Bakar, T 7993767, dorms only, clean and friendly, efficient tourist agency attached with information on all the islands, the

Sheikh Tourist Agency downstairs offers ticketing, tours, accommodation booking and up-to-date information on Tioman and other islands, ask here for details on other accommodation up the coast, eg **E** ***Farm Guesthouse***, T 7993767. **F** ***Tioman Lodging***, 2 Jln Ismail (above *Malayan Muslim Seafood Restaurant*), dorms and rooms run by young Malay couple from Tioman, clean with information about islands, ticketing.

● Places to eat

Prices: ♦♦♦♦ over RM40; ♦♦♦ RM13-40; ♦♦ RM5-13; ♦ under RM5

Restaurants seem to close quite early here.

Malay: ♦***Malayan Muslim Seafood***, 2 Jln Ismail, very cheap and unusual Malay restaurant with coconut seafood dishes, special Indonesian fish-head curry, recommended. ♦***Malaysia***, opposite the bus stop, open all night. ♦***Restoran Al-Arif***, 44 Jln Ismail (opposite *Parkson* supermarket), cheap Muslim restaurant with good rotis and curries. ♦***Sofair***, 25 Jln Ismail, Indian coffee shop serving rotis and murtabak. ♦***Sri Mersing Café***, opposite *Restoran Malaysia*. ♦***Zam-Zam***, 51 Jln Abu Bakar, more Muslim food with dosai, prata and Mersing's best murtabaks.

Chinese: ♦♦♦***New I came also***, 181 Jln Jemalang, excellent Chinese food, very friendly service. ♦♦***Embassy Hotel Restaurant***, 2 Jln Ismail, big Chinese seafood menu, reasonably priced, chilli crabs, drunken prawns, wild boar and kang-kong belacan, recommended. ♦♦***Mersing*** (Ground Floor, *Mersing Hotel*), Jln Dato Mohammed Ali, excellent seafood. ♦♦***Mersing Seafood***, 56 Jln Ismail, a/c restaurant with spicy Szechuan or Cantonese seafood dishes, try squid with salted egg yoke, spicy coconut butter prawns, big menu, reasonable prices. ♦♦***Sin Nam Kee Seafood***, 387 Jln Jemaluang (1 km out of town on Kota Tinggi road), huge seafood menu and reckoned by locals to be the best restaurant in Mersing, occasional karaoke nights can be noisy. ♦***Yung Chuan Seafood***, 51 Jln Ismail, big open coffee shop with vast selection, speciality: seafood steamboat.

Indian: ♦***Taj Mahal***, Jln Abu Bakar.

Foodstalls: there are a number of upmarket stalls and coffee shops in the new *Plaza R & R* next to the river.

● Banks & money changers

Maybank, Jln Ismail; **UMBC**, Jln Ismail, no exchange on Sat. Money changer on Jln Abu Bakar and **Giamso Safari**, 23 Jln Abu Bakar also changes TCs.

● Hospitals & medical services

Dentists: Dr Logesh, Klinik Pergigian, 28 Jln Mohd, Ali, T 7993135.

Doctors: Dr Lai Chin Lai, Klinik Grace, 48 Jln Abu Bakar, T 7992399.

● Post & telecommunications

Area code 07.

Post Office: Jln Abu Bakar.

● Shopping

Lee Arts Souvenir, 1, Gerai MDM, Jln Tun Dr Ismail, next to Malay restaurants on the corner after *R & R Plaza*. Artist Sulaiman Aziz specializes in colourful T-shirts, shorts and beachware and hand-painted batiks. There are some nick-nacky souvenir shops in the *R & R Plaza*.

● Tour companies & travel agents

There are ticketing and travel agents all over town dealing with travel to and from the islands and accommodation. They are much of a muchness and visitors are unlikely to be ripped off. Many agents are now located in the new *Plaza R & R* on Jln Tun Dr Ismail, next to the river. Competition is intense at peak season and tourists can be hassled for custom. Many agents also promote specific chalet resorts on the islands to which they offer package deals; sometimes these can be good value, but buying a boat ticket puts you under no obligation to stay at a particular place. Among the better agents are: ***Dura Tourist Agency***, 7 Jln Abu Bakar, T 7991002; ***Giamso Safari***, 23 Jln Abu Bakar, T 7992253, F 7991723 (owns *Paya Beach Resort* on Tioman); ***Island Connection***, 19 R & R Plaza (owns *Mukut Village Chalets* on Tioman); ***Sheikh Tourist Agency***, 1B Jln Abu Bakar, T 7993767.

● Tourist offices

Mersing Tourist Information Centre, Jln Abu Bakar (about 1 km from the jetty walking into town), T 7995212. Friendly and useful source of information.

● Transport

133 km north of Johor Bahru and 189 km south of Kuantan; 353 km from KL.

Local Bus: the local bus station is on Jln Sulaiman opposite the *Country Hotel*.

Road Bus: long-distance buses leave from two locations: the roundabout by the *Restoran Malaysia* and Jln Abu Bakar, not far from the jetty. Regular connections with KL, JB, Kuala Terengganu, Kuantan, Ipoh, Penang, Melaka, 5 hours, and Singapore. Passengers have reported having their bags stolen en route between Mersing and Singapore while stored in the luggage compartment of the coach. This applies, for example, to the *Johora Express* bus company. **Taxi**: taxis leave from Jln Sulaiman opposite the *Country Hotel*, next to the local bus station; KL, JB (for Singapore, change at JB), Melaka (RM25), Kuala Terengganu and Kuantan.

Sea Boat: the jetty is a 5-minute walk from the bus stop. Most of the ticket offices are by the jetty but boat tickets are also sold from booths near the bus stop. (See transport to individual islands.) **NB** The boat trip to the islands from Mersing can be extremely rough during the monsoon season; boats will sometimes leave Mersing in the late afternoon, on the high tide, but rough seas can delay the voyage considerably. During peak monsoon all ferry services are cancelled and the ferry companies move to the west coast to find work there. It is advisable only to travel during daylight hours.

PULAU TIOMAN

Tioman, 56 km off Mersing, is the largest island in the volcanic Seribuat Archipelago – it is all of 20 km by 12 km. The island is dominated by several jagged peaks (notably the twin peaks of Nenek Semukut and Bau Sirau towards the southern end of the island) and in Malay legend its distinctive profile is the back of a dragon whose feet got stuck in the coral. Tioman is densely forested and is fringed by white coral-sand beaches; with kampungs around the coast. The highest peak is Gunung Kajang (1,049m) or 'Palm Frond Mountain'. It has been used as a navigational aid for centuries and is mentioned in early Arab and Chinese sailing charts. In the mid-1970s, 12th century Sung Dynasty porcelain was unearthed on the island.

Despite the growth in hotels and guesthouses, Tioman, once rated as one of the world's 10 best 'desert island escapes' by *Time* magazine, remains a beautiful island. In the 1950s it was discovered by Hollywood and selected as the location for the musical *South Pacific* where it starred as the mythical island of Bali Hai. All this attention put Tioman on the map; tourism accelerated during the 1970s and 1980s as facilities were expanded. However, during the 90s business has not been quite so brisk and prices, which for some establishments during the 80s were absurdly high, given the level of amenities on offer, have now levelled out. Indeed most hotels have not increased their rates for 5 years or so. Even so there are various new hotels under construction and guesthouses still seem to be building new chalets or upgrading existing ones.The cheaper beach-hut accommodation is mostly to be found on the northwest side of the panhandle, and despite a growth in the number of places to stay, these little kampungs have retained their charm and are still very laid back, making them an idyllic retreat for anyone who is looking for a deserted beach, a touch of snorkeling or diving and some great seafood. Thankfully, as yet, there are no nightclubs or fastfood restaurants and the tourist-trinket shops are very low key. But the emergence of a condotel – even the name must be one of the ugliest in the English language – to the south of the *Berjaya Tioman Beach Resort* (and owned by them) is, perhaps, a sign of things to come.

NB Sandflies can be a problem on Tioman and mosquito coils are recommended.

Getting around the island There are very few trails around the island and only one road – a 2 km-long stretch from the airstrip at Tekek to the *Berjaya Tioman Beach Resort*. Plans are afoot to build a road across to the less-developed east side of the island, presently connected by a beautiful jungle trail (see trekking, below), but there has been talk of this for a number of years. To get from one kampung to another, the best way is to go by boat and a 'sea bus' service works its way around the island (see Transport, below).

Treks The **cross-island trail**, from the mosque in Kampung Tekek to Kampung Juara, on the east coast, is a 2-3 hour hike (around 4 km), which is quite steep in places. The trail is reasonably well marked: follow the path past the airport and then turn inland towards the mosque. From Juara, the trail begins opposite the

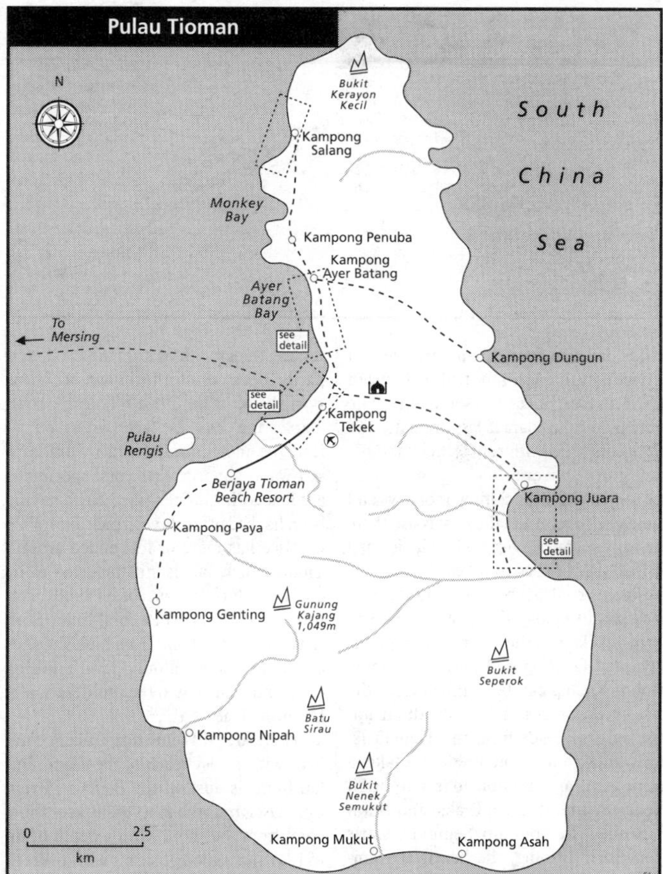

pier. It is a great walk, although for those planning to stay at Juara, it is a tough climb with a full pack. The section from Tekek is part natural path, part concrete steps. Three-quarters of the way up from Tekek there is a small waterfall – really just a jumble of rocks and water – just off the path to the right. Wonderfully refreshing after the arduous climb, but check for leeches when you emerge. Shortly after the waterfall the route levels out and works it way through an upland plateau. This is the most enchanting part of the walk: massive trees and dense forest, strangling figs – a real taste of jungle. It is not unusual to see squirrels, monkeys and various tropical insects. Some enterprising Livingstones have even carved 'Jane' and 'Tarzan' on one of the trees. Just as the path begins to descend towards Juara there is a small drinks stop – the *Rest Cross* – incongruously located amongst the giant trees. This marks the beginning of the concrete trail which

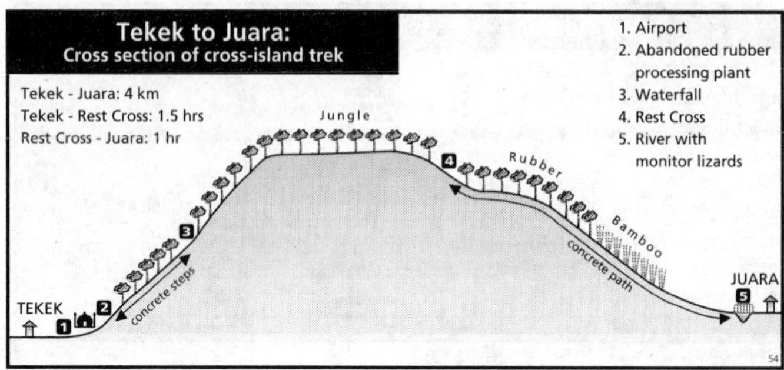

winds down to Juara. A motorcycle taxi service is available for the truly exhausted as well as fruit juices and soft drinks. The section down to Juara is less dramatic and more cultivated with rubber trees and banana groves, but even here it is common to see some wildlife, including monkeys and squirrels. To return to the west coast, there is a daily sea bus service from Juara leaving at 1500 (RM18 back to Tekek).

There are also many easier jungle and coastal walks along the west coast: south from Tekek, past the resort to kampungs Paya and Genting and north to Salang. Mount Kajang can be climbed from the east or west sides of the island; an unmarked trail leads from the Tioman Island golf course (advisable to take a guide). It is also possible to trek to Bukit Nenek Semukut (Twin Peaks) and Bukit Seperok. The trail up Semukut starts from Pasir Burong, the beach at Kampung Pasir. Guides available from *Berjaya Tioman Beach Resort* and *Happy Café*, Juara and *Zaha's Information Service* (near the jetty at Tekek) and Kampung Tekek. The trail from Kampung Juara, on the east coast, is longer and more arduous.

Diving Tioman's coral reefs are mainly on the western side of the island, although sadly large areas have been killed off. This is in part due to fishing boats dragging anchor, partly through nimble-fingered snorkellers pilfering coral stalks (this kills neighbouring corals), partly because all the boat activity kicks up sand and retards the growth or kills the coral, and partly because of the crown-of-thorns starfish (see page 295). Wholesale coral 'harvesting' has also been going on, to feed the increasingly lucrative trade in salt-water aquaria. Live coral specimens are loaded into water-filled bags, having been hacked off reefs with pick axes. This practice has more or less ended around Tioman now, but is still reported to be going on off other east coast islands. Pollution is also said to be a coral-killer. Both sewerage and effluent from building sites can alter water salinity levels, killing coral and resulting in the proliferation of harmful algae.

There are still some magnificent coral beds within easy reach of the island. Pulau Renggis, just off the *Berjaya Tioman Beach Resort*, is the most easily accessible coral from the shore, with a depth of up to 12m and a good place for new divers to find their flippers. For more adventurous dives, the islands off the northwest coast are a better bet. There is cave diving off Pulau Chebeh – 20 minutes from the *Berjaya* (up to 25m), and varied marine life off the cliff-like rocks of Golden Reef (25 minutes from the *Berjaya* and up to 20m) and nearby Tiger Reef (20 minutes from *Berjaya* and up to 50m). Off the northeastern tip of the island is Magicienne Rock (30 minutes from *Berjaya* and 25m dives) – where bigger fish have been sited. Off the southwestern coast is Bahara Rock (30 minutes from *Berjaya* and 20m), considered one of the best spots on the island. Best time to dive: mid-March to May, when visibility is at its best, but it is possible to dive through to the end of October. There are dive shops based in most of the kampung: at Salang, Tekek, Genting, Paya, Ayer Batang and at the *Berjaya Tioman Beach Resort* (see the listings under each kampung entry).

Best time to visit Many guesthouses and resorts close down between November and February when it is wet and can be windy and rough. Chinese New Year seems to be a popular time for places to open, cashing in on the Singapore market, but as Chinese New Year is a moveable feast the date can vary considerably from year to year. Transport from Mersing also becomes more difficult during the off season; ferries will only leave if there is sufficient demand to make it worth their while.

Boat tours Boats leave from Kampung Tekek: to Pulau Tulai (or Coral Island) Turtle Island; to a waterfall at Mukut, or an around-island trip. All boats must be full – otherwise prices increase. Boat trips can also be arranged to other nearby islands. Boats can be booked through *Zaha's Information Service*, near the jetty, Kampung Tekek and from many of the guesthouses.

Local information

● Accommodation

Prices: L over RM500; **A+** RM260-500; **A** RM130-260; **B** RM65-130; **C** RM40-65; **D** RM20-40; **E** RM10-20; **F** Below RM10

The *Berjaya Tioman Beach Resort* and most of the cheaper places to stay are scattered along the west coast (the island is virtually uninhabited on the southeast and southwest sides and north of Juara Beach on the east coast, apart from 1 or 2 fishing kampungs). Most of the accommodation on the island is simple: atap or tin-roofed chalets/huts (**C-E** categories), 'A'-frames (**E-F**) or dorms (**F**). Chalets with attached bathrooms fall into our **C/D** categories and upwards. Not all have electricity. Rooms are fairly spartan; expect to pay more for mosquito nets and electricity. Inevitably, beach-front chalets cost more. Due to stiff competition, many prices are negotiable depending on the season.

Kampung Lalang is not really a kampung at all but a beach devoted solely to the *Berjaya Tioman Beach Resort* and its sister condotel. **A+** *Berjaya Tioman Beach Resort*, Lalang, T 4145445, F 4145718, 400 rooms set in 200 acres of land, built on the site of the old Kampung Lalang. Bought by Tan Sri Vincent Tan in 1993, when it was dramatically expanded, this tourist class hotel is by far the biggest and most expensive resort on Tioman, with a good range of facilities and a lovely stretch of beach. This is not the place to come if you are hoping for a quiet retreat; during holiday periods, the whole place is heaving with activity. Rooms are adequately equipped but furnishings are a little dated. Choice of rooms; the cheapest have garden views and are the older one storey chalets. The deluxe and superior two storey chalets are bigger and are more suitable for families, some overlook the sea (if you crane your neck). All rooms have wooden floors and balconies, a/c, TV and mini-bar. Rather shabby bathrooms, with hot water shower only(bath tubs in deluxe rooms only). The suites are very forgettable. Several restaurants (see places to eat below). Rather cramped area for the free-form pool with children's slides and jacuzzi. Watersports centre (including scuba diving facilities, RM800 for a 6-7 day PADI certification course) with boats for diving and snorkelling parties to nearby islands, (it is possible to snorkel 100m out from the northern end of the bay and at the very southern end, near the beach) jet skis, windsurfers, 18-hole golf course (see Sports at the end of the entry for details), gym – with good range of (under used) equipment,donkey and horse riding, tennis courts. The *Condotel* is a very ugly 4 storey block perched on a rocky promontory to the south of the *Berjaya*, which opened in March 1997. All the rooms are suites, with a sitting area looking onto balconies. The drawback here is that there are no eating outlets (just a small shop with ready to eat food and pantries in all the suites). A shuttle bus service runs to the hotel at meal times. There is a large lengths pool with no shade. The best rooms face south. The *Condotel* is largely a time share affair but will also be used as an overflow place for the *Berjaya*.

Kampung Tekek is the kampung-capital of Tioman and, frankly, is nothing special. However because boats from Mersing first call at Tekek's large concrete jetty, and the airport is also here, many visitors decide to stay put rather than face another journey. Others find they have to stay a night here 'in transit'. Tekek has the longest

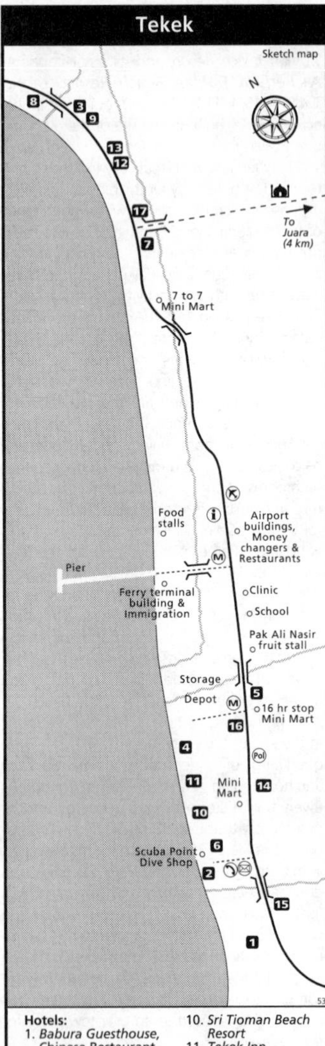

beach on the island, but for a large stretch north of the jetty it is rather dirty and with an ugly concrete breakwater. Almost all the coral is dead and broken, the river is polluted and there are rusting oil drums and other paraphernalia littering the town. There are many places to stay at Tekek, mostly south of the jetty or towards the northern end of the bay. However, much of the accommodation is run down and the place doesn't have much of a tropical island resort atmosphere. It feels like a small service centre – which is what it is. Tekek has a small post office, a police post, a clinic, a couple of money changers, the administrative HQ for the island, a few mini-marts, and an immigration post. There are two main areas of accommodation. One group of guesthouses is south of the jetty within 5-10 minutes walk of the jetty and airport. A second group begins 500m north of the jetty and airport and stretches towards the National Park office at the far end of the bay. These are quieter, cheaper, but in general do not seem to be so well run. The 'road' here is just a 1m-wide concrete path. **B** ***Persona Island Resort***, T/F 4146213 (in Kuantan T 09-3155566, F 09 5130510), some a/c, restaurant, turn right at jetty and this place is a 10-minute walk. It is the flashest place to stay in Tekek with 24 clean and functional rooms in 2-storey buildings but it is not on the beach. Large restaurant. **A-C** ***Babura Sea View***, T 011-767502, some a/c, restaurant, the last place at the south end of the beach with 23 varied rooms. It consists of 3 separately owned businesses – the resort, a good Chinese restaurant, and *Tioman Reef Divers*, a PADI/NAUI dive shop. The rooms are clean and well maintained although some can be dark; the best are in the new block on the beach front, recommended. **B-D** ***Coral Reef Holidays***, T 011-766326, some a/c, restaurant, a group of chalets all looking rather jaded and dusty, some facing onto the sea, others set back and facing one another. **B-D** ***Sri Tioman Beach Resort***, T 09-4145189, some a/c, restaurant, a popular place and one of the better places to stay in this price range in Tekek. Sea-facing chalets shaded beneath casuarina trees, good restaurant with prawn, squid and fish dishes as well as the usual range of pancakes etc. **D** ***Tekek Inn***, T 011-358395, this is perhaps the best of the cheaper places to stay. It is on the beach, rooms are OK with attached showers, the management is suitably relaxed and there are snorkels and canoes for hire. A PADI dive shop should open here in 1997/98 but there is no restaurant, just a drinks station, recommended. **C** ***Mastura***, T 011-715283, restaurant (American breakfast included in room rate) on the beach and run by Zuki. Much the same as *Tekek Inn* and *Sri Tioman Beach Resort* (the three actually share guests when they are full) although *Mastura* suffers from being next to what looks like an oil storage depot. **B-C** ***Peladang***, T 09-4146249, F 09-4146249, some a/c, a well-kept little place with clean and comfortable chalets. It's big drawback is that it is on the opposite side of the road some distance from the beach so it is neither possible to watch the sun go down over the horizon nor dash headlong from your chalet into the water. **D** ***Tioman Enterprise***, T 011-952856, lovingly cared for but very small chalets – more like Wendy Houses. The guesthouse is right at the end of the runway. **D** ***Seroja Inn II***, T 7995209, restaurant, 24 undistinguished chalets in front of beach, bicycles for hire. The following are all around RM25 and there is little to mark them out from one another: ***Faira***, ***Ramli's House***, and ***Tioman Sea View***.

Other services at Tekek: Tekek has a good range of restaurants, including some which are independent of guesthouses. The ***Babura Sea View Chinese Restaurant*** (separate ownership from the guesthouse) is recommended and so too is the ***Liza Restaurant***, which is the most sophisticated place to have a meal. Of the guesthouse restaurants the one at the ***Sri Tioman Beach Resort*** is worth trying, especially the squid and chilli prawns, while the small ***Malay No Name Restaurant*** north of the *Babura* and before the bridge is also recommended, as are the food stalls just north of the pier. There are a number of minimarts in the Kampung; ***Pak Ali Nasir's*** stall is the best place for fruit; and there is a very small market area next to the *Peladang Restaurant*. See the general entries below for details on other amenities. **Diving**: the best dive shop is reputedly ***Tioman Reef Divers*** attached to *Babura Sea View*. It offers PADI and NAUI certification courses. Other dive shops include ***Scuba Point*** (PADI) next to *Coral Reef Holidays*, and a new dive shop (PADI) attached to the *Tekek Inn*.

Kampung Penuba: **C-D** *Penuba Paradise Inn*, this place is situated just to the north of Kampung Ayer Batang, on the next promontory, and has its own jetty. Attractively laid out chalets built on stilts on the hillside, many with seaviews. Rocky beach, snorkelling in front of resort, restaurant, rather idyllic being so secluded, homely atmosphere, **F** for dorms

Kampung Ayer Batang lies to the north of Tekek. Accommodation here is spread out around the bay and is generally quite good. The beach is rocky at low tide and the sandy area quite small. On the whole, accommodation at Ayer Batang is better than at Tekek. There are said to be some monitor lizards here and the tall coconut palms are home to scores of bickering fruit bats during the day. **B-C** ***Johan's House***, big plot with small chalets on the beach and some newer and bigger rooms with a/c on the hill. Extensive travellers' food menu, snorkelling equipment for hire, library, speedboat available. **B-D** *Nazri's*, the most southerly of the guesthouses in Ayer Batang with a range of accommodation. The complex is set around a mangrove swamp (so bring your mosquito coils) reputedly home to large monitor lizards. Some rooms in rows with a running verandah (5 with a seaview), some simple 'A' frames at the back of the plot, amongst the mango trees. Spartan but clean rooms, restaurant on seafront, friendly management, good discounts available during low season, recommended. **E** *Tioman House*, 20 small huts built at right angles to the beach, a bit cramped, basic with fans. Seaside restaurant. **E** *ABC*, last place to stay at northern end of beach (good beach here), small 'A'-frames, attractive rather intimate little plot with family atmosphere, good cheap food, hammocks, volleyball, friendly service, recommended. **E** *Double Ace*, small rooms in 'A'-frames on a cramped plot. **E** *Mawar*, basic rather gloomy 'A' frames all with balconies right on the beach. Restaurant with lots of seafood, hammocks. **D-E** *TC*, 12 'A' frames, very basic, mosquito nets provided, no food here. **E** *My Friend Place*, very small rooms, fan and mosquito net. **C-E** *Mokhtar's*, huts look onto an attractive little garden, fan and mosquito nets provided, basic restaurant, unfriendly owner. **D-E** *South Pacific*, 19 basic but adequate and clean rooms with fans and mosquito nets in choice of setting, some have seaview, two restaurants with good fish (notably the owner's fresh water catfish which he rears in ponds behind the guesthouse). Plenty of fruit available from trees on plot (in the right season). Friendly owner from Kuantan will happily negotiate a good price for room, recommended. **E** *Sri Nelayan*, row of 10 small chalets. **E** *Rinda House*, small rooms with mosquito nets set around a very attractive little garden with outside café. **C** *Nazri 11* (also called *Air Batang Beach Cabanas*), the most expensive on this beach and by far the nicest, with decent, clean and not too cramped rooms with wooden floors and seaviews. A raised restaurant provides a spectacular view of the bay. Laundry service, jet ski, fishing and snorkeling available, recommended.

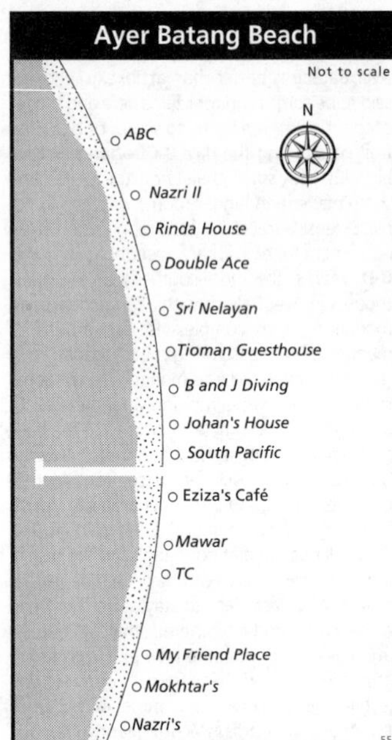

Other services at Kampung Ayer Batang: *B&J Diving Centre* next to *Johan's House* has a small pool for diving practice and can provide PADI certification. Mini market next to *Sri Nelayan's* for basic supplies and souvenirs. *Eziza's Café* near the jetty offer simple dishes.

Kampung Salang is the northernmost development on the island and is set in a sheltered cove with a beautiful beach. Development here is quite ramshackle, with a scattering of beachside restaurants and a relaxed atmosphere. The mangrove swamp to the south of the jetty, though dirty, still holds plenty of monitor lizards which cruise around like primeval monsters. Some are getting on for 2m in length. A 500-room resort, the *Tunku Adunan*, has been under construction for at least 18 months at the south end of the Bay, past *Zaid's Place*, despite a supposed ban on new developments. When it is finally completed Salang's laid back atmosphere may become part of history. **B-D** *Salang Beach Resort*, Chinese restaurant, spacious chalets with verandahs set in well-kept grounds, some with a/c. This is the northernmost development so it is quiet and the beach is virtually a private one. The management can be brusque. **C** *Zaid's Place*, a popular place, with fairly switched-on management. There's a choice of rooms, some with seaview, others which face onto a little garden, all are clean and have fans. Money changer, library, good restaurant, recommended. **B-D** *Salang Indah*, T 793155, large rather garish restaurant with seafood specialities, variety of chalets in all price brackets, some with attached bathrooms right on the sea, others with a/c and private stairs down to the sea, plus the original rather drab rooms in a 'U'-shaped barrack of a building. The guesthouse is owned by the Orang Kayah and expansion is still underway with a number of new Minang-style chalets built in 1997, provides a minimart and various other services. It is hard to avoid the conclusion that it has over-expanded. **B-D** *Khalid's Place*, 36 rooms in relatively new compound – a pleasant garden setting with fairly basic rooms. Family room available. If Khalid's girth is anything to go by, the restaurant must be good. **D** *Paklong*, 5 rooms with fan, no seaview, but friendly family management, rather fetid swamp close by.

Other services at Salang: this is a sizeable hamlet, so there are a number of restaurants independent of the guesthouses. ***Sunset Boulevard*** is built over the sea north of the *Salang Indah*. Good seafood and the best spot for a cold beer. Among the best of the warungs is the place just north of the *Sunset Boulevard* – simple dishes, breakfast served. Another good option is ***Amin's Café*** right by the jetty; it provides breakfast, lunch and dinner, simple, low key place. ***Salang Dreams*** next to the *Salang Indah Minimart* has good Malay food and a good evening seafood BBQ. There are minimarts at *Salang Indah* and at *Khalid's Place* for basic supplies such as drinks, toilet paper, nibblies, fruit etc. **Diving**: Salang is sold as a snorkellers' haven but, sadly, that is history – the coral is disappointing. It does, however, get better further out, and where the coral cliff drops off to deeper water, there is a more interesting variety of marine life including the odd reef shark. ***Ben's Diving Centre***, next to *Salang Indah* hires out equipment and can organize PADI certification and diving trips to nearby islands. A 4-day PADI course costs RM625, two dives RM110, which include equipment and boat. ***Dive Asia*** by the *Salang Beach Resort* also offers PADI certification; one dive with a full set is costed at RM70, night dives also arranged. ***Fishermen Dive Centre*** near the *Salang Indah* offer SSI (Scuba Schools International) certification, a full course costs RM750, a full day's diving, RM140. There is also ***B&J***

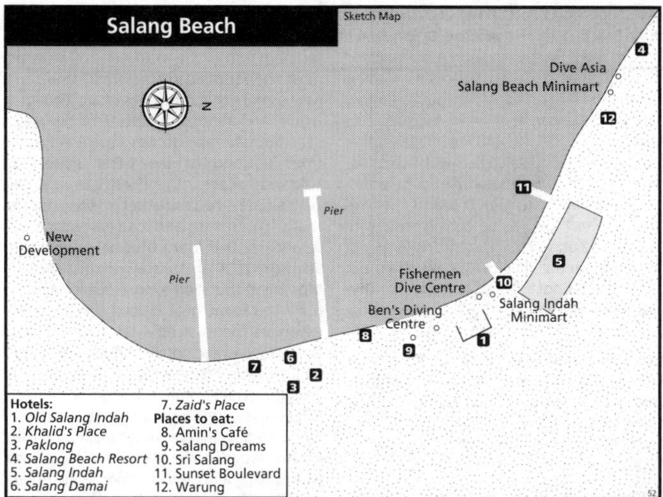

another PADI outfit, T 011-717014, F 011-954247. Snorkels and fins can be hired just about everywhere, about RM7-10/day.

Kampung Paya is south of Tekek. The jetty here has now been upgraded and the ferries from Mersing stop here. The beach is attractive enough but at low tide a belt of dead and broken coral makes swimming difficult. It is a quiet place with a small *surau* (prayer hall) and a couple of restaurants. **A** *Paya Resort* (booking office Jln Sulaiman 11, Mersing, T 07-7991432, or in Singapore at 101 Upper Cross St, 01-36 People's Park Centre, T 5341010), T 01762534, restaurant, small resort with 30 a/c rooms, which is clean and well looked-after but perhaps a little overpriced given the standard of the rooms. There is a PADI dive school attached to the hotel, the resort, is owned by the director of *Giamso Safari* tour agency in Mersing. The resort is closed Nov-Jan. **D** *Sri Paya Holiday*, 26 small bungalows in the middle of the village by the pier, little character. **B-D** *Sri Paya Tioman Enterprise*, T 011-765744, T 02 (Singapore) 3656974, 10 a/c bungalows with twin double beds so that 4 can share and attached bathrooms, 8 small fan rooms. Clean but not a place to induce that tropical island paradise feeling.

Other services at Kampung Paya: the *Mekong Restaurant* at the south end of the bay produces good Chinese seafood dishes. Dive shop at the *Paya Resort* with PADI certification courses.

Kampung Genting lies to the south of Kampung Paya and is the second largest village on the island. However it is not as popular as some of the other kampungs and has the feeling of a locals resort. The extensive jetty gives an impression that the village had hoped for greater things. The beach here is poor; rocks are exposed at low tide and the coral is largely broken and dead. There is, though, an incredibly modest 'sight': the graves of Tun Mohamad bin Tun Adbul Majid, the 6th Bendahara of Pahang, and his wife, also of royal blood being the daughter of Sultan Mahmud of Johore-Riau-Lingga-Pahang. In 1803 the Bendahara (who had assumed the position the year before) and his wife were at sea between Tioman and the mainland when their boat foundered in a thunderstorm. With their cabin locked the couple were unable to escape and both drowned. Their bodies, though, were recovered and buried here after having been washed in fresh water from the local river – which is now known as the Sungai Air Rajah. (Another version has it that the bodies were never found and the graves are purely symbolic.). There is a *surau* (prayer hall) by the jetty. **B** *Tropical Coral Inn*, a/c, restaurant, T 011-713465, this place is owned by *Sany Travel and Tour*, 545 Orchard Rd (Far East Shopping Centre), Singapore, T 4661360, F 7328137 and 70% of guests come from Singapore on package deals. The chalets are adequate, there is a good restaurant and *Sharkey's*

Dive Shop is attached. **D** ***Bayu***, at the north end of the beach, quiet and secluded. **D** ***Sun Beach Resort***, about 50 rambling bungalows built too close together, some on the seafront others piled up the hill behind. Monstrous restaurant on stilts. **D** ***Damai***, bookable in Mersing at Jln Abu Bakar, T 07 793048, about 80 rather grotty looking double chalets with balconies, restaurant, minimarket and 24-hour electricity, speedboat to Mersing. **D** ***Island Reef Resort***, set back on hillside behind jetty, with chalets side on to beach, so no views except in the restaurant. Relatively new affair, but business does not seem to be booming. **Diving**: *Sharkeys*, based at the *Tropical Coral Inn*, run SSI certificated courses.

Kampung Nipah (south of Kampung Genting): **B-D** *Desa Nipah*, beachside chalets with attached bathrooms, because this is the only accommodation available, Kampung Nipah is one of the most secluded and tranquil spots on the island.

Kampung Mukut (on south side of island): **C** ***Mukut Village Chalets***, restaurant, backed by coconut palms, traditional-style atap-roofed chalets with balconies, secluded, beautiful location with magnificent backdrop of the 'Twin Peaks', owned by *Island Connection* ticketing agency, 19 Plaza R & R, Mersing. Also at Mukut: ***Asah Resort*** and ***Mukut Waterfall Backpacker Resort***.

Kampung Juara: is the only kampung on the east coast with accommodation. It has beautiful long white beaches which sometimes have good breakers. The snorkelling though, is poor. Being on the seaward side, Juara has a completely different atmosphere from the west coast kampungs – it is quieter, friendlier, more laid-back and bucolic, thanks mainly to its seclusion. There is a path from Kampung Tekek, through the jungle, to Juara (see Treks). Alternatively, it is possible to take a boat from Tekek. Accommodation is cheaper at Juara. The Sungai Baru which flows into the sea here is home to some monitor lizards. **E** ***Paradise Point***, restaurant with extensive menu, one of only two places to stay on the northern side of the beach. Simple rooms, attached showers, the chalets siding onto the beach get the breeze, a quiet places with a relaxed atmosphere, recommended. **E-F** ***Busong***, same ownership as *Paradise Point* and close to the northern end of the beach, near a mangrove fringed lagoon which, after heavy rain, discharges into the sea. There are some simple 'A'-frame huts as well as more recently built chalets. Very quiet and right on the beach. **D** ***Juara Bay Resort***, restaurant, rather ugly series of new hillside chalets at the southern end of the main beach. This is the most sophisticated place to stay and there have even been murmerings of a/c. Though it is quiet and the chalets have attractive views over the bay they do not have the beach-front position of the other places. **E-F** ***Atan's Place***, T 7992309, restaurant (*Turtle Café* – but you don't go there for the food), 'A'-frames and chalets with small verandahs. **D-E** ***Juara Mutiara***, same management as *Atan's Place*, organizes diving trips/island tours, booking office in Mersing, 6 Jln Abu Bakar, near *Plaza R & R*. The more expensive rooms sleep 4, all have attached showes, clean and popular, some chalets right on the beach, can be noisy (for Juara) as there are other chalet operations on both sides. **E-F** ***Sunrise***, restaurant, simple and small 'A' frame huts that become airless and stuffy on still days. Good water activities: canoes, windsurfers and boats for hire. **E** ***Bushman***, near the southern end of the beach, simple 'A'-frame hus. **E-F** ***Musni Chalet***, over the headland at the southern end of the beach, isolated and quiet. **D** ***Saujana Bay Resort***, the last place to stay at the southern end of the bay. It is quite a walk from the jetty – over the headland.

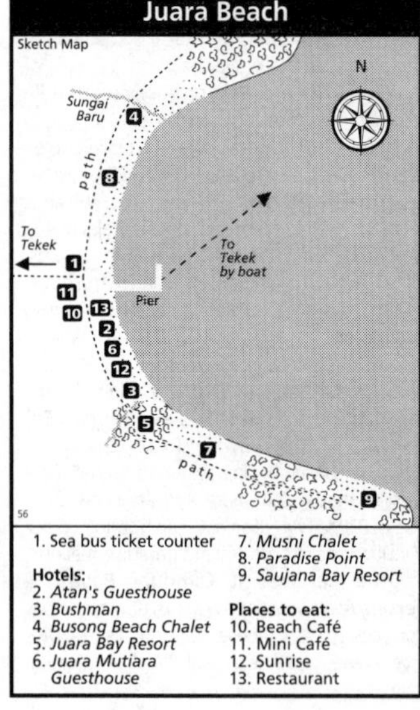

Other services at Kampung Juara: all the guesthouses here serve roughy the same dishes – curries, noodle and rice dishes, pancakes, fish, omlettes etc. There are also a couple of independent restaurants – the ***Mini Café*** and the ***Beach Café***, both near the pier. Inevitably fish is good: chilli fish, sweet and sour, or simply grilled. Snorkelling and fishing gear can be hired from most of the guesthouses.

Getting to Kampung Juara: being on the east side of the island, the ferries from Mersing rarely call here and it is necessary to catch one of the sea buses that circle the island, RM18 from Tekek to Juara, 2 hours. To walk from Tekek to Juara is a tough 2-hour walk.

● Places to eat

Prices: ♦♦♦♦ over RM40; ♦♦♦ RM13-40; ♦♦ RM5-13; ♦ under RM5

Most restaurants are small family-run kitchens attached to groups of beach huts. All provide western staples such as omelettes and French toast, as well as Malay dishes. On the whole, the food is of a high standard. Understandably it makes most sense to eat seafood – superb barbecued shark, barracuda, squid, stingray and other fish. Most restaurants are listed under each kampung entry above. **NB** Not all restaurants sell beer. ***Berjaya Tioman Beach Resort Restaurant*** offers a choice of restaurants, none of which are outstanding. The best bet is the buffet meal, which is quite good value and a huge spread is on offer. The other restaurants offer barbecue and steamboat. Service for a la carte meals is painfully slow and pretty inefficient. The golf club offers a snack bar with good pizzas and sandwiches; ***Liza Restaurant***, in Tekek serves delicious Malay food, and is the most sophisticated place to eat outside the *Berjaya*.

● Airline offices

Silk Air and Pelangi, both operate out of *Berjaya Resort*, T 4145445, F 4145718.

● Banks & money changers

There are two money changers at Tioman Airport in the new blue-roofed shopping plaza. Some shops in Salang will also change money. Travellers' cheques can be changed at the *Berjaya Tioman Beach Resort* (large surcharge). Recently, some smaller resorts have begun to accept them.

● Hospitals & medical services

There is a small clinic in Tekek.

● Post & telecommunications

Public phones in all villages, IDD calling from *Berjaya* and some guesthouses. Phones to be installed in guesthouses sometime in the near future.

Area code: 07.

Post Office: mini-post office in Kampung Tekek.

Card phones: in Tekek next to the Mini Pos (cards available at Post Office).

● Shopping

Souvenirs: Tioman is not a place to come shopping. However, there are a handful of souvenir shops in Tekek selling the usual range of sea-derived knick-knacks including shells fashioned into inprobable scenes and jewellery which most people discard immediately upon return home.

● Sports

Diving: most beaches have dive centres attached to at least one guesthouse. These are listed under the various accommodation entries. PADI, NAUI and SSI (Scuba Schools International) certification available.

Golf: *Tioman Island Golf Club*, T 445445, F 445716, most club-members are weekend trippers from KL and Singapore, beautiful 18-hole course, green fees RM80 weekdays, RM100 weekends. Equipment including clubs (full set RM50), golf shoes (RM10), and buggy (RM40 weekdays, RM50 weekends) all available for hire.

● Tour companies & travel agents

Zaha's, Tekek Pier, sells boat tickets to Mersing and round-the-island excursion tickets.

● Transport

60 km from Mersing.

Local Boat: beaches and kampungs are connected by an erratic sea-bus service, which runs roughly every hour or so from 0800 to 1800. The early-morning sea-bus goes right round the island; otherwise it is necessary to charter a boat to get to the waterfalls (on the south coast) and Kampung Juara. All the boats from Mersing take passengers to the kampungs on the west side; the first port of call is Kampung Tekek. Sea-bus fares (pp, children half price) from Kampung Tekek to: Kampung Ayer Batang/ABC (RM4), Penuba (RM6), Salang (RM9), Lalang (*Berjaya Tioman Beach Resort*) (RM6), Juara (RM20). Note that there is a slightly different schedule on Fri. The east coast is accessible by (very slow) boat or by the jungle trail.

Air Tioman Airport is in the centre of Tekek. The runway is being extended to take larger aircraft. The *Berjaya* sends a bus to meet each plane and various touts approach likely looking passengers. The jetty is just 100m or so away. Daily connections with KL's Subang Airport and

Kuantan on *Pelangi Air*, and with Subang alone on *Berjaya Air*. Multiple daily connections with Johor Bahru on *Tiram Air* and daily with Mersing. Note that the baggage allowance is 10 kg.

Sea Boat: most people arrive on Tioman by ferry from Mersing. The jetty at Mersing is 5 minutes walk out of Mersing next to the blue-roofed *R & R Plaza*. It is best to buy a one way ticket; the ferry timetable is only drawn up 1 month in advance because it depends on tides. Fast boats leave at roughly 1 hour intervals when the tide is high. A/c fast boats (eg *Seagull Express*, T 7994297, and *Damai Express* T 793048): RM25 (one way, child RM15), 1½-2 hours; moderate speed boats taking about 45 passengers: RM20 (one way), 3 hours; fishing boats can be chartered by groups of 12 or more people for RM180 (for the boat), 4-5 hours. During the monsoon season (Nov through Feb) the sea can get quite rough and it is inadvisable to leave Mersing after 1500. During these months departures can be erratic; boats may not run if there are insufficient passengers. (It can be difficult to find accommodation after nightfall and most restaurants close early.) All boats land on the west coast of Tioman and call at each of the main kampungs; occasionally they may cross to the east side of the island and call at Juara, but it is usually necessary to catch one of the 'sea buses' that circle the island. If intending to stay at Juara leave enough time to catch a sea bus – it takes around 2 hours from Kampung Tekek to Juara. There are also boats twice a day from Tanjung Gemok (Endau), just north of Mersing, to Tioman during the busy season (Mar-Oct) run by *Kuala Perlis Langkawi Ferry Service*, RM25 (one way, RM13 children), 1½ hours.

● International connections

Air Several connections a day with Seletar Airport (on north side of Singapore Island, see page 712) on *Pelangi Air* (RM191 one way) and *SilkAir*. A bus from the *Berjaya Tioman Resort* meets each arrival and transports guests to the hotel. Alternatively walk to the pier and catch one of the sea buses to the other beaches.

Sea The *Auto Tioman* leaves from Tanah Merah, Singapore 0830 and returns 1430, 4½ hours (S$85 one way, children S$55). Reservations at *Auto Batam*, 1 Maritime Square, World Trade Centre, Singapore T 2714866 (web: http://www.sembcorp.com.sg/autobatam).

PULAU RAWA

A small island, 16 km off Mersing, Pulau Rawa is owned by a nephew of the Sultan of Johor and is highly rated by lots of travellers. The island has a fantastic beach and for those in need of a desert-island break, Rawa is perfect, for there is absolutely nothing to do except mellow-out. Unfortunately the coral reef is disappointing, but more active visitors can windsurf, canoe, and fish. The island gets busy at weekends as it is close enough for day-visitors; it is also a popular getaway for Singaporeans.

Local information

● Accommodation

Rawa has no kampungs on it, and, as yet, only one resort.

A-B *Rawa Safaris Island Resort*, Tourist Centre, Jln Abu Bakar, Mersing T 7991204, some a/c, restaurant (Malay and international dishes), bungalows, chalets and 'A'-frames, watersports, Sahid mixes some mean cocktails in the bar – drink more than two Rawa specials and you'll be on the island for good.

● Transport

Sea Boat: daily connection via slow boat with Mersing, 1½ hours (RM25 return).

OTHER ISLANDS

There are a total of 64 islands off Mersing; many are inaccessible and uninhabited. There is accommodation available and boats to Pulau Babi Besar (Big Pig Island), Pulau Tinggi, Pulau (Babi) Tengah (which the government has declared a marine park because of its reef and the fact that Giant Leatherback turtles (see page 293) lay their eggs there between June and August), Pulau Sibu (the 'Island of Perilous Passage' – it used to be a pirate haunt), Pulau Aur (Bamboo Island) and Pulau Pemanggil. Pemanggil's best beaches are at Kampungs Buan and Pa Kaleh – which is fortunately where the accommodation is sited. **Pulau Babi Besar** is larger and closer to the mainland than Rawa. It is a very peaceful island and is particularly well-known for its beaches and coral. **Pulau Tinggi** is probably the most dramatic-looking island in the Seribuat group, with its 650m volcanic peak. **Pulau Tengah** (formerly a refugee camp for Vietnamese boat people) is an hour away from Mersing. The island is a marine park, as the giant leatherback turtles (see page 293) come here to lay their eggs in July/August. **Pulau Sibu** has been recommended by many travellers for its beaches and watersports. Sibu is frequented more by Singaporeans and expatriates than by western tourists. It is popular for fishing and diving and because it is larger than the other islands there is more of a sense of space and there are also some good walks.

In addition to these more established islands, there are also other places being developed. It is worth asking around in Mersing for more information and collaring people on the jetty who have just returned. Island currently under development include **Pulau Hujung** and **Pulau Aur**. The latter is the most remote.

Local information

● Accommodation

Most of the accommodation on these islands is run by small operators, who organize packages from Mersing. Resort bookings must be made in either Mersing or Johor Bahru.

Pulau Babi Besar: **A** *Radin Island Resort*, 9 Tourist Information Centre, Jln Abu Bakar, Mersing, T 7994152, restaurant, (some a/c) stylish traditional chalets with jungle hillside backdrop. **A-C** *White Sand Beach Resort*, 98 Jln Harimau Tarum, Century Garden, Johor Bahru, T (07) 7994995, runs diving packages, 4 days for 2 people. **B** *Besar Marina Resort*, 10, Tourist Information Centre, Jln Abu Bakar, Mersing, T 7993606. **B** *Hillside Beach Resort*, 5B Jln Abu Bakar, Mersing or book through Suite 125, 1st Flr, Johor Tower, 15 Jln Gereja, Johor Bahru, T (07) 7994831, F 2244329, restaurant, very attractively designed Kampung-style resort, nestling on jungled slopes above beach, watersports. **C** *Besar Beach Chalet*, new resort with government-style chalets backed by Irish jungle.

Pulau Tinggi: **A** *Smailing Island Resort*, c/o 17 Tingkat 2, Tun Abdul Razak, Kompleks (KOMTAR), Jln Wong Ah Fook, Johor Bahru, T (07) 2231694, also booking office in Mersing opposite *Plaza R & R*, Jln Abu Bakar, restaurant, pool, luxurious Malay-style wooden chalets. Also 'A'-frames (**F**), chalets (**D**) and bungalows (**C**) on the island; **A-B** *Tinggi Island Resort*, bookings from *Sheikh Tourist Agency*, 1B Jln Abu Bakar, Mersing, T 7993767/7994451, attractive chalets balanced precariously on steep hillside and next to beach, excellent range of indoor and outdoor facilities, boat trips arranged to nearby islands (Pulau Lima and Pulau Simbang) for diving.

Pulau (Babi) Tengah: more accommodation is planned on the island. **B** *Pirate Bay Island Resort*, restaurant, spacious cottages built in traditional style with full selection of amenities, watersports.

Pulau Sibu Besar: **A-D** *Sibu Island Cabanas* (c/o G105 *Holiday Plaza*, Century Garden JB), T (07) 3317216, restaurant, chalets and de luxe bungalows. **C-D** *O & H Kampung Huts* (c/o 9 Tourist Information Centre, Jln Abu Bakar, Mersing), T 7993124/7993125, good restaurant, chalets, some with attached bathrooms, clean and friendly, trekking and snorkelling, recommended. **C-D** *Sea Gypsy Village Resort*, 9 Tourist Information Centre, Jln Abu Bakar, Mersing, T 7993124, restaurant, chalets and bungalows, recommended.

Pulau Sibu Tengah: **C** *Sibu Island Resorts*, Suite 2, 14th Flr, KOMTAR, Jln Wong Ah Fook, Johor Bahru, T (07) 2231188, restaurant, bungalows only, watersports.

Pulau Aur: **F** *Longhouse* provides basic accommodation.

Pulau Pemanggil: Package deals for *Wira Chalets and longhouse* (also has dive shop). There is a small agent at the very front of Mersing's *Plaza R & R* dealing exclusively with Pemanggil travel and accommodation. **C-E** *Dagang Chalets and Longhouse*, Kampung Buau (1 longhouse room sleeps 8 at RM10 pp), restaurant serving local food, *Mara Chalet* at Kampung Pa Kaleh, on southwest side. Contact *Tioman Accommodation & Boat Services*, 3 Jln Abu Bakar, Mersing, T 7993048.

● Places to eat

All resorts have their own restaurants.

● Transport

Sea Boats: to the islands leave daily from Mersing, usually around 1100 and return 1530 (all slow boats): Tengah (RM18 return), Babi Besar (RM30 return), Sibu (RM25 return), Tinggi (RM50 return). No regular boats to Pulau Aur or Pulau Pemanggil – though this may change as the islands develop. Getting to Pulau Aur takes 4 hours or more. Also boats to Sibu from Tanjung Sedili Besar at Teluk Mahkota (23 km off the Kota Tinggi-Mersing road), south of Mersing (RM22 return).

ENDAU ROMPIN NATIONAL PARK

Endau Rompin National Park straddles the border of Johor and Pahang states and is one of the biggest remaining tracts of virgin rainforest on the peninsula; about 80,000 hectares. In the late 1980s it was upgraded to the status of a National Park to protect the area from the logging companies. Within the park, it may be possible to see Sumatran rhino, tigers, wildboars, tapir, elephant, deer and mousedeer. Birdlife includes hornbills and the argus pheasant. Amongst the flora there are fan palms (*Endau ensis*), walking stick palm (*Phychorapis singaporensis*) and climbing bamboo (*Rhopa loblaste*), pitcher plants and orchids.

Access to the park will become easier and cheaper during the next few years and accommodation is planned for upriver. (At present transport and accommodation facilities are limited.) Trips to Endau require careful planning – it is not like Taman Negara – and are best organized by tour agents (see below) who usually end up cheaper than trying to arrange it independently.

It is possible to hire boats from Endau, on the coast road, up Sungai Endau. The first 10 km to Kampung Punan is navigable by larger motor boats; from there,

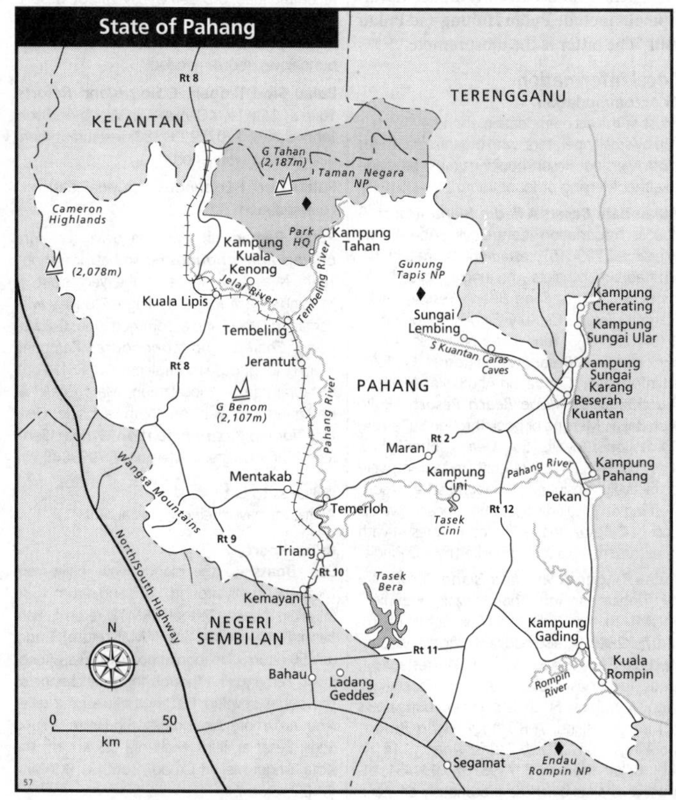

Pahang: the land of the sacred tree

A Malay legend tells of a huge, majestic Mahang (softwood) tree that once stood on the bank of the Pahang River, not far from Pekan, towering over everything else in the jungle. The tree was said to resemble the thigh of a giant and considered sacred by the Orang Asli and the Jakun tribespeople. The Malays adopted the name, which, in time, became Pahang. Perhaps not coincidentally, *pahang* also happens to be the Khmer word for 'tin' – there are ancient tin workings at Sungai Lembing near Kuantan, where traces of early human habitation have been found.

Until the end of the 19th century, Pahang, the peninsula's largest, but least populous state, had always been a vassal. It paid tribute to Siam, Melaka and then Johor. In 1607 the Dutch set up a trading post in Pahang, but the state found itself caught in the middle of protracted rivalries between Johor and Aceh, the Dutch and the Portuguese. Pekan was sacked repeatedly by Johor and Aceh in the early 17th century, before coming under the direct rule of the Sultan of Johor in 1641; it stayed that way for two centuries.

In 1858, the death of the chief minister of Pahang, resulted in a 5-year civil war. The dispute between his two sons was finally settled when the youngest, Wan Ahmad, declared himself Chief Minister and then became the Pahang's first sultan in 1863. Sultan Wan Ahmad was autocratic and unpopular, so the British entered the fray, declaring the state a protectorate in 1887. An anti-British revolt ensued, supported by the sultan, but Wan Ahmad's power was whittled away. In 1895 the state's administrative capital was moved from Pekan to Kuala Lipis, 300 km up the Pahang River and later to Kuantan. Pahang became part of the federated Malay states in 1896. It was completely cut off from the west coast states, except for a couple of jungle trails, until a road was built from Kuala Lumpur to Kuantan in 1901. Pahang remains a predominantly Malay state.

smaller boats head on upstream to Orang Asli villages. The junction of the Endau and Jasin rivers (9 hours from Endau) is a good campsite and base for trekking and fishing expeditions. Boats go further upstream, but it is advisable to take a guide. They can be hired from Endau or from the Orang Asli kampungs (RM20-30/day). At present it is necessary to take all provisions and camping equipment with you. It is inadvisable to travel during the monsoon season from November to March. Following the drowning of a Singaporean student in rapids in 1992, it has become much more difficult to visit Endau Rompin independently and it is essential to secure a permit. Permits are considered necessary because the area still falls under the Internal Security Act; in the days before the surrender of the Communist Party of Malaya in 1990, the Endau-Rompin jungle used to be part of the guerrillas' supply route through the peninsula. Visitors are strongly recommended to go to Endau with a travel agency, which can obtain permits on a visitor's behalf (see below).

Most package trips involve a 70 km jeep trip from Mersing to Kampung Peta followed by a 1½ hours longboat ride to first campsite. The rest of the trip involves trekking around the Asli trails and visiting spectacular waterfalls, the biggest of which is the Buaya Sangkut waterfall on Sungai Jasin. Fishing trips are best organized between February and August.

Permits From National Parks Johor Corporation, JKR 475 Bukit Timbalan, Johor Bahru, T 2237471, F 2237472. Applications for permits must be made at least 2 weeks in advance, in writing, with passport details, two passport photographs, and proposed length of trip. The travel agencies listed below can secure permits within 5 days, but it is advisable to leave more time if possible.

Park information

● Accommodation

Kuala Rompin: **A** *Lanjut Golden Beach Resort*, 20 km north of Kuala Rompin, a golf resort with a/c, 2 restaurants, pool, rooms and bungalows. **B** *Seri Malaysia Rompin*, Tg Gemok, T 7944724, F 7944732, 55 km from the national park, organizes tours, clean and comfortable rooms in new government chain hotel. **C** *Government Resthouse* in Kuala Rompin, clean-looking; **C** *Rumah Rehat* (*Rest House*), 122.5 Milestone, T 565245, restaurant, 2-storied resthouse, all rooms with attached bathroom. There is no accommodation available in the park: camping only. **D-E** *Watering Hole Bungalows*, 3 km south of Kuala Rompin and then 2 km or so towards the coast, T (011) 411894, quiet and clean, price including breakfast and dinner, we have had reports the Swiss-Malaysian couple who run this place could be friendlier and more welcoming but it is still a relaxing hideaway and well run – they pick up travellers twice a day from the bus station in Kuala Rompin at 1430 and 1700.

● Post & telecommunications

Area code: 09.

● Tour companies & travel agents

Organized expeditions, in which prices are inclusive of return vehicle and boat transfer, camping equipment, cooking utensils and permits, can be booked through: *Eureka Travel*, 277A Holland Ave, Holland Village, Singapore, T 65-4625077, F 4622853, offers ecologically orientated tours to Endau Rompin National Park, recommended; *Giamso Travel*, 23 Jln Abu Bakar, Mersing, T 07-7992253, approximately RM190 pp for 3 days/2 nights, RM210 pp for 4 days 3 nights. The company can supply camping equipment, or through *Shah Alam Tours*, 138 Mezz Flr, Jln Tun Sambanthan, Kuala Lumpur T 03-2307161, F 03-2745739; *Sheikh Tourist Agency*, 1B Jln Abu Bakar, Mersing, T 793767, 4 days/3 nights trips RM380 pp, all in RM100 deposit payable on booking; *Wilderness Experience*, 6B Jln SS 21/39, Damansara Utama, Petaling Jaya, T 03-7178221. Hotels and guesthouses in Kuala Rompin also usually organize trips into the park.

● Transport

130 km south of Kuantan, 37 km north of Mersing.

Road Bus: connections with JB, Terengganu and Kuantan. Buses from Johor Bahru and Kuantan stop on demand at Endau, or regular local buses from Mersing to Endau and then into the park by boat. **Taxi**: from Mersing.

Sea Speed boats to first Orang Asli village (Kampung Punan). This can cost anything from RM200-400 for a two day trip. It is possible to charter longboats (carrying up to 6 passengers) from Kampung Punan to go further upstream.

PEKAN

Pekan is the old royal capital of Pahang. *Pekan* means 'town' in Malay – it used to be known as Pekan Pahang, the town of Pahang. Even before the Melakan sultanate was established in the late 14th century, it was known by the Sanskrit name for 'town' – *Pura*. It is divided into Old Pekan (Pekan Lama) and New Pekan (Pekan Bharu); the former was the exclusive abode of the Malay nobility for centuries. Today the town has a languid feel to it. It has a reasonably picturesque row of older wooden shophouses on the busy street along the river, but is otherwise not a particularly photogenic town. Aside from its mosques, Pekan's most distinguishing feature is its bridge, which straddles the Pahang River, the longest river on the peninsula.

There are two mosques in the centre of Pekan: the **Abdullah Mosque**, Jalan Sultan Ahmad (beyond the museum) and the more modern **Abu Bakar Mosque** next door. On the north outskirts of the town is the **Istana Abu Bakar** – the royal palace – just off Jalan Istana Abu Bakar. Its opulent trimmings are visible from the road, but it is closed to the public. The small but interesting **Sultan Abu Bakar Museum**, on Jalan Sultan Ahmad is housed in a splendid colonial building and has a jet-fighter mounted Airfix-style in the front garden. The museum includes a collection of brass and copperware, royal regalia, porcelain from a wrecked Chinese junk and an exhibition of local arts and crafts. In the back garden there is a depressing mini-zoo which rarely gets visited. It is home to Malayan Honey Bears, a tapir, a collection of monkeys, a black panther and a fish eagle, all squeezed into tiny cages. Good map of Pekan provided. Admission: RM1. Open 0930-1700 Tuesday-Thursday, Saturday and Sunday; 0930-1215, 1445-1700 Friday.

Local festivals

October: *Sultan's Birthday* (24th: state holiday) celebrated with processions, dancing and an international polo championship which the sultan hosts on his manicured polo ground at the istana.

Local information

● Accommodation

Prices: L over RM500; **A+** RM260-500; **A** RM130-260; **B** RM65-130; **C** RM40-65; **D** RM20-40; **E** RM10-20; **F** Below RM10

There is a poor selection of hotels in Pekan – the government rest house is the best bet.

D *Pekan*, 60 Jln Tengku Ariff Bendahara, T 71378, a/c, restaurant, badly run, but quite friendly people. **D** *Rumah Rehat* (rest house), beside the football field (*padang*), off Jln Sultan Abu Bakar, T 421240, restaurant, it is a big, low-slung colonial building – which is in need of a lick of paint – with a cool, spacious interior and big, clean rooms, it is advisable to try to book accommodation in advance if visiting during the Sultan's birthday celebrations.

● Places to eat

♦♦*Pekan Hotel Restaurant*, 60 Jln Tengku Ariff Bendahara, nothing special. There are a couple of reasonable coffee shops in the new town. The foodstalls on Jln Sultan Ahmad, near the bus/taxi stands, are the best Pekan has to offer.

● Banks & money changers

Bumiputra, 117 Jln Engku Muda Mansur.

● Post & telecommunications

Post Office: in the middle of town.

● Sports

Polo: matches are held in season (Prince Charles is said to have played here). The polo field is surrounded by traditional Malay houses.

● Transport

47 km south of Kuantan.

Road Bus: bus stop on Jln Sultan Ahmad in the centre of town. Regular connections with Kuantan and from there onward although there are direct buses to Mersing. **Taxi**: taxis for Kuantan and elsewhere stand between Jln Sultan Ahmad and the waterfront, opposite the indoor market.

KUANTAN

The modern capital of Pahang has a population of around 100,000 and is a bustling, largely Chinese, town at the mouth of the Kuantan River. Kuantan is the main transport and business hub for the east coast; most visitors spend at least a night here. Kuantan's short on sights, but the brand new **Sultan Ahmad Shah** mosque, in the centre of town, is worth wandering around. It is an impressive building, freshly decorated in blue and white with a cool marbled interior. It has blue and yellow stained glass windows and the morning sun projects their coloured patterns on the interior walls. Kuantan has several streets of old shophouses which date from the 1920s. Most of the oldest buildings are opposite the padang on **Jalan Makhota**. The **Kuantan River** might also qualify as a sight, such is the dearth of obvious things to see. The 300 km stretch of coast between Kuantan and Kota Bharu, is comprised of long beaches, interspersed with fishing kampungs and the occasional natural gas processing plant and oil refinery.

Excursions

Teluk Cempedak is just 4 km east of Kuantan (see page 278). *Getting there*: regular connections on bus no 39 from the

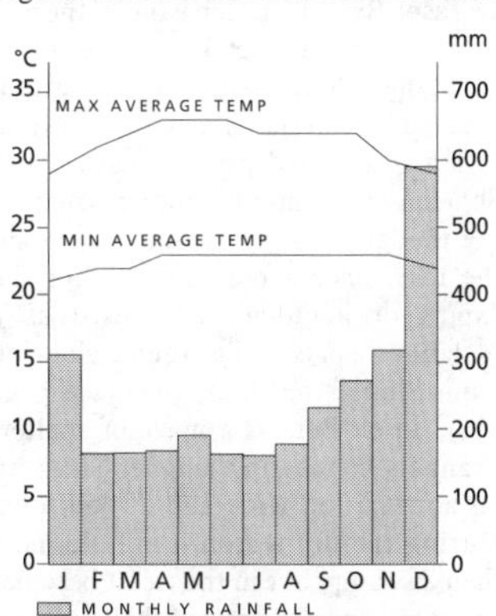

Climate: Kuantan

6

Dateline Kuantan: Churchill's Malayan nightmare

"In all the war, I never received a more direct shock," wrote former British wartime Prime Minister Winston Churchill in his memoirs. "As I turned and twisted in bed, the full horror of the news sank in upon me." On 10 December 1941 Churchill got the news that a Japanese air strike force operating from Saigon (South Vietnam) had destroyed and sunk two of the most powerful warships in the Royal Navy. *HMS Prince of Wales*, a 35,000-ton battleship, and *HMS Repulse*, a 32,000-ton battle cruiser, sank within an hour of each other, with the loss of 1,196 lives, 95 km off Kuantan.

A few days earlier the ships had arrived in Singapore, then the biggest naval operations base in the world, to underscore Britain's commitment to protecting its colonies in the East. They were soon speeding N in an effort to pre-empt and disrupt Japan's amphibious invasion of Malaya, but the flotilla, which had no air cover, was spotted by a Japanese submarine. The first wave of Japanese fighter-bombers arrived at 1100; by 1233, the *Repulse*, its thick armour-plated hull holed by five torpedoes, was sunk. The *Prince of Wales* went down 47 mins later in about 60m of water. Accompanying destroyers rescued 1,900 men from the two vessels before retreating to Singapore, which fell to the Japanese Imperial Army 8 weeks later. The wrecks of the two ships were declared war graves and in 1991, on the 50th anniversary of the Japanese attack, a team of British Navy divers laid white ensign flags on both ships to commemorate the dead.

local bus station. A short walk north of Teluk Cempedak are Methodist Bay and Teluk Pelindong, which are beyond the range of most picknickers.

Tasek Cini is an amalgam of 13 freshwater lakes about 100 km southwest of Kuantan (see page 279). *Getting there*: is not easy on public transport. See page 280 for details.

Tasek Bera Temerloh is one of the best access points for Tasek Bera – 'the lake of changing colours' – the biggest natural lake in Malaysia. There are several Jakun – so-called proto-Malays – and Semelai aboriginal kampungs (including the largest Kota Iskandar), around the lake, once a major centre for the export of jelutong resin, used as a sealant on boats and as jungle chewing gum. Similar to Tasek Cini (see page 512), Tasek Bera is a maze of shallow channels connecting smaller lakes, in all about 5 km wide and 27 km long. During the dry season it is little more than a swamp, but in the wet it becomes an interconnected array of shallow lakes. The Semelai traditionally exploited the expansion and contraction of the lake(s), fishing during the wet season and collecting non-timber forest products during the dry. When the waters reached their peak, and wild pigs became stranded on the many islands that dot the lake, the Semelai would hunt. One of the lake's resident species is the rare fish-eating 'false' gharial crocodile (*Tomistoma schlegeli*). However Asli boatmen on the lake can be hired for about RM10/day. *Getting there*: there is no scheduled public transport to the lake. It is possible to take a bus or share taxi to Triang, due south of Temerloh, and then charter a taxi to the lake. Or take a taxi the entire way from Temerloh – an expensive option which may make sense in a group. Alternatively, bus from Kemayan to Bahau, 45 minutes; bus from Bahau to Ladang Geddes, 30 minutes; hitch or taxi to Kota Iskandar on the south side of the lake (where there are bungalows with cooking facilities, bookable through the Department of Aboriginal Affairs in Temerloh). Kota Iskandar is one of the best places on the peninsula to visit Orang Asli villages. Boats can be hired to explore the lake but requires enthusiastic negotiation. **NB** Do not attempt this trip without taking adequate supplies and provisions (including basic cooking utensils).

Caras Caves lies 25 km northwest of town. Take a right fork at the 24 km mark. In 1954, the Sultan of Pahang gave a Thai Buddhist monk permission to build a temple in a limestone cave at Pancing, known as the 'yawning skull' cave. A steep climb up 200 stone steps leads into the cave which contains shrines and religious icons cut into the rock. The collection is dominated by a 9m-long reclining Buddha, set among the limestone formations. There is always a monk in residence in the cave. Admission RM2. *Getting there*: catch bus no. 48 running towards Sungai Lembing from the local bus station and get off at Panching. From here it is 5 km to the caves – although it may be possible to catch a lift on the back of a motorbike.

Beyond the caves is **Sungai Lembing**, an old tin mine and the site of some of the oldest tin workings on the peninsula. It claims to be the deepest tin mine in the world. It has now opened to visitors. *Getting there*: bus no. 48, every hour.

Gunung Tapis Park is a new state park, offering rafting, fishing and trekking 49 km from Kuantan. Arrangements have to be made through the Tourist Information Centre or the local Outward Bound Society. *Getting there*: only accessible by jeep via Sungai Lembing, from here accessible via a 12 km track.

Beserah was once a picturesque fishing kampung, 10 km north of Kuantan, but has now become a rather touristy suburb of the town. But like Teluk Cempedak to the south it does provide a slightly quieter place to stay. *Getting there*: bus nos 27, 28, 30 from the main bus terminal in Kuantan all run through Beserah (departures every 30 minutes).

Local information

● Accommodation

Prices: L over RM500; **A+** RM260-500; **A** RM130-260; **B** RM65-130; **C** RM40-65; **D** RM20-40; **E** RM10-20; **F** Below RM10

The upmarket hotels are mostly at Teluk Cempedak (4 km north of Kuantan, see page 278). **A** *Swiss-Garden Resort* is due to open towards the end of 1997 which promises "fun-in-the-sun and fully-equipped buiness facilities": it should be worth checking. There are plenty of cheap Chinese hotels in Kuantan itself, mostly on and around Jln Teluk Sisek and Jln Besar. Several smart new hotels have sprung up in the **B-C** range which offer excellent value for money. **NB** Telephone numbers have recently changed, if you have difficulty getting through to hotel, contact the Tourist Information Centre, T (09) 5135566, F (09) 5130510.

A *Hotel Grand Continental*, Jln Gambut, T 5158888, F 5159999, new addition to the *Grand Continental* chain, not much character but comfortable and smart, over 200 rooms all with a/c, TV, in-house movie, tea and coffee-making facility, other facilities include pool, coffee house, Chinese restaurant, health centre, business centre. **A-B** *Samudra River View*, Jln Besar, T 5155333, F 5100618, a/c, restaurant (good breakfasts), next to Kuantan Swimming Centre, was Kuantan's best and with a good position on the river, but new mid-market hotels are smarter and better value, carpets shabby, doubles are small, twins bigger with sitting area.

B *Classic*, 7 Bangunan LKNP, Jln Besar, T 5154599, F 5104141, a/c, scooped Tourism Malaysia's Best Hotel of the Year Award 1992 (in budget category), extremely clean, big rooms and spacious attached bathrooms, one of the best-value-for-money hotels in the country, conveniently located next to Kuantan Swimming Centre, behind the *Samudra River View* next door, recommended. **B** *Oriental Evergreen*, 157 Jln Haji Abdul Rahman, T 5130168, a/c, restaurant (Chinese), prominently advertised hotel that's clean but rather average, nightmare decor with avocado suites, clashing bedspreads and astroturf carpets. **B** *Pacific*, 60-62 Jln Bukit Ubi, T 5141980, a/c, restaurant, one step down from the *Samudra*, the 6th Flr has recently been renovated and upgraded – tasteful and recommended – good hotel in central location. **B** *Suraya*, 55-57 Jln Haji Abdul Aziz, T 5154266, F 5126728, a/c, coffee area, another **Tourism Malaysia** award-winning hotel (1990, 1992), simple, well-appointed rooms, attached bathrooms, video, catering mainly for

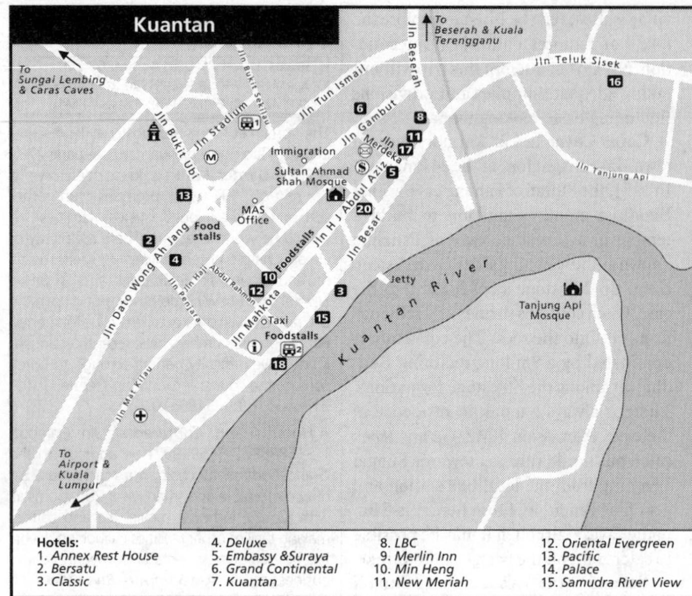

business people and domestic tourist market, good value. **B** *Le Village Beach Resort*, Lot 1260 Sungai Karang, T 5447900, F 5447899, Indian management, a pleasant enough place with a pool, getting popular with tour groups. **B-C** *Bersatu*, 2-4 Jln Darat Makbar (off Jln Wong Ah Jang), T 5112328, F 5106822, a/c, very clean, attached bathrooms, aimed at Malaysian executives.

C *Chusan*, 37-39 Jln Dato Wong Ah Jang, T 5134422, clean, friendly staff – who deliver an English language paper to your room in the morning. **C** *Deluxe*, 1st Flr, 53 Jln Wong Ah Jang (next to *Chusan Hotel*), a/c, above all-night restaurant, small rooms but clean and well-kept, caters mainly for itinerant businessmen, excellent value, recommended. **C** *LBC* (above *Loo Brothers Co*), 59 Jln Haji Abdul Aziz, T 5282582, a/c, big rooms and reasonably well-kept, can be noisy, attached showers but outside loos. **C** *New Embassy*, Jln Besar, some a/c, restaurant, clean and well looked after. **C-D** *Embassy*, 60 Jln Teluk Sisek, T 5127486, well looked after, all rooms have attached bathroom, good value, above *Tanjung Ria* coffee shop, some rooms rather noisy because of main road.

D *Tong Nam Ah*, Jln Teluk Sisek, T 5135204, basic, but conveniently located for bus station and hawker stalls and rooms are quite reasonable. **D** *New Meriah*, 142 Jln Telok Sisek, T 5125433, some a/c, some rooms with attached bathrooms and hot water, well priced.

E *Min Heng Hotel & Bakery*, 22 Jln Mahkota, T 5134885/5135885, restaurant, Kuantan's oldest hotel, opened 1926, basic, rooms partitioned with grills, entrance down side street, next to steakhouse and cake shop. **E** *Sin Nam Fong*, 44 Jln Teluk Sisek, T 5121561, restaurant, friendly management but when the traffic is heavy you might as well be camped on the central reservation.

● Places to eat

Prices: ◆◆◆◆ over RM40; ◆◆◆ RM13-40; ◆◆ RM5-13; ◆ under RM5

◆◆◆*Cheun Kee*, Jln Mahkota, large open-air Chinese restaurant, good selection of seafood.

◆◆*BKT* (also known as Restoran Malam), 53 Jln Wong Ah Jang, open coffee-shop/restaurant under *Hotel Deluxe*, best known for chicken rice and fish head curries and for being open until 0400. ◆◆*Cantina*, 16 Lorong Tun Ismail 1 (off Jln Bukit Ubi), smart a/c restaurant with waiters

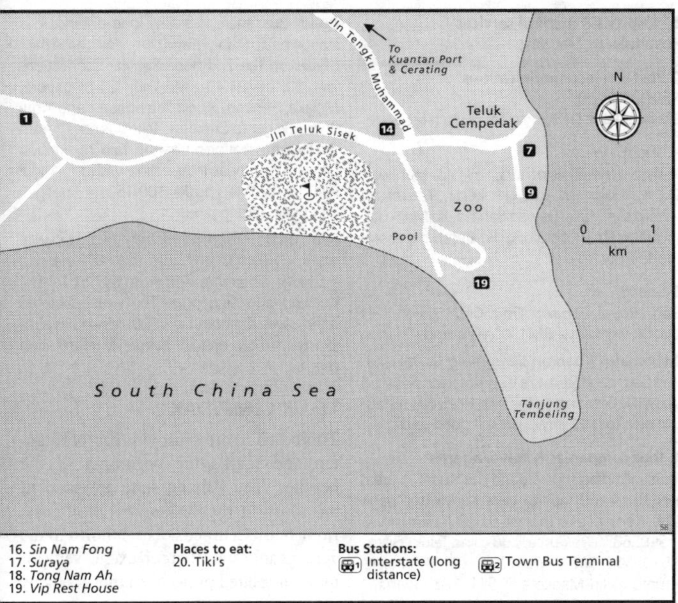

in batik bajus, Indonesian-style seafood and curries, recommended by locals. ♦♦*Kuantan* ***Seafood***, Jln Wong Ah Jong, opposite *BKT* (*Restoran Malam*), hawker-style stalls in big open restaurant, very popular. ♦***Choo Kong***, Jln Mahkota, Chinese noodles, cold beer, marble top tables, basic but good, recommended. ♦***K-heng Hup***, 17 Jln Makhota (on corner, opposite *Taman Salera Hawker Centre*, big old coffee shop with marble-top tables, raised voices and good *nasi lemak* and *nasi daggang* in the mornings, unchanged for 50 years. ♦***Salme***, 10 Jln Besar, cheap Malay dishes – *ikan bakar* (grilled fish) and *nasi campur* (pick-your-own curries). ♦***Sri Patani***, 79 Bangunan Udarulaman, Jln Tun Ismail, excellent Malay/South Thai food, recommended. ♦***Tanjung Ria Coffee Shop***, 60 Jln Teluk Sisek (below *Embassy Hotel*), good breakfasts (especially *nasi lemak*), bright and sunny and friendly. ♦***Tiki's***, Jln Mahkota (opposite Maybank), cheap western fare and local dishes, good for Western-style breakfast. ***Zul Satay***, junction of Jln Teluk Sisek and Jln Beserah (known as Kuantan Garden, between Kuantan and Teluk Cempedak), upmarket satay joint with all the usual plus rabbit, liver and offal, recommended.

Foodstalls: Malay cafés and foodstalls along the river bank, behind the long distance bus station, busy and popular, recommended – especially for seafood. There are more hawker stalls on junction of Jln Mahkota and Jln Masjid (Taman Salera), next to local bus station. ***Kuantan Garden***, junction of Jln Teluk Sisek and Jln Beserah (between Kuantan and Teluk Cempedak), large number of Chinese stalls.

● Bars

The best bars and nightlife are along the beachfront at Teluk Cempedak. ***The Sampan Bar***, on the *Hyatt Hotel* beachfront, is in the atap-roofed shell of a junk which beached in 1978 with 162 Vietnamese refugees aboard. The bar capitalizes on this slightly perverse novelty by charging more.

● Airline offices

MAS, Ground Floor, Wisma Bolasepak Pahang, Jln Gambut, T 5157055, F 5157870; **Pelangi Airways**, Sultan Ahmad Shah Airport, T 5381177, F 5381713; **Silk Air**, c/o MAS, T 5157055, F 5157870.

● Banks & money changers

Along Jln Mahkota and Jln Besar, between GPO and bus station.

● **Hospitals & medical services**
Hospitals: Jln Mat Kilau.

● **Post & telecommunications**
Area Code: 09.
General Post Office: Jln Mahkota (east end).

● **Shopping**
Books: *Hamid Brothers*, 23 Jln Mahkota; *Syarikat Ganesh*, 18C Jln Besar; *Teruntum Enterprise*, Wakil Dewan Bahasa, Jln Mahkota. Several craft shops along Jln Besar, expensive and touristy.

● **Sports**
Golf: *Royal Pahang Golf Club*, green fees RM100 weekdays, RM1500 weekends.

Swimming: *Kuantan Swimming Centre* (behind *Classic* and *Samudra View* hotels on Jln Besar) is a public pool next to the river, RM5/day, restaurant next to river, very clean and good value.

● **Tour companies & travel agents**
Tours including trips around the Kuantan area, river tours and trips to Lake Kenyir (see page 299). ***Kenyir Lake Tourist***, 01-83 Jln Tun Ismail, T 5105687; ***Reliance***, 66 Jln Teluk Sisek, T 5102566; ***SMAS Travels***, 1st Flr, Kompleks Teruntum, Jln Mahkota, T 5113888; ***Syarikat Perusahaan***, 38, 2nd Flr, Bangunan DPMP, Jln Wong Ah Jang; ***Taz Ben Travel & Tours***, 2nd Flr, Kompleks Teruntum, Jln Mahkota, T 5102255.

● **Tourist offices**
LKNP Tourist Information Centre, 15th Flr, Kompleks Teruntum, Jln Mahkota, T 5133026; **Tourist Information Centre**, Tingkat Bawah Bangunan, Jln Haji Abdul Aziz.

● **Useful addresses**
Immigration Office: Wisma Persektuan, Jln Gambut, T 5142155.

● **Transport**
219 km from Kuala Terengganu, 229 km from KL, 325 km from Johor Bahru.

Local Bus: local bus station is on junction of Jln Haji and Jln Abdul Rahman. Regular connections with Teluk Cempedak; for Cerating take bus no. 27. **Car hire**: **Budget**, 59 Jln Haji Abdul Aziz, T 5126370 or *Coral Beach Resort*, 152 Sungai Karang, Beserah, T 5447544; **Hertz**, *Samudra River View Hotel*, Jln Besar, T 5122688; **National**, 49 Jln Teluk Sisek, T 5127303.

Air Sultan Ahmad Shah Airport is 20 km south of town. Regular connections with Johor Bahru, KL and Kuala Terengganu. It is also possible to fly direct from Kuantan to Pulau Tioman daily on Pelangi Airways. Taxi to town RM10.

Road Bus: there is a new long-distance bus station on Jln Stadium and companies have their offices on the 2nd floor. Regular connections with KL (RM21.10), Mersing, JB, Singapore, Melaka, Penang, Kuala Terengganu and Kota Bharu. To get to Cherating take bus no. 27 from the local bus station on Jln Haji. **Taxi**: taxi station on Jln Besar, near intersection with Jln Abdul Rahman. KL, Mersing (RM100-150 for 4 people) and Kuala Terengganu.

Sea Boat: *Cruise Muhibbah* (*Feri Malaysia*) starts in Kuantan and goes to Kota Kinabalu, Kuching, Singapore and Port Klang. To KK, Kuching and Singapore. The well-appointed ferry leaves Kuantan Sat 1800. Schedules subject to change: enquire at tourist information centre.

TELUK CEMPEDAK

This beach resort is just 4 km east of Kuantan and marks the beginning of the beaches. The Pahang state government has reserved the 30 km stretch of coast from Teluk Cempedak beach north to the Terengganu state border exclusively for tourism-related projects, so there is likely to be much more development in the next few years. Teluk Cempedak was once the site of a quiet kampung, and is now a beach strip with a range of hotels, a string of bars and restaurants. There is a government-run handicraft shop (*Kedai Kraf*) beside the beach, specializing in batik.

● **Accommodation** Teluk Cempedak provides a more relaxed alternative to the noisier hotels in Kuantan. **A+ *Hyatt Regency Kuantan***, T 5131234, a/c, several restaurants and bars, 2 pools, low-rise hotel in landscaped gardens and a beautiful setting on the beach, good sports (including watersports) facilities, well-stocked craft shop, well-managed with good views, Sampan Bar (formerly a Vietnamese refugee boat), the hotel has recently been extended to include apartments, recommended. **A *Merlin Inn***, adjacent to *Hyatt*, T 5141388, recently renovated, not as good facilities as the *Hyatt*. **B *Samudra Beach Resort***, T 5135933, a/c, restaurant, rooms look like municipal toilets from the outside, but they have big French windows overlooking spacious gardens and the bay, nice place. **B-C *Annex Rest House***, Jln Teluk Sisek, 2 km before Teluk Cempedak, restaurant (rather inadequate), newly renovated, though we have had reports of bad service and broken down facilities, spacious grassy grounds. **B-C** ***Kuantan***, opposite *Hyatt*, T 5130026, a/c, restaurant, very clean, cheaper rooms fan only but all have attached bathroom, noisy television lounge, very pleasant terrace for sun-downers – although it now faces the new Hyatt extension, recommended. **C** ***Hill View***, T 5121555, a/c, restaurant in block of karaoke lounges, bars and restaurants, not good value for money. **D** ***Sri Pantai Bungalows***, T 5125250, some a/c, situated close to the *Hillview Hotel* this is one of the better cheaper places to stay, rooms are clean and reasonable for this price.

• **Places to eat** ♦♦♦***Nisha's Curry House***, 13 Teluk Cempedak, North Indian cuisine plus fish-head curry. ♦♦***Cempedak Seafood***, A-1122, Jln Teluk Sisek, big Chinese restaurant at the cross-roads on the way to Teluk Cempedak, specialities: chilli crab and freshwater fish. ♦♦***Pattaya***, on the beach front, good views of the beach, serves crab priced by weight, good food and good value. ♦♦***Tan's***, 29 Teluk Cempedak, Malay/Chinese, recommended fish head curry. **Foodstalls**: group of gerai makan in new brick kiosks, next to beach alongside Handicraft centre.

• **Bars** There are a number of bars along the seashore. One pub which comes recommended is the *Country Ranch* not far from the *Hilton Hotel*.

• **Post & telecommunications** **Area Code**: 09.

• **Tour companies & travel agents** *East Coast Holidays*, 33 Teluk Cempedak, T 5105228, helpful staff; ***Mayflower Acme Tours***, *Hyatt Kuantan*, Teluk Cempedak, T 5121469; ***Morahols Travel***, 11 Teluk Cempedak, T 5100851.

• **Transport** 4 km east of Kuantan. **Local Car hire**: **Avis**, *Hyatt Hotel*, Teluk Cempedak, T 5125211 and Ground Floor, Loo Bros Bldg, 59 Jln Haji Abdul Aziz, T 5123666; **Mayflower**, *Hyatt Kuantan*, Teluk Cempedak, T 5131234; **Sinat**, Lot 3, *Merlin Inn*, Teluk Cempedak, T 5141388; **Thrifty**, *Merlin Inn*, Teluk Cempedak, T 5141388. **Road Bus**: regular connections from Kuantan – bus 39 from the local bus station in Kuantan. A short walk north of Teluk Cempedak are Methodist Bay and Teluk Pelindong, which are beyond the range of most picknickers.

TASEK CINI

Tasek Cini is an amalgam of 13 freshwater lakes, whose fingers reach deep into the surrounding forested hills, 100 km southwest of Kuantan. The lake and the adjoining mountain are sacred to the Malays; legend has it that Lake Cini is the home of a huge white crocodile. The Jakun proto-Malay aboriginals, who live around Tasek Cini, believe a naga, or serpent, personifying the spirit of the lake, inhabits and guards its depths. Some commentators think that as tourism picks up there, Tasek Cini will acquire the status of Scotland's Loch Ness – although Lake Cini's monster has not been spotted now for 12 years. Locals call their monster 'Chinnie'. More intriguing still are tales that the lake covers a 12th-14th century Khmer walled city. The rather unlikely story maintains that a series of aquaducts were used as the city's defence and that when under attack, the city would be submerged. In late-1992, however, the *Far Eastern Economic Review* reported that recent archaeological expeditions had uncovered submerged stones a few metres underwater at various points around the lake. But the Orang Asli fishermen do not need archaeologists to support their convictions that the lost city exists. Between June and September the lake is carpeted with red and white lotus flowers.

Tours There are a few tour companies which run package tours to the lake. Recommended is *Malaysian Overland Adventures*, Lot 1.23, 1st Flr, Bangunan Angkasaraya, Jln Ampang, Kuala Lumpur, T 03-2413569.

• **Accommodation** **C** *Lake Cini Resort*, T 4086308/4567897, 10 chalets, some with attached bathrooms, camping (**F**), small restaurant attached to the resort serving simple dishes. **E** ***Rajan Jones Guest House***, this is the cheapest place to stay situated 30 minutes walk from the *Lake Cini Resort*, room rate includes all meals but the accommodation is very basic – no running water of electricity – tours and treks arranged.

• **Post & telecommunications** **Area Code**: 09.

• **Transport** Getting to Tasek Cini is difficult by public transport; by far the easiest way to visit the lake is on an organized tour (RM60). Contact the **Tourist Information Centre**, 15th Flr, Kompleks Teruntum, Jln Mahkota, T 505566, Kuantan. **Bus and boat**: take the KL highway (Rt 2) from Kuantan towards Maran; 56 km down the road, Tasek Cini is signposted to the left. From here there used to be buses to Kampung Belimbing, a trip of 12 km, but there are reports that this service has been suspended. If so, hitch or walk to Belimbing. At Belimbing it is possible to hire a boat across the Pahang River and onto the waterways of Tasek Cini (RM40-50). It is also possible to be dropped off at the resort and picked up at an arranged time (RM80). An alternative way to get to Tasek Cini is by catching a bus from Kuantan or Pekan for Kampung Cini (12 km from the resort). From here there is a sealed road to the resort but, again, no public transport – although people have managed to persuade local motorcyclists to take them pillion.

BESERAH

Once a picturesque fishing kampung, 10 km north of Kuantan, Beserah now sprawls and is not much more than a suburb of Kuantan. Beserah is a friendly place but aesthetically it bears little comparison with villages further north. There is, however, a local handicraft industry still; there is a batik factory to the north of the village. The village's speciality is *ikan bilis*, or anchovies, which are boiled, dried and chillied on the beach and end up on Malaysian breakfast tables, gracing *nasi lemak*. Beserah's fishermen use water buffalo to cart their catch directly from their boats to the kampung, across the middle of the shallow lagoon.

The kampung has become rather touristy in recent years, but there is a good beach, just to the north, at Batu Hitam.

Excursions Kampung Sungai Ular (Snake River Village), 31 km north of Kuantan, is a typical laid-back and very photogenic Malay fishing village. There is a small island (Pulau Ular), just offshore. The beach is usually deserted, is backed by coconut palms and has fine white sand. The Kampung is signposted to the right, just off the main road. **Accommodation A-B** *Ombak Beach Resort*, Mukim Sungai Karang (35 km north of Kuantan), T 609 5819166, F 609 5819433, 30 a/c rooms in 3 acres of land, all with own terrace and parking space so this is clearly directed mainly at people with their own transport. Right on the beach, swimming pool, limited conference facilities. *Getting there*: catch a bus running up the east coast road and asked to be dropped off at Kampung Sungai Ular.

• **Accommodation** Most of the resort hotels are around Sungai Karang, 3-6 km north of Beserah village itself. **A** ***Coral Beach Resort*** (formerly *Ramada*), 152 Sungai Karang (about 6 km north of Beserah), T 5447544, F 5447543, a/c, restaurants, pool, paddling pool, playground, good range of facilities including tennis, squash, badminton, gymnasium, jacuzzi and watersports, adjacent to fine white-sand beach, popular stop-over for cruises, hence its amphitheatre which can seat 800 people for cultural shows, all rooms spacious, a/c, TV, in-house video, mini-bar, tea and coffee-making facilities, non-smoking rooms available; *Reliance tour agency* in arcade. **A-B** ***Le Village Beach Resort***, Sungai Karang, T 5447900, F 5447899, restaurants, pool, beach front with watersport facilities, tennis, playground and paddling pool, neatly landscaped grounds with well-spaced chalets and a new 66-room extension, good atmosphere and attractive decor. **B** ***Blue Horizon Beach Resort***, Kampung Balok (5 km north of Beserah) T 5448119, F 5448117, north of Beserah on good beach, pool, clean and spruce with big wooden chalet rooms, built around central area, garden a bit of a wilderness, discounts often available. **B** ***Gloria Maris Resort*** (1 km north of Beserah), T 5447788, F 5447619, a/c, restaurant, watersports, very small pool, sandwiched between road and Pasir Hitam (not such a good stretch of beach), small chalets and friendly management. **B** ***Tiara Beserah Beach Resort***, 812 Jln Beserah, T 5448101, F 5141979, 32 rooms in new atap-roofed chalets, a/c, TV, pool, café. **E** ***La Chaumiere***, T 5447662, this is the most popular of the budget places to stay, under French management it is well run and pleasant, to get here ask to be let off at Kampung Pantai Beserah and walk towards Kampung Pelidong and the sea – about 1 km. **E-F** ***Jaffar's Place***, very rudimentary kampung accommodation, room rate includes all meals, away from the beach.

• **Places to eat** ♦♦♦*Pak Su Seafood Restaurant*, popular Chinese restaurant on terrace next to the beach, recommended. ♦♦♦*Beserah Seafood*, Malay/Chinese, speciality: buttered prawns. ♦♦♦*Gloria Maris Golden Cowrie Restaurant*, near the chalets, Malay/Indian/Thai and traditional Sunday lunch at fixed price, seafood salad by weight.

• **Post & telecommunications Area Code**: 09.

• **Transport Road Bus**: bus nos 27, 28 and 30 from Kuantan's main bus terminal all pass through Beserah – departures every 30 minutes.

TEMERLOH

Temerloh, on the Pahang River, is the halfway point on the KL-Kuantan road and a popular makan stop. The Karak Highway tunnels through the Genting Pass, to the northeast of KL and the road then runs east through Mentakab (where there is a railway station) to Temerloh. From Temerloh it is possible to take a river trip to **Pekan**, the old royal capital of Pahang (see page 272) and to **Tasek Bera** (page 274). Frankly, there's not much to bring people to Temerloh, although it is emerging as an important administrative and service centre.

• **Accommodation** The accommodation in Temerloh is basic. **B** *Hotel Green Park*, Lot 373, Jln Serendit, T 2963055, F 2962517, a/c, complimentary tea/coffee, TV, newly opened and smartly furbished, recommended. **B** *Seri Malaysia Temerloh*, Lot 370/6/92, Jln Mazmah, T 2965776, one of the new budget chain, a/c, TV, coffee/tea making facilities, money-changer, restaurant, good value, recommended. **C** *Kam San*, C-67 Jln Datuk Ngau Ken Lock, T 2965606. **C** *Rumah Rehat* (*Rest House*), Jln Datuk Hamzah, T 2961254/2963254, some a/c, restaurant, great position on the river, large rooms, recommended. **C-D** *Ban Hin*, 40 Jln Tangku, T 2962331, some a/c, better rooms with attached bathrooms, reasonable. **D** *Kwai Pan*, 66 Jln Datuk Ngau Ken Lock, T 2961431. **D-E** *Isbis*, 12 Jln Tengku Babar, T 2963126/2963136, some a/c, the best of the cheaper places to stay, more expensive rooms with attached bathrooms.

• **Post & telecommunications Area Code**: 09.

• **Transport Train** The nearest railway station is at Mentakab, 12 km west of Temerloh. Connections south with Singapore and north to Kota Bharu, see page 512 for details of timetabling. **Road Bus and taxi**: the bus terminal is close to the centre of town. Daily connections with KL's Pekeliling terminal, Melaka, Penang, Kota Bharu and Kuantan. Taxis run to KL, Kuantan, Mentakab and Jerantut.

TAMAN NEGARA (NATIONAL PARK)

Once known as King George V Park, Taman Negara was gazetted as a national park in 1938 when the Sultans of Pahang, Terengganu and Kelantan agreed to set aside a 43,000-hectare tract of virgin jungle where all three states meet. Taman Negara is in a mountainous area (it includes Gunung Tahan, the highest mountain on the peninsula) and lays claim to some of the oldest rainforest in the world. This area was left untouched by successive ice ages and has been covered in jungle for about 130 million years which makes it older than the rainforests in the Congo or Amazon basins.

Gunung Tahan (2,187m) is the highest of three peaks on the east side of the park, and marks the Pahang-Kelantan border. Its name means 'the forbidden mountain': according to local Asli folklore the summit is the domain of a giant monkey, who guards two pots of magic stones. The first expeditions to Gunung Tahan were despatched by the Sultan of Pahang in 1863 but were defeated by the near-vertical-sided Teku Gorge, the most obvious approach to the mountain, from the Tahan River. The 1,000m-high gorge ended in a series of waterfalls which came crashing 600m down the mountain. Several other ill-fated European-led expeditions followed, before the summit was finally reached by four Malays on another British expedition in 1905.

Until the park was set up, **Kampung Kuala Tahan**, now the site of the park headquarters, was one the most remote Orang Asli villages in North Pahang, at the confluence of the Tembeling and Tahan

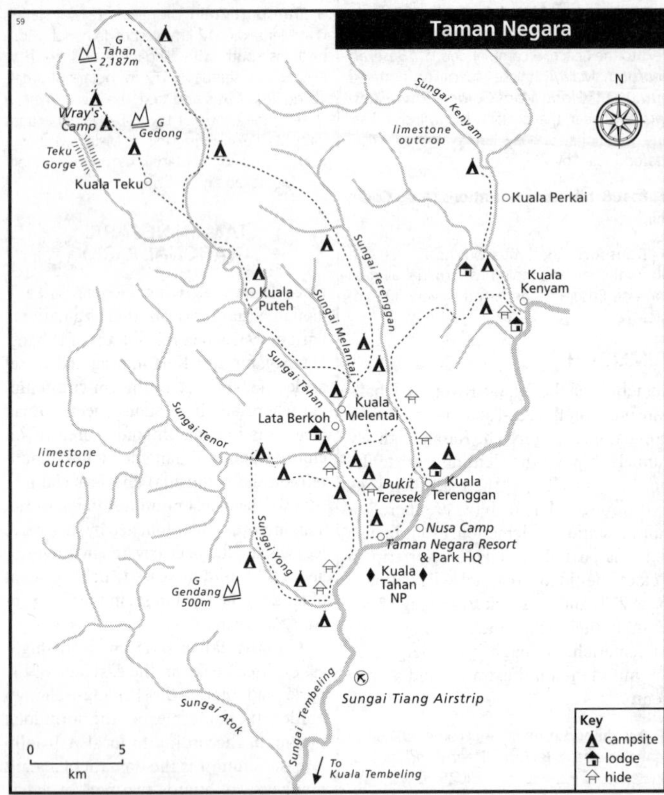

rivers. This area of the peninsula remained unmapped and mostly unexplored well into the 20th century. These days, Kuala Tahan is sometimes over-run with visitors; park accommodation has expanded rapidly under private sector management. But most visitors do not venture more than a day or two's walk from headquarters, and huge swathes of jungle in the north and east sections of the park remain virtually untouched and unvisited. Taman Negara now has scores of trails, requiring varying amounts of physical exertion; the toughest walk is the 9-days Gunung Tahan summit trek.

The range of vegetation in the park includes riverine species and lowland forest to upland dwarf forest (on the summit of Gunung Tahan). Over 250 species of bird have been recorded in Taman Negara, and wildlife includes wild ox, sambar, barking deer, tapir, civet cat, wild boar and even the occasional tiger and elephant herd. However, the more exotic mammals rarely put in an appearance – particularly in the areas closer to Kuala Tahan.

Hides Some hides or *bumbun* are close to Park HQ – as close a 5-minute walk – and nearly all are within a day's walk or boat ride. Visitors can stay overnight, but there are no facilities other than a sleeping space (sheets can be borrowed from Kuala Tahan – RM5/night) and a pit latrine. Take a powerful torch to spotlight any animals that visit the salt-licks. You are more likely to see wildlife at the hides further from park HQ, as the numbers of people now visiting Taman Negara have begun to frighten the animals away. Rats are not frightened: food bags must be tied securely at night. During popular periods and on weekends it is best to book your spot at a salt lick.

Permits The Department of Wildlife has a bureau at the Kuala Tembeling jetty (see below) and issues permits and licences. Park permit RM1; fishing licence RM10; camera licence RM5.

Fishing Fishing is better further from Kuala Tahan; there are game-fishing lodges near the confluence of the Tenor and Tahan rivers, at Kuala Terenggan (up the Tembeling from Kuala Tahan) and at Kuala Kenyam, at the confluence of the Kenyam and the Tembeling. The best months to fish are February-March and July-August; during the monsoon season. The rivers Tahan, Kenyam and the more remote Sepia (all tributaries of the Tembeling) are reckoned to be the best waters. There are more than 200 species of fish in the park's rivers including the *kelasa* which is a renowned sport fish. A permit costs RM10, rods for hire (See also Booking, Equipment and Accommodation, below).

River trips Boat trips can be arranged from Park HQ to the Lata Berkoh rapids on Sungai Tahan (near Kuala Tahan), Kuala Terenggan (several sets of rapids to be negotiated), and to Kuala Kenyam (from where a trail leads to the top of a limestone outcrop). Boats accommodating three passengers cost RM60/hour. Although this is a comparatively expensive way to see the park it is probably the most enchanting and when split between a number of people (boats carrying upto 12 people can be booked) is worthwhile.

Treks

Trails are signposted from Park HQ. Tours are conducted twice daily by park officials and these include night walks (RM15 per person), cave treks (RM35) and other treks and walks. Because most visitors tend to stick to the trails immediately around the Park HQ, even a modest day's outing will take you away from the crowds. A full listing and details on various routes can be obtained at Park HQ. Independent day treks/walks can be taken to caves, swimming holes, waterfalls, along rivers (again with swimming areas), to salt licks and hides, and, of course, through forest. Longer overnight treks are also possible although guides must be taken on all these longer forays. The most demanding is climbing Gunung Tahan.

Gunung Tahan (2,187m), is a 9-days trek to the summit and back. It is best climbed in February and March, the driest months. **Day 1**: Kuala Tahan to Kuala Melantai (4-5 hours). **Day 2**: Kuala Melantai to Kuala Puteh (8 hours). No streams en route; succession of tough climbs along the ridge, final one is Gunung Rajah; 1½ hours descent to campsite by Sungai Tahan. **Day 3**: Kuala Puteh to Kuala Teku (2½-4½ hours). Route follows Sungai Tahan, which must be crossed several times. The campsite is at the Sungai Teku confluence and was the base camp for the first successful Gunung Tahan expedition in 1905. **Day 4**: Kuala Teku to Gunung Tangga Lima Belas (7 hours). Long uphill slog (4½ hours) to Wray's Camp (named after 1905 expedition member). This is a good campsite; alternatively climb through mossy forest to Gunung Tangga Lima Belas campsite, which has magnificent views, but is very exposed. **Day 5**: Gunung Tangga Lima Belas to summit, returning to the Padang. After a scramble up the side of a rockface on Gunung Gedong, the trail leads to the Padang – a plateau area (3-4 hours). Set up tents and leave equipment at campsite; route to summit follows ridge and takes 2½ hours. Essential to take raincoat; summit often shrouded in mist. Begin descent to the Padang by 1600. **Days 6-9**: Padang to Kuala Tahan, following the same route. **Hiring a guide** A guide is necessary for this climb (RM400/week, RM50 for each additional day); maximum of 12 people with one guide. **NB** A sleeping bag and a tent are vital, all of the camps have water and firewood.

Another mountain in Taman Negara that is less frequently climbed is **Gunung Gagau** (1,377m), far to the northeast of Kuala Tahan. It is a 6-7 day trek of which 1 day is spent travelling upriver on Sungai Sat. This area of the park is rarely visited and it is advisable to take a guide.

The new **Canopy Walk**, half an hour from headquarters, is worth a visit. The walkway is suspended about 30m above the forest floor and stretches for over 400m. Admission: RM2. Open: 1100-1500 Monday-Thursday and Saturday-Sunday.

Equipment For trekking it is worth having walking boots for even the shortest of excursions as rain turns mud paths into skid patches, a thick pair of socks and long (loose) trousers. Leeches are common in the park after rain – spraying clothes and boots with insect repellent helps. Having said this, minimal clothing is needed, as it's hot work. A good torch is essential equipment for those going to hides and a water bottle is also essential on longer walks and treks. A raincover may be useful. Visitors are not permitted to carry glass into the park. The shop at Park HQ hires out torches, tents, water bottles, cooking equipment and fishing tackle – even jungle boots. Camera permit $5 (but no-one checks).

Booking Visits to the national park have to be pre-arranged at *River Park Sdn Bhd*, 260 h, 2nd Mile Jalan Ipoh, KL, T (03) 2915299 or *Malaysian Tourist Information Centre* (MATIC), Jalan Ampang, KL, T (03) 2643929 ext 113. Visitors are required to pay a RM30 deposit to confirm bookings for the park boat and accommodation at Kuala Tahan (park HQ). The boat to headquarters costs RM15 per person (one way). Those who risk turning up at the Kuala Tembeling jetty without booking may be turned away if boats are full.

Best time to visit Between March and September, during the dry season. – the park may be closed during the height of the monsoon season from the beginning of November to the end of December, when the rivers are in flood, although this isn't always the case.

Park Headquarters At Kuala Tahan, on the south boundary of the park, accessible by boat from Kuala Tembeling, a 2-3 hour – and beautiful – journey. At Kuala Tahan all visitors are required to check in at the reception desk, open 0800-2200, Monday-Sunday. Park Headquarters provide a range of facilities – although prices tend to be steep – including shop, restaurant, money changing facilities (poor rates), telephone service, equipment hire, etc.

Tours

Various companies run tours to Taman Negara. It is a more expensive way to visit the park, but permits, itineraries etc are well-organized in advance. Many visitors, particularly those unfamiliar with travelling in Malaysia, have recommended tours for their logistical advantages. Since the park has been run privately, however, it has become much more user-friendly and it is easy to visit independently. The disadvantage of independent travel is that tour groups tend to book up the hides. *Asia Overland Services*, 35M Jalan Dewan Sultan Sulaiman Satu (off Jalan Tunku Abdul Rahman), Kuala Lumpur, T 2925622, 3 days safari US$245; *Malaysia Overland Adventures*, Lot 1.23, 1st Flr, Bangunan Angkasaraya, Jalan Ampang, Kuala Lumpur, T 03-2413659; *Overland Discovery Tours*, Unit 5, 1st Podium Flr, *Shangri-La Hotel*, 11 Jalan Sultan Ismail, Kuala Lumpur, T 2302942; *Scenic Holidays and Travel*, Lot SO64, 2nd Flr Sungai Wang Plaza, Jalan Sultan Ismail, Kuala Lumpur, T 2424522; *SPKG Tours*, 16th Flr LKNP Building, Bandar Baru, Jerantut, T 262369; *Tuah*

Travel & Tours, 12 Jalan Lipis, Kuala Lipis, T 312144; *Camp Nasa*, 16 LKNP Building, New Town Jerantut, T 262369, F 264369. Packages can also be organized by Kuala Tahan Office, Taman Negara Resort, Kuala Tahan, T 263500, F 261500.

Park information

● Accommodation

Prices: L over RM500; **A+** RM260-500; **A** RM130-260; **B** RM65-130; **C** RM40-65; **D** RM20-40; **E** RM10-20; **F** Below RM10

Kuala Tahan and Kampung Kuala Tahan: The management of *Taman Negara* was handed over to the private sector in 1990. All accommodation for the Taman Negara Resort must be booked in advance, either direct to ***Taman Negara Resort***, Kuala Tahan, 27000 Jerantut, Pahang T 09-2663500, F 09-2661500 or through the sales office: Suite 1901, 19th Flr, Pernas International, Jln Sultan Ismail, 50250 KL, T 03-2634434, F 03-2610615, or at MATIC in KL (T 03 2643929, ext 113). The resort encompasses a range of rooms and types of accommodation (some with self-catering facilities): starting at the bottom of the range are bunk beds in the hostel (8 people/dorm) with communal facilities at RM18 pp. Moving up, rooms in the original accommodation centre cost RM120. Self-contained chalets and bungalows range from the standard wooden chalet at RM170, to RM260 for the deluxe chalet, to RM500+ for 2-bedroom suite bungalows. Note that it is also possible to camp (see below).

An alternative to the park is to stay in **Kampung Kuala Tahan**, on the other side of the river, where accommodation is much cheaper – albeit slightly less convenient: **D-F** *Teresek View*, T 011 911530, range of places to stay including dorm beds, basic chalets and more sophisticated bungalows with attached bathrooms. **E-F** *Liang Hostel*, basic with 4 beds/room. **E-F** *Tembeling Hostel*, much like *Liang's* in price and standard, but 2 beds/room. Upriver from Kampung Kuala Tahan is **D-F** *Nusa Camp*, restaurant, across the river from Park HQ and then 15 minutes upriver, bookable in KL at MATIC, T 03 2643929 ext 112 or T 09 2662369, offers a range of accommodation including dorms with 2 bunk beds/room, bungalows with attached bathrooms, and also tents for hire, the owner 'Byoing' is keen to help and will organize trips to the rapids (not particularly exciting). To get to *Nusa Camp* take one of the longboats from Park HQ (there is a shuttle boat every 2 hours); they also run a direct service from Kuala Tembeling.

Accommodation elsewhere in the Park: in addition, there are a number of fishing lodges in the park, in which beds and mattresses are provided; there is no bedding or cooking equipment however. These can be booked at Kuala Tahan HQ (RM8/night). Visitor Lodges (**B**)for hides at **Kuala Terenggan** and **Kuala Kenyam** can also be booked from Kuala Tahan HQ (RM5). These are right away from the crowds but are surprisingly comfortable with attached bathrooms and restaurant. There is no charge for staying in the hides themselves.

● Camping

The newly landscaped campsite can accommodate up to 200, but fortunately never does. *Taman Negara Resort* rents out tents (2/3/4-person) for RM6-12/night. There is an additional RM1 fee for use of the campsite. Tents, once hired, can be taken with you on treks. There are communal toilet facilities and lockers are available.

● Places to eat

Prices: ◆◆◆◆ over RM40; ◆◆◆ RM13-40; ◆◆ RM5-13; ◆ under RM5

The resort operates two restaurants and a bar – the rotan and bamboo ***Tembeling Lounge*** which even gets daily newspapers, it is open 1100-2400, Mon-Sun. The ***Tahan Restaurant*** and ***Teresek Cafeteria*** serve both local and western cuisine; the former is more expensive, both are open 0700-2300 Mon-Sun. Because of the cost of food at the resort, many tourists prefer to bring their own.

On the other side of the river at **Kampung Kuala Tahan** are a number of floating restaurants which serve unremarkable food but at prices considerable lower than those in the park complex. Beer, though, tends to be expensive.

● Useful services

The *Taman Negara Resort* include an overpriced mini-market (selling provisions for trekking and camping, open 0800-2230), a clinic (open 0800-1615 Mon-Sun; hospital attendant on call 24 hours, for emergencies), a mini-post office, a library and a Pelangi Air reservations and ticketing counter. There is also a jungle laundry service. In the 'Interpretative Room', there is a thrice daily film and slide-show on the park's flora and fauna (2045 Mon-Sun).

● Transport

All access to Taman Negara – other than for those who fly in – is by longboat from Kuala Tembeling.

Air Pelangi Air used to run a service between Taman Negara's Sungai Tiang airstrip

(30 minutes boat ride from Kuala Tahan)and KL and Kerteh in Terengganu. However as of mid-1997 this service had been discontinued.

Train Tembeling Halt, the nearest stop for Kuala Tembeling, is accessible from Kuala Lumpur, Kota Bharu and Singapore. It is necessary to inform the guard/conductor if you want to alight at Tembeling Halt, as it is still an unscheduled stop. From there it is a 30-minute walk to the jetty at Kuala Tembeling. From Kota Bharu: to Tembeling Halt; departures from Wakaf Bharu station (outside KB) at 1150 on Sun, Tues, Wed and Fri. From KL: trains to Tembeling Halt, via Gemas (on KL-Singapore line). The overnight sleeper departs 2200, arrives Tembeling Halt 0630. From Singapore: change at Gemas; connections to Tembeling Halt at 0530 Mon-Sun. Note that trains rarely pick up at Tembeling Halt and the nearest regular station is at Mela, a short bus journey away from the jetty.

Road Bus/taxi: the easiest way into the park is to catch one of the direct tourist minibuses from KL to Kuala Tembeling (about RM25), where the jetty for boats to the park is situated. Most guesthouses in KL can arrange tickets and also some tour companies. The nearest town to Kuala Tembeling is Jerantut where there is a range of accommodation. For those who want to use regular public transport or who are travelling from elsewhere, there are regular connections from KL via Temerloh (see Jerantut entry below for details). There is now a road all the way from Jerantut to Kampung Kuala Tahan but it is rough and requires 4WD – transport is provided by guesthouses in Jerantut but it means missing out on the river journey.

Boat It is a 59 km journey from Kuala Tembeling jetty, up the Sungai Tembeling to Kuala Tahan (Park HQ), 2½ hours, depending on river level (RM18 pp); departures at 0900 and 1400 (1430 on Fri). The return trip takes 2 hours; departures at 0900 and 1400. *Nusa Camp* also operate a boat service from Kuala Tembeling to their own resort (see Accommodation, above). Although it is now possible to go by road all the way to Kampung Kuala Tahan the boat journey is far more interesting and enjoyable.

JERANTUT

The nearest town to Kuala Tembeling, the most popular entry point into Taman Negara, is Jerantut some 16 km away. For those travelling to the Park on public transport it may be necessary to spend a night here and there is a range of accommodation on offer.

• **Accommodation** **B-C** *Sri Emas Hotel*, T 2664499, F 2664801, some a/c, the most sophisticated hotel in town, information on National Park, free transport to and from bus/rail station, organize trips to National Park, dorm beds available (**F**). **C-D** *Rumah Rehat* (*Rest House*), Jln Benta (short walk out of town), T 2664488, some a/c, restaurant, popular place with range of options including a/c rooms with attached bathrooms, simple fan rooms, and dorm beds (**F**), they organize daily trips to National Park. **E** *Chett Fatts*, adequate. **E** *Hotel Jerantut*, T 2665568, not recommended. **E** *Hotel Piccadilly*, 312 Sungai Jan.

• **Places to eat** Number of Malay-style coffee shops in town as well as the usual stalls in the market area.

• **Post & telecommunications** **Area code**: 09.

• **Transport** 16 km from Kuala Tembeling. **Train** Jerantut is accessible from Kuala Lumpur, Kota Bharu and Singapore. From Kota Bharu: to Jerantut; departures from Wakaf Bharu station (outside KB). From KL: trains to Jerantut, via Gemas (on KL-Singapore line) including the overnight sleeper. From Singapore: change at Gemas for connections to Jerantut. **Road Bus and taxi**: the bus and taxi station in Jerantut is in the centre of town. Regular connections from KL's Pekeliling terminal via Temerloh. Taxis direct to Jerantut from KL leave from the Puduraya bus terminal. From the east coast, there are hourly buses from Kuantan to Jerantut as well as taxis. For Kuala Tembeling (and Taman Negara) there are buses and taxis; some of the guesthouses also lay on minibuses. There is now a road all the way from Jerantut to Kampung Kuala Tahan but it is rough and requires 4WD – transport is provided by guesthouses in Jerantut but it means missing out on the river journey.

KUALA LIPIS AND THE KENONG RIMBA NATIONAL PARK

Kuala Lipis is a pleasant and relaxed town on the Jelai and Lipis rivers. Unlike other towns it has not been thoughtlessly redeveloped and many of the colonial buildings still survive. This is probably because Malaysia's development has passed Kuala Lipis by. At the end of the 19th century it grew to prominance as a gold mining town and, for a short period, was the administrative capital of the area. However gold fever has passed (although the mines have recently been re-opened) and the town's administrative role passed on to Kuantan in 1955. Today it is a good base from which to trek to Kenong Rimba and also has it own not inconsiderable charms.

Excursions

Kenong Rimba Park is 1½ hours east of Kuala Lipis by boat down the Jelai River to Kampung Kuala Kenong. The park, which encompasses the Kenong River valley and encompasses some 120 sq km, is the home of the *Batik Orang Asli* tribe, who are shifting cultivators. There is a network of Asli trails around the park and several caves and waterfalls. There are two campsites along the river; the first, *Kesong Campsite*, has three atap huts which serve as basic accommodation. There are also some simple huts, the *Persona Chalets*, at Gunung Kesong. The park is a good alternative to Taman Negara. Though it may not have the same variety of animal life (and especially large mammals) it is less touristed and trekking here is cheaper. Note that a registered guide is required. For tours and treks to Kenong Rimba, see Tours below. Entrance to the park is to Batu Sembilan (accessible on the jungle train), and from there by boat to Jeti Tanjung Kiara.

Tours

Mr Appu Annandaraja who runs the *Kuala Lipis Hotel* (see Accommodation) comes highly recommended as a trek organizer. He organizes a 4 day trek including food and boat transport in and out of Kenong Rimba for approx US$65. Another guesthouse which organizes trips to the park for much the same price is the *Gin Loke Hotel*, 64 Jalan Besar. Organized treks into Kenong Rimba are also run by *Tuah Travel & Tours*, 12 Jalan Lipis, Kuala Lipis, T 312144. There are other registered freelance guides who can be hired from Kuala Lipis. **NB** Travellers have warned us of one guide called 'Johnny' who is alleged to have drugged and raped several women.

Local information

● Accommodation

B *Taipan*, Jln Lipis Bentar, T 3122555, a/c, new hotel on the outskirts of town and the most expensive place to stay.

C-D *Rumah Rehat* (*Rest House*), T 3122599, some a/c, this places was formerly the home of the British Resident in Pahang, large rooms with attached bathrooms, certainly the most atmospheric of places to stay in Kuala Lipis – outside town on a hill.

D *Hotel Kuala Lipis* (aka *Appu's Guesthouse*), 63 Jln Besar, T 3121388, some a/c, shared bathrooms run by Mr Appu who runs highly recommended tours to Kenong Rimba (see tours), good source of information, recommended. **D** *Hotel Sri Pahang*, T 3122445, some a/c, clean and well-run place. **D** *Hotel Jelai*, 44 Jln Jelai, T 3121562, near the Jelai River, clean rooms and reasonable value.

E *Gin Loke*, 64 Jln Besar, T 3121388, simple rooms, shared facilities, organizes treks into Kenong Rimba. **E** *Hotel Tongkok*, Jln Besar, T 3121027, clean, good value.

● Post & telecommunications

Area code: 09.

● Transport

Train The Golden Blowpipe train, travels from Kuala Lumpur through Kuala Lipis. There are also slow jungle trains and connections with Kota Bharu and Jerantut/Tembeling Halt (for Taman Negara).

Road Bus: regular bus connections with Kuala Lumpur leave from the Pekeliling bus terminal in KL. Daily connections from Kuala Lipis with Kota Bharu and Kuantan. There are also connections with Fraser's Hill.

International connections: **Train** Connections with Singapore, either direct or via Gemas.

KAMPUNG CERATING

A quiet seaside village, set among coconut palms, a short walk from the beach, Kampung Cerating (or Cherating, as it is pronounced) has become a haven for those who want to sample kampung life or just hang out in a simple chalet-style budget resort. Cerating never was much of a kampung until the tourists arrived – there was a small charcoal 'factory', using *bakau* mangrove wood, but the local economy is now entirely dependent on sarong-clad

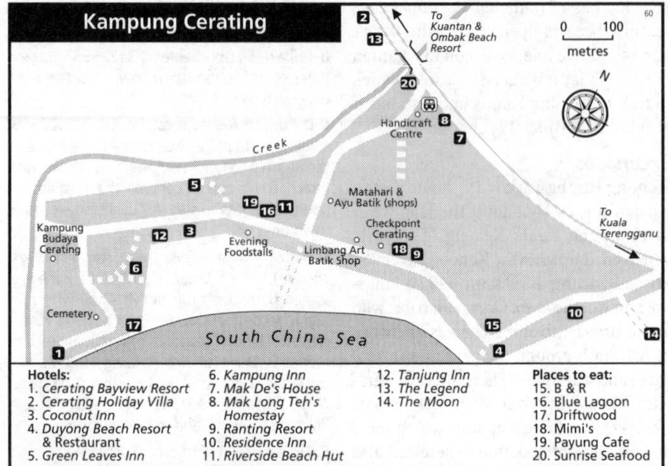

westerners and, more recently, growing numbers of Malaysian and Singaporean tourists. The beach at Cerating is big, but not brilliant for swimming because the sea is so shallow; it is also quite dirty. Cerating is named after the sand-crabs which are very common along the beach. They may look like heavily armoured tanks, but they are not dangerous. There are a couple of very private and beautiful little beaches tucked into the rocky headland dividing Cerating beach and the *Club Med* next door. These are more easily accessible from the sea (boats can be hired from the kampung) than from the steep trail leading over the promontory. This path goes right over to the *Club Med* Beach ... which is private. Bathers and sun-bathers should be prepared for periodic low-level fly-pasts by the Royal Malaysian Army whose helicopters swoop over the beaches.

Cerating has grown explosively in recent years. Big, modern resort complexes have sprung up 3 km south of the original kampung – it is known as Cerating Bharu (New Cerating). The old roadside village (together with the string of atap-roofed chalet resorts) is called Cerating Lama (Old Cerating). Although the old kampung atmosphere has been irreversibly tempered by the arrival of Anchor Beer and the population explosion, Cerating is still a peaceful haunt with some excellent places to stay and one or two of the best bars in Malaysia. Cerating's Malay residents have taken the boom stoically – although their obvious prosperity has helped them tolerate the 'cultural pollution'.

It is possible to hire boats to paddle through the mangroves of the Cerating River, to the south side of the kampung, where there is a good variety of birdlife as well as monkeys, monitor lizards and otters. For a price there are also demonstrations of silat (the Malay martial art), top-spinning, kite-flying and batik-printing in the village. There are some monkeys in the kampung which are trained to pluck coconuts. A couple of kilometres up the road, on Cendor Beach, green turtles come ashore to lay their eggs; they are much smaller than the leatherbacks which lay their eggs at Rantau Abang, further north. Cerating is also a good base to visit some of the sights in this part of the east coast including Tasek Cini (see page 279) and the Caras Caves (see page 275), for example.

Boat trips Organized from Checkpoint Cerating (see below) and by several beach hotels/chalets, 6 people are needed to fill a boat, with a full boat approximately RM8 per person, depending on distance up river.

Local information

● Accommodation

Prices: L over RM500; **A+** RM260-500; **A** RM130-260; **B** RM65-130; **C** RM40-65; **D** RM20-40; **E** RM10-20; **F** Below RM10

Many new bungalows and chalets have sprung up along the beach in the past decade; larger developments including the ***Impiana*** resort which has gone up about 2 km north of Cerating Lama. There is a good range of accommodation available, from simple kampung-style stilt-houses and 'A'-frame huts to upmarket chalets. Some of the accommodation in the kampung proper is family run; 'A'-frame and chalet accommodation is along the beach. The smarter, plusher hotels 3 km down the road at Cerating Bharu are much closer to the sea – and have a much nicer stretch of beach. 'A'-frame huts start at about RM10-15 while the more salubrious chalets cost from RM15-20. Note that the mid- and upper-range places whose guests are predominantly Malaysians and Singaporeans on weekend breaks, usually offer discounts during the week.

A+ *Impiana Resort Cherating*, km 32, Jln Kuantan, T 5819000, F 5819090, 250 rooms in spacious buildings elegantly decorated with wood and rattan, good range facilities including pool, kid's pool, outdoor jacuzzi, tennis, children's playground and playhouse with caretaker, 2 restaurants, pub with happy hour, all rooms have balconies facing sea, a/c, fan, TV, in-house movies, CNN, minibar, tea/coffee-making facilities, four poster wooden beds with nets, recommended.

L-A *Cerating Holiday Villa*, Lot 1303, Mukim Sungai Karang, T 5819500, a/c, restaurant, disco (boasts to be largest in town), pool, 2 rooms and 13 Malaysian chalets – corny but nice inside, recommended.

A+ *The Legend*, Lot 1290, Mukim Sungai Karang (Cerating Bharu), T 5819818, a/c, Italian and Thai restaurant, huge pool, villas near the beach with smartly appointed rooms, sports centre, tennis courts, watersports facilities, disco, rooms, which overlook big garden and beach, are pleasant and bright, recommended. **A** *Canoona Beach Resort* (just north of ***Holiday Villa***, Cerating Bharu), pleasant hotel with chalet blocks in grounds next to beach. **A** *Club Med* (round the headland from Kampung Cerating), T 439131/591131, a/c, restaurant, totally self contained resort designed to resemble a Malay village – private beach, watersports facilities, body-building classes and evening entertainment, minimum stay: 2 nights, closed Nov-Jan, the 'Circus Village' teaches children and adults to juggle, walk a tightrope or fly a trapeze – will be familiar to those who know Club Meds elsewhere. **A** ***Residence Inn Cerating***, on the same lane as *The Moon*, at the northern end of the village, between the main road and the 'village street', T 5819333, F 5819259, pool, kid's pool, jacuzzi, restaurant, disco, karaoke, comfortable rooms with a/c, minibar, TV, tea/coffee-making facilities. **A** ***Tanjung Inn*** turn right at bottom of lane down from main road, after *Coconut Inn*, T 5819081, attractive choice of accommodation ranging from first class big bungalows for families to budget chalets (with communal shower and toilet), restaurant, set in carefully tended and landscaped grounds with palms and two ponds, six new spacious bungalows under construction in mid-1997 and a beachfront restaurant scheduled for autumn 1997, this is a charming place to stay and has won the 2nd prize for best-kept accommodation in the state of Pahang, recommended. **A-B** *Ombak Beach Resort*, Lot 2466 Mukim Sungai Karang, T 5819166, F 5819433, friendly 30-room hotel, surrounding pool, short distance from sandy beach, restaurant, simple tiled roooms, a/c, TV, fridge, tea/coffee-making facilities, discounts offered in off-peak season making it exceptionally good value for money, managed by the *Berjaya* chain with professionalism.

B *Cerating Bayview Resort*, Cerating Lama, T 5819248, F 5819415, modern chalets on beach front, some with a/c and TV, restaurant, a good mid-range place to stay, well priced. **B-C** *Duyong Beach Resort*, Batu 28, T 5819335 (left at end of lane from main road, at far end), modern chalets at the end of the beach next to jungled hillside, mainly attracts Malaysian and Singaporean tourists, some rooms with a/c and TV. **B-C** *Ranting Resort*, T 5819068 (turn left at bottom of lane from main road bridge), restaurant (western and local dishes), extra for a/c and 2-room chalets on stilts, no TV, quite smart. **C-D** *Matahari Chalets*, T 5819126, on the southern of the two lanes from the main Juantan-Kemaman road, no phone. Two rows of attractive bungalows facing each other, with a lawn of about 30m in between. Some bungalows (with spacious verandahs) have fridges. One of the more pleasant places to stay here, recommended. **C-D** ***The Moon*** (the northernmost chalet resort on the loop off the main road), attractive, more rustic chalets in spacious leafy grounds, up a hillside, excellent bar (see below) and restaurant, chalets and longhouse (**E**), much more tranquil surroundings than chalet resorts along the beach, recommended. **C-D** ***Riverside***, some a/c, popular place with some more sophisticated rooms, recommended. **C-F** ***The Kampung Inn***, right at end of lane from main road, at far end on left, T 439344, nothing too special with very average chalet accommodation and A-frames and not much atmosphere, but advantageously located near *Boathouse Bar* and close to beach.

D ***Mak Long Teh Guesthouse***, T 503290, restaurant, like *Mak De*, this family-run operation was up-and-running long before Cerating was discovered by main-stream tourists, friendly, with excellent Malay home cooking – again, and like *Mak De's*, is can be noisy. **D-E** ***Coconut Inn***, T 5819299, run by Ilal – one of the kampung's best-known characters – and his Dutch wife, A-frames with rusting roofs, badly in need of some maintenance. **D-E** ***Mak De's House***, in the old village, next to police station, opposite bus stop (so can be noisy), T 511316, *Mak De* has been offering kampung-accommodation since the late-1970s and has an equally long-standing reputation for hospitality and good food, recommended.

E ***Green Leaves Inn***, right at end of lane from main road, on right, T 378242, tucked in among the riverside mangroves, *Green Leaves* looks like a Vietkong jungle camp, albeit with decent 'A'-frames, sheltered and shaded, close to sea and cheap, with breakfast thrown in, very clean.

● Places to eat

Prices: ♦♦♦♦ over RM40; ♦♦♦ RM13-40; ♦♦ RM5-13; ♦ under RM5

A few new restaurants have sprung up along the main road but because most chalet hotels have attached restaurants there's not much demand for outside food outlets.

♦♦♦***Sunrise Seafood Restaurant***, one of the new restaurants on main road, pleasant terrace set back from road, western and local dishes.

♦♦***Blue Lagoon*** (right at end of land from main road, after *Moonlight Lagoon* restaurant), another big neon-lit establishment offering wide selection of Chinese, Malay and western dishes, good on seafood, friendly atmosphere. ♦♦***B & R***, north end of Cerating beach road (next to *Duyong*), travellers' fare and some local dishes. ♦♦***Payung Inn 'n' Café***, next to river, opposite *Coconut Inn*, pleasant little open coffee shop, but forget the 'inn' bit. ♦♦***Restoran Dragon***, simple atap-roofed terrace at side of road in Cerating Lama, good claypot and buttered crab. ♦♦***Restoran Duyong***, T 5819578 (inside the *Duyong Beach Resort*), lovely setting on raised wooden terrace at edge of beach, lobster and prawns sold by weight, good selection of western and local dishes. ♦♦***The Deadly Nightshade*** (part of *The Moon* chalet resort at northwest end of loop off main road), also known as 'the restaurant at the end of the universe', enchantingly vague menu, mainly western with some concessions to local tastes, great atmosphere. ***Mimi's Restaurant, Services and Tours*** (left at end of lane from main road, on left) restaurant inefficient, and tours par for the course, but *Mimi's* offers useful laundry service.

Plenty of **foodstalls**.

● Bars

The Moon (part of chalet resort of same name at northwest end of loop off main road), great bar amid atap and leafy foliage, second only to the *Boathouse*, recommended; ***The Driftwood***, at southern end of beach, very laid back, serves western food; ***Nan's Beach Bar***, behind *Coconut Inn*, the most popular beach bar, with Dire Straits and Celine Dion as favourites on the CD player.

● Airline offices

Pelangi Airways, Kerteh Airport, T 8261187, F 8263972.

● Banks & money changers

(See Checkpoint Cerating, under Useful addresses, below.) The nearest bank is at Kemaman, 12 km north.

● Entertainment

Kampung Budaya Cerating (Cerating Cultural Centre), western end of the village street, before *the Cerating Bay View Resort*, pavilion-style attraction, in landscaped garden with a big rather uncosy restaurant, where shows take place. Batik painting, top spinning, songkhet weaving and other typical east coast activities can be seen in the. The work of artist Ayam is particularly worth seeing.

● Post & telecommunications

Area code: 09.

● **Shopping**

Batik: there are 3 batik shops in Cerating; all the artists offer classes; prices (which include tuition) T-shirt RM20-25, sarong RM25, singlet RM18. ***Limbang Art*** (left at bottom of lane down from main road bridge), mainly shirts, T-shirts painted by *Munif Ayu Art* (on lane down from main road bridge); ***Cerating Collection*** (in old village, next to main road and *Mak De's*), designs more colourful and abstract than its two local competitors; ***Matahari Chalets*** local artist Ayu sells his batik T-shirts here and does batik painting classes.

● **Sports**

Golf: *Kelab Golf Desa Dungun*, T 8441041, Dungun, 18 holes, green fees RM40. **A+** ***Awana Kijal Beach and Golf Resort***, Kijal, just south of Kerteh Airport, opened in 1996, same management as Genting Highlands, 5-star resort and 18-hole golf course, T (603) 262 3555, F (603) 261 6611, rather monstrous design, with extensive facilities, surrounded by golf course and the beach.

Watersports: *Cerating Beach Recreation Centre*, arranges water skiing and windsurfing, RM10 hire, RM15 lesson; *Club Med*, watersports facilities and body-building classes open to non-guests 0900-1100 and 1400-1600 Mon-Sun (RM60 for half day).

● **Useful addresses**

Checkpoint Cerating: (about 100m down on left from lane leading from main road bridge), ticketing (buses, taxis, minibuses), vehicle hire: car (RM90/day), motorbike (RM25/day), mountain bike (RM10/day), boats (RM10/day), foreign exchange (including Tcs, poor rate), mobile phone, book rental, newspapers and tourist info, also organizes tours to Lake Cini, Terengganu National Park and batik factories.

● **Transport**

50 km from Kuantan.

Local (See Checkpoint Cerating, under Useful addresses, above.)

Air Kerteh Airport is about 40 km north of Cerating. **Pelangi Airways** operate regular connections with KL.

Road Bus: regular buses from Kuantan (Kemaman bus). Bus stops at both ends of the kampung. Regular connections with Rantau Abang, Kuala Terengganu, Marang, Kota Bharu. Minibuses leave Checkpoint Cerating for Kuantan at 07.30 Mon-Sun and to Memaman, to change to northbound express buses. **Taxi**: Rantau Abang, Kuantan, Kuantan airport.

KEMASIK

On the road north from Cerating there are several stretches of beach, among the best of which is Kemasik. It is off the main road to the right (85 km north of Kuantan, 28 km north of Cerating), just before the oil and gas belt of Kerteh. Ask buses to stop shortly after windy stretch through hills. At Kemasik, the beach is deserted; there is a lagoon, some rocky headlands and safe bathing. No facilities.

KUALA ABANG

Turtles also come ashore at Kuala Abang (a few kilometres north of Dungun), which is much quieter than Rantau Abang, although there are still a few hotels. There are also several places to stay, although not right on the beach, at the small port of **Kuala Dungun** (famed for its *kuini*, a local mango). There is a weekly night-market (*pasar malam*) in Dungun on Thursdays. From there it is possible to hire a boat to Pulau Tenggol, 29 km out – popular with snorkellers.

Local information

● **Accommodation**

C-D *Kasanya*, 225-227 Jln Tambun, T 9841704, a/c; **C-D** *Sri Dungun*, K135 Jln Tambun, T 9841881, a/c, restaurant.

D *Mido*, 145-6 Jln Tambun, a/c, T 9841246; **D** *Sri Gate*, 5025 Jln Sura Gate, a/c; **D** *Sun Chew*, 10 Jln Besar Sura Gate, T 9841412, a/c, restaurant.

Tanjung Jara: **A+-A** *Tanjung Jara Beach Hotel* (6 km north of Dungun), T 8441801, F 8442653, a/c, restaurant, pool, the best known 5-star beach resort on the east coast, its Malay-inspired design won it the Aga Khan award for outstanding Islamic architecture, tour excursions, windsurfing, golf and tennis facilities, also offers local tours.

● **Post & telecommunications**

Area code: 09.

● **Transport**

Road Bus: express buses leave for Kuantan, Mersing, KL and JB/Singapore. **Taxi**: Kuala Terenganu, Kota Bharu, Dungun, and Kuantan.

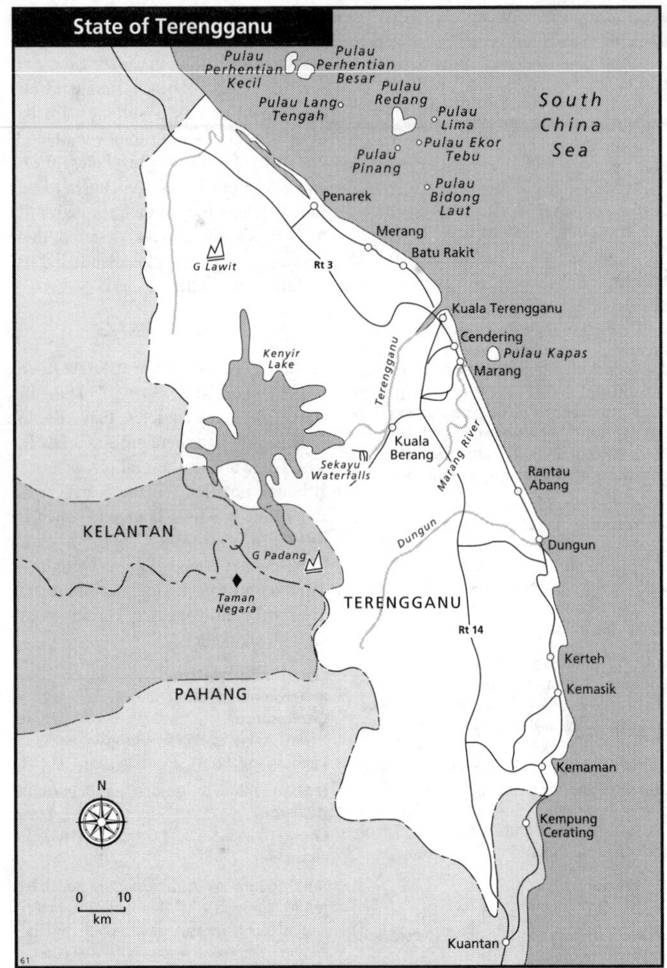

RANTAU ABANG

This strung-out beachside settlement owes its existence to turtles. Every year between May and September, five different species of turtle (*penyu* in Malay) come to this long stretch of beach to lay their eggs, including the endangered giant leatherbacks. And every year, tens of thousands of tourists also make the pilgrimage. During the peak egg-laying season, in August (which coincides with Malaysia's school holidays), the beach gets very crowded. Up until the mid-1980s the egg-laying 'industry' was poorly controlled; tourists and locals played guitars around bonfires on the beach and scrambled onto turtles' backs for photographs as

The giant leatherback turtle *(Dermochelys coriacea)*

The symbol of the old Malaysian Tourist Development Corporation, the giant leatherback turtle is so-called for its leathery carapace, or shell. It is the biggest sea turtle and one of the biggest reptiles in the world. The largest grow to 3m in length and most of the females who lumber up Rantau Abang's beach to lay their eggs are over 1.5m long. On average they weigh more than 350 kg, but are sometimes more than double that. Giant leatherbacks are also said to live for hundreds of years. They spend most of their lives in the mid-Pacific Ocean – although they have been sighted as far afield as the Atlantic – and return to this stretch of beach around Rantau Abang each year to lay their eggs, in the way salmon return to the same river. The beach shelves steeply into deeper water, allowing turtles to reach the beach easily.

They are not well-designed for the land. It requires huge effort to struggle up the beach, to above the high-tide mark. After selecting a nesting site, the turtle first digs a dummy hole before carefully scooping out the actual nest pit, in which she lays up to 150 soft white eggs between the size of a golf ball and a tennis ball. The digging and egg-laying procedure, punctuated by much groaning and heaving and several rest-stops, takes up to 2 hours, after which she covers the hole and returns to the sea. During the egg-laying period, the turtle's eyes secrete a lubricant to protect them from the sand, making it appear as if it is crying. In the course of the egg-laying season (from May to September) this exhausting slog up the beach might be repeated up to 9 times.

The gestation period for the eggs is 52-70 days. During this period the eggs are in danger from predators, so the Fisheries Department collects up to 50,000 eggs each season for controlled hatching in fenced-off sections of beach. The eggs are also believed to be an aphrodisiac and can be bought in wet markets along the east coast for about RM1 each (a small quota is set aside for public consumption). Young hatchlings are regularly released into the sea from the government hatchery. Many are picked off by predators, such as gulls and fish, and few reach adulthood. The turtles have been endangered by drift-net fishing and pollution. It is also prized for its shell which is thought to have the most beautiful markings of any sea turtle. In nature it is used to camouflage, it is thought, the turtle against a dappled coral background. The 'tortoiseshell' is fashioned into combs and cigarette boxes. In 1990 the Malaysian government announced it would start fitting radio transmitters to leatherbacks to enable satellites to monitor their movements in international waters. French satellite information is providing a stronger database on turtle populations and movements allowing the formulation of a more effective conservation strategy.

Even so, the leatherback turtle appears to be fighting a losing battle against extinction. There are just five main places in the world where these behemoths lay their eggs: South Africa's east coast, Surinam, Costa Rica, the Pacific coast of Mexico, and Rantau Abang. In the mid-1950s 10,000 turtles were arriving at Rantau Abang alone; in 1996 it was a mere 68. When one considers the odds against an egg turning into a mature adult leatherback – around one in a 1,000 (some say, 10,000) – and couple that with all the new threats that the leatherback has to contend from drift nets to pollution, it is small wonder that some marine biologists believe this magnificent creature could, by the next millenium, be on the verge of extinction.

Green turtles come ashore to lay their eggs later in the season. (For more detailed information on the green turtle, see page 484.)

they laid. Conservationists became increasingly concerned about the declining number of giant leatherbacks that chose to nest on the beach and began to press for stricter policing and management.

Parts of the beach have now been set aside by the government, and access is prohibited; there are also sections of beach with restricted access, where a small admission charge is levied by guides. The Fisheries Department does not charge. Local guides, who trawl the beach at night for leatherbacks coming ashore, charge tourists RM2 a head for a wake-up call. Turtle-watching is free along the stretch around the Turtle Information Centre. The Fisheries Department also runs three hatcheries to protect the eggs from predators and egg-hunters: they are a local delicacy. The closest is 5 minutes walk from *Awang's*. Officers from the department patrol the beach in 3-wheeler beach buggies.

NB Do not interfere with the turtles while they are laying. There is now a ban on flash photography and unruly behaviour is punishable by a RM1,000 fine or 6 months' imprisonment. Camp fires, loud music, excessive noise and littering are all illegal, although the latter is not well enforced.

Rantau Abang Turtle Information Centre, 13th Mile Jalan Dungun, T 8441533, F 8442653, opposite the big new *Plaza R & R*, has an excellent exhibition and film presentation about sea turtles, focusing on the giant leatherback. A slide-show also opened in 1993. The Fisheries Department at the centre are very helpful and friendly. Open Saturday-Thursday 0900-1300, 1400-1900, 2000-2300, Friday 0900-1200, 1500-2300 (June-August); 0800-1245, 1400-1600 Saturday-Wednesday, 0800-1245 Thursday, closed Friday (September-April).

Excursions

Kuala Abang, south of Rantau Abang, is easily accessible. See page 291.

Local information

● Accommodation

Rantau Abang's accommodation is strung-out along the main road; there are many over-priced, unpleasant little hovels. New places are opening and old ones closing all the time. Security is a problem here: it is inadvisable to leave valuables in rooms. The only up-market place to stay near here (unless new outfits have opened) is the beautiful *Tanjung Jara Beach Hotel* which is roughly half-way between Rantau Abang and Kuala Dungun, see the Kuala Abang entry above for details.

B *Rantau Abang Information Centre*, 13th Mile, Jln Dungun, T 8441533, F 8442653, a/c, beautiful chalets overlooking lagoon in land-scaped gardens, a little noisy as next to road, but by far the nicest place to stay, all chalets have hot water showers, fridges, TVs and small kitchens and at RM60-100 split between maximum of 4 people, superb value for money. **B-E** *Ismail's*, T 8441054, next to *Awang's*, good restaurant (only open in peak season), south of the Visitor's Centre, average beach-side set-up, similar to *Awang's*.

C-D *Dahimah's*, T 9835057, 1 km south of Visitor's Centre, restaurant, clean rooms in Malay wooden chalets. **D** *Awang's*, T 8443500, restaurant, some a/c, some rooms are very poor, the best are only average; *Awang's* organizes trips to nearby Pulau Kapuas and to batik factories.

Kuala Abang: **B-C** *Merantau Inn*, T 8441131, at the south end of the turtle beach, a/c, restaurant, big, clean chalets above old fish ponds, past its prime, but three decent chalets on the beach.

● Places to eat

Most hotels have their own restaurants, but there are stalls along the roadside and several coffee shops around the bus stop.

♦♦*Awang's*, right on the beach, Awang was formerly the chef at the *Tanjung Jara Beach Hotel*. *Ismail's* also has a restaurant and there are some stalls in the *Plaza R & R*; *Mikinias*, just down from *Awang's*. Big menu but service is slow if it gets busy.

● Post & telecommunications

Area code: 09.

● Transport

22 km north of Kuala Dungun, 58 km south of Kuala Terengganu and 160 km north of Kuantan. **Road Bus**: regular connections with Kuala Terengganu and Kuala Dungun from opposite Turtle Information Centre. From Kuala Dungun connections with Kuantan and other destinations.

MARANG

Marang is a colourful Malay fishing kampung at the mouth of the Marang River, although it is not as idyllic as the tourist literature suggests. To get into the town from the main road, follow signs to LKIM Komplex from the north end of the bridge. The recent rush to put up budget accommodation has placed it firmly on the tourist map. Since then it has begun to acquire a bit of a run-down look. It is still a very lovely village though, with its shallow lagoon, full of fishing boats. The best beach is opposite Pulau Kepas at Kampung Ru Muda. It was the centre of a mini-gold-rush in 1988 when gold was found 6 km up the road at Rusila. On the road north of Marang there are a number of batik workshops, all of which welcome visitors.

Excursions

Pulau Kapas is 6 km (30 minutes) off the coast, with some good beaches. Those wanting a quiet beach holiday should avoid weekends and public holidays when it is packed. The coral here has been degraded somewhat and there is much better snorkelling at **Pulau Raja**, just off Kapas, which has been declared a marine park. All the guesthouses organize snorkelling and the *Kapas Garden Resort* also has scuba equipment. **Accommodation A** *Primula Kapas Island Village Resort*, T/F 6236110, Malay-style chalets, pool. Since a change of management this place seems to have gone downhill: service is poor, the beach

The crown-of-thorns – the terminator on the reef

The crown-of-thorns starfish (*Acanthaster planci*) – a ruthlessly efficient, cold-blooded killing machine – launched an invasion of the Pulau Redang Marine Park in the early 1990s. The destructive starfish, which did serious damage to Australia's Great Barrier Reef in the 1980s, can regenerate and multiply rapidly leading to sudden infestations on coral reefs. The crown-of-thorns grazes on staghorn coral (*Acropora*) in particular and if population explosions are left unchecked, the starfish can reduce rich coral colonies into blanched skeletal debris. One crown-of-thorns can suck the living tissues from a coral in a matter of hours and, if present in large numbers, they can eat their way across a reef, devastating it in a matter of weeks or months.

The crown-of-thorns is aptly named. It measures about 50 cm across and is covered in thousands of poisonous spines, each 3-5 cm long. The spines are extremely sharp and toxic – if they puncture human skin, they cause a severe reaction, including nausea, vomiting and swelling. These short spines grow on the starfish's legs, of which it has more than 20. But marine conservationists, concerned about the threat to the coral and fish breeding grounds, face a daunting task in ridding reefs of the unwelcome echinoderms. Because of their amoeba-like regenerative abilities, the crown-of-thorns cannot simply be chopped in half *in situ* – that would create two of them. Instead, each one has to be prised off the coral, taken to the surface and buried on land.

The Malaysian Fisheries Department, with private sector backing, mounted a reef-rescue expedition to Redang in 1992 to do exactly this. The department's marine biologists were unsure as to what had triggered the infestation of crown-of-thorns starfish; it could be that they invade in natural cycles – or human interference could have something to do with it. The last major infestation was in the early 1970s. Following their difficult task of picking the starfish off the reef, the divers buried them on shore, as instructed. Perhaps they should have driven wooden stakes through their hearts too: the starfish can go for as long as 9 months without food.

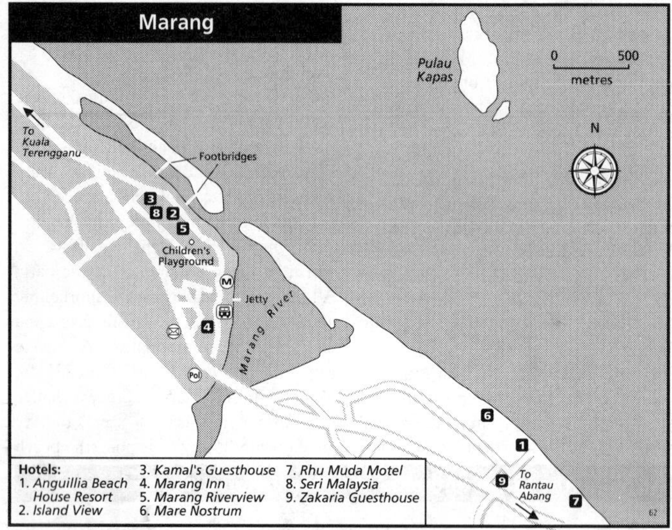

dirty, bathrooms poorly maintained, food ghastly – and therefore significantly overpriced. **B-C** *Tenggol Aqua Resort*, Pulau Tenggol, T 9861807, the only accommodation on the island. **C** *Sri Kapas Lodge*, T 6181529, simple rooms rather overpriced at this rate. **C-D** *Makcik Gemok Chalet*, T 6181221, largest outfit on the island with a range of rooms from simple huts with shared facilities through to larger chalets with attached bathrooms. **D** *Kapas Garden Resort*, T (011) 9871305, friendly place with well maintained rooms, some with attached bathrooms. **D** *Pulau Kapas Resort*, T 6132989, restaurant, snorkelling, forest tours, fishing trips (RM150/day). **D-E** *Zaki Beach Resort*, T 6120258, restaurant, chalets. *Getting there*: many hotels in Marang offer day-trips to the islands (RM15-20 return) and it is easy enough to grab a ride. The Abdul Tourist Boat Service is helpful, and will pick up even at low tide. They have fast boats.

River and island tours Half-day river tours organized by *Ping Anchorage 2* or *Marang Inn*. The same people also offer efficiently-run tours to nearby islands; most hotels in town can arrange trips to Pulau Kapas.

Local information

● Accommodation

There are hotels and guesthouses in Marang itself and in Kampung Rhu Muda, a couple of kilometres before the bridge over the Marang River.

B ***Seri Malaysia Marang***, Lot 3964 Kampung Paya, T 6182889, F 6181825, one of the *Seri Malaysia* chain, opened in 1995, good value, views of Pulau Kapas, a/c, TV, coffee/tea making facility, restaurant, launderette, organize island trips, recommended. **B-D** ***Angullia Beach House***, 12¼ milestone, Kampung Rhu Muda, T 6181322/6182403, some a/c, restaurant (with good set meal), extremely friendly, family-run chalet resort on lovely stretch of beach opposite Pulau Kapas (therefore sheltered), leafy, well-kept grounds and very clean chalets (no alcohol served), some visitors reckon it is overpriced, recommended. **B-C** ***Liza Inn Marang***, Kampung Pulau Kerengga, 10 km south of Marang, T 6132989, a/c, restaurant. **B-C** ***Marang Riverview***, T 6182928, on the seafront, in heart of the town, a/c, open air restaurant and a/c, rather weird looking new hotel, clinical rooms.

C ***Rumah Rehat Semarak*** (*Rest House*), Taman Rehat Semarak, Km 17, Jln Kuala Terengganu

(4 km south of Marang), T 6227631, chalets on the beach, formerly government-owned, past its prime, but pleasant rooms with balconies, the best ones facing the sea, small restaurant and stalls next door. **C-E** ***Mare Nostrum Holiday Resort***, Kampung Rhu Muda, T 6182417, a/c, restaurant, clean and hospitable, boat trips, pleasant little resort next door to *Angullia*, well-kept compound (if a little cramped) and clean chalets, recommended.

D ***Zakaria Guesthouse***, Kampung Rhu Muda, T 6182328, basic and further out of the village, dorm or rooms. **D-E** ***Island View***, opposite the lagoon, T 6182006, some a/c, free bicycles, chalets with attached bathrooms and some simpler rooms, popular.

E ***Marang Inn & Garden Café***, 132 Bandar Marang, T 6182132, restaurant, in decorated blue-and-orange shophouse overlooking lagoon, helpful, organizes tours around Terengganu and trips to islands. **E-F** ***Kamal's***, T 6182181, opposite the lagoon, very popular, dormitory and chalets, more upmarket than the *Inn* and the *Anchorage*, set in pleasant garden, friendly. **E-F** ***Marang Inn***, Batu 22 Rhu Muda, T 6182288, dorm and chalets.

F ***Ping Anchorage II***, 190A Bandar Marang, T 6128093, run by same people who run the *Marang Inn* and *Ping Anchorage I* in Kuala Terengganu, they also run tours and trips to islands, recommended.

● Places to eat

Most hotels have good restaurants serving Malay and international dishes. The ***Marang Inn*** restaurant is particularly good. There are cheap food stalls along the waterfront next to the market. Stalls at Taman Selera, Kampung Rhu Muda (along the roadside) are well known (particularly by long-distance bus and taxi drivers) for their Malay and Thai-style seafood, (closed Fri).

● Post & telecommunications

Area code: 09.

● Shopping

Handicrafts: market in Marang has a craft market upstairs and there are several handicraft shops along the main street. ***Balai Ukiran Terengganu*** (Terengganu Woodcarving Centre), Kampung Rhu Rendang, near Marang, master-carver Abdul Malek Ariffin runs the east coast's best-known woodcarving workshop, makes wide range of intricately carved furniture from cengal wood, carved with traditional floral geometric and Islamic calligraphic patterns, the varnished cengal wood is not to everyone's taste, but everything from mirrors to beds can be ordered for export, because most pieces are made to order there is little on show in Abdul's chaotic workshop, but carvers can be seen at work during the day. Good **batik** in Marang.

● Transport

18 km from Kuala Terengganu.

Road Bus: bus station between *Marang Inn* and *Ping Anchorage*. Connections with Kuala Terengganu, a little unpredictable, and with Kuala Dungun via Kuala Abang.

KUALA TERENGGANU

The royal capital of Terengganu state was a small fishing port (the state accounts for about a quarter of all Malaysia's fishermen) until oil and gas money started pumping into development projects in the 1980s. The town has long been a centre for arts and crafts, and is known for its *kain songket*, batik, brass and silverware.

Like neighbouring Pahang, Terengganu state was settled at least as far back as the 14th century, and over the years has paid tribute to Siam and, in the 15th century, to the sultanate of Melaka. When the Portuguese forced the Melaka royal house to flee to Johor, Terengganu became a vassal of the new sultanate. In the 18th century, Terengganu is recorded as having a thriving textile industry; it also traded in pepper and gold with Siam,

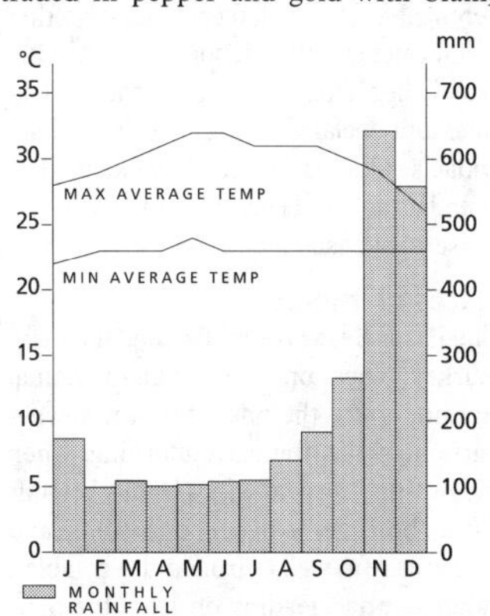

Climate: Kuala Terengganu

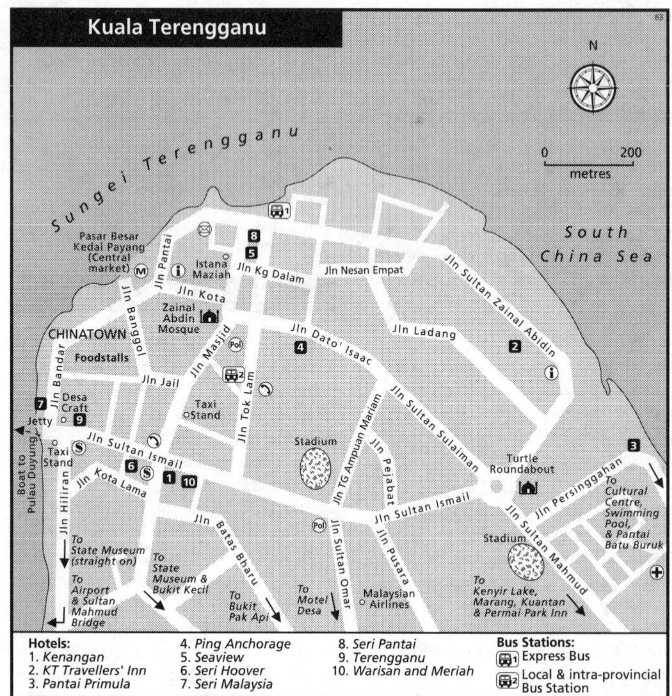

Cambodia, Brunei and China. A Chinese merchant community grew up in Kuala Terengganu. In 1724, the youngest brother of a former sultan of Johor, Zainal Abidin, established Terengganu as an independent state and declared himself its first sultan. Today's sultan is a direct descendent. The state has always been known for its ultra-conservative Islamic traditions.

Places of interest

The **Pasar Besar Kedai Payang**, the main market place on Jalan Sultan Zainal Abidin, is still the busiest spot in town – particularly in the early morning, when the fishing fleet comes in. The market sells batik, brocade, songket, brassware, and basketware as well as fruit and vegetables. **Jalan Bandar**, leading off from the market, is a street of old Chinese shophouses and there is also a busy and colourfully painted Chinese temple. Nearby is the imposing **Zainal Abdin Mosque**. Not far from the mosque (on the other side of Jalan Kota) is the apricot-coloured **Istana Maziah**, the old home of Terengganu's royal family, built in French style. It is now only used on ceremonial occasions and is not open to the public.

Some of Kuala Terengganu's older buildings have fine examples of traditional Malay carvings. One of these has been moved from the centre of town to the southern outskirts, along the seafront on Pantai Batu Buruk, and houses the **Pengkalan Budaya** (Cultural Centre), (see Entertainment page 302). Another of these traditional houses was taken apart and reassembled in Kuala Lumpur in the grounds of the National

Museum as an example of classical Malay architecture.

The **State Museum** has recently moved to Losong, a town a few kilometres south-west of the city. It is situated at the end of Jalan Losong Feri, facing Pulau Sekati. The museum exhibits rare Islamic porcelain, silver jewellery, musical instruments and weaponry – including a fine selection of *parangs* and *krises*. An eclectic collection, erratically labelled. Open 0800-1600 Saturday-Thursday. **Bukit Puteri**, near the Istana, has fortress remains on it and provides excellent views of the town.

Excursions

There is a thriving cottage industry in and around Kuala Terengganu and many of Malaysia's best-known handicrafts are made locally. Surrounding kampungs practice silverwork, batik-printing, songket-weaving and *wau* kite-building, but the best way to see these under one roof is in the Cendering handicraft centres (see below).

Pulau Duyung Besar is the largest island in the Terengganu Estuary and famed for its traditional boat-building. It now mainly survives by custom-building yachts. **Accommodation F** *Awi's Yellow House*, T 6231741, built out over the river on stilts, very popular with budget travellers, dorm and atap-roofed huts, some with balconies over river, pleasant location with cool breezes, there are some stalls at the bus stop near the bridge, but most travellers bring their own food from KT and have use of kitchen facilities, *Awi's Yellow House* is not yellow and can be hard to find but is well enough known to sniff out. *Getting there*: boat from jetty on Jalan Bandar – last boat around 2200 – or by road, via the new *Sultan Mahmud* bridge (taxis or bus from KT). The river is navigable for quite a distance upstream and it is possible to hire boats from the jetty for river trips.

Kampung Pulau Rusa, 6 km upriver, is a songket-weaving and batik centre, and is known for its traditional Petani-Terengganu wooden houses. *Getting there*: boat from the jetty on Jalan Bandar. (The village can also be reached by bus from the bus station on Jalan Syed Hussin.)

Cendering lies 7 km south of Kuala Terengganu and is home to several handicraft centres. *Kraftangan Malaysia*, with a beautifully displayed selection of silver, woodwork, silk, batik, brass and basketware as well as handicrafts from elsewhere in Malaysia, is very classy compared with *Rusila* (below), open 0830-1700 Saturday-Wednesday, 0830-1200 Thursday. Next door to *Kraftangan Malaysia* is the huge *Nor Arfa Batik Factory*, producing modern and traditional designs and readymades. Behind *Kraftangan Malaysia* is the *Sutera Semai* silk factory. *Getting there*: Marang-bound buses from Jalan Syed Hussin. The turning is clearly signposted off the main road.

Kenyir Lake 55 km south of Kuala Terengganu, is a man-made 370 km^2 lake and Kuala Terangganu's latest holiday destination. Having completed the Kenyir Dam in 1985, the state economic development board has built a 2½ km access road, a jetty and a tourist information centre at a place called Pengkalan Gawi. There are facilities for fishing, canoeing and boating. Major hotel and resort developments will be going up in the course of the next few years; luxury chalets – some of them 'floating chalets', built over the lake – and the inevitable 18-hole golf course are among projects in the pipeline. Most will be centred on Pengkalan Gawi or at Pengkalan Utama, 5 km away. (Enquire at tourist information office in Kuala Terengganu as to what stage developments have reached.) The lake is surrounded by jungled hills although the lake edge itself is still rather bare and devastated. There are plans to use Kenyir Lake as a back-door to the remote east side of Taman Negara. The lake itself has more than 300 islands. In parts swimming can be as hazardous as navigation thanks to the millions of submerged and semi-submerged trees. It has been stocked with fish and tour operators from Kuala Terengganu, some of which have houseboats on the lake, offer fishing tackle, canoeing and water-skiing as part of the package. The **Sekayu waterfalls**, with natural water-cut pools for swimming, are also 15 km from Kuala Berang. **NB** Mosquitoes are a problem around the lake. **Accommodation** There are plans to provide camping facilities in the area although currently there is no budgt accommodation. **A-B** *Primula Kenyir Lake Resort*, T (09) 6222100, Poh Island, restaurant, children's play area, pool, Malay-style chalets (and 8 floating chalets), no a/c, mosquito nets at windows, tiny shower room, no fridge or tea/coffee-making facilities, organizes activities on the lake. **B-C** *Kenyir Woods*, T (09) 6238188, chalets on a hill side overlooking the lake, comfortable and the best value accommodation here. Two other developments about 30 minutes by boat from Pengkalan Gawi are the **B** *Muping Island Resort* (T 09-6812197) and **B** *Uncle John's Resort* (T 09-6229564). *Getting there*: bus to Kuala Berang, off the inland road south at Ajil, and then taxi to the lake, or by taxi from Kuala Terengganu. From KL, buses depart at 0900 and 2100 from Putra Station. Many tour companies in Kuala Terengganu run inclusive packages to the lake.

Beaches Batu Buruk beach, running down the northeast side of KT is not safe for swimming. But there are some good beaches near Kuala Terengganu – Merang 30 km (see page 302) and Batu Rakit 20 km north. There is a (**D**) guesthouse at the latter. *Getting there*: regular buses to both beaches from Jalan Syed Hussin.

Numerous **islands** lie off shore from Kuala Terengganu including **Pulau Redang** (see page 303) and **Pulau Perhentian** (see page 304). *Getting there*: boats leave for the islands from Merang and from the Jalan Bandar jetty in Kuala Terengganu, from which there are now scheduled departures.

Tours

A number of tour agents offer tours to the offshore islands and trekking tours to the Kenyir Lake area (see page 302).

Local information

● Accommodation

Prices: L over RM500; **A+** RM260-500; **A** RM130-260; **B** RM65-130; **C** RM40-65; **D** RM20-40; **E** RM10-20; **F** Below RM10

There are only a couple of hotels at the top-end of the market but there are several cheaper hotels scattered round town, mainly at the jetty-end of Jln Sultan Ismail and on Jln Banggol, but the selection is not great. For budget travellers it is worth considering staying at *Awi's Yellow House* on Pulau Duyung (see Excursions, above, for details).

A *Permai Park Inn*, Jln Sultan Mahmud, T 6222122, F 6222121, good quality hotel offering value for money, just under 150 rooms, friendly staff, very comfortable, carpeted rooms with a/c, TV, in-house movies, mini fridge, tea/coffee-making facilities, pleasant pool and children's pool, restaurant, *SI Travel Services* organize local packages, eg Lake Kenyir, recommended. **A** ***Primula Parkroyal***, Jln Persinggahan, T 6222100, F 6233360, a new name, but not a new look unfortunately, a/c, restaurant (good Malay-food buffet for RM25), good pool, hi-rise hotel with all mod-cons but rooms are shabby and not sound-proofed, they do have a sea-view though,also organizes island excursions.

B *Kenangan*, 65 Jln Sultan Ismail, T 6222342/6222688, a/c, restaurant, reports are that this hotel has deteriorated into an expensive and dirty hovel. **B** ***Motel Desa***, Bukit Pak Api, T 6223033, F 6223863, a/c, TV, in-house video, minibar, restaurant, pool, set in gardens on a small hill overlooking the town, a possibility for those with own transport. **B-C** *Seaview*, 18a Jln Masjid Abidin, T 6221911, F 6223048, a/c, centrally located opposite Istana Maziah, good mid-range place to stay. **B** *Qurata Riverside*, Lot 175K Kuala Ibai, T 6175500, F 6175511, 7 km south of Kuala Terengganu, small and friendly hotel, 21 rooms in individual wooden chalets on stilts near the Kuala Ibai River, designed by a nephew of the local royal family to resemble a Malay village, set in meticulous garden, only marred by proximity of main road, comfortable rooms with wood floors, a/c, ceiling fans, TV and shower room, at low tide it is possible to walk across the river mouth to nearby sand beach, recommended.

B *Seri Malaysia*, Lot 1640, Jln Hiliran, T 6236454, F 6238344, a/c, restaurant (good, inexpensive), another in the well-run modern *Seri Malaysian* chain, a/c, TV, minibar, light airy rooms overlooking the river. **B-C** ***Batu Burok Chalet***, 906-A, Pantai Batu Burok, T 6221598, F 6232904, some a/c, restaurant, the only chalet-style accommodation in town, not bad, but a bit over-priced, pleasant open restaurant overlooking beach (which is dangerous for swimming). **B-C** ***Bunga Raya***, 105-111 Jln Banggol, T 6620527, bit run-down and noisy, on road. **B-C** *Seri Hoover*, 49 Jln Sultan Ismail, T 6233823, F 6233863, a/c, restaurant, big, clean rooms, although slightly musty smell. **B-C** *K.T. Travellers Inn*, 201, 1st Flr, Jln Sultan Zainal Abidin, T 6223666, F 6235378, convenient location downtown, a/c, TV, clean rooms. **B-C** *Terengganu*, 12 Jln Sultan Ismail, T 6222009/6222900, a/c, plush new foyer, rooms could do with lick of paint but clean and reasonable value, recommended.

C *Warisan*, 65 Jln Sultan Ismail, T 6222688, a/c, restaurant, attached to shopping arcade, cultural performances can be arranged. **C-D** *Meriah*, 67 Jln Sultan Ismail, T 6222655, restaurant, bar and nightclub, good, clean Malay-run hotel.

D-E *Rex*, 112 Jln Sultan Ismail, T 6221540, clean Chinese hotel, fan only, some rooms with attached bathroom.

E *Nam Tan*, 8 Jln Kota Hilir, T 6223308, fan only, some rooms with attached bath. **E** *Seri Pantai*, 35a Lot 312, Jln Sultan Zainal Abidin, T 6232141, F 6230488, close to bus station, good value. **E-F** *Ping Anchorage*, 77A Jln Dato' Issac, T 6220851, roof-top café, free breakfast, helpful with travel information, although rooms can be noisy, organizes trekking trips to Kenyir Lake area and offshore islands, now has sister hotel (*Ping Anchorage II*) in Marang, and the *Marang Inn* is part of the empire, dorm beds available, recommended.

● Places to eat

Prices: ♦♦♦♦ over RM40; ♦♦♦ RM13-40; ♦♦ RM5-13; ♦ under RM5

Nasi dagang – known as 'fishermen's breakfast' – is a speciality of the area. It is made with aromatic or glutinous rice, served with *gulai ikan tongkol* (tunafish with tamarind and coconut gravy). *Keropok* – or prawn crackers – are another Terengganu speciality.

Malay: ♦♦♦***Rhusila Coffee House***, *Primula Beach Resort*. ♦♦♦***Permai Park Inn***, Jln Sultan Mahmud, good value buffet. ♦♦***Keluarga IQ***, 74 Jln Banggol, good place for *nasi dagang* breakfast, also excellent *nasi campur* (curry buffet), open 0630-0300, closed Fri. ♦***Mali***, 77 Jln Banggol, near the bus station, popular, cheap coffee shop – *nasi lemak*, *nasi campur*, satay and good rotis. ♦***Nik***, 104 Jln Sultan Ismail, standard curries. ♦***Zainuddin***, Jln Tok Lam; ***Sri Intan***, 14 Taman Sri Intan, Jln Sultan Omar, well-appointed restaurant serving standard Malay dishes.

Chinese: ♦♦♦♦***KT Wok***, 1081 Block W, Jln Sultan Sulaiman, T 6243825, ultra modern decor, black and pink colour scheme, specialize in dim sum. ♦♦***Awana***, near public swimming pool, Jln Pantai Batu Buruk, recommended by locals. ♦♦***Golden Dragon Restaurant***, 198 Jln Bandar, good pork, interesting vegetable dishes, some tables on street, recommended. ♦♦***One-Two-Six***, 102 Jln Kampung Tiong 2 (off Jln Sultan Ismail), big open-air restaurant with hawker stalls, good seafood menu, special: fire chicken wings (comes to table in flames), recommended. ***Restaurants Good Luck, Kui Ping and Lee Kee*** all along Jln Engku Sar, standard Chinese fare.

Indian: *Taufik*, 18 Jln Masjid Abidin (opposite Istana Maziah), North and South Indian dishes, well-known for its rotis; ***Kari Asha***, 1-H Jln Air Jermh, good range of curries (including fish heads, dosai and rotis).

International: *Husni*, 954 Jln Sultan Mohammed, Thai, Malay and western dishes, vast menu.

Seafood: *Nil*, Jln Pantai Batu Buruk (near the *Pantai Primula Hotel*), view of the beach, good selection of seafood and renowned for its butter crabs in batter; *Taz*, Jln Sultan Zainal Abidin (below *Seri Pantai Hotel*).

Foodstalls: *Gerai Makanan* (foodstalls) opposite the bus station; Malay; ***Kampung Tiong*** (off Jln Bandar), excellent hawker centre with Malay food on one side, Chinese and Indian on the other, open 8 till late; *Jalan Batu Buruk*, near the cultural centre, some excellent Malay food and seafood stalls, recommended; also ***Warung Pak Maidin***, nearby on Jln Haji Busu, which is good on seafood; ***Kompleks Taman Selera Tanjung*** (1st Flr), huge area of stalls with good variety of dishes, open-air terrace; ***Majlis Perbandaran*** stalls, Jln Tok Lam; ***Pasar Besar Kedai Payang*** (Central Market), 1st Flr, Malay snacks, good views over the river. There are also some stalls next to *Stadium Negeri*.

● Airline offices

MAS, 13 Jln Sultan Omar, T 6222266/6221415; **Pelangi Airways**, No 29-D, Jln Sultan Ismail, T 6247071, F 6047072.

● Banks & money changers

There are several banks along Jln Sultan Ismail. **Bumiputra**, UMNO Jln Masjid Zainal Abidin; **Hong Kong Bank**, 57 Jln Sultan Ismail; **Maybank**, 69 Jln Paya Bunga; **Public**, 1 Jln Balas Baru; **Standard Chartered**, 31 Jln Sultan Ismail; **UMBC**, 59 Jln Sultan Ismail. There are virtually no money-changers in Kuala Terengganu.

● Entertainment

Cultural shows: *Pengkalan Budaya* (Cultural Centre), Pantai Batu Buruk. Displays of *silat* (Malay art of self-defence), traditional dances, top-spinning and sometimes *wayang kulit* (shadow puppets), 1700-1900 and 2100-2300 Fri and Sat.

● Hospitals & medical services

Hospitals: Jln Peranginan (just off Jln Sultan Mahmud).

● Post & telecommunications

Area code: 09.

General Post Office: Jln Sultan Zainal Abidin.

Telekom: Jln Sultan Ismail.

● Shopping

Batik: some of the best batik in Malaysia can be found in the central market (*Pasar Besar Kedai Payang*). ***Wan Ismail Tembaga & Batik***, near turtle roundabout, off Jln Sultan Zainal Abidin – a small, old-fashioned batik factory. There are a number of small craft and batik factories in Kampung Ladang – the area around Jln Sultan Zainal Abidin; ***Desa Craft***, 73 Jln Sultan Ismail, in the centre of town, has a good selection of silk and batik readymades and sarongs. The Central Market sells batik, silk, songket etc. Other shops selling batik can be found on Jln Bandor, including the ***Bank Gallery*** at number 194 and ***Yuleza*** at number 208.

Handicrafts: the **Central Market** is touristy, but offers a range of handicrafts, textiles, brassware etc. ***Desa Craft***, on Jln Sultan Ismail, is another good centre. Out of town, there are centres in Cendering (see **Excursions**, page 299).

● Sports

Diving: ***Merlin Enterprise***, 1-E, 1st Flr, Wisma Guru, Jln Hiliran, T 636200, manager David Chua has a reputation as one of the country's leading divers and is well known for his scuba expeditions.

Golf: *Badariah Golf Club*, south of town, 9-holes, requires special permission from the Sultan's private secretary's office, T 632456. ***Berjaya Redang Golf Club***, T 6233369.

● Tour companies & travel agents

Hedaco Travel, Ground Floor, Terengganu Foundation Bldg, Jln Sultan Ismail, T 631744; ***Ruways Travel***, 14 Bangunan Yayasan Terengganu, Jln Sultan Ismail, T 635582; ***The Little Traveller***, PO Box 117, T 673218, F 671527, trips to islands, equipped with comfortable houseboats on Lake Kenyir; ***WLO Travel & Air Cargo***, Ground Floor, *Hotel Pantai Primula*, Jln Persinggahan, T 635844.

● Tourist offices

Tourism Malaysia, 2243 Ground Floor, Wisma MCIS, Jln Sultan Zainal Abidin, T 6221433/6221893, F 6221791. **State Tourist Information Centre** (TIC), Jln Sultan Zainal Abidin, near the Istana Meziah on the jetty, T 6221553. Impressive looking place bursting with information.

● Transport

455 km from KL, 168 km from Kota Bharu, 209 km from Kuantan.

Local Bus: from the main bus terminal on Jln Masjid. **Car hire**: **South China Sea**, *Permai Park Inn*, T 6224903. **Taxi**: T 621581. **Trishaw**: RM2-3 for short trips around town.

Air The airport lies 18 km northwest of town, T 6264500 for information. Regular connections with KL, Kuantan, Penang and Johor Bahru. **Transport to town**: RM15 by taxi.

Road Bus: Kuala Terengganu has two bus stations. The express, long distance bus terminal is at Medan Selera, on the northern edge of the city centre. Local and intra-provincial buses leave from the MPKT station on Jln Syed Hussin which runs off Jln Masjid. Regular connections with KL (RM21.60), JB, Kota Bharu, Kuantan, Rantau Abang, Mersing, Singapore, Melaka, Butterworth and Marang. **Taxi**: taxis operate from next to the bus station on Jln Masjid and from the waterfront. Destinations include Kota Bharu, Rantau Abang, Marang, Kuantan, KL, JB and Penang.

MERANG

Merang is another small fishing kampung with a long white sandy beach; it is also the departure point for the many offshore islands, the biggest and best-known of which is Pulau Redang. Recently, Pulau Bidong has opened to tourists (Bidong's coral is said to be superb); throughout the 1980s it served as a Vietnamese refugee camp. The only island with accommodation is Pulau Redang.

Excursions A number of islands are accessible from Merang, notably **Pulau Redang** (see below).

Other islands, most of which are uninhabited, and all of which are endowed with good coral include Pulau Pinang, Pulau Lima, Pulau Lang Tengah, Pulau Tenggol and Pulau Ekor Tebu; fishing boats are usually happy to stop off on request. Tenggol is notable for its diving opportunities, with a sandy bay on the west coast, and good diving on the east. Tours can be organized to this island (and surrounding islands).

• **Accommodation** **A+** *Aryani Resort*, Jln Rhu Tapai-Merang, Pantai Peranginan Merang, 21010 Setiu, T 6241111, F 6248007, the original heritage timber suites have private courtyards with outdoor bath (but are in the **L** price bracket), elevated restaurant, pool, luxurious. **A-B** *Sutra Beach Resort*, Kampung Rhu Tapai, T 6696200/6233718, F 669410, a/c, restaurants, pool, 124 chalets, good sports facilities, 20 minutes from Kuala Terengganu's airport. **D** *Mare Nostrum Beach Resort*, 1 km out of town on road to *Penarik*, restaurant, rooms and 'A'-frames on beautiful stretch of beach. **D** *Kembara Resort*, 474 Pantai Peranginan Merang, 21010 Setiu, T 6238771, F 6238201, situated on an endless palm-fringed deserted white beach, running south from the jetty, set in a beautiful garden compound, very relaxed atmosphere, just 8 bungalows and 8 rooms all with attached shower and toilet, and fans. Cheap dorm accommodation. No restaurant but there's a large kitchen in the court which is well equiped and can be used freely, a little known paradise, recommended. **E** *Sugi Man's Homestay*, 500m beyond junction, on road to Penarek (signposted from the road), restaurant, basic kampung farm house, quite a walk from the beach, cooking lessons and kite making, including meals. **E-F** *Naughty Dragon's Green Planet Homestay*, popular place in the village, dorm rooms available, simple but relaxed and welcoming.

• **Post & telecommunications** **Area code**: 09.

• **Transport** 38 km north of Kuala Terengganu, on the coast road. **Road** **Bus**: two buses a day from Kuala Terengganu to Merang (RM1.70), and then on to Penarek. Minibus connections also available from Kuala Terengganu, from Jln Masjid. **Taxi**: taxis from Merang to Penarek.

PULAU REDANG

27 km off Merang; the archipelago is a marine park of nine islands and it has some of Malaysia's best reefs, making it one of the most desirable locations for divers. In the months after the monsoon, visibility increases to at least 20m but during the monsoon the island is usually inaccessible. Line-fishing is permitted and squid fishing, using bright lights, is popular between June and September; the fishermen use a special hook called a *candat sotong*. The lamps light the surrounding waters, attracting the squid. *Scuba Quest* (T/F (03) 2636032) organize diving trips to the islands.

• **Accommodation** Resorts on Redang offer competitive and flexible package deals – check with *Tourism Malaysia*. **A** *Berjaya Redang Golf and Country Resort*, T 6971111, F 6971100, 152 rooms with a/c, TV, minibar, pool, restaurants, health spa, gym, 18-hole golf course, popular destination for businessmen wishing to combine work and golf (limited business facilities), dive centre, gym, tennis courts, health spa. **A** *Redang Beach Resort*, T 6222599 (contact office: 36E, 1st Flr, Jln Dato' Isaac), full range of facilities, package deals available. **A** *Redang Pelangi Resort*, T 6223158, F 6235202. **D** *Pulau Redang Resort* (book in Kuala Terengganu, T 6227050), bungalows, 'A'-frames slightly cheaper.

• **Post & telecommunications** **Area code**: 09.

• **Transport** **Boat**: leave for the islands from Merang as well as from the jetty in Kuala Terengganu. It has, however, become very expensive to charter boats from Merang. *Tourism Malaysia* in Kuala Terengganu recommends that tourists take advantage of the package deals offered by the island's resorts; further details can be obtained from the *Tourism Malaysia* office. There are now scheduled departures to Redang from Kuala Terengganu. From Merang: RM70 return for boat (takes 8 people) or slow fishing boat for RM30 return (takes 12 people). A typical 2-days/2-nights trip costs around RM230 pp; all food, camping and snorkelling equipment included. As always, if you value a measure of privacy and seclusion, avoid weekends and public holidays. For further information contact *Coral Redang*, Wisma Awang Chick, Sultan Mahmud, T 6236200.

PULAU PERHENTIAN

Two more beautiful east coast islands – Pulau Perhentian Besar (big) and Pulau Perhentian Kecil (small) – just ovr 20 km off the coast are separated by a narrow sound with a strong current. Despite considerable development in the past 2 years, with more hotels, restaurants, bars, diving outfits and much more noise, the Perhentian islands still remain a paradise, with excellent diving and snorkelling, magnificent beaches and some of the best places for swimming on the east coast. There is a fishing village and a turtle hatchery in the middle of Long Beach (Pasir Panjang) on Perhentian Kecil. There are jungle trails across Perhentian Besar; all are well marked.

Best time to visit: travellers should be wary of risking the boat trip too close to

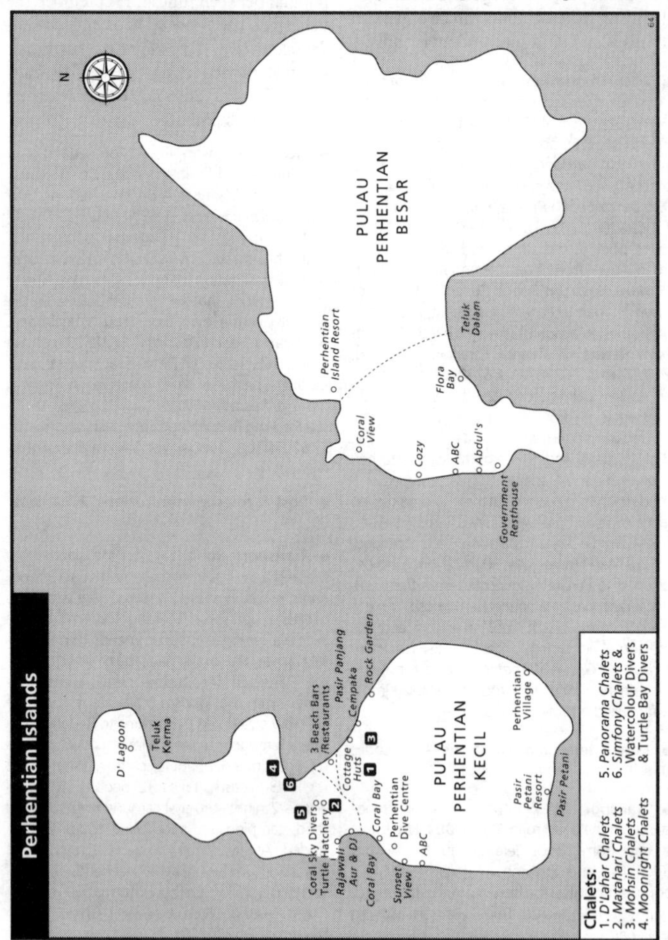

the beginning or end of the December-February monsoon season.

• **Accommodation NB** All the resorts and chalets now have their own generators; and all have fresh water from wells. Visitors are advised to bring some food and bottled water which can be purchased from the very well-stocked (and normally priced) mini market near the jetty in Kuala Besut, as restaurants are relatively expensive. **Perhentian Besar**: **A** ***Perhentian Island Resort*** (bookings c/o 25 Menara Promet, Jln Sultan Ismail, KL, T 03 2448530, F 2434984), T (09) 6910946 or (010) 9010100, 103 rooms, some a/c, licensed but expensive restaurant, some watersports facilities, tennis, swimming pool, diving equipment and courses available. **B-C** ***Coral View Island Resort*** at northern end of beach, rooms close together, bathroom attached. **B-D** ***Flora Bay Chalet***, Telok Dalam, T (011) 977266, secluded bay. **C** ***Cozy Chalet***, T (09) 6910090. **C-E** ***Abdul's***, restaurant, popular chalets. **D** ***Government Resthouse***, 4 chalets which can be booked through the District Office in Jerteh, each chalet can accommodate 4. **E** ***Coco Hut Chalets***, T 972085, restaurant, unspecial 'A'-frames. **E** ***ABC*** 8 cheap and basic huts, on the beach. **Perhentian Kecil**: there is more budget accommodation on Kecil and it is a quieter island to Besar. Accommodation is split, with some huts on the beautiful whitesandy beach of Pasir Panjang, on the east side of the island, and some on Coral Bay, on the west. There are a couple of places at the southern tip, not far from Perhentian village. **C** ***Mohsin***, Long Beach, elevated position behind *Cempaka*, steep stairs to get to the restaurant where there are great views – for the fit only. 30 rooms, mostly in rows, expensive, considering the inconvenient location. **C-D** ***Pasir Petani Resort***, at the southern end, chalets with fans and attached bathrooms. **D** ***Panorama***, Long Beach, attractive chalets with attached showers and toilets, fans and mosquito nets. **D** ***Sunset View Chalets***, Coral Bay, elevated restaurant with good seaviews. **D-E** ***D'Lagoon***, Teluk Kerma, T (09) 970105, very remote position at the northern end of the island, some rooms in a longhouse, chalets have attached bathrooms, restaurant. **D-E** ***Matahari***, Long Beach, excellent restaurant, the best place to stay on the island, often full — proof of its popularity. **E** ***Cempaka***, Long Beach, southern end, pleasantly uncramped site with seaviews for all the 10 chalets, no electricity, but lamps are provided, charcoal for cooking is provided. **E** ***Cottage Huts***, Pasir Panjang, T (011) 977252, popular restaurant on the beach, rather cramped accommodation. **E** ***Simfony***, Long Beach, simple chalets with common showers and toilets. **Camping**: RM5 at *Perhentian Island Resort*; camping is not restricted on the island.

• **Places to eat** There are a couple of restaurants on Perhentian Besar serving simple food – banana pancakes etc: ***Coral Cave Café*** and ***Isabella Coffee Shop*** (next to *Rest House*). There are also coffee shops in the kampung on Perhentian Kecil.

• **Sports Diving and snorkelling**: the coral around the Perhentian islands is some of the best off the East Coast. Most guesthouses arrange snorkelling trips and provide masks, snorkels and fins. There are also dive shops (PADI) on Pulau Perhentian Besar which run courses and arrange dives for beginners to old hands, including night dives.

• **Transport** 20 km offshore. **Road Bus**: from Kuala Terengganu (Jln Masjid): Kota Bharu-bound bus to Jerteh. Regular connections between Jerteh and Kuala Besut. From Kota Bharu: Bus 3, south-bound to Pasir Puteh (36 km south). Regular connections between Pasir Puteh and Kuala Besut. From Kuala Lumpur: *Rangkalan Mewah* bus company leaves at 0900 and 2130, T 4432805. Boats leave from here to Perhentian. **Taxi**: Kuala Terengganu; Kota Bharu. Taxis from Pasir Puteh or Jerteh to Kuala Besut. Boats leave from here to Perhentian. **Sea Boat**: fast boats leave Kuala Besut at 0930, 1030, 1430, and take 30 minutes, single fare RM30, boats carry 8-10 people. The same boats leave Pulau Perhentian for Kuala Besut between 1130-1200 and 1530-1600. Slow boats leave Kuala Besut at approximately 0930 and 1630, take 1½-2 hours and carry 12 people, single fare RM15. They return from the islands at 0900 and 1400. For further information, call *Perhentian Ferry Travel & Tours*, T 6919679. Those staying at the more remote *Pasir Petani Resort* on Perhentian Kecil should pre-arrange a pick-up time. Travellers should be wary of risking the boat trip too close to the beginning or end of the Dec-Feb monsoon season. The fishing boats are not best-equipped for rough seas and life jackets are rarely available. In Mar 1994, two passengers in a boat carrying 30 tourists died when the vessel capsized after being hit by huge waves.

KOTA BHARU

Kota Bharu is the royal capital of Kelantan, 'the land of lightning', and is situated near the mouth of the Kelantan River. The city is one of Malaysia's Malay strongholds, despite its proximity to the Thai border. The state's south and west regions include some of the most mountainous country on the peninsula, but the fertile alluvial soils of the Kelantan River valley and the coastal plain have supported mixed farming and a thriving peasant economy for centuries. Kelantan may have been part of the 2nd century kingdom of Langkasuka (see page 200), but from early in the first millennium AD, it was an established agricultural state which adopted the farming practices of the kingdom of Funan on the lower Mekong River. Because it was effectively cut off from the west coast states of the peninsula, Kelantan always looked north: it traded with Funan, the Khmer Empire and the Siamese kingdom of Ayutthaya.

By the 14th century, Kelantan was under Siamese suzerainty – although at that time it also fell under the influence of the Javanese Majapahit Empire. For a while, during the 15th and 16th centuries, Kelantan joined other peninsular states in sending tribute to the Sultanate of Melaka, and its successor, Johor. By then the state had splintered into a number of small chiefdoms; one local chief, Long Mohammed, proclaimed himself Kelantan's first sultan in 1800.

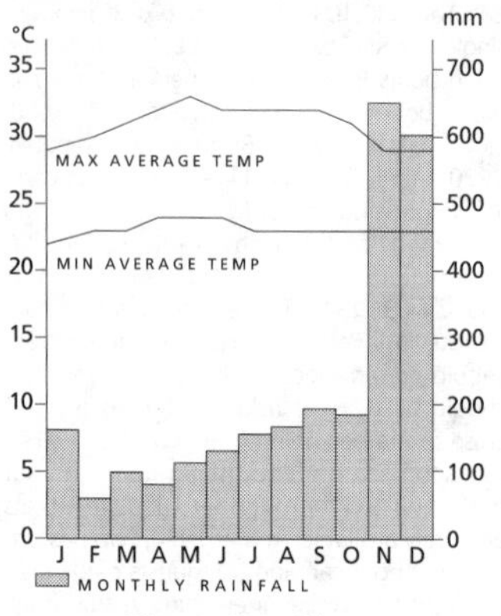

Climate: Kota Bharu

When a succession dispute erupted on the death of the heirless Sultan Mohammed, Siam supported his nephew, Senik the 'Red-Mouth' who reigned for 40 peaceful years. On the next succession crisis, in 1900, Bangkok installed its own nominee as sultan. But in 1909, a treaty between Siam and Britain pushed Bangkok to cede its suzerainty over Kelantan to the British. This severed the state from its Islamic neighbour, the former sultanate of Petani, in Southeast Thailand. British interference caused much resentment and provoked a brief revolt in 1912. After using Kota Bharu as one of their beachheads for the invasion of Malaya in December 1941, the Japanese Imperial Army won support for restoring Kelantan to Thailand. In October 1945 however, Kelantan reluctantly joined the Malayan Union, under the British colonial administration.

Today Kelantan is Malaysia's most conservative and traditional state, and since October 1990, has been ruled by the hard-line Parti Islam – or *PAS*, its Malay acronym. In 1993 the PAS-led state government voted to introduce strict Islamic – or Syariat– law. Non-Muslims in the state – mainly in Kota Bharu, where one third of the population is Chinese or Indian – were alarmed by the prospect of the '*hudud*' criminal code being implemented. It dictates that for crimes such as theft, fornication, intoxication and apostasy, 'criminals' should have their hands and/or legs severed or should be lashed until death if unrepentant. When Islamic officials broke up a rowdy Chinese New Year party in Kota Bharu in 1994, the local Chinese community thought their fears had been realized and that this was a taste of things to come. *Hudud* can't become law until it's passed by a two-thirds majority in Federal Parliament, but the whole

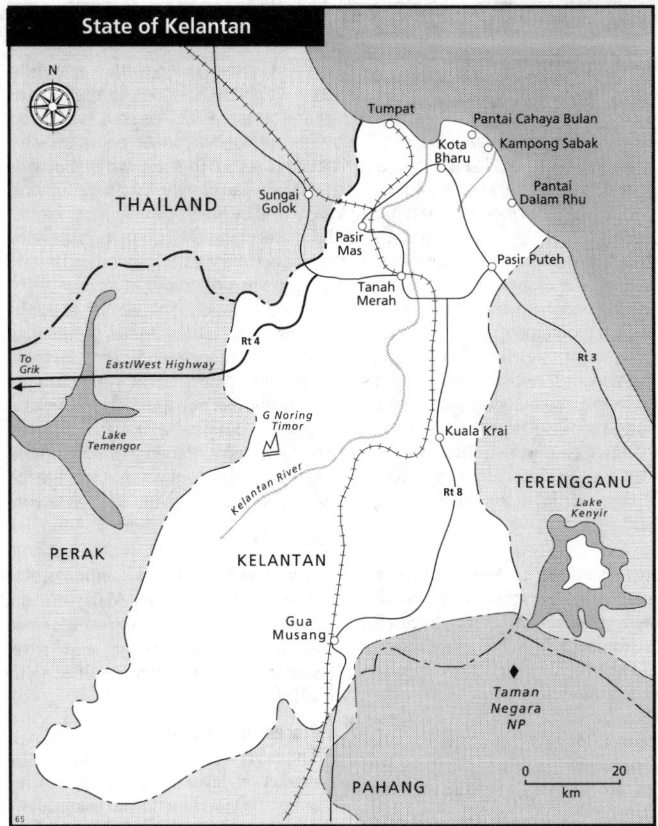

matter has become a conundrum for Muslim politicians in KL. Dr Mahathir's government does not want to be seen as un-Islamic by opposing Kelantan's move, so the Prime Minister has been busily polishing his own Islamic credentials by building new mosques and sponsoring Koran-reading competitions. For Dr Mahathir, the idea of having a mini-Iran as part of his Malaysian Federation is anathema. It totally conflicts with the vision of Islamic moderates and modernists. The Federal Government has been slow to provide much-needed development funds to Kelantan and is doing nothing to promote investment there. They point to the fact that the state has failed to attract a single foreign investment project in the past 3 years as proof that big business is scared-off by Islamic fundamentalism. Nonetheless, in the 1995 general election the PAS managed to maintain its grip on the state depsite Mahathr's landslide victory overall and the promise of massive development funds. Tunku Razaleigh Hamzah, a former member of Mahattir's UMNO party and now a bitter critic and opposition MP for the state, as well as being a prince in the Kelantan royal family, argues: "We don't have the problems that

The Pergau Dam affair – aid-for-arms

The Pergau Dam affair marred Anglo-Malaysian relations for a year from early 1994. The dam, nearing completion in Kelantan, is funded to the tune of £234mn from Britain's overseas aid budget and the aid, as it turned out, was linked to a £1.3bn arms deal. The British government, under former prime minister Margaret Thatcher's leadership, had managed to secure the *quid pro quo* deal as it tried to claw its way back into the lucrative Malaysian market. When the London *Sunday Times* alleged that backhanders were paid by British companies to prominent Malaysian politicians, Mahathir hit back. He imposed a ban on public sector contracts going to British companies and lambasted the West in general and Britain in particular as morally bankrupt, hypocritical and neo-colonialist in attitude.

In London, investigations showed that the aid-for-arms link was an abuse of the aid programme. In agreeing to the deal, ministers ignored 2 years of technical advice which showed that the dam was poor value for money and Sir Tim Lankester, permanent secretary of the Overseas Development Administration, went so far as to write a 'memorandum of dissent' to show that he had not approved the project. Just to add insult to injury, the World Development Movement, a UK-based pressure group, won a case in the High Court in London when it argued that funding the dam was an illegal use of tax-payers' money. The government was forced to make up the shortfall in the aid budget elsewhere and emerged from the affair as tawdry and dishonest.

exist elsewhere. In Malaysia's quest for industrialization, those in power accept any development, whatever the cost to the environment. In Kelantan we resist."

This highly-charged political/religious atmosphere contrasts with the Kelantanese people's laid-back, gentle manner. Tourists visiting the state should be particularly aware of Islamic sensitivities (see page 254), but the trappings of Islam rarely impinge on the enjoyment of the state's rich cultural heritage. But don't expect to find much in the way of funfairs: it was reported at the end of 1995 that the state government had banned bumper cars and Ferris wheels on the pretext that they allow teenagers too much body contact.

The crafts for which Kelantan is renowned – such as silverware, weaving and metal-working – were in part the result of the state's close relations with the Siamese kingdom of Ayutthaya in the 17th century. The *makyung*, a traditional Malay court dance, is still performed in Kelantan and *wayang kulit* (shadow puppet plays) still provide entertainment on special occasions in the kampungs. Kota Bharu is the centre for Malay arts and crafts, although batik-printing, wood-carving, songket-weaving and silver-working are more often confined to the villages.

Places of interest

The heart of Kota Bharu is the **central market** off Jalan Temenggong, which is one of the most vibrant and colourful wet markets in the country. It is housed in a 3-storey octagonal concrete complex painted green which has a glass roof and, because it's so bright, is a photographer's paradise. In the modern Buluh Kubu complex across the road on Jalan Tengku Petra Semerak, there are many shops selling Kelantanese batik and other handicrafts. Nearby is the **Istana Balai Besar**, the 'palace with the big audience hall', built in Patani-style in 1844 by Sultan Mohammed II. The istana, with its decorative panels and wood-carvings is still used on ceremonial occasions. The palace contains the throne-room and the elaborate royal barge, which the sultan only ever used

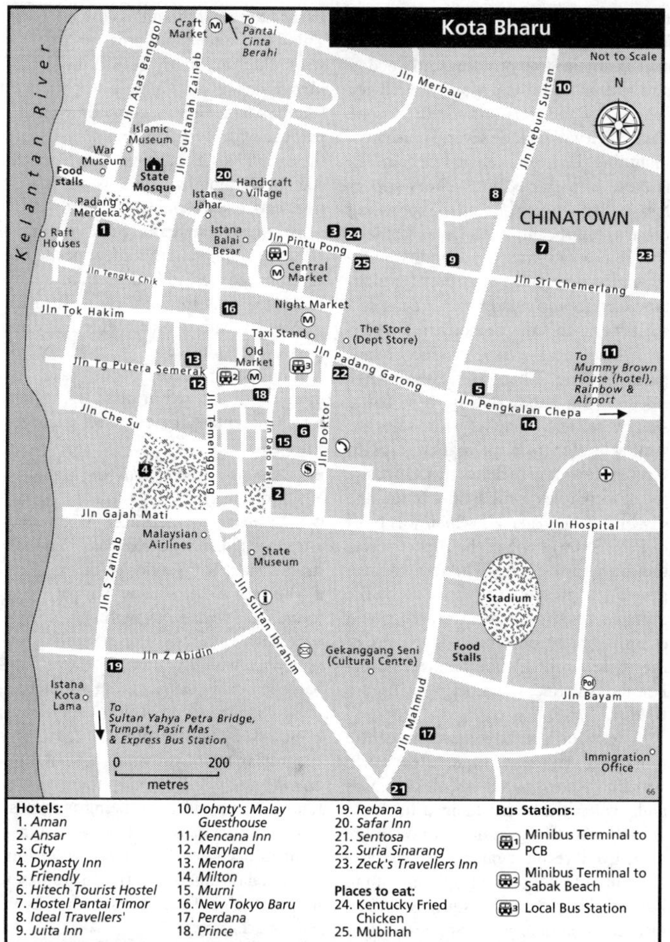

once for a joy ride on the Kelantan River in 1900. It is not usually open to the public but visitors can obtain permission to visit from the palace caretaker. Beside the old istana is the single-storey **Istana Jahar**, constructed in 1889 by Sultan Mohammed IV; it is now the 'centre for royal customs' and is part of the new cultural complex (see below). It exemplifies the skilled craftsmanship of the Kelantanese woodcarvers in its intricately carved beams and panels. There is a small craft collection including songket and silverware. Admission RM1. Open 0930-1230, 1400-1700 Saturday-Wednesday, 0930-1200 Thursday.

Kota Bharu's **Kampung Kraftangan** – or Handicraft Village is close to the central market. It aims to give visitors a taste of Kelantan's arts and crafts all under one roof. The large enclosure, in which *merbuk* birds (doves) sing in their bamboo cages, contains four buildings, all wooden and built in traditional Malay style. They are part of the Kelantan Cultural zone area which will include several museums, including the Istana Jahar. The complex is quite impressive, but visitors appear few and far between, giving the sprawling place a slightly empty, lackadaisical feel. The Handicraft Museum contains exhibits and dioramas of traditional Kelantanese crafts and customs. There is also a batik workshop and demonstration centre where local artists produce hand-painted batiks. There are several stalls, stocked with handicrafts such as batik, silverware and songket, for sale. At ground level there is a pleasant restaurant serving Kelantanese delicacies. Opposite the new complex is the **Istana Batu** – the sky-blue Stone Palace – which was built in 1939 and was one of the first concrete buildings in the state. The former royal palace was presented to the state by the Sultan for use as a royal museum and contains many personal possessions of the royal family. Admission: Kampung Kraftangan free; Handicraft Museum RM1.

A little north of the commercial centre is **Padang Merdeka**, built after World War One as a memorial. Merdeka Square is also where the British hanged Tok Janggut – 'Father Long-beard' – who led the short-lived revolt against British land taxes in 1915. Opposite (on Jalan Sultan Zainab), is the **State Mosque** completed in 1926. Next door is the State Religious Council building, dating from 1914. Next to the mosque on Jalan Merdeka is a magnificent 2-storey green-and-white mansion (with traditional Islamic lattice-work carving on eaves) which houses the **Islamic Museum**. The building itself is more noteworthy than its eclectic contents. Open 0900-1700 Saturday-Thursday; donations only.

Directly west of the mosque, running north-south along the riverbank is **Jalan Pasar Lama** (off Jalan Pos Office Lama). This is an interesting area for a gentle stroll; there are many beautiful but rapidly decaying old Chinese Shophouses (there's a large Chinese community in this part of town). Most of the buildings date to the early 1900s. Some have been rendered completely uninhabitable because vast trees have taken root inside them.

At the **Gelanggang Seni** (Cultural Centre), on Jalan Mahmud, opposite the stadium and close to *Perdana Hotel*, many traditional arts are regularly performed. The centre tends to get rather touristy but it is the best place to see a variety of cultural performances in one place. For more detail on each of these traditional forms of entertainment, see page 82. These include:

- Demonstrations of *silat* (the Malay art of self-defence).
- *Drumming* competitions (Wednesday afternoons) using the *rebana ubi* Kelantan drums, made from hollowed-out logs.
- *Wayang kulit* (shadow-puppet) performances (Wednesday nights).
- *Kite-flying* competitions (Saturday afternoons) with the famous paper-and-bamboo *wau bulan* – or Kelantan moon-kites, the symbol of MAS. This has been a Kelantanese sport for centuries; the aim is to fly your kite higher than anyone else's and, once up there, to defend your superiority by being as aggressive as possible towards other competitors' kites. Kite-flying, according to the Malay Annals, was a favourite hobby in the hey-day of the Melaka sultanate in the 15th century.
- *Top-spinning* competitions (Wednesday and Saturday afternoons).

Other cultural performances include traditional dance routines such as the royal *Mak Yong* dance and the *Menora*, both of which relate local legends. A set programme of shows (available from the Tourist Promotion Board) usually starts at 1530-1730; 2100-2245 Monday-Sunday, February-October. **NB** No shows during Ramadan.

The **State Museum**, on Jalan Sultan Ibrahim (near the clock tower and next to the Tourism Malaysia office), whose proudest boast is its big collection of krisses. There is also an assemblage of Chinese procelain. Open Saturday-Thursday 1030-1745. Admission: RM2.

Excursions

To Kong Mek, (also known as Tin Heng Keong) Chinese temple is 1 km out of town, on the road to PCB (see below). It is about 100 years old and is particularly colourful; best time to visit is 0900-1000 each day when the temple is particularly lively. (There is another smaller temple with a grotesque laughing Buddha and a grotto on the riverbank, closer to town. *Getting there*: from KB follow road to PCB; after 500m, on sharp right bend, turn left at vegetable market; go down dirt track and turn right through Chinese gateway at bottom.)

Pantai Cinta Berahi (now renamed **Pantai Cahaya Bulan**, but still known as **PCB**), KB's most famous beach, 10 km north of the city, is really only famous for its name, meaning the 'Beach of Passionate Love'. In 1994 the Islamic state government – which takes a dim view of passionate love – rechristened it the Beach of the Shining Moon, which conveniently retains the old acronym, PCB. In comparison with some other east coast beaches, it is an unromantic dump. In Malay, the word *berahi* is, according to one scholar, "loaded with sexual dynamite ... a love madness". Local Malays, alluding to this heated innuendo, used to euphemistically call it *pantai semut api* – the beach of the fire ants. Today, young Malay lovers do not even dare to hold hands on the beach, for fear of being caught by the religious police and charged with *khalwat*, the crime of 'close proximity', under *Syariat* Islamic law. The origin of the name *cinta berahi* is lost. One theory is that it was used as a code word by Malay and British commandos during the Japanese wartime occupation: the site of the Imperial Army's invasion, in 1941, is nearby, on Pantai Dasar Sabak (see page 311). Despite being rather overrated, there are several resorts along the beach. It gets crowded on weekends and rooms rates rise accordingly. **Accommodation A** *Perdana Resort* (also known as *PCB Resort*), Jalan Kuala Pa'Amat, T 7744000, F 7744980, a/c, restaurant, pool, watersports, pleasanter stretch of beach, dotted with white chalets colour schemed blue, green and pink according to room type, not very well maintained, popular with business conventions and meetings. **C-D** *Long House Beach Motel*, T 7731090, some a/c, restaurant (Thai food), not bad value really but it doesn't have a great deal of charm. **D-E** *HB Village*, T 7734993, very clean, very friendly and very big crocodiles in attached farm. *Getting there*: minibus 10 every 20 minutes from Bazaar Buluh Kubu, off Jalan Tengku Chik or from Jalan Padang Garong or by taxi.

Other beaches **Pantai Dalam Rhu** (also known as Pantai Bisikan Bayu, the Beach of the Whispering Breeze), lies 40 km southeast of KB: **Accommodation E** *Dalam Rhu Homestay*, simple kampung-style accommodation, well looked-after. *Getting there*: bus no. 3, south bound (RM2); change at Pasir Puteh. **Pantai Irama**, the 'Beach of Melody', 25 km south of KB is the best of the nearby beaches for swimming. **Accommodation B-C** *Motel Irama Bachok*, Bachok, T 7788462, clean and reasonable value. *Getting there*: bus 2A or 2B to Bachok every 30 minutes. **Pantai Dasar Sabak**, 13 km northeast of KB, is where the Japanese troops landed on 7 December 1941, 90 minutes before they bombed Pearl Harbour. Nearby Kampung Sabak is a good place to watch fishing boats come in in the morning. *Getting there*: bus 8 or 9 from old market terminal.

Waterfalls In the area round Pasir Puteh there are several waterfalls – Jeram Pasu, Jeram Tapeh and Cherang Tuli. **Jeram Pasu** is the most popular, 35 km from Kota Bharu. *Getting there*: most easily accessible by taxi or bus 3 to Padang Pak Amat (RM1.70) and taxi to the waterfalls.

Tumpat Around Tumpat, next to the border, are small Thai communities where there are a few Thai-style buildings and wats; they do not, however, compare with the Thai architecture on the other side of the border. **Wat Phothivian** at Kampung Berok (12 km east of KB, on the Malaysian side of Sungai Golok) has a 41m reclining Buddha statue, built in 1973 by chief abbot Phra Kruprasapia Chakorn, which attracts thousands of Thai pilgrims every year. *Getting there*: bus 27 or 19 to Chabang Empat and then a taxi the last 3-4 km to Kampung Jambu – this last part of the journey also make for a pleasant enough rural stroll.

Masjid Kampung Laut at Kampung Nilam Puri, 10 km south of KB, was built 300 years ago by Javanese Muslims as an offering of thanks for being saved from pirates. Having been damaged once too often by monsoon floods, it was dismantled and moved inland to Kampung Nilam Puri, which is an Islamic scholastic centre. It was built entirely of cengal, a prized hardwood, and constructed without the use of nails. It vies with Masjid Kampung Kling (in Melaka) for the title of Malaysia's oldest mosque. *Getting there*: bus 44 or express bus 5 every 30 minutes.

River trips From Kuala Kerai (a 1½-hour bus trip south from Kota Bharu, bus 5) departs 0745 Monday-Sunday, it is possible to take a boat upriver to Dabong, a small kampung nestled among the jungled foothills of the Main Range (2 hours, departs 1000 but not on Friday), where there is a resthouse and restaurant. Dabong, in the centre of Kelantan state, is on the north-south railway, so it is possible to catch the train back to Wakaf Bharu (across the river from KB), the journey takes 2 hours 45 minutes (3rd class only). Alternatively, taxi.

Tours

KTIC (Kolantan State Tourist Information Centre) organizes a number of tours – river and jungle-safari trips, staying in kampungs and learning local crafts. They also organize 3-day 'Kampung Experience' tours which are not as contrived as their name suggests. Full board and lodging provided by host families which can be selected from list including potters, fishermen, batik-makers, kite-makers, silversmiths, dance instructors, top-makers and shadow puppet-makers. Cost from RM160 (all in); minimum two people. They also run short Kelantanese cooking courses.

Local festivals

May/June: *Malaysia International Kite Festival*, Pantai Seri Tujuh (Beach of the Seven Lagoons), Turnport (adjacent to Thai border), 7 km from KB). *Getting there*: bus 43 RM1).

July: *drum festival* (movable) a traditional east coast pastime. *Sultan's birthday celebrations* (10th-12th).

August: *Bird Singing Contest* (movable) when the prized *merbuk* (doves) or *burong ketitir* birds compete on top of 8m-high poles. Bird singing contests are also held on Fri mornings around Kota Bharu.

September: *top-spinning contest* (movable) another traditional East Coast sport which is taken very seriously.

Local information

● Accommodation

Prices: L over RM500; **A+** RM260-500; **A** RM130-260; **B** RM65-130; **C** RM40-65; **D** RM20-40; **E** RM10-20; **F** Below RM10

Budget travellers are spoilt for choice in KB; there are some very pleasant cheaper hostels and guesthouses (most of them in secluded alleyways with gardens) and they are locked in fearsome competition. As a result, new ones start up all the time as old ones fold; the State Tourist Information Centre has a list of budget accommodation and is happy to make recommendations. Until recently, the selection of top-bracket and mid-range hotels was poor – however, a number of new **A-B** bracket hotels have recently opened. None of the hotels except for the *Murni* serves alcohol so minibars are usually a bleak sight.

A *Perdana*, Jln Mahmud, T 7485000, F 7447621, a/c, restaurant, pool, tennis and squash courts, bowling alley, best in town, central location, but overpriced; **A-B** ***Mawar***, Jln Parit Dalam, T 7448888, F 7476666, new and well located. **A-B** ***Murni***, Jln Datuk Pati, T 7482399, a/c, restaurant, the original 'luxury' hotel in KB but now appears rather dark and dingey, location is its only advantage. **A-B** ***Safar Inn***, Jln Hilir Kota, T 7478000, F 7479000, 31 rooms, a/c, TV, new hotel, carefully furnished rooms with wall-to-wall carpets.

B ***Ansar***, Jln Maju, T 7474000, F 7461150, new, clean hotel, conveniently located near the night market, it is an 'Islamic Hotel', so no shoes, prayers in the hallways and signs mentioning Allah in the elevators, basic breakfast included, overpriced. **B** ***Dynasty Inn***, 2865 D and E Jln Sultan Zainab, T 7473000, F 7473111, 47 rooms, a/c, TV, hot shower, rooftop coffee house. **B** ***Juita Inn***, Jln Pintu Pong, T 7446888, F 7445777, 70 rooms, a/c, TV, minibar, restaurant, room rates include breakfast, attractive new hotel. Rooms are small but clean and well furnished – note that the superior rooms have no windows. **B** ***Kencana Inn***, Jln Padang Garong, T 7447944, a/c, restaurant, reasonable value for money; do not confuse with sister hotel *Kencana Inn City Centre* which should have a health warning attached. **B-C** ***New Tokyo Baru***, 3945 Jln Tok Hakim, T 7449488, a/c, well maintained place, friendly, recommended. **B-C** ***Sentosa***, 3180-A Jln Sultan Ibrahim, T 7443200, a/c, restaurant, (formerly *Irama Baru & Apollo Hotel*), all spruced up, clean and new.

C ***Aman***, 23C/D Jln Tengku Besar, T 7443049, a/c, restaurant, not particularly good value, but no extra charge for regular alarm calls courtesy of mosque next door. **C** ***Suria Sinarang***, Jln Padan Garong, T 7446567, a/c, good value for money compared to others in this category. **C-D** ***Maryland***, 2726-2727 Jln Tok Hakim, T 7482811, a/c, reasonably priced, clean with big, airy rooms but no atmosphere. **C-D** ***New Prince***, 2953 Jln Temenggong. **C-E** ***Johnty's Malay Guesthouse***, 822 Jln Kebun Sultan, T 7448866/7478677 (off Jln Dusun Raja), some a/c, popular but past its peak, rooms and dorm, offers excursions, bike-hire, traditional massage and free breakfast to keep up with the Joneses, in a quiet corner on the outskirts of town. **C-E** ***Hostel Pantai Timor***, Lot 391 Jln Pengkalan Chepa, behind Safra Jaya supermarket, T 7483753, well kept (won cleanliness award in 1993), friendly, also dorms.

D ***Milton***, 5471a Jln Pengkalan Chepa, T 7482744, a/c. **D** ***Sri Cemerlang Hostel***, 5640 U-X Jln Sri Cemerlang, T 7449648, a/c, good value, clean. **D-E** ***Ideal Travellers' House***, 5504a Jln Padang Garong, T 7442246, quiet, friendly, pleasant verandah, rooms and dormitory. **D-E** ***Prince***, 2953 Jln Temenggong, T 7482066, situated one floor above the *New Prince Hotel* and therefore easily missed, run by a very friendly man named Fendi (who also guides groups in the National Park and takes trips to Pulau Perhentian) a/c, scrupulously clean, good value.

E ***Floating Homestay***, Raft House 70, Jln Tengku Chik, T 010-906252/011-977252 (both mobile); close to centre of town, off Jln Post Office Lama; unlicenced with tourist board but very well run and river cruises, rooms clean and simple, mozzie nets provided; unique and recommended. **E** ***KB Inn***, 1872 Jln Padang Garong, T 7441786, very close to bus station and night market, breakfast and hot drinks free, friendly and helpful owner named Nasron, recommended. **E** ***Hitech Tourist Hostel***, Tingkat 1 & 2, Bangunan Pengakap, Jln Suara Muda, T 7440961, cheap, friendly, clean, one of the older guesthouses in town. **E** ***Menora***, Wisma Chua Tong Boon, (1st Flr) Jln Sultanah Zainab, T 7481669, well kept, facilities include TV and 'strong showers', dorm (**F**), recommended. **E** ***Mummy Brown House***, 4398 Jln Pengkalan Chepa, set in an old house, garden, breakfast included. **E** ***Rainbow***, 4423 Jln Pengkalan Chepa, helpful, attractive garden but near noisy road, breakfast included. **E** ***Rebana***, 1218 Jln Sultanah Zainab, opposite the old istana, bicycle hire, garden, recommended by travellers, attractive old house but rather rundown. **E** ***Zeck Traveller's Inn***, 7088-G Jln Sri Cemerlang, T 7473422, some rooms with private shower, dorm rooms (RM6), verandah, light meals available, one of the most popular places to stay. **E** ***Zee Hostel***, 696-a Lorong Hj. Sufian, Jln Sultanah Zainab, T 7445376, brand new hostel, dormitory accommodation. **E-F** ***City***, 2nd Flr, 35 Jln Pintu Pong (next to *Kentucky Fried Chicken*), clean and helpful on local information, price including breakfast, dorm, recommended. **E-F** ***Friendly***, 4278D Jln Kebun Sultan, T 7442246, dorm and rooms, garden. **E-F** ***Town***, T 7485192, 4959B (1st Flr) Jln Pengkalan Chepa, T 7485192, roof restaurant, friendly and clean, close to the bus terminal, travel services, dorm and rooms. **E-F** ***Wann's***, Jln Sultanah Zainab, T 7485381 (behind silversmith), clean, good value, recommended. **E-F** ***Yee***, Jln Padang Garong, 2nd Flr, T 7441944, everything you need: laundry, breakfast, showers, travel information, bicycles for hire, unfortunately, the rooms are dirty.

F *DE999*, next to *Rebana*, Jln Sultanah Zainab, T 7481955, cheap and clean rooms, close to the Cultural Centre, price including breakfast, free bicycles, dorm and rooms.

● Places to eat

Prices: ◆◆◆◆ over RM40; ◆◆◆ RM13-40; ◆◆ RM5-13; ◆ under RM5

The Kelantan speciality is *ayam percik* – roast chicken, marinated in spices and served with a coconut-milk gravy. *Nasi tumpang* is a typical Kelantanese breakfast; banana-leaf funnel of rice layers interspersed with prawn and fish curries and salad. **NB** Beer and other alcoholic beverages are only available in certain Chinese coffee shops, notably along Jln Kebun Sultan. ***Kuchino Italiano***, 147 Jln Pengkalau Chepa, on Main road between city cente and the airport, family run restaurant, a poor attempt at Italian cuisine; ***Ambassador***, 7003 Jln Kebun Sultan, big Chinese coffee shop next to *Kow Lun* (below), Chinese dishes including pork satay and other iniquitous substances – like beer; ***Azam***, Jln Padang Garong, North Indian tandoori, with fresh oven-baked naan, good rotis and curry; ***Kow Lun***, 7005 & 7006 Jln Kebun Sultan, good lively Chinese coffee shop with large variety of dishes and lots of beer; ***Malaysia***, 2527 Jln Kebun Sultan, Chinese cuisine, speciality: steamboat, this is the place to sample turtle eggs – legally; ***Meena Curry House***, 3377 Jln Gajah Mati, Indian curry house, banana leaf restaurant, recommended; ***Neelavathy***, Jln Tengku Maharani (behind *Kencana Inn*), South Indian banana-leaf curries, recommended; ***Qing Liang***, Jln Zainal Abidin, excellent Chinese vegetarian, also Malay and western dishes, recommended; ***Satay Taman Indraputra***, Jln Pekeliling/Jln Hospital garden; ***Syam***, Jln Hospital, Thai-influenced.

Indian: food can be found on Jln Gajah Mati.

Chinese: food is available on Jln Kebun Sultan.

Fastfood: *McDonalds* at the bus station.

Foodstalls: *Night market* (in car park opposite local bus station, in front of Central Market), exclusively Malay food, satays and exquisite array of curries; colour-coded tables – if you eat from a certain stall and sit at a blue table, you are obliged to buy your drink from stall in blue area; excellent fruit juices, no alcohol, recommended; ***Nasi Padang Osman Larin*** (otherwise known as *Nasi Hoover* as it is outside *Hotel Hoover*) is a stall on Jln Datuk Pati (between the Tourist Information Centre and the bus station) famed locally for its curries.

Bakery: ***Mubihah Vegetarian Restaurant and Cake House***, opposite *Kentucky Fried Chicken*, 157 Jln Pintu Pong. Eat in or take away; excellent breads, pastries, cakes etc – one of the best '*kek and roti*' shops in Malaysia.

● Airline offices

MAS, Ground Floor, Komplek Yakin, Jln Gajah Mati (opposite the clock tower), T 7447000 and T 7440557 at the airport; **Pelangi Airways**, c/o MAS, T 7447000, F 7440557.

● Banks & money changers

Money changers in main shopping area. **Bumiputra**, Jln Maju; **D & C**, Jln Gajah Mati; **Hongkong & Shanghai**, Jln Sultan.

● Embassies & consulates

Royal Thai Consulate, Jln Pengkalan Chepa, T 7422545/7482545 (open 0900-1200, 1330-1530, Mon-Thur and Sat).

● Entertainment

Cultural shows: regular cultural shows at the *Gelanggang Seni* (cultural centre), Jln Mahmud (see above).

● Hospitals & medical services

Hospitals: Jln Hospital.

● Post & telecommunications

Area code: 09.

General Post Office: Jln Sultan Ibrahim.

Telegraph Office: Jln Doktor.

● Shopping

Antiques: *Lam's*, Jln Post Office Lama (in contrast to the modern town walk there are several old bamboo raft houses along this street).

Batik: ***Astaka Fesyer***, 782K (3rd Flr), recommended; ***Bazaar Buluh Kubu***, Jln Tengku Petra Semerak, just across the road from the Central Market, houses scores of batik boutiques; also in the building are tailors' shops which can turn out very cheap shirts, blouses and dresses within 24 hours.

Handicrafts: the central market is cheapest for handicrafts. There are numerous handicraft stalls, silver-workers, kite-makers and woodcarvers scattered along the road north to Pantai Cinta Berahi. At Kampung Penambang, on this road, just outside KB, there is a batik and songket centre.

Silverware: on Jln Sultanah Zainab (near *Rabana Guest House*), before junction with Jln Hamzah, there are three shops selling Kelantan silver including *KB Permai*, a family business which works the silver on the premises. The new *Kampung Kraftangan* (Handicraft Village) contains many stalls with a huge range of batik sarongs and ready-mades, silverware, songket, basketry and various Kelantanese nick-nacks.

● Sports

Golf: *Royal Kelantan Golf Club*, 5488 Jln Hospital, green fees weekdays RM80, weekends RM120, 18-hole course.

● Tour companies & travel agents

Batuta Travel & Tour, 1st Flr, Bangunan PKDK, Jln Datuk Pati, T 7442652; ***Boustead Travel***, 2833 Jln Temenggong, T 7449952; ***Kelmark Travel***, Kelmark House, 5220 Jln Telipot, T 7444211; ***Pelancongan Bumi Mars***, Tingkat Bawah, Kompleks Yakin, Jln Gajah Mati, T 7431189. The **Tourist Information Centre** also arrange tours as do several of the guesthouses in town.

● Tourist offices

Tourist Information Centre, Jln Sultan Ibrahim, T 7485534. A helpful office, which will arrange taxis and ferries to the islands, as well as booking accommodation on the islands.

● Useful addresses

Immigration Office: 3rd Flr, Federal Bldg, Jln Bayam.

● Transport

474 km from Kuala Lumpur, 168 km from Terengganu, 371 km from Kuantan.

Local Bus: city buses and many long-distance express buses leave from the Central Bus Station, Jln Hilir Pasar, so there is no need to go to the inconveniently located long-distance bus stations in the south of the city. Regional buses to places like Gua Musang and Pasir Puteh also depart from this station. **Car hire**: Avis, *Hotel Perdana*, Jln Sultan Mahmud, T 7484457, South China Sea, airport, T 7744288, F 7736288; from *Perdana Hotel*. **Trishaw**: short journeys RM2; RM10-12/hour; recommended way of touring town but they are gradually disappearing as salaries rise and people opt for motorized transport.

Air Airport is 8 km from town; RM12/taxi. Regular connections with Ipoh, KL, Penang on MAS and KL on Pelangi Airways. **Transport to town**: by taxi RM10 pp or town bus No 9.

Train Wakaf Bharu station is 5 km out of town, across the Kelantan River. Bus 19 or 27 (RM1). Daily connections with Singapore and KL via Gua Musang, Kuala Lipis, Jerantut and Gemas. The jungle railway is slow but the scenery makes the journey worthwhile. *Golden Blowpipe* departs Wakaf Bharu in the early afternoon and arrives Gemas at around midnight (connections arrive Singapore/KL early next morning). Second class a/c connections with Jerantut-Taman Negara, KL and Singapore.

Road Bus: KB has three long-distance bus stations although many express buses leave from the central terminal on Jln Hilir Pasar, saving on a trip to one of the two out of town stations. The main inter-city express bus company is the state-owned SKMK and its buses leave both from the central station on Jln Hilir Pasar and from the Langgar bus station south of town on Jln Pasir Puteh. The second out of town bus terminal is also south of town on Jln Hamzah and all bus companies other than SKMK operate vehicles from here. Regular connections with: Grik, Kuala Terengganu, Jerantut, Kuantan, KL (RM25), JB, Penang, Alor Star, Kuala Lipis, Butterworth, Melaka, Mersing, Temerloh, and many other destinations. Buses from Kuala Lumpur leave at 0900 and 2100 from Putra Station (*Mutiara Express*, T 4433655, *PPMP*, T 4445699, *Naela Express*, T 4439155). **Taxi**: taxi station next to the Central Bus Station, Jln Hilir Pasar. Destinations include Kuala Terengganu, Kuantan, KL, JB, Butterworth, Grik. Also taxis to Rantau Panjang (for Sungai Golok, Thailand).

International connections The Thai border is at the Malaysian town of Rantau Panjang; on the other side is the Thai settlement of Sungai Golok. Bus no. 29 for Rantau Panjang leaves on the hour through the day from the central bus station, off Jln Hilir Pasar (1½ hours). From here it is a shortish 1 km walk across the border to Sungai Golok's train and bus stations where there are connections to other destinations in Thailand including Hat Yai, Surat Thani (for Koh Samui) and Bangkok. Trishaws and motorbike taxis wait to assist people making the crossing. Another route into Thailand is via Pengkalan Kubor, a quieter and much more interesting crossing to Ta Ba (Tak Bai). Bus nos. 27, 27a and 43 go to Pengkalan Kubor. Small boats cross the river regularly and there is also a car ferry. Long-tails cater for the clientele of the cross-border prostitution industry only. There are also regular bus connections with Singapore.

GUA MUSANG

Gua Musang is the largest town on route 8, the road through the interior, and lies in Kelantan state close to the border with Pahang. It began life as little more than a logging camp but has now expanded into a thriving administrative centre. The jungle is studded with limestone outcrops in this area of the Peninsula and a particularly impressive one overshadows Gua Musang. There have been reports of large mammals including wild elephants, tigers and tapirs along the roads near here and this is about as wild as Peninsular Malaysia gets outside the national parks and wildlife reserves.

• **Accommodation** **C** *Kesedar Inn*, T (09) 9121229, on the edge of town, recently re-opened after building extra rooms on the rather attractive lawn, clean rooms, friendly. **E** *Rest House*, rather run down but an attractive place to stay, shared facilities.

• **Transport Road Bus**: daily buses from Kuala Lipis to Gua Musang (0800 and 1300) and Kuala Krai (1430) with onward connections to Kota Bharu.

GRIK

Grik, also spelt Gerik, was once a remote logging town just a few kilometres south of the Thai border. It is now on an important junction, and the beginning of the east-west highway. Few people stay the night there, but it is a good staging post and midday *makan* stop. (The huge Temenggor and Lenering man-made reservoirs are near-by.)

Grik can be reached from Kuala Kangsar in Perak (see page 170) or from Butterworth via either Kulim (directly east of the town) or Sungai Petani (35 km north of town) which lead first to Keroh, on the Thai border, then on to Grik. The Kuala Kangsar route is a particularly scenic drive along a 111 km road which winds its way up the Perak River valley, enclosed by the Bintang mountains to the west and the Main Range to the east. En route, the road passes Tasek Chenderoh, a beautiful reservoir, surrounded by jungled hills. At **Kota Tampan**, just north of the lake, archaeologists have unearthed the remains of a Stone Age workshop, with roughly chiselled stone tools dating back 35,000 years. The road cuts through the jungle and there are some spectacular view-points. There are often landslides along this stretch of road during the wet season.

• **Accommodation** Because Grik is not on the main tourist track, accommodation is basic. **A** *Banding Island Resort*, 35.8 km Grik East West Highway, T 7912273, F 7912076, restaurant, situated on Lake Temengor, now 10 years old, decor is dated, service is poor, rooms below par, food dull – not good value for money. Even the previously attractive views will probably have been ruined, 130 new bungalows were completed at the end of 1997 covering the pretty inlet and headland but views pleasant. **D** *Diamond*, 40A Jln Sultan Iskander, T 892388. **D** *Kong Seng*, 32 Jln Sultan Iskander, T 892180. **D** *Rumah Rehat Grik*, Jln Meor Yahaya, T 891211. **D-E** *Bee Hoon*, Jln Tan Sabah, T 892201.

• **Transport Road Bus** Connections with Butterworth, KL, Taiping and Ipoh. For Kota Bharu change at Tanah Merah. **International connections**: it is possible to cross the border into Thailand from Keroh, 50 km north of Grik. There are regular taxis from Keroh to the border post and Thai taxis and *saamlors* (trishaws) on the other side. Their are Thai taxis to Betong which is 8 km from the border.

COAST TO COAST

The **East-West highway** makes for a memorable journey. It runs from Kota Bharu to Penang, straight across the forested backbone of the peninsula and was one of the biggest civil engineering projects ever undertaken in Malaysia. During its 11-years construction, contractors had to push their way through densely jungled mountains, coping with frequent landslides and even hit-and-run attacks by Communist insurgents.

To the east of **Grik**, the highway runs close to the former bases of the Communist Party of Malaya, which, until 1989, operated out of their jungle headquarters near Betong, just across the Thai border. The area was known as 'Target One' by the Malaysian security forces. The construction of the road opened the previously inaccessible area up to timber companies; there has been much illegal logging – and cross-border drug-smuggling – in this 'cowboy country' of North Perak and Kelantan. The 200 km-long highway opened in 1982, and for the first few years was closed to traffic after 1600 because of the security threat posed by Communist insurgents; this threat has now ended. However, road maintenance is something of a hazard, and the journey is slow going with a whole series of road works and places where the road has subsided.

The *Golden Blowpipe* trundles along the railwayline which cuts a diagonal through the peninsula, running due north from Gemas (south of KL on the KL-Singapore line) to **Kota Bharu**. Much of the route is through the jungle, and the track skirts the west boundary of **Taman Negara**, the national park (see page 281). Those heading into Taman Negara must disembark at **Tembeling Halt**, to the southeast of **Kuala Lipis**, or at **Jerantut**. The train is slow, but it is an interesting journey. From **Gemas** the line goes through Jeranut, Kuala Lipis, **Gua Musang**, **Kuala Krai** and on to Kota Bharu. It is possible to catch the train at **Mentakab** (along the Karak Highway, east of KL) or at Kuala Lipis, which can be reached by road via **Fraser's Hill** and **Raub**. It is also possible to drive from Kuala Lipis via Gua Musang to Kota Bharu. There are buses from Kuala Lipis to Gua Musang and Kuala Krai.

Malaysian Borneo: Sarawak and Sabah

Borneo Horizons	319	**Sabah**	422
Sarawak	333	Kota Kinabalu	434
Kuching	354	Tunku Abdul Rahman Park	447
Bako National Park	376	South of Kota Kinabalu	448
Sibu and the Rejang River	383	The North and Gunung Kinabalu Park	463
Bintulu and Niah Caves	396	The East Coast	475
Niah National Park	400	Sipadan Island Marine Reserve	494
Miri and the Baram River	404		
Gunung Mulu National Park	410		
Bareo and the Kelabit Highlands	419		
Limbang and Lawas	420		

BORNEO has always held a mystical fascination in the imagination of Westerners. Patrick Synge, a botanist, travelled through Sarawak in 1932. "As we moved slowly up river", he writes, "Sarawak's forests were like a dream come true to me, a dream of abundance, of beauty and peace, but also of mystery alive behind this wall". Some Europeans found the island terrifying with its head hunters, interminable jungle, and monstrous insects. Others saw in it a bounteous and luxiriant land, an island where God had worked special magic. And still others a peaceful place where humans became miniscule and lost in the immensity and complexity of nature.

HORIZONS

The East Malaysian states of Sarawak and Sabah, and the Sultanate of Brunei, occupy the northern third of the island of Borneo. Sabah and Sarawak represented the 'other' Malaysia, divided by much more than 500 km of sea from the states of the 'Mainland'. Here, in East Malaysia, 'tribal' Dayaks dominate the human landscape and the local economy is sustained not by manufacturing but by the exploitation of natural resources – particularly, timber and oil and gas. Sabah and Sarawak were only integrated into the Federation of Malay States in 1963 and visitors from the mainland are still required to obtain a travel permit to come here – and a work permit if they want a job. The states maintain control over immigration, education and language issues because of the fear that without these controls the indigenous peoples of Sabah and Sarawak would be elbowed out by their more sophisticated brethren from across the South China Sea.

The name Borneo is thought to be a European mispronunciation of 'Burni' or Brunei. Early Western books variously spelt Borneo 'Burni', 'Burney', 'Burny', 'Borny', 'Borney', 'Burneo', 'Bornei', 'Bruneo', 'Porne; and 'Borneu'. This was not entirely the Europeans' fault, for as John Crawfurd points out in *A Descriptive Dictionary of the Indian Isles* (1856), the name is "indifferently pronounced by the Malays, according to the dialect they happen to speak – Brune, Brunai, Burne or Burnai". The Chinese, for good measure, referred to the island from the early 9th century as P'o-ni, or P'o-li, or Fo-ni. The sultanate itself became known as 'Borneo Proper', and its capital as Brunei Town. Crawfurd concluded that "the name of the town was not extended to the island by European writers, but by the Mohamedan navigators who conducted the carrying trade of the archipelago before the advent of Europeans". Borneo Proper was first visited by Europeans in the early 16th century, most notably by Antonio Pigafetta, the official chronicler on the Portuguese explorer Ferdinand Magellan's expedition, which called in on the Sultan of Brunei in 1521 (see page 327). The Ibans of Sarawak maintain that the name Borneo derives from the Malay *buah nyior*, meaning 'coconut', while the Malays had another, less well-known name for the island: Kalimantan. This, according to Crawfurd, was the name of a species of wild mango "and the word ... would simply mean 'Isle of Mangoes'". This was the name chosen by Indonesia for its section of the island; for some reason, it is generally translated as 'River of Diamonds' – probably because of the diamond fields near Martapura in the south.

THE LAND

Three countries have territory on Borneo, but only one of them, the once all-powerful and now tiny but oil-rich sultanate of Brunei, is an independent sovereign state in itself. It is flanked to the west by the Malaysian state of Sarawak and to the east by Sabah. Sarawak severs and completely surrounds Brunei. Sabah, formerly British North Borneo, and now a Malaysian state, occupies the northeast portion of Borneo. The huge area to the south is Kalimantan, Indonesian Borneo, which occupies about three-quarters of the island.

GEOGRAPHY

Borneo is the third largest island in the world (after Greenland and New Guinea) covering almost three-quarters of a million square kilometres. During the Pleistocene period, Borneo was joined to mainland Southeast Asia, forming a continent which geologists know as Sundaland. The land bridge to mainland Asia meant that many species – both flora and fauna – arrived in what is now Borneo before it was cut off by rising sea levels. Borneo is part of the Sunda shelf. Its interior is rugged and mountainous and is dissected by many large rivers, navigable deep into the

River roads

In Borneo, rivers are often the main arteries of communication. Although roads are being built, linking most main towns, many Dayak (tribal) longhouse communities are only accessible by river. Rivers are the mediators that divide forest dwellers from coastal settlers and this is usually expressed in terms of upriver, or *hulu* and downstream, or *hilir*. The two terms are not just geographical; they also reflect different lifestyles and economies, different religions and cultures. In Borneo, to be *hulu* is to set oneself apart from the Malay peoples of the lowlands and coasts.

Contrary to many assumptions, the tribal *hulu* peoples were never entirely isolated and self-reliant. From early times, there was a flourishing trade between the coasts and the interior. Upriver tribal peoples would exchange exotic jungle products like rattan, benzoin, camphor, skins, hornbill 'ivory', precious stones and rare dyes for products that they could not obtain in the forest – like iron, salt, dried fish (now, tinned fish), betel and gambier. They also bartered for prestige objects like brass gongs, large ceramic Chinese pots, and Dutch silver coins. Many of these prestige objects can still be seen in the longhouses of Borneo and have become precious heirlooms or *pusaka*.

interior. The two biggest rivers – the Kapuas and Mahakam – are both in Kalimantan, but there are also extensive river systems in the East Malaysian states of Sabah and Sarawak. About half of Borneo's land area is under 150m – particularly the swampy south coastal region.

Borneo's highest mountain, Gunung Kinabalu in Sabah (4,101m) is often declared the 'highest mountain in Southeast Asia' (see page 467). Despite this claim being repeated so many times that it has taken on the status of a truth, it isn't: there are higher peaks in Indonesia's province of Irian Jaya and in Myanmar (Burma). Kinabalu is a granite mound called a pluton, which was forced up through the sandstone strata during the Pliocene period, about 15 million years ago. The mountain ranges in the west and centre of the island run east-to-west and curve round to the northeast. Borneo's coal, oil and gas-bearing strata are Tertiary deposits which are heavily folded; most of the oil and gas is found off the northwest and east coasts. The island is much more geologically stable than neighbouring Sulawesi or Java – islands in the so-called 'ring of fire'. Borneo only experiences about four mild earthquakes a year compared with 40-50 on other nearby islands. But because there are no active volcanoes, Borneo's soils are not particularly rich.

CLIMATE

Borneo has a typical equatorial monsoon climate: the weather usually follows predictable patterns, although in recent years it has been less predictable – a phenomenon some environmentalists attribute to deforestation and others to periodic changes to the El Nin Southern Oscillation. Temperatures are fairly uniform, averaging 23-33°C during the day and rarely dropping below 20°C at night, except in the mountains, where they can drop to below 10°C. Most rainfall occurs between November and January during the northeast monsoon; this causes rivers to burst their banks, and there are many short, sharp cloudbursts. The dry season runs from May to September. It is characterized by dry south-easterly winds and is the best time to visit. Rainfall generally increases towards the interior; most of Borneo receives about 2,000-3,000 mm a year, although some upland areas get more than 4,000 mm. For graphs showing monthly rainfall and temperature in Kuching and Kota Kinabalu see pages 354 and 434.

FLORA AND FAUNA

Borneo's ancient rainforests are rich in flora and fauna, including over 9,000-15,000 species of seed plants (of which almost half may be endemic), 200 species of mammals, 570 species of birds, 100 species of snake, 250 species of fresh water fish and 1,000 species of butterfly. The theory of natural selection enunciated by Victorian naturalist Alfred Russel Wallace – while that other great Victorian scientist Charles Darwin was coming to similar conclusions several thousand miles away – was influenced by Wallace's observations in Borneo. He travelled widely in Sarawak between 1854 and 1862.

Despite years of research the gaps in scientists' knowledge of the island's flora and fauna remain yawning – and if anything are becoming more so. For a significant proportion of the flora of Borneo, scientists have barely any information on their geographic distribution, let alone details of their ecology. It has been estimated that around one quarter of plant species are only known from their 'type' specimen (ie the specimen on which the initial identification was based), or from one or two specimens. Even on Gunung Kinabalu, which has been intensively researched for years, there are significant knowledge gaps.

Flora

As late as the middle of the 19th century, the great bulk – perhaps as much as 95% – of the land area of Borneo was forested. Alfred Russel Wallace, like other Western travellers, was enchanted by the island's natural wealth and diversity: "ranges of hill and valley everywhere", he wrote, "everywhere covered with interminable forest". But Borneo's jungle is disappearing fast – some naturalists would say that over extensive areas it has disappeared – and since the mid-1980s there has been a mounting international environmental campaign against deforestation. The campaign has been particularly vocal in Sarawak (see page 412) but other parts of the island are also suffering rapid deforestation, notably Sabah and also Indonesia's province of East Kalimantan. Harold Brookfield, Lesley Potter and Byron state in their hard-headed book *In place of the forest* (1995):

> "Concerning those large areas of forest that have been totally cleared and converted to other uses or that lie waste [in Borneo], we can state only that there is nothing to be gained from bemoaning the past. A great resource has been squandered, and the major part of the habitat of a great range of plant and animal species has been destroyed. Moreover, this has been done with far less than adequate economic return to the two nations [Malaysia and Indonesia] concerned."

How extensive has been the loss of species as a result of the logging of Borneo's forests is a topic of heated debate. Brookfield *et al* in the volume noted above suggest that there "is very little basis in firm research for the spectacular figures of species loss rates that appear not infrequently in sections of the conservationist literature and that readily attract media attention." But they do admit that the flora and fauna of Borneo is especially diverse with a high degree of endemism and that there has been a significant loss of biodiversity as a result of extensive logging. It has been estimated that 32% of terrestrial mammals, 70% of leaf beetles, and 50% of flowering plants are endemic to Borneo – in other words, they are found nowhere else.

The best known timber trees fall into three categories, all of them hardwoods. Heavy hardwoods include *selangan batu* and *resak*; medium hardwoods include *kapur*, *keruing* and *keruntum*; light hardwoods include *madang tabak*, *ramin* and *meranti*. There are both peat-swamp and hill varieties of meranti, which is one of the most valuable export logs. *Belian*, or Bornean iron wood (*Eusideroxylon zwageri*) is one of the hardest and densest timbers in the world. It is thought that the largest belian may be 1,000 years or

Fields in the forest – shifting cultivation

Shifting cultivation, also known as slash-and-burn agriculture or swiddening, as well as by a variety of local terms, is one of the characteristic farming systems of Southeast Asia. It is a low-intensity form of agriculture, in which land is cleared from the forest through burning, cultivated for a few years, and then left to regenerate over 10-30 years. It takes many forms, but an important distinction can be made between shifting field systems where fields are rotated but the settlement remains permanently sited, and migratory systems where the shifting cultivators shift both field (swidden) and settlement. The land is usually only rudimentarily cleared, tree stumps being left in the ground, and seeds sown in holes made by punching the soil with a dibble stick.

For many years, shifting cultivators were regarded as 'primitives' who followed an essentially primitive form of agriculture and their methods were contrasted unfavourably with 'advanced' settled rice farmers. There are still many government officials in Southeast Asia who continue to adhere to this mistaken belief, arguing that shifting cultivators are the principal cause of forest loss and soil erosion. They are, therefore, painted as the villains in the region's environmental crisis, neatly sidestepping the considerably more detrimental impact that commercial logging has had on Southeast Asia's forest resources.

Shifting cultivators have an intimate knowledge of the land, plants and animals on which they depend. One study of a Dayak tribe, the Kantu of Kalimantan (Borneo), discovered that households were cultivating an average of 17 rice varieties and 21 other food crops each year in a highly complex system. Even more remarkably, Harold Conklin's classic 1957 study of the Hanunóo of the Philippines – a study which is a benchmark for such work even today – found that the Hanunóo identified 40 types and subtypes of rocks and minerals when classifying different soils. The shifting agricultural systems are usually also highly productive in labour terms, allowing far more leisure time than farmers using permanent field systems.

But shifting cultivation contains the seeds of its own extinction. Extensive, and geared to low population densities and abundant land, it is coming under pressure in a region where land is becoming an increasingly scarce resource, where patterns of life are dictated by an urban-based élite, and where populations are pressing on the means of subsistence.

more old. They are so tough that when they die they continue to stand for centuries before the wood rots to the extent that the trunk falls. On average, there are about 25 commercial tree species per hectare, but because they are hard to extract, 'selective logging' invariably results in the destruction of many unselected trees. The main types of forest include:

Lowland rainforest (mixed dipterocarp) predominates up to 600m. Dipterocarp forest is stratified into three main layers, the top one rising to heights of 45m. In the top layer, trees' crowns interlock to form a closed canopy of foliage. The word 'dipterocarp' comes from the Greek and means 'two-winged fruit' or 'two [di]-winged [ptero] seed [carp]'. The leaf-like appendages of the mature dipterocarp fruits have 'wings' which makes them spin as they fall to the ground, like giant sycamore seeds. Some species have more than two wings but are all members of the dipterocarp family. It is the lowland rainforest which comes closest to the Western ideal of a tropical 'jungle'. It is also probably the most species rich forest in Borneo. A recent study of a dipterocarp forest in Malaysia found that an area of just 50 hectares supported no less than 835 species of tree. In Europe or North America a similar area of forest would support less than 100 tree species. The red resin produced by many species of dipterocarp, and which can often be seen staining the trunk, is known as *damar* and was traditionally used as a lamp 'oil'. Another characteristic feature of the trees found in lowland dipterocarp rainforest is buttressing – the flanges of wood that protrude from the base of the trunk. For some time the purpose of these massive buttresses perplexed botanists who arrived at a whole range of ingenious explanations. Now they are thought – sensibly – to provide structural support. Two final characteristics of this type of forest are that it is very dark on the forest floor (explaining why trees take so long to grow) and that it is not the inpenetrable jungle of Tarzan fantasy. The first characteristic explains the second. Only when a gap appears in the forest canopy – after a tree falls – do light-loving pioneer plants get the chance to grow. When the gap in the canopy is filled by another tree, these grasses, shrubs and smaller trees die back once more.

Many of the rainforest trees are an important resource for Dayak communities. The jelutong tree, for example, is tapped like a rubber tree for its sap ('jungle chewing gum') which is used to make tar for waterproof sealants – used in boat-building. It also hardens into a tough but brittle black plastic-like substance used for *parang* (machette) handles.

Montane forest occurs at altitudes above 600m, although in some areas it does not replace lowland rainforest until considerably higher than this. Above 1,200m mossy forest predominates. Montane forest is denser than lowland forest with smaller trees of narrower girth. Moreover, dipterocarps are generally not found while flowering shrubs like magnolias and rhododendrons appear. In place of dipterocarps, tropical latitude oaks as well as other trees that are more characteristic of temperate areas, like myrtle and laurel, make an appearance. Other familiar flora of lowland forest, like lianas, also disappear while the distinctive pitcher plant (Nepenthes) become common.

The low-lying river valleys are characterized by **peat swamp** forest – where the peat is up to 9m thick – which makes wet-rice agriculture impossible.

Heath forest or *kerangas* – the Iban word meaning 'land on which rice cannot grow' – is found on poor, sandy soils. Although it mostly occurs near the coast, it is also sometimes found in mountain ranges, but almost always on level ground. Here trees are stunted and only the hardiest of plants can survive. Some trees have struck up symbiotic relationships with animals – like ants – so as to secure essential nutrients. Pitcher plants (Nepenthes) have also successfully colonized heath forest. The absence of bird calls and other animal noises make heath forest rather eerie, and it also indicates their general biological poverty.

Along beaches there are often stretches of **casuarina forest**; the casuarina grows up to 27m, and looks like a conifer, with needle-shaped leaves. **Mangrove** occupies tidal mud flats around sheltered bays and estuaries. The most common mangrove tree is the *bakau* (*Rhizophora*) which grows to heights of about 9m and has stilt roots to trap sediment. Bakau wood is used for pile-house stilts and for charcoal. Further upstream, but still associated with mangrove, is the *nipah* palm (*Nipa fruticans*), whose light-green leaves come from a squat stalk; it was traditionally of great importance as it provided roofing and wickerwork materials.

Mammals

Orang utan (*Pongo pygmaeus*) Walt Disney's film of Rudyard Kipling's *Jungle Book* made the orang utan a big-screen celebrity, dubbing him "the king of the swingers" and "the jungle VIP". Borneo's great red-haired ape is also known as 'man of the jungle', after the translation from the Malay: orang (man), utan (jungle).

The 'Oran-ootan' as remembered by an early European visitor.

Source: Beeckman, Daniel (1718) *A voyage to and from the island of Borneo*, London

The orang utan is endemic to the tropical forests of Sumatra and Borneo although at the beginning of the historic period is was distributed from tropical China to Java. The Sumatran animals tend to keep the reddish tinge to their fur, while the Bornean ones go darker as they mature. It is Asia's only great ape; it has four hands, rather than feet, bow-legs and has no tail. The orang utan moves slowly and deliberately, sometimes swinging under branches, although it seldom travels far by arm-swinging. Males of over 15 years old stand up to 1.6m tall and their arms span 2.4m. Adult males (which make loud roars) weigh 50-100 kg – about twice that of adult females (whose call sounds like a long, unattractive belch). Orang utans are said to have the strength of seven men but they are not aggressive. They are peaceful, gentle animals, particularly with each other. Orang utans have bluey-grey skin and their eyes are close together, giving them an almost human look. Males develop cheek pouches when they reach maturity, which they fill with several litres of air; this is exhaled noisily when they demarcate territory.

Orang utans mainly inhabit riverine swamp forests or lowland dipterocarp forests. Their presence is easily detected by their nests of bent and broken twigs, which are woven together, in much the same fashion as a sun bear's, in the fork of a tree. They are solitary animals and always sleep alone. Orang utans have a largely vegetarian diet consisting of fruit and young leaves, supplemented by termites, bark and birds' eggs. They are usually solitary but the young remain with their mothers until they are 5 or 6 years old. Two adults will occupy an area of about 2 sq km and are territorial, protecting their territory intruders. They can live up to 30 years and a female will have an average of three to four young during her lifetime. Females reach sexual maturity between the ages of 7-9 years and the gestation period is 9 months. Female orang utans usually have one only one young although twins and even triplets have been recorded. After giving birth, they do not mate for around another 7 years.

Estimates of the numbers of orang utan vary considerably. One puts the figure at 10,000-20,000 animals; another at between 70-100,000 in the wild in Borneo and Sumatra. Part of the difficulty is that many are thought to live in inaccessible and little researched areas of peat swamp. But this is just a very rough estimate, based on one ape for each 1½ sq km of forest. No one, so far, has attempted an accurate census. What is certain is that the forest is disappearing fast, and with it the orang utan's natural habitat. Orang utans' favoured habitat is lowland rainforest and this is particularly under threat from logging. The black market in young apes in countries like Taiwan means that they fetch relatively high returns to local hunters. At the village level an orang utan might command US$100; in local markets, around US$350; and at their international destination, along with all the necessary forged export permits, travel costs and so on, from US$5,000 to as much as US$60,000. In 1991, six baby apes were discovered, by chance, in a crate labelled 'live birds' at Bangkok's Don Muang Airport. They had diarrhoea and were severely dehydrated. The customs officers only opened the crate because it seemed suspiciously heavy for a box of birds.

Proboscis monkey (*Nasalis larvatus*) The proboscis monkey is an extraordinary-looking animal, endemic to Borneo, which lives in lowland forests and mangrove swamps all around the island. Little research has been done on proboscis monkeys; they are notoriously difficult to study as they are so shy. Their fur is reddish-brown and they have white legs, arms, tail and a ruff on the neck, which gives the appearance of a pyjama-suit. Their facial skin is red and the males have grotesquely enlarged, droopy noses; females' noses are shorter and upturned. The male's nose is the subject of some debate among zoologists: what ever else it does, it apparently increases their sex-appeal. To ward off intruders, the nose is straightened out, "like a party whoopee whistle", according to one description. Recently a theory has been advanced that the nose acts as a thermostat, helping to regulate body temperature. But it also tends to get in the way: old males often have to resort to holding their noses up with one hand while stuffing leaves into their mouths with the other.

Proboscises' penises are almost as obvious as their noses – the proboscis male glories in a permanent erection, which is probably why they are rarely displayed in zoos. The other way the males attract females is by violently shaking branches and making spectacular – and sometimes near-suicidal – leaps into the water, in which they attempt to hit as many dead branches as they can on the way down, so as to make the loudest noise possible. The monkeys organize themselves into harems, with one male and several females and young – there are sometimes up to 20 in a group. Young males leave the harem they are born into when the adult male becomes aggressive towards them and they rove around in bachelor groups until they are in a position to form their own harem.

Proboscis monkeys belong to the leaf monkey family, and have large, pouched stomachs to help digest bulky food – they feed almost entirely on the leaves of one tree – the *Sonneratia*. The proboscis is a diurnal animal, but keeps to the shade during the heat of the day. The best time to see them is very early in the morning or around dusk. They can normally be heard before they are seen: they make loud honks, rather like geese; they also groan, squeal and roar. Proboscis monkeys are good swimmers; they even swim underwater for up to 20m – thanks to their partially webbed feet. Males are about twice the size and weight of females. They are known fairly ubiquitously (in both Malaysian and Indonesian Borneo) as 'Orang Belanda', or Dutchmen – which is not entirely complimentary. In Kalimantan they also have other local names including *Bekantan*, *Bekara*, *Kahau*, *Rasong*, *Pika* and *Batangan*.

Other monkeys found in Borneo include various species of leaf monkey – including the grey leaf monkey, the white-fronted leaf monkey, and the red leaf monkey. One of the non-timber forest products formerly much prized was bezoar stone which was a valued cure-all. Bezoars are green coloured 'stones' which form in the stomachs of some herbivores, and in particular in the stomachs of leaf monkeys. Fortunately for the leaf monkeys of Southeast Asia though, these stones – unlike rhino horn – are no longer prized for their medicinal properties. One of the most attractive members of the primate family found in Borneo is the

Protected areas of Sabah and Sarawak

Sarawak	**Area (ha)**	**See page**
Bako National Park	2,728	page 376
Batang Ai National Park	24,040	page 381
Gunung Gading National Park	5,430	page 364
Gunung Mulu National Park	52,887	page 410
Kubah National Park	2,230	page 365
Lambir Hills National Park	6,952	page 406
Lanjak-Entimau National Park	168,755	-
Loagan National Park	650	page 406
Niah National Park	3,140	page 400
Pulau Tukong Ara-Banun Wildlife Sanctuary	1	-
Samunsam Wildlife Sanctuary	6,092	-
Similajau National Park	7,067	page 399
Semonggoh Orang Utan Sanctuary		page 361
Tanjung Datu National Park	331	page 365
Sabah		
Crocker Range National Park	139,919	page 451
Danum Valley Conservation Area	42,755	page 491
Gomontong Forest Reserve	3,297	page 479
Kinabalu National Park	75,370	page 467
Kota Belud Bird Sanctuary	12,000	page 463
Kulamba Wildlife Reserve	20,682	-
Madai-Baturong Forest Reserve	5,867	page 490
Maliau Basin Conservation Area	39,000	-
Maligan Virgin Jungle Reserve	9,240	-
Mount Silam	4,128	page 490
Pulau Tiga National Park	15,864	page 462
Sepilok Forest Reserve	4,294	page 486
Tabin Wildlife Reserve	122,530	-
Tavai Protection Forest Reserve	22,697	-
Tawau Hills Park	27,972	page 497
Tunku Abdul Rahman Park	4,929	page 447
Turtle Islands Park	1,740	page 483
Sipadan Marine Park (proposed)		page 494
Likas Swamp (proposed)		-
Semporna Marine Park (proposed)		page 492
Kinabatangan Wildlife Sanctuary (proposed)		page 487

Source: Cubitt, Gerald and Payne, Junaidi (1990) *Wild Malaysia*, London: New Holland.

tubby slow loris or *kongkang*. And perhaps the most difficult to pronounce – at least in Dusun – is the tarsier which is locally known as the *tindukutrukut*.

Elephant Borneo's wild elephants pose a zoological mystery. They occur only at the far northeast tip of the island, at the furthest possible point from their Sumatran and mainland Southeast Asian relatives. No elephant remains have been found in Sabah, Sarawak or Kalimantan. It is known that some animals were introduced into Sabah – then British North Borneo – by early colonial logging concerns. But it is certain that there were already populations established in the area. Another theory has it that one of the sultans of Sulu released a small number of animals several centuries ago. The difficulty with this explanation is that experts find it difficult to believe that just a handful of elephants could have grown to the 2,000 or so that existed by the end of the last century. Some zoologists speculate that they were originally introduced at the time of the Javan Majapahit Empire, in the 13th and 14th centuries. Antonio Pigafetta, an Italian historian who visited the Sultanate of Brunei as part of Portuguese explorer Ferdinand Magellan's expedition in July 1521, tells of being taken to visit the sultan on two domesticated elephants, which may have been gifts from another ruler.

It is possible, however, that elephants are native to Borneo and migrated from the Southeast Asian mainland during the Pleistocene when sea levels were lower and land-bridges would have existed between Borneo and the mainland. Their concentration in Northeast Borneo could be explained by the presence of numerous salt-licks between the Sandakan and Lahad Datu areas of Sabah. This would make the present population a relic of a much larger group of elephants. Borneo's male elephants are up to 2.6m tall; females are usually less than 2.2m. Males' tusks can grow up to 1.7m in length and weigh up to 15 kg each. Mature males are solitary creatures, only joining herds to mate. The most likely places to see elephants in the wild are the Danum Valley Conservation Area (see page 491) and the lower Kinabatangan basin (see page 487), both in Sabah.

Rhinoceros The 2-horned Sumatran rhinoceros, also known as the hairy rhinoceros, is the smallest of all rhinos and was once widespread throughout Sumatra and Borneo. The population has been greatly reduced by excessive hunting. The horn is worth more than its weight in gold in Chinese apothecaries, and that of the Sumatran rhino is reputedly the most prized of all. But the ravages of over-hunting have been exacerbated by the destruction of the rhino's habitat. Indeed, until quite recently it was thought to be extinct on Borneo. Most of Borneo's remaining wild population is in Sabah, and the Malaysian government is attempting to capture some of the thinly dispersed animals to breed them in captivity, for they remain in serious danger of extinction (see page 487 and page 486).

Other large mammals include the **banteng**, a wild cattle known as the *tembadau* in Sabah. These are smaller than the *seladang* of Peninsular Malaysia, and are most numerous in lowland areas of eastern Sabah where herds are encountered on country roads. The **bearded pig** is the only member of the pig family found in Borneo and is a major source of meat for many Dayak groups. Of the **deer family**, Borneo supports two species of barking deer or *kijang*, and the Greater (*npau*) and Lesser mouse deer. The latter barely stands 30 cm tall.

Birds

Hornbill There are nine types of hornbill on Borneo, the most striking and biggest of which is the rhinoceros hornbill (*Buceros rhinoceros*) – or *kenyalang*. They can grow up to 1.5m long and are mainly black, with a white belly. The long tail feathers are white too, crossed with a thick black bar near the end. They make a remarkable, resonant "GERONK" call in flight, which can be heard over long distances; they honk when resting. Hornbills are usually seen in pairs – they are believed to be monogamous. After mating, the female imprisons herself in a hole in a tree, building a sturdy wall with her own droppings. The male bird fortifies the wall from the outside, using a mulch of mud, grass, sticks and saliva, leaving only a vertical slit for her beak. She remains incarcerated in her cell for about 3 months, during which the male supplies her and the nestlings with food – mainly fruit, lizards, snakes and mice. Usually, only one bird is hatched and reared in the hole and when it is old enough to fly, the

The Iban Hornbill Festival

One of the main Iban festivals is *Gawai Kenyalang*, or the Hornbill Festival. The *kenyalang* – a carved wooden hornbill – traditionally played an important part in the ceremony which preceded head-hunting expeditions, and the often ornate, brightly painted images also made appearances at other *gawais*, or festivals. The kenyalang is carved from green wood and the design varies from area to area. A carved hornbill can be about 2m long and 1m high and is stored until a few days before the festival, when it is painted, bringing the carving to life. It is carried in procession and offered *tuak* (rice wine), before being mounted on a carved base on the *tanju*, the longhouse's open verandah. As the singing gets underway, the kenyalang is adorned with specially woven *pua kumbu* (see page 350) and then raised off the ground to face enemy territory. Its soul is supposed to attack the village's enemies, destroying their houses and crops.

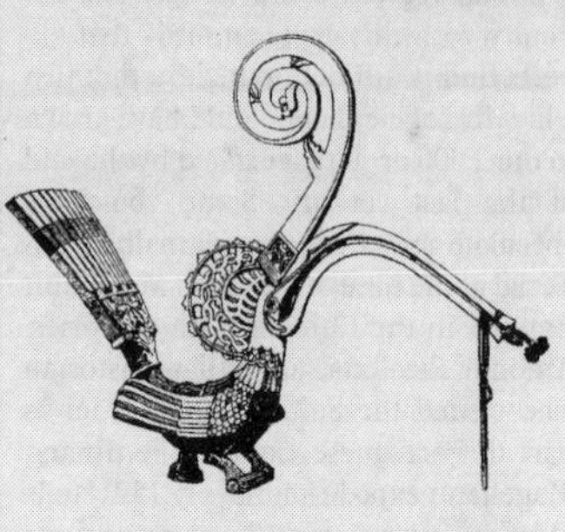

Kenyalang, hornbill image
From Roth, Henry (1896) *The natives of Sarawak and British North Borneo*, Truslove & Hanson: London

female breaks out of the nest hole. Both emerge looking fat and dirty.

The 'bill' itself has no known function, but the males have been seen duelling in mid-air during the courting season. They fly straight at each other and collide head-on. The double-storeyed yellow bill has a projection, called a casque, on top, which has a bright red tip. In some species the bill develop wrinkles as the bird matures: one wrinkle for each year of its life. For this reason they are known in Dutch, and in some eastern Indonesian languages as 'year birds'.

Most Dayak groups consider the hornbill to have magical powers and the feathers are worn as symbols of heroism. In tribal mythology the bird is associated with the creation of mankind, and is a symbol of the upper world. The hornbill is also the official state emblem of Sarawak. The best place to see hornbills is near wild fig trees – they love the fruit and play an important role in seed dispersal. The helmeted hornbill's bill is heavy and solid and can be carved, like ivory. These bills were highly valued by the Dayaks, and have been traded for centuries. The third largest hornbill is the wreathed hornbill which makes a yelping call and a loud – almost mechanical – noise when it beats its wings. Others species on Borneo include the wrinkled, black, bushy-crested, white-crowned and pied hornbills.

Reptiles

Crocodiles The largest population of estuarine crocodiles are found in the lower reaches of Borneo's rivers. However, they have been so extensively hunted that they are rarely a threat – although people do very occasionally still get taken.

HISTORY

Archaeological evidence from Sarawak shows that *Homo sapiens* was established on Borneo at least 40,000 years ago (see page 400). The outside world may have been trading with Borneo from Roman times, and there is evidence in Kaltim

(East Kalimantan) of Indian cultural influence from as early as the 4th century. Chinese traders began to visit Borneo from about the 7th century – they traded beads and porcelain in exchange for jungle produce and birds' nests. By the 14th century, this trade appears to have been flourishing, particularly with the newly formed Sultanate of Brunei. The history of the north coast of Borneo is dominated by the Sultanate of Brunei from the 14th-19th centuries (see page 536). The Europeans began arriving in the East in the early 1500s, but had little impact on North Borneo until British adventurer James Brooke arrived in Sarawak in 1839. From then on, the Sultan's empire and influence shrank dramatically as he ceded more and more territory to the expansionist White Rajahs (see page 335) and to the British North Borneo Chartered Company to the north (see page 424). Many of the upriver Dayaks were left largely to themselves.

CULTURE

PEOPLE

Borneo's population is still pretty sparse by Asian standards, but compared with the state of affairs only two centuries ago it has grown enormously. Anthony Reid in his book *Southeast Asia in the age of commerce* (1988) estimates that the total population in 1800 was just 1,500,000. The vast majority of Borneo's population is concentrated in the narrow coastal belt; the more mountainous, jungled interior is sparsely populated by Dayak tribes. It has been suggested that there was a long lasting hostile relationship between the tribal peoples of the interior and the settled coastal populations – explaining why only those people living along the main rivers like the Kapuas and Barito in Kalimantan ever converted to Islam.

Whereas the word 'native' has taken on a derogatory connotation in English – it tends to smack of colonial arrogance towards indigenous people – this is not the case in Borneo, particularly in Sarawak and Sabah. Tribespeople are proud to be called natives, with a meaning equivalent to that of *bumiputra* on the Malaysian peninsula (see page 66). Borneo's 200-odd Dayak tribes are the indigenous people; they are generally fairly light-skinned with rounded facial features and slightly slanted eyes, although physical characteristics vary from tribe to tribe. Their diverse anthropological backgrounds have defied most attempts at neat classification. In Sabah and Sarawak, Dayaks are known by their individual tribal names – except in the case of the Orang Ulu, a collective term for upriver groups. Today, Dayak cultural identity is strong, and upriver tribespeople are proud of their heritage.

Dayak groups are closely-knit communities and traditionally tended to live in longhouses. Many Dayaks are shifting cultivators (see page 322). Most are skillful hunters but few made good traders – historically, that was the domain of the coastal Malays and, later, the Chinese. The Dayaks lived in self-sufficient communities in the interior until they began to come under the influence of Malay coastal sultanates from the 14th and 15th centuries. Some turned to Islam, and more recently, many have converted to Christianity – due to the activities of both Roman Catholic and Protestant missionaries (see page 330). Few Dayaks – other than those in the remoter parts of the interior – still wear their traditional costumes. Most have abandoned them in favour of jeans and T-shirts.

Dayaks throughout Borneo have only been incorporated into the economic mainstream relatively recently – although they have always traded with settled 'down river' people (see box on page 320). Relations with coastal groups were not always good, and there was also constant fighting between groups. Differences between the coastal peoples and inland tribes throughout Borneo were accentuated as competition for land increased. The situation was aggravated by

Painted panel from a Dayak coffin of a 'Ship of the Dead'. Note the gongs and cannon

Adapted from: Hersey, Irwin (1991) *Indonesian primitive art*, OUP: Singapore

a general movement of the population towards the coasts. There was constant rivalry between tribes, with the stronger groups taking advantage of the weaker. Today however, Dayak groups have relatively good access to education and many now work in the timber and oil and gas industries, which has caused out-migration from their traditional homelands. This has completely changed the lifestyles of most Dayak communities, who used to live in what some anthropologists term 'primitive affluence'. With a few exceptions, everything the people needed came from the jungle. There was an abundance of fish and wild game and building materials; medicine and plant foods were easily obtainable. Jungle products such as rattan, tree resins, edible birds nests were traded on the coast for steel tools, salt, brass gongs, cooking pots and rice wine jars from China. Villages are now tied to a coastal cash culture and western subculture.

RELIGION

In Sabah and Sarawak, apart from the Malays, Bajaus, Illanuns and Suluks, who accepted Islam, all the inland tribes were originally animists. The religion of all the Dayak tribes in Borneo boiled down to placating spirits, and the purpose of tribal totems, images, icons and statues was to chase bad spirits away and attract good ones, which were believed to be capable of bringing fortune and prosperity. Head-hunting (see page 348) was central to this belief, and most Dayak tribes practiced it, in the belief that freshly severed heads would bring blessing to their longhouses. Virtually everything had a spirit, and complex rituals and ceremonies were devised to keep them happy. Motifs associated with the spirit world – such as the hornbill (see page 328) – dominate artwork and textiles and many of the woodcarvings for sale in art and antique shops had religious significance. Islam began to spread to the tribes of the interior from the late 15th century, but mostly it was confined to coastal districts or those areas close to rivers like the Kapuas and Barito where Malays penetrated into the interior to trade. Christian missionaries arrived with the Europeans but did not proselytize seriously until the mid-19th century. The Dutch, particularly, saw missionaries fulfilling an administrative function, drawing the tribal peoples close to the Dutch and, by implication, away from the Muslim Malays of the coast: it was a policy of divide and rule by religion means. Both Christianity and Islam had enormous influence on the animist tribes, and many converted en-mass to one or the other. Despite this, many of the old superstitions and ceremonial traditions, which are deeply ingrained, remain a part of Dayak culture today. (The traditional beliefs of Kalimantan's Dayaks is formalized in the *Kaharingan* faith, which, despite the in-roads made by Christianity and Islam, is still practiced by some Mahakam and Barito river groups. The Indonesian government recognizes it as an official religion.)

In 1973 a fanatical Christian revival spread through longhouse communities in Sarawak. In some villages people went to church up to three times a day and drinking and dancing were forbidden. Priceless family heirlooms such as beads, charms, statues, totems (including the

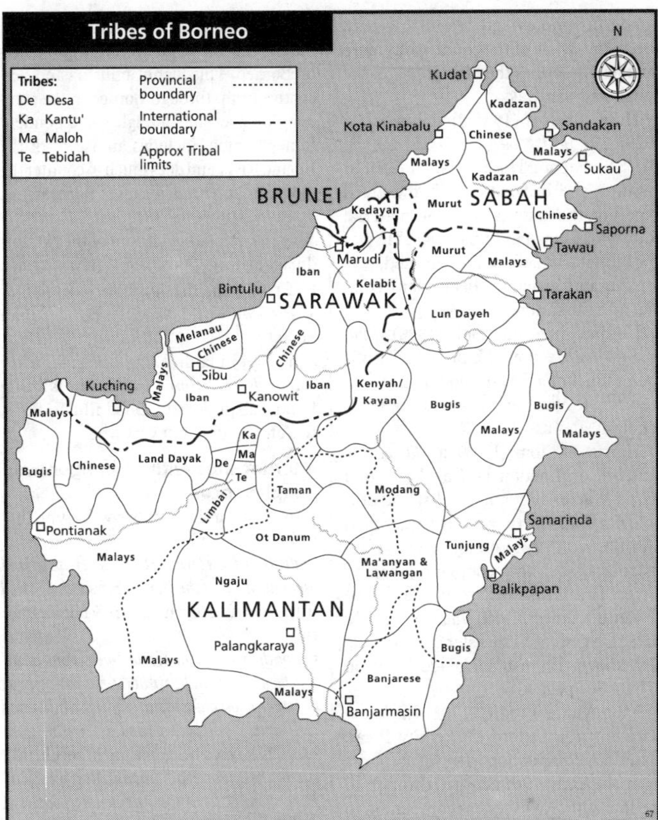

carved *tegundo* guardian spirits which traditionally stood at the entrance to villages) and old headhunting swords were thrown in the rivers or burned because of their association with magical powers. These objects are an indispensable part of animist beliefs and are considered wholly incompatible with Christian teachings.

BOOKS ON BORNEO

Bock, Carl (1985, first published 1881) *The headhunters of Borneo*, OUP: Singapore. Bock was a Norwegian naturalist and explorer and was commissioned by the Dutch to make a scientific survey of southeastern Borneo. His account, though, makes much of the dangers and adventures that he faced, and some of his 'scientific' observations are, in retrospect, clearly highly faulty. Nonetheless, this is an entertaining account.

Chapman, F Spencer: *The jungle is neutral*. An account of a British guerrilla force fighting the Japanese in Borneo — not as enthralling as Tom Harrisson's book, but still worth reading.

Cubitt, Gerald and Payne, Junaidi (1990) *Wild Malaysia*, London: New Holland. Large format coffee table book with wonderful photos and reasonable text; covers the whole of the country but more than half describes the protected areas of Sabah and Sarawak.

Hose, Charles (1985, first published 1929) *The field book of a jungle wallah*, OUP: Singapore. Hose was an official in Sarawak and became an acknowledged expert on the material and non-material culture of the tribes of Sarawak. He was one of that band of highly informed, perceptive and generally benevolent colonial administrators.

Hanbury-Tenison, Robin (1980) *Mulu, the rain forest*, Arrow/Weidenfeld. This is the product of a Royal Geographical Society trip to Mulu in the late 1970s; semi-scholarly and useful.

Harrisson, Tom (1959) *World within*, Hutchinson: London. During the Second World War, explorer, naturalist and ethnologist Tom Harrisson was parachuted into Borneo to help organize Dayak resistance against the occupying Japanese forces. This is his extraordinary account.

Keith, Agnes (1969) *Land below the wind*, Ulverscroft: Leicester. Perhaps the best-known English language book on Sabah. See page 476.

King, Victor T (edit) (1992) *The best of Borneo travel*, Oxford University Press: Oxford. A compilation of travel accounts from the early 19th century through to the late 20th. An excellent companion to take while exploring the island. Published in portable paperback.

King, Victor T (1993) *The peoples of Borneo*, Oxford: Basil Blackwell. A scholarly yet readable book written by one of the world's foremost experts on the peoples of Borneo. It includes chapters on history, economic development, culture, socio-political organization, religion and art.

O'Hanlon, Redmond (1984) *Into the heart of Borneo*, Salamander Press: Edinburgh. One of the best recent travel books on Borneo. This highly amusing and perceptive romp through Borneo in the company of poet and foreign correspondent James Fenton, includes an ascent of the Rejang River and does much to counter the more romanticized images of Bornean life.

Payne, Robert: *The white Rajahs of Sarawak*. Readable account of the extraordinary history of this East Malaysian state.

Payne, Junaidi *et al*: *Pocket guide to birds of Borneo*, World Wildlife Fund/Sabah Society.

Payne, Junaidi *et al*: *A field guide to the mammals of Borneo*, World Wildlife Fund/Sabah Society. Good illustrations, reasonable text, but very dry.

Internet sites with an indigenous peoples focus

http://www.mdx.ac.uk/www/hap/brc.html
contents of the Borneo Research Bulletin and list of members of the Borneo Research Council

http://www.halcyon.com/FWDP/help.html
site of the Centre for World Indigenous Studies; focus tends to be rather America-centric, but still a good place to start for those interested in Fourth World (tribal) issues

http://www.ics.bc.ca/ica/membert.html'l
site of the Indonesia-Canada Alliance NGO Partnerships; focus is on indigenous peoples in Indonesia and Canada – has material on Dayak of Borneo

http://www.pip.dknet.dk/~pip1917/publicat.html
site of the International Work Group for Indigenous Affairs (IWGIA); good links with related sites and good source of articles

http://www.icppgr.fao.org/links/2.html
focus on traditional and indigenous knowledge; good links with related sites

Sarawak

Horizons	335	Niah National Park	400
Kuching	354	Miri and the Baram River	404
Bako National Park	376	Gunung Mulu National Park	410
Sibu and the Rejang River	383	Bario and the Kelabit Highlands	419
Bintulu and Niah Caves	396	Limbang and Lawas	420

SARAWAK, 'the land of the hornbill', is the largest state in Malaysia, covering an area of 124,967 sq km in NW Borneo. In the mid-19th century, the naturalist Charles Darwin described Sarawak as "one great wild, untidy, luxuriant hothouse, made by nature for herself". Despite the state's rapacious logging industry, which has drawn world attention to Sarawak in recent years, more than two-thirds of its land area (roughly equivalent to that of England and Scotland combined) is still covered in jungle – much, though, degraded and a far cry from 'virgin' rainforest. Some of it is still as the Victorian naturalist, Alfred Russel Wallace (whose theories of natural selection influenced Darwin) saw it in 1855. "For hundreds of miles in every direction," he wrote, "a magnificent forest extended over plain and mountain, rock and morass". Sarawak has swampy coastal plain, a hinterland of undulating foothills and an interior of steep-sided, jungle-covered mountains. The lowlands and plain are dissected by a network of broad rivers which are the main arteries of communication. Sarawak has a population of around 1.5 million, most of which is settled along the rivers.

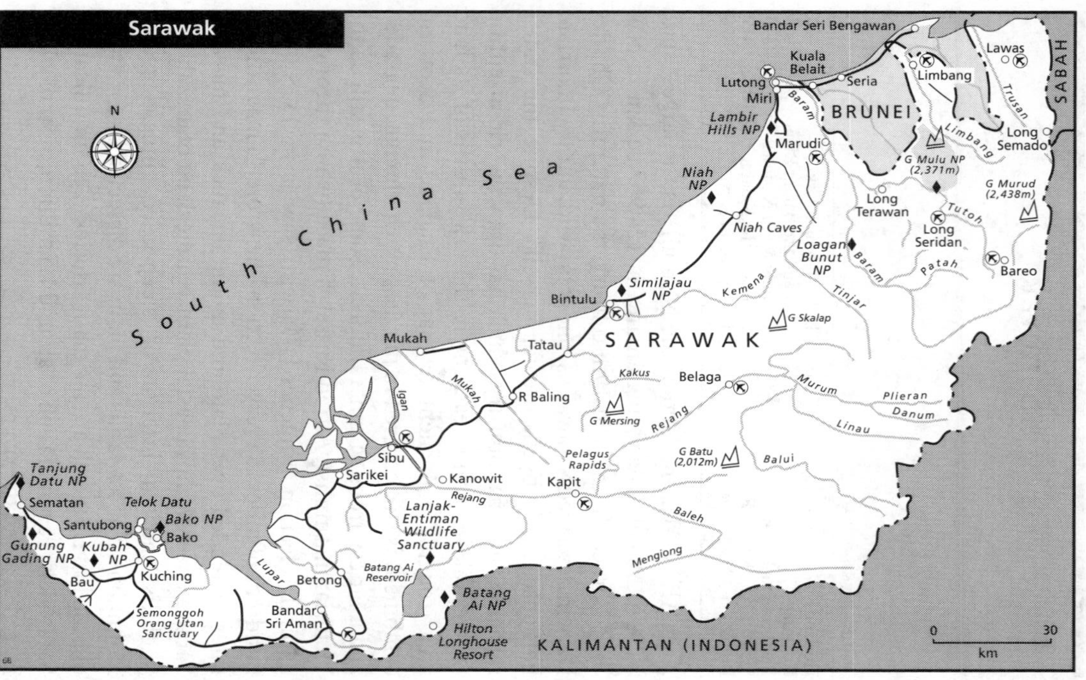
Sarawak
N
South China Sea
Bandar Seri Bengawan
Kuala Belait
Lutong
Miri
Seria
BRUNEI
Limbang
Lawas
Trusan
SABAH
Long Semado
Limbang
G Mulu NP (2,371m)
G Murud (2,438m)
Lambir Hills NP
Baram
Marudi
Niah NP
Niah Caves
Long Terawan
Tutoh
Long Seridan
Loagan Bunut NP
Baram
Patah
Bareo
Tinjar
Similajau NP
Bintulu
Kemena
G Skalap
SARAWAK
Mukah
Tatau
Kakus
Belaga
Murum
Plieran
Danum
Mukah
Igan
R Baling
G Mersing
Rejang
Linau
Sibu
Pelagus Rapids
G Batu (2,012m)
Balui
Sarikei
Kanowit
Kapit
Rejang
Tanjung Datu NP
Sematan
Telok Datu
Lanjak-Entiman Wildlife Sanctuary
Baleh
Santubong
Bako NP
Bako
Gunung Gading NP
Kubah NP
Kuching
Bau
Lupar
Betong
Batang Ai Reservoir
Mengiong
Batang Ai NP
Semonggoh Orang Utan Sanctuary
Bandar Sri Aman
Hilton Longhouse Resort
KALIMANTAN (INDONESIA)
0
30
km

About 30% of the population is made up of Iban tribespeople – who used to be known as the 'Sea Dayaks' – former headhunters, who live in longhouses on the lower reaches of the rivers. Chinese immigrants, whose forebears arrived during the 19th century, make up another 30%. A fifth of the population is Malay – most are native Sarawakians, but some came from the peninsula after the state joined the Malaysian Federation in 1963. The rest of Sarawak's inhabitants are indigenous tribal groups – of which the main ones are the Melanau, the Bidayuh and upriver Orang Ulu such as the Kenyah, Kayan and Kelabits; the Penan are among Southeast Asia's few remaining hunter-gatherers.

For over 150 years, Sarawak was under the rule of the 'White Rajahs' who tried to keep the peace between warring tribes of headhunters. The Brooke family ran Sarawak as their private country and their most obvious legacies are the public buildings in Kuching, the state capital, and the forts along the rivers. Outside Kuching, the towns have little to offer; most are predominantly Chinese, they are mainly modern, without much grace or character. One or two are boom-towns, having grown rich on the back of the logging and oil and gas industries. From a tourist's point of view, the towns are just launching-pads for the longhouses and jungle upriver.

For information on geography, climate, flora and fauna, pages 319-328.

HISTORY

Sarawak earned its place in the archaeological textbooks when a 40,000-year-old human skull – belonging to a boy of about 15 – was unearthed in the Niah Caves in 1958 (see page 400), predating the earliest relics found on the Malay peninsula by about 30,000 years. The caves were continuously inhabited for tens of thousands of years and many shards of Palaeolithic and Neolithic pottery, tools and jewellery as well as carved burial boats have been excavated at the site. There are also prehistoric cave paintings. In the first millennium AD, the Niah Caves were home to a prosperous community, which traded birds' nests, hornbill ivory, bezoar stones, rhinoceros horns and other jungle produce with Chinese traders in exchange for porcelain and beads.

Some of Sarawak's tribes may be descended from these cave people, although others, notably the Iban shifting cultivators, migrated from Kalimantan's Kapuas River valley from the 16th-19th centuries. Malay *Orang Laut*, sea people, migrated to Sarawak's coasts and made a living from fishing, trading and piracy. At the height of Sumatra's Srivijayan Empire in the 11th and 12th centuries, many Sumatran Malays migrated to North Borneo. Chinese traders were active along the Sarawak coast from as early as the 7th century: Chinese coins and Han pottery have been discovered at the mouth of the Sarawak River. Most of the coins and ceramics, however, date from the Chinese Song and Yuan periods (11th-14th centuries).

From the 14th century right up to the 20th century, Sarawak's history was inextricably intertwined with that of the neighbouring Sultanate of Brunei, which, until the arrival of the White Rajahs of Sarawak, held sway over the coastal areas of North Borneo. A more detailed account of how Sarawak's White Rajahs came to whittle away the sultan's territory and expand into the vacuum of his receding empire is given in the introduction to Brunei (see page 537).

Enter James Brooke

As the Sultanate of Brunei began to decline around the beginning of the 18th century, the Malays of coastal Sarawak attempted to break free from their tributary overlord. They claimed an independent ancestry from Brunei and exercised firm control over the Dayak tribes inland and upriver. But in the early 19th century Brunei started to reassert its power over them, dispatching Pangiran Mahkota (see page 537), from the Brunei court to govern Sarawak in 1827 and supervise the mining

Piracy: the resurgence of an ancient scourge

In February 1992, the International Maritime Bureau convened a conference on Piracy in the Far East Region in Kuala Lumpur, Malaysia. The IMB had become alarmed at the increase in piracy and by the fact that attacks were becoming more ferocious. The number of ships arriving in Singapore that had suffered pirate attacks doubled to 61 in 1991. In 1994 the IMB recorded 90 pirate attacks worldwide. Of these, 48 were in Southeast Asian waters. Some ships just suffer hit-and-run attacks; other pirates hijack entire vessels, whose cargo is removed and the ship resold under another name. On 2 May 1991, for example, the *Hai Hui I*, a Singapore-registered ship bound for Cambodia was attacked and relieved of its cargo in the Strait of Singapore. The pirates seized 400 tonnes of electronics, motorcycles and beer. Most attacks took place in the Strait of Melaka, in the Riau Archipelago, to the northwest of Sarawak in the South China Sea, and around Sabah (see page 489).

Many modern pirates use high-speed boats to escape into international waters and avoid capture by racing from one country's waters into another's. Cooperative international action offers the only way to successfully patrol the shipping lanes. Following the IMB conference, a Regional Piracy Centre was set up in Kuala Lumpur.

But while modern shipping companies might consider the rise in piracy a new and dangerous threat, there is nothing new about piracy in Southeast Asian waters. For centuries, pirates have murdered and pillaged their way along the region's coasts, taking hundreds of slaves as part of their booty. As far back as the 6th century, pirates are thought to have been responsible for the destruction and abandonment of the ancient Hindu capital of Langkasuka, in the Northwest Malaysian state of Kedah. Piracy grew as trade flourished: the Strait of Melaka and the South China Sea were perfect haunts, being on the busy trade routes between China, India, the Middle East and Europe. Most of the pirates were the Malay Orang Laut (sea gypsies) and Bugis who lived in the Riau Archipelago, the Acehnese of North Sumatra, the Ibans of the Sarawak estuaries and – most feared of all – the Illanun and Balinini pirates of Sulu and Mindanao in the Philippines. The Illanuns were particularly ferocious pirates, sailing in huge *perahus* with up to 150 slaves as oarsmen, in as many as three tiers. The name *lanun* means pirate in Malay.

of high-grade antimony ore, which was exported to Singapore to be used in medicine and as an alloy. The name 'Sarawak' comes from the Malay word *serawak*, meaning 'antimony'.

Mahkota founded Kuching, but relations with the local Malays became strained and Mahkota's problems were compounded by the marauding Ibans of the Saribas and Skrang rivers who raided coastal communities. In 1836 the local Malay chiefs, led by Datu Patinggi Ali, rebelled against Governor Mahkota, prompting the Sultan of Brunei to send his uncle, Rajah Muda Hashim to suppress the uprising. But Hashim failed to quell the disturbances and the situation deteriorated when the rebels approached the Sultan of Sambas (now in Northwest Kalimantan) for help from the Dutch. Then, in 1839, James Brooke sailed up the Sarawak River to Kuching.

Hashim was desperate to regain control and Brooke, in the knowledge that the British would support any action that countered the threat of Dutch influence, struck a deal with him. He pressed Hashim to grant him the governorship of Sarawak in exchange for suppressing the rebellion, which he duly did. In 1842 Brooke became Rajah of Sarawak. Pangiran Mahkota – the now disenfranchised former governor of Sarawak – formed an alliance with an Iban pirate chief on the Skrang River, while another Brunei prince, Pangiran Usop, joined Illanun pirates. Malaysian historian J Kathirithamby-Wells writes: "... piracy and politics became irrevocably linked and Brooke's battle against his political opponents became advertised as a morally justified war against the pirate communities of the coast."

The suppression of piracy in the 19th century became a full-time occupation for the rulers of Sarawak and Brunei – although the court of Brunei was well known to have derived a substantial chunk of its income from piracy. Rajah James Brooke believed that as long as pirates remained free to pillage the coasts, commerce would not pick up and his kingdom would never develop; ridding Sarawak's estuaries of pirates – both Iban ('Sea Dayaks') and Illanun – became an act of political survival. In his history of the White Rajahs, Robert Payne writes:

> "Nearly every day people came to Kuching with tales about the pirates: how they had landed in a small creek, spread out, made their way to a village, looted everything in sight, murdered everyone they could lay their hands on, and then vanished as swiftly as they came. The Sultan of Brunei was begging for help against them."

Anti-piracy missions afforded James Brooke an excuse to extend his kingdom, as he worked his way up the coasts, 'pacifying' the Sea Dayak pirates. Brooke declared war on them and with the help of Royal Naval Captain Henry Keppel (of latter-day Singapore's Keppel Shipyard fame), he led a number of punitive raids against the Iban 'Sea Dayaks' in 1833, 1834 and 1849. "The assaults", writes DJM Tate in *Rajah Brooke's Borneo*, "largely achieved their purpose, and were applauded in the Straits, but the appalling loss of life incurred upset many drawing-room humanitarians in Britain." There were an estimated 25,000 pirates living along the North Borneo coast when Brooke became Rajah. He led many punitive expeditions against them, culminating in his notorious battle against the Saribas pirate fleet in 1849.

In that incident, Brooke ambushed and killed hundreds of Saribas Dayaks at Batang Maru. The barbarity of the ambush (which was reported in the *Illustrated London News*) outraged public opinion in Britain and in Singapore – a commission of inquiry in Singapore acquitted Brooke, but badly damaged his prestige. In the British parliament, he was cast as a 'mad despot' who had to be prevented from committing further massacres. But the action led the Sultan of Brunei to grant him the Saribas and Skrang districts (now Sarawak's Second Division) in 1853, marking the beginning of the Brookes' relentless expansionist drive. 8 years later, James Brooke persuaded the sultan to give him what became Sarawak's Third Division, after he drove out the Illanun pirates who had disrupted the sago trade from Mukah and Oya, around Bintulu.

In 1857, James Brooke ran into more trouble. Chinese Hakka goldminers – who had been in Bau (further up the Sarawak River) longer than he had been in Kuching, had grown resentful of his attempts to stamp out the opium trade and their secret societies. They attacked Kuching, set the Malay kampongs ablaze and killed several European officials; Brooke escaped by swimming across the river from his *astana*. His nephew, Charles, led a group of Skrang Dayaks to chase after the Hakka invaders, who fled across the border into Dutch Borneo; about 1,000 were killed by the Ibans on the way; 2,500 survived. Historian Robert Payne writes: "The fighting lasted for more than a month. From time to time Dayaks would return with strings of heads, which they cleaned and smoked over slow fires, especially happy when they could do this in full view of the Chinese in the bazaars who sometimes recognized people they had known." Payne says Brooke was plagued by guilt over how he handled the

James Brooke: the white knight errant

James Brooke lived the life of a *Boy's Own* comic-book hero. To the socialites of London, many of who idolized him, he was the king of an exotic far-away country, on a mysterious jungled island, inhabited by roving tribes of headhunters. It was a romantic image, but while it was also a tough life, it was not far from the truth. The Brookes were a family of benevolent despots, characterized by historian Robert Payne as "tempestuous and dedicated men, who sometimes quarrelled violently among themselves, but closed ranks whenever the fortunes of their people were at stake. They were proud and possessive, but also humble." There were three White Rajahs, who ruled for over a century, but it was James Brooke, with his forceful personality, violent temper, vengeful instincts but compassion for his people, that set the tone and created the legend.

James was born in India in 1803, the son of a High Court judge in Benares. He joined the Indian army, and fought in the First Anglo-Burmese War as a cavalry officer, where he was mentioned in dispatches for "most conspicuous gallantry." But in 1825 he was hit in the chest by a bullet and almost left for dead on the battlefield. He was forced to return to England where any military ambitions he might have had were dashed by the severity of his injury. He recovered enough to make two trips to the East in the 1830s, on one of which he visited Penang and Singapore where he became an admirer of Sir Thomas Stamford Raffles, Singapore's founding father (see page 580). Back in England, he bought a schooner, *The Royalist*, and drew up plans to sail to Maurdu Bay (North Sabah), to explore the fabled lake at Kini Ballu (see page 463). His trip did not work out as planned.

The Royalist arrived in Singapore in 1839 and the governor asked Brooke to deliver a letter of thanks to Rajah Muda Hashim, the ruler in Kuching, who had rescued some shipwrecked British sailors. He called in briefly, as promised, was intrigued with what he found, but sailed on. When he returned a year later, the Rajah Muda was still struggling to contain the rebellion of local Malay chiefs. Hashim said that if Brooke helped suppress the rebellion, he could have the Sarawak River area as his and the title of Rajah. Brooke took him up on the offer, quelled the revolt and after leaning heavily on Hashim to keep his word, became acting Rajah of Sarawak on 24 September 1841. His title was confirmed by the Sultan of Brunei the following year.

The style of Brooke's government – which also characterized that of his successors – is described by historian Mary Turnbull as "a paternal, informal

Chinese rebellion, for so many deaths could not easily be explained away. Neither James nor Charles ever fully trusted the Chinese again, although the Teochew, Cantonese and Hokkien merchants in Kuching never caused them any trouble.

The second generation: Rajah Charles Brooke

Charles Johnson (who changed his name to Brooke after his elder brother, Brooke Johnson, had been disinherited by James for insubordination) became the second Rajah of Sarawak in 1863. He ruled for nearly 50 years. Charles did not have James Brooke's forceful personality, and was much more reclusive – probably as a result of working in remote jungle outposts for 10 years in government service. Historian Robert Payne notes that "In James Brooke there was something of the knight errant at the mercy of his dream. Charles was the pure professional, a stern soldier who thought dreaming was the occupation of fools. There was no non-

government based upon consultation with local community chiefs". Brooke realized the importance of maintaining tribal laws and observing local customs; he also recognized that without his protection, the people of Sarawak would be open to exploitation by Europeans and Chinese. He determined to keep such influences out. In 1842, shortly after he was confirmed as Rajah, he wrote: "I hate the idea of a Utopian government, with laws cut and dried ready for the natives... I am going on slowly and surely basing everything on their own laws, consulting all the headmen at every stage, instilling what I think is right – separating the abuses from the customs." Like his successors, James Brooke had great respect for the Dayaks and the Malays, whom he treated as equals. In the 1840s he wrote: "Sarawak belongs to the Malays, Sea Dayaks, Land Dayaks, Kenyahs, Milanos, Muruts, Kadayans, Bisayahs, and other tribes, and not to us. It is for them we labour, not for ourselves."

Unlike most colonial adventurers of the time, Brooke was not in it for the money. He had a hopeless head for figures and his country was constantly in debt – it would have gone bankrupt if it were not for an eccentric English spinster, Angela Burdett-Coutts, who lent him large amounts of money. In his history of *The White Rajahs of Sarawak*, Robert Payne wrote that "he was incapable of drawing up a balance sheet [and] could never concentrate upon details. He had the large view always and large views incline dangerously towards absolute power, and he had seized power with all the strength and cunning that was in him. He possessed the Elizabethan love for power, believing that some Englishmen are granted a special dispensation by God to wield power to the uttermost."

By pacifying pirate-infested coastal districts, Brooke persuaded the Sultan of Brunei to cede him more and more territory, so that towards the end of his reign, Sarawak was a sizeable country. An attack of smallpox, combined with the emotional traumas of a Chinese rebellion in 1857 and the public inquiry into his punitive ambush on the Saribas pirates, seems to have broken his spirit, however. His illness aged him, although an old Malay man, who knew him well, said his eyes remained "fierce like those of a crocodile". Rajah Sir James Brooke (he was knighted by Queen Victoria) visited Sarawak for the last time in 1863 following a succession dispute in which he disinherited his heir, Brooke Johnson. He retired to Dorset in England a disillusioned and embittered man. On Christmas Eve 1867 he had a stroke, and died 6 months later. When news of his death reached Sarawak, guns sounded a thunderous salute across the Sarawak River.

sense about him." He engendered great loyalty, however, in his administrators, who he worked hard for little reward.

Charles maintained his uncle's consultative system of government and formed a Council Negeri, or national council – comprised of his top government officials, Malay leaders and tribal headmen – which met every couple of years to hammer out policy changes. His frugal financial management meant that by 1877 Sarawak was out of debt and the economy gradually expanded. The country was not a wealthy one, however, and had very few natural resources – its soils proved unsuitable for agriculture. In the 1880s, Charles' faith in the Chinese community was sufficiently restored to allow Chinese immigration, and the government subsidized the new settlers. By using 'friendly' downriver Dayak groups to subdue belligerent tribes upriver, Charles managed to pacify the interior by 1880.

When Charles took over from his ailing uncle in 1863, he found himself in charge of a large country; but he proved to be even more of an expansionist. In 1868 he tried to take control of the Baram River valley, but London did not approve the cession of the territory until 1882. It became the Fourth Division; in 1884, Charles acquired the Trusan Valley from the Sultan of Brunei, and in 1890, he annexed Limbang ending a 6-year rebellion by local chiefs against the sultan. The two territories were united to form the Fifth Division, after which Sarawak completely surrounded Brunei. In 1905, the British North Borneo Chartered Company gave up the Lawas Valley to Sarawak too. "By 1890," writes Robert Payne, "Charles was ruling over a country as large as England and Scotland with the help of about twenty European officers." When the First World War broke out in 1914, Charles was in England, and he ruled Sarawak from Cirencester.

The third generation: Charles Vyner Brooke

At the age of 86, Charles handed the reins to his eldest son, Charles Vyner Brooke, in 1916 and died the following year. Vyner was 42 when he became Rajah and had already served his father's government for nearly 20 years. "Vyner was a man of peace, who took no delight in bloodshed and ruled with humanity and compassion," writes Robert Payne. He was a delegator by nature, and under him the old paternalistic style of government gave way to a more professional bureaucracy. On the centenary of the Brooke administration in September 1941, Vyner promulgated a written constitution, and renounced his autocratic powers in favour of working in cooperation with a Supreme Council. This was vehemently opposed by his nephew and heir, Anthony Brooke, who saw it as a move to undermine his succession. To protest against this, and his uncle's decision to appoint a mentally deranged Muslim Englishman as his Chief Secretary, Anthony left for Singapore. The Rajah dismissed him summarily from the service in September 1941. 3 months later the Japanese Imperial Army invaded; Vyner Brooke was in Australia at the time, and his younger brother, Bertram, was ill in London.

Japanese troops took Kuching on Christmas Day 1941 having captured the Miri oilfield a few days earlier. European administrators were interned and many later died. A Kuching-born Chinese, Albert Kwok, led an armed resistance against the Japanese in neighbouring British North Borneo (Sabah) – see page 425 – but in Sarawak, there was no organized guerrilla movement. Iban tribespeople instilled fear into the occupying forces, however, by roaming the jungle taking Japanese heads, which were proudly added to much older longhouse head galleries. Despite the Brooke regime's century-long effort to stamp out head-hunting, the practice was encouraged by Tom Harrisson (one of Sarawak's most famous 'adopted' sons) who parachuted into the Kelabit Highlands towards the end of World War Two and put together an irregular army of upriver tribesmen to fight the Japanese. He offered them 'ten-bob-a-nob' for Japanese heads. Australian forces liberated Kuching on 11 September 1945 and Sarawak was placed under Australian Military Administration for 7 months.

After the war, the Colonial Office in London decided the time had come to bring Sarawak into the modern era, replacing the anachronous White Rajahs, introducing an education system and building a rudimentary infrastructure. The Brookes had become an embarrassment to the British government as they continued to squabble among themselves. Anthony Brooke desperately wanted to claim what he felt was his, while the Colonial Office wanted Sarawak to become a crown colony or revert to Malay rule. No one was sure whether Sarawak wanted the Brookes back or not.

The end of Empire

In February 1946, the ageing Vyner shocked his brother Bertram and his nephew Anthony, the Rajah Muda (or heir apparent), by issuing a proclamation urging the people of Sarawak to accept the King of England as their ruler. In doing so he effectively handed the country over to Britain. Vyner thought the continued existence of Sarawak as the private domain of the Brooke family an anachronism; but Anthony thought it a betrayal. The British government sent a commission to Sarawak to ascertain what the people wanted. In May 1946, the Council Negri agreed – by a 19-16 majority – to transfer power to Britain, provoking protests and demonstrations and resulting in the assassination of the British governor by a Malay in Sibu in 1949. He and three other anti-cessionists were sentenced to death. 2 years later, Anthony Brooke, who remained deeply resentful about the demise of the Brooke Dynasty, abandoned his claim and urged his supporters to end their campaign.

As a British colony, Sarawak's economy expanded and oil and timber production increased which funded the much-needed expansion of education and health services. As with British North Borneo (Sabah), Britain was keen to give Sarawak political independence and, following Malaysian independence in 1957, saw the best means to this end as being through the proposal of Malaysian Prime Minister Tunku Abdul Rahman, who suggested the formation of a federation to include Singapore, Sarawak, Sabah and Brunei as well as the peninsula. In the end, Brunei opted out, Singapore left after 2 years, but Sarawak and Sabah joined the federation, having accepted the recommendations of the British government. Indonesia's President Sukarno denounced the move, claiming it was all part of a neo-colonialist conspiracy. He declared a policy of confrontation – *Konfrontasi*. A United Nations commission which was sent to ensure that the people of Sabah and Sarawak wanted to be part of Malaysia reported that Indonesia's objections were unfounded.

Communists had been active in Sarawak since the 1930s. The *Konfrontasi* afforded the Sarawak Communist Organization (SCO) Jakarta's support against the Malaysian government. The

Konfrontasi

The birth of the Federation of Malaysia on 31 August 1963 was not helped by the presence of heckling spectators. The Philippines was opposed to British North Borneo (Sabah) joining the federation because the territory had been a dependency of the Sultan of Sulu for over 170 years until he had agreed to lease it to the North Borneo Chartered Company in 1877. But Indonesia's objection to the formation of the federation was even more vociferous. In Jakarta, crowds were chanting "Crush Malaysia!" at President Sukarno's bidding. He launched an undeclared war against Malaysia, which became known as *konfrontasi* – confrontation.

Indonesian armed forces made numerous incursions across the jungled frontier between Kalimantan and the two new East Malaysian states; it also landed commandos on the Malaysian peninsula and despatched 300 saboteurs who infiltrated Singapore and launched a bombing campaign. Sarawakian Communists fought alongside Indonesians in the Konfrontasi and there were countless skirmishes with Malaysian and British counter-terrorist forces in which many were killed. Sukarno even managed to secure Soviet weapons, dispatched by Moscow "to help Indonesia crush Malaysia". Konfrontasi fizzled out in 1965 following the Communist-inspired coup attempt in Indonesia, which finally dislodged Sukarno from power.

SCO joined forces with the North Kalimantan Communist Party (NKCO) and were trained and equipped by Indonesia's President Sukarno. But following Jakarta's brutal suppression of the Indonesian Communists – the Partai Komunis Indonesia (PKI) – in the wake of the attempted coup in 1965, Sarawak's Communists fled back across the Indonesian border, along with their Kalimantan comrades. There they continued to wage guerrilla war against the Malaysian government throughout the 1970s. The Sarawak state government offered amnesties to guerrillas wanting to come out of hiding. In 1973 the NKCP leader surrendered along with 482 other guerrillas. A handful remained in the jungle, most of them in the hills around Kuching. The last surrendered in 1990.

CULTURE

PEOPLE

About 30% of Sarawak's population is Iban, another 30% Chinese, 20% is Malay and the remaining fifth is divided into other tribal groups. The people of the interior are classified as Proto-Malays and Deutero-Malays and are divided into at least 12 distinct tribal groups including Iban, Murut (see page 430), Melanau, Bidayuh, Kenyah, Kayan, Kelabit and Penan. In upriver Dayak communities, both men and women traditionally distend their earlobes with brass weights – long earlobes are considered a beauty feature – and practice extensive body tattooing. For the longhouse communities, the staple diet is hill rice, which is cultivated with slash-and-burn farming techniques.

NB For those intending to visit any of Sarawak's tribal peoples, see page 378.

Malay About half of Sarawak's 300,000-strong Malay community lives around the state capital; most of the other half lives in the Limbang Division, near Brunei. The Malays traditionally live near the coast, although today there are small communities far upriver. There are some old wooden Malay houses, with carved facades, in the kampongs along the banks of the Sarawak River in Kuching; other traditional Malay houses still stand on Jalan Datus in Kuching. In all Malay communities, the mosque is the centre of the village, but while their faith is important to them, the strictures of Islam are generally less rigorously enforced in Sarawak than on the peninsula. Of all the Malays in Malaysia, the Sarawak Malays are probably the most easy-going. During the days of the White Rajahs, the Malays were recruited into government service, as they were on the Malay peninsula. They were renowned as good administrators and the men were mostly literate in Jawi script. Over the years there has been much intermarriage between the Malay and Melanau communities. Traditionally, the Malays were fishermen and farmers.

Chinese Hakka goldminers had already settled at Bau, upriver from Kuching, long before James Brooke arrived in 1839. Cantonese, Teochew and Hokkien merchants also set up in Kuching, but the Brookes did not warm to the Chinese community, believing the traders would exploit the Dayak communities if they were allowed to venture upriver. In the 1880s, however, Rajah Charles Brooke allowed the immigration of large numbers of Chinese – mainly Foochow – who settled in coastal towns like Sibu (see page 383). Many became farmers and ran rubber smallholdings. The Sarawak government subsidized the immigrants for the first year. During the Brooke era, the only government-funded schools were for Malays and few tribal people ever received a formal education. The Chinese however, set up and funded their own private schools and many attended Christian missionary schools, so they formed a relatively prosperous, educated elite. Now the Chinese comprise nearly a third of the state's population and are almost as numerous as the Iban; they are the middlemen, traders, shopkeepers,

Tribal tattoos

Tattooing is practiced by many indigenous groups in Borneo, but the most intricate designs are those of the upriver Orang Ulu tribes. Designs vary from group to group and for different parts of the body. Circular designs are mostly used for the shoulder, chest or wrists, while stylized dragon-dogs (*aso*), scorpions and dragons are used on the thigh and, for the Iban, on the throat. Tattoos can mean different things; for the man it is a symbol of bravery and for women, a good tattoo is a beauty-feature. More elaborate designs often denote high social status in Orang Ulu communities – the Kayans, for example, reserved the *aso* design for the upper classes and slaves were barred from tattooing themselves at all. In these Orang Ulu groups, the ladies have the most impressive tattoos; the headman's daughter has her hands, arms and legs completely covered in a finely patterned tattoo. Designs are first carved on a block of wood, which is then smeared with ink. The design is printed on the body and then punctured into the skin with needles dipped in ink, usually made from a mixture of sugar, water and soot. Rice is smeared over the inflamed area to prevent infection, but it usually swells up for some time.

Tatooed Kenowit, with pendulous ear-lobes, *Illustrated London News*, 10 November 1849

timber *towkays* (magnates) and express-boat owners. At the last census on 30 June 1990, the Chinese population numbered 483,301 with similar numbers of Foochow and Hakka (each representing 32% of the total), being the largest groups. Hokkien constitute 13% of the Chinese population, and Teochew, 9%.

Iban Sarawak's best known erstwhile head- hunters make up nearly a third of the state's population and while some have moved to coastal towns for work, many remain in their traditional longhouses. But with Iban men now earning good money in the timber and oil industries, it is increasingly common to see longhouses bristling with television aerials, equipped with fridges, self-cleaning ovens and flush-toilets, and with Land Cruisers in the car park. Even modern longhouses retain the traditional features of gallery, verandah and doors. The Iban are an out-going people and usually extend a warm welcome to visitors. Iban women are skilled weavers; even today a girl is not considered eligible until she has proven her skills at the loom by weaving a ceremonial textile, the *pua kumbu* (see page 350). The Ibans love to party, and during the Gawai harvest festival (June), visitors are particularly welcome to drink copious amounts of *tuak* (rice wine) and dance through the night.

The Iban are shifting cultivators who originated in the Kapuas River basin of West Kalimantan and migrated into Sarawak's Second Division in the early 16th century, settling along the Batang Lupar, Skrang and Saribas rivers. By the early 19th century, they had begun to spill into the Rejang River valley. It was this growing pressure on land as more and more migrants settled in the river valleys that led to fighting and headhunting (see page 348). Probably because they were shifting cultivators, the Iban remained in closely bonded family groups and were a classless society. Historian Mary Turnbull says "they retained their pioneer social organization of nuclear family groups living together in longhouses and did not evolve more sophisticated political institutions. Long-settled families acquired prestige, but the Ibans did not merge into tribes and had neither chiefs, *rakyat* class, nor slaves."

The Ibans joined local Malay chiefs and turned to piracy – which is how Europeans first came into contact with them. They were dubbed 'Sea Dayaks' as a result – which is really a misnomer as they are an inland people. The name stuck, however, and in the eyes of westerners, it distinguished them from 'Land Dayaks' – who were the Bidayuh people from the Sarawak River area (see page 345). While Rajah James Brooke only won the Ibans' loyalty after he had crushed them in battle (see page 337), he had great admiration of them, and they bore no bitterness towards him. He once described them as "good-looking a set of men, or devils, as one could cast eye on. Their wiry and supple limbs might have been compared to the troops of wild horses that followed Mazeppa in his perilous flight." The Iban have a very easy-going attitude to love and sex (best explained in Redmond O'Hanlon's book *Into the Heart of Borneo*). Free love is the general rule among Iban communities which have not become evangelical Christians, although once married, the Iban divorce rate is low and they are monogamous.

Melanau The Melanau are a handsome, relaxed and humorous people. Rajah James Brooke, like generations of men before and after him, thought the Melanau girls particularly pretty. He said that they had "agreeable countenances, with the dark, rolling, open eye of the Italians, and nearly as fair as most of that race". The Melanau live along the coast between the Baram and Rejang rivers; originally they lived in magnificent communal houses built high off the ground, like the one that has been reconstructed at the Cultural Village in Kuching, but these have long since disappeared. The houses were designed to afford protection from incessant pirate raids (see page 337), for the Melanau were easy pickings, being coastal people. Their stilt-houses were often up to 12m off the ground. Today most Melanau live in Malay-style pile-houses facing the river. Hedda Morrison, in her classic 1957 book *Sarawak*, says: "As a result of living along the rivers in swamp country, the Melanaus are an exceptionally amphibious people. The children learn to swim almost before they can walk. Nearly all progress is by canoe, sometimes even to visit the house next door."

The traditional Melanau fishing boat is called a *barong*. Melanau fishermen employed a unique fishing technique. They would anchor palm leaves at sea as they discovered that shoals of fish would seek refuge under them. After rowing out to the leaves, one fisherman would dive off his barong and chase the fish into the nets which his colleague hung over the side. The Melanaus were also noted for their sago production – which they ate

Shifting cultivation – how to grow hill rice

Winding upriver on Sarawak's express boats, it is hard not to notice that the hillsides on either bank have been shaved of their jungle: evidence of shifting cultivation (see page 322). The Iban, who live in the middle reaches of Sarawak's big rivers, have always been shifting cultivators – the deep peat soils meant it was impossible to farm wet-rice. Any secondary forest (*belukar*) seen growing on the riverside slopes is really just fallow land, and in 8-15 years' time, it will be cut again and the *ladang* will be replanted. The Malaysian government claims there are 3 million hectares of land like this in Sarawak, left idle, through slash-and-burn cultivation. In defence of its environmental record, it says shifting cultivators are more destructive than logging firms and cause serious soil erosion.

What the government tends to overlook, however, is that the rivers were clear before the loggers arrived and that the swidden farmers – in labour terms – managed highly productive agricultural systems. As long as the land is allowed to lie fallow for long enough, the Iban can produce rice with far less effort than lowland wet rice farmers. The Iban clear their designated hillsides in the middle of the year and burn them off in August. In September, planting starts: holes are made in the soot-blackened soil with sharp-pointed dibble-sticks called *tugal*. Women drop a few grains into each hole and the rice is interplanted with maize. Harvesting is done by the women, who use special knives called *ketap*.

instead of rice. At Kuching's Cultural Village there is a demonstration of traditional sago production, showing how the starch-bearing pith is removed, mashed, dried and ground into flour. Most Melanau are now Muslim and have assimilated with the Malays through intermarriage. Originally, however, they were animists (animist Melanau are called *Likaus*) and were particularly famed for their elaborately carved 'sickness images', which represented the form of spirits which caused specific illnesses (see page 352).

Bidayuh In the 19th century, Sarawak's European community called the Bidayuh 'Land Dayaks' – mainly to distinguish them from the Iban 'Sea Dayak' pirates. The Bidayuh make up 8.4% of the population and are concentrated to the west of the Kuching area, towards the Kalimantan border. There are also related groups living in West Kalimantan. They were virtually saved from extinction by the White Rajahs. Because the Bidayuh were quiet, mild-mannered people, they were at the mercy of the Iban head-hunters and the Brunei Malays who taxed and enslaved them. The Brookes afforded them protection from both groups.

Most live in modern longhouses and are dry rice farmers. Their traditional longhouses are exactly like Iban ones, but without the *tanju* verandah. The Bidayuh tribe comprises five sub-groups: the Jagoi, Biatah, Bukar-Sadong, Selakau and Lara, all of whom live in far West Sarawak. They are the state's best traditional plumbers, and are known for their ingenious gravity-fed bamboo water-supply systems. They are bamboo-specialists, making everything from cooking pots and utensils to finely carved musical instruments (see page 351) from it. Among other tribal groups, the Bidayuh are renowned for their rice wine and sugar cane toddy. Henry Keppel, who with Rajah James Brooke fought the Bidayuhs' dreaded enemies, the Sea Dayaks, described an evening spent with the Land Dayaks thus: "They ate and drank, and asked for everything, but stole nothing."

Orang Ulu The jungle – or upriver – people encompass a swathe of different small tribal groups. Orang Ulu longhouses are usually made of belian (ironwood) and

The palang – the stimulant that makes a vas diferens

One of the more exotic features of upriver sexuality is the *palang*, or penis pin, which is the versatile jungle version of the French tickler. Traditionally, women suffer heavy weights being attached to their earlobes to enhance their sex-appeal. In turn, men are expected to enhance their physical attributes and entertain their womenfolk by drilling a hole in their organs, into which they insert a range of items, aimed at heightening their partner's pleasure on the rattan mat. Tom Harrisson, a former curator of the Sarawak Museum, was intrigued by the palang; some suspect his authority on the subject stemmed from first-hand experience. He wrote: "When the device is put into use, the owner adds whatever he prefers to elaborate and accentuate its intention. A lively range of objects can so be employed – from pigs' bristles and bamboo shavings to pieces of metal, seeds, beads and broken glass. The effect, of course, is to enlarge the diameter of the male organ inside the female." It is said that many Dayak men, even today, have the tattoo man come and drill a hole in them as they stand in the river. As the practice has gone on for centuries, one can only assume that its continued popularity proves it is worth the agony.

are built to last. They are well known swordsmiths, forging lethal *parangs* from any piece of scrap metal they can lay their hands on. They are also very artistic people, are skilled carvers and painters and are famed for their beadwork – taking great care decorating even simple household utensils. Most Orang Ulu are plastered with traditional tattoos (see page 343).

Kenyah and Kayan These two closely related groups were the traditional rivals of the Ibans and were notorious for their warlike ways. Historian Robert Payne, in his history *The White Rajahs of Sarawak* described the Kayans of the upper Rejang as "a treacherous tribe, [who] like nothing better than putting out the eyes and cutting the throats of prisoners, or burning them alive". They probably originally migrated into Sarawak from the Apo Kayan district in East Kalimantan. Kenyah and Kayan raids on downriver people were greatly feared, but their power was broken by Charles Brooke, just before he became the second White Rajah, in 1863. The Kayans had retreated upstream above the Pelagus Rapids on the Rejang River (see page 388), to an area they considered out of reach from their Iban enemies. In 1862 they killed two government officers at Kanowit and went on a killing spree. Charles Brooke led 15,000 Ibans past the Pelagus Rapids, beyond Belaga and attacked the Kayans in their heartland. Many hundreds were killed. In November 1924, Rajah Vyner Brooke presided over a peace-making ceremony between the Orang Ulu and the Iban in Kapit (there is a photograph of the ceremony on display in the Kapit Museum).

The Kenyahs and Kayans in Sarawak live in pleasant upriver valleys and are settled rice farmers. They are very different from other tribal groups, have a completely different language (which has ancient Malayo-Polynesian roots) and are class-conscious, with a well-defined social hierarchy. Traditionally their society was composed of aristocrats, noblemen, commoners and slaves (who were snatched during raids on other tribes). One of the few things the Kayan and Kenyah have in common with other Dayak groups is the fact that they live in longhouses, although even these are of a different design, and are much more carefully constructed, in ironwood. Subgroups include the Kejamans, Skapans, Berawans and Sebops. Many have now been converted to Christianity.

In contrast to their belligerent history, the Kenyahs and Kayans are much more introverted than the Ibans; they are slow and deliberate in their ways, and are very

Green pen pals: Mahathir versus Manser

Few people infuriate Prime Minister Datuk Seri Mahathir Mohamad more than Bruno Manser, green activist and self-styled defender of the tribal peoples of Borneo, and particularly the Penan. Manser, a Swiss, spent six years living with the Penan and now fights for their rights. Mahathir's views on Manser, 'green imperialism' in general, and the 'plight' of the tribals comes through nowhere clearer than in a letter he wrote to Manser in March 1992.

Herr Manser

If any Penan or policeman gets killed or wounded in the course of restoring law and order in Sarawak, you will have to take the blame. It is you and your kind who instigated the Penans to take the law into their own hands and to use poison darts, bows, arrows and parangs to fight against the Government.

As a Swiss living in the laps of luxury with the world's highest standard of living, it is the height of arrogance for you to advocate that the Penans live on maggots and monkeys in their miserable huts, subjected to all kinds of diseases. It is fine for you to spend a short holiday tasting the Penan way of life and then returning to the heated comfort of your Swiss chalet. But do you really expect the Penans to subsist on monkeys until the year 2500 or 3000 or forever? Have they no right to a better way of life? What right have you to condemn them to a primitive life forever?

Your Swiss ancestors were hunters also. But you are now one of the most 'advanced' people living in beautiful Alpine villages, with plenty of leisure and very high income. But you want to deny even a slight rise in the standard of living for the Penans and other Malaysians.

The Penans may tell you that their primitive life is what they like. That is because they are not given a chance to live a better life like the other tribes in Sarawak. Those of the Penans who have left the jungle are educated and are earning a better living have no wish to return to their primitive ways. You are trying to deny them their chance for a better life so that you can enjoy studying primitive peoples the way you study animals. Penans are people and they should be respected as people. If you had a chance to be educated and live a better life, they too deserve that chance.

Stop being arrogant and thinking that it is the white man's burden to decide the fate of the peoples in this world. Malaysians, the Penans included, are an independent people and are quite capable of looking after themselves. Swiss imperialism is as disgusting as other European imperialism. It is about time that you stop your arrogance and your intolerable European superiority. You are no better than the Penans. If you have a right to decide for yourself, why can't you leave the Penans to decide for themselves after they have been given a chance to improve their living standards.

Dr Mahathir Mohamad

(reproduced in *Far Eastern Economic Review*, 27 August 1992).

artistic and musical. They are also renowned for their parties; visitors recovering from drinking *borak* rice beer have their faces covered in soot before being thrown in the river. This is to test the strength of the newly forged friendship with visitors, who are ill-advised to lose their sense of humour on such occasions.

Penan Perhaps Southeast Asia's only remaining true hunter-gatherers live mainly in the upper Rejang area and Limbang. They are nomads and are related – linguistically at least – to the Punan, former nomadic forest-dwellers who are now settled in longhouses along the upper Rejang. The Malaysian government has long wanted the Penan to sedentarise too, but has had limited success in attracting them to expensive new longhouses. Groups of Penan hunter-gatherers still wander through the forest in groups to hunt wild pigs, birds and monkeys and search for sago palms from which they make their staple food, sago flour. The Penan are considered to be the jungle experts by all the other inland tribes. Because they live in the shade of the forest, their skin is relatively fair.

Skulls in the longhouse: heads you win

Although head-hunting has been largely stamped out in Borneo, there is still the odd reported case, once every few years. But until the early 20th century, head-hunting was commonplace among many Dayak tribes, and the Iban were the most fearsome of all. Following a head-hunting expedition, the freshly taken heads were skinned, placed in rattan nets and smoked over a fire – or sometimes boiled. The skulls were then hung from the rafters of the longhouse and they possessed the most powerful form of magic.

The skulls were considered trophies of manhood (they increased a young bachelor's eligibility), symbols of bravery and they testified to the unity of a longhouse. The longhouse had to hold festivals – or *gawai* – to appease the spirits of the skulls. Once placated, the heads were believed to bring great blessing – they could ward off evil spirits, save villages from epidemics, produce rain and increase the yield of rice harvests. Heads that were insulted or ignored were capable of wreaking havoc in the form of bad dreams, plagues, floods and fires. To keep the spirits of the skulls happy, they would be offered food and cigarettes and made to feel welcome in their new home. Because the magical powers of a skull faded with time, fresh heads were always in demand. Tribes without heads were considered spiritually weak.

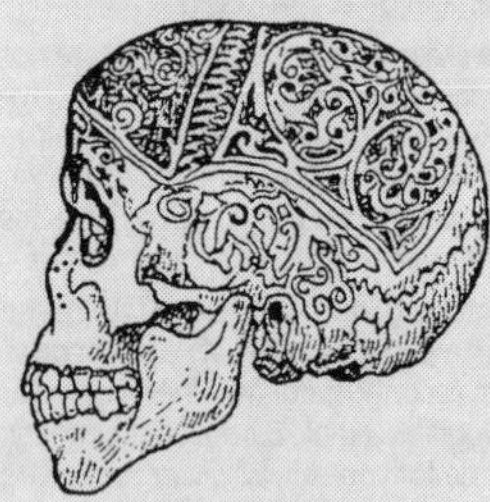

Dayak decorated human skull
Adapted from: Hersey, Irwin (1991) *Indonesian primitive art*, OUP: Singapore

Today, young Dayak men no longer have to take heads to gain respect. They are, however, expected to go on long journeys (the equivalent of the Australian aborigines' Walkabout) – or *bejalai* in Iban. The one unspoken rule is that they should come back with plenty of good stories, and, these days, as most berjalai expeditions translate into stints at timber camps or on oil rigs, they are expected to come home bearing video recorders, TV sets and motorbikes. Many Dayak tribes continue to celebrate their head-hunting ceremonies. In Kalimantan, for example, the *Adat Ngayau* ceremony uses coconut shells, wrapped in leaves, as substitutes for freshly cut heads.

They have a great affection for the coolness of the forest and until the 1960s were rarely seen by the outside world. For them sunlight is extremely unpleasant. They are broad and much more stocky than other river people and are extremely shy, having had little contact with the outside world. Most of their trade is conducted with remote Kayan, Kenyah and Kelabit longhouse communities on the edge of the forest.

In the eyes of the West, the Penan have emerged as the 'noble savages' of the late 20th century for their spirited defence of their lands against encroachment by logging companies. But it is not just recently that they have been cheated: they have long been the victims of other upriver tribes. A Penan, bringing baskets full of rotan to a Kenyah or Kayan longhouse to sell may end up exchanging his produce for one bullet or shotgun cartridge. In his way of thinking, a bullet will kill one wild boar which will last his family 10 days. In turn, the buyer knows he can sell the same rotan downstream for RM50-100. Penan still use the blowpipe for small game, but shotguns for wild pig. If they buy the shotgun cartridges for themselves, they have to exchange empties first. Some of their shotguns date back to the Second World War, when the British supplied them to upriver tribespeople to fight the Japanese. During the Brooke era, a large annual market would be held which both Chinese traders and Orang Ulu (including Penan) used to attend; the district officer would have to act as judge to ensure the Penan did not get cheated.

Those wishing to learn more about the Penan should refer to Denis Lau's *The Vanishing Nomads of Borneo* (Interstate Publishing, 1987). Lau has lived among the Penan and has photographed them for many years; some of his recent photographs appear in the photographic collection entitled *Malaysia – Heart of Southeast Asia* (published by Archipelago Press, 1991).

Kelabit The Kelabits, who live in the highlands at the headwaters of the Baram River, are closely related to the Murut (see page 430) and the Lun Dayeh of Kalimantan. It was into Kelabit territory that Tom Harrisson parachuted with Allied Special Forces towards the end of World War Two. The Kelabit Highlands, around Bario, were chosen because they were so remote. Of all the tribes in Sarawak, the Kelabits have the sturdiest, strongest builds, which is usually ascribed to the cool and invigorating mountain climate. They are skilled hill-rice farmers and their fragrant Bario rice is prized throughout Sarawak. The highland climate also allows them to cultivate vegetables. Kelabit parties are also famed as boisterous occasions, and large quantities of *borak* rice beer are consumed – despite the fact that the majority of Kelabits have converted to Christianity. They are regarded as among the most hospitable people in Borneo. For information on religion, see page 330.

DANCE, DRAMA AND MUSIC

Dance

Dayak tribes are renowned for their singing and dancing, and the most famous is the hornbill dance. In her book *Sarawak*, Hedda Morrison writes: "The Kayans are probably the originators of the stylized war dance which is now common among the Ibans but the girls are also extremely talented and graceful dancers. One of their most delightful dances is the hornbill dance, when they tie hornbill feathers to the ends of their fingers which accentuate their slow and graceful movements. For party purposes everyone in the longhouse joins in and parades up and down the communal room led by one or two musicians and a group of girls who sing." On these occasions, drink flows freely. With the Ibans, it is *tuak* (rice wine), with the Kayan and Kenyah it is *borak*, a bitter rice beer. After being entertained by dancers, a visitor is under compunction to drink a large glassful, before bursting into song and doing a dance routine themselves. The best guideline for visitors on how to handle such occasions is provided by Redmond O'Hanlon in his book *Into the Heart of Borneo*. The general rule of thumb is to be prepared to make an absolute fool of yourself, throwing all inhibition to the wind. This will immediately endear you to your hosts.

The most common dances in Sarawak are: *Kanjet Ngeleput* (Orang Ulu) dance performed in full warrior regalia, traditionally celebrating the return of a hunter or head-hunters. *Mengarang Menyak* (Melanau) dance depicting the processing of sago from the cutting of the tree to the production of the sago pearls or pellets. *Ngajat Bebunuh* (Iban) war dance, performed in full battle dress and armed with sword and shield. *Ngajat Induk* (Iban) performed as a welcome dance for those visiting longhouses. *Ngajat Lesong* (Iban) dance of the *lesong* or mortar, performed during gawai. *Tarian Kris* (Malay) dance of the *kris*, the Malay dagger, which symbolizes power, courage and strength. *Tarian Rajang Beuh* (Bidayuh) dance performed after the harvesting season as entertainment for guests to the longhouse. *Tarian Saga Lupa* (Orang Ulu) performed by women to welcome guests to the longhouse, accompanied by the *sape* (see below). *Ule Nugan* (Orang Ulu) dance to the sound of the *kerebo bulo*, or bamboo slates. The music is designed to inspire the spirit of the paddy seeds to flourish. The male dancers hold a dibbling stick used in the planting of hill rice.

Music

Gongs range from the single large gong, the tawak, to the engkerumong, a set of small gongs, arranged on a horizontal rack, with five players. An engkerumong ensemble usually involves between five and seven drums, which include two suspended gongs (*tawak* and *bendai*) and 5 hour-glass drums (*ketebong*). They are used to celebrate victory in battle or to welcome home a successful head-hunting expedition. Sarawak's Bidayuh also make a bamboo gong called a pirunchong. The jatang uton is a wooden xylophone which can be rolled up like a rope ladder; the keys are struck with hardwood sticks.

The Bidayuh, Sarawak's bamboo-specialists, make two main stringed instruments – a 3-stringed cylindrical bamboo harp called a tinton and the rabup, a rotan-stringed fiddle with a bamboo cup. The Orang Ulu (Kenyah and Kayan tribes) play a 4-stringed guitar called a sape, which is also common on the Kalimantan side of the border. It is the most common and popular lute-type instrument, whose body, neck and board are cut from one piece of softwood. It is used in Orang Ulu dances and by witch doctors. It is usually played by two musicians, one keeping the rhythm, the other the melody. Traditional sapes had rotan strings, today they use wire guitar strings and electric pick-ups. Another stringed instrument, more usually found in Kalimantan, or deep in Sarawak's interior, is the *satang*, a bamboo tube with strings around the outside, cut from the bamboo and tightened with pegs.

One of the best known instruments in Sarawak is the engkerurai (or *keluri*), the bagpipes of Borneo, which is usually associated with the Kenyahs and Kayans, but is also found in Sabah (where it is called a *sompoton*). It is a hand-held organ in which four vertical bamboo pan-pipes of different lengths are fixed to a gourd, which acts as the wind chamber. Simple engkerurai can only manage one chord; more sophisticated ones allow the player to use two pipes for the melody, while the others provide an harmonic drone. The Bidayuh are specialists in bamboo instruments and make flutes of various sizes; big thick ones are called branchi, long ones with five holes are kroto and small ones are called nchiyo.

TEXTILES

The weaving of cotton *pua kumbu* is one of the oldest Iban traditions, and literally means 'blanket' or 'cover'. Iban legend recounts that 24 generations ago the God of War, Singalang Burong, taught his son how to weave the most precious of all *pua*, the *lebor api*. Dyed deep red, this cloth was traditionally used to wrap heads taken in battle.

The weaving of *pua kumbu* is done by the women and is a vital skill for a would-be bride to acquire. There are two main methods employed in making and decorating pua kumbu: the more common is the *ikat* tie-dyeing technique, known as *ngebat* by the Iban. The other method is the *pileh*, or floating weft. The Ibans use a warp-beam loom which is tied to two posts, to which the threads are attached. There is a breast-beam at the weaving end, secured by a back strap to the weaver. A pedal, beneath the threads, lowers and raises the alternate threads which are separated by rods. The woven material is tightly packed by a beater. The material is tie-dyed in the warp.

Because the pua kumbu is made by the warp-tie-dyeing method, the number of colours is limited. The most common are a rich browny-brick-red colour and black, as well as the undyed white sections; blues and greens are used in more modern materials. Traditionally, pua kumbu were hung in longhouses during ceremonies and were used to cover images during rituals. The designs and patterns are representations of deities which figure in Iban myths and are believed to protect individuals from harm; they are passed down from generation to generation. Such designs, with deep spiritual significance, can only be woven by wives and daughters of chiefs. Other designs and patterns are representations of birds and animals, including hornbills, crocodiles, monitor lizards and shrimps, which are either associated with worship or are sources of food. Symbolic representations of trees, plants and fruits are also included in the designs as well as the events of everyday life. A typical example is the zigzag pattern which represents the act of crossing a river – the zigzag course is explained by the canoe's attempts to avoid strong currents. Many of the symbolic representations are highly stylized and can be difficult to pick out.

Malay women in Sarawak are traditionally renowned for their *kain songket*, sarongs woven with silver and gold thread.

CRAFTS

Woodcarvings Many of Sarawak's tribal groups are skilled carvers, producing everything from huge burial poles (like the Kejaman pole outside the Sarawak museum in Kuching) to small statues, masks and other decorative items and utensils. The Kenyah's traditional masks, which are used during festivals, are elaborately carved and often have large protruding eyes. Eyes are always emphasized, as they are to frighten the enemy. Other typical items carved by tribal groups include spoons, stools, doors, walking sticks, *sapes* (guitars), ceremonial shields, tops of water containers, tattoo plaques, and the hilts of *parang ilang* (ceremonial knives). The most popular Iban motif is the hornbill, which holds an honoured place in Iban folklore (see page 327), being the messenger for the sacred Brahminy kite,

Mask, from Henry Ling Roth's (1896), *The natives of Sarawak and British North Borneo.*

the ancestor of the Iban. Another famous Iban carving is the sacred measuring stick called the *tuntun peti*, used to trap deer and wild boar; it is carved to represent a forest spirit. The Kayan and Kenyahs' most common motif is the *aso*, a dragon-like dog with a long snout. It also has religious and mythical significance. The Kenyah and Kayan carve huge burial structures, or *salong*, as well as small ear pendants made of hornbill ivory. The elaborately carved masks used for their harvest ceremony are unique.

Bamboo carving The Bidayuh ('Land Dayaks') are best known for their bamboo carving. The bamboo is usually carved in shallow relief and then stained with dye, which leaves a pattern in the areas which have been scraped out. The Bidayuh carve utilitarian objects as well as ceremonial shields, musical instruments and spirit images used to guard the longhouse. The Cultural Village (Kampong Budaya) in Kuching is one of the best places to see demonstrations of Bidayuh carving.

Blowpipes Blowpipes are made by several Orang Ulu tribes in Sarawak and are usually carved from hardwood – normally belian (ironwood). The first step is to make a rough cylinder about 10 cm

Mask, from Henry Ling Roth's (1896), *The natives of Sarawak and British North Borneo.*

wide and 2.5m long. This rod is tied to a platform, from which a hole is bored through the rod. The bore is skillfully chiselled by an iron rod with a pointed end. The rod is then sanded down to about 5 cm in diameter. Traditionally, the sanding was done using the rough underside of *macaranga* leaves. The darts are made from the *nibong* and wild sago palms and the poison itself is the sap of the *upas* (Ipoh) tree (*Antiaris toxicari*) into which the point is dipped.

Beadwork Among many Kenyah, Kayan, Bidayuh, and Kelabit groups, beads have long been symbols of status and wealth; necklaces, skull caps and girdles are handed down from generation to generation. Smaller glass – or plastic – beads (usually imported from Europe) are used to decorate baby carriers, baskets, headbands, jackets, hats, sheaths for knives, tobacco boxes and handbags. Beaded baby carriers are mainly used by the Kelabit, Kenyah and Kayan and often have shells and animals' teeth attached which make a rattling sound to frighten away evil spirits. Rounded patterns require more skill than geometric patterns, the quality of the pattern used to reflect the status of the owner. Only upper-classes are permitted to have beadwork depicting 'high-class' motifs such as human faces or figures. Early beads were made from clay, metal, glass, bone or shell (the earliest have been found in the Niah Caves). Later on, many of the beads that found their way upriver were from Venice, Greece, India and China – even Roman and Alexandrian beads have made their way into Borneo's jungle. Orang Ulu traded them for jungle produce. Tribes attach different values to particular types of beads.

Sickness images The coastal Melanau, who have now converted to Islam, but used to be animists, have a tradition of carving sickness images (*blum*). They are usually carved from sago or other soft woods. The image is believed to take the form of the evil spirit causing a specific illness. They are carved in different forms according to the ailment. The Melanau developed elaborate healing ceremonies; if someone was struck down by a serious illness, the spirit medium would perform the *berayun* ceremony, using the blum to extract the illness from the victim's body. Usually, the image is in a half-seated position, with the hands crossed across the part of the body which was affected. During the ceremony, the medium attempts to draw the spirit out of the sick person and into the image, after which it is set adrift on a river in a tiny purpose-made boat or it is hidden in the jungle. These images are roughly carved and can, from time to time, be found in antique shops.

Basketry A wide variety of household items are woven from rotan, bamboo, bemban reed as well as nipah and pandanus palms. Malaysia supplies 30% of the world's demand for *manau rotan* (rattan). Basketry is practised by nearly all the ethnic groups in Sarawak and they are among the most popular handicrafts in the state. A variety of baskets are made for harvesting, storing and winnowing paddy as well as for collecting and storing other items. The Penan are reputed to produce the finest rattan sleeping mats – closely plaited and pliable – as well as the *ajat* and *ambong* baskets (all-purpose jungle rucksacks, also produced by the Kayan and Kenyah). Many of the native patterns used in basketry are derived from Chinese patterns and take the form of geometrical shapes and stylized birds. The Bidayuh also make baskets from either rotan or sago bark strips. The most common Bidayuh basket is the *tambok*, which is simply patterned and has bands of colour; it also has thin wooden supports on each side.

Hats The Melanau people living around Bintulu make a big colourful conical hat from nipah leaves called a *terindak*. Orang Ulu hats are wide-brimmed and are often decorated with beadwork or cloth appliqué. Kelabit and Lun Bawan women wear skull-caps made entirely of beads, which are heavy and extremely valuable.

Pottery Malaysia's most distinctive ceramic designs are found in Sarawak where Iban potters reproduce shapes and patterns of Chinese porcelain which was originally brought to Borneo by traders centuries ago (see page 358). Copies of these old Chinese jars are mostly used for brewing *tuak* rice wine.

MODERN SARAWAK

POLITICS

In 1957 Kuala Lumpur was keen to have Sarawak and Sabah in the Federation of Malaysia and offered the two states a degree of autonomy, allowing their local governments control over state finances, agriculture and forestry. Sarawak's racial mix was reflected in its chaotic state politics. The Ibans dominated the Sarawak National Party (SNAP), which provided the first Chief Minister, Datuk Stephen Kalong Ningkan. He raised a storm over Kuala Lumpur's introduction of Bahasa Malaysia in schools and complained bitterly about the federal government's policy of filling the Sarawakian civil service with Malays from the peninsula. An 'us' and 'them' mentality developed: in Sarawak, the Malay word *semenanjung* – peninsula – was used to label the newcomers. To many, semenanjung was Malaysia, Sarawak was Sarawak.

In 1966 the federal government ousted the SNAP, and a new Muslim-dominated government – led by the Sarawak Alliance – took over in Kuching. But there was still strong political opposition to federal encroachment. Throughout the 1970s, as in Sabah, Sarawak's strongly Muslim government drew the state closer and closer to the peninsula: it supported *Rukunegara* – the policy of Islamization – and promoted the use of Bahasa Malaysia. Muslims make up less than one third of the population of Sarawak. The Malays, Melanaus and Chinese communities grew rich from the timber industry; the Ibans and the Orang Ulu (the upriver tribespeople) saw little in the way of development. They did not reap the benefits of the expansion of education and social services, they were unable to get public sector jobs and to make matters worse, logging firms were encroaching on their native lands and threatening their traditional lifestyles.

It has only been in more recent years that the tribespeoples' political voice has been heard at all. In 1983, Iban members of SNAP – which was a part of Prime Minister Dr Mahathir Mohamad's ruling Barisan Nasional (National Front) coalition – split to form the Party Bansa Dayak Sarawak (PBDS), which, although it initially remained in the coalition, became more outspoken on native affairs. At about the same time, international outrage was sparked over the exploitation of Sarawak's tribespeople by politicians and businessmen involved in the logging industry. The plight of the Penan hunter-gatherers came to world attention due to their blockades of logging roads (see page 412) and the resulting publicity highlighted the rampant corruption and greed that characterized modern Sarawak's political economy.

The National Front remain firmly in control in Sarawak. But unlike neighbouring Sabah, or indeed any other state in the country with the exception of PAS-ruled Kelantan, Sarawak's politicians are not dominated by the centre. The chief minister of Sarawak is Taib Mahmud, a Melanau, and his Parti Pesaka Bumiputra Bersatu is a member of the UMNO-dominated National Front. But in Sarawak itself UMNO wields little power.

Today there are many in Sarawak as well as in Sabah, who wish their governments had opted out of the Federation like Brunei. Sarawak is of great economic importance to Malaysia, thanks to its oil, gas and timber. The state now accounts for more than one third of Malaysia's petroleum production (worth more than US$800mn/year) and more than half of its natural gas. As with neighbouring Sabah however, 95% of Sarawak's oil and gas revenues go directly into federal coffers.

A famous cartoon in a Sarawak newspaper once depicted a cow grazing in Sarawak and being milked on the peninsula. While Sarawak has traditionally been closer to federal government than Sabah (there has never been any hint of a seccessionist movement), discontent surfaces from time to time. In late-1989, all it took was a quarrel over a football match between Sarawak and Selangor state to touch off deep-seated resentments in Kuching.

KUCHING

Shortly after dawn on 15 August 1839 James Brooke sailed round a bend in the Sarawak River and, from the deck of his schooner, *The Royalist*, had his first view of Kuching. According to the historian Robert Payne, he saw "...a very small town of brown huts and longhouses made of wood or the hard stems of the nipah palm, sitting in brown squalor on the edge of mudflats." The settlement, 32 km upriver from the sea, had been established less than a decade earlier by Brunei chiefs who had come to oversee the mining of antimony in the Sarawak River valley. The antimony – used as an alloy to harden other metals, particularly pewter – was exported to Singapore where the tin-plate industry was developing.

By the time James Brooke had become Rajah in 1841, the town had a population of local Malays and Dayaks and Cantonese, Hokkien and Teochew traders. Chinatown dominated the south side of the river while the Malay kampongs were strung out along the riverbanks to the west. A few Indian traders also set up in the bazaar, among the Chinese shophouses. Under Charles Brooke, the second of the White Rajahs, Kuching began to flourish; he commissioned most of the

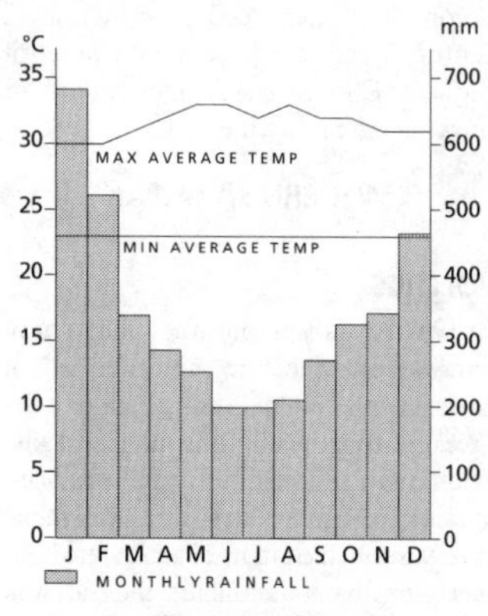

Climate: Kuching

A town called Cat

There are a number of explanations as to how Sarawak's capital acquired the name 'Cat'. (*Kuching* means 'cat' in Malay – although today it is more commonly spelt *kucing* as in modern Bahasa, '*c*' is pronounced '*ch*'.) Local legend has it that James Brooke, pointing towards the settlement across the river, inquired what it was called. Whoever he asked, mistakenly thought he was pointing at a passing cat. If that seems a little far-fetched, the Sarawak museum offers a few more plausible alternatives. Kuching may have been named after the wild cats (*kucing hutan*) which, in the 19th century, were commonly seen along jungled banks of the Sarawak River. Another theory is that it was called after the fruit *buah mata kucing* ('cat's eyes'), which grows locally. Most likely however, is the theory that the town may originally have been known as *Cochin* – or port – a word commonly used across India and Indochina.

town's main public buildings. Ranee Margaret Brooke (Charles' wife) wrote: "The little town looked so neat and fresh and prosperous under the careful jurisdiction of the Rajah and his officers, that it reminded me of a box of painted toys kept scrupulously clean by a child." Because of Kuching's relative isolation, and the fact that it was not bombed during the Second World War, the town has retained much of its 19th century charm; despite the increasing number of modern high-rise buildings, Chinese shophouses still line many of the narrow streets. Covered sampans, or *perahu tambang*, paddle back and forth across the river from the riverfront esplanade to the kampongs and the Astana on the north bank.

The city, which today has a population of about 70,000, is divided by the Sarawak River; the south is a commercial and residential area, dominated by Chinese while the north shore is predominantly Malay in character with the old kampong houses lining the river. The Astana, Fort Margherita and the Petra Jaya area, with its modern government offices, are also on the north side of the river. The two parts of the city are very different in character and even have separate mayors. Kuching's cosmopolitan make-up is immediately evident from its religious architecture: Chinese and Hindu temples, the imposing state mosque and Protestant and Roman Catholic churches.

Of all the cities in Malaysia, Kuching was worst effected by the smog associated with the fires that engulfed Indonesian Borneo (Kalimantan) in mid-1997 (see page 45). At the peak of the 'emergency' in late September – for that is what it became – the city came to a stop. It was too dangerous to drive and, seemingly, too dangerous to breathe. People were urged to remain indoors. Schools, government offices and factories closed. The port and aiport were also closed. Tourism traffic dropped to virtually zero and for ten days the city stopped. At one point there was even discussion of evacuating the population of the State of Sarawak. People began to buy up necessities and the prices of some commodities rose 500%.

Places of interest

Kuching's biggest attraction is the internationally renowned **Sarawak Museum**, on both sides of Jalan Tun Haji Openg. The old building (to the east of the main road) is a copy of a Normandy town hall, designed by Charles Brooke's French valet. The Rajah was encouraged to build the museum by the naturalist Alfred Russel Wallace, who spent over 2 years in Sarawak, where he wrote his first paper on natural selection. The museum was opened in 1891, extended in 1911, and the new wing built in 1983. Its best-known curators have been naturalist Eric Mjoberg (who made the first ascent of

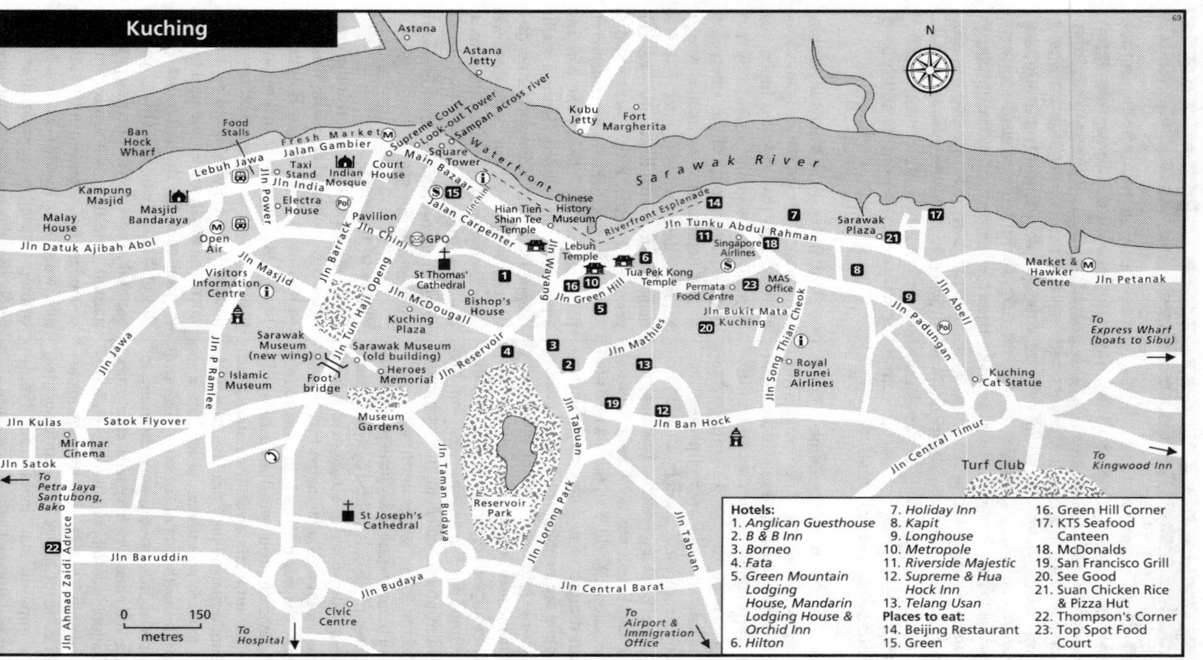
Kuching
N
Astana
Astana Jetty
Kubu Jetty
Fort Margherita
Sarawak River
Waterfront
Riverfront Esplanade
Sampan across river
Look-out Tower
Supreme Court
Ban Hock Wharf
Food Stalls
Fresh Market
Jalan Gambier
Lebuh Jawa
Taxi Stand
Indian Mosque
Court House
Square Tower
Main Bazaar
Kampung Masjid
Masjid Bandaraya
Jln India
Jln Power
Electra House
Malay House
Open Air
Pavilion
Jln China
GPO
Jalan Carpenter
Hian Tien Shian Tee Temple
Chinese History Museum
Jln Datuk Ajibah Abol
Jln Masjid
Visitors Information Centre
Jln Barrack
Jln Tun Haji Openg
St Thomas' Cathedral
Bishop's House
Jln McDougall
Kuching Plaza
Jln Wayang
Lebuh Temple
Jln Green Hill
Tua Pek Kong Temple
Jln Tunku Abdul Rahman
Singapore Airlines
Permata Food Centre
MAS Office
Jln Bukit Mata Kuching
Sarawak Plaza
Market & Hawker Centre
Jln Petanak
Jln Abell
Jln Padungan
To Express Wharf (boats to Sibu)
Jln Jawa
Jln P Ramlee
Sarawak Museum (new wing)
Islamic Museum
Foot-bridge
Sarawak Museum (old building)
Heroes Memorial
Jln Reservoir
Jln Mathies
Jln Song Thian Cheok
Royal Brunei Airlines
Kuching Cat Statue
Jln Kulas
Satok Flyover
Miramar Cinema
Museum Gardens
Jln Tabuan
Jln Ban Hock
Jln Central Timur
Turf Club
To Kingwood Inn
Jln Satok
To Petra Jaya Santubong, Bako
Jln Taman Budaya
Reservoir Park
Jln Lorong Park
St Joseph's Cathedral
Jln Ahmad Zaidi Adruce
Jln Baruddin
Jln Budaya
Jln Central Barat
Civic Centre
0 150 metres
To Hospital
To Airport & Immigration Office
Hotels:
1. Anglican Guesthouse
2. B & B Inn
3. Borneo
4. Fata
5. Green Mountain Lodging House, Mandarin Lodging House & Orchid Inn
6. Hilton
7. Holiday Inn
8. Kapit
9. Longhouse
10. Metropole
11. Riverside Majestic
12. Supreme & Hua Hock Inn
13. Telang Usan
Places to eat:
14. Beijing Restaurant
15. Green
16. Green Hill Corner
17. KTS Seafood Canteen
18. McDonalds
19. San Francisco Grill
20. See Good
21. Suan Chicken Rice & Pizza Hut
22. Thompson's Corner
23. Top Spot Food Court

Gunung Murud – Sarawak's highest peak (see page 406) – in 1922) and ethnologist and explorer Tom Harrisson, whose archaeological work at Niah made world headlines in 1957. The museum overlooks pleasant botanical gardens and the Heroes Memorial, built to commemorate the dead of World War II, the communist insurgency and the confrontation with Indonesia. Across the road, and linked by an overhead bridge, is the Dewan Tun Abdul Razak building, a newer extension of the museum.

The museum has a strong ethnographic section, although some of its displays have been superceded by the Cultural Village (see below), Sarawak's 'living museum'. The old museum's ethnographic section includes a full-scale model of an Iban longhouse, a reproduction of a Penan hut and a selection of Kayan and Kenyah woodcarvings. There is also an impressive collection of Iban war totems (*kenyalang*) and carved Melanau sickness images (*blum*), used in healing ceremonies. The museum's assortment of traditional daggers (or *kris*, see page 49) is the best in Malaysia. The Chinese and Islamic ceramics include 17th-20th century Chinese jars, which are treasured heirlooms in Sarawak (see page 358).

The natural science collection – covering the flora and fauna of Sarawak – is also noteworthy. The new Tun Abdul Razak ethnological and historical collection includes prehistoric artefacts from the Niah caves (see page 400); there is even a replica of Niah's Painted Cave – without the smell of guano.

There is a library attached to the museum as well as a giftshop, the Curio Shoppe, all proceeds of which go to charity and a bookshop. Permits to visit the Niah's Painted Cave can be obtained, free of charge, from the curator's office. Open 0900-1800 Monday, Thursday, Saturday and Sunday. Audio-visual showings: 1015, 1215, 1430, 1445, 1530. Museum open 0800-1800 Tuesday-Sunday, free admission.

Not far from the Sarawak Museum is the **Sarawak Islamic Museum**, on Jalan P Ramlee, in the restored Maderasah Melayu Building – an elegant, single storey colonial building. As its name suggests, the museum is devoted to Islamic artefacts from all the ASEAN countries, with the collection of manuscripts, costumes, jewellery, weaponry, furniture, coinage, textiles and ceramics spread over seven galleries, each with a different theme, and set around a central courtyard. Open Saturday-Thursday 0900-1800.

Apart from the Sarawak Museum, the White Rajahs bequeathed several other architectural monuments to Kuching. The **Astana** (a variant of the usual spelling *istana*, or palace) was built in 1870, 2 years after Charles Brooke took over from his uncle. It stands on the north bank of the river (almost opposite the market on Jalan Gambier). The Astana was hurriedly completed for the arrival of Charles' new bride (and cousin), Margaret. It was originally three colonial-style bungalows, with wooden shingle roofs, the largest being the central bungalow with the reception room, dining and drawing room. "How I delighted in those many hours spent on the broad verandah of our house, watching the life going on in the little town on the other side of the river," Ranee Margaret later reminisced in her book *My Life in Sarawak*. The crenellated tower on the east end was added in the 1880s at her request. Charles Brooke is said to have cultivated betel nut in a small plantation behind the Astana, so that he could offer fresh betel nut to visiting Dayak chiefs. Today it is the official residence of the governor (Yang Di Pertuan Negeri) of Sarawak and is only open to the public on Hari Raya Puasa, at the end of Ramadan. To the west of the Astana, in the traditionally Malay area, are many old wooden kampong houses.

Not far away (and also on the north shore) is **Fort Margherita** (now the Police Museum) on Jalan Sapi; it was also built by Rajah Charles Brooke in 1879 and

A ceramic inheritance

Family wealth and status in Sarawak was traditionally measured in ceramics. In the tribal longhouses upriver, treasured heirlooms include ancient glass beads, brass gongs and cannons and Chinese ceramic pots and beads (such as those displayed in the Sarawak Museum). They were often used as currency and dowries. Spencer St John, the British consul in Brunei, mentions using beads as currency on his 1858 expedition to Gunung Mulu. Jars (*pesaka*) had more practical applications; they were (and still are) used for storing rice, brewing *tuak* (rice wine) or for keeping medicines. Their value was dependent on their rarity: brown jars, emblazoned with dragon motifs, are more recent and quite common while olive-glazed *dusun* jars, dating from the 15th-17th centuries are rare. The Kelabit people, who live in the highlands around Bario, treasure the dragon jars in particular. Although some of the more valuable antique jars have found their way to the Sarawak Museum, many magnificent jars remain in the Iban and other tribal longhouses along the Skrang, Rejang and Baram rivers. Many are covered by decoratively carved wooden lids.

Chinese contact and trade with the north coast of Borneo has gone on for at least a millennium, possibly two. Chinese Han pottery fragments and coins have been discovered near the estuary of the Sarawak River and from the 7th century, China is known to have been importing birds' nests and jungle produce from Brunei (which then encompassed all of North Borneo), in exchange for ceramic wares. Chinese traders arrived in the *Nanyang* (South Seas) in force from the 11th century, particularly during the Sung and Yuan dynasties. Some Chinese pottery and porcelain even bore Arabic and Koranic inscriptions – the earliest such dish is thought to have been produced in the mid-14th century. In the 1500s, as China's trade with the Middle East grew, many such Islamic wares were traded and the Chinese emperors presented them as gifts to seal friendships with the Muslim world, including Malay and Indonesian kingdoms.

named after Ranee Margaret, although there was a fort on the site from 1841 when James Brooke became Rajah. It commanded the river approach to Kuching, but was never used defensively, although its construction was prompted by a near-disastrous river-borne attack on Kuching by the Ibans of the Rejang in 1878. Even so, until World War Two a sentry was always stationed on the lookout post on top of the fort; his job was to pace up and down all night and shout "All's well" on the hour every hour until 0800. The news that nothing was awry was heard at the Astana and the government offices.

After 1946, Fort Margherita was first occupied by the Sarawak Rangers and was finally converted into a police museum in 1971; this is a lot more interesting than it sounds. There is a large collection of armour and weaponry on the ground floor, including weapons captured during the Indonesian *konfrontasi* from 1963-65 (see page 341). Up the spiral staircase, on the second floor, there is a display of police uniforms and communications equipment used by jungle patrols. The third floor houses an exhibition on drugs, counterfeit currency and documents, supplies and weapons captured from Communist insurgents in the 1960s and 70s. From the top, there are good views across the city and up and down the Sarawak River. En route to the courtyard at the bottom, former prison cells have been set up to recreate an opium den – complete with emaciated dummy – and to reinforce the dangers of *dadah*, the courtyard itself contains the old town gallows complete with hanging dummy. (During the rule of the White Rajahs, however, death sentences were carried out by a slash of the *kris* through the heart.)

Open 1000-1800 Tuesday-Sunday. Closed public holidays. *Getting there*: sampan across the river from the Pangkalan Batu next to Square Tower on Main Bazaar to the Istana and Fort (RM2 return; the boats can be hired for around RM15-20 an hour). The **Malay kampungs** along the riverside next to Fort Margherita are seldom visited by tourists – however, they have some beautiful examples of traditional and modern Malay architecture.

On the south side of the river around Main Bazaar are some other important buildings dating from the Brooke era; most of them are closed to the public. The **Supreme Court** on Main Bazaar, was built in 1871 as an administrative centre. State council meetings were held here from the 1870s until 1973, when it was converted to law courts. In front of the grand entrance is a memorial to Rajah Charles Brooke (1924) and on each corner, there is a bronze relief representing the four main ethnic groups in Sarawak – Iban, Orang Ulu, Malay and Chinese. The clock tower was built in 1883. The **Square Tower**, also on Main Bazaar, was built as an annex to Fort Margherita in 1879 and was used as a prison. Later in the Brooke era it was used as a ballroom and is now a one-stop information centre for tourists with a video wall and an interactive video on Sarawak past and present and a Waterfront Information Counter, providing details of forthcoming events. The square tower marks one end of Kuching's new waterfront esplanade which runs alongside the river for almost 900m to the *Hilton*. Open 1000-1400, 1600-2130 daily.

The **Waterfront** has recently been transformed into a landscaped esplanade through restoration and a land reclamation project. It has become a popular meeting place, with foodstalls, restaurants and entertainment facilities including an open-air theatre. There is a restored Chinese pavilion, an observation tower, a tea terrace and musical fountains, as well as a number of modern sculptures. During the day, the waterfront offers excellent views of the Astana, Fort Margherita and the Malay kampungs which line the north bank of the river. At night, the area comes alive as younger members of Kuching's growing middle class make their way down here to relax.

The **General Post Office**, with its majestic Corinthian columns, stands in the centre of town, on Jalan Tun Haji Openg. It was built in 1931 and was one of the few buildings built by Vyner Brooke, the last Rajah.

The **Court House** complex was built in 1871 as the seat of Sarawak's government and was used as such until 1973. It remains one of Kuching's grandest structures. The buildings have belian (ironwood) roofs and beautiful detailing inside and out, reflecting local art forms. The colonial-baroque **clock tower** was added in 1883 and the **Charles Brooke Memorial** in 1924. The complex also includes the **Pavilion Building** which was built in 1907 as a hospital. During the Japanese occupation is was used as an information and propaganda centre and it is now the Education Department headquarters. The **Round Tower** on Jalan Tun Abang Haji Openg (formerly Rock Road) was originally planned as a fort (1886) but was never fully completed. The whole area is undergoing restoration for future art galleries and cultural exhibits. The **Steamship Building** was built in 1930 and was previously the offices and warehouse of the Sarawak Steamship Company. It has been extensively restored and now houses a restaurant, souvenir stalls, a handicrafts gallery and an exhibition area.

The **Bishop's House**, off Jalan McDougall, near the Anglican cathedral, is the oldest surviving residence in Sarawak. It was built in 1849, entirely of wood, for the first Anglican Bishop of Borneo, Dr McDougall. The first mission school was started in the attic – developed into St Thomas's and St Mary's School, which is now across the road on Jalan McDougall.

Kuching's Chinese population, part of the town's community since its foundation, live in the shophouses lining the narrow streets around **Main Bazaar**. This street, opposite the waterfront, is the oldest in the city. The Chinese families who live here still pursue traditional occupations such as tinsmithing and wood working. Kuching's highest concentration of antique and handicraft shops is to be found here. **Jalan Carpenter**, parallel to Main Bazaar, has a similar selection of small traders and coffee shops, as well as foodstalls and two small Chinese temples. Off **Leboh China** (Upper China Street), there is a row of perfectly preserved 19th century Chinese houses. The oldest Chinese temple in Kuching, **Tua Pek Kong** (also known as Siew San Teng), in the shadow of the *Hilton* on Jalan Tunku Abdul Rahman, was built in 1876, although it is now much modernized. There is evidence that the site has been in use since 1740 and a Chinese temple was certainly here as early as 1770. The first structure was erected by a group of Chinese immigrants thankful for their safe journey across the hazardous South China Sea. New immigrants still come here to give thanks for their safe arrival. The Wang Kang festival to commemorate the dead is also held here.

The **Chinese History Museum** stands on the Waterfront, opposite Tua Pek Kong Temple. The building itself is of interest: it was completed in 1912 and became the court for the Chinese population of Kuching. The Third Rajah was keen that the Chinese, like other ethnic groups, should settle disputes within their community in their own way and he encouraged its establishment. From 1912 until 1921, when the Chinese court was dissolved, all cases pertaining to the Chinese were heard here in front of 6 judges elected from the local Chinese population. The building itself is a simple cella with a flat roof and shows English colonial influences. In 1993 it was handed over to the Sarawak Museum and was turned into the Chinese History Museum. The museum documents the history of the Chinese in Sarawak, from the early traders of the 10th century to the waves of Chinese immigration in the 19th century. The museum building was constructed in the early 20th century as the Chinese court, officially established in 1911 by Rajah Charles Brooke, T 231520. Open Saturday-Thursday 0900-1800. **Hian Tien Shian Tee** (Hong San) temple, at the junction of Jalan Carpenter and Jalan Wayang, was built in 1897. The **Indian mosque**, on Lebuh India, originally had an atap roof and *kajang* (thatch) walls; in 1876 belian-wood walls were erected. The mosque was built by South Indians and is in the middle of an Indian quarter where spices are sold along the main bazaar. When the mosque was first built only Muslims from South India were permitted to worship here; even Indian Muslims from other areas of the sub-continent were excluded. In time, as Kuching's Muslim population expanded and grew more diversified, so this rigid system was relaxed. It is hard to get to the mosque as it is surrounded by buildings. However a narrow passage leads from Lubuh India.

The Moorish, gilt-domed **Masjid Bandaraya** (old state mosque) is near the market, on the east side of town; it was built in 1968 on the site of an old wooden mosque dating from 1852. The new **State Mosque**, which is currently being extended, is situated across the river at Petra Jaya. Its interior is of Italian marble.

Kuching's architectural heritage did not end with the White Rajahs; the town's modern buildings are often based on local styles. The new administration centre is in Petra Jaya, on the north side of the river. The **Bapak** (father) **Malaysia** building, in Petra Jaya, is named after the first Prime Minister of Malaysia and houses government offices; the **Dewan Undangan Negeri**, next door, is based on the Minangkabau style. Kuching's latest building is the ostentatious **Masjid Jamek** at Petra Jaya. Also in Petra Jaya, like a space launch overlooking the road to Damai Peninsula, is the **Cat Museum** which houses everything you ever wanted to know about cats. Open Tuesday-Sunday 0900-1700. *Getting there*: Petra Jaya Transport No 2B or 2C.

The **Timber Museum** nearby, on Wisma Sumber Alam (next to the stadium in Petra Jaya), is meant to look like a log. It was built in the mid-1980s to try to engender a bit more understanding about Sarawak's timber industry (see page 412). The museum, which has many excellent exhibits and displays, toes the official line about forest management and presents facts and figures on the timber trade, along with a detailed history of its development in Sarawak. The exhibition provides an insight into all the different forest types. It has background information on and examples of important commercial tree species, jungle produce as well as many traditional wooden implements. The final touch is an air-conditioned forest and wildlife diorama, complete with leaf-litter; all the trees come from the Rejang River area. While the museum sidesteps the more delicate moral issues involved in the modern logging business, its detractors might do worse than to brush up on some of the less emotive aspects of Sarawak's most important industry. The museum has a research library attached to it. Open 0830-1600 Monday-Thursday, 0830-1130, 1430-1630 Friday, 0830-1230 Saturday, closed Sunday.

On the south side of the river the extraordinary-looking **Civic Centre** on Jalan Taman Budaya, is Kuching's stab at the avant garde. It has a viewing platform (open 0800-0930, 1030-1200, 1400-1530, 1630-1800) for panoramas of Kuching. The Civic Centre complex houses an art gallery with temporary exhibits, mainly of Sarawakian art, there is also a restaurant and a pub-cum-karaoke bar one floor down, together with a public library. Open 0915-1730 Monday-Thursday, 0915-1800 Saturday and Sunday. Malaysia's first planetarium is also within the complex: **Sultan Iskandar Planetarium**. It opened in 1989 and has a 15m dome and a 170-seat auditorium. Admission RM2. Shows at: 1500 Monday-Sunday plus 1930 Tuesday and Thursday. On public holidays there are afternoon and evening shows. *Getting there*: bus from Lebuh Market, south along Jalan Tun Haji Openg.

Excursions

Permits for national parks and the orang utan sanctuary are available from the Sarawak Tourist Information Centre on Padang Merdeka, T 248088 or the National Parks office in Petra Jaya, Wisma Sumber Alam, T 442180.

South and west of Kuching

Semenggoh Orang Utan Sanctuary is 32 km from Kuching, on the road to Serian. Semenggoh became the first forest reserve in Sarawak when the 800 hectares of jungle was set aside by Rajah Vyner Brooke in 1920. It was turned into a wildlife rehabilitation centre for monkeys, orang utans, honey bears and hornbills in 1975. All were either orphaned as a result of logging or were confiscated having been kept illegally as pets. The aim is to reintroduce as many of the animals as possible to their natural habitat. The centre is not set up as a tourist attraction but visitors are most welcome. The feeding platform is a 5-minute walk from the park office, which is about 1 km walk from the main gates along a tarmac road. Feeding times: 0830-0900 and 1430-1530 Monday-Sunday. The star attraction is the 19-year-old orang utan called Bullet, who earned his name after being shot in the head by hunters. There are a few trails around the park including a plankwalk and a botanical research centre, dedicated to jungle plants with medicinal applications. As an orang

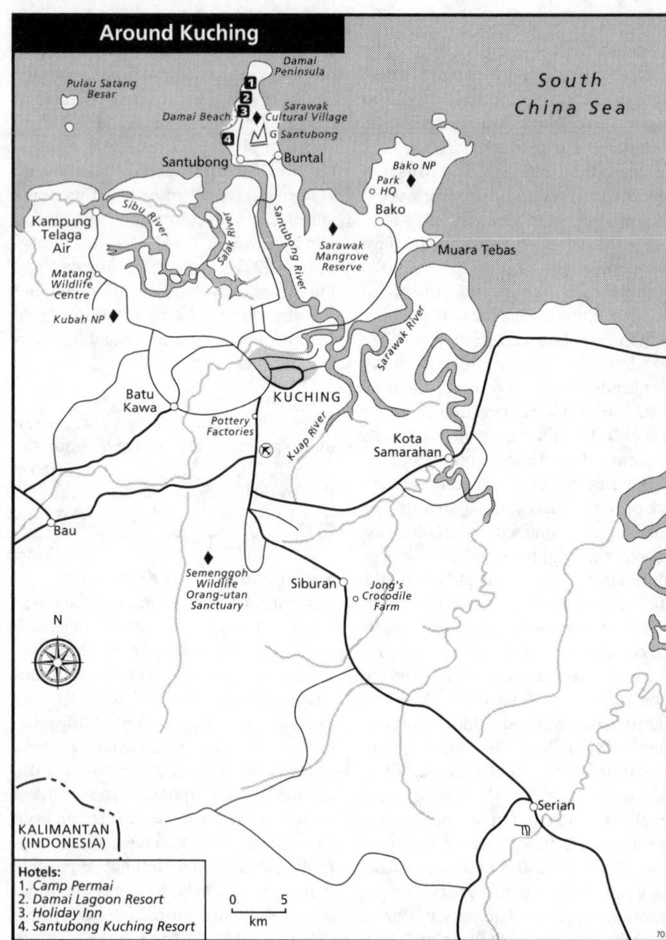

utan rehabilitation centre, however, it does not compare with Sepilok in Sabah (see page 486), which is an altogether more sophisticated affair; that said, Semonggoh gets few visitors and is a good place to watch orang utans close up. Visitors need a permit (free) to visit the sanctuary, available from Visitors Information Centre on Padang Merdeka. Open 0800-1615 Monday-Sunday. *Getting there*: Sarawak Transport Co bus 6 from Ban Hock Wharf, Jawa Street. From there, hitch a lift to the centre which is another 3 km away. **NB** There are plans to transfer the animals at Semenggoh to the Matang Wildlife Centre in the near future; check with the Visitors' Information Centre before making your way out here.

Jong's Crocodile Farm, Mile 18.5 Kuching (29 km from Kuching), Jalan Endap, off the Serian Highway, has several

The Penan – museum pieces for the 21st century?

Economic progress has altered many Sarawakians' lifestyles in recent years; the oil and natural gas sector now offers many employment prospects and upriver tribespeople have been drawn into the logging industry (see page 412). But it is logging that has directly threatened the 9,000-strong Penan tribe's traditional way of life. Sarawak's nomadic hunter-gatherers have emerged as 'the noble savages' of the late 20th century, as their blockades of logging roads drew world attention to their plight. In 1990, Britain's Prince Charles' remarks about Malaysia's "collective genocide" against the Penan prompted an angry letter of protest from Prime Minister Dr Mahathir Mohamad. He is particularly irked by Western environmentalists – Bruno Manser, who lived with the Penan in the late 1980s. "We don't need any more Europeans who think they have a white man's burden to shoulder," Dr Mahathir said.

Malaysia wants to integrate the Penan into mainstream society, on the grounds that it is morally wrong to condemn them to a life expectancy of 40 years, when the average Malaysian lives to well over 60. "There is nothing romantic about these helpless, half-starved, disease-ridden people," the Prime Minister said. The government has launched resettlement programmes to transform the Penan from hunters into fishermen and farmers. One of these new longhouses can be visited in Mulu (see page 414); it has failed to engender much enthusiasm from the Penan, although 4,000-5,000 Penan have now been resettled. Environmentalists countered that the Penan should be given the choice, but, the government asks, what choice do they have if they have only lived in the jungle?

The Cultural Village, opened by Dr Mahathir in 1990, offered a compromise or sorts – but the Penan had the last laugh. One tribal elder, called Apau Madang, and his grandson were paid to parade in loincloths and make blowpipes at the Penan hut while tourists took their snapshots. The arrangement did not last long as they did not like posing as artefacts in Sarawak's 'living museum'. They soon complained of boredom and within months had wandered back to the jungle where they could at least wear jeans and T-shirts. Today, the Penan hut is staffed by other Orang Ulu. There are thought to be only 400 Penan still following their traditional nomadic way of life.

types of crocodile – albino, saltwater, and the freshwater Malayan gharial (*Tomistoma schlegeli*) – all bred for their skins. These are 'harvested' at about 10 years of age and 2 sq cm of skin fetches about RM60; younger crocodiles are also killed for their valuable tender belly skin. In the entrance area, there is a ghoulish collection of photographs of people who have been mauled by crocodiles... and one depicting the contents of a maneater's stomach – not for the faint-hearted. There have been eight fatal attacks from crocodiles in Sarawak since the mid-1970s; thus far none of these has been at Jong's which is a rather squalid affair and does not inspire much confidence as far as security goes. Feeding times every Sunday at 1000. Admission RM5 Monday-Saturday, RM3 Sunday (RM1 for children). Open 0900-1700 Monday-Sunday. Apart from crocodiles there are also numerous species of birds and animals only found in Borneo at the **Taman Nor Badia Wildlife and Reptile Park**: monkeys, leopard-cats, sunbears, bearcats, pheasants, civets, barking deer, sambar deer, turtles, fruit bats, monitor lizards, pythons and hornbills. Admission: RM5 for adults, RM2 for children. Open daily 1000-1800 *Getting there*: Sarawak Transport Co. bus 3, 3A and 9A and 9B from

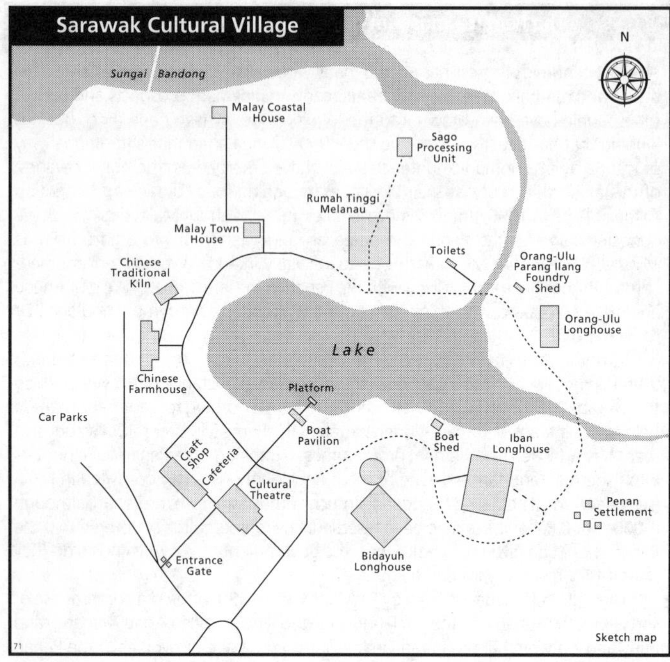

Ban Hock Wharf, every 15 minutes.

Gunung Penrissen (1,329m) is the highest peak in the mountain range south of Kuching running along the Kalimantan border. The mountain was visited by naturalist Alfred Wallace in 1855. Just over 100 years later, the mountain assumed a strategic role in Malaysia's *konfrontasi* with Indonesia (see page 341) – there is a Malaysian military post on the summit. Gunung Penrissen is accessible from Kampong Padawan on the road to Serian, to the southeast of Kuching. It is a difficult mountain to climb (requiring two long days), but affords views over Kalimantan to the south and Kuching and the South China Sea to the north. Guides – most of whom were former border scouts during *konfrontasi* – can be hired through the headman at Kampung Padawan; prospective climbers are advised to consult the detailed trail-guide in John Briggs' *Mountains of Malaysia*. (The book is usually obtainable in the Sarawak museum bookshop.)

Gunung Gading National Park was constituted in 1983 and covers 41,106 hectares either side of Sungai Lundu. There are some marked trails, the shortest of which takes about 2 hours and leads to a series of waterfalls on the Sungai Lundu. Gunung Gading and Gunung Perigi summit treks take 7-8 hours; it is possible to camp at the summit. The park is made up of a complex of mountains with several dominant peaks including Gunung Gading (906m). The Rafflesia is found in the park but if you are keen to see one in flower, it might be worth phoning the Park HQ to establish whether one is in bloom – it has a very short flowering period, T 735714. Upon arrival in the park, visitors must register at the HQ. Park fees are RM3 for adults, RM1 for children, with additional fees for cameras and videos. The HQ is small, consisting of an information centre, toilet blocks, and accommodation. **Accommodation B** two 2-room chalets, washrooms, toilets, electricity. **D** *Hostel*, 4 beds/room, bookable through the Visitors' Information Centre in Kuching. Getting there: Gunung Gading National Park is between Lundu and Semantan – regular bus connections with Kuching (see below).

Bau, about 60 km from Kuching, used to be a small-scale mining town. Nowadays, it is a market town and administrative centre. There are several caves close by; the **Wind Cave** is a popular picnic spot. The **Fairy Cave** is larger and more impressive, with a small Chinese shrine in the main chamber and varied vegetation at the entrance. A torch is essential. *Getting there*: the Fairy Cave is about 10 km from Bau; tour companies organize the trip, or take a taxi.

Lundu and **Sematan** are villages with beautiful, lonely beaches and there is a collection of deserted islands off Sematan. One of the islands, **Talang Talang**, is a turtle sanctuary and permission to visit it must be obtained from the local district officer. **Accommodation B** *Folkland Beach Bungalow*, Sematan, T 65387, call first for boat transfer from Siar Beach to Folkland Beach. **C-D** *Sematan Hotel*, T 711162, some a/c, hotel in the centre of Samatan, rooms are fine. *Getting there*: Sarawak Transport Co bus 2B to Lundu (via Bau) (2 hours); from there take a Pandan bus and ask to be dropped off at the park.

Kubah National Park is 20 km west of Kuching. This is a mainly sandstone, siltstone and shale area covering some 2,230 hectares with three mountains: Gunung Serapi, Gunung Selang and Gunung Sendok; there are at least seven waterfalls and bathing pools. Flora include mixed dipterocarp and *kerangas* (heath) forest; the park is also rich in palms (93 species) and wild orchids. Wildlife includes bearded pig, mouse deer and hornbills and numerous species of amphibians and reptiles. Unfortunately for visitors, Kubah's wildlife tends to stay deep in the forest; it is not really a park for 'wildlife encounters'. There are four marked trails, ranging from 30 minutes to 3 hours, one of which, the Rayu Trail, passes through rainforest that contains a number of bintangor trees (trees which are believed to contain two chemicals which have showed some evidence of being effective against AIDS). Visitors may be able to see some trees which have been tapped for this potential rainforest remedy. Permits can be obtained through the National Parks Booking Office, Kuching; day visitors can pay and register at the Park HQ (T 225003) or at the gate of the Matang Wildlife Centre, RM3/RM1. **Accommodation** There are five huge double storey bungalows at the Park HQ at 180Rm/night with full kitchen facilities, 4 beds (2 rooms), a/c, hot water, TV and verandah. Book through the Visitors' Information Centre in Kuching or through the National Parks Booking Office T 082 248088. *Getting to Kubah*: Matang Transport Company bus No 11 or 18 departs from outside the Saujana Car Park. Travel agents arrange tours to the park.

The **Matang Wildlife Centre** (T 225012) is part of the Kubah National Park. It is still in the process of being developed but will eventually house endangered wildlife in spacious enclosures which are purposefully placed in the rainforest. There will also be an Information Centre and education programmes, which will enable visitors to learn more about the conservation of Sarawak's wildlife. **Accommodation** Chalets at RM120 and an 8 room hostel block (**F**). *Getting to Kubah*: Matang Transport Company bus No 11 or 18 departs from outside the Saujana Car Park. Travel agents arrange tours to the park.

Tanjung Datu National Park is the newest and smallest park in the state of Sarawak, first gazetted in 1994, at the westernmost tip. The land is covered with mixed dipterocarp forest, rich flora and fauna, and beautiful beaches with crystal clear seas and coral reefs. Facilities for visitors are currently being developed and it may be worth checking with the tourist office in Kuching whether it is open to visitors. *Getting there*: bus to Sematan and boat to the park.

Tours

Most tour companies offer city tours as well as trips around Sarawak: to Semenggoh, Bako, Niah, Lambir Hills, Miri, Mulu and Bario. There are also competitively-priced packages to longhouses (mostly up the Skrang River – see page 381). It is cheaper and easier to take organized tours to Mulu, but these should be arranged in Miri (see page 404) as they are much more expensive if arranged from Kuching. Other areas are easy enough to get to independently.

Local information

● Accommodation

Prices: L over RM500; **A+** RM260-500; **A** RM130-260; **B** RM65-130; **C** RM40-65; **D** RM20-40; **E** RM10-20; **F** Below RM10

There is a good choice of international-standard hotels in Kuching (and over the next couple of years there will be an ever better choice as the *Ramada* and *Central* both have hotels being built) – most of them are along Jalan Tunku Abdul Rahman with views of the river and the Astana and Fort Margherita on the opposite bank. The choice at the lower end of the market is limited, except for the *Anglican Guesthouse*; the cheaper hotels and lodging houses are concentrated around Jalan Green Hill, near the Tua Pek Kong temple. Some newer, mid-range accommodation has grown up in the area around Jalan Ban Hock.

L-A+ ***Hilton***, Jln Tunku Abdul Rahman, PO Box 2396, T 248200, F 428984, white modern block commanding superb views of river and town, lives up to its name in providing quality and exclusive atmosphere, 322 rooms all with a/c, TV, in-room movies, mini-bar, tea and coffee making facilities, very pleasant pool with swim-up bar, shaded by palms, and separate children's pool and playground, tennis, fitness centre, 4 restaurants including good steak house (air-freighted meat from Australia), boutique, hair salon, travel agent, recommended. **L-A+** ***Riverside Majestic***, Jln Tunku Abdul Rahman, PO Box 2928, T 247777, F 417552, 5-star, high-rise glitz hotel with an adjoining, 5-storey shopping complex complete with bowling alley and cineplex. 250 a/c rooms with mini-bar, tea and coffee making facilities, personal safe, TV, in-house movies, en suite bathroom with marble vanity and good shower, plush carpets, wood furnishings carved with Sarawak designs, facilities include pool, fitness centre, squash court, patisserie, 3 restaurants including the *Sri Sarawak* on the 18th floor which has panoramic views and serves Malay and international food, regular shuttle (RM10) to sister hotel, *Damai Lagoon*, on the Damai Peninsula, recommended. **A+-A** ***Holiday Inn***, Jln Tunku Abdul Rahman, PO Box 2362, T 423111, F 412777, the first international hotel to open in Kuching and the only one right on the riverfront, popular with families, plenty of organized activities, 305 rooms with a/c, tea and coffee making facilities, TV with movies and satellite channels, mini-bar, pool, fitness centre, 3 restaurants, souvenir and bookshop. **A-B** ***Borneo***, 30 Jln Tabuan, T 244122, F 254848, a/c, restaurant, reasonable value, central location, breakfast include. **A-B** ***Grand Continental***, Lot 42, Section 46, Jln Ban Hock, T 230399, F 230339, pool and business centre. **A-B** ***Kingwood Inn***, Jln Padungan, T 330888, F 332888, pool.

B ***Hua Kuok Inn***, Lot 227, Jln Ban Hock, T 429788, F 424329, simple but clean, a/c, Chinese management. **B** ***Impiana***, Jln Tan Sri Ong Kee Hui, T 247111, a/c, restaurant, pool, bit out of town. **B** ***Metropole Inn***, 22-23 Jln Green Hill, PO Box 2202, T 412561, a/c, poor quality but offers reasonable rates. **B** ***Rajah Court***, Jln Tun Razak, T 484799, F 482750, budget hotel with good facilities for conferences, slightly out of town but pleasant place with variety of rooms, chalets and apartments, pool, squash court, good atmosphere. **B** ***Supreme***, Jln Ban Hock, T 255155, F 252522, 74 rooms in brand-new block, a/c, en suite bath or shower, mini-bar, TV with in-house videos, very comfortable – best value for money in Kuching, recommended. **B** ***Telang Usan***, Jln Ban Hock (next to *Supreme* and *Hua Hock*), T 415588, F 425316, a/c, TV, bath, restaurant, in-house travel agent, orang ulu owned and managed hotel, friendly with traditional kenyah decor, karaoke and bar, conference rooms, smart and comfortable, quiet location, excellent value.

C ***Fata***, Jln McDougall, T 248111, F 428987, a/c, restaurant, rooms in the older part of the hotel are cheaper and better value for money. **C** ***Green Mountain Lodging House***, 1 Jln Green Hill, T 416320, F 246342, a/c, reasonable value. **C** ***Kapit***, 59 Jln Padungan, T 244179, a/c, attached bathrooms, located past the *Holiday Inn*, to the east end of town. **C** ***Longhouse***, Jln Abell, T 419333, F 421563, a/c, restaurant, good value but a bit out of town (past the *Holiday Inn*). **C** ***Mandarin*** , 6 Jln Green Hill, T 418269, some a/c, shared bathrooms. **C** ***Orchid Inn***, 2 Jln Green Hill, T 411417, F 241635, a/c. **C-D** ***Anglican Guesthouse***, back of St Thomas' Cathedral (path from Jln Carpenter), T 414027, fan, old building set in beautiful gardens on top of the hill, spacious, pleasantly furnished rooms, with basic facilities, far and away the best of the cheaper accommodation in town, family rooms are big with sitting room and attached bathroom, recent visitors warn, however, of a spate of thefts from the guesthouse, so take precautions, recommended.

D ***Kuching***, Lebuh Temple, T 413985, adequate Chinese-run hotel, reasonable rates for rooms with fan and wash-hand basin, shared bathrooms.

E ***Government Resthouse***, Jln Crookshank (behind *Kikyo Tei Restaurant*), T 242042 (phone first for vacancies) typically Malaysian, dating from colonial era, spacious, simple, fan and attached bath, set in pleasant garden.

● Places to eat

Prices: ◆◆◆◆ over RM40; ◆◆◆ RM13-40; ◆◆ RM5-13; ◆ under RM5

Kuching, with all its old buildings and godowns along the river, seems made for open-air restaurants and cafes – but good ones are notably absent. However, the town is not short of hawker centres. Local dishes worth looking out for include *Umai* – a spicy salad of raw marinated fish with limes and shallots.

Malay: Malay food here seems to be less spicy than on the Peninsular. ***Rex Café***, Main Bazaar, good mixed rice, rojak and laksa. ***National Islamic Café***, Jln Carpenter. ***Sri Sarawak***, *Riverside Majestic Hotel*, gourmet food, good views. ***Glutton's Corner***, Lorong Rubber 12, wide selection, closed 1900 and on Sun. ***Home Cook***, Jln Song Thian Cheok, clean and good value, speciality assam fish. ***Suan Chicken Rice***, Jln Tunku Abdul Rahman, next to Sarawak Plaza, steamed or curried chicken. There are a handful of Malay/Indian coffee shops on India Street including ***Madinah Café***, ***Jubilee*** and ***Malaysia Restaurant***.

Chinese: all the major hotels have Chinese restaurants; most open for lunch and dinner, closing in between. ◆◆***Hot and Spicy House***, Lot 303, Section 10, Rubber Rd, T 250873, closed Tues, Chinese cooking with West Malaysian influence. Speciality is Ipoh-style *yong tau hoo* (vegetables stuffed with beancurd), just outside the city centre. ***Lok Thian***, 1st floor, Bangunan Beesan, Jln Padungan, T 331310, good food, pleasant surroundings and excellent service, booking advisable, especially at the weekends. ***Marie Café***, Jln Ban Hock (near *Liwah Hotel*), Chinese food Sarawak-style, open for breakfast and lunch only. ***Minsion Canteen***, end of Jln Chan Chin Ann, on right, speciality is *daud special* (thick noodles in herbal soup with chunks of chicken). ***Tsui Hua Lau***, Lot 321-324, Jln Ban Hock, T 414560, Shanghai-style dishes. ◆◆◆***City Tower***, top of Civic Centre, T 234396, wonderful views and gourmet food. ◆◆◆***River Palace***, *Riverside Majestic Hotel*, first class Chinese restaurant, offers regular food promotions. ◆◆◆***Hornbill Corner Cafe***, 85 Jln Ban Hock. All-you-can-eat steamboat and barbecue, popular. ***Red Eastern Cafe***, Jln Ban Hock, specializes in steamboat ◆◆***Meisan***, *Holiday Inn*, Jln Tunku Abdul Rahman, dim sum, RM12.50 set lunch; Sun eat-as-much-as-you-can dim sum special (RM13), also Sechuan cuisine, recommended. ***Lan Ya Keng***, Jln Carpenter, opposite old temple, specializes in pepperfish steak. ◆◆***Beijing Riverbank***, enjoys good location on riverfront, opposite *Riverside Majestic*, in a circular pavilion style building, serves Chinese Muslim food and coffeeshop fare, recommended.

Indonesian: ***Minangkabau Nasi Padang***, 168 Chan Chin Ann Rd, spicy Padang food including such classics as beef rendang, lunch time only.

Indian: there are several cheap Indian Muslim restaurants along Lebuh India. ***Bismillah***, Leboh Khoo Hun Reang (near Central Police Station), North Indian Muslim food, good tandoori chicken. ***Green***, 16 Main Bazaar, open all day, good choice of Southern Indian food, vegetarian, rajak, murtabak, roti canai etc. ***LL Banana Leaf***, 7G Lorong Rubber 1, T 239404, open all day, specializes in Indian banana leaf meals, reasonable prices. ***Pots 'n' Buns***, Taman Sri Sarawak Mall, opposite rear store entrance, good roti canai, murtabak, plus usual hawker stall food. ***Rahamath Café***, 19 Jln Padungan, good roti canai; ◆◆◆***Lyn's Restaurant***, Lot 62, 10G Lg. 4, Jln Nanas, a taxi-ride from the centre but worth the trip – genuine North Indian tandoori cuisine, excellent naan, locals recommend it, closed Sunday evenings. ♦♦♦***Serapi***, *Holiday Inn*, specializes in North Indian tandoori, good vegetable dishes, naan, also serves air-freighted steak and other western dishes, recommended.

Japanese: ♦♦♦♦***Robata Yaki***, 493G Jln Rambutan, T 251021, although decor is not as fancy as *Kikyo-Tei*, this is highly recommended by locals, take a taxi to get there. ♦♦♦♦***Ten-Ichi***, Bangunan Bee San, Jln Pandungan, T 331310, elegant surroundings. ♦♦♦***Kikyo-Tei***, Jln Crookshank, in front of Government Resthouse, also some Chinese and western dishes, large main room with separate Teppanyaki and Tatami rooms, recommended by locals. ♦♦♦***Minoru***, Lot 493, Section 10, Rubber Rd, T 251021, set lunch and dinner as well as an extensive menu and good service.

Thai: ♦♦♦***Steamship Restaurant***, Kuching Waterfront, wide selection of Thai-Chinese and Singaporean dishes in former building of the steamship company, trendy. ♦♦***Bangkok Thai Restaurant***, Jln Pending, maybe not up to Bangkok standards, but not bad for Sarawak, pleasant surroundings, good service, advisable to book, recommended by locals.

Seafood: excellent seafood is to be found in Kuching. ***Benson Seafood***, Lot 122/3, Section 49, Jln Abell, T 255262, full range of Sarawak seafood. ***Ah Leong***, Lot 72, Jln Pandungan, near *Kingwood Inn*, good choice of seafood. ***KTS Seafood Canteen***, 157, Jln Chan Chin Ann, excellent butter prawns and grilled stingray. ***Pending Seafood Centre***, behind Kuching Port, in industrial area, good range of stalls selling fabulous choice of seafood, if you go by taxi, arrange a pick-up time to avoid getting stranded. ***See Good***, Jln Bukit Mata Kuching, behind MAS office, extensive range of seafood and friendly owners, recommended by locals, strong flavoured sauces and lots of herbs, extensive and exotic menu, unlimited free bananas, closed 4th and 18th of every month.

International: ♦♦♦♦-♦♦♦***Serapi***, *Holiday Inn*, imported steaks, excellent selection of grills and seafood, North Indian tandoori, elegant surroundings, open lunch and dinner but not between times. ♦♦♦***Orchid Garden***, *Holiday Inn*, Jln Tunku Abdul Rahman, good breakfast and evening buffets, international and local cuisine, recommended. ♦♦♦***San Francisco Grill***, 76 Jln Ban Hock, steak house, cosy atmosphere, live piano, largely Chinese clientele which means steak is seasoned with 5 spices, meat is air-freighted, chips mediocre but nice atmosphere. ♦♦***Dulit Coffee House***, *Telang Usan Hotel*, Jln Ban Hock, pleasant terrace cafe, mix of western and eastern food, specializes in French oxtail stew and the only genuine chicken kebabs in Kuching. ♦♦***Hani's Bistro***, Jln Chan Chin Ann (near *Holiday Inn*), reasonably priced café, good mix of eastern and western cuisine, generous helpings, tasty haricot oxtail, good background music, recommended. ♦♦***Majestic Café***, *Riverside Majestic Hotel* (also accessible from Riverside Shopping Complex), western and Malay food, good value buffet. ♦♦***Trumps***, 2nd Flr, Civic Centre, Jln Taman Budaya, Malay dishes more reasonable than western and Chinese, good view. ♦♦***Waterfront***, *Hilton Hotel*, Jln Tunku Abdul Rahman, reasonably priced for the venue, the best pizzas and a family brunch buffet on Sun which is very popular.

Kampung Buntal: several seafood restaurants built on stilts over the sea, 25 km north of Kuching, very popular with Kuchingites.

Coffee Shops: Kuching has many good Chinese coffee shops, which are known for their excellent *laksa* (breakfast of curried coconut milk soup with noodles, served with prawns, shredded omelette, chicken, bean sprouts, coriander and a side plate of *sambal belacan* (chillied prawn paste). ***Fook Hoi***, Jln Padungan, old-fashioned coffee shop, famous for its *sio bee* and *ha kau* (pork dumpling). ♦***Life Cafe***, 108 Ewe Hai St (near Carpenter St, behind Main Bazaar), T 411954, closed Tues, attractive café serving mostly vegetarian food plus a good range of teas and coffees (including Sarawak tea), friendly staff and pleasant atmosphere. ***Borneo Deli***, *Borneo Hotel*, Jln Tabuan, selection of coffees, teas, cakes and pastries in a relaxing atmosphere. ***Chang Choon Café***, opposite *City Inn* Jln Abell. ***Choon Hui Café***, Jln Ban Hock. ***Green Hill Corner***, Lebuh Temple; ***Tiger Garden***, opposite Rex Cinema, Lebuh Temple. ***Wonderful Café***, opposite Miramar Theatre, Jln Palm.

Fastfood: ***McDonalds***, Jln Tunku Abdul Rahman, opposite *Sarawak Plaza*. ***Pizza Hut***, Jln Tunku Abdul Rahman, opposite side to *McDonalds*, a little further down. ***KFC***, branches in *Sarawak Plaza* and *Riverside Shopping Centre*. ***Hertz Chicken***, *Sarawak Plaza*. ***Sugar Bun***, in *Riverside Shopping Centre* with other branches throughout town.

Foodstalls and Food Centres: some of the best food centres are located in the suburbs; a taxi is essential. ***Hock Hong Garden***, Jln Ban Hock, opposite *Grand Continental*, finest hawker stall food in Kuching, little English

Footprint Handbooks

...step inside
a world other travel
guides miss

Win a 7 night Cuban Highlights Tour for two courtesy of Hayes and Jarvis

We want to hear your ideas for further improvements as well as a few details about yourself so that we can better serve your needs as a traveller.

Well established as one of the UK's leading long haul tour operators Hayes and Jarvis prides itself on providing good quality, reliable arrangements at sensible prices for the discerning traveller. Every reader who sends in the completed questionnaire will be entered in the Footprint Prize Draw.

Mr ☐ Mrs ☐ Miss ☐ Ms ☐ Age..........

First name ....

Surname..

Permanent Address..

....

....

Postcode/Zip..

Country..

Email..

Occupation..

Title of Handbook..

Which two destinations would you most like to visit in the next two years?

....

....

How did you hear about us?

Recommended	☐	Bookshop	☐
Used before	☐	Media/press article	☐
Library	☐	Internet	☐

There is a complete list of Footprint Handbooks at the back of this book. Which other countries would you like to see us cover?

....

Offer ends 31 May 1999. Prize winners will be notified by 30 June 1999 and holidays are subject to availability. Hayes and Jarvis may offer an alternative tour if the prize is no longer featured at time of travel.

If you do not wish to receive information from other reputable businesses, please tick box ☐

Footprint Handbooks
6 Riverside Court
Lower Bristol Road
Bath BA2 3DZ
T 01225 469141
F 01225 469461
handbooks@footprint.cix.co.uk
www.footprint-handbooks.co.uk

Thailand Handbook
Argentina Handbook
Sri Lanka Handbook
Andalucía Handbook
Jordan, Syria & Lebanon Handbook
Zimbabwe & Moçambique Handbook
Caribbean Islands Handbook
Goa Handbook
Indonesia Handbook
Chile Handbook
Colombia Handbook
India Handbook
Cambodia Handbook
Bolivia Handbook
Israel Handbook
Vietnam Handbook
East Africa Handbook
Tibet Handbook
Peru Handbook
South Africa Handbook
Morocco Handbook
Malaysia & Singapore Handbook
Cuba Handbook
Namibia Handbook
Myanmar (Burma) Handbook
Brazil Handbook
Egypt Handbook
Venezuela Handbook
Nepal Handbook
Ecuador & Galápagos Handbook
Mexico & Central America Handbook
Laos Handbook
South American Handbook
Tunisia Handbook

Footprint Handbooks
6 Riverside Court
Lower Bristol Road
Bath
BA2 3DZ
England

Affix
Stamp
Here

Win a 7 night Cuban Highlights Tour for two courtesy of Hayes and Jarvis

HAYES and JARVIS
HOLIDAYS WORLDWIDE

spoken. ***Chinese Food Centre***, Jln Carpenter (opposite temple), Chinese foodstalls. ***King's Centre***, Jln Simpang Tiga (bus no 11 to get there), large range of foodstalls, busy and not many tourists. ***Kubah Ria Hawker stalls***, Jln Tunku Abdul Rahman (on the road out of town towards Damai Beach, next to Satok Suspension Bridge), specialities *sop kambling* (mutton soup). ***Petanak Central Market***, Jln Petanak, above Kuching's early morning wet market, light snacks, full seafood selection, good atmosphere, especially early in the morning. ***Satok Bridge***, under the suspension bridge, very good barbecued chicken and seafood. ***Saujana Food Centre***, 5th Floor of the carpark near the mosque (take the lift), mostly Malay food but also seafood. ***Song Thieng Hai Food Centre***, between Jln Padungan and Jln Ban Hock, every type of noodle available. ***Third Mile (Central Park)***, opposite Timberland Medical Centre, difficult to get to, mainly hawker stalls. ♦♦***Permata Food Centre***, behind Malaysian Airways office, purpose-built alternative to the central market, prices are higher but the choice is better, bird-singing contests (mainly Red-Whiskered Bulbuls and White-Rumped Sharmas) every Sun morning, excellent range of fresh seafood, recommended. ***Batu Lintang Open-Air Market***, Jln Rock (to the south of town, past the hospital). ***Capital Cinema Hawker Centre***, Jln Padungan. ***Jln Palm Open-Air Market***. ***Lau Ya Keng***, Jln Carpenter, opposite temple, specializes in Chinese dishes. ***Rex Cinema Hawker Centre***, Jln Wayang/Jln Temple, squashed down an alleyway, satay recommended. ***Thompson's Corner***, Jln Palm/Jln Nanas. ***Top Spot Food Court***, Jln Bukit Mata Kuching, top floor of a carpark, wide range of stalls, popular. ***Tower Market***, Lebuh Market.

Bars: usual charge for beer is RM6-7, and most bars close around 0100-0200. ***Casablanca Lounge***, *Riverside Majestic Hotel*, cocktail lounge and karaoke. ***Cat City***, Jln Chan Chin Ann (turn left at *Pizza Hut*), happy hour 2030-2215, followed by live bands (usually Filipino) playing a mixture of western rock covers and Malay and Chinese ballads, open late. ***The Club***, *Riverside Majestic Hotel*, large video screen and private karaoke rooms. ***De Tavern***, Taman Sri Sarawak Mall (facing *Hilton* carpark), friendly kayan-run corner pub, serves good rice wine, open 1630-0130, happy hour until 2030. ***Dulit Terrace and Tuak Bar***, *Telang Usan Hotel*. ***The Fisherman's Pub***, 1st Flr, Taman Sri Sarawak Mall, karaoke, friendly staff and a pleasant crowd of regulars. ***Hornbill's Corner Cafe***, Jln Ban Hock, breezy open air pub. ***Margerita Lounge***, *Hilton Hotel*, the best cocktails and live music. ***Rejang Lobby Lounge***, *Holiday Inn*, small but popular. ***Tribes***, downstairs at *Holiday Inn*, ethnic food, tribal decor and a variety of live music, open 1600-0100.

● Airline offices

British Airways, 92 Jln Green Hill, T 242367; **Hornbill Skyways**, North Pan Hanger, International Airport, PO Box 1387, T 455737, F 455736; **MAS**, Lot 215, Jln Song Thian Cheok, T 246622, F 244563; **Merpati** ticket agent, ***Sin Hwa Travel Service***, 8 Lebuh Temple, T 246688; **Singapore Airlines**, Jln Tunku Abdul Rahman, T 240266, F 238487; **Royal Brunei**, 1st flr, Rugayah Building, Jln Song Thian Cheok, T 243344, F 244563; **Dragonair**, 1st Flr, Wisma Bukit Mata Kuching, Jln Tunku Abdul Rahman, T 233322, F 238819; **Saega Airlines**, Level 16, Wisma Ting Pek Khing, 1 Jln Padungan, T 236905-8, F 236922.

● Banks & money changers

There are money changers in the main shopping complexes which usually give a much better rate for cash than the banks – although if changing TCs the rates are much the same. **Standard Chartered**, opposite *Holiday Inn*, Jln Tunku Abdul Rahman; **Hongkong**, 2-4 Jln Tun Haji Openg (Main Bazaar end); **American Express**, 3rd floor MAS Building, Jln Song Thian Cheok (assistance with Amex traveller's cheques) T 252600; **Majid & Sons Money Changer**, 45 Jln India; **Mohamed Yahia & Sons** (money changer), Lower Ground Floor, Sarawak Plaza; **Bank of Commerce** 23 Jln Khoo Hun Yeang.

● Embassies & consulates

Consulates: **Indonesian Consulate**, 5a Jln Pisang, T 241734, RM10 for visa, only if travelling overland. *Getting there*: blue bus 5A or 6 from State Mosque; **Australian Honoray Consul**, T 330039; **British Consulate**, Rugayah Building, Jln Song Thian Cheok, T 231320; **Chinese Consulate**, Lorong 5, Jln Tan Pint Timur, T 453344; **French Consul**, c/o *Telong Usan Hotel*, T 415588.

● Entertainment

Cinemas: ***Riverside Cineplex***, Riverside Complex, T 427061, check local press for details of programme; ***Miramar***, on the corner of Jln Satok and Jln Tun Ahmad Zaidi Adruce (Palm Rd), T 411488, highest tech of the cinemas, with a ground floor karaoke lounge, a food court and a rooftop beer garden. ***Laserdisc centres***, all around town, where you can watch a scheduled film in a small cinema or rent a private room to see the film of your choice.

Cultural shows: *Cultural Village*, Damai Beach, cultural shows, with stylized and expertly choreographed tribal dance routines, 1130 and 1630, Mon-Sun.

Discos: *Peppers*, *Hilton Hotel* (downstairs), top 40 hits and pool table, very busy on ladies nights (Wed and Fri). ***Marina Fun Pub and Disco***, Jln Ban Hock, live band until 0200, then a DJ until 0330, crowded at weekends.

Exhibitions: the **Society Atelier** holds regular exhibitions at various venues in the city. Its HQ is an old government house near to the Civic Centre, 10 minutes walk from Main Bazaar. Phone for details of current and forthcoming events, Jln Taman Budaya, T 243222.

Karaoke: karaoke lounges abound, with songs in Chinese, English, Iban, Malay, Japanese and Korean. ***City Tower***, top of the Civic Centre, good views and well priced drinks. ***Palm Super Lounge***, Jln Tun Ahmad Zaidi Adruce (Palm Rd), in Miramar Cinema Building. Some private rooms, smart bar and wide range of songs, good service. ***Dai Ichi Karaoke***, Jln Tunku Abdul Rahman (above *Pizza Hut*), for connoisseurs, large choice of songs, friendly and good service.

● Hospitals & medical services

Dentist: Taman Sri Sarawak (behind *De Tavern*).

Hospitals: *Kuching General Hospital*, Jln Tan Sri Ong Kee Hui, off Jln Tun Haji Openg, T 257555; *Normah Medical centre*, across the river on Jln Tun Datuk Patinggi Hj. Abdul Rahman Yakub, T 440055, private hospital with good reputation; *Doctor's Clinic*, Main Bazaar, opposite Chinese History Museum (RM20 for consultation); *Poliklinik*, 11 Jln P Ramlee, T 240741; *Timberland Medical Centre*, Rock Rd, T 234991, recommended.

Pharmacies: *Apex Pharmacy*, 125 1st Flr, Sarawak Plaza, open 1000-2100; *YK Farmasi*, 22 Main Bazaar, open 0830-1700; *UMH*, Ban Hock Rd, open 0900-1700.

● Places of worship

Christian churches conduct services in a number of languages. The Muslim Council of Sarawak provide details of Muslim prayer times throughout the state, T 429811. **Anglican**: St Thomas' Cathedral, Jln McDougall, T 247200 for times of services, **evangelical services**: Lot 1863 Block 10, 26 Iris Gardens, T 425212. **Roman Catholic**: St Joseph's Cathedral, Jln Tun Abang Hj, T 423424. **Baptist**: Sarawak Baptist Church, Setampak, Stampin, T 413462. **Methodist**: Trinity Methodist Church, 57 Jln Ellis, T 411044.

● Post & telecommunications

Area code: 082.

General Post Office: Jln Tun Haji Openg, open Mon-Sat 0800-1800, Sun 1000-1300.

Telekom (for international telephone calls): Jln Batu Lintang (open 0800-1800 Mon-Fri; 0800-1200 Sat and Sun). International calls can also be made from most public cardphones. Major hotels all have cardphones in their lobbies.

● Shopping

When it comes to choice, Kuching is the best place in Malaysia to buy tribal handicrafts, textiles and other artifacts, but they are not cheap. In some of Sarawak's smaller coastal and upriver towns, you are more likely to find a better bargain, although the selection is not as good. If buying several items, it is a good idea to find one shop which sells the lot, as good discounts can be negotiated. It is essential to shop around: the best-stocked handicraft and antique shops in and near the big hotels are usually the most expensive; it is possible to bargain everywhere. **NB** It is illegal to export any antiquity without a licence from the curator of the Sarawak Museum. An antiquity is defined as any object made before 1850. Most things sold as antiquities are not: some very convincing weathering and ageing processes are employed.

Antiques & Curios: most of these shops are scattered along Main Bazaar, with a few in the Padungan Area.

Artwork: *Galleri M*, *Hilton* Lobby, paintings from a wide range of Sarawakian artists. **Postcards**: *Adventure Images showroom*, 55 Main Bazaar, good range of both colour and black and white postcards, also sell grettings cards and posters.

Birdsnests: mostly exported to China. ***Teo Hoe Hin Enterprise*** (next to *McDonalds*) is worth visiting to view the delicacies.

Books & maps: ***Berita Book Centre***, Jln Haji Taha, has a good selection English-language books. ***HN Mohd Yahia & Son***, *Holiday Inn*, Jln Tunku Abdul Rahman, and in the basement of the Sarawak Shopping Plaza, sells a 1:500,000 map of Sarawak. It is also possible to get good maps from the State Government offices (2nd Flr) near the end of Jln Simpang Tiga. It is necessary to obtain police clearance for the purchase of more detailed sectional maps. ***Times Books***, 1st Flr, Riverside Shopping Complex, Jln Tunku Abdul Rahman, best and biggest bookshop for foreign language books. ***Pasara Bookstore***, Jln Haji Taha.

Handicrafts: most handicraft and antique shops are along Main Bazaar, Lebuh Temple and Lebuh Wayang. Most shops are closed Sun. ***Telang Usan Hotel***, some Orang Ulu and Penan crafts, including good modern beadwork and traditional headgear. ***Sarakraf***, 14 Main Bazaar, wide range of souvenirs and handicrafts with outlets in major hotels in Kuching, Damai, Sarawak Cultural Village and Miri airport (chain set up by the Sarawak Economic Development Corporation). ***Gallerie M***, *Hilton* Lobby, exclusive jewellery, bead necklaces and antiques, best available Iban hornbill carvings. ***Bong & Co***, 78 Main Bazaar. ***Borneo Art Gallery***, Sarawak Plaza, Jln Tunku Abdul Rahman. ***Borneo Arts & Crafts***, 56 Main Bazaar. ***The Curio Shoppe*** is attached to the Sarawak Museum, prices are high but profits go to charity. There is a Sun market on Jln Satok, to the southwest of town, with a few handicraft stalls. ***Eeze Trading***, Lot 250, Section 49, Ground Floor, Jln Tunku Abdul Rahman. ***Karyaneka (handicrafts) Centre*** at Cawangan Kuching, Lot 324 Bangunan Bina, Jln Satok. ***Loo Pan Arts***, 83 Jln Ban Hock. ***Native Arts***, 94 Main Bazaar. ***Sarawak Batik Art Shop***, 1 Lebuh Temple. ***Sarawak House***, 67 Main Bazaar (more expensive). ***Syarikat Pemasarah Karyaneka***, Lot 87, Jln Rubber. ***Tan & Sons***, 54 Jln Padungan. ***Thian Seng***, 48 Main Bazaar (good for *pua kumbu*); ***Art Gallery***, 5 Wayang St, designer T-shirts with Sarawak motifs amongst other crafts. ***Fabriko***, Main Bazaar in beautifully restored Chinese shophouse, interesting souvenirs and gallery.

Markets: the ***Vegetable*** and ***Wet market*** are on the riverside on Jln Gambier; further up is the ***Ban Hock Wharf market***, now full of cheap imported clothes. The ***Sunday Market*** on Jln Satok sells jungle produce, fruit and vegetables (there are a few handicraft stalls) and all sorts of intriguing merchandise; it starts on Sat night and runs through Sun morning and is well worth visiting. There is a jungle produce market, Pasar Tani, on Fri and Sat at Kampong Pinang Jawa in Petra Jaya.

Pottery: rows of pottery stalls along Jln Penrissen, out of town, take a bus (STC 3, 3A, 9A or 9B) or taxi. Antique shops sell this pottery too.

Shopping complexes: *Sarawak Plaza*, next to the *Holiday Inn*, Jln Tunku Abdul Rahman; ***Riverside Shopping Complex***, next to *Riverside Majestic Hotel*, best complex in Kuching, has Parkson Department Store and good supermarket in basement.

● Sports

Bowling: Riverside Complex, Jln Tunku Abdul Rahman, 24-lane bowling alley.

Fishing: offshore from Santubong or deep sea game fishing at Tanjung Datu (near Indonesian border, contact Mr Johnson, Fui Lip Marketing, 15 Ground Floor, Wisma Phoenix, Jln Song Thian Cheok.

Golf: *Damai Golf Course* , Jln Santubong, T 846088, F 846044, green fees RM150 weekdays, RM180 weekends, due to its popularity bookings should be made 3 days in advance, designed by Arnold Palmer, right on the sea, 18-holes, swimming, tennis and squash courts are among the other facilities available here. ***Kelab Golf Course***, Petra Jaya, 18 holes, green fee RM84 (weekdays), RM126 (weekends), T 440966. ***Prison Golf Club***, Jln Penrissen, T 613544, 9-hole, green fees RM30. ***Sarawak Golf and Country Club***, Petra Jaya, T 440966, green fees RM100 weekdays, RM150 weekends.

Hash House Harriers: men only harriers on Tuesdays at 1730, ladies harriettes on Wednesdays at 1730, mixed city hash on Saturdays at 1630. Contact Tom Leng (T/F 363096) or Jennifer Yap (T 411694, F 413700).

Jogging: track at Reservoir Park

Mountain Biking: good trails from Kamppung Singgai, about 30 minutes from Kuching (across the Batu Kawa birdge). Beginners to intermediate – good trail near Kampung Apar. Advanced trail – Batang Ai. *Borneo Adventure* (T 245175) on Main Bazaar rent mountain bikes and can arrange specialized tours. Alternatively, hire a bike from Kuching and tour the Malay villages adjacent to the Astana and Fort Margherita. Cross the Sarawak River by sampan (RM1 for you and your bike) and then follow the small road that runs parallel to the river.

Outward bound: *Camp Permai Sarawak*, PO Box 891, Satok Post Office, T 321497, F 321500.

Spectator Sports: Malaysia Cup football matches held in the ***Stadium Negeri Sarawak***, Petra Jaya. The ***Turf Club*** on Serian Rd is the biggest in Borneo (see newspapers for details of meetings).

Swimming: ***Kuching Municipal Swimming Pool***, next to Kuching Turf Club, Serian Rd, admission RM1, open am only, another public pool is on Jln Pandungan, just past the Kuching City South Council office complex.

Watersports: Damai Beach.

● Tour companies & travel agents

Borneo Adventure, No 55 Main Bazaar, T 245175, F 422626, recommended; ***Borneo Interland Travel***, 63 1st flr Main Bazaar, T 413595, F 411619, as well as wide range of local tours, car-hire, air, bus and boat tickets – including bus tickets for Pontianak (Indonesia); ***Borneo Transverse***, 10b 1st Flr, Wayang St, T 257784, F 421419; ***CPH Travel Agencies***, 70 Ground Floor, Jln Padungan, T 243708, F 426981, also have tour desks in *Riverside Majestic Hotel* and *Damai Lagoon Resort*; ***Ibanika Expeditions***, Lot 435, Ground Floor, Jln Ang Cheng Ho, T 424022, also offers French and German-speaking guides; ***Inter-World Services***, 85 Jln Rambutan, T 252344, F 424515; ***Journey Travel Agencies***, Lobby Flr, *Hilton Hotel*, Jln Borneo, T 424934, F 240652; ***Pan Asia Travel***, 2nd Flr, Unit 217-218, Sarawak Plaza, Jln Tunku Abdul Rahman, T 419754, half day excursions from Kuching.

● Tourist offices

The state and national tourism organizations are both well informed and helpful; they can offer advice on itineraries, travel agents and up-to-date information on facilities in national parks. **National Parks and Wildlife Office**, Wisma Sumber Alam, Jln Stadium, Petra Jaya (T 442180, F 441377) for information on national parks and advance bookings (note that the office is inconveniently located and it is easier to use the National Park Booking Office in the Sarawak Tourist Information Centre); Visitors' Information Centre, 31 Jln Masjid, Padang Merdeka, T 248088, F 256301 (beside the new wing of the Sarawak Museum), it is possible to book national park accommodation and obtain permits for Bako at this office, historical exhibitions on Sarawak, open 0800-1615 Mon-Thur, 0800-1645 Fri, 0800-1245 Sat, the centre holds two shows daily (at 1000 and 1500) on the variety of attractions in the state; **Sarawak Tourism Centre**, waterfront, Main Bazaar, T 240620, F 427151 or Kuching International Airport, T 456266, good for information on bus routes, approved travel agents and itineraries; It is possible to call the STB toll-free from Kuala Lumpur (T 8009291) or from Singapore (T 800 6011043) from 0800-1245, 1400-1615 Mon-Fri and 0800-1245 Sat. **Tourism Malaysia**, Bangunan Rugayah, Jln Song Thian Cheok, T 246775, information on Sarawak and rest of Malaysia – good stock of brochures.

● Useful addresses

Immigration: 1st Flr, Bangunan Sultan Iskandar (Federal Complex) Jln Simpang Tiga, T 245661.
Police: T 241222.
Resident's Office: T 243301.

● Transport

Local Boat: sampans cross the Sarawak River from next to the Square Tower on Main Bazaar to Fort Margherita and the Astana on the north bank (RM0.30). Small boats and some express boats connect with outlying kampongs on the river. Sampans can also be hired by the hour (RM15-20) for a tour up and down the river. The Waterfront Development Office plan to take boat hire under their control so that tourists will have to purchase coupons from the Waterfront office. **Bus**: there are two bus companies around town: Chin Lian Long's blue and white buses serve the city and its suburbs. Major bus stops at Jln Mosque, the Post Office and Gambier St. The green and yellow Sarawak Transport Company (STC) buses leave from the end of Lebuh Jawa, next to Ban Hock Wharf and the market. STC buses operate on regional routes; bus 12A (RM0.80) goes to the airport, service starts at 0630 and departs every 40 minutes until 1915. Chin Lian Long blue buses 19 or 17 go to the jetty, the Bintawa Express Wharf, for boats to Sibu (RM0.40). **Car hire**: **Avis**, Ground Floor, *Holiday Inn*, Jln Tunku Abdul Rahman, T 411370; **Mahana Rent-a-Car**, 18G, Level 1, Taman Sri Sarawak Mall, Jln Borneo (opposite *Hilton Hotel*), T 411370, F 423644. **Pronto Car Rental**, 1st Flr, 98 Jln Padungan, T/F 236889, also at Kuching International Airport; **Mayflower Car Rental**, Lot 4.24A, 4th flr, Bangunan Satok, Jln Satok, T 410110, F 410115, Kuching International Airport booth, T 575233. **Taxi**: local taxis congregate at the taxi stand on Jln Market, or outside the big hotels, they do not use meters, so agree a price before setting off. 24-hour radio taxi service T 343343/342255. Short distances around town should cost RM5. 'Midnight' surcharge of 50% 2400-0600.

Air The airport is 10 km south of Kuching. Regular connections with KL (RM199 – early morning economy), JB (RM169), KK (RM228), Bintulu (RM117), Miri (RM164), Sibu (RM72), Penang (RM340), Labuan (RM199), Mukah (RM76), Bandar Seri Begawan, Brunei (RM288). **NB** MAS has advance purchase fares and 50% group discounts on certain flights (bookable only in Malaysia).SIA also operates direct flights to and from Singapore (RM267), Saenga Airlines flies to Sibu. Green bus Sarawak Transport Co, 12A (RM0.80) from Lebuh Jawa or taxi to town: RM16.50.

Road Bus: there are several different bus companies serving varying destinations. The *Sarawak Transport Company* (T 242967) operates green and yellow buses and leave from Lebuh Jawa, next to Ban Hock Wharf. They serve the Kuching area and south-west Sarawak. *Petra Jaya Transport* (T 429418) serves Bako, Damai and Santubong. Their buses (yellow with black and red stripes) depart from the open air market near Electra House. *Matang Transport Company's* yellow and orange buses depart from outside the Saujana Car Park and go to Matang and Kubah. Long distance buses depart from the Regional Express Bus Terminal on Jln Penrissen. The most convenient place to buy tickets is at the *Biaramas Express* office on Jln Khoo Hun Yeang (near Electra House), T 429418. *Biaramas* also has a 24-hour office at the terminal (T 452139). Buses to Sibu, Bintulu and Miri often involve a change of bus in Sarikei.

River Boat: express boats leave from the Marine Base, Jln Pending, 4 km east of town. *Getting there*: blue bus 19 or 17 (RM0.60) from Lubuh Jawa; taxi (RM10) from Lebuh Market. Tickets for the Kuching-Sibu express boats can be bought in advance at the *Metropole Inn Hotel*, 196 Jln Padungan or *Borneo Interland Travel*, 63 Main Bazaar. Regular connections with Sibu (involving a change to a river express boat at Sarikei); 4 hours (RM33). There are also cargo boats going to Sibu and Miri 18 hours (RM12): further information from Sarawak Tourist Association.

● International connections

Air MAS operates a twice weekly flight from Kuching to Pontianak, Kalimantan. Dragonair operates 2 direct flights weekly from Kuching to Hong Kong, with onward connections.

Bus fares and destinations, Kuching

Destination	Bus No/ Company	Duration	Departure	Fare
Kuching Airport	STC 12A	30 minutes	every 50 minutes 0630-1900	RM0.90
Bako	Petra Jaya 6 (minibuses also leave Electra House for Kampung Bako, RM3)	45 minutes	0640-1800	RM2.10
Bau	STC 2	1 hour	every 40 minutes 0600-1800	RM3 (a/c)
Bintulu	(see Sarikei)			RM52
Buntal	Petra Jaya 2B	35 minutes		RM2
Damai/Cultural Village	Shuttle bus from *Holiday Inn*, *Riverside Majestic*, *Borneo Hotel*, *Santubong Inn*, 2 pickups daily, T 846411	50 minutes	0900 and 1230	
Kubah	Matang 18	50 minutes	0600-1640	RM3
Lubok Antu	Biaramas	4 hours	departs 1300	RM20 (a/c)
Lundu (for G Gading)	STC 2B	2 hours	0800-1600	RM6.80-7.80
Miri	(see Sarikei)			RM70
Penrissen Bus Terminal	STC		0630-2100	RM0.50
Pontianak (Indonesia)		10 hours	0700-1230	RM34.50
Santubong Village	Petra Jaya 2B	40 minutes	0645-1800	RM2.30
Sarikei	Biaramas/ Borneo Express	5-6 hours	0630-2200	RM28
Sematan	STC 2B to Lundu, then connecting Lundu-Sematan bus			
Semenggoh	STC 6		every hour	RM1.50
Serian	STC 3 or 3A	1 hour	every 35 minutes 0630-1750	RM4.60-5
Sibu	(see Sarikei)	7 hours		RM35
Sri Aman	Biaramas, STC	3 hours	0730-1930	RM15 (a/c)

Road Bus: regular express buses go to Pontianak in Kalimantan, Indonesia, 10 hours (depart 0700-1230, RM34.50). It is necessary to have a valid Indonesian visa (see Consulates, above). Buses leave from Khoo Hun Yeang St. Booking office: Mile 3.5, Penrissen Rd, T 454548/454668 or through Kedai Jam Ban Poh, 130 Jln Padungan or *Borneo Interland Travel*, 63 Main Bazaar. There are now several bus companies, providing a/c, reclining seats, wc. *SJS Executive Bus Co*, leaves from 3½ mile Bus Terminal, Jln Penrissen – daily service to Pontianak, morning departure, 10 hours (so long as there is no delay at the border). Other companies include *Biaramas* and *Tebakong*. For a more adventurous route, it is possible to take Sarawak Transport Company buses 3 or 3A to Serian, 1 hour; *Mara Transport Company* bus from Serian to Tebedu, 1½ hours, and from Tebedu it is possible to trek across the border to Balai Kerangan in Kalimantan.

DAMAI PENINSULA

The Damai Peninsula, 35 km north of Kuching, has been developed over recent years by the Sarawak Economic Development Corporation, partly to create local employment and partly to open up the area to tourism. The peninsula is located at the west mouth of the Sarawak River and extends northwards as far as Mount Santubong, a majestic peak of 810m. Its attractions include the Sarawak Cultural Village, trekking up Mount Santubong, sandy beaches, a golf course, adventure camp and three resorts which are particularly good value off season when promotional rates are often available.

The village of **Santubong** itself, located at the mouth of the Sarawak River, is small and quiet. Formerly a fishing village, most of the villagers now work in one of the nearby resorts. However, some fishing still goes on, and the daily catch is still sold every morning at the quayside. Near the quayside are two or three Chinese-run grocery stores and a simple coffee shop. The rest of the village is made up of small houses strung out along the road, built in the Malay tradition on stilts – many are wooden and painted in bright colours. The only other village on the peninsula is **Buntal** which lies just off the Kuching-Santubong road. Popular with local Kuchingities who come here at the weekends for the seafood restaurants, the resort that was built here never really took off and it is planned to be turned into a hotel training centre.

The **Sarawak Cultural Village** (Kampong Budaya Sarawak) was the brainchild of the Sarawak Development Corporation which built Sarawak's 'living museum' at a cost of RM9.5mn to promote and preserve Sarawak's cultural heritage. With increasing numbers of young tribal people being tempted from their longhouses into the modern sectors of the economy, many of Sarawak's traditional crafts have begun to die out. The Cultural Village set out to teach the old arts and crafts to new generations. For the state development corporation, the concept had the added appeal of creating a money-spinning 'Instant Sarawak' for the benefit of tourists lacking the time or inclination to head into the jungle. As with any such artificial scheme, it is rather contrived, but the Cultural Village has been a resounding success and contains some superb examples of traditional architecture. It should be on the sight-seeing agenda of every visitor to Kuching, if only to provide an introduction to the cultural traditions of all the main ethnic groups in Sarawak.

Each tribal group is represented by craftsmen and women who produce handicrafts and practice traditional skills in houses built to carefully researched design specifications. Many authentic every-day articles have been collected from longhouses all over Sarawak. In one case the Village has served to preserve a culture that is already effectively dead: today the Melanau people all live in Malay-style kampongs, but a magnificent traditional wooden Melanau house has been built at the Cultural Village and is now the only such building in Sarawak. Alongside it there is a demonstration of traditional sago processing.

A resident Melanau craftsman makes sickness images (*blum*) – each representing the spirit of an illness, which were floated downriver in tiny boats as part of the healing ritual.

There are also Bidayuh, Iban and Orang Ulu longhouses, depicting the lifestyles of each group. In each there are textile or basket-weavers, wood-carvers or sword-makers. There are exhibits of beadwork, bark clothing, and *tuak* (rice wine) brewing. At the Penan hut there is a demonstration of blow-pipe making – visitors are invited to test their hunting skills. There is a Malay house and even a Chinese farmhouse with a pepper garden alongside. The tour of all the houses, seven in all (you can collect a stamp from each one for your passport!) is capped by an Andrew Lloyd Webber-style cultural show which is expertly choreographed – if rather ersatz. It is held in the on-site theatre which is fully a/c.

The Cultural Village employs 140 people, including dancers, who earn around RM300 a month and take home the profits from handicraft and tuak sales. Special application must be made to attend heritage centre workshops where courses can be requested in various crafts such as wood-carving, mat-weaving, batik-painting; also intensive day-long and 3-4 days courses. Restaurant and craft shop, *Sarakraf*. Admission RM45, child (6-12 years) RM22.50, including cultural show. Open 0900-1715 Monday-Sunday, cultural show 1130-1215 and 1630-1715.

Excursions

Gunung Santubong (810m) is on the Santubong Peninsula, and its precipitous southern side provides a moody backdrop to Damai Beach. The distinctive – and very steep – mountain is most accessible from the east side, where there is a clear ridge trail to the top. There are two trails to the summit, one of which begins opposite the *Palm Beach Seafood Restaurant and Resort*, about 2.5 km before the *Holiday Inn Damai Beach*. The conical peak – from which there are spectacular views – can be reached in 7-9 hours (the last stretch is a tough scramble), guides are not necessary (but can be provided), check with the hotel recreation counters or at the Santubong Mountain Trek Canteen (T 846153). The official *Damai Guide* provides a more detailed description of the trek. Take supplies of food and water. *Getting there*: bus to Damai Beach or (more regularly) to Santubong.

Pulau Satang Besar, north of Kampung Telaga Air, has been designated as a Turtle Sanctuary to protect the Green Turtles which come ashore here to lay their eggs. *Getting there*: inquire at the Visitor Information Centre in Kuching for departures from Santubong or Kampung Telaga Air.

Trips up the Salak River depart from the terminal at Santubong village, a 10 minute drive from the resort hotels. These river tours last about 3 hours. The journey ventures into smaller rives and a creek and it is a good introduction to the mangrove forest ecosystem. Contact hotel recreation counters or tour operators for details.

Malay villages (kampungs) in Damai and Santubong can be visited from the resort hotels – a recommended excursions. These include Kampung Santubong, Buntal, Pasir Panjong or Pasir Pandak. *Getting there*: own transportation required.

Local information

● Accommodation

Prices: L over RM500; **A+** RM260-500; **A** RM130-260; **B** RM65-130; **C** RM40-65; **D** RM20-40; **E** RM10-20; **F** Below RM10

L-A+ *Damai Lagoon Resort*, Teluk Penyuk, Santubong, PO Box 3159, T 846900, F 846901, managed by *A&A Hotels*, it is the sister of the *River Majestic* in Kuching, superbly located at the foot of Mount Santubong, on a small, well-kept, sandy beach, its 256 rooms and 30 chalets are in stylish buildings with steep, wood-shingled roofs, there are polished wood floors and decorative woodcarving throughout, a monumental, timber-roofed lobby open to the sea, and pleasant gardens dotted with tribal wooden effigies surrounding a lagoon-style pool (the largest in Sarawak) which has a sandy slope for kids at one end and a man-made cave, complete with cascade and stage for shows, at the other, the lagoon also has a circular, swim-up bar, shaded by colonial, wood-shingled roof, all rooms have a/c, TV, in-house movies, mini-bar, tea and coffee-making facilities, balcony and personal safe, other facilities including restaurant, tea-house (excellent for sunset views), bar, health club (with spa), tennis, boutique, bicycle hire, canoe hire, watersports and children's playground, stirling competition for the *Holiday Inn* and definitely better in terms of access to beach and general tranquility, recommended. **L-A+** *Holiday Inn Resort Damai Beach*, Teluk Bandung, Santubong, PO Box 2870, T 846999, F 846777, taken over from the *Sheraton* in 1987, the resort calls itself the 'Crown Jewel of Sarawak', although the real jewel in the crown is the large, private, wooden mansion at the top of the resort which belongs to the Sultan of Brunei, the new hill-top extension, directly below the Sultan's mansion, has chalets modelled on ethnic designs, such as the circular Bidayuh buildings which make this a better than average *Holiday Inn*, the beach is bigger than that at *Damai Lagoon Resort*, but less accessible if you are staying at the hill-top site, the total 302 rooms, including 179 chalets, all with a/c, colour TV, in-house movie, coffee and tea-making facilities, other facilities including 2 pools, tennis, spa pool, watersports, kiddies' club, bicycle/scooter hire, games room, restaurant (good value buffet), PV Fun Pub (a popular night spot for Kuchingites), children's playground and lobby shops. **A+** *Santubong Kuching Resort*, Jln Santubong, PO Box 2364, T 846888, F 846666, surrounded by the *Damai Golf Course*, 380 rooms all with a/c, restaurant, large pool, chalets with jacuzzis, tennis, basketball, volleyball, gym, mountain biking etc., nestling beneath Mount Santubong, a low rise resort popular with golfers, it also has the largest conference and banquet facilities in Sarawak. **A** *Damai Rainforest Resort (Camp Permai)*, Pantai Damai, Santubong, PO Box B91, Satok Post Office, T 321498, F 321500, located at the foot of Mount Santubong, near the *Damai Lagoon Resort*, this is an outward bound centre which offers a number of courses including adventure training and leadership development, other facilities include artificial climbing wall, obstacle course, abseiling, sailing, canoeing, paintball competitions, accommodation in 10 a/c tree houses or log cabins, cafeteria, tents and camping equipment for hire.

● Places to eat

Santubong Mountain Trek Canteen, 5 minutes walk from hotels, rice and noodle dishes, in nearby *Buntal village* there are excellent seafood restaurants.

● Bars

PV The Fun Pub at *Holiday Inn Damai Beach* is Damai's main night spot and very popular – an open air pub with pool and karaoke and live bands.

● Entertainment

Cultural shows: *Cultural Village*, Damai Beach, cultural shows, with stylized and expertly choreographed tribal dance routines, 1130 and 1630, Mon-Sun.

● Sports

Golf: *Damai Golf Course*, Jln Santubong, PO Box 400, T 846088, F 846044, international standard, 18-hole golf course designed by Arnold Palmer, laid out over approximately 6.5 km, 10-bay driving range, green fees weekdays RM80, weekends RM100, caddies, clubs and shoes for hire, spacious club house, restaurant, bar, pro shop, tennis, squash, pool.

● Transport

Road Bus: there are shuttle buses from the *Holiday Inn* and *Riverside Majestic* or take the public bus, operated by Petra Jaya Transport (yellow buses with black and red stripes) at a fraction of the price from the market place at the end of Jln Gambier. Tour companies offer packages for US$60, for transport on shuttle bus, entrance to the Sarawak Cultural Village and lunch. **Taxi**: from Kuching costs RM30, from the airport RM46.50.

BAKO NATIONAL PARK

Established in 1957, Bako was Sarawak's first national park. It is a very small park (2,742 hectares) but it has an exceptional variety of flora, and contains almost every type of vegetation in Borneo. Very soon the park will be privatised, which will guarantee its conservation and tourism will be more actively promoted. Bako is situated on the beautiful Muara Tebas peninsula, a former river delta which has been thrust above sea level. Its sandstone cliffs, which are patterned and streaked with iron deposits, have been eroded to produce a dramatic coastline with secluded coves and beaches and rocky headlands. Millions of years of erosion by the sea has resulted in the formation of wave-cut platforms, 'honeycomb' weathering, solution pans, arches and sea stacks. Bako's most distinctive feature is the westernmost headland – Tanjung Sapi – a 100m high sandstone plateau, which is unique in Borneo.

Flora and fauna

There are seven separate types of vegetation in Bako. These include mangroves (*bakau* is the most common stilt-rooted mangrove species), swamp forest and heath forest – known as *kerangas*, an Iban word meaning 'land on which rice cannot grow'. Pitcher plants (*Nepenthes ampullaria*) do however grow in profusion on the sandy soil (see page 38). There is also mixed dipterocarp rainforest (the most widespread forest type in Sarawak, characterized by its 30-40m-high canopy), beach forest, and *padang* vegetation, comprised of scrub and bare rock from which there are magnificent views of the coast. The rare *daun payang* (umbrella palm) is found in Bako park; it is a litter-trapping plant as its large fronds catch falling leaves from the trees above and funnel them downwards where they eventually form a thick organic mulch enabling the plant to survive on otherwise infertile soil. There are also wild durian trees in the forest – they can take up to 60 years to bear fruit.

Bako is one of the few areas in Sarawak inhabited by the proboscis monkey (*Nasalis larvatus*), known by Malays as 'Orang Belanda' – or Dutchmen, or even 'Pinocchio of the jungle' – because of their long noses (see page 325). Bako is home to approximately 150 rare proboscis monkeys. They are most often seen in the early morning or at dusk in the Teluk Assam, Teluk Paku and Teluk Delima areas (at the far west side of the park, closest to the headquarters) or around Teluk Paku, a 45 minutes walk from park HQ. The park also has resident populations of squirrels, mousedeer, sambar deer, wild pigs, long-tailed macaques, flying lemur, silver leaf monkeys and palm civet cats. Teluk Assam, in the area around park HQ, is one of the best places for birdwatching: over 150 species have been recorded in the park, including pied

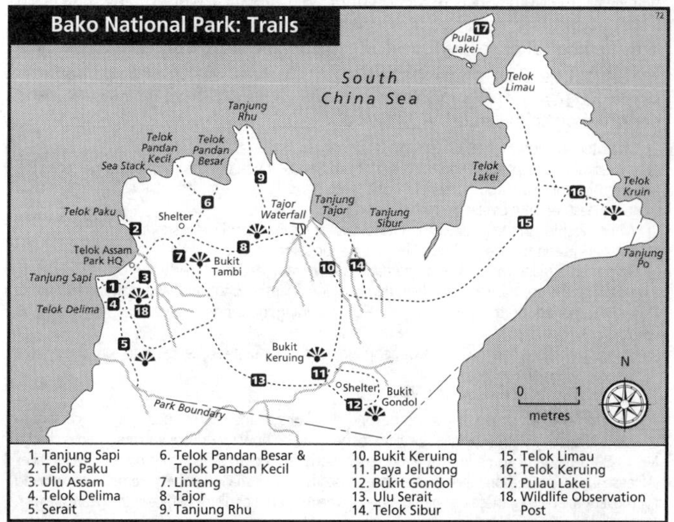

Visiting longhouses: house rules

There are more than 1,500 longhouses in Sarawak, and as the state's varied tribal culture is one of its biggest attractions, trips to longhouses are on most visitors' itineraries. Longhouses are usually situated along the big rivers and their tributaries... notably the Skrang (the most easily accessible to Kuching, see page 381), the Rejang (see page 389) and the Baram (see page 406). The **Iban**, who are characteristically extrovert and hospitable to visitors, live on the lower reaches of the rivers. The **Orang Ulu tribes** – mainly Kayan and Kenyah – live further upriver, and are generally less outgoing than the Iban. The **Bidayuh** (formerly known as the 'Land Dayaks') live mainly around Bau and Serian, near Kuching. Their longhouses are usually more modern than those of the Iban and Orang Ulu, and are less often visited for that reason. The **Kelabit** people live in the remote plateau country near the Kalimantan border around Bareo (see page 419).

The most important ground rule is not to visit a longhouse without an invitation... people who arrive unannounced may get an embarrassingly frosty reception. Tour companies offer the only exception to this rule, as most have tribal connections. Upriver, particularly at Kapit, on the Rejang (see page 389), such 'invitations' are not hard to come by; it is good to ensure that your host actually comes from the longhouse he is inviting you to. The best time to visit Iban longhouses is during the *gawai* harvest festival at the beginning of Jun, when communities throw an open-house and everyone is invited to join the drinking, story-telling and dancing sessions, which continue for several days.

On arrival, visitors should pay an immediate courtesy call on the headman (known as the *tuai rumah* in Iban longhouses). It is normal to bring him gifts; those staying overnight should offer the headman between M$10 and M$20/head. The money is kept in a central fund and saved for use by the whole community during festivals. Small gifts such as beer, coffee, tea, biscuits, whisky, batik and food (especially rice or chicken) go down well. It is best to arrive at a longhouse during late afternoon after people have returned from the fields. Visitors who have time to stay the night generally have a much more enjoyable experience than those who pay fleeting visits. They can share the evening meal and have time to talk... and drink. Visitors should note the following:

- ❑ On entering a longhouse, take off your shoes.
- ❑ It is usual to accept food and drink with both hands. If you do not want to eat or drink, the accepted custom is to touch the brim of the glass or the plate and then touch your lips as a symbolic gesture; sit cross-legged when eating.
- ❑ When washing in the river, women should wear a sarong and men, shorts.
- ❑ Ask permission to take photographs. It is not uncommon to be asked for a small fee.
- ❑ Do not enter a longhouse during *pantang* (taboo), a period of misfortune – usually following a death. There is normally a white (leaf) flag hanging near the longhouse as a warning to visitors. During this period (normally 1 week) there is no singing, dancing or music, and no jewellery is worn.
- ❑ Bow your head when walking past people older than you. It is rude to stride confidently past with head held high.
- ❑ Try not to shout or be loud and noisy.

Trips upriver are not cheap. If you go beyond the limits of the express boats, it is necessary to charter a longboat. Petrol costs M$2-4/litre, depending on how far upriver you are. Guides charge M$40-80 a day and sometimes it is necessary to hire a boatman or front-man as well. Prices increase in the dry season when boats have to be lifted over shallow rapids. Permits are required for most upriver areas; these can be obtained at the resident's or district office in the nearest town.

Interior of a Sea Dyak Long-house, from William T Hornaday's (1885) *Two years in the jungle: the experience of a hunter and naturalist in India, Ceylon, the Malay Peninsula and Borneo*

and black hornbills. Large numbers of migratory birds come to Bako between September and November. The blue fiddler crab – which has one big claw, and is forever challenging others to a fight, can also be seen in the park and mudskippers – evolutionary throw-backs (half-fish, half-frog) are common in mangrove areas. Also in the park there are two species of otter: the oriental small-clawed otter and the hairy-nosed otter (the best area to see them is at Teluk Assam). The Bornean bearded pig is the largest mammal found at the park and is usually seen snuffling around the park HQ. There are many lizards, with the water monitor being the largest – and often found near the accommodation. The only poisonous snake occasionally seen is the Wagler's pit viper. Nocturnal animals include flying lemur, pangolin, mousedeer, bats, tarsier, slow loris and palm civet (the beach by the HQ is a great place for a night time stroll).

Treks

There are a good range of well marked trails throughout the park – over 30 km in total; all paths are colour coded, corresponding with the map available from Park HQ. The shortest trek is the steep climb to the top of Tanjong Sapi, overlooking Teluk Assam, which affords good views of Gunung Santubong, on the opposite peninsula, across Tanjong Sipang, to the west. Some trails are temporarily closed – check with Park HQ. Full day treks and overnight camping expeditions can be arranged. There are plank walkways with shelters at intervals – to provide quiet watching spots particularly required for viewing the proboscis monkey in the early morning.

Beaches

The best swimming beach is at Teluk Pandan Kecil, about 1½ hours walk, northeast from Park HQ. It is also possible to swim at Teluk Assam and Teluk Paku. Enquire about jellyfish at Park HQ before swimming in the sea; it is advisable not to swim in March and April.

Transport around the park It is possible to hire boats around the park: speed boats RM85 (can accommodate 5-6).

Permits are available from the National Parks Booking Office, Sarawak Tourist Information Centre on Padang Merdeka, T 248088, F 256301. Day-trippers can pick up a day permit at the Bako boat jetty in Kampung Bako. On arrival visitors are required to register at the Park HQ.

Park Information Centre is next to park HQ, with a small exhibition on geology, flora and fauna within the park. Visitors can request to see an introductory video to Bako National Park, duration 42 minutes. Open 0800-1245 (0800-1100 on Friday) 1400-1615 Monday-Sunday.

Entrance to Park RM3/adult, RM1/child or student. Photography permit RM5, video camera RM10, professional camera RM200.

Park information

● Accommodation

All bookings to be made at the National Parks and Wildlife Booking Office, c/o Visitors' Information Centre, Lot 31, Jln Masjid, Kuching, T 248088, F 256301. The hostels are equipped with mattresses, kerosene stoves and cutlery. Resthouses have refrigerators and electricity until 2400. Unless a researcher, the recommended length of stay is 2 days/1 night. Resthouses and the hostel have fans ***Lodge***, RM40/room; ***Hostel*** RM40/room, RM10/bed, check-out time 1200.

● Camping

For those not intending to trek to the other side of the park, it is not worth camping as monkeys steal anything left lying around and macaques can be aggressive. In addition, the smallest amount of rain turns the campsite into a swimming pool. It is however necessary to camp if you go to the beaches on the Northeast peninsula. Tents can be hired RM8 (sleeps 4); campsite RM4.

● Places to eat

The canteen is open 0700-2100. It serves local food at reasonable prices and sells tinned foods and drinks. No need to take food, there is a shop available and a good seafood restaurant near the jetty.

● Transport

37 km from Kuching.

Bus & boat: Petra Jaya (yellow/red/black stripes) bus 6 or Bus Company Chin Lian Long, Regas Transport or Sarawak Transport every 15 minutes from Electra House on Lebuh Market to Kampong Bako, 45 minutes (RM3.50) every hour; also minibuses from Lebuh Market. From Kampong Bako, charter a private boat to Sungai Assam (30 minutes) which is a short walk from Park HQ, RM30/boat each way – ask price before boarding (up to 6 people). **NB** In the monsoon season, between Nov and Feb, the sea can be rough. Local tour operators also organize trips and boats to the park are operated by villagers who live nearby.

BANDAR SRI AMAN

Bandar Sri Aman, previously called Simmanggang, lies on the Batang Lupar. The river is famous for its tidal bore and divides into several tributaries: the Skrang River is one of these (see below). The Batang Lupar provided Somerset Maugham with the inspiration for his short story *Yellow Streak* in *Borneo Tales*. It was one of the few stories he wrote from personal experience: he nearly drowned after being caught by the bore in 1929.

Bandar Sri Aman is the administrative capital of the second division. **Fort Alice** is the only building of note and was constructed in 1864. It has small turrets, a central courtyard, a medieval-looking drawbridge, and is surrounded by a fence of iron spikes. Rajah Charles Brooke lived in the Batang Lupar district for about 10 years, using this fort – and another downriver at Lingga – as bases for his punitive expeditions against pirates and Ibans in the interior. The fort is the only one of its type in Sarawak and was built commanding this stretch of the Batang Lupar River as protection against Iban raids. The original fort here was built in 1849 and named Fort James; the current fort was constructed using much of the original materal. It was renamed Alice in honour of Ranee Margaret Brooke (it was her second name). It is said that every evening at 2000 until the practice was ended in 1964 a policeman would call from the fort (in Iban): "Oh ha! Oh ha! The time is now 2000. The steps have been drawn up. The door is closed. People from upriver, people from downriver are not allowed to come to the fort anymore." (It probably sounded better in Iban.)

Most tourists do not stop in Bandar but pass through on day trips up the Skrang River from Kuching. The route to Bandar goes through pepper plantations and many 'new' villages. During Communist guerrilla activity in the 1960s (see page 341), whole settlements were uprooted in this area and placed in guarded camps.

Excursions

Skrang longhouses The Skrang River (the second longest river in Sarawak) was one of the first areas settled by Iban immigrants in the 16th-18th centuries. The slash-and-burn agriculturalists originally came from the Kapual River basin in Kalimantan. They later joined forces with Malay chiefs in the coastal areas and terrorized the Borneo coasts; the first Europeans to encounter these pirates called them 'Sea Dayaks' (see page 343). They took many heads. Blackened skulls – which local headmen say date back to those days – hang in some of the Skrang longhouses. In 1849, more than 800 Iban pirates from the Batang Lupar and Skrang River were massacred by Rajah James Brooke's forces in the notorious Battle of Beting Marau. 4 years later the Sultan of Brunei agreed to cede these troublesome districts to Brooke; they became the Second Division of Sarawak.

There are many traditional Iban longhouses along the Skrang River, although those closer to Pias and Lamanak (the embarkation points on the Skrang) tend to be very touristy – they are visited by tour groups almost every day. Long Mujang, the first Iban longhouse, is an hour upriver. Pias and Lamanak are within 5 hours drive of Kuching. **Trekking**: Jungle trekking is available (approximately 2 hours), RM20. The guide provides an educational tour of the flora and fauna. **Accommodation** All longhouses along the Skrang River are controlled by the Ministry of Tourism so all rates are the same – RM40 inclusive of all meals. Resthouses at most of the longhouses can accommodate 20-40 people, mattresses and mosquito nets are provided in a communal sleeping area with few partitions, basic conditions, with flush toilet, shower, local food (visitors are sometimes allowed to sleep on the communal area), phone available and clinic nearby. If the stay is 3days/2 nights, on the second night it is possible to camp in the jungle and then get a return boatride to the longhouse. *Getting there*: bus 14 and 19 to Pias (RM4) and bus 9 to Lemanak (RM6). Self-drive car rental RM300-400 return or minibus (8-10 people) RM1000 return from Kuching to Entaban. From these points it is necessary to charter a boat, which costs around RM100 to reach the nearest longhouses. Many of the Kuching-based tour agencies offer cut-price deals for day-long or 2-day excursions to Skrang. Unless you are already part of a small group, these tours work out cheaper because of the boat costs.

Batang Ai The Batang Ai River, a tributary of the Batang Lupar, has been dammed to form Sarawak's first hydroelectric plant which came into service in 1985; it provides 60% of Sarawak's electricity supply, transmitting as afar as Limbang. The area was slowly flooded over a period of 6 months to give animals and wildlife a chance to escape, but it has effected no less than 29 longhouses, 10 of which are now completely submerged. The re-housing of the longhouse community has been the topic of controversial debate over the last 10 years. The communities were moved into modern longhouses and given work opportunities in local palmeries. However, it now seems that the housing loans that were initially given are not commensurate with local wages and will be very difficult for the longhouse communities ever to pay off. In addition, the modern longhouses were not provided with farmland, so many local people have returned to settle on the banks of the reservoir. Near the dam there is a fresh water fish nursery. These fish are exported to Korea, Japan and Europe.

Those families displaced by the flooding of the dam largely work here and many of the longhouses surrounding the dam depend upon this fishery for their own fish supply.

The Batang Ai dam has created a vast and very picturesque man-made lake which covers an area of some 90 sq km, stretching up the Engkari and Ai rivers. Beyond the lake, more than an hour's boat ride upriver from the dam, it is possible to see beautiful lowland mixed dipterocarp forest. The **Batang Ai National Park** covers an area of over 24,040 hectares and was inaugurated in 1991. It protects the much endangered orang utan, and is home to a wide variety of other wildlife, including hornbills and gibbons. As yet there are no visitor facilities, but four walking trails have been created, one of which takes in an ancient burial ground. Trips to one of the 29 longhouses surrounding the dam and to Batang Ai National Park are organized by *Borneo Adventure Travel Company* who are based in Kuching (55 Main Bazaar, T 410569, F 422626) and have a counter in the *Hilton Batang Ai Longhouse Resort*. Many of the restaurant staff in the resort are locals and discreet enquiries may get you a trip to a longhouse and/or Batang Ai National Park for considerably less than the *Borneo Adventure Travel Company* charge. **Accommodation A** *Hilton International Batang Ai Longhouse Resort*, c/o *Kuching Hilton International*, T 248200, F 428984, on the eastern shore of the lake, the *Hilton* have built a luxury longhouse resort. Opened in 1995, the resort is made up of 11 longhouses, built of the local belian (ironwood) to traditional designs. Unfortunately this means that despite its lakeside location there are no views, except from the walkways, as longhouses are built, for purposes of defence, to face landwards – in this case over the buggy track. However, compromises to modern comforts have been made with the result that the rooms are somewhat cluttered with furniture and TV sets. 100 rooms all with a/c, fan, TV, shower room, tea and coffee making facilities, mini-bar, other facilities include a pool and paddling pool, restaurant, 18 km jogging track, shuttle from *Kuching Hilton International*, tour desk. If the *Hilton* is not your style (or your pocket cannot stretch to it), there is, unfortunately, not much else. The park does not supply any rooms. However, there are some private tour companies which provide accommodation in the longhouses here, in a much more central location within the Park than the *Hiton* (which is not very close to the longhouses). *Getting there*: the park is 250 km from Kuching and takes 2 hours from the jetty by boat (RM300 return).

Bukit Saban Resort located on the rarely visited Paku River, just north of the Skrang and Lemnak rivers, about 4½ hours from Kuching. Sales office T 232351, F 245551, 50 rooms in longhouse style with traditional sago palm thatch, RM92, restaurant, a/c, TV, hot water, seminar facilities.

Local information

● Accommodation

Limited selection.

B-C *Alison*, 4 Jln Council, T 322578/9. **B-C** *Hoover*, Tiong Hua Building, 139 Jln Club, T 321985-8. **B-C** *Taiwan*, 1 Jln Council, T 322493, a/c.

C *Sum Sun*, 62 Jln Club, T 322191, a/c.

● Places to eat

♦*Alison Café & Restaurant*, 4 Jln Council, Chinese cuisine. *Chuan Hong*, 1 Jln Council, Chinese coffee shop, also serves Muslim food. *Melody*, 432 Jln Hospital, Chinese and Muslim food.

● Useful addresses

Resident's Office: T 322004.

● Transport

135 km from Kuching.

Road Bus: regular connections with Kuching (RM12) and Sibu (via Sarikei).

SIBU AND THE REJANG RIVER

SIBU

The Batang Rejang is an important thoroughfare and Malaysia's longest river at 563 km (it is, however, 12 times shorter than the Nile). Tours to upriver longhouses can be organized from Sibu, or more cheaply from Kapit and Belaga.

With a population of 150,000, Sibu is the second largest town in Sarawak. The town is sited at the confluence of the Rejang and the Igan rivers 60 km upstream from the sea. Thanks to the discovery of the Kuala Paloh channel in 1961, Sibu is accessible to boats with a sizeable draft. It is the starting-point for trips up the Rejang to the towns of Kapit and Belaga.

Sibu is a busy Chinese trading town – the majority of the population came originally from China's Foochow Province – and is the main port on the Batang Rejang (also spelt 'Rajang'). In 1899, Rajah Charles Brooke agreed with Wong Nai Siong, a Chinese scholar from Fukien, to allow settlers to Sibu. Brooke had reportedly been impressed with the industriousness of the Chinese: he saw the women toiling in the paddy fields from dawn to dusk and commented to an aide: "If the women work like that, what on earth must the men be like?"

The Kuching administration provided these early agricultural pioneers with temporary housing on arrival, a steamer between Sibu and Kuching, rice rations for the first year and tuition in Malay and Iban. The town grew quickly (its rapid early expansion is documented in a photographic exhibition in the Civic Centre), but was razed to the ground in 'the great fire' of 1828. The first shophouses to be constructed after the fire are the 3-storey ones still standing on

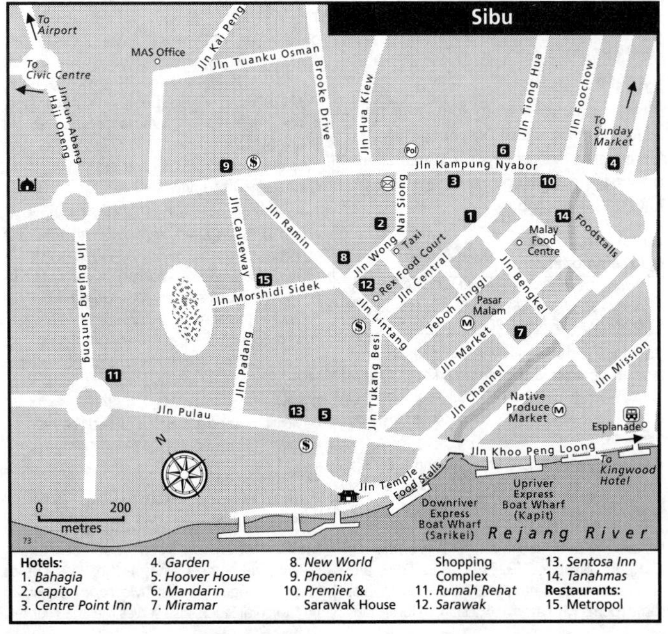

Jalan Channel. In the first few years of the 20th century, Sibu became the springboard for Foochow migration to the rest of Sarawak. Today it is an industrial and trading centre for timber, pepper and rubber. It is home to some of Sarawak's wealthiest families – nearly all of them timber towkays.

The old trading port has now been graced with a pagoda, a couple of big hotels and a smart **esplanade**, completed in 1987. The 1929 shophouses along the river are virtually all that remains of the old town. The 7-storey **pagoda**, adjacent to Tua Pek Kong Temple, cost RM1.5mn to build; there are good views over the town from the top. In the **Sibu Civic Centre**, 2.5 km out of town on Jalan Tun Abang Haji Openg, there is an exhibition of old photographs of Sibu and an unspectacular tribal display. This serves as Sibu's municipal museum. Five aerial photographs of the town, taken every 5 years or so between 1947 and 1987, chart the town's explosive growth. Open 1500-2000 Tuesday-Saturday, 0900-1200, 1400-2000 Sunday.

Tours

Most companies run city tours plus tours of longhouses, Mulu National Park and Niah Caves. It is cheaper to organize upriver trips from Kapit or Belaga (see below) than from Sibu.

Local information

● Accommodation

Prices: L over RM500; **A+** RM260-500; **A** RM130-260; **B** RM65-130; **C** RM40-65; **D** RM20-40; **E** RM10-20; **F** Below RM10

Hotels are scattered all over Sibu; cheaper ones tend to be around the nightmarket in Chinatown. A couple of the top hotels are good, but those at the lower end of the market are very mediocre.

A+-A *Kingwood*, 12 Lorong Lanang 4, PO Box 1201, T 335888, F 334559, 168 rooms, largest hotel in Sibu, views of Rejang River, all rooms with a/c, TV, mini-bar, *Riverfront Cage*, Chinese Restaurant, pool, health centre. **A** *Premier*, Jln Kampung Nyabor, T 323222, F 323399, a/c, restaurant, rooms have a/c, TV, own bath, bar, some rooms with river view, clean, helpful staff, adjoins the Sarawak House Shopping Centre, discounts often available, recommended. **A** *Tanahmas*, Jln Kampung Nyabor, T 333188, F 333288, a/c, restaurant, run to a very high standard, very well-appointed modern hotel, recommended.

B *Centre Point Inn*, Jing Hwa Building, off Jln Central, T 320222, F 320496, a/c, often offers sizeable discounts; **B** *Garden*, 1 Jln Hua Ping, T 317888, F 330999, a/c, restaurant, well-kept and efficiently run, recommended.

B-C *Phoenix*, 1 & 3 Jln Kai Peng (off Jln Kampung Nyabor), T 313877, F 320392, a/c, reasonable.

C *Bahagia*, 11 Jln Central, T 320303, a/c, restaurant, reasonable value for money. **C** *Capitol 88*, 19 Jln Wong Nai Siong, T 336444, a/c, restaurant, rooms are clean and reasonable value. **C** *Mandarin*, 183 Jln Kampung Nyabor, T 339177, F 333425, a/c, popular with travellers. **C** *Miramar*, 1st Flr, 47 Jln Channel, T 332433, some a/c, best of a bad bunch, next to the *pasar malam* (night market). **C** *New World*, 1 Jln Wong Nai Siong, T 310311, a/c, clean rooms with attached bathrooms, good value. **C** *Rumah Rehat* (*Government Resthouse*), Jln Awang Ramli Amit, T 332834 and Jln Bujang Suntong, T 330406. **C** *Sarawak*, 34 Jln Lintang, T 333455, F 320536, a/c, attached bathroom, TV, good value. **C** *Sentosa Inn*, 12 Jln Pulau, T 349875, a/c, TV, simple but good value. **C** *Wen Ya*, 1st Flr, 39 High St (Teboh Tinggi), T 321288/321290, big rooms, one of the better in this price bracket. **C** *Wisma Katolik* (Catholic Building), 1 Jln Lalang, T 337277, good location near the *Tanahmas Hotel* and bus station, large, clean rooms, recommended.

D *Emas*, 3A Foochow Lane, T 310877, some a/c, clean. **D** *Rejang*, 40 Jln Blacksmith (opposite Standard Chartered Bank), T 315590, some a/c, some rooms have attached bathrooms. **D-E** *Hoover House* (*Methodist Guesthouse*), Jln Pulau (next to church), T 332491, some a/c, fan-cooled rooms are particularly good value for money, spotlessly clean and with character – often, and understandably, full, recommended; **D-E** *Mehung*, 17 Jln Maju, T 324852, some a/c, serviceable rooms with attached bathrooms, probably the best bet if the *Hoover House* is full.

● Places to eat

Prices: ♦♦♦♦ over RM40; ♦♦♦ RM13-40; ♦♦ RM5-13; ♦ under RM5

Malay: ♦♦*Sheraton*, Delta Estate (out of town), Malay (and some Chinese), fish head curries recommended by locals. ♦*Metropol*, 1st Flr, 20 Jln Morshidi Sidek, also serves Melanau curries.

Chinese: ***♦♦♦Jhong Kuo***, 13 Jln Wong Nai Siong, Foochow. ***♦♦Blue Splendour***, 1st Flr, 60-62 Jln Kampung Nyabor (opposite *Premier Hotel*), recommended by locals. ***♦♦Golden Palace***, *Tanahmas Hotel*, Jln Kampung Nyabor, Cantonese and Schezuan. ***♦♦Hock Chu Leu***, 28 Jln Blacksmith, Foochow dishes only.

International: ***♦♦♦Peppers Café***, *Tanahmas Hotel*, Jln Kampung Nyabor, western and local food, curries particularly recommended, popular. ***♦♦♦Villa by the Grand***, Grand Meridien Building, 2nd Flr, 131 Jln Kampung Nyabor, run by a group of Canadian graduates. ***McDonalds***, Sarawak House Shopping Complex, Jln Kampung Nyabor.

Foodstalls: there is a good hawker centre on Jln Market, in the centre of town. ***Rex Food Court***, 28 Jln Cross, is new and clean, one correspondent recommends it, saying it serves an excellent selection of foods.

● Airline offices

British Airways, T 338884; **MAS**, 61 Jln Tuanku Osman, T 326166; **MAS**, 61 Jln Tunku Osman, T 326166; **Singapore Airlines**, T 332203.

● Banks & money changers

Standard Chartered, Jln Cross; **Hong Kong**, 17 Jln Wong Nai Siong Hock Hua, Jln Pulau.

● Post & telecommunications

Area code: 084.
General Post Office: Jln Kampung Nyabor.

● Shopping

Handicrafts: stalls along express boat wharves at Jln Channel, mainly selling basketware. One shop on Jln Central for a variety of handicrafts.

Markets: Pasar Malam, along High St, Jln Market and Lembangan Lane (Chinatown). Native market (Lembangan market), on Lembangan River between Jln Mission and Jln Channel, sells jungle produce.

Pottery: 2 potteries at Km 7 and 12 Ulu Oya Rd.

Supermarket: Sarawak House Shopping Complex, Jln Kg Nyabor, has Premier Department Store.

● Sports

Golf: *Sibu Golf Club*, Km 17 Ulu Oya Rd, green fees RM15.

● Tour companies & travel agents

Hornbill, 1, 1st Floor, Jln Bengkel, T 321005, F 318987; ***Equatorial Tour & Travel Centre***, 11 Raminway, T 331599; ***Golden Horse Travel***, 20B-21B Sarawak House Complex, T 323288, F 310600; ***Hornbill Holiday***, No 1, 1st Flr, Jln Bengkel, Lorong 1, T 321005, F 318987; ***Hunda Holiday Tours***, 11 Tingkat Bawah, Lorong 1, Brooke Drive, T 326869, F 310396; ***Kiew Kwong Travel***, 175B Jln Kampung Nyabor, T 315994, F 318236; ***Metropolitan Travel***, 72-4 Jln Pasar, T 322251, F 310831; ***R H Tours & Travel***, 32 Blacksmith Rd, T 316767, F 316185; ***Sazhong Trading & Travel***, 4 Jln Central, T 336017, F 338031, very efficient and courteous, recommended; ***Sibu Golden Tours***, 15 1st Flr, Jln Workshop, T 316861, F 318680; ***Sitt Travel***, 146 Ground Floor, Jln Kampung Nyabor, T 320168; ***Travel Consortium***, 14 Jln Central, T 334455, F 330589; ***WTK Travel***, Ground Floor, Bangunan Hung Ann, T 319393, F 319933.

● Tourist office

Visitors' Information Centre , Ground Floor, 32 Cross Road, T 340980, F 341280, stbsibu@tm.net.my.

● Useful addresses

Police: Jln Kampung Nyabor, T 322222.
Resident's Office: T 321963.

● Transport

Air The airport is 25 km north of town, bus 1 or taxi. Regular connections with Kuching, Bintulu, Miri, Marudi, Kapit and Belaga. There are also some connections with Kota Kinabalu. Sibu airport information centre, T 307072.

Road Bus: buses leave from Jln Khoo Peng Loong. Regular connections with Bintulu, 3 hours and Miri along a surfaced road. Best to purchase tickets the day before departure. The early morning buses to Bintulu connect with the buses direct to Batu Niah (see Bintulu). There are also connections with Kapit and Kuching via Sarikei (2 hours to Sarikei, 5-6 hours Sarikei to Kuching, RM35).

River Boat: boats leave from the wharf in front of the pagoda. Ticket agents Sibu-Kuching: Ekspress Bahagia 20 Jln Tukang Besi and *Capitol Hotel 88*; 1 Bank Rd and 14 Jln Khoo Peng Loong. There are three express boats a day between Sibu and Kuching. These boats stop off at Sarekei. It is necessary to change to an ocean-going boat at Sarekei for Sibu. Boats to Kapit leave from the Kapit wharf, a little further upriver. Regular express boats to Kapit 2-3 hours and in the wet season, when the river is high enough, they continue to Belaga, 5-6 hours. If travelling from Sibu through Kapit to Belaga, take one of the early morning boats (the first leaves at 0545), as they connect all the way through. The last Sibu-Kapit boat departs at around 1300. In the dry season passengers must change on to smaller launches to get upriver to Belaga (see below). The Sibu-Kapit boats also stop off at Kanowit and Song on their journey upriver.

KAPIT

Kapit is the 'capital' of Sarawak's seventh division, through which flows the Batang Rejang and its main tributaries, the Batang Balleh, Batang Katibas, Batang Balui and Sungai Belaga. In a treaty with the Sultan of Brunei, Rajah James Brooke acquired the Rejang Basin for Sarawak in 1853. Kapit is the last 'big' town on the Rejang and styles itself as the gateway to 'the heart of Borneo' – after Redmond O'Hanlon's book (*Into the Heart of Borneo*) which describes his adventure up the Batang Balleh in the 1980s. Kapit is full of people who claim to be characters in this book. Like O'Hanlon and his journalist companion James Fenton, most visitors coming to Belaga, venture into the interior to explore the upper Rejang and its tributaries, where there are many Iban and Orang Ulu longhouses.

There are only 20 km of metalled road in and around Kapit, but the little town has a disproportionate number of cars. It is a trading centre for the tribespeople upriver and has grown enormously in recent years with the expansion of the logging industry upstream (see page 412). Logs come in two varieties – 'floaters' and 'sinkers'. Floaters are pulled downstream by tugs in huge chevron formations. Sinkers – like belian (ironwood) – are transported in the Chinese-owned dry bulk carriers which line up along the wharves at Kapit. When the river is high these timber ships are able to go upstream, past the Pelagus Rapids. The Batang Rejang at Kapit is normally 500m wide and in the dry season, the riverbank slopes steeply down to the water. When it floods, however, the water level rises more than 10m, as is testified by the high water marks on Fort Sylvia. The highest recorded level was in 1983 when the water reached half way up the fort's walls.

Fort Sylvia, was built of belian (ironwood) by Rajah Charles Brooke in 1880, and is now occupied by government offices – it is near the wharves. It was originally called Kapit Fort but was renamed in 1925 after Rajah Vyner Brooke's wife. Most of the forts built during this time were designed to prevent the Orang Ulu going downriver; Fort Sylvia was built to

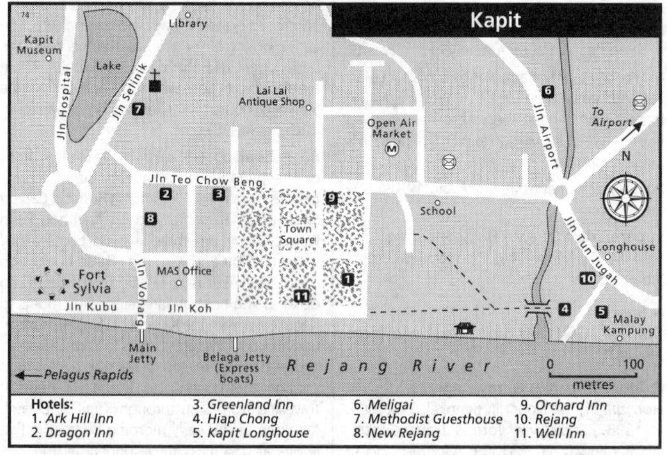

stop the beligerent Iban head-hunters from attacking Kenyah and Kayan settlements upstream.

The other main sight is the **Kapit Museum**, recently enlarged and moved to Fort Sylvia. It exhibits on Rejang tribes and the local economy. It was set up by the Sarawak Museum in Kuching and includes a section of an Iban longhouse and several Iban artifacts including a wooden hornbill (see page 328). The Orang Ulu section has a reconstruction of a longhouse and mural, painted by local tribespeople. An Orang Ulu *salong*

Sarawak's river express boats – smoke on the water

Sarawak's *Ekspres* boats, powered by turbo-charged V-12 engines, are the closest most upriver tribespeople come to experiencing supersonic flight. They look like floating aircraft fuselages, are piloted from a cockpit and have aircraft-style cabins below, complete with reclining seats and head-rests. Journeying downriver, these sleek Chinese-run bullet-boats reach speeds of 70 km/hour, and in their wake, longhouse landing rafts are left rocking in metre-high swell. On straighter stretches of river, pilots like to race each other, while the 'front-man', perched on the bows, keeps a look-out for semi-submerged logs – or 'floaters' – which regularly damage propellers. Incapsulated in the air-conditioned cabins, passengers (everyone from Chinese businessmen to tattooed Orang Ulu) are oblivious to the hazards. Most of them remain gripped, throughout the trip, by the deafening kung-fu films continuously screened on video.

Express boats are in use on most of the major rivers in Sarawak; ocean-going versions also ply the coastal waters. They have reduced travelling time dramatically: when Ranee Margaret Brooke made the most exciting trip of her life, from Kapit to Belaga and back in the 1880s, the journey upriver took 6 days. Today it can be done in 5 hours. But navigating the coffee-coloured waters of the Rejang and Baram rivers is a dangerous occupation. Free-floating logs pose an ever-present threat. Log rafts – huge chevrons of timber, up to 500m long, which are towed downstream by tugs – swing wide on meanders, leaving narrow gaps for the express boats. But a pilot can only claim to have cut his teeth once he has shot the Rejang's famous Pelagus Rapids, 45 minutes upriver from Kapit.

Over this 2½ km-long stretch of white water, he has to contend with logs, rocks, whirlpools and cataracts while keeping a look-out for express boats from the opposite direction. When Ranee Margaret Brooke shot these rapids over a century ago, she wrote: "As I stood looking at the whirlpool, Hovering Hawk [her Iban steersman], who was standing near me, pointed with his thumb to the swirling water, all flecked with foam. 'See there,' he said, 'who knows how many eyes lie buried beneath that foam!'" More eyes have been buried beneath the foam in recent years with the loss of 10 lives in June 1991 when an express boat capsized.

But accidents happen even without the rapids. In 1990, two express boats collided head-on in early morning fog just downriver from Kapit. One boat rolled and sank within seconds. Older boats have just one emergency exit, at the back, which is said to be impossible to open underwater as it opens outwards; windows are sealed. Newer boats have more exits, fitted under a more rigid safety code introduced in 1990. On the older boats it is possible to ride the gauntlet on the roof-top (tourists are strongly advised to take adequate precautions against sunburn). Other points to bear in mind when contemplating travel by express boat: first, given the number of express boat trips made daily, the actual accident rate is low; and second, flying from Kapit to Belaga is only marginally more expensive.

The Rajahs' fortresses – war and peace in the Rejang

The lower reaches of the Batang Rejang are inhabited by the Iban and the upper reaches by the Kenyah and Kayan tribes, the traditional enemies of the Iban (for details on tribes, see page 342). During the days of the White Rajahs, a number of forts were built along the river in an effort to keep the peace and prevent head-hunting (see page 348). All the forts in Sarawak had chambers where confiscated heads were stored, each with a tag detailing the name of the tribe which took it and the name of the victim. Head-hunting proved a difficult practice to stamp out. In 1904, when Vyner Brooke was based at Kapit Fort as Resident of the Third Division (before he succeeded Charles as Rajah) he reported an attack on one longhouse in which head-hunters severed the heads of 80 women and children while their men were working in the fields. Tribal head-hunting raids were regular occurrences until 1924, when wild boars were exchanged between the Iban and Orang Ulu tribes at a peace-making ceremony in Kapit, presided over by the Rajah. (There are photographs of this ceremony in the Kapit Museum.)

The river fortresses were also used as bases for punitive raids against tribal rebels in the interior. One of the first stops on the route upriver from Sibu is Kanowit, where Charles Brooke built Fort Emma. In 1859 the Rejang Resident and the fort commander were murdered there by local tribespeople. Charles Brooke swore to bathe his hands in the blood of the murderers. With 15,000 'friendly' Ibans, he went upriver in 1862, and led his expedition past the Pelagus Rapids and Belaga to the Kayan and Kenyah strongholds. Brooke then led the Ibans into a lengthy pitched battle in which hundreds died that finally broke the power of the Orang Ulu.

While the Brookes successfully forged alliances with the Rejang's Ibans, some individual groups rebelled from time to time. In her book *My Life in Sarawak*, Ranee Margaret (Charles Brooke's wife) relates the story of one Iban chief's dawn attack on the Rajah's fort at Sibu. Inside were several other 'friendly' Dayak chiefs. "...The manner in which the friendly Dyak chiefs behaved during the skirmish amused me very much," she wrote, "for they did nothing but peer through the lattice-work, and shout Dyak insults at the attacking party, most of whom they knew very well. They made unpleasant remarks about the enemy's mothers, and inquired whether the men themselves belonged to the female sex, as their efforts were so feeble."

(burial hut), totem pole and other woodcarvings are also on display. The museum also has representative exhibits from the small Malay community and the Chinese. Hokkien traders settled at Kapit and Belaga and traded salt, sugar and ceramics for pepper, rotan and rubber; they were followed by Foochow traders. Appropriately, the Chinese exhibit is a shop. There are also displays on the natural history of the upper Rejang and modern industries such as mining, logging and tourism. All exhibits are labelled in English. The museum's energetic and erudite curator, Wilfred Billy Panyau, is very knowledgeable on the area. Open 0900-1200, 1400-1600 Monday-Friday, 0900-1200 Saturday and Sunday. **NB** The museum often seems closed during opening hours and it may be necessary to actively search for the curator to open the place up.

Kapit has a particularly colourful daily **market** in the centre of town. Tribeswomen bring in fruit, vegetables and animals to sell; it is quite normal to see everything from turtles, frogs, birds and catfish to monkeys, wild boar and even pangolin and pythons.

Excursions

The **Pelagus Rapids** are 45 minutes upstream from Kapit on the Batang Rejang.

Exterior of a Sea Dyak Long-house, from William T Hornaday's (1885) *Two years in the jungle: the experience of a hunter and naturalist in India, Ceylon, the Malay Peninsula and Borneo*

The $2\frac{1}{2}$ km-long series of cataracts and whirlpools are the result of a sudden drop in the riverbed, caused by a geological fault-line. Express boats can make it up the Pelagus to Belaga in the wet season (September-April), but the rapids are still regarded with some trepidation by the pilots (see page 387). When the water is low (May-August), the rapids can only be negotiated by the smallest longboats. There are seven rapids in total, each with local names such as 'The Python', 'The Knife' and one, more ominously, called 'The Grave'. **Accommodation A** *Pelagus Resort*, set on the banks of the Rejang overlooking the rapids, T/F (084) 796050, T (082) 238033, F 238050, 40 longhouse style rooms, with restaurant, pool, bar and sun-deck, de-luxe rooms have a/c, otherwise there are fans. Trips organized from resort to longhouses, nature treks and river safaris, white water rafting on the rapids, RM80-100. *Getting there*: regular express boats pass through the rapids upstream.

Longhouses around Kapit Some longhouses around Kapit are accessible by road, and several others are within an hour's longboat ride from town. In Kapit you are likely to be invited to visit one of these (some hotels will help organize trips, or inquire at the Police Station). There are guides in Kapit who charge too much for very unsatisfactory tours. Visitors are strongly advised not to visit a longhouse without an invitation, ideally from someone who lives in it (see page 378). As a general rule, the further from town a longhouse is, the more likely it is to conform with the image of what a traditional longhouse should be like. That said, there are some beautiful traditional longhouses nearby, mainly Iban. One of the most accessible, for example is **Rumah Seligi**, about 30 minutes drive from Kapit. (Cars or vans can be hired by the half-day; RM10). Only a handful of longhouses are more than 500m from the riverbanks of the Rejang and its tributaries. Most longhouses still practice shifting cultivation (see page 345); rice is the main crop but under government aid programmes many are now growing cash crops such as cocoa.

Longhouse tours To go upriver beyond Kapit it is necessary to get a permit (no charge) from the offices in the State Government Complex. The permit is valid for travel up the Rejang as far as Belaga and for an unspecified distance up the Balleh. **NB** On our last visit, Belaga was temporarily closed. For upriver trips beyond Belaga another permit must be obtained there; however, these trips tend to be expensive and dangerous. Those planning to visit longhouses should refer to the guidelines on visiting longhouses (see page 378).

The vast majority of the population in Sarawak's 7th Division is Iban (about 72%). They inhabit the Rejang up to (and a little beyond) Kapit as well as the lower reaches of the Balleh and its tributaries.

The longhouse – prime-site apartments with river view

Most longhouses are built on stilts, high on the riverbank, on prime real estate. They are 'prestigious properties' with 'lots of character', and with their 'commanding views of the river', they are the condominiums of the jungle. They are long-rise rather than high-rise however, and the average longhouse has 20-25 'doors' (although there can be as many as 60). Each represents one family. The word *long* in a settlement's name – as in Long Liput or Long Terawan – means 'confluence' (the equivalent of *kuala* in Malay), and does not refer to the length of the longhouse.

Behind each of the doors – which even today, are rarely locked – is a *bilik*, or apartment, which includes the family living room and a loft, where paddy and tools are stored. In Kenyah and Kayan longhouses, paddy (which can be stored for years until it is milled) is kept in elaborate barns, built on stilts away from the longhouse, in case of fire. In traditional longhouses, the living rooms are simple atap roofed, bamboo-floored rooms; in modern longhouses – which are designed on exactly the same principles – the living rooms are commonly furnished with sofas, lino floors, a television and an en suite bathroom. At the front of the bilik is the *dapur*, where the cooking takes place. All biliks face out onto the *ruai*, or gallery, which is the focus of communal life, and is where visitors are usually entertained. The width of the wall which faces onto the ruai indicates the status of that family. Attached to the ruai there is usually a *tanju* – an open verandah, running the full length of the house – where rice and other agricultural products are dried. Long ladders – notched hardwood trunks – lead up to the tanju; these can get very slippery and do not always come with handrails.

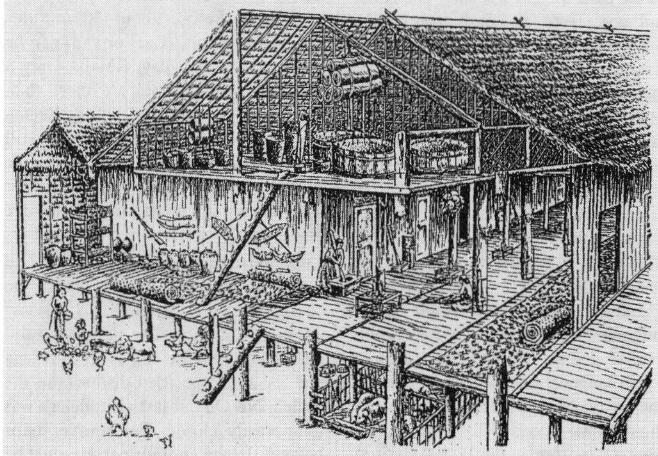

The Iban people are traditionally the most hospitable to visitors, but as a result, their longhouses are the most frequently visited by tourists. Malays and Chinese account for 5% and 3% of the population respectively. The Orang Ulu live further upriver; the main tribes are the Kayan and the Kenyah (12%) and a long list of sub-groups such as the Kejaman, Beketan, Sekapan, Lahanan, Seping, and Tanjong. In addition there are the nomadic and semi-nomadic Penan, Punan and Ukit. Many tribal people are employed in the logging industry, and with their paid jobs, have brought the trappings of modernity to even the remotest longhouses.

Longhouses between Kapit and Belaga are accessible by the normal passenger boats but these boats only go as far as Sungai Bena on the Balleh River ($2\frac{1}{2}$ hours). To go further upriver it is necessary to take a tour or organize your own guides and boatmen. The sort of trip taken by Redmond O'Hanlon and James Fenton (as described in O'Hanlon's book *Into the Heart of Borneo*) would cost more than RM1,500 a head. Longhouse tours along the Rejang and Balleh rivers can be organized by the following: *Ark Hill Inn*, Lot 451, Shop Lot 10, Jalan Airport, T 794168, F 796337, manager David Tan can organize upriver trips and tours of longhouses around Kapit, if contacted in advance, they can arrange full itinerary from Kuching or Sibu; *Dinnel Nuing*, PBDS office, Kapit, T 796494; *Rejang Hotel*, 28 New Bazaar, T 796709, recommended; *Tan Seng Hi*, Jalan Tan Sit Leong. The *Resident's office* also has some official tourist guides on its books. **WARNING** More than one reader has alerted us to Donald Ak Ding and his associate Ajim Anyie of *Hornbill Adventures* – they are said not to speak Kayan or Kenyah, they overcharge for petrol and may just disappear at any moment!

Rumah Tuan Lepong Balleh – only enter this longhouse with the local policeman who lives there – Selvat Anu (ask for him at Kapit Police Station). During the day Selvat and some members of the longhouse can take visitors on various adventure tours: river trips, visiting longhouses, jungle treks, fishing, pig-hunting, camping in the jungle, trips up to logging areas, swimming in rivers, mountain trekking ... Selvat is very knowledgeable and has good relations with the longhouse communities. Visitors can eat with the family and occasionally have the chance to experience a traditional Iban ceremony. **Accommodation** In his longhouse, RM20-25, inclusive of meals, generator until 2300, basic. *Getting there*: about 1 hour drive from Kapit; take a minibus and ask for 'Selvat and Friends Traditional Hostel and Longhouse', RM3.

Local information

● Accommodation

Prices: L over RM500; **A+** RM260-500; **A** RM130-260; **B** RM65-130; **C** RM40-65; **D** RM20-40; **E** RM10-20; **F** Below RM10

All hotels are within walking distance of the wharves.

B-C *Greenland Inn*, 463 Jln Teo Chow Beng, T 796388, F 796708, a/c, well maintained small hotel with good rooms, recommended. **B-C** *Meligai*, 334 Jln Airport, T 796817/796611, full range of accommodation from VIP suite to dingy standard rooms, has some of the accoutrements of a city hotel but the rooms are generally poor. **B-C** *Well Inn*, 40 Jln Court, T 796009/796566, a/c, variable rooms but ask to look at the range.

C *Ark Hill Inn*, 451 Jln Airport, T 796168, F 796337, a/c, friendly, clean rooms, recommended.

D *Hiap Chong*, 33 New Bazaar, T 96213, some a/c, no attached bath, top floor best bet. **D** *Kapit Longhouse*, New Bazaar, T 796415, a/c, grubby hotel with a few dubious business sidelines. **D** *Orchard Inn*, 64 Jln Airport, T 796325, a/c, restaurant, clean rooms and helpful staff, deluxe rooms with a/c, TV, bath to economy rooms (cheapest rooms have no window). **D-E** *Rejang*, 28 New Bazaar, T 796709, some a/c, basic but clean, helpful staff.

E *Dragon Inn*, Lot 467, Jln Teo Chow Beng, T 796105, central, near Express wharves, clean and well kept. **E** *Methodist Guesthouse*, sometimes budget rooms available here.

● Places to eat

Prices: ♦♦♦♦ over RM40; ♦♦♦ RM13-40; ♦♦ RM5-13; ♦ under RM5

Kapit's cuisine is predominantly Chinese.

Malay: *MI*, Jln Pedral, Malay Muslim food.

Chinese: ♦*Hua Hua*, Jln Airport/Jln Court, Chinese food. ♦*Lily Pond*, in the middle of the lily pond, off Jln Hospital, pleasant setting, plenty of mosquitoes and an unimaginative menu. ♦*S'ng Ee Ho Restaurant*, next to Metox supermarket, happy to cook anything you ask for. *Jade Garden*, Jln Pedral, local and Chinese food, smart. *99*, Jln Pedral, fresh air, clean local and Chinese food. *Seafood Restaurant*, Jln Pedral.

International: ♦♦♦*Orchard Inn*, 64 Jln Airport, T 796325, the most upmarket restaurant in Kapit, food well presented but the coffee shops taste just as good, disco from 2200-0100.

Fast food: ♦*Frosty Boy*, Jln Teo Chow Beng (below *Greenland Inn*), fast food: pizzas, burgers, ice cream. *American Fried Chicken*, Jln Pedral.

Bakeries and breakfast: ♦*Ung Tong Bakery*, opposite the market, bakery and café, good continental style breakfasts – big selection of rolls and good coffee, fresh bread baked twice daily (0600 and 1100), recommended. *Chuong Hin*, opposite the Sibu wharf, best stocked coffeeshop in town. *Sugar Bun*, near Main Square.

Foodstalls: stalls at the top end of the road opposite the market (dead end road; brightly painted on the outside). Good satay stall on Jln Hospital, next to the lily pond.

● Airline offices

MAS, in block opposite Sibu jetty.

● Banks & money changers

There are two banks which will accept TCs, one in the New Bazaar and the other on Jln Airport, but it is easier to change money in Sibu.

● Libraries

On the other side of the road from 1st Flr State Government Complex. Good selection of books on history and natural history of Borneo. Open 1615-2030 Mon-Sat, 0900-1115, 1400-1630 Sat, 0900-1100, 1400-1830 Sun.

● Post & telecommunications

Area code: 084.

● Shopping

Handicrafts: *Lai Lai Antique shop*, next road along on the right from the *Putena Jaya* (see below), small selection of woven rugs/sarongs, prices are high but they are similar to the starting prices at the longhouses. *Din Chu Café*, next to Methodist Resthouse, sells antiques and handicrafts.

● Useful addresses

Maps: Land Survey Department, Jln Beletik on Jln Airport. Maps of Kapit Division and other parts of Sarawak.

Resident's Office: 1st Flr State Government Complex (opposite the lily pond), T 796963. Permits for upriver trips. Tourists going to Baleh or upper Rejang areas must sign a form saying they fully understand they are travelling at their own risk.

● Transport

160 km from Sibu.

Air The airport is 4 km south of town. Regular connections with Sibu and Belaga. Low cloud at Kapit often prevents landing and the plane goes straight to Belaga.

River Boat: all three wharves are close together. Regular connections with Sibu from 0600-1530, 2-3 hours. Belaga is not accessible by large express boats during the dry season. Prices for the express boats start from RM20. For the smaller boats going upriver in the dry season prices are higher and start from RM50.

BELAGA

Belaga is the archetypal sleepy little town; most people while their time away in coffee shops. They are the best place to watch life go by, and there are always interesting visitors in town, from itinerant wild honey-collectors from Kalimantan to Orang Ulu who have brought their jungle produce downriver to the Belaga bazaar or are heading to the metropolis of Kapit for medical treatment. At night, when the neon lights flicker on, Belaga's coffee shops are invaded by thousands of cicadas, beetles and moths.

A few Chinese traders set up shop in Belaga in the early 1900s, and traded with the tribespeople upriver, supplying essentials such as kerosene, cooking oil and shotgun cartridges. The Orang Ulu brought their beadwork and mats as well jungle produce such as beeswax, ebony, gutta-percha (rubbery tree-gum) and,

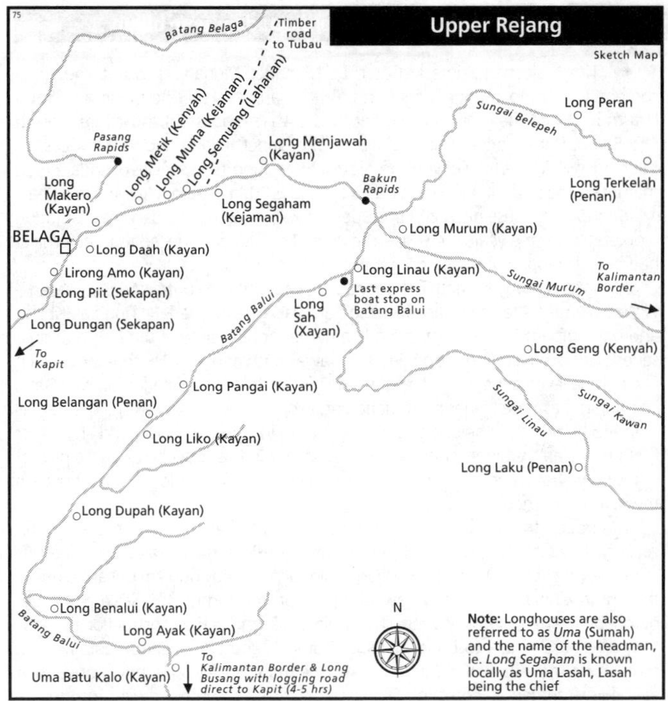

most prized of all, bezoar stones. These are gall-stones found in certain monkeys (the *wah-wahs*, *jelu-merahs* and *jelu-jankits*) and porcupines. To the Chinese, they have much the same properties as rhinoceros horn (mainly aphrodisiacal) and even today, they are exported from Sarawak to Singapore where they fetch S$300/kg.

Belaga serves as a small government administration centre for the remoter parts of the 7th Division. There is a very pretty **Malay kampung** (Kampung Bharu) along the esplanade downriver from the Belaga Bazaar. (The Kejaman burial pole on display outside the Sarawak Museum in Kuching was brought from the Belaga area in 1902).

Excursions To go upriver beyond Belaga it is necessary to obtain a permit from the Resident's office and permission from the police station. When the river is high, express boats go upstream as far as **Rumah Belor** on the Batang Balui, but for the purpose of visiting longhouses in the Belaga area, it is best to hire a boat in Belaga. Many of the longhouses around Belaga are quite modern, although several of the Kenyah and Kayan settlements have beautifully carved wooden tombstones – or *salongs* – nearby. All the longhouses beyond Belaga are Orang Ulu. Even longhouses which, on the map, appear very remote (such as Long Busang), are now connected by logging roads from Kapit – only 4 hours drive away. To get well off the beaten track, into Penan country, it is possible to organize treks from Belaga towards the Kalimantan border, staying in longhouses en route.

The Bakun hydroelectric project: dam time bomb

The Malaysian Prime Minister, Dr Mahathir Mohamad, is not known as someone prone to changing his mind. But in January 1993 he made a US$6bn U-turn by giving the green light to Southeast Asia's biggest infrastructure project. The Bakun Dam, upriver from Belaga on the Upper Rejang and 400 km east of Kuching, will flood a tract of virgin rainforest that supports 43 species of endangered mammals and birds. It will also displace around 8,000 tribespeople living in at least 14 longhouses. These displaced tribespeople will, in large part, become plantation workers. Just three years previously the Prime Minister announced that the project had been scrapped for environmental reasons.

It's not clear why Mahathir changed his mind, but the contract was awarded – without tender – to the swashbuckling Sarawakian entrepreneur Ting Pek Khiing and his company Ekran. He had made a name for himself with the PM through a series of instant-resort developments in Sarawak and Langkawi. His company, which is widely believed to be backed by Malaysia's powerful former finance minister Daim Zainnudin, has no experience in managing projects the size of Bakun. The dam is going to be twice the height of the Aswan Dam in Egypt and will flood an area of 69,000 hectares – bigger than Singapore. Mahathir has described it as "a project whose time has come". Environmentalists say it will be an ecological time bomb in the heart of Borneo.

It is hoped that Bakun will generate 2,400 MW of electricity by the early 21st century. Most of the power will be exported to Peninsular Malaysia to feed its industries, first by 670 km of overhead cables and then by 650 km of cables under the South China Sea. Experts say subaqua transmission on this scale has never before been attempted anywhere. The project will require the construction of roads through dense jungle to bring building materials and engineering equipment to the remote site, above the Bakun Rapids (see map). Malaysian lobby groups such as the Environmental Protection Society predict that the project will cause severe soil erosion in an area already suffering from the effects of logging. Ten years ago the riverwater was clear and fish abundant; now the river is a muddy brown and water levels fluctuate wildly. Nor is the project a long-term one: even the government admits its productive life is likely to be in the region of 25 years, before it silts up.

Pasang Rapids About 2 km up the Batang Belaga from Belaga. These spectacular rapids are certainly the biggest in Sarawak. It appears that no one has purposely tried to shoot them – they are too dangerous. Boats can get reasonably close, however, and in the dry season, it is possible to climb up to a picnic area, overlooking the white water. *Getting there*: hire a boat from Belaga (RM70).

Tours The *Belaga Hotel* will contact guides for upriver trips and the District Office can also recommend a handful of experienced guides. In this part of Sarawak, guides are particularly expensive – sometimes up to RM80 a day, mainly because there are not enough tourists to justify full-time work. It is necessary to hire experienced boatmen too, because of the numerous rapids. The best guide for longer trips (to jungle areas northeast of Belaga and to Penan areas along the Kalimantan border) is Ronald Bete. Such trips require at least 5 or 6 days. Prices for trips to longhouses upriver vary according to distance and the water level, but are similar to those in Kapit. As a rough guideline, a litre of petrol costs about RM10-15; a 40 hp boat uses nearly 20 litres to go 10 km. English

Two of Ekran's main shareholders are the sons of Sarawak's Chief Minister, Abdul Taib Mahmud, who is widely believed to own a third of the state's timber concessions through nominees and political allies. Another leading shareholder is James Wong, Sarawak's environment minister who doubles as a big timber concessionnaire in Limbang (the district adjacent to Mulu). In May 1994 a group of longhouse dwellers from the Long Murum area were prevented from delivering a petition opposing the Bakun project to the Sarawak state parliament. They allege that members of the government-appointed committee on Bakun do not defend their interests because, like Wong and Taib's sons, they are the very people responsible for selling tribal land they don't own to loggers.

Over recent years, 17 technical studies – including environmental impact analyses – have been carried out on Bakun. Most, though, have not been released to the public. In 1995 one study carried out by a team from Sarawak University concluded that severe environmental effects were unavoidable. *Friends of the Earth Malaysia* says: "This project is going to have a tremendous effect on the lives of natives, plants and animals and bio-diversity of the pristine forests where it is going to be built". The local tribespeople, whose ancestors battled for decades against the White Rajahs, have, it seems, finally met their match, in Malaysia's relentless thrust towards modernity.

At the beginning of 1995 the Environment Ministry approved the first stage of the project – allowing logging of the forest to be flooded to begin. But notwithstanding the powerful economic and political forces backing the Bakun project, new delays and difficulties crop up just as soon as old ones are ironed out. In mid-1997 a conflict between the main contractor, the Swiss-Swedish firm ABB, and Ekran, the Malayasian firm which manages the project, emerged. ABB insisted that all subcontract work be put out to competitive tender; while Ting Pek Khiing, who dominates Ekran, had earlier stated that his firms would get the lion's share of the work. But most of all, environmentalists are hoping that Malaysia's financial crisis will put an end to the Bakun Dam. In late 1997 it was 'shelved' as Mahathir began to look for ways to save money. Activists hope 'shelved' may become 'binned'.

is not widely spoken upriver, basic *Bahasa* comes in handy. (See page 520).

Local information

● Accommodation

C *Bee Lian Hotel*, 11 Belaga Bazaar, T 461416, a/c, rooms are fine. **C-D** *Belaga Hotel*, 14 Belaga Bazaar, T 461244, some a/c, restaurant, no hot water, particularly friendly proprietor, good coffee shop downstairs, in-house video and cicadas.

D *Sing Soon Huat*, 27 New Bazaar, T 461257, F 461346, a/c.

● Places to eat

Several small, cheap coffee shops along Belaga Bazaar and Main Bazaar, the menus are all pretty similar.

● Airline offices

MAS, c/o Lau Chun Kiat, Main Bazaar.

● Post & telecommunications

Area code: 084.

General Post Office: in the District Office building.

● Shopping

Handicrafts: *Chop Teck Hua*, Belaga Bazaar has an intriguing selection of tribal jewellery, old coins, beads, feathers, woodcarvings, blowpipes, parangs, tattoo boards and other curios buried under cobwebs and gekko droppings at the back of the shop, although the owner is noticeably uninformed about the objects he sells.

The massacre at Long Nawang

One-hundred years and three months after James Brooke was proclaimed Rajah of Sarawak, the Japanese Imperial Army invaded the country. On Christmas Day 1941, when Rajah Vyner Brooke was visiting Australia, they took Kuching; a few days earlier they had occupied the Miri oilfields. Japanese troops, dressed for jungle warfare, headed upriver. They did not expect to encounter such stiff resistance from the tribespeople. The Allies had the brainwave of rekindling an old tribal pastime – head-hunting, which successive Brooke administrations had tried to stamp out. Iban and Orang Ulu warriors were offered 'ten-bob-a-knob' for Japanese heads, and many of the skulls still hanging in longhouses are said to date from this time. The years of occupation were marked by terrible brutality, and many people fled across the border into Dutch Borneo – now Kalimantan. The most notorious massacre in occupied Sarawak involved refugees from Kapit.

Just a month after the Japanese invasion, a forestry officer stationed on the Rejang heard that a group of women and children from Kapit were planning to escape across the Iran Range into Dutch territory. He organized the evacuation, and led the refugees up the rivers and over the mountains to the Dutch military outpost at Long Nawang. The forester returned to Kapit to help organize resistance to the Japanese. But when the invading forces heard of the escape they dispatched a raiding party upriver, captured the Dutch fort, lined up the fifty women and ordered the children to climb into nearby trees. According to historian Robert Payne: "They machine-gunned the women and amused themselves by picking off the children one by one... Of all those who had taken part in the expedition only two Europeans survived."

● **Useful addresses**
District Office: (for upriver permits) on the far side of the basketball courts.

● **Transport**
At the moment Belaga is comparatively isolated and overland links are poor. It is possible to travel by road and river to Bintulu (see below), but it is drawn out and expensive. However it is likely, especially if the Bakun Dam project goes ahead (in late 1997 it was delayed/shelved due to Malaysia's financial difficulties), that road links will improve.

Air Connections twice a week on Wednesdays and Sundays with Kapit and on to Sibu.

River Express boats from Kapit only when the river level is high enough to negotiate the Pelagus Rapids, 5-8 hours (depending on season). Prices start at RM20. When the river is very low the only option is to fly to Belaga.

To Tabau and on to Bintulu It is possible to hire a boat from Belaga to Kestima Kem (logging camp) near Rumah Lahanan Laseh (RM60 pp in a group or RM260 for 2/3 people); from there logging trucks go to Tabau on the Kemena River. **NB** Logging trucks leave irregularly and you can get stuck in logging camps. It is a 3-hour drive to Tabau; this trip is not possible in the wet season. There are regular express boats from Tabau to Bintulu (RM20). This is the fastest and cheapest route to Bintulu, but not the most reliable. It is necessary to obtain permission from the Resident's office and the police station in Belaga to take this route.

To Kalimantan It is not legal to cross the border by way of Kapit, Belaga and up the Batang Balui to Long Nawang, although it has been done. You may be turned back.

BINTULU AND NIAH CAVES

BINTULU

The Niah Caves are just off the Miri-Bintulu road and are easily accessible from both towns. Trips to Similajau National Park and longhouses on the Kemena River (rarely visited) can be organized from Bintulu.

The word Bintulu is thought to be a corruption of *Mentu Ulau*, which translates as 'the place for gathering heads'.

Bintulu, on the Kemena River, is in the heart of Melinau country and was traditionally a fishing and farming centre ... until the largest natural gas reserve in Malaysia was discovered just offshore in the late 1970s, turning Bintulu into a boomtown overnight; Shell, Petronas and Mitsubishi moved to the town in force. In 1978 the town's population was 14,000; it is now over 50,000. More than RM11bn was invested in Bintulu's development between 1980 and 1990.

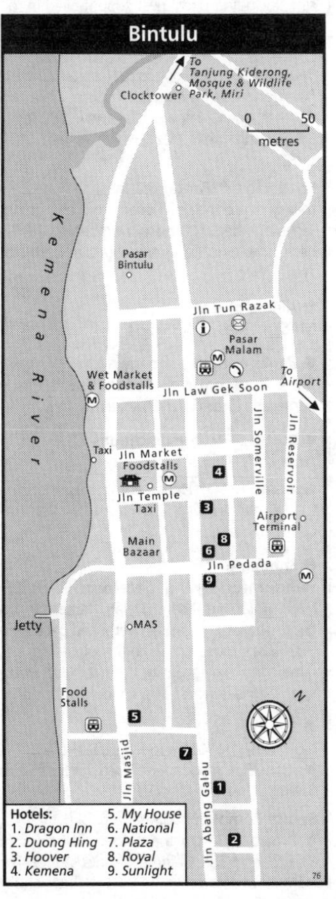

The remnants of the old fishing village at Kampong Jepak are on the opposite bank of the Kemena River. During the Brooke era the town was a small administrative centre. The **clock tower** commemorates the meeting of five representatives from the Brooke government and sixteen local chieftains, the birth of Council Negeri, the state legislative body.

The first project to break ground in Bintulu was the RM100mn crude oil terminal at Tanjong Kidurong from which 45,000 barrels of petroleum are exported daily. A deep-water port was built and the liquefied natural gas (LNG) plant started operating in 1982. It is one of the Malaysian government's biggest investment projects. The abundant supply of natural gas also created investment in related downstream projects. The main industrial area at Tanjong Kidurong is 20 km from Bintulu. The **viewing tower** at Tanjong Kidurong gives a panoramic view of the new-look Bintulu, out to the timber ships on the horizon. They anchor 15 km offshore to avoid port duties and the timber is taken out on barges.

Bintulu has a modern **Moorish-style mosque**, completed in 1988, called the **Masjid Assyakirin**; visitors may be allowed in when it is not prayer time. There is a new colourful centrally located chinese temple called **Tua Pek Kong**. **Pasar Bintulu** is also an impressive new building in the centre of town, built to house the local jungle produce market, foodstalls and limited handicrafts stalls. A landscaped **Wildlife Park** has been developed on the outskirts of town, on the way to Tanjong Batu. It is a local recreational area and contains a small zoo and a botanic garden (the only one in Sarawak). Admission RM2. Open 0800-1900 Monday-Sunday. Few tourists stay long in Bintulu, although it is the jump-off point to the Similajau National Park (which opened in 1991) and Niah Caves. The longhouses on the Kemena River are accessible, but tend not to be as interesting as those further up the Rejang and Baram rivers. The Penan and Kayan tribes are very hospitable and eager to show off their longhouses and traditions to tourists.

Excursions

Similajau National Park, see below.

Niah Caves and National Park, see page 400.

Upriver More than 20 Kemena River longhouses can be reached by road or river within 30 minutes of Bintulu. Iban longhouses are the closest; further upriver are the more traditional Kayan and Kenyah longhouses. *Getting there*: overpriced tours organized by *Similajau Adventure Tours* (see tour companies) or hire a boat from the wharf. A 2-hour river cruise RM275 per person, 5 hour Iban longhouse tour RM200 per person, 4 hour Iban longhouse tour (by boat) RM530 per person, 2 hour longhouse tour (by boat) RM345 per person.

Local information

● Accommodation

Prices: L over RM500; **A+** RM260-500; **A** RM130-260; **B** RM65-130; **C** RM40-65; **D** RM20-40; **E** RM10-20; **F** Below RM10

A ***Plaza***, Jln Abang Galau, 166 Taman Sri Dagang, T 335111, F 332742, a/c, restaurant, pool, very smart hotel, and, compared with other upmarket hotels in Sarawak, excellent value for money, recommended. **A** ***Royal Inn***, 10-12 Jln Pedada, T 332166, F 334028.

B ***Hoover***, Jln Keppel, T 337166, restaurant, smallish rooms, but well kept place. **B** ***Regent***, Kemena Commercial Complex, Jln Tanjong Batu, T 335511, F 333770, 47 rooms, a/c, TV, mini-bar, restaurant. **B** ***Sunlight***, 7 Jln Pedada, T 332577, F 334075, a/c.

C ***My House***, 2nd Flr, 161 Taman Sri Dagang, Jln Masjid, T 336399, F 332050, a/c, recommended. **C** ***National***, 2nd Flr, 5 Jln Temple, T 337222, a/c, clean and well kept, recommended. **C** ***Kemena***, 78 Jln Keppel, T 331533, a/c, refurbished and on a quiet street.

D ***Dragon Inn***, Jln Abang Galau, some a/c, a reasonable place to stay and the a/c rooms are good value; **D-E** ***Duong Hing***, 20 New Commercial Centre (off Jln Abang Galau), some rooms with a/c and bath, a small hotel with welcoming management.

● Places to eat

Prices: ◆◆◆◆ over RM40; ◆◆◆ RM13-40; ◆◆ RM5-13; ◆ under RM5

Umai, raw fish pickled with lime or the fruit of wild palms (*assam*) and mixed with salted vegetables, onions and chillies is a Melanau speciality. Bintulu is famed for its *belacan* – prawn paste – and in the local dialect, prawns are *urang*, not *udang*. Locals quip that they are 'man-eaters' because they *makan urang*.

◆◆◆***Marco Polo***, on the waterfront on the edge of town, locals recommend pepper steak. ◆◆***Fook Lu Shou***, *Plaza Hotel*, Jln Abang Galau, Taman Sri Dagang, seafood and Chinese cuisine, including birds' nest soup, boiled in rock sugar (RM45). ◆◆***River Inn***, opposite wharf, western and local food.

◆***Popular Corner***, opposite Hospital, Chinese. ◆***Kemena Coffee House***, western, Malay and Chinese, open 24 hours. ◆***Sarawak***, 160 Taman Sri Dagang (near *Plaza Hotel*), cheap Malay food.

Foodstalls: ◆◆***Pantai Ria***, near Tanjong Batu, mainly seafood, only open in the evenings, recommended. ◆***Chinese stalls*** behind the Chinese temple on Jln Temple. Stalls at both markets.

● Airline offices

MAS, Jln Masjid, T 331554.

● Banks & money changers

Bank Bumiputra and **Bank Utama** on Jln Somerville; **Standard Chartered**, Jln Keppel.

● Post & telecommunications

Area code: 086.

General Post Office: far side of the airport near the Resident's office, 2 km from town centre – called Pos Laju.

● Shopping

Handicrafts: *Dyang Enterprise*, Lobby Flr, *Plaza Hotel*, Jln Abang Dalau, Taman Sri Dagang. The latter is rather overpriced because of the Plaza's more upmarket clientele; the best handicrafts are to be found at ***Li Hua Plaza***, near the *Plaza Hotel*, in a 4 storey building.

● Sports

Golf: *Tanjong Kidurong*, new 18-hole course, north of Bintulu, by the sea (regular buses from town centre), green fees RM15.

Sports Complex: swimming pool (RM2), tennis, football. To get there, fork right from the Miri road at the Chinese temple, about 1km from town centre.

● Tour companies & travel agents
Deluxe Travel, 30 Jln Law Gek Soon, T 331293, F 334995; ***Similajau Travel and Tours***, *Plaza Hotel*, Jln Abang Dalau offers tours around the city, to the Niah caves, longhouses and Similajau National Park. ***Hunda Travel Services***, 8 Jln Somerville, T 331339, F 330445. There are half a dozen other agents in town.

● Useful addresses
National Parks Booking Office: T 331117, ext 50, F 331923.

● Transport
Air The airport is in the centre of town. Regular connections with Kuching (RM122), Miri (RM74), Sibu (RM69). There are also some connections with Kota Kinabalu.

Road Bus: there are two stations in town. The terminal for local buses is in the centre of town while the long-distance Medan Jaya station is 10 minutes by taxi from the centre. Regular connections with Miri (RM18), Sarikei (RM32), Batu Niah (RM10)and Sibu (RM16). There are several bus companies but the main one is the Syarikat Bas Suria T 334914. **Taxi**: taxis for Miri and Sibu leave from Jln Masjid. Because of the regular bus services and the poor state of the roads, most taxis are for local use only and chartering them is expensive.

River Boat: regular connections with Tabau, 2½ to 3 hours, last boat at 1400 (RM18). Connections with Belaga, via logging road, see page 396; this route is popular with people in Belaga as it is much cheaper than going from Sibu. Direct boat connections with Sibu, Miri, Kuching, Song, Kapit and Belaga (enquire at the wharf for times and prices).

SIMILAJAU NATIONAL PARK

Sarawak's most unusually shaped national park is more than 32 km long and only 1.5 km wide. Similajau was demarcated in 1978, but has only really been open to tourists since the construction of decent facilities in 1991. Lying 20 km northeast of Bintulu, Similajau is a coastal park with sandy beaches, broken by rocky headlands. **Pasir Mas** – or Golden Sands – is a beautiful 3.5 km-long stretch of coarse beach, to the north of the Likau River, where green turtles (see page 484) come ashore to lay their eggs between July and September. A few kilometres from park headquarters at **Kuala Likau** is a small coral reef, known as Batu Mandi. The area is renowned for birdwatching. Because it is so new, and because Bintulu is not on the main tourist track, the park is very quiet. Its seclusion makes it a perfect escape.

The beaches are backed by primary rainforest: peatswamp, *kerangas* (heath forest), mixed dipterocarp and mangrove (along Sungai Likau and Sungai Sebubong). There are small rapids on the Sebulong River. The rivers (particularly the beautiful **Sungai Likau**) have sadly been polluted by indiscriminate logging activities upstream.

Flora and fauna One of the first things a visitor notices on arrival at Kuala Likau is the prominent sign advising against swimming in the river, and to watch your feet in the headquarters' area: Similajau is well known for its saltwater crocodiles (*Crocodylus perosus*). Similajau also has 24 resident species of mammals (including gibbons, Hose's langurs, banded langurs, long tailed macaques, civets, wild boar, porcupines, squirrels) and 185 species of birds, including many migratory species. Marine life includes dolphins, porpoises and turtles; there are some good coral reefs to the north. Pitcher plants grow in the *kerangas* forest and along the beach.

NB In February 1994 the generators that light the Niah caves for visitors were destroyed by a fire, and the caves closed. It is believed that the Berawan tribal group sabotaged the generators to thwart attempts to develop the Baram River as a tourist attraction. The caves themselves are regarded as sacred by a number of tribes, and their development for tourism is resented by some members. Supporters of tourism development, for their part, maintain that the tribal peoples are being manipulated by outside parties. It appears unlikely that the generators will be replaced, therefore it is essential to take a good torch.

Treks Several trails have been cut by park rangers from the Park Headquarters. One path follows undulating terrain, parallel to the coast. It is possible to cut to the left, through the jungle, to the coast, and walk back to Kuala Likau along the beach. The main trail to Golden Beach is a 5-6 hour walk, crossing several streams and rivers where estuarine crocodiles are reputed to lurk. Most of these crossings are on 'bridges', which are usually just felled trees with no attempt made to assist walkers (some 'bridges' have drops of around 5m) – a good sense of balance is required.

Permits are available from the Bintulu Development Authority.

Park information centre at Park Headquarters (T (085) 737450, F (085) 737454) at the mouth of Sungai Likau, across the river from the Park. A boat is needed to cross the 5m of crocodile infested river. **NB** Because the facilities to the park are actually outside the park, visitors do not need a permit to stay there. This has led to the 'park' becoming very popular with Bintulites at the weekend.

Park information

Accommodation

(**C**) 2 chalets, 2 hostels and one 'mega' hostel – with 27 4-bedrooms. The latter has attractive polished hardwood decor. It can get block-booked. 24-hour electricity.

Places to eat

Canteen at Park Headquarters serving basic food. Picnic shelters at Park HQ.

Transport

Road A new road from Bintulu has been completed. Taxis travel the route (about RM40), (30 minutes). In 1997 there was no bus service.

River Boat: boats available from the wharf or arrange through *Similajau Tours* in Bintulu.

NIAH NATIONAL PARK

Niah's famous caves, tucked into a limestone massif called Gunung Sabis, made world headlines in 1959, when they were confirmed as the most important archaeological site in Asia. About 40,000 years ago, when the Gulf of Thailand and the Sunda Shelf were still dry ground, and a land-bridge connected the Philippines and Borneo, Niah was home to *Homo sapiens*. It was the most exciting archaeological discovery since Java man (*Homo erectus*).

Scientist and explorer A Hart Everett led expeditions to Niah Caves in 1873 and 1879, after which he pronounced that they justified no further work. 79 years later, Tom Harrisson, ethnologist, explorer and conservationist and curator of the Sarawak Museum, confirmed the most important archaeological find in Southeast Asia at Niah. He unearthed fragments of a 37,000-year-old human skull – the earliest evidence of *Homo sapiens* in the region – at the west mouth of the Niah Great Cave itself. The skull was buried under 2.4m of guano. His find debunked and prompted a radical reappraisal of popular theories about where

Niah's guano collectors: scraping the bottom

Eight bat species live in the Niah Caves, some of them more common ones such as the horseshoe bat and fruit bats. Other more exotic varieties include the bearded tomb bat, Cantor's roundleaf horseshoe bat and the lesser bent-winged bat. The ammonia-stench of bat guano permeates the humid air. People began collecting guano in 1929 – it is used as a fertilizer and to prevent pepper vines from rotting. Guano collectors pay a licence fee for the privilege of sweeping up *tahi sapu* (fresh guano) and digging up *tahi timbang* (mature guano) which they sell to the Bat Guano Cooperative at the end of the plankwalk.

modern man's ancestors had sprung from. A wide range of Palaeolithic and Neolithic tools, pottery, ornaments and beads were also found at the site. Anthropologists believe Niah's caves may have been permanently inhabited until around 1400 AD. Harrisson's excavation site, office and house have been left intact in the mouth of the Great Cave. A total of 166 burial sites have been excavated, 38 of which are Mesolithic (up to 20,000 years before present) and the remainder Neolithic (4,000 years before present). Some of the finds are now in the Sarawak Museum in Kuching.

Today, Niah National Park is one of the most popular tourist attractions in Sarawak and attracts more than 15,000 visitors every year. The caves were declared a national historic monument in 1958, but it was not until 1974 that the 3,000 hectars of jungle surrounding the caves were turned into a national park to protect the area from logging.

Permits are necessary to enter the park (and to see the Great Cave). RM3 (RM5 for a camera). A guide is not essential but they provide information and can relate legends about the paintings. But even with a guide, visitors cannot cross the barrier 3m in front of the cave wall. A guide will cost RM35.

To reach the caves, take a longboat across the river from Park Headquarters at Palangkalan Lubang to the start of the 4 km belian (ironwood) plankwalk to the entrance of the **Great Cave**. (Take the right fork 1 km from the entrance). The remains of a small kampong, formerly inhabited by birds' nest collectors (see below) and guano collectors, is just before the entrance, in the shelter of overhanging rocks. It is known as **Traders' Cave**.. Beware of voracious insects (wear long trousers and plenty of repellent). The lights in the Great Cave have not been replaced, so torches are needed.

The **Painted Cave** is beyond the Great Cave, and has been closed for preservation work since 1992. Prehistoric wall-paintings – the only ones in Borneo – stretch for about 32m along the cave wall. Most of the drawings are of dancing human figures and boats, thought to be associated with a death ritual. On the floor of the cave, several 'death-ships' were found with some Chinese stoneware, shell ornaments and ancient glass beads. These death-ships served as coffins and have been carbon-dated to between

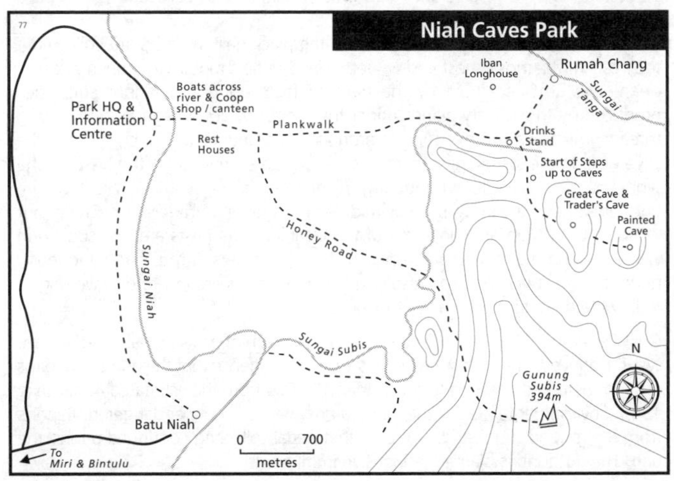

How to make a swift buck

The Malay name for Niah's Painted Cave is *Kain Hitam* – or 'black cloth' – because the profitable rights to the birds' nests were traditionally exchanged for bolts of black cloth. The Chinese have had a taste for swiftlets' nests for well over a thousand years, and the business of collecting them from 60m up in the cavernous chamber of the Great Cave is as lucrative (and as hazardous) a profession now as it was then. The nests are used to prepare birds' nest soup – they are blended with chicken stock and rock salt – which is a famous Chinese delicacy, prized as an aphrodisiac and for its supposed remedial properties for asthma and rhumatism. Birds' nests are one of the most expensive foods in the world: they sell for up to US$500/kilo in Hong Kong, where about 100 tonnes of them (worth US$40mn) are consumed annually. The Chinese communities of North America import 30 tonnes of birds' nests a year. Locally, they fetch RM150-600/kg, depending on the grade.

Hundreds of thousands – possibly millions – of swiftlets (of the *Collocalia* swift family) live in the caves. Unlike other parts of Southeast Asia, where collectors use rotan ladders to reach the nests (see Gomontong Caves, Sabah, page 479), Niah's collectors scale belian (ironwood) poles to heights of more than 60m. They use bamboo sticks with a scraper attached to one end (called *penyulok*) to pick the nests off the cave-roof. The nests are harvested three times each season (which run from August to December and January to March). On the first two occasions, the nests are removed before the eggs are laid and a third left until the nestlings are fledged. Nest collectors are now all supposed to have licences, but in reality, no one does. Although the birds nests are supposed to be protected by the National Park in the off-season, wardens turn a blind eye to illegal harvesting – the collectors also know many secret entrances to the caves. Officially, people caught harvesting out of season can be fined RM2,000 or sent to jail for a year, but no one's ever caught. Despite the fact that it is a dangerous operation (there are usually several fatal accidents at Niah each year), collecting has become such a popular pursuit that harvesters have to reserve their spot with a lamp. Nest collecting is run on a first-come, first-served basis.

Nests of the white nest swiftlets and the black nest swiftlets are collected – the nests of the mossy-nest and white-bellied swiftlets require too much effort to clean. The nests are built by the male swiftlets using a glutinous substance produced by the salivary glands under the tongue which is regurgitated in long threads; the saliva sets like cement producing a rounded cup which sticks to the cave wall. In the swifts' nest market, price is dictated by colour: the best are the white nests which are without any plant material or feathers. Most of the uncleaned nests are bought up by middlemen, agents of traders in Kuching, but locals at Batu Niah also do some of the cleaning. The nests are first soaked in water for about 3 hours, and when softened, feathers and dirt are laboriously removed with tweezers. The resulting 'cakes' of nests are left to dry over-night: if they are dried in the sun they turn yellow.

On 1 December 1993, a 2-year ban on the collection of nests in Niah's Great Cave was introduced. The authorities were swayed by evidence that the number of birds nesting there had declined to fewer than 100,000 from the estimated 4 million in 1962. Environmentalists say the *aerodramus* species is now endangered. Reports from the ground suggested, however, that illegal collecting continued during the ban. The authorities blamed Indonesian immigrants.

1 and 780 AD. By around 700 AD there is thought to have been a flourishing community based in the caves, trading hornbill ivory and birds' nests with the Chinese in exchange for porcelain and beads. But then it seems the caves were suddenly deserted in about 1400. In Penan folklore there are references to 'the ancestors who lived in the big caves' and tribal elders are said to be able to recall funeral rites using death-boats similar to those found at Niah.

Flora and fauna The Niah National Park is primarily comprised of alluvial or peat swamp as well as some mixed dipterocarp forest. Long-tailed macaques, hornbills, squirrels, flying lizards and crocodiles have all been recorded in the park. There are also bat hawks which present an impressive spectacle when they home in on one of the millions of bats which pour out of the caves at dusk.

Treks A lowland trail called Jalan Madu (Honey Rd), traverses the peat swamp forest and up Gunung Subis; it is not well marked. Return trips need a full day. The trail leads off the plankwalk to the right, about 1 km from Pangkalan Lubang (Park HQ). The left-fork on the plankwalk, before the gate to the caves, goes to an Iban longhouse, Rumah Chang (40 minutes walk), where cold drinks can be bought.

Park Headquarters at Pangkalan Lubang next to Sungai Subis. You must apply for an entry permit here before proceeding into the park. You will need your passport and pay an RM3 entry fee for each person and RM5 for camera, RM10 for video and RM200 for professional photography. (Open daily 0800-1700 – caves open daily 0800-1630). For more information on the park, contact Deputy Park Warden, Niah National Park, PO Box 81, Miri Post Office, Batu Niah, T 085 737450, F 085 737918.

Transport around the Park From Park HQ, longboats can be hired for upriver trips (RM40/day; 8 people max/boat). Crossing the river from HQ costs RM0.50.

Equipment Visitors are advised to bring a powerful torch for the caves. Walking boots are advisable during the wet season as the plankwalk can get very slippery.

Guides can be hired from Park HQ (RM35 for groups of up to 20).

Park Information Centre At Park Headquarters, has displays on birds' nests and flora and fauna. The exhibition includes the 37,000-year-old human skull which drew world attention to Niah in 1958. Also on display are 35,000-year-old oyster shells, as well as palaeolithic pig bones, monkey bones, turtle-shells and crabs which were found littering the cave floor. There are also burial vessels dating from 1600BC and carved seashell jewellery from around 400BC. Open 0800-1230, 1400-1615 Monday-Friday; 0800-1245 Saturday; 0800-1200 Sunday.

Park information

● Accommodation

Call Miri, at the Old Forestry Building, Jln Angkasa, T (085) 436637. All accommodation has 24-hour electricity and treated water. ***Family Chalet*** similar to hostel but cooker and a/c are planned for the future, 2 rooms with 4 beds in each, RM65/room. ***5 Hostels***, each with 4 rooms of 4 beds each, all rooms have private bathrooms, clean and western style with shower, toilet, electric fans, fridges, large sitting area and kitchen. No cooking facilities but kettle, crockery and cutlery can be provided upon request. Booking advisable during holiday season (June-August, December), RM42 for one room of 4 beds, or RM10.50 for one bed. ***VIP Resthouse***, RM200/room, a/c, TV, hi-fi.

Batu Niah: there are also 4 small hotels in Batu Niah (4 km from Park HQ): **A-B** ***Park View Hotel***, T (085) 737021, most expensive hotel in town with range of comfortable rooms, discounts often available. **B** ***Niah Caves Inn***, T (085) 737333, recently opened place. **D** ***Hock Seng***, T (085) 737740, some a/c, attached facilities. **D** ***Niah Caves Hotel***, T (085) 737726, some a/c, shared facilities.

● Camping

Tents can be hired from Park HQ (RM8) or from the site (RM4).

● Places to eat

The Guano Collectors' Cooperative shop at the beginning of the plankwalk sells basic food and cold drinks and camera film. There is another basic shop/restaurant just outside the park gates. There is a canteen at Park HQ, which serves good local food and full western breakfast, good value, BBQ site provided, the canteen is supposed to be open from 0700-2300, but is a little erratic. Emergency rations recommended.

● **Transport**
109 km from Miri to Batu Niah.

Road Bus: hourly connections with Miri, 2 hours (RM8.50), 7 buses a day to Bintulu, 2 hours (RM10) and Sibu via Bintulu to Batu Niah. **Taxi**: from Miri (RM20 pp) to Park HQ, will only leave when there are 4 passengers. From Bintulu to Batu Niah (RM30).

River Boat: boats from Batu Niah (near the market) to Park Headquarters at Pengkalan Lubang, Niah National Park (RM10 pp or if more than 5 people, RM2 pp) or 45 minutes walk to Park Headquarters.

MIRI AND THE BARAM RIVER

MIRI

Miri is the starting point for adventurous trips up the Barani River to Marudi, Bario and the Kelabit Highlands. Also accessible from Miri and Marudi is the incomparable Gunung Mulu National Park with the biggest limestone cave system in the world and one of the richest assemblages of plants and animals.

The capital of Sarawak's fourth division is a busy, prosperous town; more than half its population is Chinese. Many new buildings have gone up over the last few years, including two big new hotels, the *Mega* and the *Grand Palace* each of which has an adjoining shopping mall. One of the newest projects is a waterfront development with a marina – there is a pleasant walk on the peninsula here across the Miri River, and some good fishing. Another project recently completed is the *Bintang Plaza*, a large shopping complex on the edge of town on the road to the Baram River which contains *Parkson*, one of Malaysia'a largest department store chains.

In the latter years of the 19th century, a small trading company set up in Sarawak, to import kerosine and export polished shells and pepper. In 1910, when 'earth oil' was first struck on the hill overlooking Miri, the little trading company took the plunge and diversified into the new commodity – making, in the process, Sarawak's first oil town. The company's name was Shell. Together with the Malaysian national oil company, Petronas, Shell has been responsible for discovering, producing and refining Sarawak's offshore oil deposits. Oil is a key contributor to Malaysia's export earnings and Miri has been a beneficiary of the boom. There is a big refinery at Lutong to the north, which is connected by pipeline with Seria in Brunei. Lutong is the next town on the Miri River and the main headquarters for Shell.

Taman Bulatan is a scenic centrally located park with foodstalls and boats for hire on the man made lake.

The oil boom in this area began on Canada Hill, behind the town (where, incidently, this limestone ridge provides excellent views of the town). **Oil Well No 1** was built by Shell and was the first oil well in Malaysia, spudded on 10 August 1910. The well was still yielding oil 62 years later, but its productivity began to slump. It is estimated that a total of 600,000 barrels were extracted from Well No 1 during its operational life. It was shut off in 1972. There are now 624 oil wells in the Miri Field, producing 80 million barrels of oil a year.

Juxtaposed against Miri's modern boom-town image is **Tamu Muhibba** (the native jungle produce market, open 24 hours), opposite the *Park Hotel* in a purpose-built concrete structure with pointed roofs on the roundabout connecting Jalan Malay and Jalan Padang. Orang Ulu come downriver to sell their produce, and a walk round the market provides an illuminating lesson in jungle nutrition. Colourful characters run impromptu 'stalls' from rattan mats, selling yellow cucumbers that look like mangoes, mangoes that look like turnips,

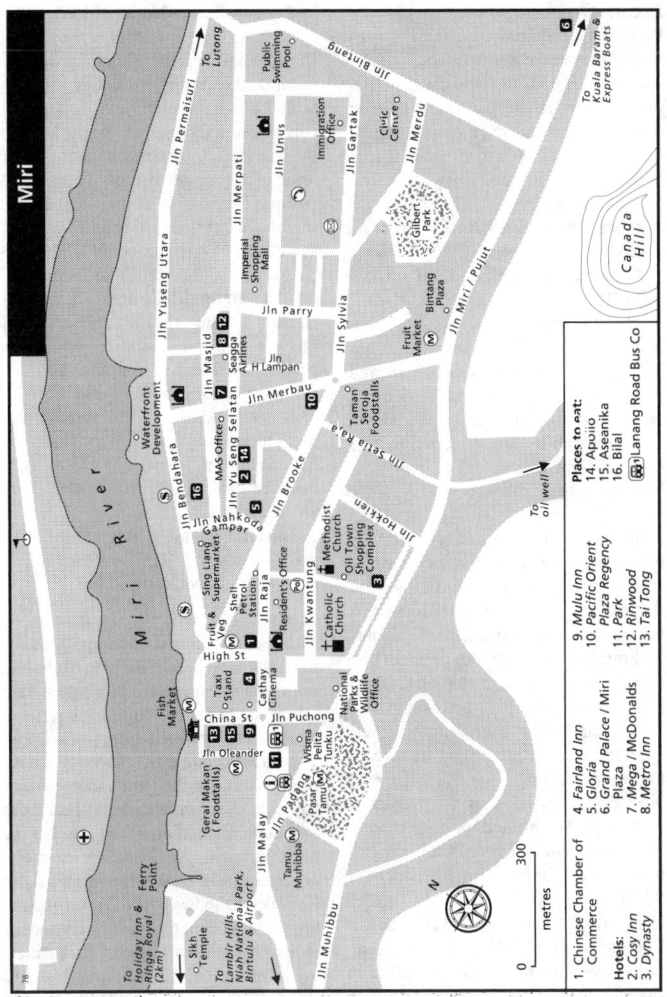

huge crimson durians, tiny loofah sponges, sackfulls of fragrant Bario rice (brown and white), every shape, size and hue of banana, *tuak* (rice wine) in old Heineken bottles and a menagerie of jungle fauna – including mousedeer, falcons, pangolins and the apparently delicious long-snouted *tupai*, or jungle squirrel. There is a large selection of dried and fresh seafood – fish and *bubok* (tiny prawns), and big buckets boiling with catfish or stacked with turtles, there are also some handicrafts.

Miri is the main centre for organizing tours up the Baram River, to Mulu National Park.

Excursions

Permits are required to go anywhere upriver. Apply at the Resident's office, Jalan Kwantung, T 433205 – with passport photocopy. Permits are also available from Marudi. After aquiring a permit, the Police Station will need to stamp it. If travelling with a tour company it will take care of the bureaucracy.

Niah Caves & National Park, see page 400.

Gunung Mulu National Park, see page 410.

Hawaii Beach is a pristine palm fringed beach, popular for picnics and barbecues. **Accommodation**: available here in chalets. *Getting there*: 15 minutes' taxi ride from Miri.

Lambir Hills The park mainly consists of a chain of sandstone hills bounded by rugged cliffs, 19 km south of Miri and just visible from the town, the park's main attraction is its beautiful waterfalls. **Flora and fauna** *Kerangas* (heath forest) covers the higher ridges and hills while the lowland areas are mixed dipterocarp forest. Bornean gibbons, bearded pigs, barking deer and over 100 species of bird have been recorded in the park. **Treks** There is only one path across a rickety suspension bridge at present, but there are numerous waterfalls and tree towers for birdwatching. The park attracts hoardes of day-trippers from Miri at weekends. **Accommodation**: 5 chalets, one with 2 rooms, 3 beds, 4 units with 2 rooms, 2 beds, RM40/room or RM80/house; A/c chalet, 2 rooms with 3 beds, RM60/room or RM120/house, **Campsite**: rental RM4. **Places to eat**: canteen provided, no cooking allowed in chalet, can cook at campsite or take food into canteen. The Park Headquarters is close to the Miri-Niah road, there is an audio visual room with seating for 30 here. Park entrance: RM3, photography RM5, video camera RM10, professional camera RM100. *Getting there*: from *Park Hotel* take Bintulu or Bakong bus (RM3).

Loagan Bunut National Park is located in the upper reaches of the Sungai Bunut and contains Sarawak's largest natural lake. At approximately 650 hectares, Loagan Bunut may not be large but it is no ordinary lake; the water level in the lake is totally dependent on the water level of the rivers Bunut, Tinijar and Baram. The level is at its lowest in the months of February, May and June and sometimes, for a period of about 2-3 weeks, the lake becomes an expanse of dry cracked mud. The main cultural attraction at the lake is the traditional method of fishing (*selambau*), which has been retained by the Berawan fishermen. The surrounding area is covered with peat swamp forest. The common larger birds found here are the darters, egrets, herons, bittern, hornbill and kites. Gibbons are also common. At present, there are no visitors facilities.

Luconia Island is surrounded by a pristine coral reef. Trips can be organized through tour operators in Miri.

Tours

Although most tour companies specialize in trips up the Baram River to Mulu National Park, some are much better than others – in terms of facilities and services offered. The best agents are *Alo Doda* and *Tropical Adventure* which have private accommodation in the Park and run an interesting selection of more off-beat treks to remote destinations; they are also the most expensive. *Alo Doda*, for example, organizes treks to the Penan areas and Kenyah longhouses of Ulu Baram – on the upper stretches of the river. Every agency in Miri has a Mulu National Park itinerary covering the caves, pinnacles, and summits. It is also possible to trek to Bario and Mount Murud, as well as to Limbang from Mulu. Most of the agencies employ experienced guides who will be able to advise on longer, more ambitious treks. The Mulu National Park is one destination where it is usually cheaper to go through a tour company than to try to do it independently. Costs vary considerably according to the number of people in a group: for the 3 days Mulu trip, a single tourist can expect to pay RM500; this drops to RM400 a head for a group of four and about RM350 each for a group of 10, all accommodation, food, travel and guide costs included. An 8-days tour of Ulu Baram longhouses, would cost RM1,800 for one person and RM1,200 per person in a group of 10. A 20-day trek will cost two people (minimum number) around RM2,000 each, and a group of 6-10, RM1,300 a head. For those who want to visit remote longhouses, tour companies present by far the best option. Tour fees cover 'gifts' and all payments to longhouse headmen for food, accommodation and entertainment.

Local information

● Accommodation

Prices: L over RM500; **A+** RM260-500; **A** RM130-260; **B** RM65-130; **C** RM40-65; **D** RM20-40; **E** RM10-20; **F** Below RM10

Most people going to Mulu will have to spend at least one night in Miri. The town has a growing selection of mid-to-upmarket hotels; many offer discounts of 30-40% off quoted prices as a matter of course. Many of the mid-range hotels are around Jln Yu Seng Selatan. But being an oil town, and close to Brunei, Miri has a booming prostitution industry. Many of the cheaper lodging houses, particularly those around Jln China, are sleezy brothels. The cheaper accommodation listed below represents the more respectable end of the market, but there is not much for anyone hoping to stay somewhere that's cheap and not a brothel.

A+-A *Holiday Inn*, Jln Temenggong Datuk Oyong Lawai, T 418888, F 419999, 2 km from town centre, at mouth of the Miri River, this 5-storey, modern, white block curves around the South China Sea, very popular with families at weekends (check for special weekend rates (**B**) price category), 168 rooms all with a/c, TV (no less than 11 channels), bathroom, tea and coffee making facilities, mini-bar, balcony, thick carpets and comfy beds, sunsets over sea, colourful but noisy river traffic, free-form pool, pleasantly surrounded by plants and palms with swim-up bar in form of traditional boat (popular with kids), jacuzzi and baby pool, sandy area for kids to play, beach too near town to be clean and sea not safe for swimming but pleasant for sunset strolls, coffee house, Chinese restaurant, bar and bakery/delicatessen, fitness centre, sauna, recommended. **A+-A** *Rihga Royal*, Lot 799, Jln Temenggong Datuk Oyong Lawai, T 421121, F 421099, Japanese-managed hotel on coast south of Miri, 5-star comforts, 225 rooms, all rooms with a/c, mini-bar, TV, tea and coffee making facilities, Japanese restaurant (the only one in Miri), Chinese restaurant and coffee house, pool, tennis, health centre. **A** *Dynasty*, Lot 683, Block 9, Jln Pujut-Lutong, T 421111, F 422222, a/c, restaurants, pool, health centre, next to Oil Town Shopping Complex. **A** *Grand Palace*, 2 km Jln Miri-Pujut, Pelita Commercial Centre, T 428888, F 427777, imposing peach and pastel building on town outskirts next to Miri Plaza Shopping Centre, 125 comfortable, carpeted rooms with a/c, TV, bathroom, mini-bar, tea and coffee making facilities, pool, fitness centre, karaoke, restuarant. **A** *Mega*, Lot 907, Jln Merbau, T 432432, F 433433/427373, the tallest and largest hotel in Miri town centre, 228 rooms with a/c, TV, bathroom, Chinese restaurant, coffee house, pool with jacuzzi, health centre, business centre, shopping mall attached. **A** *Park*, Jln Raja, T 414555, F 414488, a/c, Chinese restaurant, until the *Holiday Inn* opened, the *Park* was the best hotel in town, ranks at about a 3-star hotel, although now rather run down, it is good value for money and convenient location for bus station. **A-B** *Gloria*, 27 Jln Brooke, T 416699, F 418866, a/c, restaurant, 42 rooms, better than it looks from outside, although the economy rooms are windowless, recommended. **A-B** *Rinwood*, Jln Yu Seng Utara, T 415888, F 415009, a/c, restaurant, one of the smaller mid-range places to stay. **A-B** *Pacific Orient*, 49 Jln Brooke, T 413333, F 410003, 65 rooms, all with a/c, many with TV and fitted carpets, special rates sometimes available, tavern and café.

B *Cosy Inn*, 545-547 Jln Yu Seng Selatan, T 415522, F 415155, a/c, restaurant.

C *Metro Inn*, Lot 762, 1st Flr, Jln Merpati, T 411663, F 424663, small but comfortable rooms with a/c, TV and attached bathrooms. **C-D** *Tai Tong Lodging House*, 26 Jln China, T 411498, some a/c, Chinese guesthouse-cum-hotel with range of rooms from a/c with attached bathrooms to fan-cooled with shared facilities, dorm beds also available (**F**), although possessions left here are reputedly not very secure.

D *Fairland Inn*, Jln Raja, T 413981, a/c, small, clean rooms, friendly management, probably the best of the cheaper places in Miri.

Places to eat

Prices: ♦♦♦♦ over RM40; ♦♦♦ RM13-40; ♦♦ RM5-13; ♦ under RM5

Malay: ♦♦***Aseanika***, Jln China, also serves good Indian and Indonesian food. ♦***Nabila's***, 1st Flr, 441 DUBS Building, Jln Bendahara, also serves Indonesian and Oriental, curries, good rendang.

Chinese: ♦♦♦***Kok Chee***, 1st Flr *Park Hotel*, Jln Kingsway. ♦♦***Apollo***, Lot 394 Jln Yu Seng Selatan (close to *Gloria Hotel*), good seafood, popular. ♦♦***Sea View Café***, Jln China.

Indian: ♦♦***Bilal***, Jln Persiaran Kabor, excellent curries and rotis, coffee house.

International: ♦♦♦***Golden Steak Garden***, *Gloria Hotel*, 27 Jln Brooke, steak. ♦♦♦***Park View Restaurant*** (coffee house of *Park Hotel*), Jln Malay, most sophisticated menu in town, jellyfish, good selection of seafood and grill. ♦♦***McDonalds***, next to *Mega Hotel*. ♦♦***Bonzer Garden Steak House***, Jln Yu Seng Utara, local dishes much cheaper than burgers. ♦***Sugar Bun***, Ground Floor, Wisma Pelita Tunku, burgers, pastries, cakes etc. ***Cosy Garden*** (and in *Mega Hotel* block), pleasant restaurant, but the a/c inhibits any cosiness, limited menu but reasonable prices, steak.

Bakeries: ***Appletree***, Ground Floor, Wisma Pelita Tunku; ***Deli Corner***, *Holiday Inn*.

Foodstalls: ♦*Taman Seroja*, Jln Brooke, Malay food, best in the evenings. ***Tamu Muhibba*** (Native Market), opposite *Park Hotel* on roundabout connecting Jln Malay and Jln Padang, best during the day. ***Tanjong Seafood stalls***, Tanjung Lobung (south of Miri), best in evening. ***Gerai Makan***, near Chinese temple at end of Jln Oleander, Malay food.

Airline offices

MAS, 239 Halaman Kabor, off Jln Yu Seng Selatan, T 414144; **Royal Brunei**, Lot 263, Halaman Kabor, T 426322; **Seagga**, Jln Sim Cheng Kay, near mosque, T 439954.

Banks & money changers

All major banks are represented in Miri.

Entertainment

Miri has scores of karaoke lounges and discos, mostly along Jln Yu Seng. Check local paper for information on films and cultural events. The ***Holiday Inn*** stages regular performances of western music and theatre. ***Rig*** disco in *Regal Hotel*, very popular.

Hospitals & medical services

Hospital: opposite Ferry Point, T 420033.

Post & telecommunications

Area code: 085.

General Post Office: just off Jln Gartak.

Telecom Office: Jln Gartak, open Mon-Sun 0730-2200.

Shopping

Books: ***Pelita Book Centre***, 1st Flr, Wisma Pelita Tunku; ***Parksons Department Store***, Bintang Plaza.

Shopping Malls: ***Bintang Plaza*** Jln Miri; ***Imperial Mall***, Jln Parry; ***Soon Hup Tower***, next to *Mega Hotel* with Parkwell's supermarket and department store; ***Wisma Pelita Tunku***, near bus station, department store; ***Miri Plaza***, next to *Grand Palace Hotel* – mediocre supermarket – not worth the trek out here.

Handicrafts: ***Longhouse***, 2nd Flr, Imperial Mall, the best in town; ***Kong Hong***, Wisma Pelita, 1st Flr; ***Sarawak Handicrafts***, 2nd Floor, Soon Hup Centre; ***Joy art and fashion House***, M Flr, Wisma Pelita Tunju; ***Syarikat Unique arts and handicrafts centre***, Lot 2994; ***Morsjaya Commercial Centre***, Jln Miri; ***Royal Selangor***, 28F, High St; ***Swet Love Gift Shop***, Lot 219, 2nd Flr, Wisma Pelita Tunku. Roadside stalls at Nakat, 18 km down the southbound road to Niah (1 km before Lambir Hills National Park) also sell baskets.

Supermarket: ***Pelita***, Ground Floor, Wisma Pelita Tunku, useful for supplies for upriver expeditions; ***Sing Liang Supermarket*** on Jln Nakhoda Gampar – Chinese store; ***Parkson Grand***, Bintang Plaza; ***Ngiukee***, moving from Pelita to Imperial Mall.

Sports

Golf: ***Miri Golf Club***, Jln Datuk Patinggi, T 416787, F 417848, by the sea, green fees RM80-120.

Swimming: Public pool off Jln Bintang, close to the Civic Centre, RM1.

Fitness Centres: *Holiday Inn* and *Rihga Hotels* both have centres where non-residents can become short-term members.

Tour companies & travel agents

Borneo Adventure, *Pacific Orient Hotel*, 49 Jln Brooke, T 414935, F 419543, recommended; ***Borneo Leisure***, Lot 227, Ground Floor, Jln Maju, Beautiful Jade Centre, T 413011; ***Borneo Overland***, 37 Ground Floor, Bangunan Raghavan, Jln Brooke, T 4302255, F 416424; ***East-West***, 792 Jln Bintang, T 410717, F 411297; ***Hornbill Travel***, G26 Park Arcade, Jln Raja, T 417385, F 412751; ***JJM Tours & Travel***, Lot 3002, Ground Floor, Morsjaya Commercial Centre, 2.5 Miles,

Miri-Bintulu Rd, T 416051, F 414390, young company with some very experienced guides, recommended; ***KKM Travel & Tours***, 236 Jln Maju, T 417899, F 414629; ***Malang Sisters Agency***, 248 Jln Bendahara, T 417770, F 417123; ***Robert Ding***, Lot 556, 1st Flr, Royal Snooker Centre, Jln Permaisuri, T 416051, F 414390, recommended by National Parks Office; ***Seridan Mulu***, Lot 351, 2nd Flr, Jln Brooke, T 422277, F 415277, private accommodation within park, recommended by National Parks Office; ***Transworld Travel Service***, Jln Padang, T 422277, F 415277; ***Tropical Adventure***, Ground Floor, *Mega Hotel*, Soon Hup Tower, PO Box 2197, T 419337, F 414503, private accommodation within Mulu Park, recommended.

Tourist Information Centre: Lot 452, Jln Malay (next to bus station), T 434181, F 434179. Permits and accommodation bookings for Niah, Mulu and Lambir.

● Useful addresses

National Parks and Wildlife Office: Jln Puchong, T 436637, F 431975.
Resident's Office: Jln Kwantung, T 433205.
Immigration Office: Jln Unus, T 442100.
Area code: 085.
Hospital: T 420033.
Police Station: Jln Kingsway, T 432533.

● Transport

Local Car hire: **Mega,** No 3, Lorong 1, Sungai Krokop, T 427436. Fleet of Proton Sagas available. RM120-150/day. **Kimoto,** T411007. **Ferry**: operates every 15 minutes from 0630-2000. **Taxi**: T 432277.

Air Regular connections on MAS with Kuching (RM169), Sibu (RM120), Marudi (RM25), Bario, via Marudi (RM75), Bintulu, Limbang, Lawas, Mulu and Labuan. Also connections with Kota Kinabalu (RM109). For transport information, T 33433. *Getting to town*: fare by taxi to town from Padang Kirbua Terminal is RM20, or RM12 to the old bus station. Bus no 7 runs between town and the airport from early morning to early evening.

Road Bus: a new bus terminal has opened – Pujuk Padang Kerbau, Jln Padang. Regular connections from early morning to early/mid afternoon with Batu Niah 2-3 hours, Bintulu 3 hours, Sibu 6 hours, and Kuching. Tickets can be booked at following agents: **Lanang Road Bus Co**, next to *Park Hotel*, T 435336, **Syarikat Bas Express**, next to *Park Hotel*, T 439325. Express buses to Marudi, depart from Kuala Baram, the port area, 2 hours, RM18.

To Kuala Baram and the express boat upriver to Marudi Regular bus connections with Kuala Baram; there are also taxis to Kuala Baram, either private or shared. **Boat**: express boats upriver to Marudi from Kuala Baram, 3 hours. Roughly 1 boat every hour from 0715. Last boat 1430. This is the first leg of the journey to Mulu and the interior.

● International connections

Regular connections (Miri-Belait Transport Company, T 419129) with Kuala Belait in Brunei, 2 hours. Travelling by your own means of transport from Miri it is necessary to take the car ferry across the Baram River, then pass through immigration, before another ferry across the Belait River. At weekends and public holidays there are long queues for the ferries as well as at immigration – so be prepared for a long, hot wait. Be warned also that the ferry across the Belait River takes an unscheduled 1 hour break for lunch. Distance itself is nothing – the ferry crossings take no more than 10 minutes each and Miri to Kuala Belait is just 27 km. Bus passengers by-pass the queues because they board the ferry as foot passengers and then hop on another bus the other side of the river. From Kuala Belait regular connections with Seria, 1 hour and from Seria regular connections with Bandar Seri Begawan, 1-2 hours. It takes the best part of a day to reach BSB.

MARUDI

Four major tribal groups – Iban, Kelabit, Kayan and Penan – come to Marudi to do business with the Chinese, Indian and Malay merchants. Marudi is the furthest upriver trading post on the Baram and services all the longhouses in the Tutoh, Tinjar and Baram river basins. Most tourists only stop long enough in Marudi to down a cold drink before catching the next express boat upriver – as the trip to Mulu National Park can now be done in a day, not many have to spend the night here. Because it is a major trading post, however, there are a lot of hotels, and the standards are reasonably good.

Fort Hose was built in 1901, when Marudi was still called Claudetown, and has good views of the river. It is named after the last of the Rajah's Residents, the anthropologist, geographer and natural historian Dr Charles Hose. The fort is now used as administrative offices. Also of note is the intricately carved **Thaw Peh Kong Chinese Temple** (diagonally opposite the express boat jetty), also known as Siew San Teen. It was shipped from China and erected in Sarawak in the early 1900s, although it was probably already 100 years old by the time the temple began life in its new location.

Excursions Permits are necessary to go upriver from Marudi. Permits for Mulu and Bario are issued by the district officer in Fort Hose.

Gunung Mulu National Park, see below.

Brunei The Marudi-Kampong Teraja log walk is normally done from the Brunei end, as the return trek, across the Sarawak/Brunei border takes a full day, dawn to dusk. It is, however, possible to reach an Iban longhouse inside Brunei without going the full distance to Kampong Teraja. The longhouse is on the Sungai Ridan, about 2½ hours down the jungle trail. The trail starts 3 km from Marudi, on the airport road. A local Chinese man, who runs an unofficial taxi service to and from the trail head, may spot you before you find the trail (ask at the houses along the road). There is no customs post on the border; the trail is not an official route into Brunei. Trekkers are advised to take their passports in the unlikely event of being stopped by police, who will probably turn a blind eye. Kampong Teraja in Brunei is the furthest accessible point which can be reached by road (from Labi; see page 562).

Longhouses Three longhouses, *Long Seleban*, *Long Moh* and *Leo Mato*, are accessible by 4 wheel drive vehicle from Marudi.

Local information

● Accommodation

B-C *Zola*, Lot 14-15 Queens Sq, T 755711, a/c, restaurant next door, clean, occasionally lacking in sheets.

C-D *Alisan*, 63-5 Queen's Sq, T 755911, some a/c, the more expensive a/c rooms are spacious but the cheaper rooms are more like cells; **C-D** *Grand*, Marudi bazaar, T 755711, some a/c, large but good hotel, with clean rooms, close to jetty and plenty of information on upriver trips.

D *Marudi*, 3 Queen's Sq, T 755141, a/c; **D-E** *Hop Chong*, 1 Queen St, T 755146/755387, some a/c (a boarding house).

● Places to eat

There are several coffee shops dotted around town. The ♦*Rose Garden*, opposite *Alisan Hotel* is an a/c coffee shop serving mainly Chinese dishes.

● Banks & money changers

There are 2 local banks with foreign exchange facilities.

● Post & telecommunications

Area code: 085.

Post Office: Airport Rd.

● Useful addresses

Police station: on Airport Rd.

● Transport

Air The airport is 5 km from town. Connections with Miri (RM29) Bario (RM55), Sibu (RM100).

River Boat: boats leave from opposite the Chinese temple. Connections with Kuala Baram; 8 boats a day from 0700-1430 (RM18), Tutoh (for longboats to Long Terawan and Mulu National Park, one boat at 1200) (RM20), Long Lama (for longboats to Bario) 1 boat every hour 0730-1400.

GUNUNG MULU NATIONAL PARK

Tucked in behind Brunei, the 52,866 hectares Gunung Mulu National Park lays claim to Gunung Mulu (at 2,376m, the second highest mountain in Sarawak) and the biggest limestone cave system in the world. In short, Mulu is essentially a huge hollow mountain range, sitting on top of 180-million-year-old rainforest. Its primary jungle contains astonishing biological diversity. In Robin Hanbury-Tenison's book *The Rain Forest*, he says of Mulu: "All sense of time and direction is lost." Every scientific expedition that has visited Mulu's forests has encountered plant and animal species unknown to science. In 1990, 5 years after it was officially opened to the public, Mulu National Park was handling an average 400 visitors a month.

Gunung Mulu National Park

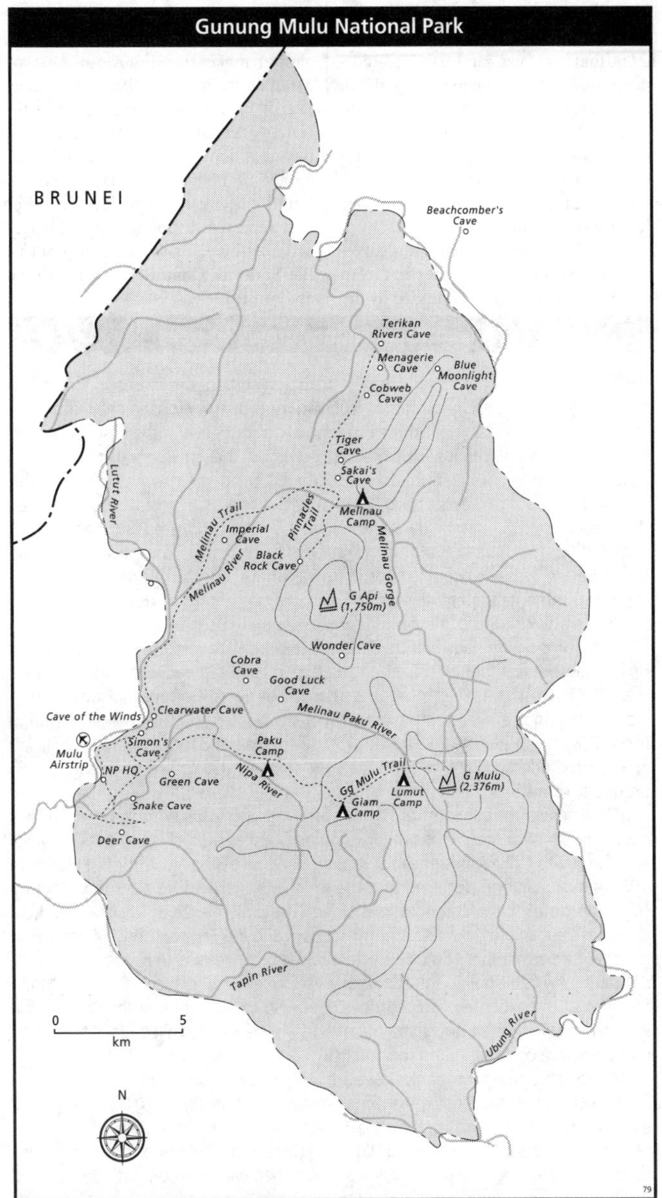

BRUNEI
Beachcomber's Cave
Terikan Rivers Cave
Menagerie Cave
Blue Moonlight Cave
Cobweb Cave
Tiger Cave
Sakai's Cave
Melinau Camp
Lutut River
Melinau Trail
Pinnacles Trail
Imperial Cave
Black Rock Cave
Melinau River
Melinau Gorge
G Api (1,750m)
Wonder Cave
Cobra Cave
Good Luck Cave
Cave of the Winds
Clearwater Cave
Melinau Paku River
Mulu Airstrip
Simon's Cave
Paku Camp
NP HQ
Green Cave
Nipa River
Gg Mulu Trail
G Mulu (2,376m)
Lumut Camp
Giam Camp
Snake Cave
Deer Cave
Tapin River
Ubung River
0
5
km
N
79

Numbers have increased markedly since then – the area is now attracting about 12,000 tourists a year – and as the eco-tourism industry has extended its foothold, local tribespeople have been drawn into confrontation with the authorities. A series of sabotage incidents in 1993 have been blamed on the Berawan tribe, who claim the caves and the surrounding jungle are a sacred site.

In 1974, 3 years after Mulu was gazetted as a National Park, the first of a succession of joint expeditions led by the British Royal Geographical Society (RGS) and the Sarawak government began to make the discoveries that put Mulu on the map. In 1980 a cave passage over 50 km long was surveyed for the first time. Since then, a further 137 km of passages have been discovered. Altogether 27 major caves have now been found – speleologists believe they probably represent a tiny fraction of what is actually there. The world's biggest cave, the **Sarawak Chamber**, was not discovered until 1984.

A land where money grows on trees

Ever since Sarawak's riverbanks were first settled, the Iban and Orang Ulu tribespeople have practiced shifting cultivation, growing crops in their clearings. Today, most of the clearing is done by commercial loggers and the cash-crop is the jungle itself. No one can travel up the Baram without feeling alarmed at the volume of logs, stockpiled like giant matchsticks, on either side of the river for mile after mile. In July 1991 members of two European environmental protest groups chained themselves to logs at Kuala Baram; they were promptly arrested and deported. In March 1992, James Barclay, author of *A stroll through Borneo*, a book about logging on the Baram, was also deported from Sarawak after a month in jail. The government says environmentalists are ill-informed and are presenting a false picture to the world. Sarawak's forests, it maintains, will be there in perpetuity.

The Borneo Company first tried logging on the Baram in the early 1900s, and built Sarawak's first timber mill at Kuala Baram in 1904 but early logging operations were not successful as the timber was attacked by pests. Commercial logging only really began in the 1950s with the arrival of the tractor and the chainsaw. During the 1980s and early 1990s, Sarawak's 130 million-year-old forests were being felled at an unprecedented rate. In 1993 the state shipped US$2bn of timber and forest products, some 9.1 million cubic metres of logs.

Who derives the benefits from the lucrative logging industry is a sensitive political issue – in Sarawak, politics is timber. Logging licences are tickets to get rich quick and the state's Chief Minister can award timber concessions to whom he wants. In 1987 a rival politician disclosed that the Chief Minister and his allies held about a ⅓ of the state's logging concessions alone. The previous Chief Minister had held nearly as much. Sarawak's Minister for Tourism and the Environment, James Wong is himself a partner in a 180,000-hectare logging concession in Limbang. Environmentalists say these politicians, together with Chinese timber tycoons, are amassing fortunes at the expense of forest tribes. The rush to extract what they can before environmental pressure puts them out of business has fuelled allegations of political manoeuvring, corruption and malpractice.

Although logging companies have provided jobs for upriver tribespeople (a total of 150,000 people are employed in Sarawak's timber industry), logging has wreaked ecological havoc and impinged on tribal lands. The traditional lifestyles of the Penan hunter-gatherers and other Orang Ulu tribes have been threatened as loggers push deeper into the jungle. In the past, Kayan tribesmen would simply have decapitated

The first attempt on Gunung Mulu was made by Spencer St John, the British consul in Brunei, in 1856 (see also his attempts on Gunung Kinabalu, Sabah, page 467). His efforts were thwarted by "limestone cliffs, dense jungle and sharp pinnacles of rock". Dr Charles Hose, Resident of Marudi, led a 25-days expedition to Gunung Mulu in 1893, but also found his path blocked by 600m-high cliffs. Nearly half a century later, in 1932, a Berawan rhinoceros-hunter called Tama Nilong guided Edward Shackleton's Oxford University expedition to the summit. (One of the young Oxford undergraduates on that expedition was Tom Harrisson, who later made the Niah archaeological discoveries, see page 400). Tama Nilong, the hunter from Long Terawan, had previously reached the main southwest ridge of Mulu while tracking a rhinoceros.

The limestone massifs of Gunung Api and Gunung Benarat were originally at the same elevation as Gunung Mulu, but their limestone outcrops were more

anyone caught trespassing on their tribal lands; these days the Orang Ulu protest against the encroachment by blockading logging access roads. Many have been jailed for such protests. The government argues that the jungle tribes are a sideshow and says they have been hijacked by Western environmental groups in a bid to give their campaigns a human face. Environmentalist groups counter that the livelihoods of the forest tribes are as important in the sustainability stakes as the trees themselves.

Since the early 1980s, the water in Sarawak's main rivers has turned brown, due to the sediment which is washed into it from the timber camps upstream. Water supplies have been contaminated by chemical pollutants and fish stocks have been depleted – few can survive in the turgid waters. In Belaga, on the upper Rejang, the price of fish has risen 10-fold in a decade. In Orang Ulu longhouses, tribespeople complain that logging operations have chased their game away, turning hunting trips for wild boar into major expeditions.

The state government is eager to allay fears that it is logging without regard to the forest ecology and the indigenous tribes. But while the state's forestry policy looks good on paper, the Enforcement Division of the Forest Department cannot cope with the vast territory it has to police; it is now using satellites to detect areas where illegal logging has occurred. The government dismisses warnings that Sarawak's logging rates (which are the highest in the world) cannot be sustained as scaremongering. But in 1991, the Japan-based International Tropical Timber Organization said that if logging rates were not halved, the state could be 'logged-out' within the decade.

In the course of the next few years, Sarawak will be cutting its log production down to a level which it claims will make its forestry sustainable by the mid-1990s. But the state will always be dependent on timber as 90% of its oil and gas revenues – its only other major resources – are diverted to federal coffers. Without logging Sarawak would be left high and dry. To ensure the survival of the industry, wood-processing industries are being promoted, because furniture and sawn timber exports will yield more money from fewer logs, and in 1994 a ban on raw log exports was imposed. For environmentalists the announcement in 1992 of the creation of the 187,000 ha Lonjak Entimau forest reserve on the border with Kalimantan was a faint ray of light in an otherwise rather gloomy situation.

prone to erosion than the Mulu's sandstone. The cliffs of the Melinau Gorge rise a sheer 600m, and are the highest limestone rockfaces between North Thailand and Papua New Guinea. Northwest of the gorge lies a large, undisturbed alluvial plain which is rich in flora and fauna. Penan tribespeople (see page 363) are allowed to maintain their lifestyle of fishing, hunting and gathering in the park. At no small expense, the Malaysian government has encouraged them to settle at a purpose-built longhouse at **Batu Bungan**, just a few minutes upriver from Park HQ – but its efforts have met with limited success. Penan shelters can often be found by river banks.

Reeling from international criticism, the Sarawak state government announced in 1994 that it had set aside 66,000 hectares of rainforest as what it called 'biosphere' – a reserve where indigenous people could practice their traditional lifestyle. Part of this lies in the Mulu National Park. In Baram and Limbang districts, the remaining 300 Penan will have a reserve in which they can continue their nomadic way of life. A further 23,000 hectares has reportedly been set aside for 'semi-nomadic' Penan. In 1994 Malaysian officials said that 16 non-governmental organizations around the world had raised US$250,000 on behalf of the Penan.

Flora and fauna In the 1960s and 70s, botanical expeditions were beginning to shed more light on the Mulu area's flora and fauna: 100 new plant species were discovered between 1960 and 1973 alone. Mulu park encompasses an area of diverse altitudes and soil types – it includes all the forest types found in Borneo except mangrove. About 20,000 animal species have been recorded in Mulu Park, as well as 3,500 plant species and 8,000 varieties of fungi (more than 100 of these are endemic to the Mulu area). Mulu's ecological statistics are astounding: it is home to 1,500 species of flowering plant, 170 species of orchid and 109 varieties of palm. More than 280 butterfly species have been recorded. Within the park boundaries, 262 species of birds (including all eight varieties of hornbill), 67 mamalian species, 50 species of reptile and 75 amphibian species have been recorded.

Mulu's caves contain an unusual array of flora and fauna too. There are three species of swiftlet, 12 species of bat, and nine species of fish, including the cave flying fish (*Nemaaramis everetti*) and blind catfish (*Silurus furnessi*). Cave scorpions (*Chaerilus chapmani*) – which are poisonous but not deadly – are not uncommon. Other subterranean species include albino crabs, huntsman spiders, cave crickets, centipedes and snakes (which dine on swiftlets and bats). These creatures have been described as "living fossils...[which are] isolated survivors of ancient groups long since disappeared from Southeast Asia."

Treks from Park Headquarters Trails around headquarters are well marked but it is illegal to go anywhere without hiring a guide.

Gunung Mulu The minimum time to allow for the climb is 4 days, 3 nights; tents are not required if you stay at Camps 1 and 2. The main summit route starts from the plankwalk at Park HQ heading towards Deer Cave. The Mulu walkway forks left after about 1 km. From Park HQ it is an easy 4-5-hour trek to Camp 1 at 150m, where there is a shelter, built by the RGS/Sarawak government expedition in 1978. The second day is a long uphill slog (8-10 hours) to Camp 4 (1,800m), where there is also a shelter. Past Camp 3, the trail climbs steeply up Bukit Tumau, which affords good views over the park, and above which the last wild rhinoceros in Sarawak was shot in the mid-1940s. There are many pitcher plants (*Nepenthes lowii*) along this stretch of trail (see page 38). From Camp 4, known as 'The Summit Camp', the path passes the helicopter pad, from where there are magnificent views of Gunung Benarat, the Melinau Gorge and Gunung

Api. The final haul to the summit is very steep; there are fixed ropes. Around the summit area, the *Nepenthes muluensis* pitcher plant is common – it is endemic to Mulu. From Camp 4 it takes 1½ hours to reach the summit, and a further 7 hours back down the mountain to Camp 1. The views from the summit are best during April and May.

Equipment Camp 1 has water, as does Camp 4 if it has been raining. (Water should be boiled before drinking). It is necessary to bring your own food; in the rainy season it is wise to bring a gas cooking stove. A sleeping bag and waterproofs are also necessary and spare clothes, wrapped in a plastic bag, are a good idea.

Mulu can also be climbed from the south ridge of Melinau Gorge (see below) – 3 hours to Camp 1, 5 hours to Camp 3, steep 4-5-hour climb to Camp 4, 2 hours to the top. Forest changes from alluvial/swamp forest through mixed dipterocarp to mossy sub-montane and summit scrub.

Treks from Camp 5 (in the Melinau Gorge, facing Gunung Benarat, about 4-6 hours upstream from Park HQ). From the camp it is possible to trek up the gorge as well as to the Pinnacles, on Gunung Api. *Getting there*: it is advisable to hire a longboat for the duration of your time at and around Camp 5. The boat has to be abandoned at Kuala Berar, at the confluence of the Melinau and Berar rivers: it is only used for the first and last hours of the trip, but in the event of an emergency, there are no trails leading back to HQ and there are grim stories of fever-stricken people being stranded in the jungle. For a 3-days trip, a longboat will cost about RM350 (bargain hard) to hire – as opposed to RM300 if you just arrange to be collected 3 days later. It takes 2-3 hours, depending on the river level, from Park Headquarters to Kuala Berar; it is then a 2-3-hour trek (8 km) to Camp 5. Visitors to the Camp 5 area are also advised to plan their itinerary carefully as it is necessary to calculate how much food will be required and to carry it up there.

Accommodation at Camp 5 There is a basic shelter (built by the RGS/Sarawak government expedition in 1978), which can house about 30 people. The camp is next to the Melinau River; river water should be boiled before drinking.

Melinau Gorge Camp 5 nestles at the south end of the gorge, across a fast-flowing section of the Melinau River and opposite the unclimbed 1,580m Gunung Benarat's stark, sheer limestone cliffs. The steep limestone ridges, that lead eventually to Gunung Api, comprise the east wall of the gorge. Heading north from Camp 5, the trail fizzles out after a few minutes. It takes an arduous 2-3 hours of endless river-crossings and scrambles to reach a narrow chute of white water, under which is a large, deep and clear jungle pool with a convenient sandbank and plenty of large boulders to perch on. Alfred Russel Wallace's *Troides brookiana* – the majestic Rajah Brooke's birdwing – is particularly common at this little oasis, deep in undisturbed jungle. The walk involves criss-crossing through waist-deep, fast-flowing water and over stones that have been smoothed to a high polish over centuries: strong shoes are recommended – as is a walking stick. Only occasionally in the walk upstream is it possible to glimpse the towering 600m cliffs.

The Pinnacles are a forest of sharp limestone needles three-quarters of the way up Gunung Api. Some of the pinnacles rise above tree-tops to heights of 45m. The trail leaves from Camp 5, at the base of the Melinau Gorge. It is a very steep climb all the way and a maximum time of 3-4 hours is allowed to reach the pinnacles (1200m); otherwise you must return. There is no source of water *en route*. It is not possible to reach Gunung Api from the pinnacles. Is is strongly recommended that climbers wear gloves as well as long-sleeved shirts, trousers and strong boots to protect themselves against cuts from the razor-sharp rocks. Explorers on Spenser St John's expedition to Mulu in

1856 were cut to shreds on the pinnacles: "...three of our men had already been sent back with severe wounds, whilst several of those left were much injured," he wrote, concluding that it was "the world's most nightmarish surface to travel over".

Gunung Api ('Fire Mountain') The vegetation is so dry at the summit that it is often set ablaze by lightning in the dry season. The story goes that the fires were so big that locals once thought the mountains were volcanoes. Some of the fires could be seen as far away as the Brunei coast. The summit trek takes a minimum of 3 days. At 1,710m, it is the tallest limestone outcrop in Borneo and, other than Gunung Benarat (on the other side of the gorge), is probably the most difficult mountain to climb in Borneo. Many attempts to climb it ended in failure; two Berawans from Long Terawan finally made it to the top in 1978, one of them the grandson of Tama Nilong, the rhinoceros-hunter who had climbed Gunung Mulu in 1932. It is impossible to proceed upwards beyond the Pinnacles.

Kerangas forest From Camp 5, cross the Melinau River and head down the Limbang trail towards Lubang Cina. Less than 30 minutes down the trail, fork left along a new trail which leads along a ridge to the south of Gunung Benarat. Climbing higher, after about 40 minutes, the trail passes into an area of leached sandy soils called *kerangas* (heath) forest. This little patch of thinner jungle is a tangle of many varieties of pitcher plants.

Limbang It is possible to trek from Camp 5 to Limbang, although it is easier to do it the other way. (See page 420).

Caves In 1961 geologist Dr G Wilford first surveyed Deer Cave and parts of the Cave of the Winds. But Mulu's biggest subterranean secrets were not revealed until the 1980s.

Clearwater Cave (*Gua Ayer Jernih*): part of the Clearwater System, on a small tributary of the Melinau River, is, at 107 km, the longest underground cavity in Southeast Asia, and the seventh longest in the world. The cave passage – 75 km of which has been explored – links Clearwater Cave with the **Cave of the Winds** (*Lubang Angin*), to the south. It was discovered in 1988 and is the longest cave system in Southeast Asia. Clearwater is named after the jungle pool at the foot of the steps leading up to the cavemouth, where the longboats moor. Two species of monophytes – single-leafed plants – grow in the sunlight at the mouth of the cave. They only grow on limestone. A lighting system has been installed down the path to Young Lady's Cave, which ends in a 60m-deep pot hole.

On the cave walls are some helictites – coral-like lateral formations – and, even more dramatic, are the photokarsts, tiny needles of rock, all pointing towards the light. These are formed in much the same way as their monstrous cousins, the pinnacles (see above), by vegetation (in this case algae) eating into and eroding the softer rock, leaving sharp points of harder rock which 'grow' at about half a millimetre a year. Inside Clearwater it is possible to hire a rowing boat for RM10 – the river can be followed for about 1½ km upstream, although the current is strong. It is illegal to fish at Clearwater, although it is possible to fish anywhere else in park waters with a hook and line. *Getting there*: Clearwater can be reached by a 30-minute longboat ride from Park HQ. Individual travellers must charter a boat for RM85 (return). Tour agents build the cost of this trip into their package – which works out considerably cheaper.

Deer Cave is another of Mulu's record-breakers: it has the world's biggest cave mouth and the biggest cave passage, which is 2.2 km long and 220m high at its highest point. Before its inclusion in the Park, the cave had been a well known hunting ground for deer attracted to the pools of salty water running off the guano. The silhouettes of some of the cave's limestone formations have been creatively interpreted; notably the profile of Abraham Lincoln. Adam's and Eve's

Showers, at the east end of the cave, are hollow stalactites; water pressure increases when it rains. This darker section at the east end of Deer Cave is the preferred habitat of the naked bat. Albino earwigs live on the bats' oily skin and regularly drop off. The cave's east entrance opens onto 'The Garden of Eden' – a luxuriant patch of jungle, which was once part of the cave system until the roof collapsed. This separated Deer Cave and Green Cave, which lies adjacent to the east mouth; it is open only to caving expeditions.

The west end of the cave is home to several million wrinkle-lipped, and horseshoe bats. Black, twisting ribbons of hundreds of thousands of these bats pour out of the cave at dusk. Bat hawks can often be seen swooping in for spectacular kills. The helipad, about 500m south of the cavemouth, provides excellent vantage points. (VIPs' helicopters, arriving for the show, are said to have disturbed the bats in recent years). From the analysis of the 3 tonnes of saline guano the bats excrete every day, scientists conclude that they make an 80 km dash to the coast for meals of insects washed down with seawater. Cave cockroaches eat the guano, ensuring that the cavern does not become choked with what locals call 'black snow'. *Getting there*: 1 hour trek along a plank walk from Park HQ.

Lang's Cave, which is part of the same hollow mountain as Deer Cave, is less well known but its formations are more beautiful, and contains impressive curtain stalactites and intricate coral-like helictites. The cave is well illuminated and protected by bus-stop-style plastic tunnels.

The Sarawak Chamber, the largest natural chamber in the world, was discovered in 1984. It is 600m long, 450m wide and 100m high – big enough, it is said, to accommodate 40 Jumbo Jets wing-tip to wing-tip and eight nose-to-tail. Unfortunately it is not open to the public as it is considered too dangerous.

For cavers wishing to explore caves not open to the public, there are designated 'adventure caves' within an hour of park HQ. Experienced cave-guides can be organized from HQ. The most accessible of these is the 1 hour trek following the river course through Clearwater Cave. Cavers should bring their own equipment.

Rapids Just outside the national park boundary on the Tutoh River there are rapids which are possible to shoot; this can be arranged through tour agencies.

Transport around the park Independent travellers will find it more expensive arranging the trip on their own. Longboats can be chartered privately from Park HQ, if required; (maximum 10 persons/boat). The cost is calculated on a rather complicated system which includes a rate for the boat, a charge for the engine based on its horsepower, a separate payment for the driver and frontman, and then fuel on top of that. The total cost can be RM100+. How far these boats can actually get upriver depends on the season. They often have to be hauled over rapids, whatever the time of year.

Equipment There is a small store at the park HQ which sells basic necessities; there is also small shop just outside the Park boundary, at Long Pala. A sleeping bag is essential for Gunung Mulu trips; other essential equipment includes good insect repellent, wet weather gear and a powerful torch.

Guides No visitors are permitted to travel in the park without an authorized guide which can be arranged from park HQ or booked in advance from the National Parks office in Miri (see above). Most of the Mulu Park guides are very well-informed about flora and fauna, geology and tribal customs. Tour agencies organize guides as part of their fee. **Guide fees** RM20/cave (or per day) and an extra RM10/night. Mulu summit trips: minimum of RM264 for 4 days, 3 nights; Melinau Gorge and Pinnacles: minimum RM110 (3 days, 2 nights). Ornithological guides cost an additional RM10 a day.

Porterage: max 10 kg and RM30/day. RM1 for each extra kilo. Mulu summit: minimum RM90; Melinau Gorge (Camp 5): minimum RM65. It is usual to tip guides and porters.

Entrance fee RM3, RM5 for camera, RM10 for video, RM200 for professional filming.

Permits can be obtained from the National Parks and Wildlife Office, Old Forestry Building, Jalan Angkasa, Miri, T 436637/431975, also from Visitors' Information Centre, Lot 452, Jalan Malay, Miri. It is necessary to book and pay a deposit for accommodation at the same time. Permits can also be picked up from the National Parks and Wildlife Office, 1st Flr, Wisma Sumber Alam, Kuching, T 36637; accommodation can be booked through Kuching too. It is also necessary to get a permit from the police and the Miri or Marudi Residents. In Marudi, both the resident's office (Fort Hose) and the police station are on the airport road. This bureaucratic mess can be avoided if travel arrangements are left to a Miri travel agent.

Park information

● Accommodation

Accommodation in the park must be booked in advance at the National Parks and Wildlife Office Forest Department in Miri or Kuching. Booking fee is RM20/party and the maximum party size is 10 people. Bookings must be confirmed 5 days before visit. Three Miri-based travel agents have private accommodation in the park: ***Seridan Mulu Tour*** (RM10/night); ***Tropical Adventure*** (RM10/night).

Park Headquarters: *annexe* (hostel) (1 room, 10/room) RM10 pp; *Annexe* (8 rooms, 5/room) RM75/room; *Chalet, class 3* (4 rooms, 4/room) RM63/room; *Chalet class 2* (2 rooms, 3/room) RM94/room or RM180/house; *VIP Chalet* (3/room), RM200, *Rumah Rehat Jenis 2,* RM210/room; *Rumah Rehat Jenis 3,* RM157/room. There is also a privately owned hostel, the *Melinau Canteen* (T 011-291641 or 085-657884) with dorm beds about 5 minutes walk downstream from the Park HQ, on the other bank of the river, RM10 pp.

Long Pala: **A+** *Royal Mulu Resort*, Sungai Melinau, Muku, Miri, T 085 421122, F 085 421088, a/c, restaurants, owned by Japan's Royal Hotel Group Rihga the resort currently has 50 chalets and plans more, also proposes to carve an 18-hole golf-course out of rainforest adjacent to parks, 35 minutes from Miri, has sparked much resentment among local tribespeople, in Aug 1993, Berawan tour guides, boat-operators and labourers in the Park went on strike for 2 weeks because they say the resort was built on land which is theirs by customary right. 20 minutes (RM5) boat ride downstream from Park HQ, 2 ***Hostels***, run and owned by tour companies but with rooms available for drop-ins if not already booked, kitchen and bathrooms, crockery and bed linen provided; ***Private guesthouses***, run by tour companies (RM10-15 plus meals). Tour agents offer private accommodation of a high standard, just outside the National Park boundary. There is 12-hour electricity supply; the water supply is treated but it is advised to boil the water before drinking.

Camping: Can only use tents provided RM8.

● Places to eat

There are stoves and cooking utensils available and the small store at Park HQ also sells basic supplies. Small canteen at park headquarters but the menu is limited and the food rather boring. As an alternative, cross the suspension bridge and walk alongside the road to the first house on the left; down the bank from here is the ***Mulu Canteen***, which fronts onto the river (so there is no sign on the road). There is also the ***Melinau Canteen***, just downriver from HQ. Small shop with basic supplies at Long Pala. All tour companies with their own accommodation offer food.

● Transport

Visitors are recommended to go through one of the Miri-based travel agents (see page 408). The average cost of a Mulu package (pp) is RM350-400 (4 days/3 nights) or RM500 (6 days/5 nights).

Air Daily flights from Miri to Marudi, 15 minutes. A new airstrip has been constructed just downriver from Park HQ and is now able to accommodate larger 50 seater planes. Currently 3 flights/day from Miri, and two daily from Marudi and Limbang. The price of a flight is only marginally more expensive than taking the bus and boat from Miri.

Road Bus/taxi/boat: bus or taxi from Miri to Marudi express boat jetty near Kuala Baram at mouth of river Baram (see page 409). Regular express boats from Kuala Baram to Marudi, 3 hours (RM15) from early morning until about

1500. One express boat per day (leaves around noon) from Marudi to Long Tarawan on the Tutoh River (tributary of the Baram), via Long Apoh. During the dry season express boats cannot reach Long Terawan and terminate at Long Panai, on the Tutoh River, where longboats continue to Long Terawan (RM20). Longboats leave Long Tarawan for Mulu Park HQ: this used to be regular and comparatively cheap; now that most people travel to Mulu by air, longboats are less frequent and sometimes need to be privately chartered – an expensive business. Mulu Park HQ is 1½ hours up the Melinau River (a tributary of the Tutoh) (RM35). As you approach the park from Long Tarawan the Tutoh River narrows and becomes shallower; there are 14 rapids before the Melinau River, which forms the park boundary. When the water is low, the trip can be very slow and involve pulling the boat over the shallows, this accounts for high charter rates. For a group of nine or 10 it is cheaper to charter a boat (RM250 one way). The first jetty on the Melinau River is Long Pala, where most of the tour companies have accommodation. The Park HQ is another 15 minutes upriver. Longboats returning to Long Terawan leave Park HQ at dawn each day, calling at jetties *en route*.

NB It is best to avoid visiting Mulu National Park during school and public holidays. In Dec the park is closed to locals, but remains open to tourists.

BARIO (BAREO) AND THE KELABIT HIGHLANDS

Bario lies in the Kelabit Highlands, a plateau, 1,000m above sea level (close to the Kalimantan border). The highlands are Sarawak's answer to the hill stations on the peninsula. The undulating Bario valley is surrounded by mountains and fed by countless small streams which in turn feed into a maze of irrigation canals. The local Kelabits' skill in harnessing water has allowed them to practice wet rice cultivation rather than the more common slash-and-burn hill rice techniques. Fragrant Bario rice is prized in Sarawak and commands a premium in the coastal markets. The Kelabit Highlands' more temperate climate also allows the cultivation of a wide range of fruit and vegetables.

The plateau's near-impregnable ring of mountains effectively cut the Kelabit off from the outside world: it is the only area in Borneo which was never penetrated by Islam. In 1911 the Resident of Baram mounted an expedition which ventured into the mountains to ask the Kelabit to stop raiding the Brooke Government's subjects. It took the expedition 17 days to cross the Tamu Abu mountain range, to the west of Bario. The Kelabit were then brought under the control of the Sarawak government. The most impressive mountain in the Bario area is the distinctive twin-peak of the sheer-faced 2,043m **Bukit Batu Lawi**, to the northwest of Bario itself. The Kelabit traditionally believed the mountain had an evil spirit and so never went near it. Today such superstitions are a thing of the past – locals are mostly evangelical Christians.

In 1945, the plateau was selected as the only possible parachute drop zone in North Borneo not captured by the Japanese. The Allied Special Forces which parachuted into Bario were led by Tom Harrisson, who later became curator of the Sarawak Museum and made the famous archaeological discoveries at Niah Caves (see page 400). His expedition formed an irregular tribal army against the Japanese, which gained control over large areas of North Borneo in the following months.

Treks around Bario Because of the rugged terrain surrounding the plateau, the area mainly attracts serious mountaineers. There are many trails to the longhouses around the plateau area, however. Treks to Bario can be organized through travel agents in Miri (see page 406). Guides can also be hired in Bario and surrounding longhouses for RM30-40/day. It is best to go through the Penghulu, Ngiap Ayu, the Kelabit chief. He goes round visiting many of the longhouses in the area once a month. It is recommended that visitors to Bario come equipped with sleeping bags and camping equipment. There are no formal facilities for tourists and provisions should be brought from Miri or Marudi. The best time to visit Bario is between March and October. **NB** There are no banks or money-changers in Bario.

Several of the surrounding mountains can be climbed from Bario, but they are, without exception, difficult climbs. Even on walks just around the Bario area, guides are essential as trails are poorly marked. The lower ('female') peak of **Bukit Batu Lawi** can be climbed without equipment, but the sheer sided 'male' peak requires proper rock-climbing equipment – it was first scaled in 1986. **Gunung Murudi** (2,423m) is the highest mountain in Sarawak; it is a very tough climb.

Permits It is necessary to have a permit to visit the Bario area, obtainable from the Resident's offices in Miri or Marudi.

• **Accommodation** *Bario Lodging House*, above the shop, or with the Penghulu in his kampong house, at Bario Bharu, 10 minutes from the airstrip. There is also another recommended place to stay, *Tarawe's*, which is a good source of information and well run, falls into our **D** category. Most visitors camp.

• **Transport Air** Bario's airstrip is very small and because of its position, flights are often cancelled because of mist and clouds. During school holidays flights are also often booked up. Connections with Miri and Marudi. **Foot** It is a 7-day trek from Marudi to Bario; accommodation in longhouses *en route*. This trip should be organized through a Miri travel agent (see page 406). *Alo Doda* recommended.

LIMBANG

Very few tourists reach Limbang or Lawas but they are good stopping-off points for more adventurous routes to Sabah and Brunei.

Limbang is the finger of Sarawak territory which splits Brunei in two. It is the administrative centre for the 5th Division, and was ceded to the Brooke government by the Sultan of Brunei in 1890. The Trusan Valley, to the east of the wedge of Brunei, had been ceded to Sarawak in 1884.

Limbang's **Old Fort** was built in 1897 (renovated 1966) and was used as the administrative centre. During the Brooke era half the ground floor was used as a jail. It is now a centre of religious instruction, *Majlis Islam*. Limbang is famous for its **Pasar Tamu** every Friday, where jungle and native produce is sold. Limbang also has an attractive small museum, **Muzium Wilayah**, 400m south of centre along Jalan Kubu (open 0900-1800, Tuesday-Sunday). Housed in a wooden villa, painted beige and white, the museum has a collection of ethnic artefacts from the region, including basketry, musical instruments and weapons. To the right of the museum, a small road climbs the hill to a park with a man-made lake.

Excursions Trek to Gunung Mulu National Park Take car south to Medamit; from there hire a longboat upriver to Mulu Madang, an Iban longhouse (3 hours, depending on water level). Alternatively, go further upriver to Kuala Terikan (6-7 hours at low-water, 4 hours at high-water) where there is a simple zinc-roofed camp. From there take a longboat 1 hour up the Terikan River to Lubang China – which is the start of a 2-hours trek along a well-used trail to Camp 5. There is a park rangers' camp about 20 minutes out of Kuala Terikan where it is possible to obtain permits and arrange for a guide to meet you at Camp 5. The longboats are cheaper to hire in the wet season.

Tours *Sitt Travel*, specializes in treks in this area and is the ticketing agent for Miri tour operators.

Festivals May: *Buffalo Racing* (movable) marks the end of the harvesting season.

Local information

• Accommodation

Prices: L over RM500; **A+** RM260-500; **A** RM130-260; **B** RM65-130; **C** RM40-65; **D** RM20-40; **E** RM10-20; **F** Below RM10

Limbang has become a sex stop for Bruneians whose government takes a more hardline attitude to such moral transgressions and consequently many hotels and guesthouses have a fair share of short time guests.

B *Centre Point Hotel*, a/c, restaurant, T 212922, newish place which tops Limbang's limited bill of hotels. **B-C** *Muhibbah*, Lot T 790, Bank St, T 213705, F 212153, located in town centre, has seen better days, but rooms are fairly clean with a/c, TV and bathroom. **B-C** *Metro*, Lot 781, Jln Bangkita, T 211133, F 211051, a fairly new addition to Limbang's mid-range accommodation, under 30 rooms, all with a/c, TV, fridge, tea and coffee making facilities, good quality beds, small but clean rooms, recommended. **B-C** *National Inn*, 62a Jln Buangsiol, T 212922, F 212282, probably the best of the 3 hotels along the river here, comfortable a/c rooms with TV, mini-bar, tea and coffee making facilities, higher rates for river view.

● **Places to eat**

Prices: ♦♦♦♦ over RM40; ♦♦♦ RM13-40; ♦♦ RM5-13; ♦ under RM5

♦♦♦*Tong Lok* a/c Chinese restaurant next to *National Inn*, gruesome pink table cloths and fluorescent lighting, but good quality Chinese food.

♦♦*Maggie's Café* on the riverside near *National Inn*, Chinese coffee shop, pleasant location, tables outside next to river in evening – braziers set up in evening too for good grilled fish on banana leaf, recommended.

♦*Hai Hong*, one block south of *Maggies*, a simple coffee shop – good for breakfast with fried egg and chips on the menu.

● **Useful addresses**

Resident's Office: T 21960.

● **Transport**

Air Daily connections with Miri, Mulu and Lawas; weekly flights to Labuan; and twice weekly connections with KK. The airport is about 5 km from town and taxis ferry passengers in.

Boat Regular connections with Lawas, departs early in the morning (2 hours, RM15). There is also an early morning express departure to Labuan.

International connections with Brunei Regular boat connections with Bandar Seri Begawan, Brunei (30 minutes, RM15).

LAWAS

Lawas District was ceded to Sarawak in 1905. The Limbang River, which cuts through the town, is the main transport route. Very few tourists visit Limbang or Lawas; they are however, on the route through to Sabah. It is possible to travel from Miri to Bandar Seri Begawan (Brunei) by road, then on to Limbang and Lawas. From Lawas there are direct buses to Kota Kinabalu in Sabah.

Local information

● **Accommodation**

A-B *Country Park Hotel*, Lot 235, Jln Trusan, T 85522, a/c, restaurant.

C *Lawas Federal*, 8 Jln Masjid Baru, T 85115, a/c, restaurant.

D *Hup Guan Lodging House*, T 85362, some a/c, above a pool hall so can be noisy but the rooms are clean and spacious and reasonable value for money.

● **Transport**

Air Connections with Miri, Limbang, Kuching, Labuan and Kota Kinabalu.

Road Bus: connections with Merapok on the Sarwak/Sabah border (RM5). From here there are connections to Beaufort in Sabah. Twice-daily connections with Kota Kinabalu, 4 hours (RM20).

River Boat: regular connections to Limbang, 2 hours.

International connections: daily morning boat departures for Brunei.

Sabah

Horizons	422	The North and Gunung Kinabalu Park	463
Kota Kinabalu	434	The East Coast	475
Tunku Abdul Rahman Park	447	Sipadan Island Marine Reserve	494
South of Kota Kinabalu	448		

SABAH occupies the northeast corner of Borneo, and is shaped rather like a dog's head. The state covers 72,500 square kilometres – about the size of Ireland – and is the second largest of Malaysia's thirteen states, after Sarawak. To the west, it faces the South China Sea and to the east, the Sulu and Celebes seas.

Malaysian Prime Minister Dr Mahathir Mohamad once called Sabah "the wild East". In the popular imagination of West Malaysians, Sabah is the land of the Bajau 'cowboys', gun-toting pirates, timber *towkays* and one-horse towns. The state does indeed have a frontier feel to it; jeeps and Land Cruisers are the only practical way of travelling long-distances overland and piracy is still rife along its east seaboard. It can be an expensive place to travel – particularly if you intend to hire a 4WD vehicle.

The name 'Sabah' probably derives from the Arabic *Zir-e Bad*, meaning 'the land below the wind'. It is an appropriate name for the state as it lies just to the south of the typhoon belt. Officially, the territory has only been called Sabah since 1963, when it joined the Malay federation, but the name appears to have been in use long before that. When Baron Gustav Von Overbeck was awarded the cession rights to North Borneo by the Sultan of Brunei in 1877 (see page 424), one of the titles conferred on him was 'Maharajah of Sabah'. And in the *Handbook of British North Borneo*, published in 1890, it says: "In Darvel Bay there are the remnants of a tribe which seems to have been much more plentiful in bygone days – the Sabahans". From the founding of the Chartered Company until 1963, Sabah was known as British North Borneo.

Sabah has a population of about 1.4 million, about half of whom are illegal immigrants (see page 431). The inhabitants of Sabah can be divided into four main groups: the Murut, the Kadazan, the Bajau and the Chinese, as well as a small Malay population. These main groups are subdivided into several different tribes (see page 426). For information on geography, climate, flora and fauna, see page 319.

In a fresh twist to Sabah's lively political scene, a new state government came

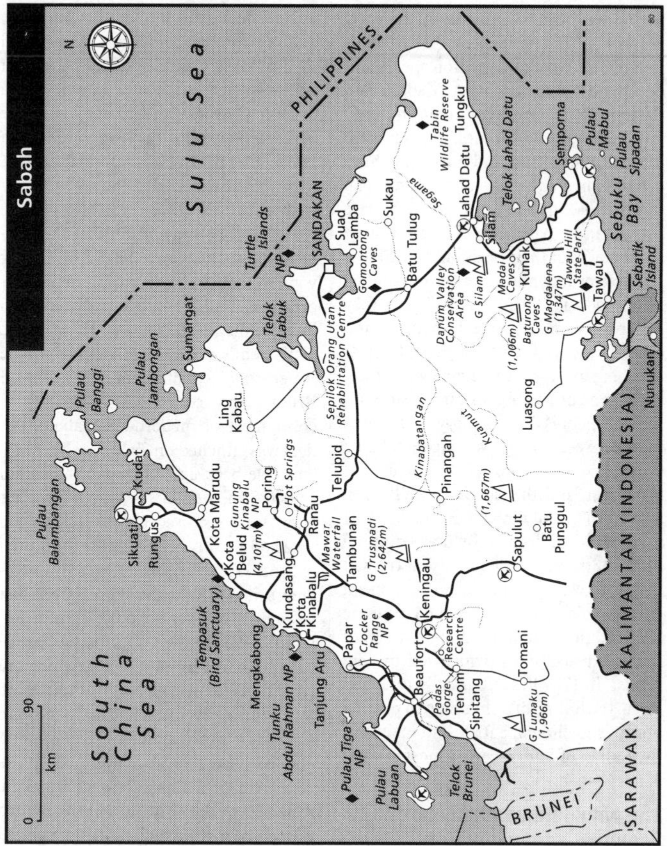

to power in March 1994 (see page 432). Unlike the former Christian-led administration, which was at constant loggerheads with the federal government, the new state government is in alliance with Dr Mahathir's ruling party. Its supporters reckon there will be an influx of development money and that the tourism sector will be the prime beneficiary. The upside of this will be the construction of new hotels and resorts and the upgrading of facilities generally; the downside will be the construction of huge new golf courses, theme parks and the arrival of more tourists. The state government wants to target tourists and golfers from Japan, Taiwan and Hong Kong in particular. This should mean an increase in the number of direct air links between Kota Kinabulu and East Asian destinations.

HISTORY

Prehistoric stone tools have been found in eastern Sabah, suggesting that people were living in limestone caves in the Madai area 17,000-20,000 years ago. The caves were periodically settled from then on; pottery dating from the late Neolithic period has been found, and by the early years of the first millennium AD, Madai's inhabitants were making iron spears and decorated pottery. The Madai and Baturong caves were lived in continuously until about the 16th century, and several carved stone coffins and burial jars have been discovered in the jungle caves (one of which is exhibited in the Sabah State Museum, see page 435). The caves were also known for their birds' nests; Chinese traders were buying the nests from Borneo as far back as 700 AD. In addition, they exported camphor wood, pepper and other forest products to Imperial China.

There are very few archaeological records indicating Sabah's early history, although there is documentary evidence of links between a long-lost kingdom, based somewhere in the area of the Kinabatangan River, and the Sultanate of Brunei, whose suzerainty once extended over most of North Borneo. By the beginning of the 18th century, Brunei's power had begun to wane in the face of European expansionism. To counter the economic decline, the sultan is thought to have increased taxation – which led to civil unrest. In 1704 the Sultan of Brunei had to ask the Sultan of Sulu's help in putting down a rebellion in Sabah, and in return, the Sultan of Sulu received most of what is now Sabah.

The would-be white rajahs of Sabah

It was not until 1846 that the British entered into a treaty with the Sultan of Brunei and took possession of the island of Labuan (see page 456) – this was in part to counter the growing influence of the Rajah of Sarawak, James Brooke. The British were also wary of the Americans – the US Navy signed a trade treaty with the Sultan of Brunei in 1845 and in 1860 Claude Lee Moses was appointed American Consul-General in Brunei Town. He was only interested in making a personal fortune and quickly persuaded the sultan to cede him land in Sabah. He sold these rights to two Hong Kong-based American businessmen who formed the American Trading Company of Borneo. They styled themselves as Rajahs and set up a base at Kimanis, just south of Papar. It was a disaster. One of them died of malaria, the Chinese labourers they imported from Hong Kong began to starve and the settlement was abandoned in 1866.

But the idea of a trading colony on the North Borneo coast interested the Austrian consul in Hong Kong, Baron Gustav von Overbeck, who, in turn, sold the concept to Alfred Dent, a wealthy English businessman also based in Hong Kong. With Dent's money, Overbeck bought the Americans' cession from the Sultan of Brunei, and extended the territory to cover most of modern-day Sabah. The deal was clinched on 29 December 1877, and Overbeck agreed to pay the sultan 15,000 Straits dollars a year. A few days later Overbeck discovered that the entire area had already been ceded to the Sultan of Sulu 173 years earlier, so he immediately sailed to Sulu and offered the sultan an annual payment of 5,000 Straits dollars for the territory. On his return, he dropped three Englishmen off along the coast to set up trading posts – one of them was William Pryer, who founded Sandakan (see page 475). 3 years later, Queen Victoria granted Dent a royal charter and, to the chagrin of the Dutch, the Spanish and the Americans, the British North Borneo Company was formed. London insisted that it was to be a British-only enterprise however, and Overbeck was forced to sell out. The first managing director of the company was the Scottish adventurer and former gun-runner William C Cowie. He was in charge of the day-to-day running of the territory, while the British government supplied a governor.

The new chartered company, with its headquarters in the City of London, was given sovereignty over Sabah and a free hand to develop it. The British administrators soon began to collect taxes from local people and quickly clashed with members of the Brunei nobility. John

Whitehead, a British administrator, wrote: "I must say, it seemed rather hard on these people that they should be allowed to surrender up their goods and chattels to swell even indirectly the revenue of the company". The administration levied poll-tax, boat tax, land tax, fishing tax, rice tax, *tapai* (rice wine) tax and a 10% tax on proceeds from the sale of birds' nests. Resentment against these taxes sparked the 6-year Mat Salleh rebellion (see page 449) and the Rundum Rebellion, which peaked in 1915, during which hundreds of Muruts were killed by the British.

Relations were not helped by colonial attitudes towards the local Malays and tribal people. One particularly arrogant district officer, Charles Bruce, wrote: "The mind of the average native is equivalent to that of a child of 4 ... So long as one remembers that the native is essentially a child and treats him accordingly he is really tractable." Most recruits to the chartered company administration were fresh-faced graduates from British universities, mainly Oxford and Cambridge. For much of the time there were only 40-50 officials running the country. Besides the government officials, there were planters and businessmen: tobacco, rubber and timber became the most important exports. There were also Anglican and Roman Catholic missionaries. British North Borneo was never much of a money-spinner – the economy suffered badly whenever commodity prices slumped – but it managed to pay for itself for most of the time up until World War Two.

The Japanese interregnum

Sabah became part of *Dai Nippon* – Greater Japan – on New Year's Day 1942, when the Japanese took Labuan. On the mainland, the Japanese Imperial Army and *Kempetai* (military police) were faced with the might of the North Borneo Armed Constabulary – about 650 men. Jesselton (Kota Kinabalu) was occupied on 9 January and Sandakan, 10 days later. All Europeans were interned and when Singapore fell in 1942, 2,740 prisoners of war were moved to Sandakan, most of whom were Australian, where they were forced to build an airstrip. On its completion, the POWs were ordered to march to Ranau – 240 km through the jungle. This became known as 'The Borneo Death March' and only six men survived (see page 478).

The Japanese were hated in Sabah and the Chinese mounted a resistance movement which was led by the Kuching-born Albert Kwok Hing Nam. He also recruited Bajaus and Sulus to join his guerrilla force which launched the 'Double Tenth Rebellion' (the attacks took place on 10 October 1943). The guerrillas took Tuaran, Jesselton and Kota Belud, killing many Japanese and sending others fleeing into the jungle. But the following day the Japanese bombed the towns and troops quickly retook the towns and captured the rebels. There followed a mass-execution in which 175 rebels were decapitated. On 10 June 1945 Australian forces landed at Labuan, under the command of American General MacArthur. Allied planes bombed the main towns and virtually obliterated Jesselton and Sandakan. Sabah was liberated on 9 September, and thousands of the remaining 21,000 Japanese troops were killed in retaliation – many by Muruts.

A British Military Administration governed Sabah in the immediate aftermath of the war, and the cash-strapped chartered company sold the territory to the British crown for £1.4mn in mid-1946. The new crown colony was modelled on the chartered company's administration and set about rebuilding the main towns and war-shattered infrastructure. In May 1961, following Malaysian independence, Prime Minister Tunku Abdul Rahman proposed the formation of a federation incorporating Malaya (ie Peninsular Malaysia), Singapore, Brunei, Sabah and Sarawak (see page 59). Later that same year, Tun Fuad Stephens, a timber magnate and newspaper publisher formed Sabah's first-ever political party, the United National Kadazan Organisation (UNKO). Two other parties were founded shortly afterwards – the Sabah Chinese Association and the United Sabah National Organization (USNO). The British were keen to leave the colony and the Sabahan parties thrashed out the pros and cons of joining the proposed federation. Elections were held in late-1962 – in which a UNKA-USNO alliance (the Sabah Alliance) swept to power – and the following August, Sabah became an independent country ... for 16 days. Like Singapore and Sarawak, Sabah opted to join the federation, to the indignation of the Philippines and Indonesia which both had claims on the territory. Jakarta's objections resulted in the *konfrontasi* – an undeclared war with Malaysia (see page 341) which was not settled until 1966.

CULTURE

PEOPLE

Sabah's main tribal communities are comprised of the Kadazan, who mostly live on the west coast, the Murut, who inhabit the interior, to the south, and the Bajau, who are mainly settled around Gunung Kinabalu. There are more than 30 tribes, more than 50 different languages and about 100 dialects. Sabah also has a large Chinese population and many illegal Filipino immigrants.

Kadazans

The Kadazans are the largest ethnic group in Sabah (comprising about a third of the population), and are a peaceful agrarian people with a strong cultural identity. Until Sabah joined the Malaysian Federation in 1963, they were known as 'Dusuns', meaning 'peasants' or 'orchard people'. This name was given to them by outsiders, and picked up by the British. It became, in effect, a residual category including all those people who were not Muslim of Chinese. Most Kadazans call themselves after their tribal place names. They can be broken into several tribes including the Lotud of Tuaran, the Rungus of the Kudat and Bengkoka Peninsular, the Tempasuk, the Tambanuo, Kimarangan and the Sanayo. Minokok and Tengara Kadazans live in the upper Kinabatangan River basin while those living near other big rivers are just known as *Orang Sungai*, or 'river people'. Most Kadazans used to live in longhouses; these are virtually all gone now. The greatest likelihood of a visitor coming across a longhouse in Sabah is in the Rungus area of the Kudat Peninsula; even there, former longhouse residents are moving into detached, kampung-style houses while one or two remain for the use of tourists.

But Kadazan identity is not that simple. The 1991 census lists both Kadazans (110,866) and Dusuns (229,194). In the 1970 census all were listed as Kadazan, while in the 1960 census they were all Dusun. In 1995 the Malaysian government agreed to add the common language of these people(s) to the national repertoire to be taught in schools. This they named Kadazandusun. (The other four are Malay, Chinese, Tamil and Iban.)

All the Kadazan groups had similar customs and modes of dress (see below). Up to World War Two, many Kadazan men wore the *chawat* loin cloth. The Kadazans used to hunt with blow-pipes,

Sabah's ethnic breakdown

	Population	%
Kadazan/Dusun	340,060	19.6
[Kadazan	110,866	6.4]
[Dusun	229,194	13.2]
Murut	50,315	2.9
Bajau	202,995	11.7
Malay	107,570	6.2
Other Muslim	235,960	13.6
Chinese	199,525	11.5
Indonesia	421,605	24.3
Filipino	142,270	8.2
Others	34,700	2.0
Total population	1,735,000	100

Source: 1991 census

Tamus – Sabah's markets and trade fairs

In Sabah, an open trade fair is called a *tamu*. Locals gather to buy and sell jungle produce, handicrafts and traditional wares. *Tamu* comes from the Malay word '*tetamu*' – 'to meet' and the biggest and most famous is held at Kota Belud, north of Kota Kinabalu in Bajau country (see page 463). Tamus were fostered by the pre-war British North Borneo Chartered Company, when district officers would encourage villagers from miles around to trade among themselves. It was also a convenient opportunity for officials to meet with village headmen. They used to be strictly Kadazan affairs, but today tamus are multiracial events. Sometimes public auction of water buffalo and cattle are held. Some of the biggest tamus around the state are:

Monday:	Tandek
Tuesday:	Kiulu, Topokan
Wednesday:	Tamparuli
Thursday:	Keningau, Tambunan, Sipitang, Telipok, Simpangan
Friday:	Sinsuran, Weston
Saturday:	Penampang, Beaufort, Sindumin, Matunggong, Kinarut
Sunday:	Tambunan, Tenom, Kota Belud, Papar, Gaya Street (KK)

and in the 19th century, were still head-hunting. Today, however, they are known for their gentleness and honesty; their produce can often be seen sitting unattended at roadside stalls, and passing motorists are expected to pay what they think fair. The Kadazans traditionally traded their agricultural produce at large markets, held at meeting points, called *tamus* (see box). The Kadazan are farmers, and the main rice-producers of Sabah. They used to be animists, and were said to live in great fear of evil spirits; most of their ceremonies were rituals aimed at driving out these spirits. The job of communicating with the spirits of the dead, the *tombiivo*, was done by priestesses, called *bobohizan*. They are the only ones who can speak the ancient Kadazan language, using a completely different vocabulary from modern Kadazan. Most Kadazans converted to Christianity (mainly Roman Catholicism) during the 1930s, although there are also some Muslim Kadazan.

The big cultural event in the Kadazan year is the **Harvest Festival** which takes place in May. The ceremony, known as the *Magavau* ritual, is officiated by a high priestess, or *Bobohizan*. These elderly women – who wear traditional black costumes and colourful headgear with feathers and beads – are now few and far between. The ceremony culminates with offerings to the *Bambaazon*, or rice spirit. After the ceremonies Catholic, Muslim and animist Kadazans all come together to play traditional sports such as wrestling and buffalo racing. This is about the only occasion when visitors are likely to see Kadazan in their traditional costumes. In the Penampang area a woman's costume consists of a fitted, sleeveless tunic and ankle-length skirt of black velvet. Belts of silver coins (*himpogot*) and brass rings are worn round the waist; a colourful sash is also worn. Men dress in a black, long-sleeved jacket over black trousers; they also wear a *siga*, colourful woven head gear. These costumes have become more decorative in recent years, with colourful embroidery. Villages send the finalists of local beauty contests to the grand final of the Unduk Ngadau harvest festival queen competition in Penampang, near Kota Kinabalu.

Bajau

The Bajau – the famous 'cowboys' of the 'wild East' – came from the South Philippines during the 18th and 19th centuries and settled in the coastal area around Kota Belud, Papar and Kudat, where they made a handsome living from piracy. The Bajau who came to Sabah joined forces with the

Tapai – Sabah's rice wine

Tapai – the fiery Sabahan rice wine – is much loved by the Kadazan and the Murut. It was even more popular before the two tribal groups' wholesale conversion to Christianity in the 1930s. Writer Hedda Morrison noted in 1957 that: "The squalor and wretchedness arising from [their] continual drunkenness made the Murut a particularly useful object of missionary endeavour. In the thirties missionaries succeeded in converting nearly all the Murut to Christianity. The Murut grasped at this new faith much as the drowning man is said to grasp at a straw. From being the most drunken people in Borneo, they became the most sober." In the Sabah State Museum (see page 435) there is a recipe for tapai – also known as 'buffalos' blood', which was taken down by an administrator during chartered company days:

"Boil 12lbs of the best glutinous rice until well done. In a wide-mouthed jar, lay the rice in layers of no more than two fingers deep, and between layers, place a total of about 20 ½-oz yeast cakes. Add two cups of water, tinctured with the juice of six beetroots. Cover jar with muslin and leave to ferment. Each day, uncover it and remove dew which forms on the muslin. On the fifth day, stir the mixture vigorously and leave for four weeks. Store for one full year, after which it shall be full of virtue and potence and most smooth upon the palate."

Tapai is drunk from communal jars – which were also used as burial urns – through bamboo straws. The jar is filled nearly to its brim with tapai. Large leaves are placed on the top just under the lower edge of the rim. These leaves are pierced with straws for sucking up the liquid and the intervening space between the leaves and the top of the jar is filled with water. Etiquette demands that one drinks till the water has been drained off the leaves. They are then flooded again and the process is repeated. There is also the distilled form of tapai, called *montaku*, which is even more potent. When North Borneo became a British crown colony after World War Two, the administration was concerned about the scourge of tapai drinking on three counts. First, it was said to consume a large portion of the natives' potential food crop, second, it usually caused a crime-wave whenever it was drunk, and thirdly, it was blamed for the high rate of infant mortality as mothers frequently gave their babies a suck at the straw.

Oscar Cook, a former district officer in the North Borneo Civil Service, noted in his 1923 book *Borneo: the stealer of hearts*, that tapai was not to everyone's fancy – and certainly not to his. "As an alternative occupation to head-hunting, the Murut possess a fondness for getting drunk, indulged in on every possible occasion. Tapai, or *pengasai*, as the Murut calls it, is not a nice drink. In fact, to my thinking it is the very reverse, for it is chiefly made from fermented rice... is very potent, and generally sour and possessed of a pungent and nauseating odour. Births, marriages, deaths, sowing, harvesting and any occasion that comes to mind is made the excuse for a debauch. It is customary for Murut to show respect to the white man by producing their very best tapai, and pitting the oldest and ugliest women of the village against him in a drinking competition." Cook admits that all this proved too much for him and when he was transferred to Keningau, he had to employ an "official drinker". "The applicants to the post were many," he noted.

Dance			
Name of Dance	**Tribe**	**District**	**Description**
Sumazau Penampang	Kadazan/ Dusun	Penampang, west coast	Performed during Annual Harvest Festival (*Pesta Kaamatan*) to honour the rice spirit (*Bambaazon*). *Sumazau* means dancing.
Angalang	Murut	Pensiangan and Tenom, interior and south	A solo warrior dance, accompanied by a group of women dancers (*angalong*). Originally performed after a victorious battle or head-hunting trip.
Mangiluk	Suluk	East coast	Performed at weddings and social events.
Magunatip	Murut and Kwijau Dusun	Interior and south	These dancers need skill and agility to dance among bamboo poles which are hit together to produce the rhythm of the dance.
Adai Adai	Brunei Malay	Sipitang and Membakut, south-west of Sabah	Evolved from a song; it tells of the activities of the local fishermen and farmers.
Mongigol Sumundai	Rungus	Kudat and Pitas, north of Sabah	Can be performed as part of certain ritual festivals. For instance, Thanksgiving to rice spirit for a bountiful harvest or moving into a new house.
Limbai	Bajau	Kota Belud, west coast	Performed at weddings, characterized by graceful wrist rotations. Accompanying music is called *bertitik*.
Dansa	Cocos	Lahad Datu, east coast	Performed at weddings. It features energetic foot stomping.
Bolak Bolak	Bajau	Semporna, east coast	*Bolak-Bolak* is Malay for castanets. The dancers hold the castanets and create the rhythm of the music.
Mongigol Sumayan	Lotud	Tuaran, west coast	Ritual dance performed during *Rumaha* ceremony to honour spirits of skulls, or the *Mangahau* ceremony for the spirits of sacred jars.
Umang-Umang Ting-Ting	Brunei Malay	Bongawan, west coast	Celebrates the birth of a newborn child.
Daling-Daling	Suluk	East coast	A 'courting' dance said to be derived from the English 'darling'. Usually accompanied by a love song.

Dance			
Name of Dance	**Tribe**	**District**	**Description**
Sumazau Papar	Kadazan Dusun	Papar, west coast	Performed at similar occasions to Sumazau Penampang. Distinctive foot work.
Titikas	Orang Sungai	Kinabatangan, east coast	Titikas is based on the *Ingki-Ingki* game, similar to hopscotch.
Liliput	Bisaya	Beaufort, west coast	*Liliput* means 'go around'. It is a dance to cast away evil spirits in a possessed person.
Kuda Pasu	Bajau	Kota Belud, west coast	Originally performed by horsemen to welcome or escort a bridegroom and his entourage to the bride's home. The female dancers hold handkerchieves as a sign of welcome.

notorious Illanun and Balinini pirates. They are natural seafarers and were dubbed 'the sea gypsies'; today they form the second largest indigenous group in Sabah and are divided into subgroups, notably the Binadan, Suluk and Obian. They call themselves 'Samah' – it was the Brunei Malays who first called them Bajau. They are strict Muslims and the famous Sabahan folk hero, Mat Salleh, who led a rebellion in the 1890s against British Chartered Company rule, was a Bajau (see page 449). Despite their seafaring credentials, they are also renowned horsemen and (very occasionally) still put in an appearance at Kota Belud's *tamu* (see page 463). Bajau women are known for their brightly coloured basketry – *tudong saji*. The Bajau build their atap houses on stilts over the water and these are interconnected by a network of narrow wooden planks. The price of a Bajau bride was traditionally assessed in stilts, shaped from the trunks of bakau mangrove trees. A father erected one under his house on the day a daughter was born and replaced it whenever it wore out. The longer the daughter remained at home, the more stilts he got through and the more water buffalo he demanded from a prospective husband.

Murut

The Murut live around Tenom and Pensiangan in the lowland and hilly parts of the interior, in the southwest of Sabah – and in the Trusan Valley of North Sarawak. Some of those living in more remote jungle areas, retain their traditional longhouse way of life – but many Murut have now opted for detached kampung-style houses. *Murut* means 'hill people' and is not the term used by the people themselves. They refer to themselves by their individual tribal names. The Nabai, Bokan and Timogun Murut live in the lowlands and are wet-rice farmers, while the Peluan, Bokan and Tagul Murut live in the hills and are mainly shifting cultivators. They are thought to be related to Sarawak's Kelabit and Kalimantan's Lun Dayeh people, although some of the tribes in the South Philippines have similar characteristics. The Murut staples are rice and tapioca, they are known for their weaving and basketry and have a penchant for drinking *tapai* (rice wine – see page 428). They are also enthusiastic dancers and devised the *lansaran* – a sprung dance floor like a trapeze (see page 453). The Murut are a mixture of animists, Christians and Muslims and were the last tribe in Sabah to give up head-hunting, a practice finally stopped by British North Borneo Chartered Company administrators.

Chinese

The Chinese accounted for nearly a third of Sabah's population in 1960; today they make up just a fifth. Unlike Sarawak, however, where the Chinese were a well-established community in the early 1800s, Sabah's Chinese came as a result of the British North Borneo Chartered Company's immigration policy, designed to ease a labour shortage. About 70% of Sabah's Chinese are Christian Hakkas, who first began arriving at the end of the 19th century, under the supervision of the Company. They were given free passage from China and most settled in the Jesselton and Kudat areas; today most Hakka are farmers. There are also large Teochew and Hokkien communities in Tawau, Kota Kinabalu and Labuan while Sandakan is mainly Cantonese – who originally came from Hong Kong.

Filipinos

Immigration from the Philippines started in the 1950s and refugees began flooding into Sabah when the separatist war erupted in Mindanao in the 1970s. Today there are believed to be upwards of 700,000 illegal Filipino immigrants in Sabah (although their migration has been undocumented for so long that no one is certain), and the state government fears they could outnumber locals by early next century. There are many in Kota Kinabalu, the state capital and a large community – mainly women and children – in Labuan, but the bulk of the Filipino population is in Semporna, Lahad Datu, Tawau and Kunak (on the east coast) where they already outnumber locals 3:1. One Sabah government minister, referring to the long-running territorial dispute between Malaysia and the Philippines, was quoted as saying "We do not require a strong military presence at the border any more: the aliens have already landed".

Although the federal government has talked of its intention to deport illegal aliens, it is also mindful of the political reality: the majority of the Filipinos are Muslim, and making them legal Malaysian citizens could ruin Sabah's predominantly Christian, Kadazan-led state government. The Filipino community is also a thorn in Sabah's flesh because of the crime-wave associated with their arrival: the Sabah police claims 65% of all crimes in the state are committed by Filipinos. The police do not ask many questions when dealing with Filipino criminal suspects – about 40-50 are shot every year. Another local politician was quoted as saying: "the immigrants take away our jobs, cause political instability and pose a health hazard because of the appalling conditions in which some of them live".

There are six different Filipino groups in Sabah: the Visayas and Ilocano are Christian as are the Ilongo (Ilo Ilo), from Zamboanga. The Suluks are Muslim; they come from South Mindanao and have the advantage of speaking a dialect of Bahasa Malaysia. Many Filipinos were born in Sabah and all second generation immigrants are fluent in Bahasa. Migration first accelerated in the 1950s during the logging boom, and continued when the oil palm plantation economy took off – the biggest oil palm plantation is at Tungku, east of Lahad Datu. Many migrants have settled along the roadsides on the way to Danum Valley; it is easy to claim land – all they have to do is simply clear a plot and plant a few fruit trees.

RELIGION

For information on religion, see page 330.

CRAFTS

Compared with neighbouring Sarawak and Kalimantan, Sabah's handicraft industry is rather impoverished. Sabah's tribal groups were less protected from western influences than Sarawak's, and traditional skills quickly began to die out as the state modernized and the economy grew. In Kota Kinabalu today, the markets are full of Filipino handicrafts and shell-products; local arts and crafts are largely confined to basketry, mats, hats, bead-work, musical instruments and pottery.

The elongated Kadazan backpack baskets (found around Mount Kinabalu National Park) are called *wakids* and are made from bamboo, rattan and bark. Woven food covers – or *tudong saji* – are often mistaken for hats, and are made by the Bajau of Kota Belud. Hats, made from nipah palm or rattan, and whose shape varies markedly from place to place, are decorated with traditional motifs. One of the most common motifs is the *nantuapan*, or 'meeting', which represents four people all drinking out of the same tapai (rice wine) jar. The Rungus people (from the Kudat peninsula) also make *linago* basketware from a strong wild grass; it is tightly woven and not decorated (see page 465 for more detail on the Rungus). At *tamus* – Sabah's big open-air markets (see page 427) – there are usually some handicrafts for sale. The Kota Belud tamu is the best place to find the Bajau horseman's embroidered turban, the *destar* (see page 463). Traditionally, the Rungus people, who live on the Kudat Peninsula, were renowned as fine weavers, and detailed patterns were woven into their ceremonial skirts, or *tinugupan*. These patterns all had different names, but, like the ingredients of the traditional dyes, many have now been forgotten.

MODERN SABAH

POLITICS

Sabah's political scene has always been lively – and never more so than in 1994 when the Malaysian Prime Minister, Dr Mahathir Mohamad, pulled off what commentators described as a democratic coup d'etat. With great political dexterity, he out-manoeuvered his rebellious rivals and managed to dislodge the opposition state government – despite the fact that it had just won a state election. The reasons why Dr Mahathir was motivated to bulldoze his own party into power there go back 10 years and the roots of Sabah's political instability go back even further.

Following Sabah's first state election in 1967, the Sabah Alliance ruled until 1975 when the newly formed multi-racial party, Berjaya, swept the polls. Berjaya had been set up with the financial backing of the United Malays National Organisation (Umno), the mainstay of the ruling Barisan Nasional (National Front) coalition on the Peninsula. Over the following decade that corrupt administration crumbled and in 1985 the Parti Bersatu Sabah (Sabah United Party) – led by the Christian Kadazan Datuk Joseph Pairin Kitingan – won a landslide victory and became the only state government in Malaysia that did not belong to the Umno-led coalition. It became an obvious embarrassment to Prime Minister Dr Mahathir Mohamad to have a rebel Christian state in his predominantly Muslim federation. Nonetheless, the PBS eventually joined Barisan Nasional, believing its partnership in the coalition would help iron things out. It did not.

When the PBS came to power, the federal government and Sabahan opposition parties openly courted Filipino and Indonesian immigrants in the state – almost all of whom are Muslim – and secured identity cards for many of them, enabling them to vote. Dr Mahathir has made no secret of his preference for a Muslim government, in Sabah. Nothing, however, was able to dislodge the PBS, which was resoundingly returned to power in 1990. The federal government had long been suspicious of Sabahan politicians – particularly following the PBS's defection from Dr Mahathir's coalition in the run-up to the 1990 general election – a move which bolstered the opposition alliance. Dr Mahathir described this as "a stab in the back", and referred to Sabah as "a thorn in the flesh of the Malaysian federation". But in the event, the Prime Minister won that national election convincingly without PBS help, prompting fears, in Sabah, of political retaliation. Those fears proved justified in the wake of the election.

Sabah paid a heavy price for its 'disloyalty'; several prominent Sabahans were arrested as seccessionist conspirators under Malaysia's Internal Security Act, which provides for indefinite detention without trial. Among them was Jeffrey Kitingan, brother of the Chief Minister head of the influential Yayasan Sabah, or Sabah Foundation (see page 437). At the same time, Joseph Pairin Kitingan himself was charged with corruption. There was a feeling in Sabah that the two Kitingans were the bearing the brunt of Dr Mahathir's personal political vendetta.

As the political feud grew more venomous, the federal government added to the fray by failing to promote Sabah to foreign investors. As investment money dried up, so did federal development funds – big road and housing projects were left unfinished for years. Many in Sabah felt that their state was being short-changed by the federal government. The political instability had a detrimental effect on the state economy and the business community began to feel that continued feuding would be economic lunacy. Politicians in the Christian-led PBS, however, continued to claim that Sabah wasn't getting its fair share of Malaysia's economic boom. They said the agreement which enshrined a measure of autonomy for Sabah when it joined the Malaysian federation had been eroded.

The main bone of contention was the state's oil revenues – worth around US$852mn a year – of which 95% disappeared into federal coffers. There were many other sore points too and as the list of grievances grew longer, the state government exploited them to the full. By 1994, anti-federal feelings were running high. The PBS continued to promote the idea of 'Sabah for Sabahans' – a defiant slogan in a country where the federal government was working to centralize power. Because Dr Mahathir likes to be in control, the idea of granting greater autonomy to a distant, opposition-held state was not on his agenda. A showdown was inevitable.

It began in January 1994. As Datuk Pairin's corruption trial drew to a close, he dissolved the state assembly, paving the way for fresh elections. He did this to cover the eventuality of his being disqualified from office through a 'guilty' verdict: he wanted to have his own team in place to take over from him. He was convicted of corruption. But the fine imposed on him was just under the disqualifying threshold, and, to the Prime Minister's fury, he led the PBS into the election. Dr Mahathir put his newly appointed deputy, Anwar Ibrahim, in charge of the National Front alliance campaign.

Datuk Pairin won the election, but by a much narrower margin than before. He alleged vote-buying and ballot rigging. He accused Dr Mahathir's allies of whipping up the issue of religion. He spoke of financial inducements being offered to Sabah's Muslim voters – some of whom are Malay, but most of whom are Bajau tribespeople and Filipino immigrants. His swearing-in ceremony was delayed for 36 hours: the governor said he was sick; Datuk Parin said his political enemies were trying to woo defectors from the ranks of the PBS, to overturn his slender majority. He was proved right.

3 weeks later, he was forced to resign – his fractious party had virtually collapsed in disarray and a stream of defections robbed him of his majority. Datuk Parin's protestations that his assemblymen had been bribed to switch sides were ignored. The local leader of Dr Mahathir's ruling party, Tan Sri Sakaran Dandai, was swiftly sworn in as the new Chief Minister.

Following this 'constitutional coup', Mahathir might reasonably have hoped that the people of Sabah would come to realize that Datuk Pairin's head was the price they had to pay for political reconciliation with Kuala Lumpur – and the financial inducements that would follow. However, in the 1995 general election the PBS did remarkably well, holding onto eight seats and defeating a number of Front candidates who had defected from the PBS the previous year. Sabah was one area – along with the East Coast state of Kelantan – which resisted the Mahathir/BN electoral steamroller.

KOTA KINABALU

Kota Kinabalu started life as a trading post in 1881 – not on the mainland, but on Gaya Island, opposite the present town, where a Filipino shanty is today. On 9 July 1897 rebel leader Mat Salleh, who engaged in a series of hit-and-run raids against the North Borneo Chartered Company's administration, landed on Pulau Gaya. His men looted and sacked the settlement and Gaya township was abandoned.

Two years later the Europeans established another township but this time located on the mainland, opposite Pulau Gaya, adjacent to a Bajau stilt village. The kampung was called '*Api Api*' – meaning 'Fire! Fire!' – because it had been repeatedly torched by pirates over the years. After the Gaya experience, it was an inauspicious name. The Chartered Company rechristened it Jesselton, after Sir Charles Jessel, one of the company directors. But for years, only the Europeans called it Jesselton; locals preferred the old name, and even today Sabahans sometimes refer to their state capital as 'Api'.

Jesselton owed its raison d'être to a plan that back-fired. William C Cowie – formerly a gun-runner for the Sultan of Sulu – became managing director of the

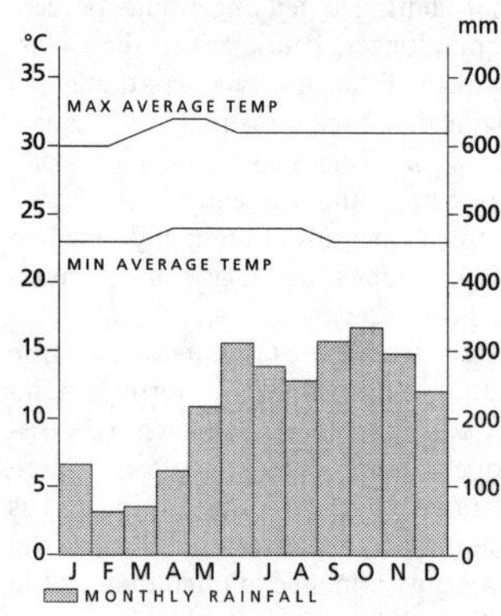

Climate: Kota Kinabalu

9

Chartered Company in 1894. He wanted to build a trans-Borneo railway (see page 454) and the narrow strip of land just north of Tanjung Aru and opposite Pulau Gaya, with its sheltered anchorage, was selected as a terminus.

Photographs in the Sabah State Museum chart the town's development from 1899, when work on the North Borneo Railway terminus began in earnest. By 1905, Jesselton was linked to Beaufort by a 92 km narrow-gauge track. By 1911 it had a population of 2,686, half of whom were Chinese and the remainder Kadazans and Dusuns; there were 33 European residents. Jesselton was of little importance in comparison to Sandakan, the capital of North Borneo.

When the Japanese Imperial Army invaded Borneo in 1942, Jesselton's harbour gave the town strategic significance and it was consequently completely flattened by the Allies during World War Two. The modern town lacks the colonial charm of Sarawak's state capital Kuching. Only three buildings – the old **General Post Office** on Gaya St, **Atkinson's Clock Tower** (built in 1905 and named after Jesselton's first district officer) and the old red-roofed **Lands and Surveys building** remain of the old town. The renovated post office now houses the Sabah Tourist Promotion Corporation. Jesselton followed Kudat and Sandakan as the administrative centre of North Borneo, at the end of World War Two.

In September 1967 Jesselton was renamed Kota Kinabalu after the mountain – its name is usually shortened to KK. The modern city, which has a population of about 180,000, is strung out along the coast, with jungle-clad hills as a backdrop. Two-thirds of the town is built on land reclaimed from the shallow Gaya Bay – during the spring tides it is possible to walk across to the island. Only light fishing boats and passenger vessels can dock at KK's wharves – heavy cargo is unloaded at Likas Bay, to the north. Jalan Pantai, or Beach Rd, is now in the centre of town. Successive land reclamation projects has meant that many of the original stilt villages, such as Kampung Ayer, have been cut off from the sea and some now stand in stinking, stagnant lagoons. The government plans to clean up and reclaim these areas in the next few years and the inhabitants of the water villages are being rehoused.

Places of interest

The golden dome of **Masjid Sabah**, on Jalan Tunku Abdul Rahman, is visible from most areas of town although it is actually about 3 km out of town (regular minibuses connect it with the town centre). Completed in 1975, it is the second biggest mosque in Malaysia and, like the Federal Mosque in Kuala Lumpur, is a fine example of contemporary Islamic architecture. It can accommodate 5,000 worshippers.

Perched on a small hill overlooking the mosque is the **Sabah State Museum** (and State Archives) on Jalan Mat Salleh/Bukit Istana Lama. The museum is designed to look like a longhouse. It has a fascinating ethnographic section which includes an excellent exhibition on the uses of bamboo. Tribal brassware, silverware, musical instruments, basketry and pottery are also on display. On the same floor is a collection of costumes and artifacts from Sabah tribes – the Kadazan/Dusun, Bajau, Murut and Rungus.

One of the most interesting items in this collection is a *sininggazanak* – a sort of totem pole. If a Kadazan man dies without an heir, it was the custom to erect a sininggazanak – a wooden statue supposedly resembling the deceased – on his land. There is also a collection of human skulls – called a *bangkaran* – which before the tribe's wholesale conversion to Christianity, would have been suspended from the rafters of Kadazan longhouses. Every 5 years a *magang* feast was held to appease the spirits of the skulls.

The museum's archaeological section contains a magnificently carved coffin

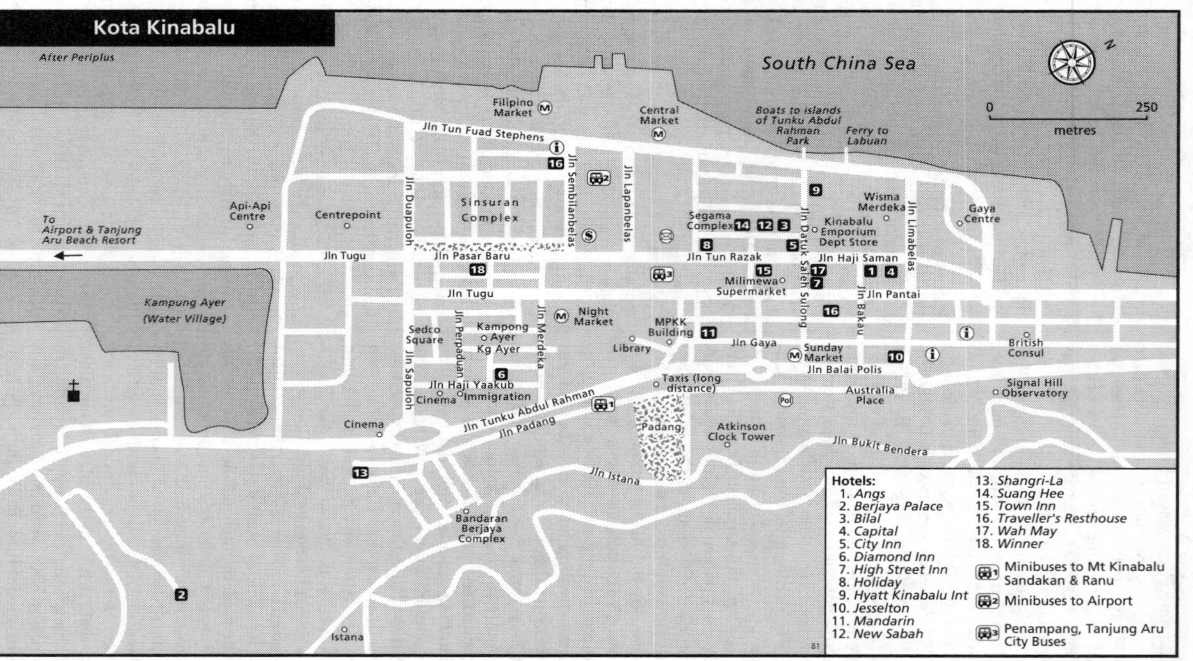
Kota Kinabalu
After Periplus
South China Sea
0
250
metres
Filipino Market
Central Market
Boats to islands of Tunku Abdul Rahman Park
Ferry to Labuan
Jln Tun Fuad Stephens
Jln Sembilanbelas
Jln Lapanbelas
Wisma Merdeka
Gaya Centre
Api-Api Centre
Centrepoint
Jln Duapuloh
Sinsuran Complex
Segama Complex
Kinabalu Emporium Dept Store
Jln Limabelas
To Airport & Tanjung Aru Beach Resort
Jln Tugu
Jln Pasar Baru
Jln Tun Razak
Jln Haji Saman
Jln Datuk Saleh Sulong
Milimewa Supermarket
Jln Tugu
Jln Pantai
Kampung Ayer (Water Village)
Night Market
MPKK Building
Jln Bakau
Sedco Square
Jln Perpaduan
Kampong Ayer
Kg Ayer
Jln Merdeka
Library
Jln Gaya
Sunday Market
British Consul
Jln Balai Polis
Jln Sapuloh
Jln Haji Yaakub
Cinema
Immigration
Taxis (long distance)
Australia Place
Signal Hill Observatory
Jln Tunku Abdul Rahman
Jln Padang
Cinema
Padang
Atkinson Clock Tower
Jln Bukit Bendera
Jln Istana
Bandaran Berjaya Complex
Istana
Hotels:
1. Angs
2. Berjaya Palace
3. Bilal
4. Capital
5. City Inn
6. Diamond Inn
7. High Street Inn
8. Holiday
9. Hyatt Kinabalu Int
10. Jesselton
11. Mandarin
12. New Sabah
13. Shangri-La
14. Suang Hee
15. Town Inn
16. Traveller's Resthouse
17. Wah May
18. Winner
Minibuses to Mt Kinabalu Sandakan & Ranu
Minibuses to Airport
Penampang, Tanjung Aru City Buses

The Sabah Foundation

The Sabah Foundation was set up in 1966 to help improve Sabahans' quality of life. The foundation has a 972,800 ha timber concession, which it claims to manage on a sustainable-yield basis. Two-thirds of this concession has already been logged. Profits from the timber go towards loans and scholarships for Sabahan students, funding the construction of hospitals and schools and supplying milk, textbooks and uniforms to school children. The Foundation also operates a 24-hour flying ambulance service to remote parts of the interior.

found in a limestone cave in the Madai area. Upstairs, the natural history section, provides a good introduction to Sabah's flora and fauna. Next door is a collection of jars, called *pusaka*, which are tribal heirlooms. They were originally exchanged by the Chinese for jungle produce, such as beeswax, camphor and bird's nests.

Next door is the **Science Museum**, containing an exhibition on Shell's offshore activities. The **Art Gallery and Multivision Theatre**, within the same complex, are also worth a browse. The art gallery is small and mainly exhibits works by local artists; among the more interesting works on display are those of Suzie Mojikol, a Kadazan artist, Bakri Dani, who adapts Bajau designs and Philip Biji who specializes in burning Murut designs onto chunks of wood with a soldering iron. The ethnobotanical gardens are on the hillside below the museum complex. There is a cafeteria at the base of the main building. Open 1000-1800 Monday-Thursday, 0900-1800 Saturday and Sunday.

Sabah has a large Christian population and the **Sacred Heart Cathedral** has a striking pyramidal roof which is clearly visible from the Sabah State Museum complex.

Further into town and nearer the coast are a series of water villages, including **Kampung Ayer**, although its size has shrunk in recent years. **Signal Hill** (Bukit Bendera), just southeast of the central area, gives a panoramic view of the town and islands. In the past, the hill was used as a vantage point for signalling to ships approaching the harbour. There is an even better view of the coastline from the top of the **Sabah Foundation (Yayasan Sabah) Complex**, 4 km out of town, overlooking Likas Bay. This surreal glass sculpture has circular floors suspended on high-tensile steel rods and houses the Chief Minister's office. The revolving restaurant on top has closed down, but may reopen. The fact that between the Yayasan Sabah and the core of the city is one of Borneo's largest squatter communities visibly demonstrates that not everyone is sharing equally in the timber boom.

Gaya street market is held every Sunday (from 0800), selling a vast range of goods from jungle produce and handicrafts to pots and pans. The market almost opposite the main minibus station on Jalan Tun Fuad Stephens is known as the **Filipino market**, as most of the stalls are run by Filipino immigrants. A variety of Filipino and local handicrafts are sold in the hundreds of cramped stalls, along winding alleyways which are strung with low-slung curtains of shells, baskets and bags. The Filipino market is a good place to buy cultured pearls (about RM5 each) and has everything from fake gemstones to camagong-wood salad bowls, fibre shirts and traditional Indonesian medicines. Further into town, on the waterfront, is the **central market** selling mainly fish, fruit and vegetables. The daily fishing catch is unloaded on the wharf near the market.

Excursions

Tanjung Aru Beach is the best beach, after those in Tunku Abdul Rahman National Park, and is close to *Tanjung Aru Resort*, 5 km south of KK (see accommodation and places to eat below). It is

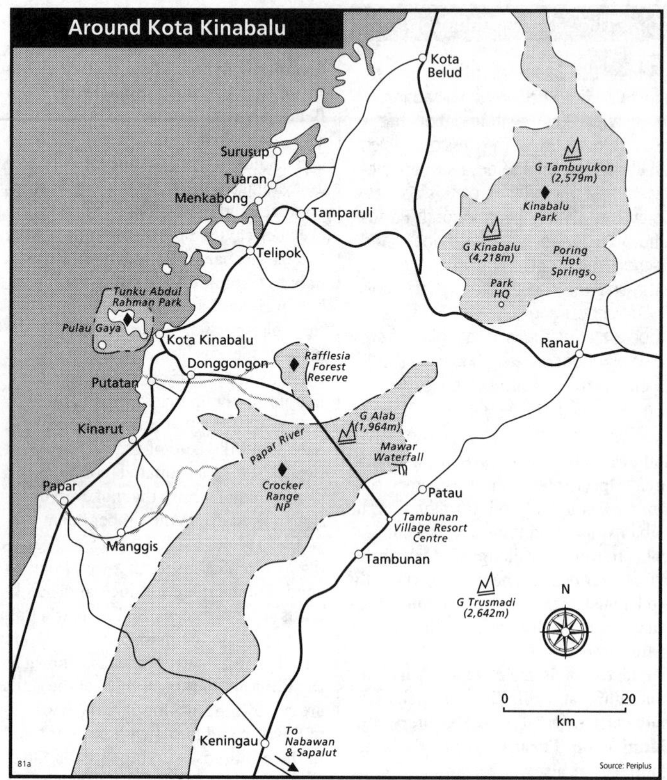

particularly popular at weekends and there is a good hawker centre. *Getting there*: minibuses from the terminus in front of the market, Jalan Tun Fuad Stephens (RM1); red and white buses to Tanjung Aru leave from outside the MPKK building, next to the State Library, or take a red bus marked 'beach' from Jalan Tunku Abdul Rahman.

Tunku Abdul Rahman Park, see page 447.

Penampang, a Kadazan district, is 13 km from KK. The old town of Donggongon was demolished in the early 1980s and the new township built in 1982. The population is mainly Kadazan or Sino-Kadazan and about 90% Christian. The oldest church in Sabah, **St Michael's** Roman Catholic church, is on a steep hill on the far side of the new town. (Turn left just before bridge – and after turn-off to the new town – through kampung and turn left again after school). It was originally built in 1897 but is not dramatic to look at and has been much renovated over the years. Services are conducted in Kadazan but are fascinating to attend and visitors are warmly welcomed; hymns are sung in Kadazan and Malay. The social focus of the week is the **market** every Sunday.

There are many **megaliths** in the Penampang area which are thought to be associated with property claims – particularly when a landowner died without a direct heir. Some solitary stones, which can be seen standing in the middle of paddy fields, are more than 2m tall. The age of the megaliths has not been determined. Wooden figures, called *sininggazanak* can also be seen in the ricefields (see page 435). **Places to eat** ♦♦*Yun Chuan*, Penampang New Town (also known as Donggongon Township), specializes in Kadazan dishes, such as *hinava* – or raw fish, the Kadazan equivalent of sushi. Tapai chicken is also recommended. See page 510 for details on Kadazan cuisine. *Getting there*: green and white Union Transport bus from in front of the MPKK building next to the State Library.

House of Skulls is in Kampung Monsopiad (named after a fearsome Kadazan warrior-cum-headhunter – Siou do Mohoing, the so-called Hercules of Sabah) just outside Penampang. There are 42 fragile human skulls in the collection, some of which are said to be 300 years old and possess spiritual powers. They are laced together with leaves of the *hisad* palm, which represents the hair of the victims. For those who have already visited longhouses in Sarawak, this collection of skulls, in the rafters of an ordinary little kampung house overlooking the village and the Penampang River, is a bit of an anti-climax. But Dousia Moujing, and his son Wennedy, are very hospitable and know much about local history and culture. They preside over their ancestor's dreaded sword (although Wennedy reckons it's not the original, even though there are strands of human hair hanging off it). A 3-day, 3-night-long feast is held at the house in May, in the run-up to the harvest festival. Visitors should remove footwear and not touch the skulls or disturb the rituals or ceremonies in progress. Opening hours: from 0930. For more information, *Borneo Legends and Myths*, 5 km Ramaya/Putaton Rd, Penampang, T 088 761336. A reconstruction of the original Monosopiad main house allows the visitor an insight into the life and times of the warrior and his descendants. There is a good restaurant here serving traditional dishes; the *kadazandusun hinara* is recommended – it consists of fresh sliced raw fish marinated in lime juice and mixed with finely sliced chilli, garlic, gourd and shallots. *Getting there*: the house is hard to find, from new town take main road east, past Shell station and turn right at sign to Jabatan Air; past St Aloysus Church, house on left about 1.5 km from turn-off; minibus from Donggongon Township to Kampung Monsopaid.

Riding at Kinarut, Kinarut Riding School, south of KK, call Dale Sinidal (an Australian lady who has run this school for over 10 years), T 225525, mobile T 0108 100233. Trail rides (approximately 2 hours) through villages and padi fields or along the beach and across to an island at low tide. Stunning surroundings, well kept and good tempered horses. RM60 for 2 hours, RM50 for 1½ hours. *Getting there*: call Ms Sinidal and she will organize transport from KK.

Tampuruli, 32 km north of KK at the junction of the roads north and east, has a suspension bridge straddling the Tuaran River. It was built by the British Army in 1922. Popular stop for tour buses. There is a good handicraft shopping centre here. *Getting there*: minibuses from the terminus in front of the market, Jalan Tun Fuad Stephens. Green buses leave for Tuaran from the padang at the foot of Signal Hill.

Mengkabong is a Bajau – or sea gypsy – fishing village within easy reach of KK (see page 434). The village is particularly photogenic in the early morning, before Mount Kinabalu, which serves as a dramatic backdrop, is obscured by cloud. The fishermen leave Mengkabong at high tide and arrive back with their catch at the next high tide. They use sampan canoes, hollowed out of a single treetrunk, which are crafted in huts around the village. Some of the waterways and fields around Menkabong are choked by water hyacinth, an ornamental plant that was originally introduced by Chinese farmers as pig-fodder from South America. *Getting there*: minibus to Tuaran, taxis to Menkabong.

For visitors wanting to escape the popular beaches close to KK, **Tuaran**, offers a quieter alternative. It lies 45 minutes north of KK and is a good access point for several different tourist destinations including the stilt village of **Mengkabong Water Village** likened to an Asian Venice. **Accommodation A+** *Rasa Ria Resort*, Pantai Dalit Beach, PO Box 600, T 792888, F 792777, rrr@po.jaring.my, top-class *Shangri-La* resort with 330 rooms, free-form pool, watersports, 18-hole golf course, driving range, spacious gardens, conference facilities, cultural events, several restaurants including an Italian and a seafood beach front restaurant, unique torch lighting ceremony, 30 hectares of forest nature reserve nearby means that orang utans are visitors to the resort, recommended. *Getting there*: local bus to Tuaran. The nearby **Karam Bunai Beach** has a good picnic area, clean beach and sea, close by is **Mimpian Jadi, accommodation**: **A-B** *Mimpian Jadi Resort*, No 1 Kuala Matinggi, Kampung Pulau, Simpangan, T 787799, F 787775, chalets, private beach, watersports, fishing, mini zoo, karaoke bar, horseriding, volleyball, children's playground, Malay/Chinese and western food. **Surusup** is another 10-15 minutes beyond Tuaran. Ask at the store in Surusup for Haji Abdul Saman – he will take visitors by boat to the lesser known Bajau fishing village, **Kampung Penambawan**, also likened to an Asian Venice, on the north bank of the river. Nearby there is a suspension bridge and rapids where it is possible to swim. **Accommodation** *Pantai Palit Resthouse*. *Getting there*: boat from Surusup will cost RM30-40.

Local festivals

May: *Magavau* (see page 525), a post-harvest celebration, carried out at Hongkod Koisaan (cultural centre). Mile 4.5, Jalan Penampang. *Getting there*: green and white bus from the MPKK Building, next to state library.

Tours

Most companies run city tours. Other tours that are widely available include: Kota Belud tamu (Sunday market), Mount Kinabalu Park (including Poring Hot Springs), Sandakan's Sepilok Orang Utan Rehabilitation Centre, train trips to Tenom through the Padas Gorge and tours of the islands in the Tunku Abdul Rahman National Park. Several companies specialize in scuba-diving tours, see page 444.

Local information

● Accommodation

Prices: L over RM500; **A+** RM260-500; **A** RM130-260; **B** RM65-130; **C** RM40-65; **D** RM20-40; **E** RM10-20; **F** Below RM10

Several new out-of-town resorts are under construction or recently completed. The scenic Karambunai peninsula, 30 km north of KK is due to be transformed by a sprawling multi million dollar golf and beach resort complex, encompassing two big hotels. South of KK, the *Borneo Golf and Beach Resort*, including two 18-hole courses – one designed by Jack Nicklaus, the other by his son – will be up-and-running. The *Shangri-La* group, which now owns the *Tanjung Aru*, has built the *Rasa Ria Resort* at Pantai Dalit, near Tuaran (see excursions above). Well-heeled tourists will seek the more refined out-of-town resorts; but in KK itself, mid-range hotels have improved immeasurably in recent years. The best bets, offering good value-for-money are those catering for itinerant Malaysian businessmen, such as the *Mandarin Palace* and *Shangri-La*.

L-A+ *Hyatt Kinabalu International*, Jln Datuk Saleh Sulong, T 221234, F 225972, a/c, 315 rooms, 3 restaurants, small pool, good central location, rooms vary in standard, business centre, live entertainment in the atrium. **L-A+** *Shangri-La Tanjung Aru Resort*, Tanjung Aru, T 225800, F 244871/217155, e-mail: star@po.jaring.my, a/c, 500 rooms, pool, one of the best hotels in Sabah, although it is now in competition with its new sister hotel the *Rasa Ria*. Tanjung Aru is a public beach, frequented by kite-flyers, swimmers, joggers, and lovers, the hotel is noticeably on the European honeymoon circuit, recommended. **A-A+** *Jesselton*,

69 Jln Gaya, T 223333, F 240401, a/c, restaurant, the first hotel to be opened in KK, dates from 1954, remains a classic – just 32 rooms. **A** ***Berjaya Palace***, 1 Jln Tangki, Karamunsing, T 211911, F 211600, a/c, restaurant, 160 rooms, pool, conference rooms, gym, proprietor James Sheng has a small resort, with chalets, on Pulau Gaya, at Maluham Bay, east of Police Bay, enquire at hotel. **A** ***Kinabalu Daya***, Lot 3 & 4, Jln Pantai, T 240000, F 263909, 68 rooms, restaurant serves Asian and western food, video in bedrooms, seminar room. **A** ***Beverly Hills 'Vanria Holiday' Apartment***, Lot A6-3, Block A, 3rd Flr, Beverly Hills, T 8212098, 10 km from city centre, suitable for family groups with 2 bedroom apartments and dorms (**E**) with breakfast included in the room rate. The apartment has fan rooms and cooking facilities. Van rentals and tours organized, swimming pool. **A** ***Promenade***, 4 Lorong Api-Api 3, Api-Api Centre, T 265555, F 246666, several restaurants, business facilities, gym with good range of equipment, pool. **A** ***Shangri-La***, 75 Bandaran Berjaya, T 212800, F 212078, a/c, restaurant, not in the international *Shangri-La* group; reasonable hotel though and the haunt of visiting businessmen. **A-B** ***Borneo Resthouse***, Mile 3.5 Jln Penampang, Taman Fraser, T 718855, F 718955, a/c, 50 rooms, restaurant, pool, garden. **A-B** ***Capital***, 23 Jln Haji Saman, T 231999, F 237222, a/c, 102 rooms, coffeeshop, central position. **A-B** ***Century***, Lot 12 Jln Masjid Lama, T 242222, F 242929, a/c, 54 rooms, good seafood restaurant.

B ***City Inn***, 41 Jln Pantai, T 218933, F 218937, a/c, good for the price, often full. **B** ***Holiday***, Jln Tun Razak, T 213116, a/c, quite good, but overpriced. **B** ***Holiday Home (B&B)***, No 6, Block 1, Taman Likas Haya, Jln Teluk Likas, Lorong Kenari, T/F 423993, close proximity to city centre, beach and sports complex within easy reach, tour and travel information provided, dorms (**E**) beds available. **B** ***Mandarin***, 138 Jln Gaya, T 225222, F 225481, a/c, restaurant, very swish, marble floors, well-fitted rooms, excellent central location, friendly staff, 6th flr rooms with good view over town; deluxe and super-deluxe particularly spacious, recommended. **B** ***New Sabah***, Block A, No 9-11 Jln Padas, Lot 394 Segama Complex, T 224698, F 235875, a/c, TV, bathroom, average hotel, very noisy. **B** ***Pantai Inn***, 57 Jln Pantai, T 217095, F 216839, a/c, good central location, well-appointed rooms, small but very clean. **B** ***Ruby***, Jln Laiman Diki, Kampung Ayer T 213222, F 2321198. **B** ***Seaside Travellers Inn***, H30 Gaya Park, Jln Penampang (20 km from Kota Kinabalu, 12 km from airport), T 750555, F 750479, http://www.infosabah.com.my/tourism/hotel/t-inn/index.htm, 22 rooms in a beach-side resort – 4 rooms in modern house, the others in more basic accommodation at the front, a/c, hot water, restaurant (Chinese food), pool, tennis court, small and homely inn, designed for families on a moderate budget. **B** ***Town Inn***, 31 & 33 Jln Pantai, T 225823, F 217762, a/c, 24 rooms, clean with excellent facilities, central location, good for the price, recommended. **B** ***Wah May***, 36 Jln Haji Saman, T 266118, F 266122, 36 clean rooms, modern Chinese hotel. **B** ***Winner***, 9 & 10 Jln Pasar Baru, Kampung Ayer, T 243222, F 217345, a/c, 36 rooms, restaurant, pleasant hotel in a central location with friendly staff and a good restaurant. **B-C** ***Ang's***, 28 Jln Bakau, T 234999, F 217867, a/c, 35 rather threadbare rooms. **B-C** ***Diamond***, Jln Haji Yaakub, T 225222, F 231198, 32 very adequate rooms. **B-C** ***High Street Inn***, 38 Jln Pantai, T 218111, F 219111, a/c, TV, in-house movies, hot water, small but comfortable rooms.

C ***Rosel***, 2nd Flr, Block B, Lot 1 & 2 Segama Complex, T 256709, F 263220, chapsel@pc.jaring.my, a/c, above the Indian Muslim restaurant *Bilal*, this centrally located hotel, although basic, is spotless and bright with friendly management, rooms have hot water showers and TV, tourist information, recommended. **C** ***Suang Hee***, Block F, 7 Segama Shopping Centre, T 254168, F 217234, a/c, restaurant, 24 rooms, clean Chinese hotel, reasonable value for money, a/c, TV and bathroom. **C** ***Golden Inn***, Sinsuran Complex, T 211510. **C-D** ***Celia's Bed & Breakfast***, 413 Jln Saga, Kampung Likas, T 35733, out of town but recommended by all who stay there. **C-D** ***Travellers' Rest Hostel***, Block L, 3rd Flr, Lot 5 & 6, Sinsuran Complex, Bangunan Pelancungan, T 224720, some a/c, no attached bath and limited toilet facilities, some rooms don't have a window, friendly, lots of travel information, cooking and laundry facilities, tours around Sabah arranged here.

D ***Government Sports Complex Hostel***, Likas (behind Signal Hill), facilities including running track, gym, swimming pool, tennis and badminton courts, takes 15 minutes by Likas-bound minibus from town, or walk over Signal Hill, dorm (**E**), a/c (**C**). **D** ***Jack's B&B***, 17, 1st Flr, Block B, Jln Karamunsing, T 232367, a/c, including breakfast, clean and friendly, jungle tours organized, recommended. **D** ***Islamic Hotel***,

Kampung Ayer, cheap accommodation with fan only rooms and separate mandis. Excellent restaurant downstairs sells very good roti. **D** ***Segama***, 2nd/3rd Flr, Block D, Lot 1, 16 Jln Labuk, Segama, T 221327, a/c, clean, but rooms are dark. **D** ***Trekkers Lodge***, 46 Jln Pantai, T 213888, F 262818. Price is per person, in a/c dorm style rooms. Breakfast is included. Recently opened, centrally located, managed by USA-trained Alex Yee, who is extremely helpful. All the staff have been well trained and the place is spotlessly clean. Laundry and storage facilities available, recommended.

E ***Backpacker Lodge***, Australia Place, T 261495, friendly, clean dorms with a good breakfast included in the room rate. **E** ***Trekkers Lodge***, 46, Jln Pantai, T 213888, F 262888, run by Alex Yee, a/c dorm rooms, price includes breakfast, tour information available, one recent visitor E-mailed us the following – "... a fantastic place, very clean, friendly, good service and, most of all, in a very convenient location, I would highly recommend it". **E-F** ***Borneo Wildlife Youth Hostel***, Lot 4, Block L, Sinsuran Complex, T 213668, F 219089, a newish place almost next door to the *Travellers' Resthouse* and above the *Borneo Wildlife Adventure Tour Company*, basic but clean.

Home away from Home, 413 Jln Saga, Mile 4½, Likas, T 428733, F 424998; kampung accommodation organized for all parts of Sabah; contact Ms Faridah Abdul Rahman, director.

● Places to eat

Prices: ◆◆◆◆ over RM40; ◆◆◆ RM13-40; ◆◆ RM5-13; ◆ under RM5

Malay: ◆◆***Copelia***, Jln Gaya, *nasi lemak* for breakfast, also does takeaway. ◆***Restoran Ali***, Segama Complex, opposite *Hyatt Hotel*, best in a string of coffee shops, all of which are good value for money.

Chinese: ◆◆◆***Hyatt Poolside Hawker Centre***, *Hyatt*, Jln Datuk Saleh Sulong, steamboat (minimum 2 people). ◆◆***Avasi Cafeteria & Garden Restaurant***, EG 11 Kompleks Kuwasa, steamboat and seafood. ◆◆***Nan Xing***, opposite the *Hyatt* and emporium, dim sum and Cantonese specialities. ◆◆***Phoenix Court***, *Hyatt*, Jln Datuk Saleh Sulong, dim sum 0700-1400. ◆◆***Tioman***, Lot 56 Bandaran Berjaya, good claypot and lemon chicken. ◆***Chuan Hin***, Jln Kolam (next to the Cottage Pub), excellent *ikan panggang*. ◆***Friendly***, Tuaran Rd, Mile 2, Likas, cheap.

Nyonya: ◆◆***Sri Melaka Restoran***, 9 Jln Laiman Diki, Kampung Ayer (Sedco Complex, near *Shiraz*).

Other Asian cuisine: ◆◆◆***Azuma***, 3rd Flr, Wisma Merdeka, Japanese. ◆◆◆***Jaws***, 4th Flr, Gaya Centre, Jln Tun Fuad Stephens, Thai/Chinese cuisine, such as *tom yam* steamboat. ◆◆◆***Nishiki***, Gaya St (opposite Wing On Life Building), Japanese. ◆◆***Korean***, Jln Bandaran Berjaya, next to *Asia Hotel*, large selection, barbecues speciality. ◆◆***Shiraz***, Lot 5, Block B, Sedco Square, Kampung Ayer, Indian, recommended. ◆***Bilal***, Block B, Lot 1 Segama Complex, Indian Muslim food, rotis, chapatis, curries, recommended. ◆***Islamic Restoran***, Kampung Ayer, the best roti in town. ***Sri Sakthi***, Mile 4.5 Jln Penampeng (opposite Towering Heights Industrial Estate), South Indian banana-leaf – good value. ***Jothy's Curry Restaurant***, Api Api Centre.

International: ◆◆◆***Gardenia***, *Jesselton Hotel*, 69 Jln Gaya. ◆◆◆***Peppino***, *Tanjung Aru Beach Resort*, tasty but expensive, Italian, good Filipino cover band. ◆◆***Sri Kapitol***, Ground Floor, *Hotel Capital*, 23 Jln Haji Saman, T 219688, European breakfasts. ◆***Fat Cat***, Jln Haji Saman, cheap slap-up breakfasts. ***MacDonalds***, Api Api Centre. ***Pizza Hut***, Centre Point, Gaya St. ***Sugarbun***, Centre Point, Gaya St. ***KFC***, in half a dozen locations around town including Centre Point, Gaya St, Tuaran, Tanjung Aru. ***Burger King***, Segama, Centre Point, Gaya St.

Seafood: seafood in KK is seasonally prone to red tide. Locals will know when it's prevalent. Avoid all shellfish if there is any suspicion. ◆◆◆***Garden Restaurant***, *Tanjung Aru Beach Resort*, tables outside. ◆◆◆***Merdeka***, 11th Flr, Wisma Merdeka, reasonably good seafood, but the view is better in this restaurant which offers 'karaoke at no extra charge'. ◆◆◆***Seafood Market***, Tanjung Aru Beach, T 238313, pick your own fresh seafood and get advice on how to have it cooked. ◆◆***Golf Field Seafood***, 0858 Jln Ranca-Ranca (better known by taxi-drivers as *Ahban's Place*), excellent marine cuisine, local favourite, recommended. ◆***Port View***, Jln Haji Saman (opposite old customs wharf), huge selection of fresh seafood and delicious chilli crab, open until 0200 weekdays and 0300 on Sat, very popular with locals. ***Golf View***, Jln Swamp (near Sabah Golf and Country Club), recommended by locals.

Coffee shops: found in most areas of KK, hot and cold drinks are served as well as a variety of local noodle and rice dishes.

Bakeries: KK bakers abound and are particularly good.

Foodstalls: ◆◆Stalls above ***central market***. ◆◆***Sedco Square***, Kampung Ayer, large square filled with stalls, great atmosphere in the evenings, ubiquitous *ikan panggang* and satay; *night market* on Jln Tugu, on the *waterfront* at the Sinsuran Food Centre and at the *Merdeka Foodstall Centre*, Wisma Merdeka. ***Tanjung Aru Beach***, mainly seafood – recommended for *ikan panggang* – and satay stalls: very busy at weekends, but on weekdays it is rather quiet, with only a few stalls to choose from.

● Bars

Hard Rock Café, Sutera Harbour; ***Cyber Café***, Gaya St, for internet surfers; ***The Cottage***, Jln Bukit Padang.

● Airline offices

British Airways, Jln Haji Saman, T 428057/428292; **Cathay Pacific**, Ground Floor, Block C, Lot CG, Kompleks Kuwasa, 49 Jln Karamunsing, T 428733; **Garuda Airways**, Wisma Sabah; **MAS**, 10th Flr, Karamunsing Kompleks (off Jln Tunku Abdul Rahman, south of Kampung Ayer), Jln Kemajuan, T 213555, also have an office at the airport; **Philippine Airlines**, Lot 3.48, Karamunsing Complex, Jln Kemajuan, T 239600; **Royal Brunei Airlines**, G13, Wisma Sabah, Jln Haji Saman, T 242193; **Sabah Air**, KK Airport, T 428733/428326; **Singapore Airlines**, 20 Jln Pantai Tempahan, T 428444/428333; **Thai Airways**, T 232896.

● Banks & money changers

There are money changers in main shopping complexes. **Hong Kong & Shanghai**, 56 Jln Gaya; **Sabah Bank**, Wisma Tun Fuad Stephens, Jln Tuaran; **Standard Chartered**, 20 Jln Haji Saman; **Maybank**, Jln Kemajuan/ Jln Pantai.

● Church services

English: *St Simon's Catholic Church*, Likas, Sun 1700; *Stella Maris* (Tanjung Aru) Sun 0700; *SIB*, Likas (Baptist), Sun 0800.

● Embassies & consulates

British Consul, Hong Kong Bank Building, 56 Jln Gaya; **Indonesian Consulate**, Jln Karamunsing, T 428100; **Japanese Consulate**, Wisma Yakim, T 428169.

● Entertainment

Cinemas: Poring and Capital cinemas, near Sedco Complex.

Cultural shows: *Kadazan-Dusun Cultural Centre* (Hongkod Koisaan), KDCA Building, Mile 4.5, Jln Penampang, restaurant open year-round, but at the end of May, during the harvest festival, the cultural association comes into its own, with dances, feasts and shows and lots of *tapai* (RM15); *Tanjung Aru Beach Hotel* on Wed and Sat, 2000.

Discos: *Shennanigan's*, *Hyatt Hotel*, the smartest in town; ***Next Door***, *Tanjung Aru Beach Hotel*; ***Tiffiny***, Tanjung Aru, opposite Sacred Heart Church. ***LA Rock***, along the left side of Tong Hing Supermarket; ***Rockies***, *Promenade Hotel*.

Karaoke: very popular in KK; found in Damai, Foh Sang and KK centre.

MTV: *Popeye's MTV* in Bandaran.

● Hospitals and medical services

Health Care: one of the better private clinics is the Damai Specialist Centre.

● Post & telecommunications

Area code: 088.

General Post Office: Jln Tun Razak, Segama Quarter (poste restante facilities).

Telekom: Block C, Kompleks Kuwaus, Jln Tunku Abdul Rahman, international calls as well as local, fax service.

● Shopping

Antiques: good antiques shop at the bottom of the Chun Eng Building on Jln Tun Razak, a couple also on Gaya St. It is necessary to have an export licence from the Sabah State Museum if you intend to export rare antiques.

Books: ***Arena Book Centre***, Lot 2, Ground Floor, Block 1, Sinsuran Kompleks; ***Rahmant Bookstore***, *Hyatt Hotel*, Jln Datuk Salleh Sulong; ***Iwase Bookshop***, Ground Floor, Wisma Merdeka, T 233757, selection of English language books and magazines.

Clothes: ***The House of Borneo Vou'tique*** Lot 12A, First Floor, Lorong Bernam 3, Taman Saon Kiong, Jln Kolam, T 268398, F 263398, for that ethnic, exotic and exclusive look for men and women – corporate uniforms, souvenir items, tablecloths, cushion covers etc.

Handicrafts: mainly baskets, mats, tribal clothing, beadwork and pottery. ***Borneo Gifts***, Ground Floor, Wisma Sabah. ***Borneo Handicraft***, 1st Flr, Wisma Merdeka, local pottery and material made up into clothes. ***Elegance Souvenir***, 1st Flr, Wisma Merdeka, lots of beads of local interest (another branch on Ground Floor of Centre Point); ***Malaysian Handicraft***, Cawangan Sabah, No 1, Lorong 14, Kg Sembulau, T 234471, F 223444, open Mon-Sat 0815-1230 and Fri 0815-1600; ***The Crafts***, Lot AG10, Ground Floor, Wisma Merdeka, T 252413; ***Filipino Market***, Jln Tun Fuad Stephens (see page 437); ***Kaandaman Handicraft Centre*** below *Seafood Market Restaurant*, Tanjung Aru Beach; ***Kampung Air Night Market***, mainly Filipino handicrafts; ***Sabah Art***

and Handicraft Centre, 1st Flr, Block B, Segama Complex (opposite *New Sabah Hotel*); ***Sabah Handicraft Centre***, Lot 49 Bandaran Berjaya (next to *Shangri-La*) good selection (also has branches at the museum and the airport). There are also several handicraft shops in the arcade at the *Tanjung Aru Beach Hotel* and one at the airport. *Api Tours*, Lot 49, Bandaran Berjaya also has a small selection of handicrafts.

Jewellery: most shops in Wisma Merdeka.

Markets: see page 437.

Shopping complexes: ***Segama*** on Jln Tun Fuad Stephens and ***Sinsuran***, **NB** Beware of pick-pocketing during the day and more particularly at night, when KK's transvestite population is at large; ***Kinabalu Emporium***, Wisma Yakim, Jln Daruk Salleh Sulong is the main department store; ***Likas Square*** Likas, pink monstrosity with two floors of shopping malls, foodstalls and restaurants. Cultural shows in central lobby.

Supermarkets: ***Kemayan*** Likas; ***Tong Hing*** KK and Damai; ***Home and Garden***, ***Merdeka***, KK; ***Milemewah***, KK.

● Sports

The sports complex at Likas is open to the general public; it provides volleyball, tennis, basketball, a gym, badminton, squash, aerobics and a swimming pool. To get there take a Likas-bound minibus from town. *Likas Square*, the monstrous pink shopping complex north of Likas Sports Complex, has a Recreation Club within it providing tennis, squash, jogging, golf, driving range, a pool and a children's playground.

Bowling: ***Merdeka Bowl***, 11th Flr, Wisma Merdeka.

Diving: snorkelling and scuba-diving in Tunku Abdul Rahman National Park. Tour operators specializing in dive trips also organize dives all over Sabah.

Golf: Green fees are considerably higher over the weekend – as much as double the week day rate. Fees range from a low of about RM50 during the week at the cheaper courses, to as much as RM200 or more over the weekend at flasher clubs. Courses at Tanjung Aru and the ***Sabah Golf and Country Club*** at Bukit Padang, T 247533, an 18-hole championship course, which affords magnificent views of Mount Kinabalu on clear days, green fees RM150 (weekdays), RM200 (weekends); ***Kinabalu Golf Club***, Tanjung Aru.

Hash: there are three hashes in KK. **1**: ***K2 H4*** (KK Hash House Harriers) – men only, T 428535, Mon, 1715. **2**: ***K2 H2*** (KK Hash House Bunnies) – women (but not exclusively), T 244333, ext 389. **3**: ***K2 H4*** (KK Hash House Harriers and Harriets) – mixed, T 217541, Fri, 1715.

Sailing: yacht club at Tanjung Aru, next to the hotel.

Roller blading: Centre Point, 3rd Floor, Gaya St.

Watersports: ***Tanjung Aru Marina***, snorkelling RM10/day, water skiing RM120/hour, fishing RM12-25/day, sailing RM20-40/hour, water scooter RM60/hour. Snorkelling equipment for rent at good prices from the *Travellers Resthouse*.

White water rafting: Papar River (Grades I & II), Kadamaian River (Grades II & III), Padas River (Grade IV). Usually requires a minimum of 3 people. Main operators including *Api Tours*, *Borneo Expeditions* and *Discovery Tours* (see page 440).

● Tour companies & travel agents

The Sabah Tourism Promotion Corporation has a full list of tour and travel agents operating in the state.

Api Tours (Borneo), No 13 Jln Punai Dekut, Mile 5, Jln Tuaran, PO Box 12851, T 421963, F 424174, e-mail: apitour@po.jaring.my. Offers a wide variety of tours, including some more unusual ones such as overnight stays in longhouses, recommended. ***Borneo Divers***, Lot 529, Mile 3.5 Tuaran Rd, T 53074 and Lot 401-412, 4th Flr, Wisma Sabah, T 222226, F 221550, bdivers@po.jaring.my, web site: http://www.jaring.my/bdivers (there is another branch in the *Tanjung Aru Beach Hotel*), operates exotic scuba diving trips and runs a dive station on Pulau Sipadan (see page 494), *Borneo Divers* also runs an excellent dive store and operates 5-days training courses with classes tailored for beginners or advanced divers (RM875-575 depending on group size), the company also has an office in Tawau T 089 761214, F 089 761691, and in Labuan T 087 415867, F 087 413454 (see page 456) which organizes 2-days dives to shipwrecks off the island, trips are seamlessly organized, but very expensive. ***Borneo Eco Tours***, Lot 12A, 2nd Floor, Lorong Bernam 3, e-mail: betsb1@po.jaring.my, web site: http://www. jaring.my/bet, ecotourist specialists – their *Sukau Rainforest Lodge* on the Kinabatangan River is highly recommended. ***Borneo Endeavour***, 2nd Flr, Lot 10, Block A, Damai Plaza, Luyang, T 249950,

Layang-Layang Atoll: OK coral

Malaysia is just one of five claimants to the countless reefs and atolls in the Spratly group. While Vietnam and China are more interested in the prospective riches from what are thought to be oil-bearing strata beneath the seabed, Malaysia is the only country to have cashed in on tourism on the reefs themselves. Layang-Layang (or 'Kite') atoll is about 250 km northwest of Kota Kinabalu – a 16 hour boat ride – and has recently been added to other coral reefs such as Sipadan Island, off Sabah's east coast (see page 494) as part of the state's growing list of fabulous dive sites. Layang-Layang – formerly known as Swallow Reef – is 7 km long and 5 km wide, with a lagoon in the middle. There is a Malaysian navy base at one end and basic tourist accommodation (in concrete and breeze block houses) next to it. The island attracts migratory birds, but is best-known as a scuba paradise. Divers visiting Layang-Layang usually stay aboard the MV *Coral Topaz* and make trips to other nearby reefs. There are reportedly several wrecks in the area, but most diving focuses on the coral walls on the outer edges of the reefs which drop sheer to the seabed 2,000m below. This area also has some of Southeast Asia's finest game fishing.

F 249946; ***Borneo Expeditions***, *Tanjung Aru Beach Resort*, Shop Lot 7, Jln Aru, T 222721, F 222720. Specialists in mountain trekking and white water rafting – mainly on the Padas River; run by a former British outward-bound school instructor, Stephen Pinfield, whose forte is safari tours. A trek to Kampung Long Pa Sia, deep in Murut country, near the Sarawak and Kalimantan borders is highly recommended. ***Borneo Sea Adventures***, 1st Flr, 8a Karamunsing Warehouse, T 230000, F 221106 also conducts scuba diving courses and runs diving and fishing trips all around Sabah. It specializes in the 'Wall Dive' off Pulau Sipadan (see page 494). ***Borneo Wildlife Adventures***, Lot 4, Block L, Ground, 2nd and 3rd Floors, Sinsuran Complex, T 213668, F 219089, one of the newer eco-tour companies. ***Coral Island Cruises***, 10th Floor, Wisma Merdeka, T 223490, F 223404, e-mail: miaovo@po.jaring.my. Specializes in boat cruises, mostly around Tunku Abdul Rahman National Park, and offers night fishing trips. *Coral Island Cruises* has teamed up with the Labuan-based dive company *Ocean Sports* to run 6-days scuba-diving trips to Layang Layang, an atol in the disputed Spratly group, 6-16 days dive packages, costing RM1,000+, leave 2-3 times a month in peak season (June-Aug) (see box). Also operates dive voyages aboard *MV Coral Topaz* to Sipadan/Ligitan islands (see page 496), recommended. ***Discovery Tours***, Lot G28, Wisma Sabah, Jln Haji Saman, T 216426, F 221600. Run by experienced tour-operator Albert Wong, recommended. ***Exotic Borneo Holidays***, Lot 24, 1st Flr, Suite B, Likas Industrial Centre, Tuaran Rd, T 429224, F 429024, organize well-run theme tours including culture, adventure and nature – at a price. ***Kota Aquatics***, AG04 Wisma Merdeka, Jln Tun Razak, T/F 218710 runs diving courses, hires scuba and snorkelling equipment and organizes diving trips. Also runs fishing trips. ***Pan Borneo Tours & Travel***, 1st Floor, Room 127, Wisma Sabah, T 221221, F 219233, panborn@po.jaring.my. ***Sabah Air***, Sabah Air Building, Old Airport Rd, T 256733, F 235195. Sightseeing by helicopter. ***Sipadan Dive Centre***, 10th Flr, Wisma Merdeka, Jln Tun Razak, T 240584, F 240415, e-mail: sipadan@po.jaring.my, web site: http://www.jaring.my/sipadan. ***Tanjung Aru Tours***, The Marina, *Tanjung Aru Beach Hotel*, T 214215/240966. Fishing and island tours – particularly to Tunku Abdul Rahman National Park. ***Transworld***, 2nd Flr, Bangunan Dewan Perniagaan, Bumiputera Sabah, Jln Gaya, T 238448, F 240866 (also an office at *Tanjung Aru Beach Resort*). Glass-bottom boat trips to Tunku Abdul Rahman National Park.

● Tourist offices

Sabah Tourist Promotion Corporation, 51 Jln Gaya, T 218620, F 212075, web site: http://www.jaring.my/sabah; **Tourism Malaysia Sabah**, Ground Floor, Wing On Life Building, Jln Sagunting, T 211698/211732 helpful office.

● Parks offices

Forestry Division, Sabah Foundation, Sabah Foundation Building, Likas, T 34596; **Innoprise Corporation Building**, Sadong Jaya, T 243251 for the Danum Valley Field Centre (see page 491); **Sabah National Parks Office Headquarters**, Ist Floor, Lot 1-3, Block K, Sinsuran Kompleks, Jln Tun Fuad Stephens, T 211652, F 211585, necessary to book accommodation for the National Parks (T 211881) – particularly Mount Kinabalu National Park or Poring Hot Springs. Also has general information on the parks, the office has a good library with reports on wildlife in the parks and natural history surveys which can be used with the permission of the office, open 0800-1600 Mon-Fri, 0830-1230 Sat.

● Useful addresses

British Council: Wing On Life Building, Jln Sagunting, 1st Flr, not very helpful.

Business centres: at the *Hyatt Hotel* and *Shangri-La Tanjung Aru Resort* and *Shangri-La Rasa Ria*.

Immigration: 4th Flr Government Building, Jln Haji Yaakub. Visas can be renewed at this office, without having to leave the country.

● Transport

77 km from Kota Belud, 128 km from Keningau, 386 km from Sandakan.

Local Buses: city buses leave from area between Jln Tun Razak and Jln Tugu. Buses from behind the Centre Point Shopping Complex go to Kapayan, Queen Elizabeth Hospital, Sembulan, Putatan, Jalan Baru and Penampang. Red and white buses go to Penampang and Tanjung Aru and leave from the bus station in front of the MPKK Building, next to the state library. Green buses go to areas north of KK (Tuaran, Likas etc) and leave from the padang at the bottom of Signal Hill. *Luen Thong* white a/c buses go from in front of the *Shangri-La Hotel*, they go to Tuaran, Telipok, Dayavila and Kampung Likas. From MPKK building, *Luen Thong* a/c buses go to Tanjung Aru and Kapayan. **Car hire**: not all roads in the interior of Sabah are paved and a 4WD vehicle is advisable. However, car hire is expensive and starts at around RM300-400/day. Rates often increase for use outside a 50 km radius of KK. All vehicles have to be returned to KK as there are no agency offices outside KK, although local car-hire is usually available. **Adaras Rent-a-Car**, Lot G03, Ground Floor, Wisma Sabah, T 222137/ 216010, F 232641; **Avis**, *Hyatt Kinabalu Hotel*, Jln Datuk Salleh Sullong, T 428577; **Borneo Car Rental**, Lot 24, 1st Flr, Suite A, Likas Industrial Centre, Tuaran Rd, T 429224, **Extra Rent-a-Car**, No 2, 1st Flr, Jln Api Api, T 218160; **E & C Limousine Services** Ground Floor, Wisma Sabah, T 57679, F 221466; **Hertz**, Block B, Sedco Complex, T 221635; **Kinabalu Rent-a-Car**, Lot 3.61, 3rd Flr, Kompleks Karamunsing, T 232602; **Sintat**, Block L, Lots 4-6, Sinsuran Complex, T 428729; **Travel Rent-a-Car**, Lot 20, Ground Floor, Wisma Sabah, T 222708, F 221751. **Minibuses**: all minibuses have their destinations on the windscreen, most rides in town are RM0.40-0.60 and they will leave when full. You can get off wherever you like. **Taxis**: there are taxi stands outside most of the bigger hotels and outside the General Post Office, the Segama complex, the Sunsuran complex, next to the MPKK building, the Milemewah supermarket, the Capitol cinema and in front of the clocktower (for taxis to Ranau, Keningau and Kudat). Approximate fares from town: RM8 to *Tanjung Aru Beach Resort*, RM10 Sabah Foundation, RM10 to the museum, RM17 airport. **NB** Most taxis are not metered.

Air The airport is 6 km from town. *Transport into town*: Taxi RM17 to town centre – coupon can be purchased in advance from the booths outside the arrivals hall. Regular connections with KL – cheaper flights if in a group of three or more, late-night flights, or book 14 days in advance. There are also connections from KK with Bintulu, Johor Bharu, Kuching, Kudat, Lahad Datu, Labuan, Miri, Penang, Sandakan, Sibu and Tawau.

Train The station is 5 km out of town in Tanjung Aru. Diesel trains run three times daily to Beaufort, 4 hours and on to Tenom, a further 3 hours. Departure times are subject to change, T 52536/54611. *Transport to town*: long distance buses stop near the train station.

Road Bus: buses around the state are cheaper than minibuses but not as regular or efficient. The large buses go mainly to destinations in and around KK itself. **Minibus and taxi**: there is no central bus station in KK. Taxis and minibuses bound north for Kota Belud, Tamparuli and Kudat and those going south to Papar, Beaufort, Keningau and Tenom leave from Bandar Berjaya opposite the Padang and clocktower. Taxis and minibuses going west to Kinabalu National Park, Ranau and Sandakan leave from Jln Tunku Abdul Rahman, next to the Padang and opposite the State Library. Tamparuli, a few kilometres east of Tuaran, serves as a mini-terminus for minibuses heading to Kinabalu National Park. Minibuses leave when full and those for long-distance destinations leave in the early morning. Long-distance taxis also leave when full from in front of the clocktower on Jln Tunku Abdul Rahman. Minibus fares from KK: Tuaran 45 minutes (RM3), Kota Belud 2 hours (RM12),

Kudat 4-5 hours (RM25), Beaufort 2-3 hours (RM15), Keningau 2-3 hours (RM20), Tenom 4 hours (RM30), Kinabalu National Park 1½ hours (RM20), Ranau 2 hours (RM15), Sandakan 8-10 hours (RM35).

Sea Boat: 3 boats a day leave for Labuan, 2½ hours (RM30). Boats leave from the jetty behind the *Hyatt Hotel*. Reservations can be made at *Rezeki Murmi Sdn Bhd*, Lot 3, 1st Flr, Block D, Segama Shopping Complex, T 236834/5, F 237390.

International Connections Air Connections with Singapore, Brunei, Hong Kong, Manila, Seoul, Jakarta, Taipei and Tokyo.

TUNKU ABDUL RAHMAN PARK

The five islands in Gaya Bay which make up Tunku Abdul Rahman Park lie 3-8 km offshore. They became Sabah's first national park in 1923 and were gazetted in an effort to protect their coral reefs and sandy beaches. Geologically, the islands are part of the Crocker Range formation, but as sea-levels rose after the last ice age, they became isolated from the massif. Coral reefs fringe all the islands in the park. The best reefs are between Pulau Sapi and Pulau Gaya, although there is also reasonable coral around Manukan, Mamutik and Sulug; the islands can be visited all year round.

Flora and fauna Some of the only undisturbed coastal dipterocarp forest left in Sabah is on Pulau Gaya. On the other islands most of the original vegetation has been destroyed and established secondary vegetation predominates, such as ferns, orchids, palms, casuarina, coconut trees and tropical fruit trees. Mangrove forests can be found at two locations on Pulau Gaya. Animal and bird life includes long-tailed macaques, bearded pig and pangolin (on Pulau Gaya), white-bellied sea eagle, pied hornbill, green heron, sandpipers, flycatchers and sunbirds.

There is a magnificent range of marine life because of the variety of the reefs surrounding the islands. The coral reefs are teaming with fish-tank exotica such as butterfly fish, Moorish idols, parrot fish, bat fish, razor fish, lion fish and stone fish – in stark contrast to the areas which have been depth-charged by Gaya's notorious dynamite fishermen.

Four of the five islands have excellent snorkelling and diving as well as jungle trails. The largest island, **Pulau Gaya**, was the site of the first British North Borneo Chartered Company settlement in the area in 1882. The settlement lasted only 15 years before being destroyed in a pirate attack. There is still a large settlement on the island on the promontory facing KK – but today it is a shanty town, populated mainly by Filipino immigrants (see page 431). On Pulau Gaya there are 20 km of marked trails including a plank-walk across a mangrove swamp. Police Bay has a beautiful shaded beach. **Accommodation A** *Gayana Resort Bay*, Lot 16, Ground Floor, Wisma Sabah, Jalan Tun Razak, T 245158, F 245168, for more information, east coast of the island, a/c chalets, restaurant (serves asian and western food), barbecue site, private beach, activities include diving, snorkelling, windsurfing, trekking in the jungle, fishing, yachting.

Pulau Sapi, the most popular of the island group for weekenders, also has good beaches and trails. It is connected to Pulau Gaya by a sandbar. A glass-bottomed boat is available here for hire for those who wish to view the coral and marine life; there are good day-use facilities. **Pulau Mamutik** is the smallest island but closer to the mainland and has a well-preserved reef off the northeast tip. **Pulau Manukan** is the site of the park headquarters and most of the park accommodation. It has good snorkelling to the south and east and a particularly good beach on the east tip; it is probably the nicest of all the islands but is heavily frequented by day trippers and rubbish is sometimes a problem. Marine sports facilities stretch to the hire of mask, snorkel and fins (RM15 plus RM50 deposit for the day); no sub-aqua gear available, swimming pool. The best reefs are off **Pulau Sulang**, which is less developed being a little bit further away. Unfortunately the beach here is full of rubbish and the island has a neglected air.

It is necessary to hire snorkel, mask and fins from boatmen at the KK jetty beforehand. Fishing with a hook and line is permitted but the use of spearguns and nets is prohibited.

Permits not necessary.

Park Headquarters on Pulau Manukan and ranger stations on Gaya, Sapi and Mamutik.

Park information

● Accommodation

Chalets and resthouses on Pulau Mamutik and Pulau Manukan. **NB** Rooms are significantly discounted during the week. **A+** (w/e)-**A** (weekdays) ***Resthouse***, Pulau Mamutik, under refurbishment, but will be open by the time this book goes to press and now managed by *Borneo Divers* of KK. **A** (w/e) **-B** (weekdays) ***Chalets***, Pulau Manukan, restaurant, pool, facilities including tennis and squash courts, football field, 1,500m jogging track and a diving centre. ***Chalets at Maluham Bay***, east of Police Bay, Pulau Gaya. Enquire at *Palace Hotel*, KK.

● Camping

It is possible to camp on any of the islands (obtain permission from the Sabah Parks Office in KK). Basic facilities on Pulau Mamutik.

● Places to eat

Excellent restaurant on Pulau Manukan. Pulau Mamutik and Pulau Sapi each have a small shop selling a limited range of very expensive food and drink. Cooked food on Pulau Sapi is sometimes in short supply. For Pulau Sulang, Sapi and Mamutik take all the water you need – there is no drinkable water supply here; shower and toilet water is only provided if there has been sufficient rain.

● Useful addresses

Park information: for reservations and more information on the park, contact *Coral Island Cruises*, Ground Floor, Wisma Sabah, PO Box 14527, KK, T 223490, F 223404; *Sea Quest Tours and Travel*, Wisma Merdeka, Phase 2, 2nd Flr, Lot B207, T 230943; or *Tanjung Aru Tours, Tanjung Aru Beach Hotel*, T 214215, F 217155.

● Transport

3-8 km offshore.

Sea Boat: most boats leave from the jetty opposite the *Hyatt Hotel*. Regular ferry services leave from the Jetty Taman Sabah (near the *Hyatt*) for Manukan at 0830, 1000, 1100, 1200, 1600 and return to KK 0730, 1030, 1130, 1700, cost of a return for adult is RM15 and for child is RM10. If you want to visit more than one island, a boat needs to be chartered, at a cost of about RM200, taking 12 passengers. It is possible to negotiate trips with local fishermen. Boats also leave from *Tanjung Aru Beach Hotel*.

SOUTH OF KOTA KINABALU

Travelling south from KK, the route crosses the Crocker Range to Tambunan. Continuing south the road passes through the logging town of Keningan and on to Tenom, where it is possible to take the North Borneo railway, which snakes down the Padas Gorge to Beaufort. The Padas River is the best place to go white-water rafting in Sabah. Few towns are worth staying in for long on this route but it is a scenic journey.

TAMBUNAN

The twisting mountain road that cuts across the **Crocker Range National Park** (see page 451) and over the Sinsuran Pass at 1,649m is very beautiful. There are dramatic views down over Kota Kinabalu and the islands beyond and glimpses of Mount Kinabalu to the northeast. The road itself, from KK to Tambunan, was the old bridle way that linked the west coast to the interior; inland communities traded their tobacco, rattan and other jungle produce for salt and iron at the coastal markets. The road passes through Penampang. Scattered farming communities raise hill rice, pineapples, bananas, mushrooms and other vegetables which are sold at road-side stalls, where wild and cultivated orchids can also be found. After descending from the hills the road enters the sprawling flood plain of Tambunan – the Pegalam River runs through the plain – which, at the height of the paddy season, is a magnificent patchwork of greens. The Tambunan area

Mat Salleh – fort-builder and folk hero

Mat Salleh was a Bajau, and son of a Sulu Chief, born in the court of the Sultan of Sulu. He was the only native leader to stand up against the increasingly autocratic whims of the North Borneo government as it sequestrated land traditionally belonging to tribal chiefs. Under the Chartered Company and the subsequent colonial administration, generations of school children were taught that Mat Salleh was a deplorable rabble-rouser and trouble-maker. Now Sabahans regard him as a nationalist hero.

In the British North Borneo Herald of 16 February 1899, it was reported that when he spoke, flames leapt from his mouth; lightening flashed with each stroke of his *parang* and when he scattered rice, the grains became wasps. He was said to have been endowed with 'special knowledge' by the spirits of his ancestors and was also reported to have been able to throw a buffalo by its horns.

In 1897 Mat Salleh raided and set fire to the first British settlement on Pulau Gaya (off modern-day Kota Kinabalu). For this, and other acts of sabotage, he was declared an outlaw by the Governor. A price tag of 700 Straits dollars was put on his head and an administrative officer, Raffles Flint, was assigned the unenviable task of tracking him down. Flint failed to catch him and Mat Salleh gained a reputation as a military genius.

Finally, the managing director of the Chartered Company, Scottish adventurer and former gun-runner William C Cowie, struck a deal with Mat Salleh and promised that his people would be allowed to settle peacefully in Tambunan – which at that time was not under Chartered Company control. After the negotiations Cowie wrote: "His manner and appearance made me aware that I was face to face with the Rob Roy of British North Borneo, the notorious Mat Salleh, whom I at once saluted with a *takek* [a greeting from an inferior]."

Half the North Borneo administration resigned as they considered Cowie's concessions outrageous. With it looking less and less likely that the terms of his agreement with Cowie would be respected, Mat Salleh retreated to Tambunan where he started building his fort; he had already gained a fearsome reputation for these stockades. West Coast Resident G Hewett described it as "the most extraordinary place and without [our] guns it would have been absolutely impregnable". Rifle fire could not penetrate it and Hewett blasted 200 shells into the fort with no noticeable effect. The stone walls were 2.5m thick and were surrounded by three bamboo fences, the ground in front of which was studded with row upon row of sharpened bamboo spikes. Hewett wrote: "...had we been able to form any idea of the external strength of the place we should never have attempted to rush in as we did." His party retreated having suffered four dead and nine wounded.

Mat Salleh had built similar forts all over Sabah, and the hearts of the protectorate's administrators must have sunk when they heard he was building one at Tambunan. A government expedition arrived in the Tambunan Valley on the last day of 1899. There was intensive fighting throughout Jan, with the government taking village after village, until at last, the North Borneo Constabulary came within 50m of Mat Salleh's fort. Its water supply had been cut off and the fort had been shelled incessantly for 10 days. Mat Salleh was trapped. On 31 January 1900 he was killed by a stray bullet which hit him in the left temple.

Rafflesia arnoldi: the largest flower in the world

The rafflesia (*Rafflesia arnoldi*), named after Stamford Raffles, is the largest flower in the world. The Swedish naturalist Eric Mjoberg wrote in 1930 on seeing the flower: "The whole phenomenon seems so amazing, so unfamiliar, so fantastic, that we are tempted to explain: such flowers cannot be real!". Stamford Raffles, who discovered the flower for Western science one hundred years earlier during his first sojourn at Bengkulu on the west coast of Sumatra, noted that it was "a full yard across, weighs fifteen pounds, and contains in the nectary no less than eight pints [of nectar]...". The problem is that the rafflesia does not flower for very long – only for a couple of weeks, usually between August and December. Out of these months there is usually nothing to see. The plant is in fact parasitic, so appropriately its scent is more akin to rotting meat than any perfume. Its natural habitat is moist, shaded areas.

is largely Kadazan/Dusun and the whole area explodes into life each May during the harvest festival when copious quantities of *lihing*, the famed local rice wine, are consumed and the Bobolians or high priestesses are still called upon to conduct various rituals. (There is a Lihing brewery inside the Tambunan Village Resort Centre.) The Tambunan District covers an area of 134,540 hectares and has a population of about 24,000. At an altitude of 650m to 900m, it enjoys a spring-like climate during much of the year.

Tambunan – or 'Valley of the Bamboo', as there are at least twelve varieties of bamboo to be found here – also lays claim to the Kitingan family. Joseph was Sabah's first Christian Chief Minister until deposed in March 1994. His brother, Jeffrey, was formerly head of the Sabah Foundation. He entered politics in 1994 on his release from detention on the peninsula. He had been charged under Malaysia's Internal Security Act of being a secessionist conspirator.

A modest plaque just outside Tambunan, among the ricefields and surrounded by peaceful kampung houses, commemorates the site of **Mat Salleh's fort**. Mat Salleh, now a nationalist folkhero, led a rebellion for 6 years against the Chartered Company administration until he was killed in 1900. There is not much left of his fort for visitors to inspect.

The Rafflesia Information Centre (T 087 774691), located at the roadside on the edge of a Forest Reserve that has been set aside to conserve this remarkable flower (see box). The Information Centre has a comprehensive and attractive display on the Rafflesia and its habitat and provides information on flowers in bloom. If trail maps are temporarily unavailable, ask the ranger to point out the site where blooms can be seen on the large relief model of the Forest Reserve at the back of the Information Centre. The blooming period of the flower is very short so to avoid disappointment, it may be worth phoning the Centre first. Open: Monday-Friday 0845-1245, 1400-1700, Saturday and Sunday 0800-1700. **Accommodation C** *Gunung Emas Highlands Resort*, Km 52 (about 7 km from the Rafflesia Centre) some dorm rooms (**E**), some very basic tree houses, a fresh climate and good views. Mini zoo and restaurant serving local food. *Getting there*: tkae the Rabunan or the Keningau minibus and then another bus from Tambunan.

Ahir Terjan Sensuron is a waterfall 4 km from Raffelesia Information Centre on the Tambunan-KK road (heading towards KK). From the road, it is a 45-minute walk to the waterfall.

A large **market** is held here every Thursday morning – on sale are tobacco, local musical instruments, clothing, strange edible jungle ferns and yeast used to make fermented rice wine. There are also bundles of a fragrant herb known as *tuhau*, a member of the ginger family that is made into a spicy condiment or sambal redolent of the jungle. A smaller market is held every Sunday in Kampung Toboh, north of Tambunan.

Excursions

Crocker Range National Park incorporates 139,919 hectares of hill and montane forest, which includes many species endemic to Borneo. It is the largest single totally protected area in Sabah. No visitors' facilities have yet been developed. But private development is taking place along the narrow strips of land each side of the KK-Tambunan road, which were unfortunately overlooked when the park was gazetted. A decrepit motel – complete with a horrifying menagerie – has sprung up at Sinsuran Pass and an outward bound school also has its headquarters here. *Getting there*: as for Tambunan. The **Mawah Waterfall** is reached by following the road north towards Ranau to Kampung Patau, where a sign beside the school on the left indicates a gravel road leading almost to the waterfall (*Mawah Airterjun*). *Getting there*: 15 minutes down road by car, 5-10 minutes walk along trail.

Gunung Trusmadi, 70 km southeast of KK, is the second highest mountain in Malaysia at 2,642m, but very few people climb it. There are two main routes to the top: the north route, which takes 4 days to the summit (and 3 days down) and the south route, which is harder but shorter – 2 days to the summit. Trusmadi is famous for its huge, and very rare, pitcher plant *Nepethes trusmadiensis*, which is only found on one spot on the summit ridge (see page 38). It is also known for its fantastic view north, towards Gunung Kinabalu, which rises above the Tambunan valley. There is a wide variety of vegetation on the mountain as it rises from dipterocarp primary jungle through oak montane forest with mossy forest near the summit and heath-like vegetation on top. The best time to climb is in March and it is advisable to take guides and porters for the tough climb (ask the District Officer in Tambunan). An expedition to Trusmadi requires careful planning – it should not be undertaken casually. A more detailed account of the two routes can be found in *Mountains of Malaysia – a practical guide and manual*, by John Briggs.

Local information

● Accommodation

Both hotels are out of town.

C *Tambunan Village Resort Centre (TVRC)*, signposted off the main road before the town located on both sides of the Pegalam River, collection of chalets and a 'longhouse' dormitory made of split bamboo. Restaurant, motel and entertainment centre (with karaoke and slot machines), hall and sports field. There are also a couple of retreat centres located about 10 minutes walk away.

C-D *Government Resthouse*, T 774339.

● Places to eat

The area is renowned for its rice wine (*lihing*). Visitors can watch it being brewed at the factory within the *TVRC (Tambunan Village Resort Centre)*.

● Shopping

Handicrafts: *Handicraft Centre* just before the Shell petrol station, for traditional weaving and basketry from the area.

Market: *Tamu* on Thur.

● Transport

90 km from KK.

Road Minibus: minibuses for Tambunan leave from the corner of Australia Place/Jln Tunku Abdul Rahman in KK. Those leaving Tambunan go from the centre of town by the mosque. Regular connections to KK, 1½ hours (RM10) and Ranau (RM10).

KENINGAU

The Japanese built fortifications around their base in Keningau during World War Two. It is now rather a depressing, shabby lumber town, smothered in smoke from the sawmills. The timber business in this area turned Keningau into a boom town in the 1980s and the population virtually doubled within a decade. The felling continues –

but there is not much primary forest left these days. There are huge logging camps all around the town and the hills to the west. Logging roads lead into these hills off the Keningau-Tenom road which are accessible by 4WD vehicles. It is just possible to drive across them to Papar, which is a magnificent route. **NB** Anyone attempting the drive should be warned to steer well clear of log-laden trucks as they make their way down the mountain.

Excursions

Murut villages: Sapulut is deep in Murut country and is accessible from Keningau by a rough road via Kampung Nabawan. At Sapulut, follow the river of the same name east through Bigor and Kampung Labang to Kampung Batu Punggul at the confluence of Sungai Palangan. **Batu Punggul** is a limestone outcrop protruding 200m above the surrounding forest, a half hour walk from the kampung; it can be climbed without any equipment, but with care; it is quite a dangerous climb but the view of the surrounding forest from the top is spectacular. Both the forest and the caves in and around Batu Punggul are worth exploring. Nearby is the recently discovered, but less impressive limestone outcrop, **Batu Tinahas**, which has huge caves with many unexplored passages. It is currently being surveyed and it is believed to have at least 3 levels of caves and tunnels. From Sapulut, it is a fairly painless exercise to cross the border into Kalimantan. A short stretch of road leads from Sapulut to Agis which is just a 4-hour boat ride from the border. There is even an immigration checkpoint at Pegalungan, a settlement en route. One particular longhouse is **Kampung Selungai**, only 30 minutes from Pegalungan. Here it is possible to see traditional boat builders at work, as well as weaving, mat making and beadwork. There are many rivers and longhouses in the area worth exploring. Given the luxury of time, it is a fascinating area where traditional lifestyles have not been much eroded. *Getting there*: it is possible to charter a minibus along the Nabawan road to Sapulut, where you can hire boats upriver. At Sapulut, ask for Lantir (the headman, or *kepala*). He will arrange the boat-trip upriver (which could take up to 2 days depending on the river) and accommodation in Murut longhouses, through the gloriously named *Sapulut Adventurism Tourism Travel Company*, run by Lantir and his mate. As in neighbouring Sarawak, these long upriver trips can be prohibitively expensive unless you are in a decent-sized group.

Local infomation

● Accommodation

A-B *Perkasa*, Jln Kampung Keningau, T 331045, F 334800, on the edge of town, a/c, Chinese restaurant, coffee house, health centre, comfortable rooms.

C *Rai*, Jln Masak, T 333188, some a/c, walking distance from the bus stop. **D-E** *Government Rest House*, T 331525, dorms (**F**) – book through Rural Development Corporation, T 088 428910.

● Places to eat

Seri Wah Coffee Shop, on the corner of the central square; selection of foodstalls.

● Shopping

Tamu on Sat.

● Transport

40 km from Tenom, 128 km from KK.

Air Connections with KK.

Road Minibus: minibuses leave from centre of town, by the market. Regular connections with KK and Tenom.

TENOM

Tenom, at the end of the North Borneo Railway, is a hilly inland town, with a population of about 4,000 – predominantly Chinese. Although it was the centre of an administrative district under the Chartered Company from the turn of the century, most of the modern town was built during the Japanese occupation in World War Two. It is in the heart of Murut country – but do not expect to see longhouses and Murut in traditional costume. Many Murut have moved into individual houses except in the remoter parts of the

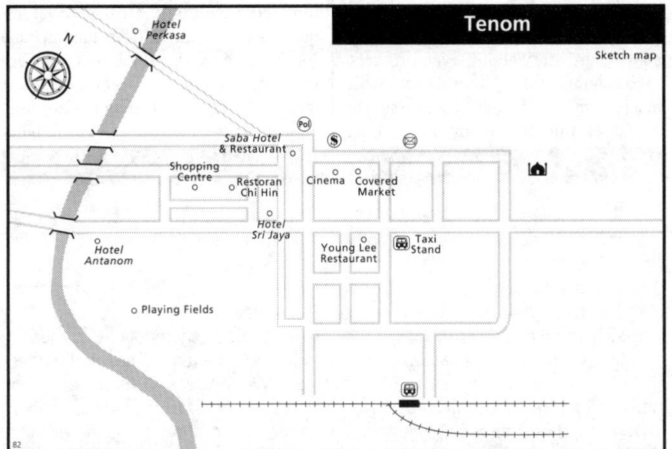

interior, and their modernized bamboo houses are often well equipped.

The surrounding area is very fertile and the main crops here are soya beans, maize and a variety of vegetables. Cocoa is also widely grown; the cocoa trees are often obscured under shade trees called *pokok belindujan*, which have bright pink flowers. The durians from Tenom (and Beaufort) are reckoned to be the best in Sabah.

Excursions

Murut villages There are many Murut villages surrounding Tenom all with their own churches. In some villages there is also an over-sized mosque or *surau*; the federal government has viewed the spread of Christianity in Sabah with some displeasure and there are financial incentives for anyone converting back to Islam. The best local longhouses are along the Padas River towards Sarawak at Kampung Marais and Kampung Kalibatang where blowpipes are still made. At Kemabong, about 25 km south of Tenom, the Murut community has a *lansaran* dancing trampoline. The wooden platform is sprung with bamboo and can support about 10 Murut doing a jig. *Getting there*: irregular minibuses.

Lagud Sebren Cocoa Research Station, 10 km northeast of Tenom, is in fact better known for its orchids, although it was originally a research centre for cocoa and rubber. Much of the work has been done by British botanist Tony Lamb who has turned the station into an important breeding centre for orchids. The flowering season is mainly between October and February. The centre also conducts research on tropical fruits and coffee. Open 0800-1300, Monday-Friday. **Accommodation E** *Rumah Rehat Lagud Sebren* (Orchid Research Station Resthouse), 5 km from the centre, a/c. *Getting there*: minibus from main road; if driving, take the road over the railway tracks next to the station and head down the valley.

Batu Bunatikan Lumuyu (rock carvings), are at Kuala Tomani near Kampung Tomani, 40 km south of Tenom. A huge boulder, now protected from the elements by a corrugated tin roof, is carved with mysterious, distorted faces. Swirling lines, etched into the rock, depict various facial features as well as feet, a bird and a snake. The rock was discovered by villagers clearing land for agriculture around the river Lumuyu in April 1971. The Sabah State Museum in KK has no idea what the patterns represent or how old they are. The local explanation is an absurd story about seven brothers, one of whom is killed; the other six doodle on a rock in their bereaved depression as they head into the mountains to bury him. Disappointing. *Getting there*: requires a 4WD vehicle: from Tenom, head south, crossing the Padas River at Tomani. After 2 km, turn right; follow this track for 20 km, through Kampung Kungkular to Kampung Ulu Tomani.

The railway which ran out of steam

In the last years of the 19th century, William Cowie, the managing director of the North Borneo Chartered Company, had a vision. With Governor Beaufort, he outlined his ambitious plans for a Trans-Borneo Railway, cutting through 200 km of dense jungle, from Brunei Bay to Sandakan, straight through the interior of North Borneo. Work started at Weston on Brunei Bay in 1896 and two years later, the stretch of line linking the new township and Beaufort triumphantly opened.

But A J West – the railway engineer who humbly named the new town after himself – somehow overlooked the fact that Weston was surrounded by an impenetrable mangrove swamp, not an ideal location for a railway terminus or port. Two alternative sites were toyed with before the stretch of narrow land opposite Pulau Gaya was finally selected as the site for the new terminus in 1899. It was thought to be a promising site for a town as it had a sheltered harbour. They called it Jesselton.

But Cowie's visionary railway project – and the innovative telegraph line that was to run alongside the track – was to be a costly undertaking. The administration, headed by Governor Beaufort, levied a new tax on rice to pay for it: a move which proved disastrously unpopular. Chinese retailers and tribal chiefs petitioned London to intervene – but to no avail. Historians believe the North Borneo Railway indirectly sparked the 6-year Mat Salleh rebellion (see page 449).

The 92 km line between Jesselton and Beaufort started operating in 1905. The track was pushed into the interior at the same time, and on 5 April 1905 the first train steamed into Tenom. The line went on to the railhead at Melalap, 16 km further up the valley. But that was as far as the 186 km 'trans-Borneo railway' ever got – it seems that after struggling up the Padas Gorge from Beaufort, the prospect of building another 200 km of track was too much to bear. The idea was abandoned. The towns of Papar, Beaufort and Tenom however, became totally dependent on the railway. The Chartered Company administration refused to build roads in an effort to force people to use it.

Oscar Cook, a former District Officer in the North Borneo Civil Service, served in Tenom in 1912, and recorded his journey from Beaufort in his 1923 book, *Borneo: the Stealer of Hearts*. "Normally the journey of about 30 miles took 3 hours, but one always considered it lucky to reach one's destination only an hour late... The route twisted and turned to such an extent, as the line followed its precarious course along the river bank, that... passengers in the front portion could almost put their hands out of the windows and shake those of passengers in the rear. On wet days up certain grades passengers have even been known to descend and help push the train over the most slippery and steepest gradients, while at one watering place chocks of wood were invariably put under the engine wheels to prevent the train from slowly slipping backwards!"

The train, now pulled by a diesel engine, still creeps along the 45 km narrow-gauge track, and the 2½ hour trip is well worth it.

Outside Kampung Ulu Tomani, turn right just before the river. Follow the track for 1½ km. At the point where a stream crosses the track, take the footpath to the rock carvings (20 minutes). An HEP station was built on the Tenom River about 15 years ago; the power it generates supplies Tenom and all the surrounding districts.

Local information

● Accommodation

Prices: L over RM500; **A+** RM260-500; **A** RM130-260; **B** RM65-130; **C** RM40-65; **D** RM20-40; **E** RM10-20; **F** Below RM10

Tenom Hotel and *Sri Jaya Hotel* are both within walking distance of the bus stop.

B ***Perkasa***, top of the hill above the town (RM3 taxi ride) (PO Box 225), T 735811, F 736134, a/c, restaurant, the *Tenom Perkasa* (one of a chain of three – the others are at Keningau and Kundasang) is a large, modern hotel, 7-storeys high, commanding superb views over Tenom and surrounding countryside. Rooms are spacious, carpeted, attractively furnished, with a/c, en suite bathroom, TV. As guests are few and far between, the restaurant has a limited but well-priced selection of Chinese and Western dishes. Staff are friendly and helpful in organizing local sightseeing, recommended.

C ***Hotel Antanom***, on the road to Tomani, slightly outside centre, recently refurbished, good selection of rooms from basic to a/c comfort, no en suite bathrooms.

D ***Sabah***, Block L, Shop No 91, Jln Datuk Yaseen, PO Box 14, T 735534, only 6 rooms in this very decent hotel, some rooms with a/c, definitely the best place to stay in budget range. **D** ***Hotel Sri Jaya***, PO Box 47, T 735077, a competitor to the *Sabah Hotel*, total 12 rooms all with a/c, shared bathroom, basic but clean and recently tiled.

D ***Sri Jaya***, Main St, T 736689, a/c. **D** ***Tenom***, Jln Tun Datu Mustapha, T 736378, fan only, restaurant, no attached bath, roof terrace.

● Places to eat

Prices: ♦♦♦♦ over RM40; ♦♦♦ RM13-40; ♦♦ RM5-13; ♦ under RM5

♦♦***Jolly***, near the station, serves western food (including lamb chops) and karaoke. ♦♦***Restaurant Curry Emas***, which specializes in monitor lizard claypot curries, dog meat and wild cat. ♦♦***Sabah***, Jln Datuk Yaseen, Muslim Indian food, clean and friendly. ♦♦***Sapong***, *Perkasa Hotel*, local and western. ♦♦***Y&L (Young & Lovely) Food & Entertainment***, Jln Sapong (2 km out of town), noisy but easily the best restaurant in Tenom, it serves mainly Chinese food: freshwater fish (steamed *sun hok* – also known as *ikan hantu*) and venison, these can be washed down with the local version of *air limau* (or *kitchai*) which comes with dried plums, there is a giant screen which was shipped in to allow Tenomese to enjoy the 1990 Football World Cup, recommended. ♦***Yong Lee Restaurant***, coffee shop serving cheap Chinese fare in town centre. ♦***Restoran Chi Hin***, another Chinese coffee shop.

Foodstalls: *Gerai Makanan*, above the market.

● Shopping

Tamu on Sun.

● Transport

140 km from KK, 45 km from Beaufort.

Train Leaves four times a day and takes about 3 hours to Beaufort and another 2½ hours to Tanjung Aru.

Road Minibus: minibuses leave from centre of town by the market. Regular connections with Keningau and KK 4 hours. Minibuses to Keningau leave from rail station after a train has arrived.

Sipitang, located on the coast, is a sleepy town with little to offer the traveller apart from a smallish supermarket and the *Shangsan Hotel* (T 821800), in the **B-C** price category, which has fairly comfortable rooms with a/c and TV. Cheaper, but much dirtier rooms are available in the *Hotel Lian Hin*, a few doors along. There is the ubiquitous coffee shop in the same street and a line of minibuses and taxis along the waterfront. The jetty for ferries to Labuan is a 10-minute walk away from the centre.

BEAUFORT

This small sleepy, unexciting town is named after British Governor P Beaufort of the North Borneo Company, who was a lawyer and was appointed to the post despite having no experience of the east or of administration. He was savaged by Sabahan historian KG Tregonning as "the most impotent Governor North Borneo

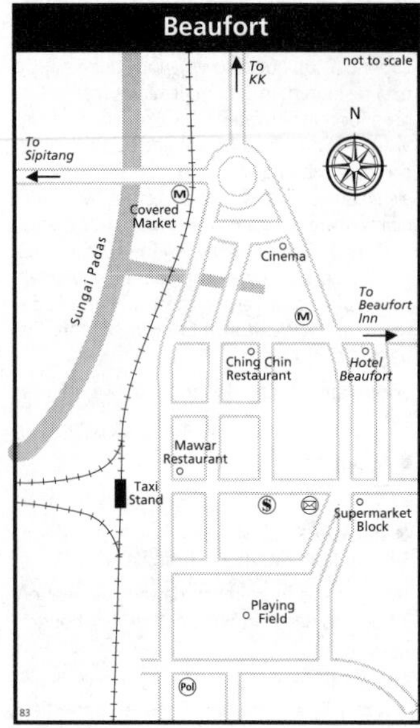

ever acquired and who, in the manner of nonentities, had a town named after him." Beaufort is a quaint town, with riverside houses built on stilts to escape the constant flooding of the Padas River.

Local information

● Accommodation

Beaufort has a poor selection of hotels, all roughly the same and slightly over-priced although rooms are a/c and have attached bathrooms.

C ***Beaufort***, centre of town, T 211911, a/c. **C** ***Beaufort Inn***, Lot 19-20 Lochung Park, T 211911, a/c. **C** ***Mandarin***, Lot 38, Jln Beaufort Jaya, T 212800, a/c. **C** ***Padas***, riverfront by the bridge (opposite the fish market), T 211441, a/c, restaurant, not as nice as the Beaufort.

● Places to eat

♦♦***Jin Jin Restaurant***, behind *Beaufort Hotel*, Chinese, popular with locals. ***Beaufort Bakery***, behind *Beaufort Hotel*, "freshness with every bite".

♦***Ching Chin Restaurant***, Chinese coffee shop in town centre.

● Banks & money changers

Hongkong Bank & Standard Chartered in centre of town.

● Post & telecommunications

Area code: 087.

General Post Office & Telekom: next to Hongkong Bank.

● Shopping

Tamu on Sat.

● Transport

90 km from KK.

Train The KK-Tenom line passes through Beaufort: Tenom, 2½ hours, KK, 3 hours.

Road Minibus: minibuses meet the train, otherwise leave from centre of town. Regular connections with KK, 2 hours.

To Sarawak Sipitang is south of Beaufort and the closest town in Sabah to the Sarawak border. It is possible to take minibuses from Beaufort to Sipitang (the road is under reconstruction, with a new stretch being added to Weston – take minibus or taxi with a/c if roadworks are still underway as it is too dusty to travel with windows open) and from there on to Merapok in Sarawak, 1 hour. There is an immigration checkpoint at Sipitang. From Sipitang there are also regular boats to Labuan, for reservations T 087 822350/422124.

PULAU LABUAN

The Sultan of Brunei ceded the 92 sq km island to the British crown in 1846 (see page 538). The island had a superb deep water harbour. Labuan promised an excellent location from which the British could engage the pirates which were terrorizing the Northwest Borneo coast. Labuan also had coal, which could be used to service steamships. Sarawak's Rajah James Brooke became the island's first governor in 1846; 2 years later it was declared a free port. It also became a penal colony: long-sentence convicts from Hong Kong were put to work on the coal face and in the jungle – clearing roads. The island was little more than a malarial swamp and its inept colonial administration was perpetually plagued by fever and liver disorders. Its nine drunken civil servants provided a gold mine of eccentricity for the novelists Joseph Conrad and Somerset Maugham.

By the 1880s ships were already by-passing the island, and the tiny colony began to disintegrate. In 1881 William Hood Treacher moved the capital of the new territory of British North Borneo from Labuan to Kudat. And 8 years later, the Chartered Company was asked to take over the administration of the island. In 1907 it became part of the Straits Settlements, along with Singapore, Malacca (Melaka) and Penang. In 1946 Labuan became a part of British North Borneo and was later incorporated into Sabah as part of the Federation of Malaysia in 1963.

Datuk Harris is thought to own half the island (including the *Hotel Labuan*). As Chief Minister, he offered the island as a gift to the federal government in 1984 in exchange for a government undertaking to bail out his industrial projects and build up the island's flagging economy. The election of a Christian government in Sabah in 1986 proved an embarrassment to Malaysian Prime Minister Dr Mahathir Mohamad: making it Malaysia's only non-Muslim-ruled state. As a result, Labuan has assumed strategic importance as a Federal Territory, wedged between Sabah and Sarawak. It is used as a staging post for large garrisons of the Malaysian army, navy and air force.

In declaring Labuan a tax haven – or, more properly, an International Off-shore Financial Centre – the Malaysian government set out its vision of Labuan becoming the Bermuda of the Asia-Pacific for the 21st century. More than 250 off-shore banks, insurance firms and trust companies had set up operations on the island by mid-1994. The island has attracted loans and deposits of more than US$1.6bn. Critics and sceptics have long pointed to the fact that the standard trimmings of a tax haven are still hundreds of millions of dollars away, but a new Financial park complex with four 16-flr office towers has recently been completed. And with new hotels including the Sheraton and the Waterfront which overlooks a brand new marina, springing up too, it seems that Labuan's days of being a sleepy rural backwater are over.

Today the island has a population of about 30,000 – not including 10,000 Filipino refugees, with about 21 different ethnic groups. The island is the centre of a booming 'barter' trade with the South Philippines – the island is home to a clutch of so-called string vest millionaires, who have grown rich on the trade. In Labuan, 'barter' is the name given to smuggling. The Filipino traders leaving the Philippines simply over-declare their exports (usually copra, hardwood, rotan and San Miguel beer) and under-declare the imports (Shogun jeeps, Japanese hi-fi and motorbikes) – all ordered through duty-free Labuan. With such valuable cargoes, the traders are at the mercy of pirates in the South China Sea. To get round this, they arm themselves with M-16s, bazookas and shoulder-launched missiles. This ammunition is confiscated on their arrival in Labuan, stored in a marine police warehouse, and given back to them for the return trip.

Away from the bustling barter jetty, Labuan Town (this name has largely superseded its name of Port Victoria) is a dozy, unremarkable Chinese-Malaysian mix of shophouses, coffee shops and karaoke bars. There is a new US$11mn mosque, and a manicured golf course. Illegal cockfights are staged every Sunday afternoon. There is an old brick coal chimney at Tanjung Kubong – or coal point – with a good view of the east coast. It was built in 1847 by the British who needed fuel for their steamships on the Far Eastern trade route. On the west coast there are pleasant beaches, mostly lined with kampungs. There is a large Japanese war memorial on the east coast and a vast, and well tended, Allied war cemetery

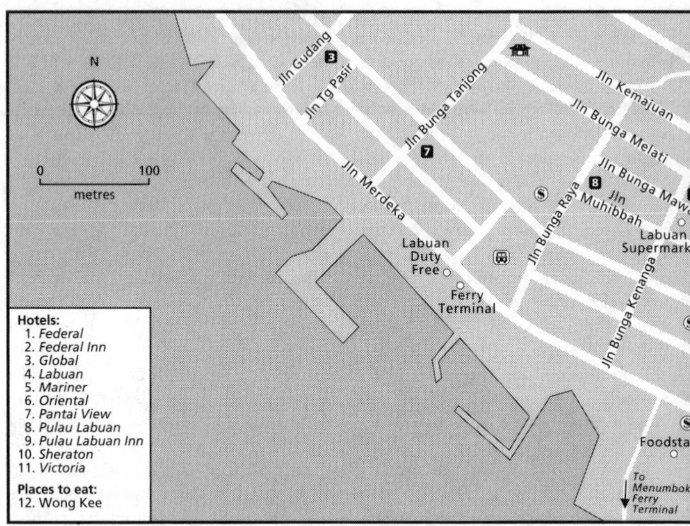

between the town and the airport with over 3,000 graves most of which are unknown soldiers. In 1995 a commemoration service was held at the cemetery to mark the 50th anniversary of Allied Forces landing in Labuan. It was attended by veterans from the US, Australia and Britain.

Excursions

Boat trips can be made to the small islands around Labuan, although only by chartering a fishing vessel. The main islands are Pulau Papan (a boring island between Labuan and the mainland), Pulau Kuraman, Pulau Rusukan Kecil (known locally as '*the floating lady*' for obvious reasons) and Pulau Rusukan Besar ('*floating man*'). The latter three have good beaches and coral reefs (see *Diving*, below) but none has any facilities.

Local information

● Accommodation

Prices: L over RM500; **A+** RM260-500; **A** RM130-260; **B** RM65-130; **C** RM40-65; **D** RM20-40; **E** RM10-20; **F** Below RM10

A+ ***Manikar Beach Resort***, Jln Batu Manikar, T 418700, F 418740, 20 minutes from town centre (complimentary shuttle) on the northwest tip of Labuan, although local ex-pats like to comment that things have slipped since it was taken over by the *Sheraton*, it is a stylish reosrt built with polished wood (the owner is a timber tycoon), set in 15 ha of gardens, dotted with tall palms which reach down to the beach. The 235 rooms, all sea-facing with generous balconies, are very spacious, paved with stone, tastefully furnished, complete with a/c, mini-bar, TV, in-house video, tea and coffee making facilities. Large pool set at sea level with swim-up bar, separate children's pool, fitness centre, tennis, play-room, business centre, duty-free shop. The beach is regularly cleaned and sprayed so sandflies are not a problem, but the sea is not recommended for swimming due to jellyfish. Restaurant with indoor and outdoor dining areas, excellent quality food, good value theme buffet nights. Enquire about discounts offered on room rates – 50% discount for bookings and payment 14 days in advance. **A+** ***Tiara Labuan***, Jln Tanjung Batu, PO Box 80537, T 414300, F 410195, on the west coast next to the golf course, 5-minute taxi ride from town centre, beautiful hotel and serviced apartments surrounding a large lotus pond and deep blue pool complete with jacuzzi. Built onto Adnan Kashoggi's old mansion, the property has an Italian feel with terracotta

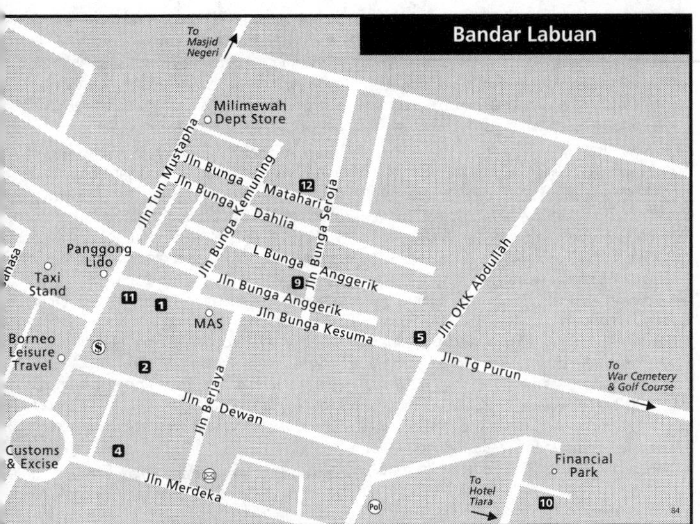

tiles, putty pink stone, a glorious gilt fountain, and long shady arcades. The original mansion now holds the reception, restaurant (food mediocre), and acres of opulent lounge including an Arab lounge which has low sofas, hubbly-bubbly pipes and a marble fountain. All 25 rooms, and also the 48 serviced apartments (one or two bedroom) are complete with a/c, TV, mini-bar, ring electric hob, cooker hood and sink, and a living room. The Tanjung Batu beach, just across the road, is rather muddy, but good for walks when the tide is out. The *Labuan Beach Restaurant* is here too. On the whole, holiday-makers opt for the larger hotels, especially families, as the *Tiara* has no organized activities nor kiddy pool, but this is partly what makes it a haven of tranquility, recommended. **A+** ***Waterfront Labuan Financial Hotel***, 1 Jln Wawasan, T 418111, F 413468, this new property, overlooking the new yacht marina (and also an industrial seascape) has cultivated a marina-look combined with the atmosphere of being on a luxury cruise. It has over 200 rooms, all with a/c, mini-bar, TV, tea and coffee making facilities and opulent fittings. The main restaurant, in sea-faring spirit, called the Clipper, serves western and local food, there is also a bar, the Anchorage, which has live entertainment every evening except Mon. Other facilities include pool, tennis and health centre. The hotel also manages the marina with its total of 50 berthing spaces each of which has internationally rated facilities. The Harbour Master not only oversees the running of the Marina but also organizes yacht charters and luxury cruises, recommended.

A *Sheraton Labuan*, Lot TL 462, Jln Merdeka, T 422000, F 422222, another new block, cream with green roofs, built opposite the Financial Park complex, this deluxe city hotel has 183 rooms all with spacious bathrooms, a/c, TV, in-house movies channel, mini-bar, tea and coffee making facilities, iron and ironing board. Other facilities include pool with whirlpool and swim-up bar, business centre (in-room personal computer and faxes also available). Decor has all the opulence of a Sheraton with a vast lobby, clad in marble and dripping with chandeliers, which resounds to live pianoforte in the afternoons, and classy food outlets including Victoria's Brasserie for European fare and The Emperor Chinese Restaurant which specializes in Cantonese food. Staff are professional and offer top service with a smile, recommended. **A** *Labuan*, Jln Merdeka, T 412502, F 415355, a/c, restaurant, large concrete block on edge of town, grand lobby with an arcade of shops, rooms have seen better days but have a/c, in-house video and attached bathroom, Chinese and Japanese restaurants, coffee house and the Rock Café Fun Pub, pool. **A-B** *Mariner*,

Jln Tg Purun (on crossroads opposite police HQ), T 418822, F 418811, a/c, restaurant, opened 1993, so among Labuan's newest offerings, rooms well-equipped (including mini fridge, a/c, TV, in-house video and attached bathroom), good coffee house; generous discounts available on request.

B *Federal Inn*, Jln Dewan, T 411711, F 411337, new, smart hotel, clean and reasonable, 39 rooms with a/c, attached bathroom, TV, in-house video and mini-bar. **B** ***Oriental***, U0123-4, Lot 33 and 34, Jln Bunga Mawar, T 419019, F 419408, reception on 1st Flr, clean, tiled rooms with a/c, TV, private bathroom. **B** *Pulau Labuan*, 27-28 Jln Muhibbah, T 416288, F 416255, a/c, restaurant (*Golden Palace Restaurant* downstairs). ***Global***, U0017, Jln OKK Awang Besar (near market), T 425201, F 425180, brand new and best value for money in town, a/c, mini-bar, tea and coffee, TV, in-house video, complimentary shuttle to ferry and airport, recommended. **B-C** ***Federal***, Jln Bunga Kesuma, T 411239, F 411337, a/c, restaurant, all rooms have a/c, TV, in-house video, mini-bar fridge, complimentary tea and coffee maker, pink and pastels colour scheme, Chinese-run catering mainly for business people, clean, good value, run by same management as *Federal Inn*. **B-C** ***Pantai View***, Lot 119 and 120, Jln OKK Awang Besar, T 411339, F 412793, a/c, basic, not very clean and not much of a view of the *pantai*. **B-C** ***Pulau Labuan Inn***, Lot 8, Jln Bunga Dahlia, T 416833, F 441750, the down-market sister of the *Pulau Labuan*, spotlessly clean but small a/c rooms. **B-C** ***Victoria***, Jln Tun Mustapha, T 412411, F 412550, one of the oldest hotels in Labuan, pale pink exterior with white stucco decorated lobby, 46 rooms, a/c, private bath, recommended.

C ***Kelab Golf***, Jln Tanjung Batu, a/c, restaurant, 6 simple but pleasant rooms in the clubhouse, 3 have a view down the manicured fairways. **C** ***Pertama***, Hujong Pasir, Jln OKK Awang Besar (next to fish market), T 413311, a/c.

● Places to eat

Prices: ♦♦♦♦ over RM40; ♦♦♦ RM13-40; ♦♦ RM5-13; ♦ under RM5

Malay: ♦♦***Restoran Zainab***, Jln Merdeka (opposite duty free shop), Indian/Muslim. ***Seri Malindo***, next to *Federal Inn*, mixture of Malay and western food.

Chinese: ♦♦♦♦***The Emperor Chinese Restaurant***, Sheraton Labuan, top-class Chinese cuisine, Cantonese specialities, fresh seafood, special *dim sum* on Sun and public holidays, recommended. ♦♦♦***Golden Palace***, 27 Jln Muhibbah. ♦♦♦***Wong Kee***, Lot 5 and 6, Jln Kemuning, large, brightly lit restaurant with a/c, good steamboat, recommended. ♦***Café Imperial***, Chinese coffee shop behind *Federal Hotel*, better than average coffee shop fare.

International: ♦♦♦***Country Deli Restaurant and Wine Bar***, Lot 25, Block D, Jati Commercial Centre, T 410410, Malaysian pizza, take-aways possible. ♦♦♦***Labuan Beach***, Jln Tanjung Batu, T 415611, International and local cuisine, breezy location on sea shore, food not special but ambience makes up for it, as does very well chilled draft Carlesberg, recommended. ***Victoria's Brasserie***, *Sheraton Labuan*, European brasserie-style, good theme buffets as well as á la carte, prides itself on its 'show kitchen concept', recommended. ***The Clipper***, *Waterfront Labuan Financial Hotel*, 24-hour up-market coffee shop with local and western cuisine, recommended.

Seafood: ♦♦♦***Restaurant Pulau Labuan***, Lot 27-28, Jln Muhibbah, smart interior complete with chandeliers, a/c, fresh fish sold by weight – good tiger prawns, recommended. ♦♦♦***Sung Hwa Restaurant***, 2nd Flr, Ujong Pasir, Jln OKK Awang Besar (across from fish market and above Kedai Kopi South Sea, recommended. ♦♦***New Sung Hwa Seafood***, Jln Ujong Pasir, PCK Building, among best value seafood restaurants in Malaysia, chilli prawns, grilled stingray steak recommended, no menu, recommended.

Foodstalls: above wet market and at the other end of town, along the beach next to the *Island Club*. There is an area of stalls on Jln Muhibbah opposite the end of Jln Bahasa, next to the cinema and there are a few hawker stalls behind *Hotel Labuan*.

● Airline offices

MAS, Wisma Kee Chia, Jln Kesuma, T 412263.

● Banks & money changers

Hongkong, Jln Merdeka; **Standard Chartered**, Jln Tanjung Kubang (next to *Victoria Hotel*); **Syarikat K Abdul Kader Money-changer**.

● Post & telecommunications

Area code: 087.
General Post Office: Jln Merdeka.

● Sports

Diving: *Borneo Divers*, Lot 28, Lazenda Commercial Centre, Phase II (next to waterfront), T 415867, F 413454. Specializes in 2-days packages diving on shipwrecks off Labuan for certified scuba divers, there are four wrecks in total, each wreck costs about RM100, 2 day packages with accommodation at the Manikar are possible; *Ocean Sports*, 134 Jln OKK Awang Besar, T 415389, F 411911/415844. Offers 5-days full-time scuba courses for RM700 and reef dives on the nearby islands of Pulau Kuraman, Pulau Rusukan Kecil and Pulau Rusukan Besar. These islands have good beaches but no facilities. Diving around Pulau Papan is not very exciting and the water is often cloudy because of river silt. The reefs around Labuan suffer from the after-effects of the Allied bombing during WW2 and from Filipino dynamite fishermen. *Ocean Sports*, in association with Coral Island Cruises in KK takes groups of divers 18 hours into the South China Sea to Terumba Layang Layang, an atoll on the edge of the disputed Spratly group, reputed to be "even better than Sipadan". A 6-days package costs around RM2,000 pp (see also page 445).

Golf: *Kelab Golf*, Jln Tanjung Batu. Magnificent 9-hole golf course. Visitors may be asked to see proof of handicap or a membership card from your own club. Non-members pay RM30 a round on weekdays, RM50 on weekends. There are also tennis courts at the golf club and a swimming pool which can be used by visitors for a modest fee.

● Shopping

Labuan Duty Free, Bangunan Terminal, Jln Merdeka, T 411573. 142 years after Rajah James Brooke first declared Labuan a free port, *Labuan Duty Free* opened in Oct 1990. The island's original duty free concession did not include alcohol or cigarettes, but the new shop was given special dispensation to sell them. 2 months later the government extended the privilege to all shops on the island, which explains the absurd existence of a duty free shop on a duty free island. The shop claims to be the cheapest duty free in the world, however, you will find competitively priced shops in town too, including Monegain. It can undercut most other outlets on the island due to the volume of merchandise it turns over: more than RM1mn a month. The shop owes its success to Filipino 'barter traders' who place bulk purchase orders for VCRs or hundreds of thousands of dollars' worth of Champion cigarettes. These are smuggled back to Zamboanga and Jolo and find their way onto Manila's streets within a week. Brunei's alcohol-free citizens also keep the shop in business – they brought nearly RM2mn worth of liquor from Labuan into Brunei within the first 3 months of the shop opening. **NB** If you plan to take duty-free goods into Sabah or Sarawak, you have to stay on Labuan for a minimum of 72 hours. Behind Jln Merdeka and before the fish market, there is a congregation of corrugated tin-roofed shacks which houses a small ***Filipino textile and handicraft market*** and an interesting ***wet market***.

Supermarkets *Milimewah*, Lot 22-27 Lazenda Commercial Centre, Phase II, Jln Tun Mustapha, department store with supermarket on ground floor; ***Financial Park***, Jln Merdeka, shopping complex with Milimewah supermarket; ***Thye Ann Supermarket***, central position below *Federal Inn*; ***Labuan Supermarket***, Jln Bunga Kenanga, centre of town.

● Transport

7 km from the mainland.

Local Bus: local buses around the island leave from Jln Bunga Raya. **Taxi**: old Singapore NTUC cabs are not in abundant supply, but easy enough to get at the airport and from outside *Hotel Labuan*. It is impossible to get a taxi after 1900.

Air 5 km from town. Regular connections with KK, Miri. The MAS office is in the *Federal Hotel* block, T 412263.

Sea Boat: from the Bangunan Terminal Feri Penumpang (T 411573) next to the duty free shop on Jln Merdeka. Regular connections with Memumbuk every 45 minutes. Speedboats leave every few minutes. There are two speedboats every day to Limbang (Sarawak); enquiries, T 22908. Three boats a day to Kota Kinabalu, 2½ hours. One express boat daily to Sipitang (Sabah mainland, see page 455).

International connections: on weekends and public holidays in Brunei the ferries are packed-out and it is a scramble to get a ticket. It is possible to reserve tickets to Brunei at the following agents: ***Victoria Agency House*** (T 412332) (next to the *Federal Hotel* in Wisma Kee Chia), ***Borneo Leisure Travel***, T 410251, F 419989 (opposite Standard Chartered) and the booking office at the back of the Sports Toto on Jln Merdeka all deal with advanced bookings to Brunei. ***Broadwin Agency***, also on Jln Merdeka, takes bookings for ferries to Malaysian destinations. Five express boats leave Labuan for Brunei (Bandar Seri Begawan). They depart at 0800, 1300, 1400, 1500 Mon-Sat, 0800, 1000 and 1200, Sun, 1½ hours.

PAPAR

Formerly a sleepy Kadazan village, about 40 km south of KK, Papar is developing fast. In *bandar lama* (the old town) there are several rows of quaint wooden shophouses, painted blue and laid out along spacious boulevards lined with travellers' palms. There is a large market in the centre of town. The Papar area is famous for its fruit and there is a good *tamu* every Sunday.

There is a scenic drive between Papar and KK, with paddy fields and jungle lining the roadside. The nearby beach at Pantai Manis is good for swimming and can be reached easily from Papar; it is also possible to make boat trips up the Papar River, which offers gentle rapids for less-energetic white-water-rafters. White-water rafting trips can be organized through tour agents in KK (see page 440).

Excursion

Pulau Tiga National Park is 48 km south of KK. Declared a Forest Reserve in 1933, the 15,864 hectares park is made up of three islands, Pulau Tiga, Kalampunian Damit and Kalampunian Besar. Pulau Tiga's three low hills were all formed by mud volcanoes. The last big eruption was in 1941, which was heard 160 km away and covered the island in a layer of boiling mud. The dipterocarp forest on the islands is virtually untouched and they contain species not found on other west coast islands, such as a poisonous amphibious sea snake (*Laticauda colubrina*), which comes ashore on Pulau Kalampunian Damit to lay its eggs. Rare birds such as the pied hornbill (*Anthracoceros convexus*) and the megapode (*Megapodus freycinet*) are found here, as well as flying foxes, monitor lizards, wild fruit trees and mangrove forest. A network of trails, marked at 50 meter intervals leads to various points of interest. *Best time to visit*: between February and April, when it is slightly drier and the seas are calmer. **Park Headquarters** on the south side of Pulau Tiga, is mainly used as a botanical and marine research centre and tourism is not vigorously promoted; as a result there are no special facilities for tourists. **Accommodation**: 2 cabins (2 people/cabin) at RM60/cabin; there is also a hostel **(D)** that can accommodate 32 people. Accommodation must be booked in advance through the Sabah Parks Office in KK; no food is provided. It is possible to camp. *Getting there*: boats from Kuala Penyu fishing village (at the tip of the Klias Peninsula), 45 minutes.

Pantai Manis, just outside Papar, is a 3 km-long stretch of golden sand, with a deep lagoon.

Local information

● Accommodation

A ***Beringgis Beach Resort***, Km 26, Jln Papar, Kampung Beringgis, Kinarut, T 752333, F 752999, a/c, hot baths, car rental, conference halls, private beach, pool, watersports, tours and sports facilities.

C ***Seri Takis Lodging House***, Papar New Town, T 219173, a/c, very clean, friendly management. **C-D** ***Sea Side Travellers Inn***, Km 20 Papar Highway, Kinarut (no T/F), some a/c, restaurant, range of accommodation from dorms to detached bungalows; breakfasts included, pleasant location off the beach, 500m way KK-Papar. ***Papar Lodging House***, Papar New Town.

● Places to eat

Several run-of-the-mill coffee shops and restaurants in the old town.

♦***Seri Takis***, Papar New Town (below the lodging house), Padang food; ***Sugar Buns Bakery***, old town.

● Shopping

Tamu on Sun.

● Transport

40 km south of KK.

Road Minibus: leave from Bandar Lama area. Regular connections with KK, 1 hour and Beaufort, 1 hour.

THE NORTH AND GUNUNG KINABALU PARK

From KK, the route heads north to the sleepy Bajau town of Kota Belud which wakes up on Sunday for its colourful *tamu* market. Near the northernmost tip of the state is Kudat, the former state capital. The region north of KK is a more interesting area with Gunung Kinabalu always in sight. From Kota Belud, the mountain looks completely different. It is possible to see its tail, sweeping away to the east and its western flanks, which rise out of the rolling coastal lowlands.

KOTA BELUD

The town is in a beautiful location, nestling in the foothills of Mount Kinabalu on the banks of the Tempasuk River. It is the heart of Bajau country – the so-called 'cowboys of the East'. The first Bajau to migrate to Sabah were pushed into the interior, around Kota Belud. They were originally a seafaring people but then settled as farmers in this area. The famed Bajau horsemen wear jewelled costumes, carry spears and ride bareback on ceremonial occasions. The ceremonial headdresses worn by the horsemen – called *dastars* – are woven on backstrap looms by the womenfolk of Kota Belud. Each piece takes 4 to 6 weeks to complete. Traditionally, the points of the headdress were stiffened using wax – these days, strips of cardboard are inserted into the points. Modern Kota Belud is a busy little town, but of little obvious interest to most tourists.

The largest **tamu** (traditional open air market) in Sabah is held every Sunday in Kota Belud (behind the mosque), starting at 0600. Visitors are strongly recommended to get there early. A mix of races – Bajau, Kadazan/Dusun, Rungus, Chinese, Indian and Malay – come to sell their goods and it is a social occasion as much as it is a market. Aside from the wide variety of food and fresh produce on sale, there is a weekly water buffalo auction at the entrance to the tamu.

This is the account of a civil servant, posted to the KB district office in 1915:

"The tamu itself is a babel and buzz of excitement; in little groups the natives sit and spread their wares out on the ground before them; bananas, langsats, pines and bread-fruit; and, in season, that much beloved but foul-smelling fruit the Durian. Mats and straw-hats and ropes; fowls, ducks, goats and buffaloes; pepper, *gambia sirih* and vegetables; rice (padi), sweet potatoes, *ubi kayu* and indian-corn; dastars and handkerchiefs, silver and brass-ware. In little booths, made of wood, with open sides and floors of split bamboos and roofs of atap (sago palm-leaf) squat the Chinese traders along one side of the Tamu. For cash or barter they will sell; and many a wrangle, haggle and bargain is driven and fought ere the goods change hands, or money parted with."

Excursions

Tempasuk has a wide variety of migrating birds and is a proposed conservation area. More than 127 species of birds have been recorded along this area of the coastal plain and over half a million birds flock to the area every year, many migrating from north latitudes in winter. These include 300,000 swallows, 50,000 yellow longtails

Tamus in Kota Belud District

Tuesday: Pandasan (along the Kota Belud to Kudat road).
Wednesday: Keelawat (along the Kota Belud to KK road).
Thursday: Pekan Nabalu (along the Kota Belud to Ranau road).
Friday: Taginambur (along the Kota Belud to Ranau road, 16 km from Kota Belud.
Monday and Saturday: Kota Belud.

Market time: 0600-1200. All tamus provide many places to eat.

and 5,000 water birds. The best period for bird watching is from October to March.

Between Kota Belud and the sea, there are mangrove swamps with colonies of proboscis monkeys. It is possible to hire small fishing boats in the town to go down the Tempasuk River (RM10/hour).

Local information

● Accommodation

C ***Kota Belud***, 21 Lebuh Francis (just off the central square), T 976576, a/c, noisy. **C** ***Tai Seng***, also on Central Square, some a/c, minimalist but adequate.

E ***Government Resthouse***, Jln Ranau (on hill north of town, signed from the main road), T 967532, some a/c, often full of officials.

Homestay programme in Kota Belud village: there is no limit to your length of stay. Live with and be treated as part of the family, getting invited to celebrations such as weddings etc. Activities include buffalo riding, jungle trekking, river swimming, cultural dancing, visits to local tamus, padi planting ... The basic price is RM10/week. Arrange through *Borneo Expedition and Exotic Borneo*; for more information contact Terisah Yapin, PO Box 13337, T 242433, F 223443, very affordable for young travellers and an excellent way to learn the language and gain an indepth knowledge of the culture.

● Places to eat

There are several Indian coffee shops around the main square.

♦♦***Bismillah Restoran***, 35 Jln Keruak (main square), excellent *roti telur*. ***Indonesia Restoran***, next to the car park behind the *Kota Belud Hotel*.

● Banks & money changers

Public Bank Berhad, Jln Kota Kinabalu; ***Sabah Finance***, Jln Ranau; ***Bank Pertanian***, Jln Kudat.

● Churches

There are no English churches but people are happy to interpret. Catholic Church, Jln Ranau; Basel Christian Chruch of Malaysia, off Jln Kota Kinabalu; SIB (Evangelical Church of Borneo), off Jln Ranau; SIB Taginambur, Jln Ranau (20 minutes drive from Kota Belud and the centre of a religious revival).

● Entertainment

The annual Tamu Besar includes a parade and equestrian games by the Bajau Horsemen; a very colourful event.

● Shopping

Market in main square every day, fish market to the south of the main market. Large *tamu* every Sun and an annual Tamu Besar, with a wide variety of local handicrafts on offer.

Handicraft Centre: just outside town.

● Transport

77 km from KK.

Road Minibus: leave from main square. Regular connections with KK, Kudat and Ranau.

KUDAT

Kudat town, surrounded by coconut groves, is right on the northern tip of Sabah, 160 km from KK. The local people here are the Rungus, members of the Kadazan tribe. The gentle, warm and friendly Rungus have clung to their traditions more than other Sabahan tribes and some still live in longhouses, although many are now building their own houses. Rungus longhouses are built in a distinctive style with outward-leaning walls (the Sabah State Museum incorporates many of the design features of a Rungus longhouse). The Rungus used to wear coils of copper and brass round their arms and legs and today the older generation still dress in black. They are renowned for their fine beadwork and weaving. A handful of Rungus longhouses are dotted around the peninsula, away from Kudat town.

The East India Company first realized the potential of the Kudat Peninsula and set up a trading station on Balambanganan Island, to the north of Kudat. The settlement was finally abandoned after countless pirate raids. Kudat became the first administrative capital of Sabah in 1881, when it was founded by a Briton, AH Everett. William Hood Fletcher, the protectorate's first governor, first tried to administer the territory from Labuan, which proved impossible, so he moved to the newly founded town of Kudat which was nothing more than a handful of atap houses built out into the sea on stilts. It was a promising location, however, situated on an inlet of Marudu Bay, and it had a good harbour. Kudat's glory-years were short-lived: it was displaced as the capital of North Borneo by Sandakan in 1883.

Today it is a busy town dominated by Chinese and Filipino traders (legal and illegal) on the coast, and prostitutes trading downtown. Kudat was one of the main centres of Chinese and European migration at the end of the 19th century. Most of the Chinese who came to Kudat were Christian Hakka vegetable farmers: 96 of them arrived in April 1883, and they

The Rungus of Kudat

Arts and crafts The Rungus are renowned in Sabah as highly skilled artisans who traditionally make colourful beaded necklaces from local plant seeds and clay. The most notable Rungus beadworks are the *pinakol* or shoulder bands which are long and broad with multi-strands and worn diagonally across the chest. The beadwork motifs are drawn from traditional designs and usually tell legends from Rungus folklore. Rungus women are also highly skilled in the arts of weaving and basketry. Their traditional attire is made from home-grown, hand spun cotton which is woven on a back strap loom. Their black cotton sarongs are decorated with an intricate and colourful border, created using a type of needle weaving. Again, traditional motifs and designs are employed. All this requires painstaking hours of time and attention.

Rungus men can be easily distinguished by their richly embroidered traditional headgear or *sigal tinohian*, traditionally worn as part of their daily attire. The *sigal* plays an important part in social life, distinguishing between ranks at festivals and other celebrations. The traditional colour of the Rungus is black. Aside from the different patterns and designs of their beadwork and headgear, Rungus women also used to adorn their necks, arms and legs with heavy brass coils. This tradition is likely soon to disappear as many young girls today opt not to wear these coils and the skills needed to make them are dying out.

Beliefs, Rites and Rituals Despite conversion to Islam and Christianity, the Rungus have maintained their cultural and traditional beliefs through the practice of traditional Rungus rites and rituals, mainly performed through ritual specialists known as *Bobolizan*. For example, when selecting a site for a longhouse, the Rungus will invite a male *Bobolizan* to initiate a ritual known as the *mamabat*. Prayers (*moguhok*) are chanted and a four-string puzzle known as a *mongumbang* is used to protect the longhouse residents from evil spirits. Other rituals involve the use of paddy grains, clam shells and prayers recited in ancient Rungus. To contact spiritual beings, the *kamagi*, a special beaded necklace, is worn and the *Bobolizan* shakes a rattle or *gonding* at the start of the ritual to summon the 'good' spirits. These rituals may last anything from a day to a week.

Part of the female *Bobolizan's* task is healing the sick by fighting off 'angry' spirits. The ritual specialists also take the role of the local 'doctor' and have an intimate knowledge of medicinal herbs and other forest remedies. Certain ceremonies also include traditional ritualistic dances, which are sometimes also performed at special festivities.

The Longhouse The Rungus align their longhouses west-east, facing Mount Kinabalu, in the belief that a cool, airy atmosphere is attained for ideal living and good health. Rungus builders choose only trees that bring good luck; brittle plants and those with red sap (which signifies blood) are considered to bring bad luck and are avoided.

were followed by others, given free passages by the Chartered Company. More Europeans, especially the British, began to arrive on Kudat's shores with the discovery of oil in 1880. Frequent pirate attacks and an inadequate supply of drinking water forced the British to move their main administrative offices to Sandakan in 1883.

Kudat is dotted with numerous family farms cultivating coconut trees, maize, ground nuts and keeping bees. Being surrounded by the sea, seafood is also an important element in the diet and fisheries an important industry. Kudat is inhabited by many other ethnic groups: Bonggi, Bajau, Bugis, Kadazandusun, Obian, Orang Sungei and Suluk.

Excursions

Beaches There are some beautiful and extensive unspoilt white sand beaches north of town, the best known is **Bak-Bak**, 11 km from Kudat. This beach, however, can get crowded at weekends and there are plans to transform it into a resort. It is signposted off the Kota Belud-Kudat road. *Getting there*: minibus.

Sikuati is 23 km west of Kudat, with a good beach. Every Sunday (0800) the Rungus come to the tamu in this village, on the northwest side of the Kudat peninsula. Local handicrafts are sold. *Getting there*: minibus (RM2).

Between Kota Belud and Kudat there is a marsh and coastal area with an abundance of birds. Costumed Bajau horsemen can sometimes be seen here.

The **'Longhouse Experience'** is possibly the most memorable thing to do in Kudat. A stay at a longhouse enables visitors to observe, enjoy and take part in the Rungus' unique lifestyle. There are two Baranggaxo longhouses with 10 units. Nearby there are the village's only modern amenities – toilets and showers. During the day, the longhouse corridor is busy with Rungus womenfolk at work stringing elaborate beadworks, weaving baskets and their traditional cloth. Visitors can experience and participate in these activities. Longhouse meals are homegrown; fish and seafood come from nearby fishing villages, drinks consist of young coconuts and local rice wine. Evening festivities consist of the playing of gongs with dancers dressed in traditional Rungus costume. *Getting there*: tour companies organize trips; look at Longhouse Rules for advice on visiting longhouses (see page 378).

For those wanting a less touristy visit to a longhouse, **Matunggong** is an area found on the road south of Kudat best known for its longhouses.

At **Kampung Gombizau**, visitors get to see bee-keeping and the process of harvesting beeswax, honey and royal jelly. While **Kampung Sumangkap**, an enterprising little village, offers visitors traditional gong-making and handicraft-making by the villagers.

Local information

● Accommodation

The *Sunrise* and *Oriental* hotels are within walking distance of the bus stop.

B-C *Greenland*, Lot 9/10, Block E, Sedco Shophouse (new town), T 612212, a/c, standard rooms, shared bath.

C *Kinabalu*, Kudat Old Town, T 613888, a/c, clean enough, average value. **C** *Sunrise*, 21 Jln Lo Thien Hock, T 611517, a/c, restaurant (*Silver Inn*).

E *Government Resthouse*, T 61304. *Oriental*, Jln Lo Thien Chock, T 61677/61045, a/c, big, clean rooms, some shared bathrooms.

● Places to eat

Malay: ♦*Restoran Rakyat*, Jln Lo Thien Hock. *Cahaya Timur*, Jln Lo Thien Hock (next to *Kudat Hotel*).

Chinese: ♦♦*Silver Inn*, Jln Lo Thien Hock (below *Sunrise*).

● Banks & money changers

Standard Chartered, Jln Lo Thien Hock.

● Transport

122 km north of KK.

Air Connections with KK, Sandakan.

Road Minibus: minibuses leave from Jln Lo Thien Hock. Regular connections with KK, 4 hours.

GUNUNG KINABALU PARK

Gunung Kinabalu is the pride of Sabah, the focal point of the national park and probably the most magnificent sight in Borneo. In the first written mention of the mountain, in 1769, Captain Alexander Dalrymple of the East India Company, observing the mountain from his ship in the South China Sea, wrote: "Though perhaps not the highest mountain in the world, it is of *immense* height." During World War Two Kinabalu was used as a navigational aid by Allied bombers – one of whom was quoted as saying "That ... thing ... must be near as high as Mount Everest". It's not, but at 4,101m, Gunung Kinabalu is the highest peak between the Himalayas and New Guinea. It is not though, the highest mountain in Southeast Asia: peaks in Northern Burma and the Indonesian province of Irian Jaya are higher.

Although Mount Kinabalu has foothills, it's dramatic rockfaces, with cloud swirling around them, loom starkly out of the jungle. The view from the top is unsurpassed and on a clear day you can see the shadow of the mountain in the South China Sea, over 50 km away.

There are a number of theories about the derivation of its name. The most convincing is the corruption of the Kadazan *Aki Nabulu* – 'the revered place of the spirits'. For the Kadazan, the mountain is sacred as they consider it to be the last resting place of the dead, and the summit was believed to be inhabited by their ghosts. In the past the Kadazan are said to have carried out human sacrifices on Mount Kinabalu, carrying their captives to the summit in bamboo cages, where they would be speared to death. The Kadazan guides still perform an annual sacrifice to appease the spirits – today they make do with chickens, eggs, cigars, betel nuts and rice – on the rock plateau below the Panar Laban Rockface.

The Chinese also lay claim to a theory. According to this legend, a Chinese prince arrived on the shores of Northern Borneo and went in search of a huge pearl on the top of the mountain, which was guarded by a dragon. He duly slew the dragon, grabbed the pearl and married a beautiful Kadazan girl. After a while he grew homesick, and took the boat back to China, promising his wife that he would return. She climbed the mountain every day for years on end to watch for her husband's boat. He never came and in desperation and depression, she lay down and died and was turned to stone. The mountain was then christened *China Balu* – or Chinaman's widow.

In 1851, Sir Hugh Low, the British colonial secretary in Labuan made the first unsuccessful attempt at the summit. 7 years later he returned with Spencer St John, the British Consul in Brunei. Low's feet were in bad shape after the long walk to the base of the mountain, so St John went on without him, with a handful of reluctant Kadazan porters. He made it to the top of the conical southern Peak, but was "mortified to find that the most westerly [peak] and another to the east appeared higher than where I sat." He retreated, and returned 3 months later with Low, but again failed to reach the summit – now called Low's Peak. It remained unconquered for another 30 years. The first to reach the summit was John Whitehead, a zoologist, in 1888. Whitehead spent several months on the mountain collecting birds and mammals and many of the more spectacular species bear either Low's or Whitehead's name. More scientists followed and then a trickle of tourists but it was not until 1964, when Kinabalu Park was gazetted, that the 8.5 km trail to the summit was opened. Today the mountain lures around 200,000 visitors a year. Although the majority are day visitors who do not climb the peak, the number of climbers is steadily increasing, with around 30,000 making the attempt each year.

In plan, the top of the mountain is U-shaped, with bare rock plateaux. Several peaks stand proud of these plateaux, around the edge of the U; the space between the western and eastern arms is the spectacular gully known as Low's Gully. No one has ever scaled its precipitous walls, nor has anyone climbed the Northern Ridge (an extension of the eastern arm) from the back of the mountain. From Low's Peak, the eastern peaks, just 1½ km away, look within easy reach. As John Briggs points out in his book *Mountains of Malaysia*, "It seems so close, yet it is one of the most difficult places to get to in the whole of Borneo."

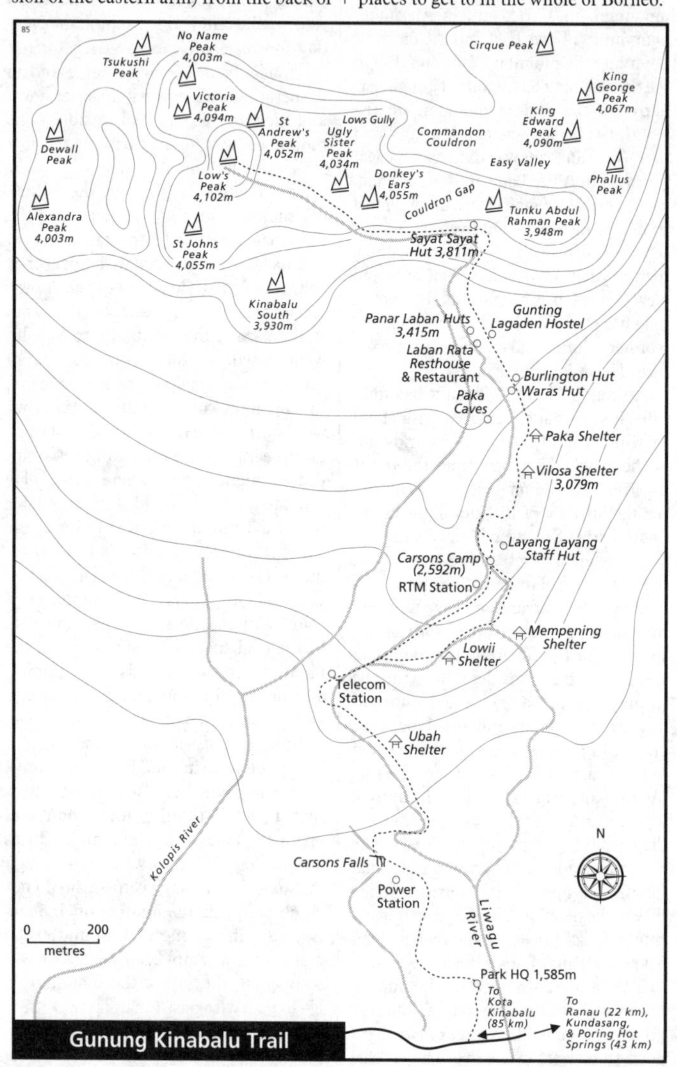

Gunung Kinabalu Trail

Mountain rescue: five soldiers and seven white chickens

Anyone who has peered from Kinabalu's summit into the seemingly bottomless depths of Low's Gully will appreciate the special sort of lunacy exhibited by two groups of British and Hong Kong soldiers who decided to abseil down it. One group emerged traumatised and exhausted a week later than they said they would. The other team got lost in the jungle below and were not found for three weeks. The dramatic jungle mountain rescue story – which took place in March 1994 – catapulted the name Kinabalu into the British media, where it was mispronounced with gay abandon.

For the five soldiers who tackled the precipitous walls of the Gully which plunge a sheer 1,600m from Kinabalu's summit, Sabah's much-touted "paradise" turned into a living hell. Having abseiled down the rock faces (which have yet to be scaled) they disappeared. More than 300 troops, rangers and mountain rescue specialists were involved in the search. When they were finally discovered, it emerged that they had been unable to move from their little jungle encampment at the foot of the gully; the terrain was too hostile even for them. Although their rations had run out, the soldiers recovered quickly after spending a night in hospital in Kota Kinabalu.

They were lucky men. Irene Charuruks, the head of Sabah's Tourism Promotion Corporation, was quick to point out that "*Aki Nabalu* means the resting place of the dead in Kadazan". She said that because the five soldiers had been entering an area of the mountain never trodden before, they would have been well advised to have sacrificed seven white chickens so as to avoid offending the spirits of the mountain. Whether or not the spirits were involved, the men owe their lives to a Malaysian helicopter rescue team. The rescue effort was a successful story of cooperation between Malaysia and Britain – which at the time were still embroiled in an acrimonious trade dispute over British press allegations that Malaysian politicians are corrupt. Sadly the happy ending at the resting place of the dead was not enough to prompt the resurrection of Anglo-Malaysian relations.

The 754 sq km Gunung Kinabalu Park was established in 1964 to protect the mountain and its remarkably diverse flora and fauna. Gunung Kinabalu is an important watershed: eight major rivers originate on the mountain.

Flora and fauna The range of climatic zones on the mountain has led to the incredible diversity of plant and animal life. Kinabalu Park is the meeting point of plants from Asia and Australasia and has one of the richest assemblages of flora in the world, with over 2,000 species of flowering plants. There are thought to be over 1200 species of orchid alone. And this does not include the innumerable mosses, ferns and fungi. These flowering plants of Kinabalu are said to represent more than half the families of flowering plants in the world. Within the space of 3 km, the vegetation changes from lowland tropical rainforest to alpine meadow and 'cloud' forest. The jungle reaches up to 1300m; above that, to a height of 1800m, is the lower montane zone, dominated by 60 species of oak and chestnut; above 2,000m is the upper montane zone with true cloud forest, orchids, rhododendrons and pitcher plants. Above 2600m, growing among the crags and crevices of the summit rock plateau are gnarled tea trees (*Leptospermums*) and stunted rhododendrons. Above 3300m, the soil disappears, leaving only club mosses, sedges and Low's buttercups (*Ranunculus lowii*), which are alpine meadow flowers.

Among the most unusual of Kinabalu's flora is the world's largest flower, the rust-coloured *Rafflesia pricei*. They can usually only be found in the section of the park closest to Poring Hot Springs. Rafflesia are hard to find as they only flower for a couple of days; the main flowering season is from May to July.

Kinabalu is also famous for the carnivorous pitcher plants, which grow to varying sizes on the mountain. (A detailed guide to the pitcher plants of Kinabalu can be bought in the shop at park headquarters). Nine different species have been recorded on Kinabalu. The largest is the giant Rajah Brooke's pitcher plant; Spencer St John claimed to have found one of these containing a drowned rat floating in 4 litres of water. Insects are attracted by the scent and when they settle on the lip of the plant, they cannot maintain a foothold on the waxy, ribbed surface. At the base of the pitcher is an enzymic fluid which digests the 'catch' (see page 38).

Rhododendrons line the trail throughout the mossy forest (there are 27 species in the park), especially above the Paka Cave area. One of the most beautiful is the copper leafed rhododendron, with orange flowers and leaves with coppery scales underneath.

It is difficult to see wildlife on the climb to the summit as the trail is well used, although tree shrews and squirrels are common on the lower trails. There are, however, more than 100 species of mammal living in the park. The Kinabalu summit rats – which are always on cue to welcome climbers to Low's Peak at dawn – and nocturnal ferret badgers are the only true montane mammals in Sabah. As the trees thin with altitude, it is often possible to see tree-shrews and squirrels, of which there are over 28 species in the park. Large mammals – such as flying lemurs, redleaf monkeys, wild pigs, orang-utan and deer are lowland forest dwellers. Nocturnal species include the slow loris (*Nycticebus coucang*) and the mischievous-looking bug-eyed tarsier (*Tarsius bancanus*).

Over half of Borneo's 518 species of birds have also been recorded in Kinabalu Park, but the variety of species decreases with height. Two of the species living above 2500m are endemic to the mountain: the Kinabalu friendly warbler and the Kinabalu mountain blackbird.

More than 75 species of frogs and toads and 100 species of reptile live in the park. Perhaps the most interesting frog in residence is the horned frog, which is virtually impossible to spot thanks to its mastery of the art of camouflage. The giant toad is common at lower altitudes; he is covered with warts, which are poisonous glands. When disturbed, these squirt a stinking, toxic liquid. Other frogs found in the park include the big-headed leaf-litter frog, whose head is bigger than the rest of its body, and the green stream shrub frog, who has a magnificent metallic green body, but is deadly if swallowed by any predator.

The famous flying tree snake (the subject of an early film by the British nature documentary-maker David Attenborough) has been seen in the park. It spreads its skin flaps, which act as a parachute when the snake leaps blindly from one tree to another.

There are nearly 30 species of fish in the park's rivers – including the unusual Borneo sucker fish (*Gastomyzon borneensis*), which attaches itself to rocks in fast-flowing streams. One Sabah Parks publication likens them to 'underwater cows', grazing on algae as they move slowly over the rocks.

Walkers and climbers are more likely to come across the park's abundant insect life than anything else. Examples include pill millipedes, rhinoceros beetles, the emerald green and turquoise jewel beetles, stick insects, 'flying peapods', cicadas, and a vast array of moths (including the giant atlas moth) and butterflies (including the magnificent emerald green and black Rajah Brooke's birdwing).

The climb Mount Kinabalu is a tough, steep climb but requires no special skills or equipment. The climb to the summit and back should take 2 days – 4-6 hours from park HQ at 2,580m to the *Laban Rata Resthouse* (3,550m) on the first day and then 3 hours to the summit for dawn, returning to the park headquarters at around noon on the second day. Gurkha soldiers and others have made it to the summit and back in well under 3 hours. For the really keen, or the really foolhardy, depending on one's perspective and inclination, there is also the annual Kinabalu Climbathon which is held in early October. In 1997 the race was hampered by the fires which ravaged Indonesian Borneo and created such dangerous atmospheric conditions in Sabah and Sarawak.

A jeep for 12 people can take groups from headquarters to the power station at 1,829m where the trail starts (RM10-20). A minibus also makes the 5.5 km run to the power station from park headquarters on a regular basis (RM2). It is a 25 minutes walk from the Power Station to the first shelter, Pondok Lowi. The trail splits in two soon afterwards, the left goes to the radio station and the helipad and the right towards the summit. The next stop is Layang Layang staff headquarters (drinking water, cooking facilities, accommodation) – also known as *Carson's Camp* (2,621m), named after the first warden of the park. There is one more shelter, Ponkok Villosa (2,942m, and about 45 minutes from Carson's Camp) before the stop at the path to Paka Caves – really an overhanging rock on the side of a stream. Paka is a 10-minute detour to the left, where Low and St John made their camps.

From the cave/fifth shelter the vegetation thins out and it is a steep climb to Panar Laban huts – which includes the well equipped *Laban Rata Resthouse*, affording magnificent views at sunset and in the early morning. The name *Panar Laban* is derived from Kadazan words meaning 'place of sacrifice': early explorers had to make a sacrifice here to appease the spirits – this ritual is still performed by the Kadazan once a year. Sayat Sayat (3,810m) hut – named after the ubiquitous shrubby tea tree – is an hour further on, above the Panar Laban Rockface. Most climbers reach Panar Laban (or the other huts) in the early afternoon in order to rest up for a 0300 start the next morning in order to reach the summit by sunrise. The trail is well laid out with regular half mile resting points. Ladders, handrails and ropes are provided for the steeper parts. The first 2 hours after dawn are the most likely to be cloud-free. For enthusiasts interested in alternative routes to the summit, John Briggs's *Mountains of Malaysia* provides a detailed guide to the climb.

Equipment A thick jacket is useful, but at the very least you should have a light waterproof or windcheater to beat the windchill on the summit. Remarkably, no one appears to have set up rental facilities; contrary to rumour, it is not possible to hire jackets or windcheaters from park HQ. It is also necessary to bring a sweater or some thick shirts. Walking boots and a sleeping bag are recommended, but not essential. The latter can be hired from HQ. Many people climb the mountain in training shoes. Carry food and a few sweets as a precaution. Essential items include: torch, toilet paper, water bottle, plasters, headache tablets and suntan lotion. A hat is also a good idea – as protection against the sun and the cold. Gloves can be bought in the *Perkasa Hotel* shop. Lockers are available, free of charge, at the park headquarters reception office. The *Laban Rata Resthouse* has welcome hot-water showers, but soap and towels are not provided. The hostel is well heated and bedding is provided.

Guides Hiring a guide is compulsory: RM25 per day (1-3 people), RM28 per day (4-6), RM30 per day (7-8), RM3.50 per person for insurance is required. Porter's available for RM25 per day, maximum load 11 kg. Guides and porters should be reserved at least a day in advance at the park headquarters or at the parks office in KK. On the morning of your climb, go to the HQ and a guide will be assigned to you. A guide is not compulsory if you want to walk the trail only as far as Laban Rata, below the rockface. A small colour pamphlet, '*Mount Kinabalu/A Guide to the Summit Trail*' published by Sabah Parks and widely available, serves as a good guide to the wildlife and the trail itself.

Permits RM10 per person (RM2 for students) to climb Gunung Kinabalu, no permit necessary if just visiting the park. It is necessary to obtain permission to visit the park by visiting the Sabah Parks Office in Kota Kinabalu (see page 446). Compulsory insurance costs RM3.50.

Treks there is a map of trails around the park available from Park HQ. Most are well-used and are easy walks, but the Liwagu Trail is a good 3-4 hour trek up to where it joins the summit trail and is very steep and slippery in places – not advised as a solo trip. Guided trail walk 1100 Monday-Sunday from park administration building.

Mountain Garden (behind park administration building) The landscaped garden has species from all over the mid-levels of the mountain, which have been planted in natural surroundings. Open 0730-1630 Monday-Friday, 0800-1700 Saturday, 0900-1600 Sunday.

Museum At headquarters with information on local flora and fauna. Beetles "as large as Tom Jones' medallions" and foot-long stick insects. There is also a slide show introducing some of the park's flora and fauna at 1930.

Poring Hot Springs *Getting there*: take a minibus to Ranau and taxi from there to Poring (see page 474).

Park Headquarters A short walk from the main Ranau-KK road and all the accommodation and restaurants are within 15 minutes walk from the main compound. **Souvenir and bookshop**: next to the park headquarters has good books on the mountain and its flora and fauna. **Slide and film shows** are held in the mini-theatre in the Administration Building at weekends and public holidays in the evening, while naturalists give escorted trail walks every morning.

Best time to visit The average rainfall is 400 cm a year, with an average temperature of 20°C at park headquarters but at Panar Laban it can drop below freezing at night. With the wind chill factor on the summit, it feels very cold. The best time to climb Gunung Kinabalu is in the dry season between March and April when views are clearest. The worst time has traditionally been November to December during the monsoon – although wet or dry periods can occur at any time of the year. The forest fires of August, September and October 1997 also presented climbers with particular health problems, not to mention rather truncated views. Avoid weekends, school and public holidays if at all possible.

Park information

● Accommodation

(Also see Ranau and Kundasang below). **NB** It is necessary to book in advance: by either writing to The Director, Gunung Kinabalu Park, Sabah Parks Office, First Floor, Lot 1-3, Block K, PO Box 10626, T 211881, F 221001, or visit the office while in KK. During weekends and school holidays visiting the park is very popular – make reservations well in advance at the counter of Sabah Parks Head Office in Sinsuran Shopping Complex, KK.

Park Headquarters: Each cabin is provided with a fireplace, kitchen, shower, gas cooker, refrigerator and cooking and eating utensils. Electricity, piped water and firewood are all provided free of charge. The rates quoted below are reduced on weekdays: ***Annex suite***, 4 people, RM160/night; ***Basement room***, 2 people, RM80/night; ***Double storey deluxe cabin***, 7 people, RM250/night; ***Duplex chalet***, 6 people, RM200/night; ***Kinabalu Lodge***, 8 people, RM360/night; ***Nepenthes Villa***, 4 people, RM250/ night; ***New Hostel***, RM10/night; ***Old Hostel***, RM10/night; ***Single storey deluxe cabin***, 5 people, RM200/night; ***Twin bed cabin***, 2 people, RM80/night.

A ***Haleluyah Retreat Centre***, Jln Linouh, Km 61, Tuaran-Ranau Highway, PO Box 13337,

T 011 817937, F 088 223443, reservations at Sinsuran Complex, Block A, Lot 8, Second Floor, KK. This Christian centre is open to all and is located at 1,500m close to the foot of Mount Kinabalu. It makes a good stop off point before climbing the mountain. Set amidst 2 acres of natural jungle and approximately 15 minutes walk from the Park Headquarters, it is isolated but safe, clean, friendly and with a relaxing atmosphere. Cooking and washing facilities, camping area, multi-purpose hall and meeting rooms makes it a suitable venue for seminars, meetings, youth camps or family holidays. Food is available at a reasonable price from a canteen, dorms beds also available (**F**).

Gunung Kinabalu: *Laban Rata Resthouse*, Panar Laban, 54 rooms, canteen (but sometimes rather limited food – it all has to be walked up the mountain) and hot water shower facilities plus electricity and heated rooms, bedding provided. RM25/night pp. **Huts**: RM10 pp shared rooms with wooden bunks, mattresses, and sleeping bags, gas cylinder cooking stoves supplied and limited eating utensils; no heating provided. Climbers may want to bring their own food for cooking, although there is a restaurant just below the Panar Laban Huts. *Rosie's Cabin*, not far from Park HQ, newish Chinese run hotel and restaurant. *Gunting Lagandan Hut*; *Panar Laban Hut*; *Sayat Sayat Huts*; *Waras Hut*, all RM4 and unheated.

● Places to eat

Park Headquarters: the best places to stay are here although the restaurants are rather spread out requiring a walk between buffet and bed. ♦♦*Club Canteen*, decent meals. ♦♦*Steak & Coffee House*. Cooking facilities at *Kinabalu Lodge*, *Double storey*, *Single storey*, *Duplex chalet*, *Nepenthes villa*, *New hostel*, *Old hostel*.

● Transport

60 km northeast of KK. **Road Minibus**: regular connections from KK to Ranau, ask to be dropped at the park, 2 hours. Return minibus must be waved down from the main road. Chartered 28-seater minibus from the National Parks office: RM300. **Bus**: scheduled a/c bus from Kota Kinabalu to Ranau at 0800 and 1230 (RM7), slower than the minibus but more luggage space. **Taxi**: at least RM100/taxi from KK.

RANAU AND KUNDASANG

The Ranau plateau, surrounding the Kinabalu massif, is one of the richest farming areas in Sabah and much of the forest not in the park has now been devastated by market gardeners. Even within the national park's boundaries, on the lower slopes of Mount Kinabalu itself, shifting cultivators have clear-felled tracts of jungle and planted their patches. More than 1,000 hectares are now planted out with spinach, cabbage, cauliflower, asparagus, broccoli and tomatoes, supplying much of Borneo.

Kundasang and Ranau are unremarkable towns a few kilometres apart; the latter is bigger. The **war memorial**, behind Kundasang, which unfortunately looks like Colditz, is in memory of those who died in the 'death march' in World War Two (see page 478). In September 1944, the Japanese marched 2,400 Allied prisoners of war through the jungle from Sandakan to Kundasang. The march took 11 months and only six men survived to tell the tale. The walled gardens represent the national gardens of Borneo, Australia and Britain.

Excursions

Mentapok and Monkobo are southeast of Ranau. Both are rarely climbed. Mentapok, 1581m, can be reached in 1½ days from Kampung Mireru, a village at the base of the mountain. A logging track provides easy access half way up the south side of the mountain. Monkobo is most easily climbed from the northwest, a logging track from Telupid goes up to 900m and from here it is a 2-hour trek to the top. It is advisable to take guides, organized from Ranau or one of the near-by villages.

Local information

● Accommodation

Kundasang: **A** *Kinabalu Pines Resort*, T 088 889388, F 088 889288. **A** *Perkasa*, visible on the hill above Kundasang, T 889511, F 889101, a/c, restaurant, slightly run down but a good view of the mountain, organizes tours to Kinabalu National Park and surrounding area. **B** *Sonny's Village*, T 088 750555, 6 bedrooms with spectacular views. *Kinabalu Rose Cabin*, Kundasang, a/c, restaurant, towards gold course (30% discount to golfers); range of rooms, suites. **E** *Mountain View Motel*, located 5 km east of the Kinabalu National Park on the Ranau-Tamparuli Highway, T (088) 889819, F (088) 231359, price includes breakfast, hot water, restaurant, local tours, climbing gear available for rent.

Ranau: **B-C** *Ranau*, on the bottom side of the square, nearest the main road, T 876176, some a/c. **D** *Sapati*, top left side of the square, no attached bath. **E** *Government Rest House*, half a mile out on the Sandakan Rd, T 875229.

● Places to eat

Kundasang: there are several restaurants along the roads serving simple food, open 0600-2100. ♦♦♦*Perkasa Hotel Restaurant*, local and western dishes, service good and food excellent.

Ranau: **Chinese**: ♦*Five Star Seafood Restaurant*, opposite the market; ♦*Sin Mui Mui*, top side of the square near the market.

● Shopping

Cheap sweaters and waterproofs for the climb from *Kedai Kien Hin*, Ranau. A *tamu* is held near Ranau on the first of each month and every Sat. Kundasang tamu is held on the 20th of every month and also every Fri.

● Sports

Golf: *Kundasang Golf Course*, 3 km behind Kundasang in the shadow of the mountain is one of the most beautiful courses in the region, became 18-hole course in Jan '94 when new clubhouse also opened. Club hire from the *Perkasa Hotel*, Kundasang, RM25/round. The *Perkasa* offer golfing packages to include golf fees, accommodation, breakfast and lunch, transfer from hotel to course.

● Transport

113 km from KK.

Road Minibus: minibuses leave from the market place. Regular connections to park headquarters, to KK, to Sandakan 8 hours.

PORING HOT SPRINGS

Poring lies 43 km from Gunung Kinabalu Park Headquarters – and is actually part of the national park. The **hot sulphur baths** were installed during the Japanese occupation of World War Two, for the jungle-weary Japanese troops. There are individual concrete pools with taps (which can fit two people), one for the hot spring mineral water and the other for cold; once in your bath you are in complete privacy. The springs are on the other side of the Mamut River, over a suspension bridge, from the entrance. They are a fantastic antidote to tiredness after a tough climb up Gunung Kinabalu. There is also a cold water rock pool. The pools are in a beautiful garden setting of hibiscus and other tropical flowers, trees and thousands of butterflies. There are some quite luxurious private cabin baths available; a standard cabin costs RM15 for the first hour or part thereof, then RM25 for every additional hour. There are also large baths capable of accommodating eight people. The deluxe cabins have lounge areas and jacuzzis and cost RM20 for the first hour then RM30 for each additional hour. The Kadazans named the area Poring after the towering bamboos, of that name, nearby. (These big bamboos were traditionally used as water-carriers and examples can be seen in the museum in KK). Admission RM2. A new Information Centre has been built here, plus a rafflesia centre, orchid centre, aviary and tropical garden.

The **jungle canopy walk** at Poring is a rope walkway 35m above the ground, which provides a monkey's eye view of the jungle; springy but quite safe. Guides are available. The entrance is 5 minutes walk from the Hot Springs and the canopy walkway is 15 minutes walk from the entrance.

Kipungit Falls are only about 10 minutes walk from Poring and swimming is possible here. Follow the trail further up the hill and after 15 minutes you come to bat caves; a large overhanging boulder povides shelter and a home for the bats.

The **Langanan Waterfall** trail takes 90 minutes one way and is up hill all the way – but it is worth it. There is another hard 90 minute trail to Bat Cave (inhabited, would you believe, by what seems to be a truly stupendous number of bats) and a waterfall. The **Butterfly Farm** was established by a Japanese-backed firm in 1992 and is very educational in the descriptions of butterflies and other insects.

If the weather is clear at Ranau, it is generally safe to assume that the canopy walk will also be clear. The warmer climate at lower altitudes means there is an abundance of wild fruit in the park, which attracts flying lemur, red leaf monkeys; even orang-utans have occasionally been seen here. The bird life is particularly rich and diverse and provides a complete contrast to the montane birds seen round the Park Headquarters. There are also numerous butterflies. Admission 1030-1430 RM2 per person; 1830-2230 RM10 per person; 2230-1030 RM20 per person if in group of four or more, otherwise RM30 for 1-3 persons. No admission charge if you have already been to Mount Kinabalu. An inside bath can be rented for RM15-20/hour. If staying at Poring then there is no admission charge, and the baths can be used all night long.

Permits Not necessary.

Local information

NB Booking is recommended, see page 472, Park information.

● Accommodation

E *Youth Hostel*, 24 people in a dorm, RM8 adult, RM2 student; ***Mamutik Resthouse***, 8 people, RM180/night; ***Manukan Chalet***, 4 people, RM220/night; ***Poring New Cabin***, 4 people, RM95/night; ***Poring Old Cabin***, 6 people, RM115/night.

Camping: RM5.00.

● Places to eat

♦♦*Restaurant*, quite good Chinese and Malay food at the springs and other stalls outside the park.

● Transport

No minibuses to Poring. **Road Taxi**: available.

THE EAST COAST

From Ranau it is possible to reach Sandakan by road – although the road is not metalled and is a quagmire in the wet season. Several key sights are within reach of **Sandakan**: the **Turtle Islands National Park**, 40 km north in the Sulu Sea, **Sepilok Orang Utan Rehabilitation Centre**, and the **Kinabatangan Basin**, to the southeast. From Sandakan, the route continues south to the wilds of Lahad Datu and Danum Valley and onto Semporna, the jumping off point for Pulau Sipadan. This island has achieved legendary status among snorkellers and scuba divers in recent years.

SANDAKAN

Sandakan is at the neck of a bay on the northeast coast of Sabah and looks out to the Sulu Sea. For the Sulu traders, the Sandakan area was an important source of beeswax and came under the sway of the Sultans of Sulu. William Clarke Cowie, a Scotsman with a carefully waxed handlebar moustache, who ran guns for the Sultan of Sulu across the Spanish blockade of Sulu (and was later to become the managing director of the North Borneo Chartered Company), first set up camp in Sandakan Bay in the early 1870s. He called his camp, which was on Pulau Timbang, 'Sandakan', which had been the Sulu name for the area for about 200 years – but it became known as Kampung German as there were several German traders living there, and early gun-runners tended to be German. The power of the Sulu sultanate was already on the wane when Cowie set up. In its early trading days, there were many nationalities living in Sandakan – Europeans, Africans, Arabs, Chinese, Indians, Javanese, Dusun and Japanese. It was an important gateway to the interior and used to be a trading centre for forest produce like rhinoceros horn, beeswax, and hornbill ivory along with marine products like pearls and sea cucumbers (*tripang* – valued for their medicinal properties). In 1812 an English visitor, John Hunt, estimated that the Sandakan/Kinabatangan area produced an astonishing 37,000 kg of wild beeswax and 23,000 kg of bird's nests each year.

The modern town of Sandakan was founded by an Englishman, William Pryer, in 1879. Baron von Overbeck – the Austrian consul from Hong Kong who founded the Chartered Company with businessman Alfred Dent – had signed a leasing agreement for the territory with

Agnes Keith's house

American authoress Agnes Keith lived with her English husband in Sandakan from 1934 to 1952. He was the Conservator of Forests in North Borneo and she wrote three books about her time in the colony. *The Land Below the Wind* relates tales of dinner parties and tiffins in pre-war days; *Three Came Home* is about her three years in a Japanese internment camp during the war (on Pulau Berhala, off Sandakan and in Kuching) and was made into a film. *White Man Returns* tells the story of their time in British North Borneo. The Keiths' rambling wooden house on the hill above the town was destroyed during the war but was rebuilt by the government to exactly the same design when Harry Keith returned to his job after the war. The house, near Sandakan Viewpoint and *Ramada Renaissance Hotel*, has been unoccupied for a number of years and its garden neglected.

the Sultan of Brunei, only to discover that large tracts on the east side of modern-day Sabah actually belonged to the Sultan of Sulu. Overbeck sailed to Sulu in January 1878 and on obtaining the cession rights from the Sultan, dropped William Pryer off at Kampung German to make the British presence felt. Pryer's wife Ada later described the scene: "He had with him a West Indian black named Anderson, a half-cast Hindoo named Abdul, a couple of China boys. For food they had a barrel of flour and 17 fowls and the artillery was half a dozen sinder rifles." Pryer set about organizing the three existing villages in the area, cultivating friendly relations with the local tribespeople and fending off pirates. He raised the Union Jack on 11 February 1878.

Cowie tried to do a deal with the Sultan of Sulu to wrest control of Sandakan back from Pryer, but Dent and Overbeck finally bought him off. A few months later Cowie's Kampung German burned to the ground, so Pryer went in search of a new site, which he found at Buli Sim Sim. He called his new settlement Elopura – meaning 'beautiful city' – but the name did not catch on. By the mid-1880s it was recalled Sandakan and, in 1884, became the capital of North Borneo when the title was transferred from Kudat. In 1891 the town had 20 Chinese-run brothels and 71 Japanese prostitutes – according to the 1891 census there were three men for every one woman. The town quickly established itself as the source of birds' nests harvested from the caves at Gomontong (see page 479) and shipped directly to Hong Kong – as they are today.

Timber was first exported from this area in 1885 and was used to construct Beijing's Temple of Heaven. Sandakan was, until a few years ago, the main east coast port for timber and it became a very wealthy town. In its heyday, the town is said to have boasted one of the greatest concentrations of millionaires in the world. The timber-boom days are over: the primary jungle has gone, and so has the big money. In the mid-1990s the state government adopted a strict policy restricting the export of raw, unprocessed timber. The hinterland is now dominated by cocoa and oil palm plantations.

Following the Japanese invasion in 1942, Sandakan was devastated by Allied bombing. In 1946 North Borneo became a British colony and the new colonial government moved the capital to Jesselton (later to become Kota Kinabalu).

Sandakan is a post-war town, much of it rebuilt on reclaimed land. It is Malaysia's biggest fishing port – and even exports some of its catch to Singapore.

Sandakan is often dubbed 'mini Hong Kong' because of its Cantonese influence; its occupants are well-heeled and there are many prosperous businesses. It is now also home to a large Filipino community, mostly traders from Mindanao and the

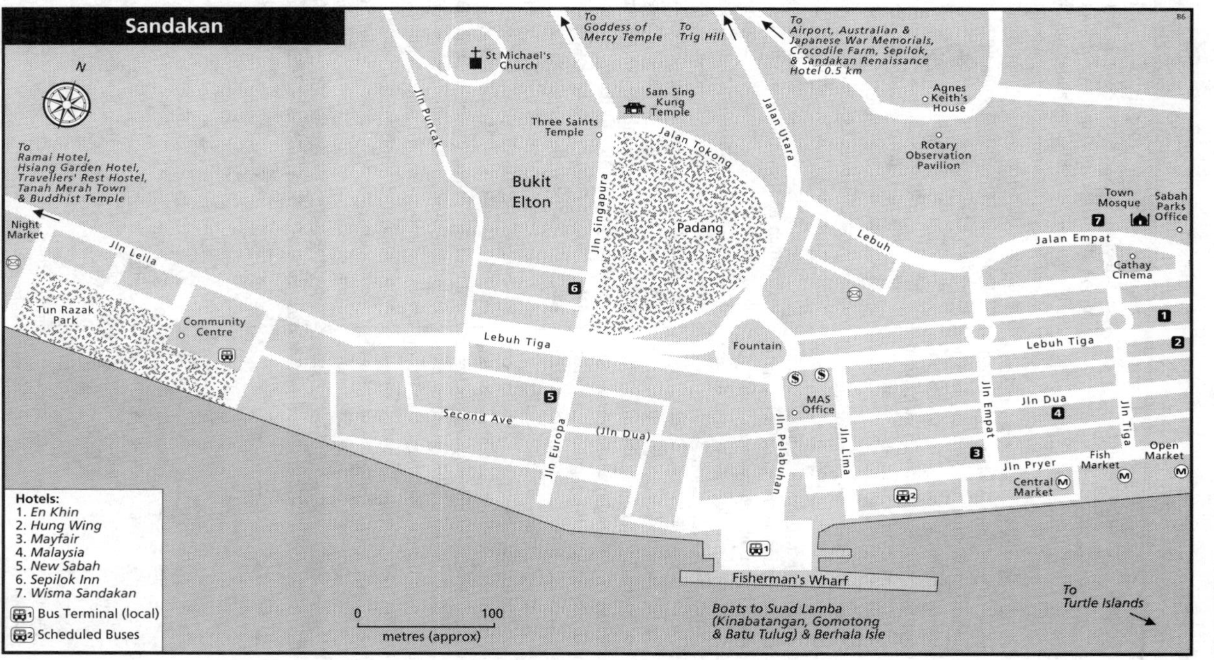
Sandakan
N
To Ramai Hotel, Hsiang Garden Hotel, Travellers' Rest Hostel, Tanah Merah Town & Buddhist Temple
Night Market
Jln Leila
Tun Razak Park
Community Centre
Jln Puncak
St Michael's Church
To Goddess of Mercy Temple
To Trig Hill
To Airport, Australian & Japanese War Memorials, Crocodile Farm, Sepilok, & Sandakan Renaissance Hotel 0.5 km
Sam Sing Kung Temple
Three Saints Temple
Bukit Elton
Jalan Tokong
Jalan Utara
Jln Singapura
Padang
Agnes Keith's House
Rotary Observation Pavilion
Town Mosque
Sabah Parks Office
Lebuh
Jalan Empat
Cathay Cinema
Lebuh Tiga
Fountain
Lebuh Tiga
Second Ave
Jln Europa
(Jln Dua)
MAS Office
Jln Pelabuhan
Jln Lima
Jln Empat
Jln Dua
Jln Tiga
Jln Pryer
Central Market
Fish Market
Open Market
Fisherman's Wharf
Boats to Suad Lamba (Kinabatangan, Gomotong & Batu Tulug) & Berhala Isle
To Turtle Islands
0
100
metres (approx)
Hotels:
1. En Khin
2. Hung Wing
3. Mayfair
4. Malaysia
5. New Sabah
6. Sepilok Inn
7. Wisma Sandakan
Bus Terminal (local)
Scheduled Buses

Sulu Islands. The Philippines only recently relaxed its posturing in its claim to Sabah – Sandakan is only 28 km from Philippines' territorial waters.

Places of interest

Sandakan is strung out along the coast but in the centre of town is the riotous **daily fish market**, which is the biggest and best in Sabah. The best time to visit is at 0600 when the boats unload their catch. The **Central Market** along the waterfront, near the local bus station, sells such things as fruit, vegetables, sarongs, seashells, spices and sticky rice cakes.

The **Australian war memorial**, near the government building at Mile Seven on Labuk Rd, between Sandakan and Sepilok, stands on the site of a Japanese prison camp and commmemorates Allied soldiers who lost their lives during the Japanese occupation. *Getting there*: Labuk bus service nos 19, 30 and 32 (60¢). The Japanese invaded North Borneo in 1942 and many Japanese also died in the area. In 1989 a new **Japanese war memorial** was built in the Japanese cemetery, on Red Hill (Bukit Berenda), financed by the families of the deceased soldiers.

St Michael's Anglican church is one of the very few stone churches in Sabah; it is an attractive building, designed by a New Zealander in 1893. Most of Sandakan's stone churches were levelled in the war and, indeed, St Michael's is one of the few colonial-era buildings still standing. It is just off Jalan Singapura, on the hill at the south end of town. In 1988 a big new **mosque** was built for the burgeoning Muslim population at the mouth of Sandakan Bay. The main Filipino settlements are in this area of town. The mosque is outside Sandakan, on Jalan Buli Sim Sim where the town began in 1879, just after the jetty for Turtle Islands National Park and is an imposing landmark. There is also a large water village here, offering a glimpse of traditional culture and life.

Pertubuhan Ugama Buddhist (Puu Jih Shih Buddhist temple), overlooks Tanah Merah town. The US$2mn temple was completed in 1987 and stands at the top of the hill, accessible by a twisting road which hairpins its way up the hillside. The temple is very gaudy, contains three large Buddha images and is nothing special, although the 34 teakwood supporting pillars, made in Macau, are quite a feature. There is a good view of Sandakan from the top, with Tanah Merah and the log ponds directly below, in Sandakan Bay. The names of local donors are inscribed on the walls of the walkway.

There are a couple of other notable Chinese temples in Sandakan. The oldest one, the **Goddess of Mercy Temple** is just off Jalan Singapura, on the hillside. Originally built in the early 1880s, it has been expanded over the years. Nearby is **Sam Sing Kung Temple** which becomes a particular focus of devotion during exam periods since one of its deities is

The Borneo Death March

The 4 years of Japanese occupation ended when the Australian 9th division liberated British North Borneo. Sandakan was chosen by the Japanese as a regional centre for holding Allied prisoners. In 1942 the Japanese shipped 2,750 prisoners of war (2,000 of whom were Australian and 750 British) to Sandakan from Changi Prison, Singapore. A further 800 British and 500 Australian POWs arrived in 1944. They were ordered to build an airfield (on the site of the present airport) and were forced to work from dawn to dusk. Many died, but in September 1944 2,400 POWs were force-marched to Ranau – a 240 km trek through the jungle which only six Australians survived. This 'Death March', although not widely reported in World War Two literature, claimed more Australian lives than any other single event during the war in Asia – including the notorious Burma-Siam railway.

reputed to assist those attempting examinations. The **Three Saints Temple**, further down the hill at the end of the padang, was completed in 1887. The three saints are Kwan Woon Cheung (a Kwan clan ancestor), the goddess Tien Hou (or Tin Hou, worshipped by seafarers – see the box on page 651) and the Min Cheong Emperor.

The only **Crocodile Farm** in Sabah is a commercial licensed enterprise, set up in 1982 when the government made the estuarine crocodile a protected species. The original stock were drawn from a population of wild crocodiles found in the Kinabatangan River. Visitors can see around 2,000 crocs at all stages of maturity waiting in concrete pools for the day when their skins are turned into bags and wallets and their meat is sold to local gourmets. The farm, at Mile 8, Labuk Road, is open to the public and has about 200 residents. Feeding time (and the only active time) is at 1000. Admission RM2. Open 0800-1700 Monday-Sunday. Labuk Rd bus. The **Forest Headquarters** (*Ibu Pejabat Jabatan Perkutanan*) is on Labuk Rd next to the Sandakan Golf Course and contains an exhibition centre and a well laid out and interesting mini-museum showing past and present forestry practice.

Excursions

Sepilok Orang-utan Sanctuary, see page 486.

Turtle Islands National Park, see page 483.

Kinabatangan River, see page 487.

The Gomontong Caves are 32 km south of Sandakan Bay, between the road to Sukau and the Kinabatangan River, or 110 km overland on the Sandakan-Sukau road. The name Gomontong means 'tie it up tightly' in the local language and the caves represent the largest system in Sabah. They are contained within the 3,924 hectares Gomontong Forest Reserve. There are sometimes orang-utan, many deer, mouse deer, wild boar and wild buffalo in the reserve, which was logged in the 1950s. There are several cave chambers. The main limestone cave is called Simud Hitam – or the *Black Cave*. This cave, with its ceiling soaring

Edible nests

The edible nests of black and white swiftlets are collected from the cave chambers, but the trade is now strictly controlled by Wildlife Department wardens. The white nests (of pure saliva) fetch more than US$500/kilo in Hong Kong; black nests go for around US$40/kg. The nest-collectors pick about 250 kg a day in the lower chamber and about 50 kg a day in the upper chamber. They earn about M$25 a day. The collectors use 60m-long rotan ladders. Heavy bundles of wood are lashed to the ladders to minimize swaying – but fatal accidents do occur. On average, a collector is killed once every 4 or 5 years in a fall. Bat guano is not collected from the floor of the cave so that it can act as a sponge mattress in the event of a serious fall.

The nests, which are relished as a delicacy by the Chinese (see page 402), are harvested for periods of 10 days, twice a year. The nests are first harvested just after the birds have made them (between February and April). The birds then build new nests, which are left undisturbed until after the eggs have been laid and hatched; these nests are then gathered, sometime between July and September. Harvesting contracts are auctioned to wholesalers who export the nests to Hong Kong, where their impurities are taken out and they are sold at a huge mark-up. Of the profits, about half go to the state government, and more than a third to the contractor. Less than a fifth goes to the collectors. It is possible to buy the birds nests in Sandakan restaurants, although they are all re-imported from Hong Kong.

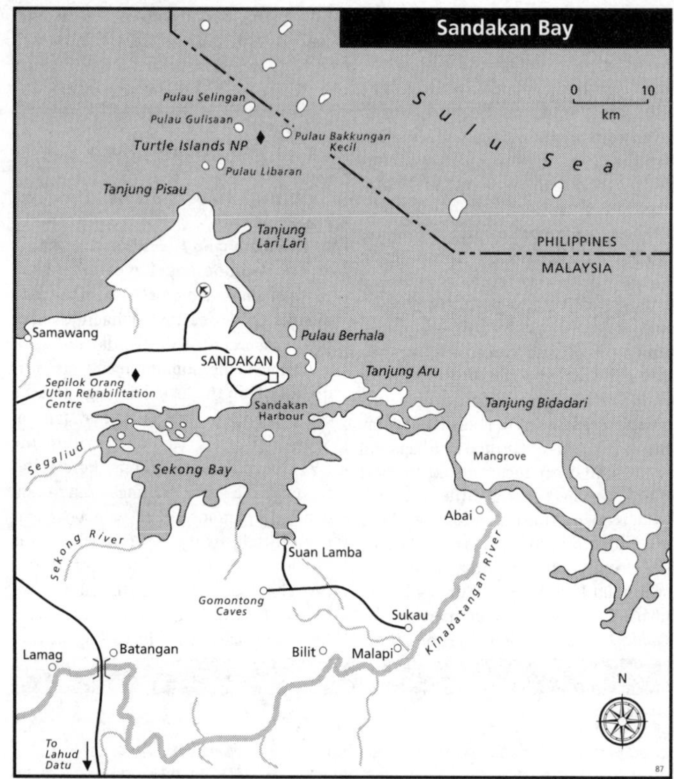

up to 90m overhead, is just a 5 minute walk from the registration centre and picnic area. The smaller and more complex *White Cave* or (Simud Putih) is above. It is quite dangerous climbing up as there is no ladder to reach the caves and the rocks are slippery. Over 2 million bats of two different species are thought to live in the caves: at sunset they swarm out to feed. 64 species of bat have been recorded in Sabah – most in these caves are fruit and wrinkled-lipped bats whose guano is a breeding ground for cockroaches. The squirming larvae make the floor of the cave seethe. The guano can cause an itchy skin irritation. The bats are preyed upon by birds like the bat hawk, peregrine falcon and buffy fish owl. There are also an estimated one million swiftlets which swarm into the cave to roost at sunset – these are the birds of bird's nest soup fame. The swiftlets of Gomontong have been a focus of commercial enterprise for perhaps 400 or 500 years. However it was not until 1870 that harvesting bird's nests became a serious industry here. The caves are divided into five pitches and each is allocated to a team of 10-15 people. Harvesting periods last 15 days and there are three each year (February-April, July-September, and December). Collecting the nests from hundreds of feet above the ground is a dangerous business and deaths are not uncommon. Before each harvesting period a chicken or goat is sacrificed to the cave spirit – it is thought that deaths are not the result of human error, but an angry spirit. The birdlife around the caves is particularly rich, with crested serpent eagles, kingfishers, Asian fairy bluebirds, and leadbirds all often sighted. Large groups of richly coloured butterflies are also frequently sighted drinking from pools along the track leading from the forest into the caves. The Niah Caves (see page 400) are on an even larger scale and yet more interesting. At the park headquarters there is an information centre, a small cafeteria where drinks and simple dishes are sold, and a pit latrine. If you arrive independently then one of the nest workers, a person from the information centre, or a ranger will show you around. The caves are open: 0800-1600, Monday-Sunday. The bats can be seen exiting from the caves between 1800 and 1830 – to request to see this it is necessary to ask at the information centre (Wildlife Department). **Accommodation** *Proboscis Lodge*, Sukau (T 240584 or F 240415, Kota Kinabalu), 2 hours by road from Sandakan, wooden stilt cabins set in the heart of the jungle, restaurant. **A** *Gomantong Rainforest Chalet*, this place is owned by *Sabah Travel* and opened in 1997; chalets are clean, with shared bathrooms and guides are provided. *Getting there*: it is easiest on a tour (see page 481). The caves are accessible by an old logging road, which can be reached by bus from the main Sandakan-Sukau road. The timing of the bus is inconvenient for those wishing to visit the caves – although an alternative is to charter a Labuk/Leila bus from Pryer St, opposite the bus station (RM100-200). It is much easier to take the 1100 boat from Sandakan's fish market to Suad Lamba, 1½ hours (RM3). From there it is possible to take a minibus to Gomontong (RM10/head, if there are a reasonable number of passengers). Visitors can stay overnight in the resthouse at nearby Sukau (see below). There are plans afoot to build a chalet and restaurant at Gomontong. Minibuses will pick up passengers for the return trip to Suad Lamba by arrangement – the daily boat back to Sandakan leaves Suad Lamba at 0530.

Pulau Berhala is ideal for picnicking and swimming. It has 200m rust-coloured sandstone cliffs on the south end of the island, with a beach at the foot, within easy reach by boat. The island was used as a leper colony before World War Two and as a prisoner of war camp by the Japanese. Agnes Keith (see page 476) was interned on the island during the war. *Getting there*: boats from the fish market (RM10).

Tours

Most tour companies operate tours to Turtle Islands, Sepilok, the Gomontong Caves, Sukau and the Kinabatangan River. See Tour companies and travel agents, page 483.

Local information

● Accommodation

Prices: L over RM500; **A+** RM260-500; **A** RM130-260; **B** RM65-130; **C** RM40-65; **D** RM20-40; **E** RM10-20; **F** Below RM10

A+ *Sandakan Renaissance* (formerly the *Ramada Renaissance* and before that the *Sabah Hotel*), Mile 1.5, Jln Leila, PO Box 537, T 213299, F 271171, a/c, restaurants, attractive pool, Sandakan's top hotel has been refurbished to 5-star standard with 120 rooms, fitness centre, tennis, pool and squash courts.

B *Hsiang Garden*, Mile 1.5, Jln Leila, Hsiang Garden Estate, Lot 7 & 8, Blok C, PO Box 1003, T 273122, F 273127, a/c, restaurant, all facilities, good bar. **B** *Malaysia*, 32 Jln Dua, T 218322, F 271249, clean and more spacious than *Hung Wing*, rooms have TVs. **B** *New Sabah*, 18 Jln Singapura, T 218949/218711, F 273725, a/c, well kept. **B** *Ramai*, Km 1.5, Jln Leila, Hsiang Gardens, T 273222, F 271884, a/c, restaurant, recommended. **B** *Sepilok Inn*, Blok 46, Lot 9, Tingkat 1,2,3, Jln Sekolah, T 271222, F 273831, a/c, clean rooms with attached bathrooms and Tvs, good value.

C *En Khin*, Jln Tiga (next to Maybank), T 217300, a/c, clean, reasonable value. **C** *Hung Wing*, Lot 4, Block 13, Jln Tiga, T 218855, F 271240, some a/c, probably the best of the middle-bracket hotels, clean rooms with own bathroom. **C** ***Mayfair***, 24 Jln Pryer, a/c, central location, good value.

D-E *Uncle Tan's*, Mile 17.5 (Km 29), Labuk Rd (5 km beyond Sepilok junction), T 089 531639, F 089 271215, set in fruit plantation; bicycle hire RM3/day, all meals included, tours arranged (see Tour companies), very cheap but not very clean and being on the main road, it's noisy from the logging trucks which continue to thunder past all night long. One redeeming feature is Uncle Tan himself who is a great raconteur, the other is Susie, a Filipino who runs the place and provides excellent food. **D-E** ***Travellers Rest Hostel***, 2nd Floor, Apt 2, Block E, Jln Leila, Bandar Ramai-Ramai, T 221460, some a/c, no attached bathrooms and limited toilet facilities, friendly with lots of travel information. Cooking and washing facilities.

● Places to eat

Prices: ◆◆◆◆ over RM40; ◆◆◆ RM13-40; ◆◆ RM5-13; ◆ under RM5

Sandakan is justifiably renowned for its inexpensive and delicious seafood.

Malay: ◆◆***Jiaman***, 1st Flr, Wisma Khoo Siak Chiew, serves interesting selection of Malay and Bajau dishes, no alcohol. ◆◆***Perwira***, *Hotel Ramai*, Jln Leila, Malay and Indonesian, good value, recommended.

Chinese: four Chinese seafood restaurants on Trig Hill overlooking the harbour. The seafood is fantastic. ◆◆◆***Golden Palace***, Trig Hill (2 km out of town), fresh seafood, specializes in drunken prawns, crab and lobster, and steamboats,(owners will provide transport back to Sandakan if there are no taxis available, recommended. ◆◆◆***Ming Restaurant***, *Sandakan Renaissance Hotel*, T 213299, Km 1, Jln Utara, Cantonese and Szechuan cuisine, particularly renowned for *dim sum* (breakfast). ◆◆◆***Japanese Corner***, *Hotel Hsiang Garden*, Jln Leila, Hsiang Garden Estate, T 273122, lobster and tiger prawns, good value and a popular local lunch venue. ***See Lok Yum***, next door to *Sea View Garden*, also very popular with locals.

Coffee Shops: ***New Bangsawan***, next to New Bangsawan cinema, just off Jln Leila, Tanah Merah, no great shakes, but best restaurant in Tanah Merah (where there are stacks of coffee shops). ***Silver Star Ice Cream and Café***, Third Ave, popular coffee shop with on-site satay stall in the evenings, particularly friendly and helpful management, recommended. ***Union Coffee Shop***, 2nd Flr Hakka Association Building, Third Ave, budget.

Foodstalls: Malay foodstalls next to minibus station, just before the community centre on the road to Ramai Ramai, also at summit of Trig Hill.

Trig Hill: this is a collection of semi-outdoor restaurants situated at the top of Trig (Trigonometry) Hill. Great views of Sandakan and also good food – especially seafood and steamboat.

Indian: ◆***Restoran Awalia***, Roti and curry.

Korean: ◆◆◆-◆◆***Korean Restaurant***, Hsiang Garden Estate, 1.5 km, Jln Leila, T 43891.

International: ◆◆◆***X O Steak House***, Lot 16, Hsiang Garden Estate (opposite the *Hsiang Garden Hotel*), Mile 1.5, Jln Leila, T 44033, lobster and tiger prawns and a good choice of fresh fish as well as Australian steaks, buffet barbecue on Fri nights, recommended. ◆◆***Hawaii***, *City View Hotel*, Lot 1, Block 23, Third Ave, western and local food, set lunch, recommended. ◆◆***Sandakan Recreation Club***, just off the Padang. ◆◆***Seoul Garden***, Hsiang Garden Estate, Mile 1.5, Leila Rd, Korean. ◆***Apple Fast Food***, Lorong Edinburgh, good spot for breakfasts. ◆***Fat Cat***, 206 Wisma Sandakan, 18 Jln Haji Saman, several branches around town, breakfasts recommended.

Vegetarian: ◆◆***Supreme Garden Vegetarian Restaurant***, Block 30, Bandar Ramai Ramai, Jln Leila, T 213292.

Fastfood: ◆◆***Fairwood Restaurant***, Jln Tiga, an inexpensive, a/c fastfood place with all the local favourites, situated in the centre of town.

● Airline offices

MAS, Ground Floor, Sabah Building, Jln Pelabuhan, T 273966; **Sabah Air**, Sandakan Airport, T 660527, F 660545.

● Banks & money changers

Most around Lebuh Tiga and Jln Pelabuhan. **Hong Kong & Shanghai**, Jln Pelabuhan/Lebuh Tiga; **Standard Chartered**, Jln Pelabuhan.

● Churches

St Michael's (Anglican) and *St Mary's* (RC) are on the hill at the south end of Sandakan town. There is also the *True Jesus Church*, *St Joseph's Catholic Church*, the *SIB Baptist Church*, the *All Saints Anglican Church* and the *Basel Church*.

● Entertainment

Cinemas: *Cathay Cinema*, next to Wisma Sabah and town mosque.

Discos and Karaoke: there is a karaoke parlour on just about every street. ***Tiffany Discotheatre and Karaoke***, Block C, 7-10, Ground and 1st Floors, Jln Leila, Bandar Ramai-Ramai.

● **Sports**

Bowling: *Champion Bowl*, Jln Leila, Bandar Ramai Ramai.

Recreation Clubs: *Sepilok Recreation Club*, Bandar Ramai Ramai, with snooker, sauna and darts as well as karaoke.

● **Post & telecommunications**

Area code: 089.

General Post Office: Jln Leila. Parcel post off Lebuh Tiga.

● **Shopping**

Almost everything in Sandakan is imported. There are some inexpensive batik shops and some good tailors. ***Wisma Sandakan***, next to the town mosque and the *Cathay*, is the trendiest place in town and offers 3-floors of a/c Singapore-style shopping.

● **Sports**

Golf: *Sandakan Golf Club*, 10 km out of town, open to non-members.

● **Tour companies & travel agents**

Alexander Ng Sandakan Adventure Tours, Pejabat Pos Jln Utara, Batu 1.5, T 212225, F 219959 caters for specialist interests and offers individually-tailored tours; ***Uncle Tan's***, Mile 17.5 (Km 29), Labuk Rd (5 km beyond Sepilok junction), T 216227, F 271215, inexpensive tours to his 'Utan Wildlife Camp' on the Kinabatangan (max 20 people), there are guides and a cook at the camp, daily departures during peak season (RM130 transport, RM15/night – all meals inclusive), also runs reasonably priced tours to Turtle Islands and Gomontong Caves, advance bookings can be addressed to PO Box 620, 90007 Sandakan, recommended; ***Unique Tours***, Lot 6, Block 1, Bandar Kim Fung, Batu 4, Jln Utara, T 212150; ***Wildlife Expeditions***, Room 903, 9th Flr, Wisma Khoo Siak Chiew, Lebuh Tiga, Sim Sim Rd, T 219616, F 214570 (branches in *Ramada Renaissance Hotel*), the most expensive, but also the most efficient, with the best facilities and the best guides, recommended; ***Discovery Tours***, 1008 10th Flr, Wisma Khoo Siak Chiew, T 274106, F 274107; ***Borneo Ecotours***, c/o *Hotel Hsiang Garden*, Jln Leila, PO Box 82, T 220210, F 213614.

● **Tourist offices**

National Parks Office, Jln Leila, T 42188.

● **Useful addresses**

Immigration: Federal Building, Jln Leila.

Sabah Parks Office: Room 906, 9th Flr, Wisma Khoo, Lebuh Tiga, T 273453. Bookings for Turtle Islands National Park (see below).

Wildlife Department: 6th Flr, State Secretariat Building, Mile 7 (on road to the airport), T 666550, permits for Gomontong caves and Sepilok.

● **Transport**

386 km from KK, 160 km from Lahad Datu.

Local Local minibuses from the bus stop between the Esso and Shell stations on the sea front on Jln Pryer.

Air The airport is 11 km from the town centre (RM10-12 by taxi into town). Early morning flights from KK to Sandakan allow breath-taking close-up views of Mount Kinabalu as the sun rises. Connections with Tomanggong, Miri, Lahad Datu, Kudat, Semporna, Tawau, KK.

Road Minibus: Sandakan's a/c long distance minibuses leave from the footbridge over Lebuh Tiga or from the minibus station just before the community centre on the Ramai-Ramai road. Be prepared for a long wait before departure, whilst the bus fills up. Regular connections from both stops with most towns in Sabah including Kota Kinabalu, 8 hours (RM35), Ranau, 3.5 hours (RM25), Lahad Datu (RM15), Tawau (RM25). An a/c coach from KK takes about 7 hours (RM25).

TURTLE ISLANDS NATIONAL PARK

40 km north of Sandakan, the Turtle Islands are at the south entrance to Labuk Bay. The park is separated from the Philippine island of Bakkungan Kecil by a narrow stretch of water. These eight tiny islands in the Sulu Sea are, together, among the most important turtle breeding spots in all Southeast Asia. The turtle sanctuary is made up of three tiny islands (Pulau Selingaan, Pulau Bakkungan Kecil and Pulau Gulisaan) and also encompasses the surrounding coral reefs and sea, covering 1,700 hectares. On Pulau Bakkungan Kecil there is a small mud volcano.

The islands are famous for their green turtles (*Chelonia mydas*) – which account for about four-fifths of the turtles in the park – and hawksbill turtles (*Eretmochelys imbricata*) – known locally as *sisik*. Most green turtles lay their eggs on Pulau Selingaan. The green turtles copulate about 50-200m off Pulau Selingaan and can often be seen during the day, their heads popping up like submarine periscopes. Hawksbills prefer to nest on Pulau Gulisaan.

Both species come ashore, year-round, to lay their eggs, although the peak season is between July and October. Even during the off-season between 4 and 10 turtles come up the beach each night to lay their eggs. Pulau Bakkungan Kecil and Pulau Gulisaan can only be visited during the day but visitors can stay overnight on Pulau Selingaan to watch the green turtles.

The numbers of visitors are restricted to 20/night in an effort to protect the female turtles, which are easily alarmed by noise and light when laying. Visitors are asked not to build camp fires, shine bright torches or make noise at night on the beach. The turtles should be watched from a distance to avoid upsetting the nesting process. Only the females come

The tough life of a turtle

Historically, green and hawksbill turtles have been hunted for their meat, shells and their edible eggs (a Chinese delicacy). They were a favourite food of British and Spanish mariners for centuries. Japanese soldiers slaughtered thousands of turtles for food during World War Two. Dynamite fishermen are also thought to have killed off many turtles in both Malaysian and Philippines waters in recent years.

Malaysia, Japan, Hong Kong, Japan and the Philippines, where green turtle meat and eggs are much in demand, are all signatories of the Convention in International Trade in Endangered Species (CITES), and trading in sea turtles has been proscribed under Appendix 1 of the Convention since 1981. However, the eggs are still sold illegally in Sandakan's wet market and can be bought for about RM1 each.

In his book *Forest Life and Adventures in the Malay Archipelago*, the Swedish adventurer and wildlife enthusiast Eric Mjoberg documents turtle egg-hunting and shell collecting in Sabah and Sarawak in the 1920s. He tells of how the Bajau would lie in wait for hawksbills, grab them and put them on the fire so their horny shields could be removed. "The poor beasts are put straight on the fire so that their shield may be more readily removed, and suffer, in the process, the tortures of the damned. They are then allowed to go alive, or perhaps half-dead into the sea, only to come back again after a few years and undergo the same cruel process." The Bajau, he says, used an 'ingenious contrivance' to hunt their prey. They would press pieces of common glass against their eyes 'in a watertight fashion' and would lie face-down on a piece of floating wood, dipping their faces into the water, watching for hawksbills feeding on seaweed. They would then dive in, armed with a small harpoon and catch them, knocking them out with a blow to the head.

The British North Borneo Company first introduced conservation measures in 1927 limiting the turtle hunting seasons. In 1964, eight islands in the Selingaan area were constituted as turtle farms; the rights to collect turtle eggs were only granted to contractors, who bid for them at auction. In 1964, the highest bid was RM20,000, which gives some idea of the profitability of the egg-collecting industry. Egg collecting was a hazardous profession: the first (and last) egg collector on Pulau Selingaan was murdered by pirates in 1964. Even today staff at the government hatchery on Pulau Selingaan have to be periodically withdrawn because of the threat posed by pirates. Selingaan always had the richest harvest of about 285,000 eggs a year. Pulau Bakkungan Kecil yielded about 127,000 eggs a year and Pulau Gulisaan, 63,000.

In August 1966 the first turtle hatchery in Malaysia was set up on Pulau Selingaan and in 1971 the three islands now comprising the park were compulsorily acquired by the Sabah state government. See page 293 for a box on the giant leatherback turtle.

ashore; the male waits in the sea nearby for his mate. The females cautiously come ashore to nest after 2000, or with the high tide. The nesting site is above the high tide mark and is cleared by the female's front and hind flippers to make a 'body pit', just under a metre deep. She then digs an egg chamber with her powerful rear flippers after which she proceeds to lay her eggs. The clutch size can be anything between 40 and 200 (batches of 50-80 are most common).

When all the eggs have been laid, she covers them with sand and laboriously fills the body pit to conceal the site of the nest, after which the exhausted turtle struggles back to the sea, leaving her Range Rover-like tracks in the sand. The egg-laying process can take about an hour or two to complete. Some say the temperature of the sand effects the sex of the young, if it is warm the batch will be mostly female and if cold, mostly male. After laying her eggs, a tag reading "If found, return to Turtle Island Park, Sabah, East Malaysia" is attached to each turtle by the rangers, who are stationed on each island. Over 27,000 have been tagged since 1970; the measurements of each turtle are recorded and the clutches of eggs are removed and transplanted to the hatchery where they are protected from natural predators – such as monitor lizards, birds and snakes.

The golf ball-sized eggs are placed by hand into 80 cm-deep pits, covered in sand and surrounded by wire. They take up to 60 days to hatch. The hatchlings mostly emerge at night when the temperature is cooler, breaking their shells with their one sharp tooth. There are hatcheries on all three islands and nearly every night a batch is released into the sea. More than 2.6 million hatchlings were released between 1977 and 1988. They are released at different points on the island to protect them from predators: they are a favoured snack for white-bellied gulls and only a fraction – about 3 to 5% – survive to become teenage turtles.

Permits are required by all visitors, RM30 from the Sabah Parks Office in Sandakan: Room 906, 9th Floor, Wisma Khoo, Lebuh Tiga (Third Avenue), T 273453. It is necessary to acquire special permits to visit Pulau Bakkungan Kecil and Pulau Gulisaan. Unofficially, however, it is possible to make the 5-minutes boat-trip to Pulau Bakkungan Kecil where there is some excellent coral. **NB** Visitors are advised to wait for the Park Ranger in their chalets; he will tell them when their turtle is laying eggs. Visitors should **not** walk on the beach after dark unaccompanied.

Tours

The average cost of a 1-night tour is RM150-200. Most tour companies (see page 481) operate tours to Turtle Islands and have their own boats, which makes the trip a bit cheaper. An expedition to the islands needs to be well-planned; vagaries such as bad weather, which can prevent you from leaving the islands as planned, can mess up itineraries. Most visitors to the islands book their trips in advance.

Best time to visit The driest months and the calmest seas are between March and July. The peak egg laying season is July-October. Seas are rough between October and February.

Park information

● Accommodation

The number of visitors to the islands is restricted, even at peak season. There are three cabins (one with two double bedrooms, two with six double bedrooms) on Pulau Selingaan (RM150/night/room). It is necessary to book in advance through the Sabah Parks office, Room 906, 9th Flr, Wisma Khoo, Lebuh Tiga (Third Ave), Sandakan, T 273453, F 274718.

● Places to eat

Chalets are equipped with cooking facilities and visitors can bring their own food. Restaurant in the Information Centre building.

● Transport

40 km northeast of Sandakan.

Sea Ferries: daily 50-60 seater ferry, 2-3 hours (RM33 return). The National Parks office in Sandakan can recommend speedboats of licensed tour companies.

SEPILOK ORANG-UTAN SANCTUARY AND REHABILITATION CENTRE

Sepilok, a reserve of 43 sq km of lowland primary rainforest and mangrove was set up in 1964 to protect the orang-utan – *Pongo pygmaeus* – from extinction. It is the first and largest of only three orang-utan sanctuaries in the world and now welcomes around 40,000 visitors a year. Logging has seriously threatened Sabah's population of wild orang-utan, as has their capture for zoos and as pets. The orang-utan (for details, see page 321) lives on the islands of Borneo and Sumatra and there are estimated to be perhaps as few as 10,000 still in the wild. In Sabah there are populations of orang utan in the Kinabatangan basin region (see page 487) and in the Danum Valley Conservation Area (see page 491 as well as in a few other isolated tracts of jungle.

Sepilok is an old forest reserve (it was gazetted as a forestry experimentation centre as long ago as 1931, and by 1957 logging had been phased out), where orphaned or captured orang-utans which have become too dependent on humans through captivity (many are captured by the oil palm planters, because they eat the young oil palm trees) are rehabilitated and protected under the Fauna Conservation Ordinance and eventually returned to their natural home. Initially, the animals at the Centre and in the surrounding area are fed every day but as they acclimatize, they are sent further and further away or are re-released into the Tabin Wildlife Reserve (near Lahad Datu). In 1996, researchers placed microchip collars on the orang-utans enabling them to be tracked over a distance of up to 150 km so that a better understanding of their migratory habits and other behaviour could be acquired.

After an initial period of quarantine at Sepilok, newly arrived orang-utans are moved to Platform A and taught necessary survival skills by the rangers. At the age of seven they are moved deeper into the forest to Platform B (about half an hour walk from Platform A and now not open to the public). At Platform B, they are encouraged to forage for themselves. Other animals brought to Sepilok include Malay sun bears, wild cats and baby elephants

Small and hairy: the Sumatran rhinoceros

Although not as rare as its Javan brother, the Sumatran, or lesser 2-horned rhino (*Didermoceros sumatrensis*) is severely endangered. It was once widespread through mainland and island Southeast Asia but has now been hunted to the point of extinction; there are probably less than 1,000 in the wild, mostly in Sumatra but with small populations in Borneo, Peninsular Malaysia and Vietnam. Only on Sumatra does it seem to have a chance of surviving. The situation has become so serious that naturalists have established a captive breeding programme as a precaution against extinction in the wild. Unfortunately this has been spectacularly unsuccessful. Around one third of animals have died during capture or shortly thereafter and, according to Tony and Jane Whitten, the only recorded birth was in Calcutta – in 1872. The species has suffered from the destruction of its natural habitat, and the price placed on its head by the value that the Chinese attach to its grated horn as a cure-all. Should the Sumatran rhino disappear so too, it is thought, will a number of plants whose seeds will only germinate after passing through the animal's intestines.

The Sumatran rhino is the smallest of all the family, and is a shy, retiring creature, inhabiting thick forest. Tracks have been discovered as high as 3,300m in the Mount Leuser National Park in Sumatra. It lacks the 'armoured' skin of other species and has a soft, hairy hide. It also has an acute sense of smell and hearing, but poor eyesight.

Feeding times Platform A: 1000 and 1500 (Friday 1000 only). Orang-utans undergo training exercises on Monday, Tuesday and Friday at 0800-0900 and 1400-1500.

Sepilok also has a rare Sumatran rhinoceros (*Didermoceros sumatrensis*) – also known as the Asian 2-horned rhinoceros (see box page 486). This enclosure is closed to the public.

The **Mangrove Forest Trail** takes 2-3 hours, one way. The walk takes in transitional forest, pristine lowland rainforest, a boardwalk into a mangrove forest, water-holes and a wildlife track. All enquiries at the Visitors Reception Centre.

The Information Centre, next to park headquarters, runs a nature education exhibition with replicas of jungle mammals and educational videos (video viewing times 0910, 1040 and 1115). The Park is open from 0900-1100, 1400-1530. Admission RM10, video camera RM10. It is worth getting to the park early.

Excursions

The new **Rainforest Interpretation Centre** on the road to Sepilok provides detailed and informative displays about the vegetation in the area. It is run by the Forest Research Centre (also found on this road). Great emphasis is given to participation, with questionnaires, games and so on; it offers a wide range of information about all aspects of tropical rainforests and the need for their conservation. The centre is located in the Forest Research Centre's arboretum and in addition to the exhibits there is a 0.8 km rainforest walk around the lake. Open: Monday-Thursday 0815-1215, 1400-1600, Friday 0815-1135, 1400-1600, Saturday 0815-1215. No admission fee and a free booklet is available. For more information contact the Forest Research Centre, PO Box 14-07, T 531522, F 531068.

Local information

● Accommodation

B-C *Wildlife Lodge*, Mile 14, Labuk Road, Sepilok Orang Utan Sanctuary, PO Box 2082, 100m behind the *Government Resthouse*, T 089 533031, F 089 533029, office in Sandakan: Ground Floor, Lot 1 and 2, Block C, Taman Grandview, Sim Sim Highway, T 089 273711, F 089 273010, some a/c, some dorm beds for RM20, cheaper rooms have shared bathrooms, with hot water showers, cafeteria. *The Lodge* is the realization of a dream for John and Judy Lim, who have gradually purchased all the land on the edge of the forest and over the past 3 years have been landscaping the area surrounding three man-made lakes and clearing the fruit orchards they inherited. They have planted lots of flowering and fruiting trees, attracting butterflies and birds in the process. Pleasant restaurant, great setting, clean and comfortable, boats for fishing available, recommended.

B *Chalet Resort* a new establishment for which we have no details, but understand that it is 3-4 star.

C *Orang Utan Rehabilitation Centre Rest House (Government Resthouse)*, Mile 14 Labuk Rd, T 089 215189, F 089 225189. Basic and characterless.

C-D *Sepilok B&B*, Jln Sepilok, of Mile 14, PO Box 155, T 089 532288, F 089 217668.

Camping: campsite at *Sepilok Wildife Lodge*.

● Places to eat

There is a good restaurant at the Centre.

● Useful information

Further information about Sepilok can be obtained from: Co-ordinator, Sepilok Orang Utan Rehabilitation Centre, Sabah Wildlife Department, WDT 200, 95000 Sandakan, T 089 531180, F 089 531189.

● Transport

23 km from Sandakan.

Road Bus: 8 daily public buses from Sandakan, from the central mini-bus terminal in front of *Nak Hotel*. Ask for the Sepilok Batu 14 line. From the airport, the most convenient way to reach Sepilok is by taxi. Sepilok is 1.9 km from the main road.

KINABATANGAN RIVER

At 560 km, this river is Sabah's longest. Much of the lower basin is gazetted under the Kinabatangan Wildlife Sanctuary and meanders through a flood plain, creating numerous ox-bow lakes and an ideal environment for some of the best wildlife in

Malaysia. One of the principal reasons why the Kinabatangan has remained relatively unscathed by Sabah's rapacious logging is because much of the land is permanently waterlogged and the forest contains only a small number of commercially valuable trees. Just some of the animals include: tree snake, crocodile, civet cat, otter, monitor lizard, long-tailed and pig-tailed macaque, silver-, red- and grey-leaf monkey and proboscis monkey. It is the most accessible area in Borneo to see the proboscis monkey which are best viewed from a boat in the late afternoon, when they converge on tree tops by the river banks to settle for the night. Sumatran rhinoceros have also been spotted (see box) and herds of wild elephant often pass through the park. The birdlife is particularly good and includes oriental darter, egret, storm's stork, osprey, coucal owl, frogmouth, bulbul, spiderhunter, oriole, flowerpecker and several species of hornbill. (For details on Borneo's flora and fauna, see page 321.)

Because of the diversity of its wildlife, the Kinabatangan riverine forest area has been proposed as a forest reserve. In addition, there has been little disturbance from human settlements: the Kinabatangan basin has always been sparsely inhabited because of flooding and the threat posed by pirates. The inhabitants of the Kinabatangan region are mostly Orang Sungai or people of mixed ancestry including Tambanua, Idahan, Dusun, Suluk, Bugis, Brunei and Chinese. The best destination for a jungle river safari is not on the Kinabatangan itself, but on the narrow, winding Sungai Menanggol tributary, about 6 km from Sukau. The Kinabatangan estuary – largely mangrove

The Long John Silvers of Sabah's east coast

In August 1986 a group of pirates invaded Lahad Datu one Friday afternoon when the Muslims were at prayer. Twenty-two of them, dressed in army fatigues and led by a 'beautiful woman' landed at the wharf and made straight for the blue and white-painted wooden police station on the hill behind the town. They hit it with several mortar rounds. They then entered the Standard Chartered Bank firing wildly as they went. One civilian was killed and the bank's security guard was shot dead. They made off with M$80,000 in cash, crossed the road and raided the MAS office on the ground floor of the *Mido Hotel*, which yielded another M$8,000 in cash. They escaped in Miami-Vice-style speed boats to one of the outer islands in Kennedy Bay, close to Philippines' waters.

Malaysian police field forces, reinforced by Royal Malaysian Air Force fighter-bombers from Labuan took on the pirates outside Malaysian territorial waters. They bombed a fishing village on one island where the Lahad Datu raiders were suspected of taking refuge. The Malaysian government claimed that most of the pirates had been killed and the Philippines government stayed silent. Corpses of seven of those killed were later brought back to Lahad Datu for identification.

The word on the local rumour mill was that the pirates would retaliate. A fortnight after the pirate attack, an enterprising robber pulled off a gold heist in town. He detonated a smoke bomb outside a goldsmith's and then calmly walked into the abandoned gold shop. No one raised an alarm. Instances of piracy are still common in the Lahad Datu area. In January 1993, a Malaysian marine police patrol sank a hijacked trawler and speedboat after a gun-battle with pirates. The Malaysian news agency reported: "Eight policemen sank the trawler with a canon shot. The pirates from the trawler jumped into the speedboat, and, when it too was sank, all jumped into the sea and were presumed to have escaped. The trawler skipper swam ashore and reported to police."

– is also rich in wildlife, and is a haven for migratory birds. Boats can be chartered from Sandakan to Abai (at the mouth of the river).

Batu Tulug (also known as Batu Putih, or White Stone) on the Kinabatangan River (100 km upstream from Sukau), is a cave containing wooden coffins dating back several hundred years (some of the better examples have been removed to the Sabah State Museum in KK). The caves are about 1 km north of the Kinabatangan Bridge, on the east side of the Sandakan-Lahad Datu road. *Getting there*: take the Sukau bus from Sandakan, 1400.

Exploring the Kinabatangan Visitors who prefer an in depth look at the area's wildlife can stay overnight at Sukau, 2 hours by road from Sandakan, where accommodation is provided by local tour operators. Tour operators take visitors by boat in the late afternoon through the freshwater swamp forest to see proboscis monkeys and other wildlife. There are also walks through the jungle. Because of the lack of public transport to Sukau, the only way to visit the area is with a tour; all tours must be booked in Sandakan or KK.

Local information

● Accommodation

Most companies running tours to the Kinabatangan put their guests up in Sukau. The one exception is *Borneo Eco Tours* (see above for address in Sandakan). ***Sukau Rainforest Lodge (SRL)***. *SRL*, accessible by boat from Sukau, provides eco-friendly accommodation for 40 visitors, in traditional Malaysian-style chalets, on stilts. All 20 rooms have solar-powered fans, twin beds, mosquito netting, and attached tiled bathroom with hot water. Other facilities include an open dining and lounge area (good restaurant), garden and sundeck overlooking the rainforest, and gift shop. Friendly and efficient service. All in all, a shining example of eco-tourism at its best, highly recommended.

● Tour companies & travel agents

(All Sandakan telephone numbers are prefixed with 089.) ***Borneo Eco Tours***, *c/o Hotel Hsiang Garden*, Jln Leila, PO Box 82, Sandakan, T 220210, F 213614; ***Discovery Tours***, 1008, 10th Flr, Wisma Khoo Siak Chiew, Sandakan, T 274106, F 274107; ***S.I. Tours***, Lot 3B, 3rd Flr, Yeng Ho Hong Building, Sandakan, T 213502, F 271513; ***Wildlife Expeditions***, Room 903, 9th Flr, Wisma Khoo Siak Chiew, Sandakan and Ground Floor, *Ramada Renaissance Hotel*, Jln Utara, Sandakan, T 219616, F 214570; ***Sukau Rainforest Lodge (SRL)***, owned and managed by ***Borneo Eco Tours***, Shoplot 12A, 2nd Flr, Lorong Bernam 3, Taman Soon Kiong, Kota Kinabalu, T 234009, F 233688, e-mail: betsbl@po.jaring.my. This last establishment is the most expensive tour operator but is worth it, as it can provide much more than the others (it has won several awards for excellence). It is situated at the edge of the sanctuary in a secluded spot on the Kinabatangan River. Qualified guides use wooden boats built by local orang sungai craftsmen, powered by electric engines to minimize noise disturbance to wildlife.

● Transport

Road It is possible to charter a minibus to take you from Suad Lamba to Gomontong and on to Sukau. It will pick passengers up again at a set time, by arrangement (RM70-100 return). A bus leaves from Sandakan to Sukau (via Gomontong turn-off) at 1100 and 1400, 115 km 3½ hours (RM20). The return bus leaves Sukau for Sandakan at 0600.

Sea Boat: to Suad Lamba, on the far side of Sandakan Bay leaves from the rear of Sandakan's wet market at 1100 every day, 1½ hours (RM3). (The return boat leaves Suad Lamba at 0530).

LAHAD DATU

Lahad Datu is Malaysia's 'wild East' at its wildest, and its recent history testifies to its reputation as the capital of cowboy country. The population is an intriguing mixture of Filipinos, Sulu islanders, migrants from Kalimantan, Orang Bugis, Timorese – and a few Malays. Most came to work on the oil palm plantations. Nowadays there are so many migrants, few can find employment. There are reckoned to be more illegal Filipino immigrants in Lahad Datu than the whole official population put together. Piracy in the Sulu Sea and the offshore islands in Kennedy Bay is rife – local fishermen live in terror.

The town itself is grubby and uninteresting. During World War Two, the Japanese made Lahad Datu their naval headquarters for East Borneo. After the war, the timber companies moved in: the British Kennedy Bay Timber Company built the Lahad Datu's first plywood mill in the early 1950s. Oil palm plantations grew up in the hinterland after the timber boom finished in the 1970s. As for the town, what it lacks in aesthetic appeal is made up for by its colourful recent history.

Kampung Panji is a water village with a small market at the end of Jalan Teratai, where many of the poorer immigrant families live.

Excursions

Beaches and islands The only good beaches are on the road to Tungku; Pantai Perkapi and Pantai Tungku. They can be reached by minibus from Lahad Datu or by boat from the old wharf. It is possible to get to the nearby islands from the old wharf behind the *Mido Hotel*, but at the moment it is too dangerous for tourists.

Danum Valley, see page 491.

Madai Caves are about 2 km off the Tawau-Lahad Datu road, near Kunak. The caves are an important archaeological site – there is evidence they were inhabited over 15,500 years ago. The birds' nests are harvested three times a year by local Idahan people whose lean-to kampung goes right up to the cave mouth. Own transport is required for this trip as it doesn't really cater for tourists.

Another 15 km west of Madai is **Baturong**, another limestone massif and cave system in the middle of what was originally Tingkayu Lake. The route is not obvious, so it is advisable to take a local guide. Stone tools, wooden coffins and rock paintings have been found there. Evidence of humans dating from 16,000 years ago, after the lake drained away can be found at the huge rock overhang. Take a torch. It is possible to camp here. *Getting there*: minibus from Lahad Datu.

Gunung Silam, 8 km from Lahad Datu on the Tawau road, a track leads up the mountain to a Telekom station at 620m and from there, a jungle trail to the summit. There are good views over the bay (when it isn't misty) and out to the islands beyond. It is advisable to take a guide. **Accommodation B** *Silam Lodge*, Silam, T 088 243245, F 088 254227, owned by the *Borneo Rainforest Lodge* and mostly used by people in transfer to the Danum Valley. *Getting there*: minibus from Lahad Datu.

Local information

● Accommodation

Prices: L over RM500; **A+** RM260-500; **A** RM130-260; **B** RM65-130; **C** RM40-65; **D** RM20-40; **E** RM10-20; **F** Below RM10

Lahad Datu is not a popular tourist spot and accommodation is poor and expensive. The *Perdana* and *Venus hotels* on Jln Seroja are worth avoiding.

B *Permaisaba*, Block 1, Lot 3, 1/4 Jln Tengah Nipah, T 883800, F 883681, 5 minutes drive from the airport and from town, seafood restaurant, Malaysian and Indian food, conference hall, free transfers to/from the airport and town. Big rooms with bathroom attached and hot water, information on the Danum Valley, characterless but convenient. **B** *Mido*, 94 Jln Main, T 881800, a/c, restaurant, the façade (facing the Standard Chartered Bank) is pock-marked with M-16 bullet holes – the result of over-curious residents watching the 1986 pirate raid on the bank, the *Mido* comes with all the sleaze of 'the wild East' and fails miserably to live up to its reputation as the best hotel in town.

C *Full Wah*, Jln Anggrek (opposite Chinese temple), T 883948, a/c, clean enough and probably a better bet than the Mido. **C** *Ocean*, Jln Teratai (just past the Esso Station), T 881700, a/c.

Government Resthouse, T 81579.

● Places to eat

Prices: ♦♦♦♦ over RM40; ♦♦♦ RM13-40; ♦♦ RM5-13; ♦ under RM5

Seafood: ♦♦♦*Melawar*, 2nd Flr, Block 47, off Jln Teratai (around the corner from the *Mido Hotel*), seafood restaurant, popular with locals. ♦♦♦*Ping Foong*, 1 mile out of Lahad Datu, on Sandakan Rd, open-air seafood restaurant, highly recommended. by locals. ♦♦*Evergreen Snack Bar and Pub*, on 2nd Flr, Jln Teratai, opposite the Hap Seng Building, a/c, excellent fish and chips and best-known for its tuna steaks, recommended. ♦♦*Golden Key*, on stilts over the sea opposite the end of Jln Teratai, it is really just a tumble-down wooden coffee shop, but is well known for its seafood. ♦♦*Good View*, just over 500m out of town on Tengku Rd, recommended by locals. ♦♦*Seng Kee*, Block 39, opposite *Mido Hotel* and next to Standard Chartered Bank, cheap and good. ***Restoran Ali***, opposite *Hotel New Sabah*, Indian, good roti.

Foodstalls: ♦*Pasar Malam* behind *Mido Hotel* on Jln Kastam Lama. Spicy barbecued fish (*ikan panggang*) and skewered chicken wings recommended.

● Airline offices

MAS, Ground Floor, *Mido Hotel*, Jln Main, T 881707.

● Banks & money changers

Standard Chartered, in front of *Mido Hotel*.

● Entertainment

The ***Lacin cinema*** (which usually screens violent kung-fu movies) is next to the post office on Jln Kenanga.

● Post & telecommunications

Area code: 089.

Post Office: Jln Kenanga, next to the Lacin cinema.

● Shopping

There is a new ***Central Market*** on Jln Bungaraya and a spice market off Jln Teratai where Indonesian smugglers tout Gudang Garam cigarettes and itinerant dentists and bumohs draw large crowds.

● Tour and travel agents

Borneo Nature Tours, Block 3, Fajar Centre, T 880207, F 885051.

● Useful addresses

Sabah Foundation: 2nd Flr, Hap Seng Building, Jln Main, T 881092. Bookings for Danum Valley. Bookings can also be made at the Sabah Foundation headquarters in Kota Kinabalu (T 354496).

● Transport

Air connections with Tawau, Sandakan, Semporna, KK and Kudat.

Road Minibus: minibuses leave from the bus station on Jln Bunga Raya (behind Bangunan Hap Seng at the mosque end of Jln Teratai) and from opposite the Shell station. Regular connections with Tawau, 2½ hours, Semporna, Sandakan, Madai.

Sea Boat: fishing boats take paying passengers from the old wharf (end of Jln Kastam Lama) to the Kennedy Bay islands, Tawau and Semporna, although time-wise (and, more to the point, safety-wise) it makes much more sense to go by road or air.

DANUM VALLEY CONSERVATION AREA

Danum Valley's 438 sq km of virgin jungle is the largest expanse of undisturbed lowland dipterocarp forest in Sabah. The field centre, which is 65 km west of Lahad Datu – and 40 km from the nearest habitation – was set up by the Sabah Foundation (Yayasan) in 1985 for forest research, nature education and recreation; when we last visited the centre, it was only open to Malaysian school trips. Tourists are allowed to visit *only* through the *Borneo Rainforest Lodge*. The Segama River runs through the conservation area, and past the field centre. The Danum River is a tributary of the Segama joining it 9 km downstream of the Field Centre. Gunung Danum (1093m) is the highest peak, 13 km southwest of the Field Centre. Within the area is a Yayasan Sabah timber concession, which is tightly controlled.

This area has never really been inhabited, although there is evidence of a burial site which is thought to be for the Dusun people who lived here about 300 years ago. There is also growing evidence of pre-historic cave-dwellers in the Segama River area. Not far downstream from the field centre, in a riverside cave, two wooden coffins have been found, together with a copper bracelet and a tapai jar, all of uncertain date. There is evidence of some settlement during the Japanese occupation – townspeople came upstream to escape from the Japanese troops. The area was first recommended as a national park by the World Wide Fund for Nature's Malaysia Expedition in 1975 and designated a conservation area in 1981. The field centre was officially opened in 1986.

The main reason for this large conservation area is to undertake research into the impact of logging on flora and fauna and to try and improve forest management, to understand processes which maintain tropical rainforest and to provide wildlife management and training opportunities for Sabahans. Many are collaborative projects between Malaysian and foreign scientists. The Sabah state tourism promotion board has recently thought to capitalize on this remote tract of jungle though. Following the opening of the Borneo Rainforest Lodge, Danum Valley will be promoted as a high-style expedition centre.

Flora and fauna Because of its size and remoteness, Danum Valley is home to some of Sabah's rarest animals and plants. The dipterocarp forest is some of the oldest, tallest and most diverse in the world, with 200 species of tree per hectare; there are over 300 labelled trees in the conservation area. The conservation area is teeming with wildlife: Sumatran rhinoceroses have been recorded, as have elephants, clouded leopards, orang-utans, proboscis monkeys, crimson langur, pig-tailed macaques, sambar deer, bearded pigs, western tarsier, sunbears and 275 species of bird including hornbills, rufous picolet, flowerpeckers and kingfishers. (For details on Borneo's flora and fauna, see page 321). A species of monkey, which looks like an albino version of the red-leaf monkey, was first seen on the road to Danum in 1988, and appears to be unique to this area. There are guided nature walks on an extensive trail system. Features include a canopy walkway, ancient Dusun burial site, waterfalls and a self-guided trail.

What to take: Leech socks are essential here.

Local information

● Accommodation

A ***Danum Valley & Borneo Rainforest Lodge***, PO Box 61174, Lahad Datu, T 088 709106/880207, F 088 709105, KK office: *Innoprise Jungle Lodge*, Block D, Lot 9 & 10, 2nd & 3rd Flr, Sadong Jaya Complex, T 244100, F 254227, e-mail ijl@po.javing.my. One of the most recent and finest tourism developments in Sabah. Eighteen bungalows in a magnificent setting beside the Danum River, built on stilts from belian (ironwood) and based on traditional Kadazan design with connecting wooden walkways. There are 28 rooms, each with private bathroom and balcony overlooking the Danum River, good restaurant, jacuzzi (solar-heated water). Based on *Tiger Tops* in Nepal and designed by naturalists, the centre hopes to combine a wildlife experience in a remote primary rainforest with comfort and privacy and provide high quality natural history information. There is a conference hall, excellent guides (including a very good woman called Mizy), who pre-plan their routes so that visitors don't bump into each other while thinking they are latter day Indiana Jones'; day visits to a forest management centre, good library of resource books, after dinner slide shows, a gift shop, rafting is available and night drives can be organized. Mountain bikes, fishing rods and river tubes all available for hire. Electricity available all day; the lodge is being marketed internationally in association with *Tiger Tops*. Expensive but well worth it.

Forest Cabin (built by Operation Raleigh), 18 km from field centre; ***Hostel***, 30 beds; ***Resthouse***, 5 double rooms, often booked up with visiting scientists.

● Transport

85 km west of Lahad Datu (left along the logging road at Km 15 on the Lahad Datu-Tawau road to Taliwas and then left again to field centre. The *Borneo Rainforest Lodge* is 97 km from Lahad Datu; they provide a transfer service (2 hours), telephone the *Lodge* for details.

Air 2 flights daily with MAS from Kota Kinabalu to Lahad Datu.

Road Bus: Lahad Datu is 7 hours from KK, 3 hours from Sandakan, 3 hours from Semporna, 2 hours from Tawau.

SEMPORNA

Semporna is a small fishing town at the end of the peninsula and is the main departure point for Sipidan Island (see below). Semporna has a lively and very photogenic market, spilling out onto piers over the water. It is a Bajau town and is known for its seafood. There are scores of small fishing boats, many with outriggers and square sails. There is a regatta of these traditional boats every March. The town is built on an old coral reef – said to be 35,000 years old – that was exposed by the uplift of the sea bed.

Many illegal Filipino immigrants pass through Semporna, as it is only 2 hours from the nearest Philippine island, which gives the place quite a different feel to other Malay towns.

Excursions

Sipadan, see below.

Other islands The islands off Semporna stand along the edge of the continental shelf, which drops away to a depth of 200m to the south and east of Pulau Ligitan, the outermost island in the group. Darvel Bay, and the adjacent waters, are dotted with small, mainly volcanic islands all part of the 73,000 acre Semporna Marine Park. The bigger ones are Pulau Mabol, Pulau Kapalai, Pulau Si Amil, Pulau Danawan and Pulau Sipadan. The coral reefs surrounding these islands have around 70 genera of coral – placing them in terms of their diversity, on a par with Australia's Great Barrier Reef. More than 200 species of fish have also been recorded in these waters.

Locals live in traditional boats called *lipa-lipa* or in pilehouses at the water's edge and survive by fishing. In the shallow channels off Semporna, there are three fishing villages, built on stilts: Kampung Potok Satu, Kampung Potok Dua and Kampung Larus. There are many more islands than are marked on the map; most are hilly, uninhabited and have beautiful white sandy beaches.

Reefs in the 73,000 acre Semporna Marine Park include Bohey Dulang, Sibuan Ulaiga, Tetugan, Mantabuan Bodgaya, Sibuan, Maigu, Selakan and Sebangkat. Pulau Bohey Dulang is a volcanic island with a Japanese-run pearl culture station. Visitors can only visit it if there is a boat from the pearl culture station going out. The Kaya Pearl company leases part of the lagoon and Japanese pearl oysters are artificially implanted with a core material to induce the growth of pearls. The oysters are attached to rafts moored in the lagoon. The pearls are later harvested and exported directly to Japan. *Getting there*: the islands can be reached by local fishing boats from the main jetty by the market, including Sibun, Sibankat, Myga and Selakan.

Local information

● Accommodation

B *Dragon Inn*, T 781088, hotel built on stilts over the sea, a/c, restaurant, very poor.

C *Semporna Hotel*, more expensive rooms have a/c and attached mandi.

E *Government Resthouse*, T 7718709. **E** *Sulabayan Lodging House*, 500m from town, at the entrance to Semporna, behind a Shell Station, cheapest in town with fan rooms and shared mandi, basic but OK.

● Places to eat

*******Floating Restoran dan Bar*, attached to *Dragon Inn*, pile house with good seafood, verify prices before ordering. There is an excellent Muslim restaurant at the top end of town, furthest from the market, and a number of coffee shops.

● Post & telecommunications

General Post Office: next to minibus station.

● Shopping

Cultured pearls are sold by traders in town. Filipino handicrafts.

● Sports

The Semporna Ocean Tourism Centre has recently been built, with a marina from where all sea sports can be organized.

● Transport

106 km north of Tawau.

Air Regular connections with Sandakan.

Road **Minibus**: minibus station in front of USNO headquarters. Regular connections with Tawau and Lahad Datu.

Sea **Boat Charter**: RM200 to Sipadan. There are day trips from Tawau to Sipadan with bigger boats, cutting the price down to RM50 (weekends only); the local papers supply information.

SIPADAN ISLAND MARINE RESERVE

The venerable French marine biologist Jacques Cousteau 'discovered' Sipadan in 1989 and after spending 3 months diving around the island from his research vessel *Calypso* had this to say: "I have seen other places like Sipadan 45 years ago, but now no more. Now we have found ... an untouched piece of art. "Since then Sipadan has become a sub-aqua Shangri-La for serious divers. In September 1990 Australia's *Sport Diving* magazine called the island "one of the most exciting dive spots imaginable ... an absolutely bewildering underwater experience." The reef is without parallel in Malaysia. But Sipadan Island

Lines on the map: sensitive territory

There's a new distraction on the horizon for scuba divers and sun-worshippers on Sipadan Island: warships. Because Sipadan – along with the neighbouring island of Ligitan – is disputed by the Indonesian and Malaysian governments, frigates from the alternate navies regularly make their presence felt by prowling around the turquoise waters like cats sniffing out their territorial boundaries. The issue of the overlapping claims lay dormant for decades but things changed with the discovery of Sipadan's incomparable underwater charms. With Malaysia giving the go-ahead to the construction of resorts on Sipadan, the government in Jakarta has been pressing harder for an urgent diplomatic solution to the dispute.

Under an agreement signed in 1969, Malaysia has been allowed to retain control of the islands until a solution is found. But Indonesia now says that agreement is being flouted. The two sides agreed to halt any developments until the dispute is settled by negotiation, but even the presence of the Indonesian frigates does not appear to have discouraged Malaysian developers. A joint commission has recently been studying the competing claims; both sides have reportedly produced further evidence to substantiate their claims. But a successful resolution of the dispute – which, thanks to good neighbourly relations, is extremely unlikely to escalate – could pave the way to the resolution of other similar disputes in the region.

Another long-standing dispute is the Philippine claim to the whole of Sabah, which Manila has never officially recognized as a legal part of the Malaysian Federation, formed in 1963. The Philipppines' historic claim to the territory rests on Sabah's original status as a dependency of the Sultanate of Sulu, in the Philippine islands, southwest of Mindanao. The sultan leased the land to the British North Borneo Chartered Company in 1877 and the British government inherited the lease when Sabah became a crown colony after the Second World War. Manila maintains that London had no right to then seed that lease to Kuala Lumpur and has never relinquished its claim, to the chagrin of Malaysia's federal government.

The very existence of the Association of Southeast Asian Nations (ASEAN) puts the brakes on the escalation of such disputes. Today, trade and investment deals have helped paper over cracks in bilateral relations, formalising the characteristically non-confrontational Asian way of doing things. But there is one outstanding territorial quarrel which is yet to really raise its ugly head: the Spratly Islands – an archipelago of 250 atolls dispersed over 800,000 sq km in the middle of the South China Sea. They are claimed by China, Vietnam, The Philippines, Malaysia and Taiwan; Indonesia and Brunei also stake claims to various islands but have not yet occupied them. Because the atolls straddle shipping lanes to Japan and lie on top of what are thought to be oil and mineral-rich strata, the Spratlys represent Southeast Asia's hottest potential flashpoint.

is not just for scuba divers: it is a magnificent tiny tropical island with pristine beaches and crystal clear water and its coral can be enjoyed by even the most amateur of snorkellers.

Pulau Sipadan is the only oceanic island in Malaysia – it is not attached to the continental shelf, and stands on a limestone and coral stalk, rising 200m from the bed of the Celebes Sea. The limestone pinnacle mushrooms out near the surface, but a few metres offshore drops off in a sheer underwater cliff to the seabed. The reef comes right into the island's small pier, allowing snorkellers to swim along the edge of the coral cliff, while remaining close to the coral-sand beach. The edge is much further out around the rest of the island. The tiny island has a cool forested interior and it is common to see flying foxes and monitor lizards. It is also a stop-over point for migratory birds, and was originally declared a bird sanctuary in 1933. It has been a marine reserve since 1981 and three Wildlife Department officials are permanently stationed on the island. The island is also a breeding ground for the green turtle; August and September are the main egg-laying months (see page 484).

Sipadan is known for its underwater overhangs and caverns, funnels and ledges, all covered in coral. 5m down from the edge of the precipice there is a coral overhang known as the Hanging Gardens, where coral dangles from the underside of the reef. The cavern is located on the cliff right in front of the island's accommodation area. Its mouth is 24m wide and the cave, which has fine formations of stalactites and stalagmites, goes back almost 100m, sometimes less than 4m below the surface. Visibility blurs where fresh water mixes with sea water. Inside, there are catacombs of underwater passages.

The island is disputed between the Indonesian and Malaysian governments. Indonesia has asked Malaysia to stop developing marine tourism facilities on Sipadan. Malaysia's claim to the island rests on historical documents signed by the British and Dutch colonial administrations. Periodically the two sides get around the negotiating table, but it appears that neither is prepared to make a big issue of Sipadan. Occasionally guests on the island see Indonesian or Malaysian warships just off- shore and in 1994 rumours were circulating in Sabah that the Governor of the neighbouring Indonesian province of Kaltim wanted to send settlers to the island. A third party also contests ownership of Sipadan: a Malaysian who claims his grandfather, Abdul Hamid Haji, was given the island by the Sultan of Sulu. He has the customary rights to collect turtles eggs on the island – although the Malaysian government disputes this.

The island's tourist facilities are run by three tour companies, who control everything. They are required to restrict the number of visitors allowed on the island at any one time to about 40 and on arrival visitors have to sign a guarantee that they will do nothing to spoil the island. One of the directors of the Sipadan Dive Centre – a lawyer from Kota Kinabalu – has presented proposals to the state government concerning future environmental safeguards for the island. These have the support of the other resort owners on Sipadan who have agreed to bear the costs together. The proposals recommend that human activity be carefully controlled by further restricting the number of visitors (particularly day-trippers and weekenders), limiting the size and speed of boats using the jetty, the introduction of a bio-digester to dispose of all waste and a scale-down of all diving and snorkelling activities during the height of the northeast and southwest monsoons, to allow the island a recovery period. These proposals have yet to be endorsed by the state government.

Tours

Each operator rents out equipment (RM75-100/day) and provides all food and accommodation. Pre-arranged packages operated by the companies include air transfer to and from Kota Kinabalu. 'Walk-in' rates marginally cheaper. *Borneo Divers*, Rooms 401-412, 4th Flr, Wisma Sabah, Kota Kinabalu, T 222226, F 221550. Run monthly trips, 8-20 divers for any trip, packages (all in) approx: US$1065 (5 days/4 nights); *Pulau Sipadan Resort*, 484, Block P, Bandar Sabindo, T 765200, F 763575, organizes dive tours, food and lodging and diving instruction, snorkelling equipment is also available, maximum of 30 divers at any one time; *Sipadan Dive Centre*, A1103, 10th Flr, Wisma Merdeka, Jln Tun Razak, Kota Kinabalu, T 240584, F 240415, sipadan@po.jaring.my, packages (all in) approx: US$740 (5D/4N), recommended. **NB** *Borneo Divers* and *Sipadan Dive Centre* both provide 4-days PADI training courses. The PADI Divemaster Scuba courses – conducted off KK's TAR Park islands – cost US$250-US$330. The *Coral Island Cruises tour company* (based in KK see page 445) also operates a small ship, the MV *Coral Topaz*, which makes special diving voyages to the Sipadan/Ligitan island group. The 'live-on-board' dive vessel features a/c accommodation, bars, lounges and buffet meals. 5 days/4 nights cruises cost US$760 per person (diving equipment included).

Best time to visit Best diving season from mid-February to mid-December when visibility is greater (20-60m); mostly drift diving; night diving is said to be spectacular.

Local information

● Accommodation & places to eat

Sipadan Longhouse Resort, fan rooms with shower, buffet western food, RM390 for 2 days and nights, full board. ***Sipadan Lodge***, a/c, hot water, local, Chinese and western food, private boats available. The island's drinking water is brought in from Semporna. *Sipadan Dive Centre*'s facilities are marginally better. It is the most recent operator to set up on the island and its chalets have attached bathrooms and hot water.

● Sports

Deep sea fishing: for tuna, marlin, barracuda and bonito can be organized from Sipadan. Trawler operated by *Pulau Sipadan Resort* is charged per person and per hour. Early mornings and evenings are best. Because the island and the reef are protected, line fishing from the shore is illegal.

● Transport

32 km from Semporna in the Celebes Sea.

Sea Boat: organized by the two tour companies from Semporna, including in price of trip. Also boats from Tawau once a week from the main dock (much rougher journey as have to go more on the open sea). **Speedboat**: hired, 1½ hours from Semporna.

MABUL ISLAND

Located between Semporna and Sipadan, this island of 21 hectares is considerably larger than Sipadan and is partly home to Bajau fishermen who live in traditional palm thatched houses. In contrast to Sipadan's untouched forest, the island is predominantly planted with coconut trees. Diving has been the most recent discovery; an Australian diver claims it is "one of the richest single destinations for exotic small marine life anywhere in the world". It has already become known as the world's best 'muck diving'. The island is surrounded by gentle sloping reefs with depths from 3-35m and a wall housing numerous species of hard corals. Visibility is usually at least 12m.

● Accommodation Mabul was chosen to provide more upmarket accommodation than that found on Sipadan, offering exclusive private chalets. For people diving off Sipadan, Mabul is a convenient place to stay and considerably less crowded. There are two resorts on the island. **A+** ***Sipadan Water Village***, for reservation PO Box 62156, T 089 751777, F 089 752997, swvill@tm.net.my, general sales agent: *Pan Borneo Tours and Travel*, constructed on several wharves in Bajau water village-style on ironwood stilts over the water. 35 chalets with private balconies, hot water showers, restaurant serving good range of cuisine, dive shop and centre, deep sea fishing tours available. Budget or student travellers are sometimes given large discounts. **L** ***Sipadan Mabul Resort***, located at the southern tip of the island, overlooking Sipadan, PO Box 14125, T 088 23000, F 088 242003, mabul@po.jaring.my, 25 beach chalets with a/c, hot water showers, balcony, pool and jacuzzi, restaurant serving Chinese and western food in buffet style, all inclusive price, padi diving courses, snorkelling, windsurfing, deep sea fishing, volleyball, private diving boats.

• **Transport Air and Sea**: flight to Tawau, met upon arrival and then taken to Semporna (1½ hours), from where it is a 30-minute boat ride to Mabul Island.

TAWAU

Tawau is a timber port in Sabah's south-eastern corner. The town was developed in the early 19th century by the British who planted hemp. The British also developed the logging industry in Sabah, using elephants from Burma. The Bombay Burma Timber Company became the North Borneo Timber Company in 1950; a joint British and Sabah government venture.

Tawau is surrounded by plantations and smallholdings of rubber, copra, cocoa and palm oil. The local soils are volcanic and very fertile and palm oil has recently taken over from cocoa as the predominant crop; Malaysian cocoa prices dropped when its quality proved to be 20% poorer than cocoa produced in Nigeria and the Ivory Coast. In addition, the cocoa plants became diseased. As a result of the decline, many of the cocoa growers emigrated to the Ivory Coast. KL is now an established research centre for palm oil and recently it has been discovered that palm oil can be used as a fuel.

Now that the Sandakan area has been almost completely logged, Tawau has taken over as the main logging centre on the east coast. The forest is disappearing fast but there are ongoing reafforestation programmes. At Kalabakan (west of Tawau) there is a well established, large scale reafforestation project with experiments on fast-growing trees such as *Albizzia falcataria*, which is said to grow 30m in 5 years. There are now large plantation areas. The tree is processed into, among other things, paper for paper money. Tawau is a busy commercial centre and the main channel for the entry of Indonesian workers into Sabah. Kalimantan is visible, just across the bay.

Excursions Tawau Hills State Park lies 24 km north-west of Tawau; it protects Tawau's water catchment area. The Tawau River flows through the middle of the 27,972 hectares park and forms a natural deepwater pool, at Table Waterfall, which is good for swimming. There is a trail from there to some hot water springs and another to the top of Bombalai Hill, an extinct volcano. Most of the forest in the park below 500m has been logged. Only the forest on the central hills and ridges is untouched. The park is a popular away-day destination for locals at weekends, Admission: RM2. **Camping** is possible but bring your own equipment. For further information on the park, contact Ranger Office, Tawau Hills Park, T 011 810676, F 011 884917. *Getting there*: access to the park is via a maze of rough roads through the Borneo Abaca Limited agricultural estates. Probably best to hire a taxi.

• **Accommodation** Hotels in Tawau are not great value for money. The cheaper lodging houses, around Jln Stephen Tan, Jln Chester and Jln Cole Adams should be avoided. **A** *Emas*, Jln Utara, T 762000, F 763569, a/c, restaurant. **A-B** *Belmont Marco Polo*, Jln Abaca/Jln Clinic, T 777988, F 763739, a/c, restaurant, best hotel in Tawau. **C** *Merdeka*, 3023 Jln Masjid, T 776655, F 761743, a/c, restaurant. **B** *Royal*, 177 Jln Bilian, T 773100/772856, a/c, restaurant. **C** *Tawau*, 72-3 Jln Chester, T 771100, cheaper rooms without attached bathroom and rather smelly and dirty. **D** *Pan Sabah*, Jln Stephen Tan, behind local minibus station, T 762488, a/c, TV, attached bathrooms, clean rooms and very good value.

• **Places to eat Malay**: ♦♦*Asnur*, 325B, Block 41 Fajar Complex, Thai and Malay, large choice. ♦♦*Venice Coffee House*, *Marco Polo Hotel*, Jln Abaca/Jln Clinic, 'hawker centre' for late night eating, Malay and Chinese. **Chinese**: ♦♦*Dragon Court*, 1st Flr, Lot 15, Block 37 Jln Haji Karim, Chinese, popular with locals, lots of seafood. **International**: ♦♦*Dreamland*, 541 Jln Haji Karim, also good local selection. ♦♦*The*

Hut, Block 29, Lot 5 Fajar Complex, Town Extension II, western, Malay and Chinese, large menu. ***Kublai Khan***, *Marco Polo Hotel*, Jln Abaca/Jln Clinic. **Seafood**: *May Garden*, 1 km outside town on road to Sempcrna, outside seating. ***Maxims***, Block 30, Lot 6 Jln Haji Karim. **Foodstalls**: stalls along the seafront.

• **Airline offices** MAS, Lot 1A, Wisma SASCO, Fajar Complex, T 765533; **Merdeka Travel**, 41 Jln Dunlop, T 772534/1, booking agents for Bouraq (Indonesian airline); **Merpati** 47A Jln Dunlop, 1st Flr, next to Borneo Divers, T 752323; **Sabah Air**, Tawau Airport, T 774005.

• **Banks & money changers** Bumiputra, Jln Nusantor, on seafront; **Hong Kong**, 210 Jln Utara, opposite the padang; **Standard Chartered**, 518 Jln Habib Husein (behind Hongkong Bank). Exchange kiosk at wharf.

• **Embassies & consulates** Indonesian Consulate, Jln Apas, mile 1.5.

• **Entertainment** Cinema is on Jln Stephen Tan, next to central market. There are karaoke bars on every street corner. Several of the hotels have nightclubs and bars.

• **Post & telecommunications Area code**: 089. **Post Office**: off Jln Nusantor, behind the fish market.

• **Shopping** General and fish market at the west end of Jln Dunlop, near the Custom's Wharf.

• **Sport Diving**: Borneo Divers, 46 1st Flr, Jln Dunlop, T 762259, F 761691. **Golf**: 9-hole golf course, modest green fees, even cheaper during the week.

• **Tour companies & travel agents** *GSU*, T 772531, booking agent for Kalimantan; ***Pulau Sipadan Resort Tours***, 1st floor, no 484, Bandar Sabindo, T 242262, F 213036.

• **Useful addresses Immigration**: Jln Stephen Tan.

• **Transport** 110 km from Semporna. **Air** The airport is 2 km from town centre. Regular connections with KK, Lahad Datu and Sandakan. **Road Bus**: station on Jln Wing Lock (west end of town). Minibus station on Jln Dunlop (centre of town). It is now possible to take a bus from Tawau to Kota Kinabalu direct, leaving at 0700, 11 hours, RM45 **4WD**: it is possible to drive from Sapulut (south of Keningau, see page 452) across the interior to Tawau on logging roads but a 4WD vehicle is required.

• **International connections** The Indonesian town of Tarakan is not a visa-free entry point; it is necessary to obtain a 1-month visa in advance (takes 1 day). There is an Indonesian consulate in Tawau and in KK. The cost is RM75 (1 photograph needed), 2 month tourist visa provided without hassle. **Air** It is possible to fly to Tarakan from Tawau: Indonesian Bouraq and MAS operate flights. **Sea Boat**: packed boats leave Tawau's Customs Wharf (behind Pasar Ikan) twice daily at 0800 and 1600 for Pulau Nunukan Timur – in Kalimantan, Indonesia – 2 hours, RM25/16,000Rp. It is possible to get a direct boat from Tawau to Tarakan at 0800 (RM45). Tickets available from the offices opposite Pasar Ikan. From there it is possible to get a boat to Tarakan the next day, or a direct boat to Pare Pare (Sulawesi) 48 hours (45,000Rp). There are no longer direct boats to Tarakan and travellers must stop over at Nunukan (see next entry).

NUNUKAN

Travellers making the journey between Tawau and Tarakan (in Indonesia) need to stop-over in Nunukan as there are no longer any direct boats. Nunukan offers very little for the visitor: there are no beaches and it seems to be impossible to arrange even a canoe trip. On the plus side the people are friendly. There is one bank – *BNI* – on the main square but it gives very poor exchange rates.

• **Accommodation** There are several losmen (guesthouses) in town including: **E** ***Losmen Monaco***, 5 minutes walk from the port, clean and reasonable value with shared mandis. **E** ***Losmen Arena***, on the main square, a step down from the *Monaco*. **F** ***Losmen Nunukan***, on main square, bottom of the range and just about tolerable.

• **Transport Sea Boat**: daily ferry connections (which are packed) with Tawau in Sabah, Malaysia, 2 hours (16,000Rp). Also daily ferries to Tarakan.

Information for travellers

Before travelling	499	Getting around	510
Getting there	502	Communications	520
On arrival	504	Entertainment	522
Where to stay	507	Holidays and festivals	522
Food and drink	508	Further reading	526

BEFORE TRAVELLING

ENTRY REQUIREMENTS

● Visas

Passports should be valid for 6 months beyond the period of intended stay in Malaysia.

No visa is required for citizens from Commonwealth countries (except India, Bangladesh, Sri Lanka and Pakistan), Albania, Algeria, Austria, Bahrain, Belgium, Britain, Czech Republic, Denmark, Egypt, Finland, Germany, Hungary, Germany, Iceland, Republic of Ireland, Italy, Japan, Jordan, South Korea, Kuwait, Lebanon, Liechtenstein, Luxembourg, the Netherlands, Norway, Morocco, Oman, Qatar, San Marino, Saudi Arabia, Republic of Slovakia, Sweden, Switzerland, Tunisia, Turkey, United Arab Emirates, USA, and North Yemen for a stay of 3 months, if they are not working.

Citizens of France, Greece, Poland and South Africa, as well most African and Latin American countries, are permitted to stay for 1 month without a visa.

On arrival visitors normally receive a 1 or 2 month visitor's permit (Commonwealth citizens get 2 months). Usually those arriving by air get 2 months; overland, 1 month. If you intend to stay longer, permits can be painlessly extended to 3 months at immigration departments in Kuala Lumpur, Penang or Johor Bahru.

Citizens of ASEAN countries (Brunei, Indonesia, Laos, Myanmar/Burma, Philippines, Singapore, Thailand, Vietnam), do not need visas for visits not exceeding a month – they are issued on arrival. Nationals of most other countries including Afghanistan, Iran, Iraq, Libya, Syria and South Yemen may stop over in Malaysia for up to 14 days without advance visas but it is preferable to have proof of outward bookings. Citizens of Bulgaria, Rumania and Russia may stay for 7 days without a visa. Applications for visas should be made well in advance to the nearest Malaysian diplomatic mission, or, in countries where there are no Malaysian representatives, to the British Consular Representative.

Visit passes issued for entry into Peninsular Malaysia are not automatically valid for entry into the East Malaysian states of Sabah and Sarawak. On entry into East Malaysia from Peninsular Malaysia visitors have to go through immigration even though the flight is an internal one. You get a new stamp in your passport and it may actually reduce the time you can stay in Malaysia. A month's stamp is usual – if you want more, then you must ask the official. (The reason for this odd state of affairs is that Sabah and Sarawak maintain control over immigration and even Malaysian visitors from the 'mainland' are required to obtain a travel permit to come here.) Apply to the immigration offices in Kota Kinabalu and Kuching for an extension. There are certain areas where permits are necessary in East Malaysia, eg for upriver trips in Sarawak permits are obtained from the residents' offices (see appropriate sections). All national parks in Peninsular and East Malaysia require permits from the national or state parks offices.

● Vaccinations

A certificate of vaccination for Yellow Fever is necessary for those coming from endemic zones except for children under 1 year of age.

Dr Watson solves the Malayan malaria mystery

The word 'malaria' was first used in the 18th century and comes from the Italian *mala aria* – or 'bad air' – because it was thought to be caused by unwholesome air in swampy districts. It was not until 1899 that Dr Ronald Ross, a medical officer in Panama during the construction of the canal, discovered that the real culprit was not the air, but the swamp inhabitants themselves – mosquitos. The following year a young Scotsman, Dr Malcolm Watson, was appointed as a government medical officer in Malaya, where malaria was the biggest killer. Dr Watson was posted to Klang where a malarial epidemic was wreaking havoc. In September 1901 nearby Port Swettenham (now Port Klang) opened for business; by Christmas 118 out of the 176 government employees had been struck down by the disease.

Armed with the knowledge of the recent Panama discovery, Dr Watson set about draining the coastal swamplands, spraying them and improving the water-flow in streams. It worked, and the doctor became known as the 'White Knight of Malaria Control'. Historian Mary Turnbull writes that "it was said of Watson that 'he could probably have claimed to have saved more lives than any other physician in history', and Ronald Ross described his work in Malaya as 'the greatest sanitary achievement ever accomplished in the British Empire'". The methods used in his battle against the *nyamuk* – the menacing and almost onomatopoeic Malay word for mosquito – became standard practice in the colony. Combined with the increased use of quinine, malaria was controlled, which is one of the reasons why colonial Malaya's plantation economy began to take off in the early 1900s. The planting of rubber estates in the coastal lowlands – greatly encouraged by the zealous director of Singapore's Botanic Gardens, 'Mad' Henry Ridley (see page 660) – would otherwise have been a much more hazardous occupation.

● Tourist information

Tourism Malaysia (headquarters), 24-27 Flr, Menara Dato' Onn, Putra World Trade Centre, 45, Jln Tun Ismail, 50480 Kuala Lumpur T(03) 2935188, F (03) 2935884. There is an information centre on Level 2 of the Putra World Trade Centre (in the convention centre). For practical advice, visitors are better advised to contact Malaysian Tourist Information Centre (MATIC), 109 Jln Ampang, Kuala Lumpur T 2423929. There are several other tourist information bureaux in KL (see page 138) and regional tourism offices in state capitals, all of which are reasonably efficiently run.

Tourism Malaysia has tourist information bureau in most large towns; it is very efficient and can supply further details on tourist sights, advise on itineraries, help place bookings for travel and cultural events and provide updated information on hotels, restaurants and air, road, rail, sea and river transport timetables and prices. If there is no Tourism Malaysia office in a town, travel agents are usually helpful.

WHEN TO GO

● Best time to visit

The rainy seasons should be borne in mind when planning itineraries in Malaysia; the best time to visit the Peninsula's east coast is between March and September. Trips along the east coast and interior jungles are not advisable between November and February, during the north-east monsoon. The east coast suffers flooding at this time of year, and it is inadvisable and also impossible to take fishing boats to offshore islands such as Pulau Tioman as the sea can be very rough. Taman Negara (the National Park) is closed from November to the end of January. Other parts of Peninsular Malaysia can be visited year round as the rainy season is not torrential, although it is fairly wet during the north-east monsoon period. Rainfall is worst from May to September on the west coast of the Peninsula, but it is never very heavy. In East Malaysia March and June are the best times to visit the interior, the worst rains are usually from November to February and some roads are impassable in these months. Conversely, in the dry season, some rivers become unnavigable. In recent years the onset of the wet and dry seasons in both Sabah and Sarawak have become less predictable; environmentalists ascribe this to deforestation, although there is no scientifically proven link. **NB** School holidays run from mid- to late February, mid-May to early June, mid- to late August and late November to early January. During these periods it is advisable to book hotels. For more information on climate and cross references to rainfall and temperature graphs see page 36.

HEALTH

● Vaccinations

Visiting the peninsula's west coast does not require any medical precautions other than some insect repellent. Those travelling to national parks, rural areas and to Sabah and Sarawak are advised to have vaccinations against cholera, typhoid and polio, hepatitus A, tetanus and Japanese Encephalitus.

● Malaria

This is not a problem in main cities but it is advisable to take malaria pills if you are going to rural areas. Malaria is more prevalent in East Malaysia, particularly in the jungled interior of Sabah.

● Food and water

Water is clean and safe to drink in major cities on the peninsula but in other areas it should be boiled or sterilized. Mineral water can be bought fairly easily. With food, normal precautions should be taken with shellfish; ensure stall food is properly cooked and avoid unpeeled fruits.

● Medical facilities

Malaysian health care is excellent and private clinics are found in most small towns and there are good government hospitals in major cities. All state capitals have general hospitals and every town has a district hospital. On the whole it is inexpensive to visit a private doctor (about RM20-40), and a sojourn in a government hospital is cheaper than most hotels (no a/c or pool). Big hotels have their own in-house doctors – who are extremely expensive. Other doctors are listed in the telephone directory. Pharmaceuticals are available from numerous outlets including shopping centres, supermarkets and hotels. Most pharmacists are open 0900-1800 Mon-Sat. A number of drugs that can only be obtained on prescription in western countries can be bought over the counter in Malaysia. Traditional Chinese pharmacies – mostly found in Chinatowns – also dispense Chinese medicines, and will advise on traditional remedies for most ailments. Facilities in East Malaysia are not as good as those on the Peninsula.

MONEY

● Cash

The Malaysian dollar (RM), is called the **ringgit**, and is divided into 100 **sen** (cents). Bank notes come in denominations of RM1, 5, 10, 20, 50, 100, 500 and 1,000. Coins are issued in 1, 5, 10, 20 and 50 cent denominations. As a rough guideline, US$1= RM3.2 (November 1997). Note that the ringgit took a hammering over 1997 as the fallout from the Thai financial crisis and Mahathir's response to this crisis led to a sharp devaluation – and to an even steeper fall in the stock market.

● Cost of living

While the average inflation rate is about 5%, the cost of living in the main cities – particularly KL – is rising much faster. This has affected the cost of not only consumer durables but also hotels and restaurants. In theory the sharp fall in the value of the ringgit in 1997 should mean that Malaysia is much cheaper for foreigners, relative to 1996. However hotels, and particularly the higher grade hotels which quote their room rates in US$, may well increase their ringgit prices to account for the fall.

Malaysia is no longer a cheap place to live. But it is still possible to travel on a relatively low budget. Cheaper guesthouses charge around RM15-50 a night for two – which at the late 1997 rate of exchange translates into a US$ figure of about US$5-16. Dorm beds are available in most towns, and these are priced at around RM10-15, or US$3-5. It is usually possible to find a simple a/c room for RM50-80 or US$16-26. Eating out is also comparatively cheap: a good curry can be had for as little as RM2-4, or around US$1. Finally, overland travel is a bargain. Although private car ownership is rapidly spreading, many ordinary Malaysians still travel by bus and consequently the bus network is not only extremely good, but fares are very good value.

● Credit cards

Most of the bigger hotels, restaurants and shops accept international credit cards, including American Express, BankAmericard, Diners, MasterCard and Visa. Visa and MasterCard are the most widely accepted. Cash advances can be issued against credit cards in most banks, although some banks – notably Bank Bumiputra

– limit the amount that can be drawn. A passport is usually required for over-the-counter transactions. It is also possible to draw cash from ATMs (Automatic Teller Machines) if you have a PIN number (Personal Identification Number). Maybank, with branches in most towns, will accept both Visa and MasterCard at its ATMs.

● **Travellers' cheques**
These can be exchanged at banks and money-changers and in some big hotels (often guests-only). Money-changers often offer the best rates, but it is worth shopping around. Banks charge commission on TCs.

TCs from all major issuing companies, and denominated in just about any major currency, are widely accepted. But, as elsewhere, US$ are probably best.

GETTING THERE

AIR

The main airport for Malaysia is Kuala Lumpur's Subang International Airport, 24 km from the city centre. However, the construction of a new international airport is well underway at Sepang, 45 km south of KL. It is scheduled for completion in 1998. Note that the information provided below on airport facilities and transport to and from the airport applies to Subang. Some international flights also go direct to Penang, Kota Kinabalu and Kuching. Smaller airlines also run services between Singapore and island resorts such as Langkawi and Tioman. More than 25 international carriers serve Kuala Lumpur. Terminal 1 is the main international terminal. Terminal 3 is for domestic flights only.

Connections by air in the region with Kuala Lumpur

	Connections/ week
Kuala Lumpur-Bangkok	numerous
Kuala Lumpur-Rangoon	2
Kuala Lumpur-Hanoi	2
Kuala Lumpur-Saigon	Daily
Kuala Lumpur-Manila	twice daily
Kuala Lumpur-Phnom Penh	3
Kuala Lumpur-Singapore	numerous
Kuala Lumpur-Jakarta	numerous
Kuala Lumpur-Bali	numerous

Non-Malaysian passport holders are eligible for the **Discover Malaysia Pass**, if they fly into the country on Malaysian Airlines (MAS). It offers significant savings on domestic air travel. The pass is valid for any five sectors within the peninsula (US$99), or within Sabah or Sarawak as well as the peninsula (US$199). It must be purchased outside Malaysia.

Terminal 2 operates a shuttle service between KL and Singapore with MAS or Singapore Airlines planes departing nearly every hour (more during peak hours). **NB** Flights between Singapore and Malaysia cost the same dollar figure whether bought in Malaysia or Singapore; it saves money buying a return ticket in Malaysia. There are flights from KL to most Asian destinations. With the fall in the ringgit, this may change.

● **From Europe**
Approximate time from London to Kuala Lumpur (non-stop): 12½ hours. From London Heathrow: British Airways and Malaysia Airlines (in a joint service with Virgin) are two carriers. From Amsterdam: Malaysia Airlines and KLM. From Frankfurt: Malaysia Airlines, Lufthansa and China Airlines. You can fly from Zurich with Malaysia Airlines, Royal Brunei and China Airlines. From Paris: Malaysia Airline. From other cities a change of plane is often necessary en route.

● **From the USA and Canada**
Approximate time from LAX (Los Angeles): 20 hours. Malaysia Airlines fly from LA via Tokyo and Canada.

● **From Australasia**
You can fly direct from Sydney, Melbourne, Brisbane, Darwin, Cairns and Perth (flight times range between 5 and 9 hours), with Qantas, British Airways, Malaysia Airlines and many others. From Auckland, Malaysia Airlines.

● **From South Asia**
Malaysia Airlines and Air India fly from Delhi. From Colombo, Air Lanka. You can fly from Dhaka with Biman Bangladesh Airlines and from Karachi (PIA and Malaysia Airlines). Flights via other cities available from Male and Kathmandu.

● **From the Far East**
Many flights from Hong Kong, Manila and Tokyo.

TRAIN

Keretapi Tanah Melayu (KTM) runs five express trains daily between Singapore and the major cities on the west coast of Malaysia. There is a daily express train between Bangkok and Butterworth (RM92.80 for first class, RM42.30 for second class), which connects with Kuala Lumpur (RM58.50, RM25.40, RM14.40); KL-Singapore (RM60, RM26, RM14.80). Bangkok to Singapore via Malaysia (RM206.80, RM91.70). Another railway line runs from Gemas (half way between KL and Johor Bahru) to Kota Bharu, on the northeast coast (see map page 516).

The most luxurious way to journey by train to Malaysia is aboard the *Eastern & Oriental (E&O) Express*. The a/c train of 22 carriages including a salon car, dining car, bar and observation deck and carrying just 132 passengers runs once a week from Singapore to Bangkok and back. Luxurious carriages, fine wines and food designed for European rather than Asian sensibilities make this not just a mode of transport but an experience. The journey takes 43 hours with stops in Kuala Lumpur, Butterworth and Padang Besar. But such luxury is expensive: up to, and over, US$3,000 for the most expensive ticket. For information call Bangkok 2514862; London (0171) 9286000; USA (800) 5242420; Singapore (065) 2272068.

Transport to town Taxis from KL's magnificent Moorish railway station also run on a fixed-price coupon system; coupons must be bought in advance from the booth next to the taxi rank.

ROAD

It is possible to travel to and from Malaysia by bus or share taxi from Thailand and Singapore. Direct buses and taxis are much easier than the local alternatives which stop at the borders. Singapore is 6 hours by taxi from KL (via Johor Bahru) and about 7 hours by bus (see page 140). Taxi fares are approximately double bus fares.

There are direct buses and taxis to destinations in Thailand from most major towns in northern Malaysia (see relevant sections) and 6 border crossing points. For those using the north-south highway – which is most people – the crossing point is at Bukit Kayu Hitam, which links up with the Thai city of Hat Yai. On the western side of the Peninsula there are also crossings at Wang Kelian and Padang Besar. The Wang Kelian crossing (to Satun in Thailand) is convenient if driving oneself; it is quiet and usually pretty rapid. The Padang Besar is an easy crossing on foot and makes sense if travelling to or from Pulau Langkawi. In Perak the crossing is at Pengkalan Hulu, and in Kelantan, on the eastern side of the Peninsula there are two more crossing points, the more important at Pengkalan Kubar, and the second from Kota Bahru to Rantau Panjang/Sungai Golok (see page 306). The more popular of this is the Rantau Panjang crossing; few people cross at Pengkalan Kubar. Local buses and taxis terminate at the border crossing points, but there are regular connections to towns and cities from each side.

It is also possible to cross overland from the East Malaysian states of Sarawak and Sabah to Kalimantan (Indonesian Borneo) and Brunei. The main crossing point is in the west, between Kuching in Sarawak and Pontianak in Kalimantan and regular buses run between these two towns.

SEA

Most passenger ships/cruise liners run between Port Klang, west of Kuala Lumpur, Georgetown (Penang), Singapore, Kuantan, Kuching and Kota Kinabalu. Feri Malaysia connects these Malaysian ports and Singapore. Deluxe cabins are also available. Schedules change annually; contact Tourism Malaysia for bookings.

There are also regular ferry services from Melaka to Dumai in Sumatra and from Georgetown (Penang) to Medan, also in Sumatra (see relevant sections). Passenger boats connect Langkawi Island with Satun in South Thailand (see page 199). High-speed catamarans connect Singapore with Pulau Tioman (off the east coast of Peninsular Malaysia), 4½ hours. Small boats also run between Johor state and Singapore's Changi Point (see page 666). In East Malaysia, there are connections between Tawau and Tarakan via Nunukan (see page 498).

CUSTOMS

● Duty free allowance

200 cigarettes, 50 cigars or 250g of tobacco and 1 litre of liquor or wine. Cameras, watches, pens, lighters, cosmetics, perfumes, portable radio/cassette players are also duty-free in Malaysia. Visitors bringing in dutiable goods such as video equipment may have to pay a refundable deposit for temporary importation. It is advisable to carry receipt of purchases to avoid this problem.

● Currency regulations

Visitors are allowed to import RM10,000 and export RM5,000. There is no limit imposed on other currencies or TCs.

● Prohibited items

The trafficking of illegal drugs into Malaysia carries the death penalty (see page 86).

● Export restrictions

Export permits are required for arms, ammunition, explosives, animals and plants, gold, platinum, precious stones and jewellery (except reasonable personal effects), poisons, drugs, motor vehicles. Unlike Singapore, export permits are also required for antiques (from the Director General of Museums, Muzium Negara, Kuala Lumpur).

ON ARRIVAL

● Airport information

Subang International Airport is 24 km southwest of Kuala Lumpur. There are banks in the departure and arrivals halls, a good selection of duty-free shops, a tourist information desk, hotel reservation service and car hire offices as well as an international telecoms office. Because Subang is running down while the new airport is being completed, it is not on a par with the glitzy Southeast Asian norm, but nonetheless runs pretty efficiently and has all the facilities one would expect. Subang airport enquiries/flight confirmation: T 7461235. For details of other international airports (Penang, Kota Kinabalu and Kuching), see relevant sections. **NB** During 1998 a new international airport will open at Sepang, 45 km south of KL. The information provided here relates to the existing airport at Subang. For up-to-date details on Sepang T (03) 2538588 or F (03) 2535671.

Transport to town **Bus**: buses 47 and 343 connect the airport and central KL (RM1.60); there is also the slightly more expensive Indrakota a/c bus (RM1.90). Buses leave about every 20 minutes from 0630 to 2230. **Car hire**: major car hire firms have desks in the terminal. **Hotel pick-up service**: hotel transport must be arranged in advance or at the office just outside the terminal exit. **Taxi**: the price is fixed for taxi rides into KL and it is necessary to buy a coupon at the taxi booth in the airport (RM25-30). The coupon system was introduced to prevent tourists being overcharged. The drive into KL takes about 45 minutes.

● Airport tax

Airport departure tax is RM5 for domestic flights, RM20 for Singapore and Brunei and RM40 for all other countries.

● Clothing

Malaysians dress for the heat – clothes are light, cool and casual most of the time; but they also dress fairly smartly. Some establishments – mainly exclusive restaurants – require a long sleeved shirt with tie (or local batik shirt) and do not allow shorts in the evening. Those visiting the Cameron Highlands or other upland areas are advised to bring a light sweater. For those planning to go on jungle treks, a waterproof is advisable, as are canvas jungle boots, which dry faster than leather.

Although many Malaysian business people have adopted the western jacket and tie for formal occasions, the batik shirt, or *baju*, is the traditional formal wear for men, while women wear the graceful *sarung kebaya*. It is worth bearing Islamic conservatism in mind when visiting east coast states (see page 254).

● Conduct

Dress Malaysians dress smartly, particularly in cities; tourists in vests, shorts and flip-flops look out of place in modern cosmopolitan KL. Dress codes are important to observe from the point of view of Islamic sensitivities, particularly on the peninsula's east coast. In some places such as Marang, bikinis are banned and wearing them will cause great offence. Topless bathing is completely taboo in Malaysia; this should be remembered even where tourists have started doing it, such as on Pulau Tioman. Dress modestly out of respect for Muslim tradition.

Malaysia's cross-cultural differences are most apparent on the streets: many Chinese girls think nothing of wearing brief mini-skirts and shorts, while their Malay counterparts are clad from head to toe. The *tudung* (or *telukung*) veil signifies adherence to the puritanical lifestyle of the fervently Islamic *dakwah* movement; during the 1980s, this almost became a fashion among women at universities as well as among blue-collar workers in factories. Some women began to dress in the full black purdah until it was forbidden by the government. Much of this was the result of peer pressure and reflected a revival of strict Islamic values in Malaysia during and after the 1970s.

Eating When picking up and passing food, do not use the left hand in Muslim company. It is worth remembering that Malays do not make pork satay and that Hindus do not make beef curries.

Pointing Using the index finger to point at people, even at objects, is regarded as insulting. Use the thumb or whole hand to indicate something, or to wave down a taxi, for example.

General Everywhere in Southeast Asia, 'losing face' brings shame. You lose face if you lose your temper, and even in a situation like bargaining, using a loud voice or wild gesticulations will be

Malaysian manners – as learned from a princess

In modern, cosmopolitan Malaysia, traditional customs and cultural conventions are alive and well and rigorously adhered to. In Malaysia's multi-ethnic melting pot, Malays, Chinese, Indians, Eurasians and expatriates have discovered that cross-cultural etiquette and the art of obliging another's sense of decorum is the essence of racial harmony. The trouble is that for many visitors, commiting a Malaysian-style *faux pas* is one of life's inevitabilities. Or it was, until Datin Noor Aini Syed Amir published her practical handbook to Malaysian customs and etiquette in 1991. As a Malay princess, Datin Noor – Malaysia's Miss Manners – should know. "While the Malays are very generous and forgiving with foreigners who make Malay *faux pas*, those who do not make such blunders will be highly admired and respected," the Datin says.

Her catch-all advice to visitors is to utter "a profuse apology *in advance* to the person you may offend". For those who forget to absolve themselves before they slip up, her social observations cover every conceivable situation *mat sallehs* – the local nickname for foreigners – might find themselves in. When eating with chopsticks, warns Datin Noor, avoid crossing them and never stick them vertically into your ricebowl so they resemble joss sticks. Do not be offended by enthusiastic belches and slurps around the dinner table either: Malaysians live to eat and like to share their appreciation.

Visitors must also learn to distinguish between flabby handshakes and Malay *salams*. "Unlike the Western handshake, which is a rather vigorous up and down movement... the Malay handshake is a simple palm-to-palm touch", she writes. The most important part of the gesture is immediately touching your hand to your heart as a signal of sincerity. And, she adds, "never use your left hand in Malay company!" Datin Noor goes on to warn newcomers not to touch people's heads, when to take their shoes off and to think before they kiss a lady's cheek – in greeting. Dazzling, long-sleeved batik shirts are what you wear to formal dinners and black is taboo for happy occasions. She explains what Tunkus, Tuns, Datuks, Dato's and Datins are and notes that the King's title 'Yang Di-Pertuan Agong' means 'He Who is Made Supreme Lord'.

Malaysian Customs & Etiquette A Practical Handbook by Datin Noor Aini Syed Amir. Times Books International, 1991.

taken to signify anger. By the same token, the person you shout at will also feel loss of face too, particularly if it happens in public. It should also be noted that in Muslim company it is impolite to touch others with the left hand and other objects – even loose change. Although men shake hands, for a man to shake a woman's hand is not the norm outside KL. Indeed excessive personal contact should be avoided: Malays, especially, do not tend to slap one another on the back!

Private homes Remove shoes before entering a private home; it is usual to bring a small gift for the host.

Religion Remove shoes before entering mosques and Hindu and Buddhist temples; in mosques, women should cover their heads, shoulders and legs and men should wear long trousers.

Visiting longhouses in Sarawak See page 378.

● Emergencies

Ambulance, police or fire, T 999.

● Hours of business

Banks: 0930-1500 Mon-Fri and 0930-1130 Sat. **NB** For Kedah, Perlis, Kelantan and Terengganu banks are open 0930-1130 on Thur and closed on Fri. **Government**: 0800-1245, 1400-1615 Mon-Thur, 0800-1200, 1430-1615 Fri, 0800-1245 Sat. In the states of Kedah and Terengganu, goverment offices are open 0800-1615 Sat-Wed, 0800-1245 Thur, and are shut on Fri. In Kelantan government offices are open 0800-1645 Sun-Wed, 0800-1245 Thur, and closed on Fri and Sat. **Shops**: generally open from 0930-1900 (department stores often later) and supermarkets and department stores from 1000-2200.

In the former Federated States, which were under the British (Selangor, Melaka, Penang, Perak, Pahang and Negri Sembilan), there is a half day holiday on Sat and full day holiday on Sun. The former Unfederated States of Kelantan and Terengganu retain the traditional half day holiday on Thur and full day holiday on Fri. Sat and Sun are treated as weekdays. In the other former Unfederated States – Johor, Kedah and Perlis, the half day on Thur is often observed, but most businesses now observe the Sat/Sun weekend.

● Official time

8 hours ahead of GMT.

● Safety

Normal precautions should be taken with passports and valuables such as cameras; many hotels have safes. Pickpocketing is a problem in some cities. Women – if not accompanied by men – usually attract unwarranted attention, particularly in more Islamic areas, such as the east coast. Mostly this is bravado, however, and there have been no serious incidents involving foreign tourists.

● Shopping

Most big towns now have modern shopping complexes as well as shops and markets. Department stores are fixed-price, but nearly everywhere else it is possible – and necessary – to bargain. In most places, at least 30% can be knocked off the asking price; your first offer should be roughly half the first quote.

The islands of Langkawi (see page 205) and Labuan (see page 456) have duty-free shopping; the range of goods is poor, however. In addition to the duty-free shops, cameras, watches, pens, lighters, cosmetics, perfumes and portable radio/cassette players are all duty-free in Malaysia. Film and camera equipment are still cheaper in Singapore, which offers a wider selection of most products – especially electronics and computer products.

Kuala Lumpur and most of the state capitals have a Chinatown which usually has a few curio shops and nearly always a *pasar malam*. Indian quarters, which are invariably labelled 'Little India', are only found in bigger towns; they are the best places to buy *sarungs*, *longuis*, *dotis* and *saris* (mostly imported from India) as well as other textiles. Malay handicrafts are usually only found in markets or government craft centres.

Handicrafts The Malaysian arts and crafts industry used to enjoy much more royal patronage, but when craftsmen went in search of more lucrative jobs, the industry began to decline. The growth of tourism in recent years has helped to reinvigorate it – particularly in traditional handicraft-producing areas, such as the east coast states of Terengganu and Kelantan. The Malay Arts and Crafts Society has also been instrumental in preventing the decline of the industry. In 1981, Malaysian Handicraft and Souvenir Centres (*Karyaneka* centres), were set up to market Malaysian arts and crafts in KL and some state capitals. Typical Malaysian handicrafts which can be found on the peninsula include woodcarvings, batik, *songket* (cloth woven with gold and silver thread), pewterware, silverware, kites, tops and *wayang kulit* (shadow puppets). For more detail on Malaysian arts and crafts, see page 81.

Other than the peninsula's east coast states, Sarawak is the other place where the traditional handicraft industry is flourishing (see page 351). The state capital, Kuching, is full of handicraft and antique shops selling tribal pieces collected from upriver; those going upriver themselves can often find items being sold in towns and even longhouses *en route*. Typical Sarawakian handicrafts include woodcarvings, *pua kumbu* (rust-coloured tie-dye blankets), beadwork and basketry. Many handicraft shops on Peninsular Malaysia also sell Sarawakian handicrafts – particularly those in KL – although there is a considerable mark-up.

● Tipping

Tipping is unusual in Malaysia as a service of 10% is added automatically to restaurant and hotel bills, plus a 5% government tax. Nor is tipping expected in smaller restaurants where a service charge is not automatically added to the bill. For personal services – porterage for example – a modest tip may be appropriate.

● Voltage

Malaysia's current is 220-240 volts, 50 cycle AC. Some hotels supply adaptors.

● Weights and measures

Malaysia has gone metric although road distances are marked in both kilometres and miles.

WHERE TO STAY

Accommodation

Malaysia offers a good selection of international class hotels as well as simpler hotels, rest houses and hostels. Room rates are subject to 10%+5% taxes. Many of the major international chains have hotels in Malaysia, such as *Hilton, Regent, Holiday Inn* and *Hyatt* plus local and regional chains such as *Merlin, Ming Court* and *Shangri-La*; most of these are on the west coast. Room rates in the big hotels – particularly in Kuala Lumpur – rose steeply during the early and mid-1990s but are now set for a period of stability: there may even be a decline in room rates. The number of 4 and 5 star hotel rooms will double between 1997 and 2000/2002 and analysts believe that falling occupancy rates will lead to a fall in room (price) rates by between 5% and 20%. By world standards, even the most expensive hotels are good value for money. It is also possible to rent condominiums in some cities – mainly KL and Georgetown. Whether the fall in the value of the ringgit will mean cheaper hotels (in US$ terms) is not clear. It is likely that budget and mid-range places which tend to rely on local custom as much as foreigners will not re-cost their rooms; however, more expensive hotels which have a largely international clientele may do so. If rooms are priced in US$ then the fall in the ringgit will not apply be relevant.

Hotel prices and facilities

L: RM500+ **Luxury**: hotels in this bracket are few and far between. Kuala Lumpur's splendid *Carcosa Seri Negara* is one such hotel. The *Datai* on Langkawi is another and the *Pangkor Laut Resort* on the private island of Pangkor Laut is also in the top league. Most **A+** grade hotels have luxury presidential suites.

A+: RM260-500 **International class**: impeccable service, beautifully appointed offering a wide array of facilities and business services. Malaysia's **A+** grade hotels – most of which are grouped towards the bottom end of the price category – are regarded as among the best value in the region.

A: RM130-260 **First class**: good range of services and facilities. Very competitively priced, given the standards of service.

B: RM65-130 **Tourist class**: hotels in this category will have swimming pools; most provide just a basic range of services and facilities although all will have a/c.

C: RM40-65 **Economy**: while there are some excellent economy hotels in this category, few provide much in the way of services. Guests will usually have the option of a/c or fan-cooled rooms and a choice of attached/shared bathrooms. Government rest-houses (*rumah rehat*) offer the best value for money in this grade.

D: RM20-40 **Budget**: most hotels in the budget class are Chinese-run and located in town centres (they are therefore often noisy – and not just because of the traffic; they also seem to be busy much later into the night because of the arrival and departure of the long-distance drivers who use them). At the upper end, rooms have a/c and attached bathrooms; cheaper rooms have fans and communal bathrooms (with *mandi*). Some fine old tumbledown colonial relics in this range offer good value for money. Youth hostels also fall into this price-range.

E: RM10-20 **Lodging house/guesthouse/hostel**: rooms are rarely a/c; shared *mandi* with squat toilet; few facilities. Lodging houses (*rumah tumpangan*) sometimes double as brothels. Tourist-oriented guesthouses usually offer better value and a better atmosphere; there are a few exceptionally good places in this category.

F: under RM10: there is little accommodation in this price bracket in Malaysia, although many guesthouses and hostels in the **D** and **E** categories provide the option of bottom-dollar, cramped dormitory accommodation. In some beach resort areas it is sometimes possible to find simple 'A'-frame accommodation in this range.

There are Youth Hostels in KL, Georgetown (Penang), Port Dickson, Fraser's Hill, Cameron Highlands, Kuantan, Kota Bahru, Kota Kinabalu and Pulau Pangkor. There are also scores of government rest houses (*rumah rehat*) around the country; these often offer well-maintained, reasonably priced rooms, although they can become heavily booked, particularly during public holidays. On the east coast of Peninsular Malaysia and in East Malaysia, it is often possible to stay with families in Malay *kampungs* (villages), the so called Homestay programme (contact local tourist office or travel agent for more information). The most popular place to do this is at Kampung Cerating, north of Kuantan, although it has become increasingly touristy in recent years; it is also possible to stay in a kampung house in Merang. Along many of Malaysia's beaches and on islands, there are simple atap-roofed 'A'-frame bungalows.

Accommodation in East Malaysia does not offer such value for money as hotels on the peninsula, although, again, there are some bargains. As on the peninsula, there are government rest houses in many of the main towns. For accommodation in National Parks, see relevant sections: it is necessary to book in advance. In Sarawak it is possible to stay in longhouses, where rates are at the discretion of the visitor (see page 378).

NB In the more popular holiday destinations like the Cameron Highlands, accommodation can become scarce during the school holidays – April, August and December. During these months it is worth booking ahead.

● Camping

There are not many camping sites in Malaysia, but 'wild camping' is easy. In Sabah, especially, camping is a much cheaper option and you get to stay exactly where you want to be, for example at Tunkul Abdul Rahman Marine Park, Danum Valley, and the islands around Semporna.

FOOD AND DRINK

FOOD

Malaysians, like neighbouring Singaporeans, love their food, and the dishes of the three main communities – Malay, Chinese and Indian – comprise a hugely varied national menu. Even within each ethnic cuisine, there is a vast choice – every state has its own special Malay dishes and the different Chinese provincial specialities are well represented; in addition there is North Indian food, South Indian food and Indian Muslim food. Nyonya cuisine is found in the old Straits Settlements of Penang and Melaka. Malaysia also has great seafood – which the Chinese do best – and in recent years a profusion of restaurants, representing other Asian and European cuisines, have set up, mainly in the big cities. In the East Malaysian states of Sabah and Sarawak, there are tribal specialities.

As in Singapore, good food is not confined to restaurants – some of the best local dishes can be sampled at hawker centres, which are cheap and often stay open late into the night. Hotels regularly lay on buffet spreads, which are good value at about RM20-30, often much cheaper than the price of a room would suggest.

NB1 Many restaurants charge an extra 15% service and tax. **NB2** During Ramadan many Malay restaurants close during daylight hours.

● Malay

The best Malay food is usually found at stalls in hawker centres. The staple diet is rice and curry, which is rich and creamy due to the use of coconut milk. Herbs and spices include chillis, ginger, turmeric, coriander, lemon grass, anise, cloves, cumin, caraway and cinnamon.

Rice dishes

nasi campur – Malay curry buffet of rice served with meat, fish, vegetables and fruit.
nasi goreng – rice, meat and vegetables fried with garlic, onions and *sambal*.
nasi lemak – a breakfast dish of rice cooked in coconut milk and served with prawn sambal, *ikan bilis*, a hard boiled egg, peanuts and cucumber.

Restaurant prices

♦♦♦♦	RM40+	Hotel restaurants and exclusive restaurants
♦♦♦	RM12.50-40+	Restaurants in tourist class hotels & more expensive local restaurants
♦♦	RM5-12.50	Coffee shops (*kedi kopi*) and basic restaurants
♦	under RM5	Hawker stalls

nasi padang – plain rice served with a selection of dishes.
nasi puteh – plain boiled rice.
nasi dagang – popular on the east coast for breakfast; glutinous rice cooked in coconut milk and served with fish curry, cucumber pickle and *sambal*.

Soup
soto ayam – popular for breakfast in Johor and Sarawak, a spicy chicken soup served with rice cubes, chicken and vegetables.
lontong – popular in the south, particularly for breakfast. Cubed compressed rice served with mixed vegetables in coconut milk. *Sambal* is the accompaniment.

Meat
satay – chicken, beef or mutton marinated and skewered on a bamboo, barbecued over a brazier. Usually served with *ketupat*.

Noodles
kway teow – flat noodles fried with seafood, egg, soy sauce, beansprouts and *kuchai* (chives).
laksa johor – noodles in fish curry sauce and raw vegetables.
mee goreng – fried noodles.
mee jawa – noodles in gravy, served with prawn fritters, potatoes, tofu and beancurd.
mee rebus – noodles with beef, chicken or prawn with soybean in spicy sauce.

Curries
rendang – dry beef curry (a Sumatran dish).
longong – vegetable curry made from rice cakes cooked in coconut, beans, cabbage and bamboo shoots.

Salad
rojak – Malaysian's answer to Indonesia's *gado gado* – mixed vegetable salad served in peanut sauce with *ketupat*.

Vegetables
sayur manis – sweet vegetables; vegetables fried with chilli, *belacan* and mushrooms.

Sweets *(kueh)*
apam – steamed rice cakes.
pulut inti – glutinous rice served with sweetened grated coconut.
nyonya kueh – Chinese kueh, among the most popular is *yow cha koei* – deep fried kneaded flour.

● Chinese

Cantonese and Hainanese cooking are the most prevalent Chinese cuisines in Malaysia (for details on these and other Chinese cuisines found in Malaysia and Singapore, see page 713). Some of the more common Malaysian-Chinese dishes are Hainanese chicken rice (rice cooked in chicken stock and served with steamed or roast chicken), *char kway teow* (Teochew-style fried noodles, with eggs, cockles and chilli paste), *or luak* (Hokkien oyster omelette), *dim sum* (steamed dumplings and patties) and *yong tow foo* (beancurd and vegetables stuffed with fish). Good Chinese food is available in restaurants, coffee shops and from hawker stalls.

● Indian

Indian cooking can be divided into three schools: northern and southern (neither eat beef) and Muslim (no pork). Northern dishes tend to be more subtly spiced, use more meat and are served with breads. Southern dishes use fiery spices, emphasize vegetables and are served with rice. The best-known North Indian food are the *tandoori* dishes, which are served with delicious fresh *naan* breads, baked in ovens on-site. Other pancakes include roti, thosai and chapati. Malaysia's famous *mamak*-men are Indian Muslims who are highly skilled in everything from *teh tarik* (see Drink below) to *rotis*.

Other dishes include:
roti canai – pancakes served with lentils and curry.
murtabak – a thick *roti*-pizza with minced meat, onion and egg.
nasi biriyani – rice cooked in ghee with spices and vegetable and served with beef or chicken.
nasi kandar – Mamak's version of nasi campur.
daun pisang – a Malay/South Indian *thali* – curry and rice, with poppadoms and chutneys all served on a banana leaf.

● Nyonya

Through inter-marriage with local Malays a unique culture evolved (see page 230 for information on the history of the Nyonyas), and with it, a cuisine that has grown out of a blend of the two races. Nyonya food is spicier than Chinese food, and it uses pork. Nyonya dishes in Penang have adopted flavours from neighbouring Thailand, whereas Melaka's Nyonya food has Indonesian overtones. In traditional Straits Chinese households, great emphasis was placed on presentation and the fine-chopping of ingredients.

Typical dishes include:
kapitan – chicken cooked in coconut milk.
otak otak – minced fish, coconut milk and spices, steamed in a banana leaf.
laksa – rice noodles in spicy coconut-milk and prawn-flavoured gravy blended with spices and served with shellfish, chicken, beancurd and belacan.

assam laksa – the specialized Penang version – rice noodles served in fish gravy with shredded cucumber, pineapple, raw onions and mint.

● Sabahan

The Kadazans form the largest ethnic group in Sabah. Their food tends to use mango and can be on the sour side.

Popular dishes include:
hinava – marinated raw fish.
sup manuk on hiing – chicken soup with rice wine.
tapai – chicken cooked in local rice wine.
pakis – ferns, which are fried with mushrooms and *belacan*. Sometimes ferns are eaten raw, with a squeeze of lime (*sayur pakis limau*)
sup terjun – jumping soup – salted fish, mango and ginger.
hinompula – a dessert made from tapioca, sugar, coconut and the juice from screwpine leaves.

● Sarawakian

Dishes peculiar to Sarawak include:
Ternbok – fish, either grilled or steamed.
pan suh manok – chicken pieces cooked in bamboo cup and served with *bario* (Kelabit mountain rice).

COOKERY COURSES

For those wishing to learn more about Malaysian cuisine, several state tourist boards offer short courses in curry-making, etc. Enquire at Tourism Malaysia information centres. Tourism Malaysia publishes a glossy pamphlet called *Malaysian Common Recipes* providing an introduction to spices and ingredients and easy-to-follow recipes to 16 succulent dishes. A wide variety of Malaysian cookery books is available at leading bookshops.

DRINK

Fizzy soft drinks, mineral water and freshly squeezed fruit drinks are available. Anchor and Tiger beer are widely sold – except in the more Islamic states of the east coast, especially Kelantan – and is cheapest at the hawker stalls (RM5/bottle). A beer will cost RM8-12/bottle in coffee shops. Malaysian-brewed Guinness is also popular, mainly because Chinese believe it has medicinal qualities as it has been successfully sold on the "Guinness Stout is good for you" line. Malaysian tea is grown in the Cameron Highlands and is very good. One of the most interesting cultural refinements of the Indian Muslim community is the Mamak-man, who is famed for *teh tarik* (pulled tea), which is thrown across a distance of about a metre, from one cup to another, with no spillages. The idea is to cool it down for customers, but it has become an art form; mamak-men appear to cultivate the nonchalant look when pouring. Malaysian satirist Kit Leee says a tea-stall mamak "could 'pull' tea in free fall without spilling a drop – while balancing a *beedi* on his lower lip and making a statement on Economic Determinism". Most of the coffee comes from Indonesia, although some is locally produced. Malaysians like their coffee strong and unless you specify *kurang manis* (less sugar), *tak mahu manis* (don't want sugar) or *kopi kosong* (empty coffee – black, no sugar), it will come with lashings of sweet condensed milk.

GETTING AROUND

Transport around the East Malaysian states of Sabah and Sarawak is not as easy as it is on the peninsula – there are fewer roads and they are not in a good state of repair. There are excellent coastal and upriver express boat services in Sarawak and the national airline, MAS, has an extensive network in both states; flying is relatively inexpensive.

AIR

Malaysia Airlines (MAS) operates an extensive network to domestic destinations: Kuala Lumpur, Ipoh, Penang, Alor Star, Langkawi, Kota

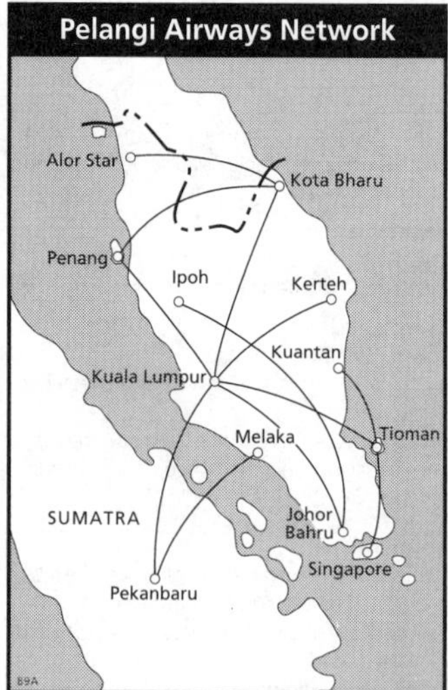

MAS domestic network (1997)

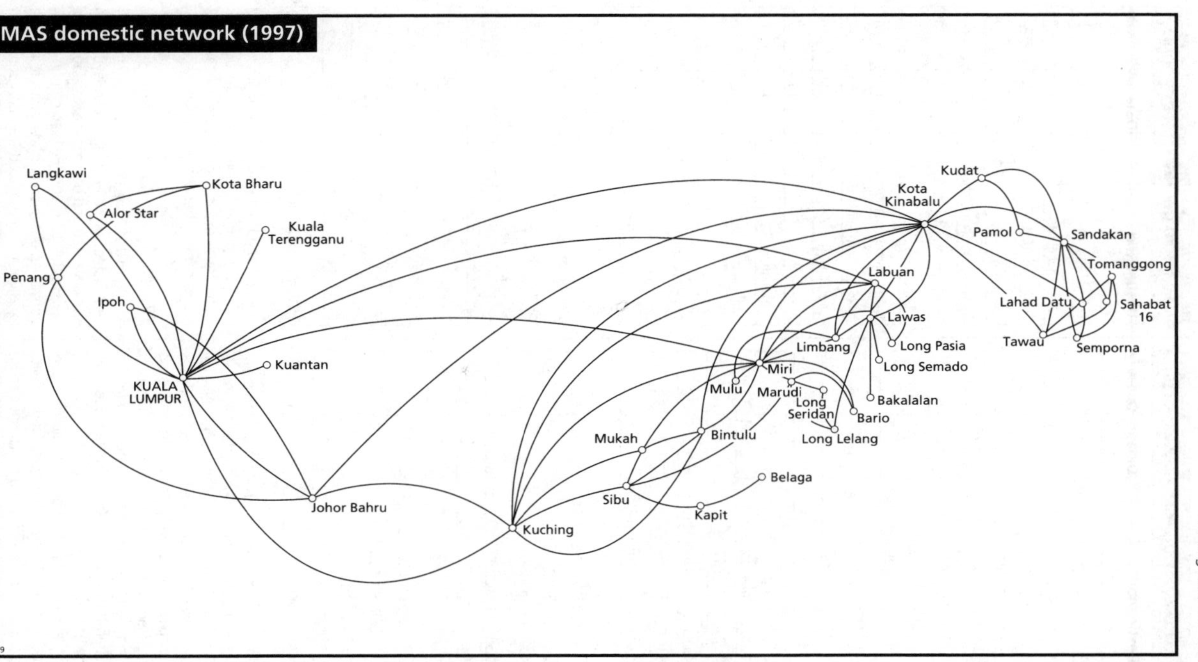

Guide to domestic Mas air fares

Destination	Distance (km)	One-way (RM)
Alor Star-Kota Bharu	215	71
Johor Bahru-Kota Kinabalu	1,502	347
Johor Bahru-Kuala Terengganu	-	149
Johor Bahru-Kuching	757	169
Kota Kinabalu-Kudat	141	50
Kota Kinabalu-Lahad Datu	272	106
Kota Kinabalu-Labuan	115	52
Kota Kinabalu-Lawas	140	47
Kota Kinabalu-Miri	294	104
Kota Kinabalu-Sandakan	226	83
Kota Kinabalu-Tawau	280	96
Kuala Lumpur-Alor Star	368	113
Kuala Lumpur-Ipoh	178	66
Kuala Lumpur-Johor Bahru	354	93
Kuala Lumpur-Kota Bahru	352	104
Kuala Lumpur-Kota Kinabalu	1,678	437
Kuala Lumpur-Kuala Terengganu	318	104
Kuala Lumpur-Kuantan	224	74
Kuala Lumpur-Kuching	1,035	262
Kuala Lumpur-Langkawi	-	135
Kuala Lumpur-Penang	283	104
Kuantan-Johor Bahru	261	93
Kuching-Bintulu	354	117
Kuching-Kota Kinabalu	811	228
Kuching-Miri	519	164
Kuching-Mukah	250	76
Kuching-Sibu	191	72

Guide to domestic Mas air fares

Destination	Distance (km)	One-way (RM)
Lahad Datu-Tawau	100	40
Lawas-Bekelalan	100	46
Lawas-Labuan	54	31
Lawas-Limbang	44	25
Lawas-Long Semadoh	74	40
Long Seridan-Long Lellang	59	35
Marudi-Bario	135	55
Marudi-Long Lellang	135	46
Marudi-Long Seridan	85	42
Marudi-Sibu	344	100
Miri-Bario	180	70
Miri-Bintulu	168	69
Miri-Labuan	180	66
Miri-Lawas	168	59
Miri-Limbang	123	45
Miri-Marudi	42	29
Penang-Kota Bharu	246	87
Penang-Kuala Terengganu	317	151
Penang-Langkawi	131	51
Sandakan-Kudat	177	54
Sandakan-Lahad Datu	102	40
Sandakan-Semporna	170	50
Sandakan-Tawau	185	61
Sandakan-Tomanggong	85	42
Sibu-Bintulu	163	64
Sibu-Kapit	128	48
Sibu-Mini	326	112

NB Late 1997 fares quoted

Bharu, Kuala Terengganu, Kuantan, Johor Bahru, Singapore, Kota Kinabalu, Sandakan, Lahad Datu, Labuan, Kuching, Sibu, Bintulu, Tawau, and Miri (plus many more internal flights in Sabah and Sarawak). Local MAS offices are listed under each town; the head office is at Bangunan MAS (opposite *Equatorial Hotel*), Jln Sultan Ismail, 50250, Kuala Lumpur. See table for 1997 fares.

Pelangi Air, a solely domestic airline, operates services to certain resorts and smaller towns. It flies to/from: Kuala Lumpur, Ipoh, Penang, Alor Setar, Melaka, Kerteh, Kuantan, Tioman Island, Johor Bahru, Kota Bharu, and Kuala Terengganu. There are reductions for night flights, group and advance bookings. **NB** Flights get very booked up on public holidays.

TRAIN

In August 1992 the Peninsular Malaysian Railway System or Keretapi Tanah Melayu (KTM) was privatized and became the Keretapi Tanah Melayu Berhad or KTMB. Their corporate mission statement declared: "We strive to provide excellent rail and related transport services in Malaysia, utilising our resources to optimize

Pelangi air fares	
Destination	**Single** (RM)
Alor Star-Kota Bharu	71
Ipoh-Johor Bahru	159
Kuala Lumpur-Johor Bahru	91
Kuala Lumpur-Kerteh	125
Kuala Lumpur-Kota Bharu	104
Kuala Lumpur-Penang	96
Kuala Lumpur-Tioman	141
Penang-Kota Bahru	87
Singapore-Tioman	$S115
Tioman-Kuantan	79
Tioman-Singapore	151
NB 1997 fares quoted: return ticket is double price quoted	

financial performance whilst meeting stakeholder expectations."

Notwithstanding the tendency to hyperbole in any mission statement, the KTMB is an economical and comfortable way to travel round the peninsula. Privatization has pumped much needed investment into the system which, in 1981, the *New Straits Times* was predicting would "collapse into one mass heap of worthless metal".

There are two main lines. One runs up the west coast from Singapore, through KL, Ipoh and Butterworth, connecting with Thai railways at Padang Besar (where one half of the extra-long platform is managed by Malaysian officials and the other half by Thais) and from there continues to Hat Yai in Southern Thailand and north to Bangkok. The other line branches off from the west coast line at Gemas (half way between KL and Singapore) and heads north-east to Kota Bahru. From Kota Bahru it is possible to take buses/taxis to Rantau Panjang/Sungai Golok for connections with Thai railways. The express service (Ekspres Rakyat or Ekspres Sinaran) only stops at major towns; the regular service stops at every station but is slightly cheaper. All 1st class and 2nd class coaches have sleeping berths on overnight trains and all classes have a/c. Reservations can be made for both classes. Visitors should note that the a/c on Malaysian trains is very cold. 1st and 2nd class carriages are equipped with videos. In East Malaysia there is only one railway line, running from Kota Kinabalu to

Wau Express

Kuala Lumpur-Tumpat-Kuala Lumpur

Type/Train No	XW/16	Dep ↓	Arr ↑	XW/17
Kuala Lumpur	2020			0610
Kajang	2040			0531
Seremban	2118			0445
Tampin	2201			0400
Gemas	2246			0253
Bahau	2343			0218
Mentakab	0057			0042
Jerantut	0151			2355
Kuala Lipis	0245			2303
Gua Musang	0414			2138
Krai	0604			1948
Tanah Merah	0635			1916
Pasir Mas	0659			1852
Wakaf Baharu	0713			1840
Tumpat	0735	Dep	Arr	1830

Timuran Express

Singapore-Tumpat-Singapore

Type/Train No	XST/14	Arr ↑	Dep ↓	XST/15
Singapore	2020			0735
Johor Bahru	2045			0643
Kluang	2202			0538
Labis	2253			0454
Segamat	2319			0431
Gemas	2345			0405
Bahau	0028			0330
Triang	0117			0240
Mentakab	0207			0156
Jerantut	0259			0051
Kuala Lipis	0353			2359
Gua Musang	0524			2238
Dabong	0625			2136
Krai	0718			2048
Tanah Merah	0750			2016
Pasir Mas	0816			1952
Wakaf Bahru	0832			1940
Tumpat	0854	Dep	Arr	1930

NB 1997 schedule; subject to change

Langkawi Express fares

Kuala Lumpur-Hat Yai-Kuala Lumpur

Kuala Lumpur to:	1st class		2nd class			1st class		2nd class		
	Lower Berth	Upper Berth	Seat	Lower Berth	Upper Berth	Lower Berth	Upper Berth	Seat	Lower Berth	Upper Berth
	-	-	-	-	-	100.00	90.00	40.00	46.00	43.50
Tapah Road	54.00	44.00	19.00	25.00	22.50	77.00	67.00	30.00	36.00	35.50
Ipoh	62.00	52.00	22.00	28.00	25.50	70.00	60.00	27.00	33.00	30.50
Taiping	75.00	65.00	28.00	34.00	31.50	56.00	46.00	21.00	27.00	24.50
BT Mertajam	87.00	77.00	33.00	39.00	36.50	44.00	34.00	16.00	22.00	19.50
Sg Petani	92.00	82.00	35.00	41.00	38.50	44.00	34.00	16.00	22.00	19.50
Alor Star	92.00	82.00	35.00	41.00	38.50	44.00	34.00	16.00	22.00	19.50
Arau	92.00	82.00	35.00	41.00	38.50	44.00	34.00	16.00	22.00	19.50
P Besar	92.00	82.00	35.00	41.00	38.50	38.00	28.00	13.00	19.00	16.50
Hat Yai	100.00	90.00	40.00	46.00	43.50	-	-	-	-	-

Timuran Express fares

Singapore to:	2nd Class Berth		2nd Class Seating	Economy Class
	Lower	Upper		
Bahau	30.00	27.50	20.00	14.00
Triang	33.00	30.50	23.00	16.00
Mentakab	35.00	32.50	25.00	17.00
Jerantut	38.00	35.50	28.00	19.00
Kuala Lipis	41.00	38.50	31.00	21.00
Gua Musang	47.00	44.50	37.00	25.00
Krai	47.00	44.50	37.00	29.00
Tenah Merah	49.00	46.50	39.00	30.00
Pasir Mas	51.00	48.50	41.00	31.00
Wakaf Bahru	51.00	48.50	41.00	32.00
Tumpat	51.00	48.50	41.00	32.00

Wau Express: sleeper fares

	1st class		2nd class		Economy Class	1st class		2nd class		Economy Class
	Lower Berth	Upper Berth	Lower Berth	Upper Berth	Seating	Lower Berth	Upper Berth	Lower Berth	Upper Berth	Seating
Kuala Lumpur	-	-	-	-	-	88.00	80.00	49.00	46.50	29.00
Kajang	-	-	-	-	4.00	85.00	77.00	48.00	45.50	28.00
Seremban	-	-	-	-	5.00	79.00	71.00	45.00	42.50	26.00
Tampin	-	-	-	-	7.00	74.00	66.00	43.00	40.50	24.00
Gemas	-	-	-	-	9.00	68.00	60.00	40.00	37.50	24.00
Bahau	-	-	-	-	11.00	64.00	56.00	38.00	35.50	23.00
Mentakab	-	-	-	-	14.00	65.00	47.00	35.00	32.50	20.00
Jerantut	56.00	48.00	35.00	32.50	15.00	-	-	-	-	18.00
Kuala Lipis	64.00	56.00	39.00	36.50	18.00	-	-	-	-	16.00
Gua Musang	76.00	68.00	44.00	41.50	21.00	-	-	-	-	12.00
Krai	78.00	70.00	45.00	42.50	25.00	-	-	-	-	8.00
Tanah Merah	83.00	75.00	47.00	44.50	27.00	-	-	-	-	6.00
Pasir Mas	85.00	77.00	48.00	45.50	28.00	-	-	-	-	5.00
Wakaf Bahru	86.00	78.00	48.00	45.50	28.00	-	-	-	-	5.00
Tumpat	88.00	80.00	49.00	46.50	29.00	-	-	-	-	-

NB 1997 fares quoted in RM, subject to change

Express train fares									
	Butterworth			Kuala Lumpur			Singapore		
	1	2	3	1	2	3	1	2	3
	RM	RM	RM	RM	RM	RM	$S	$S	$S
Padang Besar	34.00	20.00	11.00	-	-	-	-	-	-
Arau	30.00	18.00	10.00	-	-	-	-	-	-
Alor Star	24.00	15.00	8.00	-	-	-	-	-	-
Sungai Petani	15.00	11.00	6.00	-	-	-	-	-	-
Butterworth	-	-	-	67.00	34.00	19.00	127.00	60.00	34.00
Bt Mertajam	10.00	9.00	5.00	65.00	33.00	19.00	125.00	59.00	33.00
Parit Buntar	14.00	11.00	6.00	61.00	31.00	17.00	121.00	57.00	32.00
Taiping	23.00	15.00	8.00	53.00	28.00	16.00	112.00	53.00	30.00
K Kangsar	28.00	17.00	9.00	49.00	26.00	14.00	107.00	51.00	29.00
Ipoh	36.00	21.00	11.00	40.00	22.00	12.00	100.00	48.00	27.00
Batu Gajah	38.00	21.00	12.00	38.00	21.00	12.00	97.00	47.00	26.00
Kampar	41.00	23.00	13.00	34.00	20.00	11.00	94.00	46.00	26.00
Tapah Road	44.00	24.00	13.00	32.00	19.00	10.00	92.00	45.00	25.00
Kuala Lumpur	67.00	34.00	19.00	-	-	-	68.00	34.00	19.00
Seremban	79.00	39.00	22.00	20.00	13.00	7.00	58.00	30.00	17.00
Tampin	85.00	42.00	23.00	27.00	17.00	9.00	50.00	27.00	15.00
Gemas	94.00	46.00	26.00	35.00	20.00	11.00	43.00	23.00	13.00
Segamat	97.00	47.00	26.00	40.00	22.00	12.00	38.00	21.00	12.00
Kluang	110.00	53.00	30.00	52.00	27.00	15.00	26.00	16.00	9.00
Johor Bahru	122.00	58.00	33.00	64.00	33.00	18.00	13.00	10.00	6.00
Singapore	127.00	60.00	34.00	68.00	34.00	19.00	-	-	-

Ordinary train fares									
	Butterworth			Kuala Lumpur			Singapore		
	1	2	3	1	2	3	1	2	3
	RM	RM	RM	RM	RM	RM	$S	$S	$S
Padang Besar	25.50	11.10	6.30	81.00	35.10	20.00	139.50	60.50	34.40
Arau	21.80	9.50	5.40	76.50	33.20	18.90	136.50	59.20	33.60
Alor Star	15.30	6.70	3.80	70.50	30.60	17.40	130.50	56.60	32.20
Butterworth	-	-	-	58.50	25.40	14.40	118.50	51.40	29.20
Bt Mertajam	1.80	0.80	0.50	57.00	24.70	14.10	117.00	50.70	28.80
Taiping	14.40	6.30	3.60	45.00	19.50	11.10	103.50	44.90	25.50
K Kangsar	19.50	8.50	4.80	40.50	17.60	10.00	99.00	42.90	24.40
Ipoh	27.80	12.10	6.90	31.50	13.70	7.80	91.50	39.70	22.60
Tapah Road	36.00	15.60	8.90	23.30	10.10	5.80	84.00	36.40	20.70
Kuala Lumpur	58.50	25.40	14.40	-	-	-	60.00	26.00	14.80
Seremban	70.50	30.60	17.40	11.10	4.90	2.80	49.50	21.50	12.20
Tampin	76.50	33.20	18.90	18.80	8.20	4.70	42.00	18.20	10.40
Gemas	85.50	37.10	21.10	27.00	11.70	6.70	34.50	15.00	8.50
Segamat	88.50	38.50	21.80	31.50	13.70	7.80	30.00	13.00	7.40
Kluang	102.00	44.20	25.10	43.50	18.90	10.80	17.30	7.50	4.30
Johor Bahru	114.00	49.40	28.10	55.50	24.10	13.70	4.20	1.90	1.10
Singapore	118.50	51.40	29.90	60.00	26.00	14.80	-	-	-
Hat Yai	34.20	14.90	-	-	-	-	-	-	-
Bangkok	99.20	44.90	-	-	-	-	-	-	-

NB 1997 fares quoted

Tenom, via Beaufort (see page 446). See table for 1997 fares.

10-day and 30-day rail passes are available to foreign visitors for every class and there are no restrictions (other than availability of seats). Passes are available from railway stations in Singapore, KL, Johor Bahru, Butterworth, Padang Besar, Rantau Panjang, Wakaf Bahru (Kota Bahru). A 30 day pass in 1997 cost US$120 (adult), US$60 (child); and a 10 day pass, US$55 (adult), US$28 (child). There are also concessions offered (including foreigners) to family groups (4 people or more), 25%; groups of 10 or more, 25%; handicapped persons, 50%; and senior citizens (65 years+), 50%.

Train information: T (03) 2738000 (03) 2747435, (03) 2747442, 0630-2230. E-mail: passenger@ktmb.com.my. Web site: http://www.ktmb.com.my.

International Express

Butterworth-Bangkok-Butterworth

Type/Train No	Arr	IE/48	Dep	IE/49
Butterworth	↑	1425	↓	1244
Bukit Mertajam		1435		1218
Sungai Petani		1509		1144
Alor Star		1559		1054
ARAU		1632		1021
Padang Besar		1705		1000
Hat Yai		1810		0702
Bangkok	**Dep**	0950	**Arr**	1515
NB 1997 schedule; subject to change				

BUS

Peninsular Malaysia has an excellent bus system with a network of public express buses and several privately run services. A/c express buses (and VIP buses on the more popular routes) connect the major towns, seats can be reserved and prices are reasonable. Prices quoted are for a/c buses (see relevant sections). (The a/c on Malaysian buses is, like the trains, very cold.) There are also cheaper non-a/c buses that ply between the states and provide an intra-state

Ekrwres Nasional bus fares (1997)

Destination	Fare (RM)	Time of Departure
Alor Star		
Ipoh	11.90	1100, 1800
Kuala Lumpur	21.20	0900, 1100, 1400, 2200, 2230
Johor Bahru	37.70	1800
Butterworth		
Kuala Lumpur	17.10	0900
Johor Bahru	33.50	2000
Kota Bharu	16.50	1000, 2200
Kuala Kangsar	5.60	1045, 1430, 1545, 1700
Batu Pahat		
Kuala Lumpur	10.90	0830, 1000, 1400, 1530, 1830
Ipoh		
Alor Star	11.90	1330
Butterworth	7.10	1000, 1630
Johor Bahru	25.80	1300
Kangar	14.00	1230
Kota Bharu	17.10	2200
Kuala Perlis	14.00	1230
Kuala Lumpur	9.40	0830, 1030, 1230, 1330, 1430, 1530, 1630, 1830
Sungai Petani	8.80	1000, 1630
Johor Bahru		
Alor Star	37.70	1800
Butterworth	33.50	1800
Ipoh	25.80	
Kuala Lumpur	16.50	0900, 1000, 1100, 1300, 1600, 2230, 2300, 2400
Kangar		
Ipoh	14.00	0830
Kuala Lumpur	23.40	0830, 2100
Kuantan		
Kuala Lumpur	21.10	0930, 1030, 1130, 1230, 1430, 1630, 1730, 2400
Kuala Terengganu		
Kuala Lumpur	21.60	0930, 1000, 1200, 1400, 2130, 2200
Kota Bharu		
Kuala Lumpur	25.00	0900, 2000, 2100
Kuala Lumpur		
Alor Star	21.20	0930, 1030, 1200, 2200, 2230, 2300, 2400
Butterworth	17.10	1000, 1400, 2200, 2230
Batu Pahat	10.90	0900, 1030, 1400, 1500, 1830
Ipoh	9.40	0830, 1100, 1230, 1430, 1630, 1830
Johor Bahru	16.50	0930, 1100, 1300, 1400, 1630, 2230, 2300, 2400
Kangar	23.40	0900, 2100, 2130
Kemaman	13.50	1000, 1100, 1200, 2130, 2200, 2300
Kota Bharu	25.00	0900, 2030, 2130
Kuantan	12.10	0900, 1030, 1130, 1230, 1430, 1630, 1730, 2400
Kuala Terengganu	21.60	0900, 1100, 1200, 2130, 2200, 2300
Kuala Perlis	23.40	0900
Muar	8.50	1000, 1300, 1730
Penang	18.50	0900, 2200
Singapore	17.80	0900, 2200
Taiping/KK	13.20	0900, 1000, 1300, 1500, 1600, 2230
Muar		
Kuala Lumpur	8.50	0830, 0930, 1100, 1430, 1500, 1530, 1700, 1930
Penang		
Kuala Lumpur	18.50	1000, 2200
Singapore		
Kuala Lumpur	17.80*	0900, 2200
Taiping		
Butterworth	3.80	0830, 1200, 1600, 1930
Kuala Lumpur	13.20	0900, 1000, 1230, 1430, 1600, 2230
Sungai Petani	5.50	0830, 1200, 1600, 1930

NB These fares are indicative only. They were correct at time of going to press in late 1997 and apply to one bus company only, Ekspres Nasional.

* Fare in S$

service. Prices vary according to whether the bus is a/c or non a/c, express or regular, and between companies. The largest bus company is MARA, the government service. In larger towns there may be a number of bus stops; some private companies may also operate directly from their own offices. Travelling up the east coast of the peninsular is often quicker as the roads are less congested; west coast travel is very slow but will be improved with the completion of the north-south highway.

Buses in East Malaysia are more unreliable because of the poorer road conditions. But even in East Malaysia, roads are a good deal better than in Indonesian Borneo (Kalimantan). In Sarawak, the Sibu-Bintulu and Bintulu-Miri roads are rough and often impassable in the wet season, as is the road connecting Kota Kinabalu and Sandakan in Sabah.

NB During school holiday time, it can be difficult to get bus tickets and it is worth booking ahead.

CAR AND MOTORBIKE HIRE

Car hire companies are listed in individual towns under **Local transport**. Visitors can hire a car provided they are in possession of an international driving licence, are over 23 and not older than 65 and have at least 1 year's driving experience. Car hire costs from RM100 to RM250/day (approximately) depending on the model and the company. Cheaper weekly/monthly rates and special deals are available.

Driving is on the left; give way to drivers on the right. Within towns the speed limit is 50 km/hour; the wearing of seat belts is compulsory for front seat passengers and the driver. Most road signs are international but *awas* means "caution". Petrol costs a little over RM1 a litre. Road maps are on sale at most petrol stations; Petronas (the national oil company) produces an excellent atlas: *Touring Malaysia by Road*. Road conditions are good when compared with Indonesia and Thailand: most are kept in good repair and local drivers are generally safe. However during the monsoon season, heavy rains may make some east coast travel difficult and the west coast roads can be congested. In Sarawak the road network is extremely limited: air or water transport are the only option in many areas. In Sabah, 4WD vehicles are *de rigeur*; they are readily available, but expensive. On some islands, such as Penang, Langkawi and Pangkor, motorbikes are available for hire, for around RM20-25/day. If bringing your own car into the country, no carnet or deposit is required. The vehicle is allowed to stay in the country as long as the owner has permission to stay.

Important road signs to note:

awas	caution
beri laluan	give way
berhenti	stop
dilarang berhenti	no stopping
dilarang meletak kereta	no parking
dilarang memotong	no overtaking
ikut kiri	keep left
jalang bahaya	dangerous road ahead
jalan licin	slippery road
jalan sehala	one way
kawasan kemalangan	accident area
kurangkan laju	slow down
utara/selatan	north/south
timur/barat	east/west

OTHER LOCAL TRANSPORT

● Bicycling

We have had a number of letters from people who have bicycled through various parts of Southeast Asia. The advice below is collated from their comments, and is meant to provide a general guideline for those intending to travel by bicycle. There may be areas, however, where the advice does not hold true. (Some of the letters we have received even disagree on some points).

Bike type: touring, hybrid or mountain bikes are fine for most roads and tracks in Malaysia – take an ordinary machine; nothing fancy.

Spares: are readily available for most machines. Mountain bikes have made a big impact in the country, so accessories for these are also widely available. What is less common are components made of unusual materials – titanium and composites, for example. It is best to use common accessories.

Attitudes to bicyclists: bicyling is becoming more common in Malaysia, and clubs are springing up across the country. Unlike Indonesia and Thailand, a foreigner on a bike is not such an object of interest.

Road conditions: the maps in this guide are not sufficiently detailed for bicycling and a good, colour map is useful in determining contours and altitude, as well as showing minor roads.

	Alor Star	Bukit Fraser	Butterworth	Brinchang	Ipoh	Johor Bahru	Kota Bharu	Kuala Lumpur	Kuala Selangor	Kuala Terengganu	Kuantan	Lumut	Melaka	Mersing	Padang Besar	Port Dickson	Seremban
Bukit Fraser	443																
Butterworth	93	350															
Brinchang	378	195	285														
Ipoh	257	186	164	121													
Johor Bahru	830	467	737	582	573												
Kota Bharu	409	406	386	512	391	689											
Kuala Lumpur	462	99	369	214	205	368	474										
Kuala Selangor	446	166	352	214	189	435	541	67									
Kuala Terengganu	521	453	498	633	503	521	168	455	522								
Kuantan	684	253	591	436	427	325	371	259	326	209							
Lumut	278	269	170	204	83	656	453	288	272	586	510						
Melaka	606	243	513	358	349	224	607	144	211	508	292	432					
Mersing	815	436	722	567	558	134	568	353	420	401	191	641	255				
Padang Besar	82	525	175	460	339	912	491	544	528	603	760	360	688	897			
Port Dickson	552	189	459	304	295	318	564	90	162	503	291	384	94	321	634		
Seremban	526	163	433	478	269	304	538	64	131	471	259	352	80	289	608	32	
Taiping	183	272	90	207	86	659	369	291	275	481	513	104	435	644	265	387	355

Malaysia distance chart (Km)

Road users attitude to bicyclists: cars and buses rarely give way to a bicycle. Be very wary, especially on main roads.

Taking bikes on buses: non-a/c, cheaper buses are more accommodating of bicycles; a/c tour buses may refuse to carry a bike.

Bicycles on airlines: many international airlines take bicycles free-of-charge, provided they are not boxed. Take the peddles off and deflate the tyres.

In general: Avoid major roads. Avoid major towns.

Useful equipment
Unlike Indonesia and Thailand, camping grounds do exist pretty widely in Malaysia – both in Peninsular Malaysia and in Sabah and Sarawak. If intending to camp, then all the usual equipment is necessary – a tent, stove, cooking utensils, sleeping bag etc. Also take:

Pollution mask if travelling to large cities.
Basic tool kit – including a puncture repair kit, spare tubes, spare tyre, pump.
Good map of the area.
Bungee cords.
First aid kit.
Water filter.

● Hitch-hiking

It is easy for foreigners to hitch in Malaysia; look reasonably presentable and it shouldn't be long before someone will stop. Hitching is not advisable for single women to hitch-hike alone.

● Taxi

There are two types of taxi in Malaysia – local and 'out-station' – or long distance. The latter – usually Mercedes or Peugeot – connect all major towns and cities. They operate on a shared-cost basis – as soon as the full complement of four passengers turns up the taxis set off. Alternatively, it is possible to charter the whole taxi (for the price of four single fares). Taxi stands are usually next-door to major bus stations. Fares are fixed by the government and posted at stands, so there is no need, or point, in bargaining. If shared, taxi fares usually cost about twice as much as bus fares, but they are much faster. For groups travelling together taking a taxi makes good sense. Note that it is easier to find passengers going your way in the morning than later in the day.

Local taxi fares in Malaysia are among the cheapest in Southeast Asia. Most local taxis in major towns are now metered and a/c. Turning the a/c on costs an additional 20%. If there is no meter – or, as is more often the case, the meter is broken – fares should be negotiated in advance.

● Trishaws

In Kuala Lumpur it has long been too dangerous for trishaws, apart from around Chinatown and suburban areas. In towns such as Melaka, Georgetown and Kota Bharu, as well as in many other smaller towns, they remain one of the best – and certainly most pleasant – ways of getting around, particularly for sightseeing. It is necessary to negotiate fares in advance. As Malaysia becomes more affluent, so trishaws are disappearing; before long, presumably, it will be like Singapore: an expensive way to travel for well-heeled tourists.

BOAT

Local water transport comes into its own in Sarawak, where lack of roads makes coastal and river transport the only viable means of communication. On the larger rivers in Sarawak – such as the Rajang and the Baram – there are specially adapted express boats (see page 387). If there is no regular boat, it is nearly always possible to charter a local longboat, although this can be expensive. In the dry season the upper reaches of many rivers are unnavigable (except by smaller boats). In times of heavy rain, logs and branch debris can make rivers unsafe. Some river transport still operates on rivers on the peninsula's east coast.

Feri Malaysia runs two routes, both on a weekly schedule. 1) Port Klang – Singapore – Kuching – Kota Kinabalu – Singapore – Kuantan – Port Klang. 2) Kuantan – Kota Kinabalu – Kuching – Singapore – Port Klang. **Tourism Malaysia** offices have information on Feri Malaysia and can place bookings. (For price guidelines, see page 278).

There are regular scheduled ferry services between the main islands – Pulau Pangkor, Penang and Pulau Langkawi – and the mainland. There are services from Mersing and Singapore to Pulau Tioman. There are passenger/car ferries between Butterworth and Georgetown (Penang) every 20 minutes. For other offshore islands, mostly off the east coast, fishing boats (and sometimes regular boats) leave from the nearest fishing port.

COMMUNICATIONS

● Language

Bahasa Melayu (the Malay language – normally just shortened to *bahasa*) is the national language; it is very similar to Bahasa Indonesia – which evolved from Malay – and can be understood in southern Thailand, throughout Borneo and as far afield as the Moro areas of the southern Philippines. All communities – Malay, Chinese and Indian, as well as tribal groups in Sabah and Sarawak – speak Malay, as most are schooled in the Malay medium. Nearly everyone in Malaysia speaks some English – except in remoter rural areas – although the standard of English has declined markedly in the past 10 years. Realizing this, and because good English is essential for business, the government has sought to reverse the decline. The other main languages spoken in Malaysia include the Chinese dialects of Mandarin, Cantonese and Hokkien as well as Tamil and Punjabi.

● Postal services

Malaysia's post is cheap and reasonably reliable, although incoming and outgoing parcels should be registered.

International postal charges: postcards and aerograms cost RM0.50, letters, RM0.90.

Post office opening hours: 0800-1700 Mon-Fri, 0800-1200 Sat.

Fax and telex services: available in most state capitals.

Poste Restante: reliable services at general post offices in major cities.

● Telephone services

Local: there are public telephone booths in most towns; telephones take RM0.10 and RM0.20 coins. Card phones are now widespread. There are two types of card: Kadfon and Unicard. Kadfon can only be used at Telekom phone-booths, Unicard can be used at Uniphone phone-booths. Cards are available from airports, petrol stations and most outlets of '7-eleven' and 'Hop-In'. Telekom cards are sold at post offices, Telekom offices, and some shops. On most public phones it is necessary to press the release button once the other person responds.

Operator: for 'outstation' (trunk) calls T 101; enquiries T 102; directory T 103; international IDD assistance and details on country codes T 108.

Learning the language – a practical alternative

Malaysian English – which has been dubbed "Manglish", as opposed to Singaporean English ("Singlish") – has evolved its own usages, abbreviations and expressions. Its very distinctive pronunciation can be almost unintelligible to visitors when they first arrive. The first thing many visitors notice is the use of the suffix "lah" which is attached to just about anything and means absolutely nothing. English has been spoken in the Malay world since the late 18th century, but over time, it has been mixed with local terms. The converse has also happened: English has corrupted Malay to such a degree that it is now quite common to hear the likes of "you *pergi-mana*?" for "where are you going?" In abbreviated Malaysian-Chinese English, "can" is a key word. "Can-ah?" (inflection) means "may I?"; "can-lah" means "yes"; "cannot" means "no way"; "also can" means "yes, but I'd prefer you not to" and "how can?" is an expression of disbelief.

The man who first applied the term Manglish to mangled Malaysian English was Chinese-Malaysian satirist Kit Leee, in his book *Adoi* (which means "ouch") which gives an uncannily accurate and very humorous pseudo-anthropological run-down on Malaysia's inhabitants. His section on Manglish, which should be pronounced exactly as it is written is introduced: "*Aitelyu-ah, nemmain wat debladigarmen say, mose Malaysians tok Manglish... Donkair you Malay or Chinese or Indian or everyting miksup... we Malaysians orways tok like dis wan-kain oni...*" Below are extracts from his glossary of common Manglish words and phrases (which will help decipher the above).

atoyu (wat) gentle expression of triumph: "What did I tell you?"

baiwanfriwan ploy used mainly by shop assistants to promote sales: "If you buy one you'll get one free".

betayudon mild warning, as in "You'd better not do that".

debladigarmen contraction of "the bloody government"; widely used scapegoat for all of life's disappointments, delays, denials, and prohibitions.

hauken another flexible expression applicable in almost any situation, eg "That's not right!", "Impossible!" or "Don't tell me!".

izzenit from "isn't it?" but applied very loosely at the end of any particular statement to elicit an immediate response, eg "Yused you will spen me a beer, izzenit?"

kennonot request or enquiry, contraction of "can or not": "May I?" or "Will you?" or "Is it possible?"

nola a dilute negative, used as a device to interrupt, deny or cancel someone else's statement.

oridi contraction of already.

sohau polite interrogative, usually used as a greeting, as in "Well, how are things with you?"

tingwat highly adaptable expression stemming from "What do you think?"

wan-kain adjective denoting uniqueness... contraction of "one of a kind". Sometimes rendered as "*wan-kain oni*" ("only").

watudu rhetorical question: "But what can we do?"

yala non-committal agreement, liberally used when confronted with a bore.

yusobadwan expression of mild reproach: "That's not very nice!"

(With thanks to Kit Leee and his co-etymologists: Rafique Rashid, Julian Mokhtar and Jeanne MC Donven. Leee, Kit (1989) *Adoi*, Times Books International: Singapore.)

International: there is an international telephone exchange in KL and calls can be booked to most countries in the world. Calls may be booked in advance. Collect calls can be linked to destination countries without delay (the operator will call you back). Direct calls can be made from telephones with IDD (international direct dialling) facility (007 plus country code plus area code plus number). Direct international calls can be made from most Kedai Telekom and telephone booths in major towns.

ENTERTAINMENT

MEDIA

● Newspapers

The main English-language dailies are *The New Straits Times*, *Business Times*, *The Star*, *The Daily Express* and *The Malay Mail* (afternoon). The main Sunday papers are *The New Sunday Times*, *The Sunday Mail* and *The Sunday Star*. The English-language dailies are government-owned and this is reflected in their content which tends to be relentlessly pro-government. *Aliran Monthly* is a high-brow but fascinating publication offering current affairs analysis from a non-government perspective. *The Rochet* is the Democratic Action Party's opposition newspaper, and also presents an alternative perspective. Both are available at news outlets. International editions of leading foreign newspapers and news magazines can be obtained at main news stands and book stalls, although some of these are not cleared through customs until mid-afternoon (notably *The Asian Wall Street Journal*).

In East Malaysia the main English language newspapers are the *Sabah Daily News* and the *Sarawak Tribune*.

● Radio

There are six government radio stations which broadcast in various languages including English. Radio 1 broadcasts in Bahasa Melayu; Radio 2 is a music station; Radio 3 is mainly Bahasa but broadcasts a special programme for tourists every day at 1800; Radio 4 is in English; Radio 5, Chinese; Radio 6, Tamil. In KL you can tune into the Federal Capital's radio station and elsewhere in the country there are local stations. The BBC World Service can be picked up on FM in southern Johor, from the Singapore transmitter. Elsewhere it can be received on shortwave. The main frequencies are (in kHz): 11750, 9740, 6195 and 3915.

● Television

RTM1 and RTM2 are operated by Radio Television Malaysia, the government-run broadcasting station. Apart from locally produced programmes, some American and British series are shown. Three other channels, are commercially run. There is a broad mixture of content, from Chinese kung-fu movies to Tamil musicals and English-language blockbusters and series. On the three commercial stations, all programmes are liberally interspersed with advertising, most of it for cigarettes, and leading tobacco companies sponsor film shows. Programmes for all channels are listed in daily newspapers. Singapore Broadcasting Service programmes can be received as far north as Melaka and are often listed in Malaysian papers. The government has long resisted the arrival of satellite TV, believing it to be a cultural polluter. To supplement local TV news, CNN was rebroadcast for an hour every night and since March 1994, BBC World Service Television has also been allowed in. It too is rebroadcast however, enabling government censors to review the output.

HOLIDAYS AND FESTIVALS

Tourism Malaysia has dates of movable holidays and festivals. Note that Islamic holidays may vary significantly in their timing during the year. Chinese, Indian (Hindu) and some Christian holidays are also movable. To make things even more exciting, each state has its own slate of public holidays when shops close and banks pull down their shutters. This makes calculating public holidays in advance a bit of a quagmire of lunar events, assorted kings' birthdays, and tribal festivals.

January: *New Year's Day* (1st: public holiday except Johor, Kedah, Kelantan, Perlis and Terengganu).

January/February: *Thaipusam* (movable: public holiday Johor, Negeri Sembilan, Perak, Penang and Selangor only) celebrated by many Hindus throughout Malaysia in honour of their deity Lord Subramanian (also known as Lord Muruga); he represents virtue, bravery, youth and power. Held during full moon in the month of Thai, it is a day of penance and thanksgiving. Devotees pay homage to Lord Subramanian by piercing their bodies, cheeks and tongues with sharp skewers (*vel*) and hooks weighted with oranges and carrying *kevadis* (steel structures bearing the image of Lord Muruga). There are strict rules the devotee must follow in order to

Cinema: Dr Mahathir, Mr Schindler and the censors'

In March 1994 the Malaysian government scored a spectacular own goal in international public relations by banning the Oscar-winning film *Schindler's List*. The film tells the true story of a German businessman who saved hundreds of Jews from the Nazi holocaust. The government defended the decision by the Board of Censors which branded Stephen Spielberg's epic "Jewish propaganda". In their list of reasons for banning the film, the board ruled that it reflected the virtues of one race only with the purpose of asking for sympathy and tarnishing the other race. The banning order provoked international outrage. Two weeks later, it was finally overturned by the cabinet on the condition that scenes with nudity and violence be cut.

In appealing against the ban, the film's distributors said Malaysia had missed the whole point; *Schindler's List* was about humanity, they said, and with ethnic cleansing still being practiced today, it needed to be widely seen. Jewish groups around the world called the ban "shameful" and "deplorable". The Malaysian Prime Minister, Dr Mahathir Mohamad, who maintained that his country had the right to ban any film, was accused of "long-standing anti-Semitism".

When an Indonesian cleric called for similar action there, because the film, in his view, was "nothing but Zionist propaganda", the American State Department entered the fray. Alarmed at the upsurge of such sentiments in Malaysia and Indonesia – particularly following the massacre of Palestinian worshipers at a mosque in Hebron on the West Bank – Washington sought to support the film's historical accuracy. In a face-saving formula, the two countries' reservations about the film were finally passed off as part of their standard practice of excising nudity from celuloid. Censors in the Philippines had earlier attempted to stop *Schindler's List* being shown there because portions of the film "showed too much breast". Their decision was over-ruled by President Fidel Ramos. Not a murmur, though, from normally flesh-shy Singapore, where the uncut version packed cinemas across the island.

purify himself before carrying the kevadi – he becomes a vegetarian and abstains from worldly pleasures. Women cannot carry kevadis as they are not allowed to bare their bodies in order to be pierced. Although a kevadi carrier can have as many as a hundred spears piercing his flesh he only loses a small amount of blood in his trance. Each participant tries to outdo the others in the severity of his torture. At certain temples fire-walking is also part of this ceremony. Many Hindus disapprove of the spectacle and believe that their bodies are a gift from Siva; they should serve as a temple for the soul and should not be abused. This festival is peculiar to Hindus in Malaysia, Singapore and Thailand and is a corruption of a Tamil ceremony from South India. The biggest gatherings are at Batu Caves just outside KL, when thousands of pilgrims from all over the country congregate in a carnival-like atmosphere (see page 114); there are also festivals held in Melaka, Penang and Singapore.

Chinese New Year (movable: public holiday, 2 days in most states, 1 day in Kelantan and Terengganu) a 15-days lunar festival celebrated in late January/early February (for more details, see page 721). Chinatown streets are crowded for weeks with shoppers buying traditional oranges which signify luck. Lion, unicorn or dragon dances welcome in the New Year and, unlike in Singapore, thousands of fire crackers are let off to ward off evil spirits. *Chap Goh Mei* is the 15th day of the Chinese New Year and brings celebrations to a close; it is marked with a final dinner, another firecracker fest, prayers and offerings. The Chinese believe that in order to find good husbands, girls should throw oranges into the river/sea on this day. In Sarawak the festival is known as *Guan Hsiao Cheih* (Lantern Festival).

March-April: *Easter* (movable) celebrated in Melaka with candle-lit processions and special services (see page 237). *Good Friday* is a public holiday in Sabah and Sarawak.

May: *Labour Day* (1st: public holiday).
Kurah Aran (1st) celebrated by the Bidayuh tribe in Sarawak (see page 345) after the paddy harvest is over.
Wesak Day (movable: public holiday except Labuan) the most important day in the Buddhist calendar, celebrates the Buddha's birth, death and enlightenment. Temples throughout the country are packed with devotees offering incense, joss-sticks and prayers. Lectures on Buddhism and special exhibitions are held. In Melaka there is a procession at night with decorated floats, bands, dancers and acrobatics.

June: *Birthday of His Majesty the King* (1st Saturday of the month: public holiday) mainly celebrated in KL with processions.
Dragon Boat Festival (movable) honours the suicide of an ancient Chinese poet hero, Qu Yuan. He tried to press for political reform by drowning himself in the Mi Luo River as a protest against corruption. In an attempt to save him fishermen played drums and threw rice dumplings to try and distract vultures. His death is commemorated with dragon boat races and the enthusiastic consumption of rice dumplings; biggest celebrations are in Penang.

August: *Hari Kebangsaan* or *National Day* (31st: public holiday) commemorates Malaysian independence (*merdeka*) in 1957. Big celebration in KL with processions of floats representing all the states; best places to see it: on the Padang (Merdeka Square) or on TV. In Sarawak, Hari Kebangsaan is celebrated in a different divisional capital each year.
Mooncake or *Lantern Festival* (movable). This Chinese festival marks the overthrow of the Mongol Dynasty in China; celebrated, as the name suggests, with the exchange and eating of mooncakes. According to Chinese legend secret messages of revolt were carried inside these cakes and led to the uprising. In the evening, children light festive lanterns while women pray to the Goddess of the Moon.

August-September: *Festival of the Hungry Ghosts* (movable) on the seventh moon in the Chinese lunar calendar, souls in purgatory are believed to return to earth to feast. Food is offered to these wandering spirits. Altars are set up in the streets and candles with faces are burned on them (for more detail see page 723).

October: *Festival of the Nine Emperor Gods* or *Kiew Ong Yeah* (movable) marks the return of the spirits of the nine emperor gods to earth. The mediums whom they are to possess purify themselves by observing a vegetarian diet. The gods possess the mediums, who go into trance and are then carried on sedan chairs whose seats are comprised of razor-sharp blades or spikes. Devotees visit temples dedicated to the nine gods. A strip of yellow cotton is often bought from the temple and worn on the right wrist as a sign of devotion. The ceremonies usually culminate with a fire walking ritual.

October-November: *Deepvali* (movable: public holiday except Sarawak and Labuan) the Hindu festival of lights commemorates the victory of light over darkness and good over evil: the triumphant return of Rama after his defeat of the evil Ravanna in the Hindu epic, the Ramayana. Every Hindu home is brightly lit and decorated for the occasion.

December: *Christmas Day* (25th: public holiday) Christmas in Malaysia is a commercial spectacle these days with fairy lights and decorations and tropical Santa Clauses – although it does not compare with celebrations in Singapore. Mostly celebrated on the west coast and ignored on the more Muslim east coast. Midnight mass is the main Christmas service held in churches throughout Malaysia.

● Islamic holidays

December: *Awal Ramadan* (movable: public holiday Johor and Melaka, 31 December 1997) the first day of Ramadan, a month of fasting for all Muslims – and by implication, all Malays. During this month Muslims abstain from all food and drink (as well as smoking) from sunrise to sundown – if they are very strict, Muslims do not even swallow their own saliva during daylight hours. It is strictly adhered to in the conservative Islamic states of Kelantan and Terengganu. Every evening for 30 days before breaking of fast, stalls are set up which sell traditional Malay cakes and delicacies. The only people exempt from fasting are the elderly as well as women who are pregnant or are menstruating.

January: *Hari Raya Puasa* or *Aidil Fitri* (movable: public holiday, 30-31 January 1998) marks the end of the Muslim fasting month of Ramadan and is a day of prayer and celebration. In order for Hari Raya to be declared, the new moon of Syawal has to be sighted; if it is not, fasting continues for another day. It is the most important time of the year for Muslim families to get together; Malays living in towns and cities balek kampung (return home to their village), where it is 'open house' for relatives and friends, and special Malay delicacies are served. Hari Raya is also enthusiastically celebrated by Indian Muslims.

Festivals in East Malaysia

Besides those celebrated throughout the country, Sabah and Sarawak have their own festivals. Exact dates can be procured from the tourist offices in the capitals. State public holidays are listed on page 522.

Kadazan Harvest Festival or ***Tadau Keamatan*** (movable: public holiday Sabah and Labuan only) marks the end of the rice harvest in Sabah; The ***magavau*** ritual is performed to nurse the spirit back to health in readiness for the next planting season. Traditionally, the ritual would have been performed in the paddy fields by a *bobohizan* (high priestess). Celebrated with feasting, *tapai* (rice wine) drinking, dancing and general merry-making. There are also agricultural shows, buffalo races, cultural performances and traditional games. The traditional *sumazal* dance is one of the highlights of the festivities.

Gawai (movable: public holiday Sarawak only) this is the major festival of the year for the Iban of Sarawak; longhouses party continuously for a week. The Gawai celebrates the end of the rice harvest and welcomes the new planting season. The main ritual is called *magavau* and nurses the spirit of the grain back to health in advance of the new planting season. Like the Kadazan harvest festival in Sabah, visitors are welcome to join in, but in Sarawak, the harvest festival is much more traditional. On the first day of celebrations everyone dresses up in traditional costumes and sings and dances and drinks *tuak* rice wine until they drop.

Gawai Burung (Sarawak) biggest of all the gawais and honours the war god of the Ibans. *Gawai Kenyalang* is one stage of Gawai Burung and is celebrated only after a tribesman has been instructed to do so after a dream.

Gawai Antu (Sarawak) also known as *Gawai Nyunkup* or *Rugan*. Iban tribute to departed spirits. In simple terms a party to mark the end of mourning for anyone whose relative had died in the previous 6 months.

Gawai Batu (Sarawak) whetstone feast held by Iban farmers sometime in June.

Gawai Mpijog Jaran Rantau (Sarawak) celebrated by the Bidayuh before the cutting of grass in new paddy fields.

Gawai Bineh (Sarawak) Iban festival celebrated after harvest. Welcomes back all the spirits of the paddy from the fields.

Gawai Sawa (movable) celebrated by the Bidayuh in Sarawak to offer thanksgiving for the last year and to make the next year a plentiful one.

Nuzul Quran (movable, Kelantan, Pahang, Perak, Perlis, Selangor and Terengganu, 15 January 1998).

April: *Hari Raya Haji* (movable: public holiday, 7 April 1998, in Kedah, Kelantan, Perlis and Terengganu the 8 April 1998 – *Hari Raya Qurban* – is also a public holiday) celebrated by Muslims to mark the 10th day of Zulhijgah, the 12th month of the Islamic calendar when pilgrims celebrate their return from the Haj to Mecca. In the morning, prayers are offered and later, families hold 'open house'. Those who can afford it sacrifice goats or cows to be distributed to the poor. Many Malays have the title Haji in their name, meaning they have made the pilgrimage to Mecca; men who have been on the Haj wear a white skull-hat. The Haj is one of the five keystones of Islam.

Maal Hijrah (*Awal Muharram*) (movable: public holiday, 28 April 1998) marks the first day of the Muslim calendar, marking the Prophet Muhammad's journey from Mecca to Medina on the lunar equivalent of 16 July 622 AD. Religious discussions and lectures commemorate the day. Wesak Day (movable, public holiday).

July: *Birthday of the Prophet Muhammad* (*Maulidur Rasul*) (movable: public holiday, 7 July 1998) to commemorate Prophet Muhammad's birthday in 571 AD. Processions and Koran recitals in most big towns.

November: *Hari Hol Almarhum Sultan Ismail* (movable, Johor, 31 October 1998).

December: *Israk and Mikraj* (movable, Kedah and Negeri Sembilan, 18 November 1998).

● State holidays

Only sultans' and governors' birthday celebrations are marked with processions and festivities; state holidays can disrupt travel itineraries – particularly in east coast states where they may run for several days.

January: *Sultan of Kedah's birthday* (2nd Sunday of the month, Kedah).

February: *Federal Territory Day* (1st, KL and Labuan).

March: *Sultan of Selangor's birthday* (2nd Saturday of the month, Selangor); *Installation of Sultan of Terengganu Day* (21st, Terengganu); *Sultan of Kelantan's birthday* (30th & 31st, Kelantan).

April: *Sultan of Johor's birthday* (8th, Johor); *Declaration of Melaka as Historic City* (15th, Melaka); *Sultan of Perak's birthday* (19th, Perak); *Sultan of Terengganu's birthday* (29th, Terengganu).

May: *Pahang Hol Day* (7th, Pahang); *Harvest Festival* (30th and 31st, Sabah and Labuan).

June: *Dayak Day* (1st and 2nd, Sarawak); *Rajah of Perlis' birthday* (17th, Perlis).

July: *Governor of Penang's birthday* (2nd Saturday of the month, Penang); *Yang Di-Pertuan Besar of Negri Sembilan's birthday* (19th, Negri Sembilan).

September: *Governor of Sarawak's birthday* (16th, Sarawak); *Governor of Sabah's birthday* (16th, Sabah).

October: *Governor of Melaka's birthday* (2nd Saturday of the month, Melaka); *Sultan of Pahang's birthday* (24th, Pahang).

● School holidays

Schools in Malaysia have five breaks through the year, although the actual dates vary from state to state. They generally fall in the months of January (1 week), March (2 weeks), May (3 weeks), August (1 week), and October (4 weeks).

FURTHER READING

● Novels

Burgess, Anthony: Burgess lived in Malaysia between 1954 and 1957, learnt Malay, and mixed with the locals to a far greater extent than Maugham or Conrad, and this is reflected in a much more nuanced understanding of the Malay character. After leaving Malaya in 1957, he taught in Brunei until 1960. Among his books are *Time for a tiger* (1956), *The enemy in the blanket* (1958) and *Beds in the east* (1959) which were later published together by Penguin as *Malayan trilogy*.

Conrad, Joseph: Perhaps the finest novelists of the Malay archipelago, books include *Lord Jim* and *Victory*, both widely available in paperback editions from most bookshops.

Keith, Agnes (1969) *Land below the wind*, Ulverscroft: Leicester. Perhaps the best-known English language book on Sabah. See page 476.

Maniam, KS (1983) *The return*, Skoob Books: London. The novel, by a Indian Malaysian, is about the difficulties a Hindu has in finding a home in Malaysia, especially since the Indian in question is educated at a British colonial school.

Maugham, West Somerset (1969) *Maugham's Malaysian stories*, Heinemann: London and Singapore. Another English novelist who wrote extensively on Malaysia. These stories are best for the insight they provide of colonial life, not of the Malay or Malay life.

Theroux, Paul (1979) *The consul's file*, Penguin. A selection of short stories based on Malaysia.

● Travel

Bird, Isabella (1883 and reprinted 1983) *The Golden Chersonese*, Murray: London, reprinted by Century paperback. The account of a late 19th century female visitor to the region who shows her gumption facing everything from natives to crocs.

Bock, Carl (1985, first published 1881) *The headhunters of Borneo*, OUP: Singapore. Bock was a Norwegian naturalist and explorer and was commissioned by the Dutch to make a scientific survey of south-eastern Borneo. His account, though, makes much of the dangers and adventures that he faced, and is some of his ' scientific' observations are, in retrospect, clearly highly faulty. Nonetheless, this is an entertaining account.

Charles, Hose (1985, first published 1929) *The field book of a jungle wallah*, OUP: Singapore. Hose was an official in Sarawak and became an acknowledged expert on the material and non-material culture of the tribes of Sarawak. He was one of that band of highly informed, perceptive and generally benevolent colonial administrators.

King, Victor T (edit). (1992) *The best of Borneo travel*, Oxford University Press: Oxford. A compilation of travel accounts from the early 19th century through to the late 20th. An excellent companion to take while exploring the island. Published in portable paperback.

Mjoberg, Eric: *Forest life and adventures in the Malay archipelago*, OUP: Singapore.

O'Hanlon, Redmond (1984) *Into the heart of Borneo*, Salamander Press: Edinburgh. One of the best recent travel books on Borneo. This highly amusing and perceptive romp through Borneo in the company of poet and foreign correspondent James Fenton, includes an ascent of the Rejang River and does much to counter the more romanticised images of Bornean life.

● History

Harrisson, Tom (1959) *World within*, Hutchinson: London. During the Second World War, explorer, naturalist and ethnologist Tom Harrisson was parachuted into Borneo to help organize Dayak resistance against the occupying Japanese forces. This is his extraordinary account.

Barber, Noel (1971) *The war of the running dogs: Malaya 1948-1960*, Arrow Books. This is one of numerous accounts of the Malayan Emergency and the successful British attempt to defeat the Communist Party of Malaya.

Turnbull, Mary C (1989) *A history of Malaysia, Singapore and Brunei*, Allen and Unwin. A very orthodox history of Malaysia, Singapore and Brunei, clearly written for a largely academic/student audience.

Chapman, F Spencer: *The jungle is neutral*. An account of a British guerrilla force fighting the Japanese in Borneo — not as enthralling as Tom Harrisson's book, but still worth reading.

Payne, Robert: *The white Rajahs of Sarawak*. Readable account of the extraordinary history of this East Malaysian state.

● Natural history

Briggs, John (1988) *Mountains of Malaysia: a practical guide and manuel*, Longman: London. He has also written *Parks of Malaysia*, useful for anyone intending to especially visit the country's protected areas (Longman: Kuala Lumpur).

Cranbrook, Earl of (1987) *Riches of the wild: land mammals of South-East Asia*, OUP.

Cubitt, Gerald and Payne, Junaidi (1990) *Wild Malaysia*, London: New Holland. Large format, coffee table book, lots of wonderful colour photos, reasonable text, short background piece on each national park.

Hanbury-Tenison, Robin (1980) *Mulu, the rain forest*, Arrow/Weidenfeld. This is the product of an Royal Geographical Society trip to Mulu in the late 1970s; semi-scholarly and useful.

Payne, Junaidi *et al*: *Pocket guide to birds of Borneo*, World Wildlife Fund/Sabah Society.

Payne, Junaidi *et al*: *A field guide to the mammals of Borneo*, World Wildlife Fund/Sabah Society. Good illustrations, reasonable text, but very dry.

Tweedie, MWF and Harrison, JL (1954 with new editions) *Malayan animal life*, Longman.

Wallace, Alfred Russel (1869) *The Malay Archipelago*. A classic of Victorian travel writing by one of the finest naturalists of the period. Wallace travelled through all of island Southeast Asia over a period of some years. The original is now re-printed.

● Other books

Leee, Kit (1989) *Adoi*, Times Books: Singapore. An amusing book of Malaysian attitudes to most things.

Craig, Jo Ann: *Culture shock Malaysia*. One in a series of Culture Shock books, this examines and assesses the do's and don't of Malaysian and Singapore society. Useful for those going to live or spend an extended period in the region.

Lat: Lat is Malaysia's foremost cartoonist. His images of the effects of social and economic change on a simple kampung boy are amusing and highly perceptive. His cartoons are compiled in numerous books including *Kampung boy* and *Town boy*, published by Straits Times Publishing.

● Maps and guides

Malaysia Nelles Map; Shell Map of Malaysia (available from Shell stations in Malaysia). Concertina Road Maps – Peninsula Malaysia and Sabah, Sarawak and Brunei, published by Falcon Press.

Brunei

Horizons	530	Parks and walks	562
Bandar Seri Begawan	549	Information for travellers	564
Around Brunei	559		

THE MICROSCOPIC Sultanate of Brunei lays claim to one of the most dramatic rags-to-riches stories of all time. Its now-legendary oil-wealth rests on a stroke of geological luck. Had it not been for oil, the Sultan of Brunei would probably be struggling to make ends meet as a member of the Federation of Malaysia's minor nobility. In the early 1900s, the kingpin of Brunei's industrial economy was the Kampong Subok cutch (or gambier) factory, hidden in the mangrove swamps on the shores of Brunei Bay. This obscure dye produced at Subok – extracted from the bark of the *bakau* mangrove tree, and used in the tanning of leather – accounted for 90% of Brunei's exports. For the average Bruneian, life had changed little in centuries. The once-great trading empire, which in its heyday held sway over vast tracts of Borneo and beyond, had crumbled. For generations, the sultanate had been sandwiched, squeezed and bullied by marauding pirates and successive colonial and commercial adventurers.

Horizons

Today, the citizens of this oil-rich sultanate are the wealthiest people in the Asia-Pacific region after the Japanese. The paternalistic government directly employs a third of the workforce, and ensures they are the best-paid bureaucrats in the world. Few Bruneian Malays want to work in the private sector and certainly none as manual labourers – but foreign migrants willingly flock to Southeast Asia's El Dorado to fill the gap.

Bruneians bask in the munificence of their autocratic monarch – whose personal fortune was estimated in 1997 at US$38bn – and his government, whose treasury is overflowing with the profits of Brunei Shell Petroleum. The sultanate has been dubbed a 'Shell-fare state': Bruneians do not pay income tax, enjoy free education, medical care and old-age pensions.

Sultan Hassanal Bolkiah, who celebrated his 50th birthday in 1996, has kept the lid on political dissent – which has not erupted since an abortive revolt in 1962 – by, according to some commentators, buying the loyalty of his subjects. The monarch (see profile, page 534) appears to have no trouble reconciling his extravagant, cosmopolitan lifestyle with the strictures of Islam – as ruler, he is the head of the Islamic faith. Good salaries and creature comforts have, however, politically lobotomized a people who might otherwise rebel against a monarchical system which appears to be out of step with the 20th century.

Negara Brunei Darussalam – the country's official name – means 'Brunei, Abode of Peace' and life is indeed very peaceful in the sultanate. In some diplomatic and governmental circles, the capital, Bandar Seri Begawan, is known as the 'Geneva of ASEAN', ostensibly because of its generous hospitality budget; but most people also find Brunei dull and expensive.

The Sultan's fiefdom has featured on seafarers' maps of Southeast Asia for over a millennium, the first documented mention of Brunei being a Chinese trader's account of P'o-ni (Brunei) in the 9th century. The name 'Brunei' is said to derive from the Sanskrit *Varunai*, meaning 'sea-people'. In the 19th century, when the White Rajahs of Sarawak had their eyes on the Sultan's territory, Brunei was known as 'Borneo Proper'. The name 'Borneo' itself may be a European cartographer's corruption of the word Brunei – although Iban folklore has it that 'Borneo' derives from the Malay *buah nyiur* – meaning coconut.

THE LAND

Brunei Darussalam lies about 400 km north of the equator, between 4° and 5° north, on the northwest coast of Borneo. The sultanate has a 160 km-long coastline, facing the South China Sea. The country is divided into four districts: Brunei/Muara, Tutong, Belait and Temburong.

GEOGRAPHY

Territorially, modern Brunei is the rump of what was once a sprawling empire. Today the sultanate has a land area of 5,769 sq km – a pinprick on the map, about

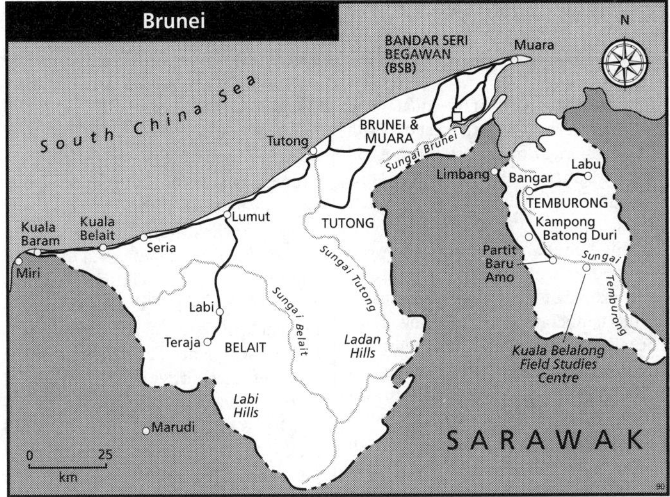

twice the size of Luxembourg. In 1981 the government bought a cattle ranch at Willeroo, in Australia's Northern Territory, which is larger than the whole of Brunei. As a country, it is a geographical absurdity; its two wedges of territory are separated by Limbang, ceded to the expansionist Charles Brooke, Rajah of Sarawak in 1890. Bruneians commute between the Temburong district and Bandar Seri Begawan in speedboats nicknamed 'flying coffins'.

Most of Brunei occupies a low alluvial coastal plain. There are four main rivers, flowing north into the South China Sea. The coastal lowlands and river valleys are characterized by a flat or gently undulating landscape, rarely rising more than 15m above sea level. The coastline is mainly sandy except for a stretch of rocky headlands between Muara and Pekan Tutong. These cliffs rise to a height of about 30m, where the north coastal hills meet the South China Sea. Further west, the Andulau Hills stand at the north end of a watershed separating the Belait and Tutong drainage basins.

Towards the interior of West Brunei, along the border with Sarawak and in South Temburong district, it gets much hillier. In West Brunei there are two upland areas: the Ladan Hills run north to south between the Tutong and Limbang basins. Bukit Bedawan is the highest of these, at 529m. In Belait district, near the border with Sarawak, are the Labi Hills – the highest being Bukit Teraja at 417m. The south half of Temburong district is much more mountainous, with deep, narrow valleys and several hills of over 600m. The highest of these is Bukit Pagon at 1,850m, although the summit itself is actually outside Brunei.

Geology

The Seria oilfield, the source of Brunei's liquidity, lies on a narrow anticline, a quarter of which is submerged by the sea. All the oil comes from a strip just 13 km long and 2.5 km wide. The oil is in fractured blocks of sandstone between 240m and 3,000m below the surface. Some of the oil under the sea is accessed by wells drilled from the shore which reach more than 1.5 km out to sea. The oil has a low sulphur content (see page 547).

Brunei's upland areas are comprised of sandstones and shale.

CLIMATE

Brunei is only 5° north of the equator and so is characterized, like the rest of North and West Borneo, by consistently hot and sticky weather: uniform temperature, high humidity (average 82%) and regular rainfall.

Daily temperatures average between 22°C and 28°C. Mid-day temperatures rarely exceed 35°C; at night it is unusual for the temperature to dip below 21°C. The average daily minimum temperature is 23°C, the maximum 32°C.

Rainfall is well distributed throughout the year but two seasons are distinguishable: there is less rainfall between February and August, and the rainy season sets in during September and runs through to the end of January. The northeast monsoon peaks in December and January and is characterized by short-lived, violent downpours. Even during the monsoon season, though, there is a 50% chance of it not raining each day and a daily average of 7 hours of sunshine. The annual average rainfall is over 2,500 mm a year, nearly five times that of London or more than double New York's annual rainfall. The south interior region, including Temburong district, is wetter, with up to 4,060 mm a year. The west coast areas get between 2,540 and 3,300 mm of rainfall a year. In Bandar Seri Begawan, the average annual rainfall is 2,921 mm. For rainfall and temperature graphs for Kuching and Kota Kinabalu, in neighbouring Sarawak and Sabah, see pages 354 and 434.

FLORA AND FAUNA

(For more detail on jungle flora and fauna, see Introduction to Borneo, page 321.) Like much of the neighbouring Malaysian state of Sarawak, the low-lying areas of Brunei are characterized by peat swamp forest which is unsuited to agriculture. In parts the peat is up to 9m thick and cannot support permanent agriculture. About 60% of Brunei is still covered in lush virgin jungle. If secondary forest – known as *belukar* – is included, about 80% of Brunei's land area is still forested.

Apart from the peat swamp forest, Brunei has areas of heath forest (*kerangas*) on sandy soils near the coast, and mangrove, which grows on the tidal mudflats around Brunei Bay and in the Belait and Tutong estuaries. The most common mangrove tree is the bakau, which grows to a height of about 9m and has stilt roots to trap sediment. The bakau was the source of cutch – a dye made from boiling its bark, and used in leather-tanning – which was produced at Brunei Bay until the 1950s. Bakau wood also made useful piles for stilt-houses in Bandar Seri Begawan's Kampong Ayer as it is resistant to rotting, and excellent charcoal. Also on the coast, between Kuala Belait and Muara, are stretches of casuarina forest.

Away from the coastal plain and the river valleys, the forest changes to lowland rainforest – or mixed dipterocarp forest – which supports at least eight commercial hardwood species. The *Dipterocarpacae* family forms the jungle canopy, 30-50m above the ground. Timber from Brunei's jungle is used locally – none is exported. By 1990, logging firms were required to use sustainable management techniques and within a year, felling was cut to half the 1989 level. Forest reserves have been expanded and cover 320,000 hectares. Indeed, Brunei has some of Southeast Asia finest forests – despite its small size when compared with the neighbouring Malaysian states of Sabah and Sarawak, and with Indonesian Borneo (Kalimantan). The reason for this is not difficult to fathom: Brunei's oil wealth has meant that there has been no pressure to generate foreign exchange through the export of tropical timber and timber products.

Wildlife

Brunei's jungle has been left largely intact – thanks to Brunei's oil wealth there is no need to exploit the forest. Loggers and shifting cultivators have been less active than they have in neighbouring territories and the forest fauna have been less disturbed. Their only disruptions come from a few upriver tribespeople, a handful of wandering Penan hunter-gatherers, the odd scientist and the occasional platoon of muddied soldiers enduring jungle warfare training exercises. Tourists rarely venture into Brunei's jungle as Sarawak's nearby national parks are much more accessible and better known. 1996, however, marked the opening of the Ulu Temburong National Park with its network of wooden walkways – some as high as the forest canopy. For those who have access to a car, there are also several jungle trails on Brunei's doorstep (see **Parks and walks**, page 562).

Brunei boasts most of Borneo's jungle exotica. For oil explorers and their families in the early 1900s, some local residents proved more daunting than others. Up until the 1960s, encounters with large crocodiles were commonplace in Brunei, and in the oil town of Seria they posed a constant menace to the local community. In August 1959 Brunei Shell Petroleum was forced to recruit a professional crocodile-catcher. Mat Yassin bin Hussin claimed to have caught and destroyed more than 700 crocodiles in a career spanning four decades, the largest being a highly unlikely 8.5m long man-eater which had devoured 12 Ibans south of Kuala Belait.

Mat Yassin's technique was to sprinkle gold dust into the river as part of a magic ritual, then to dangle chickens over bridges on baited rattan hooks. According to GC Harper, a Seria oilfield historian, Mat Yassin would wait until a crocodile jumped for the bait and then he would "blow down its snout with the aid of a blowpipe to make the strong reptile weak. It could then be dragged up the river bank and its jaws tied before it was destroyed." Mat Yassin silenced cynics when he landed two maneaters in as many days and said he had come across an old white crocodile which was considered sacred; he refused to touch it because it "could never be destroyed either by bullets or by magic".

HISTORY

Brunei's early history is obscure – but although precise dates have been muddied by time, there is no doubt that the sultanate's early prosperity was rooted in trade. As far back as the 7th century, China was importing birds' nests from Brunei, and Arab, Indian, Chinese and other Southeast Asian traders were regularly passing through. Links with Chinese merchants were strongest: they traded silk, metals, stoneware and porcelain for Brunei's jungle produce: bezoar stones, hornbill-ivory, timber and birds' nests. Chinese coins dating from the 8th century have been unearthed at Kota Batu, 3 km from Bandar Seri Begawan. Large quantities of Chinese porcelain dating from the Tang, Sung and Ming dynasties have also been found. A Chinese trader mentioned P'o-ni – a Sinified transliteration of Brunei – in an account of his travels in the 9th century. The sultanate was on the main trade route between China and the western reaches of the Malayan archipelago and by the Chinese Sung Dynasty, in the 10th to 13th centuries, trade was booming. By the turn of the 15th century there was a sizeable Chinese population settled in Brunei.

With the decline of the Srivijayan Empire (based at Palembang, Sumatra) in the late 13th century, the Siamese (Thai) kingdom of Sukhothai and the Hindu empire of Majapahit, centred on East Java, were on the rise. Brunei and West Borneo became tributary states of the Majapahit Empire in the 1300s. As the Brunei royal chronicles only list the names of rulers and not their dates, it is impossible to establish specific dates for

The Sultan of Brunei – living by the profit

When Hassanal Bolkiah was crowned the 29th Sultan of Brunei, in August 1968, at the age of 21, a barrel of oil cost US$1.33. As oil prices rocketed in the wake of the 1973 oil crisis, so did the Sultan's fortune. *Fortune* magazine and *The Guinness Book of Records* rate him the richest man in the world. His personal wealth was recently assessed at US$37bn – three times that of Queen Elizabeth II. It is believed that he earns more than US$100 a second – or US$2bn a year.

As befitting the man with the biggest bank account in the world, the biggest palace in the world, and head of the second oldest dynasty in the world (after Japan), Sultan Bolkiah also has a long name. The official version, even when condensed, is an alphabet soup of acronyms and honorifics:

> His Majesty Paduka Seri Baginda Sultan and Yang Di-Pertuan, Sultan Hassanal Bolkiah Mu'izzaddin Waddaulah Ibni Al-Marhum Sultan Haji Omar Ali Saifuddien Sa'adul Khairi Waddien, DKMB, DK, PSSUB, DPKG, DPKT, PSPNB, PSNB, PSLJ, SPMB, PANB, GCMG, DMN, DK (Kelantan), DK (Johor), DK (Negri Sembilan), Collar of the Supreme Order of the Chrysanthemum, Grand Order of the Mugunghwa, DK (Pahang), BRI, Collar of the Nile, the Order of Al-Hussein bin Ali, the Civil Order of Oman, DK (Selangor), DK (Perlis), PGAT, Sultan and Yang Di-Pertuan Negara Brunei Darussalam.

Sultan Hassanal Bolkiah was named after the fifth Sultan of Brunei, who presided over Brunei's golden age. He was sent to boarding school at Kuala Lumpur's Victoria Institution, which was modelled on the British public school. He was not academically inclined, and in 1965, on his return from Malaysia, married his cousin, Princess Saleha. A year later, he was dispatched to the Royal Military Academy at Sandhurst in England, but was unable to attend his own passing-out parade, due to his father's sudden abdication in Oct 1967. He was gazetted as a captain and returned, unwillingly, to Brunei to become Sultan. 5 years later, he was knighted by Queen Elizabeth II, and on independence in 1984, was awarded the rank of major-general.

The Sultan now has a second wife, Queen Mariam Bell, whom he married against his father's wishes in 1981. Sceptics, cynics, or muckrakers, depending on their perspective, say that it is a ploy to increase the size of the royal family and therefore power. Certainly, the number of princes and princesses is going up at such a rate that it seems a private school will be built specifically to educate them.

The Sultan insists that the assertions about his wealth are an exaggeration. But it is very difficult to separate his private fortune from that of the state. His unauthorized – and generally critical – biographer James Bartholomew writes: "Brunei is a private country run like a private possession ... The line between his personal wealth and that of the state is far from clear." A government committee determines the Sultan's salary – as Head of State, Prime Minister and Minister of Defence – which is separate from his family inheritance, private funds and investments. However, state funds were allegedly used to purchase London's Dorchester Hotel in 1985 for £88mn, and to fund the construction of the Sultan's palace, the Istana Nurul Iman in Bandar Seri Begawan. He is also said to own a fleet of 350 cars and a veritable squadron of private aircraft – including a private Airbus, Gulfstream executive jet and a helicopter. Sultan Hassanal Bolkiah also has a penchant for glitzy hotels, of which he has several around the world including the *Bel*-Air in Beverley Hills and in mid-1996 was alleged to be close to buying the *George V* in Paris. Diplomatic sources claim that Elton John, Diana Ross, Stevie Wonder and even the rap singer MC Hammer have entertained the Sultan and his family in the Istana. In 1995 Tina Turner was flown in to sing at his daughter's birthday party – well, that is what was rumoured – it was never publicly announced.

He has not always been so successful in his forays onto the world stage. In 1986, at the request of former US President Ronald Reagan, the Sultan agreed to contribute 'humanitarian aid' of US$10mn to the right-wing Nicaraguan Contra rebels. The funds were wired to a Swiss bank account set up by Colonel Oliver North. The money was accidentally deposited in the wrong account; that of a Swiss businessman, who promptly moved his windfall to another bank. Because the Sultan forgot to notify Washington that the money had been sent, its loss went unnoticed for 3 months. It was finally returned to the embarrassed Sultan in mid-1987, amid much publicity.

Sultan Hassanal Bolkiah seems genuinely bemused by the attention accorded him by gossip columnists in the West who have consistently cast him as a spendthrift, polygamous, polo-playing Oriental potentate with dubious acquaintances – among them, Adnan Khashoggi, the Al-Fayed brothers (of Harrods fame) and an Indian swami. To counter their muck-raking tendencies, he hired Shandwick plc, a British public relations firm, in 1987 to bolster Brunei's image abroad. He also commissioned Shandwick's director, Lord Alun Chalfont to write a hagiography: *By God's Will: a portrait of the Sultan of Brunei*. Chalfont writes: "He has had to put up with the routine distortions, and sometimes straight inventions, of Fleet St gossip columnists and others who trawl the fashionable shopping areas of London collecting rumours and anecdotes."

Recently the Sultan has undergone a change of image – possibly orchestrated by Shandwick. The *Far Eastern Economic Review* says he has been moving to assert himself as a religiously inclined, caring monarch. He has even abandoned polo in favour of the less-elitist games of badminton and golf. Sultan Hassanal Bolkiah celebrated 25 years on the throne in Oct 1992. He was pulled through the streets of BSB on a 23m-long chariot made of gilded teak to the strains of 'Colonel Bogey'. In the evening he hosted a banquet at his palace for 5,000 guests. In a speech to mark the occasion, he said Brunei "has proven that the system of monarchy, which we have practised all along, is strong and has been successful in bringing benefits to the people". In 1996, the Sultan celebrated his 50th birthday with as much pomp and splendour as one would expect. A TV documentary, broadcast on Star and reaching out to a potential audience of over 200 million viewers, provided a glowing portrait of the Sultan and his kingdom. Britain's Prince Charles joined in the celebrations and Michael Jackson provided the background music.

the origin of the Sultanate. However, it is thought that some time around 1370 Sultan Mohammad became first Sultan.

In the mid-1400s, Sultan Awang Alak ber Tabar, married a Melakan princess and converted to Islam. Brunei already had substantial trade links with Melaka and exported camphor, rice, gold and sago in exchange for Indian textiles. But it was not until an Arab, Sharif Ali, married Sultan Awang Alak's niece, that Islam spread beyond the confines of the royal household. Sharif Ali – who is said to have descended from the Prophet Mohammad – became Sultan Berkat, and was responsible for consolidating Islam, converting the townspeople, building mosques and setting up a legal system based on Islamic Sharia law. Trade flourished and Brunei assumed the epithet 'Darussalam' – 'the abode of peace'. The oldest tombstone in Brunei dates from 1432 – or the Islamic Hijra equivalent – indicating that by then, Islam had already made its mark.

The golden years

The very first rajahs of Brunei are likely to have been Bisayas or Muruts. Bruneians only became known as 'Malays' as they converted to Islam – there is no evidence to suggest that Malays migrated to North Borneo from Sumatra. The coastal Melanaus quickly embraced the Muslim faith, but tribal groups in the interior were largely unaffected by the spread of Islam and retained their animist beliefs. As Islam spread along the coasts of North and West Borneo, the sultanate expanded its political and commercial sphere of influence. By the 16th century, communities all along the coasts of present-day Sabah and Sarawak were paying tribute to the Sultan. The sultanate became the centre of a minor empire whose influence stretched beyond the coasts of Borneo to many surrounding islands, including the Sulu archipelago and Mindanao in the Philippines. Even Manila had to pay tribute to the Sultan's court.

The first half of the 16th century, under Sultan Bolkiah and Sultan Hassan, was Brunei's golden age. The latter was the 9th sultan; he vigorously resisted European territorial encroachments. One of the ways he did this was by formalizing Brunei's political and hierarchical administrative system – based on the tenets of Islam – which lent the Sultanate internal cohesion. Sultan Hassan's system still forms the basis of Brunei's government.

On 8 July 1521 Antonio Pigafetta, an Italian historian on Portuguese explorer Ferdinand Magellan's expedition, visited the Sultanate of Brunei and described it as a rich, hospitable and powerful kingdom with an established Islamic monarchy and strong regional influence. Pigafetta published his experiences in his book, *The First Voyage Around the World*. He records the existence of a sophisticated royal court and the lavishly decorated Sultan's palace. Brunei Town was reported to be a large, wealthy city of 25,000 households. The townspeople lived in houses built on stilts over the water. Returning today, Pigafetta would find Kampong Ayer little changed – apart from the addition of new schools and mosques, air-conditioned housings and electricity cables.

When Melaka fell to the Portuguese in 1511, Muslim merchants turned to Brunei instead, although the Sultan was careful to maintain good relations with the Portuguese. In 1526 the Portuguese set up a trading post in Brunei, and from there conducted trade with the Moluccas – the famed Spice Islands – via Brunei. At the same time, more Chinese traders immigrated to Brunei, to service the booming trade between Melaka and Macau and to trade with Pattani on the South Thai isthmus.

But relations with the Spaniards were not so warm; the King of Spain and the Sultan of Brunei had mutually exclusive interests in the Philippines. In the 1570s Spaniards attacked several important

Muslim centres and in March 1578, the captain-general of the Philippines, Francesco de Sande, led a naval expedition to Brunei, demanding the Sultan pay tribute to Spain and allow Roman Catholic missionaries to proselytize. The Sultan would have none of it and a battle ensued off Muara, which the Spaniards won. They captured the city, but within days the victors were stopped in their tracks by a cholera epidemic and had to withdraw. In 1579 they returned and once again did battle off Muara, but this time they were defeated.

The sun sets on an empire

Portugal came under Spanish rule in 1580, and Brunei lost a valuable European ally: the sultanate was raided by the Spanish again in 1588 and 1645. But by then Brunei's golden age was history and the Sultan's grip on his further-flung dependencies had begun to slip. The Sultan of Sulu had asserted his independence and Brunei was even losing its influence over its Borneo territories. It was to go downhill for a further 2 centuries.

In the 1660s, civil war erupted in Brunei due to feuding between princes and together with additional external pressures of European expansionism, the once mighty sultanate all but collapsed. Only a handful of foreign merchants dealt with the sultanate and Chinese traders passed it by. Balanini pirates from Sulu and Illanun pirates from Mindanao posed a constant threat to the Sultan and any European traders or adventurers foolhardy enough to take them on (see page 336). In return for protection from these sea-borne terrorists, the Sultan offered the British East India Company a base on the island of Labuan in Brunei Bay in the late 1600s – although the trading post failed to take off.

For 150 years, Brunei languished in obscurity. By the early 1800s, Brunei's territory did not extend much beyond the town boundaries, although the Sarawak River, and the west coastal strip of North Borneo officially remained under the Sultan's sway. Historian Mary Turnbull writes: "Brunei town was little more than a centre for pirates' loot and slaves, a shrunken shadow of its former self." Within a period of 50 years, its population had been reduced by three-quarters: by the 1830s it was just 10,000, compared to Penang's 125,000.

James Brooke – the man who would be king

The collection of mini-river states that made up what was left of the Sultanate were ruled by the *pangeran*, the lesser nobles of the Brunei court. In the 1830s Brunei chiefs had gone to the Sarawak valley to organize the mining and trade in the high-grade antimony ore which had been discovered there in 1824. They recruited Dayaks as workers and founded Kuching. But, with the support of local Malay chiefs, the Dayaks rebelled against one of the Brunei noblemen, the corrupt, Pangeran Makota, one of the Rajah's 14 brothers. By all accounts, Makota was a nasty piece of work, known for his exquisite charm and diabolical cunning.

It was into this troubled riverine mini-state, in armed rebellion against Makota, that the English adventurer James Brooke sailed in 1839 (see box, page 338). Robert Payne, in his book *The White Rajahs of Sarawak*, describes Makota as a "princely racketeer" and "a man of satanic gifts, who practised crimes for pleasure". Makota confided to Brooke: "I was brought up to plunder the Dayaks, and it makes me laugh to think that I have fleeced a tribe down to its cooking-pots." With Brooke's arrival, Makota realized his days were numbered.

In 1837, the Sultan of Brunei, Omar Ali Saiffuddin, had dispatched his uncle, Pengiran Muda Hashim, to contain the rebellion. He failed, and turned to Brooke for help. In return for his services, Brooke demanded to be made Governor of Sarawak. After vacillating for several years, Hashim abdicated, ceding Sarawak and its dependencies to "the well-born James Brooke" in September

1841. The new Rajah promptly left for Brunei Town to have the transfer of power rubber stamped by the Sultan of Brunei, Omar Ali Saifuddin II, whom he mistook as a harmless lunatic. In reality, Sultan Omar was cool and cunning. This is how Robert Payne describes him:

> "Like Prince Makota, the Sultan was one of those men who appear to belong to legend rather than to history. He was the incarnation of murderous imbecility. He was over 50, a small, thin, bald man, who could neither read nor write; he had three thumbs, having an extra thumb, like a small claw, on his right hand. He suffered from cancer of the mouth, his arms and legs were painfully thin, and he wore an expression of permanent confusion. He was dressed in purple satin and cloth-of-gold, and wore a gold-headed kriss at his waist. James was fascinated by the monster, who talked continually, often joked, and was unable to concentrate on a serious matter for more than a few seconds. Given handsome presents, he kept asking for more."

After he had been formally installed in his new role by Sultan Omar, Brooke set about building his own empire. In 1848 he said: "I am going in these revolutionary times to get up a league and covenant between all the good rivers of the coast, to the purpose that they will not pay revenue or obey the government of Brunei ..." Brooke exploited rivalries between various aristocratic factions of Brunei's royal court which climaxed in the murder of Pengiran Muda Hashim and his family.

No longer required in Sarawak, Hashim had returned to Brunei to become Chief Minister and heir apparent. He was murdered along with 11 other princes and their families, by Sultan Omar. The Sultan and his advisers had felt threatened by their presence, so they disposed of Hashim to prevent a coup. The massacre incensed Brooke. In June 1846, his British ally, Admiral Sir Thomas Cochrane bombarded Brunei Town, set it ablaze and chased the Sultan into the jungle.

Cochrane wanted to proclaim Brooke Sultan of Brunei, but decided, in the end, to offer Sultan Omar protection if he cleaned up his act and demonstrated his loyalty to Queen Victoria. After several weeks, the humiliated Sultan emerged from the jungle and swore undying loyalty to the Queen. As penance, Sultan Omar formally ceded the island of Labuan to the British crown on 18 December 1846. The brow-beaten Sultan pleaded proneness to sea sickness in an effort to avoid having to witness the hoisting of the Union Jack on Labuan Island. Although Brunei forfeited more territory in handing Labuan to the British, the Sultan calculated that he would benefit from a direct relationship with Whitehall. It seemed that London was becoming almost as concerned as he was about Brooke's expansionist instincts. A Treaty of Friendship and Commerce was signed between Britain and Brunei in 1847 in which the Sultan agreed not to cede any more territory to any power, except with the consent of the British government.

The Sultan's shrinking shadow

The treaty did not stop Brooke. His mission, since arriving in Sarawak, had been the destruction of the pirates who specialized in terrorising Borneo's coastal communities. Because he knew the Sultan of Brunei was powerless to contain them, he calculated that their liquidation would be his best bargaining chip with the Sultan, and would enable him to prise yet more territory from the Sultan's grasp. Over the years he engaged the dreaded Balanini and Illanun pirates from Sulu and Mindanao as well as the so-called Sea-Dayaks and Brunei Malays, who regularly attacked Chinese, Bugis and other Asian trading ships off the Borneo coast.

At the battle of Batang Maru in 1849, Brooke annihilated a Saribas Dayak pirate fleet, sinking 87 of their 98 boats and killing more than 1,500 pirates. As a result of this, Sultan Abdul Mumin of

Brunei ceded to him the Saribas and Skrang districts, which became the Second Division of Sarawak in 1853. 8 years later, the Sultan was in trouble with the Illanun pirates, who were wreaking havoc with the profitable sago trade west of Bintulu. Brooke successfully persuaded the Sultan to hand the region over to him and it became the Third Division of Sarawak. The Illanun raided for the last time in 1862. From 1868, James Brooke's successor, Rajah Charles Brooke, attempted to further erode the Sultan's territory, but by this stage even the British were becoming wary of the White Rajahs' expansionism. London rejected Brooke's 1874 proposal that it should make the Sultanate a protectorate.

But by now the Sultan was as worried about territorial encroachment by the British as he was about the Brookes and as a counterweight to both, granted a 10-year concession to much of what is modern-day Sabah to the American consul in Brunei, Charles Lee Moses. This 72,500 sq km tract of North Borneo later became British North Borneo and is now the East Malaysian state of Sabah, see page 424.

With the emergence of British North Borneo, the British reneged on their agreement with the Sultan of Brunei again and the following year approved Brooke's annexation of the Baram river basin by Sarawak – which became its Fourth Division. The Sarawak frontier was advancing ever-northwards.

In 1884 a rebellion broke out in Limbang and Rajah Charles Brooke refused to help the Sultan restore order. Sultan Hashim Jalilul Alam Aqamaddin, who acceded to the throne in 1885, wrote to Queen Victoria complaining that the British had not kept their word. Sir Frederick Weld was dispatched to mediate; he sympathized with the Sultan, and his visit resulted in the Protectorate Agreement of 1888 between Brunei and Britain, which gave London full control of the Sultanate's external affairs. When Brooke annexed Limbang in 1890 and united it with the Trusan valley to form the Fifth Division of Sarawak, while the Queen's men looked on, the Sultan was reduced to a state of disbelief. His sultanate had now been completely surrounded by Brooke's Sarawak. Some years later the British labelled this a cession by default and recognized Limbang as part of Sarawak.

From sultanate to oilfield

In 1906 a British Resident was appointed to the Sultan's court to advise on all aspects of government except traditional customs and religion. In his book *By God's Will*, Lord Chalfont suggests that the British government's enthusiastic recommitment to the Sultanate through the treaty may have been motivated by Machiavellian desires. "More cynical observers have suggested that the new-found enthusiasm of the British Government may not have been entirely unconnected with the discovery of oil ... around the turn of the century." Oil exploration started in 1899, although it was not until the discovery of the Seria oilfield in 1929 that it merited commercial exploitation. Historian Mary Turnbull notes the quirk of destiny that ensured the survival of the micro-sultanate: "It was ironic that the small area left unswallowed by Sarawak and North Borneo should prove to be the most richly endowed part of the old sultanate."

The Brunei oilfield fell to the Japanese on 18 December 1942. Allied bombing and Japanese sabotage prior to the sultanate's liberation caused considerable damage to oil and port installations and urban areas, necessitating a long period of reconstruction in the late 1940s and early 1950s. Australian forces landed at Muara Beach on 10 July 1945. A British Military Administration ruled the country for a year, before Sultan Sir Ahmad Tajuddin took over.

In 1948 the Governor of Sarawak, which was by then a British crown colony, was appointed High Commissioner for Brunei, but although never a colony itself, the Sultanate remained what one commentator describes as "a constitutional anachronism". In September 1959 the United Kingdom resolved this by withdrawing the Resident and signing an agreement with the Sultan giving Whitehall responsibility for Brunei's defence and foreign affairs.

Because of his post-war influence on the development of Brunei, Sultan Omar was variously referred to as the 'father' and 'architect' of modern Brunei. He shaped his sultanate into the anti-Communist, non-democratic state it is today and, being an Anglophile, held out against independence from Britain. By the early 1960s, Whitehall was enthusiastically promoting the idea of a North Borneo Federation, encompassing Sarawak, Brunei and British North Borneo. But Sultan Omar did not want anything to do with the neighbouring territories – he felt Brunei's interests were more in keeping with those of peninsular Malaysia. The proposed federation would have been heavily dependent on Brunei's oil wealth. Kuala Lumpur did not need much persuasion that Brunei's joining the Federation of Malaysia was an excellent idea – probably because Brunei's Malays presented a convenient ethnic counterweight to Singapore's Chinese.

Democrats versus autocrat

In Brunei's first-ever general election in 1962, the left-wing Brunei People's Party (known by its Malay acronym, PRB) swept the polls. The party's election ticket had been an end to the Sultan's autocratic rule, the formation of a democratic government and immediate independence. Aware that there was quite a lot at stake, the Sultan refused to let the PRB form a government. The Sultan's emergency powers, under which he banned the PRB, which were passed in 1962, remain in force, enabling him to rule by decree.

On 8 December 1962, the PRB, backed by the Communist North Kalimantan National Army – effectively its military wing – launched a revolt. The Sultan's insistence on British military protection paid off as the disorganized rebellion was quickly put down with the help of a Gurkha infantry brigade, and other British troops. Within 4 days the British troops had pushed the rebels into Limbang, where the hard core holed up. By 12 December, the revolt had been crushed and the vast majority of the rebels disappeared into the interior, pursued by the 7th Gurkha Rifles and Kelabit tribesmen.

Early in 1963, negotiations over Brunei joining the Malaysian Federation ran into trouble, to the disappointment of the British. The Malaysian Prime Minister, the late Tunku Abdul Rahman, wanted the Sultanate's oil and gas revenues to feed the federal treasury in Kuala Lumpur and made the mistake of making his intentions too obvious. The Tunku envisaged central government exercising absolute control over oil revenues – in the way it controls the oil wealth of Sabah and Sarawak today. Unhappy with this proposal and unwilling to become 'just another Malaysian sultan', Omar abandoned his intention to join the Federation.

Meanwhile, Indonesia's Sukarno was resolute in his objective of crushing the new Federation of Malaysia and launched his *Konfrontasi* between 1963 and 1966. Brunei offered itself as an operational base for the British army. But while Brunei supported Malaysia against Indonesia, relations between them became very strained following the declaration of the Federation in September 1963. 10 years later, Malaysian intelligence services allegedly supported the breakout, by eight political detainees from the 1962 revolt, from Berakas internment camp. They were given asylum in Malaysia, and were allowed to broadcast anti-Brunei propaganda from Limbang. Libya's Colonel Gadaffi reportedly offered military training to PRB members.

In 1975 Kuala Lumpur sponsored the visit of a PRB delegation to the UN, to propose a resolution calling on Brunei to hold elections, abolish restrictions on political parties and allow political exiles to return. In 1976 Bruneian government supporters protested against Malaysian 'interference' in Bruneian affairs. Nonetheless, the resolution was adopted by the UN in November 1977, receiving 117 votes in favour and none against. The United Kingdom abstained. Relations with Malaysia warmed after the death of Prime Minister Tun Abdul Razak in 1976, leaving the PRB weak and isolated. The party still operates in exile, although it is a spent force. Throughout the difficult years, the Sultan had used his favourite sport to conduct what was dubbed 'polo diplomacy', fostering links with like-minded Malaysian royalty despite the tensions in official bilateral relations.

By 1967, Britain's Labour government was pushing Sultan Omar to introduce a democratic system of government. Instead, however, the Sultan opted to abdicate in favour of his 21-year-old son, Hassanal Bolkiah. In November 1971, a new treaty was signed with Britain. London retained its responsibility for Brunei's external affairs, but its advisory role applied only to defence. The Sultan was given full control of all internal matters. Under a separate agreement, a battalion of British Gurkhas was stationed in the Sultanate. As Bruneians grew richer, the likelihood of another revolt receded.

Independence

Britain was keen to disentangle itself from the 1971 agreement: maintaining the protectorate relationship was expensive and left London open to criticism that it was maintaining an anachronistic colonial relationship. Brunei did not particularly relish the prospect of independence as without British protection, it would be at the mercy of its more powerful neighbours. But in January 1979, having secured Malaysian and Indonesian assurances that they would respect its independence, the government signed another agreement with London, allowing for the Sultanate to become independent from midnight on 31 December 1983 after a century-and-a-half of close involvement with Britain and 96 years as a protectorate.

At a Commonwealth Heads of Government Meeting in 1985 Hassanal Bolkiah explained the sultanate's position:

> "There can be few instances in the history of a relationship between a protecting power and a protected state where the protector applied pressure on the protected to accept early independence, and this pressure was vigorously resisted by the latter. That was precisely what happened between Britain and Brunei."

The role of the 900-odd remaining Gurkhas is primarily to guard the oil and gas fields in the Seria district – for which Brunei pays £3mn a year.

Population

In the days of Charles Brooke, the sultanate had a population of about 20,000. A hundred years on, it stood at 283,500 (1994). The city-state of Singapore has 10 times as many people. Today 60% of the country's population lives in towns; more than half is aged under 20, a third under 14. With the population growing at 2.5% a year, Brunei has one of the fastest-growing populations in the region; it also has the region's lowest death rate and second lowest infant mortality rate after Singapore. Bruneians' average life expectancy, at 71, is also second only to Singaporeans'. About 40% of the population is Malay, 30% Chinese and 29% indigenous tribal groups (see **Culture and life**, below); there are also approaching 100,000 expatriate workers – both professionals and labourers. The average density of population is low: about 34 people per sq km; most are concentrated along the narrow coastal belt.

CULTURE

PEOPLE

Brunei 'Malays', who make up 68% of the sultanate's population, are indigenous to North Borneo – most are Kedayans or Melanaus. There was no great migration of Malays from the peninsula. Similarly, few Iban migrated into what is modern Brunei, although in the 19th century, they pushed up to the middle-reaches of Sarawak's rivers, which in those days came under the sultanate's ambit. Ibans, Muruts, Kedayans, Dayaks and even Dusuns are, however, all represented in the 29% of the population labelled 'indigenous tribal groups' (for more detail on individual tribal groups, see page 329).

Today most Bruneian Malays are well off and well-educated; more than half of them have secure government jobs. The increase in car-ownership in Brunei is a telling indicator of Bruneians' growing affluence: the number of cars trebled in the decade to 1981, and now Brunei has one of the highest car population ratios in the world. Recognizing that things might get out of hand, in 1995 the authorities introduced a new car tax to try and curb Brunei's love affair with the automobile. The standard of living is high by Southeast Asian standards although there are poorer communities living in Kampong Ayer and Kampong Kianggeh (near the open market). Many of these are recent immigrants – there is a high level of illegal immigration from the neighbouring states of Sabah and Sarawak as well as from Kalimantan.

The government policy of 'Bruneization' discriminates positively in favour of the Malays and against the Chinese, who make up 30% of the population. Most of the Chinese are fairly wealthy as they account for the vast majority of Brunei's private sector businessmen.

Unlike the Malays, the Chinese did not automatically become citizens of Brunei at independence – even if they could trace their ancestry back several generations. The question of citizenship is very important as only citizens of Brunei can enjoy the benefits of the welfare state – free education, health care, subsidized housing and government jobs.

Only about 6,000 Chinese presently have citizenship; the rest hold British 'protected person' passports – which, like the situation in Hong Kong, does not give them the right to live in the UK. At independence the Sultan decreed that it would only be possible for a Chinese to qualify for citizenship if he or she had lived in Brunei continuously for 25 years in the 30 years prior to the application. Candidates for citizenship are tested in their ability to speak Malay and in their cultural understanding of the country.

Brunei Shell Petroleum was forced to freeze the promotion of Chinese employees to allow Malays access to top jobs. Foreign businesses have trouble filling vacancies because of this so-called 'Bruneization' policy – there are simply not enough skilled Bruneian Malays. A leading international business intelligence publication reports that this policy is "sapping morale, with an adverse impact on output and efficiency." It adds that the policy "is a source of considerable resentment among non-Malays." The Chinese would think that an understatement: their emigration rate of about 3,000 a year suggests that they have begun to vote with their feet.

RELIGION

Brunei is a Sunni Muslim monarchy; the state motto is 'Always render service by God's guidance' which is emblazoned on the crescent on Brunei's national flag. Islam appears to have been firmly established in the Sultanate by the mid 15th century. Today it is the official religion, and a religious council advises the Sultan, who is head of the Islamic faith in Brunei, on all Islamic matters. The minister of Religious Affairs, Yang Berhormat Pehin

Orang Kaya Ratna Deraja Dato Seri Utama Dr Ustaz Haji Awang Mohammad Zain bin Haji Serudin, holds a cabinet post. His ministry is in charge of maintaining Brunei's growing number of mosques, paying religious teachers and subsidizing pilgrimages to Mecca.

CRAFTS

Brassware

Brass casting is said to have been introduced into Brunei Darussalam at the end of the 15th century, when the Sultanate became particularly famous for its brass cannon. Italian historian Antonio Pigafetta – who visited Brunei in 1521 – describes "a fortress with 56 brass cannons and six of iron in front of the king's house". The cannon were also used to decorate boats and were prominently displayed in longhouses: brassware is a traditional symbol of wealth and power in Brunei. Cannon were used in battle and to convey messages from one village to another about deaths, births and festivities – such as the beginning and end of Ramadan. The collection of 500 cannon and guns (not all on display) in the Brunei Museum is largely of local manufacture. Brass cannon and gongs were items of currency and barter and often used in dowries, particularly among the tribal Belaits and Dusuns. Brassware is a prized family heirloom, and was the basis of fines in the traditional legal system.

In 1908 there were more than 200 brass workers in Brunei, but by the mid-1970s their numbers had reportedly fallen to fewer than 10. Today, traditional casting by the 'lost wax' technique is being revived.

Silver and goldware

Silversmiths have a good reputation for their intricate designs, betelnut boxes being a speciality. Brunei is a reasonable place to buy gold jewellery, mostly 22 and 24 carat.

Textiles

The best known local fabric is *Kain Jong Sarat*, a cotton sarong, usually about 2m in length, woven with more than 1,000 gold threads on a handloom. Another textile is the *Sukma-Indera* which is distinguished by its multi-coloured floral patterns. Jong Sarat are said to have been brought to Brunei from Java by the consort of Sultan Bolkiah, Princess Laila Menchanai, who occupied herself on the voyage by weaving them; Jong Sarat means 'fully laden junk'. Today they are only used on ceremonial occasions. The *tenunan*, a special cloth woven with gold thread and worn by men round the waist on Hari Raya Aidil Adha can cost up to B$1,000.

MODERN BRUNEI

POLITICS

On independence in January 1984, Sultan Hassanal Bolkiah declared Brunei a 'democratic' monarchy. 3 years later, he told his official biographer Lord Chalfont: "I do not believe that the time is ripe for elections and the revival of the legislature. What I would wish to see first is real evidence of an interest in politics by a responsible majority of the people ... When I see some genuine interest among the citizenry, we may move towards elections." But his well-heeled subjects are not particularly interested in politics or elections.

Independence has changed nothing: absolute power is still vested in the Sultan, who mostly relies on his close family for advice. One of his brothers holds the most sensitive cabinet portfolio: Prince Mohammed is foreign affairs minister. Another brother, Prince Jefri used to head the critical finance ministry but resigned, surprisingly, in February 1997. Following independence, the Sultan took up the offices of Prime Minister, Minister of Finance and Minister of Home Affairs. In 1986, he relinquished the latter two, but appointed himself Minister of Defence. He also took over responsibility for Finance on the resignation of his brother, Prince Jefri.

In May 1985 the Brunei National Democratic Party (BNDP) was officially registered. Its aim was to introduce a parliamentary democracy under the Sultan.

The Flag of Brunei Darussalam

Brunei's rather avant garde flag is riddled with symbolizm and was adopted in 1906 when Brunei accepted the first British Resident. The colours – yellow, black and white – symbolize the colours of the three principal Bruneian signatories to the agreement with Britain: the Sultan (yellow), and two senior state officials, the Pengiran Bendahara (white) and the Pengiran Pemancha (black). The odd-looking and rather cumbersome red concoction in the middle consists of a flag (*bendera*), the royal umbrella (*payung ubor-ubor*), two wings (*sayap*), a pair of hands (*tangan*), and the crescent (*bulan*). The flag and umbrella are symbolic of royalty; the wings symbolize justice, prosperity and peace; the hands symbolize the government's intent to bring welfare, peace and prosperity (again) to the people of Brunei; and the crescent symbolizes the state religion, Islam. On the crescent is inscribed, in Arabic script, 'Always render service by God's guidance', while the scroll beneath reads 'Brunei Darussalam [Abode of Peace]'.

But just before the Malays-only party came into being, the government announced that government employees would not be allowed to join it – or any other political party. In one stroke, the BNDP's potential membership was halved. In early 1986, the Brunei United National Party – an offshoot of the BNDP – was formed. Unlike its parent, its manifesto was multi-racial. The Sultan allowed these parties to exist until 27 January 1988 when he proscribed all political parties and imprisoned, without trial, two of the BNDP's leaders.

In the early 1990s, the Sultan was reported to have become increasingly worried about internal security and about Brunei's image abroad – the information and views contained in this anodyne introduction are even viewed as beyond the pale in many quarters. In 1992 he brought the security division of the Brunei police force under his direct control. The *Far Eastern Economic Review* also quoted sources as saying that the Brunei army is kept under the discreet surveillance of the Gurkha battalion personally employed by the Sultan. Eight long-term political detainees, in prison since the abortive 1962 coup, were released in 1990. The last political detainee, the former deputy leader of the Brunei People's Party (PRB), Zaini Ahmad, is said to have written to the Sultan from prison following the releases. He apparently apologized for the 1962 revolt and called for the democratically elected Legislative Council – as outlined in the 1959 constitution – to be reconvened. To coincide with the Sultan's 50th birthday in 1996, Zaini Ahmad was released from prison. The exiled PRB has been greatly weakened and increasingly isolated since Brunei's relations with Malaysia became more cordial following the sultanate's accession to the Association of Southeast Asian Nations (ASEAN) in 1984 and clearly the Sultan and his adviser no longer feel threatened by the party.

Foreign relations

Brunei joined ASEAN on independence in 1984. Prince Mohammed, the foreign affairs minister, is said to be one of the brightest, more thoughtful members of the royal family, but in foreign policy,

Brunei is 'timid' and goes quietly along with its ASEAN partners. Relations with Malaysia are greatly improved, but the sultanate's closest ties in the region, especially in fiscal and economic matters, are with Singapore. Their relationship was initially founded on their mutual distrust of the Malaysian Federation, which Brunei never joined and Singapore left 2 years after its inception in 1965. Singapore provides assistance in the training of Brunei's public servants and their currencies are linked.

As a member of ASEAN, on good terms with its neighbours, Brunei does not have many enemies to fear. But if its Scorpion tanks, Exocet rockets, Rapier ground-to-air missiles and helicopter gunships seem a little redundant, it is worth considering the recent experience of another oil-rich Islamic mini-state. As *The Economist* wrote, in October 1992, "substitute jungle for desert and Brunei is uncannily like Kuwait."

Economy

Whenever a world oil glut depresses petroleum prices, Brunei suffers – relatively speaking. Brunei is wealthy enough not to have to worry too much about fluctuating oil prices. Because Bruneians' incomes are directly dependent on oil, per capita incomes also tend to fluctuate. In 1980 Brunei's oil exports earned it US$6bn; by 1988 they were worth US$1.6bn. Even so, the average personal income level in 1990 was slightly less than Japan's, more than Australia's, and double Singapore's.

Economic growth stagnated in the 1980s – for several years Brunei registered a negative growth rate. While the economy will continue to be dominated by the oil and natural gas industries for the foreseeable future, other sectors, such as services, have assumed greater importance in recent years – partly because the government has tried to diversify the economy. In 1979, hydrocarbons accounted for 83% of the GDP; in 1993 for 60% of the sultanate's GDP, while government spending contributed another 24%.

Thanks to its unrivalled liquidity, Brunei is a huge international investor. Economists reckon that should the oil and gas run dry tomorrow, Brunei would have no trouble financing all its needs from the Brunei Investment Agency's foreign investment yields. Brunei's foreign reserves stood at US$36.5 bn in 1993 – well over five times those of Indonesia and more than the entire GDP of neighbouring Malaysia. When Nick Leeson brought the blue-blooded British merchant bank Barings to the brink of bankruptcy in 1995, the Bank of England turned to Brunei to bail the institution out. Brunei's terms, though, proved too tough and Barings toppled.

At the end of 1995, Prince Jefri Bolkiah purchased the troubled but equally blue-blooded royal jewellers Asprey's. Even if the Sultan could not rescue Barings, his brother found the readies to to put Asprey's on an even keel – and to return to the nation three coronation crowns and a coronation Bible. The crowns of George I (1714), George IV (1821) and Queen Adelaide (1831) would have fetched an estimated £1.5 million at auction.

The most recent financial ambulance foray was the Sultan's purchase – through the Brunei Investment Agency – of large amounts of Singapore dollars and Malaysian ringgit in August 1997. Following the collapse of the Thai economy and the devaluation of the Thai baht (and Philippine peso) foreign currency speculators turned their attention to Malaysia, Singapore and Indonesia. The Sultan not only contributed to the US$16.7 billion IMF rescue package for Thailand but also clearly ordered the Brunei Investment Agency to shore-up the collapsing currencies.

As oil-rich Brunei's per capita income exceeds Britain's or Italy's, it does not have to resort to **tourism** promotion to generate foreign exchange. Visiting Brunei can be quite expensive and because the country is not geared to tourism, it has successfully kept itself off the

Southeast Asian tourist map. In 1990, for example, just 8,000 tourists visited the Sultanante. That said, the government has shown some interest in developing ecotourism, for, unlike the neighbouring Malaysian states of Sabah and Sarawak, Brunei has never had to resort to commercial logging either. Its ancient rainforest remains unscathed by the 20th century – except for the odd wandering band of heavily armed and camouflaged soldiers. (The elite 22nd Special Air Service (SAS) regiment is one of the British army units which conducts its jungle warfare training exercises in Brunei. The Singapore defence force also has a jungle training school in the Sultanate.) The growing importance of tourism, though admittedly from a very low base, is reflected in the number of hotel rooms in the capital, BSB: in 1980 there were just 230; in 1994, some 650. With the opening of a large new hotel in Jerudong in 1996/97 (to be managed by the Hyatt group) this number will increase by another 50% or so. On paper it may seem as though this expansion in facilities is being followed by an increase in visitors – one recent study put the number of visitors at nearly 30,000 (still just 0.5% of the number visiting Malaysia). However, it is more likely that this increase is related to two other factors. First, the change in the embarkation card; and second the cheap fares that Royal Brunei Airlines was offering to Hong Kong at the time, enticing Malaysians from Sabah and Sarawak to travel to Brunei.

Nonetheless, **ecotourism** is, for Brunei, seen as the answer to its fears of tourism. It is perceived (why, is not quite clear) that ecotourists will be more sensitive to Brunei's moral and religious codes and will be more respectful of Islam. The new Ulu Temburong National Park (see page 559) is being readied for an influx of ecotourists, and there are also other chalets, forest walkways and observation platforms. The fact that Brunei has little to offer the tourist except forests is also a firm reason to move in this direction.

Diversification drive

Aware of Brunei's over-dependence on oil and gas revenues, the Sultan has put increasing emphasis on economic diversification. But despite the continued stated aim of the government to build up a more diversified economy, commentators have been sceptical, saying the policy has more to do with national pride than economic sense. One visiting foreign journalist was told: "It makes more sense to keep handing out cheques than setting up factories." Petroleum revenues still comprise 95% of Brunei's export earnings. The government has, however, identified pioneer industries which it wants to develop for the day the oil runs out. These include pharmaceuticals, cement, aluminium, steel, chemicals, ceramics and other hi-tech industries. In 1995 Brunei applied for membership of the World Bank and the International Monetary Fund, and joined in 1996. (At the time of its application, Brunei and North Korea were the only two Asian countries not to be members of the WB and IMF.) The motivation for this step was not because Brunei wishes, or needs to borrow money; but because the Sultanate wants advice on how to promote diversification. The upshot, though, will be that Brunei's national accounts will be opened up to public scrutiny.

5% of Brunei's land area is cultivated and agriculture accounts for about 1% of GDP. Most Bruneians consider themselves above working the land. Four-fifths of Brunei's rice requirements are imported. The government is trying to encourage local agricultural production but rice grown at the government rice project outside Bandar Seri Begawan costs three times as much to produce as rice imported from Thailand.

Rubber was introduced to Brunei in 1908. By the 1950s it was Brunei's chief export, but with the discovery of oil and natural gas, rubber planting declined rapidly. In 1980 the area under rubber was just 4,600 hectares. Pepper was introduced in the 19th century–although, today there are only 30 hectares under pepper cultivation – mainly by Chinese commercial farmers. The pepper is grown on terraced hillsides and the vines yield for about 15 years. The red berries are soaked in water to remove their pericarps (skins) and then dried in sun for 3 days to make white pepper. For black pepper, the berries are dried with their skins, not soaked.

Most of Brunei's meat comes from its huge state-owned farm in Australia which the sultanate bought in 1981. Even some fruit and vegetables come from Australia, instead of neighbouring Sabah and Sarawak. A cargo plane arrives from Australia every Thursday with food requirements for the next week.

Brunei's hydrocarbonated economy

Brunei's oil reserves were estimated in 1990 to be 1.4 billion barrels–enough to last until 2018 at the current rate of extraction. The sultanate also has 322 billion m^3 of natural gas, which at present extraction rates, should keep the economy ticking over until 2027. Given the probability of there being new finds, and the government's conservation policy, production should continue well into the 21st century. Brunei Shell Petroleum is now producing about 150,000 barrels per day (b/d), down from 243,000 b/d in the late 1970s.

In 1899 Brunei's first oil well was drilled at Ayer Bekunchi, near Brunei Town, at the site of a natural oil seepage. The bore went down 260m but amazingly failed to strike oil. By 1923 Shell had drilled eight exploratory holes around Tutong and several other companies – including the British Borneo Petroleum Syndicate and others from Singapore and the Netherlands – had drilled wells. All were dry. Only Shell persevered, and with the aid of modern survey methods drilled a further 17 exploration wells before hitting the Seria field in 1929.

By the time the Japanese invaded in 1941, the Seria field was already producing 17,000 b/d. During their World War Two occupation, the Japanese did everything they could to repair war-damaged oil installations and step up production at Seria. They managed to get 11.5 million barrels out before the Australian 9th Division liberated Seria on 21 June 1945. Threatened by the Allied advance however, the Japanese did exactly what Saddam Hussein did in Kuwait nearly half a century later: they torched 38 well-heads and dug defensive pits which they flooded with blazing oil. The fires took several months to extinguish.

It was not until the 1970s that Brunei hit the jackpot; oil prices rose ninefold through the '70s, and the price increases coincided with a series of new finds. By 1980, Brunei's oil and gas revenues were 35 times higher than they had been in 1970. Today, the government, which has a 50% stake in Brunei Shell Petroleum, taxes oil and gas revenue at 55%.

In 1973, the year oil prices increased fourfold, the liquified natural gas (LNG) plant at Lumut came on-stream. It is the gas that has given Brunei the licence to print money. Brunei is now the world's second largest exporter of LNG. It produces 3 million tonnes of liquified gas a year, which is sold exclusively to Japan. The gas is taken by a tanker fleet directly to Tokyo: one of the partners in the Lumut plant is the Mitsubishi Corporation. About a third of Brunei's oil exports also go directly to Japan. The Sultanate uses only about 3% of its oil for domestic purposes.

After more than 50 years, Seria's 'nodding donkeys' are still pumping oil, although 80% of it now comes from the five offshore fields which began production in 1963. The oil is piped to Seria's terminal via the 84 km-long Champion underwater pipeline.

Brunei: fact file

Geographic

Land area	5,769 sq km
Arable land as % of total	0.6
Average annual rate of deforestation	na
Highest mountain Bukit Pagon	1,850m
Average rainfall in BSB	2,921 mm
Average temperature in BSB	27.5°C

Economic

GNP/person (1989)	US$15,390
GDP/person (PPP*, 1992)	US$20,589
GNP growth (/capita, 1980-1991)	na
% labour force in agriculture	na
Total debt (% GNP)	na
Debt service ratio (% exports)	na
Military expenditure (% GNP)	6%

Social

Population	0.3 million
Population growth rate (1960-92)	3.8
Adult literacy rate	88%
Mean years of schooling	5.0 years
Tertiary graduate as % of age group	na
Population in absolute poverty	na
Rural population as % of total	42
Growth of urban population (1960-92)	0.9
Urban population in largest city	na
Televisions per 1,000 people	241

Health

Life expectancy at birth	75 years
Population with access to clean water	na
Calorie intake as % of requirements	na
Malnourished children under 5 years old	na
Contraceptive prevalence rate†	na

* PPP = Purchasing Power Parity (based on what it costs to buy a similar basket of goods and services in different countries).

† % of women of childbearing age using contraception.

Source: World Bank (1997) *World development report 1997*, OUP: New York; and other sources.

Employment

Out of a total population of 270,000, nearly 100,000 are estimated to be foreigners or, as they are politely termed, 'guest workers'. Like so much in Brunei – except relating to the oil and gas industry – management expertise and manual labour has to be imported. Apart from contracted migrant workers, there are many illegal immigrant labourers: mainly from Indonesia and the Philippines. More than a third of the local workforce is employed by the government, and Brunei Shell Petroleum employs about another 8,000. The private sector is dominated by the Chinese. But because government jobs offered such attractive salaries and fringe benefits, private sector firms were having trouble tempting Malays into jobs. In 1989 the government became worried about rising unemployment – because people were becoming too choosy – and listed a range of jobs in which only Bruneians could be employed. The government hopes to create 40,000 private sector jobs for Bruneian Malays.

University Brunei Darussalam, better known simply as UBD, opened in 1988, and about 500 students enrolled in 1990. One of the ideas behind the university was to discourage students from attending universities abroad – the government is wary of 'less-desirable western habits' – one of the few commodities it does not want to import. In the past, students have been detained for several months on their return from studying overseas. The Sultan has vigorously promoted the concept of Melayu Islam Beraja (MIB – Malay tradition, Islam and the monarch) as a national ideology in an effort to stem social problems such as alcoholism and drug abuse – which have been attributed to these foreign influences and sparked off by rising unemployment. All students at the university are required to attend courses in MIB, which is styled to give the sultanate a sense of national identity.

Bandar Seri Begawan

BANDAR SERI BEGAWAN, informally dubbed BSB or just Bandar – 'town' in Malay, but of Sanskrit origin, meaning 'port' – is the capital of Brunei Darussalam and is sited on a natural inlet of Brunei Bay. It is a fraction of the size of neighbouring Asian capitals and had a population at the last census in 1993 of just 56,300. It used to be called Brunei Town, but was renamed in 1970 in honour of the present Sultan's father, Sir Omar Ali Saifuddien III, who modernized the town and is regarded as the architect of modern Brunei. Following his abdication in 1967, Sir Omar took the title Seri Begawan, which, roughly translated, means 'blessed teacher'. Built on the wide Brunei River, BSB used to be the sultanate's main port – the oldest parts of town run along the waterfront – but the port declined as ships got bigger and navigating the narrow channels became more hazardous.

BSB is a modern city, rapidly changing and expanding. Unlike other Southeast Asian cities, there is a noticeable absence of motorbikes, dogs, roadside stalls, brothels, bars, beggars and nightclubs. But in common with many of them, BSB still has a sprawling maze of wooden houses, built on stilts over the river. Healthy bank balances, and the trimmings of capitalism have not tempted Kampong Ayer's 30,000 residents to abandon their traditional lifestyles.

Kampong Ayer is one of the more interesting elements in this otherwise rather unexciting, modern city: most of its buildings are low-slung and modern and government buildings stand out. BSB is split into three main areas: the 'old' 1950s-built central area with a row or two of shophouses, which is now complete with an opulent shopping mall, the Yayasan, near the elegant Omar Ali Saifuddien Mosque; the Seri Complex – a commercial area on the way out to the Sultan's palace, which dates from the 1970s; and Gadong with its newly built shopping centre, 'Centrepoint', and numerous restaurants. The latter stands on the site of an old rubber plantation from the days when the economy ran on latex rather than oil.

PLACES OF INTEREST

Although the city is relatively spread out, the list of sights is short: it is easy to walk round them in a day.

The golden dome of **Omar Ali Saifuddien Mosque** on Jalan Pretty features on most postcards of Brunei. Named after the current Sultan's father, a devout Muslim, it was designed by British architects and built in 1958 in classical Islamic style and cost US$5mn to complete. The mosque is impressive enough from the outside but rather unimaginative within. Its 44m minaret has a lift and the top affords a good view of the city. The floors are made of Italian marble, the stained glass windows and chandeliers were made in England, the carpets in Iran and Belgium and the granite imported from Hong Kong. Linked to the mosque and built in the middle of a lake is a concrete reconstruction of a 16th century royal barge. Open 0800-1200, 1300-1500, 1630-1730 Saturday-Wednesday, 1630-1730 Friday. Closed to non-Muslims on Thursday. Opening times apply to non-Muslims only. Dress in appropriate (modest) clothes and remove shoes on entering.

The mosque overlooks the 500-year-old **Kampong Ayer**, once the centre of a trading empire and still the world's biggest stilt village. In 1521, Italian historian, Antonio Pigafetta, who was travelling with Ferdinand Magellan's expedition, described "a city that is entirely built in salt water". He estimated that there were 25,000 dwellings, implying a population of well over 100,000. Most historians believe his estimate to be an exaggeration. James Brooke, the Rajah of Sarawak, described Brunei's aquapolis as "a very Venice of hovels, fit only for frogs". Visitors to modern Brunei might consider that rather harsh – it is the sultanate's most picturesque tourist attraction. The government, however, is said to be aware of its health hazards and has been trying to lower its profile as a tourist destination. However, in 1987 it was declared a national monument and rates as the most interesting 'sight' in BSB.

Francesco de Sande, Spain's Captain-General in the Philippines in the 1770s, appears to have been the source of the 'Oriental Venice' cliché. Following his naval expedition to Brunei in 1578, he wrote to King Philip II of Spain that "the city was very large and rich and was built over a very broad and deep river that had the appearance of another Venice. The buildings were of wood, but the houses were excellently constructed

'A street in Bruni', *Illustrated London News,* 13 October 1988

of stonework and gilded, especially the king's palaces, which were of huge size. That city contained a very sumptuous mosque, a very large and interesting building, quite covered with half relief and gilded." It seems that little has changed.

Even though many families have been resettled on the mainland in recent years, the 40 separate Kampongs on the north

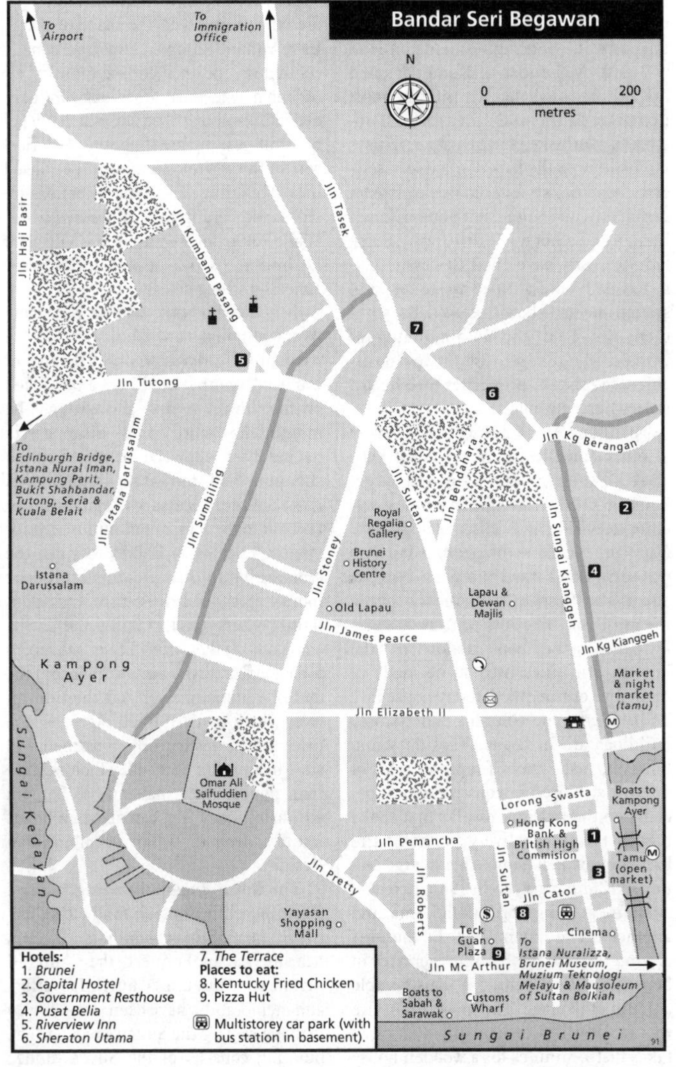

and south banks of the river, which make up Kampong Ayer, probably house about 30,000 people – mostly Malays; each Kampong has its own chief (*tua kampong*) and council. The government has attempted to encourage the residents to move onto dry land, but they have been unsuccessful. Settling residents on land will destroy the idea of Kampongs and the culture associated with it. The most upmarket district is the area furthest upstream, overlooked by the palace. This is mainly due to the lack of a modern sewerage disposal system: houses upstream do not have to contend with quantities of human and other waste drifting by. Some families now have their sewerage collected daily and a piped waste disposal system may soon be introduced. But until then, the Thai and Filipino migrant workers who rent some of the less desirable downstream properties face health risks when bathing.

Kampong Ayer's houses are not short of other amenities however: most have electricity, air-conditioning and street lighting. Others have fax machines, satellite television and cellular telephones. Many are owned by prosperous families whose cars are parked bumper to bumper along Jalan Residency (on the way out to the museum). The 20th century has also influenced the construction of the houses. Stilt piles used to be made of mangrove or iron wood: today houses are built on concrete columns and 2-storey buildings are in vogue. This does not, however, make them fireproof: a lot of wood is still used in construction, especially on the rickety catwalks that snake around the village. Every so often a fire breaks out which demolishes a large section of Kampong Ayer. In 1981 there was a big fire at Kampong Sultan Lama, and another broke out in 1990 in the area around the mosque. Two further fires in September 1993 caused a considerable amount of damage. The most recent fire was in 1995. According to statistics, it takes just 7 minutes for a wooden house to burn to the ground – or in this instance, to the water. It is consequently feared that before long there will be little left of the historical Kampong Ayer.

Some traditional cottage industries such as weaving, silverware and brassware, are still practised in the maze of alleys. Each of the 40 Kampongs was traditionally centred on one such cottage industry, although now they are either long gone or in decline. Kampong Saba Darat, a district of five villages representing the historical core of the whole community, specialized in boat building – and some water taxis are still made here from local *meranti* wood. While Kampong Pandai Besi – Village of the Ironsmiths – was, as its name suggests, a metal-working village.

It is safe to walk around Kampong Ayer – although care should be taken on some of the older catwalks. The area of water village that could once be visited on foot linked to dry land, around the mosque, has more or less disappeared, having been replaced by the Yayasan shopping mall. To visit the water village, it is therefore necessary to catch a water taxi out to the larger community in midstream. Locals pay B$0.50 to make the crossing but tourists are usually charged more – agree the price before setting out if this bothers you (B$1.00 is usual). Boats can also be taken from any of the jetties for a 'tour' up to the Sultan's palace at the end of Kampong Ayer and then downriver which costs B$10-20. Agree on the price before setting off – boatmen will start by quoting B$30-40, which is more than double the usual rate, so bargain enthusiastically. You can also hail boats, like taxis, from the waterfront along Jalan Residency.

The **Royal Regalia Building**, with its gleaming white dome, is sandwiched between Jalan Stoney and Jalan Sultan, near the Lapau. Formerly the Churchill Memorial Museum, Churchill's effigy and memorabilia have been stowed away to make way for the Sultan's regalia. The building consists of the Silver Jubilee

Gallery, the Royal Exhibition Hall and the Constitutional History Gallery. The Royal Exhibition Hall features the massive litter that was used to carry the Sultan through the streets of BSB in 1968 to celebrate his coronation – and all the paraphernalia that went along with it – including the golden hand used to support the Sultan's chin while he was being crowned. The Silver Jubilee Gallery has a similar litter that was used during the jubilee and an opulent maquette of the Royal Audience Hall. The Constitutional History Gallery has documents and video recordings of strategic moments in Brunei's recent history, leading up to its independence. The entrance is on Jalan Sultan, through glass automatic doors to the right of the dome. Leave shoes outside and deposit bags and cameras at desk inside on right. Open 0830-1700 Monday, Thursday, Saturday, Sunday 0900-1130, 1430-1700 Friday.

Next door, is the **Brunei History Centre**. This was opened in 1984 to mark Brunei's full independence. It was founded to undertake research into the history of Brunei. Exhibitions are held here, usually to coincide with national celebrations. The exhibition space is small and labels are generally in Malay. Of greater interest is the collection of memorial stones in the old Lapau next door. This low white building, built by the British in the 1950s, served as the Lapau (or ceremonial hall), before the much grander version on the opposite side of the road was built. Most of the memorial stones housed inside (all of which are replicas) are from Brunei Sultans' tombs. The frequent appearance of the lotus motif at the top of a tombstone is to indicate royal birth. The showpiece is the replica of the Bolkiah Mausoleum. Also of interest is the 'geneological stone' in the entrance, which is inscribed in Arabic script, dating from 1807, and describes the origins of the Sultanate. Open 0900-1200, 1330-1630 Monday, Tuesday, Wednesday, Thursday, Saturday.

The nearby **Lapau and Dewan Majlis** on Jalan Sungai Kianggeh stand side by side. The **Lapau** (Royal Ceremonial Hall) with its distinctive golden roof and **Dewan Majlis** (Parliament House) are a blend of Malay and western architectural styles. The Lapau contains Brunei's throne (the Patarana). Neither building is open to the public.

The **Chinese temple** is situated on the corner of Jalan Sungai Kianggeh and Jalan Elizabeth II, opposite the market (tamu). On religious occasions, Chinese operas and dragon dances are sometimes staged at the temple. The temple is open to visitors. The **market** (or *tamu*) opens from early morning along the Kianggeh River. But it is best visited in the evening when it becomes a night food market selling cheap and tasty local dishes.

The **Arts and Handicraft Training Centre**, a tall modern building on the banks of the Brunei River along Jalan Residency, is about 1 km out of BSB (an easy walk along the river or take a water taxi). It was established to preserve Brunei's craft industry and is funded by the government. There are occasionally training demonstrations and assorted crafts are on sale: the most important item they make are sarongs woven from gold and silver thread (B$3,000-5,000/m). Other handicrafts include silverware, basketware, finely woven textiles and traditional drums. The basketware is affordable, otherwise prices tend to be steep. These handicrafts can also be bought at the airport. Open 0745-1200, 1330-1630 Monday-Thursday and Saturday; 0800-1200, 1330-1630 Sunday, closed Friday. A further 800m beyond the Arts and Handicrafts along Jalan Residency, just after the left turn, Jalan Subok, is the **Taman Rekrearsi Hutan Simpan Bukit Subok**. This newly created park area is one of the most panoramic viewing points in the city. It involves a stiff climb up a series of wooden stairways from the layby, but the view warrants the effort.

EXCURSIONS

Istana Nurul Iman His Majesty's official residence is on Jalan Tutong (4 km from Bandar Seri Begawan) overlooking the river. The palace was designed by a prominent Filipino architect, Leandro V Locsin. The main feature of the design is the long sloping roofs like those of the traditional longhouses and the Islamic-style domes, covered with 22 carat gold leaf. It is said to be the world's biggest palace – it is bigger than both Buckingham Palace and the Vatican – and cost between US$350mn and US$600mn to build.

In Lord Alan Chalfont's biography of the present Sultan, *By God's Will*, he writes: "In the western press the palace has attained a certain notoriety thanks to the efforts of a succession of excitable reporters who have set out to evoke images of vulgar and conspicuous expenditure. Bruneians on the other hand, see the Istana as a symbol of national pride ..."

The following is a collection of trivia about the Istana – which Lord Chalfont dismisses as "routine gee-whizzery" – which was collated by James Bartholomew, author of *The Richest Man in the World*. It may be legitimately argued that this is just journalistic excess, and there is little way to confirm Bartholomew's statistics. They could be accurate, or exaggerated, or apocryphal. Illuminating the 1,780 rooms requires 51,490 light bulbs. Altogether, the palace's floorspace adds up to more than 20 hectares – roughly the area of 30 football pitches. Construction materials came from 31 countries. There is enough marble (38 different kinds were used) to cover 5.6 hectares – The Privy Council Chamber has a wall carved from a single slab of Moroccan onyx marble. The palace reportedly has 18 lifts and 44 staircases. The throne hall is furnished with four thrones – the extras are in case royal couples drop by. It is garnished with 12 chandeliers, each weighing a tonne, and backed by a 20m-high Islamic arch, adorned with 22-carat gold tiles. Among other palace facilities, there is a 4,000-seat banqueting hall, 257 toilets and a sports complex – including the essential polo practice field.

The palace was completed in only 2 years for the celebration of full independence from Britain in 1984. Today it is the home of the Sultan's first wife, Queen Saleha. In keeping with tradition, the ruler's Istana is also the seat of government and it is here that the council of cabinet ministers meet. It is open to the public on Hari Raya Puasa (at the end of Ramadan) when the palace doors are open for 3 days and hoards of local people flock to shake hands with royalty and receive a Hari Raya gift. *Getting there*: bus from underneath the multi-storey car park on Jalan Cator (B$1 or by taxi).

Nearby the Istana Nural Iman is **Damuan Park**, on the banks of the Brunei River. There are sculptures here by artists from the ASEAN countries; they were created for the Fourth ASEAN Symposium in 1986 and the theme of the work is 'Harmony in Diversity'. The park is popular in the evening. There is an open-air steam-boat restaurant here and a children's playground.

The Sultan's second wife, Queen Mariam, lives in the smaller, but no less grand, **Istana Nurul Izza**, 24 km from BSB, not far from the polo club in Jerudong district. Built to mark Brunei's independence in 1984, it also has a throne room and five swimming pools. The Nurul Izza cost only US$60mn to build. It is not open to the public.

Brunei Museum, Jalan Kota Batu (continuation of Jalan Residency), is located in Kota Batu, the original site of the capital, past the Arts and Handicrafts Training Centre, 5 km from the centre of BSB. It is a modern building, overlooking the Brunei River. The museum houses exhibits depicting life in Brunei, archaeology, history and natural history as well as a section on the oil industry, sponsored by Shell. The New Islamic Art gallery is made up from the Sultan's personal collection and is on permanent loan to the museum. The museum also has a large gallery used for art exhibitions. It is one of the few art galleries in Brunei, and certainly the largest. Open: 0900-1700 Tuesday-Thursday and Saturday-Sunday, 0930-1130 and 1430-1700 Friday. Closed Monday. *Getting there*: bus from underneath the multi-storey car park on Jalan Cator (B$0.50); a taxi will cost B$6-8; or hitch.

Muzium Teknologi Melayu (Malay Technology Museum) is about 1 km on up the road from the Brunei Museum and about 500m off Jalan Kota Batu below the Brunei Museum. (The two museums are connected by a footpath through the trees on the hillside.) Opened in 1988, the museum's three galleries focus on traditional house construction from 1850-1950. It contains models (virtually full-size) of the traditional Malay homes of Kampong Ayer, Kedayan and Dusun houses, and a Murut longhouse. The models are meticulous recreations, built by villagers with first-hand knowledge of age-old building skills. There are also exhibits of traditional technology, such as gold and silversmithing, iron-founding techniques, fishing and boat making.

The third gallery contains exhibits of Brunei's indigenous people showing how they lived as nomadic hunter-gatherers (as in the case of the Penan), as shifting cultivators or as settled agriculturalists like the Dusuns, Murut and Kedayan. Open Wednesday-Thursday and Sunday-Monday 0930-1700, Friday 0900-1130, 1430-1700, closed Tuesday. *Getting there*: bus from station below the car park on Jalan Cator (B$0.50), by taxi B$10, or 10 minutes walk from Brunei Museum.

Mausoleum of Sultan Bolkiah, 650m along Jalan Kota Batu from the Brunei Museum in the direction of the town centre. It is reached by a path from a layby, where there is a sign. Bolkiah was fifth Sultan of the dynasty (1473-1521) and one of Brunei's most colourful rulers. The mausoleum is surrounded by a peaceful garden dotted with gravestones, beneath a canopy of frangipani trees. The site of an old fort on the left, as you head down the footpath to the mausoleum, is currently being excavated. The mausoleum is about 4 km from BSB. *Getting there*: bus from station below multi-storey car park on Jalan Cator (B$0.50).

Jame 'Asr Hassanil Bokiah Mosque, the largest mosque in Brunei, is located on the crossroads at Kg Kiarong. Built in 1992 by the Sultan, the mosque is clad in tiles and has a ponderous golden dome and 4 chunky minarets.

TOURS

A handful of travel agents (see below for addresses) organize coach tours of the city on request. They will also organize excursions to Jerudong, the Seria oil fields and to Temburong. River cruises operate three times a day from Queen Elizabeth Jetty, on Kota Batu, 8 km from BSB. Departure times are 0900, 1300 and 1700. The tour takes 1½-2 hours and visits the Bolkiah Mausoleum, Kampong Ayer, Omar Ali Saifuddien Mosque and the palace Istana Nurul Iman. Tickets cost B$20 per person and are booked through Titian Travel and Tours (see address below). The Sheraton Hotel also operate river cruises every Saturday. There is the sunset cruise at 1745 which costs B$15 per person and a dinner cruise at 1930 which costs B$39 pp and includes a buffet dinner. Contact the *Sheraton Hotel* for bookings and further details.

LOCAL INFORMATION

● Accommodation

Prices: A+ over B$175-320; **A** B$70-175; **B** B$30-70; **C-F** B$30-10

If you want to avoid the high costs of staying in Brunei, Limbang or Miri in Sarawak are the nearest accessible towns with more reasonable accommodation. (For Transport to and from Sarawak, see page 502.) Hotels in Brunei cost upwards of B$70/night except for the *Pusat Belia* (Youth Centre) which is often full and in any case may refuse entry if you are not a student. The most recent a'ddition to accommodation in Brunei is the large resort at Jerudong, managed by the *Hyatt* group.

A+ *Brunei*, 95 Jln Pemancha, T 242372-9, F 226196, a/c, restaurant (has a poor reputation, serves European and local cuisine), free transfer to airport, business centre, guests can make use of the nearby private sports club, *Mabohai*, where facilities include a pool, tennis courts, badminton courts and fitness rooms, transport is provided. **A+** ***Riverview Inn***, Jln Gadong, T 238238, F 236688, a/c, annexe with pool, open air dining-room and fitness centre, shopping centre, coffee shop and restaurant, private clinic, situated on the road to the airport so not exactly a city centre location. **A+** ***Sheraton Utama***, Jln Tasek, T 244272, F 221579, a/c, restaurant, pool, 154 rooms and business centre, professionally-run, Sheraton-style decor on the severe side rather than opulent, good central location. **A+** ***The Centrepoint***, Abdul Razak Complex Km 4, Jln Gadong, T 430430, F 430200, a/c, restaurants, pool, sports centre, business centre, serviced apts also available, large adjoining shopping complex.

A ***Jubilee***, Jubilee Plaza, Jln Kampong Kianggeh, T 228070, F 228080, a/c, small restaurant and coffee shop (good capuccino), 5 minutes stroll into town and the open market, the best value of the mid-range places and a step up in terms of comfort from the *Princess Inn* and *Terrace* hotels – discounts sometimes on offer, so ask. **A** ***Princess Inn***, Seri Complex, Km 2, Jln Tutong (PO Box 109), T 241128, F 241138, a/c, restaurant, reasonably comfortable place but situated out of the city centre so a little inconvenient for those who want to walk around town. **A** ***Terrace***, Jln Tasek Lama 1, T 243553/4, F 227302, a/c, restaurant, pool, this was formerly *Ang's Hotel*, it has undergone a name change, refurbishment and a face lift, free transfer to airport.

B ***Bradoo Inn***, Jln Sungai Akar, T 336723, situated near the airport so not much use for enjoying the splendiforous sights of BSB, but fine if it is just a stop-over. Rooms are clean, with attached bathrooms. **B** ***Capital Hostel***, 7 Simpang 2, Jln Berangan (behind the Youth Centre), T 223561, F 228789, a/c, restaurant, cheapest hotel in town.

D *Government Rest House*, Jln Cator, T 223571, a/c, this place is for the use of people on government or other official business and ordinary tourists cannot usually stay here, but a letter to the Municipal Chairman (Bandar Seri Begawan 2031) at least 1 week before your arrival, stating your purpose and intended length of stay can do the trick, if you're on a tight budget this is worth trying as a room here costs only B$20.

E *Pusat Belia* (Youth Centre), Jln Sungai Kianggeh, T 229423, a/c, restaurant, pool, dorm only, proof of membership of some youth or student organization is required before you can register – although a passport listing occupation as student may suffice, swimming pool open to public 0900-1800, B$1 entrance. It can be full if there is some visiting youth group in town; otherwise it is a morgue.

● Places to eat

Prices: ♦♦♦♦++ over B$30; ♦♦♦♦ B$20-30; ♦♦♦ B$8-15; ♦♦ B$3.50-10; ♦ B$2.50-6

Chinese: ♦♦♦♦***Jade Garden***, *Riverview Inn*; ♦♦♦♦***Szechuan Dynasty***, ground flr, Centrepoint, Gadong; ♦♦♦♦***Phongmun***, 2nd Flr, Teck Guan Plaza, good seafood, also specializes in birds' nest, view over Kampong Ayer.

♦♦***Rose Garden***, 8 Block C, Abdul Razak Complex, Gadong; ***Chin Lian***, 20 Grd Flr, Jln Sultan; ***Emperor's Court***, Wisma Hj Mohd Taha; ***Harini***, 5th Flr, Bangunan Guru Gurumelayu, Jln Sungai Kianggeh; ***Lucky***, 1st Flr, PAP Umi Kalthum Bldg, Seri Complex Jln Tutong; ***QR Restaurant***, 4 1st Flr Block C, Abdul Razak Complex, Gadong; ***Rasa Sayang***, 5th Flr, Bangunan Guru Guru Melayu, Jln Sungai Kianggeh.

Fastfood: ***Kentucky Fried Chicken***, 22/23 Jln Sultan and G15-G16 Plaza Athirah, Seri Complex; ***Jollibee (fast food)***, Yaohan Megamart, Centrepoint, Gadong; ***McDonalds***, Block H, Abdul Razak Complex, Gadong; ***Pizza Hut***, Block J, Abdul Razak Complex, Gadong and Teck Guan Plaza, Jln Sultan. All more expensive than equivalent in Malaysia.

Foodstalls: at riverfront near bridge, where Jln McArthur/Jln Residency cross the creek, satay recommended. At intersection of Jln Sungai Kianggeh and Jln Pemancha, on the other side of the creek, there is a night market and one of the few places where you can buy food from stalls. Excellent barbecued fish.

Indian: ♦♦♦***Regent***, 3a Mas Panca Warna Bldg, Seri Complex, Jln Tutong – good buffet on Sat evening. ♦♦♦***Tenaga***, 1st Flr, 6 Hasbollah Bldg; ♦♦***Popular Restaurant***, 5 Hajjah Norain Bldg, Seri Complex, Jln Tutong.

Sino Malaysian: ***Nyonya Restaurant***, 3 Hasbollah Bldg 1, Gadong – clean, well air-conditioned, try the buttermilk chicken or fish slices with garlic.

Japanese: ♦♦♦♦***Taraka***, Centrepoint, Gadong (entrance at back of building) – pricey but has a good reputation – take away also available. For take away sushi try the *sushi bar* on ground flr of Centrepoint next to Jollibee.

Indonesian: *Keri*, Seri Complex, Jln Tutong; *Pondok Sari Wangi*, 12 Block A, Abdul Razak Complex, Gadong, good Gado Gado.

International: ♦♦♦*Café Melati*, *Sheraton*, Jln Tasek, also serves local food; ♦♦♦*Frattini's*, Yayasan Shopping Mall, Italian pizza, pasta, capuccino and ice cream; ♦♦♦*Mawar Coffee Garden*, *Brunei Hotel*, 95 Jln Pemancha, buffet lunch; ♦♦♦*Seasons*, 2nd Flr, Centrepoint, Gadong; ♦♦*Coffee Tree*, Mabohai Shopping Complex, Jln Kebangsaan, real coffee, excellent home-made pizzas; *Deals*, *Sheraton*, Jln Tasek, expensive French and Italian cuisine; *Rainbow*, 110 Jln Batu Bersurat, Gadong.

Lebanese: *Ghawar*, Hasbollah Bldg, Gadong, T 421205, buffet recommended on Thur and Sat.

Malay: ♦♦*Isma Jaya*, Jln Sultan, also Indian and Chinese dishes; ♦♦*Wisma Bahru Dan Anak-Anak*, Jln Sultan (opposite Brunei Shell), Malay and Indian food; *Mohammed's Coffee Shop*, Jln Sultan; *Rindurasa*, 3 Bangunan Hasbollah 4, Jln Gadong; *Rosanika*, Jln Roberts; *Seri Indah*, Jln McArthur.

Thai: ♦♦♦*Aumrin*, 1 Hasbollah Bldg, Gadong.

● Bars

Since Jan 1991, Brunei's bars have ceased to exist (see Food and Drink, page 567).

● Airline offices

British Airways (part of Jasra Harrisons), Jln Kianggeh, T 243911, F 243904; **Cathay Pacific**, c/o Royal Brunei Airlines, RBA Plaza, Jln Sultan, T 242222; **Malaysia Airlines**, 144 Jln Pemancha, T 224141; **Philippine Airlines**, 1st Floor, Wisam Hajjah Fatimah Building, Jln Sultan, T 222970; **Royal Brunei Airlines**, RBA Plaza, Jln Sultan, T 242222 (reservations), F 244737; **Singapore Airlines**, 49-50 Jln Sultan, T 244901/227253, F 243608; **Thai International**, 4th Flr, Complex Jln Sultan, 51-54 Jln Sultan, T 242991, F 242871.

● Banks & money changers

Citibank, Jln Sultan, T 243983; **Hong Kong & Shanghai Bank**, Jln Sultan/Jln Pemancha, T 242305; **Islamic Bank of Brunei**, Jln Pemancha, T 235686, F 235722; **Standard Chartered**, 51-55 Jln Sultan, T 242386. Money changers don't officially exist, but some local shops will change money. Residents advise sticking to the banks or change money at the airport.

● Churches

Anglican: *St Andrew's*, Jln Kumbang Pasang, T 222768.

Roman Catholic: *St George's*, Jln Kumbang Pasang, T 224458.

● Embassies & consulates

Australia, 4th Flr, Teck Guan Plaza, Jln Sultan, T 229435, F 221652; **France**, 3rd Flr, UNF Bldg, Jln Sultan, T 220960, F 243373; **Germany**, 49-50, 6th Flr, UNF Bldg, Jln Sultan, T 225547, F 225583; **Indonesia**, Simpang 528, Lot 4498, Sungai Hanching, Jln Muara, T 330180, F 330646; **Japan**, Kampong Mabohai, Jln Kebangsaan, T 229265, F 229481; **Malaysia**, 437 Kampong Pelambayan, Jln Kota Batu, T 228410, F 228412; **Netherlands**, Brunei Shell Petroleum Sdn Bhd, Seria, T 03-773999; **Philippines**, Room 1-2, 4th Flr, Badi'ah Complex, Jln Tutong, T 241465, F 237707; **Singapore**, 5th Flr, RBA Plaza, T 227583, F 220957; **Thailand**, LB241, Kampong Kiarong, T 429653, F 421775; **UK**, 3rd Flr, Hong Kong Bank Chambers, T 222231, F 226002; **USA**, 3rd Flr, Teck Guan Plaza, Jln Sultan, T 229670, F 225293.

● Entertainment

BSB is not the place to come if you are after a wild nightlife. It is rather tame by Southeast Asian standards – alcohol is banned, entertainment is restricted and what night life there is shuts down by 2200. Islamic codes of conduct are rigorously adhered to. Although illegal nightclubs come and go, for a good night out, locals take the short boat ride to Labuan.

Cinemas: *Hassanal Bolkiah Theatre*, Jln Kianggeh, sometimes shows films in English (T 222176), B$3 for a deluxe seat.

Cultural centres: **British Council**, 5th Flr, Hongkong Bank Building. Open: 0800-1215 and 1345-1630 Mon-Thur, 0800-1230 Fri and Sat. For those who really are short on things to do.

● Hospitals & medical services

Raja Isteri Pengiran Anak Saleha Hospital (RIPAS), Jln Tutong, T 242424, state-subsidized hospital, *Jerudong Park Medical Centre*, Jerudong, T 671433, private hospital, brand new, good but pricey – and it has left RIPAS impoverished as all the best doctors have moved out here! If you need to see a doctor it is best to go to one of the private GPs in Bandar (B$30 consultation) *Hart Medical Clinic*, 1st Flr, 47 Jln Sultan, T 225531, *Riverview Medical Centre*, River view Inn, Dr Reynolds, T 238238.

● Post & telecommunications

Area code: 02.

Central Telegraph Office: Jln Sultan, telephone, telex and fax services here. Open: 0800-2400, Mon-Sun.

General Post Office: corner of Jln Elizabeth II and Jln Sultan. Open: 0745-1630 Mon-Thur and Sat; 0800-1100 and 1400-1630 Fri.

● Shopping

Shopping in BSB is spread out over several locations. Each location has a department store, a myriad of small shops, banks and restaurants. The principal areas are Downtown (Jln Sultan) which now boasts the salubrious Yayasan Complex, Seri Complex (Km 1 Jln Tutong) and Gadong which has Centrepoint and the Abdul Razak Complex. There is nothing that cannot be bought cheaper in neighbouring countries, but the small shophouses are interesting for a browse.

Books: *Best Eastern*, 3rd Flr, Teck Guan Plaza Bldg, Jln Sultan; *Bluestone Bookstore*, 18 Block 1, Abdul Razak Complex, Gadong; *Booker International*, 12 Block J, Abdul Razak Complex, Gadong; *Jademan Bookshop*, 1st Flr Plaza Athirah, Seri Complex.

Handicrafts: *Brunei Arts and Handicrafts Centre* on Jln Residency, a 1-km walk along the Brunei River, see page 553 airport boutique.

Markets: open air market facing Jln Sungai Kianggeh is the closest thing you will get to a Southeast Asian market. Some open air food stalls. Worth a wander but not much to buy.

● Sports

The Hassanal Bolkiah National Stadium Complex also has a sports centre with facilities for badminton, squash, football, table tennis and athletics, as well as a pool.

Bowling: *Utama Bowling Centre*, ten pin bowling (2 km out of BSB), Jln Tutong, at Seri Complex next to Yaohan, recently overhauled with computerized score boards and bumpers for children's bowling alleys, T 242578.

Hash House Harriers: expats of all varieties and some more Westernized locals run in the local version of Hash House Harriers. It is really just an excuse to let off steam and have a good time – and, in other parts of Asia, to consume large quantities of ice cold beer, although Brunei has rather put the kaybosh on this element of the sport. The club are more than happy to welcome visitors to their runs. Visit the British Council in the Hongkong Bank building for run times. See the box on page 105 for further details on what's involved.

Golf: driving range near the International Airport.

Sailing: *Royal Brunei Yacht Club*, Pantai Serasa, Muara, T 772011 (members only).

Scuba diving: *Brunei Sub-Aqua Diving Club*, PO Box 432, Seri Complex, BSB 2604.

Swimming: public swimming pool at the Youth Centre, Jln Sungai Kiangngeh, open 0900-1800, Mon-Sun, (B$1). Swimming pool at *Hassanal Bolkiah National Stadium Complex*, Jln Berakas, T 240700, open daily 0900-2000 except Fri 1430-2000. *Anggerek Desa Swimming Pool*, Jln Berakas, T 330279, open Mon 1130-2030, Tues, Wed, Sat and Sun 0830-2030, Fri 0830-1100, 1430-2030. All public swimming pools close for the month of Ramadan.

Tennis: *Brunei Tennis Club*, Jln Tapak Kuda, T 225344.

Windsurfing: *National Windsurfing Association*, Serasa Beach, next to Yacht Club (open weekends only).

● Tour companies & travel agents

Antara Travel & Tours, G11 Bangunan, GP1, Jln Gadong, T 448805, F 448817; *Borneo Leisure Travel*, Britannia House, Jln Cator, T 223407, F 240990; *Freme Travel*, 4th Flr, Wisma Jaya, Jln Pemancha, T 234277, F 234284; *Intan*, Unit 1-6 Gadong Properties, Mile 3, Jln Gadong, T 427340, F 443235; *Jasra Harrisons*, Jln McArthur/Kianggeh, T 236675, F 243904; *Ken Travel*, 1st Flr Teck Guan Plaza, Jln Sultan, T 223127, F 244066; *Sunshine Borneo Tours and Travel*, Block A, 1st Flr, Abdul Razak Complex, T 441791, F 441790; *Zura*, 101 Ground Flr, Bangunan, Guru-Guru Melayu, T 225813, F 225204.

● Tourist offices

Tourist information desk at the airport – but not much use to the independent traveller. **Public Relations Office**, Tourist Section, Economic Development Board, Room 13, Customs Wharf, Jln McArthur.

● Transport

See **Information for travellers**, page 567 and Around Brunei section below.

Local Bus: a regular bus service (the Northern Line) has recently been introduced with a fleet of small purple buses. The 3 main stations are at Berakas, the Airport and at the bus terminal in the basement of the multi-storey carpark on Jln Cahor. Buses run every 15 minutes but tend to depart when full, irrespective of the schedule. The Circle Line, another new service, operated by the purple bus, makes a circuit from the Jln Cahor terminal, to Sheraton, Stadium Gadong, Jame-Asr Hassanal Bolkiah Mosque, Ripas, Seri Complex and back to terminal again. For long distance bus and minibus connections see the 'getting to Brunei' entry in the Information for travellers section (page 565). **Car hire**: Avis, 16 Ground Flr, Haji Dand Complex (behind Hua Ho's), Jln Gadong, T 426345, F 442285, or at the *Sheraton Utama Hotel*, T 227100, or the *Riverview Hotel*, T 238238; **Budget U-Drive**, E17 1st Flr, Bangunan GP Satu, T 445846; **El Sie**, 3a 1st Flr, Bangunan Gadong Properties, T 427238; **Ramza Enterprise**, 7 Bangunan Hasbollah, Gadong, T 445474; **Sabli Development & Engineering Co**, 21 Lambak Kanan Industrial Estate, T 391122; **Zarinah Car Rental Enterprise**, 509 Plaza Athirah, Mile 1, Jln Tutong, T 243669. **Hitchhiking**: an easy way to get around, even on short trips, although women should never hitchhike alone. At the very least, women should hitch in pairs or in a group with a man. **Taxis**: congregate at the taxi stand under the multi-storey car park on Jln Cator. They do not cruise BSB looking for fares. Flag fall is B$3 and there are numerous surcharges for putting luggage in the boot, travelling out to the airport, or picking up fares between 2100 and 0600. **Boat**: water taxis or flying coffins provide transportation for the inhabitants of Kampong Ayer. There are fixed fares for most trips ranging from B$0.50 upto B$2 but it is rare to meet a visitor who has actually paid the stipulated rate. Expect to pay double what the locals are charged.

AROUND BRUNEI

Brunei only has a handful of towns, all situated on, or near the coast and easily accessible from BSB in a day. Public transport is slow and irregular and hiring a car is probably the best way to get around Brunei, particularly if you want to get off the beaten track.

TEMBURONG DISTRICT

Temburong district is isolated from the rest of Brunei and is surrounded by Sarawak-Limbang, the land in between, was ceded to Sarawak in 1884. It is the most mountainous area of Brunei. In the south are the inaccessible ridges of Bukit Pagan. Temburong can only be reached by boat or air. It is possible to take a boat through the mangrove swamps up to Bangar (48 km to the southeast of BSB). **Bangar**, whose population just tops 1,000, is the main town and administrative centre for the Temburong district and is sited on the Temburong River, about 15 km upriver from Brunei Bay. It is comprised of a row of shophouses, a market, hospital, school and a collection of longhouses – all with cars and televisions. There is a road going further upstream to **Batang Duri**, a 'resort' with a riverside picnic area. Along this reach of river are several Iban longhouses (the nearest is 13 km from Bangar).

The **Batu Apoi Forest Reserve** covers 50,000 hectares concentrated in the southern part of Temburong District. The reserve is currently being upgraded to National Park status – and in the process will become the country's first National Park. The highest point in the Reserve is Gunung Pagon at 1,850m, a week's hike from the Kuala Belalong Field Studies Centre (see below). The vegetation in Batu Apoi ranges from lowland mixed dipterocarp forest to montane forest. Located within the boundaries of the Reserve is the **Kuala Belalong Field Studies Centre**, established by the Univerisiti Brunei Darussalam (UBD) in 1991 as a base for research into rainforest flora, fauna and ecosystems, and also as a teaching and training centre for schools and institutes of higher education. (In 1995 the centre was found to have deteriorated in the damp conditions and overnight stays were suspended while the centre was renovated.) Surrounding the Centre are virgin stands of lowland Dipterocarp, riverine, heath, and ridge Dipterocarp forest. Fauna include gibbons, macaques, langur monkeys, civets and sun bears. The nearest montane forest to the Centre is on Bukit Belalong (995m), a 2 day hike away. The facilities at the Centre include 6 chalets linked by walkways at the waters edge (with accommodation for 24 visitors), a laboratory, kitchen, dining hall, filtered water supply and generator. There is also a recently constructed 60m-high observation tower for observing the forest canopy and an aerial walkway across a deep ravine. *Getting there*: all visitors to the Centre must take a longboat up the Temburong River from Kampong Batang Duri, a journey of 45 minutes to 2 hours, depending on the state of the river. Guides are available for hire, and there are also well marked, self-guided trails for those who wish to venture out on their own. Although the Centre is specifically for teaching and research purposes (which receive priority), it is open to other interested visitors. For further information contact: The Co-ordinator, Kuala Belalong Field Studies Centre, Department of Biology, Universiti Brunei Darussalam, Gadong 3186, Brunei, T 427001, F 427003; or The Ministry of Industry and Primary Resources, BSB, T 382822, F 383811.

Limbang (Sarawak) – see page 420 – can be reached by road from Bangar.

• **Transport Boat** It is possible to take either a slow ferry from the Customs Wharf in BSB or the faster and more dangerous 'Flying Coffins' from the jetty, just across the bridge over Sungai Kianggeh, on Jln Residency, also in BSB. It is an interesting boat ride; it may be possible to see monkeys and the flora and fauna on the banks of the river are worth a glance, as the boat weaves from one muddy channel to another. (B$7-12) 45 minutes. From Temburong, the last boat back to BSB leaves at 1630. If you are forced to stay overnight you are obliged to report to the district officer.

MUARA

The small centre of Muara has a few simple eating places and a daily fish market. There are two beaches nearby. The first, Pantai Serasa, has only a narrow and littered sandy strip, overlooked by the port. But it is possible to hire wind surfs and sailing boats here, and on a clear day there are fine views across to Mount Kinabalu. The second beach is much better and is on the seaward side, out of sight of the port. It is known as Crocodile Beach which some say is named after the sandflies here which have a bite like a crocodile. Sandflies can be a problem, so take insect repellent and swimming in the sea is not advised without clothes on, due to jellyfish. However, the beach is spectacular, littered with vast timbers that have drifted down the coast from the logging areas in Sarawak.

• **Accommodation** *Hyatt International* have begun construction of an international beach resort at Pantai Meragong.

• **Transport** 28 km east of BSB. **Road Bus**: regular connections with BSB from the main bus terminal on Jln Cator (B$2).

RECREATIONAL PARKS

Berakas Forest Recreation Park is a 199 hectares reserve, 19 km from BSB, which backs a long white sand beach. There is an observation tower, picnic tables, and a marked trail through the forest which is typically Kerangas, heath forest.

Bukit Shahbandar 15 km from BSB is a 70 hectares park in kerangas (heath) forest with an observation tower. The park is between Pantai Tungku and Jerudong on the coast road. There are trails, picnic sites and a good view over BSB.

Jerudong Park 22 km from BSB, is Brunei's answer to Disneyland. It consists of a large outdoor amusement park, which grows larger every year, and is complete with roller coaster, simulators, bumper cars, pedaloes, children's playgrounds and an extensive area of eating places. There is also a vast outdoor arena being built which everyone hopes will be a venue for live concerts. It is a must for children and has the added attraction of being free of charge. To get there continue westwards for a few kilometres beyond the Berakas Forest Recreation Park until the fair ground comes into sight on your left. On the right of the road are the Sultan's stables, golf club and polo club. The new resort to be opened by Hyatt is also at Jerudong. Plans are afoot too to build a mega shopping mall here.

Kampong Parit (also known as Taman Mini Perayaan or Celebration Mini Park) is 26 km from BSB. More than 20 traditional-style houses have been built on the site as part of an effort to preserve the country's traditional construction techniques. They range from rural villages, to a mini-water village with houses like those in Kampong Ayer, built as they would have been a century ago. There is a restaurant in the Kampong. *Getting there*: buses go to Kampong Parit from Tutong (B$2); taxi B$30 from Jalan Cator, BSB. It is situated just off the BSB-Seria road.

TUTONG

This agricultural area, 48 km southwest of BSB, is the focus of government efforts to diversify the economy. For strategic reasons, it has invested heavily in commercial agricultural projects: Brunei imports most of its food supplies. There is a coffee plantation at Kampong Bukit Udal, tapioca and cinnamon are grown at Kampong Sinaut, and Birau Agricultural Station conducts research into cereals.

Tutong itself doesn't offer much more than a Standard Chartered Bank and a couple of sawmills. It is, however, fairly picturesque; the food in the open-fronted shops next to the river, is cheap and tasty and the nearby beach is quite unspoiled. Known as Pantai, Seri Kenangan ('Unforgettable Beach'), Tutong's beach lies on a spit of land, with the South China Sea on one side and the Tutong River on the other. There is a small children's playground at one end and picnic tables.

Excursion Tasek Merimbun, 27 km inland from Tutong is a shallow, freshwater lake, about 500m long and 150m wide. It has been developed as a recreation area with long plankwalks out over the water to the small islands in the centre and beyond. There are pavilions dotted along the way for picnicking and sheltering from the sun. There are signs warning of crocodiles – so beware! There are also jungle trails in the area.

SERIA

Seria lies 64 km southwest of BSB; it has a population of around 25,000 and is the economic heart of the country. It is a Shell oil town and the source of much of the country's wealth. The town was originally called Padang Berawa – 'wild pigeon's field' – and apart from the beach was a virtually inaccessible mangrove swamp. Early accounts relate the terrible problems encountered by explorers – not least the fact that the brackish, muddy red water was undrinkable and turned cooked rice into sticky paste. Even the Dayaks could not stomach it; one report stated they would "drink the little rain water contained in the chalices of the Nepenthes leaves (pitcher plants) after fishing out the dead insects".

Anyone posted to Seria right up to the 1960s was almost guaranteed to contract malaria – in 1941 the hospital in Kuala Belait was treating 200 cases a month. It is now malaria-free and booming; it has a large expatriate community mostly involved with the oil industry (see page 547).

Although Seria is the second biggest metropolis in the country. The town is built on a grid iron pattern of *lorongs* (lanes): the centre comprising lorongs 1-3, while lorongs 4-14 are lined with military bungalows – for the Brunei garrison and the Gurkhas – and oil workers' quarters. To the east of town lies the industrial area with the refinery, oil storage tanks and power stations.

• **Accommodation** **B** *Rumah Tumpangan Seria*, Jln Sharif Ali, some a/c, an old wooden place with some charm.

• **Post & telecommunications** **Area code**: 03. **General Post Office**: Jln Sultan Omar Ali.

• **Transport** **Local** **Taxis**: T 223255. **Road** **Bus**: regular connections with BSB, roughly hourly until 1500 (B$4). Green Line bus from Jln Cator, under multi-storey car park. **Taxi**: from BSB (B$100 full car).

KUALA BELAIT

Kuala Belait is situated on the east bank of the Belait estuary and traffic still crosses by ferry. It is a small port with a population of around 20,000. Like neighbouring Seria, KB is laid out on a grid-iron pattern of shophouses, centred on Jln Pretty, the central business district. From Kuala Belait there are boats up river to Kuala Balai. Just outside the town is the Panaga Club and Golf course, members only.

• **Accommodation** The best place to stay – if it is possible – is the *Government Rest House* on Jln McKerron (T 334288) but access seems to be jealously guarded and only the very occasional visitor without *bone fide* documentation seems to be able to corner a room which are charged out at rock bottom prices (**E-F**). With that possibility in all likelihood closed off, there is: **B** *Sea View*, Lot 3678, Km 2.6, Jln Maulana, T 332651, F 336139, a/c, pool, recreation centre, Brunei's first and, until recently, only beach resort, Avis car hire desk; **B** *Sentosa*, 92-3 Jln McKerron, T 334341, F 331129, a/c, expensive for what you get – plain rooms with barely a smidgeon of character.

• **Churches** **Anglican**: *St James's Church*, Jln McKerron T 336139; **Roman Catholic**: *St John's Church*, Jln Bunga Raya, T 334546.

• **Hospitals & medical services** *Suri Seri Begawan Hospital*, Jln Panglima, T 335331.

• **Post & telecommunications** **Area code**: 03. **General Post Office**: Jln Bendahara.

• **Transport** **Local** **Taxis**: T 334581. **Road** **Bus**: regular connections via Seria (BSB-Seria B$4, Seria-Kuala Belait B$1). Buses to Miri: five connections daily, first 0730, last 1530 (B$9.50). **Taxi**: to/from BSB (B$100 full car).

For those travelling to Miri, there is a regular bus which avoids queuing in the car lane – quite a consideration at weekends and public holidays when queues can be 6 to 10 hours long. The problem is that there are two rivers to cross by ferry, the Belait River and the Baram River, as well as the Sungai Tujoh immigration to clear. Sungai Tujoh is being expanded, but the river ferries do not cope with the amount of traffic even though the crossing is no more than 5 minutes. It would be logical for there to be a bridge – and indeed there are plans for one to be built over the Baram – however, it seems that politics do not encourage a crossing point over the Belait River – the bridge that currently exists further upriver is not open to the public. Both would seem to be bridges too far, albeit for rather different reasons.

PARKS AND WALKS

Rampayoh Waterfall, Labi (**NB** There is no public transport to this area, so it is necessary to hire a car from BSB or KB.) From Tutong drive to Labi (about 40 minutes) – which is as far as it is possible to drive. After Labi, the road turns to laterite, and there are several walks from various points along this road, two of which are signposted. The first starts 300m after the end of the metalled road. A 2-hour walk brings you to a large waterfall, which has a picnic site. The second walk starts 10 minutes further down the road from Labi: there is a waterfall and a rock pool for swimming. A third walk begins at Kampong Teraja, at the end of the road to Labi – about a 30 minutes drive. At Teraja longhouse, follow the stream eastwards for about 45 minutes to another waterfall. The Teraja villagers are usually delighted to help lost *orang putehs* to find the trail.

The Marudi Log Walk starts from Kampong Teraja, at the end of the Labi road (see above) and takes you across to

Marudi, the trading town on the Baram River in Sarawak. It is best to set aside 2 days for the return trip, although one-way it's just a 4-6-hour walk. It is officially illegal to cross from Brunei into Malaysia as there is no customs post at the Sarawak border, which is not even marked in the jungle. It is essential to carry a passport, however, in the event of being stopped by police in Marudi.

The local Ibans have laid a log trail across the swampy sections of the trail. You pass an impressive Iban longhouse on Sungai Ridan, which is surrounded by paddy fields. If you are constrained by time, the log-trail to the longhouse (which takes between 1½-2 hours) is a pleasant jungle walk in itself. For those venturing across the border, the trail ends about 3 km from Marudi. A local Chinese has set up a Hyundai van 'taxi' service into and out of town for about M$1 each way. If you do not bump into him as you emerge from the jungle, stop at one of the houses next to the road and he will find you. It is best to stay overnight in Marudi (for accommodation, see page 409). The Hyundai man is happy to pick you up at your hotel the following morning to take you back to the trail head.

Information for travellers

Before travelling	564	Getting around	567
Getting there	565	Communications	568
On arrival	566	Entertainment	568
Where to stay	567	Holidays and festivals	569
Food and drink	567	Further reading	569

BEFORE TRAVELLING

ENTRY REQUIREMENTS

● Visas

Citizens of the UK, USA, Malaysia, Indonesia and Singapore can visit Brunei for up to 30 days without a visa. Citizens of Thailand, Philippines, Japan, Denmark, France, Luxembourg, the Maldives, Liechtenstein, the Netherlands, Belgium, Sweden, Norway, Switzerland, Canada, South Korea and Germany do not need visas for visits of up to 14 days. Because of a history of misunderstanding between the Sultan and the Australians, it can be more difficult for Australian citizens to acquire a visa. If you arrive in Brunei without a visa, you will only be given a 72-hour transit visa, even if you are in possesion of an onward ticket and adequate cash. All others, including British Overseas Citizens and British Dependent Territories Citizens, must have visas which are usually issued for 14 days but can be renewed in Brunei. In countries where there is no Brunei Darussalam diplomatic mission, visas can be obtained from British consulates or from the Immigration Department on arrival. Visa exemption is granted with a confirmed onward ticket, valid passport and sufficient funds. **NB** Visas cannot be obtained in the neighbouring Malaysian states of Sabah and Sarawak.

Brunei has overseas missions in the following countries: Abu Dhabi, Australia, Belgium, China, Egypt, France, Germany, India, Indonesia, Iran, Japan, Malaysia, Oman, Pakistan, Philippines, Singapore, Saudi Arabia, South Korea, Swizerland, Thailand, UK, and USA.

● Vaccinations

Certificates of vaccination against yellow fever and cholera are necessary for those over 1 year of age coming from infected countries within the last 6 days.

● Tourist information

There is a tourist information desk at the airport, but there is no real tourist office in Brunei. ***The Tourism Section***, Economic Development Board, PO Box 2318, Jln James Pearce, BSB 2011, T 220243, is listed as the official tourist board but its ***public relations office***, Room 13, 2nd Flr, Customs Wharf, Jln MacArthur/Jln Sungai Kianggeh is a (slightly) better bet. The office is not geared up for tourists although it does print brochures and pamphlets and even a map. These are hard to come by and are not particularly helpful.

WHEN TO GO

● Best time to visit

Brunei is hot and sticky all year round – but to avoid the rainy season do not visit between November and March. For rainfall graphs in nearby cities see page 357 (Kuching, Sarawak) and page 435 (Kota Kinabalu, Sabah).

HEALTH

● Vaccinations

The usual injections for this part of the world are unnecessary for those just visiting Brunei. Malaria was eliminated in 1970.

● Food and water

About 90% of Brunei's water supply is treated so there is no need to boil water or use sterilizing tablets, except in remote areas. That said, many residents do take the precaution of boiling drinking water and filtering it.

● Medical facilities

There are five main hospitals in Brunei, several clinics and dispensaries and a flying doctor service for outlying areas. Emergency treatment (including emergency dental treatment) is available free for citizens at the casualty department of the *RIPAS General Hospital* in BSB. Visitors probably have to pay. Treatment is also available at a low cost from private doctors. Pharmaceuticals are available from the main shopping complexes in BSB. The *Guardian Pharmacy* in Yaohan, Seri Complex is one of the best stocked.

MONEY

The sultanate does not have a Central Bank – the money supply is managed by Singapore.

● Currency

The Brunei dollar (B$) is the official currency and is linked to the Singapore dollar. In November 1997, B$1 = US$1.57. In Brunei, Singapore currency is interchangeable with the Brunei dollar. Dollar notes are available in denominations of B$1, 5, 10, 50, 100, 500, 1000, 5000 and 10,000. Coins are in 1, 5, 10 and 50 cent denominations. (Singapore $2 notes are also legal tender.) Foreign currencies and TCs can be exchanged at banks, big hotels and some department stores.

● Credit cards

Most credit cards are accepted.

GETTING THERE

AIR

Flights with **Royal Brunei Airlines** (RBA), the national carrier, make regular connections with the following destinations: Singapore, Kuala Lumpur, Bangkok, Hong Kong, Jakarta and Bali, Manila, Dubai, Taipei, Darwin and Perth (Australia), London, and Frankfurt. There are daily connections with Kuching and Miri (Sarawak), Kota Kinabalu and Labuan (Sabah). Other destinations include Brisbane, Balikpapan (Kalimantan, Indonesia), Osaka and Zurich. **Singapore Airlines**, **Thai**, **Philippines** and **Malaysia Airlines** also fly regularly to and from Bandar Seri Begawan. RBA does not serve alcohol on its flights but they do allow you to take alcohol on board to drink. In February 1996 the Sultan also announced that the air crew would henceforth observe strict Muslim dress code and prayers would be broadcast during flights.

OTHER LAND TRANSPORT

● Motoring

The main highway in Brunei runs from Muara at the east end of the coast to Kuala Belait at the west end. Muara is a dead end, but from Kuala Belait car ferries transport vehicles across the Belait and Baram rivers into Sarawak where the coastal road continues to Miri and beyond. Be warned that the car ferries, which are generally very frequent, do not operate at lunchtime, from 1200-1300. The coastal highway from Muara to Kuala Belait is serviced by buses calling via Seria. To travel by road into Sabah is not as simple.

Before reaching Sabah you cross several borders, first into Sarawak, then into Brunei (Temburong), back into Sarawak and finally to the Sabah border. This involves some very lengthy form filling at each border crossing, and will fill about 2 pages of your passport for the return trip with stamps. An additional difficulty is that at the Sabah border there is a very steep gradient hill to get over, which is also impossibly muddy in wet weather. It is suitable for 4WD vehicles only. By public transport use a combination of buses and boats.

BUS

There are private minibus connections between BSB and Miri. These minibuses pick-up and drop-off at hotels in BSB, which is handy. For those who want to travel by public bus, it is necessary to catch a bus from the main terminal on Jln Cator in BSB (see the BSB transport section) to Seria, from there to Kuala Belait, and then from Kuala Belait to Miri. There are about five bus departures a day from Kuala Belait to Miri, the last at 1530.

BOAT

There are regular connections with **Limbang** in Sarawak (B$10). The Limbang ticket office is opposite the Plaza Sumber Mulia on the wharf, boats leave from the wharf. There are also regular connections with **Labuan** in Sabah (B$20) from the same wharf. Boats from Labuan to BSB leave twice daily (M$22, B$20). Alternatively, there are two ferries daily from **Lawas** (Sarawak) to BSB (B$15). The agent for the Labuan ferry tickets is between two goldsmith shops opposite the Limbang ticket office: *Borneo Leisure Travel*, No 63 Jln McArthur, T 222805. It is essential to book the day before you travel – otherwise you will not be allowed to board. Book tickets well in advance if travelling at weekends or on public holidays as seats are quickly filled. Cruise ships dock at Muara, northeast of BSB.

CUSTOMS

● **Duty free allowance** (for non-Muslims)
200 cigarettes, 50 cigars or 250 grammes of tobacco, 'any two bottles of any alcoholic beverage' (about a litre each) and perfume for personal use.

● **Currency**
There are no restrictions on the import or export of foreign currency or TCs.

● **Prohibited items**
The death penalty applies to anyone caught smuggling narcotics. Certain books are banned if they are regarded as offensive to Muslims or critical of Brunei. Any video tapes will be inspected and returned if they are not offensive.

ON ARRIVAL

● **Airport information**
Brunei International Airport is at Berakas, about 15 minutes (11 km) north from Bandar Seri Begawan (BSB). The airport was given a facelift in 1987 by the Dutch firm that built Singapore's Changi Airport and has all the modern facilities including shops, offices, restaurants, banks and car rental desks. There is also a small tourist information desk at the airport. **Flight information**: T 331747.

Transport to town **Bus**: ADBS (yellow and red) buses leave every 15 minutes in theory, but every 30 minutes in practice, for the central bus station in BSB on Jln Cator (B$1). **Taxi**: the ride into town costs around B$20, taxis are metered. **Car hire**: Avis and **Hertz** have desks at the airport.

● **Airport tax**
B$5 on flights to Malaysia and Singapore, B$12 for all other international destinations.

● **Clothing**
Dress in Brunei is informal – for big occasions, a long-sleeved batik shirt is appropriate. Yellow should be avoided on formal occasions if there is any possibility of a member of the royal family being present. Light cotton clothing is recommended, but bear in mind Islamic sensitivities to skimpiness (bikinis, for example, are out of the question). Women should keep their arms and legs covered; men should wear trousers except when playing sport or at the beach. However, there is a large enough Chinese population and also ex-pat community who wear 'normal' summer clothes, so t-shirts and shorts are not uncommon.

● **Conduct**
Religion When visiting a mosque remove your shoes and avoid passing in front of someone who is praying. Bruneians adhere closely to the strictures of Islam. Muslims are forbidden to eat pork or drink alcohol, although the former is available in hotels and Chinese restaurants. During *Ramadan* it is an offence for Muslims to eat or smoke during daylight hours.

Forms of address Shoes should be removed before entering private houses. Avoid showing the soles of feet when sitting. Only the right hand should be used when offering or receiving something. It is considered impolite for members of the opposite sex to shake hands and it is discourteous to refuse a drink, wear revealing clothing or to point the index finger.

● **Emergencies**
Ambulance: T 222366.
Fire brigade: T 222555.
Police: T 222333.

● **Hours of business**
Government offices: 0800-1200, 1300-1630 Mon-Thur and Sat. The working day is shortened during Ramadan. **Banks**: 0900-1500 Mon-Fri, 0900-1100 Sat. **Post Offices**: 0745-1630 Mon-Thur and Sat; 0800-1100 and 1400-1630 Fri. **Shops**: 0800-1900 Mon-Sat and some on Sun. Larger department stores tend to open at 0900 but may stay open as late as 2100, inlcuding Sun.

● **Official time**
8 hours ahead of GMT.

● **Safety**
BSB is a very safe city – but take the usual precautions.

● **Shopping**
There is almost nothing to buy in Brunei that you cannot get cheaper elsewhere. There is little or no duty on watches and electronic goods but prices are lower in Singapore. Almost everything is imported. Handicrafts are available from the *Arts and Handicrafts Centre* on the waterfront in BSB but stock tends to be limited and expensive. The main handicrafts are **brassware**, **silverware**, **weaving** and **basketry**.

● **Tipping**
Tipping is not necessary in Brunei – except in the case of porters at hotels. Some restaurants impose a service charge.

● **Voltage**
220/240 volts, 50 cycles. Most plugs are 13 amp, 3 pin (UK style).

Hotel prices and facilities

A+: B$175-320; international-class hotel with usual 5-star services.

A: B$70-175; better value than **A+** category.

B: B$30-70 economy; average and over-priced compared with similar accommodation elsewhere in the region.

C-F: B$30-under B$10; does not really exist in Brunei, other than the *Youth Hostel* and *Government Rest House* in BSB.

● Weights and measures

Metric.

WHERE TO STAY

With a small population and no tourist industry to speak of, there are very few places to stay. Facilities for campers and low-budget travellers are virtually non-existent. There is a cheapish youth centre but no down-market Chinese-run hotels, so expect to pay upwards of B$70 a night. In BSB it is advisable to book accommodation in advance.

FOOD AND DRINK

● Food

As in Malaysia, there is a plethora of Chinese, Malay and Indian restaurants and foodstalls to choose from. But the quality of food in Brunei is particularly high as most of it is imported from Australia. All its meat is imported from a government- owned cattle ranch in Australia which covers a larger area than the country.

Kalupi is peculiar to Brunei: individually packaged, steamed sweet cake made from rice or cassava. Other traditional dishes are *kueh koci* (rice flour dumplings with sweetened coconut filling wrapped in banana leaves) and *cucur ubi* (sweet potato fritters).

Fish is the Bruneians' biggest source of protein, although the sultanate imports 40% of its needs. The barbecued fish sold in food stalls by the river (off Jln Sungai Kianggeh) is excellent. The most common fish found there are mackerel (*rumahan* or *tenggiri*), red snapper (*ikan merah*), garoupa (*kerapu*) and pomfret (*duai puteh*).

● Drink

To the obvious regret of some Bruneians – particularly hoteliers, bar tenders and liquor-shop owners – the Sultanate dried up on New Year's Day 1991. Chinese restaurants can no longer sell their 'special tea'. In chic restaurants, wine buffs now sniff the bouquet of alcohol-free Californian Ariel Blanc and beer-drinkers have to content themselves with alcohol-free Buckler, Tourtel and Lowenbrau.

Prohibition was introduced by the Department of Religious Affairs because of the increasing influence of radical Islam in Brunei. Bruneians regularly run the gauntlet of the Department of Religious Affairs and anyone guilty of giving or selling alcohol to a Malay, which is *haram*, or forbidden, risks a hefty fine or arrest. Alcohol flows in from Malaysia's strategically located duty-free island of Labuan, and non-Muslims can bring in 2 bottles of spirits and 12 cans of beer for personal consumption. It can also be procured discreetly on the black market – with a 500% mark up. For tourists however, this is an inadvisable pursuit. The authorities have recently stepped up their patrols in an effort to stamp out liquor-smuggling.

But although it may be difficult to get an (alcoholic) drink in Brunei at least it is (theoretically) possible to drink water straight from the tap. Many locals, though, continue to drink bottled water.

GETTING AROUND

BUS

Most people have cars and so the public transport system is not highly developed – it is one of the only countries in Asia where the buses are not crowded. Buses run between the capital

Restaurant prices

♦♦♦♦++	B$30.00+	hotel restaurants and exclusive restaurants
♦♦♦♦	B$20.00+	upmarket restaurants
♦♦♦	B$8.00-15.00	basic restaurant
♦♦	B$3.50-10.00	Chinese coffee shops
♦	B$2.50-6.00	hawker centres

and other main centres and with the newly introduced Northern Lines the service has improved although it has done little to change the growing problem of traffic congestion in the city. The central bus station – where all local and long-distance buses leave from – is underneath the multi-storey car park on Jln Cator. Buses are not all air-conditioned.

CAR HIRE

Cars can be rented by those aged between 23 and 60 who have an international driving licence. Hire cost is upwards of B$65/day. Driving is on the left and speed limits are 50 km/hour in town, 80 km/hour out of town. The wearing of seatbelts is compulsory. Brunei's roads are well maintained: there is a good network of sealed roads – although they are largely confined to coastal areas. A single main road runs the full 135 km length of the sultanate; there are just over 1,000 km of paved roads in the country although this is increasing as new roads, particularly around BSB, are being built all the time. Car-ownership levels are high in Brunei: there are about 90,000 privately owned cars in a population of 260,000. A road map of BSB is available from the information office at the airport. There is also a new map, Bandar Seri Begawan dan Sekitar, published by the government, with a 1:25,000 scale which is available in bookshops. Parking in BSB is difficult – although the multi-storey car park next to the Jln Cator bus station always has spaces. The Yayasan Shopping Mall has also provided a new carpark with almost 1000 spaces. Beware of black limousines while driving: never overtake one. An expatriate wife recently sped past one and an expulsion order was delivered to her home the same evening.

OTHER LAND TRANSPORT

● Hitchhiking

It is surprisingly easy to hitch in Brunei: local businessmen travelling south to Seria, Kuala Belait and Sarawak make sure you are not left standing for long.

● Taxi

Taxis charge B$2/mile, with a minimum fare of B$4. Taxis are metered, but they are expensive by Southeast Asian standards and are also thin on the ground (they do not cruise around town hoping to pick up fares). There is a taxi rank next to the bus station, underneath the multi-storey car park on Jln Cator. They also congregate at the international airport. Many hotels have their own free car services to ferry guests into and around BSB. Long distance taxis are expensive: for example, it costs B$100 for the whole car from BSB to Seria. A new city taxi system is said to be in the pipeline charging a flat rate of B$3.

BOAT

Boats are still the most common means of transport in Brunei; the largest waterways are Sungai Belait, Sungai Tutong and Sungai Brunei. There are regular boat services from BSB to Bangar, Limbang (Sarawak), Labuan (Sarawak) and some towns in Sabah. **Water taxis** – open longboats with outboard engines – are fast and widely used. On longer routes, larger boats with covered cabins, accurately dubbed 'flying coffins', operate. **Ferries** leave from the Customs Wharf, BSB to Labuan, Tutong, Temburong and Limbang. There are also flying coffins to many of the above; they leave when full. It is also possible to take smaller river and coastal boats to destinations in Sabah and Sarawak.

COMMUNICATIONS

● Language

Malay (Bahasa Melayu) is the official language but English is widely spoken and taught in schools. Chinese is also spoken, mainly Hokkien but also Cantonese, Hakka and Mandarin.

● Postal services

Brunei's postal service is efficient and reliable. **Local postal charges**: B$0.20. **International postal charges**: B$0.90/10g, aerogrammes B$0.40. **Post Office opening hours**: 0800-1530 Mon-Thur and Sat.

● Telephone services

Local: free unless made from a telephone box, where a cardphone is needed. **Area codes**: there are four area codes: 02 for Brunei/Muara district (including BSB), 03 for Belait district, 04 for Tutong district and 05 for Temburong district. **International**: IDD code: 673; dial 0124 for the operator. International calls can be made through the operator or using IDD country codes. International calls can be made from cardphones and from the public telephones in the Central Telegraph Office, the main Post Office, Jln Sultan, BSB and from the airport, which operates 24 hours a day. There is a telex and fax service here as well. Telecom phone cards can be purchased from Telecom offices.

ENTERTAINMENT

● Newspapers

The *Borneo Bulletin* is the only local English newspaper and comes out daily Mon to Sat. It is owned by royalty and avoids reporting any news that might be domestically sensitive. International newspapers and magazines can be purchased at hotel news stands. The *Straits Times* (Singapore), *Borneo Post* and *Borneo Mail* are relatively widely available. The *Daily Express* (Sabah) and *Sabah Times* are also on sale.

● Radio

There are two radio networks, one in Malay and one in English (95.9 MHz) and Chinese. Recently it has also been possible to pick up Capital FM.

● Television

TV programmes in Malay and English, viewing starts at 1600 most days, earlier on Fri and Sun. There is an English-language news bulletin, covering local and foreign news, at 2200. 60% of the programmes are imported, mostly from ASEAN, the UK and USA. Satellite TV is now available, with a choice of 9 channels (BBC, CNN, Star movies, sport etc). Malaysian TV broadcasts can also be received in Brunei.

HOLIDAYS AND FESTIVALS

January/February: *New Year's Day* (1st: public holiday). *Chinese New Year* (movable, late January/February: public holiday) a 15-day lunar festival. See Malaysia, Information for travellers, page 523.

February: *Hari Kebangsaan Negara Brunei Darussalam (National Day)* (23rd: public holiday) processions in BSB, parades and firework displays.

May: *Armed Forces Day* (31st: public holiday), celebrated with the help of the Royal Brunei Armed Forces who parade their equipment around town.

July: *Sultan's Birthday* (15th: public holiday – but celebrations go on until the end of the second week in August). Birthday procession, with lanterns and fireworks and traditional boat race in BSB.

December: *Christmas Day* (25th).

● Islamic holidays

December: *Awal Ramadan* (movable, 31 December 1997) the first day of Ramadan, a month of fasting for all Muslims. During this month Muslims abstain from all food and drink (as well as smoking) from sunrise to sundown – if they are very strict, Muslims do not even swallow their own saliva during daylight hours. The only people exempt from fasting are the elderly as well as women who are pregnant or are menstruating.

January: *Hari Raya Aidil Fitri (Eid)* (movable: public holiday, 30-31 January 1998). Puasa celebrates the end of Ramadan, the Islamic fasting month. Families keep themselves to themselves on the first day – on the second, they throw their doors open. Everyone dresses up in their Friday-best; men wear a length of *tenunan* around their waist, a cloth woven with gold thread.

February: *Israk Mekraj* (movable, public holiday) celebrates the Prophet's trip to Jerusalem.

March: *Nuzul Al-Quran (Anniversary of the Revelation of the Koran)* (movable: public holiday). Includes various religious observances, climaxing in a Koran-reading competition.

April: *Hari Raya Haji* (movable: public holiday, 7 April 1998), celebrated by Muslims to mark the 10th day of Zulhijgah, the 12th month of the Islamic calendar when pilgrims perform their Haj to Mecca. In the morning, prayers are offered and later families hold an 'open house'. Those who can afford it sacrifice goats or buffalo to be distributed to the poor. Unlike in neighbouring Islamic states, the cost of a trip to Mecca is affordable by many in Brunei, so there is a large population of Hajis. Every year 4,000 Bruneians go on the Haj. If any pilgrim has difficulty making ends meet, the Ministry of Religious Affairs provides a generous subsidy.

April: *Maal Hijrah* (movable, 28 April 1998) is the day the Muslim calendar began, when the Prophet Mohammad journeyed from Mecca to Medina on 16 July 622 AD (lunar based). Religious discussions and lectures commemorate the day.

July: *Maulud Nabi* (Prophet Mohammad's birthday, movable, 7 July 1998), celebrated with public gatherings and coloured lights in BSB.

FURTHER READING

● Suggested reading

For books on Borneo see page 526.

Bartholomew, James: *The World's Richest Man the Sultan of Brunei*, Viking: London. This book is a bit of a hatchet job on the Sultan and his entourage, but interesting nonetheless. For a 'balanced view' it should be read in conjunction with Lord Chalfont's book.

Chalfont, Lord: *By God's Will: a portrait of the Sultan of Brunei*. This book was written as a riposte to Bartholomew's volume. Chalfont is chairman of the PR firm Shandwick's, engaged by the Sultan to promote his image. The book, not surprisingly, therefore glosses over the seamier side to the Sultan's life but in some ways it is more accurate. Chalfont, at least, had access to the Sultan and numerous sources that Bartholomew was denied.

Singapore

Horizons	574	Little India	654
Places of interest	627	Arab Street	657
The colonial core and the Singapore River	631	Around Singapore Island	659
		Singapore's islands	670
The port	641	Tours and tour operators	676
Orchard Road	643	Local information	678
Chinatown	646	Information for travellers	707

SINGAPORE is, without doubt, a remarkable place – and not just in the sense that it has gone from destitution to affluence in what amounts, historically, to the snap of two fingers. With an incomparable range of cuisines, excellent museums and other entertainments, first class shopping, and wonderful public amenities from clean streets to hyper-efficient public transportation, this is a micro-state that visitors can enjoy. Easily.

A few years ago the Singapore Tourist Promotion Board was marketing this green and clean republic with the line 'Surprising Singapore'. Perhaps deciding that for many visitors the only surprising thing was the lack of surprises, the STPB adroitly changed tack and went for the more fulsome 'New Asia-Singapore: so easy to enjoy, so hard to forget'. Warming to the theme, posters then began to trumpet, in mixed fonts, 'I saw a city with its head in the future and its soul in the past', the faceless tourist adding for good measure, 'I saw ancient operas performed on modern streets. I saw a dozen races co-exist as one. I didn't see an unsafe street. Was it a dream I saw?'

Well, what to make of that, lah! It's easy to see where the STPB are coming from. You can drink the water, walk the streets and the buses run on time. Just like home – but safer and even more efficient. But then they've interleaved the efficiency/modernity line with the 'ancient opera' and 'melting pot of races' hook. In a sense the STPB are right. But only in the sense that the English Tourist Board market quaint villages and traditional pubs in the West Country and Cockneys in sequins in London. Singapore is more modern than it is traditional, more new than old, and what is old and traditional is firmly embedded in the late 20th century. The street operas are thoroughly commercialised; the shophouses have been converted into boutiques, eateries and bars; and the Chinese, Indian and Malay inhabitants of this remarkable island state will more likely be tapping on a computer keyboard than tapping rubber.

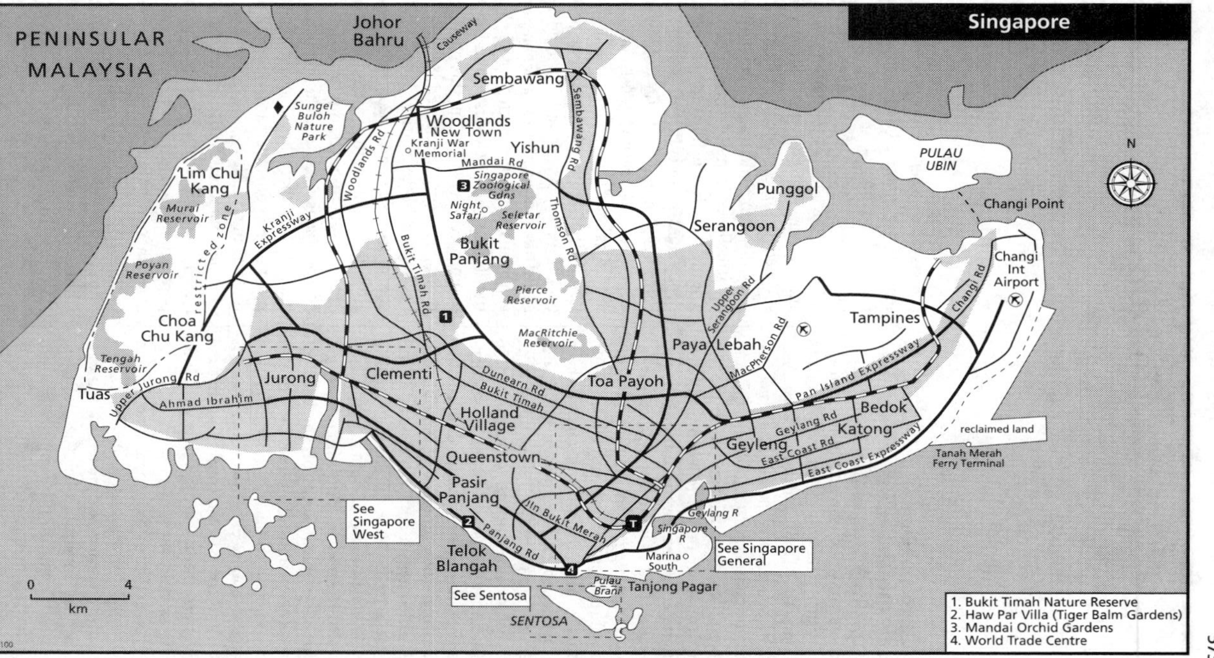
Singapore
PENINSULAR
MALAYSIA
Johor
Bahru
Causeway
Sembawang
Sungei
Buloh
Nature
Park
Woodlands
New Town
Kranji War
Memorial
Yishun
Woodlands Rd
Sembawang Rd
Mandai Rd
Singapore
Zoological
Gdns
Night
Safari
Seletar
Reservoir
Lim Chu
Kang
Murai
Reservoir
Kranji
Expressway
restricted zone
Bukit Timah Rd
Bukit
Panjang
Thomson Rd
Pierce
Reservoir
MacRitchie
Reservoir
Poyan
Reservoir
Choa
Chu Kang
Tengah
Reservoir
Tuas
Upper Jurong Rd
Ahmad Ibrahim
Jurong
Clementi
Dunearn Rd
Bukit Timah
Holland
Village
Queenstown
Pasir
Panjang
Panjang Rd
Jln Bukit Merah
Telok
Blangah
See
Singapore
West
See Sentosa
SENTOSA
Pulau
Brani
Tanjong Pagar
Marina
South
Singapore
R
Geylang R
See Singapore
General
Toa Payoh
Paya Lebah
Upper
Serangoon Rd
MacPherson Rd
Serangoon
Punggol
PULAU
UBIN
Changi Point
N
Changi
Int
Airport
Changi Rd
Tampines
Pan Island Expressway
Bedok
Geylang Rd
Katong
Geyleng
East Coast Rd
East Coast Expressway
reclaimed land
Tanah Merah
Ferry Terminal
0
4
km
1. Bukit Timah Nature Reserve
2. Haw Par Villa (Tiger Balm Gardens)
3. Mandai Orchid Gardens
4. World Trade Centre

Horizons

Singapore is difficult to fathom, especially from afar. Reading, watching and listening to the Western media it is hard not to come away with the impression that the city state is the closest that civilization has come to Aldous Huxley's *Brave New World*: eugenics is applauded, the government sponsors parties for unmarried couples, chewing gum is banned, people who fail to flush public toilets are publicly humiliated, the government hounds dissidents. The litany of stories from scary to downright barmy that the Western media like to recount is apparently endless. With this in mind, first time visitors who have done a spot of homework may step out from their planes with some trepidation. It comes as a surprise to many, then, to find that Singapore is not one-dimensional, nor is it crushingly dull, or overbearing. Entertainment is plentiful, with excellent restaurants, a good nightlife and stacks to do. Most Singaporeans have a well-honed sense of humour, especially about themselves and their country, and the government keeps off the backs of most people most of the time. Indeed, with its tangible affluence, clean and safe streets, and excellent public services it is easy to come to the conclusion that the Western media have a vendetta against this tiny city state.

Nonetheless, Singapore is not just an Oriental Switzerland. Beneath its slick veneer of westernized modernity, many argue that Singapore's heart and soul are Asian. Behind all the computers, hi-tech industries, marble, steel and smoked-glass tower blocks, highways and shopping centres is a society with an ingrained sense of conservative Confucian values. In 1992, an editorial in the pro-government *Straits Times* said: "Values are the software which makes the nation's social and economic hardware tick." Singapore still believes in extended families, filial piety, discipline and respect and most of all, it believes in the Asian work ethic. The man who has instilled and preserved these values is former Prime Minister Lee Kuan Yew – a man that Jim Rohwer in his book *Asia rising* variously characterized as the 'Thomas Jefferson of the Pacific Rim' and 'Asia's Moses' (see page 604). But, to some – and it should be added that most of these are non-Singaporeans – his far-sighted vision has transformed his clockwork island into a regimented city-state. In this view of things, modern, automated Singapore has spawned a generation of angst-ridden, over-programmed people who have given their country the reputation of being the most crushingly dull in Asia. But now, all that is changing. The architect of modern Singapore has allowed a new generation of Singaporeans to step up to the drawing board.

When Stamford Raffles first set foot on Singapore in 1819, the island had a population of about 150 – mostly pirates and fishermen. By the time of the first census, 5 years later, the population was 10,683 and growing fast. It included 3,317 Chinese, 4,850 'Malays', 756 Indians (Muslim, Hindu and Sikh), 74 Europeans, 15 Arabs and 16 Americans; there were also Javanese, Bugis, Minangkabau,

Filipinos and Terengganu and Kelantan Malays. The Bugis comprised one fifth of the population in the 1820s, but they gradually merged with the Malay and Javanese communities. By 1827, due to massive immigration (see page 584), half the population was Chinese; by 1860 this had risen to 65% and today they make up more than three-quarters of the population (see page 595). At the turn of the 19th century, Singapore was the most polyglot city in Asia.

The island now has a population of just under 3 million and one of the highest population densities in the world, with over 4,600 people per sq km. Because most people live in tower blocks, about 61% of the population lives on just 17% of the land area. Around 30% of Singaporeans are under 20 years of age, and another 37% are aged between 20 and 40.

THE LAND

GEOGRAPHY

Singapore is a small, roughly diamond-shaped island at the end of peninsular Malaysia and is not much bigger than Britain's Isle of Wight. It occupies a strategic position at the turning-point for shipping on the shortest sea-route between the Indian Ocean and the South China Sea. It is separated from Malaysia by the narrow Strait of Johor, but the two are linked by a 1.2 km-long causeway. To the south, Singapore is separated from the north islands of the Indonesian Riau Archipelago by the Strait of Singapore, which has been a favoured pirate haunt for centuries (see page 336). The country includes 58 other small islands, islets and reefs which lie a little over one degree (137 km) north of the equator. The biggest of Singapore's other islands are Pulau Tekong (18 sq km) and Pulau Ubin (10 sq km), both to the northeast. Singapore island itself measures 22.9 km north to south and 41.8 km east to west and has an area of around 600 sq km, although this is increasing, thanks to ambitious land reclamation schemes. After 1961 large areas of land were reclaimed from mangrove swamps to provide the Jurong industrial estate. There has been further reclamation along the east coast and at Marina Bay.

Singapore's skyscrapers are mostly taller than the island's highest point, Bukit Timah Peak (Tin Hill), whose summit is just 165m. (The three tallest buildings are the UOB Plaza, the OUB Centre and the Republic Plaza which all rise to 280m.) Most of the island is about 10m above sea-level, although there are scattered undulating hillocks and ridges – such as the one ending at Mount Faber, where the cable car goes across to Sentosa. The hillier areas at the centre of the island are mainly made up of granite and

Facts about Singapore you could do without

- The highest recorded wind speed in Singapore is 144 mph.
- The longest recorded drought (rain free) was just 31 days – between 17 February and 19 March 1983.
- The hotel with the largest number of rooms is the *Westin Stamford* (1,251).
- The only surviving large mammal, other than the ubiquitous *Homo sapiens*, is the wild pig – found on Pulau Ubin and Pulau Tekong.
- The highest buildings in Singapore (three, at present) are 280m tall – government regulations stipulate that anything higher is a risk to airliners.
- One in five households speak English at home.
- In 1995 there were 504 dairy cows in Singapore.

other igneous rocks. The west of the island is composed of sedimentary shales and sandstones while alluvial deposits cover the east end. Singapore's foreshore provides a superb, sheltered deep-water anchorage, in the lee of two islands – Sentosa (formerly Pulau Blakang Mati) and Pulau Brani (now a naval base).

CLIMATE

Singapore's climate is uniformly hot and sticky throughout the year, although the northeast monsoon, which blows from November to January, gives some respite. These 'winter' months are also the wettest. The average daily maximum temperature is 30.7°C which drops to an average minimum of 23°C. The hottest months are March to July; the highest temperature on record was 35.8°C in April 1983. The coolest month is January and the coldest temperature recorded this century was 19.4°C. Relative humidity peaks at over 96% (just before dawn), while the daily average is about 84%. Most Singaporeans prefer their air-conditioned microclimates to their balmy equatorial air and frequently catch colds from rushing between the two.

It rains throughout the year, but the northeast monsoon, brings the most prolonged downpours. The average annual rainfall is 2,369 mm; the wettest month is December, with an average of 277 mm and the driest is July with 159 mm. The most rain ever recorded in a single day fell on 2 December 1978, when Singapore received 512 mm of rain. Sometimes it rains for several days continuously and on these occasions there is often serious flooding. Between monsoons, from April to November, there are regular pre-dawn thunderstorms which strike with frightening intensity 3 or 4 times a month; they are called Sumatras (see page 38). Dramatic thunderstorms are fairly common at other times of year too; Singapore has an average of 180 lightning days a year. The sunniest month is February and the cloudiest, December.

Flower power

The Vanda Miss Joaquim orchid was named after an Armenian woman, Agnes Joaquim, who found the orchid – a 'natural hybrid' – growing in her garden in 1893 and presented it to the Botanic Gardens. In 1981 it was chosen as Singapore's national flower and then became the motif on Singapore's national costume – the flowery shirts sported by politicians. The purple and white orchid is on sale in all Singapore florists and can also be seen at the orchidarium in Singapore's botanic gardens (see page 643) and at Mandai Orchid Gardens (see page 668).

FLORA AND FAUNA

When Stamford Raffles first arrived, Singapore was blanketed in dense jungle and skirted by mangroves. An 1825 account of Bukit Timah (in the centre of the island), which appeared in the *Singapore Chronicle*, gives a graphic impression of what Singapore must have been like in those days. "Bukit Timah, although not above 7 or 8 miles from the town, has never been visited by a European, seldom by a native; and such is the character of the intervening country, that it would be almost as easy a task to make a voyage to Calcutta as to travel to it." Originally the island was 83% forested; but by the 1880s, about 90% of that had already been cleared. Today virtually all the jungle has disappeared and 49% of Singapore's land area is concreted over. Many endemic plant species have disappeared too, including more than 50 species of mangrove orchid. Bukit Timah Nature Reserve has 62 hectares of mature rainforest however, and there is a total of 2,796 hectares of forest reserve under management – including 15 sq km of mangrove along the north coastline.

Singapore is one of only two cities in the world to have genuine tropical rainforest – the other being Rio de Janeiro in Brazil. Although few tourists come to

Singapore to see wildlife, the tourism board is promoting ecotourism at Bukit Timah Nature Reserve and at Kranji, MacRitchie, Seletar and the Upper and Lower Peirce reservoirs. All have areas of primary rainforest and contain more plant species than the whole of North America – a mere 45 minutes from the centre of the city. Modern Singapore is a big, carefully planned landscaped garden. About 80% of its trees and shrubs are imported however: even frangipani – with its fragrant white blossoms – was originally introduced from Mexico. Bougainvillaea was imported from South America and the travellers' palm, so often associated with old Singapore, is a native of Madagascar. It is not actually a palm, being related to the banana tree and was introduced to Singapore in the early 1900s.

Despite the name Singapura – 'Lion City' – there have been no reported sightings of lions since the 13th century, when, according to the *Sejara Melayu* (the 16th century Malay Annals), Sri Tri Buana, the ruler of Palembang (Sumatra) mistakenly thought he saw one while sheltering from a storm on the island. He named the nearby settlement accordingly. Many of Singapore's bigger mammals and more exotic species have long-since disappeared, along with their habitat. The largest mammal still surviving in the 'wild' – other than the ubiquitous human – is the wild pig (found on Pulau Ubin and Pulau Tekong).

Man-eating tigers provoked a national emergency in 1855 and created a furore in the *Raffles Hotel* in 1902; but the last wild tiger was shot in Singapore by a Mr Ong Kim Hong in October 1930. Sambar deer, barking deer, wild boars and wild cats, which were once common, have all now gone. But flying lemurs (*Cynocephalus cariegatus*), flying squirrels (*Callosciurus notatus* and *Sandasciurus tenuis*), flying lizards and flying foxes still inhabit the protected forests where there are also small populations of mouse deer, porcupines and pangolins (scaly anteaters). Singapore also has many reptiles – the most common being lizards and snakes – but there are also crocodiles, whose fertilized eggs have been found in Seletar Reservoir. In 1989 a Thai construction worker was bitten by one while fishing. More than 300 bird species have been recorded in Singapore; the government has established a small bird sanctuary in mangrove swamps at Sungei Buloh (near Lim Chu Kang on the north coast) where there are many migratory birds.

HISTORY

Early records

Although Singapore has probably been inhabited for the past 2 millennia, there are few early records. In the 3rd century, Chinese sailors mention *Pu-luo-chung* – 'the island at the end of the peninsula' – and historians speculate that this may have been Singapore. Even its name, Singapura, from the Sanskrit for 'Lion City', is unexplained – other than by the legendary account in the *Sejara Melayu* (see page 577). It was originally called Temasek – or 'Sea Town' – and may have been a small seaport in the days of the Sumatran Srivijayan Empire. Following Srivijaya's decline at the end of the 13th century, however, Singapore emerged from the shadows.

Marco Polo, the Venetian adventurer, visited Sumatra in the late 1200s and referred to 'Chiamassie', which he says was a 'very large and noble city'. Historians believe this was probably Temasek. According to the 16th century *Sejara Melayu*, Temasek was a thriving entrepôt by the 14th century, when it changed its name to Singapura. Another contemporary account, however, by the Chinese traveller, Wang Ta-yuan, noted that the island was a dreaded pirate haunt. Whatever prosperity it may have had did not last. In the late 1300s, it was destroyed by invading Siamese and Javanese, for Singapura fell in the middle ground between the expanding Ayutthaya (Siamese) and

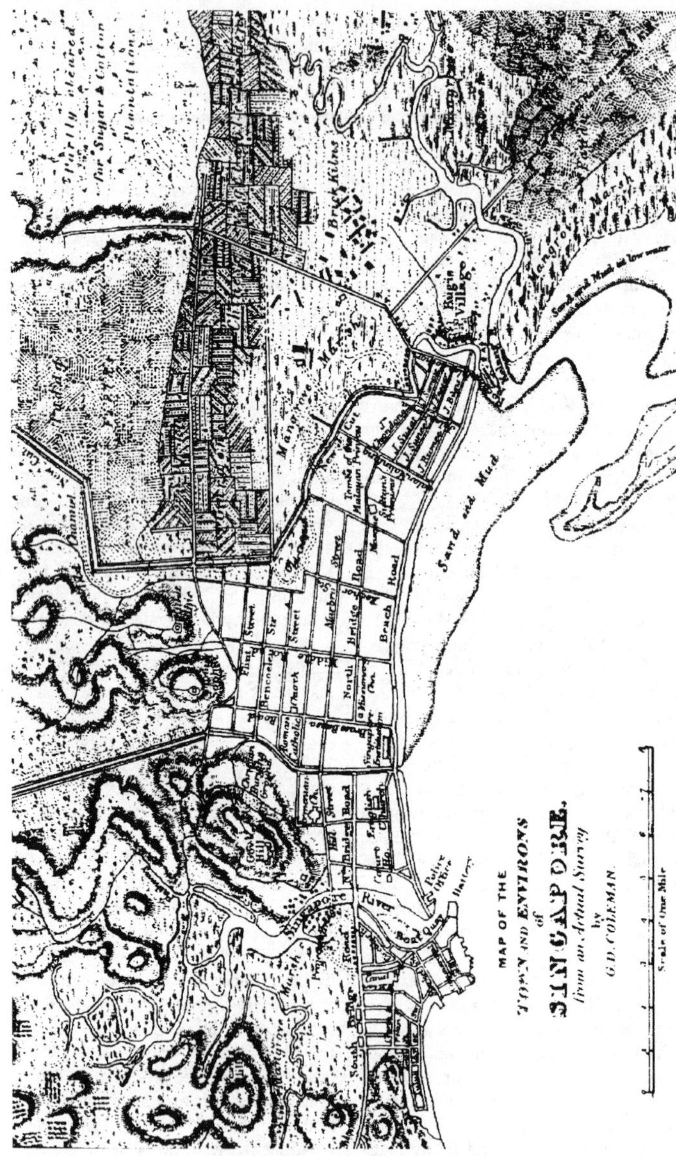

Map of Singapore town and surrounds
based on an 1839 survey by GD Coleman

Unimportant dates in Singapore's history, 1822-1988	
1822	Singapore's first market, Telok Ayer, opens for business as does the first school (with 12 pupils – a gender balanced twin-six)
1824	The first gas street lamps begin to glow and Singapore's first newspaper, *The Singapore Chronicle*, hits the streets
1828	The first two executions are carried out in Singapore, on 26 June
1831	Signor Masoni gives Singapore's first public performance – a violin recital – and *The Singapore Chronicle* records the first sighting of a tiger
1833	The first notice of stray dogs liable to be destroyed was posted in April and the first earth tremour is recorded (2100 on 24 November)
1839	The first boat to be built in Singapore, the 100-tonne schooner *Sree Singapura*, is launched in May
1852	The first cricket match is played on the Padang
1876	The first five rubber saplings from Brazil are planted
1880	The rickshaw makes its first appearance
1906	Singapore town is turned on by electric lights
1910	The first Scout troop of 30 boys is established
1915	The first Singapore Sling is slung
1931	Singapore experiences its first aviation accident on 17 February – two fatalities
1934	Joe Thunderface from Pasadena, California, dies during a boxing match at the New World Stadium – the first such fatality in Singapore
1949	Planned parenthood hits the island with the opening of the Singapore Family Planning Association
1971	Singapore goes metric (February)
1976	Fax machines arrive
1983	Singapore's first 3 cases of AIDS are diagnosed and, even more tragically, karaoke arrives
1988	Singapore Airlines inaugurates its first no smoking flight

Majapahit (Javanese) Empires. The ruler – called Parameswara, who was said to be a fugitive prince from Palembang in Sumatra – fled to Melaka, where he founded the powerful Malay sultanate in the 1390s (see page 220). Following Parameswara's hasty departure, Singapura was abandoned – other than for a few *Orang Laut* ('Sea People'), who made a living from fishing and piracy. While trade flourished elsewhere in the region, the port which today is the busiest in the world, was a jungled backwater and it remained that way for 4 centuries.

Raffles Steps Ashore

In the early 1800s, the British East India Company occupied Dutch colonies in the east to prevent them falling into French hands: Napoleon had occupied Holland and the Dutch East India Company had gone bankrupt. In January 1819 Sir Thomas Stamford Raffles arrived in Singapore with the hope that he could set up a trading post at the mouth of the Singapore River. He was relieved to hear that the Dutch had never been there and promptly struck a deal with the resident *temenggong* (Malay chief) of the Riau-Johor Empire. To seal this agreement he had to obtain official approval from the Sultan of Riau-Johor.

Due to a succession squabble following the previous sultan's death in 1812, there were two claimants, one on Pulau Lingga (far to the south), who was recognized by the Dutch, and one on Pulau Bintan. Realizing that the Dutch would

Thomas Stamford Raffles: architect of Singapore

"It is a pity to my mind that when Thomas Stamford Raffles... was knighted by his friend the Prince Regent in 1817, he chose to be dubbed Sir Stamford," writes Jan Morris in her introduction to Maurice Collis' biography of Singapore's founding father. "Tom Raffles was much more his style." He was the son of an undistinguished sea-captain, and was born in 1781 aboard his father's West Indian slaving ship somewhere in the mid-Atlantic. Raffles joined the East India Company as a clerk aged 14 when his father could no longer afford his school fees. 10 years later, in 1805, he was posted to Penang as an assistant secretary to the government, getting a 21-fold salary rise in the process. On the journey out, he learned Malay and because no other colonial official had bothered, he was an accepted expert within a few months.

In 1808, while working for the High Court in Penang, he took a holiday in Melaka and prevented the final destruction of the old Portuguese fortifications (see page 223). On a visit to Calcutta 2 years later, the Governor-General of India appointed him Governor of Java, a post he held from 1811-1816, while the British occupied Dutch colonies during the Napoleonic Wars in Europe. The old British Governor of India was impressed by him; he described Raffles as "a very clever, able, active and judicious man". In 1814 his wife, Olivia, died. Raffles was devastated by her death, but occupied himself researching *A history of Java*, which, was published in 1817, and is considered a landmark study of the island's history, culture and zoology.

As an administrator, Raffles was well-liked. He was known as a fair and reasonable man; he had a forceful character and opportunistic streak but few social pretentions. He was cheerful despite a succession of personal tragedies (he lost three of his children as well as his first wife). He battled to suppress piracy and slavery (he was a close friend of William Wilberforce, the social reformer, who forced the abolition of slavery in Britain). Raffles' aim was to bring prosperity to a region whose development had been hampered by the Dutch monopoly on trade in the Indonesian archipelago. He became convinced of the virtues of free trade, and later applied these principles to Singapore. Raffles was a great admirer of Napoleon (and actually met the exiled emperor on St Helena in 1823) but he never took part in any military campaign himself. He believed it was important for Britain to have a power base on the China trade route, at the south end of the Indo-Chinese land mass, and seems never to have questioned the forcible extension of the British Empire. In the words of Jan Morris, that would have happened anyway and "he was only the instrument of inexorable geo-political forces ... [although] he believed in his country as the chief agent of human progress."

After 5 years in Java, Raffles returned to England, where, in 1817 he married for the second time to an Irish woman, Sophia Hull, who he loved dearly but described as "affectionate and sensible, though not very handsome". He took her

bar the Lingga sultan from sanctioning his settlement on Singapore, Raffles conveniently approached the other one, flattering him, offering him money and pronouncing him Sultan of Johor. He agreed to pay Sultan Hussein Mohammad Shah 5,000 Spanish dollars a year in rent and a further 3,000 Spanish dollars to the temenggong. The Union Jack was raised over Singapore on 6 February 1819 and Raffles set sail again the next day – having been there less than a week – and left the former Resident of Melaka, Colonel William Farquhar, in charge. It was back to the East, where he was appointed Lieutenant-Governor of Bencoolen (Sumatra) in 1818. The same year, while on a visit to Calcutta, Raffles persuaded the Governor-General of India, Lord Hastings, to sanction a mission to set up a trading post at the southern tip of the Strait of Melaka, on the condition it did not bring the East India Company into conflict with the Dutch. Raffles had his eye on the Riau archipelago, but discovered that the Dutch had already re-established themselves on Riau's Pulau Bintan. On 28 January 1819, after casting around some other islands in the area, he headed for Singapore, anchoring off St John's Island (see page 674) before sailing up the Singapore River the next day.

After stepping ashore, he reportedly snacked on rambutans before visiting the *temenggong* (Malay chief) of the Riau-Johor Empire, to seek his permission to set up a trading post. Having formalized the agreement with the sultan, Raffles left the island and did not return to Singapore again until Sep 1822, by which time it was a booming port with 10,000 inhabitants. Raffles noted with satisfaction that in the first 2½ years, 2,839 vessels had entered and cleared the harbour; the total turnover was 8 million Spanish dollars. In 1822 itself, an even greater number of ships arrived and in that year alone, trade was worth 8.5 million Spanish dollars. It was an omen of things to come. Raffles allowed unrestricted immigration and free trade. During this second (and final) visit, Raffles quarrelled with Farquhar, took over the administration himself, wrote a constitution, drew up a street plan and 3 days before he left in 1823, he laid the foundation stone of what later became the Raffles Institution. Many prominent Singaporeans were educated at the college over the next 150 years, including the first Prime Minister Lee Kuan Yew. (The grand old building was demolished in 1984 to make way for Raffles City.)

Sir Stamford returned to England and having founded Singapore, he went on to found London Zoo. But he was far from well; for some time he had been suffering from terrible, unexplained headaches. He fell out with the East India Company over Farquhar's repeated claims to have founded Singapore himself and died the day before his 45th birthday in his home in Hendon, North London from a suspected brain tumour. His funeral was virtually ignored by London society and the local vicar refused permission for a plaque to be erected in his memory. 8 years later, his friends and admirers commissioned a marble statue of him which was placed in the north aisle of Westminster Abbey. There is another statue of Raffles, which still stands on the bank of the Singapore River, near where he landed in 1819. When Lee Kuan Yew first came to power in 1965, his Dutch economic adviser Dr Albert Winsemius told him to get rid of the Communists but to "let Raffles stand where he is today. Say publicly that you accept the heavy ties with the West because you will very much need them in your economic programme". Jan Morris writes that despite Raffles' short sojourn in Singapore, "he is honoured still in the Lion City as no other western imperialist is honoured in the East". On 30 January 1990, Singapore celebrated the 175th anniversary of Raffles' first landing.

this act of Raffles' that led to him being accorded the title 'Founder of Singapore'. Yet some historians would give the title to another great, although lesser known, British colonialist, Sir John Crawfurd. Ernest Chew, professor of history at the National University of Singapore, argues that all Raffles secured in his negotiations was permission to establish a trading post. It was not until Crawfurd became the second Resident of Singapore in 1824 that Britain acquired the island by treaty. Such details of history could not, however, dampen or detract from the celebrations marking the 175th anniversary of the 'founding' of Singapore by Sir Stamford Raffles in 1994.

The Dutch were enraged by Raffles' bold initiative and the British government was embarrassed. But after a protracted diplomatic frisson, the Treaty of London was finally signed in 1824 and the Dutch withdrew their objection to the British presence on Singapore in exchange for the British withdrawal from Bencoolen (Benkulu) in Sumatra, where Raffles had served as governor. 7 years later, the trading post was tied with Penang (which had been in British hands since 1786 – see page 175) and Melaka (which the Dutch had swapped with Bencoolen). They became known as the Straits Settlements and attracted traders and settlers from all over Southeast Asia – and the world.

Although Sir Thomas Stamford Raffles only actually visited Singapore three times, his vision for the city can still be seen today. "Our object is not territory but trade; a great commercial emporium and a fulcrum whence we may extend our influence politically as circumstances may hereafter require." Each time Raffles departed he left strict instructions as to how the city was to evolve. He wanted the streets to be laid out on a grid structure wherever possible. Houses were to have a uniform front and "a verandah open at all times as a continued and covered passage on each side of the street" (the so-called 'five-foot ways') – stipulations which resulted in the unique character of Singapore and later Malaya. During his second visit in 1819, he divided the town into distinct districts or 'kampungs' (the Malay word for village). Raffles firmly believed that the different ethnic groups should be segregated. The Europeans were to live in the Beach Road area between Stamford canal and Arab Street, the Chinese were to live south of the river (and in fact, Chinatown was divided into three separate areas for the different dialect groups), the Temenggong and the 600-odd Malays were to live along the upper reaches of the river. To the north-east of the European enclave, Kampung Glam housed Sultan Hussein and his Arab followers. The land on the north side of the river was set aside for government buildings. A mere 6 months after Raffles had landed, more than 5,000 people had settled around the mouth of the river. Much of the area to the south was mangrove swamps, but that was reclaimed and settled too.

European merchants soon realized that the beach area was inappropriate as a landing area because of the swell. In agreement with Farquhar, they started to unload from the north bank of the river. When Raffles returned for his third and final visit in October 1822, he was horrified by the chaos of the town. He fell out with Farquhar and had him replaced by John Crawfurd.

It wasn't very many years after Singapore had been established that a flourishing red light district had also appeared. The reasons are pretty clear: in 1824, Singapore had a recorded population of 2,956 Chinese men but just 361 women, a ratio of 8:1. 10 years later the combined population had risen to 10,767, of who some 10% were women. Amongst the Europeans, the ratio was slightly more equitable, but even so there were 51 men as against 23 women. With such an imbalance, the area around Krete Ayer quickly became a service centre of the red light variety and boatloads of young girls were brought in from China and Hong Kong to provide entertainment for the male population.

From fishing village to international port

Within 4 years of its founding, Singapore had overshadowed Penang in importance and grew from a fishing village to an international trading port. Thanks to its strategic location, it expanded quickly as an entrepôt, assuming the role Melaka had held in earlier centuries. But by 1833, the East India Company had lost its China trade monopoly and its interest in Singapore and the other Straits Settlements declined. Their status was downgraded and their administration trimmed. But while Penang and Melaka declined, Singapore boomed, having benefited from the abolition of the East India Company's monopoly. When the Dutch lifted trade restrictions in the 1840s, this boosted Singapore's economy again. New trade channels opened up with the Brooke government in Sarawak (see page 335) and with Thailand. The volume of trade increased fourfold between 1824 and 1868. However, the lack of restrictions and regulation developed into a state of commercial anarchy and in 1857 the merchants, who were dissatisfied with the administration, petitioned for Singapore to come under direct British rule.

10 years later, the Colonial Office in London reluctantly made Singapore a crown colony. Then in 1869 the Suez Canal opened which meant that the Strait of Melaka was an even more obvious route for EW shipping traffic than the Sunda Strait, which was controlled by the Dutch. 5 years after that, Britain signed the first of its protection treaties with the Malay sultans on the peninsula (see page 54). The governor of Singapore immediately became the most senior authority for the Straits Settlements Colony, the Federated Malay States and the British protectorates of Sarawak, Brunei and North Borneo. In one stroke, Singapore had become the political capital of a small empire within an empire. As Malaysia's plantation economy grew (with the introduction of rubber at the end of the 19th century – see page 660) and with tin-mining also expanding rapidly, Singapore emerged as the financing and administrative centre and export outlet. By then Singapore was the uncontested commercial and transport centre of Southeast Asia. Between 1873 and 1913 there was an eightfold increase in Singapore's trade. Joseph Conrad dubbed it "the thoroughfare to the East".

Historian Mary Turnbull writes: "Growing Western interests in Southeast Asia and the expansion of international trade, the liberalizing of Dutch colonial policy in the Netherlands East Indies, the increasing use of steamships (which from the 1880s replaced sailing ships as the main carriers) and the development of telegraphs all put Singapore, with its fine natural sheltered harbour, at the hub of international trade in Southeast Asia. It became a vital link in the chain of British ports which stretched from Gibraltar, through the Mediterranean Sea and the Indian Ocean to the Far East. The 60 years from the opening of the Suez Canal to the onset of the Great Depression in 1929 were a time of unbroken peace, steady economic expansion and population growth in Singapore, with little dramatic incident to ruffle the calm."

Though Singapore quickly made the transition from colonial outpost to commercial entrepot, conditions for many people were harsh. Sanitation and health were abysmal for all except the wealthy, education was limited, and work was hard and poorly paid. In 1910 the infant mortality rate was 345 per 1,000 – or, to put it another way, over one third of children born died before their first birthday. Death rates, even by the standards of other colonial outposts, were high. Brenda Yeoh observes that Singapore's population during the late 19th and early 20th centuries was only sustained by immigration – the 'appallingly high mortality rates' outstripped the birth rate. Needless to say, it varied considerably between the races. Among Europeans the death rate averaged 14 per 1,000 between 1893 and 1925. But for Malays and Chinese it was three times higher at 40 per 1,000. The diseases that wrought such havoc represent a veritable compendium of tropical ailments and included malaria, smallpox, beri-beri, cholera, enteric fever and bubonic plague. By the mid-19th century it was accepted by some people that only a clean and safe water

Chinese immigration: Singapore's life-blood

Today, Singaporeans attach great social prestige to claims to be third or fourth generation Singaporeans. Immigrants flooded into Singapore from virtually the day it was founded and within months the local Malay Orang Laut population was outnumbered. The first junk arrived from Xiamen (Amoy) in February 1821. By 1827 the Chinese had become the biggest community on the island and by the turn of the century, they made up three-quarters of the population. The first Chinese immigrants came from the neighbouring Straits Settlement of Melaka. But most came from the south Chinese provinces of Guangdong, Fujian and later Hainan; the different dialect groups included Fukien, Cantonese, Teochew, Hakka and Hainanese. One observer in the 1820s listed the Chinese as being involved in 110 separate occupations, but mostly they were concentrated in trade and merchandising and agriculture (vegetable farming and pepper and gambier cultivation). They also worked as coolies.

Most immigrants were young men and a big prostitution industry sprang up to service them. As late as 1911 there were more than 240 men to every 100 women. That same year there were reported to be 48 races living in Singapore, speaking 54 languages. Despite China's Ch'ing government outlawing emigration, they continued to arrive, driven by overpopulation and civil war. The new immigrants were known as *sinkheh*. Most were illiterate and penniless; for their first year, while paying off the cost of their passage, they received no wages. Immigrant groups from different countries settled in particular districts, and were administered by local community leaders, or *kapitans*. But in the Chinese community, real power was vested in the *hui*, or secret societies. The most powerful of these was the Triad – the Heaven and Earth Society – which had political roots in Fujian province. These societies remained legal in Singapore until the 1890s; only their membership and

supply would make Singapore a healthier place to live and the Straits Times and medical men like Dr WRC Middleton, the Municipal Health Officer, began to press the municipal authorities to make improvements. The first municipal water works was opened in 1878 near Thomson Road. This was financed with a gift of S$13,000 from Tam Kim Seng, a wealthy Straits Chinese merchant, who gave the money in 1857 on the condition that the water would be available to all, free of charge.

For the colonial authorities and most Europeans the poor health of the Chinese and Malay populations was due, in large part, to 'Asiatic' habits. As Brenda Yeoh has uncovered in documents from the end of the 19th century, it was widely accepted that the Asiatics had 'incurably filthy and disorderly habits' and 'a scant love for water and soap'. With such ingrained beliefs it took many years before the authorities saw a need to provide a comprehensive system of urban sanitation and water supply. As a result, it was not until the late 1920s that mortality rates began to show a sustained decline.

The Japanese occupation

World War One gave Singapore a measure of strategic significance and by 1938 the colony was bristling with guns; it became known as 'Fortress Singapore'. Unfortunately, the impregnable Fortress Singapore had anticipated that any attack would be from the sea and all its big guns were facing seawards. The Japanese entered through the back door. Japan attacked Malaya in December 1941 and having landed on the northeast coast, they took the entire peninsula in a lightning campaign, arriving in Johor Bahru at the end of January 1942.

rituals were kept secret. They organized the division of labour – including prostitution – and ran a crude judicial system; the societies were locked in competition.

The wealthiest of the Chinese immigrant communities were the Straits-born Chinese (the Peranakans – see page 230), many of whom came to Singapore from Melaka, where their extraordinary Chinese-Malay culture had taken root in the 15th century. Most spurned Chinese-vernacular education for English-language schooling, and many went on to university in Britain. They were set apart from the *sinkheh* immigrants because of their wealth. Although they were among the first to arrive in Singapore, they only accounted for about a tenth of the population by the turn of the century. But they continued to make money in the tin, timber and rubber trades and were unabashedly ostentacious with their wealth.

By the early 1900s the transitory nature of Singapore's population was beginning to change as immigrants married, settled and raised families. This encouraged the immigration of more women. Immigration peaked in 1927 when 360,000 Chinese landed in Singapore. Three years later the government began to impose restrictions following the onset of the Great Depression. In 1933 the Aliens Ordnance imposed a monthly quota for male immigrants, which was aimed at balancing the skewed sex ratio. Politically, Chinese immigrants were more attuned to what was happening in China. In the mid-1920s a local legislative councillor, Tan Cheng Lock, began to call for elected representation for the Straits-born population, on the governing council. Its local members were nominated by the governor – the first local nominee had been an immigrant Chinese merchant called Hoo Ah Kay (but nicknamed Whampoa, after his birthplace) who was appointed in 1869. Despite Tan's efforts to raise their political consciousness, the immigrant communities remained more interested in trade than politics until after World War Two.

The Japanese invasion of Singapore was planned by General Tomoyuki Yamashita and was coordinated from the Sultan Ibrahim tower in Johor Bahru, which afforded a commanding view over the strait and North Singapore. Yamashita became known as the Tiger of Malaya for the speed with which the Japanese 25th Army over-ran the peninsula. The northeast coast of Singapore was heavily protected but the northwest was vulnerable and the Japanese attacked in a 3-pronged offensive by the 18th Division, 5th Division and the Imperial Guards. About 20,000 Japanese landed on the northwest coast, surrounding the Australian 22nd Brigade and wiping them out. The 27th Australian Brigade fared much better and was beating back the Japanese at Kranji when orders were misunderstood and the Australians retreated, to the bemused delight of the Japanese. There were three main battlefronts at Sarimbum Point, Bukit Timah, Mandai and Pasir Panjang; in each case, the Allies were out-manoeuvred, out-numbered and out-gunned. Towards the end, the battle became increasingly desperate and degenerated into hand-to-hand combat. On 13 February 1942 the Japanese captured Kent Ridge and Alexandra Barracks on Alexandra Road. They entered the hospital where they bayoneted the wounded and executed doctors, surgeons and nurses. The Allies and the local people were left in little doubt as to what was in store.

With their water supplies from the peninsula cut off by the Japanese, and facing an epidemic because of thousands of rotting corpses, British Lieutenant-General Arthur Percival was forced to surrender in the Ford Motor Company boardroom on Bukit Timah Road at 1950 on 15 February 1942. The fall of Singapore, which was a crushing humiliation for the British, left 140,000 Australian, British and Indian troops killed, wounded or captured. Japan had taken the island in one week. Following the defeat there were accusations that Churchill had 'abandoned' Singapore and let it fall to the Japanese when reinforcements were diverted elsewhere.

The Japanese ran a brutal regime and their occupation was characterized by terror, starvation and misery. They renamed Singapore 'Syonan' – meaning "light of the south". The intention was to retain Syonan as a permanent colony, and turn it into a military base and a centre in its 'Greater East Asia Co-Prosperity Sphere'. During the war Singapore became the base of the collaborationist Indian National Army and the Indian Independence League.

In the fortnight that followed the surrender, the Japanese required all Chinese males aged 18-50 to register. 'Undesirables' were herded into trucks and taken for interrogation and torture by the Kempetai military police to the old YMCA building on Stamford Road or were summarily bayoneted and shot. The purge was known as *sook ching* – or 'the purification campaign'. Thousands were killed (Singapore says 50,000, Japan says 6,000) and most of the executions took place on Changi Beach and Sentosa. The sand on Changi Beach is said to have turned red from the blood.

Allied prisoners-of-war were herded into prison camps, the conditions in which are accurately described in James Clavell's book *King Rat*; the author was himself a Changi POW. Many of the Allied troops who were not dispatched to work on the Burma railway or sent to Sandakan in North Borneo, where 2,400 died (see page 478), were imprisoned in Selarang Barracks on the northeast side of the island. On the site of Changi Airport's Runway No 1, 4 men, who attempted to escape were summarily executed. 3½ years later, a Japanese commander, Major General Shempei Fukuei was sentenced to death for ordering the killings and executed on the same site.

Following the dropping of atomic bombs on Hiroshima and Nagasaki, the Japanese surrendered on 12 September 1945. The Japanese fifth and 18th Divisions which had spear-headed the invasion of Singapore and had carried out the massacres of civilians were from the towns of Hiroshima and Nagasaki respectively. The bombs saved Singapore from an Allied invasion. Lord Louis Mountbatten, who took the surrender, described it as the greatest day of his life.

In the wake of the war, the Japanese partially atoned for their 'blood debt' by extending 'gifts' and 'special loans' to Singapore of US$50 million. But Japanese war crimes were neither forgiven nor forgotten. When the head of Sony, Morita Akio and Japanese parliamentarian Ishihara Shintaro wrote in their 1990 book *The Japan that can say "No"* that the countries that Japan occupied during the war had become the best performing economies in Asia, it caused outrage and old wounds were reopened. They wrote: "We have to admit that we have done some wrong there ... but we cannot deny the positive influence we had". Older Singaporeans also noted with dismay and concern how Japan had rewritten its historical text-books to gloss over its wartime atrocities and many Singaporeans harbour a deep-seated mistrust of the Japanese. Among the most outspoken of them is former Prime Minister Lee Kuan Yew. This mistrust remains despite former Japanese Prime Minister Toshiki Kaifu's public apology in 1991 for what his countrymen had done half a century before.

After the war

Following a few months under a British military administration, Singapore became a crown colony and was separated from the other Straits Settlements of

Penang, Melaka and Labuan. The Malay sultanates on the peninsula were brought into the Malayan Union. The British decision to keep Singapore separate from the Malayan Union sparked protests on the island and resulted in the founding of its first political party, the Malayan Democratic Union (MDU), which wanted Singapore to be integrated into a socialist union. In Malaya, the Union was very unpopular too, and the British replaced it with the Federation of Malaya in 1948. Singapore was excluded again because Malaya's emergent Malay leaders did not want to upset the peninsula's already delicate ethnic balance by incorporating predominantly Chinese Singapore.

The same year, elections were held for Singapore's legislative council. The MDU, which had been heavily infiltrated by Communists, boycotted the election, allowing the Singapore Progressive Party (SPP) – dominated by an English-educated élite – to win a majority. The council was irrelevant to the majority of the population however and did nothing to combat poverty and unemployment and little to promote social services. When the Communist Emergency broke out on the peninsula later the same year (see page 604), the Malayan Communist Party of Malaya (CPM) was banned in Singapore and the MDU disbanded.

In 1955 a new constitution was introduced which aimed to jolt the island's apathetic electorate into political life. Two new parties were formed to contest the election – the Labour Front under lawyer David Marshall (descended from an Iraqi Jewish family) and the People's Action Party (PAP), headed by Lee Kuan Yew (see page 604). These two parties routed the conservative SPP and Marshall formed a minority government. His tenure as Chief Minister was marked by violence and by tempestuous exchanges in the Legislative Assembly with Lee. Marshall resigned in 1956 after failing to negotiate self-government for Singapore by his self-imposed deadline. His deputy, Lim Yew Hock (who later became a Muslim) took over as Chief Minister and more Communist-instigated violence followed.

The influence of the PAP grew rapidly, in league with the Communists and radical union leaders, through the trades unions and Chinese-language schools. For Lee, who hated Communism, it was a Machiavellian alliance of convenience. The Communists came to dominate the PAP central committee and managed to sideline Lee before their leaders were arrested by Marshall's government. At the same time, Singapore's administration was localized rapidly: the four main languages (Malay, Chinese, Tamil and English) were given parity within the education system and locals took over the civil service. In 1957, as Malaya secured independence from the British, Singapore negotiated terms for full self-government. In 1959 the PAP swept the polls, winning a clear majority, and Lee became Prime Minister, a post he was to hold for more than 3 decades.

The PAP government began a programme of rapid industrialization and social reform. Singapore also moved closer to Malaysia, which Lee considered a vital move, to guarantee free access to the Malaysian market and provide military security in the run-up to its own independence. But the PAP leaders were split over the wisdom of this move, and the extreme left wing, which had come to the forefront again, was becoming more vociferous in its opposition. Malaysia, for its part, felt threatened by Singapore's large Chinese population and by its increasingly Communist-orientated government. Tunku Abdul Rahman, independent Malaysia's first Prime Minister, voiced concerns that an independent Singapore could be 'a second Cuba', a Communist state on Malaysia's doorstep. Instead of letting the situation deteriorate, however, Tunku Abdul Rahman cleverly proposed Singapore's inclusion in the Federation of Malaysia.

He hoped the racial equilibrium of the Federation would be balanced by the inclusion of Sarawak, Brunei and North Borneo. Lee liked the idea, but the radical left wing of the PAP were vehemently opposed to it, having no desire to see Singapore absorbed by a Malay-dominated, anti-Communist regime, and in July 1961 they tried to topple Lee's government. Their bid narrowly failed and resulted in the left-wing dissenters breaking away to form the Barisan Sosialis (BS), or Socialist Front. Despite continued opposition to the merger, a referendum showed that a majority of Singapore's population supported it. In February 1963, in *Operation Coldstore*, more than 100 Communist and pro-Communist politicians, trades unionists and student leaders were arrested, including half the BS Central Executive Committee.

On 31 August 1963, Singapore joined the Federation of Malaysia. The following month, during a delay in the implementation of the Federation while the wishes of the Borneo states were being ascertained, Singapore declared unilateral independence from Britain. The PAP also won another resounding victory in an election and secured a comfortable majority. Almost immediately, however, the new federation ran into trouble, due to Indonesian objections, and Jakarta launched its *Konfrontasi* – or Confrontation (see page 341). Indonesian saboteurs infiltrated Singapore and began a bombing spree which severely damaged Singapore's trade. In mid-1964 Singapore was wracked by communal riots which caused great concern in Kuala Lumpur, and Lee and Tunku Abdul Rahman clashed over what they considered undue interference in each others' internal affairs. Tensions rose still further when the PAP contested Malaysia's general election in 1964, and Lee attempted to unite all Malaysian opposition parties under the PAP banner. Finally, on 9 August 1965, Kuala Lumpur forced Singapore to agree to pull out of the Federation, and it became an independent state against the wishes of the government. At a press conference announcing Singapore's expulsion from the Federation, Lee Kuan Yew wept.

As a footnote to Singapore's expulsion, in June 1996 Lee Kuan Yew suggested in an interview with local and foreign journalists that the island republic might rejoin the Federation should certain conditions be met – like no racial favoritism. Few other politicans, either in Singapore or Malaysia, took the proposal seriously. The Malaysian cartoonist Lat drew an image of the managers of a Malaysian chewing gum factory pounding the board room table as they considered the possibility of Singapore's chewing gum ban being extended to Malaysia.

ART AND ARCHITECTURE

Among the first things a visitor notices on arrival in Singapore – indeed even before arrival, on the final approach to Changi International Airport – are the towering modern high-rise buildings. Many of these are public Housing Development Board (HDB) blocks, but there are countless luxury condominium developments and, in the city, huge, office towers. The rush to modernise the city skyline and clear the urban slums resulted in what is now dubbed the 'architectural holocaust' of the 1960s and 1970s. When Singapore's older colonial buildings fell into disrepair, and the old shophouses had become squalid, decaying wrecks, they were demolished, instead of being gutted and restored. Other old buildings – perhaps most notably, the Raffles Institution – were torn down to make way for gleaming skyscrapers.

That Singapore at independence was a squalid place where a large number of people lived unhealthy lives in cramped conditions with poor sanitation is beyond question. The Housing Development Board was established soon after self government to deal with the problem and is a model of its type: between 1960 and 1990, 630,000 apartments were built and today 86% of the Republic's population live in HDB housing. They are still being built at a rate of 30,000 a year. Over time the HDB's building rationale has changed. To begin with it was a case of building cheap, basic accommodation as quickly as possible. Almost all these original developments have since been torn down although a few older HDB blocks are used to house Singapore's army of guest workers. As Singapore has made the transition from poor, to middle income, to affluent, so the HDB has moved upmarket. Its mission is now to meet the needs and aspirations of a population which is among the highest paid in Asia.

However, the HDB building frenzy did have one side effect which only the luxury of affluence revealed. During the 1980s the government began to realize that in tearing down the squalid it was also tearing down the old. The turning point came with the impending demolition of the Raffles Institution set up by Sir Stamford Raffles in 1823. Perhaps not coincidentally, Lee Kuan Yew was educated here between 1936 and 1939. Almost before it was too late, the Urban Redevelopment Authority (URA) was set up to identify and gazette buildings of historic and architectural value. In one of its pamphlets the URA intones: "A nation must have a memory to give it a sense of cohesion, continuity and identity. A sense of a common history is what provides the links to hold together a people who came from the four corners of the earth". It is typically Singaporean that the preservation of the island's architectural heritage is primarily justified not on artistic grounds, but as an exercise in nation-building.

Since the URA was established, great effort has been put into restoring shophouses to their former glory. By 1996 the URA had gazetted 5,320 buildings in 10 different areas of the city for conservation. These included four separate areas of Chinatown, the former Malay quarter of Kampung Glam, Little India and several of the quays along the Singapore River. Among the buildings declared national monuments are many old churches, temples, mosques, markets and even hotels (notably the *Raffles Hotel* – see page 634 – and the *Goodwood Park Hotel*). About a quarter of the 5,000-odd listed buildings have so far been renovated although given that shophouses are changing hands for up to S$2 million there seems to be money and profit in climbing aboard the architectural aesthetes' bandwagon.

To the cursory observer, Singapore is doing much to restore the past and to protect the architecturally valuable. Some conservationists, however, argue that this rush to renovate and conserve Singapore's fast-disappearing architectural heritage is surface treatment. The façades may have been restored, but the interiors are ripped out in the interests of efficiency and economy. (The URA stipulates that the original façade and roof form must be preserved, but the interior can be changed in any way.) The former functions of the buildings as brothels, warehouses and trading emporia are lost from view as advertising agencies, fancy restaurants and trendy bars take over. To the purist, this is Micky Mouse restoration for the Singapore yuppie who likes to sip beer in tasteful surroundings. Other renovation efforts have notably lacked even good taste. The Convent of the Holy Infant Jesus on Victoria Street is a classic example: it has been renovated and turned into a shopping complex with 70 retail units. Plans to turn the chapel into a disco were abandoned. Nor do all gazetted buildings have a copper-bottomed guarantee of protection. In March 1993, a contractor demolished a pre-war row of shophouses – earmarked by the URA for conservation – 'by mistake'. His defence was that because he could not read English, he could not understand the URA's plans or instructions. He was fined S$2,000.

Singapore is being 'museumized' or 'spectacle-ized'; it is becoming a showcase. Boat Quay, Bugis Street, Lau Pa Sat (Telok Ayer) Market, Clarke Quay – these historic places, having been turned into conservation areas, and turned over to new owners and functions, have had their historical links severed. Heritage and history are manipulated and transformed. Radicals would say that this is ideologically driven, and that it cannot be divorced from what the government would like Singaporeans (and visitors) to think about themselves and about their roots. Brenda Yeoh and Lily Kong, two geographers at the National University of Singapore, wrote in a paper in 1994 that:

> "The re-creation of the past in a place gives the state the opportunity to filter out what it deems undesirable and to retain what it considers beneficial to cultivating a sense of cohesion and national identity. History is thus recycled as nostalgia."

In the mid-1990s Koh-Lim Wen Gin, the Urban Redevelopment Authority's director of conservation and urban design, has accused the architectural 'purists' who have criticized the URA's efforts as simply living in Wonderland. As she points out, to have returned the warehouses and godowns of Boat Quay back into places to store rubber and rice is patently barmy. The companies that have invested in renovating this previously run-down area must be given some latitude when it comes to deciding on their use and this will be driven by that use which yields the highest return. Defenders of the policy also point out that few 'ordinary' people – who were the original residents of these shophouses – wish to live there, even if they could afford the sky-high rents. Times have moved on, the people have moved on and out to HDB developments, and the notion that these buildings could be restored not just to their former glory but also to their former use does not stand up to scrutiny.

In 1823, when the British administration decided to make Singapore a penal station, several hundred Indian convicts were shipped in to work as labourers. At any one time, there were as many as 1,000 convicts in Singapore. They built St Andrew's Cathedral, the Sri Mariamman Temple and the Istana. The British also imported indentured labourers – who were exclusively Tamils – to build roads, bridges, canals and wharves.

Among the more interesting decorative innovations at this time was *Madras chunam*, devised by Indian labourers to conceal deficiencies of building materials. The recipe for Madras chunam was egg white, egg shell, lime and a coarse sugar (called jaggery), mixed with coconut husks and water into a paste. Once the paste had hardened, it was polished to give a smooth surface, and moulded to give many of the buildings their ornate fronts.

Colonial architects

The first architect to make an impression on Singapore was the Irishman **George Coleman**. He was employed first by Raffles as a town planning consultant in Batavia (now Jakarta), but in 1826 moved to Singapore to take up the position of Town Surveyor. The beautiful little **Armenian Church** (see page 634), **Caldwell House** and **Maxwell House** (now **Parliament House**) were all built to his specifications. His own fine villa was sadly demolished in 1969 to make way for the *Peninsula Hotel*, but the road retains his name. Coleman skilfully adapted the Palladian style of architecture to suit the tropical climate – Doric columns, high ceilings, open floor plans and wide verandahs to provide relief from the heat. In addition to his building programme, Coleman oversaw the draining of the marshes and created the network of roads which is still evident today.

Following Coleman's death in 1844, **John Thomson** became Town Surveyor. He continued where Coleman had left off, embracing many of his ideas and in particular the tropical Palladian style. As Singapore became more affluent through the 1830s and 1840s many of the flimsy constructions that had been flung together in the early years of the settlement made way for more permanent brick buildings. **St Andrew's Cathedral**, and the **Cathedral of the Good Shepherd** both went up at this time, as did the **Thian Hock Keng Temple** and the **Hajjah Fatimah Mosque**.

Traditional house styles

The Shophouse The shophouse is the definitive Singaporean building. The shophouse evolved as a business premises with living quarters on the upper floors. The distinctive covered passageway – known as the Five-foot Way – was Raffles' innovation, and was created to provide a continuous covered way, to shelter from the rain.

The URA (Urban Redevelopment Authority) have identified five distinct shophouse styles. Chinatown, Little India and Arab Street all have their idiosyncratic styles, with the Arab Street buildings being the most flamboyant. The Chinatown styles are described and illustrated below and the Indian varieties in a box describing a walking tour of Little India on page 649. Although there are important differences between these various shophouse styles, the adoption of classical elements on the façades remained consistent, while additional ornamentation became very popular later on. Until the arrival of modern building techniques, the width of the shophouse was determined by the length of felled timber available. Shophouses were painted in pastel shades, reminscent of the colours of the finely stitched kebayas, worn by the Nonyas.

The Chinese shophouse The URA have identified five different shophouse styles – Early, First Transitional, Late, Second Transitional and Art Deco. The **Early style** were built between 1840 and 1900 and are very simple in design with two

Late Shophouse
(No 21 Bukit Pasoh Road)

Second Transitional Shophouse
(No 10 Stanley Street)

Chinese shophouses (Reproduced with kind permission of the URA)

storeys, simple Doric columns and very little ornamentation. The **First Transitional** is less stolid in appearance and in many cases boasts a third storey. In addition, there is a little more ornamentation, with the use of vents and some Chinese petal designs. However the most significant difference with the Early shophouse is that the First Transitional is significantly taller and therefore more vertically elongated. The **Late shophouse**, examples of which were built between 1900 and 1940, is much more fussy in appearance with three windows to each shopfront (instead of two). This reduces the wall space but made for cooler houses with better ventilation. Columns in Late shophouses are Corinthian rather than Doric and ornamental and plaster 'swags' decorate any remaining wallspace. Ceramic tiles were also used on the columns. The **Second Transitional** style dates from the late 1930s. The look is more austere, and although it retains the three window openings much of the ornamentation is lost. Perhaps this

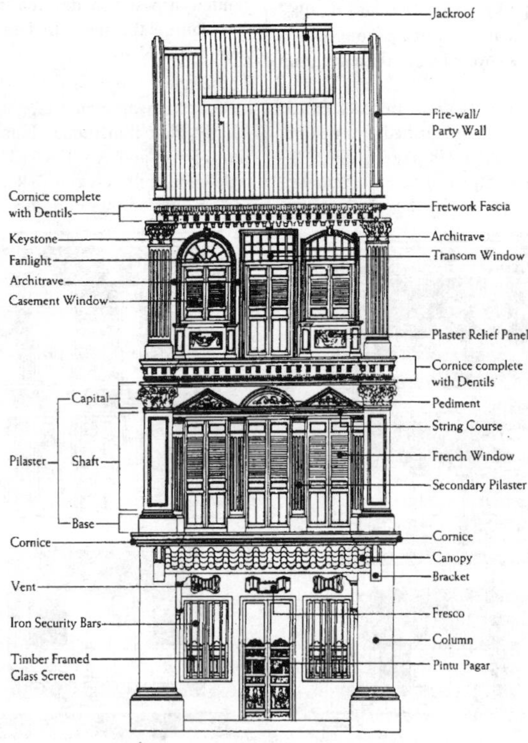

This is not an actual façade. It is drawn with the purpose of explaining the common architectural elements that can be found in shophouse façades.
(Reproduced with kind permission of the URA)

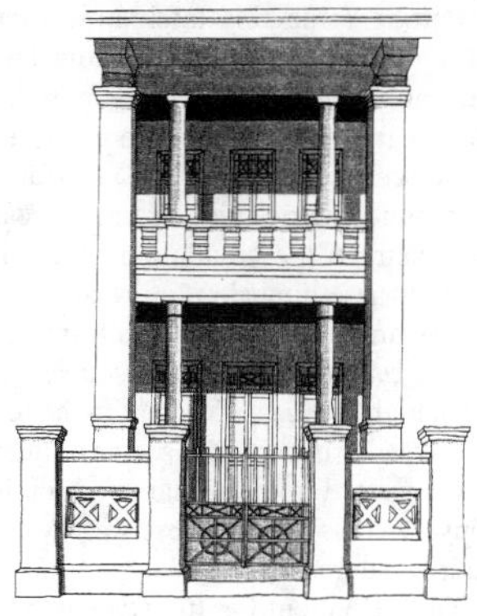
Art Deco Shophouse
(No 30 Bukit Pasoh Road)

Early Shophouse
(Nos 7-13 Erskine Road)

Chinese shophouses

was a reaction to the flamboyant exuberance of the Late Shophouse style or, perhaps, architects were starting to be influenced by Art Deco. The **Art Deco** style also dates from the 1930s and buildings in this style continued to be built into the1960s. Geometric elements were employed and many of these buildings had plaques dating them, which makes identification that much simpler.

The Peranakan house The houses of the Peranakan or Straits Chinese (Babas) were distinct from those of the Chinese. A traditional Peranakan house was long and thin. The first room on entering was the reception hall, where guests were received and the household shrine was kept. Traditionally the room was decked out with heavy blackwood chairs and tables set around the walls. Walking deeper into the house the next room was the ancestral hall, a private place where only close family and friends could enter. The ancestral shrine was housed here. As a family rather than a formal room, the mixture of furniture might well have been eclectic – a clutter of tables, chairs, photographs, portraits and mirrors. Beyond the airwell, there was a living room, where the family could relax and sit and create their distinctive embroidery pieces. Again, the furniture would have been varied with, for example, planters' chairs, Art Deco furniture and Chinese blackwood cabinets. At the back of the house was the kitchen (or *perot rumah* – the stomach of the house) and beyond the kitchen, the bridal chamber, the focal point of the 12-day wedding celebrations. The bridal chamber housed elaborately carved 'red and gold' namwood furniture. Three important ceremonies take place here during the 12 days of celebration. The first is known as *chin pang*, when the veiled bride leads her groom into the bridal chamber and he unveils her. The second is the *makan choon tok*, when the bride serves food and drink to her groom. When weddings were the result of matchmaking, this would have been the first occasion the bride and groom would have had contact with each other. The third ceremony is the *chianh sia*, when friends of the groom gather to tease the bride in an attempt to make her laugh. If they succeed, the groom must provide some sort of treat to all present. The clothes of the traditional Peranakan bride were works of art. For example the *sapu tangan*, an ornamental handkerchief worn on the

Bungalows

bride's finger, is exquisitely embroidered and embellished with metallic beads and sequins, silk and velvet applique.

The **bungalow** Apart from the plethora of shophouses, there are a few remaining examples of one and (later) 2-storey bungalows. The word is derived from the Bengali word *bangla* or *bangala*. However there is some dispute over the meaning of *bangla*. The URA maintains that it refers to the traditional mud-walled houses of Bengal, but other sources hazard that it only means "Bengali House". They point out that the adjective 'of or belonging to Bengal' is often pronounced *bangla* and it is unlikely that *bangla* was used by local people to describe their own houses.

Putting aside this fascinating foray into the origins of the word, bungalows were built by the British in Singapore and Malaya from the 1830s. The early versions were one storey affairs, raised off the ground on brick piers or timber posts to encourage the circulation of air. In general these bungalows were arranged on a symmetrical plan, with a front portico (*anjung*) and verandah (*serambi gantung*), high ceilings, a kitchen to the rear (the *kapor* or *dapor*), and servants' quarters separated from the main body of the house. Access to the house was by two external staircases.

The URA identifies five styles of bungalow corresponding (roughly) with five periods of construction. The simple **Early Bungalow** had its heyday during the 1860s and it shows clear links with British protoypes, though with various tropical environment adaptations including a verandah and timber or brick supporting piers. The **Victorian Bungalow** emerged in the 1870s. These were more solidly built, incorporating load-bearing brick walls, and were also usually considerably larger. Decorative flourishes became more pronounced with turrets, ornamental columns, iron work and fussy plasterwork. The beginning of the 20th century saw the emergence of the so-called **Black & White Bungalow**, named after the black exposed half timbers. This type of bungalow excluded all ornamentation and reverted to the use of a verandah encircling the house. The **Art Deco Bungalow** emerged in the late 1920s. This style saw the use of concrete, with classical motifs. The layout of the house changed during this period. With an emphasis on family living, the kitchen and the servants' quarters were brought into the main house. Both this and the final **Early Modern style**, which appeared in the 1950s, were strongly horizontal in design, sometimes with flat roofs and curved corners. Examples of these distinctive bungalow styles, combining European Classical, Chinese and

Malay elements, can be seen behind Orchard Road and on River Valley Road.

Chinese temples

The Chinese temple form is based on that of a traditional Chinese house or palace and is a grouping of pavilions around open courtyards – this method of constructing Chinese temples has changed little over the centuries. Chinese builders are also bound by the strict principles of Yin and Yang, and the complicated nuances of Chinese geomancy or *feng shui*. To do otherwise is to court catastrophe. Even in modern Singapore, feng shui plays an important role in architectural design. *Feng* means 'wind' and *shui* means 'water'. Chinese superstition dictates that the 'dragon' must be able to breathe life into any building and that doors, walls and furniture must be aligned according to the principles of geomancy to prevent good spirits, wealth and harmony flowing out. There must be running water nearby too. If a building in Singapore does not meet the feng shui criteria it is extremely rare for a Chinese to live there. All the big hotels and office blocks are designed with feng shui in mind; expensive alterations are made to buildings that do not have the required qualities. New buildings are also opened on auspicious days. The classic case of this was the towering OUB Centre in Raffles Place. Its construction was completed in 1986, but its official opening was delayed until 8 August 1988 (8-8-88), which translated into quadruple good luck.

Promotion of the arts

As part of its effort to transform Singapore into Southeast Asia's Centre for the Arts, the government announced a plan at the end of 1994 to invest US$300 million in a new arts centre (on the waterfront by the Padang), to be opened by 2000. This is unlikely to mean that the City State will become a centre for avant-garde art – mainstream artistic endeavour is likely to be the emphasis. Nonetheless, Singapore is not the artistic wilderness that some present it to be and some literature is daring and faintly subversive. For example, in September 1994 Philip Jeyaretnam published *Abraham's promise*, an excellent novel about a teacher whose life is ruined when he falls foul of the ruling party. It is hard to believe that the fact that Philip Jeyaretnam's father is Joshua Jeyaretnam, better known as the opposition politician JBJ who was bankrupted by former prime minister Lee Kuan Yew and publicly disgraced, is a coincidence. The book, though, has been published by a Singaporean publisher (Times Books), and it has been favourably reviewed – even by the *Straits Times*, which the novel caricatures critically.

CULTURE

PEOPLE

"Probably at no other place in the world are so many different nationalities represented as at Singapore, where one hears a babel of tongues, although Malay is the lingua franca, and rubs shoulders 'with all sorts and conditions of men' – with opulent Chinese Towkays in grey felt hat, nankeen jacket, and capacious trousers; Straits-born Babas as proud as Lucifer; easy-going Malays in picturesque sarong and baju; stately Sikhs from the garrison; lanky Bengalis; ubiquitous Jews in old-time gabardine; exorbitant Chetties with closely-shaven heads and muslin-swathed limbs; Arabs in long coat and fez; Tamil street labourers in turban and loin cloth of lurid hue; Kling hawkers scantily clad; Chinese coolies and itinerant vendors of food; Javanese, Achinese, Sinhalese, and a host of others – in fact, the kaleidoscopic procession is one of almost endless variety."

Wright (1908) *Information for tourists*.

Today, 77% of Singapore's population are of Chinese extraction, 14% are Malay, 7% Indian, and the remaining 2% belong to other races, including Eurasian. The government has worked hard to stop

Population policies and designer genes

One of the government's key social programmes during the 1970s was an effort to slow the country's spiralling birth rate by family planning. The policy proved to be so successful, however, that declining fertility rates forced a policy U-turn in the mid-1980s. The government is concerned that by 2030, one fifth of Singapore's population will be aged 65 or over. But racial concerns appear to have been an even greater motivating factor. Apparently driven by fears that the Malay population was growing faster than the Chinese population, the government scrapped the old slogan 'Stop at Two', and replaced it with 'Go for Three'. It offered generous tax incentives to induce Singaporeans to have more children. At the same time, former Prime Minister Lee Kuan Yew instigated the selective 'breeding for brilliance' campaign, which sought to mobilize the latent talent in Singapore's limited gene-pool. He promoted procreation among the more prosperous and better-educated members of Singapore society. In 1983 he warned that if something was not done: "Levels of competence will decline, our economy will falter, the administration will suffer and society will decline." These were ominous portents of the future but Lee's genetic engineering policy was very unpopular and prompted mocking disbelief abroad. Once, when regaling Britain's Princess Royal on the virtues of eugenics, she reportedly retorted: "Very interesting Prime Minister, but I can tell you, it doesn't work with horses".

The policy was officially shelved in 1985, but this did not stop Lee continuing to propound it. Lee himself got a double first at Cambridge (with a distinction) and his wife got a first; together they have produced highly intelligent offspring. In his landmark national day speech before stepping down as Prime Minister in 1990 Lee noted with satisfaction that more male graduates had married female graduates during the 1980s. He remained concerned, however, that highly educated women were not having superior babies because of Singapore men's apparent "immature" preference for younger, less-well educated girls. He said that Singapore's female graduates face "the stark option of marrying downwards, marrying foreigners or staying unmarried." Despite the fact that the smart baby policy was officially withdrawn, the pairing-off of educated people has remained an unofficial objective on the government agenda.

Singapore's drive to reverse its declining birth rate has had its amusing moments. Senior government ministers regularly attend baby shows and talk of procreation

Singaporeans thinking of themselves as Chinese, Malays or Indians; it wants them to think of themselves as Singaporeans. The republic's 'ambassador-at-large', Professor Tommy Koh (who also heads the government think-tank) wrote in 1991: "The primordial pull of race dominates ... group identity, but for most Singaporeans, especially the younger Singaporeans, their racial identity is weaker than their group identity as Singaporeans. The fact that this has been achieved in 25 years is a remarkable example of nation-building." As Prime Minister Goh Chok Tong once pointed out, in the space of 25 years, Singaporeans have been British subjects, Japanese subjects, Malaysians and now Singaporeans.

Singapore likes to take Switzerland as its model, because Switzerland has a Swiss identity that supersedes the separate German, French and Italian ethnic and cultural influences. The difference is that Switzerland has been a confederation for 700 years. Critics of the Singapore government have voiced concern as if it were an industry. Baby output is currently estimated to be about 50,000 units a year. Meanwhile, the local press has continued to sing the joys of parenthood and the Social Development Unit – the government funded computer match-making agency – is forever dreaming up new schemes for getting people (particularly, bright people) together. The head of the SDU – better known as 'Chief Cupid' – organizes discos, barbecues, computer courses and harbour cruises in the SDU 'love boat'. The SDU – which wags have dubbed Single, Desperate and Ugly – has 13,000 clients.

Each client is offered 90 computer dates over 5 years. In 1991, 1,643 pairs of college graduates married, up from 704 pairs in 1984. More than half of male graduates now marry fellow graduates, compared with 38% 10 years ago. One of the hottest-selling books in 1993 has been the Ministry of Community Development's *Preparing for Marriage*. In Jun, a Chinese-language edition rolled off the presses, offering tips on how to woo in the vernacular. The government is behind the matrimonial rush in more ways than one. Women have to be 35 or over to qualify for their own Housing Development Board flats. Marriage therefore offers a means of escaping parental homes.

From time to time the SDU organizes mass-weddings, with young couples with 'O' level qualifications in one batch, and 'A' level couples in the next. These ceremonies involve the newly weds promenading down red carpets with dry ice billowing around them for that 'head-in-the-clouds' effect. Singapore Broadcasting has chipped in with a local version of *Blind Date*. Yet despite the substantial tax incentives on offer to parents who produce more babies, Singapore's population is only growing slowly.

As if to underscore his residual angst over his breeding hang-ups, Lee raised the whole subject again in May 1994 during a tour of Australia. He said in Sydney that he regretted ever giving Singaporean women equal educational and employment status way back in 1960. He said the price for having a generation of highly qualified, confident female graduates, was that men won't marry them. It was a stinging condemnation of the Asian male who, said Lee, "does not like to have a wife who is seen to be equal at work and who may be earning as much if not more than he does. He is not wearing the pants. That is an enormous loss of face." Apoplectic Singaporean women graduates bombarded *The Straits Times* with letters, saying Singapore ought to be proud of this achievement.

over the 'Sinification' of Singapore and fear that in the long term, resentment in minority communities could turn Singapore into a Sri Lanka instead. The spectre of ethnic unrest, however, is far from being a reality. Today, Singaporeans are affluent and their prosperity has largely distracted them from ethnic prejudices. Even the Malays (see below) are, on average, better off in Singapore than they are in Malaysia, and the Indians have no doubts. Goh Chok Tong said in 1991: "So long as the economy is growing, there is plenty for everybody, I don't think people will fight over small things. But if the pie is shrinking, that will be the real test of whether we are cohesive, solid or whether we are fragile".

Historian Mary Turnbull writes that "as a largely Chinese city state in an alien region [Singapore] could not afford to build up a cultural Sino-nationalism. Its salvation lay in a secular, multi-racial statehood, encouraging communities to take pride in their cultural roots and language but conforming to a common national character." The government's efforts at forging this national character have been professionally stage-managed. On National Day every year crowds of cheer-leaders repeatedly sing "One people, one nation, one Singapore" as if trying to convince themselves that they do have a national identity. But as the older first-generation immigrants have died off, the proportion of Singapore-born Singaporeans has risen, which has helped towards building a sense of nationhood. More than 80% of the population is now Singapore-born. Today, national pride is not in question: Singaporeans rarely tire of boasting to visitors that they have the best airline in the world, the best airport in the world, the busiest port in the world and one of the fastest growing economies in the world.

Although it is common to read that Singapore is a (largely) Chinese city state, the **Chinese population** is not homogeneous in its origins. The four main dialect groups to set sail from China and settle in Singapore were the Hokkiens, Teochews, Cantonese and Hakkas. But before them came the so-called **Straits Chinese** or **Peranakan Cina** – popularly known as the Babas. The Peranakan Chinese are Singapore's – and Malaysia's – most distinctive group and were labelled "Straits Chinese" because of their association with the Straits settlements of Singapore, Melaka and Penang. Today, however, 'Baba' is largely used with reference to the Singapore and Melaka populations. Tan Chee-Beng in *Chinese Peranakan heritage in Malaysia and Singapore* (1993) sums up the Peranakan identity in these words:

> "The image of 'Baba' is really one of both acculturation and cultural persistence, best symbolized by speaking Malay and practising or taking pride in Chinese customs such as 'old-fashioned' Chinese weddings. Thus the Baba identity is really an indigenized Chinese identity. The Baba experience is one of both being indigenous and being Chinese at the same time."

For more details on the history and culture of the Peranakan Cina see page 62.

The **Malays** in modern Singapore are considered a downtrodden minority, despite the government's stated efforts to build a multi-racial society. While Malay is still the country's official language, the Malays themselves have been subsumed by the dominant Chinese culture and they complain of feeling alienated in their own country. Malays have not taken to living in tower blocks – they are kampung people by nature – and within Singaporean society, they are regarded as under-achievers, particularly in business and finance, where the Chinese reign supreme. This becomes most obvious when an embarrassing fuss is made of Malays who succeed in the academic world or as professionals. Today Singapore's Malay community has a poorer academic record in school, a higher drug addiction rate and less economic muscle than any other community. Malay (and Indian) community leaders have criticized the government's 'Speak Mandarin' campaign as racially divisive.

Ironically, however, the roots of Malay nationalism, that led eventually to calls for independence from the British, were first planted in Singapore. In 1926 the *Kesatuan Melayu Singapura* (KMS), or Singapore Malay Union, was founded by the 'father of Malay journalism' Mohammad Eunos bin Abdullah. He was Singapore's first Malay legislative councillor and magistrate, having been educated at the élite English-language Raffles Institution. The KMS set up branches in the peninsula and was the forerunner of the United Malays National Organization (UMNO) which has been at the helm of the Malaysian government since independence.

Of Singapore's population, 7.2%, or 215,000 (1995) are **Indian**. In 1824 when the first census was undertaken 7% of the (much smaller – just 10,683) population were also Indian and Indians have always played an important role in economy and society. When Raffles stepped ashore in 1819 he did so with 120 Indian sepoys and several Indian clerks in tow. An Indian trader also accompanied Raffles. To begin with Indian immigrants arrived under their own initiative from Penang, or directly from Sri Lanka or India. They took up jobs in the civil service, but also played roles as traders, teachers and engineers.

Kiasu and Kiasuism

From the early 1990s Singaporeans began to talk about the trait of *kiasu* and kiasuism. The word comes from the Hokkien, the most widely spoken Chinese dialect, and means 'fear of losing out' or 'scared to lose'. In *Singapore state of the art* it is defined as a "pathological fear of losing even the most minute of advantages". As the cartoon character Mr Kiasu explains "Better grab first, later no more". This philosophy of life can be seen in action in buffets across the city. Plates are piled high with food, far too much to eat, yet the fear of missing something, of not having as much as the next person, drives the average Singaporean to defy gravity as they build their edifices of victuals. Mr Kiasu is not just scared of missing out. He is also brash, obnoxious and rude. Yet the cartoons are required reading in Singapore and the cartoon books – the first was titled *Everything also I want* – repeatedly top the best seller lists. Mr Kiasu is a commercial success. Companies use him to promote their products. McDonald's designed a kiasuburger – where the chicken pattie was larger than the bun (and even had extra sesame seeds): 1.2 million were sold in 8 weeks.

Even the government has embraced Mr Kiasu in road safety and other public service campaigns – while at the same time urging people not to over-load their buffet plates. David Chan argues, though, that *kiasu* means more than just a fear of missing out. It is also equals conformity; the herd instinct where if the person next door is rushing out to buy some electronic gadget then it must be good and must be bought, preferably several times. In the *Not the Singapore song book* (see page 611) there is a song titled *Oh my kiasu*, sung to the tune of *Oh my Clementine*. It runs:

Mr Kiasu, Kiasu King,
Scared to lose out, always must win;
Number One in everything!
Grab first; don't talk,
Always jump queue,
Help yourself to sample things.
Look for discounts, free is better,
Never mind what they all think!
Must not give face,
Winner takes all,
Hamtam [Singlish for pulverize]
  everyone you know.
Take but don't give, hide the best things;
Get there first or else don't go!
Always quit while you are ahead.
Pushing helps to set the pace.
I want! Give me! First in all things!
That's the way to win the race!

Within 4 years of its establishment Singapore became a penal colony and several hundred Indian convicts arrived and laboured on public works projects. Many more, mostly from South India, came under the system of indentured labouring. This was banned in 1910 after widespread criticism of its abuses. From 1910 until the early 1950s when controls on immigration were introduced, there was a continuing flow of migrants from the subcontinent. Today something like 80% of Singapore's Indian population are South Indian in origin.

Singapore, unlike all the other countries of the region, was an 'artificial' creation. There was no great kingdom, no indigenous civilization, no tradition on which the colonial power could build. Singapore, as the anthropologist KW Kwok has put it "was born into modernity". The cultures that made up the entrepôt initially looked over their shoulders to China, India or Britain for cultural inspiration. Gradually their children learned other languages and, arguably, a new Singaporean emerged from the formerly plural society. This is reflected in the government's emphasis on the '4 Ms' – multiracialism, multilingualism, multiculturalism and multireligiosity. The communities that make up the Republic are allowed to maintain their identity and distinctiveness, and each is equal to the next. But, individual identity is allied with the discipline of national interest.

Most accounts of Singapore maintain the 'ethnic melting pot' angle to the country's population. However, there is also a sense in which a 'new' Singaporean is emerging, one who is a product of the years since independence and who has been moulded into a distinctive personality. Philip Jeyaretnam, one of Singapore's most talented young novelists and author of *Abraham's promise* (1994), argues:

> "... the true subject in Singapore is fear: of being thought different, of our true selves, of our neighbours, of those in power ... This fear has found its natural ally in materialism. The accumulation of goods has been both a bribe for political conformity, as well as the only approved outlet for expression."

As a visitor, it is comparatively easy to see Jeyaretnam's views being played out on the streets, in the shopping plazas, and in the restaurants of the city. In the region, Singaporeans are often considered pushy and rude. Never a place to eschew a buzzword to support some public programme or other, the latest cry from the top is that Singaporeans should learn to be more 'gracious'. Graciousness, presumably, is meant to counteract the supposed Singapore trait of *kiasu* (see box).

RELIGION

Nearly 60% of Singapore's population follow what is usually termed **'Chinese religion'**. This is an amalgum of **Mahayana Buddhism**, **Taoism** (Taoists follow the teachings of Mencius and Lao Zi and practice ancestor worship), some Confucianism, all seasoned with a good dash of spirit worship. But this is not to say that every Chinese worships these religions in equal amounts and there is considerable variation in practise, reflecting the influence of other religions and growing secularization, not to mention the different traditions of the regions of China.

Although the bulk of Singapore's Chinese population can be grouped under the loose heading 'Chinese religion', other religions have had a significant impact. Of these, Islam has made the shallowest inroads among the Chinese (although the Malay population as well as a significant proportion of Indians are Muslim) probably because it is hard for the polytheistic Chinese to embrace a strictly monotheistic religion, especially one with dietary prohibitions against the eating and drinking of pork and alcohol. Hinduism has made rather deeper inroads, but most important has been the influence of Christianity which has gained many converts, especially among the better educated. Evangelical and charismatic Christianity are particularly strong in Singapore.

Chinese **popular folk religion** is based on the premise that the spirits of the dead who throng the heavens in countless numbers are controlled and governed by a judicial bureaucracy that mirrors the earthly bureaucracy of Imperial China. Multiple gaudy images of these officials – usually denoted 'gods' by most Westerners – are found in Chinese temples. Historically they may have been folk heroes, figures from Chinese mythology or history, or even emperors. They are imbued with divine powers and wisdom and these powers can be harnessed to bring good fortune, cure illnesses, or ward off evil, for instance. However the gods are also sufficiently 'human' to become upset or annoyed by events and therefore need to be assiduously cultivated and their egos continuously massaged. The 'gods' reflect life in Imperial China in another sense: a commoner couldn't possibly deal face-to-face with a real emperor and the same is true of haughty celestial emperors. This is where the cosmic officials come in: they act as go-betweens, conveying the wishes of earthly worshippers to the emperors.

There are two groups of emperor gods worshipped in Chinese temples. First, there are the figures from Chinese mythology. These include the **Three Mythical Sage Emperors**, Fu Xi (the Emperor of Heaven), Shen Nong (the Emperor of Earth) and Huang Di (the Emperor of Humanity). **Fu Xi** is said to have ruled China between 2953 and 2838 BC and brought order to a chaotic world. He was effectively the foundation emperor of China, socialising the people of the kingdom. **Shen Nong** took over from Fu Xi in 2838 BC and he reigned for an improbable 140 years until 2698 BC. Shen Nong's reputation lies in his agricultural abilities. These helped change China from a land of hunter-gatherers to a kingdom of farmers and as a result he is regarded as the patron god of farmers. For the record, Shen Nong is also the patron god of herbalists, potters, restauranteurs and dung dealers. Fu Xi and Shen Nong are usually depicted as clean-shaven Oriental cavemen, crouching down on rocks with unkempt hair (or bald) and dressed in skirts of leaves. They sometimes have a scar running down the middle of their heads and often two protrusions as if horns are about to burst through their skulls.

Huang Di is also known as the **Yellow Emperor** and he gained the throne after Shen Nong's death in 2698. He reigned for a comparatively modest 101 years – until 2597 BC. He is also reputed to have imbibed the elixir of everlasting life after the vital essence of no less than 1,200 women had been distilled into a peculiarly effective high proof drug. This gave him the time to invent a whole host of useful inventions from the compass to the wheeled-vehicle. Fortunately for China's womanhood he died before the country had been completed depopulated of the female sex. Huang Di is usually represented as one would expect an earthly emperor: rich, gilded clothes, usually with a flat-topped crown, and a beaded veil hanging down over his eyes.

Fu, Shen and Huang were succeeded by a second group of rulers known as the **Three Emperors from the Dawn of History – Shun, Yao** and **Yu**. These men are regarded as almost without flaw and the first two were creatures of myth and legend. In Chinese temples there are usually grouped together as the Three Rulers. Of the three, Yu is probably the most important and he is usually depicted bearded, sitting on a throne, and holding two stone tablets, one in each arm. Yu is probably a real historic figure, the first emperor of the Xia Dynasty, coming to the throne in 2202 BC and ruling for just 8 years.

In addition to these emperors from Chinese mythology, temples also contain images of **dynastic emperors from Chinese history**. These are many and varied and date from the dawn of Chinese history through to the 20th century. Although Mao Zedong and Chiang Kai-shek have not been deified they are 'worshipped' in mainland China and Taiwan respectively. The importance of these emperors is that they can bestow gifts or good fortune on supplicants.

The forebears of the majority of Chinese in Singapore (and Malaysia) came from southern China, particularly Fukien and Guangdong provinces, and the brand of religion practised in Singapore shows clear links with this region of China. One of the most characteristic aspects of Chinese religion in Singapore is the custom of ***chih poeh*** – divination using bamboo or wooden spatulas. It is thought that this custom originated during the Han or T'ang dynasties when coins were used instead of sticks.

Among the gods worshipped in Chinese temples in Singapore one of the more important is ***Ta-po-kung***, the **God of the Soil**. It is thought that *Ta-po-kung* was a local god worshipped by the Hakka of Kwangtung. Statues of the god were placed in homes and he brought luck and good fortune to the family members. In Singapore (and Malaysia) he is sometimes worshipped in conjunction with a Malay god, *Datok* (meaning, approximately, 'chief' in Malay). This confused character is named *Datok Kung* and he is usually found at the foot of a large tree. The best known *Datok Kung* temple in Singapore is on Kusu Island (see page 674). In the past it was not uncommon to see images of *Datok Kung* in rubber plantations and at tin mines. He is usually depicted bearded and smiling.

Islam is practised by virtually all Malays as well as many Indians – in total, Muslims comprise 15% of the population. Singaporean Muslims are under the authority of the *Majlis Ugama Islam Singapura* (MUIS) – the Islamic Religious Council of Singapore – which advises the government on all matters Islamic. For details on Islam as practised in the Malay archipelago, see page 72.

Christians account for nearly 13% of the population, about 60% of whom are Protestants. Christian missionaries arrived in Singapore within a year of Raffles founding the city. Hindus make up 4% of the population and the most important Hindu shrine is the Sri Mariamman Temple in South Bridge Road, which was built in 1827 (see page 649). There are also nine Sikh *Gurdwara* (temples) in Singapore and two Jewish synagogues.

Following the government's allegations in 1988 that the Roman Catholic church had been infiltrated by Marxists (see page 604), the government introduced the Maintenance of Religious Harmony Act, which totally barred the mixing of politics and religion. It also introduced very strict rules regarding inter-religious proselytization. Evangelical Christians, for example, were banned – on pain of imprisonment – from any sort of missionary work in the Muslim community, which had been outraged by Christians passing Muslims tracts and leaflets on Christianity. The bill also banned the teaching of any religion in schools. The government is acutely aware of the need to remain a secular state and is extremely wary of anything it perceives as 'fundamentalist' and as a threat to ethnic harmony.

LANGUAGE

There are four official languages in Singapore: Malay, English, Chinese and Tamil. Malay is still officially the national language. English is the language of administration and business. This means there are very few Singaporeans who do not speak it – although Singaporean English (commonly known as 'Singlish') is virtually a dialect in itself (see page 720). Since 1979, the government has enthusiastically promoted the use of Mandarin – probably in the hope that Singaporeans who are bilingual in Mandarin and English will provide a bridge between the west and China. Mandarin is increasingly being used instead of Chinese dialects.

Although minority communities might regard the 'Speak Mandarin' campaign as evidence of Chinese cultural dominance, it is not uncommon to find even Tamil children in Singapore who are fluent in Mandarin. Today 46% of the population is literate in two or more languages. The main Chinese dialects still spoken in Singapore include Hokkien, Teochew, Cantonese, Hakka, Hainanese and Foochow. About 80% of Singapore's Indians are Tamil, but other Indian languages are spoken, including Punjabi, Malayalam, Telegu, Hindi and Bengali.

DANCE, DRAMA AND MUSIC

The Ministry for Information and the Arts was created in 1990; it was immediately dubbed 'the ministry of fun' and is presided over by a senior cabinet minister. The intention is to make Singapore into a cultural and entertainment hub and no expense has been spared in bringing art exhibitions and top stage acts – theatre, dance and music – to the republic as well as promoting the arts within Singapore.

The Singapore Symphony Orchestra gives regular performances – including many free open-air shows in the Botanic Gardens – and the National Theatre Trust promotes cultural dance performances and local theatre as well as inviting international dance and theatre groups to Singapore.

Traditional Chinese street operas (*wayang*) mostly take place during the seventh lunar month, following the Festival of the Hungry Ghosts (see page 723). Wayangs are regularly staged on makeshift wooden platforms which are erected in vacant lots all over the city. To the sound of clashing cymbals and drums, the wayang actors – adorned in ornate costumes and with faces painted – act out the roles of gods, goddesses, heroes, heroines, sages and villains from Chinese folklore. Many professional wayang troupes are freelancers who come from Malaysia and Hong Kong to perform.

MODERN SINGAPORE

POLITICS

In 1965, the newly independent Republic of Singapore committed itself to non-Communist, multi-racial, democratic socialist government and secured Malaysian cooperation in trade and defence. The new government faced what most observers considered impossible: forging a viable economy in a densely populated micro-state with no natural resources. At first Singapore hoped for readmission to the Malaysian Federation, but as Lee surprised everyone by presiding over one of the fastest-growing economies in the world, the republic soon realized that striking out alone was the best approach. Within a few years, independent Singapore was being hailed as an 'economic miracle'. Nonetheless, the government had to work hard to forge a sense of nationhood (see page 598). Because most Singaporeans were still more interested in wealth creation than in politics, the government became increasingly paternalistic, declaring that it knew what was best for the people, and because most people agreed, few raised any objections.

Singapore's foreign policy has been built around regional cooperation. It was a founder member in 1967 of the Association of Southeast Asian Nations (ASEAN) and has also been a leading light in the wider Asia-Pacific Economic Cooperation (APEC) grouping. Friendly international relations are considered of paramount importance for a state which relies so heavily on foreign trade and which, in terms of size and population, is a minnow among giants. Although Singapore continued to trade with the former Communist states of Eastern Europe and the Soviet Union throughout the period of the Cold War, Lee had a great fear and loathing of Communism. At home, 'Communists' became bogeymen; 'hard-core' subversives were imprisoned without trial, under emergency legislation enshrined in the Internal Security Act, a legacy of the British colonial administration.

Singapore's political stability since independence, which has helped attract foreign investors to the island, has been tempered by the government's tendency

Harry Lee Kuan Yew – the father of modern Singapore

British political scientist Michael Leifer once described Lee Kuan Yew – better known as 'Harry' or 'LKY' – as "a political superman of his time, albeit in charge of a metropolis". The father of modern Singapore, who finally stepped down after 31 years as Prime Minister in 1990, believed he knew what was best for his country. Partly because of the Confucian ethic of respect for one's elders, and partly because his policies worked wonders, Singaporeans, by and large, assigned their fate to Harry Lee's better judgement. To western observers, Lee was variously cast as a miracle-worker, a classic benevolent dictator, and, in some quarters, as a tyrant. British newspaper columnist Bernard Levin (who writes for *The Times*, London) became one of Lee's most outspoken critics. Just a few months before his resignation, Levin wrote "Today, his rule is based on a frenzied determination to allow no one in his realm to defy him, from which it follows that those who dare to do so, even in the smallest particular, must be crushed and having been crushed must be indefinitely pursued with an implacable and crazed vindictiveness". To a point, what Levin wrote was true – Lee did not suffer his critics or political opponents gladly.

But by his own hand, Lee turned tiny Singapore into a by-word for excellence, efficiency and high-achievement. In his 3 decades in power, Lee built Singapore into a powerful economy, but his authoritarian style also turned Singaporeans – western commentators often say – into timid citizens. In 1991 London's *Financial Times* wrote that Lee's laudable achievements had been "at the cost of creating an antiseptic and dull society which leaves little room for individual creativity or imagination..." *The Economist* put it more succinctly, saying that "Lee ran Singapore like a well-managed nursery". He has been compared with a master-watchmaker who built the perfect timepiece, but could not resist the temptation of constantly taking it apart again and rebuilding it, to see if it could be improved. By the late 1980s, the electorate's swing against Lee's ruling People's Action Party and its controversial policies (such as the 'breeding for brilliance' campaign – see page 596) suggested that the people were sick of the constant retuning. They were ready for change.

Harry Lee Kuan Yew was born on 16 September 1923. While his family was of Hakka Chinese origin, his parents were Straits-born Peranakan Chinese (see page 230) who had lived in the Straits Settlements for several generations. At home he grew up speaking English, Malay and Cantonese. He was the eldest son and was accorded all the privileges of a male first-born. But despite ingraining Singaporeans with the Confucian ethic of filial piety, Lee Kuan Yew himself did not like his father. In 1936 he attended the prestigious Raffles Institution. Even as a schoolboy, Lee was known for his aggressive streak and his domineering personality, according to his unauthorized biographer, James Minchin, in *No Man is an Island*. Minchin wrote: "Since coming to office, Lee has tended to indulge his instinct to bully and demolish ... Power mostly removes the humiliation of being bested. Within this dominant characteristic of aggression we may trace elements of rage, fear and self-aggrandisement".

In World War Two Lee worked as a functionary for the Japanese occupying forces, but by the end of it he had become determined that Singapore should never to stifle criticism. The media are state-owned and are so pro-government that they have become self-censoring. Foreign publications are summarily banned or their circulation restricted if they are deemed to be meddling in (ie critical of) Singapore's internal affairs. Probably because Lee Kuan Yew's People's Action

again be ruled by foreigners. After the war he went to London (which he hated), and soon abandoned an economics degree at the London School of Economics. He was then accepted by Cambridge University to study law – the same department as his future wife, Kwa Geok Choo. They both graduated in 1949 with first class honours, although Lee got a distinction. On returning to Singapore they married and set up a law firm, Lee and Lee. He became increasingly involved in politics and resigned as a partner in the firm when he became Prime Minister in 1959. His brother Denis took over and the company is still operating today. Lee proved to be a shrewd political operator – characterizing himself as an 'Anglified Chinaman' – and quickly became known for his traits of honesty, efficiency, firmness and intolerance. As a political leader, he was able to inspire both confidence and fear.

Lee was known for his disciplined, austere lifestyle; he exercises regularly (ever since his days at Cambridge, he has enjoyed playing golf); he watches his diet carefully and steers clear of anyone with a cold. He has fetishes about cleanliness and health. His private residence on Oxley Rise is guarded by Gurkha soldiers. One of Lee's most telling speeches, which gives some insight into his personal philosophy was given in 1973. He said: "The greatest satisfaction in life comes from achievement. To achieve is to be happy. Singaporeans must be imbued with this spirit. We must never get into the vicious cycle of expecting more and more for less and less ... Solid satisfaction comes out of achievement ... It generates inner or spiritual strength, a strength which grows out of an inner discipline."

Despite stepping down as Prime Minister in 1990, Lee retains the post of Senior Minister in Prime Minister Goh Chok Tong's cabinet. He is now Southeast Asia's best-known elder statesman and Singapore is too small for him. There has been joking speculation that he wanted to be a mercenary prime minister somewhere else: what better for China than to have Lee Kuan Yew at the helm?

In the run-up to his 'retirement', Lee pushed through a controversial constitutional amendment allowing for Singapore's future presidents to be elected, rather than appointed. As President Wee Kim Wee's term neared expiry in late 1993, speculation mounted that Lee would stand. In the event, he didn't; former deputy prime minister Ong Teng Cheong got the job. Some say Lee did not contest the election because he had been stung by criticism that the change was simply a device for him to retain his grip on power. But he has not ruled out standing in future elections. The next presidential election will be in 1999 when Lee will be 75 – by Asian standards that would still be an acceptable age to assume office. But whether he decides to run or not is almost irrelevant; few doubt that he will remain the power behind the throne. In his 1988 National Day speech, the old puppet master gave his most definitive statement on his future intentions. "Even from my sickbed, even if you are going to lower me into the grave and I feel that something is wrong, I'll get up". Singaporeans joked that with his new threat of resurrection, the old visionary had begun to cast himself in the messianic mould.

The Asian way

There has been a great deal of debate recently about the so-called 'Asian Way'. The low crime levels in Singapore are favourably contrasted with the war zones that constitute the centres of some US cities, and it has been asked whether the West in general has allowed the rights of individuals to undermine those of wider society to such an extent that the protection of the majority has been ignored. In short, an abstract principle has got in the way of common sense.

The inability to stop, let alone reverse, the seeming inexorable rise in crime in the West is contrasted with the apparent peaceful situation in Asia. Have Asians got it right? Is the West, as former Prime Minister of Singapore Lee Kuan Yew appears to believe, decadent and rotten to its very core? It is on this basis that Asian values are promoted and a great deal of collective navel gazing has ensued.

Asian values – often thought to be Confucianist – are seen to embody such things as respect for elders and the law, hardwork, and recognition that the needs of society may transcend those of the individual. Former Singapore Prime Minister Lee Kuan Yew, for example, has explained: "A Confucianist view of order between subject and ruler – this helps in the rapid transformation of society ... in other words, you fit yourself into society – the exact opposite of the American rights of the individual." These values are reflected, so the argument goes, in rapid economic growth, low crime rates, stability and rising prosperity. Unfortunately, or perhaps fortunately, this view of Asia, and of the Asian success story, is hugely simplistic.

First, Asia is so diverse that to talk about a single set of Asian values is nonsense. Even 'Confucianism' as currently presented bears little relation to the sage's *The Analects* written in the 5th century BC. When Asian politicians try to summarize what Asian Values are all about they risk descending into pronouncements of such crassness as to be almost embarrassing. Second, Asia is not crimeless. Singapore has a low crime rate (Asian commentator Ian Buruma defines the city state as a "huge tropical boarding school", easy to police by the 'nanny' state there), but the murder rate in Thailand is, in fact, higher than in the US. While at the same time

Party (PAP) has been so successful at bringing about the economic miracle, no credible political opposition has emerged. Politicians who have stood out against Lee's and since 1990 Goh Chok Tong's benevolent but autocratic style of government, have been effectively silenced as the government sets about undermining their credibility in the eyes of the electorate. For 13 years, between 1968 and 1981, the PAP held every single seat in parliament. The London-based Economist Intelligence Unit says: "Opposition to the ruling party and its ideals of strength through economic achievement is welcomed in theory but not in practice. Those who criticise the government are, in such a small community, both visible and vulnerable."

Through the late 1980s and into the 1990s the PAP did lose support, however – although it has always maintained a large majority in Parliament. In the 1984 election there was a 13% swing against the PAP, and support declined further in the elections of 1988 and 1991. The general election in October 1991 – which was meant to provide an endorsement for Goh's 'more caring' brand of government – saw the election of four opposition candidates to parliament, up from just one in 1988. Perhaps another sign that the PAP was in danger of losing its way came with the presidential election of August 1993, which was billed as a PAP stitch-up. Virtually all observers predicted that the result would be a foregone conclusion. In the event, the favoured candidate, former countries like China, Hong Kong and Japan face organized crime syndicates that are far more influential than any which operate in Europe, and corruption is endemic in some countries. Ian Buruma argues that in some of Asia's authoritarian states murder, theft, torture and larceny are institutionalized: rather than individuals doing these things to other individuals, the state does it to those members of its population who try and buck the trend. Events in Burma in 1988, and in Indonesia and Thailand in 1991 go to show, in Buruma's view, that "crime" has become a "state enterprise". Although this does not mean that the Asian experience should be rejected out of hand as fraudulent, all is not roses in the Asian garden and many Americans would find it suffocating to live in Singapore, for example, where the press is lack-lustre and one-dimensional in the extreme and chewing gum is outlawed for its supposed anti-social tendencies. As Buruma wrote, referring to the caning of American 18-year-old Michael Fay in Singapore in 1994 for vandalism, "the firm smack of discipline always sounds sweeter when it lands on someone else's bum".

Despite the claims that Asia is different, some Asian politicians are actively trying to prevent westernization occurring. At the end of May 1994, the Singapore parliament debated the Maintenance of Parents Bill which would allow parents to sue their children if they did not support them financially in retirement. As the *Straits Times* put it in an editorial supporting the Bill, there is a danger that the younger generation "will grow up self-absorbed, middle-class and very likely, westernized in reflex. In that milieu, financial support for parents as a time-honoured tradition would whither". There are many other signs that Asia is not impervious to the social trends evident in the West: divorce, crime, drug addiction and so on are all on the rise, just as incomes, level of education and life expectancy are too. Nonetheless, the government of Singapore may have taken some comfort from a survey of 700 Singaporean schoolchildren which revealed that they viewed the most important values to be, in order, filial piety, honesty, responsibility, and self-control.

deputy prime minister Ong Teng Cheong (Lee Kuan Yew, despite much speculation, decided not to stand) did win, but he managed to attract less than 60% of the vote, against more than 40% won by his virtually unknown challenger, a former government accountant, Chua Kim Yeoh. Chua even adopted the novel electoral strategy of admitting that his opponent was a better man than he. As he did not actively campaign, analysts attributed his sudden popularity not to genuine support but to a protest against the PAP which had barred two opposition candidates from standing. One of them, J B Jeyaretnam – better known simply as JBJ – said the result was a 'clear rebuff' to the PAP. Singapore's most recent general election was held at the beginning of 1997 and some commentators were predicting a further erosion of PAP support as the republic's increasingly sophisticated electorate bristled at the restrictions placed upon them. This, though, is not what happened and Goh Chok Tong and the PAP won a huge – and surprising in terms of its scale – victory (see below).

A kinder, but still sensitive Singapore

As Lee Kuan Yew came to be regarded as one of the region's 'elder statesmen', questions were raised over his succession. The PAP's old guard gradually made way for young blood, but Lee clung on until November 1990. Three months after Singapore's extravagant 25th anniversary, he

Asian Values: how foreign managers rate corruption in Southeast Asia

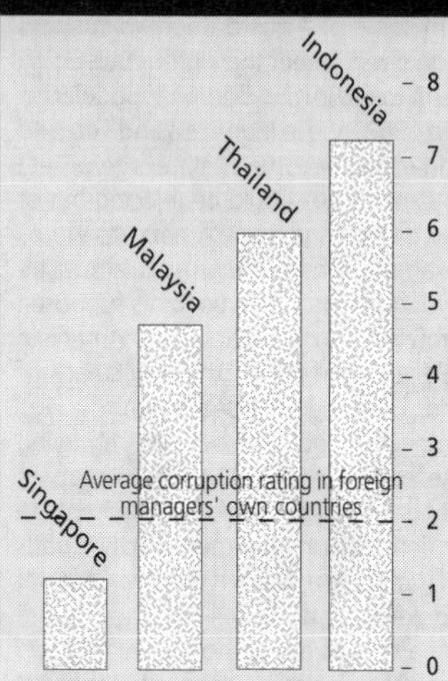

Source: Political & Economic Risk Consultancy, adapted from *The Economist*, 1995.

In 1995, the Hong Kong-based firm *Political and Economic Risk Consultancy* asked managers working in the Asian region – mainly of European and North American nationality – how they rated levels of corruption in Asian countries compared with their own, on a scale from 0-10. Singapore scored well, with levels of corruption well below those in the managers' own countries.

finally handed over to his first deputy prime minister **Goh Chok Tong**. Lee, though, remained chairman of the PAP and became 'senior minister without portfolio' in Goh's cabinet.

Although Singapore has been run as a meritocracy since independence, Goh is widely assumed to be a seat-warmer for Lee Kuan Yew's eldest son, **Brigadier-General Lee Hsien Loong**, better known locally as 'B G Lee' or 'The Rising Son'. B G Lee, like his father, got a first at Cambridge, returned to Singapore, joined the army as a platoon commander and within 8 years was a Brigadier-General in charge of the Joint Operations Planning Directorate. During that period he obtained a Masters degree at Harvard and then in 1984, at the age of 32, was elected to parliament. The following year he became a cabinet minister and is now Deputy Prime Minister. But the seemingly inexorable rise of BG Lee was dashed by the announcement in May 1993 that Lee junior had made a recovery from cancer. In November 1992 he had been diagnosed as having lymphona. In a newspaper interview, his father said: "Singapore needs the best it can get. If Singapore can get a man who has never had cancer and who is better than [Lee Hsien] Loong, then that man is the answer. But if it can't, take the best man that is available." Significantly, Prime Minister Goh Chok Tong said the younger Lee remained his choice as a successor.

When Lee senior stepped down at the end of 1990, a new era began; it became known as "The Next Lap" and the government-sponsored book of that title outlines the general directions of national development over the next 25 years. Goh promised to usher in a more open, 'people-oriented', consensus-style of government. Among his first acts was the creation of a new ministry for the arts and to underscore his faith in Singapore's maturity, he permitted the showing of blue movies, which proved very popular (see page 697). The rationale behind the new openness was to create a more cultured and less restrictive environment aimed at dissuading Singapore's brightest and best from emigrating due to boredom and concern about the country's authoritarian government. Goh's government heralded a more relaxed atmosphere; he made moves towards encouraging a freer press (particularly in regard to foreign publications), released long-term political prisoners and allowed ageing exiles to return home. But this evidence of a relaxation in government attitudes should not be regarded as a shift to Western-style liberalism (see page 617). Indeed, analysts have perceived a slight hardening of attitude as Goh's premiership has worn on. The way in which the PAP won the most recent election confirmed, for some, the willingness of the government to play hard ball to win the game.

The 1997 elections

Singapore's most recent elections were held in January 1997. First, the result: the ruling PAP under Goh Chok Tong took 65% of the vote, up from 59% in 1991, and won 81 out of 83 parliamentary seats. Opposition MPs won just two seats, down from four. Prime Minister Goh, reasonably enough, took this as a massive endorsement of his style of government. He also interpreted it to mean a rejection of Western-style liberal democracy. Critics, of course, read the tea leaves in a slightly different way. They noted that Goh had made it clear that those constituencies who voted for opposition politicians would find their Housing Development Board blocks last on the list for upgrading under the government's S$20 billion renovation programme. They might also forgo other infrastructural improvements. With their hands firmly on their wallets, people voted for the PAP. This was classic pork barrel politics – a long and noble tradition in many Western countries, it should be added. But it was not just a case of economic arm-twisting, as some publications in the West tried to portray it. The divided opposition scarcely put together a convincing programme of policies and in a sense they did not offer voters an reasonable alternative to voting for the PAP.

Although it was never in any doubt that the PAP would win the election (opposition candidates did not run in more than half of the constituencies making overall victory impossible), those standing against the PAP nonetheless found themselves under sustained attack. Tang Liang Hong was portrayed as a 'Chinese chauvinist' and then found himself the subject of a slew of law suits – 11 in all – when he accused several PAP leaders of defaming him and, allegedly, lying. Shortly after the election, Mr Tang fled to Malaysia.

Singapore's General Elections (1955-1997)

Date	Winning party	% of the vote
Apr 1955	Labour Front	27%
May 1959	PAP	53%
Sep 1963	PAP	46%
Apr 1968	PAP	84%
Sep 1972	PAP	69%
Dec 1976	PAP	72%
Dec 1980	PAP	76%
Dec 1984	PAP	63%
Sep 1988	PAP	62%
Aug 1991	PAP	59%
Jan 1997	PAP	65%

NB The elections between 1955 and 1963 inclusive were for the Legislative Assembly; elections for Parliament commenced with the 1968 general elections.

The PAP's massive majority in Parliament – holding nearly 98% of seats – vastly exaggerates the true measure of the government's support. This is because, like the British system on which it is based, the first-past-the-post system greatly favours popular parties. After all, although the majority of the population did vote for the PAP around one in three voters did not. Their voices are scarcely heard.

The August 1997 libel case which pitted veteran opposition politician JB Jayaretnam, or 'JBJ', against the current Prime Minister, Goh Chok Tong, former Prime Minister Lee Kuan Yew, along with nine other PAP leaders nicely illustrates the chasm that separates the Singapore government's view of how things should be done, and that of the West (or at least the Western media). The 11 ministers sued JBJ for announcing at an election rally in

January 1997 that another opposition candidate, Tang Liang Hong, had filed police reports against certain PAP leaders alleging 'lying and criminal conspiracy'. This, they argued, amounted to defamation by innuendo. George Carman QC represented JBJ. He adopted a tough approach to the case, treating government ministers to withering and aggressive questioning. To Prime Minister Goh he stated: "You pay lip service only to the full rights of democracy". "You say you believe in the principles of freedom of speech and freedom of the courts, but there comes a time when you adapt them for your own purposes to stay in power and stifle opposition." He also accused Goh of being 'economical with the truth'. The judge delivered his decision on the case at the end of September 1997. He found for the Prime Minister, awarding him S$20,000 damages and also ruling that JBJ should pay 60% of the plaintiff's costs. The decision vindicated Goh in the sense that he 'won', but the damages were only a fraction of those claimed by the Prime Minister. Goh also found himself paying a proportion of his costs. The case was widely covered in the media in the West. The London-based *Economist* argued on 4 October 1997:

> "... they [the PAP] might be wise to kick their litigious habit. It risks ridicule: would not the People's Action Party be better named the Libel Action Party, it will be asked? It is certainly unbecoming for a mighty government to break butterflies on the wheel, especially when there is such a strong correlation between might and right: no Singaporean leader has ever lost a libel action. Above all, it is foolish, because by stifling criticism Mr Goh & Co risk stifling useful debate and, in time, confidence and even investment."

Subversion, Singapore-style

Coinciding with the introduction of Singapore's long-promised more relaxed style of government, a cartoon book appeared on bookshelves in late 1990 entitled *Hello Chok Tong, Goodbye Kuan Yew*. The new cabinet was portrayed as a football team with former Prime Minister Lee Kuan Yew as the goal-keeper, shouting things like "Just try it!". The cartoonist was reported as saying that Singapore's 'glasnost', a result of Goh's 'kinder, gentler Singapore', allowed him to get away with it. The former Prime Minister's son, Lee Hsien Loong, was portrayed as the would-be striker on the team's right wing. The script reads: "Fans and opponents alike are watching carefully how quickly he matures in an attacking role ... Tends to over-react under pressure. Would do a lot better if he relaxed".

There have been signs that Singapore is easing up a bit politically, although following the republic's political tradition, Goh has been tough on anyone vaguely construed as a political enemy or perceived as a possible threat. Lee had assured the electorate that his successor would be "no softie". Goh has done his best to prove himself, saying he could be "a little deaf" to people in opposition constituencies.

More recently still, at the end of 1994, there was a fascinating exchange in Singapore's *Sunday Times*. In an article entitled the 'Great affective divide' author Catherine Lim (see Suggested reading, page 724) criticized Prime Minister Goh for reneging on his commitment to a 'kinder, gentler' style of government. The Prime Minister's Office responded in true style, blasting off a reply stating that "A gentler, more open political style does not mean allowing crudity and obscenity to pass off as avant-garde theatre, or ignoring political criticism which masquerades as political expression." There are limits to the politically possible even in a more open Singapore. Allowing Ms Lim to write and have published an article is one thing; to expect a sympathetic and measured response is another. Prime Minister Goh welcomes "well-meaning people who put forth their views in a very well-meaning way", but anything presumed to be snide or mocking would be dealt a "very, very hard blow from the government in return". In the bars and taxis of the Republic people are a lot more critical than the rather colourless local media might lead one to believe. One joke doing the rounds shows the ability of Singaporeans to laugh at themselves:

> An American remarks to a Somali, a Ukrainian and a Singaporean that food seems to cost a lot of money in the city state, and asks their opinion of this state of affairs. The Somali replies, "What's food?" The Ukrainian demands, "What's money?" To which the Singaporean quietly asks, "What's an opinion?"

Nor is Singapore quite the downtrodden place that the Western media might lead one to believe. In 1988 the Psychological Defence Division (sounds Brave New World-esque, lah!) of the Ministry of Communications and Information published a book called *Sing Singapore*. The largely inane songs in this official publication were to be taught in schools and transmitted on television and radio. As Dr Yeo Ning Hong of the Ministry explained in the introduction: "Singing the songs [in this book] will bring Singaporeans together, to share our feelings one with another. It will bring back shared memories of good times and hard times, of times which remind us of who we are, where we came from, what we did, and where we are going." *We are Singapore* gives a flavour of the lyrics:

This is my country
This is my flag
This is my future
This is my life
This is my family
These are my friends
We are Singapore Singaporeans
Singapore our homeland
It's here that we belong

Fortunately, a few years later, the *Not the Singapore song book* appeared to cock a paradonic snook at the original by borrowing some of the tunes and putting them to new lyrics. It represents popular resistance Singapore-style. *Count! Mummies of Singapore* pokes fun at Singapore's family planning policy:

We have the ova in our bodies,
We can conceive,
We can conceive.
We have a role for Singapore,
We must receive,
We must receive.

Then there is the *SDU March*, sung to the tune of *Colonel Bogey*:

Hey girl!
Why aren't you married yet!
You girl!
A man's not hard to get!
Now's the time for you to choose
your mate!
Don't delay! Do not procrastinate!

Other subversive songs include *Babies keep formin' in my bed* (sung to *Raindrops keep falling on my head*), *Three Cees* (condominium, credit card and car), *Gold card blues*, and *Oh my kiasu* (sung to *Oh my darling Clementine*). As Lily Kong explains, Singapore's political culture does not permit overt expressions of dissent, so Singaporeans have to find alternative avenues for opposition. The *Not the Singapore song book* is just one of many forms of covert popular resistance.

Singapore and the Internet

The conflict between control and freedom is being played out in microcosm in the debate over what to do about the Internet. Singapore, as government blandishments like to emphasize, is a place at the cutting edge of computer technology and the forefront of the information revolution. There is talk of creating an 'intelligent island' where 9 out of 10 homes are plugged into the Internet. Already there are twice as many Internet accounts held by Singaporeans (about 150,000 in late 1996 and rising fast) than by individuals in the People's Republic of China with a population 400 times larger. Yet by surfing the Net, Singapore's growing number of cybernauts not only show the world how deft the city state is at reinventing itself as technology advances; they can also read things about their own government and society that are taboo at home. So the government is faced with something of a dilemma: the Internet is the future/the Internet is destabilizing and corrosive. What to do?

They are responding in a number of ways. First the Singapore government is trying to re-make the Internet its own image by encouraging sanitized rebellion. There is, for example, a Board for On-line Graffiti where angry young men and women can scrawl faintly daring ditties without being hauled in front of the local magistrate. Second they are hoping to encourage self-policing to keep the cyber-waves free of offensive material, whether that be of a sexual, religious or political nature. Third, Cyber Cafés are required to have 'Net Nannies' to maintain a 'Surf Watch' so anything deemed beyond the pale can be nipped in the bud at Cyber Birth. Moreover, net providers are held responsible for the content of the material that they channel while local political and religious groups have to register if they want to use the Net Waves.

The key question, of course, is whether the government can successfully keep something so anarchic under control. Sites in Singapore should be fairly easy to police; the ones based abroad, especially in the US, will be much harder to control. As Nicholas Negroponte, head of the Massachusetts Institute of Technology's Media Lab put it: "The Internet is a decentralized medium ... There is no head-end, hierarchy, or point of control. People who try to 'control' the Net don't realize this. They don't understand it is more like phone conversations than print publications." Anyone willing to pay the price of an international call to Hong Kong, for example, will be able to circumvent these controls.

Defence

Singapore spends more than US$2 billion a year on defence – over a third of government expenditure. It promotes the idea of 'total defence', meaning that everyone, plays some role in protecting the country, economically and militarily. Regular emergency exercises are conducted involving the civilian population, which is designed to instill preparedness. This policy is probably influenced by memories of Singapore's inglorious surrender to the Japanese in February 1942 (see page 586). Men have to serve a compulsory 24-30 months in the Singapore Defence Forces, followed by annual 40-day training exercises for reservists, who undergo twice-yearly physical fitness tests until they are 40 years old. Being a predominantly Chinese state in the middle of the Malay world, Singapore feels very vulnerable, and government ministers have expressed their fears of a 'Kuwait situation', despite Singapore's good relations with its Malaysian and Indonesian neighbours. The armed forces are known to be trained by Israelis. Singapore is also the biggest arms manufacturer in the region and is an entrepôt for the arms trade. The island is the venue for Southeast Asia's biggest airshow every February, which has become the region's main show case for new civilian and military aircraft as well as military hardware. Many defence ministers from around the region arrive on shopping trips; with defence spending rising markedly in just about every country in Southeast Asia, defence analysts are already talking in terms of an arms race.

Singapore and its neighbours

Singapore is a member of the Association of Southeast Asian Nations (ASEAN) and enjoys generally good relations with its neighbours. However there have been times of friction, particularly during the mid-1960s when Singapore left the Malaysian Federation and had a diplomatic spat with President Sukarno of Indonesia. As a minute city state with a population less that 2% of Indonesia's, Singapore's leaders have always been acutely aware of the need to build and maintain good relations with its regional neighbours.

Even so, Singapore has not always managed to avoid offending its neighbours.

This particularly applies to Malaysia, a country with which it shares a common colonial history, but with which it is divided in so many other ways. Malaysia's majority are Malay and Muslim; Singapore's are Chinese. Malaysia has a national policy of positive discimination in favour of ethnic Malays or *bumiputras*; Singapore is a meritocracy. Malaysia is still a developing country, albeit a so-styled economic 'miracle'; Singapore has a standard of living amongst the highest in the world. This makes for a fierce competitiveness between the two countries which disguises a lingering bitterness that some commentators trace back to the ejection of Singapore from the Malaysian Federation in the mid-1960s. Malaysia is quick to take offence at anything that smacks of Singaporean superiority.

In 1996 and 1997 relations between Malaysia and Singapore sunk to their lowest level for some years. In June 1996 Lee Kuan Yew offered the thought that Singapore could, conceivably, merge once more with Malaysia. Two months later Goh Chok Tong seemed to use this as a threat when he warned that if Singapore slipped up, "we will have no option but to ask Malaysia to take us back". The Malaysian government took this as a slight. In their view, the prime minister was threatening the electorate with the possibility that they might be absorbed into Malaysia. During 1997 bilateral relations got even worse. In March, Senior Minister Lee Kuan Yew put his foot in his mouth when he suggested that the Malaysian state of Johor Bahru was "notorious for shootings, muggings and car-jackings" (this was in relation to opposition politician Tang Liang Hong's decision to flee there from Singapore). The Malaysian press and some sections of the government reacted with outrage. The Youth head of the ruling United Malays National Party (UMNO) accused Lee of being 'senile and uncouth'. Singapore's Senior Minister apologized 'unreservedly' but the damage, so to speak, had already been done. Singapore's *Straits Times* then compounded Lee's insensitivity by publishing an article listing recent crimes in Johor – which Malaysians saw as a crass attempt to justify his comments. Although the spat over Johor seems to have run its course, the growing economic competition between Singapore and Malaysia (see below) is likely to mean that bilateral relations are entering a period of instability.

ECONOMY

Singapore is a developed country – or so everyone from *The Economist* to Prime Minister Goh Chok Tong thought at the beginning of 1996. Although the nuances of whether Singapore can be defined as 'developed' or not may keep academics and journalists tapping away at their word processors, for most visitors the proof of the pudding, so to speak, is in the eating. With a per capita income of US$26,730 in 1995, higher than that of Britain (US$18,700) and France (US$24,990) – glistening tower blocks, a state-of-the-art transportation system and much else besides, it is hard to leave the island state thinking that this could in any way be placed in the same bracket as other 'developing' countries. Singapore is affluent – and this alone should be counted an enormous achievement. The fact that Western politicians should come to Singapore in order to learn from the island state, rather than lecture to it – as Britain's Prime Minister Tony Blair did at the beginning of 1996 – is evidence that the place has come an awfully long way since independence which, it is all too easy to forget, is just 30 years ago.

It is when raw income statistics are converted into 'standard of living' estimates that Singapore slips down the world income league. The London based National Institute of Economic and Social Research placed Singapore 16th in the world in terms of GDP per person (based on 1992 data). When this was converted into GDP per hour worked the republic slipped to 21st, and when the

The Central Providence Fund – saving for a rainy day

Thanks to Singapore's compulsory savings scheme, the country has the highest savings rate in the world. In 1994 Singapore saved an incredible 49.5% of GDP; 32% was invested leaving a whopping 17.5% to be lent to other countries. The Central Provident Fund (CPF) was set up in 1955 to provide pensions for workers, health care and to help people put down-payments and pay off mortgages on flats. It now covers insurance schemes and education as well. Employees below 55 years of age have to contribute 20% of their monthly income (older workers pay less) to the CPF and their employers contribute a further 20%. At the end of 1995, the CPF's 2.7 million members had S$66bn (US$46bn) under management. Members' balances are divided between three accounts. The bulk, about 75%, goes into an ordinary account where it can be used to buy property, pay school fees and purchase some designated unit trusts. A further 15% goes into a Medisave account to cover the cost of any health care needs during retirement. The last 10% goes into a sort of contingency or 'emergency' account. Originally members can start drawing on their accounts at the age of 55, although this has now been raised to 60. What does the government do with this S$66bn? It is hard to say for sure, because the great bulk goes into special government bonds or is simply deposited with the central bank. Returns on investment compared with commercial pension schemes are poor. Interest is calculated on the basis of the 12-month fixed deposit and month-end saving rates of the four major local banks. Thus for July to December 1995 interest averaged a comparatively measley 3.82%.

figures were adjusted once more to arrive at a 'quality of life' index (notoriously slippery) Singapore dropped to 24th – the bottom of the table.

The roots of growth

Singapore has natural advantages: its strategic location and an excellent harbour. It also owes a debt to its founding father, Stamford Raffles and to former Prime Minister Lee Kuan Yew. Raffles allowed unrestricted immigration and free trade, declaring Singapore a free port. In this respect, Singapore was the first place to adopt 18th century Scottish economist and philosopher Adam Smith's principle of *laissez-faire*. This policy was enshrined as the *modus operandi* of Singapore's flourishing merchant community and was the most important factor influencing the commercial growth of Raffles' trading centre. It quickly eclipsed the other, more venerable, Straits Settlement of Georgetown (Penang) and for more than a century-and-a-half, Singapore boomed as a regional trans-shipment centre.

For his part, Lee Kuan Yew gave Singapore political stability unrivalled in the region, making the island republic a magnet for multinational investment. His pragmatic and far-sighted government ploughed the profits of the booming economy into the island's physical and social infrastructure. It also concentrated on building Singapore up as a financial centre. Following independence, Singapore maintained its *laissez-faire* image only when it came to international trade; in every other sector of the economy the government has been interventionist. For Singapore's vitality is based as much on government intervention as it is on the mysterious workings of the 'market'.

The economy remained largely in the hands of the private sector but the government set up strategic public sector firms to direct and catalyse rapid industrialization. The Republic's remarkable development represents a challenge to Western free-market recipes for success. The government plays a dominant role in planning the island's development. For example: it subsidizes public housing, health and education; manipulates wages through the National Wages Council; controls trades unions by means of the National Trades Unions Congress; and owns large chunks of land. For potential foreign investors, the government has created a honey pot state with an enviable combination of an open trading economy

Singapore traffic – no more for the road

Singapore now has a highly efficient local and international transport network, with the Mass Rapid Transit railway, the splendid Changi Airport and an urban road system unrivalled in Asia. The latest addition has been the underground Central Expressway (CTE), which makes it possible to drive into the heart of the city without encountering a single red light. Above ground, Singapore is internationally renowned for its 'Restricted Zone' system, which controls traffic flows into the Central Business District at rush-hour. To enter the CBD between 0730 and 1830 on weekdays costs S$3 a day. The average speed of vehicles during peak hours is 30 kph compared with 16 kph in Hong Kong, 15 kph in London and 5 kph in Bangkok.

Singapore has one of the highest automobile densities in the world (81 per km of roadway, against 43 in Japan and 27 in the US). Yet its ultra-efficient, visionary urban planners have avoided the gridlock typical of most other capitals in the region. Part of this is to do with the CBD restrictions, but more importantly, the government has ruled that the car population cannot grow any faster than the road network. Due to this policy, Singapore's cars are about the most expensive in the world. A typical mid-size car costs about S$150,000, while an equivalent vehicle in Hong Kong would cost just a fifth as much. There is a 45% import tariff, a 150% registration fee and an annual road tax linked to engine size. For an average-sized Japanese car the tax is S$1,400. Even petrol costs substantially more than in neighbouring countries.

Because all this was still not deterring Singaporeans from buying cars, the government introduced a Certificate of Entitlement in 1990, which would-be car owners must obtain before they purchase a car. These are sold through a complex auction system. Prices of cars vary each month depending on how many people are bidding for them and how much they bid. The government sets the cut-off price for each model according to the bids, and anyone below that price does not get their car. In February 1997 a certificate of Entitlement for a Mercedes E200 cost S$64,000, making its total on the road price almost S$250,000 (US$180,000). In addition, all new cars are now legally required to have catalytic converters fitted, which increases the price still further. And because Singapore does not want its roads clogged with old bangers, owners of cars which are more than 10 years old have to pay a road tax surcharge of 10% which rises to 50% on a car's 14th birthday.

The latest ploy is the installation of an electronic system from 1997 for charging cars (or rather their owners) when they enter certain areas: a fee will be deducted from a smart card inserted into a sensor which every car will carry. The cost of the whizz-bang electronics? S$197mn. In Jan 1996 the government released a new transport white paper which detailed plans to spend S$20bn over the next 10-15 years making an already excellent transport system even better, doubling the length of the MRT system and adding new expressways and interchanges. The result, of course, is that only the republic's most affluent citizens can afford to buy a car. And when people do get their hands on a car they drive it into the ground. The average local driver covers 18,600 km a year – more than the average American driver does.

Criticism, libel and punishment

Scarcely a year goes by without Singapore's government trying to set down the limits of public debate. There can be no doubt that the country has a great deal to boast about: clean and safe streets, a booming economy, high wages, considerable equality of opportunity and reward, corruption-free government, an efficient civil service, zero unemployment, good health and education provision, an efficient public transport system. ... Many people would dearly love to be born into such a paradise. In the government's view, these undoubted successes are linked to 'discipline' in the widest sense of the word, and the avoidance of the excesses of Western-style democratic free-for-all (see page 606 for a discussion of 'Asian values').

A recent example of Singapore's attempt to deal firmly with those who cross the line was the trial of an American academic, Christopher Lingle, formerly a member of staff at the National University of Singapore. In October 1994, Dr Lingle wrote an article for the *International Herald Tribune* in which he suggested that governments in some Asian countries use a "compliant judiciary to bankrupt opposition politicians". Although Singapore was not specifically named the Singapore government filed a contempt-of-court action, and former prime minister Lee Kuan Yew, a civil libel action. In Dec the *International Herald Tribune* backed down, offering an unreserved apology. Nonetheless, the contempt case was heard and the government won in January 1995. As the government has sued and made bankrupt 11 opposition politicians between 1971 and 1993 there could be little doubt that the piece referred to Singapore, even if not by name.

Tang Liang Hong, who stood as a Worker's Party candidate in the January 1997 general elections, faced no less than 11 defamation suits from various senior figures in the PAP. His crime was to have reportedly accused them of lying when they charged that he was a 'Chinese chauvinist'. Tang fled Singapore for Malaysia soon after the election, but his wife who stayed behind had her passport confiscated. Tang believes, and he has reasonably good grounds for doing so, that Goh Chok Tong and Lee Kuan Yew want to 'bury him politically and financially'. (See page 610 for an account of the JBJ libel suit that resulted from Tang's accusations.)

It seems clear that the Singapore government will continue to pursue and attempt to punish anyone who crosses the line that they have metaphorically drawn in the sand. Lee's own civil case has yet to be heard. That Singapore is serious about such things is reflected in the number of international publications that have had their circulations restricted by the Singapore government due to some slur or perceived inaccurate report: *Time Magazine*, the *Asian Wall Street Journal*, *The Economist*, *Asiaweek* and the *Far Eastern Economic Review*. The government insists on a 'Right of Reply' and the alacrity with which the permanent secretary of the Ministry of Information and the Arts and other government functionaries send missives to various publications means that scarcely a week seems to go by without some defence, explanation or invective appearing in the international press. At the beginning of May 1995 a reader of *The Economist* had a letter published in the journal asking: "Why ... must you continue to subject the whole world to the ceaseless barrage of banal blather from the Singapore High Commission [in London]? ... If you caved in to every government as demanding and petty as Singapore's, the letters section would no doubt dwarf the rest of the magazine." Singapore's leaders have responded to their critics offering the challenge of a public debate. William Safire, a virulent American critic of the government, has said he will take up the challenge, but only on neutral ground: Switzerland.

Salary games: the highest (legally) paid: politician in the world?

At the beginning of 1995 it was announced by Singapore's government led by Goh Chok Tong that its top politicians would receive a hefty pay rise and, already among the most highly paid in the world, would become even richer. Even before the salary rises Singapore's prime minister was receiving a pay cheque four times larger than the president of the United States, and seven times larger than that of Britain's prime minister. Now the differentials have widened to 7 and over 10 times. (Although Britain's Prime Minister received a large pay rise in Summer 1996.) Mr Goh's salary is a whopping S$1.5mn. Even these comparisons pale into insignificance when compared with the salary of the president of the Philippines, who receives just US$1,000 a year. In many democracies, it might be expected that this would lead to a public outcry over politicians lining their own nests. In the debate in Singapore's parliament, the rise was justified in two ways. First, it was argued that good salaries are the only way to keep corruption at bay – such a feature of neighbouring countries. Second, that growing differentials between public and private sector pay was making it increasingly difficult to attract and then keep good people in place. As ever, the logic and the mechanics are, apparently, faultless. Ministers' salaries are pegged to the top four earners in six professions and then discounted by a third.

However, the government's own 'feed-back unit' reported deep voter dissatisfaction with the rises and the opposition leader Chiam See Tong quoted former US president Jack Kennedy when he remarked "Ask not what your country can do for you, but what you can do for your country". Prime Minister Goh and Senior Minister Lee Kuan Yew shrugged off the barbs, the latter asking, in true style, whether ordinary people were in a position to judge such things. With an election looming, the voters may decide to show that although they may not be in a position to judge, they still have some power to decide. Perhaps as a sop to public concerns, Prime Minister Goh said that he would forego his own increase for 5 years – leaving him with a comparatively measly S$1.1mn to scrape by on.

and social stability. Bi-lingualism and vocational training focussing on the skills required by targeted industries has also helped to make Singapore the chosen location for many foreign companies. Singapore's public housing policies are now legendary. New high-rise towns have sprung up around the island and the government demolished village after village, moving people into tower blocks. Something like nine-tenths of the population live in Housing Development Board flats, of which three-quarters are now owner-occupied (see page 588). Singaporeans are encouraged to use their compulsory savings in the Central Provident Fund (CPF) to purchase their flats from the government. The government has been careful to keep these blocks racially mixed: if, for example, you are a Chinese and want to move out, you cannot sell to another Chinese.

Making a miracle

When Singapore became an independent country in 1965 it had a per capita income of US$700 a year. It had virtually no natural resources and even had to import its water from Malaysia. To compound the problem, the British military withdrew from their bases in Singapore in 1971; they had contributed a fifth of Singapore's GDP and employed nearly a fifth of the labour force. Within 12 years of independence, however, per capita income had risen to US$2,500 and by the early 1980s Singapore had the third highest per capita income in Asia after Japan and Brunei. In

The Asian miracle: why it happened – the story according to the World Bank

In 1993, the World Bank published a study which tried to make sense of the Asian economic success story, with the title *The East Asian miracle: economic growth and public policy*. The unprecedented rate of economic growth in Asia, including in a number of Southeast Asian countries, demanded an explanation so that other, less fortunate regions of the world might also embark on this road to fortune. Of course, not everyone is so sanguine about Asia's success, past or future. These critics point to, for example, human rights violations, poor working conditions, widening rural-urban disparities, environmental degradation on a monumental scale, the exploitation of child labour, and corrupt and corrosive government. The mid-1997 collapse in the Thai, Indonesian and Malaysian economies seemed to support the view that the miracle economies were riding for a fall.

Although the World Bank study begins by pointing out that there is no 'recipe' for success, it does highlight a number of critical elements which countries and governments need, in their view, to get right. As the World Bank puts it, the so-called High Performing Asian Economies or HPAEs (including Singapore, Malaysia, Thailand and Indonesia) "achieved high growth by getting the basics right". Not all the below can be applied to all the countries in question all of the time; nonetheless, they represent a checklist of 'right' policies and government.

- **The principle of shared growth**: although the countries of Asia are not, in most cases, democracies, their governments have tried to ensure that the fruits of development have been relatively widely shared. This is particularly true in the case of the 'dragons' (including Singapore) where rapid growth has been achieved with relative equity. This has helped to establish the legitimacy of their governments and usually won the support of the populations at large – despite the fact that those governments may still be authoritarian in complexion.
- **Investment in physical capital**: the countries of Asia have, in general, been saving and investing a greater proportion of their total wealth than countries in

1995, the World Bank estimated that Singapore had a per capita income of nearly US$27,000 – considerably higher than Britain's, the former colonial power. It is now, in terms of personal wealth, one of the richest nations in the world: the World Bank places it 8th. Britain lies 18th. Singapore is also rated the least-risky Asian country for foreign investment after Japan (attracting almost S$7 billion in 1995); it earned the top ranking in the 1996 World Competitiveness Yearbook; and overall has been judged the world's second best economic performer.

Singapore's economy has expanded by an average of 9% a year since independence in 1965. In 1995 the growth rate was 8.8%, in 1996 6.2%, and the economy was expected to grow by 7% in 1997. 1996 proved to be a tough year for exporters. The international slump in the electronics market hit one of Singapore's key sectors. (Electronics account for 58% of the value of non-oil exports.) However looking at the performance of the economy over the medium term, the picture is extraordinarily rosy and the prediction is that growth will average 7% per year until the end of the century. It is hard not to conclude that government policies have been instrumental in forging this litany of success. The only periods of slow growth were during the early 1970s when Singapore was badly hit by the world recession associated with the first oil price hike, and in the mid-1980s when a any other region of the world. This includes both private and public investment, but is most dramatic in terms of private investment (the World Bank, as one might expect, views private investment as more efficient and effective in promoting growth).

- **Investment in human capital**: although the proportion of spending allotted to education is not very much higher in Asia than elsewhere in the developing world, this money has been primarily allocated to primary and secondary schooling, not to higher education. Among developing countries, the families of most of those entering higher education can pay for it anyway, and need little government support; the best way to improve general levels of education is by targetting primary and secondary schooling. Asian governments have also tended to educate girls nearly as well as boys.
- **Allowing the market to determine prices**: as one might expect from the World Bank, the report also highlights the importance of allowing the market to determine the price of labour, capital and goods. The Bank skipped around the tendency for Asian governments to intervene in economic decision-making (with the exception of Hong Kong) by arguing that this was judicious intervention which reinforced, rather than tried to buck, the market.
- **That vital intangible**: Lee Kuan Yew, former prime minister of Singapore, visited Vietnam – one of the poorest countries in the world with a per capita income of US$220 – and pronounced that the country's prospects were bright because it had that 'vital intangible'. Economists talk rather less poetically in terms of Total Factor Productivity (TFP). In effect, this is what cannot be explained in a country's growth by looking at such variables as investment in physical and human capital. The former Soviet Union, on paper, should have grown as fast as Singapore and S Korea. As is now abundantly clear, it did not. The problem is identifying this ghostly missing catalyst.
- **Creating a business-friendly environment**: the countries have usually welcomed foreign investment and have sought to create the conditions in which foreign companies can thrive. They have also created a cadre of efficient technocrats to manage the economy.

contraction in a number of the Republic's key export sectors caused the economy to shrink by 1.7%. Singapore has no external debt and a healthy balance of trade surplus. In 1988 the United States removed Singapore from its list of preferential developing country trading partners, which was the first official sign that Singapore had ascended – in the eyes of the industrialized West – to the status of a Newly Industrialized Economy (NIE), along with the other 'Tiger Economies' of Hong Kong, Taiwan and South Korea.

In 1965, when the government was still reeling at separation from Malaysia, the top priority was job creation and basic industrialization. During the 1970s, when more sophisticated industries set up, the government focused on diversifying the economy and upgrading skills. Export promotion, aimed at finding new markets, coupled with the intensive campaign to attract foreign investment, meant that Singapore became less and less dependent on entrepôt trade. The services sector was expanded to build up financial services and the tourism industry. Great emphasis was placed on mechanizing and increasing productivity. By the end of the 1970s, Singapore's scarcity of labour was beginning to bite and the government began to switch from labour-intensive industries to capital-intensive and hi-tech industries, including aerospace, biotechnology, information technology and petrochemicals. This was called, rather grandiosely, the Second Industrial Revolution. Instead of assembling radios for example, production line workers began making disk drives – of which Singapore is currently the world's largest producer. Corporations were given tax incentives to facilitate their use of Singapore as a regional headquarters and international purchasing centre. Within Singapore the buzzword was 'excellence'.

The recession which hit Singapore in 1985 and 1986 came as a shock to a country which had experienced fast and furious growth for 2 decades. But it allowed for a stock-taking exercise and the government carefully drew up a recovery strategy. The recipe for recovery – cooked up by a specially created committee headed by Lee Kuan Yew's son Lee Hsien Loong – was to reverse the policy of pushing up wage rates ahead of inflation (which had been used as a means to force companies to upgrade), lower employers' costs, liberalize the economy, and de-emphasize manufacturing in favour of services.

By 1987 the economic growth rate was nearly 10% again and the following year it topped 11%. The efforts put into promoting Singapore as the financial hub of Asia quickly bore fruit; by the early 1990s, the financial services industry was growing by more than 20% a year. Then, in 1990 the Gulf Crisis erupted and the US suffered an economic downturn. To the delight of the Singapore government however, its economy – although dented – did not slide into recession too. The *Economist Intelligence Unit* notes that " ... this demonstrated that the Singaporean economy had finally come of age and was no longer vulnerable, in the classic newly industrialized country manner, to sharp slowdowns in world trade".

This view has been vindicated, or at least it had been up to the time that this book went to press, by the degree to which Singapore was insulated from the economic crises afflicting other countries in the region. In mid-1997 the economic optimism that had characterized Southeast Asia since the late 1980s was shaken by a financial crisis that began in Thailand, and spread to Indonesia, Malaysia and the Philippines. The Thai baht, Philippine peso, Indonesian rupiah and Malaysian ringgit were all effectively devalued as their pegs to the US$ were shattered by heavy selling. The IMF stepped in with a US$15 billion rescue package for Thailand, and another for Indonesia. Though Thailand's problems were uniquely serious there were enough commonalities to cause concern in many of Southeast Asia's financial quarters. In Malaysia, Prime Minister Mahathir ran a characteristically uncompromising campaign against currency speculators but most analysts believe he was misguided in doing so (see page 96). However, Singapore survived the economic onslaught comparatively intact – certainly when set against events in Bangkok, Jakarta, Manila and Kuala Lumpur. But even in rock solid Singapore there has been economic fall out. The Singapore stock exchange's *Straits Times* Index fell from a high of over 2,200 in February 1997 to under 1,500 by the end of October. In addition, the traditionally stable Singapore dollar weakened against the US$ as speculators attacked it.

Sausage makers and paper tigers

Foreign investors have continued to flock to Singapore because of its unrivalled infrastructure and international communications links. This is despite the fact that Singapore is no longer a cheap place to locate. Land is expensive and so is labour: employers have to contribute 20% of workers' salaries to the Central Provident Fund (the compulsory state savings scheme – see page 614) as well as paying a skills development tax. But while the costs of locating in Singapore have continued to rise markedly, there has not been a corresponding rise in productivity, which has made analysts question how long the investors will keep coming. Productivity in other 'tiger economies' is growing much faster.

This observation that so-called Total Factor Productivity (economic expansion after account has been made of labour force growth and that associated with investments in labour and capital) in Singapore has not grown caused the American economist Paul Krugman to argue that Singapore's success was built on 'perspiration rather than inspiration'. Between 1966 and 1990 the economically active proportion of the labour force expanded from 27% to 51%. It is this sheer expansion in the numbers of people in work, Krugman argued, which explains Singapore's success leading him to suggest that when Singapore's labour force stops growing – as it will do fairly soon given low fertility rates – then so too will the economy. In 1995 *The Economist* framed the same argument rather more prosaically in terms of the 'Myth of the Sausage-makers': "If you invest in more sausage machines and employ more sausage-makers, of course you will make more sausages. Where's the miracle? Growth will slow down when you run out of extra sauage-makers" (1995: 71). The paper caused considerable consternation in Singapore – and other economists retorted that Krugman had been cavalier in his assessment of TFP – which, as a residual, is notoriously hard to estimate.

Although Krugman's paper elicited the greatest response his views are really a development of Japanese economist Yoshihara Kunio's observation that Southeast Asia is characterized by what he termed 'technologyless industrialization'. Singapore has no great entrepreneurs and no great inventors. It is, he argues, merely a production centre for multinational firms – albeit a highly efficient one. He coined the term 'ersatz capitalism' to explain growth in Singapore and the other growth economies of Southeast Asia.

In 1997 there were an estimated 4,000 multinationals operating in Singapore and these account for more than three-quarters of total investment in manufacturing. The failure of Singapore's domestic industry to take-off is bothering the government and there has been much debate in the newspapers about why a country with educational levels apparently higher than Britain's spawns so few entrepreneurs and inventers. (The number of patents lodged by Singaporeans is miniscule compared with those lodged by Western countries, even accounting for differences in population. There is virtual no world class research being undertaken, save for one or two exceptions like medicine and some facets of economics.) The Ministry of Education's own research has revealed that Singapore's graduates are competent when it comes to standard problems, but when a task requires creativity, they lag behind. The head of research at a local bank explained to the *Far Eastern Economic Review* in 1996: "If you give [Singapore workers] a handbook, they'll follow the procedures meticulously. But you tell them about a problem and ask them to think of an alternative solution, and they can't do it."

Not only does it seem that Singapore has still to make the leap from being a mere production base to becoming a leader in manufacturing but the government also worries that over-dependence on potentially footloose foreign companies has created an environment of dependency and vulnerability. There is nothing stopping these companies simply upping sticks and shifting to other locations should conditions require it. As James Clad wrote a few years ago, foreign companies seem to view Singapore more as a parking lot than a country. The government is trying to change this state of affairs by – characterisitically – intervening. In 1996 Prime Minister Goh announced the creation of a 'thinking skills programme' while the Economic Development Board (EDB) established an 'innovation development scheme'. As Chow Tat Kong, the director of the EDB's Industrial Development Division put it, the scheme is designed to 'kick-start the whole process of innovation'. Singapore is to become an 'intelligent island' with a telecommunications infrastructure which is second to none and where everyone is computer literate. Already Singapore is one the world's most competitive economies in these terms.

Labour squeeze

With no mineral wealth, oil or timber, people are Singapore's only true resource and, despite the government's efforts, people are in short supply. The government says tight labour supply will continue to limit Singapore's economic growth, and that rising labour costs will curb its exports. Manufacturers report difficulty in recruiting production workers and there is a continuing exodus of professionals. A poll published in August 1997 revealed that 37% of adults had contemplated, or were contemplating emigrating. Because of Singapore's race to industrialize, demand for labour has always exceeded supply. It got round this by importing labour from Malaysia, Indonesia, Thailand and the Philippines. There is virtually no unemployment in Singapore – everyone who wants to work can and because the labour market is so tight, skilled white collar workers have been able to demand higher and higher salaries. Labour costs rose in 1995 by 7.1% – far ahead of inflation. The government plans to raise the mandatory retirement age to help fill the labour gap, to introduce more labour-saving technology and allow an even greater influx of migrant workers. In early 1993 the head of the International Manpower Policy section of the Economic Development Board (EDB) announced that Singapore would be attempting to recruit researchers and scientists from the former Soviet Union in an effort to bolster its high-tech industries. In 1995 the EDB arranged recruitment drives to Britain, the US, India and Australia. They have placed advertisements in newspapers in Madras and Moscow and have set up a web site for prospective migrants. For the interested or inquisitive, log onto: http://www.singapore-careers.com.

Today approaching one in five of the republic's workforce is a non-Singaporean. There are around 200,000 unskilled and semi-skilled migrant workers, up 60% on 1980. Quota restrictions on the number allowed into each sector of the economy have been relaxed, but the government is alarmed that foreigners now represent nearly half the workforce in certain sectors. Singapore wants to avoid them settling on the island – it says it cannot absorb or accommodate too many unskilled workers.

The drive to increase labour efficiency has been a major policy thrust in recent years. Industrial robots have helped trim the workforce in many manufacturing plants. Manufacturers who are unable to automate their operations have gone to cheaper locations in nearby Indonesia or Malaysia, which have both benefited from the overspill. Prime Minister Goh Chok Tong, appears to have found a solution of sorts in his 'Growth Triangle', which includes the city state, Johor (the southernmost state on the Malaysian peninsula) and Pulau Batam (the northernmost island in Indonesia's Riau Archipelago).

The Growth Triangle is seen as a strategy that can exploit the economic complementarities that exist between Singapore, Malaysia and Indonesia. Singapore has technical excellence, marketing muscle, an excellent communications and financial infrastructure, good skills, and represents an excellent base for firms. Johor and Riau have cheap land and labour and less stringent environmental regulations and planning controls. Put the two together, some analysts believe, and you get yet more of the economic miracle. Over recent years, scores of transnational investors have stampeded across the causeway to Johor, and investment in Batam is picking up. Singapore benefits enormously from its new found hinterland and unskilled foreign workers can be kept conveniently at arm's length so that they do not upset the flavour of the city-state's racial cocktail. Further afield, Singapore has been investing in Vietnam, India and China. Economically speaking, Singapore is a comfortable 10-15 years ahead of its neighbours and intends to stay ahead. The Economic Development Board is training people with a vengeance and has labelled them 'thinking workers'. Policy makers believe that once they are in place, no labour crisis will ever be insurmountable.

At the other end of the labour market, in the professional, white-collar sector, there have been problems too. The government has become particularly concerned about 'the emigration problem' in which thousands of highly skilled Singaporeans have been choosing to live and work abroad. Many are Malays and Indians, who claim their long-term opportunities are limited in Singapore. Emigration peaked in 1988 when nearly 5,000 families left Singapore, and this came as a double blow to a government already facing a serious labour shortage. To stem the 'brain drain' an aggressive overseas recruitment campaign was launched for white-collar workers and this was matched by the liberalization of immigration regulations for foreign professionals. In an effort to ensure that there is a continued supply of **skilled labour**, Singapore offered tens of thousands skilled Hong Kong workers and their dependants permanent residence status in 1989. By 1995 about 40,000 applicants had been approved although only a fraction of this number – 6,500 – have actually moved to the city state. The Singapore government hoped to cash in on fears arising from the colony's reversion to Chinese rule in 1997. Singapore was secretly banking on poaching Hong Kong's brainiest emigrés before they went to Canada or Australia. The government has been careful, however, to assure Singapore's other ethnic communities that should this distort the current racial mix, it will permit the immigration of Malays and Indians to maintain the balance.

Singapore and its competitors

"We are like someone being chased by tigers with a cliff in front. The tigers are closing in fast but the cliff is difficult to scale. The tigers are the dynamic economies like Thailand, Malaysia, Indonesia and China. The cliff is the formidable challenge posed by the developed countries" (Prime Minister Goh Chok Tong, 1992).

Singapore has always been worried about its future as a small and vulnerable Chinese city state surrounding by larger and more populous countries with a Malay/Muslim cultural heritage. Now that Malaysia – not to mention places like Thailand, Indonesia and China – is challenging Singapore economically the issue of the sustainability of Singapore's economic miracle has taken on even greater resonance. Kuala Lumpur's new airport is aiming to take business away from Changi while the upgrading of Port Klang is already eating into the dominance of Singapore's ports. In 1997 Malaysia's Prime Minister Mahathir Mohamad unveiled an ambitious prgramme to create a multimedia corridor south of KL and even Indonesia has plans to expand air and port facilities in the Riau islands of Batam and Bintan. Taken together, and combined with Singapore's high labour costs, it is not hard to see why the republic's leaders constantly urge Singaporeans to strive to maintain their edge.

Singapore in the computer and telecommunications stakes (rank out of 49 countries)

Telecommunications infrastructure	6th
Technological infrastructure	2nd
Science training in schools	1st
Computer literacy	2nd
Information technology	3rd

Source: Global Competitivenes Report, 1996

Singapore tops the Asian honesty stakes

Singapore all too often comes in for critcism in the Western press for its supposed authoritarian government, overweening society, and lack of liberal credentials. However Singaporeans do seem to have a more developed sense of civic duty and responsibility than most societies, and it would not be too far-fetched to put this down, partially at least, to the emphasis on what tends to be rather loosely described as 'Asian values' (see the box on page 608). In 1997 the Readers' Digest decided to drop ten wallets filled with money, addresses, photographs and all the other paraphenalia one would expect in each of 14 Asian cities to see how many were returned. After 4 months they checked to see what had happened. The results are tabulated below.

Singapore	9	Mumbai (Bombay)	5
Inchon (Korea)	8	Kajang (Malaysia)	5
Tivandrum (India)	8	Tainan (Taiwan)	5
Kamakura (Japan)	7	Taipei	5
Chiang Mai (Thailand)	6	Lapu Lapu City (Philippines)	4
Seoul	6	Metro Manila	4
Bangkok	5	Hong Kong	3

This type of thing has also been tried in the US and Europe. Surprisingly perhaps, the average rate of return was lowest in Asia at 57% and highest in the US which scored a return rate of 67%. The figure for Europe was 58%. This goes against another leg of the Asian values thesis – that the West's emphasis on individual rights has eroded citizens' sense of community values. Nonetheless, The *Straits Times* proudly led with the headline 'S'pore tops regional honesty test'.

The contest between **Singapore and Hong Kong**, Asia's two super-successful island states, has intensified in recent years. At the end of 1995 the Singapore government ran a series of advertisements on Hong Kong television reminding viewers what a green, clean, safe and prosperous place the republic was. The subliminal message seemed to be: come while you can. But although to the outside world Hong Kong and Singapore may appear to be virtual Siamese twins – they came second and first respectively in the World Economic Forum's 1997 competitiveness league – on the ground the differences are palpable. For a start, Hong Kong is populated largely by people from Guangdong (Canton), while Singapore's Chinese are mostly Hokkien. Perhaps even more significantly, Hong Kongers relish the racey and slightly anarchic atmosphere of their territory. By comparison, Singapore appears dull, constraining and authoritarian. This is probably why so many Hong Kong residents who decided to secure another passport before the hand-over at the end of June 1997 opted for places like Canada and Australia: hardly Asian – although both have large Asian populations – but in terms of life style probably more like Hong Kong than Singapore. Singapore has been careful not to offend China. To have plucked all the best people from the colony before it was handed over would not have gone down too well in Beijing. For this reason the hard sell was disguised.

While Hong Kong Chinese may not relish the idea of relocating to Singapore, many multinationals show less reticence. A survey conducted among 6,000 Asian executives at the end of 1996 revealed that three-quarters believed Singapore to be a better regional base than Hong Kong. Compaq, Levi Strauss and Reuters all shifted their Asian headquarters from

Hong Kong to Singapore ahead of 1997. What is significant though is that the obvious reason – the handover of the colony to China – was not always the key factor. Quality of life (low crime rate, clean streets, green environment) and efficient infrastructure (public transport, telecommunications), seemed to play as great a role in the decision. Not that the game is only going Singapore's way. Hong Kong still has a much larger and more sophisticated financial sector and it also has an incomparable entrée into China.

While Singapore has achieved considerable success enticing foreign multinationals to invest in the republic, Singaporean companies have also been busy investing overseas in an effort to escape high labour costs at home. By the end of 1994 Singapore's cumulative foreign investment totalled nearly US$40 billion. In 1995 the republic was Thailand and Myanmar's (Burma) second largest investor, lay in third place in Russia, fourth in Vietnam, fifth in China and sixth in Indonesia.

Tourism

Tourism is now one of Singapore's most important industries; over 7 million visitors entered the country in 1996 – well over two times the island's population – staying an average of 3.3 days. Between them, they spend US$551 each or around US$4 billion a year and tourism contributes about 16% of Singapore's foreign exchange earnings. More than a quarter of visitors come from neighbouring ASEAN countries, and another third from the rest of Asia. Nearly a million Japanese visit Singapore every year, about half a million Australasians, 300,000 Britons and just over a quarter of a million Americans.

Why do so many people come to Singapore? It is hard to believe that it is for 'exoticism'. Singapore may be 'in the East', but it is hardly 'of the East' – despite what the Singapore Tourist Promotion Board might lead one to believe before arrival. Guide books have been extolling the virtues of Singapore as the

Singapore: fact file

Geographic	
Land area	600 sq km
Arable land as % of total	11%
Average annual rate of deforestation	na
Highest point, Bukit Timah	165m
Singapore:	
Average rainfall	2,369 mm
Average temperature	26.5°C
Economic	
GNP/person (1995)	US$26,730
GDP/person (PPP*, 1995)	US$22,770
GNP growth (/capita, 1985-1995)	6.2%
GDP growth 1996	6.2%
GDP growth 1997	7.0%
% labour force in agriculture	0.5%
Total debt (% GNP)	na
Debt service ratio (% exports)	na
Military expenditure (% GDP)	5.4%
Social	
Population (1995)	3.0 million
Population growth rate (1980-90)	1.7%
Population growth rate (1990-95)	2.0%
Total fertility rate (1995)	1.7
Adult literacy rate	95%
Mean years of schooling	na
Tertiary graduate as % of age group	na
Population below poverty line	na
Rural population as % of total	0%
Growth of urban population (1980-95)	1.8%/year
Urban population in largest city (%)	100%
Televisions per 1,000 people	378
Health	
Life expectancy at birth	76 years
Population with access to clean water	100%
Calorie intake as % of requirements	144%
Malnourished children less than 5 years	nil
Contraceptive prevalence rate†	74%

* PPP = Purchasing Power Parity (based on what it costs to buy a similar basket of goods and services in other countries)

† % of women of childbearing age using a form of modern contraception

Source: United Nations Development Programme (1995) *Human development report 1995*, OUP: New York; World Bank (1997) *World development report 1997*, OUP: New York; and other sources.

cultural and geographic crossroads of the world almost since the genre was invented. In *Information for tourists* published in 1908, Wright wrote that:

> "a curious combination of Orientalism and Occidentalism is to be observed on every side. From the midst of tawdry-looking native shops rise modern European establishments of commanding appearance; hand-drawn rickshaws and lumbering ox-waggons move side by side with electric tramcars, swift automobiles, and smart equipages; and the free and unfettered native goes on his way regardless of the conventionalities which are so strictly observed by the European. East and West meet, and the old is fast giving way to the new but there is, nevertheless a broad line of demarcation between them."

But the reality is that, compared with all its neighbours, modern Singapore is distinctly lacking as an exemplar of the Exotic East. So, to pose the question once again, why the multitudes of tourists? Many arrive merely as a stop-over en route elsewhere, taking advantage of the Republic's strategic location and excellent airport; others visit to revel in the city's reputation (now largely undeserved) as a 'shopper's paradise'; more come with the knowledge that the hotels are excellent and you can drink the water; the food is also an undoubted plus; while there are also large numbers of businesspeople who visit for conferences or on incentive breaks. Or perhaps it is simply that the Singapore Tourist Promotion Board, like the rest of the economy, is doing an excellent job.

It is significant that the STPB has recently changed its campaign slogan from 'Surprising Singapore' to the rather more verbose 'New Asia-Singapore: so easy to enjoy, so hard to forget'. Presumably on the basis that Singapore is more like the rest of the developed world than it is different from it, the STPB found it hard to promote the island on the grounds that it was 'surprising'. Instead, the marketing rationale is that it is 'easy'. Everyone speaks English, public transportation is painless, it is safe and clean ... and so on. There is also a great deal to do in Singapore and the 'attractions' (most are modern and man-made) are well run and some are world class. Perhaps the most revealing aspect of Singapore's tourism industry is that expatriates in other Southeast Asian countries visit Singapore for their R&R. In other words, this is where people resident in Asia come to escape from Asia.

Singapore

FROM first arrival to last impressions, Singapore is a neat, clean, green and prosperous place. The government want it to be known as the Garden of the Orient, but if so then it is a Metropolitan Garden for among the potted plants and carefully tended verges are futuristic skyscrapers, condominiums, multi-lane highways, hotels – and tens of thousands of shops. It is almost like being miniaturized and trapped in one of those urban models that architectural firms so like to produce to give a rosy vision of their buildings and surroundings. In Jakarta or Bangkok the models are so divorced from the reality that they are little more than castles in the sky. In Singapore the model and the reality merges. Streets and pavements are uncommonly clean, cars are parked in straight lines, people cross the road in orderly groups – and trees and flower-filled beds really do line the streets. And into this model land come 7 million tourists each year, many open-mouthed with admiration at this remarkable country.

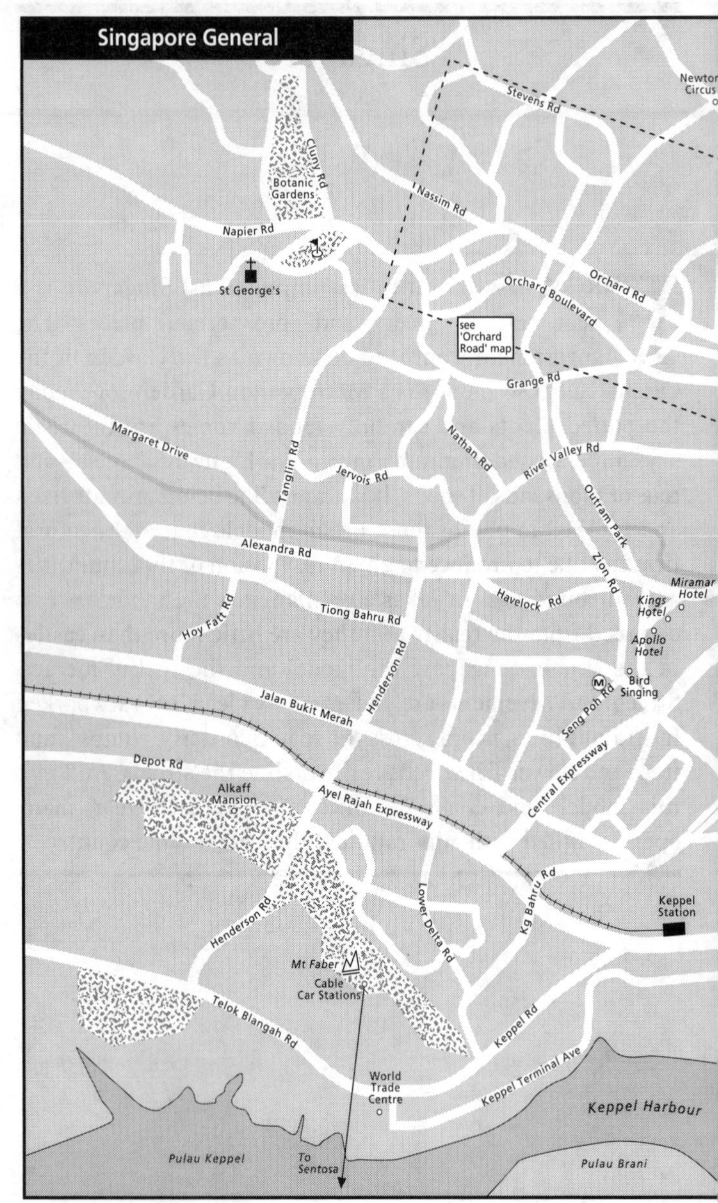
Singapore General
Newton Circus
Stevens Rd
Cluny Rd
Botanic Gardens
Nassim Rd
Napier Rd
St George's
Orchard Rd
Orchard Boulevard
see 'Orchard Road' map
Grange Rd
Margaret Drive
Tanglin Rd
Nathan Rd
River Valley Rd
Jervois Rd
Outram Park
Alexandra Rd
Zion Rd
Miramar Hotel
Havelock Rd
Kings Hotel
Hoy Fatt Rd
Tiong Bahru Rd
Apollo Hotel
Henderson Rd
Bird Singing
Seng Poh Rd
Jalan Bukit Merah
Central Expressway
Depot Rd
Alkaff Mansion
Ayel Rajah Expressway
Kg Bahru Rd
Keppel Station
Lower Delta Rd
Henderson Rd
Mt Faber
Cable Car Stations
Telok Blangah Rd
Keppel Rd
World Trade Centre
Keppel Terminal Ave
Keppel Harbour
Pulau Keppel
To Sentosa
Pulau Brani

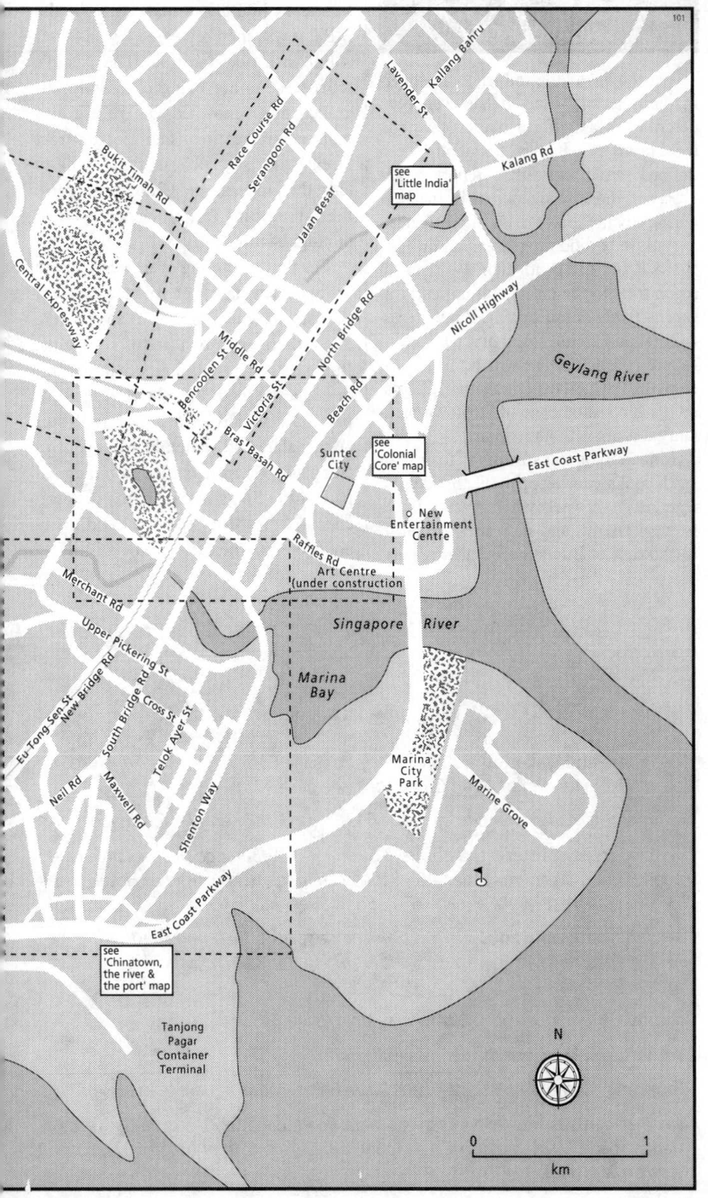

101
Kallang Bahru
Lavender St
Race Course Rd
Serangoon Rd
Kalang Rd
Bukit Timah Rd
see 'Little India' map
Jalan Besar
Central Expressway
Nicoll Highway
North Bridge Rd
Middle Rd
Bencoolen St
Victoria St
Beach Rd
Geylang River
Bras Basah Rd
Suntec City
see 'Colonial Core' map
East Coast Parkway
New Entertainment Centre
Raffles Rd
Art Centre (under construction
Merchant Rd
Singapore River
Upper Pickering St
Marina Bay
New Bridge Rd
South Bridge Rd
Cross St
Eu Tong Sen St
Telok Ayer St
Marina City Park
Neil Rd
Maxwell Rd
Shenton Way
Marine Grove
East Coast Parkway
see 'Chinatown, the river & the port' map
Tanjong Pagar Container Terminal
N
0
1
km

PLACES OF INTEREST IN SINGAPORE CITY

To some, it has all the ambience of a supermarket checkout lane. It has even been described as "a Californian resort-town run by Mormons". It has frequently been dubbed sterile and dull: a report in *The Economist* judged Singapore to be the most boring city in the world. For those who fail to venture beyond the plazas that line Orchard Road, or spend their 3½ days on coach-trips to the ersatz cultural extravaganzas, this is not surprising. But there is a cultural and architectural heritage in Singapore beyond the one which the government tries so hard to manufacture. Despite its brash consumerism and toytown mentality, it is not without its charm.

Singapore is transforming faster than guidebooks can be printed; the skyline changes every week, whole streets disappear overnight, and new ones are built. In the case of Bugis Street, having been bulldozed in 1985 to make way for the MRT, it was then recreated 7 years later – but in a new location. The island's tourist sights are being constantly upgraded and renovated. There are also many new recreational facilities to attract foreign tourists, such as Tang Dynasty City, the Japanese and Chinese Gardens, the Jurong Bird Park, the open zoo and Sentosa Island.

For those stopping over in Singapore for just a few days – en route, as most of the island's tourists are, to somewhere else – there are a handful of key sights. But in Singapore it is far more important to enjoy the food: the island has an unparalleled variety of restaurants to suit every palate and wallet. Hawker centres (see page 692) are a highly recommended part of the Singapore epicurean experience – they are inexpensive, and many are open into the early hours.

Singapore highlights

Museums and galleries *National Museum* (page 636), *Singapore Art Museum* (page 636), *Museum of Asian Civilisations* (see page 635).

Temples *Sri Mariamman Temple* (page 649), *Thian Hock Keng Temple* (page 650).

Historic areas of interest *Arab Street* (see page 657), *Serangoon Road/Little India* (page 654), *Chinatown* (page 646), *Padang area* (see below), *Raffles Hotel* (page 634), *Singapore River Area* (page 631), *Bugis Street* (page 658).

Gardens, parks and zoos *Botanic Gardens* (see page 643), *Jurong Bird Park* (page 661), *Singapore Zoological Gardens and Night Safari* (page 667), *Bukit Timah Nature Reserve* (page 668).

Islands *St Johns* (see page 674), *Pulau Ubin* (page 675).

Adventure playgrounds *Sentosa* (page 670).

Shopping *Orchard and Scotts roads* (page 643), *Marina Square* (page 684).

Hawker centres and food courts *Adam Road* (page 692), *Lau Pa Sat Festival Market* (page 692), *Newton Circus* (page 693), *Amoy Street* (page 692), *Funan Centre* (page 693).

THE COLONIAL CORE AND THE SINGAPORE RIVER

The heart of Singapore is around the mouth of the Singapore River, where Stamford Raffles first set foot in 1817. The grand colonial architecture, though physically dwarfed by the skyscrapers of the modern city, still holds its own in terms of style and majesty. Many of the early buildings were designed by the Irish architect, George Coleman (the Armenian church, Caldwell House and Maxwell House). Singapore's other main architect of the period was Alfred John Bidwell – responsible for the main wing of *Raffles Hotel*, the *Goodwood Park Hotel*, Stamford House, St Joseph's Church, the Singapore Cricket Club and Victoria Memorial Hall.

The **Padang** ('playing field' in Malay), the site of most big sporting events in Singapore – including the National Day parades – is at the centre of the colonial area. It originally fronted on to the sea, but due to land reclamation now stands a kilometre inland. After the founding of Singapore in 1819, English and Indian troops were quartered here and the area was known as the Plain. The name was only later changed to Padang. The **Cricket Club**, at the end of the Padang, was the focus of British activity. A sports pavilion was first constructed in 1850 and a larger Victorian clubhouse was built in 1884 with two levels, the upper level being the ladies' viewing gallery. A new addition is an exclusive Recreation Club, at the northern end of the Padang. The Padang is flanked by the houses of justice and government – the domed **Supreme Court** (formerly the *Hôtel de l'Europe*) and the **City Hall**. The neo-classical **City Hall** was built with Indian convict labour for a trifling S$2 million and was finished in 1929. On 12 September 1945 the Japanese surrendered here to Lord Louis Mountbatten and on the same spot, former-Prime Minister Lee Kuan Yew declared Singapore's independence in 1959.

Between the High Street and Singapore River there are other architectural legacies of the colonial period: the **clock tower**, **Parliament House, the Victoria Memorial Hall and Victoria Theatre**. It was in this area that the Temenggongs, the former Malay rulers of Singapore, built their kampung – the royal family was later persuaded to move out to Telok Blangah. The **Victoria Theatre** was originally built as the Town Hall in 1856 but was later adapted by Swan and Maclaren, to celebrate Queen Victoria's jubilee, integrating a new hall (the Memorial Hall) and linking the two with a central clock tower. The buildings are still venues for Singapore's multi-cultural dance, drama and musical extravaganzas.

Parliament House, built in 1827, is the oldest government building in Singapore, having been designed by George Coleman for the wealthy Javanese merchant John Maxwell, who was appointed by his friend Raffles as one of Singapore's first three magistrates. He never lived here however, because of a dispute over the legal rights to the land, and he later leased it out to the government as a Court House. With the construction of a Supreme Court in St Andrew's Road in 1939, the building stood empty for a decade, before becoming the Assembly Rooms in the 1950's and later, Parliament House. It is possible to see the House in session from the Strangers' Gallery, but only if there is room available. Seats are often taken by press, student groups and civil servants, so phone ahead (T 3368811). The building was undergoing renovation on our last visit. The bronze elephant in front of Parliament House was a gift to Singapore from the King of Siam, Rama V, in 1872. **Empress Place**, nearby, on the river, was one of Singapore's first conservation projects. Built as the East India Company courthouse in 1865, it later housed the legislative assembly. In its grounds stands the **Dalhousie Memorial**, an obelisk erected

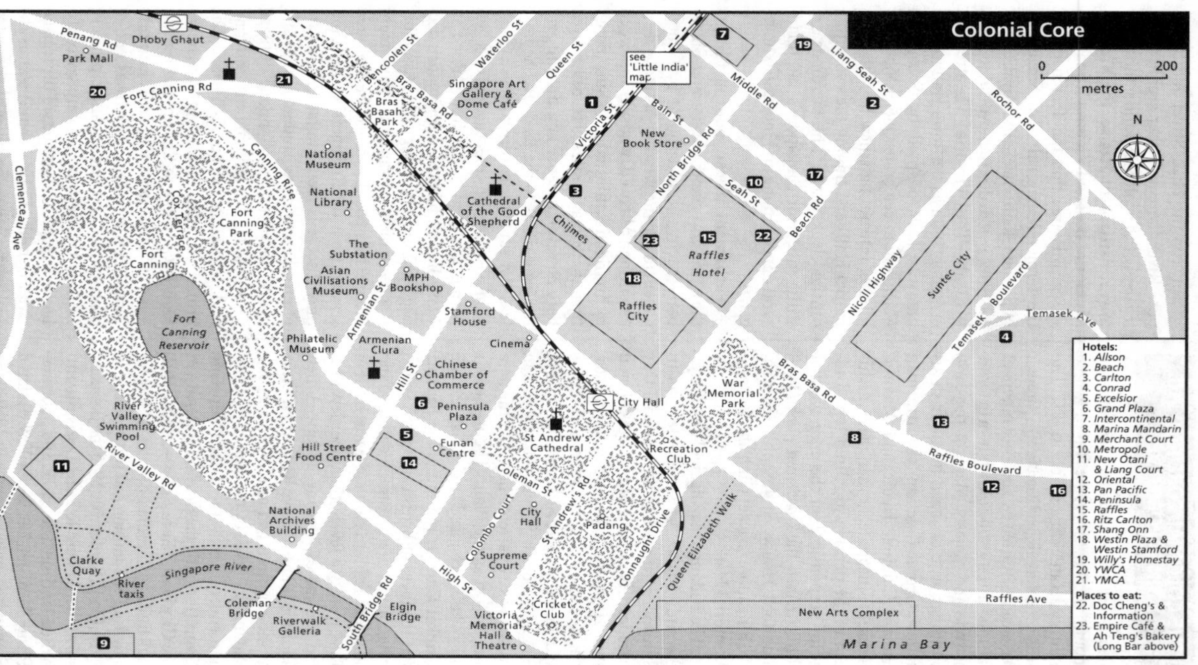
Colonial Core
0
200
metres
N
Hotels:
1. Allson
2. Beach
3. Carlton
4. Conrad
5. Excelsior
6. Grand Plaza
7. Intercontinental
8. Marina Mandarin
9. Merchant Court
10. Metropole
11. New Otani & Liang Court
12. Oriental
13. Pan Pacific
14. Peninsula
15. Raffles
16. Ritz Carlton
17. Shang Onn
18. Westin Plaza & Westin Stamford
19. Willy's Homestay
20. YWCA
21. YMCA
Places to eat:
22. Doc Cheng's & Information
23. Empire Café & Ah Teng's Bakery (Long Bar above)
Penang Rd
Park Mall
Dhoby Ghaut
Fort Canning Rd
Clemenceau Ave
Bencoolen St
Waterloo St
Queen St
see 'Little India' map
Liang Seah St
Middle Rd
Rochor Rd
Bras Basa Rd
Bras Basah Park
Singapore Art Gallery & Dome Café
Victoria St
Bain St
New Book Store
North Bridge Rd
Seah St
Beach Rd
Canning Rise
National Museum
National Library
Cathedral of the Good Shepherd
Chijmes
Raffles Hotel
Raffles City
Fort Canning Park
Cox Terrace
Fort Canning
The Substation
Asian Civilisations Museum
MPH Bookshop
Armenian St
Stamford House
Nicoll Highway
Suntec City
Temasek Boulevard
Temasek Ave
Fort Canning Reservoir
Philatelic Museum
Armenian Clura
Cinema
Hill St
Chinese Chamber of Commerce
Bras Basa Rd
War Memorial Park
City Hall
Peninsula Plaza
River Valley Swimming Pool
St Andrew's Cathedral
Funan Centre
Hill Street Food Centre
Recreation Club
Raffles Boulevard
River Valley Rd
Coleman St
St Andrew's Rd
City Hall
Padang
Colombo Court
National Archives Building
Supreme Court
Connaught Drive
Queen Elizabeth Walk
Clarke Quay
Singapore River
River taxis
High St
Coleman Bridge
Riverwalk Galleria
South Bridge Rd
Elgin Bridge
Victoria Memorial Hall & Theatre
Cricket Club
New Arts Complex
Raffles Ave
Marina Bay

in honour of Lord James Dalhousie, Governor-General of India, who visited Singapore for 3 days in 1850. He is credited on the plaque as having "emphatically recognized the wisdom of liberating commerce from all restraints".

Queen Elizabeth Walk, running from Raffles Avenue to the river-mouth, once ran along the waterfront but is now in danger of being swallowed up by the new opera house/theatre complex which is under construction here. Further upstream is a marble replica of the original **statue of Raffles**, founder of modern Singapore, on the spot where he is first believed to have stepped on to the swampy shore in 1819. The plaque on the base of the statue reads:

> "On this historic site Sir Thomas Stamford Raffles first landed in Singapore on 28 January 1819 and with genius and perception changed the destiny of Singapore from an obscure fishing village to a great seaport and modern metropole."

The original, sculpted in bronze by Thomas Woolner in 1887, stands in front of the Victoria Theatre.

Beyond the Padang is the world's tallest hotel, the *Westin Stamford*, part of the huge **Raffles City Complex** on Stamford Road. Designed by the Chinese-American architect, I M Pei (famous for the glass pyramid in front of the Louvre, Paris and the Bank of China building in Hong Kong), it contains two hotels, offices and a shopping complex.

Just down the road are the four tapering white pillars of the **War Memorial** in Memorial Park on Beach Road – better known as the four chopsticks – symbolizing the four cultures of Singapore: the Chinese, Malays, Indians and 'others'. It was built in memory of the 50,000-odd civilians who died during the Japanese occupation. A memorial service is held at the monument on 15 February each year.

The revamped ***Raffles Hotel***, with its 875 designer-uniformed staff (there is a ratio of 2½ staff to every guest) and 104 suites (each fitted with Persian carpets), eight restaurants (and a Culinary Academy) and five bars, playhouse and custom-built, leather-upholstered cabs, is the jewel in the crown of Singapore's tourist industry. In true Singapore-style it manages to boast a 5,000 sq m shopping arcade. There's even a museum of Rafflesian memorabilia on the 3rd Floor. (Open 1000-2100 Monday-Sunday. Admission free.) Next to the museum is the **Jubilee Hall Theatre** – named after the old Jubilee Theatre demolished to make way for the Raffles' extension (see below).

Raffles Hotel's original (but restored) billiard table still stands in the Billiard Room. Palm Court is still there and so is the Tiffin Room, which still serves tiffin. Teams of restoration consultants undertook painstaking research into the original colours of paint, ornate plasterwork and fittings. A replica of the cast-iron portico, known as 'cad's alley' was built to the original 19th century specifications of a Glasgow foundry.

Although just about anyone who's anyone visiting Singapore still makes a pilgrimage to the hotel, there has been a vigorous debate over whether in the process of its lavish restoration Raffles has not lost some of its atmosphere and appeal. (The same complaint has been levelled at the renovated *Railway Hotel* in Hua Hin in Thailand and the *Strand Hotel* in Rangoon, Burma.) There is no doubt that it has been done well – architecturally it can hardly be faulted and the lawns and courtyards are lush with foliage. There is also no doubt that it is an immensely comfortable and well-run hotel. But critics say they've tried a little too hard. The month after it reopened (on former Prime Minister Lee Kuan Yew's birthday, 16 September 1991), *Newsweek* said that in trying to roll a luxury hotel, a shopping mall and national tourist attraction into one, "The result is synergy run amok ... great if you need a Hermes scarf, sad if you'd like to imagine a tiger beneath the billiard table." Other critics have asked whether the hotel should really be viewed

The *Raffles Hotel* – immortalized and sanitized

"Tiger shot in *Raffles Hotel*!" blazed a *Straits Times* headline in August 1902. The wild tiger was shot while cowering among the stilts under the Billiard Room. It was one more exotic claim to fame for an already legendary institution. The hotel's magnificent teak staircases, big verandahs, bars and palm courtyards had made it the haunt of the rich and famous. It had the first electric lights, lifts and ceiling fans on the island and a French chef, which at the turn of the century was quite a novelty. To use Somerset Maugham's oft-quoted cliché, the old hotel "stood for all the fables of the exotic East ... immortalized by writers and patronized by everyone".

The main building was completed in 1889, but the hotel began life as a bungalow on the beach front, belonging to an Arab trader (today Beach Road is a long way from the sea due to land reclamation). An Englishman, Captain Dare, established a tiffin house (tiffin is the Anglo-Indian term for a light lunch) there before he expanded it into a hotel. It was then bought by the Armenian hoteliers, the Sarkies brothers, in 1885 who had just set up the *Eastern and Oriental (E&O) Hotel* in Penang and went on to establish the *Strand Hotel* in Rangoon in 1892. Under the Sarkies' management, the Raffles and its sister hotels were the epitome of British colonialism – even though the brothers were refused entry to the Singapore Cricket Club because they weren't 'white'.

Today Raffles boasts of its former guests like a public school would list its famous sons. They include celebrities, writers, kings, sultans, politicians, comedians and what one local journalist called "the flotsam and jetsam of a newly-mobile world". The hotel's literary tradition became its trump card: Somerset Maugham, Rudyard Kipling, Noel Coward and Herman Hesse all visited the hotel at one time or another. Not all were particularly impressed: Kipling said the rooms were bad and recommended that travellers go to the late great *Hôtel de l'Europe* on the Padang instead. Though the hotel claims that Joseph Conrad stayed here too, some people dispute this and say that he only visited the hotel. But the *Raffles* was *the* social epicentre of Singapore – if not the region.

as a 'national' monument. While the hotel was undergoing expansion in 1990-91, the old Jubilee Theatre was torn down to make space for it. The Jubilee Theatre was not only genuinely old – and architecturally just as significant – but also the forebears of far more Singaporeans had been to the Jubilee than had ever set foot in the *Raffles*. As local writer Heng put it in 1991, "But it is Raffles and Coward *et al* which are being preserved as heritage and not [the] Jubilee where mothers, aunts and cousins cried their hearts out for actress Ng Kuan Lai and her misfortunes by the banks of the Li-Jiang [referring to one of the Hong Kong actress' best known films, *Blood debt by the banks of Lijiang River*]."

South of *Raffles* lies **St Andrew's Cathedral**, designed by Colonel Ronald MacPherson and built in the 1850s by Indian convict labourers in early neo-gothic style. Completed in 1862, its interior walls are coated with a plaster called 'Madras chunam', a mixture of shell, lime, egg whites and sugar. Note the window commemorating Raffles as the founder of modern Singapore. The cathedral is often packed out – 13% of Singapore's population is Christian – and there are several services a day in different languages (see the notice board in the northwest corner of the plot for times of service).

Built in 1835, and the spire added in 1850, the **Armenian Church of St Gregory the Illuminator** on Hill Street is the

By the late 1920s, Arshak Sarkie – who had taken over the management of the *Raffles* and was known for his party-trick of waltzing around the Grand Ballroom with a whisky glass perched on his bald head – started gambling at the Turf Club. He got heavily into debt and at the same time launched into an expensive renovation programme at the hotel. By the turn of the decade, the bottom had fallen out of the Malayan rubber industry and the local economy collapsed into the Great Depression, taking the *Raffles* with it. Arshak Sarkies died in 1931, bankrupt and miserable. Two years later the hotel was taken over by a new company, but its golden years had died with the Sarkies'. During the war, the Japanese turned Palm Court into a drill ground. At the end of the war, patriotic British POWs gathered in the Ballroom to sing "*There'll always be an England*". The hotel served as a transit camp for them after the Japanese surrender.

By the mid-1980s the hotel had become a quaint, but crumbling colonial relic, which, like the back-packers who had taken to staying there, looked increasingly out of place in the brave new Singapore of glass and steel. The *Raffles* was rusting, peeling and mouldering. The Long Bar, the home of the Singapore Sling – first shaken by bar-tender Ngiam Tong Boon in 1915 – became a tourist gimmick. The record for Sing-Sling-slinging was set by five Australian visitors in 1985. They downed 131 inside 2 hours. Then suddenly the government woke up to the fact that it had unwittingly bulldozed half its cultural heritage. The hotel's neighbour, the Raffles Institution, had been demolished to make way for Raffles City. To save the old hotel from going the same way, it was declared a protected monument in 1987. Its recognition as an architectural treasure immediately put *Raffles* on the shortlist for a facelift. The developers spent S$160mn on consultants, white paint and fake Victorian trimmings. Shortly afterwards the group built the Raffles Hotel Arcade – from scratch – a pastiche with no history. Architect Richard Ho was appalled, writing in a letter to the *Straits Times* that it was "an atrocious and blatant falsification of our architectural heritage" adding the rebuke that it was "very much like tarting up your grandmother".

island's oldest church, designed by Irish architect George Coleman. This diminutive church seats 50 people at a squeeze. The design is said to have been influenced by London's St Martin's-in-the-Fields and Cambridge's Round Church. Agnes Joaquim is buried here – she discovered what is now the national flower of Singapore, the Vanda Miss Joaquim orchid (see page 224). Also on Armenian Street, close to Stamford Road, is a newly restored school. Tao Nan School was built in 1910 and became one of the first Chinese schools in Singapore. It has been taken over by the Singapore Museums Department and in 1997 opened as the **Asian Civilisations Museum**. As its name suggests, the focus of the museum is Chinese culture and civilisation. It consists of 12 galleries housed on 3 storeys, and along with a small permanent collection (which will be expanded) there are various temporary exhibits. The aim is for the museum to become a regional centre for Southeast Asian art history. Open 0900-1730 Tuesday-Sunday. Free guided tours Tuesday-Friday 1100, Saturday and Sunday 1100 and 1430. Admission: $3 adults, $1.50 children.

Nearby at 23B Coleman Street is the **Singapore Philatelic Museum** or **SPM** which opened to the public in 1995. It is a small but extremely well-run museum and is not just of interest to philatophiles. Children especially will find it a wonderful place to follow up on their stamp collections. Its aim is to educate the general public on the history of Singapore's – and, more widely, the world's – postal system. Children (or adults for that matter) can design their own stamps and print them out, use touch screen computers to test their knowledge of philately, tackle puzzles, or just admire the collection of stamps and envelopes. There is a good 'History Thru Stamps Gallery' which uses stamps to recount aspects of Singapore's history. Children and adults can become members of the SPM and there is also a good resource centre where visitors can access the museum's book collection and data base. Admission: S$2 (S$1 for children). Open 0900-1630 Tuesday-Sunday. *Getting there*: 5 minutes walk from the City Hall MRT station or take bus Nos 7, 14, 16, 97, 103, 166, 167, 171, 174, 182, 190 and 952.

One of George Coleman's pupils, Denis McSwiney, designed the **Roman Catholic Cathedral of the Good Shepherd**, on the junction of Queen Street and Bras Basah Road. It was used as an emergency hospital during World War Two. The building has been gazetted as a national monument, but even so looks as though it could do with a lick of paint. **CHIJMES** or the **Convent of Holy Infant Jesus**, opposite the Cathedral on Victoria Street is a complex consisting of the convent, chapel and **Caldwell House** (designed by George Coleman). It has been redeveloped by a French architect into a sophisticated courtyard of shops, pubs and restaurants. Originally, the convent was run by four French Catholic nuns, opening its doors to 14 fee paying pupils, 9 boarders and 16 orphans in 1854. As well as being an orphanage and school for older girls, Chijmes became a home to discarded babies, who were often left at the gates of the convent at the point of death. The gothic-style church, designed by French Jesuit priest Father Beurel, was added at the turn of the century. The church is now used for concerts and wedding ceremonies (and photo opportunities). Even the stained glass was painstakingly dismantled and renovated to a high standard. The former Catholic boys' school, **St Joseph's Institution**, opposite the RC Cathedral at 71 Bras Basah Road, is also a good example of colonial religious architecture. Built in 1867, it is now home to the **Singapore Art Museum**, where there are several changing exhibitions every 3 months or so. It can be a welcome break from the heat to wander through the wondrously cool galleries. On the ground floor there are inter-active multi-media presentations. While St Joseph's was being renovated a feature wall was discovered behind a row of built-in cupboards. Two supporting columns bear an entablature emblazoned with the words *Santa Joseph Ora Pro Nobis* (Saint Joseph pray for us) and it is presumed that the school chapel was located here. Admission S$3 adults, S$1.50 children and senior citizens. Open 0900-1730 Tuesday-Sunday. Bras Basah Road was so called because wet rice – *bras basah* in Malay – was dried here on the banks of the Sungai Bras Basah (now Stamford Canal).

Across the green on Stamford Road is the **National Museum and Art Gallery**. The idea of setting up a museum was first mooted by Stamford Raffles in 1823; it was finally built in 1887 and named the Raffles Museum. It was most recently renovated in 1991, after which it was renamed. As a whole, the museum is rather disappointing given the quality of Singapore's other attractions. There is little coherence between its varied exhibits and little sense of narrative. Nor are the pieces displayed terribly interesting or beautiful. Only the 20 dioramas on the left of the main entrance are a permanent exhibition. These scenes visually recount 20 important episodes in the history of Singapore from the first landing on a jungled island inhabited by fisherfolk through to Independence. They are interesting enough – especially for children – and provide an easy to digest, stoccato view of Singapore over the last two centuries or so. All the other exhibits are temporary. For example, in 1997 the interior of a Peranakan home had been reconstructed, with detailed information on the contents of each room, and there was also a toy exhibition. The attached **Children's Discovery Gallery** has changing exhibits every 6 months. During the week it is closed for 2 hours every morning and afternoon for school groups. Plenty of hands on activity for children. Admission S$3, children S$1.50. Open 0900-1730, closed Monday. Conducted tours from the information counter at 1100, Tuesday-Friday. Slide shows through the day in the AV Theatre.

The **National Art Gallery**, next to the museum, is disappointing, although from time to time there is a more invigorating visiting exhibition on show. The permanent collection contains mediocre works by Singaporean and Asian artists. Admission incorporated in entry fee to National Museum. Open 0900-1730 Tuesday-Sunday. The **National Library** is on the other side of the museum. It is open daily until 1700 and is a good place to browse, either on one of the many computers or in the bookshelves.

Where Stamford Road meets Orchard Road, just up from the museum and next to the *YMCA*, is the **Presbyterian church**, built in 1878 and now a protected monument. The church's caretaker's house was the centre of the 1984 'Curry Murder Horror'. The Tamil caretaker was dismembered and his body disposed of by cooking it up with curry and rice. It was then discarded in rubbish bins around Singapore, masquerading as the remains of a hawker-stall takeaway. Six people, including a butcher and a mutton curry stall holder, were arrested in 1987, but later released for lack of evidence.

Behind the museum is **Fort Canning Park**. The British called it Singapore Hill, but its history stretches back centuries earlier. It is known as Bukit Larangan or 'Forbidden Hill' by the Malays as this was the site of the ancient fortress of the Malay kings and reputedly contains the tomb of the last Malay ruler of the kingdom of Singapura, Sultan Iskandar Shah (see page 579). Archaeological digs in the area have discovered remains from the days of the Majapahit Empire. Also in the 20 hectares park are the ruins of Fort Canning – the Gothic gateway, derelict guardhouse and earthworks are all that remain of a fort which once covered 3 hectares – and an old Christian cemetery where the first settlers including the architect George Coleman were buried. Sir Stamford Raffles lived here for a while, in a simple attap hut, though he was not buried here. He suffered an ignominious death and funeral in North London and it was only later that he was reburied in Westminster Abbey. Fort Canning Park has been restored and redeveloped; the Ministry of National Development intends to include a museum, underground bunkers and a house to tell the story of Sir Stamford Raffles.

On the other side of the park is the Hindu **Chettiar Temple** on Tank Road. The original temple on this site was built by wealthy Chettiar Indians (money lenders). It has been superseded by a modern version, finished in 1984, and is dedicated to Lord Subramaniam. The ceiling has 48 painted glass panels, angled to reflect sunset and sunrise. Its *gopuram*, the 5-tiered entrance, aisles, columns and hall all sport rich sculptures depicting Hindu deities. Many Hindu temples close in the heat of the day, so are best seen before 1100 and after 1500.

The **Singapore River**, separates the high-rise, hi-tech financial district from the colonial heart of town. Despite modernization, the waterfront area still bears some resemblance to pre-war Singapore. Perhaps it is for this reason that engaged couples choose to have videos made (usually on Sunday) with this part of the city as the backdrop. Most hire their suits and dresses and have the videos made before they are married and the attention to detail is impressive.

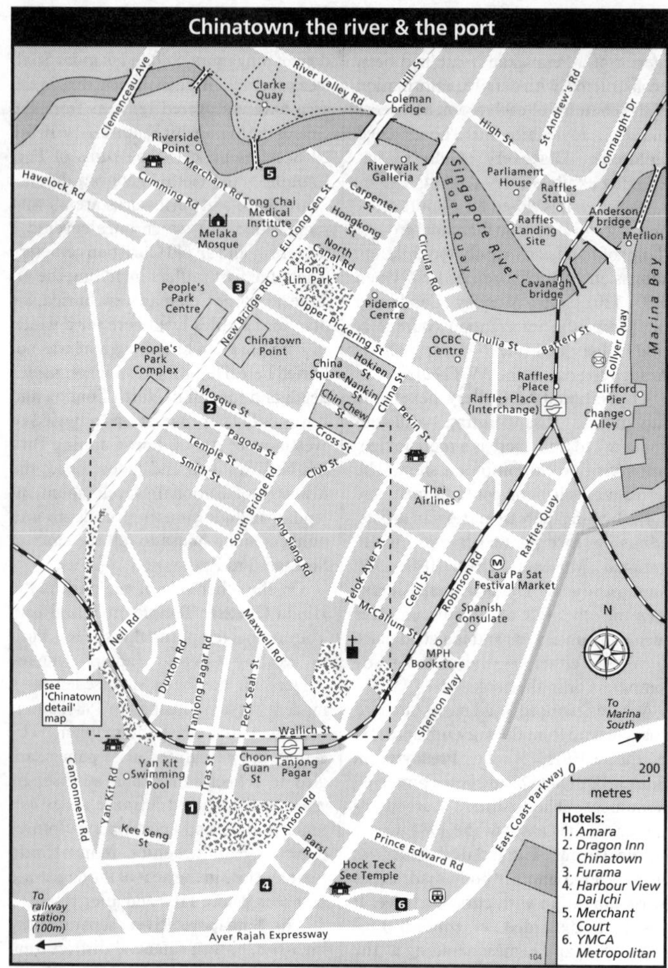

Standing guard at the mouth of the river – though rather dwarfed now by the construction of a new bridge – is the mythical **Merlion**, half-lion, half-fish, the grotesque saturnine symbol of Singapore (sculpted by local artist Lim Nang Seng in 1972 and best viewed from the Padang). It is inspired by the two ancient (Sanskrit) names for the island: *Singa Pura* meaning 'lion city', and *Temasek* meaning 'sea-town'. The confused creature is emblazoned on many a trinket and T-shirt.

Cavenagh Bridge erected in 1869 by convict labourers (the last big project undertaken by convicts here) was originally called Edinburgh Bridge to commemorate the visit of the Duke of

Edinburgh. It was later renamed Cavenagh in honour of Governor WO Cavenagh. It was built to provide a link between the government offices on the north side of the river and Commercial Square to the south. It became a footbridge in 1909 when the Anderson Bridge superseded it. It still bears its old sign that forbids bullock carts, horses and heavy vehicles from crossing. Bumboats (or *tonkangs*, a wooden lighter), barges and sampans once littered the river, but they were cleared out to Marina Bay, or destroyed and scuttled, as part of the government's river-cleaning programme over a period of 10 years. Singapore River is now said to be 'pollution-free' (although it only takes a quick glance to see that this is blatent rubbish) but what it gained in cleanliness, it has lost – some would argue (see page 588) – in aesthetics.

Along the south bank of the river, facing Empress Place, is **Boat Quay** – one of the Urban Redevelopment Authority's restoration projects. The shophouses were restored and renovated, and the original businesses were forced to moved out. Viewing Boat Quay from the north bank gives the impression of a row of brightly coloured Lego constructions set against the immensity of the CBD. The strip now provides a great choice of drinking holes and restaurants for Singapore's upwardly mobile young, expats and tourists alike. They congregate here in the evening to eat and drink *al fresco*, overlooking the river. (In 1994, *al fresco* dining was banned by the authorities after 4 expats decided to swim across the river – the loser paid the bill. The restaurants and bars shrilly claimed that they depended on their outside business and after a while the government relented.) It is perhaps the most attractive place to eat or drink in Singapore: a sort of Fisherman's Wharf comes to Covent Garden, and consequently very popular with tourists. What is disturbing to the purist is that 'conservation areas' such as Boat Quay, although they may have been meticulously restored on the outside, are now utterly divorced from their original purpose. Material fabric is painstakingly preserved or recreated; social fabric is torn down without an apparent second thought. These sorts of concerns are unlikely, though, to worry the visitor. Boat Quay is lively and fun, attractive and atmospheric – and the bars and restaurants are generally excellent. The formerly famous *Harry's Bar* is yet more famous still: this is where Barings trader Nick Leeson would buy the rounds before he bankrupted his employer. The river front opposite Boat Quay is being repiled and developed.

Clarke Quay, further upriver, has been redeveloped too. This was once godown country – in colonial days, the streets around the warehouses would have been bustling with coolies. It is now a pleasant pedestrian area with 150-odd shops, restaurants and bars. However, Clarke Quay is very different from Boat Quay; while the latter consists of individual enterprises, the former is controlled by a single company who keep close tabs on which shops and F&B outlets open. The atmosphere is more ersatz, more managed and controlled, and less vivacious. Unsurprisingly, this is more of a family place, while young, single people tend to congregate downriver at Boat Quay. In the pedestrian lanes overpriced hawker stalls and touristy knick-knack carts set up from lunchtime onwards selling all manner of goods that people could do without.

The big family attraction at Clarke Quay is the **Clarke Quay Adventure Ride**, a Singaporean Pirates of the Caribbean in which visitors take bumboats along an underground river, floating past 80 animated figures, and the noises and sights of Old Singapore. The history begins when Singapore was little more than a jungled island infested with monster snakes, crocodiles and – zoogeographically improbably – lions (presumably because this is the Lion City). It then passes

Bankers' rising aspirations

Singapore's big-four banks are obsessed with reaching for the sky. The city skyline is dominated by the banks' corporate pyramids. In the 1970s, the Oversea-Chinese Banking Corporation (OCBC) invited American-Chinese architect IM Pei to design its so-called 'vertical calculator'. DBS Bank occupies a drab building on Shenton Way, but in the 1980s funded the construction of Raffles City, which boasts the tallest hotel in the world at 220m – again built by Pei.

More recently, Overseas Union Bank (OUB) glossed its corporate image with a 280m-high aluminium triangle designed by distinguished Japanese architect Kanzo Tange and became, for a while, the tallest building in the world, outside America. Not to be out-done, United Overseas Bank (UOB) also commissioned Kanzo Tange to dream up the S$500mn, 66-storey UOB Plaza which now presides over Boat Quay and Chinatown. UOB had long suffered a loss of face in the local financial community, thanks to its squat HQ on Bonham Street – a trifling 32 storeys. A picture of the new building appeared on a UOB Visa card as early as 1988, showing it towering over the nearby OUB building. But in fact, Singapore law states that 280m is the highest a building can go without becoming an aviation hazard and both buildings are exactly 280m high. A third building also reaches this magical height: the Republic Plaza.

UOB's move to its new premises may prove too much for Singapore's vertical marathon runners: the Singapore Adventurers' Club organizes an annual race to the top of the old UOB building and down again, the marathon consisting of six round trips – or 4,692 steps. The record is just under 27 minutes.

through a series of vignettes including Singapore as a haven for pirates, its growth into one of the British Empire's most important entrepots, the ignominious fall of the city to the invading Japanese, and ending with its liberation in 1945 when Lord Louis Mountbatten took the surrender. Admission S$5, S$3 for children, family tickets available, open 1100-2230 Monday-Sunday. On the waterfront a makeshift theatre provides **wayang performances** from Wednesday-Saturday at 1930. The performers prepare themselves from 1800 onwards and onlookers are welcome to watch the making-up process. Wayang was traditionally performed in tents like this one by travelling artists who would move from town to town, performing for special occasions. The tongkangs moored alongside the quay are now used as floating restaurants. Traditionally they were used as lighters, to transport cargo from larger ships. The eyes painted on them were so that they could see where they were going.

A good way of seeing the sights along Singapore River is on a bumboat cruise, which can be taken from Clarke or Boat Quay. A rather banal recorded commentary points out the godowns, shophouses, government buildings and skyscrapers lining the riverbank. Bumboats operate 0900-2300, S$7 (S$3 for children). A river taxi also operates from here, S$1 (morning) and S$3 (afternoon).

Next to the Merlion is **Clifford Pier**, built in the 1930s. It is possible to hire boats to cruise up and down the river and around Marina Bay from the pier (see page 676). Marina Bay is dotted with small craft and ferries and framed by Benjamin Sheares Bridge.. Bumboats and junks also go to the south islands from Clifford Pier. Behind it (across the shopping arcade/footbridge) is **Change Alley** – once a crowded bazaar and the cheapest spot in Singapore. Appropriately, Change Alley has changed more than anywhere else in Singapore – it has been knocked down and anything that remains has disappeared into the void between 2 tower blocks.

Shenton Way (Singapore's equivalent of Wall Street), Raffles Place, Robinson Road and Cecil Street, all packed-tight with skyscrapers, form the **financial heart** of modern Singapore. These streets contain most of the buildings that give the city its distinctive skyline, which is best seen from the Benjamin Sheares Bridge or from the boat coming back from Batam island. The first foreign institutions to arrive on the island still occupy the prime sites – the Hong Kong and Shanghai Banking Corporation and Standard Chartered Bank. The **Lau Pa Sat Festival Market**, once known as Telok Ayer, between Robinson Road and Raffles Quay, was the first municipal market in Singapore, commissioned by Stamford Raffles in 1822 and built in cast-iron shipped out from a foundry in Glasgow in 1894. It is the last remaining Victorian cast-iron structure in Southeast Asia and was made a national monument in 1973 but had to be dismantled in 1985 to make way for the MRT, and was then rebuilt. It is now a thriving Food Centre.

Marina South, east of the city proper, is a vast expanse of land reclaimed from the sea in the 1970s and 1980s as an overspill area for the envisaged spread of Singapore's financial district. To make something out of nothing, Marina Village was built, complete with restaurants, bars, concert venues, discos, a night bazaar, and a bowling alley. It was, however, a complete flop, and the ebullient Moroccan businessman who financed it has fled the country. The fate of the development remains uncertain: one proposal is to turn it into a honeymoon village. A couple of the restaurants there are superb, however, and it is a good place to eat seafood under the stars.

THE PORT

Singapore is strategically located at the southern end of the Strait of Melaka, half way between China and India. It is a free port, open to all maritime nations. The port, largely sheltered from the city, has seven gateways; the biggest – the container port – is the **Tanjong Pagar terminal**. In 1820 the first resident, Colonel William Farquhar, realising the advantages of Keppel Harbour's deep and sheltered water, began to develop it as a port. In 1864 the Tanjong Pagar Dock Company was formed and in 1972 the first container terminal was established.

There are usually 800 or more ships in port at any one time – one arrives, on average, every 5 minutes. In 1995 104,014 vessels called at the port making it, in terms of shipping tonnage, the busiest port in the world (overtaking Rotterdam). It is also the world's busiest container port, overtaking Hong Kong in 1990. In 1995 11,850,000 TEUs (Twenty-Foot Equivalent Units) passed through the port. The container handling system is computerized and fully automated and ships are unloaded using Artificial Intelligence. These so-called 'expert-systems', designed and built in Singapore, have reduced the processing time to about 30 seconds per container. The Port of Singapore Authority operates six terminals: Tanjong Pagar is the main terminal for handling containers, Keppel Wharves and Sembawang Wharves (on the north of the island) are for conventional cargoes, Jurong Port is for dry bulk cargoes, and there is a new billion-dollar container terminal at Pulau Brani as well as the Pasir Panjang terminal. Singapore port has attracted admiring comment for almost as long as the place has existed. In 1934, Roland Braddell described the harbour as a "Clapham Junction of the World" – referring to the world's busiest railway junction in southern England. For the best views of the port, the *Harbour View Dai-Ichi Hotel* must win the prize.

South Boat Quay c1900

To the west of Tanjong Pagar port, on Keppel Road, is the **World Trade Centre**. Most people visit the World Trade Centre either to get to Sentosa (see page 670) or to take the boat to Batam and Bintan islands in Indonesia's Riau Archipelago, or to climb aboard the cable car which connects Sentosa with Mount Faber. Also here is the **Singapore Maritime Showcase**. This is really a museum devoted to Singapore's role as one of the world's largest and most efficient ports. A 12-minute 'Maritime Odyssey' transports you rather jerkily in a container through past, present and future Singapore. An extensive model of the port gives some idea of its size, a video wall describes the process of loading and unloading, there are banks of computers providing touch screens for maritime information and a rather difficult game, and there's a children's area with basic Lego available. Neptune Topaz provides a bridge and control panels for potential naval recruits and a short unexciting film about key ports of the world. The wooden models of ships are more fun. A cheap way to spend a rainy afternoon with bored children, but not worth a special visit. Admission: S$4 (S$2 for children). Open 1030-1830 Tuesday-Friday, 1030-2030 Saturday and Sunday. *Getting there*: by bus 10, 30, 61, 65, 84, 93, 97, 100, 131, 143, 145 and 166.

Opposite the exhibition halls of the World Trade Centre, lies the **Telok Blangah Johor State Mosque**, dating from the 1840s. It was the focal point of the pre-Raffles Malay royalty in Singapore. The tomb of the Temenggong Abdul Rahman – the *Tanah Kubor Rajah* or *Tanah Kubor Temenggong* – is nearby; he was partly responsible for negotiating Singapore's status as a trading post with Stamford Raffles. The Johor royal family lived at Telok Blangah until 1855 when the town of Iskandar Putri was founded on the other side of the straits; it was renamed Johor Bahru in 1866.

ORCHARD ROAD

In the mid 1800s the Orchard Road area was one vast nutmeg plantation before being cleared for the construction of colonial mansions. Until the 1970s, *Raffles' Place*, in the colonial core, was the core of Singapore's shopping district. Choon Keng Tang, a rags-to-riches immigrant from Swatow who in the 1920s sold linen door-to-door from a rickshaw, bought a plot of land on Orchard Road in 1945 and built *CK Tang's* Oriental curio store, in Chinese imperial style. In 1982 the old shop was demolished and the new hotel and department store complex went up; the eye-catching pagoda-style *Marriott Hotel* (once the *Dynasty*), with *Tang's* still next to it, is one of the last remaining remnants of Oriental style in an otherwise Occidental street. Today, for hundreds of metres on either side of *Tang's*, there are scores of multi-storey shopping complexes.

Orchard Road is the Singapore's catwalk, where young (and not so young) trendies strut, showing off their latest purchases. It is a shoppers' paradise and is said to have the highest density of shops in the world as well as being one of the world's most expensive shopping streets (see box on page 644 for plaza guide).

Peranakan Place, Cuppage Road and the pleasant Emerald Hill with its bars and street cafés have managed to escape demolition and the Peranakan (Straits Chinese) shophouses have been carefully restored to their original condition. Most were constructed between 1918 and 1930 and combined European and Chinese designs). **Emerald Hill** was laid out by 30 different owners between 1901 and 1925: conforming to the established theme was considered good manners, which has resulted in a charming street of shophouses.

The **Peranakan Place Museum** on Emerald Hill gives some idea of what Straits Chinese townhouses were originally like inside, although this recreation is a poor example (there is a much better one in Melaka, see page 230). For a detailed background on Peranakan culture, see page 230. Admission S$10 (S$5 for children). Open 1500-1600 Monday-Friday, minimum 4 people per entry.

About three-quarters of the way southeast down Orchard Road, towards Bras Basah Road, are the gates that lead along an inviting shady avenue to the **Istana Negara Singapura**, the residence of the former British governors of Singapore (from 1869-1959) and now home to the President of the Republic. The Istana was designed by the colonial architect Captain McNair, in Malay-cum-colonial style – with overhanging roofs blended with classical details. Like other colonial houses of this era (see page 594), it was raised off the ground to provide a cooling effect. It has been much altered over the years and is not open to the public. **Dhoby Ghaut**, at the end of Orchard Road, got its name from the Bengali and Madrasi dhobies who used to wash the clothes of local residents in the stream which ran down the side of Orchard Road and dry them on the land now occupied by the *YMCA*. This area has been earmarked for redevelopment in 1998.

On Tank Road is **Tan Yeok Nee Mansion**, one of the very few remaining traditionally designed Chinese houses, built in 1885 by a wealthy Teochew merchant. The building was badly damaged during the Japanese occupation but later restored by the Salvation Army. It has been designated a national monument but remains unrestored and boarded up.

At the western end of Orchard Road are the **Botanic Gardens**, on Cluny Road, not far from Tanglin and at the top end of Orchard Road (T 4709900). The gardens contain almost half a million species of plants and trees from around the world in its 47 hectares of landscaped parkland, primary jungle, lawns and lakes. The Botanic Gardens also houses an orchid garden where 2,000 perennial species of Singapore's favourite flower

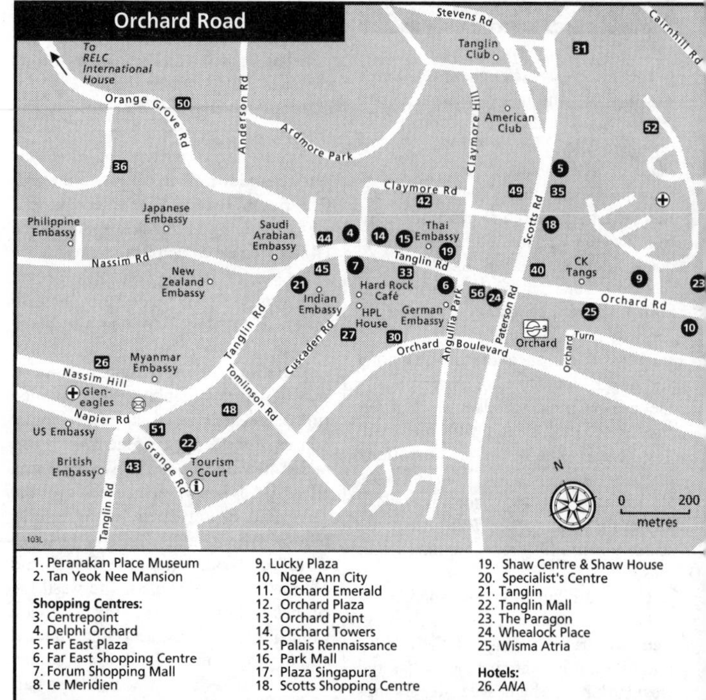

Shopping centres on Orchard Road

Centrepoint (3), dominated by *Robinsons* department store, *Mothercare*, *Lacoste*, large *Times Bookshop* and an *MPH Bookshop*, Art Gallery on top floor: *Art Focus*.
Far East Plaza (4), 14 Scotts Road: good for leather goods, camera and watch shops. Money-changers, tailors and several reasonable restaurants and a small food court; also some good electronics shops. Local department store, *Metro*, in the basement, sells clothes, household goods, shoes and accessories. Probably stays open the longest.
Lucky Plaza (5), one of Singapore's first big complexes, now rather down-market. Reasonably good for electronics and cameras, jewellery and watches, scores of tailors; at ground level, along the front there are a number of opticians offering good deals on Raybans and designer sunglasses. Copy-watch touts at the bottom. Bargaining is possible in most of the stores here.
Meridien (31), by *Meridien Hotel*, *DFS Collections* in basement for duty free goods, large very good quality furniture store – old and new wooden products.
Orchard Point, large Australian cut price textiles, *B&N*.
Factory Outlet, whole of top floor has art galleries and jade shops.
Whealock Place, brand new store, so far it only has a big *Marks & Spencer* in it.

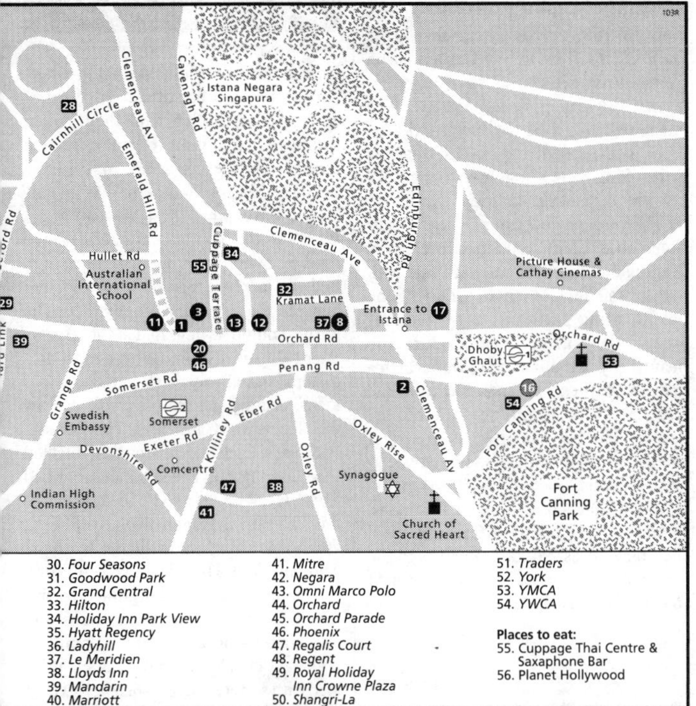

Forum, predominantly children's clothes and a *Toys 'R' Us* is here.

Hilton Shopping Plaza – connects *Hilton* and *Four Seasons Hotel – top* haute couture designers. Escalators state "Ladies watch your gowns".

Ngee Ann City (7), this massive new complex houses the *Takashimaya* department store, and over 100 speciality stores, mainly fashion boutiques – *Burberrys*, *Louis Vuitton*, *Tiffanys*, *Chanel*, *Charles Sourdain* and several restaurants. *Sparks*, a disco, is on the top floor. Popular with the rich and famous and a hang out for the young and trendy.

Palais Renaissance (9),hideously trendy design, the best in designer-boutiques and branded goods (Versace, DKNY, etc.).

Plaza Singapura (10), *Yaohan* department store and several music shops – both for CDs and for instruments.

Scotts (11), 6 Scotts Road: department store, 'Picnic' food court in basement, smart female boutiques with contemporary designers. Good electronics shops.

Shaw Centre (12), corner of Scotts Road and Orchard Road: Massive hi-tech block, with a large *Isetan* department store with all the concessions (including *Laura Ashley*), big bookshop – *Kinokuniya*, with a good range of English books and Lido Cineplex on top floors.

Specialists' Centre (13), just across from Centrepoint; downmarket department store.

Continued overleaf

are lovingly cultivated (open 0830-1800, admission $2), the closest entrance to the Gardens for the Orchid Garden is on Tyersall Avenue.

In 1963 former Prime Minister Lee Kuan Yew launched the successful Garden City campaign and most of the trees lining Singapore's highways were supplied by the Botanic Gardens.

The gardens now cater for the recreational needs of modern Singapore. Every evening and morning the park fills with joggers and Tai Chi fanatics. During the day, wedding parties pose for pictures among the foliage. The gardens are beautifully laid out and are well worth a visit. A map can be acquired from the Ranger's office, 5 minutes walk into the garden. The bandstand in the centre of the gardens is popular for live music at the weekends. Open 0530-2300 Monday-Friday, 0530-2400 Saturday and Sunday. *Getting there*: take MRT to Orchard Road, then take buses 7, 106, 174 or 123 to the junction of Cluny and Napier roads, next to Gleneagles Hospital.

CHINATOWN

Immigrants from China settled in Singapore in the latter half of the 19th century, and recreated much of what they had left behind. Clan groups began migrating from the Southern provinces of China to the *Nang Yang* or 'Southern Seas' in successive waves from the 17th century on. By 1849 the Chinese population had reached 28,000, but the area they inhabited was largely confined to a settlement between Telok Ayer and Amoy streets. The greatest numbers migrated in the 40 years after 1870, mostly coming from the south-eastern coastal provinces, with the Hokkiens forming the majority, followed by the Teochews, Cantonese, Hakkas and Foochows. Each dialect group established their own temple. The Hokkiens founded Thian Hock Keng in 1821, the Cantonese founded Fu Tak Chi on Telok Ayer Street around the same time as did the Teochews who built Wak Hai Cheng Bio on Philip Street. Streets too were occupied by different Chinese groups, with clubs and clan houses – or *kongsi* – aiding family or regional ties. The *kongsi* were often affiliated with secret societies – or *tongs* – which controlled the gambling and prostitution industries and the drug trade.

The area known as **Kreta Ayer** encompasses **Smith**, **Temple**, **Pagoda**, **Trengganu** and **Sago streets**. This was the area that Raffles marked out for the Chinese kampong and it became the hub of the Chinese community, deriving its name from the ox-drawn carts that carried

Tanglin (17), top end of Orchard Road: a treasure trove of Asian antiques and curios, Persian rugs, closes between 1800 and 1900.

The Paragon (14), one of the best places for boutique browsers, particularly mens fashions; branded names, but not that exclusive.

Wisma Atria (15), *Isetan* department store, smart fashion boutiques, an *MPH bookshop*, and small food court.

Park Mall, Penang Road one of the newer piazzas, full of interior design items: furniture, textiles, lamps. Food in basement.

Orchard Emerald, Quirky little individual shops – jewellery, unusual boutiques, etc.

Tangs, next to *Marriott Hotel*. Very smart department store; the *Harrods* of Singapore.

water to the area. Renovation by the URA has meant that these streets still retain their characteristic baroque-style shophouses with weathered shutters and ornamentation. The typical Straits Chinese house accommodated the family business on the ground floor; the second and third floors were family living quarters, sometimes accommodating two families (and in later years, as Chinatown became desperately overcrowded, up to five families). A few wealthy Chinese merchants – or *towkays* – built their houses according to traditional Chinese architectural conventions, but these have long since been demolished. However, one such example is Tan Yeok Nee's mansion on Tank Road, at the eastern end of Orchard Road (see page 643). Another is the **Thong Chai Medical Institute** on Eu Tong Sen Street, at the corner of Merchant Road. It was built in southern Chinese palace style with three halls, two inner courts and ornamental gables and was completed in 1892. By the end of the 19th century it had become a centre for traditional medicine, offering its services free to the poor – '*thong chai*' means 'benefit to all'. In 1911, during a malaria outbreak, it distributed free quinine. The building also became a focal point for the Chinese community, being the headquarters for the Chinese guilds. The Chinese Chamber of Commerce began life here. The building was made a national monument in 1973 and is in the process of renovation.

Today, Chinatown is overshadowed by the 200m-high skyscrapers of the financial area and indoor markets have replaced the many street stalls and night markets that made the area a favoured tourist spot in days gone by. (These night markets – known by their Malay name, *pasar malam*, *pasar* from the Arabic, bazaar – still reappear in the run-up to Chinese New Year). Expansion of the financial district meant that Chinatown was being demolished so rapidly that by the time the authorities realized that tourists actually wanted to see its crumbling buildings,

many of the streets had already been destroyed. In any case, Chinatown had become a slum, with overcrowding and poor sanitation being very real problems. A clean up campaign was undertaken. Its markets were cleared out, shops and stalls relocated, shophouses refurbished and the smells and noises of Chinatown banished to a world that only a few confused grandparents care to remember. Many residents have moved out to new modern flats in the Housing Development Board estates scattered around the island. Despite all the refurbishment and 'urban renewal', Chinatown remains one of the most interesting parts of town, retaining something of the original atmosphere. The rows of shophouses – once derelict – have been bought up, redeveloped and rented out as office space for small design companies, publishing companies, art galleries and so on. (For more detailed information on the rights and wrongs of redevelopment, see page 589.)

In Sago Street (or 'death house alley' as it was known in Cantonese, after its hospices for the dying), **Temple Street** and **Smith Street**, there are shops making paper houses and cars, designed to improve the quality of the after-life for

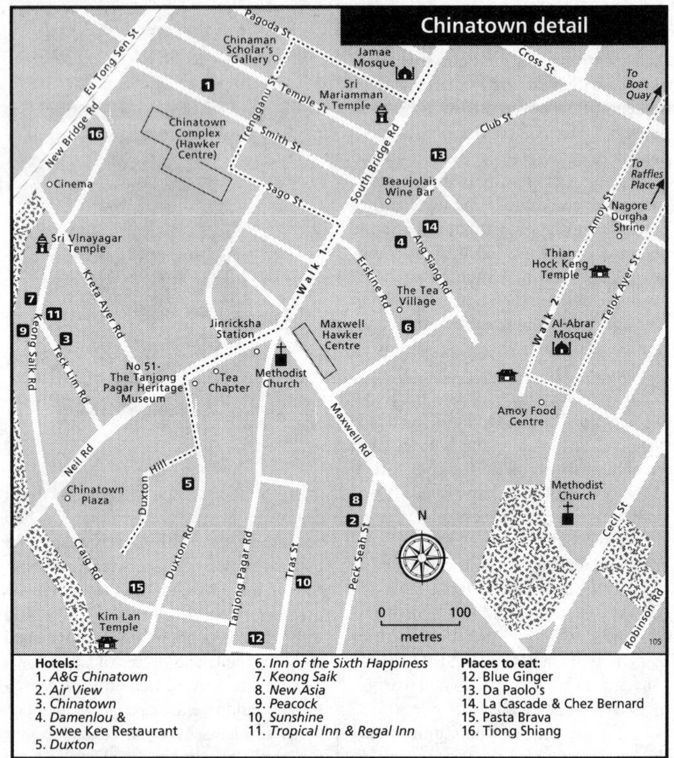

dead relatives (by burning the models after the funeral, it is believed that one's worldly wealth hurries after you into the next world). Also on these streets, shops sell all the accoutrements needed for a visit to a Chinese temple. At No 36 Smith Street a 3-storey building was originally home to a famous Cantonese opera theatre – Smith Street was also known as 'Hei Yuen Kai' or Theatre Street. The English may have given Sago Street that name as Singapore became a centre for producing high quality sago for export to India and Europe. By 1849 there were 15 Chinese and 2 European sago factories here. Chinese temple-carvers still live on **Club Street** – which also has a number of *kongsi* along it. Many of the buildings along **Mosque Street** were originally stables. It was also home to Hakkas, who traded in second-hand paper and scrap metal – today it is better known for its Chinese restaurants. No 37 Pagoda Street was one of the many coolie quarters in the area – home to Chinese immigrants, who lived in cramped conditions, sleeping in bunk spaces. Chinese traditional medicine halls still do a roaring trade, despite the advantages of Medisave schemes and 21st century pharmaceuticals. The Hong Lim complex on **Upper Cross Street** has several such medicine halls. There are also a few skilled Chinese calligraphers still around Upper Cross Street.

Walking tour of Chinatown

Chinatown is sufficiently compact and interesting to explore on foot. Set out below are two suggested walking tours, taking in many of the more interesting streets and sights of interest in the area.

Walk 1 Start at the **Jamae Mosque** on the corner of Mosque Street and South Bridge Road. Walk one block down South Bridge Road to Pagoda Street and the **Sri Mariamman Temple**. Turn into Pagoda Street and left down Trengganu Street to the **Chinaman Scholar's Gallery**, and then chicken foot through Temple, Smith and Sago Streets, to get a taste of the heart of Chinatown, to the **Jinricksha Station**, on the corner of Tanjong Pagar and Neil roads. From here, walk down **Neil Road** past **Tea Houses**, then turn left onto **Duxton Road** and right again into **Duxton Hill** – a quiet cul-de-sac of attractive restored shophouses. If you time this right, you could end up on Duxton Hill for an early evening drink in one of the bars here. Duxton Hill lies in the midst of the Tanjong Pagar conservation area, and is surrounded by streets of restored shophouses – Craig and Keong Saik roads display good examples of the Transitional Shophouse style (see page 591).

Walk 2 For a more modest stroll, start at Raffles Place (MRT station here) and wander through the high-rise blocks to the northern end of Telok Ayer Street. Walk the full length of Telok Ayer Street (see illustration), taking in the various temples, mosques and churches along the way (see page 650 for details), ending up at the Amoy Food Centre to experience an original hawker centre. Walk north again up Amoy Street, which shows you how the shophouses look pre- and post-restoration and make your way back to Raffles Place or, if you have the energy, to Boat Quay for a drink or a bite to eat.

First Traditional shophouse style
No 120 Telok Ayer Street

In the heart of Chinatown (14b Trengganu Street), up a narrow staircase, next to a herbal medicine shop is the **Chinaman Scholar's Gallery**, a mini-museum of life in the merchants' and scholars' houses in the 1920s. The gallery is run by antique dealer Vincent Tan, and visitors can sip Chinese tea as they wander around the kitchen, bedroom, dining and living areas, and flick through photographs. Mr Tan gives musical interludes with demonstrations of instruments from China, such as the lute, *pipa* (mandolin) and *yang chin* (harp). Admission S$4 (S$2 for children). Open 0900-1600 Monday-Friday, but sometimes it's inexplicably closed.

As if to illustrate Singapore's reputation as a racial and religious melting-pot, the Hindu **Sri Mariamman Temple** is situated nearby at 244 South Bridge Road. This particular temple dates from 1923, although there was a temple on this site by 1827. The temple shop is piled high with books on Hindu philosophy and cosmology and, unsurprisingly, is run by a Chinese family. Although recently renovated, this gaudy, Dravidian-style temple dates from 1823, when Stamford Raffles first granted the land to Narian Pillai, a Tamil who arrived in Singapore at the same time as its founder and set up Singapore's first brickworks. The building, in its present form, opened in 1863 and is dedicated to Sri Mariamman, a manifestation of Siva's wife Parvati. The temple is the site of the annual Thimithi festival which takes place at the end of October or the beginning of November (see page 724). To the north of the temple, also on South Bridge Road, is the **Jamae Mosque**, built in 1826 by the Chulias from southern India. It harnesses an eclectic mix of Anglo-Indian, Chinese and Malay architecture.

Telok Ayer Street is another street full of shophouses and fascinating temples of different religions. This street was once one of the most important steets in Singapore, packed with temples, businesses and clan associations. The city's oldest Chinese temple, the Taoist **Thian Hock Keng Temple** or Temple of Heavenly Happiness is on Telok Ayer Street and is a gem. Telok Ayer Street was the perfect place for merchants and traders to establish themselves as it was right on the sea. (It also became notorious for its slave trade in the 1850s.) The temple was funded by a wealthy merchant of the same name and building commenced in 1839. Skilled craftsmen and materials were all imported from China – the sculpted granite columns and the elaborate carved roof forms bear testament to their skill. The cast-iron railings came from Glasgow and the decorative tiles from Holland. The building was modelled on 19th century southern Chinese architectural traditions, with a grouping of pavilions around open courtyards, designed to comply with the dictates of geomancy (*feng shui*) (see page 595). The main deity is Tien Hou, the Goddess of Seafarers, and she is worshipped in the central hall (see box). It soon became a focal point for the newly arrived Hokkien immigrants who would gather to thank this deity for granting them a safe journey, The temple used to be on the waterfront before land reclamation projects in the 1880s moved the harbour several blocks east. Well worth a visit.

The Al-Abrar Mosque, also on Telok Ayer Street, was built from 1850-55 by Indian Muslims, who were also responsible for the fancy turrets of the **Nagore Durgha Shrine** – a little further up the street – which was built in 1829. Designated a national monument, it is a blend of architectural styles – Palladian doors and Doric columns combined with a more

Thian Hock Keng Temple

Tien Hou – Goddess of Seafarers

Tien Hou, or Thien Hau Thanh Mau (also Ma Tsu), is the goddess of the sea and protector of seafarers. She first appeared, so to speak, in Fukien province in China during the 11th century. Folklore has it that she was the daughter of a fisherman named Lin and that she died while a virgin. She appears to seafarers in times of extreme peril and saves their lives. Tien Hou is usually represented seated, with a flattened crown. But the real giveaway are her two companions, who go by the great names of Thousand-mile Eye and Follow the Wind Ear. These are both tamed demons who the goddess uses to provide long range weather forecasts to fisherman. Thousand-mile Eye is red-skinned and peers towards the horizon, hand shading his eyes; Follow the Wind Ear is green-skinned and is usually depicted cupping his hand to his ear as he listens for minor climatic changes.

traditional Islamic style and plenty of fairy lights. An intriguing architectural sight is the **Telok Ayer Chinese Methodist Church**, which is to be found at 235 Telok Ayer Street. It combines a mixture of eastern and western influences – a flat roof with a Chinese pavilion and a colonnaded ground floor. During World War Two it was used as a refugee camp.

The conservation area of **Tanjong Pagar** lies southwest of **Telok Ayer Street**. It is bordered by Tanjong Pagar Road and Neil Road and contains some of the best examples of pre-war shophouse architecture on the island. In the early 19th century this area was dominated by nutmeg plantations. Neil Road was laid in the 1830s and at that time was just a track meandering through the nutmeg groves. It was originally called Salat Road and was renamed in 1858 after one of the heroes of the Indian mutiny in Calcutta in 1857. In the early 19th century this area was inhabited by orang-laut, simple fisherfolk. The name Tanjong (cape or promontory) Pagar (wooden fence or palisade) may have derived from the fishing stakes that were commonly used to catch fish. With the arrival of the Europeans, it became an area of fruit and nutmeg cultivation. With the expansion of cultivation, planters and pickers were needed and subsequently hawkers and shopkeepers moved in to supply their needs. The community became dominated by Hokkien and Tamil coolies, with the wealthy merchants living on Duxton and Neil roads. Later in the century Tanjong Pagar was ruled by the Triads – or *tongs*. The imbalance of men to women provided a fertile breeding ground for prostitutes, and with them came their pimps. Teahouses provided 'singing girls' and opium dens were commonplace (opium smoking was not prohibited until 1964). Fires were frequent – the tinder box houses were constructed of flimsy wood with cardboard partitions. In 1830 a disastrous fire raged for 3 days (there were no fire hoses) and in 1917 another fire almost completely destroyed the area. Between 1900 and 1940 Tanjong Pagar became the 'gateway' for Chinese immigrants and clansmen took over almost all the shophouses in the area. By the 20th century Tanjong Pagar had become desperately overcrowded, with houses originally built for one family housing up to 5 or 6. This was also the constituency where Lee Kuan Yew successfully stood in a by-election in 1957 – opening the way for a full democratic election in 1959.

Tanjong Pagar was one of the first major projects undertaken by the Urban Redevelopment Authority. They acquired the area in the early 1980's, realising that this was a precious piece of Singapore's heritage which should be retained at all cost. And just in time: the government wished to demolish the area as it had become, by then, little more than a slum. Initially, thirty shophouses were

Opium smoking

restored and sold off. Then the URA changed its strategy, selling off the properties unrestored and providing the new owners with guidelines for restoration. The façades had to remain the same, but they could do almost what they wanted with the interior, provided the airwells (an area open to the sky in the middle of the shophouse, which provided light to the back rooms) were retained. Critics believe that this 'sanitization' process has destroyed the character of the area, yet it could not have remained as it was. The URA do not believe that it is their job to recreate the character of the place – the labour intensive industries which were originally here (such as the charcoal makers) simply could not operate. They want these shophouses to become viable business enterprises. One disappointment for the URA is that the 'shophouse' concept, where a business is run on the ground floor and the owners live upstairs, has not really taken off. As a result, the area is dead at night. This is something the URA are now addressing, trying – like so many other urban planners worldwide – to encourage people to live in the heart of the city. Many of the plots along Tanjong Pagar remain vacant – suggesting that rates are high. Even so, there are now a number of tea houses, mahjong-makers, reflexologists, calligraphers, lacquer-painters and mask-makers who have set up among the advertising agencies, smart restaurants and bars. **The Tanjong Pagar Heritage Exhibition** in the development at 51 Neil Road has a small display of photographs of old Chinatown, which are quite intriguing. The accompanying 'mall' and foodcourt, complete with authentic bare brickwork is a little tacky. More interesting is the **Tea Chapter**, almost next door at 9A-11A, where visitors are introduced to the intricacies of tea-tasting in elegant surroundings. As the brochure rather extravagantly puts it "it is a mythical dream come true for those seeking solace from a harsh and unfeeling existence". This is a popular place for young Singaporeans to visit on a Sunday afternoon (see afternoon tea, page 694). The white building on the corner of Tanjong Pagar and Neil Road was the **Jinriksha Station**, built in 1903. It served as the administration centre for the jinriksha pullers. Jinrickshas arrived from Japan via Shanghai in the 1880s and soon became the most popular way to travel. By 1888 there were 1,800 in use, pulled by immigrants who lived in Sago and Banda streets. At the turn of the century, the fare for a half hour trip would have been 3 cents, 20 cents for an hour.

Tiong Bahru's singing birds

For visitors who are interested in finding out more about conservation areas in the city, the URA are developing their headquarters at 45 Maxwell Road into an Exhibition and Visitors' Centre, where there will be a large model of the city and various interactive displays. The centre should open towards the end of 1998.

On Sunday mornings many bird lovers gather at the corner of **Tiong Bahru** and Seng Poh roads for traditional **bird singing competitions**, where row upon row of thrushes, merboks and sharmas sing their hearts out, in antique bamboo cages with ivory and porcelain fittings, hung from lines. The birds are fed on a carefully designed diet to ensure the quality of their song. Owners place their younger birds next to more experienced songsters to try to improve their voices and pick up new tunes. Birds start twittering at 0730 and are spent by 1000. On the opposite side of the road, there's a shop selling everything you need for your pet bird – including porcelain cage accoutrements. Walk on down Seng Poh Road to a fabulous wet market; every conceivable vegetable, fruit, fish, meat, beancurd you could ever want to purchase is available here. *Getting there*: take the MRT to Tiong Bahru or Outram Park or the bus stops right opposite this spot – bus nos 16, 16E and 33.

LITTLE INDIA

The beginning of **Serangoon Road** (named after the Rongong stork which used to inhabit swampland in the area) and its colourful side streets make up the community of Little India. By 1828, Serangoon Road was established as 'the road leading across the island', but the surrounding area remained swampland until the 1920s when its brick kilns and lime pits attracted Indian (mainly Tamil) labourers to the area. In 1840 the race course was completed, which drew Europeans to settle in the area. (The road names Cuff, Dickson and Clive would have been private lanes to the European residences.)

The Indians introduced a traditional technique of external plasterwork, *Madras chunam* (see page 590), which gave Serangoon Road's shophouses their ornate plasterwork façades (see Late Shophouse style, page 654). Some of the best examples of this can be found on Jalan Besar and along the roads which link up with Serangoon Road. This style of shophouse has come to be known as Singapore Eclectic. Nos 61-69 Syed Alwi Road display some of the finest plasterwork in Singapore and a few roads further north, Nos 10-14 Petain Road, built in the 1930s, show exceptionally ornate tiles and plasterwork. This latter row of shophouses is possibly the last intact group of eclectic style terracing remaining in Singapore.

A Little India architectural walkabout

The shophouses of Little India have a character of their own, with the earliest examples being some of the plainest and humblest on the island. This **Early Shophouse Style** spans the period between 1840 and 1900. The buildings were generally 2-storey, with doric columns and minimal ornamentation; there are examples at 127 and 159 Dunlop Street. The early 1900s saw the emergence of the so-called **First Transitional Shophouse**. These were less squat in design and incorporated more decorative elements. Vents, often quite elaborate, were now included above or between the windows, while columns were Corinthian rather than Doric. Examples of this style can be seen at 61 Serangoon Road and 39 Campbell Lane. The **Late Shophouse Style** (1900-1940) over-lapped with the First Transitional; of all the styles to be found in Little India these are without doubt the most interesting. The entire surface is elaborately decorated with plasterwork and ceramic tiles, the upper floor is divided into three, making a greater window area, and there are balustrades on the upper floor, creating shade for these rooms. Some of the best examples can be seen at 109-117 Jalan Besar and at the eastern end of Jalan Petain. The **Second Transitional Style** was relatively short-lived, dating essentially from the late 1930s. Architects and art historians have seen the Second Transitional as something of a reaction to the exuberance of the **Late Shophouse Style**. Designs were much simpler, though they still used ceramic tiles and some ornamentation. It is also possible to see the beginnings of Art Deco influences in these buildings. An example of a Second Transitional shophouse can be seen at 15 Cuff Road. Finally, the **Art Deco Style** emerged at the beginning of the 1930s and shophouses continued to be built in this style into the 1960s. Art Deco shophouses represent a logical progression from the Second Transitional style. Designs were simpler still, with proportions being more important than detail. In addition architects began to design groups of buildings rather than individual structures – with particular interest in corner sites. Many of these buildings were dated, so they are easily identified. An example can be found at 22 Campbell Lane.

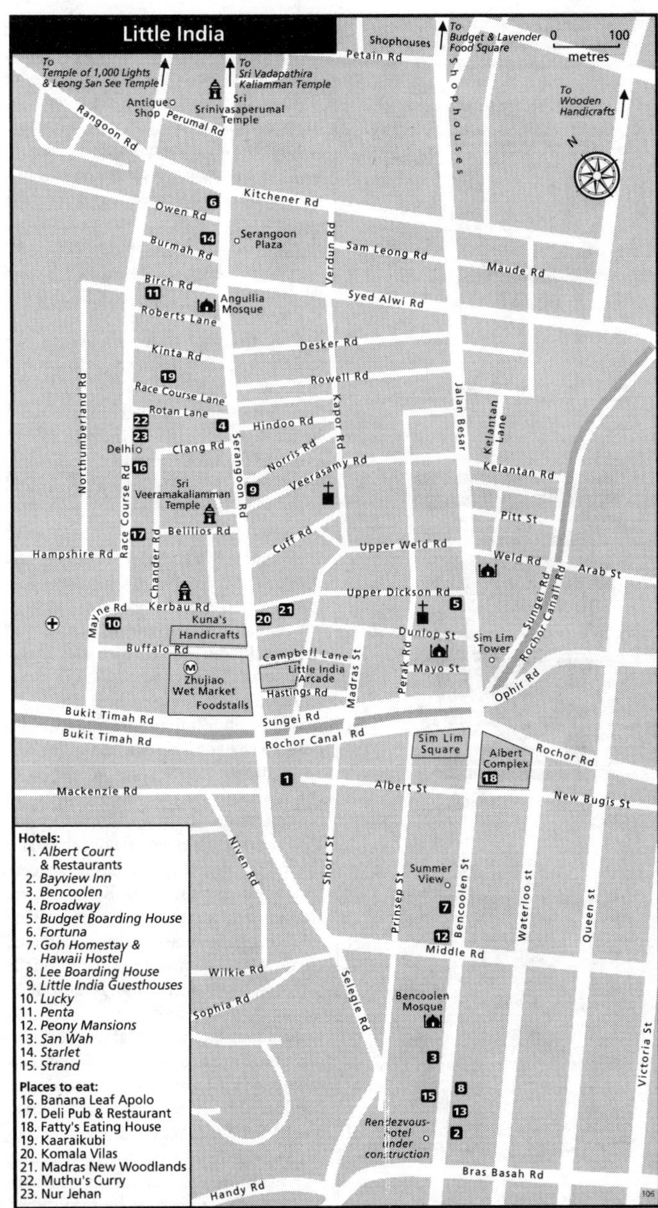

Hotels:

1. *Albert Court & Restaurants*
2. *Bayview Inn*
3. *Bencoolen*
4. *Broadway*
5. *Budget Boarding House*
6. *Fortuna*
7. *Goh Homestay & Hawaii Hostel*
8. *Lee Boarding House*
9. *Little India Guesthouses*
10. *Lucky*
11. *Penta*
12. *Peony Mansions*
13. *San Wah*
14. *Starlet*
15. *Strand*

Places to eat:

16. Banana Leaf Apolo
17. Deli Pub & Restaurant
18. Fatty's Eating House
19. Kaaraikubi
20. Komala Vilas
21. Madras New Woodlands
22. Muthu's Curry
23. Nur Jehan

Indian shophouse syles
(reporduced with kind permission of the URA)

Early shophouse,
nos 127 and 159 Dunlop Street

Late shophouse,
nos 109-117 Jalan Besar

Art Deco shophouse,
No 22 Campbell Lane

The ceramic tiles were imported from Europe and are a distinct feature of the Straits Chinese house. The majority of Indians in this area are Chettiars – a money-lending caste from South India (and there are still money changers in many of the shops on Serangoon Road – one optimistically advertises 'gold bars accepted' – but there are also Tamils, Bengalis and Sikhs, among other groups.

The fragrance of incense and freshly cut jasmine hangs over the area and with the sound-tracks of Tamil epic-musicals blaring from the video shops, the *pan* salesmen on the sidestreets and colourful milk-sweets behind the glass counters of *dosai* restaurants, Serangoon Road, with its hustle and bustle, is India in microcosm. Every Indian product imaginable is for sale: lunggyis, dotis, saris and spices, sweetmeats, flower garlands, nostril studs, bidis and stalls with mounds of dried beans, rice and back-copies of *India Today*. Look out for the birdmen who practice parrot astrology. They whisper your name and birth date to the bird, who then picks out a card with the 'right' fortune on it. Little India is also an excellent area to eat (see page 685).

The lively **Zhujiao (previously Kandang Kerbau or KK) Market** on the corner of Buffalo and Serangoon roads is an entertaining spot to wander. Spices can be ground to your own requirements. Upstairs there is a maze of shops and stalls; the wet market is beyond the hawker centre, travelling west along Buffalo Road. New legislation introduced in 1993, which ruled that no animals could be slaughtered on wet market premises, saw the end of the chicken-plucking machine. It used to do the job in 12.4 seconds.

Kandang Kerbau – Malay for corral – was the centre of Singapore's cattle-rearing area in the 1870s. The cattle trade was dominated by Indians and among them was IR Belilios, a Venetian Jew from Calcutta who gave his name to a road nearby. The roads around KK have names connected to the trade: Lembu (cow) Road and Buffalo Road. With the boom in the cattle trade, related activities established themselves in the area; the cattle provided power for wheat-grinding, pineapple preserving and so on. Opposite the market on Serangoon Road is the Little India Arcade, another URA project and full of Indian knick-knacks.

The **Sri Veeramakaliamman Temple** on Belilios Road, just off Serangoon Road, was built by the Bengali community and is dedicated to Kali, a ferocious incarnation of Siva's wife. This small, gaudy temple with its polychromed gods was built by indentured Bengali workers in 1881. It is similar in composition to most other temples of its kind and has three main elements: a shrine for the gods, a hall for worship and a *goporum* (or tower), built so that pilgrims can identify the temple from far off. Further up Serangoon Road is another Indian temple, **Sri Perumal**, with its high goporum sculptured with five manifestations of Vishnu. The temple was founded in 1855, but much of the decoration is more recent. This carving was finished in 1979 and was paid for by local philanthropist Govindasamy Pillai.

On Race Course Road (parallel to Serangoon Road) is the Buddhist **Sakayamuni Buddha Gaya Temple** or Temple of One Thousand Lights dominated by a 15m-high, 300 tonne, rather crude, statue of the Buddha surrounded by 987 lights. Devotees come here to worship the branch of the sacred Bodhi tree – under which the Buddha gained enlightenment – and the mother-of-pearl footprint of the Buddha. Under renovation during 1997. Open 0900-1630 Monday-Sunday. Across the road is the Chinese **Leong San See Temple**, Dragon Mountain Temple, with its carved entrance. It is dedicated to Kuan Yin (the goddess of mercy) who had 18 hands, which are said to symbolize her boundless mercy and compassion.

ARAB STREET

Originally this area was a thriving Arab village known as Kampong Glam (Eucalyptus Village). The area got its name from the Gelam tribe of sea-gypsies who once lived there. Singapore's Arabs were among its earliest settlers, the first being a wealthy merchant called Syed Mohammad bin Harum Al-Junied who arrived in 1819, a couple of months after Stamford Raffles. The Alkaffs were another important local Arab family, who built their ostentatious mansion on Mount Faber. Arab merchants began settling in the area around Arab Street in the mid 19th century. Arab Street is still the main artery of Muslim Singapore, and is the name applied to the district between the Rochor Canal Road and Jalan Sultan.

The focal point is the Middle Eastern-looking **Sultan Mosque**, with its golden domes, on North Bridge Road. Completed in 1928 and designed by colonial architects Swan and Maclaren, it is Singapore's largest mosque and attracts thousands of faithful every Friday. The original building, constructed in the 1820s, was part of a deal between the Temenggong of Johor and the East India Company in return for sovereignty over Singapore. Next door is the old **Kampong Glam Istana**, built in the early 1840s as the Temenggong Ali Iskander Shah's palace.

In the maze of side streets around the Sultan Mosque there is a colourful jumble of Malay, Indonesian and Middle Eastern merchandise: a good selection of batik (which is sold in sarong lengths of just over 2m), silk and Indian textiles (especially along Arab Street), wickerware, jewellery, perfumes and religious paraphernalia. In the weeks before Hari Raya Puasa, Bussorah Street is lined with stalls selling all kinds of traditional foods – after dark it is a favourite haunt of famished Muslims during Ramadan. Tombstone-makers are based along Pahang Street. Nearby at the junction of Jalan Sultan and Victoria Street is the **old**

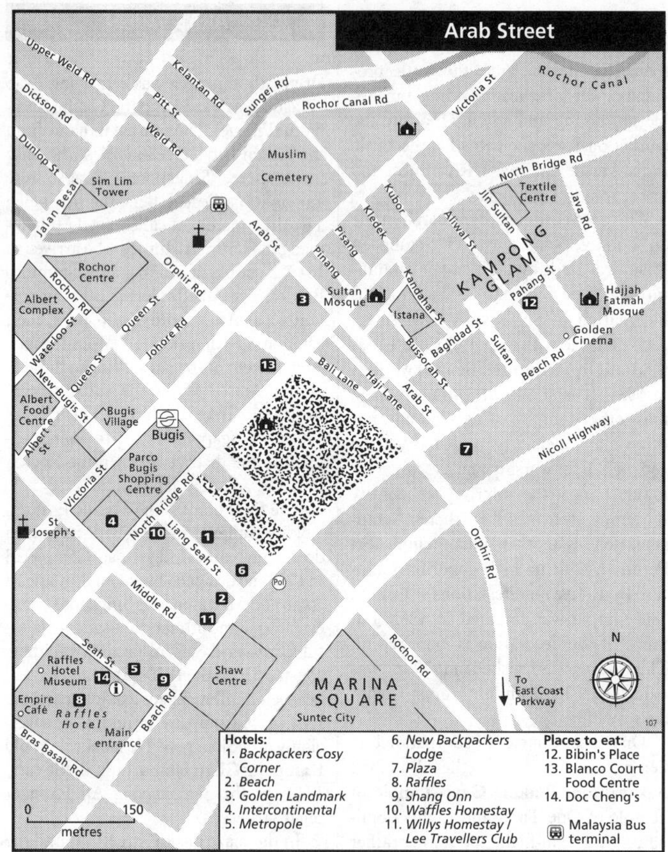

royal cemetery. Much of Kampong Glam has been renovated by the Urban Redevelopment Authority in an attempt to retain some of its architectural heritage.

Bugis Street is right across the road from the Bugis Street MRT station. It is packed with stalls selling cheap T-shirts, copy watches, handicrafts – like a street market you might see in Thailand or Malaysia, but something that seems rather out of place in modern day Singapore. For those who like to see Singapore not just as a giant shopping plaza but also as a real life experiment in ersatz existence, then Bugis Street offers more than key rings and Oriental flim-flam. The whole street has been re-created from a road that was demolished to make way for the MRT. Some people maintain that why it was demolished, and how it has been brought back from the dead, sums up Singapore's approach to life (see box). On the opposite side of Victoria Street is the new Parco Bugis Centre, a high-tech shopping plaza (in reconstructed air-conditioned shophouses) bustling with life containing restaurants, shopping malls and a mesmerizing fountain.

Another popular mosque in the area is the **Hajjah Fatimah Mosque** on Java Road. It was financed by a wealthy Melakan-born Malay woman, Hajjah Fatimah (Hajjah is the female equivalent of Haji, meaning someone who has made the pilgrimage to Mecca). It was designed by an unknown British architect and the work contracted to a French construction company. It was completed in 1846 and has, as a result of its cosmopolitan history, a distinctive flavour. Unfortunately, it is now dwarfed by surrounding Housing Development Board (HDB) blocks, but inside there are photographs of its HDB-less hinterland in 1959.

AROUND SINGAPORE ISLAND

WEST OF THE ISLAND

Haw Par Villa (formerly Tiger Balm Gardens) is at 262 Pasir Panjang Road, on the way out to Jurong. Built by Aw Boon Haw and Aw Boon Par, brothers of Tiger Balm fame, it was their family home until they opened it to the public. The delightful estate was finally sequestrated by the Singapore government in 1985 and turned into the island's most revolting theme park, a gaudy adventureland of Chinese folklore – the biggest Chinese mythological theme park in the world. Boon Haw originally designed the gardens for his

Return from the dead: Bugis Street

One of Singapore's more famous sights used to be Bugis Street, a street where by day hawkers and stalls would congregate but where, at night, transvestites would strut their wares and noisy bars would stay open until the early morning. Bugis Street was, in a sense, the nemesis of all that Lee Kuan Yew's squeaky-clean Singapore was aiming to become: it was unplanned, anarchic, wild, outrageous. Then, in 1985, Bugis Street was demolished to make way for the Mass Rapid Transit system. As *The Economist* put it at the time, this was perhaps more than mere coincidence because "Bugis Street represents all that the authorities seem to want to erase". But the arrival of the demolition ball was not to be the end of Bugis Street. In 1989 it was proposed that the street be recreated in a new, but nearby location. As the project consultant was quoted as saying in the *Singapore Bulletin*, the new creation would be "right down to the toilet building ... it will be back with smell and all". But, it would, at the same time, be "absolutely safe in terms of hygiene and personal safety". The buildings were rebuilt to the same dimensions and style, even posters from the 1960s were painted onto walls to give the ambience of the old street. But as this was a place for families and wholesome entertainment, the transvestites that made the old Bugis Street what it was, were banned. The irony, though, was that the upmarket 'retail and food and beverage outlets' that occupied the reconstructed shophouses complained of poor business and were allowed to hire transvestites as customer relations officers to explain the history of the street. But, the *Straits Times Weekly* reassured its readers, they would be watched by closed circuit television and plain clothes men to ensure that they did not solicit. When the Singapore Tourist Promotion Board put on a show in Hong Kong to promote the Republic they used transvestites. Local journalists asked how this could be justified in Singapore terms, and they were told that the performers were not transvestites but "female impersonators, professional artistes". Bugis Street has, in the process of this transformation, become more authentic of modern Singapore than the old Bugis Street was of the Singapore of the 1960s and 1970s. The latter was anachronistic ... an oddball place that had to be worn down.

'Mad Ridley' – the rubber missionary

The Botanic Gardens were founded by an agri-horticultural society in 1859. In the early years they played an important role in fostering agricultural development in Singapore and Malaya by collecting, growing and distributing plants with economic potential, the most famous of which was rubber. Henry Ridley, director of the gardens from 1888-1912, pioneered the planting of the Brazilian para rubber tree (*Hevea brasiliensis*). In 1877, 11 seedlings brought from Kew Gardens in London were planted in the Singapore gardens. One rubber tree, an immediate descendant of one of the 11 originals is still alive in the Botanic Gardens today, near the main entrance. By the lake at the junction of Tyersall and Cluny rds there is a memorial to Ridley on the site where the original trees were planted. Ridley was known as 'Mad Ridley' because of the proselytizing zeal with which he lobbied Malaya's former coffee planters to take up rubber instead.

His first convert was Melakan planter Tan Chay Yan, who planted out 1,200 hectares in 1896. Ridley devised a way of tapping the rubber trees for latex without hampering their growth. By 1920 the Botanic Gardens had distributed over 7 million seeds and the Malayan rubber industry was producing 210,000 tonnes of sheet rubber a year, accounting for half the world's rubber production. Only in 1990 did Malaysia lose its place as the world's largest producer.

family's enjoyment. His gory sculptures have instilled a sense of traditional morality in generations of Singaporeans. Sequences depict wrongdoers being punished in creative ways, most notably in the Ten Courts of Hell (which is reached along what can only be described as the Alley of the Ten Shops of Tack): one is having his tongue cut out, another is galled by a spear, others are variously impaled on spikes, gnawed by dogs, boiled in oil, bitten by snakes, sliced in two, drowned in the Filthy Blood Pond or ground into paste by enormous millstones. Some of the allegories and stories are obscure to say the least: a pig dressed in what appears to be a forerunner to the 'Y' front; acrobatic mermaids; and tangoing fowl. Though doubtless highly significant to the cognoscenti of Chinese mythology, many of the stories will be lost on the uninitiated.

Consider the story of the great Jiang Zi Ya who can be seen bearded and clasping a fishing rod towards the top of the complex. Apparently Zi Ya held the unbaited rod above a river for 8 years because, so he said to a perplexed passer-by, he was not trying to catch fish but was awaiting 'the arrival of a great leader'. His patience was rewarded when King Wen chanced upon Zi Ya still fishing after almost 100 months. Rather than being appalled at the man's foolhardiness, King Wen was singularly impressed and appointed him his Prime Minister. The moral of this story, unsurprisingly, is that "All good things come to those who wait". Perhaps it should be, "When you go fishing with Zi Ya, remember to take lots of sandwiches and orange squash".

Its 9 hectares site is five times the size of the original villa and its grounds. There is a large section on ancient China, with pagoda-roofed buildings, arts and crafts shops and restaurants serving authentic cuisine as well as traditional theatre – in which lion dances and wayangs are performed. The 'Creation of the World Theatre' tells classic tales from the Qin Dynasty; in the 'Legends and Heroes Theatre' a life-like robot is programmed to relate stories, and a video in the 'Spirit of the Orient Theatre' explains Chinese folklore, customs, traditions and festivals. Normal admission S$16 (S$10 for children). Reduced admission: S$5 (S$2.50 for children) (The 'rack rate' for

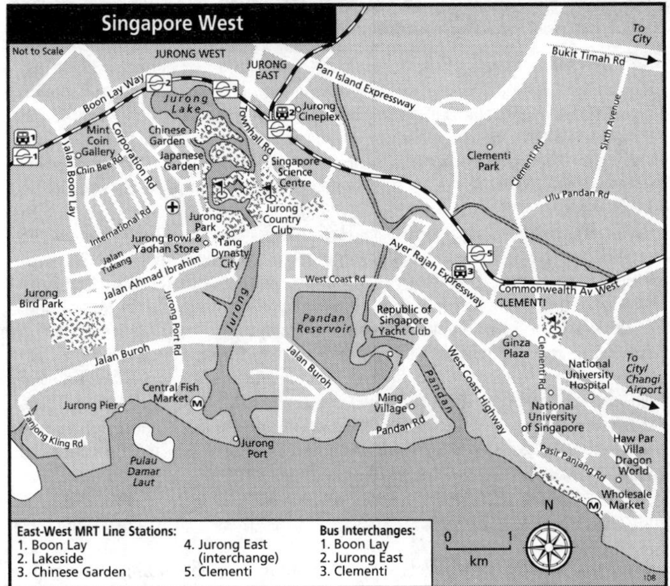

the Haw Paw Villas is S$16, but because of a lack of demand and complaints that the gardens are overpriced, entrance has been significantly reduced for some time. As of mid-1997 it was possible to buy reduced tickets from some outlets in town for as little as S$3.50.) Open 0900-1800 Monday-Sunday. **NB** Do not even think about visiting Haw Par Villa over Chinese New Year – each year about 12,000 people saunter around it in the space of about 4 days. *Getting there*: MRT west-bound to Buona Vista, then bus 200; buses 10, 30, 51 and 143 to Pasir Panjang Road.

The west coast is dominated by the industrial district of **Jurong**, where about two-thirds of the island's industrial workforce is employed. Jurong is the product of Singapore's first big state-supported industrialization programme in the 1960s and early 1970s. It now supports a large shopping complex, complete with cinemas, bowling alleys, skating rinks, hawker stalls etc.

Jurong Bird Park, on Jl Ahmad Ibrahim (T 2650022), is a beautifully kept 20 hectares haven for more than 8,000 birds of 420 species from all over the world, including a large collection of Southeast Asian birds and 600 species from Africa, South America, Europe and Asia. As it is now difficult to see most of these birds in the wild in Southeast Asia, a trip here is well worthwhile. Highlights include the world's largest collection of Southeast Asian hornbills and South American toucans, an entertaining air-conditioned penguin corner, complete with snow. One of the main attractions is one of the largest walk-in aviaries in the world, with a 30m high man-made waterfall and 1500 birds. There is also an interesting nocturnal house with owls, herons, frogmouths and kiwis. Bird shows through the day (the birds of prey show – at 1000 and 1600 – is particularly good). There is a monorail service round the park for those who find the heat too much (S$2.50, S$1 for children). Admission S$10.30 (S$4.12 for

The Tiger Balm story

In the latter years of the 19th century, a Chinese herbal doctor called Aw Chu Kin left China for Burma, where he hoped to make his fortune. In Rangoon he peddled his concoctions to ailing Burmese. Before his death in the early 1920s he invented a balm which he claimed was a miracle-cure for insect bites, stomach aches, colds, headaches, bronchial problems and muscle strain. Nobody believed him and when old Mr Aw died, his wife had to pawn all her jewellery to cover his funeral costs.

The only thing his sons Boon Haw (Haw means 'tiger') and Boon Par inherited was his secret recipe, but being entrepreneurs, they decided to market their birthright and rename it Tiger Balm. It became so well known in Rangoon that Boon Haw decided to try his luck in Singapore while Boon Par struck out for Hong Kong. Within years, the balm empire expanded to Malaysia, Hong Kong and China. In 1926 he built a magnificent villa on Nassim Road, Singapore, which the Urban Redevelopment Authority demolished in 1990. In 1931 he began work on Haw Par Villa, commissioning an artist from Swatow, China to landscape the gardens. The Japanese wrecked the place during the war and Boon Haw died in Honolulu in 1950 before it was restored to its lurid splendour. Tiger Balm, which is manufactured by the company Haw Par Brothers (despite the fact that the family no longer has any interests in it), now cures people all over the world. A small dab of it on a mosquito bite works wonders.

children under 12), family tickets available for $20. Open 0900-1800 Monday-Friday, 0800-1800, weekends and public holidays. *Getting there*: MRT west-bound to Boon Lay then SBS bus 194 or 251.

Jurong Crocodile Paradise Jalan Ahmed Ibrahim is next to Jurong Bird Park but was closed for 'updating' on our last visit. *Getting there*: MRT west-bound to Boon Lay; buses 194, 251 or 255 from Boon Lay Interchange.

Tang Dynasty City, Jalan Ahmad Ibrahim/Yuan Ching Road, Jurong (T 2611116), covers 12 hectares and is a recreation of the ancient Chinese capital of Chang An. Developers worked for 3 years to build this S$70 million theme park. The City includes 100 shophouses and a temple, with carvings by workmen from China and a 600m-long, 10m-high model of the Great Wall of China, built with bricks imported from Shenzhen. There is also a 7-storey pagoda, housing the monkey god and an impressive artificial waterfall. The main attraction, though, is an 'underground palace', with replicas of the 1,500 terracotta warriors found in the tomb of Shih Huang Ti in Xian, China. Visitors are ushered into a small theatre where a short and bloody film of the emperor's life provides a simple historical background before an entirely irrelevant earthquake ends the film show and visitors enter the reconstruction of the tomb to view the arrayed ranks of warriors illuminated by lasers. (One can only presume that the earthquake machinery was a cheap job lot from some other attraction and the management of the Tang Dynasty Village have tried to shoe horn it into an unrelated story from Chinese history.) Other key attractions include a ghost mansion and a tacky and rather musty museum where notables from Chinese history are poorly modelled from wax. There are also various shows and events staged through the day from noodle making demonstrations to juggling and martial arts and a traditional wedding procession. The City doubles as a huge movie studio and the Tang Dynasty Motion Picture company plans to make three feature films a year. The place has been half finished for years and judging by the undergrowth at the back of the lot it seems as though the enterprise is running low on funds. Indeed the general tenor is one of over-ambition: though S$70 million may have been spent on the place, it would have been better to have envisaged something less grandiose and at least done it well. There is a restaurant on site and a better and cheaper food court across the road in the Jurong Bowl complex. Given these quibbles the entrance fee is steep for something still half baked. Open 1000-1830, Monday-Sunday. Admission S$15.45 (S$10.30 for children) but advance tickets at slightly reduced rates available from travel agents and other outlets in town. *Getting there*: MRT to Lakeside station and then either bus 154 or 240, or a taxi – or a 2 km walk.

Chinese and Japanese Gardens are on Yuan Ching Road, Jurong (T 2643455). The Chinese garden gives some idea of what an imperial Sung Dynasty garden would have been like, although the biggest attraction is the giant rocking horse. Yu-Hwa Yuan, as the gardens are known in Chinese, are actually a series of theme gardens, based on the classical style of Beijing's Summer Palace. The latest attraction is the Penjing Garden ('Yun Xin Yuan – or Garden of Beauty'), a large landscaped area costing S$6 million to develop and containing 3,000 miniature penjing (bonsai) trees, from all over Asia. Two of the Chinese ones are thought to be 200 years old. On the whole the gardens are colourful but disappointingly commercial. Just across the stream is the more peaceful Japanese garden, one of the largest outside Japan. Situated on a man-made island on Jurong Lake, it is designed to mirror the natural order (typical of Japanese tradition). The *Seiwaen* (or 'garden of tranquility') is based on Japanese landscaping techniques that were practised from the 14th to 17th centuries, characterized by sweeping lawns and gently flowing streams. Combined admission for both gardens: S$4.50 (S$2 for children). Open 0900-1900 Monday-Saturday, 0830-1900 Sunday and public holidays. *Getting there*: bus Nos 335, 180 and 154 or MRT to Chinese Gardens (much easier) or taxi (S$12 from Orchard Road).

Science Centre, on Science Centre Road, Jurong, might be aimed more at children than adults – but there is plenty of fun for grown-ups too. The centre succeeds in its mission to make science come alive and with plenty of gadgets and hands-on exhibits. The museum is divided into four galleries covering social and life sciences. Admission S$15 (S$7 for children). Open 1000-1800 Tuesday-Sunday. In the **Omni-theatre** and **Planetarium** (T 5603316/5641432) next door, the marvels of science, technology and the universe can be viewed in a 284-seat amphitheatre with a huge hemispherical (3-D) screen and a 20,000 watt sound system. Take a seat-of-your-pants journey down the Grand Canyon, explore exploding volcanoes or walk in space. Excellent films and very popular. Admission S$9 (S$4 for children) for Omninax movies (screened 1200-2000, Tuesday-Sunday); S$6 (S$3 for children) for Planetarium show at 1000 and 1100. Open Tuesday-Sunday 1000-2100, T 5689100 for film schedules. *Getting there*: take the MRT to Jurong East, and walk the last 500m. Bus nos 66, 198, 335 and TIBS bus No 178 run direct to the the museum. Alternatively get bus nos 51, 78, 97 or 147 to the Jurong East Interchange and then change to a 335 or walk.

Ming Village, 32 Pandan Road (T 2657711) (not to be confused with the Tang Dynasty City) is one of the last factories in the world that faithfully reproduces Chinese porcelain antiques using traditional methods – from mould-making to hand-throwing – dating from Sung, Yuan, Ming and Qin dynasties. All the pieces are painted by hand and the factory blurb maintains that traditional methods of craftsmanship are scrupulously followed. Guides conduct tours around the factory premises. Seeing the work that goes into the pots helps explain why the prices are so high in the showroom. The shop has an export department which will pack items for shipment. The Village also runs traditional pottery and painting classes for long-stay and short-stay group visitors – telephone for details. The **Pewter Museum** has moved to the Ming Village, open 0900-1730, admission free. Daily demonstrations of traditional pewter making processes. Open 0900-1730 Monday-Sunday. Admission free. *Getting there*: MRT to Clementi, then bus 78. Or take the free 'Trolley Ming Village Shuttle Service' which picks up at Paragon By Sogo (opposite the *Crown Prince Hotel*) at 0900, 1015 and 1130 and at Marina Square (opposite the *Pan Pacific Hotel* bus stop) at 0915, 1030 and 1145.

EAST COAST

The eastern part of the island used to be dotted with small Malay fishing kampungs (most have now been demolished and replaced by Housing Development Board tower blocks). Great chunks of land have been reclaimed from the sea and carefully landscaped beaches now line the coast up to Changi. Just off the city end of the East Coast Parkway is the National Sports Stadium.

Although the east coast may not be what it was, those who want a change from the order and glitz of Orchard Road could do worse than simply hop on the 16/14 bus which runs along Joo Chiat Road and then onto the East Coast Road. There are good eating places, side streets and interesting shops (antiques, crafts etc), and even a village feel.

The suburbs of **Katong** and **Geylang Serai** are an enclave of Peranakan architecture; there are still streets of well-preserved shophouses and terraced houses in their original condition. Joo Chiat Road gives a good feel of old Singapore, sandwiched between the upmarket residential districts and government housing development projects. On Koon Seng Road, many of the houses have been carefully restored – and it is less touristy than Emerald Hill and Tanjong Pagar. Katong was also the haven for weekenders from the civil services: European and Straits Chinese mandarins had grand houses along the waterfront, a handful of which still stand today among the HDB blocks and condominiums. A little further away is Geylang Serai (on Geylang Road), considered the heart of Malay culture in Singapore; it was once an agricultural area but has been transformed into a modern industrial zone. Geylang market is well-stocked with Malay food.

Malay Cultural Village, Geylang Serai (T 7484700, F 7411662), is on a 1.7 hectares site between Geylang Serai, Sims Avenue and Geylang Road. But the Malay answer to the new Tang Dynasty City, with its mock-kampung houses, Malay foodstalls and shops has failed to draw many visitors. The irony of it is not lost on Singapore's Malay community, who have been resettled from their kampungs into HDB flats over the past 20 years. Malay cultural identity is better characterized in the stalls at Geylang market than in the cultural village. *Getting there*: by bus, SBS 2, 7; MRT to Paya Lebar, followed by 5 minutes walk. **Joo Chiat Road**, which runs south down to the sea, is interesting for its unchanged early 20th century shophouse fronts. The extravagant façades, found both here and on Koon Seng Road are an excellent example of the Singapore Eclectic Style which evolved in the 1930s. **Peter Wee's Katong Antique House** at 208 East Coast Road is well worth a visit if you are in the area, with its unsurpassed collection of Peranakan antiques and an owner who is probably the most knowledgeable person in Singapore on the Peranakan culture. (See page 699 for more details.)

East Coast Park is a popular recreation area with beaches and gardens as well as a tennis centre, driving range, sailing centre (see page 704), the **Big**

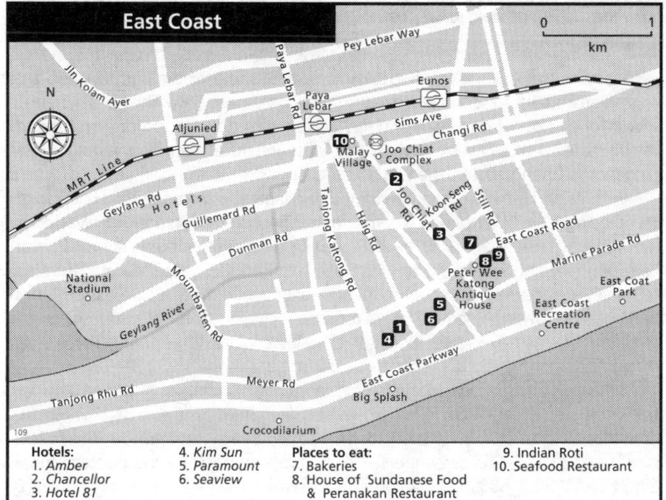

Splash admission S$3, S$2 for children, open 1200-1745 Monday-Friday and 0900-1745 Saturday and Sunday and a food centre. The sand along these beaches was imported from near-by Indonesian islands. The **East Coast Recreation Centre**, in East Coast Park, has the usual array of crazy golf, foodstalls, canoes, fun rides. *Getting there*: bus 16 goes direct from Orchard Road. On weekends and public holidays bus No 401 runs to East Coast Park from the Bedok MRT station. The **Crocodilarium**, 730 East Coast Parkway, T 4473722, has over 1,200 inmates, bred in pens. The best time to visit is at feeding times (1100 Tuesday, Thursday and Saturday) – the Crocodilarium also stages crocodile-wrestling bouts; ring for times. Crocodile-skin goods are for sale. Admission S$2 (S$1 for children). Open 0900-1700 Monday-Sunday. *Getting there*: no direct buses. Take the MRT to Paya Lebar or Eunos and then take a taxi. The **Singapore Crocodile Farm**, 790 Upper Serangoon Road, is a similar set-up, where visitors can learn more about skinning techniques. This farm, with its population of about 800 crocodiles, has been on the same site since 1945, importing crocodiles from rivers in Sarawak. Open 0830-1730 Monday-Sunday. *Getting there*: buses 81, 83, 97, 111 from Serangoon Road. **Accommodation** If you are looking for cheaper places to stay away from the city centre, this is a good area, with plenty of choice. The Tourist Office provides a budget hotel guide listing hotels in the area. **C** *Hotel 81*, 305 Joo Chiat Road, T 3488181, F 3461970. Very average rooms. **C** *Chancellor*, 181 Joo Chiat Road, T 7422222, F 3488677. Smallish rooms in shophouses, but nice showers and clean and efficient. Pastel shades and a huge TV in each room. Good value but 10 minutes walk from the MRT; **B** *Sea View*, 26 Amber Close, T 345222, F 3484335, ugly great block and not particularly friendly. Note that this place is considerably cheaper if a room is booked at the airport hotel desk. **Places to eat** Several good restaurants and bakeries on the East Coast Road.

Changi Prison is on Upper Changi Road. The prison, as featured on the 'Go to Jail' square in the Singapore version of

Changi Airport: prisoner of war camp: to international travel hub

Changi gets its name from *changi ular*, a climbing shrub. But Changi is mainly associated with the World War Two POW camp based here, where 12,000 American, Australian and British servicemen were interned (see page 586). The name Changi, which for one generation meant misery and squalor, now stands for comfort and the ultimate in efficiency. International business and travel magazines regularly rate Singapore's Changi airport the world's best.

With its two rambling, marble-floored terminals, it was thought big enough to merit being called Airtropolis when Terminal Two opened in 1991. It was even mooted that it was about to be rechristened LKY Airport (after former Prime Minister Lee Kuan Yew, and Singapore's answer to New York's JFK). The spacious, uncluttered terminals are adorned with cool fountains, luxuriant plants and tropical fish tanks and boast an array of executive leisure facilities, including saunas and squash courts, to help jet-lagged executives unwind. The airport's stress-free terminals belie its status as one of the world's most hectic transit hubs.

Because of its strategic location, Singapore has long been a refuelling stop for trans-continental jetliners. Today 67 carriers link Singapore to 131 cities in 56 countries, with around 2,900 scheduled movements each week. In 1995 the airport processed 23,196,242 passengers – eight times more than the population of Singapore. About 80% of Singapore's tourists arrive by air and it takes only 20 minutes from touch down to baggage claim – characteristically called accelerated passenger throughflow. True to form, Singapore's far-sighted government planners have already got a third terminal on the drawing board, which will cater for a further 10 million.

Monopoly, is where Singapore's hangman dispenses with drug traffickers – with gruesome regularity. It was originally built to house 600 prisoners; during the war, more than 3,500 civilians were incarcerated. In 1944, POWs were moved into the prison, and 12,000 American, Australian and British servicemen were interned in and around it. Many contracted ulcers, beriberi, dysentery and fevers. It is mostly visited by World War Two veterans – there is a small museum with reproductions of WRM Haxworth's paintings and the then 17-year-old trooper George Aspinall's photographs, which record the misery of internment. A replica of the atap-roofed Changi Prison chapel stands in the prison yard. The memorial chapel's original altar cross, whose base was made from a Howitzer shell casing, was returned to the chapel in 1992. James Clavell's novel *King Rat* is more enlightening than a visit to Changi. Open 0930-1230, 1400-1630 Monday-Saturday. Chapel holds a service on Sunday evening, 1730, T 5451411, presided over by Rev Henry Khoo, prison chaplain for the past 25 years. The Prison Museum has an interesting display. *Getting there*: bus 2 or 14 from Orchard Road.

Less than a generation ago, **Changi Village** was a sleepy backwater of Singapore, with a good beach and a few sailors' bars. Now it is dwarfed by its housing estate and has one of Asia's busiest airports in its back yard. The photo shop, *George Photo*, on Changi Village Road, is named after wartime photographer George Aspinall, who learned how to process film in the shop's darkroom in 1941. There is also a wet market and a hawker centre here. **Changi Beach** is packed at weekends. Singaporeans come to enjoy the beach, pitching their tents, setting up barbecues and turning it into an Oriental Malaga for 48 hours. From **Changi Point**, bumboats leave for Pulau Ubin every 15 minutes, $2 (see page 675) and for various destinations in Johor, just across the straits. There are also boats to Singapore's northeast islands. *Getting there*: bus 2 or MRT to Tampines and then bus 29.

NORTH OF THE ISLAND

The north of the island is Singapore's back garden: in between the sprawling new housing estates there are areas of jungly wilderness, mangroves, lakes and landscaped gardens. Immediately north of the city is the modern suburb of Toa Payoh with its Siong Lim temple. The Housing Development Board has built a string of new towns outside the central area: Queenstown and Toa Payoh in the 1960s, Ang Mo Kio and Bedok in the 70s and Hougang and Tampines in the 80s. (Ang Mo Kio – literally 'bridge of the red-haired foreign devil' – was named after John Turnbull Thomson, a government surveyor in the 19th century, who was responsible for extending Singapore's road network into the interior.)

Kong Meng San Phor Kark See Chinese Temple Complex (Bright Hill Drive) has, since its construction in 1989, grown into a sprawling, million dollar religious centre whose golden roofs spread over 7½ hectares. The temple complex has been the backdrop for many kung-fu movies and is one of the largest such complexes in Southeast Asia. There are halls for prayer and meditation, a pool containing thousands of turtles, a Buddhist library, an old people's home (and, appropriately, a crematorium), as well as a 9m-high marble statue of Kuan Yin, the 15-headed goddess of mercy, carved by Italian sculptors. Resident geriatrics spend their last days making paper cars and other worldly symbols which are torched after their deaths and, hopefully, follow them into the next world. *Getting there*: buses 4, 56, 74, 93, 104, 125, 130, 132, 143, 157, 163, 165, 166.

Singapore Zoological Gardens, 80 Mandai Lake Road (T 2693411), is one of the world's few open zoos (moats replace bars), making it one of the most attractive zoos in the world, with animals in environments vaguely reminiscent of their habitats. In its promotional brochure, the 20 hectares zoo claims that its open-design concept has paid off: "Our reward is happy animals. The proof lies in the zoo's good breeding record: unhappy animals do not make love!". Only the polar bears and the tigers seemed unhappy in their surroundings. It contains over 170 species of animals (about 2,000 actual animals), some of them rare – like the dinosauric Komodo dragons and the golden lion tamarin – as well as many endangered species from Asia, such as the Sumatran tiger and the clouded leopard. The pygmy hippos are relatively recent newcomers – they live in glass-fronted enclosures (as do the polar bears), so visitors can watch their underwater exploits. Animals are sponsored by companies – *Tiger Beer*, for example, sponsors the tigers and *Qantas* the kangaroos. Animal shows throughout the day with a strong ecological message – primates and reptiles (at 1030 and 1430) and elephants and sealions (at 1130 and 1530). Animal feeding times are provided upon arrival. There is a children's area too with farm animals, a miniature train and play equipment. There are tram tours for those too weary to walk ($2.50 and $1), with recorded commentaries and several restaurants. Elephant, camel and pony rides are on offer at various times each afternoon. A shop sells environmentally sound T-shirts and cuddly toy animals. Overall, a well-managed and informative zoo, is well worth the trip out there (check it out on the Web at http://www.asianconnect.com/zoo/). Video cameras can be hired ($10/hour). Admission $10.30, $4.60 for children. Open 0830-1800 Monday-Sunday, T2693411. *Getting there*: MRT to Ang Mo Kio and then SBS 138 from the Ang Mo Kio interchange (Ang Mo Kio is the only MRT station from which there is a direct bus to the zoo). Alternatively take bus

No 171 to Mandai Road and then cross the road to board the SBS 138 to the zoo. On Sunday and public holidays Trans-island bus service (TIBS) No 926 runs from the Woodlands bus interchange direct to the zoo. Taxis cost about S$10 to the zoo from the Orchard Road area. A bus service runs every 30 minutes from 0730 until 2300 from Orchard and Scott Roads (ask at your hotel), $5 one way. Another option is to book a ticket on the air-con Zoo Express which provides guided tours on demand (contact Elpin, T 7322133).

The unique **Night Safari** is situated adjacent to the zoo, covering 40 hectares of secondary growth tropical forest. The area has been cunningly converted into a series of habitats populated with wildlife from the Indo-Malayan, Indian, Himalayan and African zoogeographical regions. The park supports 1,200 animals belonging to 110 species including the tiger, Indian lion, great Indian rhinoceros, fishing cat, Malayan tapir, Asian elephant, bongo, striped hyaena, Cape buffalo, and giraffe. Visitors can either hop on a tram to be taken on a 40-minute guided safari through the jungle lit by moonglow lighting and informed by a rather earnest commentary, or they can walk along three short trails at their own pace – or they can do both. The whole affair is extremely well conceived and managed, and the experience is rewardingly authentic – possibly because the night-time ambience hides the seams that are usually so evident in orthodox zoos. Children love the safari experience believing that they truly are chancing upon animals in the jungle. **Places to eat** At the entrance 'lodge' there is a good noodle bar as well as a *Burger King*. There is also another small café at the East Lodge. Open: 1830-2400. Safaris start at 1930 but restaurants are open from 1630. The last tram leaves at 2315. **NB** No flash cameras permitted. Admission S$15.45, children S$10.30. *Getting there*: by bus take the trans island bus number 171 to Mandai Road and then cross the road and board the SBS 138 which goes direct to the Night Safari. By MTR, either get off at Ang Mo Kio and then board the SBS 138, or alight at Choa Chu Kang and board the TIBS 927. A taxi from the city will cost around S$12 and takes 30 minutes.

Mandai Orchid Gardens, Mandai Lake Road (T 2691036), next to the zoo, Singapore's largest commercial orchid farm, started life in 1960 as a hobby for orchidologists John Ede and John Laycock. The rare black orchid of Sumatra blossoms in July. Admission S$2, S$0.80 for children. Open 0830-1730 Monday-Sunday. *Getting there*: take the MRT to Ang Mo Kio, and bus 138 from the interchange.

Bukit Timah Nature Reserve, on Hindhede Drive off Upper Bukit Timah Road (T 4709900), nestles in the centre of the island and has a resident population of wild monkeys, pythons and scorpions. It was one of the first Forest Reserves established in 1883 for the purposes of protecting the native flora and fauna. The naturalist Alfred Russel Wallace collected beetles at Bukit Timah in 1854. Jungle trails go through the forested terrain (130 million-year-old tropical rainforest) that once covered the whole island. The artificial lakes supply the city with much of its water. Clearly marked paths (one of them metalled) in the 81-hectare reserve lead to Singapore's highest point (164m) for scenic views. A visitor centre includes an informative exhibition on natural history (open 0830-1800). The nature reserve is at its quietest and best in the early mornings. It is a wonderful contrast to the bustle of modern Singapore. *Getting there*: take the MRT to Newton Station, then SBS bus 171 or TIBS bus 182. At **Bukit Batok**, there is what little remains of a Japanese Syonan Shrine, built by Australian and British POWs. All that remains are the 125 stone steps leading up to the shrine sight. The shrine's demise is attributed to the termites which the POWs reportedly placed in the materials they used to build it. From here you can walk to the rock formations known as Little Guilin. Entrance is at Bukit Batok on top of the hill at Larong Sesuan off Upper Bukit Timah Road. *Getting there*: buses 171, 179, 182 from Orchard Boulevard or Scotts Road.

MacRitchie and Seletar Reservoirs on Lornie and Mandai roads, are popular for joggers and weekend picnickers. Jungle paths surround the reservoirs. *Getting there*: MacRitchie, buses 104, 132, 167 from Scotts Road or Orchard Boulevard. Also 171 outside *Holiday Inn*, Scotts Road. **Sungei Buloh Nature Park**, Neo Tiew Crescent (T 6690377), is Singapore's first designated wetland nature reserve. It is an important stop-over point for birds migrating along the East Asian Flyway. Best time to visit is in November. Carefully constructed hides throughout 87 hectares provide excellent observation points for visitors to view sea eagles, kites, tree-dwellers. There is also a mangrove swamp to walk through. Open 0700-1900 Monday-Friday, weekends and public holidays. Admission S$1, children S$0.50. Binoculars for hire. *Getting there*: take MRT to Choa Chu Kang, or TIBS bus 170 from Queens Street to Woodlands interchange and then TIBS bus 925 to Kranji Reservoir, then a 20-minute walk. **NB** Bus 925 runs to Park entrance on weekends only.

Kranji War Memorial and Cemetery, Woodlands Road, is where the Allied soldiers killed in Singapore in World War Two are buried. In the heart of the cemetery is the War Memorial, bearing the names of 24,346 servicemen who died in the Asia-Pacific region during the war. The design of the memorial is symbolic, representing the three arms of the services – the army, navy and airforce. The upright section was designed to represent a conning tower, the lateral elements are wings, and the walls symbolize army lines. Flowers are not allowed to be placed on graves, in case tiger mosquitoes breed in the jars. *Getting there*: bus 182 goes direct from Orchard Boulevard or Scotts Road. Alternatively, take 171, 179, 190 from Scotts Road or 171, 174, 179, 190 from Orchard Boulevard and change to 170 on Bukit Timah Road after Farrer Road.

SINGAPORE'S ISLANDS

Singapore's islands are not all of the tropical dream variety, although no expense has been spared, in the case of **Sentosa**, trying to make it into a tropical paradise.

The harder-to-get-to islands are a welcome break from the city and offer a pleasing contrast to everything that modern Singapore stands for. There are around 40 neighbouring small islands, the largest of which is **Pulau Tekong**. The group of islands west of Sentosa – **Pulau Brani**, **Bukom** and **Sambol** – are industrial adjuncts of Singapore proper. Pulau Brani was the site of Singapore's first tin smelter, built in 1890 by the Straits Trading Company. Later, it became popular as a coaling depot for British naval vessels, due to its sheltered position. You can get a scenic view of the oil refinery on Pulau Bukum from Sentosa's swimming lagoon. Ferries link the city with all its surrounding islands but for more obscure spots it's necessary to hire a boat from Clifford Pier. **NB** Avoid going to them on public holidays.

SENTOSA

A British military base until 1970, Sentosa – formerly Pulau Belakang Mati – is now an elaborate 'pleasure' resort. With four hotels, a youth hostel and camp site it is possible to by-pass reality and spend days in a fantasy land of exploding volcanoes, ferro cement geology and enchanted groves.

The name chosen for the island is hardly appropriate: 'Sentosa' means "peace and tranquility". In 1990, Sentosa had a million visitors, about 45% of whom were foreign tourists. On weekends, Sentosa can be a nightmare, as crowds converge on the island's attractions. It is not the sort of island escape one would choose to 'get away from it all'. It is guaranteed, however, to provide plenty of entertainment for children, and adults may be pleasantly surprised with one or two attractions. Sentosa is open 0730-2300, Monday-Thursday, 0730-2400 Friday-Sunday and public holidays. Note that some attractions close before 2300 – many at 1900. A second word of warning is that a day at Sentosa tends to be an expensive as well as an entertaining experience. A family of 4, for example, can easily get through S$200. Basic admission at Sentosa S$5 (S$3 for children). There are various combination tickets that include admission to Sentosa and to selected attractions. It is slightly cheaper to buy tickets this way at the World Trade Centre or on Mount Faber at the cable car entrance, rather than purchasing tickets at individual attractions after arrival (see each entry for admission charges). The disadvantage of purchasing tickets in this way is that it commits you before seeing what is on offer and some tie you in to a tour.

Images of Singapore, **Pioneers of Singapore** and the **Surrender Chambers**: a well-displayed history of Singapore focusing on key figures from the origins of the city state as an entrepot through to the modern period and also telling the traumatic World War Two story. The wax models are not up to Madame Tussaud's standard but the history is well told for those interested in such things. Admission S$5 (S$3 for children). Open 0900-2200 Monday-Sunday. *Getting there*: monorail station 4, bus Nos 2 and A. **Fort Siloso**: Singapore's only preserved fort, built to guard the narrow west entrance to Keppel Harbour has been recently renovated and is a very informative visit, especially if you are interested in the fall of Singapore. It is possible to explore the underground tunnels, artillery nests and bunkers. Also in the fort is a permanent exhibition, '*Behind Bars – Life as a Prisoner of War*', which features the work of wartime artist Stanley Warren, a model of a wartime Changi prison cell and a video of life in the internment camps. Admission S$3 (S$2 for children). Open 0900-1900 Monday-Sunday. *Getting there*:

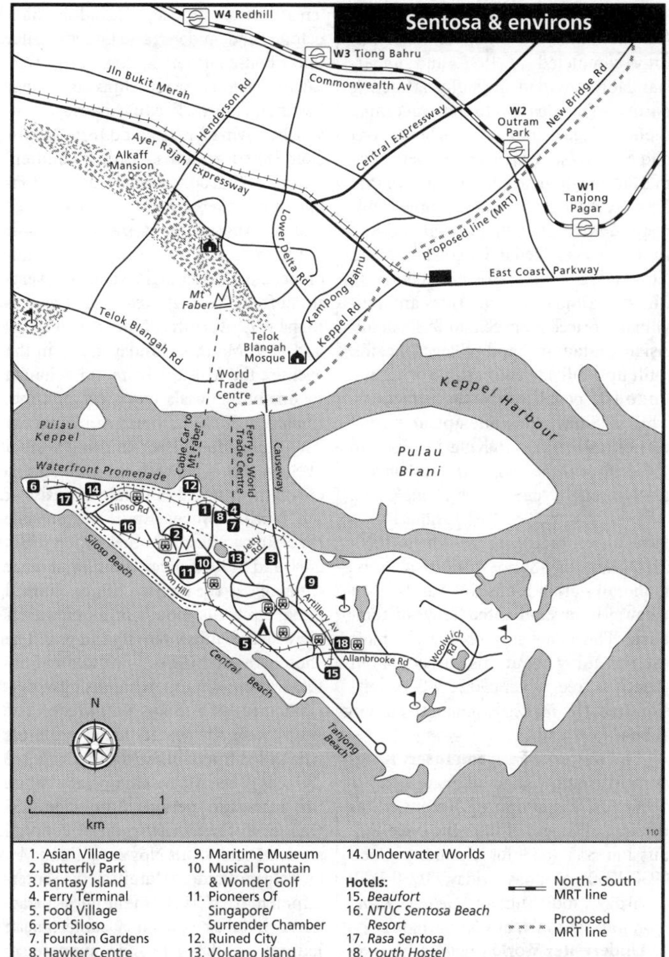

monorail station 3, bus Nos 2 and A. **Maritime Museum**: this museum, housed in a building in the shape of a boat, traces the development of marine vessels from the earliest fishing boats through to modern ships. It also tells the history of Singapore as a port. Admission S$2 (S$0.50 for children). Open 1000-1900 Monday-Sunday. *Getting there*: monorail station 7, bus Nos A, C, E and M. There is also a **Ruined City** and a **Lost Civilization** on the waterfront although these sound more exciting than they really are – just modest attempts at creating the 'Lost City in the Jungle' out of concrete with the requisite idols, ruins and runic stones. *Getting there*: monorail station 1, bus Nos 2 and C.

Asian Village, is a short walk from the ferry terminal. It opened before it was fully completed in 1993, and understandably has had difficulty attracting patrons. The idea was to construct three theme villages – for East Asia, South Asia and Southeast Asia. They're pretty dismal, although some quality souvenirs are for sale. Adventure Asia – a rather half-hearted attempt at an all-Asian kiddies' funfair – was added in for good measure. This part of the village is open 1000-1900, Monday-Sunday and the rides are individually priced from S$2 to S$3. An all-Asian restaurant and village theatre, built up a hillside and capable of seating up to 800 people, are other attractions. This is Singapore's attempt at virtual reality: rather than having to travel to these places, the sights are all conveniently brought together on a single site. Admission is free but the various shows have an entrance charge. Open 1000-2100, Monday-Sunday. *Getting there*: monorail station 1, bus Nos 2 and C. Not far away is the **Enchanted Grove of Tembusu**. The name is probably the most exciting thing about this attraction; but then it is free. Open 0900-2300. Admission free. *Getting there*: monorail station 1, bus Nos 2 and C.

The Butterfly Park and Insect Kingdom Museum (monorail station 4): a 1 hectare park containing 2,500 butterflies through all stages of their life cycle. Admission S$5 (S$3 for children). Open 0930-1730 Monday-Friday, 0930-1830 Saturday and Sunday. *Getting there*: monorail station 4, bus Nos 2 and A.

Underwater World (monorail station 2): this walk-through oceanarium is the largest in Asia and is highly recommended. A 100m tunnel, with a moving conveyor, allows a glimpse of some of its 350 underwater species and 5,000 specimens. Giant rays glide overhead while thick-lipped garoupa and spooky moray eels hide in caves and crevices. In 1997 a large additional tank was under construction which will contain so-called 'creatures of the deep' including giant octopus and spider crabs. Other smaller tanks house cuttlefish, turtles, reef fish, sawfish, corals, sea urchins and other marine creatures. Feeding times are well-worth arriving for: 1130 and 1630. Admission S$12 for adults, S$6 for children. Open 0900-2100 Monday-Sunday. *Getting there*: monorail station 2, bus Nos 2 and A. **Musical fountains** are disco-lit fountains which gyrate, with rather unorchestrated laser light show, to everything from *Joan Jett and the Blackhearts* to the *1812* overture. Shows at 1630, 1700 and 1730 Monday-Sunday. Later in the evening the Musical Fountain is joined by one of Sentosa's more recent attractions – a 37m, 12 storey-tall **Merlion**. This stupendous, laser-emitting symbol of Singapore joins with the fountains to create the Musical Fountain and Rise of the Merlion Show. Each performance lasts 30 minutes and they run at 1930, 2030 and 2130 Monday-Sunday. At other times of day the merlion can be climbed either up to its mouth or its crown for views over Sentosa, the city and port. The shop here (nothing can be built on Sentosa without some merchandising outlet) is themed as a Bugis shipwreck. The Bugis were the feared Malay seafarers who sailed from Sulawesi and controlled the seas of the Malay archipelago before the European period. Admission S$3 (S$2 for children). *Getting there*: monorail station 1 and 4, bus Nos 2, A, C and M.

Volcanoland, a 'multimedia entertainment park', is one of the latest attractions: it takes you on a subterranean journey into the earth and is supposed to trace the evolution of life – although your children will pass no exams with this rubbish. The main show is entertaining enough, but the rest of the complex is rather disappointing and, as with so much on Sentosa, the visitor exits from the multi media extravaganza, no doubt filled with grand thoughts about the origins of life, straight into a shop. There are also occasional Mayan dances although these are in no sense authentic; time your visit to coincide with these shows if desired. Open 1000-2000 Monday-Sunday. Admission S$10 (S$6 for children). *Getting there*: bus Nos A, C and M.

Sentosa Orchid Gardens, very close to the ferry terminal, is planted out with a vast variety of orchids. Within the gardens is a restaurant, a fish pond full of gobi fish and *Ranwatei,* a Japanese tea room. Open 0900-1900 Monday-Sunday. Admission S$2 (S$1 for children). *Getting there*: monorail stations 1 and 7; bus Nos 2, A, C, E, and M.

Sun World Sunbathing or swimming at the lagoons and nearby 'beach'. You can hire pedal boats, windsurfers, canoes or aqua bikes. Siloso Beach, at the west end of the island has been redeveloped by the Sentosa Development Corporation. Tens of thousands of cubic metres of golden sand were shipped in, as were 300 mature coconut palms and over 100 ornamental shrubs and flowering trees. The island has four **beaches**: Central, Beach Monkeys, Siloso and Tanjong. *Getting there*: Monorail station 5 for Central and Beach Monkeys, station 2 for Siloso, bus nos 2, A and M or the Beach Train.

Fantasy Island: advertised as the "ultimate water adventure" this is a must for children: white water river rapids, play areas in the water and aquatic slides are fun and well-designed. The various slides and chutes are graded from 1 to 4 and there is an area reserved purely for smaller children with life guards keeping a wary eye out. Public lockers and changing rooms, but no towels provided. Various snack bars on site. A sunny day here can turn a pallid European into a lobster in less time than it takes to say thermador. At weekends it is packed. Open 1000-1900 Monday-Sunday. Admission S$16 (S$10 for children). *Getting there*: monorail stations 1 and 7; bus Nos 2, A, C, E, and M.

Close to Fantasy Island is Sentosa's latest attraction: **Cinemania**. This is a high tech movie extravaganza. Combining high definition film with state of the art sound and seats raised on hydraulic jacks, it creates what is rather ambitiously called hyper reality. Shows every 30 minutes, 1100-2000 Monday-Sunday. Admission S$10 (S$6 for children). *Getting there*: monorail stations 1 and 7, bus Nos 2, A, C, E and M.

Fun World Cycling, roller-skating or golf on the 18-hole course, also a maze. The **WonderGolf** course is fun: 45 mini-holes each with some novel obstruction to surmount. Open: 0900-2100. Admission S$8 (S$4 for children). There is a suitably sanitized hawker centre at Rasa Sentosa or there is the *Newfun Kelong Restaurant* at the end of the old jetty. There is also a rather staged night market.

Sentosa Island Tour S$28 from the following hotels: *Sheraton Towers*, *Mandarin*, *Boulevard*, *Shangri-La*, *Orchard*, *Hilton International*.

● Accommodation

Prices: L+ over S$400; **L** S$300-400; **A+** S$200-300; **A** S$150-200; **B** S$100-150; **C** S$50-100; **D** S$25-50; **E** Below S$25

Contrary to first impressions, it is possible to escape from Sentosa's hoardes, thanks to the construction of two new hotels. **L** ***Beaufort***, Bukit Manis Rd, T 2750331, F 2750228, e-mail: Beaufort@singnet.com.sg, a/c, restaurants, large pool, the most refined of the hotels on Sentosa, smaller than the Rasa Sentosa, more elegant and quieter; **A+** ***Rasa Sentosa (Shangri-La)***, 101 Silosa Rd, T 2750100, F 2750355 (or from UK on T 0181 747 8485), on southern tip of island, a/c, restaurant, freeform pool, sports facilities, creche, clean beach (sterilized sand imported from Indonesia) and the water is OK for swimming. The hotel is built in a curve, behind Fort Siloso, it has 1st class facilities and an unsurpassed view of the oil refinery just across the water, competitive weekend package deals available – though it can get very busy then. **A** ***Sijori Resort***, situated close to the action by the 37m-high Merlion. This hotel/resort opened in early 1997 and is clearly positioned to attract those people who wish to make full use of Sentosa's attractions. ***Sentosa Youth Hostel*** (next to the lagoon), bookings at the World Trade Centre, the hostel is really meant for local youth and community groups, but an a/c room accommodating up to 12 costs

S$80 a night during the week and S$100 on weekends, non a/c rooms S$5 pp, tents can be hired by the day (4-man S$12; 6-man S$14.50; camp bed S$0.50); ***NTUC Sentosa Beach Resort***, Singapore's first 5-star campsite, with chalets and attap huts overlooking Siloso Beach.

● Places to eat

Prices: ♦♦♦♦++ over S$30; ♦♦♦-♦♦♦♦++ S$15-25; ♦♦-♦♦♦ S$6-15; ♦-♦♦ under S$6

There are fast-food outlets and restaurants dotted around the island. The ***Sentosa Food Centre*** close to the ferry terminal is a squeaky-clean hawker centre, serving Malay, Chinese, Peranakan, Indian and Western cuisine, the dishes are pricier than elsewere in Singapore and the food is sometimes disappointing, open 1100-2200. Other restaurants at the ferry terminal include a ***Burger King***, ice cream parlour, the ***Singapore Riverboat*** (a paddlewheel steamer) and the ***Carmelia Restaurant***. Beside the Merlion is ***Sir Basil's Café and Bar*** and there are also several burger outlets and snack bars at Siloso, Central and Tanjong beaches as well as associated with many of the individual attractions. In short, visitors will not starve during their visit. There are more elegant restaurants at the hotels.

● Transport

Local Bicycles, **tandems** and **trishaws** for hire from the ferry terminal or take the free buses (run from 0900-1930 Mon-Sun, every 10 minutes) which link the ferry terminal, Underwater World, Fort Siloso, and Images of Singapore. The free night bus (1930-2230 Mon-Sun) runs between the Beaufort and NTUC hotels and the Musical Fountain and ferry terminal. The monorail links all the island's attractions (runs at 10-minute intervals from 0900-2200 Mon-Sun, free). **Transport to the island Road** Special Sentosa bus 'A' leaves from the World Trade Centre, stopping at Underwater World, Images of Singapore, the Musical Fountain and Siloso Beach. The service runs 0700-2230 Mon-Sun. To get to the World Trade Centre take buses 65, 167 or 143 from Orchard Rd; 61, 84, 143, 145, 166 and 167 from Chinatown (the nearest MRT station is at Tanjong Pagar, from which buses 10, 97, 100 and 125 go to World Trade Centre). Sentosa bus service 'C' leaves from the Tiong Bahru MRT station for the ferry terminal and Musical Fountain and operates 0700-2330 Mon-Sun while bus 'M' continues on to Central Beach and runs 1600-2300 Mon-Fri, 0800-2300 Saturday and Sun. Service 'E' picks up at the Somerset, Dhoby Ghaut and City Hall MRT stations, at the Lucky Plaza on Orchard Rd, at Marina Square, the NTUC Income building, and at the *Mandarin* and *Le Meridien* hotels. The service operates 1000-2315 Mon-Sun. Bus services 'A', 'C' and 'M' cost S$6 (S$4 for children). Bus service 'E' is S$7 (S$5 for children). These are return fares and include entrance to Sentosa (normally priced at S$5). **Cable Car**: an alternative way to reach Sentosa is via the Cable Car. There are three stops: Mount Faber (the highest point in Singapore, with scenic views and seafood restaurants – worthwhile), the Cable Car Tower adjacent to the World Trade Centre, and the Cable Car Plaza on Sentosa. Fares: one stop S$5, 2 stops S$5.50, 4 stops S$6.50. Admission to Sentosa is in addition to these fares. Cable car operates: 0830-2100 Mon-Sun. **Taxis**: are charged a toll of S$3 and can only drop off/pick up at the hotels. **Ferry** The ferry from the World Trade Centre leaves every 20 minutes from 0930-2100, every 15 minutes 0830-2100 Sat and Sun. Fare USS$1.30 return (with entrance to Sentosa, USS$6.30).

ST JOHN'S AND KUSU ISLAND

Happily, developers have been less active on Singapore's other south islands, although they are popular city escapes. **St John's** is the larger with a few holiday camps and swimming lagoons. It used to be a quarantine station and an opium treatment centre. When Stamford Raffles first approached Singapore, his six ships anchored off Street John's. The Malays called it Pulau Si-Kijang – barking deer island. The English sailors could not pronounce it, and corrupted it to St John's. **Accommodation** A few holiday bungalows and camping is permitted; there is a cafeteria and shop; contact the World Trade Centre T 2707888 or 2707889.

It is possible to walk around **Kusu**, or Turtle Island, in a few minutes. *Kusu* means turtle in Malay and according to legend, a giant turtle turned itself into an island in order to save two shipwrecked sailors, a Malay and a Chinese, who lived here peacefully until they died. Kusu has a Chinese temple and Malay shrine (see Festivals, page 724) where the Malay/Chinese god *Datok*

Kung is worshipped. This god is an amalgum of the Chinese God of the Soil, *Tapo-kung*, and a Malay spirit, *Datok*. Like most such gods, he is thought to bring good fortune to his supplicants and is depicted bearded and smiling. *Getting there*: there is a ferry to both islands from the World Trade Centre, 30 minutes to Kusu, 1 hour to St John's (USS$6.20 return, S$3.10 for children). Monday-Saturday ferries leave the World Trade Centre at 1000 and 1330; on Sunday and public holidays there are departures about every hour between 0945 and 1715. The last boat back from St John's leaves the jetty at 1445 (Monday-Saturday), and at 2030 on Sunday and public holidays.

OTHER ISLANDS TO THE SOUTH

Pulau Hantu, **Sister's Island** (Subar Laut and Subar Darat) and **Lazarus Island**, like Pulau Biola near Raffles Lighthouse, are popular for snorkelling and fishing. **Pulau Seking** is slightly further away and village life here is still just about intact although the population of less than 50 inhabitants, living in a traditional fishing village on stilts, is rapidly dwindling. *Getting there*: There are no regular ferry services to these islands. Charter a boat from Clifford Pier (from around USS$40 per hour for 6-12 passengers) and stock up on food and water before you go. Many tour operators have snorkelling equipment for hire.

ISLANDS TO THE NORTHEAST

Pulau Ubin A great – but little-known – awayday from concrete and capitalism. This island is the source of granite for the causeway and Singapore's earlier buildings and skyscrapers. Its name derives from the Javanese word for 'squared stone'. Ubin village affords a taste of Singapore in bygone days, with dilapidated wooden shophouses, coffee-shops and community spirit. The island, with its beaten-up cars and old taxis, quarry pits, jungle tracks, hills and beaches, is a mountain-biker's paradise and has become a popular destination for that reason, as the trails are quite challenging; it is possible to hire bicycles in the village. There is an outward bound centre on the island.

The best restaurant on the island – which doubles as one of the best restaurants in Singapore – is *Ubin Seafood*, on the northeast shore at the end of a potholed jungle track (see below).

● Accommodation

D *Nature Traveller House*, 8Y Pulau Ubin, T 5426154 – ask for Thian, run by the owner of the biggest mountain-bike shop, fan-cooled only, kitchen facilities. **Camping**: tents available for rent on the island.

● Places to eat

♦♦♦*Ubin Seafood*, T 5458202/5426215 (ask for Liang), is on the northeast shore of Pulau Ubin, at the end of a jungly track, and is one of the best seafood restaurants in Singapore. It is best to book – not because it is always crowded, but to ensure they have stocked up on all the crabs, fish, mussels and Tiger beer you need, recommended. Sport Canoes, kayaks and mountain bikes all available for hire on the island.

● Transport

From Changi Point it costs S$2 to go to Pulau Ubin; bumboats go when they're full – very frequently at the weekends – and operate between 0600 and 2200. It is possible to charter the whole vessel if you want to be alone, or are bored waiting for it to fill up. (For transport to and from Changi Village, see page 666.)

Tours and tour operators

For those constrained by time, there is a big choice of organized tours which cover everything from cultural heritage to island-hopping, eating and shopping. Most city and island tours take about 3½ hours, and depending on admission fees to various sights, cost between S$20 and S$40. For a full day tour expect to pay around S$60-70.

City tours Most popular are the city tours which involve coach rides along Orchard Road, past the Istana, through Little India and visit Shenton Way, Raffles Place, Chinatown, Mount Faber and the Botanic Gardens. 3½ hours (S$20) 0900 and 1400 Monday-Sunday. Main operators: *RMG Tours, Singapore Sightseeing Tour East*, *Grey Line Tours*, *Singapore Explorers* (who run a trolley/tram service for S$9, S$7 for children, providing all day, unlimited travel tickets).

Eco-tours *Eureka Travel*, 277A Holland Avenue, Holland Village, T 4625077, F 4622853, organizes local and regional tours with an environmental bias. It is the only such company in Singapore and guides are all highly qualified naturalists. Offers everything from ornithological tours of Singapore to trips to national parks in East and West Malaysia, recommended.

Guides For private guided tours, call the Registered Guides Association, T 3383441; S$50 for a minimum of 4 hours. Licenced tourist guides wear official badges and should produce ID on request.

BOAT TRIPS

Harbour A variety of harbour and island cruises are available from Clifford Pier – but not during Kusu festival. Craft vary from bumboats to catamarans to imperial Chinese vessels (with modern facilities) and luxury cruise boats, prices range from S$20-50. Buffets and twilight or starlit dinners are served on some of the more elaborate tours for S$37-82.Harbour and island cruises depart from Clifford Pier or from the World Trade Centre. Companies operating this service include *Amaril* T 4759688, *Fantasy* T 2840424, *J&N* T 2707100 and *Pacific Seacrafts* T 2706665.

Singapore River Tours leave from three points – Raffles Landing Pier, which is next to Parliament House, Boat Quay and Clarke Quay. Most are 30-minute bumboat tours of the river with a banal commentary in English. Tours run at regular intervals from 0900-2100 Monday-Sunday (S$7, S$3 for children). The nearest MRT stop to the landing steps is Raffles Place (Standard Chartered Bank exit). For further information, call enquiries at *Singapore River Cruises*, T 2279228 or *Singapore Explorer Plc Ltd* T 3396833, F 3389205. Singapore Explorer also organize twilight cruises, with buffet dinner or longer junk cruises. Most companies provide a private charter service.

Longer cruises For longer cruises and trips into Indonesian and Malaysian waters, the main operators are *J&N Cruises*, T 2707100, *Watertours* T 5339811 (for cruises to Kusu and the southern islands only), *Amaril Cruises* T 4759688, *Fantasy*

Cruises T 2832182, F 3825293, *World Express* T 3363877, *Tour East* T 2202200, *American-Orient* T 7320488, *Commonwealth Travel Service* T 5320532, *P&O* T 2247433, *Pacific World* T 2910288, *Star Cruise* T 7336388.

Round-the-island tours There are quite a few to choose from, ranging from history tours of the colonial buildings, to west coast and Sentosa tours, Singapore by night or zoo tours. See Tour Operators listing below.

Singapore 4 Kids There is plenty on offer here for children and one tour company has identified a market; *Tour East* organize a day tour from S$66 per child, T 3323755.

Tour Operators Singapore's leading tour operators are: *Holiday Tours*, T 7341818; *RMG Tours*, T 7321432; *Singapore Explorer*, T 3396833; amongst others.

There are many other and varied tours available in Singapore. The Peninsula Plaza, on the corner of Coleman Street and North Bridge Road contains a plentiful supply of travel agents offering discount prices on air tickets. Check in the Singapore Tourist Board's Official Guide for what's currently on offer.

Local information

● Accommodation

In 1995 Singapore welcomed over 7 million tourists, and the number of hotels on the island is rather overwhelming. The vast majority are clean and well-appointed by Asian standards – although they are expensive compared with prices in other Southeast Asian capitals (even the *YMCA* falls within the '**A**' category in Singapore). Nearly all the top-end hotels offer a full range of amenities and for that reason, are fairly homogenous. The main differentiating factor is location and the hotels listed below are arranged by area, with each section beginning with a brief description of its main features, advantages and disadvantages. As there are so many hotels, this listing is not comprehensive. At the bottom end, there are a few cheap Chinese hotels (some of those in Geylang quote room rates by the hour) and crashpads where backpackers can still find dormitory accommodation, with no frills attached. The *STPB* publishes two accommodation guides available from *STPB* offices (see page 720), one covering luxury and 'tourist-class' hotels and another for budget hotels. Visitors arriving by air who do not have hotel reservations can contact the hotel counter at Changi Airport; it is worth inquiring about any special rates that might be available. Some visitors have told us that prices quoted at the airport are better than at the hotels.

Colonial Core

Prices: L+ over S$400; **L** S$300-400; **A+** S$200-300; **A** S$150-200; **B** S$100-150; **C** S$50-100; **D** S$25-50; **E** Below S$25

Accommodation in this area is well placed for exploring the sights of the colonial city on foot, including the restaurants and bars of Clarke and Boat quays. Many of Singapore's museums are also found here. The main shopping area (Orchard Rd) and the CBD are both a short taxi ride away.

L+ *Raffles*, 1 Beach Rd, T 3371886, F 3397650, e-mail: raffles@pacific.net.sg, 9 restaurants and a Culinary Academy, 5 bars (see separate entries under Places to eat and Bars) and surrounded by 70 shops, much has been said about Raffles and despite the criticisms that it has become rather sterile, it is still a great place to stay – if you can afford it. The 104 suites have been immaculately refurbished, with wooden floors, high ceilings, beautiful colonial-style furniture and plenty of space. Bathrooms are fantastic and the other facilities are excellent – lovely rooftop pool, with jacuzzis, state of the art fitness centre, both open 24 hours. About half their clients are visiting on business; corporate rates available. Very exclusive and highly recommended. **L** ***Carlton***, 76 Bras Basah Rd, T 3388333, F 3396866, pretty average 477-room hotel with business facilities, good sized pool including a children's pool, fitness centre with sauna and jacuzzi, mostly corporate guests from Australia and Japan, good location. **L** ***Intercontinental***, 80 Middle Rd, Bugis Junction, T 3387600, F 3387366, extremely attractive renovated and extended block of Art Deco shophouses, with a high rise block behind. Over 400 good sized rooms with spacious bathrooms and every luxury provided, attractive rooftop pool area with jacuzzi and state of the art fitness centre. Business centre with small meeting room. Only drawback is the distance of some rooms from the lifts (for the more expensive rooms in the renovated shophouses). Beautifully designed to a high standard and one of the best hotels in Singapore. The *Shophouse Room* is a bit of a showpiece and costs an extra $60 – for which you get original colonial furniture and parquet flooring. **L** ***Westin Stamford and Westin Plaza***, 2 Stamford Rd, e-mail: westin1@singnet.com.sg, http://www.westin.com.sg, T 3396633, F 3365117, 13 restaurants, attractive triple circular pool (great for children), high-tech fitness centre, listed in the Guinness Book of Records as the tallest hotel in the world, this 2-tower complex was designed by Chinese architect IM Pei who also designed the futuristic Bank of China building in Hong Kong. The *Compass Rose Restaurant* on the top floor, provides stunning views over three countries – Singapore, Malaysia and Indonesia. With over 2,000 rooms and a vast echoing lobby it is all a little overwhelming – and too large for that personal touch. However, it has a good reputation in the business world. On our last visit they were too busy to let us see a room. **L-A+** ***Grand Plaza***, 10 Coleman St, T 3363456, F 3399311, 2 restaurants, attractive but smallish pool and jacuzzi, gym and health spa to be open by the time this edition goes to press – all on 3rd floor. Large ballroom and 2 smaller meeting rooms, business centre with computers for guests' use. Although the outside of this building is pretty hideous, with its marble cladding, the interior is not so ostentatious and despite its size (340 rooms) it feels quite intimate. The lobby area is backed by a water garden with fishponds and also contains a sunken restaurant area. The rooms have been designed to a high standard and are not so run-of-the-mill. Attractive local prints line the walls of the corridors. Recommended.

A+ ***Allson***, 101 Victoria St, T 2260911, F 3397019, Chinese in character with heavy furniture, rooms are adequate, average pool but fitness facilities are limited to a running machine, live band in the bar, quite a friendly place slightly off the beaten track. **A+** ***Excelsior***, 5 Coleman St, T 3387733, F 3396236, several restaurants but the hotel coffee shop is in the Excelsior Plaza next door, open 0600-2230. Small pool and no gym, limited business facilities. Guests may use all the facilities of the *Peninsula Hotel* next door, which is under the same management. There is talk of these two hotels merging. Rooms are Art Deco in style and are of average size. Personal safe in every room. Cramped lobby and dreary corridors, definitely a tour group place. **A+** ***New Otani***, 177A River Valley Rd, T 3383333, F 3392854, right next to Clarke Quay, this makes the *New Otani* a lively place to be. The rooms are average, with a good sized pool for lengths and a decent fitness centre. Not surprisingly it is popular with Japanese – location is its strength. **A+** ***Peninsula***, 3 Coleman St, T 3372200, F 3393580, rooms are quite small and frayed at the edges, small pool, with adequate fitness centre, limited business facilities, 24-hour coffee shop, night club, cramped lobby area, friendly and in the heart of the Colonial Core.

B ***Metropole***, 41 Seah St, T 3363611, F 3393610, a smallish business hotel with no frills.

D ***Willy's Homestay***, 494 North Bridge Rd, T3370916, willys@mbox2.singnet.com.sg, dorms available (**E**), breakfast included, central and clean.

Orchard Road

Prices: L+ over S$400; **L** S$300-400; **A+** S$200-300; **A** S$150-200; **B** S$100-150; **C** S$50-100; **D** S$25-50; **E** Below S$25

You could be forgiven for mistaking Orchard Rd for the US; it retains little that is Asian in character. This is the catwalk of Singapore, where young trendies hang out in their droves. It is a shoppers' paradise, with at least 20 plazas to choose from (see page 643), all with their individual characters. There are many 4-5 star hotels here, with little to differentiate between them.

L+ ***Four Seasons***, 190 Orchard Boulevard, T 7341110, F 7330682. This intimate hotel of 250 rooms (and 400 staff) provides exceptional personal service; there's no check-in desk and all guests are greeted by name. Rooms are elegantly decorated in a traditional European style, with feather pillows, writing desk, multi-disc player, modem/fax hook up and spacious bathrooms. The hotel has a unique Asian art collection, with attractive artwork in all the rooms. There are 2 pools – one is for lengths, they boast the only air-conditioned tennis courts in Singapore, a golf simulator, and a state-of-the-art health and fitness centre, with attendants on hand all day. Restaurants include Cantonese and Contemporary American cuisine, with buffet provided. Although this is primarily a business hotel, children are well catered for and a special children's lunch is layed on at the weekends. For service and general ambience, this hotel is hard to beat, recommended. **L+** ***Hyatt Regency***, 10-12 Scotts Rd, T 7381234, F 7321696, sales@hyatt.com.sg, http://www.travelweb.com/hyatt.htm, owned by the Sultan of Brunei, unusual lobby area with bird prints on the walls, bustling atmosphere, stunning flower arrangements, bigger than average rooms, all with an alcove sitting area (some with poolside view) and separate showers. Spectacular large 5th floor garden, with roaring waterfall and a very attractive pool area, poolside bar and restaurant. The executive class rooms have their own private Balinese garden (good for families). Squash courts, 2 tennis courts, huge fitness centre with aerobics classes, fabulous jacuzzi and sauna. Very popular bar in basement – *Brannigans*. Its selling point must be its garden and fitness facilities. 85% corporate clients and good discounts available, recommended. **L+ *Goodwood Park***, 22 Scotts Rd, T 7377411, F 7328558, apart from *Raffles*, this is the only other colonial hotel in Singapore. It has had a chequered history, beginning life in 1856 as the German Recreation Club, the Teutonia. During World War One it was declared enemy property and was seized by the government. In 1929 it was converted into a hotel, but then during World War Two, it was occupied by the Japanese. After the war it became a War Crimes Trial Court and did not resume functioning as a hotel until 1947. The exterior is looking a little scruffy and the lobby area isn't very encouraging, but the rooms are exceptional. Of the 235 rooms, there is a choice of colonial or modern style. The former have ceiling fans and windows that can be opened, with very stylish simple decor and lots of space. The modern rooms are slightly smaller, but they overlook the Mayfair pool and some rooms on the ground level lead straight out onto this area. All rooms are fitted with the latest electronic equipment. Lovely pool area, set in a garden with pagodas, and another larger lengths pool. Several restaurants (see **Places to eat**), recommended. **L+-A+ *Melia at Scotts*** 45 Scotts Rd, T 7325885, F 7321332, this Spanish hotel has an unusual feel, with attractive modern art on the walls. The rooms are well appointed and bigger than average with high ceilings (unusual in modern hotels). There is a smallish pool and the only Spanish restaurant in Singapore. The hotel is popular with Japanese, rather off the main drag but close to Newton MRT and near the huge Hawker centre there, hospitable service, recommended. **L *Regent***, 1 Cuscaden Rd, T 7338888, F 7328838, huge rather ostentatious lobby with bubble lifts, rather sterile atmosphere reminiscent of tenement blocks. Gloomy corridors and 440 large but quite plain rooms. Excellent fitness centre but boring circular pool and barren sunbathing area. Quiet location at western end of Orchard Rd. **L *Shangri-La***, 22 Orange Grove Rd, T 7373644, F 7373257, one of Singapore's finest hotels set in a beautifully maintained, spacious landscaped garden, 300 plus rooms, the standard ones are nothing exceptional, but what is lovely about this hotel is its leisure facilities: spacious pool area, surrounded by greenery and waterfalls, jacuzzi, indoor pool, good fitness centre, squash and tennis courts, and a three hole pitch and putt 'course'. Three restaurants – *Shang Palace* for dim sum, *Tanti Bacis* for poolside Italian and a Japanese restaurant, all go towards making this hotel the winner of Singapore Tourism Promotion Board's award for best hotel year after year, recommended. **L *Hilton***, 581 Orchard Rd, T 7372233, F 7322917. *Tradewinds* restaurant serves local and North Indian food in al fresco atmosphere at the poolside, the *Inn of Happiness* serves Chinese food, *Harbour Grill* for French cuisine (different French chefs visit every month), the *Checkers Deli* on the ground floor sells chocolates and desserts and has a reputation for its Philadelphia cheesecake. The *Kaspia Bar* has the largest range of vodkas in Singapore (jazz singer performs here). Small old-style pool, good facilities in the fitness centre (and a large area). The *Hilton* was the first international hotel in Singapore. Its 434 average-sized rooms were renovated a couple of years ago, and despite its age it maintains a good reputation and is particularly popular with businessmen and women (with its function rooms constantly in demand), and with Japanese tour groups.

L *Holiday Inn Park View*, 11 Cavenagh/Orchard Rd, T 7338333, F 7324757. Grand entrance, quite attractive airy triangular layout of rooms around an atrium. Good pool and large children's pool. Good fitness centre. Rooms provided for handicapped people. 300 plus rooms in quiet spot just off the main drag. **L *Le Meridien***, 100 Orchard Rd, T 7338855, F 7327886. Open plan lobby with 4 terraces of rooms and garlands of orchids spilling over. Good sized rooms (corner rooms are larger), queen sized beds, attractive decor, ask for a room overlooking the pool, as these rooms have a balcony. Good pool for lengths, but bare seating area. Fitness centre with dance floor for classes. **L *Mandarin***, 333 Orchard Rd, T 7374411, F 7322361, http://www.singnet.com.sg, rather disjointed lobby area, with nowhere comfortable to sit in this enormous 2-towered hotel (1,200 rooms). Rooms are large and well designed, univiting pool area but large lengths pool. *Top of the M* restaurant on the 39th Flr revolves. No outstanding features to this hotel, but the service seems pretty good. **L *Marco Polo***, 247 Tanglin Rd, T 4747141, F 4710521, 600 rooms in this hotel but it has an attractive low-key lobby. The hotel is almost 25-years-old, so it's holding up well. Rooms are fairly standard but the pool area is exceptional – sunken bar, very attractive pool with gardens and a waterfall and mature trees, all on the 2nd Flr. For fitness freaks, this is the place as it has an excellent fitness centre. It's a short hop from

Orchard Rd and a short jog from the Botanic Gardens. Corporate discounts of up to 50% may be possible. *La Brasserie*, their French restaurant, is very popular and booking is needed. Excellent bakery. **L *Negara***, 10 Claymore Rd, T 7370811, F 8316617. This 200-room hotel prides itself on an intimate atmosphere. It pampers the businessman or woman away from home with personalized service (no reception counters here) and a very high standard throughout. There are no 'club' floors; all the rooms are to the same standard with larger than average and unusual rooms. Spacious bathrooms and separate showers, large pool but rather a bare sitting area. Very sophisticated fitness centre and jacuzzi. It's slightly off Orchard Rd, making it queiter and away from the crowds, recommended. **L *Orchard***, 442 Orchard Rd, T 7347766, F 7335482. For the *Drake Restaurant*, see International food (page 690). The black marble lobby is thankfully about to be ripped out. The rooms are also being renovated – they are decent sized, all with personal safes and the bathrooms have separate showers; a luxury not many hotels stretch to in Singapore. Large pool but no shade, excellent fitness centre and sauna. Its claim to fame is its magnificent ballroom which seats 1,000 for dinner and 1,500 for conference. **L *Sheraton Towers***, 39 Scotts Rd, T 7376888, F 7371072, quietly sophisticated lobby, with waterfalls and beautiful flowers everywhere. 400 rooms with bare corridors but good rooms. The more expensive rooms, known as the *Towers* rooms provide an exceptional service, with lots of extras thrown in. The *Cabana* rooms on the rooftop overlook the pool. Attractive pool area with bar. 80% business guests and popular with US visitors, Italian restaurant open evenings only and exclusive Chinese restaurant, the hotel has won the SPTB service award for 6 years. **L-A+ *ANA***, 16 Nassim Hill, T 7321222, F 732222, e-mail: ANAhotel@singnet.com.sg, restaurants (including excellent Japanese, of course), pool, formerly the *Sheraton*, a short walk from Orchard Rd.

A+ *Boulevard*, 200 Orchard Blvd, T 7372911, F 7378449, a/c, restaurants including a 24-hour coffee shop serving good value buffets. Rather bare pooldeck with average kidney shaped pool overlooked by ugly blocks of the hotel. Semi-circular open atrium and functional lobby makes it all rather uninviting, obviously popular with tour groups. **A+ *Garden***, 14 Balmoral Rd, northwest from Newton Circus, T 2353344, F 2359730, a/c, restaurant, pool. **A+ *Holiday Inn Crowne Plaza***, 25 Scotts Rd, T 7377966, F 7376646, 500-room in an ugly block, built in 1974, renovation is under way so it is difficult to know how it will look upon completion. Quite pleasant pool area, big fitness centre. Owned by the Sultan of Brunei, for whom an entire floor of suites is permanently reserved, *surau* provided for Muslims to pray, popular with Japanese and US visitors. **A+ *Marriott***, 320 Orchard Rd, T 7355800, F 7359800, another 350-room monster, which was once the *Dynasty*. Its distinguishing feature is its rather ridiculous pagoda 'hat' at the top of the tower block. Unusual lobby with 10m-high palm trees and the usual array of facilities. Good fitness centre and large swimming pool with separate whirlpool and *Garden Terrace Café*, extensive business services, efficient but unwelcoming, very central. **A+ *Novotel Orchid Singapore***, 214 Dunearn Rd, T 2503322, F 2509292, 446 rooms unexceptional rooms in an unexceptional hotel. The pool is rather old fashioned and right next to a busy road. The hotel has the added disadvantage of an inconvenient location. **A+ *Orchard Parade***, 1 Tanglin Rd, htttp://www.singnet.com.sg/~webworld/hotels/orchardp/orchardp.html, T 7371133, F 7330242, another featureless block but the rooms have an unusual layout and the bathrooms are refreshingly different. Other than that, it's all quite bland. Decent sized pool with a large bare sitting area. Smallish gym under renovation, as was the entire lobby area in 1997. The hotel is planning an extensive 3-year expansion programme which will probably improve it, but in the meantime, it's a bit of a mess. **A+ *Phoenix***, 277 Orchard Rd, T 7378666, F 7322024. Major refurbishment is taking place here in a futile attempt to go upmarket. Built as a hospital, it consequently has no pool, no gym, and provides no business centre. Selling points are steps machines and internet in every room so you can surf the web and firm up your thighs simultaneously. Mostly twin bedrooms, popular with corporate clients. **A+ *Traders***, 1A Cuscaden Rd, T 7382222, F 314314, lavish pots of orchids at the entrance makes it feel special, but there isn't much to mark this hotel apart from the competition. It has 547 rooms with about three-quarters of their guests being business people. The rooms are average but there is an attractive pool area with a large pool. It has a fitness centre and a business centre and 3 restaurants. No frills. **A+-A *Asia*** 37 Scotts Rd, T 7378388, F 7333563, ugly block with basic rooms, discounts available. **A+-A *Equatorial***, 429 Bukit Timah Rd, T 7320431, F 7379426, very average establishment with a rather public pool and a small coffee house, not a good location either. **A+-A** *Grand Central*, 22 Orchard Rd, T 7379944, F 7333175. Restaurant and pool, nothing special but its name provides its key selling point – it's central. **A** *VIP*, 5 Balmoral Crescent, T 2354277, F 2352824, a/c, restaurant, pool, situated in quiet area of the city close to *Garden Hotel* and west of the Newton MRT station, good rooms with TV, minibar etc.

B *Lloyd's Inn*, 2 Lloyd Rd, T 7377309, F 7377847, a/c, restaurant, scrupulously clean, well-appointed rooms – if a little cramped – quiet location in suburban road near River Valley Rd/Somerset MRT, off Killiney Rd. **B** ***Regalis Court***, 64 Lloyd Rd, T 7347117, F 7361651, this attractive renovated colonial style boutique hotel used to be a school. It provides 43 beautifully appointed rooms, decked out with Indonesian furniture and decor and wooden floorboards. The standard rooms have no windows, but they are well lit. The price is so reasonable because there is no pool or fitness centre. *Peranakan* restaurant on the ground floor and self service breakfast, this is one of the nicest new places around, set in a quiet street behind Orchard Rd, it's hard to beat, highly recommended. **B** ***RELC International House***, 30 Orange Grove Rd, T 7379044, F 7339976, basic no nonsense hotel with no extras, ugly featureless block but quite a good deal for businesswomen and men, conference rooms attached. **B** *YWCA*, Fort Canning Rd, T 3384222, F 3374222. Large new building with 200 plus rooms, pool, tennis courts, ballroom, exhibition hall. It is not clear why it's called a *YWCA* – it is not what you would expect from a so called 'Youth Hostel'. Dorms **B**.

C *Metropolitan YMCA*, 60 Stevens Rd, T 7377755, F 2355528, all rooms are a/c, this newly renovated no frills place provides an efficient service and clean serviceable rooms. The added bonus is a large swimming pool. Very good value, recommended. **C** ***YMCA International House***, 1 Orchard Rd, T 3366000, F 3373140, the old *YMCA* which stood on Stamford Rd was used by the Japanese during the war as their dreaded interrogation and torture centre. The new one's facilities are well above the usual *YMCA* standards, a/c, restaurant, rooftop pool, squash courts, badminton, billiards and fitness centre. Looks rather grotty from the outside, but it is very clean and efficient. Good value for this location, *MacDonald's* on the ground floor, $25 for 4 bed a/c dorm, recommended.

D *Mitre*, 145 Killiney Rd (up side lane, parallel to Lloyd Rd), T 7373811, this place is on the verge of extinction, or is ripe for redevelopment. The building is best described as 'crumbling colonial' so has heaps of character, but resembles a junk yard and the rooms are very run down. Not long to live, nicer than the cheap places on Bencoolen St because of its character.

Chinatown

Prices: L+ over S$400; **L** S$300-400; **A+** S$200-300; **A** S$150-200; **B** S$100-150; **C** S$50-100; **D** S$25-50; **E** Below S$25

Chinatown is probably the most culturally interesting area to be based, but if you are in Singapore to shop or to enjoy the night-life, then look elsewhere. It also provides more unusual accommodation, with several 'boutique' hotels in converted shophouses. These come as a refreshing change from the high-rise anonymity of Orchard Rd or the Colonial Core. If you can do without a pool and fitness centre (though some of the new blocks have such facilities), but appreciate a little more individuality, then try here.

L *Duxton*, 83 Duxton Rd, T 2277678, F 2271232, duxton@singnet.com.sg, restaurant (*L'Aigle d'Or*, page 691), guests can use the large pool at the *Amara Hotel*, intimate, stylish 50-room hotel in refurbished shophouses. The only hotel in Southeast Asia to be accepted into the '*Relais et Chateaux*' family, price including breakfast. Deluxe rooms are built in twin tiers, which are very nice, but none of the rooms are large, mainly frequented by business people as it's convenient for the financial district. Overpriced on the rack rate but good discounts available either from hotel or from travel agents, recommended.

A+ *Amara*, 165 Tanjong Pagar Rd, T 2244488, F 2243910, reserv@amara.com.sg, several restaurants (with one of the best Thai restaurants in town – *Than Ying* – see **Places to eat**) and a coffee shop serving a good buffet spread (♦♦♦), decent sized pool, with café area for steamboat and BBQs. Well maintained with average sized rooms (338 of them) and good extras such as self-service launderette. 4 tennis courts, jogging track and a gym soon. Business centre with conference room and secretaries on hand. Right next door to Amara Plaza, with a good range of shops and restaurants. Good location for those wishing to explore Chinatown or for businessmen, as it lies on the edge of the CBD. **A+** *Furama*, 60 Eu Tong Sen St,

T 5333888, F 5341489, restaurant, grand lobby belies rather scruffy featureless rooms, it all looks as though it could do with a facelift; the 5th Flr pool is a little alarming for children as the ralings around the edge of the building are not very high. The gym is very basic. The building itself stands out from the crowd for its unusual but rather ugly and dated design. **A+** ***Harbour View Dai Ichi***, 81 Anson Rd, T 2241133, F 2220749, http://www.harbourview.com.sg, good Japanese restaurant, average sized pool, over 400 rooms in this highrise block, request a harbour view as the view of Tanjong Pagar container port is worth an hour or two's quiet attention. Good location for business district and access to Chinatown. Large but quite basic rooms. Health centre but no gym, personal safes in more expensive rooms. Business centre with limited secretarial assistance. Meeting room available. Popular with Japanese clients. **A+** ***Merchant Court***, 20 Merchant Rd, T 3372288, F 3340606, mchotel@singnet.com.sg, http://www.raffles.com/ril, brand new, 500-room hotel, owned by *Raffles* group, this is a welcome addition to the mid-range bracket, many of which are looking rather tired. Attractive freeform pool with slides and a separate jacuzzi overlooking the river. Excellent fitness centre managed by *Lifestyles*. Great location makes it an appealing choice. **A** ***Inn of the Sixth Happiness***, 37 Erskine Rd, T 2233266, F 2237951, in the 1860s these buildings housed rickshaw stables and later became a row of 40 shophouses, now the upper floor is an original little hotel of 62 rooms and the ground floor holds some interesting shops, teahouses and restaurants. Unfortunately none of the standard rooms have any windows. Rooms are quite small but characterful; it's a pleasant hotel with wood-beamed ceilings, tasteful interior decor – including replica Peranakan furniture made specially in Fujian province, China. Discounts available. **A-B** ***Chinatown***, 12-16 Teck Lim Rd, T 2255166, F 2253912, a/c, no restaurant but breakfast is provided. 40 rooms in another shophouse renovation. Small shower rooms and rather bland, but, like *Keong Saik* and *The Royal Peacock*, it's an intimate place in an attractive street in the heart of Chinatown. It benefits from a small 'business centre' with a meeting room and secretarial assistance.

B ***Damenlou***, 12 Ann Siang Rd, T 2211900, F 2258500, a/c, attached bathroom, TV, minibar, cheaper rooms are very small but neat and clean and well presented. Very friendly management and located in an attractive street of shophouses, recommended. **B** ***Dragon Inn Chinatown***, 18 Mosque St, T 2227227, F 2226116, a/c. New hotel spreading over 4 shophouses on the 2nd and 3rd floors, making it a bit of a warren of a place. Attractive low rise location, but rooms are small and basic. For rooms onto the street with windows, you need to book in advance. *Homely kitchen* next door is soon to open, providing complimentary breakfast. **B** ***Keong Saik***, 69 Keong Saik Rd, T 2230660, F 2250660, a/c, opened early '97, 25 rooms in a sensitively restored shophouse, wooden floors throughout, attractive all-wood furniture, immaculately presented but rooms are very small, with little room for anything other than the bed. Standard rooms have no windows or windows are skylights (attic rooms). An intimate little 'business' hotel, let down by its room sizes. **B** ***The Royal Peacock***, 55 Keong Saik Rd, T 2233522, F 2211770, a/c, charming little restaurant, *Butterfly Pub* (with Karaoke), 79 rooms spread along 10 shophouses, similar standard to *Keong Saik*, rooms might be marginally larger, but again standard rooms have no natural light and showers only. Price includes continental breakfast. Attractively presented rooms and interesting fresh design in lobby and restaurant. Avoid rooms over the pub which stays open till 0100 or 0200. Recommended for general feel of the hotel but not for room size. **B** ***Sunshine***, 51-57 Tras St, T 2210330, F 2211178, a/c, situated in renovated shophouse, 40 rooms, immaculately presented, some rooms without windows, well decorated, quite small but comfortable. Friendly manager, attractive location and close to MRT, no restaurant but there's one next door.

C ***A&G Chinatown***, 68A Smith St, T 2221218, F 2221220. 20 pokey rooms with a shower but no hand basin and outside toilets. Good location in Chinatown but pretty basic. **C** ***Air View***, 10 Peck Seah St, T 2257788, F 2256688. Not much to differentiate this from *New Asia*, although it might be marginally cleaner. Outside toilet and unimpressive shower arrangement. **C** ***New Asia***, 2 Peck Seah St, T 2211861, F 2239002, a/c, similar to *Air View* but dingier – lino floors, smelly rooms, battered furniture ... bleak. **C** ***YMCA***, 70 Palmer Rd, T 2224666, F 2226467. A/c and basic hot water showers in 50 rooms, mostly singles (with no toilets) – doubles have toilets and are rented to women. Rather out of the way, at the southern end of Chinatown and the business district, but the rate is good and the rooms are spacious if basic. At 40 years, this must be one of the oldest establishments in

Singapore. Friendly manageress – much nicer than other places in this price range.

West of Chinatown

Prices: L+ over S$400; **L** S$300-400; **A+** S$200-300; **A** S$150-200; **B** S$100-150; **C** S$50-100; **D** S$25-50; **E** Below S$25

Between Chinatown and Orchard Rd, along Havelock Rd, there are five 3-4 star hotels in an area that some rather optimistic locals call 'Riverside'. All these hotels are undergoing facelifts in a desperate bid to win customers. Unfortunately, location is a bit of a drawback: the area is rather isolated (although it is only a few minutes by taxi or bus to Clarke and Boat Quays, Chinatown and Orchard Rd), it is overlooked by some particularly unsightly HDB blocks, and there are no shops or restaurants on the doorstep. However, the whole riverside area from here to Clarke Quay is in the process of being 'upgraded' and before long, there will be walkways and shopping malls linking these hotels with Clarke Quay.

A+ *Apollo*, 405 Havelock Rd, T 7332081, F 7331588, 3 restaurants. Built in 1972, this hotel was showing its age in 1997 but is undergoing major cosmetic surgery with a new extension of 135 rooms (making it a 400-room hotel), construction of a sizeable pool, tennis court, gym and jacuzzi, the redesign of the lobby area, and renovation of existing rooms. It needs it – this will lift it above 3-star status (and presumably will lift the price too). Good business centre facilities and larger than average rooms (but featureless). This will be quite a good place to stay in the future – probably by the time this book reaches the shelves. **A+** *Concorde*, 317 Outram Rd, T 7330188, F 7330989, 3 restaurants, pool closed for renovation at time of writing, tennis court but no gym. By far the most stunning design of the hotels in this area, with a huge circular atrium, with exterior bubble lifts. The rooms themselves are being gradually renovated as they have become tatty – ask for a new room. Popular tour group hotel, especially for Japanese visitors. **A+** *King's*, 403 Havelock Rd, T 7330011, F 7325764, Kingstel@singnet.com.sg, http://www.asianconnect.com/sha/king.shtml. 300 plus rooms in another ugly high-rise block. Initial impressions are favourable but the rooms are an anticlimax. Deluxe rooms have balconies and all rooms have personal safes. Family rooms available. Barren but large pool and paddling pool. Live band every evening, Japanese and Chinese restaurants, business centre with computer available and meeting rooms. **A+** *Miramar*, 401 Havelock Rd, T 7330222, F 7334027, restaurants including a 24-hour coffee shop, big pool and paddling pool. Built in 1971, but renovated in 1995, 340 spacious rooms in tower block overlooking the river. **A+-A** *River View*, 382 Havelock Rd, T 7329922, F 7321034, a/c, average restaurant, pool, run by Robert Pregarz, a former Italian sailor and ex-manager of the pre-theme park *Raffles*.

Marina Square

Prices: L+ over S$400; **L** S$300-400; **A+** S$200-300; **A** S$150-200; **B** S$100-150; **C** S$50-100; **D** S$25-50; **E** Below S$25

With Singapore bulging at the seams, this whole area has been built on reclaimed land. Three hotels were constructed 10 years ago, but with the arrival of two 5-star hotels, the opening of Suntec City (a high-tech conference centre), 4 new office blocks, hundreds of new shops and over 75 restaurants and an entertainment centre almost completed, this area has become a self-contained district which, because of its proximity to the airport, is proving popular with business travellers or anyone in transit. It all 'works' well but there is absolutely no sense of Singapore here.

L+ *Conrad*, 2 Temasek Boulevard, T 3388830, F 3388164, this is the latest 5-star hotel to open in Singapore. It is the closest to Suntec City, so a good choice for the business traveller and provides an excellent service, with 509 beautifully designed contemporary style rooms, lots of space, big windows and a large desk. Excellent meeting rooms, and an impressive mezzanine level for functions, with its 24 carat gold leaf chandelier and 500 light bulbs. US$1.3m investment in almost 3,000 artworks makes this hotel stand apart from the competition. As yet the pool area is a little bare and the fitness centre is adequate. Recommended. **L+** *Ritz Carlton*, 7 Raffles Ave, T 3378888, F 3380001, this and the *Conrad* are the most recent additions in this area of town. They share designers (Hirsch Bedner of the US), and this shows in the high quality of finish in both hotels. The furnishings are very contemporary; considerable investment has been made in artworks (notably the Frank Stella constructions and the Dele Chihuly glass balls below the lobby area) and rooms are very attractive, with wooden floors and big bathrooms (the bath is situated next to a large circular window, providing stunning views of the harbour and river areas). Big pool area with jacuzzi in well landscaped grounds, huge fitness centre. Good business facilities. Each room cost a staggering US$520,000 to build and the *Ritz Carlton* likes to think of itself as a '6-star' hostelry. Geomancy seems to play an important role in this hotel, with no non-auspicious room numbers, recommended. **L** ***Marina Mandarin***, 6 Raffles Blvd, Marina Sq, T 3383388, F 3394977, e-mail: mms888@singnet.com.sg, http://www.commerceasia.mandarin, a/c, restaurants, pool, well equipped fitness centre, good business facilities, large rooms. The hotel consists of 3 giant blocks arranged in a triangle enclosing a vast atrium which rises to the very top of the building, filled with cascades of plants and caged birds giving the aural impression of a jungle. **L** ***Oriental***, 5 Raffles Ave, T 3380066, F 3399537, another central atrium, this time triangular, with exterior lifts, its black marble and limited natural light makes it all a little sombre in feel. This is one of the older hotels in the Marina area, with 522 bigger than average rooms with attractive bathrooms. Harbour views are more expensive. It has a large lengths pool and a separate children's pool and quite a big area for children to play. There's also a fitness centre. Restaurants include the *Chinese Cherry Garden*, Californian cuisine at *Liana's* and an outdoor Italian restaurant by the pool. All very efficient, but nothing exceptional. **L-A+** ***Pan-Pacific***, 7 Raffles Blvd, T 3368111, F 3391861, yet another open triangular atrium which, strangely, has a rather claustrophobic feel. Bubble lifts both exterior and interior – the exterior one provides stunning views of the city and leads to a Chinese restaurant. There are 800 rooms and about 70% of the guests are business travellers. The rooms are large and pleasantly laid out, with three views. Attractive fan-shaped pool, rather overlooked, two tennis courts and a *Clark Hatch* fitness centre. Famous Japanese restaurant *Keyaki*, with a Japanese garden on the 4th Flr. Efficient service, yet lacking in atmosphere.

Arab Street and Little India

Prices: L+ over S$400; **L** S$300-400; **A+** S$200-300; **A** S$150-200; **B** S$100-150; **C** S$50-100; **D** S$25-50; **E** Below S$25

Most of the budget accommodation (such as it is in Singapore) is to be found in the Arab St or Little India areas to the north of town. Little India is probably a more interesting place to stay. Cheap accommodation is very limited in Singapore and many of the backpackers haunts are to be found in apartment blocks and do not have much to recommend them – other than price.

A+ ***Golden Landmark***, 390 Victoria St, T 2972828, F 2982038, this 400-room tower block (with Arabic overtones) is looking older than its 7 year life. It has an Indonesian restaurant, a big pool, corporate floors and a business centre. Caters mainly for tours and corporate clients – not many Europeans stay here. **A+-A** ***Albert Court***, 180 Albert St, T 3393939, F 3393252, http://www.fareast.com.sg/hotels. This new hotel lies behind a courtyard of renovated shophouses. An unusual design (a mixture of western and Peranakan), this is an intimate place built to high specifications, with attractive extras. Ask for a room with big windows. Restaurant but no other facilities, which accounts for its price. Right next to a good range of restaurants in Albert Court, recommended. **A** ***City Bayview***, 30 Bencoolen St, T 3372882, F 3382880, a/c, restaurant, leafy rooftop pool. Neat little hotel block with business facilities, personal safes in rooms, attentive service, popular with tour groups.

B ***Dickson Court***, 3 Dickson Rd, at Jl Besar end, T 2977811, F 2977833, price includes simple buffet breakfast. New, clean, smart, with friendly management. **B** ***Summer View***, 173 Bencoolen St, T 3381122, F 3366346. Compact, quite well designed modern block. 80 very small rooms. No restaurant. Popular with local (regional) businessmen. **B-C** ***Broadway***, 195 Serangoon Rd, T 2924661, F 2916414, a/c, restaurant, ugly hotel block stuck on its own, Indian-run, Indian-frequented hotel with clean rooms and friendly management, excellent Indian restaurant downstairs (*New Delhi Restaurant*): 'we know the way to your heart is through your stomach'. **B-C** ***Penta***, 33 Birch Rd, T 2996311, F 2999539. Adequate place but there are other better places to stay at this price.

C ***Beach***, 95 Beach Rd, T 3367712, F 3367713, a/c. Basic but clean rooms in a block. **C** ***Bencoolen***, 47 Bencoolen St, T 3360822, F 3362250, a/c, complimentary breakfast. It calls itself 'your home away from home' but I hope your home doesn't look like this. Corridors and bedrooms have been tiled to above waist level, making it more like a public toilet than a hotel. Scruffy bathrooms. **C** ***Little India Guesthouse***, 3 Veerasamy Rd, T 2942866, F 2984866, some a/c, no private bathrooms, but spotless male/female shower areas and immaculate rooms. No food served here, but plenty on the street. Good location if you want to be in the heart of Little India, recommended. **C** ***Lucky***, 18 Race Course Rd, T 2919122, F 2919391, small rooms, basic but clean. Good price for location; **C** ***Strand***, 25 Bencoolen St,

T 3381866, F 3381330, a/c, attractive café and refurbished rather trendy lobby raises expectations which are then dashed by grotty rooms; they are big though and it's quite good value. **C** *Tai Hoe*, 163 Kitchener Rd, T 2939122, F 2984600, a/c, hot water bath, not visited on our last visit but recommended by a traveller. **C** *Waterloo Hostel*, 4th, 5th and 7th Flr, 55 Waterloo St, T 3366555, F 3362160, a/c, centrally located, big rooms with TVs and telephones, complimentary tea/coffee and basic breakfast, very pleasant, friendly atmosphere, run by Catholic Welfare Centre, recommended. If the hostel is full and you are offered rooms in their 'homestay' – avoid, as the rooms are noisy and not recommended. **C-D** *Peony Mansion Travellers' Lodge*, 4th Flr, 46-52 Bencoolen St (lift round back of building), T 3385638, F 3391471, another in the same block as *Lee Boarding House*, marginally better than the other *Peony Mansions* across the road. **C-D** *San Wah*, 36 Bencoolen St, T 3362428, F 3344146, some a/c, public showers, 10 rooms in one of the very few remaining family-run Chinese hotels, more than 50 years old, run by old gentleman, Mr Chao Yoke San and his son, lovely old house, set incongruously amongst the tower blocks, not very clean and very noisy but so much nicer, in terms of character, than the others at this price.

D *Goh's Homestay*, 4th Flr (no lift), 169D Bencoolen St, T 3396561, F 3398606, tiny rooms with separate showers but immaculately clean, friendly place with nice snack bar and fax/storage/washing facilities, only 20 rooms so booking is advisable, recommended. **D** *Hawaii Hostel*, 2nd Flr, 171B Bencoolen St, T 3384187, in same block as *Goh*, but not quite as good, 27 small and rather dirty rooms (and an 8 bed dorm for $18). Simple breakfast included in room rate, washing facilities available, friendly manageress. **D** *Lee Boarding House*, 7th Flr, 52 Peony Mansion, 46-52 Bencoolen St, T 3383149, F 3365409, calls itself 'the exclusive club for travellers' but it seems pretty grim, 100 rooms, some a/c, some with bathrooms, complimentary breakfast of sorts, pretty grotty, travel information service, **E** for dorm beds. **D** *Shang Onn*, 37 Beach Rd, T 3384153, 10 rooms in another ugly apartment block, no breakfast, but efficient service and rooms are adequate (fan only), no dorms, long term visitors encouraged, not very friendly but recommended. **D-E** *Lee Travellers' Club*, 6th Flr of an apartment block, 75 Beach Rd, T 3395490, some a/c, breakfast included, short on bathrooms, but clean rooms, cooking facilities, storage facilities, owner prides himself on security, **E** for dorms. **D-E** *Peony Mansions*, 2nd Flr, 131A Bencoolen St, T 3385638, F 3391471, windowless rooms with only beds in them (no space for anything else). Outside cold (broken?) showers. Dirty. For double the money you can have same size room and a/c (of sorts) and a hot shower (also broken?). A plus is the good roti man on street below. **D-E** *Waffles Homestay*, 2/F, 490 North Bridge Rd, great little place, friendly management, lovely roof terrace, access through an Indian restaurant, recommended. **D-E** *Willy's Homestay*, 3rd Flr, 75 Beach Rd, T 3388826, **E** for dorm, only 15 rooms, looked clean.

E *Backpackers Cozy Corner*, 2a Liang Seah St, T 3348761, dorms, this is a cheap option, but it is cramped and sardines come to mind; one dorm room doubles up as the reception, pretty grotty. **E** *New Backpackers Lodge*, 18 Liang Seah St (off Beach Rd), a/c and fan, dorms available, as well as range of private rooms. Nice, clean place to stay which is regularly sprayed for bed bugs – although a few of the critters sneak back. Breakfast included in room rate.

● Camping

Camping on Sentosa Island and Pulau Ubin, where there are pre-erected tents available (see page 670).

● Places to eat

Prices: ♦♦♦♦++ over S$30; ♦♦♦-♦♦♦♦++ S$15-25; ♦♦-♦♦♦ S$6-15; ♦-♦♦ under S$6

The Singapore Tatler publishes *'Singapore's Best Restaurants'* annually, so if you are a bit of a foodie, it would probably be worth investing in one of these (S$10.30). It provides detailed descriptions of over 100 restaurants and is widely available in bookstores. **NB** Smoking is prohibited in all a/c restaurants.

Chinese

♦♦♦♦*Canton Garden*, *Westin Stamford* and *Westin Plaza*, 2 Stamford Rd, T 4315312, dim sum recommended. ♦♦♦♦*Chinese Swimming Club*, 34 Amber Rd, T 3447184, described by one regular as 'very Chinese food with a very Chinese atmosphere', recommended. ♦♦♦♦*Dragon City*, *Novotel*, 214 Dunearn Rd, T 2547070, popular Szechuan restaurant renowned for its spicy seafood, booking recommended, recommended. ♦♦♦♦*Imperial Herbal*, *Metropole Hotel*, 3rd Flr, 41 Seah St, T 3370491, Dr Li, an in-house herbalist, takes your pulse and recommends a meal, food prepared using ancient Chinese remedies, pricey, booking recommended for dinner. ♦♦♦♦*Lei Gardens*, Ground

Floor, CHIJMES, 30 Victoria St, T 3393822, F 3342648, also at Orchard Shopping Centre, 321 Orchard Rd, T 7343988 and Orchard Plaza, 150 Orchard Rd. Outstanding Cantonese food – dim sum, silver codfish etc. Tasteful decor and a 2-tier aquarium displaying the day's offerings, worth every penny, despite seating for 250 you need to book in advance, recommended. ♦♦♦♦*Min Jiang, Goodwood Park Hotel*, 22 Scotts Rd, T7301704, large, noisy room, expansive menu with delicious Szechuan hot and sour soup, and good choice of seafood, 7 private rooms as well. ♦♦♦♦*Red Lantern Revolving Restaurant*, 60a, Change Alley Aerial Plaza, Collyer Quay, T 2993577, high-priced, low-rise revolver, with a view over the harbour.

♦♦♦*Beng Thin Hoon Kee*, 05-02 OCBC Centre, 5th Floor, 65 Chulia St (Financial district) good Hokkien cuisine, has been in business for 47 years; ♦♦♦*Grand City*, 7th Flr, Cathay Building, 2 Handy Rd, T 3383622, big Chinese restaurant convenient for cinemas, better value with bigger groups, good Szechuan (spicy) soup, unusual creations include prawn and apple roll and Australian emu served Chinese style with spring onions on a sizzling hot plate, reservations recommended. ♦♦♦*Nomads*, Fountain Court, CHIJMES, 30 Victoria St, T 3346466, Mongolian BBQ – choose your raw food (as much as you can eat) and your sauces and then it's cooked for you. Very trendy. ♦♦♦*Prima Tower Revolving Restaurant*, 201 Keppel Rd, T 2728822, revolving restaurant atop a huge silo looks out over the harbour and city, established 20 years ago and with the same chef still working here, but still going strong, Beijing cuisine, particularly good Peking Duck, book in advance. ♦♦♦*Swee Kee*, 12 Ann Siang Rd, T 2211900, this restaurant has acquired some degree of local reknown due to the owner Tang Kwong Swee – known to his friends as 'Fish-head' – having run the same place for 60 years (although the location has changed). Recommended are the deep fried chicken, Hainanese style, fish head noodle soup and prawns in magi sauce, very popular, recommended. ♦♦♦*Tsui Hang Village*, 37 Scotts Rd, T 7373140, in the *Asia Hotel*, good Cantonese food.

♦♦*Orchard Garden*, 4th Flr, Lucky Chinatown shopping centre, New Bridge Rd, dim sum at lunchtime; ♦♦*Tinsel Moon*, 47 Circular Rd (behind Boat Quay) T 5369919, cheap and cheerful, Hong Kong-style cuisine in a refurbished shophouse, dishes including deep fried *bee tai mak*, deep fried crab, fried prawns in honey sauce and braised beencurd with egg white, recommended. Alternatively, try the ***Westlake Eating House***, opposite at Nos 139 or 141, the duck is delicious. ♦♦*Long House*, Jl Besar Stadium, good chicken rice and duck rice. ♦♦*Tiong Shiang*, corner of Keong Saik and New Bridge Rd (Chinatown), very popular Hainanese corner café with tables spilling out onto the street. ♦♦*Wing Seong Fatty's Eating House*, 01-33 Albert Complex, T 3381087, established in 1926, excellent steamed garoupa, roast duck and pork, peeled chilli prawns and other Cantonese dishes, recommended.

Indian

For North Indian cuisine, the best option is to trot down to the southern end of Race Course Rd, where there are 6 good restaurants in a row, all competing for business.

♦♦♦♦++*Hazara*, 24 Lorong Mambong (behind the front row of shophouses, Holland Village), T 4674101, sister restaurant to *Kinara* (below), specializing in northwest Frontier cuisine (tandooris etc), particularly good tandoori leg of lamb, splendid decor with genuine frontier feel, service can be slow. ♦♦♦♦*Annalakshmi*, 02-10 *Excelsior Hotel* and Shopping Centre, 5 Coleman St (Colonial Core), T 3399993,(also at Terminal 2, Changi Airport, T 5420407)vegetarian cuisine, the *Annalakshmi* is run on the same basis as KL's *Annapoorna*, it is staffed by unpaid housewives and profits go to the Kalamandair Indian cultural group, the health drinks are excellent – especially Mango Tharang (mango juice, honey and ginger) and Annalakshmi Special (fruit juices, yoghurt, honey and ginger), Sun lunchtime buffet recommended S$25++; daily lunchtime buffet $20++ and evening buffet $24.50++, cultural show once a year, the restaurant, which sprawls out onto the verandah overlooking the tennis courts, serves North and South Indian food, Samy's banana-leaf and fish-head curries are unrivalled, recommended. ♦♦♦♦*Kinara*, 57 Boat Quay, T 5330412, sister restaurant to *Hazara* (above) serving coconutty seafood using North Indian spices, *Kinara* means 'riverbank', the food is bettered only by the decor – magnificent Rajastani-style with carved pillars and *jharoka* window niches, book for upper room with river view, look out for the Rajastani swing outside the front of the restaurant, booking advisable, recommended; *Khazana* is close by at No 61 and is very similar. ♦♦♦♦*Moghul Mahal*, Basement level Columbo Court, North Bridge Rd, T 3387794, great food, shame about the decor and cramped tables, North Indian tandoori food, reasonably priced.

♦♦♦+*Bombay Woodlands*, 19 Tanglin Rd, Tanglin Shopping Centre, Orchard Rd, T 2352712.

Very reasonably priced for the area, vegetarian food. ♦♦♦*Maharani*, 05-36 Far East Plaza, Scotts Rd, T 2358840, rated as one of the best for North Indian cuisine – tandoori chicken and kormas are specialities, Indian music accompaniment. ♦♦♦*Muthu's Curry*, corner of Rotan and Race Course Rd, T 2937029, North Indian food, reckoned by connoisseurs to be among the best banana leaf restaurants in town, *Muthu's* fish-heads are famous, recommended. ♦♦♦*Orchard Maharajah*, Cuppage Terrace, T 7326331, excellent North Indian food – tandoori and Kashmiri, conveniently located next door to Saxophone (see page 690) in converted shophouse, 7 different types of bread to choose from. ♦♦♦*Ramu's*, 246-F Upper Thomson Rd (opposite Thomson Post Office, north of Orchard Rd), T 4549962, Melakan-Indian specialities such as deep-fried yoghurt chicken, sizzling prawns, claypot fish-head, mutton Mysore and fish curries, recommended by locals. ♦♦♦*Samy's*, Civil Service Club, Tanglin Club House, Dempsey Rd (off Napier Rd), diners are obliged to become temporary members of the Civil Service Club for $1 ... but Samy makes it worth your while, excellent banana leaf curries in relaxed atmosphere, recommended. ♦♦♦-♦♦*Babataher*, 1 Maritime Square, Harbour Promenade, World Trade Centre, T 2781330, very good value set menu.

♦♦*Banana Leaf Apolo*, 56 Race Course Rd, T 2938682, North Indian food, another popular fish-head curry spot. ♦♦*Hakim*, 91 Pasir Panjang Rd (west of World Trade Centre), 24 hours Indian Muslim coffee shop serving rotis, murtabaks and curries of all descriptions, cheap and very friendly, recommended. ♦♦*Madras New Woodlands*, 12 Upper Dickson Rd (off Serangoon Rd), T 2971594, thalis, masala dosa and vegetarian curries, good and cheap, recommended; ♦♦*New Delhi*, *Broadway Hotel*, 195 Serangoon Rd (Little India), good, cheap vegetarian and non-vegetarian North Indian food in Little India, specialities are chicken and almond, and seafood curries. ♦♦-♦*Komala Vilas*, 76-78 Serangoon Rd, T 2936980, South Indian thalis and masala dosas, bustling café, with a little more room upstairs, recommended.

Indonesian

♦♦♦♦++*Alkaff Mansion*, Mount Faber Ridge, 10 Telok Blangah Green, T 2786979, built in the 1920s, this huge house has undergone a S$3mn refurbishment and makes a magnificent restaurant surrounded by parkland. Go here for the atmosphere, not the food, which is very average, if you do eat the continental cuisine is better than the Indonesian. ♦♦♦♦*Diandin Leluk*, Riverside Point, 30 Merchant Rd, opposite Clarke Quay, T 4382890. Newish restaurant, with special deals and plenty of seafood, good and attractive location. ♦♦♦♦*Kintamani*, *Apollo Hotel*, 405 Havelock Rd, T 7332081, Balinese style interior, extensive buffet spread available at lunch and dinner. ♦♦♦♦-♦♦♦*Bumbu*, Orchard Shopping Centre, Orchard Rd, trendy new spot. ♦♦♦♦-♦♦♦*Riverside Indonesian Restaurant*, Riverside Point, 30 Merchant Rd, opposite Clarke Quay, T 5350383, bright functional interior, but some al fresco dining overlooking the river, baked pomfret, chilli crabs, grilled chicken – good menu and attractive location.

♦♦♦+*House of Sundanese Food*, several outlets spread around town eg Suntec City Marina Sq, 55 Boat Quay, T 5343775, 218 East Coast Rd, T 3455020, typical Sundanese (from West Java) dishes including spicy salad (*keredok*), charcoal-grilled seafood (*ikan Sunda*, *ikan emas*) and curries, simply decorated non-a/c restaurant, with a real home-cooked taste. ♦♦♦+*Tambuah Mas*, 4th Flr, Tanglin Shopping Centre, T 7332220 (another branch at Level 5, Shaw Centre), a/c restaurant, very popular and cramped, what it lacks in ambience, it more than makes up for with the food, specialities include ayam goreng istimewa (marinated fried chicken), recommended. ♦♦♦*Ramayana*, 7th Flr, Plaza Singapura, with specialities including baked pomfret and baked prawns. ♦♦♦*Sanur*, 17/18, 4th Flr, Centrepoint, 176 Orchard Rd, T 7342192, and at 3rd Flr, 133 New Bridge Rd and in the basement at 930 Yishun Ave, cramped Malay/Indonesian restaurant ideally placed for shoppers, specialities including fish-head curries and spicy grilled chicken or fish.

Japanese

♦♦♦♦++*Inagiku*, 3rd Flr, *Westin Stamford and Westin Plaza*, 2 Stamford Rd, T 4315305, clientele including the Raffles City corporate dinner brigade, so pricey, booking advisable. ♦♦♦♦+*Masakatsu*, 80 Middle Rd, Ground Floor, Parco Bugis Junction, T 3348233. Known for its hotpot. Book at weekends. ♦♦♦♦+***Migen***, Ground Floor, CHIJMES, 30 Victoria St (Colonial Core), T 3323003. Full choice of Japanese food in this attractive courtyard. Booking at weekends is recommended. ♦♦♦♦+*Suntory*, 06-01 Delfi Orchard, 402 Orchard Rd, T 7325111, for sushi, tempura, teppanyaki and shabu-shabu-lovers with a serious yen (or two). ♦♦♦♦*Izakaya Nijumaru*, 5 Koek Rd, 02-10/12 Cuppage Plaza, T 2356693, reasonably priced Japanese robatayaki restaurant.

♦♦♦*Kushi-Zen*, 3rd Flr, *Hotel Royal*, 36 Newton Rd (north of Orchard Rd) T 2565987, set menus are good value, lunch: kushi-katsu is Kushi-Zen's *pièce de résistance* – a Nipponese version of satay. ♦♦♦*Shabushin*, 4th Flr, Tanglin Shopping Centre, Tanglin Rd, T 7349908, popular restaurant offering set lunches and dinners at reasonable prices. ♦♦♦*Sushi Dokoro Yoshida*, 58 Boat Quay, T 5341401, another riverfront restaurant specializing in *izakaya* (barbecued fish), upstairs, designed around sushi bar, branch in Lucky Plaza, Orchard Rd. ♦♦♦*Yushiada Ya*, basement of Lucky Plaza, serves the best sushi in town.

Korean

♦♦♦*Korean Restaurant*, Specialists' Centre, Orchard Rd, T2350018, this imaginatively-named restaurant is well known for its *bulgogi* meat barbecues.

Malay

♦♦♦*Aziza's*, 02-05 Albert Court, 180 Albert St, T 2351130, finally after a long battle with the Emerald Hill Conservation authorities, moved their old shophouse to the present site, but still renowned for excellent home-cooked food, apparently the Sultan of Brunei eats here when in town.

♦♦*Bintang Timur*, 14 Scotts Rd, 02-08/13 Far East Plaza, T 2354539, excellent satays and curries, the ambience allows you to forget that you're in a shopping centre.

Nonya (Straits Chinese)

♦♦♦*Bibin's Place*, Pahang St, Arab St area, upmarket little place but rather poor location (unless you are staying in this area). ♦♦♦*Blue Ginger*, 97 Tanjong Pagar Rd, T 2223928, in restored shophouse – good home cooked food and relaxed atmosphere. ♦♦♦*Nonya and Baba*, 262/264 River Valley Rd, for those wanting a Peranakan theme to the evening, owner is an Elvis fan, the *Next Page pub*, in a refurbished shophouse, is nearby.

♦♦*Ivin's*, 19/21 Binjai Park, out of town, off Dunearn Rd (north of Orchard Rd), very good, cheap food in hectic atmosphere, popular restaurant serving all main Nonya dishes. Top price is $4.80 except for two fish-head dishes which cost S$13, recommended.

Thai: ♦♦♦♦+*Chao Phaya Thai Seafood*, Block 730, 2nd Flr, Ang Mo Kio Ave 6, enormous informal restaurant with huge choice of authentic Thai dishes including chilli crab, *Tom yam kung* and green, yellow or red curried fish. ♦♦♦♦+*Sukhothai*, 47 Boat Quay, T 5382422, good choice of Thai cuisine, speciality is deep fried garoupa, booking recommended for dinner. ♦♦♦♦*Bangkok Garden*, Keck Seng Tower, 133 Cecil St (financial district), T 2207310, almost anything Thai is available, even if it's not on the menu, speciality fruit juices and crab dishes are very popular.

♦♦♦*Cuppage Thai Food*, 49 Cuppage Terrace, T 7341116, popular Thai restaurant with outside tables and photographs of the food to aid decision making, makes for a good evening if combined with a visit to *Saxophone bar*, just a few doors down, recommended. ♦♦♦*Parkway Thai*, 02-08, 80 Marine Parade Rd, T 3458811, unimpressive looking restaurant belies an excellent restaurant with an extensive menu at moderate prices, pandan leaf chicken is the speciality, more central second restaurant in Centerpoint Building, Orchard Rd, T 7378080. ♦♦♦*Siam's Fins*, 45 Craig Rd (and at other outlets), Hang Khim is a Bangkok chef and he produces the very best shark's fins – along with an assortment of other seafoods. ♦♦♦*Thanying, Amara Hotel*, T 2224688 and at Clarke Quay (T 3368146) provides the best Thai food in town, extensive menu and superb food (the chef/owner is said to have cooked for the Thai royal family), deep fried garoupa is a speciality and durian served on a bed of sticky rice is available from May-Aug, booking necessary, recommended.

Vietnamese

♦♦♦♦*Saigon*, Cairnhill Place, 15 Cairnhill Rd, spacious and relaxed surroundings, superb food, with very helpful waiters to give advice, pan-fried beef recommended and innovative and tasty dishes such as crab in beer.

International

Prices: ♦♦♦♦++ over S$30; ♦♦♦-♦♦♦♦++ S$15-25; ♦♦-♦♦♦ S$6-15; ♦-♦♦ under S$6

♦♦♦♦++++**Raffles Grill**, *Raffles Hotel*, 1 Beach Rd (main building, first floor), T 3371886, elegant colonial surroundings, serving breakfast, lunch and dinner, continental cuisine, French windows open onto Palm Court, Chippendale furniture. ♦♦♦♦+++*Harbour Grill, Hilton Hotel*, 581 Orchard Rd, T 7303393, contemporary surroundings, oysters are a speciality, but other delicacies include caviar and smoked salmon, impeccable service. ♦♦♦♦++*Gordon Grill*, Lobby, *Goodwood Park Hotel*, 22 Scotts Rd, T 2358637, one of the last Grills in town, Singapore's only Scottish Restaurant with haggis on the menu ... at 24 hours' advance notice, plenty of choice cuts of meat to choose from. ♦♦♦♦++*Seasons, Four Seasons Hotel*, 190 Orchard Blvd, T 8317250, sophisticated surroundings and unusual food combinations makes this a relaxed and pleasurable gastronomic experience, at weekends they cater for children. ♦♦♦♦+*Le Chalet*, *Ladyhill Hotel*, 1 Ladyhill Rd (off Orchard Rd), T 7372111, opened in 1968 this Swiss restaurant is still the place to eat fondue in Singapore. ♦♦♦♦*Bobby Rubinos*, Fountain Court, CHIJMES, 30 Victoria St, T 3375477, good menu of ribs, burgers, chicken, booking recommended. ♦♦♦♦*Brazil Churrascaria*, 14-16 Sixth Ave, T 4631923, if carnivore-style is your thing, this restaurant – with its huge skewers of barbecued meat – is for you, as much meat as you can eat. ***Esmirada***, No 01-01/02, 180 Orchard Rd, Peranakan Place, T 7353476, Mediterranean food and always packed, reservations recommended. ♦♦♦♦*The Drake Restaurant*, basement of *Negara Hotel*, 10 Claymore Rd, off Orchard Rd, T 8316688, it is certainly a novel experience eating here, with duck decoys, duck noises, duck prints and an all-duck menu. ♦♦♦♦*Tony Romas'*, Orchard Rd Shopping Centre, Orchard Rd, good ribjoint. ♦♦♦♦-♦♦♦*Pennsylvania Country Oven*, Stamford House, Stamford Rd (Colonial Core), for all those craving some good homely New England cooking, but the interior decor is rather overdone making it a bit kitsch.

♦♦♦*Bar and Billiard Room*, *Raffles Hotel*, 1 Beach Rd (corner block), contains many of Raffles' original furnishings, serves business lunches. ♦♦♦*Blaze Café*, Ground Floor, The Cannery, Clarke Quay, pizza, pasta, hotdogs, fish and chips, burgers – a good place to bring the children. ♦♦♦*Chilis*, 75 Boat Quay for American fare – burgers, grills, sandwiches – a good menu and reasonably priced for this location. ***Chilli Buddy's***, 180 Orchard Rd, Peranakan Place, outside dining under umbrellas, informal and relaxed. ***Papa Joes***, 01-01/02, 180 Orchard Rd, Peranakan Place, T 7327012, owned by the same people as *Chilli Buddy's* and *Esmirada*, serves Caribbean food at lunch and from 1800-2230 in the evenings, but is better known for its disco (see page 697). ***Que Pasa***, 7 Emerald Hill, next door to No 5 bar, serves tapas to accompany the drinks, quite pleasant. ♦♦♦*Empire Café*, Ground Floor, *Raffles Hotel*, 1 Beach Rd, not bad for pork chops and oxtail stew, prepared by Chinese cooks and served on marble-top tables, also serves chicken rice, burgers and ice-creams, open 24 hours, *Ah Teng's Bakery* joins on, it sells pricey pastries, pies and biscuits – mostly local favourites. ♦♦♦*Hard Rock Café*, 02-01 HPL House, 50 Cuscaden Rd, one of the best bets for a decent steak, buffalo wings or a bacon cheeseburger, open until 0200. ♦♦♦*Hot Stones*, 22 Lorong Mambong (behind front row of shophouses, Holland Village), another restaurant at 53 Boat Quay (T 5355188), speciality: cooking slabs of meat or seafood on baking-hot Serpentine rock at the table. ♦♦♦*Hot Stones Steak and Seafood Restaurant*, 22 Lorong Mambong, Holland Village, T 4684688. ♦♦♦*Planet Hollywood*, 541 Orchard Rd, this restaurant opened to much fanfare in 1997, but it isn't up to much. There's a limited menu – pizza, pasta and burgers – you come for the surroundings (leopard and zebra skin walls and carpets), and the shop, not for the food. No booking available. ♦♦♦*Saxophone*, 23 Cuppage Terrace, Singapore's best live-music joint also has an excellent French restaurant: the menu is select, eat at the bar or on the terrace, escargots and chocolate mousse recommended. ♦♦♦*Singapore Polo Club*, 80 Mount Pleasant Rd (just off Thomson Rd), if you're not put off by the polo set or visiting sultans, the Polo Club is a great place to dine (or drink Pimms!) on the verandah – especially on match days (Tues, Thur and Sat) when there's plenty to look at, there is a snack menu (steak sandwich, fish and chips etc) on the verandah overlooking the turf ($8-15) and a smarter restaurant inside ($20-30), recommended. ♦♦♦*The Tavern*, 229 River Valley Rd, T 7376995, swiss chalet-style shophouse serves particularly good raclette. ♦♦♦*Tradewinds*, Top Floor, *Hilton International*, 581 Orchard Rd, T 7303395, don't be put off by the fact it's in the *Hilton* – *Tradewinds* is a reasonably priced, poolside restaurant, with delicious food and serenading Spanish guitarists, the local dishes are particularly good, recommended. ♦♦♦-♦♦*Han's*, 8 branches around the city including Raffles Link Marina Square, Harbour Promenade World Trade Centre (WTC), Park Mall, Far East Plaza, and The Arcade. This chain of restaurants is Singapore's answer to the Greasy Spoon – cafés without the acute accent on the 'e', single dish Chinese meals, simple (largely fried) breakfasts, some European food including such things as steaks, burgers and fries all served in large helpings at very competitive prices.

♦♦*Charlie's*, Block 2, 01-08, Changi Village, Charlie's folks, who were first generation immigrants from China, set up the *Changi Milk Bar* in the 1940s, then Charlie's Corner became the favoured watering hole and makan stop for sailors and riggers for decades, his mum still fries up the chips that gave them the reputation as the best chippies east of London's Isle of Dogs, excellent chilli-dogs, spicy chicken wings and 70 beers to choose from, closed weekends, recommended. *Getting there*: bus to Changi Point from Tampines MRT. ♦♦*Duxtons*, 21 Duxton Hill (Tanjong Pagar), T 2275322, bar and coffee house serving deli food, pleasant converted shophouse in a quiet pedestrianized terrace.

French

♦♦♦♦+++*L'Aigle d'Or, Duxton Hotel*, 83 Duxton Rd, T 2277678, French, a few Oriental touches and a good vegetarian selection, extensive, expensive menu with wine list to match, sophisticated atmosphere, popular as a business venue at lunch time, booking recommended. ♦♦♦♦+++*Maxim's de Paris, The Regent*, 1 Cuscaden Rd, T 7393091, French extravaganza, booking recommended, excellent food and the most extensive wine list in Singapore, pay through the nose for this spot of sophistication. ♦♦♦♦*Chez Bernard*, 7 Ann Siang Rd, 1st Flr, French bistro with snack food. ♦♦♦♦*La Cascade*, 7 Ann Siang Rd, T3241808, attractive sophisticated little French restaurant, serving snails, veal, duck – good menu, recommended. ♦♦♦♦*Les Amis*, 02-16 Shaw Centre, 1 Scotts Rd, T 7332225, fabulous innovative French restaurant in elegant surroundings, friendly sommelier and good wine list. ♦♦♦♦*Vis-à-vis*, 12 Chun Tin Rd, T 4687433, owned by Jeremy and Christine, great Francophiles, highly rated, reasonably priced French cuisine, can buy French cheeses, wine and foie gras to take away.

Italian

♦♦♦♦+++*Ristorante Bologna, Marina Mandarin Hotel*, 6 Raffles Blvd, Marina Square, T 3318470, award winning restaurant, house specialities include spaghetti alla marinara and baked pigeon, diners lounge amidst sophisticated decor and wandering minstrels strum. ♦♦♦♦++*Paladino di Firenze*, 7 Mohammed Sultan Rd, T 7380917, interesting food in a restored shophouse setting – try the broschetta. ♦♦♦♦*Da Paolo*, 66 Tanjong Pagar Rd, T 2247081, one of the 2 Italian restaurants in Tanjong Pagar in restored shophouse, contemporary decor, popular with expats, home-made pasta, overpriced. ♦♦♦♦*Pasta Fresca da Salvatore*, 30 Boat Quay and at several other outlets including Shaw Centre (convenient for movies upstairs at Shaw Lido Complex), and Suntec City, fresh, tasty pizzas and a good range of pasta, open 24 hours. ♦♦♦♦*Grappas*, CHIJMES, 30 Victoria St, T 3349928. Large restaurant in this trendy courtyard. Extensive menu, booking advisable, recommended. ♦♦♦♦-♦♦♦*Portofino*, Ground Floor, The Cannery, Clarke Quay, extensive menu. ***Tigellas***, International Plaza, Anson Rd, lunchtime pasta joint – calls itself a 'deli' – and sells fresh pasta etc to take out.

♦♦♦*Al Dente*, 70 Boat Quay for pizzas, pasta etc. ♦♦♦*Al Forno Trattoria*, 275 Thomson Rd, 01-07 Novena Villa, T 2562838, tastiest pizzas in town in bustling, very Italian eatery. ♦♦♦*Michelangelos*, 01-60 Chip Bee Gardens, T 4759069, the girth of the Oz/Italian chef here testifies to the size of the portions. Honest pasta of the highest order. ♦♦♦*Pasta Brava*, 11 Craig Rd, Tanjong Pagar, tastiest Italian in town in an equally tasty shophouse conversion, fairly expensive but good choice of genuine Italian fare, recommended.

♦♦*Fratini*, 1 Neil Rd, T 3238088, cheap and cheerful pasta joint in a restored shophouse.

Mexican

♦♦♦♦*Cha Cha Cha*, 32 Lorong Manbong, Holland Village, T 4621650, small and informal with some outdoor seating, extensive menu. ♦♦♦♦+*Chico's N Charlie's*, 05-01 Liat Towers, 541 Orchard Rd, T 7341753, an expat hang-out, good atmosphere, good hacienda food and good value. ♦♦♦♦*El Felipe's* (2 branches) – 360 Orchard Rd 02-09, International Building; 34 Lorong Mambong, Holland Village (behind front row of shophouses), T 4681520, *El Felipe's* frozen margaritas are even more delicious than the burittos, recommended.

♦♦♦*Margarita's*, 108 Faber Drive, T 7771782, appropriately named after the Tequila cocktails it's best at. ♦♦♦*Wala-Wala*, 31 Lurong Mambong, Holland Village T 4624288, buzzy atmosphere and pretty tiles on the tables, good, honest, no pretentions place.

New Asia

See page 716 for further information on this cuisine. ♦♦♦♦++*Nutmegs, Hyatt Regency Hotel*, 10-12 Scotts Rd, off Orchard Rd, T 7307112, a well established New Asia cuisine restaurant, guest chefs means that the menu changes regularly, recommended. ♦♦♦♦-♦♦♦*Doc Cheng's, Raffles Shopping Arcade*, Seah St, unusual combinations but rather irritating blurb on menu. High standard of cuisine though.

Seafood

Several seafood restaurants on Mount Faber hill, with a good view – they are not that popular and the seafood is far from being the best in town, but it's a pleasant location. ♦♦♦*Beng Hiang*, 112 Amoy St, T 2216684, Hokkien seafood menu. ♦♦♦*Jumbo Garden 1000*, East Coast Parkway, T 4490111, recommended, especially their drunken prawns (open evenings only). ♦♦♦*Kim's Seafood Restaurant*, 39 Sim's Ave, northeast of town, by Kallang MRT, T 7419838, claypot pepper crabs are the speciality in Mr Tan's cheap and informal seafood restaurant, open to 0130 weekdays and 0230 on Sat. ♦♦♦*Long Beach Seafood*, Marina South, T 2410196, one of the island's most famous seafood restaurants, specializing in pepper and chilli-crabs, drunken prawns and baby squid cooked in honey, 'Derek' is an outstanding host. ♦♦♦*Palm Beach Seafood Restaurant*, Palm Beach Leisure Park, 1st and 2nd floors, 01-16 Stadium Walk, T 3443088, located near the International Building and the National Stadium, good shellfish at a fair price, not much in the way of decor. ♦♦♦*Yu Kong Choon*, Riverside Point, 30 Merchant Rd, opposite Clarke Quay, T 4385880, good location and good looking food, open until 0400.

♦♦*Holland Beer Garden*, on junction of Clementi and Holland rpads, fairly difficult to find, but worth it, excellent steamed prawns and other good seafood, seating outside with tablecloths, popular with locals and expats alike, do not be put off by its name.

♦*Dotty Café*, Bukit Chermin Rd, off Keppel Marina, T 270 7884 and Telok Blangah Rd, just west of where the cable car goes over the road, call Dorothy before you go and plan your menu to get the best catch of the day, eat under fairlights, right on the sea, and admire yachts moored next door, very quiet and peaceful. ***UDMC Seafood Centre***, 1000 East Coast Parkway, there are a number of outlets here and they're all good. In particular – ***Gold Coast Live Seafood***, T 4482020 and ***Jumbo Seafood***, T 4423435. ***International Seafood Centre***, also on the ECP, provide trollies to choose your fish pre-cooking. Not for the squeemish, recommended.

Fastfood cafés

Despite Singapore's gourmet delights, fast-food outlets do a roaring trade in Singapore. As well as the standard names in fastfood restaurants, there are now chains of more sophisticated 'cafés', selling a larger range of European food (and less junkie).In particular, there is *Spinellis* (who provide a very good range of fresh coffees, ground or beans, which can be purchased) and *Delifrance*(who's speciality are croissants and danish pastries. Ask whether the pastries are made today, as they weren't on the occasions we sampled their food). Check *Yellow Pages* for branch addresses of the various fastfood restaurants. They include: ***A&W*** (which in 1968 became the first fast-feeder in town), ***Burger King***, ***Denny's***, ***KFC***, ***McDonalds***, ***Milano Pizza***, ***Orange Julius***, ***Pizza Hut***, ***Shakey's Pizza*** and one called ***Fat Mama's***. The best, beyond doubt, is ***Delifrance***, which is rapidly expanding in Singapore. There are Delifrance restaurants at: Clifford Centre, Marina Square, The Dynasty, Wisma Atria, The Promenade, Holland Village and Changi Airport. They also run several bistros at Holland Village and Tanglin Mall.

Hawker Centres and Food Courts

Quite a few of the old-style hawker centres have closed down to make way for new urban developments of one sort or another. But fortunately this style of eating has not been lost – hawker centres have gone underground and metamorphosed into 'Food Courts'. These are to be found in the basements of many of the plazas and shopping centres (as well as in HDB blocks) and are essentially just a sanitized version of the old hawker centre. They have the advantage of being air-conditioned and generally have higher levels of hygiene than the hawker centres. The food is good too – by far the best value for money food to be had in Singapore – although there is no doubting that they lack the vitality of the older style centres. Eating in a food court or hawker centre is easy: peruse the assorted kitchens and their menus and then order and pay at whichever takes your fancy, grabbing some implements and condiments before you go. If the food takes a few minutes to prepare, saunter off and get a beer or fruit shake, or some sticky concoction, or just grab a table. Eat anywhere – and leave the plates and cutlery to be cleared away by one of the roving table wallahs.

♦♦*Lau Pa Sat Festival Market* (formerly the Telok Ayer Food Centre) at the Raffles Quay end of Shenton Way in the old Victorian market (see page 641), good range of food on offer: Chinese, Indian, Nonya, Korean, Penang, icecreams, fruit drinks – it's well worth a browse. ♦♦*Satay Club*. In the evening a series of stands open up in the pedestrian streets of Clarke Quay. The food is good but, being a tourist trap, it's almost double the price of other food courts. ♦♦*Suntec City*, Marina Square, holds a very trendy foodcourt under the enormous fountain.

♦*Adam Road*, open all night, excellent Indian food – including one of the best roti stalls in Singapore, safest hawker centre in Singapore – adjacent to the police station. ♦*Albert Court*, between Waterloo and Queen sts, there's a huge area of hawker stalls here. ♦*Amoy Street Food Centre*, just south of Al Abrar Mosque at southern end of Amoy St, Chinatown, excellent little centre, worth a graze. ♦*Chinatown Complex Hawker Centre*, Block 335, 1st Flr, Smith St, recommended stall: *Ming Shan* (No 179), for its kambing (mutton) soup, famed for decades, though a pretty scruffy food centre. ♦*Funan Centre*, South Bridge Rd, this big shopping plaza contains one of the best food courts in Singapore in its basement, with a huge range of foods to choose from, in particular, an excellent Indian stall; both **Cuppage Plaza** and **Orchard Point** have extensive foodcourts in their basements. ♦*Hill Street Food Centre*, west side of Hill St, Colonial Core, 3 floors of hawker stalls, lots of Muslim food and plenty of everything else, very popular. Recommended stall is 01-08 for good noodles. ♦*Lavender Food Square*, Lavender Rd, north of Little India, is one of the best hawker centres in town. ♦*Maxwell Road Hawker Centre* (corner of Maxwell and South Bridge roads), Tanjong Pagar, Chinatown, mainly Chinese, best known for its two chicken rice stalls. ♦*Paradiz Centre Basement Food Centre*, 1 Selegie Rd, recommended stall: *Mr Boo's Teochew Mushroom Minced Meat Mee* (No 34). ♦*Quayside Food Court*, Basement of Liang Court, next door to Clarke Quay, good choice of Asian stalls and a *Burger King*, play area for children. ♦*Taman Serasi*, Cluny Rd, opposite entrance to Botanic Gardens, small centre but well known for Roti John and superb satay, mainly Malay stalls, excellent fruit juice stall. ♦*Zhujiao or Kandang Kerbau (KK) Food Centre*, in the same complex as the wet market, on the corner of Buffalo and Serangoon roads, big range of dishes, and the best place for Indian Muslim food: curries, rotis, dosai and murtabak are hard to beat (beer can be bought from the Chinese stalls on the other side). ***Newton Circus***, Scotts Rd, north of Orchard Rd – despite threats of closure by the government, this huge food centre of over 100 stalls is still surviving and dishing up some of the best food of its kind.

Tiffin

An English word meaning afternoon meal. The word originated in India during the heyday of the East India Company. It came to refer to special containers in which lunch is packed and sent to work places by special couriers. ♦♦♦♦-♦♦*Tiffin Room*, *Raffles Hotel*, 1 Beach Rd (main building, ground floor), tiffin curry buffet (plus à la carte menu) in pristine white, over-lit ersatz Victorian grandeur, it's good food, but at S$35 for the buffet, you're paying a lot more for the surroundings than for the curry, reservation recommended, no singlets or shorts admitted. ♦♦♦*Alkaff Mansion*, Mount Faber Ridge, 10 Telok Blangah Green, tiffin curry lunches, recommended.

Cafés

♦♦♦*Café Les Amis*, Asian Civilisations Museum, Armenian St, new offshoot of Les Amis, Shaw Centre, exotic international menu. ♦♦♦*Café Oriel*, ground floor of Selegie Arts Centre, off Prinsep St (Little India), popular for its pizzas. ♦♦♦*Dôme*, several outlets at Lane Crawford House, Orchard Rd, The Promenade on Orchard Rd, next door to the Singapore Art Museum on Bras Basah Rd, and in the heart of the business district on Cecil St, all serve delicious foccaccia sandwiches, patisseries and some of the best coffee in town, good café atmosphere and a pleasant stop for a midmorning break. ♦♦♦*Fat Frog*, The Substation, Armenian St, attractive leafy courtyard, serving wholefood snacks, sandwiches and soups. ♦♦♦-♦♦*Café Aria*, Young Musicians' Society Arts Centre, Waterloo St (Little India), popular for a coffee stop.

Tea, cakes and coffee shops

Taking Sun afternoon tea – whether it be a Chinese tea ceremony or an English tea – are popular past-times in Singapore these days. Coffee shops have also become incredibly popular in recent months. New chains to spring up have been *Delifrance*, *Spinellis* and most recently the American chain *Starbucks* (in Raffles City and Scotts Rd), which is already doing a roaring trade. All top hotels offer competitive deals for afternoon tea for less than S$15. Check the newspapers for special offers. ***Zhong Guo Hua Tuo Guan***, this traditional Chinese tea house has quite a few outlets including an atmospheric one at 52 Queen St (name above the tea house is in Chinese characters), just by the Albert and Waterloo sts roadside market, sells Hua Tuo's ancient recipes helpful for 'relieving of heatiness' and 'inhibiting the growth of tumor cells' amongst other things, very friendly proprietress will introduce you to wild ginseng and showfrog, or longan herbal jelly and tell you why you will feel better (that's if you can get any of the concoctions down!).

♦♦♦*Compass Rose Lounge*, *Westin Stamford Hotel*, 2 Stamford Rd, best views in Singapore, strict dress code, expect to queue. ♦♦♦*Goodwood Park Hotel*, Scotts Rd, sophisticated buffet tea, served on the lawn by the pool. ♦♦♦*Shangri-La Hotel*, 22 Orange Grove Rd, is said to offer the best tea in town, recommended. ***Bar Gelateria Bellavista***, Clarke Quay (see page 639), delicious Italian ice cream, indoor and outdoor seating. ***Polar Café***, B1-04 OUB Centre, Raffles Place (also branch in Lucky Plaza), the original home of the curry puff, first created at its former premises on Hill St in

1926, S$0.70 each, recommended. ***Seah Street Deli***, Ground Floor, *Raffles Hotel*, North Bridge Rd, New York-style deli serving everything, from corned beef and smoked-salmon to cheese cakes and Turkish pastries. ***Tea Chapter***, 9A-11A Neil Rd, Chinatown, ☎ 2261175, is an excellent little place on 3 floors with a choice of seating (on the floor or at tables) and a peaceful atmosphere, plenty of choice of teas and the director, Lee Peng Shu, and his wife enthusiastically talk you through the tea tasting ceremony (if you wish), recommended. ♦♦♦*Ah Teng's Bakery*, Raffles Arcade. Pricey but it has all the goodies you dream about at the end of a long trip away from home. Complimentary second cup of coffee. ♦♦♦-♦♦*Pao Pao Cha Vegetarian Restaurant*, Riverside Point, 30 Merchant Rd, on river, opposite Clarke Quay, camp little place with a good range of teas and small eats, strange decor.

Cybercafé

Café Boat Quay, 82 Boat Quay, T 2300140, a refurbished shophouse. A dozen computers available for surfing the worldwide web, S$10/hour. Built in NetNanny prevents any sleaze, if you let your children loose here. International 'snack' food, live music some nights. ***Cyberheart Café***, basement of Orchard Shopping Centre, Orchard Rd, pizzas, pasta and sandwiches and lots of fun with the net.

● Bars

NB Alcohol is expensive in Singapore (see page 717). Coffee shops and hawker centres present a cheaper option for beer-drinkers. ***Alkaff Mansion***, Mount Faber Ridge, 10 Telok Blangah Green, perfect for sundowner 'stengahs' on the terrace with an excellent view of the harbour. ***Bar and Billiard Room***, *Raffles Hotel*, Beach Rd, relocated from its original position, the bar is lavishly furnished with teak tables, oriental carpets and two original billiard tables. ***Brannigan's*** (underneath *Hyatt Regency*), 10/12 Scotts Rd, open until 0100, 0200 on Fri and Sat, American style, touristy bar with loud live music and video screens, haunt of the infamous SPG (Singapore Party Girl), very popular. ***Canopy Bar***, *Hyatt Regency*, 10/12 Scotts Rd, Singapore's only champagne bar for the more sophisticated *bon viveur*. ***Changi Sailing Club***, Changi Village, pleasant and, surprisingly, one of the cheapest places for a quiet beer, overlooking the Strait of Johor. ***Charlie's***, Block 2, 01-08, Changi Village, Charlie Han describes his bar as "the pulse of the point", tucked away behind the local hawker centre, he is a teetotaller but serves 70 brands of beer from all over the world, which you can sip as you watch the red-eyes touchdown on runway one, Charlie's is best known for its fish and chips (see *Restaurants*), recommended; several quiet bars on **Duxton Hill**, Chinatown, in a pleasant area of restored shophouses – a retreat from the hustle and bustle of Boat Quay or the city. **Duxton Road** and **Tanjong Pagar Road** (both in Chinatown) also provide a dozen or so bars in restored shophouses. ***Escobar***, 36 Boat Quay, a Latin American bar. ***Espana***, 45 Boat Quay, marguerítas, daiquiris and jugs of Heineken, accompanied by Latin music. ***Hard Rock Café***, Cuscaden Rd, west end of Orchard Rd, complete with limo in suspended animation and queues to enter. ***Harry's Quayside***, 28 Boat Quay, big bar with seating outside overlooking river, popular with City boys, serves food, pricey, jazz band. ***Ice Cold***, 9 Emerald Hill, if you like heavy music and girlie calendars on the wall, this is your place. ***Molly Malone's***, 42 Circular Rd, off Boat Quay, T 5345100, Irish pub (complete with stout, Irish folk music etc) with a restaurant upstairs, usually pretty packed. ***Beaujolais Winebar***, 1 Ann Siang Hill, T 2242227, very pleasant winebar in restored shophouse, serves reasonably-priced wine, candles in winebottles on the window-sills, atmospheric, good cheese and charcuterie platters, recommended. ***Jack's Place***, Yen San Building (opposite *Mandarin Hotel*), Orchard Rd, cellar bar with live music, squashed and not very sophisticated. ***Lone Star Bar***, 54 Tanjong Pagar Rd, run by Mike Brenders, a Texan (ex-US Navy), country and western music, darts, friendly and fun. ***Next Page Pub***, 15 Jl Mohamed Sultan, a converted shophouse, great decor – salon style with opium beds, cubby holes and cushions, makes for a good evening if combined with a meal at the nearby *Nonya and Baba* restaurant on River Valley Rd, recommended; there are a strip of pubs on Jl Mohamed Sultan – ***Wong San's*** at No 12 and ***Zens*** at No 10. The building site opposite makes the outlook rather less attractive. ***Number 5 Emerald Hill***, 5 Emerald Hill (north side, midway point of Orchard Rd), surprising mixture of decor, in this retro-chic restored shophouse bar and restaurant (upstairs), popular with young expats and Chuppies (Chinese yuppies), great music, recommended. ***Observation Lounge***, *Mandarin Hotel*, 333 Orchard Rd, circular cocktail bar on 38th Flr; *Riverbank Bar*, 68 Boat Quay, live music. ***Saxophone***, 23 Cuppage Terrace, T 2358385, on of Singapore's most popular bars – particularly with expats, offers the good live music (usually rhythm and blues) and pleasant open-air terrace, opens at 1800, recommended. ***Somerset's***, *Westin Stamford*, Raffles City, large pleasant bar with frieze of the padang in the days before Raffles City, live music. ***The Long Bar***, *Raffles Hotel*, 1-3 Beach Rd, the home of the Singapore Sling, originally concocted by bar-tender Ngiam Tong Boon in 1915 (see page 635), now on two levels and extremely popular with tourists and locals alike, gratuitous tiny dancing mechanical punkawallahs sway out of sync to the cover band. ***The Yard***, 294 River Valley Rd, the Singaporean version of a London pub complete with darts, dominos, fish 'n' chips and Newcastle Brown Ale. ***Trader Vics***, 5th Flr, *New Otani Hotel*, River Valley Rd, Hawaii 5-0 decor and Chin-Ho's favourite cocktails – try a few goblets of Tikki Puka Puka for something violently different. ***Woodstock***, Rooftop, 06-02 Far East Plaza, 14 Scotts Rd, take the bullet lift up the outside of the building, expect to meet long-hairs and hear hard rock, open until 0200. ***Writers' Bar***, *Raffles Hotel*, 1 Beach Rd (just off the main lobby), in honour of the likes of Somerset Maugham, Rudyard Kipling, Joseph Conrad, Noel Coward and Herman Hesse who were said either to have wined, dined or stayed at the hotel, bar research indicates that other literary luminaries from James A Michener to Noel Barber and the great Arthur Hailey are said to have sipped *Tigers* at the bar – as the bookcases and momentoes suggest. ***Zouk's***, 17 Jiak Kim St (off Kim Seng Rd), pleasant streetside bar affording perfect opportunity to pose with a Sol, a yuppy favourite, packed at the weekends recommended. ***Kaspia Bar***, Hilton Hotel, Orchard Rd, for the biggest selection of vodkas in Singapore and live jazz.

● Airline offices

(The first number in the address refers to the floor level within the building.)

Aeroflot Soviet Airlines, 01-02 Tan Chong Tower, 15 Queen St, T 3361757; **Air Canada**, UOB Travel, 101 Thomson Rd, No 01-10, T 2561198; Tan Chong Tower, 15 Queen St, T 3361757; **Air France** 400 Orchard Rd 14-05, Orchard Towers, T 2354233; **Air India**, 17-01 UIC Building, 5 Shenton Way, T 2259411; **Air Lanka**, 02-00 PIL Building, 140 Cecil St, T 2236026; **Air Mauritius**, 01-00 LKN Building, 135 Cecil St, T 2223033; **Air New Zealand**, 24-08 Ocean Building, 10 Collyer Quay, T 5358266; **Alitalia**, 20-01 Wisma Atria, 435 Orchard Rd, T 7373166; **All Nippon Airways**, 01-01 Cecil House, 139 Cecil St, T 2283222; **American Airlines**, 108 Middle Rd, No 04-01, T 3390001; **Bangladesh Biman**, 01-02 Natwest Centre, 15 McCallum St, T 2217155; **British Airways**, 56 United Square, 101 Thomson Rd, T 2538444; **Cathay Pacific Airways**, 16-01 Ocean Building, 10 Collyer Quay, T 5331333; **China Airlines**, 08-02 Orchard Towers, 400 Orchard Rd, T 7372211; **Czechoslovak Airlines**, 1 Scotts Rd, 18-02, T 7379844; **El Al Israel Airlines**, 03-33 *Golden Landmark Hotel*, 390 Victoria St, T 2933622; **Emirates**, 19-06 Wisma Atria, 435 Orchard Rd, T 2353535; **Finnair**, 18-01 Liat Towers, 541 Orchard Rd, T 7333377; **Garuda**, 13-03 United Sq, 101 Thompson Rd, T 2502888; **Indian Airlines**, 01-03 Marina House, 70 Shenton Way, T 2254949; **Japan Airlines**, 01-01 Hong Leong Building, 16 Raffles Quay, T 2210522; **Korean Air**, 07-08 Ocean Building, 10 Collyer Quay, T 5342111; **KLM**, 391A Orchard Rd, 12-06/07, 108 Ngee Ann City, Tower A, T 7377622; **Kuwait Airways**, 391A Orchard Rd, 12-05, T 7359989; **Lufthansa**, 05-01/02 Palais Renaissance, 390 Orchard Rd, T 7379222; **MAS (Malaysian Airline System)**, 02-09 Singapore Shopping Centre, 190 Clemenceau Ave, T 3366777; **Northwest Airlines**, 08-06 Odeon Towers, 331 North Bridge Rd, T 3363371; **Olympic Airways**, 10-05 Parkmall, 9 Penang Rd, T 3366061; **Pakistan International**, 01-01 United Sq, 101 Thomson Rd, T 2512322; **Philippine Airlines**, 01-022 Parklane Shopping Mall, 35 Selegie Rd, T 3361611; **Qantas**, 04-02 The Promenade, 300 Orchard Rd, T 7373744; **Royal Brunei**, 01-4a Royal Holiday Inn Shopping Centre, 25 Scotts Rd, T 2354672; **Royal Jordanian**, 01-05 Beach Centre, 15 Beach Rd, T 3388188; **Royal Nepal**, 03-07, 3 Coleman St, T 3395535; **SAS**, 23-01 Gateway East, 152 Beach Rd, T 2941611; **Saudi**, 035-24 Changi Airport, Passenger Terminal 1, T 5457041; **Silk Air**, 6 Shenton Way, 07-10 DBS Building, Tower 2, T 3226850; **Singapore Airlines**, SIA Building, 77 Robinson Rd, T 2238888; *Mandarin Hotel*, Orchard Rd, T 2297293; Raffles City Shopping Centre, T 2297274; **Swissair**, 18-01 Wisma Atria, 435 Orchard Rd, T 7378133; **Thai**, 01-00 and 02-00 The Globe, 100 Cecil St, T 2249977; **Trans World Airlines (TWA)**, 08-01, 391A Orchard Rd, T 7354718; **Turkish Airlines**, 06-11, 300 Orchard Rd, T 7324556; **United Airlines**, 44-02 Hong Leong Building, 16 Raffles Quay, T 2200711.

● Banks & money changers

Singapore has 13 local banks but the big four are **DBS Bank**, **United Overseas Bank**, **Overseas-Chinese Banking Corporation** and

Overseas Union Bank. Most leading foreign banks are well represented in Singapore, although some in the financial district are offshore branches only and may not provide services to the public. All local banks and the majority of big names have foreign exchange facilities and most have branches within easy access of main tourist areas. Check *Yellow Pages* for lists of branches. There are also licenced moneychangers in all main shopping centres; many give better rates than the banks for TCs – but it's worth shopping around. Others: **Bank of Singapore**, Tong Eng Building, 101 Cecil St; **Chase Manhattan Bank NA**, Shell Tower, 50 Raffles Place; **Citibank NA**, Robina House, 1 Shenton Way; **DBS Bank**, DBS Building, 6 Shenton Way; **Deutsche Bank AG**, 15-08 DBS Building Tower 2; **Far Eastern Bank**, 156 Cecil St; **Hong Kong and Shanghai Banking Corporation**, Ocean Building, 10 Collyer Quay; **Keppel Bank**, 10 Hoe Chiang Rd, 06-00; **Oversea Chinese Banking Corporation**, OCBC Centre, 65 Chulia St; **Overseas Union Bank**, OUB Centre, 1 Raffles Place; **Standard Chartered Bank**, 0900/1100 Plaza by the Park; **United Overseas Bank**, UOB Plaze 1.

● Churches

Anglican: ***St Andrew's Cathedral***, Coleman St, T 3376104, services at 0700, 0800, 0930 and 1100; ***St George's***, Minden Rd, opposite the entrance to Botanic Gardens, very popular evangelical church, services at 0800 and 1000.

Roman Catholic: ***Cathedral of the Good Shepherd***, Victoria St, mass at 0800, 1000 and 1800 on Sun, Mon-Fri at 0700 and 1315, Sat at 0700 and 1830; ***St Joseph's Church***, Victoria St, mass on Sun at 0830, 1000 and 1700, weekday at 1745.

Others: ***Wesley Methodist***, 5 Fort Canning Rd (Dhoby Ghaut MRT), T 3361433; ***Fairfield Methodist***, on corner of Tanjong Pagar and Maxwell roads. Services at 0830 and 1030 on Sun, with communion on 1st Sun of the month; ***Orchard Road Presbyterian***, 3 Orchard Rd, T 3376681, services at 0900 and 1800; ***Prinsep St Presbyterian***, 144 Prinsep St, T 3384571; ***Queenstown Baptist***, 495 Margaret Drive; ***Calvary Charismatic Centre***, 179 River Valley Rd (5th Flr, former SISIR Building), T 3392955.

● Embassies & consulates

Australia, 25 Napier Rd, T 7379311; **Austria**, Shaw Centre, 1 Scotts Rd, 24-05/06, T 2354088; **Belgium**, International Plaza, 10 Anson Rd, T 2207677; **Brunei**, 325 Tanglin Rd, T 7339055; **Canada**, 15th Storey IBM Towers, 80 Anson Rd, T 3253200; **China, People's Republic of**, 70-76 Dalvey Rd, T 7343273; **Denmark**, 13-01 United Sq, 101 Thomson Rd, T 2503383; **Finland**, 21-03 United Sq, 101 Thomson Rd, T 2544042; **France**, 5 Gallop Rd, T 4664866; **Germany**, 14-01 Far East Shopping Centre, 545 Orchard Rd, T 7371355; **Greece**, 11-25 Anson Centre, 51 Anson Rd, T 2208622; **India**, 31 Grange Rd, T 7376777; **Indonesia**, 7 Chatsworth Rd, T 7377422; **Ireland**, 08-06 Tiong Bahru Plaza, 298 Tiong Bahru Rd, T 2768935; **Israel**, 58 Dalvey Rd, T 2350966; **Italy**, 27-02 United Sq, 101 Thomson Rd, T 2506022; **Japan**, 34th Storey IBM Towers, 80 Anson Rd, T 2358855; **Malaysia**, 301 Jervois Rd, T 2350111; **Myanmar (Burma)**, 15 St Martin's Drive, T 7350209; **Netherlands**, 13-01 Liat Towers, 541 Orchard Rd, T 7371155; **New Zealand**, 15th Storey, Ngee Ann City, Tower A, 391A Orchard Rd, T 2359966; **Norway**, 44-01 Hong Leong Building, 16 Raffles Quay, T 2207122; **Philippines**, 20 Nassim Rd, T 7373977; **Poland**, 33-11 Shaw Towers, 100 Beach Rd, T 2942513; **South Africa**, 15-00 Odeon Towers, 331 North Bridge Rd, T 3393319; **Spain**, 05-08/09 Thong Teck Building, 15 Scotts Rd, T 7329788; **Sweden**, 05-08 PUB Building, 111 Somerset Rd, T 7342771; **Switzerland**, 1 Swiss Club Link, T 4685788; **Thailand**, 370 Orchard Rd, T 7372644, open 0915-1215, 1500-1645, applications for visa am only; **UK**, 100 Tanglin Rd, T 4739333; **USA**, 27 Napier Rd, T 4769100; **Vietnam**, 10 Leedon Park, T 4625938.

● Entertainment

Hotels and nightclubs are the main source of night time entertainment in Singapore. Refer to the *What's On* section in the *Straits Times* or the *New Paper* for details on concerts, dance and theatre. The tourist magazine *This Week* has a 'What's On' section.

Cabaret: ***Neptune Theatre Restaurant***, Collyer Quay; ***Studebakers***, Penthouse of Pacific Plaza, Orchard Rd. Live performances and dancing.

Chinese Street Operas (wayang): dramatizations of Chinese legends (the heroes wear red or green, the emperor, yellow and the villains, black). *Clarke Quay* now has a permanent (though it looks deliberately temporary) stage, where there are 30-minute performances on Wed, Thur and Fri. The audience is encouraged to watch the artists apply their make-up backstage from 1815 and the performance starts at 1930. Subtitles are projected onto a screen.

Cinema: with more than 50 cinemas, Singapore gets most of the blockbusters and they arrive quickly. These will be more entertaining now that the censors are easing up; there's a new RA category for those over 21 years of age, which means a little more sex and violence hits the screens. The *Straits Times* Life section publishs listings daily. When the ***Cathay***, at the southeastern end of Orchard Rd, opened in 1939 and became the first air-conditioned public building in Singapore, local celebrities turned up in fur coats. There are several brand new cinemas, showing 3 or 4 films at any one time, these include the complex at *Riverside Point* opposite Clarke Quay, *Parco Bugis Junction* on Victoria St, opposite Bugis MRT, the *Lido Cineplex* at the Shaw Centre, Orchard Rd and, most recently, there is a new complex at *Suntec City*, Marina Square.

Cultural shows and activities: the *Substation* on Armenian St (Colonial Core), runs courses in yoga, appreciating opera, screen-writing and calligraphy, batik and dance, T 3377800 for information. ***Mandarin Hotel***, 333 Orchard Rd, T 7374411, ASEAN Night, songs and dances from the Philippines, Malaysia, Thailand and Indonesia as well as Singapore, dinner at 1900, show starts 1945, admission: show (without dinner) S$23, show (including dinner) S$46; ***Singa Inn Seafood Restaurant***, 920 East Coast Parkway, T 3451111, Instant Asia Show, lion dance, Malay harvest dance and Indian snake charmers, 2000-2045 Mon-Fri (dinner from 1800) – no charge for diners.

Discos/nightclubs: most big hotels have house discos – they all have a cover charge; usually S$25-30 (which normally include a drink or two) – and dress is 'smart-casual'. Good hotel discos include: *Boiler*, basement of *Mandarin Hotel*, Orchard Rd; ***Ridleys***, *ANA Hotel*, Nassim Hill, ***Chinoiserie***, *Hyatt Regency*, 10-12 Scotts Rd, off Orchard Rd; ***Scandals***, *Westin Plaza Hotel*, Raffles City Complex, Colonial Core; ***Xanadu*** *Shangri-La Hotel*, Orange Grove Rd, northwest end of Orchard Rd; ***The Reading Room***, *Marina Mandarin Hotel*, Marina Square, is smart, expensive and pretentious and attracts a younger crowd; ***Fabrice's World Music Bar***, Basement, *Singapore Marriott*, 320 Orchard Rd, run by Fabrice De Barcy,

Joshua (aged 6) and Ella's (aged 4) guide to fun and scary Singapore

Ride/attraction	Fun	Scary	Entrance ($)	
			Adult	Child
Clarke Quay Adventure Ride	5	5	$5	$3
Fantasy Island	9	up to 9	$16	$10
Haw Par Villas	2	0*	$5	$2.50
Jurong Bird Park	9	na	$10.30	$4.12
Maritime Museum	5	2	$4	$2
Night Safari	10**	0	$15.45	$10.30
Philatelic Museum	10***	na	$2	$1
Singapore Zoo	10	na	$10.30	$4.60
Tang Dynasty City	4	6	$15.45	$10.30
Underwater World	6	na	$12	$6
Volcanoland	4	7	$10	$6

Grading system

Marks out of 10. No adult intervention bar buying tickets and ice creams.

Adult footnotes

* Very gruesome. ** From an animal-crazed 6-year-old. *** This was a surprise considering that the postage stamp is not considered high on most children's wish lists, but the appraisers would not budge from their decision.

the Belgian of *Saxophone* fame, Arabesque decor with low tables, candles and Persian rugs, live music and dance tracks, open 1700-0300 Mon-Sun, no cover before 2200, S$25 thereafter, recommended; ***Fire***, Orchard Plaza, T 2350155, two levels of music, very popular, admission charges vary; ***Moondance***, Tanjong Pagar Rd, Chinatown, $13 cover charge ($16 at the weekends), 25% off happy hour from 1900-2100, karaoke from 1900-2200; ***Rumours***, Level 3, Forum Gallaria, 583 Orchard Rd, once it was the trendiest spot in town ... now it has gone off the boil; ***Sparks***, Ngee Ann City, Orchard Rd, the biggest disco in all of Asia, very glitzy with KTV rooms and jazz bar, packed at weekends, open 1700-0200 (to 0300 on Sat and Sun). Cover: S$15 Mon-Thur, S$20 Fri-Sun, recommended; ***Top Ten Club***, Orchard Towers, 400 Orchard Rd, huge converted cinema, often has live black-American or Filipino disco bands, recommended; ***Club 392*** is also in Orchard Towers; ***The Warehouse***, 332 Havelock Rd, an old godown on the Singapore River, large dance hall mainly frequented by teenagers; ***Velvet Underground***, Jiak Jim St (off Kim Seng Rd) next door to *Zouk's* bar, owned by Zouk's, small nightclub, open until 0300, cover S$25, free for women on Wed nights, recommended.

Karaoke is very popular in Singapore and KTV lounges abound, at about S$15/hour for a private room.

Music: there are live music bars all over Singapore (see bars above). The Singapore Cultural Theatre and the Victoria Hall host most of the **classical** shows – the Singapore Symphony Orchestra gives regular performances and there are often visiting orchestras, quartets and choirs. Bands play in the gazebo in the centre of Clarke Quay every evening – dubious quality – and in the Botanic Gardens at weekends. **Chinese classical and folk music** organized by the Nanyang Academy of Fine Arts (NAFA), T 3376636, for performance details.

Instruction in music and dance: *Kala Mandhir* is at the Temple of Fine Arts, 1st Flr, Excelsior Hotel Shopping Centre, T 3390492. Classes available in dance, instrumental music, percussion and singing. Fabulous array of Indian instruments. It might be possible to take a 1 week course, although most of their courses are longer.

Theatre/dance: most performances are held at ***Victoria Hall*** and are advertised in the newspapers and tourist publications. The latest offering on the thespian and artistic scene is ***The Substation***, 45 Armenian St, set up in a former power station, has an intimate little theatre where it stages plays and shows avante garde films. It also holds drama workshops. Call T 3377800 for details on what's on when. *Raffles Jubilee Hall*, 328 North Bridge Rd holds occasional theatrical performances, for information T 3311732.

● Hospitals & medical services

Singapore's medical facilities are excellent, with many overseas-trained doctors and dentists. Registered pharmacists work from 0900-1800, with some shops open until 2200.

Ambulance: T 995.

Hospitals: *East Shore Hospital*, T 3447588; *Gleneagles Hospital*, T 4737222; *Mount Elizabeth Hospital*, T 7372666; *National University Hospital*, T 7725000;*Singapore General Hospital*, T 2223322.

● Libraries

National Library, Stamford Rd (next to the National Museum). Plenty of English books and travel guides and an array of computers providing information on just about anything – an excellent place to spend a rainy afternoon.

● Post & telecommunications

General Post Office: Ground Floor, Fullerton Building, Fullerton Rd, just off Collyer Quay and Battery Rd.

Comcentre: main public telephone office, 31 Exeter Rd, just south of Somerset MRT, Orchard Rd. 24 hours facilities.

● Shopping

Singapore is a shopper's paradise. There is an endless variety of consumer items and gimmicks, with no import duty or sales tax on most items. The choice is almost unlimited. But don't be deluded that there are bargains galore with rock bottom prices to match the variety. Prices are, in fact, much the same as anywhere else. High wages, soaring rents and a strong dollar have all eaten into the country's price advantage. Singapore's retailers have had to weather several years of stagnant demand. Local shoppers seem to be spending their disposable income in other ways (or themselves go shopping abroad) and tourists no longer come with empty suitcases to stuff full of goodies. Even the people who used to come here from places like Manila, Bangkok and Jakarta can buy just about everything at home.

Probably the best area for window shopping is the **Scotts** and **Orchard Road** area, where many of the big complexes and department stores are located (see page 644). This area comes alive after dark and most shops stay open late. The towering **Raffles City complex, Parco** at Bugis Junction and **Marina Square**, are the other main shopping centres. The East Coast shopping centres are not frequented by tourists. **Serangoon Road** (or Little India), **Arab Street** and **Chinatown** offer a more exotic shopping experience.

For specific goods, certain places are better than others and many of the plazas have become 'specialist centres' – see the box with this information.

Shopping trends For many years Singaporeans seemed to be most concerned with fashion – clothes, jewellery and so on. But with the spread of private home ownership (HDB apartments can now be bought), their has been an upsurge of interest in interior design. As a result, there are many shops selling beautiful products from colonial style furniture to candlesticks. However, nothing comes cheap.

Touts Although the government has come down hard on copy-watch touts, tourists can still occasionally be accosted (and ripped off) along Orchard Rd – particularly outside Lucky Plaza.

Tips on buying It does not take long to get the feel of where you can bargain and where you cannot. Department stores are fixed-price, but most smaller outfits – even those in smart shopping complexes – can be talked into discounts. As ever, it is best not to buy at the first shop; compare prices; get an idea of what you should be paying from big department stores – *Tang's* department store is a good measuring rod, which you can nearly always undercut. In ordinary shops, 20-30% can be knocked off the original asking price – sometimes more. Keep smiling, joking and teasing when bargaining and never believe a shopkeeper who tells you he is giving you something at cost or is not making a profit. The golden rule is to keep a sense of humour. If you lose face, they've won.

- For big purchases, ask for an international guarantee (they are often extra), although sometimes you will have to be content with Singapore-only guarantees.
- Once goods are sold they are not returnable, unless faulty, make sure you keep your receipt.
- Deposits, not usually more than 50% of the value of the goods, are generally required when orders are placed for custom-made goods.
- Make sure electrical goods are compatible with the voltage back home.
- Complaints about retailers (who from time to time exhibit aggressive tendencies when selling merchandise to tourists) can be registered at the Consumers' Association of Singapore, T 2224165.

The **Good Retailers Scheme** has been set up by the Singapore Tourist Promotion Board and has 500 shops on its books. Retailers who belong to this scheme are expected to abide by a code of conduct. The mark of a 'good retailer' is the red and white merlion emblem, and it is valid for the year it displays. The STPB produce a booklet listing all their members.

Best buys: Singapore has all the latest electronic gadgetry and probably as wide a choice as you will find anywhere. It also has a big selection of antiques (although they tend to be over-priced), arts and crafts, jewellery, silks and batiks. For branded goods, Singapore is still marginally cheaper than most other places but for Asian produced products it is no longer the cheapest place in the region.

Antiques: Singapore's antique shops stock everything from opium beds, planters' chairs, gramophones, brass fans, porcelain, jade, Peranakan marble-top tables and 17th century maps to smuggled Burmese Buddhas, Sulawesian spirit statues and Dayak masks. There are few restrictions on bringing antiques into Singapore or exporting them. Many of the top antique shops are in the **Tanglin Shopping Centre** – including the old map shop, ***Antiques of the Orient***, on the first floor, T 7349351. This is probably the best place to buy antique maps and prints in Southeast Asia and is a wonderful place to browse – they also have a library; ***Apsara***, Tanglin Shopping Centre, for lacquerware chests; ***Tiepolo***, also in Tanglin, T 7327924, was established over 20 years ago and David Mun has a fabulous range of Chinese and Indonesian porcelain, wooden pieces and bronze. Well worth a visit – Mr Mun is a mine of information and is fascinating to talk with; ***Kensoon*** also in Tanglin, exclusive Asiatic pieces; ***Tatiana***, also in Tanglin, is a long established treasure trove of mostly 'primitive' art – a considerable proportion from Indonesia: antiques, great wooden sculptures and textiles, baskets, Vietnamese drums and jewellery; ***Mata-Hari*** (in Tanglin), Indo Chinese lacquerware and a range of silver jewellery and silver pieces and textiles (as well as some good books for reference). ***Tong Mern Sern Antiques***, at 51 Craig Rd, Chinatown and at Block D, on the waterfront at Clarke Quay (also called *Keng's*, after its inimitable owner), is a treasure trove. Keng's adage: "We buy junk and sell antiques; some fool buy and some fool sell"; ***Eng Tiang***

Huat, is at 282 River Valley Rd, west from Clarke Quay, as is ***Hua Shi Oriental Arts***, at number 278 and *Vivaldi Collection* at number 296. For general antique shops, there are others dotted around **Cuppage Terrace** behind Centrepoint (upstairs, above *Saxophone*, there are several good shops, selling antique Melaka furniture, porcelain, and Peranakan pieces), **Dempsey Road**, off Holland Rd, is a great place to browse amongst the furniture warehouses in some of the old army barracks there. Furniture from Indonesia, plantation chairs, opium couches, Burmese buddhas and so on, are all available. Warehouse shops include: ***Asian Passion***, block 13, T 4731339, good for tables and cabinets; ***Renaissance***, Block 15, T 4740338, range of restored Chinese furniture; ***Pasardina***, Block 13, T 4720228, good range of new and old – cabinets, planters chairs, beds and some small scale Indonesian pieces (spice boxs and baskets); ***Journey East***, Block 13 T 4731693 for chests, planters chairs – old and new; ***Eastern Discoveries***, Block 26, T 4751814, for wooden sculptures, amongst other things; ***Abanico***, 5th Flr, Centrepoint shopping centre, antique and modern Asian pieces. There are also some good shops (selling antiques and restored/imitation items) at Binjai Park, off Bukit Timah Rd, which is rather off the beaten track to the north of Orchard Rd. Among the best is the oxymoronic ***Young Antique Co***. **Geylang** (East coast area) has a number of good antique junk shops where occasional treasures can be found. ***Peter Wee's Katong Antique House*** at 208 East Coast Rd (half museum, half shop) has one of the best selections of Peranakan antiques. The shop has been established for 20 years and has become a focal point for Peranakan culture. He has established a Peranakan Association and publishes a newsletter. Groups from the National Museum visit him. He has a considerable collection of beaded shoes and holds classes to learn how to make them every Wed. *A Guide to Buying Antiques, Arts and Crafts in Singapore* by Anne Jones is recommended, available in most bookshops.

Art Galleries: with the arrival of both *Christie's* and *Sotheby's* and the increased interest in home decorating, art has taken on a new meaning for Singaporeans. There are a good number of galleries scattered around the city. ***Eagle's Eye***, Stamford House, 39 Stamford Rd, Colonial Core, T 3398297, little gallery packed with Asian contemporary artwork (70% Singaporean work); ***Gauguin Gallery***, Orchard Hotel Shopping Arcade, 442 Orchard Rd, T 7334268. Changing exhibitions of international artists. ***Tzen Gallery***, Tanglin Shopping Centre, 19 Tanglin Rd (Orchard Rd), T 7344339, mainland Chinese watercolours and pen and ink drawings and wide selection of scrolls, reasonable prices. ***Art-2***, The Substation, 45 Armenian St, Colonial Core, T 3388713, tiny gallery, but they work more as consultants than as an exhibiting gallery; ***Asian contemporary Art***, The Substation, has a good exhibition space, where they display changing exhibitions of local artists' work; ***Art Focus***, Top floor, Centrepoint, Orchard Rd, T 7338337, F 7320448, good range of work, an attractive gallery. The top floor of ***Orchard Point***, Orchard Rd, is dedicated to art galleries. ***Wetterling Teo Gallery***, 11 Kim Yam Rd, off River Valley Rd, T 7382872, specializes in contemporary American art.

Batik and silk: Malaysian and Indonesian batiks are sold by the metre or in sarong lengths. **Arab Street** and Serangoon Rd are the best areas for reasonably priced batik and silk lengths – but you should bargain; big department stores usually have batik ready-mades. Ready-made Chinese silk garments can be found all over Singapore in Chinese emporia. If you want silk without the hassle, at reasonable prices, big department stores (such as ***Tangs***) have good selections. The best known of the silk boutiques, with fine silks at high prices, is ***China Silk House***, which has shops in Tanglin, Scotts, Centrepoint and Marina Square shopping centres. China Silk House designers come up with new collections every month. There is also a ***Jim Thompson Thai Silk*** shop on Tanglin Rd next to Tanglin Shopping Centre.

Books: there is a good selection of English language literature available in Singapore, including specialist books on the region. Either ***Times***, ***Kinokuniya*** or ***MPH*** bookshops can be found in most shopping complexes. ***MPH*** in Stamford Rd is the largest bookshop in Singapore and was built in 1908 to house the Methodist Publishing House; ***Sogo*** department store (Raffles City and Wisma Atria) also has a books section. ***Select Books***, Tanglin Shopping Centre, Orchard Rd, sell a good range of coffee table glossies of the region; ***FP Bookstore***, 56 Amoy St, Chinatown, T 2254763, for a good range of financial books; ***Christian Bookshop***, next to *MPH* on Stamford Rd, Colonial Core. There is a good selection of **second-hand bookshops**: ***New Bookstore***, west side of North Bridge Rd, just south of the *Intercontinental Hotel* buy and sell second-hand books; ***Books Paradiz***,

Paradiz Centre, 1 Selegie Rd, south of Little India, second-hand books for sale or rent; ***Sultana Bookstore***, Paradiz Centre, 1 Selegie Rd, south of Little India, have a huge range of second-hand books including a good assortment of Penguin fiction; ***Bookmark***, Marina Square; the ***atrium*** of The Cannery, Clarke Quay sell second-hand books every Sat 1600-2100.

Cameras: there are several shopping centres which are dedicated to electronic equipment and they usually provide camera shops (see plaza box for information). ***Cathay Photo***, Marina Square, the 3rd floor of Centrepoint or Peninsula Plaza all provide a good range and good advice. ***Cathay*** also sell the cheapest slide film.

Camping gear: *Campers' Corner*, 1, Selegie Rd, 01-11 Paradiz Centre, T 3374743. Stocks good range of camping and trekking equipment for sale and hire. Also organizes trekking expeditions around Singapore and Malaysia.

Children: *Paw Marks*, 1st Flr, The Cannery, Clarke Quay, every conceivable type of teddy bear for sale; ***Rainforest Shops***, 1st Flr, The Cannery, Clarke Quay, emporium of children's goodies from teddies to clock, mobiles and furniture; ***The Toy Place***, 3rd Flr, Liang Court, River Valley Rd (next door to Clarke Quay) for a toy shop – there is also a good model train shop in Liang Court; ***The Forum***, corner of Orchard Rd and Cuscaden Rd, an entire shopping plaza given over to children, with an enormous *Toys 'R' Us* on the top floor and lots of other individual shops on the other 3 floors; ***Papermoon***, Millenia Walk, Marina Square, T 3378403, for pretty children's clothing.

Chinese porcelain: *Ju-I Antiques* and ***Moon Gate***, both at Tanglin Shopping Centre and ***Toh Foong*** and ***Soon Thye Cheang***, both on Temple St in Chinatown are all good shops for porcelain; ***Ming Village***, 32 Pandan Rd. Visitors can watch reproduction Ming bases being made. Holland Village, west of the Botanic Gardens has quite a number of porcelain shops.

Computers: the **Funan Centre** on North Bridge Rd is computer city; even the Japanese buy here. **Sim Lim Tower** (upper floors) and the nearby **Albert Complex**, both just off Bukit Timah on Rochor Canal Rd, are also good.

Fashion: Singapore boasts all the international designer labels – many of the shops are strung out along **Orchard Road**, although there are now quite a few shops in Marina Square. Designer fashion comes a bit cheaper in Singapore than other Southeast Asian capitals, as no duty is levied. ***Emporio Armani***, with a big choice of younger designerwear is in ***HPL House***, behind *The Forum* on Cuscaden Rd (Orchard Rd). Locally-designed clothes keep up with the trends and are very reasonably priced, look out for work by Benny Ony, Celia Lo and Tan Yoong; for exceptional value, slight damaged clothes – factory seconds – can be purchased from ***B&N Factory Outlet***, which has branches in several shopping centres and at The Cannery, Clarke Quay.

Children's clothes: the best choice is to be found at ***The Forum***, corner of Cuscaden and Orchard roads, where there must be at least 20 shops selling childrens clothes.

Electronic goods: Singapore has all the latest electronic equipment – hot from Japan at duty free prices. Prices are still cheaper than UK, but prices can vary enormously, check for international guarantees. The centres for electronic goods are ***Sim Lim Tower*** (corner of Jl Besar, Little India), ***Sim Lim Square*** (corner of Rochor Canal Rd, south of Little India) – of these two Sim Lim Tower does not have a very good reputation; ***Funan Centre*** (between North Bridge Rd and Hill St); ***Peninsular Plaza***, next to *Grand Plaza Hotel*, Coleman St (colonial core) has dozens of shops dedicated to cameras, phones, walkman, video camera; ***Lucky Plaza*** (Orchard Rd) and ***Far East Plaza*** (Scotts Rd). The ***Changi Airport duty free*** is also very competitive.

Fabrics: *Moutain Looms*, Blk 16 Dempsey Rd, west of Orchard Rd, T 4767629, very fine pieces of cloth from all over the region.

Furniture: Singapore now has a plentiful range of old (or distressed) and new furniture, thanks to the boom in interest in Interior Design. Dempsey Rd is a good place to start, as there are half a dozen warehouses there, with a good range of products (see the Antique section above for a listing). ***Rustic Charm***, 1st Flr, The Cannery, Clarke Quay, T 3343713, is a treasure trove of Asian reproduction furniture (both large and small) ranging from spice chests to Javanese benches to planters chairs, well worth a browse and it's not too expensive; ***Renee Hoy Fine Arts***, 1st Flr, Tanglin Shopping Centre, 19 Tanglin Rd (western end of Orchard Rd), T 2351596, for a wide choice of Korean chests and some Thai furniture; ***Babazar***, 31-35A Cuppage Terrace, off Orchard Rd, T 2357866, F 7348665, excellent selection of beautiful Indian furniture; ***A2 Atelier***, Le Meridien Shopping Centre, 100 Orchard Rd, T 7375081,

F 7359912, extensive choice of reproduction furniture including 4-poster beds and some attractive chairs and chests, pacific Link shopping centre, Marina Square, sells a range of contemporary furniture and furnishings. Antique furniture in varying states of decay can be found at Upper Paya Lebar Rd, just north of Macpherson Rd. ***Chin Yi Antique House***, ***Mansion Antique House***, ***Tech Huat Antique House*** can all be found here. ***Just Anthony*** is also on this road, south of Upper Serangoon Rd – it sells antiques and makes reproductions. **River Valley Road**, just up from Tank Rd, has several antique and second-hand furniture dealers (see the antiques section). Mock antique furniture can also be found on Kelantan Lane.

Gold: see jewellery.

Handicrafts: assorted Chinese knick-knacks including kites, lanterns, silk dressing gowns, opera masks, incense sticks, candle holders, lucky money and all the paraphernalia required for visiting a Chinese temple and attending a funeral can be found in several shops in Chinatown, notably on Smith and Sago streets; it is cheap and prices are not negotiable. The biggest Chinese Emporia are in the ***People's Park Complex***, Eu Tong Sen St, and ***Katong Shopping Centre***, East Coast Rd; ***Singapore Handicraft Centre***, at Chinatown Point Shopping Centre on New Bridge Rd specializes in small handicrafts – all a bit naff, but a good place to browse for small Asian gifts; Kuna's on Buffalo Rd at the southern end of Little India sells Indian handicrafts. There are other shops around here where Indian knick-knacks can be found. The ***Substation***, 45 Armenian St, Colonial core, runs a market on the last Sun of every month where some arts and crafts are on sale; there is also a flea market every Sun at Clarke Quay, where anyone can hire a pitch for $25 for the day – there might be some bargains to be found.

Interior Decorating: *Rustic Charm*, 1st Flr, The Cannery, Clarke Quay for a good range of small, quirky pieces; ***Pennsylvania House***, Stamford House, Stamford Rd (colonial core) for New England knick knacks; ***Peter Hoe***, CHIJMES, 30 Victoria St T/F 3396880, for an interesting assortment of small scale pieces, some Indonesian.

Jade: *Kwok Gallery*, Far East Shopping Centre; and in *The Cannery*, Clarke Quay.

Jewellery: gold (mostly Asian, 18, 22 or 24 carat), precious stones, pearls (freshwater and cultured); good value here, are all easily found in Singapore. **NB** Styles and designs are quite different from the west. Gold is a good buy but it too looks different. The Singapore Assay Office uses a merlion head as a hallmark. Most of the jewellery shops are in **South Bridge Road**; Pidemco Centre on South Bridge Road, Chinatown, is known as Jewellery Mart; North Bridge Rd and People's Park, both in Chinatown, have reputable goldsmiths selling items by the weight set for the day's prices; for Indian goldsmiths, go to **Serangoon Road**; ***Zero Gravity***, Ground Floor, Merchant Court, Clarke Quay for unusual contemporary jewellery; an un-named shop in the basement of Raffles City Complex (Colonial core) has some perspex jewellery and strange puzzles, quirky key rings and mobiles etc; ***Peter Hoe***, CHIJMES, 30 Victoria St (Colonial Core) for a good range of Indonesian jewellery. Don't be taken in by shops along Orchard Rd advertising 'incredible reductions' – usually they're not. Bargaining is *de rigeur*, and it requires much shopping-around to gain an appreciation of what the true price should be. ***Singapore Gems & Metals Co***, 7 Kung Chong Rd, T 4759733, organize tours around their processing workroom to see gems cut, polished and set.

Markets: the most accessible market of interest is **the Zhujiao (formerly KK) Market** on the corner of Bukit Timah and Serangoon roads, at the southern end of Little India. It is a hive of activity and sells everything from flowers to fish and meat to spices, and every conceivable vegetable and fruit. There's a good hawker centre next door. An excellent **Sunday market** is on Seng Poh Rd, Tiong Bahru, between Tiong Bahru and Outram Rd MRT stations – worth taking in if you go to see the Singing Birds (see page 653). A good place to buy orchids is in **Holland Village's** small wet market; this stall is much cheaper than the more touristy flower shops downtown and will pack them for shipment.

Optical goods: leading makes of sunglasses, hard and soft contact lenses and designer spectacles frames are all available in Singapore at reasonable prices. Unless you have stigmatic complications, contact lenses can usually be fitted on the spot and glasses should be ready within the day. Singapore is one of the cheapest places in the world to buy Rayban sunglasses.

Paper: Thai handmade mulberry paper – *sa* paper – available from ***Paper Tree***, Tanglin Mall, 163 Tanglin Rd, Orchard Rd, good choice of colours and textures.

Shopping centres and plazas in Chinatown and the Colonial core

Chinatown Point Eu Tong Sen Street, Chinatown, specializes in small handicrafts.

Funan Centre Squeezed in between the *Excelsior* and *Peninsula* hotels in the Colonial Core, with five floors of shops. A good place for electrical equipment – in particular notebooks and software. One of the best and biggest foodcourts in the area in the basement. Huge screen in central atrium shows cartoons, opera, and pop concerts; makes a good stopping off spot if the children are tired.

Liang Court Opposite Riverside Point, and dominated by a large *Diamaru* department store, although there is also a big toy shop here – *The Toy Place* – as well as a good diving equipment shop. The Quayside Food Court in the basement is recommended (with a children's play area). There is also a *Swensen's* on the ground floor.

Marina Square and Millenia Walk A huge area of shops with a wide range of exclusive designer labels. There is also an Asian furniture and furnishings area and quite a few carpet shops. *Suntec City* close by has more shops of the same, a wide choice of restaurants and a big foodcourt.

Parco Bugis Junction This very trendy a/c shophouse mall is on Victoria St, north of the colonial core. It is packed with international names, as well as some quirky little shops and cafes, and is more fun to visit than most shopping centres. Mesmerising fountain in the centre.

Peninsula Plaza Next to the *Peninsula Hotel* this is an old style shopping centre, mostly dedicated to electrical goods – cameras, videos and mobile phones.

Pidemco Centre South Bridge Road, Chinatown, good for traditional jewellery.

Raffles City Complex Opposite the *Raffles Hotel*, this huge glitzy, noisy and trendy shopping complex holds all the international (but not designer) labels – including M&S, Max Mara, Body Shop and Knickerbox. There are upmarket foodstalls on the lower level, with another mesmerising fountain.

Riverside Point On the south side of the river, overlooking Clarke Quay. This brand new dockside development is reminiscent of London's Docklands or San Franscisco's Canary Wharf. Totally un-Asian in design, and quite attractive. Cinema on the top floor, restaurants along the riverfront but with many plots still vacant in mid-1997.

Sim Lim Tower and Sim Lim Square Both these shopping centres are on the edge of Little India on Jalan Besar and both sell the same range of electrical equipment – cameras, hi fi and desktop computers.

Stamford House Situated on the corner of Stamford Road and Hill Street this is a renovated and ornate colonial building with a range of upmarket shops. These include the *Eagle's Art Gallery*, an exclusive lighting shop, and the *Pennsylvania Country Oven Restaurant* and *Pennsylvania House* on the first floor for all your New England needs, nutritional and otherwise.

For details on shopping plazas on Orchard Road, see page 644.

Persian rugs: *Pardisan*, Orchard Shopping Centre, Orchard Rd, good selection; ***Mohammed Akhtar***, Tanglin Shopping Centre, Orchard Rd; ***Leila Carpets***, Tanglin Shopping Centre, Orchard Rd; ***Jehan Gallery***, Block 26, Dempsey Rd (west of Orchard Rd), T 4750003, huge choice but quite pricey; ***Tandis Gallery***, Blk 26, Dempsey Rd, west of Orchard Rd, T 475220. Good choice of fine rugs.

Pewter: *Selang* or *Pewter Showroom*, 356W Alexandra Rd (west on Havelock Rd from Chinatown), watch craftsmen at work, fixed price goods. There is also a **Pewter Museum** at the Ming Village, where craftsmen can be observed (see page 664).

Pharmacists/Medical requirements: there are plenty of Watson's stores scattered throughout the city, but if you require more traditional Chinese medicine, try the '*Medicine Halls*' down Eu Tong Sen St or along Temple or Smith streets.

Tailoring: quick, efficient and usually high-quality tailoring can be found in most shopping centres. The tailors in the main tourist shopping belt along Orchard and Scotts roads, notably **Far East** and **Lucky plazas**, are as good a bet as any. You can design virtually what you want for yourself, but it is worth shopping around for the best deal. For more upmarket tailoring, hotel tailors are recommended.

Watches: a huge range of watches are available at duty free prices in most shopping centres. Copy watches do not officially exist in Singapore, where most people prefer the real thing. No amount of fines or embarrassing newspaper reports have managed to clear the precincts of **Lucky Plaza** of fake watch touts who approach you as if they're peddling heroin.

Singapore knick-knacks: although considered rather twee by many, the most popular Singapore souvenirs have been ceramic models of shophouses in the '*Little Island Collection*', which first came out in 1991. Five local artists make and paint each house and come out with two new designs a month. The miniatures cost from S$60-300 and can be bought from any of the big department stores or leading handicraft shops.

Indian/Southeast Asian goods: for Indian silks, sarees, gold jewellery and trinkets try Serangoon Rd, otherwise known as **Little India**, but by far the best shop for Indian exotica is ***Natraj's Arts & Crafts***, 03-202 Marina Sq shopping centre, which is in a row of Far Eastern handicraft shops. Natraj's specialities are the *papier mâché* Bharata Natayam dancing girl dolls which wobble and shake just like the real thing. For **Malay handicrafts** there's a handicraft centre in a reconstruction of a Malay kampung at Malay Village on Geylang Serai (east of the city).

● Sports

Bicycling: this is not a bicycle-friendly city. Bicycles are available for hire at a number of public parks. ***East Coast Bicycle Centre***, East Coast Parkway, bikes for rent – including tandems – (S$3/hour), open 0800-1830; ***Sentosa Island Bicycle Station***, near Ferry Terminal S$3/hour, Mon-Fri 0900-1800, Sat and Sun 0900-1900.

Bowling: most alleys charge from S$3.00-$4.00 a game; bowling after 1800 and on weekends is more expensive. Shoe hire, S$0.50. Some recommendations out of the 16 alleys in Singapore: ***Jackie's Bowl***, 542B East Coast Rd; ***Kallang Bowl***, 5 Stadium Walk; ***ODS Bowl***, 269 Pasir Panjang Rd; ***Orchard Bowl***, 8 Grange Rd; ***Plaza Bowl***, Textile Centre, Jl Sultan; ***Super Bowl***, 15 Marina Grove. Contact the ***Singapore Tenpin Bowling Congress***, T 3550136, for more information.

Canoeing: *Canoe Centre*, 1390 East Coast Parkway (just along the beach from the Lagoon Food Centre). Mon, Tues, Fri 1000-1800, Sun 0930-1830. Closed on public hols, S$15 for 2 hours. Also possible to hire canoes at the swimming lagoon on Sentosa Island and at Changi Point.

Flying: *Republic of Singapore Flying Club*, T 4810502, book 1 month in advance; S$300/hour.

Golf: there is no shortage of courses; they are beautifully kept and non-members can play at most of the private club courses on weekdays. Green fees are expensive and increase significantly at weekends. ***Changi Golf Club***, Nethavon Rd, 9-hole, par 68, green fees S$50, Mon pm-Fri, caddy S$14-19, T 5455133; ***Keppel Club***, Bukit Chermin. 18-hole, par 72, green fees: S$90 Mon-Fri, S$150 weekends, caddy S$18-25, T 2735522; ***Raffles Country Club***, Jl Ahmad Ibrahim, Tengah Reservoir, two 18-holers, par 71 and 69, green fees S$100 weekdays, S$160 weekends, T 8617655; ***Seletar Country Club***, Seletar Airbase, 9-hole, par 70, green fees, S$80 Tues-Fri only, caddy, S$15-20; ***Sembawang Country Club***, Sembawang Rd, 18-hole, par 70, green fees S$60 Mon-Fri, S$100 weekends, caddy S$18-24, T 2570642; ***Sentosa Golf Club***, Sentosa Island, 18-hole, par 72, green fees S$60 Mon-Fri, S$120 weekends;

Wondergolf on Sentosa provides a choice of courses for young and old, one 9-hole course and two 18-holes. Admission: S$8, S$4 for children, open 0900-2115 (last entry). Take monorail to station 4. ***Singapore Island Country Club***, Upper Thompson Rd, two 18-holers, both par 72, green fees S$130 Mon-Fri only, caddy S$18-21, T 4592222; ***Warren Golf Club***, Folkstone Rd, 9-hole, par 70, green fees S$50 Mon-Fri only, caddies compulsory, S$18-25, T 7776533.

Golf Driving ranges: *Green Fairways*, Fairways Drive, off Eng Neo Ave, S$3 for 48 balls. Open 0700-2200 Mon-Sun, T 4688409; ***Marina Bay Golf and Country Club***, 6 Marina Greens, 150 bays, 230m fairway, S$9 for 100 balls, open 0700-2300 Mon-Sun, T 2212811; ***Parkland***, 920 East Coast Parkway, 60 bays, 200m fairway, S$6 for 95 balls (S$5 weekdays before 1530), open 0700-2200 Mon-Sun, T 4406726.

Horse riding: *Polo Club*, 80 Mount Pleasant Rd, T 2564530 for details, courses Mon-Sun 0700-1000 and 1630-1900; ***Green Dale Riding School***, 0830-2130 daily, T 4602209.

Roller skating: *Sentosa Roller Skating*, Jelly Rd, Sentosa Island.

Sailing and windsurfing: *Changi Sailing Club*, Changi Village, for those interested in crewing yachts, the club has a noticeboard listing possibilities; ***East Coast Sailing Centre***, East Coast Park Swimming Lagoon, 1210 East Coast Parkway, T 4495118, 2-day courses in small craft: Lasers (S$270) and windsurfers (S$80), rental rates: Lasers and windsurfers, S$20/hour, barbecue restaurant.

Scuba diving: PADI have now opened an office in Singapore where you can get all the latest information on the best dive spots in the region and can also acquire certification, 39 Tampines St 92, #05-00 Form Building, T 7859896, F 7858168. Most diving schools will run courses (PADI and/or NAUI) and many offer rental of equipment and dive guides. ***Asia Aquatic***, T 5368116; ***Great Blue Dive Shop***, T 4670767; ***Mako Sub-Aquatics***, T 7741440; ***Marsden Bros*** T 7788287; ***Pro Diving Services***, T 2912261; ***Sentosa Sports Centre***, Eastern Lagoon, rents out diving gear and snorkels. Equipment hire and open water scuba diving instruction; ***Sentosa Water Sports Centre*** (Scuba Schools International), World Trade Centre.

Snooker: Singapore has several huge snooker halls, where dress code is casual-smart. Prices between S$5 and S$9/hour. ***Academy of Snooker***, Albert Complex, Albert St, T 2862879; ***King's Leisurium***, Marina Sq, T 3393811; ***King's Snookerium***, *Amara Hotel Shopping Complex*; ***Kings Snookerium***, Marina Sq, S$6.60-9.80/hour, open 1000-1400 Mon-Fri, 1000-1500 Sat-Sun.

Squash: ***200***, Yio Chu Kang Rd, S$6/hour. 0700-2300 Mon-Sun; ***National Stadium***, S$6/hour. 0700-2200.

Swimming: most of the big hotels have swimming pools, some of which are open to non-residents for a fee. ***River Valley Swimming Pool***, River Valley Rd, opposite Clarke Quay. Open Mon-Sun until 2200, admission $1, $1.20 at the weekends, enormous lengths pool and a children's pool, good place for the serious swimmer; ***Yan Kit Swimming Pool***, Yan Kit Rd, southern end of Chinatown, open Mon-Sun 0800-2130, admission $1, $1.20 at the weekends, probably the oldest public pool in Singapore but still popular and a good place to do lengths; ***Big Splash***, East Coast Parkway, wave pool, current pool and the longest water-slides in Southeast Asia, admission S$3, S$2 for children, open 1200-1800 Mon-Fri, 0900-1800 weekends; ***CN West Leisure Park***, 9 Japanese Garden Rd, wave pool and 15m-long water-slide, admission S$4, S$2 for children, open 1200-1800 Tues-Fri, 0930-1800 weekends. Singapore has 20 public swimming pools listed in the *Yellow Pages*.

Tennis: all charge about S$6-10/hour and are open 0700-2300 Mon-Sun. ***Burghley Squash and Tennis Centre***, 43 Burghley Drive; ***Clementi Recreation Centre***, 12 West Coast Walk; ***Dover Tennis Centre***, Dover Rd; ***Farrer Park Tennis Courts***, Rutland Rd; ***Kallang Tennis Centre***, Stadium Rd; ***Singapore Tennis Centre***, 1020 East Coast Parkway; ***St Wilfrid Squash and Tennis Centre***, St Wilfrid Rd.

Water skiing: *Bernatt Boating and Skiing*, T 2575859, S$80/hour; ***William Water Sports***, Ponggol Point, T 2826879, S$60-80/hour.

Spectator sports: see newspapers for listings. Most games of any significance take place on the Padang or the National Stadium which seats up to 60,000 and regularly stages Malaysia Cup football matches and the occasional exhibition match with touring league sides from abroad (buses 14 and 16 go direct from Orchard Rd).

Cricket: *Singapore Cricket Club*, Connaught Drive, most weekend afternoons.

Horse racing: at the *Singapore Turf Club*, Bukit Timah Rd, Malaysian racing is broadcast on huge 18x16m screens. No jeans, T-shirts, flip-flops etc, weekend only Admission S$5.

Polo matches: *Singapore Polo Club* on Thomson Rd, every Tues, Thur and Sat.

● Tour companies & travel agents

There are over 500 registered licenced travel agents in Singapore; the STPB publish a booklet listing them all, and we provide a few names in the section entitled Tours and Tour Operators, see page 676.

Tourist Information: the most convenient place to pick up leaflets on Singapore is at the STPB office on the 1st Flr of Raffles Shopping Arcade, best reached from Seah St (near the restaurant, Doc Cheng's), T 18003341335 (toll free), open 0830-2000 Mon-Sun. They are well informed and have all the publicity. The main tourist information office is at Tourism Court, on Orchard Spring Lane, at the west end of Orchard Rd, T 7366622, F 7369423, open 0830-1800 Mon-Sun.

Information for travellers

Before travelling	707	Getting around	717
Getting there	708	Communications	719
On arrival	711	Entertainment	721
Where to stay	713	Holidays and festivals	721
Food and drink	713	Further reading	724

BEFORE TRAVELLING

ENTRY REQUIREMENTS

● Visas

No visa is required for citizens of the Commonwealth, USA or Western Europe. On arrival in Singapore by air, citizens of these countries are granted a 1 month visitor's permit. Tourists entering Singapore via the causeway from Johor Bahru in Malaysia or by sea, are allowed to stay for 14 days. Nationals of most other countries (except India, China and the Commonwealth of Independent States) with confirmed onward reservations may stop over in Singapore for up to 14 days without a visa. It is necessary to keep the stub of your immigration card until you leave.

Visas can be extended for up to 3 months (although it's a time-consuming process) at the **Immigration Department**, 7th Flr, Pidemco Centre, 95 South Bridge Rd, Singapore 0105, T 5301814. Alternatively, it can be just as easy to nip across the causeway to Johor Bahru (in Malaysia) then re-enter Singapore on a 2 week permit.

Immigration Dept: Pidemco Building, South Bridge Rd, Chinatown.

● Vaccinations

A certificate of vaccination against cholera and yellow fever is necessary for those coming from endemic areas within the previous 6 days.

WHEN TO GO

● Best time to visit

There is no best season to visit Singapore. It gets even hotter and stickier before the monsoon breaks in November, and wetter (but cooler) in December and January.

HEALTH

● Vaccinations

None required for Singapore. Vaccination services are available at the *Tan Tock Seng Hospital*, Moulmein Rd, T 3595958 or 3595929 (telephone beforehand).

● Malaria

Malarial mosquitoes have long been banished from the island – although there are regular outbreaks of dengue (transmitted by the Aedes, or tiger, mosquito).

● Food and water

The water in Singapore, most of which is pumped across the causeway from Johor, but is treated in Singapore, is clean and safe to drink straight from the tap.

● Medical facilities

Singapore's medical facilities are amongst the best in the world. See the *Yellow Pages* for listing of public and private hospitals. Medical insurance is recommended. Hospitals are experienced in dealing with obscure tropical diseases and serious cases are flown here from all over the region. Most big hotels have their own doctor on 24 hours call. Other doctors are listed under 'Medical Practitioners' in the *Yellow Pages*, or a medical centre in the building. Pharmaceuticals are readily available over the counter. The ***Singapore Medical Centre***, on the 6th Flr of Tanglin Shopping Centre houses a large community of specialist doctors. Local **Chinese cures** can be found in traditional clinics in Chinatown where there are medical halls and acupuncture centres. Acupuncturists and herbalists are listed in the Yellow Pages.

MONEY

● Currency

Local currency is dollars and cents. Bank notes are available in denominations of S$2, 5, 10, 20, 50, 100, 500, 1,000 and 10,000. Coins are in 1, 5, 10, 20 and 50 cent and 1 dollar denominations. During 1997 the S$ weakened against the US$. In December 1997, the Singapore dollar was valued at 1.63 to the US dollar. Brunei currency is interchangeable with Singapore currency; the Malaysian Ringgit is not.

It is possible to change money at banks, licenced money changers and hotels – although they sometimes add on a service charge. Licenced money-changers often give a better rates than banks, but it is worth shopping around. Passports are required for cashing TCs or getting cash-advances on credit cards. Singapore is one of the major banking centres of Southeast Asia so it is relatively easy to get money wired from home. Bank opening hours: 1000-1500 Mon-Fri, 1100-1300 Sat. There is no black market.

● Credit cards

Most of Singapore's hotels, shops, restaurants and banks accept the big international credit cards, and many cash machines allow you to draw cash on Visa or Mastercard. After bargaining, expect to pay at least 3% for credit card transactions; most shops insist on this surcharge although you do not have to pay it. **Notification of credit card loss**: American Express, T 2358133; Diners Card, T 2944222.

● ATMs

It is possible to withdraw money from Automatic Teller Machines if your credit card has a PIN or Personal Identification Number.

● Goods and Services Tax refund

In 1994 a 3% tax was levied on most goods and services. Shops displaying a 'Tax Refund' sign will give all qualifying visitors a refund on goods being taken out of the Republic. The Singapore Tourist Promotion Board publishes a brochure, *Tax refund for visitors to Singapore*.

GETTING THERE

AIR

As an international crossroads, Singapore is within easy reach of all key points in the region and there are flights from Changi (Singapore's airport) to destinations throughout Southeast Asia. Over 70 airlines service Singapore flying to 131 cities in 56 countries. In 1995 there were 156,334 aircraft movements – or over 400 a day – and Changi processed over 23 million passengers, nearly eight times Singapore's population. Because of the number of carriers serving Singapore, it is easy to buy a ticket out. Long-haul prices are not as competitive as London bucket shops, although they undercut some other Asian capitals. Tickets to Southeast Asian destinations are subject to minimum selling price restrictions imposed by a cartel of regional airlines. It is still possible to get special deals to selected destinations from the discount travel agents (see page 720 and Singapore *Yellow Pages*) but tickets bought in Bangkok and Penang are now a bit cheaper.

The **Singapore-Kuala Lumpur** air shuttle (operated jointly by SIA and MAS) runs every 50 minutes from Changi Terminal 1. Singapore-KL shuttle tickets can be bought on a first-come-first-served basis at Changi Airport for S$147. For timetables, call SIA on T 2238888 or MAS on T 3366777. For return flights to Kuala Lumpur, just buy a single ticket. It costs S$132, while the Kuala Lumpur-Singapore leg costs M$132. Agents do not differentiate between the two currencies.

Long haul flights from Kuala Lumpur, particularly on MAS, can be considerably cheaper than outbound flights from Singapore. It is also much cheaper when flying between Singapore and other points in Malaysia to use Johor Bahru's airport across the causeway. Johor Bahru is well connected to the Malaysian domestic network. Chartered express coaches ply between Singapore and JB airport; they leave Singapore from the *Novotel Orchid Inn* on Dunearn Rd and cost S$10 one way. The courier ensures express clearance of Malaysian customs and immigration. Details from MAS office in Singapore: 190 Clemenceau Ave, T 3366777.

● From Australasia

Flights from Sydney, Perth and Melbourne (4-8 hours) with Qantas, Singapore Airlines, JAT and British Airways. From Auckland, Air New Zealand (approx 10½ hours) and Singapore Airlines.

● From Europe

Approximate time from London to Singapore (non-stop): 13 hours. From London Heathrow Singapore Airlines, British Airways and Qantas have flights. From Amsterdam Singapore Airlines, KLM and Garuda Indonesia. From Frankfurt Singapore Airlines, Lufthansa and Garuda

Indonesia. You can fly from Zurich with Singapore Airlines and Swissair. From Paris Singapore Airlines, Air France and Garuda. Singapore Airlines, Qantas and Alitalia all serve Rome. Singapore also flies from Athens. Olympic Airways also leave from Athens. From Moscow Aeroflot. There are also flights to Singapore from Helsinki on Finnair.

● From the Far East

Singapore Airlines, Japan Air Lines, United and Northwest Airlines have flights from Tokyo. From Hong Kong Singapore Airlines, Cathay Pacific, China Airlines, Qantas and United Airlines. Singapore Airlines and Philippine Airlines fly from Manila.

● From the Middle East

You can fly from Bahrain with Gulf Air. Singapore Airlines and Egypt Air flies from Cairo. From Dubai, Royal Brunei, Singapore Airlines and Emirates.

● From South Asia

Singapore Airlines, Aeroflot and Air India fly from Delhi. Both Air Lanka, Emirates and Singapore Airlines have flights from Colombo. You can fly from Dhaka with Biman Bangladesh Airlines or Singapore Airlines. PIA and Singapore Airlines flies from Karachi. Singapore Airlines has flights from Male and Kathmandu. Emirates also serve Male and Royal Nepal Airlines leave from Kathmandu.

● From the USA and Canada

Approx time from LAX (Los Angeles): 22 hours. Singapore Airlines and United Airlines have flights from Los Angeles and San Francisco. Travel via Los Angeles from New York. Singapore Airlines has flights from Vancouver.

TRAIN

The railway station is on Keppel Rd, T 2225165. Singapore is the last port of call for the Malaysian railway system (Keretapi Tanah Melayu – KTM). The cavernous, domed station – apparently inspired by Helsinki's – opened in 1932 and was renovated in 1990. Malaysian immigration and customs clearance for inbound and outbound passengers is taken care of in the Singapore station (sometimes with the help of sniffer dogs). **Transport to town**: from the station, buses 100, 107 and 87 go to Beach Rd and 148 to Serangoon Rd.

There are two main lines connecting Singapore and Malaysia: one up the west coast to KL and Butterworth and on to Thailand and another line which goes through the centre of Peninsular Malaysia and on to Kota Bahru on the northeast coast. Some travellers use the train to go to Johor Bahru to avoid the long wait going through customs at the border (S$1.50). There are four fully air-conditioned express trains daily between Singapore and Malaysia: Kuala Lumpur, 5-7 hours (S$40-120), Butterworth, opposite Penang, 13 hours (S$29.20-118.50). Departure times: 0730 to Butterworth and 1430, 2110, 2210 to Kuala Lumpur. The overnight sleeper arrives in Kuala Lumpur at 0655. There are also express trains 3 times a week to/from Bangkok crossing the Malaysian/Thai border at Padang Besar (S$91.70, 2nd class) (see page 205). There are cheaper, but slower, mail trains which stop at every station en route. Trains are clean and efficient and overnight trains have cabins in first class, sleeping berths in second class and restaurants.

Orient-Express Hotels, which operates the Venice Simplon Orient-Express runs the new luxury *Eastern & Oriental Express*, making three return trips every 2 weeks between Singapore, Kuala Lumpur and Bangkok. The journey takes 41 hours (2 nights, 1 day) to cover the 2,000 km one-way trip. Passengers will be able to disembark at Kuala Lumpur, Butterworth (Penang), and Hua Hin. A single fare from Singapore to Bangkok starts from US$1150pp in a shared cabin; departs Singapore 1445 and arrives Bangkok 0920 Tues. Reservations can be made at Orient-Express Hotels, Sea Containers House, 20 Upper Ground, London SE1 9PF, UK T (071) 928 6000; *Orient-Express Hotels* also has agents in Singapore, Kuala Lumpur and Bangkok to handle reservations – in Singapore contact: 90 Cecil St 14-03, Carlton Building, T 2272068; in Kuala Lumpur T 232 9615; and in Bangkok T 251 4862.

ROAD

The new Express Highway into Malaysia makes for a more efficient bus service and faster travel. Beware of traffic police, who clamp down on speeding vehicles. Long distance **buses** to and from **Malaysia** operate out of the terminal at the junction of Lavender St and Kallang Bahru. There are connections every few minutes to Johor Bahru. Bus 170 goes to Woodlands immigration point and across the causeway to Johor Bahru bus station; leaves every 15 minutes from Queen St or Bukit Timah Rd. Most travel agents sell bus tickets to Malaysia: KL (S$17), Melaka (S$11), Butterworth (S$30), Mersing (S$11), Kota Bahru (S$30). **Buses to Thailand** leave from the Golden Mile Complex on Beach

Rd: Hat Yai (S$35, S$45 for VIP coach), Bangkok (S$55). There are several agents selling tickets close to the station. Buses to **Johor Bahru** leave from the Ban San Terminal at the junction of Arab and Queen streets (79c). Long distance bus companies: *A&S Bus Services* T 2816161, *WTS* T3370337, *TransIsland* T 4823888, SBS T 2848866.

Car rental: **Avis**, Cuscaden Rd, Suntec City and Changi Terminals 1 and 2, T 1800 7379477; **Hertz**, Ngee Ann City Tower B and Changi Airport, T 1800 8393388; **Budget**, 24 Raffles Place, Clifford Centre, T 5324442.

Long distance **taxis** to Malaysia leave from the Rochor Rd terminus. Taxis go as far as Johor Bahru ($7), from here there are Malaysian taxis onto Melaka (M$80), Kuantan (M$120-150), KL (M$100), Butterworth (M$180-200).

BOAT

A small fraction of Singapore's visitors arrive in the world's busiest port by ship – although cruising has become fashionable again and sea arrivals are growing by nearly 50% a year. Passenger lines serve Singapore from Australia, Europe, USA, India and Hong Kong. Ships either dock at the World Trade Centre or anchor in the main harbour with a launch service to shore. Entry formalities as above. **Star Cruises** are one of the biggest companies operating in the region, T 7336988, F 7333622. **Orient Lines, Pearl Cruises, Seabourn Cruise Lines, Silversea Cruises, Seven Seas Cruise Lines** also dock at Singapore.

It is possible to travel by sea between Singapore and Indonesia via the Riau Archipelago .

It is also possible to take a high-speed catamaran from Tanah Merah to Pulau Tioman, off the east coast of Peninsular Malaysia (see page 268), 4½ hours (S$120 return). Ferry operators have their offices at the World Trade Centre.

It is possible to enter Singapore from Malaysia by fishing boat from Johor Bahru (S$5), Tanjung Pengileh or Tanjung Surat (S$6) in southern Johor to Changi Point, on the northeast tip of Singapore – a good way of beating the bottleneck at the causeway. First boat 0700, last at 1600. Boats depart as soon as they have a full complement of 12 passengers. There is also a ferry from Changi to Tanjung Belungkor, east of JB. Passengers, S$15; cars S$20; journey time 45 minutes. Ferry times 0900, 1200, 1615 Singapore to Tanjung Belungkur; 1030, 1330 and 1745, Tanjung Belungkor to Singapore.

A timetable of all shipping arrivals and departures is published daily in the *Shipping Times* (a section of the *Business Times*). According to some travellers freighter operators are reasonably amenable to marine hitchers who want lifts to Vietnam (although it is difficult to enter Vietnam by sea), the Philippines or Indonesia. Some passenger-carrying cargo ships are booked-out well in advance, but fare-paying travellers can expect high standards, usually including comfortable single or double cabins. Passengers often eat at the Captain's table and the ships are usually well equipped with leisure facilities. Those who have travelled by freighter say the experience is unbeatable. The Australian publication *Slow Boats Freighter Travel News* (Sydney International Travel Centre, 8/F, 75 King St, Sydney, NSW 2000, Australia) lists worldwide freighter-passenger services for subscribers.

CUSTOMS

Singapore is a free port.

● Currency

There is no limit to the amount of Singapore and foreign currency or TCs you can bring in or take out.

● Duty free allowance

1 litre of liquor.

● Export restrictions

There is no export duty but export permits are required for arms, ammunition, explosives, animals, gold, platinum, precious stones and jewellery, poisons and drugs. No permit is needed for the export of antiques.

● Prohibited items

Narcotics are strictly forbidden in Singapore and, as in neighbouring Malaysia, trafficking is a capital offence which is rigorously enforced. Dawn hangings at Changi prison are regularly reported. Trafficking in more than 30g of morphine and 15g of heroin or cocaine is punishable by death. Anyone trafficking in more than 10 kg of cannabis faces 20-30 years in Changi and 15 strokes of the rotan, a punishment devised by the British colonial administration. Passengers arriving from Malaysia by rail have to march, single-file past sniffer dogs.

NB Tobacco products, including cigarettes and cigars are dutiable goods in Singapore.

In 1992, the Singapore Government banned the importation and sale of chewing gum, after the MRT Corporation claimed the substance threatened the efficient running of its underground trains. Cleaners complained about gum stuck under seats, and drivers cited incidents of train doors being gummed up. Officially, therefore, any person travelling to Singapore is prohibited from bringing gum into the country, even if it is intended for personal use.

ON ARRIVAL

Airport information

Almost all visitors arrive at Singapore's Changi Airport. The old British military base at Seletar is used for small plane arrivals and departures, notably flights from/to Pulau Tioman, off the east coast of Malaysia (see below for details).

Changi airport is at the extreme eastern tip of the island, about 20 km from town. Facilities are excellent and include banks, hotel reservation and Singapore Tourist Promotion Board desks, a medical centre, business centre, children's discovery corner, internet centre (open 24 hours) for addicted surfers, day rooms, restaurants, left-luggage facilities, mail and telecommunications desks, shopping arcades, supermarkets, sports facilities and accommodation which are all open from 0700-2300. Changi has been voted the world's leading or favourite airport by *Business Traveller International* (USA), *Business Traveller* (UK), *PATA Travel News* (Pacific), and many other publications. Everything is clearly signposted in English and the two terminals are connected by a monorail. A third terminal is already planned – the intention being that it will be completed before terminal 2 has reached capacity. **Computerised flight information**, T 5424422 for all arrivals and departures (give flight number). If flight number is not known, T 5426988. There is an excellent canteen/food centre in Terminal 2, which you reach via the multi-deck car park, recommended. An 'information pack' is available just after Immigration, near the Customs Hall.

Free city tours for transit passengers: for those who are here in transit and want a snifter of what Singapore has to offer, the Singapore Tourist Promotion Board has begun offering Free City Tours – the 'Heartlands of New Asia-Singapore' tour and the 'Spirit of New Asia-Singapore' tour. They are run on a first come, first served basis, but for those with time on their hands and who do not want to bankrupt themselves wandering the shops of Changi they offer an excellent interlude. Passengers need to show their boarding pass and are then ushered through immigration to a waiting bus. Passports are kept by the officials until they return – and there's no need even to pay the airport departure tax. The tours themselves are rather banal – 'Singapore is a nice place full of happy and smiling people' – but it is a great idea and works without a hitch, as one might expect. The logic, presumably, is that having seen what the pristine city state has to offer, next time they pass through Changi the transit passengers will stop over for a night or two. For more details and to book yourself onto a tour visit one of the Free City Tour desks on arrival.

Accommodation at Changi: **A+** *Le Meridien Changi*, 1 Netheravon Rd, T 5427700, F 5425295. Very well run, first class hotel, situated on Changi Beach, just north of the airport. Recommended for efficiency. **A** *Transit Hotel 1*, level 3 Changi Airport Terminal 1, T 5430911, F 5458365. Short term rate quoted (6 hours). A good place to take a break if you are stuck at Changi for an extended period. **B** *Transit Hotel 2*, departure/transit lounge south, Terminal 2 T 5428122, F 5426122, airport@pacific.net.sg, excellent hotel on the airport property, with short stay facility (price quoted is for 6 hours). Booking recommended as it is so popular. Business centre. They also provide a 'freshen up' service – use of showers, sauna and gym from $5.

Transport to town Hotels will only meet guests with a previous arrangement; some charge but others offer the service free. The car pick up area is outside the arrivals halls of both terminals. **Bus**: the most convenient bus is the 'airbus'. There are three services which connect Changi with most of the major hotels. Buses run every 20 minutes from 0620-2300 to the airport and from 0700-1200 from the airport to the city, S$5, S$3 for children. The special feature of the airbus is that it 'kneels', allowing elderly people, or those carrying heavy bags, easier access in the door. Tickets available from the driver (exact change in S$ only) or in the arrivals area of the airport; an efficient, comfortable service, T 5421721 for information. A number of buses run between the airport and nearby bus interchanges. Bus 16 into the city takes less than 1 hour and costs S$1.40. It is easy to catch from Orchard Rd. 16E (express) is faster but only operates for 3 hours in the morning (from city to airport) and from 1800-2100 from airport to city. Bus 24 goes to Orchard Rd (and the main hotel area) (S$1.20); exact fare needed. **Car rental**: Avis and **Hertz** desks are in the arrivals hall (close 1800). **Taxi**: taxis queue up outside the arrival halls. They are metered plus there is an airport surcharge of S$3.

Seletar Airport is a military airport – which opened as Singapore first civil airfield in 1928 – which is also used for connections with Pulau Tioman off Malaysia's east coast and for some charter flights. Although the authorities do not allow photographs on the tarmac, checking-in is all very relaxed and informal – very different from the rather brusque efficiency of Changi. Seletar was used by th British military in Singapore before they withdrew from East of Suez. The base was taken over by the Singapore Defence Force but the road names have been kept: Oxford St, Edgware Rd, Sussex Gardens and the like. **Transport to town from Seletar**: there are no public buses to Seletar, although one does run to the military base, shuttle buses are available from there to the commercial terminal. Most people take taxis, and as at Changi there is a S$3 surcharge. When a scheduled flight is arriving from Tioman the airline usually calls so that the required number of taxis are waiting.

● Airport tax

Payable on departure – S$15 for all flights to all countries. A PSC (Passenger Service Charge) coupon can be purchased at most hotels, travel agencies and airline offices in town before departure, which will save time at the airport.

● Clothing

Singapore is smart but casual dress-wise. It is rare to find places insisting on jacket and tie – although jeans and T-shirts are taboo at some nightclubs. Flip-flops, singlets and denim cut-offs look out of place in Singapore, where the locals treat Orchard Rd like the national catwalk.

● Conduct

Private homes Most Singaporeans remove their shoes at the door – more to keep their homes clean than out of any deep religious conviction. No host would insist his visitors do so, but it is the polite way to enter a home.

Eating Chinese meals are eaten with chopsticks and Malays and Indians traditionally eat with their right hands. It is just as acceptable, however, to eat with spoons and forks. In Malay and Indian company, do not use the left hand for eating.

Religion Make sure shoulders and legs are covered when entering a mosque and always take your shoes off. It is also necessary to remove shoes before entering Indian temples and many Chinese ones.

● Emergencies

Police: T 999. **Ambulance/Fire brigade**: T 995.

● Hours of business

Banks: normal banking hours are from 1000-1500 Mon-Fri, 1100-1300 Sat. Most banks handle TCs and currency exchange. Some, however, do not offer foreign exchange dealings on Sats. **Shops**: most shops in the tourist belt open around 0930-2100. In the Orchard and Scotts roads area, Sun is a normal working day.

● Official time

8 hours ahead of GMT.

● Prohibited in Singapore

The old joke is that Singapore is a 'fine' place to live; you get a fine for smoking, spitting, breeding mosquitoes, not flushing the toilet and road hogging. From time to time Singapore, which is totally dependent for its water supplies from Malaysia, tries to 'conserve water'. At such times, stickers appear in toilets saying conserve water. These are plastered next to the stickers reading "Penalty for not flushing $500". Much worse is the fate awaiting people who urinate in lifts and are stupid enough to get caught: they have their pictures printed on the front of the next day's *Straits Times*. In January 1991 chewing gum was prohibited. *The Economist* noted: "The nanny of Southeast Asia has swooped again." Chewing gum was said to be a "perennial nuisance", jamming doors in the MRT and glueing pedestrians to the pavement. Wrigley's traffickers now face a year's jail or a fine of up to S$6,200. The fact that you can now buy T-shirts ridiculing all this might suggest that things have eased up a bit. But in Singapore, it is never wise to jump to hasty conclusions. In 1993, the government managed to shock many Singaporeans with a new, vindictive campaign which commentators compared with China's Cultural Revolution. Litterbugs were forced to wear fluorescent vests and pick up rubbish in the full glare of TV lights and in front of jeering onlookers. They had added humiliation heaped on them on the front page of *The Straits Times*, whose editor was unapologetic. Some of his journalists disagreed with him in the paper's pages, government MPs spoke out and concerned citizens phoned in complaints. The story has a 2-pronged moral: (1) Singapore has still not outgrown its toytown mentality, and (2) unless you are a self-publicist, it is inadvisable to drop litter.

In 1997 the government once more tried to polish Singapore's rather tarnished reputation for spontaneity: busking was de-prohibited after a 2-year ban. But this was undermined by the regulations that any prospective busker has to negotiate before s/he can busk without fear of summary arrest. 1. Any busker must first obtain a licence. 2. To obtain a licence s/he must be a member of a government approved arts group. 3. The busker must convince a committee of their artistic merit. 4. Having jumped through these hoops, the licence awarded stipulates where a busker can work and during what hours. 5. While busking, the busker must not involve the public or perform in a busy area. 6. Before they begin they must obtain the permission from local shopkeepers and the police. 7. All money earned must be donated to charity, although expenses can be subtracted. 8. Foreigners are forbidden from busking.

There are several rules and regulations visitors should note: **Drugs**: see page 710 for details. **Smoking**: is discouraged and prohibited by law in many public places – such as buses, cinemas, theatres, libraries and department stores – and all air-conditioned restaurants. You can be fined up to S$500 for lighting up in prohibited places. Many hotels now provide non-smoking floors. **Litter**: Littering means a fine of up to S$1,000. **Jaywalking**: although less rigorously enforced than it used to be, crossing the road where you're not meant to – ie within 50m of a pedestrian crossing, bridge or underpass – could cost S$500.

● Safety

Singapore is probably the safest big city in Southeast Asia – women travelling alone need have few worries. It is wise, however to take the normal precautions and not wander into lonely places after dark.

● Shopping

See page 698 for details.

● Tipping

Tipping is unusual in Singapore. In cheaper restaurants it is not expected, although in more upmarket places when a service charge is not automatically added to the bill, a tip is usual. Most international hotels and restaurants however add 10% service charge and 4% government tax to bills. An additional tip is not expected in such instances. In general, only tip for special personal service such as porters.

● Voltage

220-240 volts, 50 cycle AC, most hotels can supply adaptors.

● Weights and measures

Metric.

WHERE TO STAY

At the end of 1996 Singapore had almost 100 gazetted hotels (approved by STPB) with 29,824 rooms. There are scores more that are not gazetted. Many of the excellent international class hotels are concentrated in the main shopping and business areas, including Orchard and Scotts roads, and near Raffles City and the Marina complexes. They are all run to a very high standard and room rates range between S$250 and S$550 – although discounts are almost always on offer and few people pay the full rack rate. Enquire at the airport hotel desk on arrival whether there are any special offers. It is advisable to book in advance. After a room glut in the early 1980s, Singapore's hotel industry is now suffering a room shortage and when a large convention or two hits town, rooms can be hard to find.

Singapore offers an excellent choice of hotels in our upper categories – from luxury to tourist class. Though rooms may be more expensive than equivalent classes of hotels elsewhere in the region, they try to make up for this in terms of service. It is rare to stay in a hotel which does not offer attentive and professional care. Budget hotels are thin on the ground and expensive and budget travellers find that money which may last a week in neighbouring Indonesia or Malaysia disappears in a day or two. However there are a few cheaper places to stay.

Taxes: of 10% (government) plus 3% (goods) plus 1% (services) are added to bills in all but the cheapest of hotels.

FOOD AND DRINK

● Food

Eating is the national pastime in Singapore and has acquired the status of a refined art. The island is a tropical paradise for epicureans of every persuasion and budget. While every country in the region boasts national dishes, none offers such a delectably wide variety as Singapore. Fish-head curry must surely qualify as *the* national dish but you can sample 10 Chinese cuisines, North and South Indian, Malay and Nonya (Straits Chinese) food, plus Indonesian, Vietnamese, Thai, Japanese, Korean, French, Italian (and other European), Russian, Mexican, Polynesian, and Scottish. There's a very respectable selection of western food at the top end of the market, a few good places in the middle bracket and swelling ranks of cheaper fastfood restaurants like *Kentucky Fried Chicken* and *McDonalds'*, not to mention a smattering of

Hotel prices and facilities

L+ (S$400+) and **L** (S$300-400) Singapore has some of the very best hotels in the world. These offer unrivalled personal service, sumptuous extras, luxury rooms and bathrooms, and just about every amenity that you can think of. Most of the top hotels now provide two in-room phone lines (for modems and calls), 24-hour business facilities, several pools, jacuzzis, health spas, tennis courts, numerous restaurants, and much else besides.

A+ (S$200-300) Most of the middle to upper range hotels in this category will provide a business centre (although it is worth checking whether these operate around the clock). Coupled with this, there will be an executive floor or two, with a lounge for private breakfast and evening cocktails, or for entertaining clients. Most of these hotels will provide a personal safe in each room. There will be a fitness centre and swimming pool and they may have a health centre as well as several restaurants.

A (S$150-200) and **B** (S$100-150) Hotels in this category will range from very comfortable to functional. Rooms in the 'A' category will have most extras – like a minibar, television, and tea and coffee making facilities. They may also have a swimming pool but it is likely to be small. They will have a coffee shop and perhaps a restaurant. Rooms in the 'B' category may be lacking some, or most, of these amenities but should still be clean and serviceable.

C (S$50-100) There are not many hotels in this category in Singapore. Rooms may be air-conditioned with a hot water shower attached; there might also be a coffee shop. These are no-frills, functional affairs. Although there are some bargains to be had, there are also hotels which are pretty sordid.

D (S$25-50) and **E** (S$ less than 25) Hotels and guesthouses in these two categories (and there aren't many) are mostly pretty squalid places, with shared bathroom facilities and box-like rooms. There are a few that are clean and perfectly adequate, and these are the registered establishments. The places on third or fourth floors of apartment buildings usually have no licence and they are often the dirtiest and least well run. Most of these places provide a basic breakfast in the price of a toom.

Burger Kings and *A&Ws* and an explosion of pizza outlets. For young, trendy Singaporeans, the favoured spots are now the numerous 'coffee bars' that have opened. *Delifrance*, *Spinelli's* and *Starbuck's* are all doing a roaring trade.

There are so many excellent restaurants in Singapore that everyone has their own recommendations – there is rarely agreement on 'the best'. New restaurants open every other day and in this gourmet paradise chefs are eminently poachable. In recent years there has been a gluttonous trend towards value-for-money, where quantity rules and patrons are encouraged to cram their plates. Hotel buffets compete to offer the biggest and cheapest spread of sumptuous savouries, salads and sweets: ads in *The Straits Times* announce the latest offers and the tourist magazine *This Week*, also notes all on-going food promotions in its *This Week* section. Typical 'teas' include everything from dim sum to Black Forest Gateaux

Do not be put off by characterless, brightly lit restaurants in Singapore: the food can be superb. Eating spots range from high-rise revolving restaurants to neon-lit pavement seafood extravaganzas. A delicious dinner can cost as little as S$3 or more than S$100 – and the two may be just yards away from each other. For example, it is possible to have a small beer in one of the bars of the *Raffles Hotel* for S$8 or more and then stagger 10m across the road and indulge in a huge plate of curry and rice for S$2. And in Singapore, because of its rigorously enforced hygiene standards, it is possible to eat just about anywhere. For a listing of over 100 restaurants, *Singapore's Best Restaurants* might be worth purchasing; it gives a description of the food and a price guideline and is available from most bookstores for $10.30. It is updated annually. The *Secret Food Map* (available at most bookstores – S$5) is a good buy.

Durians One local favourite, is durian fruit (see page 740). During the Malaysian and South Thai *montong* durian seasons (June/July and November/December), fleets of trucks ferry durians over the causeway; about 8 million are sold in Singapore each year. The roadside market on the junction of Albert and Waterloo streets is probably the best durian centre, but Smith St (Chinatown), Lavender St and Geylang Serai market are also well known by durian-lovers. An average-sized durian costs around S$10, big Thai ones command more than S$100, expect to bargain.

Hawker centres and **Food Courts** The government might have cleared hawkers off the streets, but there are plenty of hawker centres in modern Singapore.(Food Courts have become the modern, air-conditioned, sanitized version of hawker centres). They provide the local equivalent of café culture and the human equivalent of grazing. Large numbers of stalls are packed together under one roof – and for Food Courts they are usually in the basement of a shopping plaza. The seats and tableware may be basic (hygiene regulations demand plastic cutlery and polystyrene plates), but the food is always fresh and diners are spoilt for choice. Customers claim themselves a table, then graze their way down the rows of Chinese, Malay and Indian stalls. It is not necessary to eat from the stall you are sitting next to. Vendors will deliver to your table when the food's ready and payment is on receipt. The food is cheap and prices are non-negotiable.

Coffee shops Mainly family concerns, Singaporean coffee shops or *kopi tiam* are located in the older part of the city, usually in old Chinese shophouses. They serve breakfast, lunch and dinner, as well as beer, at prices only marginally higher than those at hawker centres.

Chinese cuisines Each province of China has its own distinct cuisine. A balanced meal should contain the five basic taste sensations: sweet, bitter, salty, spicy and acidic to balance the yin and yang.

Cantonese – light and delicately-flavoured dishes are often steamed with ginger and are not very spicy. Shark's fin and birds' nest soups, *dim sum* (mostly steamed delicacies trollied to your table, but only served until early afternoon) are Cantonese classics. Other typical dishes include fish steamed with soya sauce, ginger, chicken stock and wine, wan ton soup, blanched green vegetables in oyster sauce and suckling pig.

Hainanese – simple cuisine from the southern island of Hainan; chicken rice with sesame oil, soy sauce and a chilli and garlic sauce is their tastiest contribution.

Hakka – uses plenty of sweet potato and dried shrimp and specializes in stewed pigs' trotters, *yong tau foo* (deep fried bean curd), and chillis and other vegetables stuffed with fish paste.

Hokkien – being one of Singapore's biggest dialect groups means Hokkien cuisine is prominent, particularly in hawker centres, although there are very few Hokkien restaurants. Hokkien Chinese invented the spring roll and their cooking uses lots of noodles and in one or two places you can still see them being made by hand. Hokkien cuisine is also characterized by clear soups and steamed seafood, eaten with soya sauce. Fried Hokkien *mee* (yellow wheat noodles stir-fried with seafood and pork), *hay cho* (deep fried balls of prawn) and *bee hoon* (rice vermicelli cooked with prawns, squid and beansprouts with lime and chillies) are specialities.

Hunanese – known for its glutinous rice, honeyed ham and pigeon soup.

Peking (Beijing) – chefs at the imperial court in Peking had a repertoire of over 8,000 recipes. Dumplings, noodles and steamed buns predominate since wheat is the staple diet, but in Singapore, rice may accompany the meal. *Peking duck* (the skin is basted with syrup and cooked until crisp), *shi choy* (deep fried bamboo shoots), hot and sour soup are among the best Peking dishes. *Crispy Peking duck* is another typical dish; it is usually eaten rolled into a pancake and accompanied by *hoisin* sauce and spring onions. Fish dishes are usually deep-fried and served with sweet and sour sauce.

Shanghainese – seafood dominates this cuisine and many dishes are cooked in soya sauce. Braised fish-heads, braised abalone (a shellfish) in sesame sauce and crab and sweetcorn soup are typical dishes. Wine is often used in the preparation of meat dishes – hence drunken prawn and drunken crab.

Steamboat – the Chinese answer to fondue – is a popular dish in Singapore and can be found in numerous restaurants and at some hawker centres. Thinly sliced pieces of raw meat, fish,

Restaurant prices

Prices:

♦♦♦♦++	S$30+	Hotel restaurants and exclusive restaurants
♦♦♦-♦♦♦♦+	S$15-25	Upmarket restaurants
♦♦-♦♦♦	S$6-15	Chinese coffee shops
♦-♦♦	<S$6	Hawker centres

prawns, cuttlefish, fishballs and vegetables are gradually tossed into a bubbling cauldron in the centre of the table, then dunked into hot chilli and soya sauces. The resulting soup provides a flavoursome broth to wash it all down at the end.

Szechuan – very spicy (garlic and chilli are dominant) is widely considered the tastiest Chinese cuisine. Szechuan food includes heaps of hot red peppers – traditionally considered to be protection against cold and disease. Among the best Szechuan dishes are: smoked duck in tea leaves and camphor sawdust, minced pork with bean curd, steamed chicken in lotus leaves, fried eels in garlic sauce.

Teochew – famous for its *muay* porridges – a light, clear broth consumed with side dishes of crayfish, salted eggs and vegetables.

Indian There is probably as wide a selection of Indian edibles in Singapore as there is on the entire Indian sub-continent – from scorching-hot Madrasi curries to the mild, creamy kormas of the north. There is also the Indian Muslim food that is special to Singapore and Malaysia – *prata kosong* (*roti prata*, the skillfully stretched Indian dough-bread, fried and served with a thin curry sauce) and fish-head curry (do not be put off by the idea: the tenderest, most succulent flesh is on and around the head) are both local specialities. Other typical Indian dishes include *murtabak* (*paratha* filled with meat, onion and egg), southern Indian vegetarian food such as *masala dosa* (Indian pancake) and *thali* (several curries eaten with rice and served on a banana leaf).

Malay In Singapore Malay cooking is overshadowed by the Chinese gastronomic array, and because Malay curries take much longer to prepare, they do not lend themselves so easily to instant hawker food. But Malay hawkers' trump card is satay. Islam bans the use of pork (Chinese hawkers have a monopoly in pork satay) and Malay stalls and restaurants rarely serve alcohol. Coconut milk and flesh, *belacan* (pungent dried shrimp paste) and fresh chillies are vital ingredients. There are a handful of upmarket Malay restaurants but *makanan Melayu* is mostly found in hawker centres. *Roti John* (a French loaf, sliced open and fried with mutton, egg and onion) is the Malay interpretation of a European breakfast. For other Malay dishes, see page 508.

New Asia, trans-ethnic or 'fusion' cuisine This is a blending of cuisines and ingredients from East and West. So far the foodies have not agreed on a single name. It is sometimes termed 'Fusion' cuisine, sometimes Trans-ethnic, and sometimes New Asia. Perhaps this confusion over what to call the food is because people don't seem to be able to agree what constitutes the cuisine(s) in the first place. Some chefs and food critics maintain that it involves cooking Eastern ingredients using Western cooking techniques. Others see it as a combination of two styles of cooking and two sets of ingredients – a sort of 'East meets West'. One chef believes you should be able to drink wine with New Asia cuisine – something that you cannot do with Chinese food, as soy sauce kills the taste of wine. But like most things, you'll know it when you see it – though so far they don't seem to have chanced upon that gastronomic winner: black pudding and chillis in a leek and durian coulis.

Nonya *(Peranakan)* The cuisine of the Straits Chinese blends tastes from China and the Malay peninsula. Coconut, candlenut, turmeric and lemon grass are essential ingredients. *Poh piah* (savoury spring rolls filled with shredded turnip and bamboo shoots, beancurd, prawns and pork), and *otak-otak* (coconut milk with spices, prawns and fish, wrapped in a banana leaf) are typical Nonya dishes. Nonya desserts and snacks, many based on rice and coconut, are if anything more popular than the rest of the cuisine.

Seafood Singapore offers a vast variety of seafood. There are specialist seafood centres in which to sample fish from all cuisines. Chilli or pepper crabs, 'drunken' prawns (cooked in rice wine) and deep-fried squid (*sotong*) dishes are Singaporean favourites.

● Drink

Every hawker centre has at least a couple of stalls selling fresh fruit juice – a more wholesome alternative to the ubiquitous bottles of fizzy drink. A big pineapple or papaya juice costs S$2. You can choose any combination of fruits to go in your fruit punch. Freshly squeezed fruit juices are widely available at stalls and in restaurants. Fresh lime juice is served in most restaurants, and is a perfect complement to the banana-leaf curry, tandoori and dosai. Carbonated soft drinks, cartons of fruit juice and air-flown fresh milk can be found in supermarkets. For local flavour, the Malay favourite is *bandung* (a sickly-sweet, bright pink concoction of rose essence and condensed milk), found in most hawker centres, as well as the Chinese thirst quenchers, soya bean milk or chrysanthemum tea. *Red Bull* (*Krating Daeng*), the Thai tonic is also widely available – and is the toast of Singapore's army of Thai building site labourers.

Tiger and Anchor beer are the local brews and Tsingtao, the Chinese nectar, is also available. Tiger Beer was first brewed at the Malayan Breweries with imported Dutch hops and yeast on Alexandra Rd in 1932 and was the product of a joint venture between Singapore's Fraser & Neave and Heineken. Recently Tiger Beer has produced two new brews: Tiger Classic is a strong bottled beer and Tiger Light, which is now available on draught in some bars. Anchor was the result of German brewers Beck's setting up the rival Archipelago Brewery. Because of its German roots, Archipelago was bought out by Malayan Breweries in 1941 and is today part of the same empire. Popular western lager beers can also be found in supermarkets, bars and restaurants, and Guinness, brewed in Kuala Lumpur and popular with the Chinese (for medicinal purposes) is available everywhere. Some bars (such as Charlie's at Changi) specialize in imported beers but even local beer is expensive (around S$6 a bottle in hawker centres and S$8 a glass in bars and pubs). International selection of drinks at top bars but they're often pricey. Coffee houses, hawker centres and small bars or coffee shops around Serangoon Rd, Jl Besar and Chinatown have the cheapest beer. Expect to pay around S$8-10 for a half pint of beer in most smart bars. One of our correspondents, who went apoplectic at the price of a pint, pointed out some artful ploys. He noted that adjacent bars and hotels have different 'happy hours' allowing one "to gravitate from one to another". It is also possible to order several rounds of drinks before 'happy hour' expires. Once rung up on the till before the deadline, drinks can be consumed at any stage during the evening. There is no shortage of wine available in Singapore but it is expensive; Australian wines are generally a better deal than imported European ones. Supermarkets all have good wines and spirits sections; the best is probably at ***Jason's***, behind Orchard Towers, 400 Orchard Rd.

The **Singapore Sling** is the island's best known cocktail. It was invented in the Raffles Hotel in 1915 and contains a blend of gin, cherry brandy, sugar, lemon juice and angostura bitters. There are lounge bars in all main hotels and many pubs, bars and nightclubs. Coffee shops – traditionally in Chinese shophouses – serve as community bars, where locals talk business over bottles of stout.

GETTING AROUND

In an attempt to discourage Singaporeans from clogging the roads with private cars, the island's public transport system was designed to be cheap and painless. Cars can now, however, cruise from the suburbs straight into the city on the underground expressway, the CTE, which opened in 1991. Buses go almost everywhere, and the Mass Rapid Transit (MRT) underground railway provides an extremely efficient subterranean back-up. Smoking is strictly banned on all public transport – transgression is punishable by a large fine. In addition, Big Macs and durians are not allowed on the MRT.

NB The **Singapore Council of Social Services** publishes *Access Singapore*, a guidebook especially for physically disabled visitors, which gives information on easily accessible tourist attractions and facilities for the disabled. Copies can be picked up from the SCSS offices at 11 Penang Lane.

MASS RAPID TRANSIT (MRT)

Since November 1987 Singapore has had one of the most technologically advanced, user-friendly light railway systems in the world – about a third of the system is underground. The designer-stations of marble, glass and chrome are cool, spotless and suicide-free – thanks to the sealed-in, air-conditioned platforms. Nine of the underground stations serve as self-sufficient, blast-proof emergency bunkers for Singaporeans, should they ever need them.

The US$5bn MRT is indeed a rapid way of transiting – it is electrically driven and trains reach 80 km/hour. Within minutes of leaving the bustle of Orchard Rd passengers hear the honey-toned welcome to the Raffles City interchange. The MRT's 66 fully automated trains operate every 3-8 minutes, depending on the time of day, between 0600 and 2400. The two main lines run NS, with a connecting loop round to the west and east-west and cover the main tourist belt. Fare stages are posted in station concourses, and tickets dispensed, with change, from the vending machines. Fares range from 60¢ to S$2. Stored value tickets, in various denominations, can be bought at all stations from ticket dispensing machines.(There are note changing machines which will change S$2 into coins.) **NB** Children pay the same price as adults. It is also possible to buy Transitlink cards for MRT and buses, prices from S$10 to S$50 (including a S$2 refundable deposit) from the Transitlink

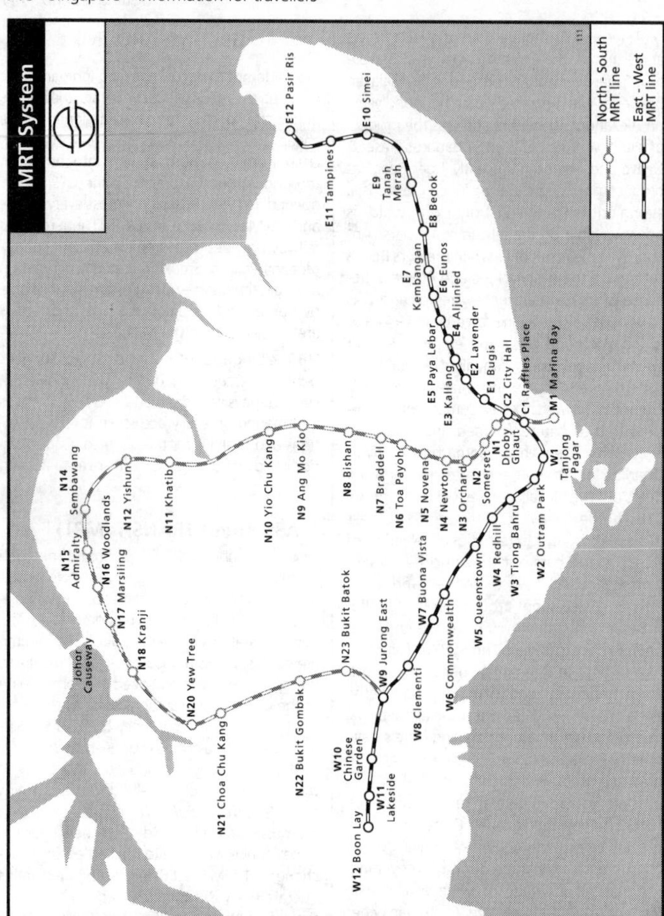

ticket booths in the MRT stations. Buses are armed with 'validator machines'. Transitlink guides are available from the booths at MRT stations – very useful source of information on bus and MRT services, fares and maps, $1.40.

BUS

For anyone visiting Singapore for more than a couple of days, the bus must be the best way of getting around, as you can get anywhere on the island at very reasonable prices, SBS (Singapore Bus Service) is efficient, convenient and cheap. Routes for all the buses are listed (with a special section on buses to tourist spots) in an SBS guide (S$1.40) available at news outlets, bookshops and MRT stations, as well as at many hotels and if you intend to do much bus travel, then this guide is well worth buying. The Singapore Tourist Promotion Board's *Official Guide* (free-of-charge from STPB offices) also carries a tourist-friendly synopsis of the service. All buses are operated by a driver only, so it is necessary to have the exact fare to hand. Fares range from 50¢ (non a/c) to S$1.40 and buses run from 0630 to 2330 Mon-Sun.

CAR HIRE

One of the most expensive ways to get around. It is not worth it unless travelling to Malaysia, as parking is expensive in Singapore (parking coupons can be bought in shops and daily licence booths). If travelling to Malaysia it is cheaper to hire a car in Johor Bahru. Rental agencies require a licence, passport and for the driver to be over 20 with a valid driver's licence (preferably international but national is usually sufficient) and passport. Car rental cost is anything from S$60 to S$350/day, depending on size and comfort, plus mileage. Vans and pickups are much cheaper as they are classified as commercial vehicles and are taxed at a lower rate.

Driving is on the left, the speed limit 50 km/hour (80 km/hour on expressways) and wearing a seat-belt is compulsory. Remember that to drive into the restricted zone a licence must be purchased (S$3). Petrol is cheap, about S$1.20/litre. In addition to car hire counters at the airport and booking offices in some top hotels, the Singapore *Yellow Pages* lists scores of local firms under 'Motorcar Renting and Leasing'. Some of the main companies are: **Avis**, Cuscaden road, Suntec City and Changi Terminals 1 and 11, T 7379477; **Budget**,24 Raffles Place and Clifford Centre, T 5324442; **Hertz** Ngee Ann City, Tower B and Changi Airport.

OTHER LOCAL TRANSPORT

● Taxis

Taxis are the fastest and easiest way to get around in comfort. More than 12,000 taxis, all of them metered and air-conditioned, ply the island's roads. Taxis cannot be stopped everywhere; it's best to go to a taxi stand or about 50m from some lights. The taxis' bells are an alarm warning cabbies once they're over the 80 km/hour expressway speed limit. Fares start at S$2.40, for the first 1.5 km, and rise 10¢ for every subsequent 300m up to 10 km. If there are more than two passengers there is a 50¢ surcharge; luggage costs S$1 extra and there's a 50% 'midnight charge' from 2400 to 0600. There's also a S$3 surcharge for journeys starting from Changi International airport or Seletar, a S$2-3 flat fee for calling a radio taxi, and S$2 extra for all trips going into or through the Central Business District (CBD). TIBS taxis now has a fleet of London cabs which may be hired by the hour, and have the advantage of accommodating five passengers. Singapore's taxis are still excellent value for money and are certainly worth considering if in a group of 3 or 4. Not only do they provide a view of Singapore which is absent from the MTR (at least in the city centre), but taxi drivers, like their brothers (and a few sisters) in most cities, are a great source of information, from political opinion to tourist practicalities.

The CBD area scheme restricts all cars and taxis from entering the area between 0730-1900 Mon-Fri, 0730-1015 Sat, unless they purchase an area licence (S$3 cars, $1 for motorbikes). Passengers entering the restricted zone are liable unless the taxi is already displaying a licence. Taxis are usually plentiful; there are stands outside most main shopping centres and hotels. Smoking is illegal in taxis. For taxi services ring: T 2825545/6/7, T 4525555, T 4686188, T 2541117, T 5521111. That may seem a lot of options, but when it rains and taxis are in heavy demand, it is difficult to find a number which is not permanently engaged.

● Trishaw

Trishaws, descendants of the rickshaw, have all but left the Singapore street-scene. A few genuine articles can still be found in the depths of Geylang or Chinatown, Serangoon Rd, by Bugis Village, off Victoria St, or outside Raffles City, but most now cater for tourists and charge accordingly, making trishaws the most expensive form of public transport in town. As ever, agree a price before climbing in. Top hotels offer top dollar trishaw tours. Off-duty trishaw drivers hang out in a large pack at the bottom of Bras Basah Rd, near the Singapore Art Museum.

● Hitchhiking

There is no law against hitchhiking, but the idea is anathema to most Singaporeans and those trying are unlikely to have any success.

BOAT

Ferries to the southern islands – Sentosa, Kusu, St John's etc – leave from the World Trade Centre or it is possible to hire a **sampan** from Jardine Steps on Keppel Rd or Clifford Pier. Boats for the northern islands go from Changi Point or Ponggol Point.

COMMUNICATIONS

● Language

No English-speaking visitor to Singapore need fear that they will not be able to make themselves understood. The official languages are Malay, Chinese (Mandarin), Tamil and English. Interestingly, Malay is the national language and English, the language of administration. Because of the republic's importance as an international trade centre, there is a high standard of English in business. Many dialects of Chinese are also spoken although the government's 'Speak Mandarin' campaign has begun to change this. Most Singaporeans speak their own lilting and musical version of English, which is dubbed '**Singlish**', and is an English patois full of curious Chinese (largely Hokkien and Cantonese) and Malay-inspired idiosyncracies and phonetic peculiarities.

As in neighbouring Malaysia, "*lah*" is a favourite suffix to just about any sentence. The words "*izzit*" and "*izzinit*" also figure prominently at the end of sentences – albeit for no particular reason. "*Wah!*" is a typical Singlish expression of surprise, horror, delight and disappointment. Singlish is generally spoken at high speed and incorporates numerous syntactical contortions, designed to make the language virtually unintelligable to the first-time visitor. Some Singaporeans object to Singlish, regarding it as crude – a perversion of the English language. They fear that it may undermine Singapore's reputation and should be stamped out. Singlish has been banned, for example, from TV and radio commercials and the *Straits Times* occasionally intones to the effect that Singlish may be bad for business. For most, though, it is a badge of national identity to be relished. A few examples: – "You makan (eaten) already or not?" – "Why you Kaypoh (busybody) lah!" – "Why you so acksi borak (show-off) like that, man?"

The most commonly used words and phrases of Singapore's lingua-franca are linguistically related to 'Manglish', the mangled English dialect spoken across the causeway. Malaysian satirist Kit Leee has unravelled its complex vocabulary and phraseology in his book *Adoi* (see page 521).

● Postal services

The **General Post Office** is on Fullerton Rd, and offers a basic service round the clock. **Local postal charges**: start at 20¢, aerograms, 35¢. **International postal charges**: 50¢ (postcard), S$1 (letter 10 grammes). **Post Office opening hours**: 0830-1700 Mon-Fri, 0830-1300 Sat. Changi Airport, 0800-2000 Mon-Sun. **Fax and telex services**: all post offices and almost all hotels have facilities for outgoing messages. The Singapore Post Office provides four sizes of sturdy carton, called Postpacs, for sending parcels abroad. These can be bought cheaply at all post offices. **Poste Restante**: Poste Restante Service, General Post Office, Fullerton Building, Singapore 0104. Correspondents should write the family name in capital letters and underline it to avoid confusion.

● Telephone services

Local: in public phones the minimum charge is 10¢ for 3 minutes. Card phones are quite widespread – cards can be bought in all post offices as well as in supermarkets and newsagents. **Directory enquiries**: T 103, for operator-assisted and international calls, T 104. **Calls to Malaysia**: T 109 for operator-assisted calls. Operators all speak English. All numbers use prefix '02' before local code and number. **International**: in contrast to many other countries in the region, Singapore Telecom offers a very efficient service. Singapore's IDD code is 65. For long distance calls dial 162 for details on country codes. International calls can be made from public phones with the red 'Worldphone' sign; these phones take 50¢ and S$1 coins or phonecards. Credit card phones are also available.

● Tourist information

To see the money invested in 'Tourism Court' makes one realize how serious Singapore is about tourism. It's a lavish block of some 20 floors, but for most visitors all they will need is the Information Desk on the ground level: Singapore Tourist Promotion Board, Tourism Court, 1 Orchard Spring Lane, Singapore 247729, T 7366622. There is also an STPB tourist information centre upstairs at the Raffles Hotel Shopping Centre, 02-34 Raffles Hotel Arcade, accessed by Seah St T 3341335/3341336 (open 0830-2000). They are all very helpful, supplying brochures and maps. Complaints can also be registered at these offices.There is now a 24 Touristline which gives automated information in English, Mandarin, Japanese and German, T18008313311 (tollfree) **Indonesian Tourist Board**, Ocean Building, 11 Collyer Quay, T 5342837; **Malaysian Tourist Board**, Ocean Building, 11 Collyer Quay **Maps**: *American Express/Singapore Tourist Board Map of Singapore* and The *Map of Singapore* endorsed by the Singapore Hotel Association are both available from the STPB office and many hotels. **Guides**: *The Singapore Official Guide* and the STPB's *Singapore Tour it Yourself* are available from STPB offices. STA Travel in the *Orchard Parade Hotel* on Tanglin Rd, T 7345681, or at the Singapore Polytechnic (next to Canteen 5), Dover Rd, T 7742270, is Singapore's top student and youth (under 26) travel centre, offering student fares, discounted tours and budget accommodation. *Street Smart Singapore*, David Brazil.

ENTERTAINMENT

MEDIA

● Newspapers/Magazines

The press is privately owned and legally free but is carefully monitored and strictly controlled. The Singapore press runs on Confucianist principles – respect for one's elders – which translates as unwavering support of the government. In the past, papers that were judged to have overstepped their mark, such as the former *Singapore Herald*, have been shut down. English language dailies are: *The Straits Times* (and *The Sunday Times*) which runs better foreign news pages than any other regional newspaper (available on the Web at http://www.asial.com.sg/straitstimes). *The Business Times* and *The New Paper* – Singapore's very own tabloid. A recent addition is *The Asian Times* – printed in Singapore, Bangkok and Hong Kong; it is an independently-run and owned newspaper with high standards of reporting and photography. So far it has escaped the censors. In 1989 the *The Straits Times* banned the use of pseudonyms on its letters page, and all would-be correspondents are vetted for authenticity before their letters are published. This has proved an effective form of censorship although as Singaporeans have got braver, with the emergence of a more relaxed government, more letters, critical of the government, have appeared. Walter Woon, an outspoken law lecturer at the National University of Singapore, believes the Singapore media is now entering a new period of *glasnost*, although it is extremely unlikely that the government will allow a truly free press.

The international press is rigorously monitored and, due to its aversion to criticism, the government has traditionally kept foreign journalists on a short leash. Having watched correspondents being unceremoniously expelled and a number of legal battles go the government's way, some foreign publications have given up caring about their Singapore circulation. A rift between the government and the New York-based Dow Jones meant that *The Asian Wall Street Journal's* circulation was heavily restricted until 1991; and only a few officially pirated copies of the *Far Eastern Economic Review* are on sale in NTUC supermarkets. *Asiaweek* and *Time* have both had their circulations curtailed in the past, although the former kowtowed sufficiently to the government and was allowed unrestricted circulation of its English and Chinese-language editions. International editions of most leading foreign newspapers are available however. Most international news and business magazines can be found in bookshops and on news stands. Many other US, Australian and European general interest glossies are also on sale. Pornographic publications are strictly prohibited under Singapore's Obscene Publications Act.

● Radio

Daily services in English and Chinese from 0600-2400, in Malay from 0445-2400 and Tamil from 0500-2100. There are five local radio stations and 2 on nearby Batam Island which blast rock music across the Straits of Singapore. **The BBC World Service**: broadcasts 24 hours a day on FM 88.9 thanks to an old British forces transmitter. The 'London Calling' programme guide is available from bookshops.

● Television

Channels 5, 8 and 12 show English, Chinese, Malay and Tamil programmes; most sets also receive Malaysian channels. Many large hotel TV sets are linked with the teletext system which has information on entertainment, sports, finance, aircraft arrivals and departures, and special events from 0700-2400. Programmes for all channels are listed in the daily newspapers. CNN international news is broadcast daily at 1900 on SBC 12. BBC World Service TV is also negotiating for some air-time on the SBC network.

HOLIDAYS AND FESTIVALS

Singapore's cultural diversity gives Singaporeans the excuse to celebrate plenty of festivals, most of which visitors can attend. The Singapore Tourist Promotion Board produces a brochure every year on festivals, with their precise dates. The *Monkey King* by Timothy Mo is very descriptive of Chinese customs and festivals, although it is set in Hong Kong.

January/February: *New Year's Day* (1st January: public holiday). *Chinese New Year* (movable: public holiday). This 15-day lunar festival celebrated in late January or early February is the most important event in the entire Chinese calendar. Each new year is given the name of an animal in 12-year rotation and each has a special significance. The seasonal Mandarin catchphrase is *Gong Xi Fa Chai* (happy new year).

The new year celebration derives from a legend in which Chinese villagers were snatched by a monster who turned out to be terrified of noise, bright lights and the colour red. Little squares of red paper, decorated with good wishes in Chinese calligraphy, are plastered on to doors and walls. New Year's eve is a family occasion with a special reunion dinner. It is the time to exchange good wishes and *hong bao* – little red envelopes containing good luck money. Employees receive a hong bao at work – usually with a symbolic 10 cent-piece inside – and unmarried children get little treats too. Chinese New Year is not a good time to visit Singapore as the city is ominously quiet (most of the shops are closed) and tourist attractions are seething.

Traditionally, the celebrations should continue for 2 weeks but Chinese shops reopen after 4 or 5 days. Compared to the celebrations in other neighbouring countries, Singapore's are rather tame and a lot quieter. Fire-crackers were banned in Singapore because of the number of injuries and deaths resulting from their indiscriminate use. Lunar New Year is publicly celebrated with the *Chingay parade* – which has lion and dragon floats, acrobats, stiltwalkers, skateboarders and dancers. Chingay translates as 'the art of masquerading'. It is now more of a multi-racial affair and not particularly Chinese. The parade is colourful and entertaining and makes its way slowly down Orchard Rd – see press for details of times.

Thaipusam (movable – January/February in the Hindu month of *Thai*) in honour of the Hindu deity Lord Subramaniam – or Murgham. Penitents pierce their bodies, cheeks and tongues with sharp skewers and weighted hooks and in trance carry *kavadi* (steel structures decorated with flowers, fruits, peacock feathers, pots of milk and pious images) on their shoulders from the Sri Perumal Temple on Serangoon Rd to the Chettiar Sri Thandayuthapani temple on Tank Rd. Penitents are accompanied by chanting well-wishers. (See page 522.)

Jade Emperor's Birthday (movable) crowds converge on the Giok Hong Tian Temple on Havelock Rd to celebrate the Jade Emperor's birthday. A Chinese opera is performed in the courtyard of the temple and lanterns are lit in the doorways of houses. *T'se Tien Tai Seng's (the monkey god) Birthday* (movable, but celebrated twice a year, in February and October). Participants go into trance and pierce their cheeks and tongues with skewers before handing out paper charms. Celebrated at the Monkey God Temple, Eng Hoon St, near Seng Poh market.

March/April: *Kwan Yin's Birthday* (movable) Chinese visit temples dedicated to the goddess of Mercy (like the one on Waterloo Rd). Childless couples come to pray for fertility. *Qing Ming* (movable – early April) is a Chinese ancestor-worship extravaganza in which family graves are spruced up and offerings of food and wine placed on tombs to appease their forebears' spirits. *Songkran* (movable) this Buddhist water festival is celebrated in Thai Buddhist temples. To welcome the New Year, the image of the Buddha is bathed and celebrants are sprinkled – or doused – with water, as a sign of purification. Offerings of flowers, incense and candles are brought to the temples – the Anada Metyarama Temple on Silat Rd is the best place to see this. *Hari Raya Puasa* or *Aidil Fitri* (movable) marks the end of Ramadan, the month of fasting for Muslims and is a day of celebration. Once the Muftis have confirmed the new moon of *Syawal*, the 10th Islamic month, Muslims don traditional clothing and spend the day praying in the mosques and visiting friends and family. During Ramadan, Muslims gather to eat at stalls after dark; Geyland Serai and Bussorah St (near Arab St) are favourite makan stops. *Tamil New Year* (movable – April-May) begins at the start of the Hindu month of *Chithirai*. *Pujas* are held at Singapore's main temples to honour *Surya*, the sun god. An almanac, containing the Hindu horoscope is published at this time. *Easter* (movable – Good Friday is a public holiday) services are held in the island's churches. There is a candlelit procession in the grounds of St Joseph's Catholic Church, Victoria St.

May: *Labour Day* (1st: public holiday). *Vesak Day* (movable – usually in May, on the full moon of the fifth lunar month) commemorates the Buddha's birth, death and enlightenment and is celebrated in Buddhist temples everywhere (Kong Meng San Phor Kark See temple in Bright Hill Drive and the Temple of a Thousand Lights in Race Course Rd are particularly lively). In Singapore celebrations begin before dawn: monks chant *sutras* (prayers) and lanterns and candles are lit to symbolize the Buddha's enlightenment. Statues of the Buddha are ritually bathed. Some temples also stage special exhibitions, conduct initiation ceremonies and present lectures on the Buddha's teachings. Buddhists release captive animals and fish, make offerings to monks and nuns and meditate. Vegetarian meals are served, Buddhists take part in a mass blood-donation exercise and cash and food are distributed to the poor and various charities.

Birthday of the Third Prince (movable) festivities to mark the birthday of this child-god, who carries a magic bracelet in one hand and a spear in the other, while riding wheels of wind and fire. Chinese mediums go into trance, slashing themselves with swords and spikes.

Hell Money - Festival of Hungry Ghosts

Dragon Boat Festival (movable) honours the suicide of an ancient Chinese poet-hero, Qu Yuan. He drowned himself in protest against corrupt government. In an attempt to save him, fishermen played drums and threw rice dumplings to try and distract predators. His death is commemorated with dragon boat races and the eating of rice dumplings.

Hari Raya Haji (movable – falls on the 10th day of *Zulhijjah*, the 12th month of the Muslim calendar) to celebrate Moslems who have made the pilgrimage to Mecca (the men are known as *haji* – identifiable by their white skull caps – and the women as *hajjah*). The feast-day is marked by prayers at mosques and the sacrificial slaughter of goats and buffalo for distribution to the poor as a sign of gratitude to Allah.

August/September: *National Day* (9th August: public holiday) to celebrate the Republic's independence in 1965. The highlight of the day is the military parade, airforce fly-past and carnival procession on and around the Padang or National Stadium. It is necessary to have tickets to get into the Padang area, but the whole thing is televised live, and broadcast again on the weekend. Cheer leaders twirl to a "Singapore we love you" chant. Political dignitaries and honoured guests look on from the courthouse steps.

Festival of the Hungry Ghosts (Yu Lan Jie): (movable: runs for 30 days after the last day of the sixth moon). It is the second most important festival after the lunar new year. Banquets given by stallholders, lavish feasts are laid out on the streets, there are roving bands of Chinese street opera singers, puppet shows and lotteries. Then there is the ritual burning of huge incense sticks and paper 'hell money' to appease the spirits, who are believed to wander around on earth for a month after the annual opening of the gates of hell. The souls of the dead, who have been murdered or wronged or just bugged by their relatives, return to torment and haunt them. Because these spirits continue to wander around for several weeks, the seventh lunar month is known as 'the devil's month' – an inauspicious month to get married.

Another legend relates that the festival commemorates Buddha's suggestion to one of his disciples, Mu Lien, that in order to save his mother from hell, he must offer food to 'the ancestors of seven generations'. Whatever its derivation, the side streets and car parks in housing estates are the venue for the festivities, which have now degenerated into noisy auctions – the goods are believed to have been blessed by the gods. Bidders for items such as ceremonial charcoal (which, thanks to its supernatural powers can command up to S$20,000 a stick) do not have to pay up until the following year. It is extremely unusual that these creditors forget to pay – it is considered unlucky to do so. The festival affords the best opportunity to see *wayang* – street opera – and the best place to catch one is in Chinatown.

Mooncake or Lantern Festival (movable – mid-way through the Chinese eigth moon). This Chinese festival commemorates the overthrow of the Mongul Dynasty in China. Children parade with elaborate candlelit lanterns and eat mooncakes filled with lotus seed paste. According to Chinese legend, secret messages of revolt were carried inside these cakes and led to the uprising which caused the overthrow of their oppressors. A gentler interpretation is that the round cakes represent the full moon, the end of the farming year and an abundant harvest –

a bucolic symbolism that must be lost on most city-born Singaporeans. Lantern competitions are held and winning entries are exhibited at the Chinese Garden (see page 663).

Pilgrimage to Kusu Island (movable) around 10,000 Taoist and Muslim pilgrims, over a month, crowd onto ferries to this sacred but ugly little island, ½-hour south of Singapore. There they make offerings at the Malay Kramat (shrine) or the Chinese temple dedicated to Ta-po-kung (Tua Pekong) also known as Datok Kung.

Navarathri Festival (movable) 9 days of prayer, temple music and classical dance honour the consorts of Siva, Vishnu and Brahma (the Hindu trinity of Gods). The festival is celebrated notably at the Chettiar Temple on Tank Rd, ending with a procession on the 10th day along River Valley Rd, Killiney Rd, Orchard Rd, Clemenceau Ave and returning to the temple.

October/November: *Deepavali* (movable – usually in October in the Hindu month of *Aipasi*) the Hindu festival of lights commemorates the victory of Lord Krishna over the demon king Narakasura, symbolizing the victory of light over darkness and good over evil. Indian mythology tells that as Narakasura lay dying he asked Krishna to grant him one last favour – to commemorate their battle as a day of fun for all the family. Every Hindu home is brightly lit and decorated for the occasion. Shrines are swamped with offerings and altars piled high with flowers. Row upon row of little earthen oil lamps are lit to guide the souls of departed relatives in their journey back to the next world, after their brief annual visit to earth during Deepavali.

Guru Nanak's Birthday (movable) the first of the 10 gurus of the Sikh faith. The domed Gurdwara in Katong (Wilkinson Rd) is buzzing on the Sikh holy day.

Thimithi Festival (movable: around end October/beginning November, in the Hindu month of *Aipasi*) this Hindu festival often draws a big crowd to watch devotees fulfil their vows by walking over a 3m long pit of burning coals in the courtyard of the Sri Mariamman Temple on South Bridge Rd. Fire walking starts at around 1600 on the arrival of the procession from Perumal Temple on Serangoon Rd. The priests walk the pit first, followed by devotees.

December: *Christmas Day* (25th: public holiday) Christmas in Singapore is a spectacle of dazzling lights, the best along Orchard Rd, where the roadside trees are bejewelled with strings of fairy lights. Shopping centres and hotels compete to have the year's most extravagant or creative display. These seasonal exhibitions are often conveniently designed to last through Chinese New Year. It would not be untypical, for example, to find Santa riding on a man-eater in the year of the tiger. In shopping arcades, sweating tropical Santa Clauses dash through the fake snow. Choirs from Singapore's many churches line the sidewalks and Singaporeans go shopping.

FURTHER READING

● Suggested reading

Singaporean novelists writing in English: Baratham, Gopal (1991) *A candle or the sun*, Times Books: Singapore. A book which deals with some of the less savoury aspects of living in Singapore, the story is based on the experience of a novelist who is asked by the government to spy on his lover.

Jeyaretnam, Philip (1987) *First loves*, Times Books: Singapore. A collection of sharply observed short stories, with an emphasis on material accumulation in a society whose soul is lost in the quest for money.

Jeyaretnam, Philip (1994) *Abraham's promise*, Times Books: Singapore. An excellent novel about a teacher whose life is ruined when he falls foul of the ruling party. It is hard to believe that the fact that Philip Jeyaretnam's father is Joshua Jeyaretnam (JBJ), the opposition politician who was bankrupted by former prime minister Lee Kuan Yew and publicly disgraced, is a coincidence. The book, though, has been published by a Singaporean publisher.

Lim, Catherine (1978) *Little ironies*, Heinemann Asia: Singapore. Lim is another of Singapore's younger breed of novelists, more introspective and critical of the Republic's progress, and more concerned with getting beneath the façade of unity and success. *Little ironies* is a collection of short stories. Her other books include *They do return*, a collection of ghost stories and *Or else, the lightning God* (1982), another set of short stories. Her work is very popular in Singapore.

Shelley, Rex (1991) *The shrimp people*, Times Books: Singapore. A novel about the experiences of the Eurasian community in Singapore during the 1950s, when the Communists were in the ascendancy.

Soh, Michael (1973) *Son of a mother*, Oriental Press: Singapore. Singaporean novelist Michael Soh recounts the story of a grocer threatened with eviction, in the process showing the emphasis on filial duty and respect.

Other Singaporean writers with a considerable local following, and whose books can be easily purchased in Singapore, include Ho Min Fong and Lim Thean Soo.

Novels about Singapore by non-Singaporeans: Conrad, Joseph (1988) *Lord Jim*, Everyman Classic: Dent. Conrad visited Singapore during his years as a seaman and the 'eastern port' in Lord Jim is unmistakably Singapore.

Anderson, Patrick (1955) *Snake wine: a Singapore episode*, Chatto and Windus: London. Patrick Anderson taught at the University of Malaya in Singapore during the 1950s and this novel is semi-autobiographical, tracing life on the campus during a particularly volatile period.

Clavell, James: *King Rat*. Perhaps the single most widely read novel based in Singapore, it tells of life in the Japanese prisoner of war camp at Changi, where Singapore's airport is located.

Farrell, JG (1979) *The Singapore grip*, Fontana: London. A best-selling thriller about Singapore during the months leading up to the Japanese invasion and occupation.

Theroux, Paul (1973) *Saint Jack*, Penguin. Paul Theroux taught in the English Department at the University of Singapore and this novel is set in Singapore. Its main character is Jack Flowers who sets up a boat-brothel to meet the demands of American GIs visiting the island.

Theroux, Paul (1977) *The consul's file*, Penguin. This is a collection of short stories, mainly based in Malaya but also drawing on Singapore material.

History, culture and politics: Barber, Noel: *Sinister twilight*, Arrow: London. Another book about the fall of Singapore, a well-respected account.

Wurtzburg, CE: *Raffles of the Eastern Isles*: OUP (1954), comprehensive story of Raffles' life in this dense volume.

Pastel Portraits, Singapore's Architectural Heritage. (1984) a coffee table book with good pictorial record of the variety of shophouses to be found around the city and descriptions of the evolution of the different sections of town.

Collis, Maurice: *Raffles*, Century: London. An easy to read biography of Raffles, fascinating for those with an interest in the history, not just of Singapore, but the Dutch East Indies too.

Craig, Jo Ann: *Culture Shock Singapore!*, Times Books: Singapore. Another book in a series, this one recounting the do's and don'ts of living in Singapore. Useful for those intending to live in Singapore, but pretty superfluous for the short-term visitor.

Minchin, James: *No man is an island*, Allen and Unwin: Sydney. A biography of Lee Kuan Yew, and none too laudatory in places. Best to buy it before arrival, or in Malaysia – Singapore's bookshops do not stock it.

Turnbull, Mary, C (1989) *A history of Malaysia, Singapore and Brunei*, Allen and Unwin. A very orthodox history of Malaysia, Singapore and Brunei, clearly written for a largely academic/student audience.

Business: the Barings collapse: following the collapse of Barings a number of books have appeared which examine the calamity. Although they are more about Barings and Nick Leeson than about Singapore and doing business there the event did, nonetheless, occur in the island state. Leeson, Nick (1996) *Rogue trader*, London: Little Brown. The story from the horse's mouth, so to speak, and not surprisingly the author (Leeson) ends up being an apologist for the subject (Leeson). Rawnsley, Judith (1995) *Going for broke: Nick Leeson and the collapse of Barings Bank*, London: Harper Collins. This book is written by a former employer of Barings in Tokyo and so has perhaps the best feel for the company and its business ethos – an ethos which created the environment in which Leeson could have got away with so much for so long and at so great a cost. Rawnsley's book, though, was published before the London and Singapore authorities published their reports on the débâcle. Fay, Stephen (1996) *The collapse of Barings*, London: Richard Cohen Books. Fay's book is probably the most detailed of the three and although it may not have the 'insider' feel of Rawnsley's volume does have the opportunity to pick over the bones of the Singapore and London reports.

Government publications The Singapore government's *Ministry of Information and the Arts* publishes a wide range of useful information on the country. They produce, for example, an annual volume called *Singapore facts and figures* as well as a more detailed yearbook entitled *Singapore 1996* (or *Singapore 1997*).

Transport guides Invaluable for making the most of Singapore's incomparable public transportation is the annual *TransitLink Guide* which lists all bus and MRT routes and stops. A snip at S$1.40 for 392 pocket-sized pages.

Maps: *Nelles Map of Singapore*; *Secret Map of Singapore*; *Secret Food Map of Singapore*;Singapore *Street Directory* is useful for driving. Various free maps can also be picked up from many hotels and tourist offices.

Rounding up

Acknowledgements	727	Health	742
Reading and listening	727	Travelling with children	749
The Internet	729	Weights and measures	752
Short wave radio	731	Glossary	753
Useful addresses	732	Tinted boxes	761
Malaysian words and phrases	737	Illustrations	768
Food glossary	740	Index	769
Distinctive fruits	740	Maps	782

ACKNOWLEDGEMENTS

BRUNEI

John Banks, UK.

MALAYSIA

Samantha Hand, UK; Kathie Summers, UK; Steven Thompson, UK; Anne McLachlan, UK; Emma Nicherson, UK; John Banks, UK; T Van Hille, Brugge; Stephanie Lee-Raby, Taipei; Serena Miazzo and Paolo Roverani, Italy; Eugenio Serrano, Indonesia; Jenny Cook, UK; Patrick and Nicole Millischer, France; Michel J van Dam, the Netherlands; Arthur Tan, Australia; Janette Eccott and Mike Hall, UK; Stefano Magistretti, Italy.

SINGAPORE

Samantha Hand, UK; Elizabeth Philips, Singapore; B Rumage, UK; Kathie Summers, UK; Patrick and Nicole Millischer, France; Janette Eccott and Mike Hall, UK; Robert Leverton, Singapore.

READING AND LISTENING

Magazines

Asiaweek (weekly). A lightweight *Far Eastern Economic Review*; rather like a regional *Time* magazine in style.

The Far Eastern Economic Review (weekly). Authoritative Hong Kong-based regional magazine; their correspondents based in each country provide knowledgeable, in-depth analysis particularly on economics and politics, sometimes in rather a turgid style.

Books

Buruma, Ian (1989) *God's dust*, Jonathan Cape: London. Enjoyable journey through Burma, Thailand, Malaysia and Singapore along with the Philippines, Taiwan, South Korea and Japan; journalist Buruma questions how far culture in this region has survived the intrusion of the West.

Caufield, C (1985) *In the rainforest*, Heinemann: London. This readable and well-researched analysis of rainforest ecology and the pressures on tropical forests is part-based in the region.

Clad, James (1989) *Behind the myth: business, money and power in Southeast*

Asia, Unwin Hyman: London. Clad, formerly a journalist with the *Far Eastern Economic Review*, distilled his experiences in this book; as it turned out, rather disappointingly – it is a hotch-potch of journalistic snippets – but is worth taking along to dip into.

Conrad, Joseph (1900) *Lord Jim*, Penguin: London. The tale of Jim, who abandons his ship and seeks refuge from his guilt in Malaya, earning in the process the sobriquet Lord.

Conrad, Joseph (1915) *Victory: an island tale*, Penguin: London. Arguably Conrad's finest novel, based in the Malay Archipelago.

Conrad, Joseph (1920) *The rescue*, Penguin: London. Set in the Malay Archipelago in the 1860s; the hero, Captain Lingard, is forced to choose between his Southeast Asian friend and his countrymen.

Dingwall, Alastair (1994) *Traveller's literary companion to South-east Asia*, In Print: Brighton. Experts on Southeast Asian language and literature select extracts from novels and other books by western and regional writers. The extracts are annoyingly brief, but it gives a good overview of what is available.

Dumarçay, Jacques (1991) *The palaces of South-East Asia: architecture and customs*, OUP: Singapore. A broad summary of palace art and architecture in both mainland and island Southeast Asia.

Fraser-Lu, Sylvia (1988) *Handwoven textiles of South-East Asia*, OUP: Singapore. Well-illustrated, large-format book with informative text.

King, Ben F and Dickinson, EC (1975) *A field guide to the birds of South-East Asia*, Collins: London. Best regional guide to the birdlife of the region.

Miettinen, Jukko O (1992) *Classical dance and theatre in South-East Asia*, OUP: Singapore. Expensive, but accessible survey of dance and theatre, mostly focusing on Indonesia, Thailand and Burma.

Osborne, Milton (1979) *Southeast Asia: an introductory history*, Allen & Unwin: Sydney. Good introductory history, clearly written, published in a portable paperback edition and recently revised and reprinted.

Reid, Anthony (1988) *Southeast Asia in the age of commerce 1450-1680*, Yale University Press: New Haven. Perhaps the best history of everyday life in Southeast Asia, looking at such themes as physical well-being, material culture and social organization meticulously researched.

Reid, Anthony (1993) *Southeast Asia in the age of commerce 1450-1680: expansion and crisis*, Yale University Press: New Haven. Volume 2 in this excellent history of the region.

Rigg, Jonathan (1991) *Southeast Asia: a region in transition*, Routledge: London. A thematic geography of the ASEAN region, providing an insight into some of the major issues affecting the region today. Recently reprinted.

SarDesai, DR (1989) *Southeast Asia: past and present*, Macmillan: London. Skilful but at times frustratingly thin history of the region from the 1st century to the withdrawal of US forces from Vietnam.

Savage, Victor R (1984) *Western impressions of nature and landscape in Southeast Asia*, Singapore University Press: Singapore. Based on a geography PhD thesis, the book is a mine of quotations and observations from western travellers. Hard to get hold of as it is out of print.

Sesser, Stan (1993) *The lands of charm and cruelty: travels in Southeast Asia*, Picador: Basingstoke. A series of collected narratives first published in the *New Yorker* including essays on Singapore, Laos, Cambodia, Burma and Borneo. Finely observed and thoughtful, the book is an excellent travel companion.

Steinberg, DJ *et al* (1987) *In search of Southeast Asia: a modern history*, University of Hawaii Press: Honolulu. The best standard history of the region; it skilfully examines and assesses general processes of change and their impacts from the arrival of the Europeans in the region.

Tarling, Nicholas (1992) *Cambridge History of Southeast Asia*, CUP: Cambridge. Two volume edited study, long and expensive with contributions from most of the leading historians of the region. A thematic and regional approach is taken, not a country one, although the history is fairly conventional.

Vatikiotis, Michael (1996) *Political change in Southeast Asia: trimming the banyan tree*, London: Routledge. This *Far Eastern Economic Review* correspondent argues that political change in Southeast Asia must be viewed through a Southeast Asian lens and not as a mirror of Western processes.

Wallace, Alfred Russel (1869) *The Malay Archipelago: the land of the orang-utan and the bird of paradise; a narrative of travel with studies of man and nature*, MacMillan: London. A classic of natural history writing, recounting Wallace's 8 years in the archipelago and now reprinted.

Waterson, Roxana (1990) *The living house: an anthropology of architecture in South-East Asia*, OUP: Singapore. Illustrated, academic book on Southeast Asian architecture, fascinating material for those interested in such things.

Young, Gavin (1991) *In search of Conrad*, Hutchinson: London. This well-known travel writer retraces the steps of Conrad; part travel-book, part fantasy, it is worth reading but not up to the standard of his other books.

MAPS

A decent map is an indispensable aid to travelling. Although maps are usually available locally, it is sometimes useful to buy a map prior to departure to plan routes and itineraries, especially in Malaysia, where even the locals admit that their maps are not very accurate. Below is a select list of maps (the scale is provided in brackets).

Regional maps Bartholomew Southeast Asia (1:5,800,000); Nelles Southeast Asia (1:4,000,000); Hildebrand Thailand, Burma, Malaysia and Singapore (1:2,800,000); ITM (International Travel Map) Southeast Asia.

Country maps Bartholomew Singapore and Malaysia (1:150,000); Nelles Malaysia (1:1,500,000); Nelles West Malaysia (1:650,000); Periplus Sabah and Kota Kinabalu; Periplus Sarawak and Kuching; Nelles Singapore (1:22,500); Periplus Singapore.

City maps Nelles Singapore; Bartholomew Singapore; Periplus Singapore; Periplus Kuala Lumpur.

Other maps Tactical Pilotage Charts (TPC, US Airforce) (1:500,000); Operational Navigational Charts (ONC, US Airforce) (1:500,000). Both of these are particularly good at showing relief features (useful for planning treks); less good on roads, towns and facilities.

Locally available maps Maps are widely available in Malaysia and Singapore. Both the Singapore and Malaysian tourist boards produce good maps of their respective capital cities and in the case of Malaysia a series of state maps, rather poorer in quality. The Sabah and Sarawak tourist boards also publish reasonable maps.

Map shops In London, the best selection is available from Stanfords, 12-14 Long Acre, London WC2E 9LP, T (0171) 836-1321; also recommended is McCarta, 15 Highbury Place, London N15 1QP, T (0171) 354-1616.

THE INTERNET

Listed below are Internet addresses which access information on Asia generally, the Southeast Asian region, or individual countries within Southeast Asia. **Newsgroups** tend to be informal talking shops offering information from hotels and sights through to wide-ranging discussions on just about any topic. **Mailing Lists** have a more academic clientele, and probably are not worth plugging into unless you have a specific interest in the subject concerned.

Web sites offer a whole range of information on a vast variety of topics. Below is only a selection.

Newsgroups on USENET with a Southeast Asian focus

Newsgroups are discussion fora on the USENET. Not every computer linked to the Internet has access to USENET – your computer needs Net News and a News reader. Newsgroups are informal fora for discussion; they are occasionally irreverent, usually interesting.

Asia general

alt.asian.movies
alt.buddha.short.fat.guy
rec.travel.asia
soc.religion.eastern
talk.religion.buddhism

Southeast Asia

soc.culture.asean

Malaysia

soc.culture.malaysia

Singapore

soc.culture.singapore

Mailing lists

These are discussion groups with a more academic content; some may be moderate – ie the content of messages is checked by an editor. Mailing lists communicate using E-mail. The focus of the groups is in italics.

Asia general

actmus-1@ubvm.bitnet
Asian Contemporary Music Discussion Group
apex-1@uhccvm.bitnet
Asia-Pacific Exchange
buddha-1@ulkyvm.bitnet
Buddhist Academic Discussion Forum

Southeast Asia

seanet-1@nusvm.bitnet
Southeast Asian Studies List
seasia-1@msu.bitnet
Southeast Asia Discussion List

Malaysia

misg-l@psuvm.bitnet
Malaysian Islamic Study Group
wacana-l@american.edu
Malaysian scholarly discussion group

Southeast Asia on the World Wide Web – Web sites

Below are some web sites with an Asian focus. The address is in Roman, and the subject of the site in italics, after the address.

Asia general

http://none.coolware.com/infoasia/
run by Infoasia which is a commercial firm that helps US and European firms get into Asia
http://pears.lib.ohio-state.edu/asianstudies/asian studies.html
huge range of links with information on topics from sports and travel to economics and engineering
http://webhead.com/asergio/asiaregion.html
travel information on Asian region
http//www.clark.net/pub/global/asia.html
mostly Japan and China, but also links with Southeast Asian countries
http://www.yahoo.com/Regional Countries/[name of country]
insert name of country to access practical information including material from other travel guides
http://coombs.anu.edu.au/WWWVLPages/WhatsNewWWW/asian-www-news.html
assortment of material from across Asian region
http://www.city.net/regions/asia
pointer to information on Asian countries
http://www.branch.com:80/silkroute/ *information on hotels, travel, news and business in Asia*
http://www.singapore.com/pata
Pacific Asia Travel Association – stacks of info on travel in the Pacific Asian region including stats, markets, products etc

Southeast Asia

http://emailhost.ait.ac.th/asia/asia. html
clickable map of mainland Southeast Asia with pointer to sources of other information on the region
http://libweb.library.wisc.edu/guides/SEA

sia/library.htm
'Gateway to Southeast Asia' from University of Wisconsin, numerous links
http://www.pactoc.net.au/index/resindex.htm
covers all Pacific, but good links into Southeast Asian material; emphasis on academic issues rather than travel
http://www.leidenuniv.nl/pun/ubhtm/mjkintro.htm
library of 100 slides of Pagan (Burma), Thailand (Phimai, Chiang Mai, Lamphun), Cambodia (Angkor) and Vietnam (Myson)

Malaysia
http://www.sphere.net.my/sphere
good links to Malaysian web sites and Malaysian-related sites elsewhere
http://www.mdx.ac.uk/www/hap/brc.html
contents of the Borneo Research Bullentin and list of members of the Borneo Research Council
http://www.jaring.my/
general information on the country
http://www.sarawak.gov.my/stb
The Sarawak Tourism Board's own website, with 20 pages of information – mostly commercial

Singapore
http://www.sg/
links to homepage with good information on events, health, sports, business and more
http://www.ste.com.sg
Provides a bulletin board for businesses to post notices and advertisements and to market their products; also a directory of licensed travel agents

Terms
E-mail = Electronic mail
WWW = World Wide Web or, simply, the Web
HTML = Hypertext Markup Language

Source: the above was collated from *Internet news* published in the *IIAS Newsletter* [International Institute for Asian Studies Newsletter], Summer 1995, updated from the *IIAS Newsletter* no 8 (Spring 1996 and from the *Asian Studies Newsletter* (June/July 1996). The IIAS publish a guide, *IIAS Internet guide to Asian Studies '96* which can be ordered from the IIAS Secretariat, PO Box 9515, 2300 RA Leiden, the Netherlands (Dfl, 20-) or accessed at: http://iias.leidenuniv.nl

SHORT WAVE RADIO (Khz)

British Broadcasting Corporation (BBC, London) *Southeast Asian service* 3915, 6195, 9570, 9740, 11750, 11955, 15360; *Singapore service* 88.9MHz; *East Asian service* 5995, 6195, 7180, 9740, 11715, 11750, 11945, 11955, 15140, 15280, 15360, 17830, 21715.

Voice of America (VoA, Washington) *Southeast Asian service* 1143, 1575, 7120, 9760, 9770, 15185, 15425; *Indonesian service* 6110, 11760, 15425.

Radio Beijing *Southeast Asian service (English)* 11600, 11660.

Radio Japan (Tokyo) *Southeast Asian service (English)* 11815, 17810, 21610.

Useful addresses

EMBASSIES AND CONSULATES ABROAD

BRUNEI

Australia
16 Bulwarra Close, O'Malley ACT 2606, Canberra, T 2901801, F 2901832.

France
4 Rue Logelbach, 75017 Paris, T 42674947, F 42675365.

Germany
Koblenzer Str 99 (4th Flr), 5300 Bonn-Bad Godesberg, Bonn 2, T 672044, F 687329.

Indonesia
Wisma Bank Central Asia Building, 8th Flr, Jln Jendral Sudirman, KAV 22-23, Jakarta, T 5712180, F 5712205.

Japan
5-2 Kitashinagawa 6-Chome, Shinagawa-ku, Tokyo 141, T (03) 34477997, F (03) 34479260.

Malaysia
Wisma SHC, Jln Tun Razak, 50400 Kuala Lumpur, T 2612800, F 2612898.

Philippines
11th Flr, BPI Building, Ayala Ave, Makati, Metro Manila, T 8162836, F 8152872.

Singapore
325 Tanglin Rd, Singapore 1024, T 7339055, F 73752754.

Thailand
154, Soi 14, Ekamai, Sukhumvit 63, Bangkok 10110, T 3916017, F 3016017.

UK
High Commission, 19-20 Belgrave Square, London, SW1X 8PG, T (0171) 5810521, F (0171) 2359717.

USA
Watergate Suite 300, 3rd Flr, 2600 Virginia Ave, Washington DC 20037, T 3420159, F 3420158 and 866 United Nations Plaza, New York, NY 10017, T 8381600, F 9806478.

MALAYSIA

Australia
High Commission, 7 Perth Ave, Yarralumla, Canberra, ACT 2600, T (06) 2731-543.

Austria
Prinz Eugenstrasse 18, A-1040 Vienna, T 505-1042.

Bangladesh
High Commission, No Four Rd No 118, Gulshan Model Town, Dhaka-12, T 600-291.

Belgium
414A Ave de Tervuren, 1150 Brussels, T 762-67-67.

Brunei
High Commission, No 473 Kg Pelambayan, Jln Kota Batu, PO Box 2826, Bandar Seri Begawan, T 228410.

Canada
High Commission, 60 Boteler St, Ottawa, Ontario KIN 8Y7, T (613) 237-5182.

China
13 Dong Zhi Menwai Dajie, San Li Tun, Beijing, T 5322531.

CIS
Mosfilmovskaya Ulitsa 50, Moscow, T 147-1514.

France
2 Bis Rue Benouville, Paris, T 4553-1185.

Germany
Mittelstrasse 43, 5300 Bonn 2, T (0228) 37-68-03.

Hong Kong
24th Flr, Malaysia Building, 50 Gloucester Rd, Wanchai, T 5270921.

India
High Commission, 50-M Satya Marg, Chanakyapuri, New Delhi 110021, T 601291; No 287 TTK Rd, Madras – 600018, T 453580.

Indonesia
17 Jln Imam Bonjol, 10310 Jakarta Pusat, T 336438; Consulate: Medan, T 511233.

Italy
Via Nomentana 297, Rome, T 8415764.

Japan
20-16 Nanpeidai-Machi, Shibuya-ku, Tokyo 150, T 3476-3840.

Laos
Route That Luang, Quartier Nong Bone, PO Box 789, Vientiane, T 2662.

Myanmar (Burma)
82 Diplomatic Quarters, Pyidaundsu Yeikhta Rd, Yangon (Rangoon), T 20248.

Netherlands
Runtenburweg 2, 2517 KE The Hague, T (070) 3506506.

New Zealand
High Commission, 10 Washington Ave, Brooklyn, Wellington, T 852439.

Pakistan
224 Nazimuddin Rd, F-7/4, Islamabad T 210147.

Singapore
301 Jervois Rd, Singapore 1024, T 235-0111.

Spain
Paseo de La Castellano 91-50, Centro 23, 28046 Madrid, T (341) 555 0684.

Sri Lanka
High Commission, 47/1 Jawatta Rd, Colombo 7, T 94-1-508973.

Sweden
Engelbrektsgatan 5, PO Box 26053, 100 41 Stockholm, T (08) 6795990.

Switzerland
Laupenstrasse 37, 3008 Berne, T 25-21-05.

Thailand
35 South Sathorn Rd, Bangkok 10120, T 286-1390; Consulate: Songkhla, T 311062.

UK
High Commission, 45, Belgrave Square, London SW1X 8QT, T (0171) 235 8033.

USA
2401 Massachusetts Ave NW, Washington DC 200008, T (202) 328-2700; Consulates: New York, T (212) 490-2722; Los Angeles, T (212) 621-2991.

Vietnam
Block A-3, Van Phuc, Hanoi, T 53371.

SINGAPORE

Australia
High Commission, 17 Forster Crescent, Yarralumla, Canberra ACT 2600, T (6) 273 3944.

Austria
c/o Embassy in Bonn; Consulate: Raiffeisen Zentral Bank, Osterreich AG, Am Stadtpark 9, 1030 Vienna, T (222) 71707 1229.

Belgium
198 Ave Franklin Roosevelt, 1050 Brussels, T (2) 660-30908.

Brunei
High Commission, 5th Flr, RBA Plaza, Jln

Sultan, Bandar Seri Begawan, T (2) 22 7583.

Canada
1305-999 Hastings St, Vancouver, T (604) 669 5115.

China
4 Liangmahe Nanlu, Sanlitun, Beijing 100600, T (1) 432 3926.

CIS
Per Voyevodina 5, Moscow, T (095) 241 3702.

Denmark
c/o High Commission in London.

Finland
c/o Embassy in Moscow.

France
12 Square de l'Ave Foch, 75116 Paris, T 4500 3361.

Germany
Sudstrasse 133, 5300 Bonn 2, T (228) 31 2007.

Greece
10-12 Kifissias Ave, 151 25 Maroussi, Athens, T (1) 683 4875.

Hong Kong
Units 901-2, Admiralty Centre Tower 1, 9th Flr, 18 Harcourt Rd, Hong Kong, T 527 2212.

India
High Commission, E-6 Chandragupta Marg, Chanakyapuri, New Delhi 110021, T (11) 60 4162. Consulates: Bombay T (2) 204 3205; Madras T (44) 47 6637.

Indonesia
Block X/4 KAV No 2, Jl HR Rasuna Said, Kuningan, Jakarta 12950, T (21) 520 1489. Consulate: Medan, North Sumatra, T (61) 51 3366.

Japan
14th Flr, Osaka, Kokusai Building, 3-13 Azuchimachi 2-Chome, Chuo-Ku, Tokyo T (6) 261 5131.

Luxemburg
c/o Embassy in Brussels.

Malaysia
209 Jln Tun Razak, Kuala Lumpur 50400, T (03) 261 6277.

Maldives
c/o High Commission, New Delhi.

Myanmar (Burma)
287 Prome Rd, Yangon (Rangoon), T 33200.

Nepal
c/o High Commission in New Delhi.

Netherlands
Rotterdam Plaza, Weena 670 3012 CN, Rotterdam, T (20) 404 2111.

New Zealand
17 Kabul St, Khandallah, Wellington, T (4) 79 2076.

Norway
c/o High Commission in London. Consulate: Oslo, T (47) 2 485000.

Pakistan
Lakson Square Building, 2 Sarwar Shaheed Rd, Karachi-1, T (21) 52 6419.

Philippines
6th Flr, ODC Building, International Plaza, 219 Salcedo St, Legaspi Village, Makati, Metro Manila, T (2) 816 1764.

Portugal
Lusograin, Rua dos Franqueiros 135-1, 1100 Lisbon, T (1) 87 8647.

Spain
Huertas 13, Madrid 28012, T (1) 429 3193.

Sri Lanka
High Commission, c/o High Commission in New Delhi.

Sweden
c/o Embassy in Bonn. Consulate: Stockholm T (8) 663 7488.

Switzerland
c/o Embassy in Bonn.

Thailand
129 South Sathorn Rd, Bangkok, T (2) 286 2111.

UK
9 Wilton Crescent, London, SW1X 8SA, T (0171) 235 8315.

USA
1824 R St NW, Washington DC 20009-1691, T 202 667 7555. Consulates: Los Angeles T 714 760 9400; Minneapolis T 612 332 8063.

TOURIST BOARD OFFICES

BRUNEI

UK
20 Belgrave Square, London SW1X 8PG, T (0171) 581 0521.

MALAYSIA

Australia
65 York St, Sydney, NSW 2000, T (02) 2994441/2/3, F (02) 262 2026; 56 William St, Perth, WA 6000, T (09) 481 0400, F (09) 321 1421.

Benelux Countries
c/o Malaysia Airlines System Bhd, Westeringschans 24A, 1017 SG Amsterdam, Netherlands, T (020) 6381146, (020) 6381189.

Canada
830 Burrard St, Vancouver, BC, Canada V6Z 2K4, T (604) 689 8899, F (604) 689 8804.

France
Office National du Tourisme de Malaisie, 29 Rue des Pyramides, 75001 Paris, T (331) 42974171, F (331) 4297 4169.

Germany
Rossmarkt 11, 60311 Frankfurt Am Main, T (069) 283782, F (069) 285215.

Hong Kong
Ground Floor, Malaysia Building, 47-50 Gloucester Rd, T 2528 5810, F 2865 4610.

Italy
Secondo Piano, Piazza San Babila 4/B, 20122 Milano, T (02) 796 702, F (02) 796 806.

Japan
5F Chiyoda Building, 1-6-4 Yurakucho, Chiyoda-Ku, Tokyo 100, T (03) 3501 8691, F (03) 3501 8692; 10th Flr, Cotton Nissay Building, 1-8-2 Utsubo-Honmachi, Nishi-Ku, Osaka 550, T (06) 444 1220, F (06) 444 1380.

Singapore
10 Collyer Quay, 01-06 & 18-02, Ocean Building, Singapore 049313, T (02) 532 6321, F (02) 535 6650.

South Africa
1st Flr, Hutton Court, corner of Jan Smuts Ave and Summit Rd, Hyde Park 2196, Johannesburg, T (2711) 327 0400, F (2711) 327 0205.

South Korea
1st Flr, Han Young Building, 57-9 Seosomun-dong, Chung-ku, Seoul, T (02) 779 4422, F (02) 779 4254.

Sweden
Sveavagen 18, Box 7062, 10386 Stockholm, T (46) 8 249 900, F (46) 8 242 324.

Taiwan
Unit C, 8th Flr, Hung Tai Centre, 170 Tun Hwa North Rd, Taipei, T (02) 514 9704, F (02) 514 9973.

Thailand
Unit 902, Liberty Square, 287 Silom Rd, Bangkok, T (662) 631 1994, T (662) 631 1998.

UK
57 Trafalgar Square, London WC2N 5DU, T (0171) 930 7932, F (0171) 930 9015.

USA
818 Suite 804, West Seventh St, Los Angeles, CA 90017, T (213) 6899702, F (213) 689 1530; 595 Madison Ave, Suite 1800, New York, NY 10022, T (212) 754 1113, F (212) 754 1116.

SINGAPORE

Australia
Level 11, AWA Building, 47 York St, Sydney, T (61-2) 9290 2888, F (61-2) 9290 2555, and 8th Flr, St George's Court, 16 St George's Terrace, Perth, T (09) 3258578, F (09) 2213864.

Canada
Standard Life Centre, 121 King St West, Suite 1000, Toronto, Ontario, T (416) 3638898, F (416) 3635752.

France
Centre d'Affaires Le Louvre, 2 Place du Palais-Royal, Paris, T (01) 42971616, F (01) 42971617.

Germany
Hochstrasse 35-37, Frankfurt, T (069) 920 7700, F (069) 297 8922.

Italy
c/o Theodore Trancu & Associates, Corso Plebisciti 15, 20129 Milano, Italy, T (39-2) 7000 3981, F (39-2) 738 1032.

Japan
1st Flr, Yamato Seimei Building, 1 Chome, 1-7 Uchisaiwai-cho, Chiyoda-ku, Tokyo 100, T (81-3) 3593 3388, F (81-3) 3591 1480; and Osaka City Air Terminal, 4F, 1-4-1, Minato-Machi, Naniwa-ku, Osaka 556, T (81-6) 635 3087, F (81-6) 635 3089.

Hong Kong
Room 2003, Central Plaza, 18 Harbour Rd, Wanchai, T 5989290, F 5981040.

New Zealand
3rd Flr, 43 High St, Auckland, PO Box 857, T (64-9) 3581191, F (64-9) 3581196.

Switzerland
Löwenstrasse 51, CH-8044, Zurich, T (01) 2117474, F (01) 2117422.

South Africa
52 3rd Ave, Parktown North 2193, PO Box 81260, T (27-11) 788 0701, F (27-11) 442 7599.

Thailand
c/o MDK Consultants, Ruamrudi Building, 4th Flr, 566 Ploenchit Rd, Lumpini, Bangkok 10330, T (66-2) 252 4117, F (66-2) 252 4118.

UK
1st Flr Carrington House, 126-130 Regent St, London W1R 5FE, T (0171) 4370033, F (0171) 7342191.

USA
Two Prudential Plaza, 180 North Stetson Ave, Suite 1450, Chicago, T 312 9381888, F 312 9380086; 8484 Wilshire Blvd, Suite 510, Beverley Hills, CA 90211, T (213) 8521901, F (213) 8520129; 590 Fifth Ave, 12th Flr, New York, NY 10036, T (212) 3024861, F (212) 3024801.

The Singapore Tourist Promotion Board also has offices in Seoul, South Korea, in Bombay, India, and in Shanghai, China. There are representative offices in Buenos Aires, Argentina; Sao Paulo, Brazil; Santiago, Chile; and Mexico City, Mexico.

Malaysian words and phrases

BASIC Malay grammar is very simple: there are no tenses, genders or articles and the structure of sentences is straight-forward. Plurals are also easy: one "man", for example is *laki*, "men" is *laki-laki*, often denoted as *laki*[2]. Pronunciation is not difficult as there is a close relationship between the letter as it is written and the sound. Stress is usually placed on the second syllable of a word. For example *restoran* (restaurant) is pronounced res-TO-ran. See page 521.

Vowels

a is pronounced as *ah* in an open syllable, or as in *but* for a closed syllable.
e is pronounced as in *open* or *bed*.
i is pronounced as in *feel*.
o is pronounced as in *all*.
u is pronounced as in *foot*.
The letter *c* is pronounced as in *ch* as in *change* or *chat*.
The *r*'s are rolled.
Plural is indicated by repetition, *bapak-bapak*[2].

A brief, essential list of words and phrases is provided below. For those wanting to get a better grasp of the language, it is possible to take courses in Kuala Lumpur (enquire at Tourism Malaysia offices) and other big cities. The best way to take a crash-course in Malay is to buy a "teach-yourself" book; there are several on the market, but one of the best ones is *Malay in 3 Weeks*, by John Parry and Sahari bin Sulaiman (Times Books, 1989), which is widely aβvailable. A Malay/English dictionary or phrase book is a useful companion too; these are also readily available in bookshops.

Useful words and phrases

Yes/No	*ia/tidak*
Thank you	*Terimah kasih*
You're welcome	*Sama-sama*
Good morning/Good afternoon (early)	*Selamat pagi/Selamat tengahari*
Good afternoon (late)/Good evening/night	*Selamat petang/Selamat malam*
Welcome	*Selamat datang*
Goodbye (said by the person leaving)	*Selamat tinggal*
Goodbye (said by the person staying)	*Selamat jalan*
Excuse me / sorry	*Ma'af saya*
Where's the...?	*Dimana...*
How much is this...?	*Ini berapa?*

I [don't] understand	*Saya [tidak] mengerti*
I want...	*Saya mahu*
I don't want	*Saya tak mahu*
My name is...	*Nama saya...*
What is your name?	*Apa nama anda?*

The hotel

How much is a room?	*Bilik berapa?*
Does the room have air-conditioning?	*Ada bilik yang ada air-con-kah?*
I want to see the room first please	*Saya mahu lihat bilik dulu*
Does the room have hot water?	*Ada bilik yang ada air panas?*
Does the room have a bathroom?	*Ada bilik yang ada mandi-kah?*

Travel

Where is the railway station?	*Stesen keretapi dimana?*
Where is the bus station?	*Stesen bas dimana?*
How much to go to...?	*Berapa harga ke...?*
I want to buy a ticket to...	*Saya mahu beli tiket ke...*
How do I get there?	*Bagaimanakah saya*
Is it far?	*Ada jauh?*
Turn left / turn right	*Belok kiri / belok kanan*
Go staight on!	*Turus turus!*

Time and days

Monday	*Hari Isnin (Hari Satu)*	Sunday	*Hari Minggu (Hari Ahad)*
Tuesday	*Hari Selasa (Hari Dua)*	Today	*Hari ini*
Wednesday	*Hari Rabu (Hari Tiga)*	Tomorrow	*Esok*
Thursday	*Hari Khamis (Hari Empat)*	Week	*Minggu*
Friday	*Hari Jumaat (Hari Lima)*	Month	*Bulan*
Saturday	*Hari Sabtu (Hari Enam)*	Year	*Tahun*

Numbers

1	*satu*	20	*dua puluh*
2	*dua*	21	*dua puluh satu...etc*
3	*tiga*	30	*tiga puluh*
4	*empat*	100	*se-ratus*
5	*lima*	101	*se-ratus satu*
6	*enam*	150	*se-ratus limah puluh*
7	*tujuh*	200	*dua ratus...etc*
8	*lapan*	1,000	*se-ribu*
9	*sembilan*	2,000	*dua ribu...*
10	*sepuluh*	100,000	*se-ratus ribu*
11	*se-belas*	1,000,000	*se-juta*
12	*dua-belas...etc*		

Basic vocabulary

airport	*lapangan terbang*	broken	*tak makan / rosak*
a little	*sedikit*	bus	*bas*
a lot	*banyak*	bus station	*setsen bas*
all right/good	*baik*	bus stop	*Perhentian bas*
and	*dan*	buy	*beli*
bad	*tidak bagus*	can	*boleh*
bank	*bank*	cannot	*tak boleh*
bathroom	*bilek mandi*	cheap	*murah*
beach	*pantai*	chemist	*rumah ubat*
beautiful	*cantik*	cigarette	*rokok*
bed sheet	*cadar*	clean	*bersih*
big	*besar*	closed	*tutup*
boat	*perahu*	coffee	*kopi*

cold	*sejuk*
crazy	*gila*
day	*hari*
delicious	*sedap*
dentist	*doktor gigi*
dirty	*kotor*
doctor	*doktor*
drink	*minum*
eat	*makan*
excellent	*bagus*
expensive	*mahal*
fruit	*buah*
good	*bagus*
he/she	*dia*
hospital	*rumah sakit*
hot (temperature)	*panas*
hot (chilli)	*pedas*
I/me	*saya*
ice	*air batuais*
island	*pulau*
male	*lelaki*
man	*laki*
market	*pasar*
medicine	*ubat ubatan*
milk	*susu*
more	*lagi/lebeh*
open	*masuk*
please	*sila*
pillow	*bantal*
police	*polis*
police station	*pejabat polis*
post office	*pejabat pos*
railway station	*stesen keretapi/tren*
restaurant	*restoran/kedai makanan*
room	*bilik*
sea	*laut*
ship	*kapal*
shop	*kedai*
sick	*sakit*
sleep	*tidur*
small	*kecil*
stand	*berdiri*
stop	*berhenti*
sugar	*gula*
taxi	*teksi*
tea	*teh*
that	*itu*
they	*mereka*
ticket	*tiket*
toilet (female)	*tandas perempuan*
toilet (male)	*tandas lelaki*
town	*bandar*
trishaw	*beca*
very	*sangat*
wait	*tunggu*
water	*air*
we	*kami*
what	*apa*
when	*bila*
woman	*perempuan*
you	*awak/anda*

A MALAY FOOD GLOSSARY

assam	sour
ayam	chicken
babi	pork
belacan	hot fermented prawn paste
daging	meat
garam	salt
gula	sugar
ikan	fish
ikan bakar	grilled fish
ikan bilis	anchovies
ikan panggang	spicy barbecued fish
kambing	mutton
kerupak	prawn crackers
ketupat	cold, compressed rice
kueh	cakes
lemang	glutinous rice in bamboo
limau	lime
makan	food
manis	sweet
mee	noodles
minum	drink
nasi	rice
roti canai	pancakes served with lentils and curry
roti john	baguette filled with sardine/egg mixture
roti kosong	plain pancake
sambal	spicy paste of pounded chilli's, onion and tamarind
sayur	vegetables
sayur manis	sweet vegetables
sayur masak lemak	deep fried marinated prawns
sejuk	crab
soto ayam	spicy chicken soup
sotong	squid
tahu	beancurd
telur	egg
udang	prawn

DISTINCTIVE FRUITS

Custard apple (or sugar apple) Scaly green skin, squeeze the skin to open the fruit and scoop out the flesh with a spoon.

Durian (*Durio zibethinus*) A large prickly fruit, with yellow flesh, about the size of a football. Infamous for its pungent smell. While it is today regarded by many visitors as simply revolting, early Europeans (16th-18th centuries) raved about it, possibly because it was similar in taste to western delicacies of the period. Borri (1744) thought that "God himself, who had produc'd that fruit". But by 1880 Burbridge was writing: "Its odour – one scarcely feels justified in using the word 'perfume' – is so potent, so vague, but withal so insinuating, that it can scarcely be tolerated inside the house". Banned from public transport in Singapore and hotel rooms throughout the region, and beloved by most Southeast Asians (where prize specimens can cost a week's salary), it has an alluring taste if the odour can be overcome (it has been described as like eating blancmange on the toilet). Some maintain it is an addiction. Durian-flavoured chewing gum, ice cream and jams are all available.

Jackfruit Similar in appearance to durian but not so spiky. Yellow flesh, tasting slightly like custard.

Mango (*Mangifera indica*) A rainforest fruit which is now cultivated. Widely available in the West; in Southeast Asia there are hundreds of different varieties with subtle variations in flavour. Delicious eaten with sticky rice and a sweet sauce (in Thailand). The best mangoes in the region are considered to be those from South Thailand.

Mangosteen (*Garcinia mangostana*) An aubergine-coloured hard shell covers this small fruit which is about the size of a tennis ball. Cut or squeeze the purple shell to reach its sweet white flesh which is prized by many visitors above all others. In 1898, an American resident of Java wrote, erotically and in obvious ecstasy: "The five white segments separate easily, and they melt on the tongue with a touch of tart and a touch of sweet; one moment a memory of the juiciest, most fragrant apple, at another a remembrance of the smoothest cream ice, the most exquisite and delicately flavoured fruit-acid known – all of the delights of nature's laboratory condensed in that ball of *neige parfumée*". Southeast Asians believe it should be eaten as a chaser to durian.

Papaya (*Carica papaya*) A New World Fruit that was not introduced into Southeast Asia until the 16th century. Large, round or oval in shape, yellow or green-skinned, with bright orange flesh and a mass of round, black seeds in the middle. The flesh, in texture and taste, is somewhere between a mango and a melon. Some maintain that it tastes 'soapy'.

Pomelo A large round fruit the size of anything from an ostrich egg to a football, with thick, green skin, thick pith, and flesh not unlike that of the grapefruit, but less acidic.

Rambutan (*Nephelium lappaceum*) The bright red and hairy rambutan – *rambut* is the Malay word for 'hair' – with its slightly rubbery but sweet flesh is a close relative of the lychee of southern China and tastes similar. The Thai word for rambutan is *ngoh*, which is the nickname given by Thais to the fuzzy-haired Negrito aboriginals in the southern jungles.

Salak (*Salacca edulis*) A small pear-shaped fruit about the size of a large plum with a rough, brown, scaly skin (somewhat like a miniature pangolin) and yellow-white, crisp flesh. It is related to the sago and rattan trees.

Tamarind (*Tamarindus indicus*) Brown seedpods with dry brittle skins and a brown tart-sweet fruit which grow on a tree introduced into Southeast Asia from India. The name is Arabic for 'Indian date'. The flesh has a high tartaric acid content and is used to flavour curries, jams, jellies and chutneys as well as for cleaning brass and copper. Elephants have a predilection for tamarind balls.

Health

WITH THE following advice and precautions, you should keep as healthy as you do at home. In Southeast Asia the health risks are different from those encountered in Europe or the USA, especially in the tropical regions, but the region's medical practitioners have particular experience in dealing with locally occurring diseases. There is an obvious difference in health risks between the business traveller who tends to stay in international class hotels in large cities and the backpacker trekking through rural areas. There are no hard and fast rules to follow; you will often have to make your own judgements on the healthiness or otherwise of your surroundings.

Medical care

In Singapore, medical care is first class but expensive. Health care in Malaysia and Brunei is also of a high standard. Most doctors speak English, but the likelihood of finding this and a good standard of care diminishes very rapidly as you move away from the big cities. In some of the countries – and especially in rural areas – there are systems and traditions of medicine wholly different from the western model and you may be confronted with less orthodox forms of treatment such as herbal medicine and acupuncture. At least you can be sure that local practitioners have a lot of experience with the particular diseases of their region. If you are in a city it may be worthwhile calling on your embassy to provide a list of recommended doctors.

Medicines

If you are a long way away from medical help, a certain amount of self administered medication may be necessary and you will find many of the drugs available have familiar names. However, always check the date stamping (sell-by date) and buy from reputable pharmacists because the shelf life of some items, especially vaccines and antibiotics, is markedly reduced in hot conditions. Unfortunately, many locally produced drugs are not subjected to quality control procedures and so can be unreliable. There have, in addition, been cases of substitution of inert materials for active drugs. With the following precautions and advice you should keep as healthy as usual. Make local enquiries about health risks if you are apprehensive and take the general advice of European, Australian or North American families who have lived or are living in the area.

BEFORE YOU GO

Take out medical insurance. You should also have a dental check-up, obtain a spare glasses prescription and, if you suffer from a long-standing condition, such as diabetes, high blood pressure, heart/lung disease or a nervous disorder, arrange for a check-up with your doctor who can at the same time provide you with a letter explaining details of your medical disorder. Check the current practice for malaria prophylaxis (prevention) for the countries you intend to visit.

Vaccination and immunisation

Smallpox vaccination is no longer required. Neither is cholera vaccination, despite the fact that the disease occurs – but not at present in epidemic form – in some of these countries. Yellow fever vaccination is not required either, although you may be asked for a certificate if you have been in a country affected by yellow fever immediately before travelling to Southeast Asia.

The following vaccinations are recommended:

Typhoid (monovalent) One dose followed by a booster 1 month later. Immunity from this course lasts 2-3 years. An oral preparation is also available.

Poliomyelitis This is a live vaccine generally given orally but a full course consists of three doses with a booster in tropical regions every 3-5 years.

Tetanus One dose should be given, with a booster at 6 weeks and another at 6 months. 10 yearly boosters thereafter are recommended.

Meningitis and Japanese B encephalitis (JVE) There is an extremely small risk of these rather serious diseases; both are seasonal and vary according to region. Meningitis can occur in epidemic form; JVE is a viral disease transmitted from pigs to man by mosquitos. For details of the vaccinations, consult a travel clinic.

Children should, in addition to the above, be properly protected against diphtheria, whooping cough, mumps and measles. Teenage girls, if they have not had the disease, should be given a rubella (German measles) vaccination. Consult your doctor for advice on BCG inoculation against tuberculosis: the disease is still common in the region.

Infectious hepatitis (jaundice) This is common throughout Southeast Asia. It seems to be frequently caught by travellers. The main symptoms are stomach pains, lack of appetite, nausea, lassitude and yellowness of the eyes and skin. Medically speaking there are two types: the less serious but more common is *hepatitis A* for which the best protection is careful preparation of food, the avoidance of contaminated drinking water and scrupulous attention to toilet hygiene. Human normal immunoglobulin (gammaglobulin) confers considerable protection against the disease and is particularly useful in epidemics. It should be obtained from a reputable source and is certainly recommended for travellers who intend to travel and live rough. The injection should be given as close as possible to your departure and as the dose depends on the likely time you are to spend in potentially infected areas, the manufacturers' instructions should be followed. A vaccination against hepatitis A has recently become generally available and is safe and effective. Three shots are given over 6 months and confer excellent protection against the disease for up to 10 years. Eventually this vaccine is likely to supersede the use of gammaglobulin.

The other, more serious, version is *hepatitis B* which is acquired as a sexually transmitted disease, from a blood transfusion or an injection with an unclean needle, or possibly by insect bites. The symptoms are the same as hepatitis A but the incubation period is much longer.

You may have had jaundice before or you may have had hepatitis of either type before without becoming jaundiced, in which case it is possible that you could be immune to either hepatitis A or B (or C or a number of other letters). This immunity can be tested for before you travel. If you are not immune to hepatitis B already, a vaccine is available (three shots over 6 months) and if you are not immune to hepatitis A already, then you should consider having gammaglobulin or a vaccination.

AIDS

AIDS in Southeast Asia is increasingly prevalent. Thus, it is not wholly confined to the well known high risk sections of the population ie homosexual men, intravenous drug abusers, prostitutes and the children of infected mothers. Heterosexual transmission is probably now the dominant mode of infection and so the main risk to travellers is from casual sex. The same precautions should be taken as when encountering any sexually transmitted disease. In some Southeast Asian countries, Thailand is an example, almost the entire population of female prostitutes is HIV positive and in other parts intravenous drug abuse is common. There is less of a problem in Singapore and – possibly – Malaysia. The AIDS virus (HIV) can be passed via unsterile needles which have been previously used to inject an HIV positive patient, but the risk of this is very small indeed. It would, however, be sensible to check that needles have been properly sterilized or disposable needles used. The chance of picking up hepatitis B in this way is much more of a danger. Be wary of carrying disposable needles. Customs officials may find them suspicious. The risk of receiving a blood transfusion with blood infected with the HIV virus is greater than from dirty needles because of the amount of fluid exchanged. Supplies of blood for transfusion are supposed to be screened for HIV in all reputable hospitals so the risk should be small. Catching the virus which causes AIDS does not necessarily produce an illness in itself; the only way to be sure if you feel you have been put at risk is to have a blood test for HIV antibodies on your return to a place where there are reliable laboratory facilities. However, the test does not become positive for many weeks.

MALARIA

Malaria is prevalent in Southeast Asia (but not in Singapore). Malaria remains a serious disease and you are advised to protect yourself against mosquito bites as above and to take prophylactic (preventative) drugs. Start taking the tablets a few days before exposure and continue to take them 6 weeks after leaving the malarial zone. Remember to give the drugs to babies and children, pregnant women also.

The subject of malaria prevention is becoming more complex as the malaria parasite becomes immune to some of the older drugs. In particular, there has been an increase in the proportion of cases of falciparum malaria which are resistant to the normally used drugs. It would not be an exaggeration to say that we are near to the situation where some cases of malaria will be untreatable with presently available drugs.

Before you travel you must check with a reputable agency the likelihood and type of malaria in the countries which you intend to visit. Take their advice on prophylaxis but be prepared to receive conflicting advice. Because of the rapidly changing situation in the Southeast Asian region, the names and dosage of the drugs have not been included. But Chloroquine and Proguanil may still be recommended for the areas where malaria is still fully sensitive. Doxycycline, Metloquine and Quinghaosu are presently being used in resistant areas. Halofantrine Quinine and tetracycline drugs remain the mainstays of treatment.

It is still possible to catch malaria even when taking prophylactic drugs, although this is unlikely. If you do develop symptoms (high fever, shivering, severe headache, and sometimes diarrhoea) seek medical advice immediately. The risk of the disease is obviously greater the further you move from the cities into rural areas, with primitive facilities and standing water.

OTHER COMMON PROBLEMS

HEAT AND COLD

Full acclimatization to tropical temperatures takes about 2 weeks and during this period it is normal to feel relatively apathetic, especially if the humidity is high. Drink plenty of water (up to 15 litres a day are required when working physically hard in the tropics). Use salt on your food and avoid extreme exertion. Tepid showers are more cooling than hot or cold ones. Large hats do not cool you down but do prevent sunburn. Remember that, especially in highland areas, there can be a large and sudden drop in temperature between sun and shade and between night and day so dress accordingly. Loose-fitting cotton clothes are best for hot weather. Warm jackets and woollens are often necessary after dark at high altitude.

INSECTS

These can be a great nuisance. Some, of course, are carriers of serious diseases such as malaria, dengue fever or filariasis and various worm infections. The best way of keeping mosquitos away at night is to sleep off the ground with a mosquito net and to burn mosquito coils containing Pyrethrum. Aerosol sprays or a 'flit gun' may be effective as are insecticidal tablets which are heated on a mat which is plugged into the wall socket (if taking your own, check the voltage of the area you are visiting so that you can take an appliance that will work; similarly, check that your electrical adaptor is suitable for the repellent plug; note that they are widely available in the region).

You can, in addition, use personal insect repellent of which the best contain a high concentration of diethyltoluamide (DET). Liquid is best for arms and face (take care around eyes and make sure you do not dissolve the plastic of your spectacles). Aerosol spray on clothes and ankles deter mites and ticks. Liquid DET suspended in water can be used to impregnate cotton clothes and mosquito nets. The latter are now available in wide mesh form which are lighter to carry and less claustrophobic to sleep under.

If you are bitten, itching may be relieved by cool baths and antihistamine tables (take care with alcohol or when driving), corticosteroid creams (great care – never use if any hint of septic poisoning) or by judicious scratching. Calamine lotion and cream have limited effectiveness and antihistamine creams have a tendency to cause skin allergies and are therefore not generally recommended. Bites which become infected (a common problem in the tropics) should be treated with a local antiseptic or antibiotic cream such as Cetrimide, as should infected scratches. Skin infestations with body lice, crabs and scabies are unfortunately easy to pick up. Use gamma benzene hexachloride for lice and benzyl benzoate for scabies. Crotamiton cream alleviates itching and also kills a number of skin parasites. Malathion lotion is good for lice but avoid the highly toxic full strength Malathion which is used as an agricultural insecticide.

INTESTINAL UPSETS

Practically nobody escapes intestinal infections, so be prepared for them. Most of the time they are due to the insanitary preparation of food. Do not eat uncooked fish, vegetables or meat (especially pork), fruit without the skin (always peel fruit yourself), or food that is exposed to flies (particularly salads). Tap water may be unsafe, especially in the monsoon seasons and the same goes for stream water or well water. Filtered or bottled water is usually available and safe but you cannot always rely on it. If your hotel has a central hot water supply, this is safe to drink after cooling. Ice should be made from boiled water but rarely is, so stand your glass on the ice cubes instead of putting them in the drink. Dirty water should first be strained through a filter bag (available from camping shops) and then boiled or treated. Bringing the water to a rolling boil at sea level is sufficient. In the highlands, you have to boil the water a bit longer to ensure that all the microbes are killed (because water boils at a lower temperature at altitude). Various sterilizing methods can be used and there are proprietary preparations containing chlorine or iodine compounds. Pasteurized or heat-treated milk is now fairly widely available as is ice cream and yoghurt produced by the same methods. Unpasteurized milk products, including cheese, are sources of tuberculosis, brucellosis, listeria and food poisoning germs. You can render fresh milk safe by heating it to 62°C for 30 minutes followed by rapid cooling or by boiling. Matured or processed cheeses are safer than fresh varieties.

Fish and shellfish are popular foods throughout island Southeast Asia but can be the source of health problems. Shellfish which are eaten raw will transmit food poisoning or hepatitis if they have been living in contaminated water. Certain fish accumulate toxins in their bodies at certain times of the year, which give rise to illness when they are eaten. The phenomenon known as 'red tide' can also affect fish and shellfish which eat large quantities of tiny sea creatures and thereby become poisonous. The only way to guard against this is to keep as well informed as possible about fish and shellfish quality in the area you are visiting. Most countries impose a ban on fishing in periods when red tide is prevalent, although this is often flouted.

Diarrhoea

Diarrhoea is usually the result of food poisoning, but can occasionally result from contaminated water. There are various causes – viruses, bacteria, protozoa (like amoeba), salmonella and cholera organisms. It may take one of several forms coming on suddenly or rather slowly. It may be accompanied by vomiting or severe abdominal pain, and the passage of blood or mucus (when it is called dysentery).

All kinds of diarrhoea, whether or not accompanied by vomiting, respond favourably to the replacement of water and salts taken as frequent small sips of some kind of rehydration solution. There are proprietary preparations consisting of sachets of oral rehydration electrolyte powder which are dissolved in water, or make up your own by adding half a teaspoonful of salt (3.5 grams) and 4 tablespoons of sugar (40 grams) to a litre of boiled water. If it is possible to time the onset of diarrhoea to the minute, then it is probably viral or bacterial and/or the onset of dysentery. The treatment in addition to rehydration is Ciprofloxacin (500 mgs every 12 hours). The drug is now widely available as are various similar ones.

If the diarrhoea has come on slowly or intermittently, then it is more likely to be protozoal, ie caused by amoeba or giardia, and antibiotics will have no effect. These cases are best treated by a doctor as should any diarrhoea continuing for more than 3 days. If there are severe stomach cramps, the following drugs may help: Loperamide (*Imodium*, *Arret*) and Diphenoxylate with Atropine (*Lomotil*). The drug usually used for giardia or amoeba is Metronidazole (*Flagyl*) or Tinidazole (*Fasigyu*).

The lynchpins of treatment for diarrhoea are rest, fluid and salt replacement, antibiotics such as Ciprofloxacin for the bacterial types, and special diagnostic tests and medical treatment for amoeba and giardia infections. Salmonella infections and cholera can be devastating diseases and it would be wise to get to a hospital as soon as possible if these were suspected. Fasting, peculiar diets and the consumption of large quantities of yoghurt have not been found useful in calming travellers' diarrhoea or in rehabilitating inflamed bowels. Oral rehydration has, especially in children, been a lifesaving technique and as there is some evidence that alcohol and milk might prolong diarrhoea they should probably be avoided during, and immediately after, an attack. There are ways of preventing travellers' diarrhoea for short periods of time when visiting these countries by taking antibiotics but these are ineffective against viruses and, to some extent, against protozoa. This technique should not be used other than in exceptional circumstances. Some preventatives such as Enterovioform can have serious side effects if taken for long periods.

SUNBURN AND HEAT STROKE

The burning power of the tropical sun is phenomenal, especially in highland areas. Always wear a wide-brimmed hat, and use some form of sun cream or lotion on untanned skin. Normal temperate zone suntan lotions (protection factors up to 7) are not much good. You need to use the types designed specifically for the tropics or for mountaineers or skiers, with a protection factor between 7 and 15 or higher. Glare from the sun can cause conjunctivitis so wear sunglasses, particularly on beaches.

There are several varieties of heat stroke. The most common cause is severe dehydration. Avoid this by drinking lots of non-alcoholic fluid, and adding salt to your food.

SNAKE AND OTHER BITES AND STINGS

If you are unlucky enough to be bitten by a venomous snake, spider, scorpion, centipede or sea creature, try (within limits) to catch or kill the animal for identification. Reactions to be expected are shock, swelling, pain and bruising around the bite, soreness of the regional lymph glands, nausea, vomiting and fever. If in addition any of the following symptoms should follow closely, get the victim to a doctor without delay: numbness, tingling of the face, muscular spasms, convulsions, shortness of breath or haemorrhage. Commercial snake-bite or scorpion-sting kits may be available but these are only useful against the specific type of snake or scorpion for which they are designed. The serum has to be given intravenously so is not much good unless you have had some practice in making injections into veins. If the bite is on a limb, immobilize it and apply a tight bandage between the bite and the body, releasing it for 90 seconds every 15 minutes. Reassurance of the victim is very important because death from snake bite is very rare. Do not slash the bite area and try to suck out the poison because this sort of heroism does more harm than good. Hospitals usually hold stocks of snake-bite serum. The best precaution is not walk in long grass with bare feet, sandals or in shorts.

When swimming in an area where there are poisonous fish such as stone or scorpion fish (also called by a variety of local names) or sea urchins on rocky coasts, tread carefully or wear plimsolls/trainers. The sting of such fish is intensely painful. This can be relieved by immersing the injured part of the body in water as hot as you can bear for as long as it remains painful. This is not always very practical and you must take care not to scald yourself, but it does work. Avoid spiders and scorpions by keeping your bed away from the wall, look under lavatory seats and inside your shoes in the morning. In the rare event of being bitten, consult a doctor.

WATCH OUT FOR

Remember that **rabies** is endemic in many Southeast Asian countries. If you are bitten by a domestic or wild animal, do not leave things to chance. Scrub the wound with soap and water and/or disinfectant, try to have the animal captured (within limits) or at least determine its ownership where possible, and seek medical assistance at once. The course of treatment depends on whether you have already been satisfactorily vaccinated against rabies. If you have (and this is worthwhile if you are spending lengths of time in developing countries) then some further doses of vaccine are all that is required. Human diploid cell vaccine is the best, but expensive: other, older kinds of vaccine such as that derived from duck embryos may be the only types available. These are effective, much cheaper and interchangeable generally with the human derived types. If not already vaccinated then anti-rabies serum (immunoglobulin) may be required in addition. It is wise to finish the course of treatment whether the animal survives or not.

Dengue fever is present in most of the countries of Southeast Asia. It is a viral disease transmitted by mosquito and causes severe headaches and body pains. Complicated types of dengue known as haemorrhagic fevers occur throughout Asia but usually in persons who have caught the disease a second time. Thus, although it is a very serious type it is rarely caught by visitors. There is no treatment, you must just avoid mosquito bites.

Intestinal worms are common and the more serious ones, such as hook worm can be contracted by walking barefoot on infested earth or beaches.

Influenza and **respiratory diseases** are common, perhaps made worse by polluted cities and rapid temperature and climatic changes – accentuated by air-conditioning.

Prickly heat is a very common itchy rash, best avoided by frequent washing and by wearing loose clothing. It can be helped by the use of talcum powder, allowing the skin to dry thoroughly after washing.

Athlete's foot and other **fungal infections** are best treated by sunshine and a proprietary preparation such as Tolnaftate.

WHEN YOU RETURN HOME

On returning home, remember to take anti-malarial tablets for 6 weeks. If you have had attacks of diarrhoea, it is worth having a stool specimen tested in case you have picked up amoebic dysentery. If you have been living rough, a blood test may also be worthwhile to detect worms and other parasites.

BASIC SUPPLIES

You may find the following items useful to take with you from home: suntan cream, insect repellent, flea powder, mosquito net, coils or tablets, tampons, condoms, contraceptives, water sterilizing tablets, anti-malaria tablets, anti-infective ointment, dusting powder for feet, travel sickness pills, antiacid tablets, anti-diarrhoea tablets, sachets of rehydration salts, a first aid kit and disposable needles (also see page 744).

FURTHER INFORMATION

Information regarding country-by-country malaria risk can be obtained from the World Health Organization (WHO) or in Britain from the Ross Institute, London School of Hygiene and Tropical Medicine, Keppel Street, London WClE 7HT which also publishes a highly recommended book: *The preservation of personal health in warm climates*. The Centres for Disease Control (CDC) in Atlanta, Georgia, USA will provide equivalent information. The organization MASTA (Medical Advisory Service for Travellers Abroad) also based at the London School of Hygiene and Tropical Medicine (T 0171 631-4408) will provide up-to-date country-by-country information on health risks. Further information on medical problems overseas can be obtained from the new edition of *Travellers health, how to stay healthy abroad*, edited by Richard Dawood (Oxford University Press, 1992). This revised and updated edition is highly recommended, especially to the intrepid traveller. A more general publication, with hints on health and much more besides, is John Hatt's new edition of *The tropical traveller* (Penguin, 1993).

The above information has been compiled by Dr David Snashall, Senior Lecturer in Occupational Health, United Medical Schools of Guy's and St Thomas' Hospitals and Chief Medical Adviser, Foreign and Commonwealth Office, London.

Travelling with children

MANY PEOPLE are daunted by the prospect of taking a child to Southeast Asia. Naturally, it is not something to be taken on lightly; travelling is slower and more expensive and there are additional health risks for the child or baby. But it can be a most rewarding experience, and with sufficient care and planning, it can also be safe. Children are excellent passports into a local culture. You will also receive the best service, and help from officials and members of the public when in difficulty.

Children in Southeast Asia are given 24-hours attention by parents, grandparents and siblings. They are rarely left to cry and are carried for most of the first 8 months of their lives – crawling is considered animal-like. A non-Asian child is still something of a novelty and parents may find their child frequently taken off their hands, even mobbed in more remote areas. This can be a great relief (at meal-times, for instance) or most alarming. Some children love the attention, others react against it; it is best simply to gauge your own child's reactions.

PRACTICALITIES

Accommodation

At the hottest time of year, air-conditioning may be essential for a baby or young child's comfort. This rules out many of the cheaper hotels, but air-conditioned accommodation is available in all but the most out-of-the-way spots. When the child is bathing, be aware that the water could carry parasites, so avoid letting him or her drink it.

Food and drink

The advice given in the health section on food and drink (see page 745) should be applied even more stringently where young children are concerned. Be aware that expensive hotels may have squalid cooking conditions; the cheapest street stall is often more hygienic. Where possible, try to watch food being prepared. Stir-fried vegetables and rice or noodles are the best bet; meat and fish may be pre-cooked and then left out before being re-heated. Fruit can be bought cheaply right across Southeast Asia: papaya, banana and avocado are all excellent sources of nutrition, and can be self-peeled ensuring cleanliness. Powdered milk is also available throughout the region, although most brands have added sugar. But if taking a baby, breast-feeding is strongly recommended. Powdered food can be bought in most towns – the quality may not be the same as equivalent foods bought in the West, but it is perfectly adequate for short periods. Bottled water and fizzy drinks are also sold widely. If your child is at the 'grab everything and put it in mouth' stage, a damp cloth and some *dettol* (or equivalent) are useful. Frequent wiping of hands and tabletops can help to minimize the chance of infection.

Transport

Public transport may be a problem; trains are fine but long bus journeys are restrictive and uncomfortable. Hiring a car is undoubtedly the most convenient way to see a country with a small child. Back-seatbelts are rarely fitted but it is possible to buy child-seats in capital cities.

ESSENTIALS

Disposable nappies These can be bought in Malaysia, Singapore and Brunei, but are often expensive. If you are staying any length of time in one place, it may be worth taking Terry's (cloth) nappies. All you need is a bucket and some double-strength nappy cleanse (simply soak and rinse). Cotton nappies dry quickly in the heat and are generally more comfortable for the baby or child. They also reduce rubbish – many countries are not geared to the disposal of nappies. Of course, the best way for a child to be is nappy-free – like the local children.

Baby products Many western baby products are now available in Southeast Asia: shampoo, talcum powder, soap and lotion. Baby wipes can be difficult to find.

HEALTH

Younger travellers seem to be more prone to illness abroad, but that should not put you off taking them. More preparation is necessary than for an adult and perhaps a little more care should be taken when travelling to remote areas where health services are primitive. This is because children can become more rapidly ill than adults (they often recover more quickly however).

Diarrhoea and vomiting are the most common problems so take the usual precautions, but more intensively. Make sure all basic childhood **vaccinations** are up to date as well as the more exotic ones. Children should be properly protected against diphtheria, whooping cough, mumps and measles. If they have not had the disease, teenage girls should be given rubella (german measles) vaccination. Consult your doctor for advice on BCG inoculation against tuberculosis: the disease is still common in the region. Protection against mosquitos and drug prophylaxis against malaria is essential. Many children take to "foreign" food quite happily. Milk in Southeast Asia may be unavailable outside big cities. Powdered milk may be the answer; breast feeding for babies even better.

Upper respiratory infections such as colds, catarrh and middle ear infections are common – antibiotics could be carried against the possibility. **Outer ear infections** after swimming are also common – antibiotic ear drops will help. The treatment of **diarrhoea** is the same as for adults except that it should start earlier and be continued with more persistence. Children get dehydrated very quickly in the tropics and can become drowsy and uncooperative unless cajoled to drink water or juice plus salts. Oral rehydration has been a lifesaving technique in children.

Emergencies

Babies and small children deteriorate very rapidly when ill. A travel insurance policy which has an air ambulance provision is strongly recommended. When planning a route, try to stay within 24 hours' travel of a hospital with good care and facilities. Many expatriats fly to Singapore for medical care, which has the best doctors and facilities in the region.

Sunburn

NEVER allow your child to be exposed to the harsh tropical sun without protection.

A child can burn in a matter of minutes. Loose cotton-clothing, with long sleeves and legs and a sun-hat are best. High-factor sun-protection cream is essential.

CHECKLIST

Baby wipes
Child paracetamol
Disinfectant
First aid kit
Flannel
Immersion element for boiling water
decongestant
Instant food for under-one-year-olds
Mug/bottle/bowl/spoons
Nappy cleanse, double-strength
ORS/ORT (Oral Rehydration Salts or Therapy) such as *Dioralyte*, widely available in the countries covered here, and the most effective way to alleviate diarrhoea (it is not a cure)
Portable baby chair, to hook onto tables; this is not essential but can be very useful
Sarung or backpack for carrying child (and/or light weight collapsible buggy)
Sterilizing tablets
Cream for nappy rash and other skin complaints
Sunblock, factor 15 or higher
Sunhat
Terry's (cloth) nappies, liners, pins and plastic pants
Thermometer
Zip-lock bags

FURTHER INFORMATION

Pentes, Tina and Truelove, Adrienne (1984) *Travelling with children to Indonesia and South-East Asia*, Hale & Iremonger: Sydney. Wheeler, Maureen *Travel with children*, Lonely Planet: Hawthorne, Australia.

TEMPERATURE CONVERSION TABLE

°C	°F	°C	°F
1	34	26	79
2	36	27	81
3	38	28	82
4	39	29	84
5	41	30	86
6	43	31	88
7	45	32	90
8	46	33	92
9	48	34	93
10	50	35	95
11	52	36	97
12	54	37	99
13	56	38	100
14	57	39	102
15	59	40	104
16	61	41	106
17	63	42	108
18	64	43	109
19	66	44	111
20	68	45	113
21	70	46	115
22	72	47	117
23	74	48	118
24	75	49	120
25	77	50	122

The formula for converting °C to °F is:

(°C x 9 ÷ 5) + 32 = °F

and for converting °F to °C:

(°F -32) x 5 ÷ 9 = °C

WEIGHTS AND MEASURES

Metric

Weight
1 Kilogram (Kg) = 2.205 pounds
1 metric ton = 1.102 short tons

Length
1 millimetre (mm)= 0.03937 inch
1 metre = 3.281 feet
1 kilometre (km) = 0.621 mile

Area
1 heactare = 2.471 acres
1 square km = 0.386 sq mile

Capacity
1 litre = 0.220 imperial gallon
= 0.264 US gallon

Volume
1 cubic metre (m^3) = 35.31 cubic feet
= 1.31 cubic yards

British and US

Weight
1 pound (lb) = 454 grams
1 short ton (2,000lbs) = 0.907 m ton
1 long ton (2,240lbs) = 1.016 m tons

Length
1 inch = 25.417 millimetres
1 foot (ft) = 0.305 metre
1 mile = 1.609 kilometres

Area
1 acre = 0.405 hectare
1 sq mile = 2.590 sq kilometre

Capacity
1 imperial gallon = 4.546 litres
1 US gallon = 3.785 litres

Volume
1 cubic foot (cu ft) = 0.028 m^3
1 cubic yard (cu yd) = 0.765 m^3

NB 5 imperial gallons are approximately equal to 6 US gallons

Glossary

A

Adat
custom or tradition

Amitabha
the Buddha of the Past (see Avalokitsvara)

Atap
thatch

Avalokitsvara
also known as Amitabha and Lokeshvara, the name literally means "World Lord"; he is the compassionate male Bodhisattva, the saviour of Mahayana Buddhism and represents the central force of creation in the universe; usually portrayed with a lotus and water flask

B

Bahasa
language, as in Bahasa Malaysia

Barisan Nasional
National Front, Malaysia's ruling coalition comprising UMNO, MCA and MIC along with seven other parties

Batik
a form of resist dyeing common in Malay areas

Becak
three-wheeled bicycle rickshaw

Bodhi
the tree under which the Buddha achieved enlightenment (*Ficus religiosa*)

Bodhisattva
a future Buddha. In Mahayana Buddhism, someone who has attained enlightenment, but who postpones nirvana in order to help others reach the same state

Brahma
the Creator, one of the gods of the Hindu trinity, usually represented with four faces, and often mounted on a hamsa

Brahmin
a Hindu priest

Budaya
cultural (as in Muzium Budaya)

Bumboat
small wooden lighters, now used for ferrying tourists in Singapore

Bumiputra
literally, 'sons of the soil'; Malays as opposed to other races in Malaysia (see page 90)

C

Cap
batik stamp

Chedi
from the Sanskrit *cetiya* (Pali, *caitya*) meaning memorial. Usually a religious monument (often bell-shaped) containing relics of the Buddha or other holy remains. Used interchangeably with stupa

Cutch
see Gambier

D

Dalang
wayang puppet master

DAP
Democratic Action Party, Malaysia's predominantly Chinese opposition party

Dayak/Dyak
collective term for the tribal peoples of Borneo

Dharma
the Buddhist law

Dipterocarp
family of trees (Dipterocarpaceae) characteristic of Southeast Asia's forests

Durga
the female goddess who slays the demon Mahisa, from an Indian epic story

E

Epiphyte
plant which grows on another plant (but usually not parasitic)

F

Feng shui
the Chinese art of geomancy

G

Gambier
also known as cutch, a dye derived from the bark of the bakau mangrove and used in leather tanning

Gamelan
Malay orchestra of percussion instruments

Ganesh
elephant-headed son of Siva

Garuda
mythical divine bird, with predatory beak and claws, and human body; the king of birds, enemy of naga and mount of Vishnu

Gautama
the historic Buddha

Geomancy
or *feng shui*, the Chinese art and science of proper placement

Goporum
tower in a Hindu temple

Gunung
mountain

H

Hamsa
sacred goose, Brahma's mount; in Buddhism it represents the flight of the doctrine

Hinayana
'Lesser Vehicle', major Buddhist sect in South-east Asia, usually termed Theravada Buddhism (see page 72)

I

Ikat
tie-dyeing method of patterning cloth

Indra
the Vedic god of the heavens, weather and war; usually mounted on a 3 headed elephant

J

Jataka(s)
birth stories of the Buddha, of which there are 547; the last ten are the most important

K

Kajang
thatch

Kala (makara)
literally, 'death' or 'black'; a demon ordered to consume itself; often sculpted over entrance-ways to act as a door guardian, also known as kirtamukha

Kerangas
from an Iban word meaning 'land on which rice will not grow'

Keraton
see kraton

Kinaree
half-human, half-bird, usually depicted as a heavenly musician

Kongsi
Chinese clan house

Kris
traditional Malay sword (see page 49)

Krishna
an incarnation of Vishnu

Kuti
living quarters of Buddhist monks

L

Laterite
bright red tropical soil/stone sometimes used as a building material

Linga
phallic symbol and one of the forms of Siva. Embedded in a pedestal shaped to allow drainage of lustral water poured over it, the linga typically has a succession of cross sections: from square at the base through octagonal to round. These symbolize, in order, the trinity of Brahma, Vishnu and Siva

Lintel
a load-bearing stone spanning a doorway; often heavily carved

Lokeshvara
see Avalokitsvara

Lunggyi
Indian sarong

M

Mahabharata
a Hindu epic text written about 2,000 years ago (see page 74)

Mahayana
'Greater Vehicle', major Buddhist sect (see page 72)

Mandi
Malay bathroom with water tub and dipper

Maitreya
the future Buddha

Makara
a mythological aquatic reptile, somewhat like a crocodile and sometimes with an elephant's trunk; often found, along with the kala, framing doorways

Mandala
a focus for meditation; a representation of the cosmos

MCA
Malaysian Chinese Association

Meru
the mountain residence of the gods; the centre of the universe, the cosmic mountain

MIC
Malaysian Indian Congress

Mudra
symbolic gesture of the hands of the Buddha

N

Naga
benevolent mythical water serpent, enemy of Garuda

Naga makara
fusion of naga and makara

Nalagiri
the elephant let loose to attack the Buddha, who calmed him

Nandi/Nandin
bull, mount of Siva

NDP
New Development Policy (see page 91)

Negara
kingdom and capital, from the Sanskrit

Negeri
also negri, state

NEP
New Economic Policy (see page 90)

Nirvana
'enlightenment', the Buddhist ideal

O

Orang Asli
indigenous people of Malaysia

P

Paddy/padi
unhulled rice

Pantai
beach

Pasar
market, from the Arabic 'bazaar'

Pasar malam
night market

Perahu/prau
boat

Peranakan
'half caste', usually applied to part Chinese and part Malay people

Pradaksina
pilgrims' clockwise circumambulation of a holy structure

Prang
form of stupa built in the Khmer style, shaped rather like a corncob

Prasat
residence of a king or of the gods (sanctuary tower), from the Indian prasada

Pribumi
indigenous (as opposed to Chinese) businessmen

Pulau
island

Pusaka
heirloom

R

Raja/rajah
ruler

Raksasa
temple guardian statues

Ramayana
the Indian epic tale (see page 74)

Ruai
common gallery of an Iban longhouse, Sarawak

Rumah adat
customary or traditional house

S

Sago
multi-purpose palm

Sal
the Indian sal tree (*Shorea robusta*), under which the historic Buddha was born

Sakyamuni
the historic Buddha

Silat
or bersilat, traditional Malay martial art

Singha
mythical guardian lion

Siva
one of the Hindu triumvirate, the god of destruction and rebirth

Songket
Malay textile interwoven with supplementary gold and silver yarn

Sravasti
the miracle at Sravasti when the Buddha subdues the heretics in front of a mango tree

Sri Laksmi
the goddess of good fortune and Vishnu's wife

Stele
inscribed stone panel or slab

Stucco
plaster, often heavily moulded

Stupa
see chedi

Sungai
river

T

tamu
market

Tanju
open gallery of an Iban longhouse, Sarawak

Tara
also known as Cunda; the four-armed consort of the Bodhisattva Avalokitsvara

Tavatimsa
heaven of the 33 gods at the summit of Mount Meru

Theravada
'Way of the Elders'; major Buddhism sect also known as Hinayana Buddhism ('Lesser Vehicle')

Tiffin
afternoon meal – a word that was absorbed from the British Raj

Timang
Iban sacred chants, Sarawak

Tong
or *towkay*, a Chinese merchant

Totok
'full blooded'; usually applied to Chinese of pure blood

Towkay
Chinese merchant

Triads
Chinese mafia associations

Tunku
also Tuanku and Tengku, prince

U

Ulama
Muslim priest

Ulu
jungle

UMNO
United Malays National Organization (M)

Urna
the dot or curl on the Buddha's forehead, one of the distinctive physical marks of the Enlightened One

Usnisa
the Buddha's top knot or 'wisdom bump', one of the physical marks of the Enlightened One

V

Vishnu
the Protector, one of the gods of the Hindu trinity, generally with four arms holding the disc, the conch shell, the ball and the club

W

Waringin
banyan tree

Wayang
traditional Malay shadow plays

Notes

Notes

Notes

Notes

Tinted boxes
(in page order)

INTRODUCTION

Exchange rates (December 1997) 17
Tourism development guidelines 24
A tourism checklist 26

MALAYSIA

Biggest = best: Malaysia's race for the skies 33
Putting Malaya on the map 34
Climatic variations: yes, we have no monsoons 36
The universal stimulant – the betel nut 37
Nepenthes – the jungle's poisoned chalice 38
Durian: king of fruits 39
Fireflies – flashers in the forest 42
Environment – mud-slinging in the greenhouse 43
Diving seasons in Malaysia 47
The kris: martial and mystic masterpiece of the Malay world 49
Malaysia's monarchs – the public swings against the sultans 52-53
Pityamit one: from guerrilla camp to holiday camp 60
The Malay istana – royals on the riverside 63
Running amok 65
The new breed: farewell to the old Malaise 67
Malay magic and the spirits behind the prophet 69
The practice of Islam: living by the Prophet 70-71
In Siddhartha's footsteps: a short history of Buddhism 72-73
The Ramayana and Mahabharata 74
Tikus Rahmat: Malaysian racial relations in rat form 76
Making a wayang kulit puppet 77
1995 Election results 85
Drugs trafficking – stiff punishment 86
Mahathir Mohamad – recalcitrance rules OK 88-89
The new economic policy – Malaysia's recipe for racial harmony 90-91
Malaysia: fact file 97
Calling names 98
Kuala Lumpur highlights 100
The only legal Hash in Malaysia 105
Kuala Lumpur's golden triangle 112
Proton: driving the flag 116-117
Light Rail Transit (LRT) fares (1997) 140
Selected Ekspres National bus fares from KL 141
Cameron Highlands tea plantations 149
Jungle walks: Cameron Highlands 150-151
Perak: the silver state that grew rich on tin 159
Penang highlights 176

Brand-name Satay from the source 214
Minangkabau – the 'buffalo-horn' people from across the water 217
The Flor de la Mar: sunken treasure beyond measure 224-225
The Nyonyas and the Babas 230-231
Modern Johor: riding on the merlion's tail 246
Islam on the east coast: fundamental pointers 254
Pahang: the land of the sacred tree 271
Dateline Kuantan: Churchill's Malayan nightmare 274
The giant leatherback turtle (*Dermochelys coriacea*) 293
The crown-of-thorns – the terminator on the reef 295
The Pergau Dam affair – aid-for-arms 308
River roads 320
Fields in the forest – shifting cultivation 322
Protected areas of Sabah and Sarawak 326
The Iban Hornbill Festival 328
Piracy: the resurgence of an ancient scourge 336
James Brooke: the white knight errant 338-339
Konfrontasi 341
Tribal tattoos 343
Shifting cultivation – how to grow hill rice 345
The palang – the stimulant that makes a vas diferens 346
Green pen pals: Mahathir versus Manser 347
Skulls in the longhouse: heads you win 348
A town called Cat 355
A ceramic inheritance 358
The Penan – museum pieces for the 21st century? 363
Bus fares and destinations, Kuching 373
Visiting longhouses: house rules 378
Sarawak's river express boats – smoke on the water 387
The Rajahs' fortresses – war and peace in the Rejang 388
The longhouse – prime-site apartments with river view 390
The Bakun hydroelectric project: dam time bomb 394-394
The massacre at Long Nawang 396
Niah's guano collectors: scraping the bottom 400
How to make a swift buck 402
A land where money grows on trees 412-413
Sabah's ethnic breakdown 426
Tamus – Sabah's markets and trade fairs 427
Tapai – Sabah's rice wine 428
Dance 429-430
The Sabah Foundation 437
Layang-Layang Atoll: OK coral 445
Mat Salleh – fort-builder and folk hero 449
Rafflesia arnoldi: the largest flower in the world 450
The railway which ran out of steam 454
Tamus in Kota Belud District 463
The Rungus of Kudat 465
Mountain rescue: five soldiers and seven white chickens 469
Agnes Keith's house 476
The Borneo Death March 478
Edible nests 479
The tough life of a turtle 484
Small and hairy: the Sumatran rhinoceros 486
The Long John Silvers of Sabah's east coast 488

Lines on the map: sensitive territory 494
Dr Watson solves the Malayan malaria mystery 500
Connections by air in the region with Kuala Lumpur 502
Malaysian manners – as learned from a princess 505
Hotel prices and facilities 507
Restaurant prices 508
Guide to Domestic MAS Air Fares 512
Pelangi Air Fares 513
Express and ordinary train fares 513-516
Ekrwres Nasional bus fares (1997) 517
Important road signs to note 518
Learning the language – a practical alternative 521
Cinema: Dr Mahathir, Mr Schindler and the censors' 523
Festivals in East Malaysia 525

BRUNEI

The Sultan of Brunei – living by the profit 534-535
The Flag of Brunei Darussalam 544
Brunei's hydrocarbonated economy 547
Brunei: fact file 548
Hotel prices and facilities 567
Restaurant prices 567

SINGAPORE

Facts about Singapore you could do without 575
Flower power 576
Unimportant dates in Singapore's history, 1822-1988 579
Thomas Stamford Raffles: architect of Singapore 580-581
Chinese immigration: Singapore's life-blood 584-585
Population policies and designer genes 596-597
Kiasu and Kiasuism 599
Harry Lee Kuan Yew – the father of modern Singapore 604-605
The Asian way 606-607
Asian values: how foreign managers rate corruption in Southeast Asia 608
Singapore's General Elections (1955-1997) 609
The Central Providence Fund – saving for a rainy day 614
Singapore traffic – no more for the road 615
Criticism, libel and punishment 616
Salary games: the highest (legally) paid: politician in the world? 617
The Asian miracle: why it happened – the story according to the World Bank 618-619
Singapore in the computer and telecommunications stakes (rank out of 49 countries) 623
Singapore tops the Asian honesty stakes 624
Singapore: fact file 625
Singapore highlights 630
The Raffles Hotel – immortalized and sanitized 634-635
Bankers' rising aspirations 640
Shopping centres on Orchard Road 644
Walking tour of Chinatown 649
Tien Hou – Goddess of Seafarers 651
A Little India architectural walkabout 654
Return from the dead: Bugis Street 659
'Mad Ridley' – the rubber missionary 660
The Tiger Balm story 662
Changi Airport: prisoner of war camp: to international travel hub 666
Joshua (aged 6) and Ella's (aged 4) guide to fun and scary Singapore 697
Shopping centres and plazas in Chinatown and the Colonial core 703

Tinted boxes
(alphabetical order)

1995 Election results 85
A ceramic inheritance 358
A land where money grows on trees 412-413
A Little India architectural walkabout 654
A tourism checklist 26
A town called Cat 355
Agnes Keith's house 476
Asian values: how foreign managers rate corruption in Southeast Asia 608
Bankers' rising aspirations 640
Biggest = best: Malaysia's race for the skies 33
Brand-name Satay from the source 214
Brunei's hydrocarbonated economy 547
Brunei: fact file 548
Bus fares and destinations, Kuching 373
Calling names 98
Cameron Highlands tea plantations 149
Changi Airport: prisoner of war camp: to international travel hub 666
Chinese immigration: Singapore's life-blood 584-585
Cinema: Dr Mahathir, Mr Schindler and the censors' 523
Climatic variations: yes, we have no monsoons 36
Connections by air in the region with Kuala Lumpur 502
Criticism, libel and punishment 616
Dance 429-430
Dateline Kuantan: Churchill's Malayan nightmare 274
Diving seasons in Malaysia 47
Dr Watson solves the Malayan malaria mystery 500
Drugs trafficking – stiff punishment 86
Durian: king of fruits 39
Edible nests 479
Ekrwres Nasional bus fares (1997) 517
Environment – mud-slinging in the greenhouse 43
Exchange rates (December 1997) 17
Express and ordinary fares 513-516
Facts about Singapore you could do without 575
Festivals in East Malaysia 525
Fields in the forest – shifting cultivation 322
Fireflies – flashers in the forest 42
Flower power 576
Green pen pals: Mahathir versus Manser 347
Guide to Domestic MAS Air Fares 512
Harry Lee Kuan Yew – the father of modern Singapore 604-605
Hotel prices and facilities 567
Hotel prices and facilities 507
How to make a swift buck 402

Important road signs to note 518
In Siddhartha's footsteps: a short history of Buddhism 72-73
Islam on the east coast: fundamental pointers 254
James Brooke: the white knight errant 338-339
Joshua (aged 6) and Ella's (aged 4) guide to fun and scary Singapore 697
Jungle walks: Cameron Highlands 150-151
Kiasu and Kiasuism 599
Konfrontasi 341
Kuala Lumpur highlights 100
Kuala Lumpur's golden triangle 112
Layang-Layang Atoll: OK coral 445
Learning the language – a practical alternative 521
Light Rail Transit (LRT) fares (1997) 140
Lines on the map: sensitive territory 494
'Mad Ridley' – the rubber missionary 660
Mahathir Mohamad – recalcitrance rules OK 88-89
Making a wayang kulit puppet 77
Malay magic and the spirits behind the prophet 69
Malaysia's monarchs – the public swings against the sultans 52-53
Malaysia: fact file 97
Malaysian manners – as learned from a princess 505
Mat Salleh – fort-builder and folk hero 449
Minangkabau – the 'buffalo-horn' people from across the water 217
Modern Johor: riding on the merlion's tail 246
Mountain rescue: five soldiers and seven white chickens 469
Nepenthes – the jungle's poisoned chalice 38
Niah's guano collectors: scraping the bottom 400
Pahang: the land of the sacred tree 271
Pelangi Air Fares 513
Penang highlights 176
Perak: the silver state that grew rich on tin 159
Piracy: the resurgence of an ancient scourge 336
Pityamit one: from guerrilla camp to holiday camp 60
Population policies and designer genes 596-597
Protected areas of Sabah and Sarawak 326
Proton: driving the flag 116-117
Putting Malaya on the map 34
Rafflesia arnoldi: the largest flower in the world 450
Restaurant prices 567
Restaurant prices 508
Return from the dead: Bugis Street 659
River roads 320
Running amok 65
Sabah's ethnic breakdown 426
Salary games: the highest (legally) paid: politician in the world? 617
Sarawak's river express boats – smoke on the water 387
Selected Ekspres National bus fares from KL 141
Shifting cultivation – how to grow hill rice 345
Shopping centres and plazas in Chinatown and the Colonial core 703
Shopping centres on Orchard Road 644
Singapore highlights 630
Singapore in the computer and telecommunications stakes (rank out of 49 countries) 623
Singapore tops the Asian honesty stakes 624

Singapore traffic – no more for the road 615
Singapore's General Elections (1955-1997) 609
Singapore: fact file 625
Skulls in the longhouse: heads you win 348
Small and hairy: the Sumatran rhinoceros 486
Tamus – Sabah's markets and trade fairs 427
Tamus in Kota Belud District 463
Tapai – Sabah's rice wine 428
The Asian miracle: why it happened – the story according to the World Bank 618-619
The Asian way 606-607
The Bakun hydroelectric project: dam time bomb 394-395
The Borneo Death March 478
The Central Providence Fund – saving for a rainy day 614
The crown-of-thorns – the terminator on the reef 295
The Flag of Brunei Darussalam 544
The Flor de la Mar: sunken treasure beyond measure 224-225
The giant leatherback turtle (*Dermochelys coriacea*) 293
The Iban Hornbill Festival 328
The kris: martial and mystic masterpiece of the Malay world 49
The Long John Silvers of Sabah's east coast 488
The longhouse – prime-site apartments with river view 390
The Malay istana – royals on the riverside 63
The massacre at Long Nawang 396
The new breed: farewell to the old Malaise 67
The new economic policy – Malaysia's recipe for racial harmony 90-91
The Nyonyas and the Babas 23(-231
The only legal Hash in Malaysia 105
The palang – the stimulant that makes a vas diferens 346
The Penan – museum pieces for the 21st century? 363
The Pergau Dam affair – aid-for-arms 308
The practice of Islam: living by the Prophet 70-71
The Raffles Hotel – immortalized and sanitized 634-635
The railway which ran out of steam 454
The Rajahs' fortresses – war and peace in the Rejang 388
The Ramayana and Mahabharata 74
The Rungus of Kudat 465
The Sabah Foundation 437
The Sultan of Brunei – living by the profit 534-535
The Tiger Balm story 662
The tough life of a turtle 484
The universal stimulant – the betel nut 37
Thomas Stamford Raffles: architect of Singapore 580-581
Tien Hou – Goddess of Seafarers 651
Tikus Rahmat: Malaysian racial relations in rat form 76
Tourism development guidelines 24
Tribal tattoos 343
Unimportant dates in Singapore's history, 1822-1988 579
Visiting longhouses: house rules 378
Walking tour of Chinatown 649

Writing to us

Many people write to us - with corrections, new information, or simply comments. If you want to let us know something, we would be delighted to hear from you. Please give us as precise information as possible, quoting the edition and page number of the Handbook you are using and send as early in the year as you can. Your help will be greatly appreciated, especially by other travellers. In return we will send you details about our special guidebook offer.

For hotels and restaurants, please let us know:

- each establishment's name, address, phone and fax number
- number of rooms, whether a/c or air-cooled, attached (clean?) bathroom
- location - how far from the station or bus stand, or distance (walking time) from a prominent landmark
- if it's not already on one of our maps, can you place it?
- your comments - either good or bad - as to why it is distinctive
- tariff cards
- local transport used

For places of interest:

- location
- entry, camera charge
- access - by whatever means of transport is most approriate, eg time of main buses or trains to and from the site, journey time, fare
- facilities - nearby drinks stalls, restaurants, for the disabled
- any problems, eg steep climb, wildlife, unofficial guides
- opening hours
- site guides

Illustrations

A street in Bruni **550**
A woodcut depicting Admiral Cornelis Matelieff's 1606 siege of Melaka **51**
Brunei flag **544**
Bungalows **594**
Chinese shophouses:
  Late Shophouse **591**
  Art Deco Shophouse **593**
  Early Shophouse **593**
  Second Transitional Shophouse **591**
Dayak decorated human skull **348**
Explanation of the common architectural elements that can be found in shophouse façades **592**
Exterior of a Sea Dyak Long-house **389**
Hell Money – Festival of Hungry Ghosts **723**
Indian shophouses:
  Art Deco shophouse **656**
  Early shophouse **656**
  Late shophouse **656**
Interior of a Sea Dyak Long-house **379**
Jinrickshaw **647**
Kenyalang, hornbill image **328**
Longhouse **390**
Malaysia distance chart (Km) **519**
Map of Singapore town and surrounds based on an 1839 survey **578**
Masks **351-352**
Melaka in 1679, from *Borts voyage* **226**
Mr Kiasu **599**
Opium smoking **652**
Painted Panel from a Dayak coffin of a 'Ship of the Dead' **330**
Petaling Street on a quiet day; the processional route of Chinese feast days **109**
Shophouses:
  First Traditional shophouse style **649**
South Boat Quay c1900 **642**
Tattooed Kenowit, with pendulous ear-lobes **343**
The 'Oran-ootan' as remembered by an early European visitor **324**
The Chinese admiral Cheng Ho **223**
The town resisdence (in jalan Pudu) of the last Captain China **104**
Thian Hock Keng Temple **650**
Tiong Bahru's singing birds **653**

CLIMATE

Cameron Highlands **147**
Johor Bahru **243**
Kota Bharu **306**
Kota Kinabalu **434**
Kuala Lumpur **99**
Kuala Terengganu **297**
Kuantan **273**
Kuching **354**
Melaka **221**
Mersing **255**
Penang **175**

Index

A

A Famosa, Melaka 228
Accommodation
See also under individual towns
Brunei 567
Malaysia 507
Singapore 678
Acknowledgements
Brunei 727
Malaysia 727
Singapore 727
AIDS 744
Air discounts 18
Air passes 18
Air travel
to Brunei 565
to Malaysia 502
to Singapore 708
within Malaysia 510
Al Arqam 75
Al-Abrar Mosque, Singapore 650
All Saints' Church 173
Alor Star 199
amok 65
Ampang Tower 113
Anjung 62
Api, Gunung 416
Arau 205
Armenian Church, Singapore 634
Around Singapore Island 659
Art and architecture
Malaysia 61
Singapore 588
Art Deco Bungalow 594
Art Deco style shophouse 593
Arts and Handicraft Training Centre 553
Ashaari Muhammed 75
Asian Civilisations Museum 635
Asian Village, Singapore 672
Astana, Kuching 357
athlete's foot 748
atlas moth 42
Ayer Itam Dam 186
Ayer Keroh 235

B

Baba-Nyonya Heritage Museum, Melaka 232
Babas 66, 230
Babi Besar 47
Babi Besar, Pulau 268
Babi Hujung 47
Babi Tengah 47
Bahasa Melayu 76
Bajau, Sabah 428
Bak-Bak 466
Bakkungan Kecil 48
Bako National Park 376
Balai Seni Negeri 200
Balik Pulau 187
Bamboo carving 351
Bandar Seri Begawan 549
accommodation 555
airline offices 557
banks 557
embassies 557
entertainment 557
excursions 554
Hospitals 557
places of interest 550
places to eat 556
post 557
shopping 558
Tour companies 558
tourist offices 558
tours 555
transport 558
Bandar Sri Aman 380
Bangar 559
Bario and the Kelabit Highlands 419
Barisan Nasional (National Front) 58
Barisan Titiwangsa and Hill Stations 35, 142
Basketry 352
Batang Ai 381
Batang Ai National Park 382
Batang Duri 559
Batik 82
Batu Apoi Forest Reserve 559
Batu Bunatikan Lumuyu 453
Batu Bungan 414
Batu Buruk 300
Batu Caves 114
Batu Ferringhi 194
Batu Maung 187
Batu Niah 403
Batu Punggul 452
Batu Tinahas 452
Batu Tulug 489
Baturong caves 490
Bau 365
Beaches 13
See also individual entries
Beadwork 352
Beaufort 455
Belaga 392
Berakas Forest Recreation Park 560
Beras Besar, Pulau 209
Beremban, Gunung 151
Besar, Pulau 235
Beserah 275, 280
best time to visit 16
Brunei 564
Malaysia 500
Singapore 707
Betel Nut 37
Bharata Natyam dance 80
Bicycling 518
Bidayuh, Sarawak 345
Big Splash, Singapore 665
Bike hire
Malaysi 518
Bintulu 396
Birch Memorial 159
bird singing competitions,

Singapore 653
Birds
Malaysia 40
Borneo 327
Black & White Bungalow 594
Blowpipes 351
boat 21
Boat Quay 639
Boat travel
to Brunei 565
to Singapore 710
within Brunei 568
within Malaysia 520
Boat trips, Singapore 676
Botanic gardens, Singapore 643
Botanical Gardens, Bukit Jambul 188
Penang 185
brassware, Brunei 543
Brigss Plan 57
Brinchang 156
Brinchang, Gunung 150
British Malaya 50
Brooke, Charles 338, 539
Brooke, Charles Vyner 340
Brooke, James 335, 338, 537
BRUNEI 59, 529-569
airport information 566
before travelling 564
communications 568
customs 566
departure tax 566
entertainment 568
entry requirements 564
food and drink 567
further reading 569
getting around 567
getting there 565
health 564
holidays and festivals 569
money 565
on arrival 566
other land transport 565, 568
parks and walks 562
recreational parks 560
shopping 566
vaccinations 564
water 564
weights and measures 567
when to go 564
where to stay 567
Brunei History Centre Museum 553
Brunei Investment Agency's 545
Brunei Museum 554
Brunei National Democratic Party (BNDP) 543
Brunei People's Party (PRB) 540
Bruneization 542
Buddhism 72, 600
Malaysia 75
Bugis Street, Singapore 658
Bujang Valley 200
Bukit Anak Takun 114
Bukit Batok, Singapore 668
Bukit Batu Lawi 419
Bukit Bendera 437
Bukit Cina, Melaka 233
Bukit Fraser 145
Bukit Jambul 188
Bukit Larut 174
Bukit Perdah 151
Bukit Saban Resort 382
Bukit Shahbandar 560
Bukit Takun 114
Bukit Timah Nature Reserve, Singapore 668
Bukit Timah Peak 575
Bukom 670
bumbung panjangi 61
bumiputra 63
Bunbun, Pulau 209
Buntal 374
Bus travel
See also individual towns
Brunei 565, 567
within Malaysia 516
buses 20
Butterfly garden, Brinchang 158
Butterfly Park, Singapore 672
Butterworth 174

C

Caldwell House 590
Cameron Highlands 147
camping 19
See also individual towns
Candi Bukit Batu Pahat 202
Canopy Walk, Gunung Gagau 284
canopy walk, KL 115
Cape Rachado 219
Car hire
See also individual towns
Brunei 568
Malaysia 518
Singapore 719
Caras Caves 275
Cash
Brunei 565
Malaysia 501
Singapore 708
Cathedral of the Good Shepherd 591
Cave of the Winds 416
Cavenagh Bridge 638
Cenering 299
Central Market, KL 108
Central Providence Fund 614
Cerating 287
Chan Kongsi, KL 110
Chan See Shu Yuen Temple, KL 110
Change Alley, Singapore 640
Changi 586
Changi airport, Singapore 711
Changi Point, Singapore 666
Changi Prison, Singapore 665
Changi Village, Singapore 666
Checklist 17
Cheng Hoon Teng Temple, Melaka 232
Cheong Fatt Tze Mansion 184
Chettiar 68
CHIJMES 636
Children's Discovery Gallery 637
Chinaman Scholar's Gallery 649
Chinatown, KL 109
Melaka 231
Singapore 645
Chinatown Point 703
Chinese 66, 542, 584
Chinese and Japanese Gardens, Singapore 663
Chinese immigrants 51
Chinese shophouse 591
Chinese temples 553, 595
Chinese, Sabah 431
Chinese, Sarawak 342
Christ Church, Melaka 228
Christians 602
Cinemania 673
City Hall, Singapore 631
Clan Piers, Penang 183
Clarke Quay Adventure Ride, Singapore 639
Clarke Quay, Singapore 639
Clearwater Cave 416
Clifford Pier, Singapore 640
Climate
Malaysia 36
Borneo 320
Brunei 532
Kuala Lumpur 99
Singapore 576
climate charts 38
Clothing
Brunei 566
Malaysia 504
Singapore 712
Club Street 648
cobra 41

Coleman, George 590
Colonial Core and Singapore River 631
colonials 50
Commonwealth War Cemetery, Maxwell Hill 174
communism, Malaysia 57
Conduct
- Brunei 566
- Malaysia 504
- Singapore 712

Confidence tricksters 18
Confrontation 59, 588
Confucianism 600
Consulates
- Brunei 732
- Malaysia 732
- Singapore 733

Convent of Holy Infant Jesus 636
Cookery courses, Malaysia 510
Coral Bay 168
corruption 88
Cost of living
- Malaysia 501

Crafts
- Malaysia 81
- Sabah 431
- Sarawak 351
- Brunei 543

Crawfurd, Sir John 581
Credit cards
- Brunei 565
- Malaysia 501
- Singapore 708

Cricket Club, Singapore 631
Crocker Range National Park 451
Crocodilarium, Singapore 665
crocodiles 40, 328
Crocodile Farm, Sabah 479
Crocodile Farms, Singapore 662, 665
Cuisine 15
- *See also places to eat*

Culture 14
- Borneo 329
- Malaysia 63
- Brunei 542
- Sabah 426
- Sarawak 342
- Singapore 595

Currency
- Brunei 565
- Malaysia 501
- Singapore 708

Custard apple 740
cycling 21

D

Dalhousie Memorial, Singapore 631
Damai Peninsula 374
Damuan Park 554
Dance
- Malaysia 78, 79
- Sarawak 349
- Singapore 603

Danum Valley, Sabah 491
- Sarawak 349

Dapur 62
Datai Bay 208
Dayabumi Complex, KL 108
Dayang, Pulau 208
Deer Cave 416
Defence, Singapore 612
Democratic Action Party (DAP) 59
Dengue fever 748
Desaru 245
Dewan Majlis 553
Dhoby Ghaut, Singapore 643
Di, Huang 601
Diarrhoea 746
Diversification 546
Diving 14
- *See also Marine Parks*
- Malaysia 46
- Labuan 48
- Pemanggil 268
- Peninsular Malaysia's West Coast 46
- Pulau Aur 268
- Pulau Kapas 47, 295
- Pulau Layang-Layang 48
- Pulau Mantanani 48
- Pulau Mengalum 48
- Pulau Pangkor 166
- Pulau Paya 47, 209
- Pulau Perhentian 48, 304
- Pulau Redang 47, 295, 303
- Pulau Sembilan 168
- Pulau Sibu 47
- Pulau Sipadan 48
- Pulau Tenggol 47
- Pulau Tiga 48
- Pulau Tioman 47, 260
- seasons 47
- Tunku Abdul Rahman Park 48
- Turtle islands National Park 48

Drama 78
Drink
- Brunei 567
- Malaysia 510
- Singapore 716
- Singapore sling 717

drugs 19
- Malaysia 86

Durian 39, 740
Durian Perangin waterfall 208
Dutch 50
Duty free allowance
- Brunei 566
- Malaysia 503
- Singapore 710

Duyung Besar, Pulau 299
dynastic emperors from Chinese history 601

E

Early Bungalow 594
Early Modern style bungalow 594
East Coast 664
East Coast Park, Singapore 664
East Coast Recreation Centre, Singapore 665
Economy
- Malaysia 92
- Brunei 545
- Singapore 613

ecotourism 546
elections
- 1995 general 85
- 1997 609

Elephant 326
Embassies
- Brunei 732
- Malaysia 732
- Singapore 733

Emerald Bay 167
Emerald Hill 643
emigration 623
Employment, Brunei 548
Empress Place, Singapore 631
Enchanted Grove of Tembusu 672
Endau Rompin National Park 270
Environment
- Borneo 319
- Malaysia 43
- cost of growth 44

environment and tourism 24
exchange rates 17
Export promotion 619

F

fact file
- Brunei 548
- Malaysia 97
- Singapore 625

Fantasy Island, Singapore 673

Fax services 520
Federation of Malaysia 588
feng shui 595
ferries 719
festivals
Brunei 569
harvest 427
Kota Bharu 312
Melaka 237
Singapore 721, 723
Filipinos, Sabah 431
fireflies 42
fires 45
First Transitional shophouse 592
flight times 18
Flora & fauna
Borneo 321
Brunei 532
Malaysia 38
Singapore 576
Food
Chinese cuisines 715
coffee shops 715
durians 715
glossary 740
Indian 716
Malay 716
Malaysia 508
New Asia, trans-ethnic and 'fusion' cuisine 716
Nonya 716
Seafood 716
Singapore 713
food and drink 20
Foreign investors 620
foreign relations
Brunei 544
Malaysia 92
Singapore 612
foreign workers 622
forest 532
Fort Alice 380
Fort Altingberg 118
Fort Canning Park, Singapore 637
Fort Cornwallis, Penang 182
Fort Hose 409
Fort Margherita, Kuching 357
Fort Siloso, Singapore 670
Fort St John, Melaka 233
Fort Sylvia 386
Fraser's Hill 145
Fruits 740
Fun World, Singapore 673
Funan Centre 703
fungal infections 748
further reading
Borneo 331
Brunei 569
Maps 729
Singapore 724
Southeast Asia 727

G

Gagau, Gunung 284
gaur 39
Gaya Island 48
Gaya, Pulau 447
Gedung Rajah Abdullah warehouse 118
Gelanggang Seni 310
Genting Highlands 142
Geography
Borneo 319
Brunei 530
Malaysia 35
Singapore 575
Georgetown 179
Gerakan 59
Gerik 316
getting around 20
air 20
boat 21
car hire 20
hitchhiking and cycling 21
language 21
road 20
train 20
getting there
air 18
overland 18
sea 18
Geylang Serai, Singapore 664
gibbon 39
Glossary 753
God of the Soil 602
Goddess of Mercy Temple, Penang 183
Goh Chok Tong 608
Golden Sands 168
Gomontong Caves 479
gongs 81
Great Cave, Niah 401
Greater East Asia Co-prosperity Sphere 55
Grik 316
Growth Triangle 622
Gua Cerita 208
Gua Langsir 209
Gua Musang 315
Gua Tambun 162
Gulisan Island 48
Gunung Api 416
Gunung Beremban 151
Gunung Brinchang 150
Gunung Gading National Park 364
Gunung Gagau 284
Gunung Jasar 151
Gunung Jerai 202
Gunung Mulu National Park 410
Gunung Murudi 420
Gunung Penrissen 364
Gunung Tahan 281
Gunung Tapis Park 275
Gunung, Tahan 281
gunungan 78

H

Hajjah Fatimah Mosque, Singapore 659
Hang Li Poh Well 233
Hantu, Pulau, Singapore 675
Hassanal Bolkiah 541
Hats 353
Haw Par Villa, Singapore 659
Hawaii Beach 406
Head-hunting 348
health 16, 742
basic supplies 748
before you go 743
fish and shellfish 746
further information 748
other common problems 745
when you return home 748
heat and cold 745
heat stroke 747
Highlights
Beaches 13
culture 14, 15
Diving 14
Hill Stations 13
Kuala Lumpur 100
Natural features 13
nightlife 15
Penang 176
shopping 15
Wildlife and Jungle 13
Hikayat Abdullah 77
Hill stations 13
See also individual towns
Bukit Larut 174
Cameron Highlands 147
Fraser's Hill 145
Genting Highlands 142
Hinduism 75
Historical sites 14
See also individual entries
History
Borneo 328
Brunei 533

Malaysia 48
Sabah 423
Sarawak 335
Singapore 577
Hitch-hiking 21
Brunei 568
Malaysia 519
Singapore 719
Holidays
See festivals
Hornbill 327
Hornbill Festival 328
Hospitals
See also individual towns
Brunei 565
BSB 557
Kuching 370
Malaysia 501
Penang 192
Singapore 698
Hotels
See accommodation
Hours of business
Brunei 566
Malaysia 505
Singapore 712
House of Skulls 439
Housing Development Board 588
How to go 16

I

Ibans, Sarawak 343
Ibrahim, Anwar 86
images of Singapore, Singapore 670
immunisation 743
Independence, Brunei 541
Indian 598
Indians 68
infectious hepatitis 743
influenza 748
Insect Kingdom Museum 672
Insects 41, 745
Internet 611, 729
intestinal upsets 745
intestinal worms 748
investment 614
Ipoh 158
Ipoh Town Hall, Ipoh 160
ISIC 17
Islam 70, 72, 542, 602
Istana 63
Abu Baker 272
Alam Shah 117
Balai Besar 308
Batu 310
Besar 243
Bukit Serene 245
Iskandariah 170
Jahar 309
Kampong Glam 657
Lama Sri Menanti 216
Maziah 298
Negara Singapura 643
Nurul Iman 554
Nurul Izza 554

J

Jackfruit 740
Jade Museum 114
Jalan Ampang, KL 111
Jalan Hang Jebat 231
Jalan Pasar Lama 310
Jalan Tun Tan Cheng Lock, Melaka 232
Jamae Mosque 650
Jame 'Asr Hassanil Bokiah Mosque 555
Japanese B encephalitis (JVE) 743
Japanese Gardens, Ipoh 160
Japanese occupation 55, 539, 584
Jasar, Gunung 151
Jawi 76
Jefri, Prince 543
Jerai, Gunung 202
Jerak Warisan Heritage Trail 227
Jeram Pasu waterfall 311
Jerantut 286
Jerudong Park 560
joget dance 80
Johor Bahru 241
accommodation 247
banks 249
excursions 245
nightlife 249
places of interest 243
places to eat 247
shopping 249
Transport 250
Johor Lama 245
Johor State 642
Kampung Kling 233
Malay 184
Masjid Bandaraya 360
Masjid Jamek 361
Masjid Kampung Laut 312
Masjid Sabah 435
Masjid Tranquerah 233
Masjid Zahir 199
Omar Ali Saifuddien 550
State 186
Sultan Abu Bakar 245
Sultan Ahmad Shah 273
Ubudiah 170
Zainal Abdin 298
Jong's Crocodile Farm 362
Jonkers Street, Melaka 231
Joo Chiat Road 664
Jubilee Hall Theatre, Singapore 633
jungle canopy walk, Poring 474
Jurong Bird Park, Singapore 661
Jurong Crocodile Paradise, Singapore 662
Jurong, Singapore 661

K

Kadazans, Sabah 426
Kain songket 83
Kala 209
Kampong Ayer 550
Kampong Parit 561
Kampung Ayer 437
Kampung Ayer Batang 263
Kampung Cerating 287
Kampung Genting 265
Kampung Gombizau 466
Kampung Juara 266
Kampung Kraftangan 309
Kampung Kuala Tahan 281
Kampung Lalang 261
Kampung Morten 228
Kampung Mukut 266
Kampung Nipah 266
Kampung Panji 490
Kampung Paya 265
Kampung Penuba 263
Kampung Pulau Rusa 299
Kampung Salang 264
Kampung Selungai 452
Kampung Sumangkap 466
Kampung Sungai Ular 280
Kampung Tekek 261
Kanching Falls 114
Kandang Kerbau (KK) wet market, Singapore 656
Kangar 204
Kapit 386
Kapitan Kling Mosque, Penang 183
Karyaneka Handicraft Centre, KL 113
Katong, Singapore 664
Kea Farm 158
Kedah Peak 202
Kek Lok Si Temple, Ayer Itam 186
Kelabit, Sarawak 349

Kellie's Castle, Ipoh 161
Kemasik 291
Keningau 451
Kenong Rimba National Park 286, 287
Kenyah and Kayan, Sarawak 346
Kenyir Lake 299
Kerangas forest 416
Ketam, Pulau 118
Khoo Kongsi, Penang 183
kiasu 600
kijang 39
Kinabalu 467
Kinabatangan River 487
Kipungit Falls 474
Kites 81
Klang 117
KLCC 112
Konfrontasi 59, 341, 540, 588
Kong Mek 311
Kong Meng San Phor Kark See Chinese Temple Complex, Singapore 667
kongsis 68, 110, 450
Kota Belanda 168
Kota Belud 463
Kota Bharu 306
  accommodation 312
  excursions 311
  festivals 312
  places of interest 308
  places to eat 314
  shopping 314
  tours 312
  transport 315
Kota Kinabalu 434
  accommodation 440
  airline offices 443
  banks 443
  embassies 443
  entertainment 443
  excursions 437
  festivals 440
  places of interest 435
  places to eat 442
  shopping 443
  tours 440
  transport 446
Kota Lukut 219
Kota Tampan 316
Kota Tinggi 245
Kra Isthmus 35
krait 41
Kranji War Memorial and Cemetery, Singapore 669
Kreta Ayer 645
kris 49
Kuah 206
Kuala Abang 291, 294
Kuala Belait 562
Kuala Belalong Field Studies Centre 559
Kuala Dungun 291
Kuala Kangsar 170
Kuala Kedah 204
Kuala Likau 399
Kuala Lipis 286
Kuala Lumpar Butterfly Park 111
KUALA LUMPUR 99
  accommodation 120
    Chow Kit 122
    city centre 120
    Golden Triangle 123
    homes away from home 126
    Jalan Ampang 125
    Little India 126
    other areas 126
  airline offices 131
  art galleries 133
  banks 132
  bars 131
  bus fares 141
  Chinatown 109
  churches 132
  cinemas 133
  City area 113
  Colonial core 106
  cultural shows 133
  embassies 132
  Excursions, east 119
  Excursions, north 114
  Excursions, South 119
  Excursions, west and southwest 115
  history 99
  Hospitals 134
  Jalan Ampang 111
  Lake Gardens 110
  language schools 133
  local information 120
  nightlife 133
  places of interest 106
  places to eat 126
  post 134
  shopping 134
  tour companies 137
  tourist office 138
  tours 120
  transport 138
KL Tower 113
Kuala Lumpur City Centre project 112
Kuala Perlis 205
Kuala Rompin 272
Kuala Selangor 118
Kuala Selangor Nature Park 118
Kuala Sepetang 173
Kuala Terengganu 297
Kuala Woh 152
Kuantan 273
Kuantan River 273
Kubah National Park 365
Kuching 354
  airline offices 369
  banks 369
  embassies 369
  entertainment 369
  excursions 361
  local information 366
  places of interest 355
  places to eat 367
  post 370
  shopping 370
  tour companies 372
  tourist office 372
  tours 366
  transport 372
Kudat 464
kudu Kepang dance 80
Kukup 245
Kundasang 473
Kusu Island, Singapore 674

L

Labour squeeze, Singapore 622
Labuan 48
Labuan, Pulau 456
Lagud Sebren Cocoa Research Station, Sabah 453
Lahad Datu 489
laissez-faire 614
Lake Garden 172
Lake Gardens, KL 110
Lambir Hills 406
Lang's Cave 417
Langanan Waterfall 474
Langkawi 205
language 21
  Brunei 568
  Malaysia 520
  Singapore 602
  words and phrases 737
Language and literature 76
Language schools, KL 133
Lapau 553
Lata Iskandar Waterfall 152
Late shophouse 592
Lau Pa Sat Festival Market 641
Lawas 421
Lazarus Island, Singapore 675
Ledang, Gunung 236

Lee Kuan Yew 587, 604
Lembu 209
Leong San See Temple, Singapore 657
Liang Court 703
Light, Captain Francis 51
Lim Kit Siang 87
Limbang 416, 420
Lion dance 80
Loagan Bunut National Park 406
Lombong 245
Long Pala 418
Longhouses
  Batu Bungan 414
  Kapit 389
  Marudi 410
  Rumah Seligi 389
Loong, Brigadier-General Lee Hsien 608
Lost Civilization, Singapore 671
Loy, Yap Ah 100
Lumut, Malaysia 165
Lundu 365

M

Mabul Island 496
MacRitchie Reservoir 669
Madai Caves 490
Madras chunam 654
Mahabharata 74
Mahathir Mohamad 84, 88
Main Range 35
Mak Yong dance 79
Makam Mahsuri 206
Malacca 220
malaria 501, 744
Malay Cultural Village, Singapore 664
Malay food glossary 740
Malay, language 602
Malayan Chinese Association (MCA) 58
Malayan Communist Emergency 57
Malayan Communist Party 56
Malayan Democratic Union (MDU) 587
Malayan Indian Congress (MIC) 58
Malays 64, 542, 598
Malays, Sarawak 342
MALAYSIA 29-527
  airport information 504
  before travelling 499
  communications 520
  customs 503
  departure tax 504
  entertainment 522
  entry requirements 499
  food and drink 508
  further reading 526
  getting around 510
  getting there 502
  health 501
  holidays and festivals 522
  money 501
  on arrival 504
  shopping 506
  water 501
  when to go 500
  where to stay 507
Malaysia Agreement 59
Malaysian Armed Forces Museum, KL 119
Malaysian Communist Party 57
Malaysian Federation 540
Malaysian Indian Congress (MIC) 70
Malaysian Tourist Information Centre (MATIC) 112
Mammals
  Malaysia 39
  Borneo 323
Mamutik Island 48
Mamutik Pulau 447
Mandai Orchid Gardens 668
mango 740
Mangosteen 740
Mangrove Forest Trail 487
Manukan Island 48
Manukan Pulau 447
Marang 295
Marco Polo 577
Marina South, Singapore 641
Marina Square 684, 703
marine Reserve, Sipadan Island 494
Maritime Museum, Singapore 671
Marshall, David 587
Marudi 409
Marudi Log Walk 562
Masjid Jamek, KL 106
Masjid Kampung Laut 312
Masjid Negara, KL 108
Mass rapid Transit (MRT), Singapore 717
Mat Salleh 449
Mat Salleh's fort 450
Matang Wildlife Centre 365
Mausoleum of Sultan Bolkiah 555
Maxwell Hill 174
Maxwell House 590
Medical facilities
  See hospitals
medicines 742
Melaka 50, 220
  accommodation 237
  banks 240
  festivals 237
  nightlife 240@
  places of interest 227
  places to eat 238
  shopping 240
  tours 236
  town square 228
  transport 241
Melaka Zoo 235
Melanaus, Sarawak 344
Melinau Gorge 415
Menara KL 113
Mengkabong, Sabah 439
Meningitis 743
Mentinggi 47
Merang 302
merdeka 58
Merdeka Stadium, KL 110
Merlion 672
Merlion, Singapore 638
Mersing 255
Mile, 19th 152
Millenia Walk 703
Mines Wonderland 119
Ming Village, Singapore 663
Mini-Malaysian Complex 235
Miri 404
Modern Brunei 543
Modern Kuala Lumpur 101
Modern Malaysia 84
Modern Sabah 432
Modern Sarawak 353
Modern Singapore 603
Mohamad, Dr Mahathir 84, 88
Mohammed, Prince 543
Money 17
  See also information for travellers
money politics 88
monsoons 36, 576
Mosques
  Abdullah 272
  Abu Baker 272
  Hajjah Fatimah 659
  Indian 360
  Jame 'Asr Hassạnil Bokiah 555
  Sultan 657
Mosque Street 648
Mountains
  Barisan Titiwangsa 35
  Bintang Range 35
  Kedah-Singgora Range 35

Tahan Range 35
mouse deer 39
Muara, Brunei 560
Muka Head 195
Mulu National Park 410
Murudi, Gunung 420
Murut villages, Tenom 453
Murut, Sabah 430
Museums
See also individual towns
Abu Baker 272
Art, Singapore 636
Baba-Nyonya Heritage 232
Brunei History Centre 553
Brunei 554
Budaya, Melaka 229
cat 361
Chinese History 360
di Raja 170
Geological, Ipoh 161
Insect Kingdom 672
Islamic 310
Kapit 387
Kinabalu 472
Kota Bharu 311
Mangrove Forest 173
Maritime, Singapore 671
Maritime 234
Muzium Negara 110
National History 108
National, Singapore 636
Orang Asli, KL 115
Penang Museum 182
Perak Darul Ridzuan, Ipoh 161
Perak 173
Peranakan Place 643
Pewter 664
Philatelic,Singapore 635
Royal Malaysian Navy 234
Sabah State 435
Sarawak Islamic 357
Sarawak 355
Science 437
State, Losong 299
Teknologi Melayu 555
Textile 106
Timber 361
Universiti Sains Malaysia 187
Wilayah 420
Music
Malaysia 78, 80
Sarawak 350
Muzium Budaya Museum, Melaka 229
Muzium Negara, KL 110

N

Nagore Durgha Shrine, Singapore 650
nappies 750
National Art Gallery, KL 108
National Art Gallery, Singapore 637
National History Museum 108
National Library 637
National Monument, KL 110
National Museum and Art Gallery, Singapore 636
National Parks
Bako 376
Batang Ai 382
Crocker Range 451
Endau Rompin 270
Gunung Gading 364
Gunung Mulu 410
Gunung Tapis 275
Kenong Rimba Park 287
Kenong Rimba 286
Kinabalu 467
Kubah 365
Mulu 410
Niah 400
Pulau Tiga 462
Similajau 399
Taman Negara 281
Tunku Abdul Rahman Park 447
Turtle Islands 483
National Planetarium, KL 111
National Zoo & Aquarium, Malaysia 119
NEP 90
Nepenthes 38
New Development Policy 94
New Economic Policy 90
Newly Industrialized Economy (NIE) 619
Newspapers
Brunei 568
Malaysia 522
Singapore 721
Niah National Park 400
Night Safari, Singapore 668
Nightlife 15
See also individual towns
JB 249
KL 133
Melaka 240
Penang 192
Singapore 696
Nong, Shen 601
Nunukan 498
Nyonyas 66, 230

O

oil 545, 547
Old Fort, Limbang 420
old Royal cemetery, Singapore 658
Omar Ali Saiffuddin 537
Omni-theatre 663
Ophir, Mnt 236
Orang Asli, Malaysia 71
Orang Asli Museum, KL 115
Orang Ulu, Sarawak 345
Orang utan 323
Orchid Gardens, Singapore 673

P

Padang Besar 205
Padang Merdeka 310
Padang, Singapore 631
Painted Cave, Niah 401
Palang 346
Pangkor Laut 167, 169
Pangkor, Pulau 166
pangolin 40
Pantai Acheh Forest Reserve 187
Pantai Air Papan 255, 256
Pantai Cahaya Bulan 311
Pantai Cenang 207, 210
Pantai Cinta Berahi 311
Pantai Dalam Rhu 311
Pantai Dasar Sabak 311
Pantai Datai 211
Pantai Irama 311
Pantai Kok 208, 211
Pantai Kundor 234
Pantai Rhu 208, 211
Pantai Tengah 207, 210
Papar 462
Papaya 741
Parameswara 579
Parco Bugis Junction 703
Parit Falls 151
Parks Offices, Kota Kinabalu 445
Parliament House, KL 111
Parliament House, Singapore 631
Parti Islam 85
PAS 85
Pasang Rapids 394
Pasar Besar Kedai Payang 298
Pasir Bogak 168
Pasir Hitam 208
Pasir Mas 399
Paya, Pulau 209
PBS 85
PCB 311
Pekan 272

Pelagus Rapids 388
Penampang, KK 438
Penan, Sarawak 347, 363
Penang 175
accommodation 188
airline offices 191
banks 191
bars 191
embassies 192
festivals 188
Hospitals 192
nightlife 192
places to eat 189
post 192
shopping 192
sports 193
Tour companies 193
tourist office 193
tours 188
transport 193
Penang Bird Park 187
Penang Bridge 184
Penang Buddhist Association 184
Penang Hill 185
Penang Museum & Art Gallery 182
Peninsula Plaza 703
Penrissen, Gunung 364
People
Borneo 329
Brunei 542
Malaysia 63
Sabah 426
Sarawak 342
Singapore 595
People's Action Party (PAP 587
People's Movement 59
Perak Darul Ridzuan Museum, Ipoh 161
Perak Tong 162
Peranakan 62
See also art & architecture
Peranakan house 593
Peranakan houses 62
Peranakan Place Museum, Singapore 643
Peranakans 66, 230
Perhentian, Pulau 304
Petaling Jaya, KL 115
Peter Wee's Katong Antique House 664
Petronas Twin Towers 113
Pewter Museum 664
Pewterware 83
Philatelic Museum, Singapore 635
Pidemco Centre 703
pile houses 61
Pinang, Pulau 175
Pinnacles, The 415
Piracy 336
Planetarium, Singapore 663
plantation 68
police 19
poliomyelitis 743
Politics
Brunei 543
Malaysia 84
Sabah 432
Sarawak 353
Singapore 603
Pomelo 741
popular folk religion 601
Population, Brunei 541
Population policies 596
Poring Hot Springs 472, 474
Port Dickson 218
Port Klang 118
Porta de Santiago, Melaka 228
Portuguese 50
Portuguese Settlement, Melaka 233
Poste Restante, Malaysia 520
Postal services
Brunei 568
Malaysia 520
Singapore 720
Pottery 353
Pre-colonial Malaya 48
Presbyterian church, Singapore 637
prickly heat 748
prisoners abroad 19
Proboscis monkey 325
Proclamation of Independence Memorial 230
prohibited items
Brunei 566
Malaysia 503
Singapore 710
Proton 116
pua kumbu 350
public debate 616
Pulau Aur 48, 269
Pulau Beras Besar 209
Pulau Berhala 481
Pulau Besar 235
Pulau Brani 670
Pulau Bunbun 209
Pulau Chebeh 47
Pulau Gaya 447
Pulau Hujung 269
Pulau Kapas 47
Pulau Labas 47
Pulau Labuan 456
Pulau Langkawi 205
Pulau Layang-Layang 48
Pulau Mamutik 447
Pulau Mantanani 48
Pulau Manukan 447
Pulau Mengalum 48
Pulau Pangkor 47, 166
Pulau Pangkor Laut 47
Pulau Paya 47, 209
Pulau Pemanggil 48
Pulau Perhentian 48
Pulau Raja 295
Pulau Rawa 47
Pulau Rebak Kecil 207
Pulau Redang 47
Pulau Sapi 447
Pulau Satang Besar 375
Pulau Selingaan Island 48
Pulau Sembilan 47
Pulau Sepoi 47
Pulau Sibu 47
Pulau Singa Besar 209
Pulau Sipadan 48
Pulau Sulang 448
Pulau Tekong 670
Pulau Tenggol 47
Pulau Tiga 48
Pulau Tiga National Park 462
Pulau Tulai 47
Putra World Trade Centre, KL 113

Q

Queen Elizabeth Walk, Singapore 633

R

rabies 747
Race
See People
racial politics 59
racial relations 92
Radio
See Short wave radio guide
Brunei 569
Malaysia 522
Singapore 721
Raffles 579
Raffles City Complex 703
Raffles City Complex, Singapore 633
Raffles Hotel, Singapore 633
Raffles, Thomas Stamford 580
Rafflesia flower 450
Rahman, Tunku Abdul 58, 587
Railway Station, KL 108
Rajah Brooke's birdwing 41

Ramayana 74
Rambutan 741
Rampayoh Waterfall, Labi 562
Ranau 474
Ranau and Kundasang 473
Rantau Abang 292
Rantau Abang Turtle Information Centre 294
Rawa, Pulau 268
Razaleigh Hamzah, Tunku 84
Rebana 81
Redang, Pulau 303
Rejang River 383
Religion
Borneo 330
Brunei 542
Malaysia 72
Sabah 431
Singapore 600
Reptiles
Borneo 328
Malaysia 40
respiratory diseases 748
Restaurants
See places to eat
Rhinoceros 327
rhinoceros beetle 42
rhinoceros, Sumatran 486
Ridley, Henry 'Mad' 660
ringgit 501
Ringlet 152
Riverside Point 703
Road travel
to Brunei 565
to Malaysia 503
to Singapore 709
Robinson Falls 151
Roman Catholic Cathedral of the Good Shepherd 636
Rose garden, Brinchang 158
Royal Abu Bakar Museum 243
Royal Boat House 200
Royal Malaysian Navy Museum 165, 234
Royal Regalia Building 552
Royal Selangor Club 106
Royal Selangor Complex 119
Ruined City, Singapore 671
Rumah Belor 393
rumah berpangung [i] 62
Rumah ibu 62
Rumah Tuan Lepong Balleh 391
Rungus 465

S

SABAH 422
Sabah Foundation 437
Sabah State Museum 435
Safety
Brunei 566
confidence tricksters 18
drugs 19
Malaysia 506
police 19
Singapore 713
theft 19
Sago Street, Singapore 647
Sakayamuni Buddha Gaya Temple, Singapore 657
Salak 741
Salak River 375
Sam Poh Tong 162
Sam Sing Kung Temple 478
sambar 39
Sambol 670
Sandakan 475
Santubong 374
Santubong, Gunung 375
Sapi Island 48
Sapi, Pulau 447
Sapulut 452
SARAWAK 333-421
Sarawak Chamber 412
Sarawak Cultural Village 374
Sarawak Museum 355
Science Centre, Singapore 663
Sea travel
to Malaysia 503
Second Transitional style shophouse 592
Segantan 209
Sejara Melayu 77
Sekayu waterfalls 300
Seking, Pulau, Singapore 675
Seleta Reservoir 669
Semangat '46 85
Sematan 365
Sembilan, Pulau 168
Semonggoh Orang Utan Sanctuary 361
Semporna 492
Sentosa 670
Sepilok Orang Utan Sanctuary and Rehabilitation Centre 486
Serambi gantung 62
Serangoon Road 654
Seremban 216
Seria 561
shadow puppet 78
Shah Alam 117
Sharif Ali 536
Shenton Way 641
Shifting cultivation 322
Shifting cultivation, Sarawak 345
Shophouses 591, 654
Shopping 15
See also individual towns
Brunei 566
BSB 558
Central market, KL 108
JB 249
KL 134
Kota bharu 314
Kuching 370
Malaysia 506
Melaka 240
Penang 192
Singapore 698
Short Wave Radio Guide 731
Shun 601
Sibu 47, 383
Sibu, Pulau 269
Sickness images 352
Signal Hill 437
Sikuati 466
Silam, Gunung 490
Silat dance 79
silver and goldware, Brunei 543
Silverware 84
Sim Lim Square 703
Sim Lim Tower 703
Similajau National Park 399
Singa Besar, Pulau 209
SINGAPORE 571-725
accommodation 678
accommodation, colonial core 678
accommodation, Orchard Road 679
airline offices 695
airport information 711
Ararb Street 657
ATMs 708
banks 695
bars 694
before travelling 707
boat 719
camping 686
car hire 719
cash 708
clothing 712
communications 719
conduct 712
credit cards 708
currency 708, 710
customs 710
departure tax 712
duty free allowance 710

embassies 696
Emergencies 712
entertainment 696, 721
entry requirements 707
export restrictions 710
food 707
food and drink 713
further reading 724
getting around 717
getting there 708
getting there by bus 718
Goods Tax 708
health 707
hitchhiking 719
holidays and festivals 721
Hospitals 698, 707
hours of business 712
language 719
Little India 654
malaria 707
money 708
official time 712
on arrival 711
Orchard Road 643
other local transport 719
places to eat 686
Port, The 641
post 698
Postal services 720
prohibited items 710, 712
radio 721
religion 712
safety 713
Shopping 698, 713
suggested reading 724
taxis 719
telephone services 720
television 721
tipping 713
tour companies 706
tourist information 720
trishaw 719
vaccinations 707
voltage 713
water 707
weights and measures 713
when to go 707
where to stay 713
Singapore Art Museum 636
Singapore Malay Union 54
Singapore Maritime Showcase 642
Singapore Progressive Party (SPP) 587
Singapore River 637, 676
Singapore Zoological Gardens 667
Singapore's Islands 670
Singapore:Golf 704
Singlish, language 602
Sipadan Island Marine Reserve 494
Sipitang 455
Sister's Island, Singapore 675
Skrang 381
snake bites 747
Snake Temple, Penang 187
Spectator sports, Singapore 705
Sports, KL 136
Sri Mahamariamman Temple, KL 110
Sri Mariamann Temple, Penang 183
Sri Mariamman Temple, Singapore 649
Sri Menanti 216
Sri Pantai 255
Sri Perumal, Singapore 657
Sri Veeramakaliamman Temple, Singapore 657
St Andrew's Cathedral 591
St Andrew's Cathedral, Singapore 634
St George's Church, Penang 182
St John's 674
St John's, Singapore 674
St Joseph's Institution 636
St Paul's Church, Melaka 228
St Paul's Hill, Melaka 228
St Peter's Church, Melaka 233
Stadthuys, Melaka 228
Stamford House 703
State Museum 200
Kota Bharu 311
State Museum, Losong 299
State of Emergency 59
statue of Raffles 633
stings 747
Straits Chinese 66, 230, 598
Straits Settlements 54, 582
street operas 79
Sulang Pulau 448
Sultan Abdul Mumin 538
Sultan Awang Alak ber Tabar 536
Sultan Bolkiah 536
Sultan Hashim Jalilul Alam Aqamaddin 539
Sultan Hassan 536
Sultan Iskandar Planetarium 361
Sultan Mosque, Singapore 657
Sultan of Brunei 534
sultans 52
Sulug Island 48
Sun World, Singapore 673
Sunburn 747
Sungai Lembing 275
Sungai Likau 399
Sungai Petani 200
Sungai Teroi Forest Recreation Park 202
Sungei Buloh Nature Park 669
Supreme Court, Singapore 631
Suria KLCC 113
Swettenham, Frank 100
Sze Ya Temple, KL 110

T

Ta-po-kungu 602
Taiping 171
Taiping Zoo 172
Talang Talang 365
Taman Burung (Bird Park), KL 111
Taman Negara (National Park) 281
Taman Rekrearsi Hutan Simpan Bukit Subok 553
Taman Tasek Titiwangsa 115
Taman Tasik 172
Tamarind 741
Tambun Hot Springs 162
Tambunan 448
Tamil 68
Tampuruli, Sabah 439
tamu 463
Tamu Muhibba 404
tamus 427
Tan Yeok Nee Mansion 643
Tanah Rata 153
Tang Dynasty City, Singapore 662
Tanjong Pagar 651
Tanjong Pagar Heritage Exhibition, Singapore 652
Tanjong Pagar terminal 641
Tanjong Pagar, Singapore 651
Tanjung Aru Beach, Sabah 437
Tanjung Bidara 235
Tanjung Bungah 196
Tanjung Datu National Park 365
Tanjung Jara 291
Tanjung Kling 234
Taoism 600
Tapah 152
Tapai 428
tapir 39
Tapis, Gunung 275
Tarakan 498
Tasek Bera 274
Tasek Cini 274
Tasek Cini, Kuantan 279

Tasek Merimbun 561
Tattoos 343
Tawau 497
Tawau Hills State Park 497
Taxi
- Brunei 568
- Malaysia 519
- Singapore 719

Tea Chapter 652
tea plantations 149
Teknologi Melayu Museum 555
Telaga Air Hangat 208
Telaga Tujuh waterfalls 208
Telephone services
- Brunei 568
- Malaysia 520
- Singapore 720

Television
- Brunei 569
- Malaysia 522
- Singapore 721

Telok Ayer Chinese Methodist Church 651
Telok Ayer Street 650
Teluk Bahang 195, 196
Teluk Batik 165
Teluk Cempedak 273
Teluk Cempedak, Kuantan 278
Teluk Ketapang 167
Teluk Mahkota 246
Teluk Nipah 168
Teluk Rubiah 165
Temburong, Brunei 559
Temburong District 559
Temerloh 281
Tempasuk 463
Temple of the Goddess of Heaven, KL 114
Temple Street, Singapore 647
Templer Park, KL 114
Templer, Sir Gerald 57
temples
- Bat 186
- Burmese 184
- Chan See Shu Yuen 110
- Cheng Hoon Teng 232
- Chettiar 637
- Chinese 553
- Foo Lin Kong 168
- Goddess of Mercy Temple, Penang 183
- Goddess of Mercy 478
- Hian Tien Shian Tee 360
- Kek Lok Si 186
- Kong Meng San Phor Kark See 667
- Ling Nam Temple 173
- Nattukotai Chettiar 185
- Perak Tong 162
- Pertubuhan Ugama Buddhist 478
- Sam Poh Kong 233
- Sam Poh Tong 162
- Sam Poh 156
- Snake 187
- Sri Mahamariamman 110
- Sri Mariamann, Penang 183
- Sri Mariamman 649
- Sri Pathirakaliaman 168
- Sri Poyyatha Vinayagar Moorthi 232
- Sri Veeramakaliamman 657
- Sze Ya 110
- Thaw Peh Kong Chinese 410
- Thian Hock Keng 650
- Three Saints 479
- Tua Pek Kong 360
- Wat Chayamangkalaram 184
- Wat Phothivian 312

Tengah Pulau 268
Tenom 452
tetanus 743
Textile Museum 106
Textiles
- Brunei 543
- Sarawak 350

The land
- Brunei 530
- Malaysia 35
- Singapore 575

theft 19
Thian Hock Keng Temple, Singapore 650
Thomson, John 590
Thong Chai Medical Institute, Singapore 647
Three Emperors from the Dawn of History 601
Three Mythical Sage Emperors 601
tiger 39
Tiger Balm Gardens, Singapore 659
Tiger Balm Story, S 662
timetabling a visit 12
Tinggi 47
Tinggi, Pulau 268
Tioman, Pulau 258
Tiong Bahru 653
tipping
- Brunei 566
- Malaysia 506
- Singapore 713

Tishaws, Malaysia 520
Titi Kerawang 187
Tops 82
Tour companies
- KL 137
- Kuching 372
- Melaka 240
- Penang 193
- Singapore 706

Tourism 22
- *See further reading*
- Art 23
- Brunei 545
- checklist 26
- Culture 22
- development guidelines 24
- Environment 24
- Guide Books 25
- Malaysia 95, 500
- pressure groups 27
- the traveller 25
- Singapore 625
- suggested reading 27

Tourist Board offices (overseas)
- Brunei 735
- Malaysia 735
- Singapore 736

Tourist information
- Brunei 564

Tourist offices
- BSB 558
- KL 138
- Kuching 372
- Penang 193

tours
- Kuala Terengganu 300
- Singapore 676

Touts, Singapore 699
Traders' cave, Niah 401
traditional house styles 591
- *See art & architecture*

traffic
- Singapore 615

Train travel
- to Malaysia 502
- to Singapore 709
- within Malaysia 512

Transport
- BSB 558
- JB 250
- Kota Bharu 315
- Kota Kinabalu 446
- Kuching 372
- Melaka 241
- Penang 193

transport and travelling 11
- East Malaysia (Sarawak and Sabah) and Brunei 12
- Singapore and the Peninsula 11

Travel agents
travellers cheques 17
  KL 137
  Malaysia 502
Travelling with Children and Babies 19, 749
  health 750
Treaty of London 51, 582
Treaty of Pangkor 54
Trekking 13
  Bako National Park 379
  Bario 419
  Gunung Mulu 414
  Gunung Tahan 283
  Kinabalu 470
  Lambir Hills 406
  Limbang 420
  Marudi Log Walk 562
  Marudi-Kampong Teraja log walk 410
  Mentapok and Monkobo 473
  Niah National Park 403
  Pulau Gaya 447
  Pulau Tioman 258
  Similajau National Park 400
Trusmadi, Gunung 451
Tuaran 440
Tumpat 312
Tun Razak Memorial 111
Tunku Abdul Rahman Park 48, 447
Turtle Islands National Park 48, 483
Tutong 561
typhoid 743

U

Ubin, Pulau, Singapore 675
UMNO Baru 84
Underwater World, Singapore 672
Union of Young Malays 54
United Malays National Organization (UMNO) 56, 84
Upper Cross Street 648

V

vaccination 501, 743
  Brunei 564
  Malaysia 499
  Singapore 707
Victoria Theatre, Singapore 631
Victorian Bungalow 594
Visas
  Brunei 564
  Malaysia 499
  Singapore 707
Vision 2020 96
Volcano Land, Singapore 672
Voltage
  Brunei 566
  Malaysia 506
  Singapore 713

W

Wah Aik Shoemaker Shop, Melaka 232
walking tour, Chinatown 649
War Memorial, Singapore 633
Wat Chayamangkalaram 184
water 20
  Brunei 564
  Malaysia 501
  Singapore 707
Wawasan 2020 96
Wayang Kulit 78, 84
weights and measures 506
what to take 16
Where to go 11
where to stay 19
White Rajah, The 338
Wildlife
  See also National Parks and Sanctuaries
  Brunei 533
  Malaysia 38
Women travelling alone 19
Woodcarving 82
  sarawak 351
Working abroad 18
World Trade Centre 642

X

Xi, Fu 601

Y

Yao 601
Yellow Emperor 601
Youland Nursery 152
Yu 601

Z

zapin dance 80

Maps

INTRODUCTION

Malaysia, Singapore & Brunei 7
Malaysian Borneo and Brunei 14
Peninsular Malaysia and Singapore 12

MALAYSIA

Alor Star 201
Ayer Keroh 237
Bako National Park: Trails 377
Bandar Labuan 458-458
Beaufort 456
Bintulu 397
Brinchang 157
Cameron Highlands 148
Forest fires and extent of the 'haze', October 1997 45
Georgetown 180-181
Gunung Kinabalu Trail 468
Gunung Mulu National Park 411
Ipoh 161
  Detail 163
Johor Bahru 244
Kampung Cerating 288
Kangar 204
Kapit 386
Kota Bharu 309
Kota Kinabalu 436
  Around Kota Kinabalu 438
Kuah 210
Kuala Kangsar 170
Kuala Lumpur 102-103
  Around Chinatown 121
  Around Kuala Lumpur 115
  Around the Golden Triangle 124
  City Centre 107
  detail 123
  Light Rail Transit (LRT) 139
Kuala Terengganu 298
Kuantan 276-277
Kuching 356
  Around Kuching 362
Lumut 165
Malaysia 30
  East Coast Malaysia 253
  Malaysian Railways 516
  MAS domestic network (1997) 511
  Pelangi Airways Network 510
  Peninsular Malaysia 32
  Southern Peninsular Malaysia 215
Marang 296
Melaka 222
  detail 229
Miri 405
Niah Caves Park 401
North of Kuala Lumpur 143
Penang 177
  Beaches 196
  Hill 186
Perhentian Islands 304
Port Dickson 219
Pulau Langkawi 207
Pulau Pangkor 167
Pulau Tioman 259
  Ayer Batang Beach 264
  Juara Beach 266
  Salang Beach 265
Tekek 262
Tekek to Juara: cross section of cross-island trek 260
Sabah 423
Sandakan 477
  Bay 480

Sarawak **334**
Sarawak Cultural Village **364**
Seremban **218**
Sibu **383**
State of:
Johor **242**
Kedah **200**
an **307**
a **221**
i Sembilan **216**
ng **270**
k **160**
is **206**
ngor **145**
ngganu **292**
ng **172**
an Negara **282**
ah Rata **154**
om **453**
es of Borneo **331**
er Rejang **393**

BRUNEI

Bandar Seri Begawan **551**
Brunei **531**

SINGAPORE

Arab Street **658**
Chinatown detail **648**
Chinatown, the river & the port **638**
Colonial Core **632**
East Coast **665**
Little India **655**
MRT System **718**
Orchard Road **644-645**
Sentosa & environs **671**
Singapore General **628-629**
Singapore West **661**
Singapore **573**

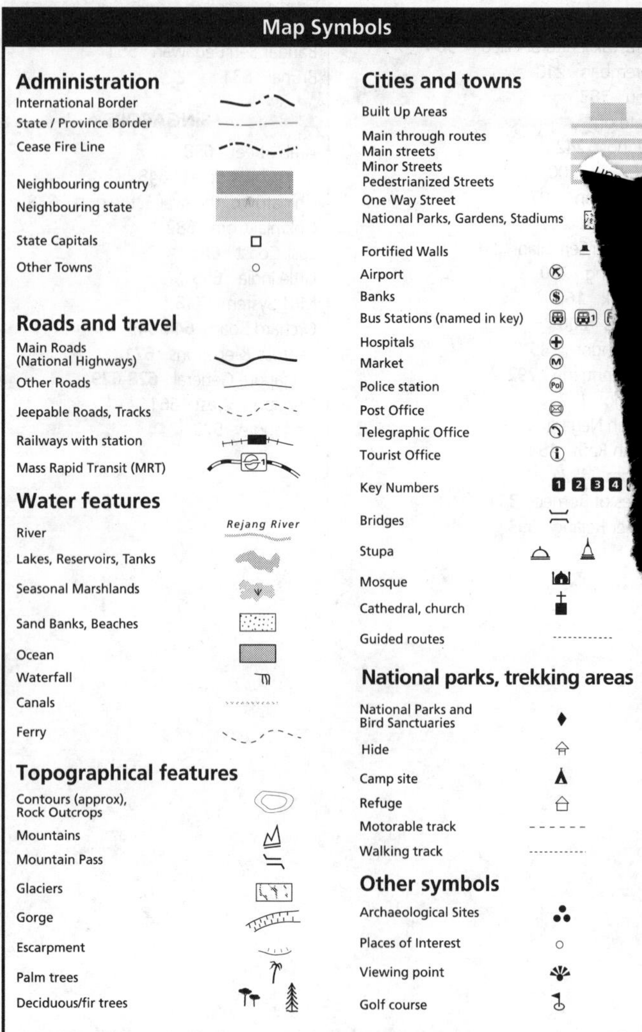
Map Symbols
Administration
International Border
State / Province Border
Cease Fire Line
Neighbouring country
Neighbouring state
State Capitals
Other Towns
Roads and travel
Main Roads
(National Highways)
Other Roads
Jeepable Roads, Tracks
Railways with station
Mass Rapid Transit (MRT)
Water features
Rejang River
River
Lakes, Reservoirs, Tanks
Seasonal Marshlands
Sand Banks, Beaches
Ocean
Waterfall
Canals
Ferry
Topographical features
Contours (approx),
Rock Outcrops
Mountains
Mountain Pass
Glaciers
Gorge
Escarpment
Palm trees
Deciduous/fir trees
Cities and towns
Built Up Areas
Main through routes
Main streets
Minor Streets
Pedestrianized Streets
One Way Street
National Parks, Gardens, Stadiums
Fortified Walls
Airport
Banks
Bus Stations (named in key)
Hospitals
Market
Police station
Post Office
Telegraphic Office
Tourist Office
Key Numbers
Bridges
Stupa
Mosque
Cathedral, church
Guided routes
National parks, trekking areas
National Parks and
Bird Sanctuaries
Hide
Camp site
Refuge
Motorable track
Walking track
Other symbols
Archaeological Sites
Places of Interest
Viewing point
Golf course

Footprint Handbooks

All of us at Footprint Handbooks hope you have enjoyed reading and travelling with this Handbook. As our story starts back in the early 1920s we thought it would be interesting to chronicle our development.

It all started 75 years ago in 1921, with the publication of the Anglo-South American Handbook. In 1924 the South American Handbook was created. This has been published each year for the last 74 years and is the longest running guidebook in the English language, immortalised by Graham Greene as "the best travel guide in existence." Celebrations, presumably, next year as we hit the 75th annual edition!

One of the key strengths of the South American Handbook over the years has been the extraordinary contact we have had with our readers through their hundreds of letters to us in Bath. From these letters we learnt that you wanted more Handbooks of the same quality to other parts of the world.

In 1989 my brother Patrick and I set about developing a series modelled on the South American Handbook. Our aim was to create the ultimate practical guidebook series for all travellers, providing expert knowledge of far flung places, explaining culture, places and people in a balanced, lively and clear way. The whole idea hinged, of course, on finding writers who were in tune with our thinking. Serendipity stepped in at exactly the right moment: we were able to bring together a talented group of people who know the countries we cover inside out and whose enthusiasm for travelling in them needed to be communicated.

The series started to steadily grow as we brought out new guides to the Indian sub-continent, Southeast Asia, Africa and Europe. At this stage we were known as Trade & Travel Publications, or "the people who publish the Handbooks!" In 1995 we felt that the time was right to look again at the identity that had brought us all this way and one year later Footprint Handbooks hit the bookshelves.

There are now well over 30 Handbooks in the series and many more in the pipeline but central to all of this is to maintain contact with our readers. Do continue to write to us with all your news, comments and suggestions and in return we will keep you up to date with developments here in the West Country.